Iran

IRAN

A Modern History

Abbas Amanat

Yale

UNIVERSITY

PRESS

New Haven & London

به اسیران قفس مژده گلزار بیار

To the captives in the cage,
Convey the glad tidings of blooming meadows.
Hafez

To Maryam

CONTENTS

Plates follow page 176

PREFACE

Covering half a millennium of history of any country or region is a formidable task. When it comes to the history of early modern and modern Iran, it becomes daunting. It took nearly two decades for me to try to cover a complex period that witnessed five dynastic changes, at least three revolutions, three civil wars, four episodes of foreign occupation, and the inception of a new Islamic government. I hope I have produced a coherent narrative that threads the events of this past into meaningful themes, just as every knot feeds into the larger pattern of a Persian carpet. Yet history, as historians are anxious to caution their readers, has many random twists and turns, which seldom lend themselves to an orderly design. What emerges, as in this book, may seem to be disarray up close, but from afar, with the benefit of hindsight, it reveals a pattern with many discernable paths.

I have tried in this book to trace the roots of Iranian modernity, or more accurately, modernities, over a half millennium. To many readers, the rise of a potent messianic movement five centuries ago may seem a far cry from any notion of modernity, at least the way it is often understood. Yet there is in fact a relationship between the rise of a state with an enforced religious creed—in this case, the Safavid Empire upholding Shiʻism—and emergence of a modern nation state in later centuries. Encounters with Europe in the nineteenth and the twentieth centuries and the adoption of Western-style modernity, in all its permutations, only reinforced Iran's own sense of identity and its distinct pattern of continuity. Despite territorial losses at the periphery and its inherent material disadvantages, Iran was among very few non-Western countries that preserved its sovereignty and much of its territorial integrity in the age of high imperialism. It did so, it can be argued, in part because it rendered, and still is rendering, its own Persianized version of modernity, not without many trials and errors.

In this book, by and large I have respected a dynastic periodization, not only because changes of dynasties mattered in and of themselves, but also because many times they were emblematic of sociopolitical, economic, and cultural shifts. Emphasis on members of the elite I also deemed inevitable, for such personalities often proved agents of important, and at times disastrous, changes. Understanding personality traits of Isma'il I and 'Abbas I of the Safavid dynasty were as crucial in the shaping of modern Iran as were those of Aqa Mohammad Khan Qajar, Reza Shah Pahlavi, and, more recently, Ayatollah Khomeini. Yet invariably I have tried to balance these political and biographical narratives with attention to socioeconomic and cultural trends. Likewise, I have tried, to the extent possible, to locate the Iranian past in broader regional landscapes. This is as much an effort to look at Iranian history inclusively or to deter perceptions of exceptionalism as it is an effort to display the vibrant bonds that tied Iran to both neighboring lands and prevailing global trends. Yet I resisted globalizing the Iranian past beyond reasonable limits. We cannot ignore shared patterns that tie Iran to its neighboring lands. Nor can we deny the dictates of geography, religion, and political culture that set Iran apart from South Asia and from Central Asia, Anatolia, Mesopotamia, or Arabia.

The book consists of an introduction, four parts, and an epilogue. Part I (1501–1797) covers the early modern era, from the rise and then shaping of the Safavid Empire to the end of the eighteenth century. Part II (1797–1911) covers the long nineteenth century, from the consolidation of the Qajar dynasty and encounters with European powers to the Constitutional Revolution at the turn of the twentieth century. Part III (1914–1977) covers developments from World War I and its aftermath to the end of the Pahlavi era. Part IV (1977–1989) is devoted to the shaping of the Islamic Revolution during its first phase. In this final part, wherever I deemed it necessary, I have made brief observations about the post-1989 period in the hope of bringing the narrative to a close. I tried to strike a balance between early modern and modern periods, even though in practice about two-thirds of the book is devoted to the twentieth century, given the weight of the events between the Constitutional Revolution and the Islamic Revolution.

Attention to long-term themes also helped determine the book's size and organization. I strived to trace overarching themes and articulate arguments while still preserving a narrative. The famous verse by the Persian poet Rumi often echoed in my mind: "The secret of the beloved is best to be told in the stories of the others." The reader will notice throughout such recognized, and stubborn, themes as natural resources and the limits of human habitat, the tension between the sedentary center and the nomadic periphery, the interplay between the state and the urban elite (including the clerical establishment), tension between rulers and ministers, the chronic resurgence of alternative socioreligious movements, and the persistence of cultural and artistic memories. In the nineteenth and twentieth centuries, a greater engagement with European imperial powers, greater awareness of material weaknesses, dilemmas of reform and development, the ideal and realities involved in becoming modern, evolving notions of national identity, and the mastery of internal economic resources all loomed large. Finally, greater reliance on exportable natural resources helped the state consolidate and further its modernizing project. Yet over time, an autocratic vision of transforming Iran lost its popular mandate, generated nostalgia for a fast-disappearing world, and fostered a revolutionary aptitude with strong Islamic undercurrents.

There are topics and personalities that are absent from this book, or appear in passing, and others who take up perhaps more than their fair share. Men far more than women dominate this narrative. Rewriting an essentially patriarchal history is formidable, if not at times impossible. The same can also be said about the silenced multitudes of the downtrodden, the marginalized, the nonconformists, and the powerless in a master narrative, often penned by agents of political power and compilers of hagiographies. I have tried, nevertheless, to retrieve some of these voices and incorporate them into my story.

In retrospect, debates about gender and ethnicity, everyday life, popular culture, public and private spheres, ecology and environment, and complexities of cultural identities could have received greater attention. Yet I hope I have shown at least historical glimpses of a society and a culture more diverse and more complex than often appear in monolithic and monotonous accounts of Iran. Reference to poetry and literary trends, for instance, is one way to enrich our understanding of those recesses of collective memory that the official narrative often ignores or denies. These are the contours of a collective memory that connects the Safavid times to the Qajar era, and to the Constitutional Revolution and the rise of Pahlavi state, the National Movement of the postwar era, and eventually to contemporary times.

The presence of my own voice in the style and substance of this book is undeniable, and this is not foreign to those students of history who seek to strike a balance between historical objectivity and the deeper traits of authorial subjectivity. What can playfully be called "history with attitude" does not aim to unfairly interrogate the past, or pass ahistorical judgments, but instead to raise critical questions, to problematize the conventional wisdom, and perhaps to render some uninhibited though subtle answers. As a child of a generation who witnessed an age of heady Westernism and the furious responses to it—that is, the latter decades of the Pahlavi era and the dawn of the Islamic Revolution—I find it almost imperative to address *problematiques* that were crucial, and still are, to the shaping of Iran (and the rest of the Middle East): frustrated struggles for democracy and tolerance, the transforming face of nationalism, the rise and fall of autocratic regimes, disillusionment with ideologies, and, of course, contentious grappling with Western powers and a globalizing culture. At the end of many years, one afterthought may best sum up these feelings: "a sorrowful stroll in the garden of memories," as the poet Forough Farrokhzad has it.

This interpretive approach allowed for only a few endnotes. Likewise, engaging the scholarly literature directly proved beyond the scope of this project. The annotated bibliography at the end of the book addresses such a need. To sustain the flow of the narrative, direct citations were also kept to minimum. Maps and illustrations are intended to enrich the text and enhance its arguments.

The transliteration system is that of the *International Journal of Middle East Studies*, but with several important modifications. First, in today's Persian, the vowels *e* and *o* represent sounds similar to those in the English language and thus have been substituted for the Arabicized *i* and *u* in the IJMES system; hence *Mohammad* and not *Muhammad* (unless in an Arabic phrase or Arabic book title) and *mojtahed* and not *mujtahid*. If some place-names and technical terms have acquired a universal currency, they are preferred over literal transliteration; hence *Isfahan* and not *Esfehan*. Likewise, the Persian attributive *ezafeh* finds its true voice. It is no longer awkwardly rendered as -*i* but as -*e*, hence *Bagh-e Shah* and not *Bagh-i Shah*. In some other instances, the Persian pronunciation of well-known proper names and place-names was preferred; hence *Azarbaijan* and not *Azerbaijan* or *Adharbaijan*, and *Alborz* and not *El-burz*. Iran is preferred over Persia throughout, but Persian culture and literature is preferred over Iranian, unless the latter attribute is specifically intended. Finally, no diacritical symbols were employed except on a very few occasions when the lack of a diacritical mark on a long *a* would have caused confusion—hence *ā* instead of *a* in 'Abd al-'Āli al-Karaki. All the translations, prose and verse, are mine unless noted otherwise.

Over the years many friends and colleagues helped with research and preparation of this book. I am grateful to Haynie Wheeler for helping to revise the manuscript. My thanks are also due to Behrouz Afagh, Aref Amanat, Hossein Amanat, Mehrdad Amanat, Assef Ashraf, Mohsen Ashtiyani, Oliver Bast, Hushang Chehabi, Joan Cole, Joanna De Groot, Farhad Diba, Roberta

Dougherty, Kevin Gledhill, John Gurney, Linda Komaroff, Jane Lewisohn, Katie Manbachi, Ulrich Marzolph, Afshin Matin-Asgari, Mahnaz Moazzami, Iman Raad, Siavush Ranjbar-Daemi, Saeed Sanjabi, Mohamad Tavakoli-Targhi, Fereydun Vahman, and Denis Volkov. I am also grateful to the Andrew Carnegie Fellows Program for the fellowship I received while researching this book. I am indebted to my mother, Besharat Khavari-Amanat, and to my family for their moral support, and I honor the memory of my father, Mousa Amanat, who first nurtured in me an interest in history. My wife, Maryam Sanjabi, has been a continuous source of support and encouragement throughout the years.

Iran

Map I.1. Contemporary Iran

INTRODUCTION

Long before Iran came to be known in the mid-twentieth century as one of the countries of the Middle East, for nearly two and a half millennia it was known to the Western world as Persia. An ancient land in western Asia, it is strategically located between the Indian subcontinent, Central Asia, and China to its east; Mesopotamia and the Mediterranean world to its west; Russia to the north; and the Persian Gulf and the Arabian Peninsula to its south. At the cross-roads of two major trade routes—the "Silk Road," passing through northern and central Iran, and the so-called the spice route, from South Asia through the Persian Gulf—for many centuries Iran, as a regional empire, was fertile ground for cultural, commercial, and population exchanges with its neighbors. As early as the second millennium BC, when the Indo-European pastoralists first entered the Iranian plateau, and as late as the twentieth century, Iran was host to a diverse ethnic, cultural, and linguistic population, either through conquest or through peaceful settlement. Despite prolonged political lapses, for two and a half millennia Iran remained a cultural entity distinguished by its indigenous characteristics and recognized as such by the world around it. Since the early sixteenth century, when the Safavid state came into being, Iran has maintained an uninterrupted political identity.

For most of the period up to the mid-seventh century, when the Sasanian Empire fell to the conquering Arab armies of Islam, Iran (or, more accurately, the Persian Empire) managed to outlive as a political community a number of its rivals to the west, starting with the Greeks and continuing with the Romans and then the Byzantine Empire of late antiquity. This despite devastating defeats, nomadic invasions, ethnic hegemonies, changes in its religious identity, and recurring domestic upheavals. Iran perhaps is one of the most invaded and

1

most revolution-prone countries in world history, a debatable merit with lasting consequences. In between the Islamic conquest and the rise of the Safavid state, Iran survived more as a cultural than a unified political entity, in part because of geography and ecology, but also because of the prevalence of the Persian language and high culture. In adopting the Arabic script in the early ninth century, Iran preserved much of its key cultural paradigms, myths, and memories.

The Perso-Islamic renaissance that occurred soon thereafter in the eleventh century, and long remained at the heart of Muslim cultural efflorescence, helped shape Iran's cultural identity. Yet classical Persian language coexisted with a wide range of other languages and dialects, regional cultures, and customs and ethnicities within and beyond Iran proper. The Persianate world—as Marshall Hodgson, the historian of Islamic civilization called it—stretched throughout eastern Islamic lands, from Central Asia and Xinjiang (Khotan in Persian) to Hindustan, and spread from the Caucasus, Anatolia (today's Asian Turkey), and the southern Balkans to Mesopotamia.

MEMORIES OF AN ANCIENT PAST

The Persians, and before them the Medes, were among the first people known to the ancient Greeks outside their own geographic sphere. As early as the sixth century BC, when Cyrus the Great, the founder of the Achaemenid Empire (c. 550 BC–330 BC) conquered Asia Minor, the Persians came to occupy in the Greek mind the place of a formidable Other. For more than two centuries the Persians inspired in the Greek imagination a mixture of awe and fear toward an imperial power, which, in contrast to the vulnerable Greek city-states, was based on a centralized state and ruled by the King of Kings. It was admired as a vast multinational empire with legendary wealth and economic power, universal currency, as well as an efficient administration, army, and communication (long-distance carriage roads and horse couriers rather than barefoot runners). It had a belief system totally different from that of the Greeks' own quarreling Olympian deities. Herodotus, himself a Greek subject of the Persian Empire living in Asia Minor, embarked on *The Histories*, with the chief aim of answering one major question: how was the only "superpower" of his time, the empire of Cyrus and Darius, resisted and eventually defeated in the Persian Wars (499 BC–449 BC) by the seemingly vulnerable Greeks? His flattering answer, a blend of fact and fiction, greatly influenced ancient historical consciousness and even helped shape Western ambivalence toward Iran in modern times.

The Greeks called this civilization "barbarian" (*barbaros*), which in the original sense of the term meant "alien," or more specifically, a person who mumbles, presumably because the Greeks could not understand the languages of Iran, whether ancient Persian or Aramaic. The term implied Persian inferiority to the Greek, and later, Roman sense of superiority. Such a condescending attitude was a predictable reaction, one could argue, to the Greeks' fear of succumbing in real life to the Persians and their material superiority. Aeschylus's *The Persians*, the first surviving Greek historical tragedy, written by a soldier who himself had fought in the Persian Wars, celebrated the Greek victory by imagining the impact of the devastating news of the Persian defeat in the war on the Persian royalty and the court—a clever ploy, no doubt reflective of the Greeks' jubilant mood at being saved from Persian hegemony.

It was not an accident that the Athenian Parthenon, the architectural representation of a rare moment of Greek solidarity, was built to celebrate victory in the Persian Wars. As has been related, on the famous shield of Athena, whose huge statue was worshipped in the Parthenon, the Persians were depicted as barbarians clad in effeminate dress, about to be humbled by the masculine and victorious Greeks. In this case, Occidental artistic representation seems to have determined long ago its choice depiction of Persia as the Orient par excellence: feminine and exotic. Nor was it an accident that the chief target of Alexander's world-conquering ambition should have been the Persian Empire.

The Macedonian adventurer, whom the Zoroastrian sources of pre-Islamic Iran labeled as "evil Alexander," no doubt exploited these anti-Persian sentiments, rampant among the Greeks of Asia Minor, as a pretext to reclaim Greek lands after more than two centuries under Persian rule. When Alexander conquered the Achaemenid Empire in 330 BC, he was too anxious—to the dismay of some of his generals, and against the advice of his teacher, Aristotle, who viewed the Persian state as tyrannical—not only to adopt Persian costumes and courtly manners, but also to create a universalistic Greco-Persian political hybrid. In this vision, as far as can be recovered from the Greek narratives, greater weight was given to the realties of the Persian model of government than to the Greek ideals. The Greek conquest nevertheless resulted in infusion of Hellenistic culture into the Iranian world that lasted for hundreds of years afterward and well into the Islamic era.

Resonating through the early modern and modern centuries, the victory against the Persian Empire was celebrated in post-Enlightenment Europe and during the Western imperial expansion in the nineteenth century as a turning point in the history of Western civilization. For modern Europeans who "rediscovered" Persia, these memories were alive and hugely reinforced by the retrieval of classical texts, and later by archeological findings in the Near East and in Iran.

References in the Hebrew Bible were far more favorable to the Persians. Cyrus the Great (Heb. *Koresh,* taken from the Old Persian), in particular, fared well. He was the "anointed one" (messiah, or *mashiah*) who delivered the Israelites from their Babylonian captivity and allowed them to return to their homeland and later, under the Achaemenid successors, to rebuild their temple in Jerusalem. He was the only historical figure in the Hebrew Bible to be recognized as the Lord's "messiah" and his "shepherd" (Isaiah 44–45), and one of the very few rulers to be praised for his tolerance and compassion. Furthermore, the story of the book of Esther—whereby the Jewish concubine of the Persian King of Kings saves his coreligionists from massacre at the hands of a sinister minister—is largely a composite narrative pieced together to reassure the Jews of their ultimate redemption against later occurrences of anti-Semitism, it nonetheless demonstrates the Israelites' favorable attitude and loyalty toward their Persian overlords in exchange for Achaemenid royal protection.

The positive attitude of the Bible toward the Persians may also be attributed to the affinity the Israelites felt between their own omniscient God and the Persian Wise Lord, the Ahura Mazda of Iranian religion and later of Zoroastrianism. Unlike the Babylonian deities, Ahura Mazda was compassionate and predictable, a supporter of the righteous and an enemy of the wicked. A distant memory of such an affinity can be seen in the book of Daniel, which, though a composite product of later centuries, represented in its apocalyptic imagery a just and mighty Persian King of Kings who redeems the saved and eliminates the damned, an image that may well have been colored by the Zoroastrian apocalyptic tradition of Iran.

AS A POLITICAL COMMUNITY

Both Greek and Hebrew portrayals represented ancient Iran as an alternative space, as the land of the Other, which should be dealt with on its own terms. To this extent, they were not far from the idea of Iran as a political community, a geopolitical entity with a centralized state and a dominant religion. The name *Iran,* as is often noted, is derived from the Iranian term *Aryanum,* the land of the Aryans, the branch of Indo-European pastoralists who settled in the Iranian plateau some four thousand years ago and gave their name to the land. Although in our time *Aryan* has been besmirched beyond recovery, etymologically it implied something benign. *Iran* and its origin, as the brilliant French philologist

Émile Benveniste has argued, essentially meant "we who are next of kin" or "we cousins," a term of kinship identification implying "us," by which these pastoralists distinguished themselves presumably from the indigenous inhabitants of the plateau or from other Indo-Europeans.

This sense of kinship solidarity is stressed in the *Shahnameh*, the great Persian epic of the tenth century, whereby the term *Iran* as a political community is contrasted with *aniran* (in Middle Persian), the "non-Iranians" or the "aliens." Like other ancient nations who employed similar kinship terms for their homelands, *Iran* came to be the sole name by which Iranians signified their own land and their state. Iran as a cultural identity persisted through the Islamic period and later was fully revived in the thirteenth century by the great Persian ministers of the Ilkhanid dynasty.

Ancient Greeks, and later their Western cultural heirs, however, continued to refer to Iran by the name of the original homeland of the prevailing Achaemenid Empire. The Greek *Persica* (or *Perses*), as well as the Hebrew *Paras*, was Anglicized to *Persia*, a reference to the heartland of the Iranian plateau, the Pars region (and today's Fars province) from which the Achaemenid Persians rose to power and came to dominate the entire Iranian plateau and beyond. For many centuries *Persia* was the name of the country to the outside world, and *Persian* a reference to its people, language, and culture while the term *Iran* was consistently used by Iranians in reference to their country. It was only in 1935 that the Iranian government adopted *Iran* instead of *Persia* as the official name of the country, a choice that made uniform the nomenclature but effectively obliterated beyond recovery the historical and cultural memory that the old name invoked.

As in most ancient states, power in Persian political culture was primarily built on a patriarchal model, one that replicated itself at royal, regional, local, tribal, and family levels. In conjunction with the institution of kingship, but still separate from it, the clerical authority demanded that its followers comply with the legal interpretation of the sacred text, be it Zoroastrian law or Islamic shari'a. For most of the early modern and modern times, the ulama (the class of the learned), or more specifically the jurists (*faqihs*), remained a semi-independent institution tangential to the authority of the state.

Yet the clerical establishment, and even state power, was occasionally challenged by the prophetic paradigm, a third force in the Persian tripartite model of authority. Over the centuries, numerous such figures—from the third-century Mani and the sixth-century Mazdak in the Sasanian era to the twelfth-century Isma'ili leader Hasan Sabbah, the fourteenth-century Noqtavi prophet Mahmud Pasikhani, and the nineteenth-century Sayyed 'Ali Mohammad the

Bab—called for the reform of religious norms and eventually the prevailing sociopolitical order by means of moral reconstruction and, at times, apocalyptic revolution. It is the interplay of these three sources of authority that punctuates Iran's narrative: violent revolts, contested historical memories, religious paradoxes, norms of gender and social divide, but also cultural florescence and fluidity. Whether by design or accident, such a narrative of anguished and volatile complexity persisted over centuries.

Crucial to the rudiments of political authority in Iran, and perhaps the oldest in its political culture, is the idea of the *shah*, the universal title for Iranian kings up to modern times. With no etymological equivalent in other Indo-European languages, *shah* is of Old Persian origin, *xshay*, which basically means the "one who deserves [to rule] on his own merit," which implies innate merit as the qualifying criterion for power. Rendered in Greek as *basiliocus*, originally in reference to Persian kings (and *Basilus Basilcus* for "King of Kings"), the term *shah* also implied autocratic independence from any priestly or other human legitimizing agency. This is depicted well, for example, in reliefs from the third century CE of the investiture of Sasanian kings, who received their divine mandate directly from a deity and not from a Zoroastrian priest. In contrast to *rex* in European languages and *raj* in Sanskrit—both of which referred to rulers who were essentially priest-kings leading their people along the "right" path of religion—the shah possessed kingly "charisma" (*farr* or *farrah*). The royal "charisma" radiating from the king's countenance (the term *charisma* in European languages probably is derived from the Persian *xoreh*, "sun ray") was divinely bestowed upon the ruler of the right "quality" (Persian *gohar*), but it could be taken away from him if he lost the art of governing (in Persian *honar*, a word of the same origin as "honor"). Deprived of charisma, the shah would ultimately be deposed by popular revolt, dynastic contestants, or foreign invaders.

The contingency of preserving the royal charisma thus served, at least in theory, as a tempering mechanism against tyranny. Despotic rulers who lose their charisma would not endure, as the prototypical example of mythical Jamshid in the *Shahnameh* reminded the historical rulers (pl. I.1). At the outset Jamshid is the founder of the cities, the teacher of new crafts, the initiator of the Persian Nowruz festival, and a great empire builder, but he loses his *farr* because of his arrogance and self-glorification, failings that came with material power and despotic behavior. Western observers, from Aristotle to Montesquieu, were only too anxious to point to these pitfalls of Persian despotism, perhaps for reasons that had to do more with the threat of despotic rulers in their own societies than with the realities of Persian kingship.

The Persian theory of government envisioned certain checks and balances to restrain the brute and unbridled exercise of power. A functional model of government known as the "circle of equity" was the ideal by which the manuals of government, a much-revered genre in Persian political writing, reminded the rulers of their duty to administer "justice." Essentially, the shah was required to maintain social balance by honoring each constituency with its due protection and reward: by keeping at bay the army and the state administration (*divan*) so as to inhibit their oppressive intrusion into the life of the subjects (fig. I.1). If the subjects are oppressed and plundered, so the circular model explains, they cannot produce and prosper, as a result of which the land will become impoverished and the state will be weakened, and eventually the ruler's power base will crumble and he will be deposed and destroyed. This cyclical model of power, inspired no doubt by the precariousness of the agrarian cycle in which it developed, seldom corresponded to the realities of power.

The reality was more like the infinite complexity of a game of chess (from the Middle Persian *shatrang*, from the original Sanskrit *chaturanga*), with the shah often in a position of checkmate (from the Persian *shah-mat*), itself a concept

Figure I.1. A nineteenth-century French presentation of the "circle of equity" based on a story in Sa'di's *Golestan*. Here depicted on a Qajar hunting excursion, the king safeguards the property of his subjects from intrusion by his entourage.
Nineteenth-century postcard. Author's collection.

in chess that developed in the Persian environment when the game was first imported from India during late antiquity. The political symbolism of the game can hardly be missed. Few shahs over the long course of Iranian history managed to maintain the formidable "balance" of both the polity and society at large without being isolated to the point of checkmate. The analogy of chess as a discourse of moves and countermoves in Persian political culture and the chessboard as the political arena is further evident in the introduction to the game of another piece, *farzin* (Persian for "sage," and later minister, or *vazir*), which later was identified in the European version as the queen. The mobility and versatility of the minister or queen (including his or her revivification to the stage from the position of a negotiating pawn) as opposed to the shah's isolated vulnerability is a telling commentary on the hazards of ministerial office as head of the divan.

The uneasy collaboration for control of the government between insecure shahs and shrewd chief ministers (sing. *sadr-e a'zam*) is a recurring theme in Iran's political history, with frequently fatal outcomes for the ministers. Fragile alliances within the divan and maneuvering for privilege and influence, moreover, made it impossible for the ministerial institution to withstand the onslaughts of its royal master. Over the long term, the divan never created an independent base free from royal intrusion, remaining instead the servant of the shah and subject to his whims and wishes.

Employing a chess analogy, the great Persian poet Hafez gives us the skeptic's ambivalence toward the institution of kingship and its volatile dependency on the minister's skilled maneuvers:

Waiting for the rook to make a move, we drive a pawn,
On the skeptics' chessboard there is no room for a king.

When the endgame comes, a pawn, symbolizing the often humble origins of the ministers, still has a chance to turn into a minister (or queen) and change the fortunes of the game, depending on how the rook (from Persian *rokh*), perhaps a symbol of peripheral power, decides to move. Otherwise, the king has no future, for he is about to be checkmated.

CENTER AND PERIPHERY

Even when the structural deficiencies in the Persian model of government were to be overcome by the ruler or his ministers, there were marginal forces outside the state's immediate reach. Most prevalent, perhaps, were the tribal landlords—the khans—on the periphery of the kingdom who, taking advan-

tage of the difficult Iranian terrain, resisted full control of the central authority. The expediency of coming to terms with peripheral powers, the rooks of
Hafez's verse, was generally acknowledged by the Persian central government,
which, instead of costly and often ineffective methods of direct rule, resorted to
granting khans of the periphery a semiautonomous status. By allowing oversight
through princely rule or other agencies, nurturing parallel leaderships within
tribal confederacies, and using the dual means of persuasion and punishment,
the state held sway over the geographical periphery.

Iran's geographical realities hence determined its administrative structure, a
legacy that lasted throughout premodern times and up to the beginning of the
twentieth century. In European languages, the terms *satrap* for "provincial governor" and *satrapy* for "provincial administration" are from the ancient Persian
term for the protector of frontier dominion in the Achaemenid Empire, who
acted as a semiautonomous agent of the King of Kings. The term *ustan*, the
provincial administrative unit of the Sasanian Empire, in contrast, became the
standard suffix for all districts (the suffix *-stan*, as in *Uzbekistan*, for example),
and later sovereign states, of the Persianate world from the Balkans and Caucasus to Central and South Asia.

The delicate arrangement between the center and the periphery was at the
core of the idea of the King of Kings (*shahan-shah*), a key notion in Persian political culture. Beyond the vainglory that was attached to the term—especially
in the twentieth century—the title of the King of Kings was an acknowledg-
ment of a pyramid of power that made the imperial "shah of the shahs" superior
to the "guardian kings," the *padshahs*, of the provincial divisions. Originally
the title of the Persian imperial sovereign of antiquity, the King of Kings was
revived both in Persian epic and court poetry and as an official title of rulers of
the Persian dynasties from the tenth century CE onward, and with even greater
regularity from the Safavid period.

The efficacy of guarding vulnerable frontiers through provincial agents prolonged the idea of a multinational system. The "Guarded Domains of Iran"
(Mamalik-e Mahruseh-e Iran), which became the official title of the country,
perhaps as early as the thirteenth century, implied decentralized autonomy and
acknowledged diversity of cultures and ethnicities. The idea of the "guarded
domains" implied the presence of contesting powers at the frontiers. In this
notion of Iran, one may argue, there was a realistic recognition not only of its
complexity but also of the inherent necessity for the central state.

The confines of sovereignty were expressed in another definitive term. The
word *Iranshahr*, the official name of Iran proper in the Sasanian period (224–
651), reinforced the idea of Iran as a protected political entity dominated by the

state and with a definite geographic space. The term *shahr*, the standard word in Persian for a walled city, etymologically denotes a "domain within which the authority of the shah is enforced." The *shahr*, in effect, is the centralized state as it crystallized within the space of the city, a concept close to that of the Greek polis. In the historical sense it referred to the ten provinces of Iran proper of the Sasanian period, through which the authority of the central government was directly enforced.

The interplay between Iranshahr and its periphery generated a central theme in pre-twentieth-century Iran and was a decisive force in shaping political authority even in the Islamic classical period, when the land of Iran became fragmented or was annexed to a larger Islamic empire. Caving under pressure, the crumbling central authority was overridden periodically by a new and more dynamic peripheral power. Since the first of the Turkic dynasties of Central Asia who came to the Iranian plateau in the tenth century, for an entire millennium nearly all dynastic states of Iran were originated in the nomadic periphery or supported by it.

IRANSHAHR AS A PHYSICAL SPACE

The delicate interplay within the Guarded Domains finds a natural, almost ideal, locale within the confines of Iran's geography. The high-altitude Iranian plateau in western Asia serves as a natural four-cornered fortress, or a walled garden, as the Persian mythology of the Sasanian era imagined the Iranshahr, dominated by mountain ranges on its northern and western ridges and large bodies of water on its fringes. The contrast with the lowlands of Mesopotamia to the southwest and with Central Asia to the northeast is even more pronounced when we look at the dramatic topography of Iran's interior, or at its geological formation, diverse climates, limited rainfall, sparse vegetation, and clusters of human habitat. Decisive though they were in shaping Iran as a country, natural geography neither seriously hindered contact with the outside world nor repulsed the conquering armies from Central Asian steps or the interiors of Arabia. It did not stop the trade caravans coming from all directions either.

The massive and seemingly impenetrable Zagros range, stretching from the northwest to the southeast of today's Iran, separated the heartlands of the Iranian world from Mesopotamia and beyond, and historically functioned as Iran's natural defense line. Significant chasms throughout the Zagros system, however, allowed not only the passage of victorious Arab armies of Islam in the seventh century but also major incursions by the Ottoman armies in early modern times (and, most recently, the Iraqi invasion of 1980–1983). The high-altitude Alborz (Elburz) range, part of a mountain system stretching from the Alps to the Himalayas, extends from northwestern Iran to northern Khorasan, eventually linking to the Hindu Kush range in Afghanistan.

Iran's most serious geostrategic weakness, however, was the passageway into the plains of Central Asia, through which waves of Turkic and Mongolian hordes swept through since the eleventh century. The profound impact of these nomadic invasions, which continued in one form or another up to the end of the eighteenth century, is notable in virtually all aspects of Iran's history and ethnicity. The prevalence of Azarbaijani Turkish and other Turkic dialects in northern Iran is but one indication. The Caucasus and the Alborz ranges, stretching across Azarbaijan and the lush but impenetrable mountain barrier on the Caspian shores, however, proved a more formidable defense against the northern threat. These natural barriers were overcome only in the nineteenth century by Russia's modern armies. Similarly, the coasts of the Persian Gulf never posed a serious strategic threat to the Iranian interior before the arrival of the Portuguese in the fifteenth century and, more effectively, British naval incursions in the nineteenth century.

The maritime trade with Hindustan, Southeast Asia, East Africa, and later Western Europe gave rise to the Persian Gulf as a vital alternative to the overland Central Asian trade with northern China or to the Mediterranean and Black Sea routes in the northwest. Since late antiquity the Persian Gulf had been incorporated into the maritime trade of the south, reaching the western shores of the Indian subcontinent and southern Arabia as far south as Yemen. Lack of forests along the Persian Gulf coasts did, though, handicap Iran's naval predominance in the region. Before the arrival of the European maritime powers, the Persian Gulf trade thus relied mostly on the Omani and Sindhi seafarers.

Being in the global arid zone, Iran is deprived of substantial rainfall at lower elevations, except for a narrow strip of the Caspian coast. In the Iranian interiors the most significant feature shaping the human habitat has been the narrow margin for survival between topographic and climatic extremes. Of the 636,296 square miles of today's Iran, close to half is mountain and desert. Of the remaining 50 percent, less than 15 percent is cultivated, another 15 percent is potentially arable, 10 percent is forest and woodland, and the remaining 10 percent is pasture. The mountainous regions, both on the periphery and throughout the plateau, are sparsely populated. The desert plains of central Iran, separating Khorasan and the southeastern provinces from western Iran, are dotted by agricultural oases and small towns on the internal trade routes that connect them to large population centers on the margins of deserts and foothills of mountain ranges. It has always been a challenge for any central government to hold sway over deserts or the high mountains in the center or on the periphery.

The horizontal and perpendicular dictates of the Iranian landscape, the deserts and the mountains, are further augmented by the limits of temperature and climate, and even more so by the scarcity of accessible water resources, perhaps the single most important contributor to sustainable life on the plateau. Although the annual rainfall on the plains does not exceed twelve inches, there are wide local vacillations. While the deserts and the Persian Gulf littoral receive only five inches on average, the Caspian littoral has an annual rainfall of forty to sixty inches. Heavy snowfalls on the mountain peaks (at least before recent global climate changes) served as the principal source of water for irrigation of the plains. The changing of the seasons is precise, with the Persian festival Nowruz announcing spring and the ancient feast of Mehregan declaring the coming of autumn. Though most of the central plains on the Iranian plateau have a predictable seasonal climate, temperature throughout the plateau at any time of the year can vary by as widely as forty degrees Celsius. These factors further condition human habitats, whether nomadic, agrarian, or urban, to clusters largely on the low-elevation foothills and mountain slopes and in the adjacent fertile plains on the edge of the desert, where drainage from the surrounding ridges is just enough to allow for irrigated cultivation, dry farming, and seasonal pasturing at higher altitudes.

In contrast to the river valleys of Egypt, Mesopotamia, and elsewhere, Iranian river valleys historically played less of a role in the country's food production. Instead, there was heavy reliance on the laborious hydrological marvel of subterranean water recovery. The *qanat* (or *kariz*) sustainable water system, a Persian invention with wide usage from Japan to Morocco, was an ingenious water-delivery system employed throughout the central Iranian plains (before the days of deep-well and river-dam technologies). The subterranean canal, some as long as thirty miles, connected numerous shafts from the mountain slopes, where water was in abundance, to the thirsty plains, where it could irrigate agricultural land and keep inhabitants of towns and villages alive (fig. I.2). Yet it could sustain only a limited population in any given locale. In areas with access to shallow aquifers, lifting water by beasts of burden was an alternative to *qanat* (fig. I.3). Thus, availability of water largely determined the geographical distribution of nearly thirty thousand villages and hamlets throughout the Iranian landscape, where the aridity of the wilderness sharply contrasted to the precious vegetation of a controlled environment.

Moreover, water explained the feasibility of the growth of major Iranian cities at strategic crossroads at the edges of watered plains, where a fertile cluster

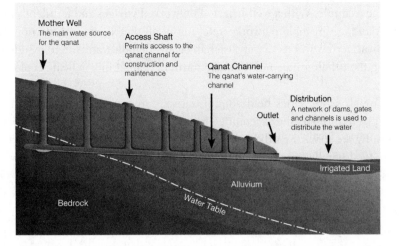

Figure I.2. Cross-section of a *qanat*.
By Sam Baily. https://commons.wikimedia.org/wiki/File:Qanat_cross_section.svg.

Figure I.3. An 1822 sketch of Persian farming tools and irrigation methods.
The World in Miniature: Persia, ed. F. Shoberl, 3 vols. (London, n.d.), opp. 159.

of villages in the hinterlands would supply the cities with food. The cites were connected to one another within and outside the plateau via a network of caravan routes, which passed through strings of smaller market towns, villages, and oases. Within this web of urban, rural, and pastoral habitats, each unit preserved a fair degree of subsistence but also maintained a delicate interdependence with the whole. The Isfahan region, with a metropolis at its heart, is but one example. With a well-irrigated network of villages and farmlands in its hinterland, a vast trade network stretching in all directions, and the nomadic Bakhtiyari territory in its vicinity, Isfahan clearly demonstrates interdependence among the urban, rural, and nomadic forms of habitat in a delicate ecological system.

As much as the cities held administrative, commercial, and cultural sway over the countryside, they accounted for only a small fraction of the total population. By the 1900s the urban population of Iran was no more than 10 percent of the total population of nine million to ten million. The vast numbers of villages, in contrast, which contained the bulk of the sedentary population (perhaps as much as 50 percent before the end of the nineteenth century), were the most vulnerable and economically impoverished sector of the population. Although villagers were not bound by serfdom and there was a fair amount of self-governance within villages, as well as freedom of mobility to other regions, the ancient agrarian regime overseeing the sharecropping system allowed absentee landlords to control the means of agricultural production and a substantial share of the crop (usually three-fifths), leaving the peasants to subsist at best and starve at worst. With the demise (or rather the impoverishment) of the Persian *dehqan* class—the closest equivalent is the English gentry—in the early Islamic centuries, Iran's villages and the land around them often came to be squeezed between the urban elites and the tribal landlords. By means of resistance, peasants' moves from one village to another were not uncommon, nor was a switch between agrarian and pastoral modes of subsistence.

Far more mobile than the peasantry and less subordinate to the city, the tribal pastoralists constituted probably as much as 40 percent of the Iranian population at the turn of the twentieth century. Their nomadic or semisedentary life in regions generally beyond irrigated lands, dictated a subsistent, at times harsh, lifestyle that largely relied on herding. Yet their use of pastures in the vicinity, caused clashes with the sedentary population and disrupted trade, especially during seasonal migrations. Consisting of smaller kinship units within the fluid confederacy of a tribe, the participating subtribes shared a common language and ethnicity, even though some confederacies, such as the Khamseh (meaning "consisting of five") in Fars province, were of diverse origins.

The vast territories under tribal control were virtually off limits to the state's direct jurisdiction and governments invariably appointed, or endorsed, leaders of the tribes from within the tribal elite. At times, strong governments also broke up tribes, organized new ones, or removed and incorporated clans into existing tribes at will for reasons of domestic security and defense of the frontiers. Numerous Kurdish tribes of the northwest were settled along Iran's northeastern borders to safeguard against Uzbek and Turkmen raids during the seventeenth and eighteenth centuries. The tribes depended on the cities as venues for offering their livestock and animal products for sale and replenishing their supplies but also to seek allies in the conflicts with rival tribes or to prevail in internecine power struggles. The tribes' flexible superstructure, however, neither diminished their patriarchal ethos nor sapped their military potency.

Major tribes on the northern Iranian periphery, at least from the mid-Safavid period, were Turkish speaking (such as the Shahseven of Azarbaijan) or Kurdish. The Turkmens (such as the Yamut and Kuklan) roamed the northeastern periphery, whereas the tribes on the southern periphery were largely Arab and Baluch. In the interior the major tribal formations mostly were of Iranian stock (such as the Bakhtiyari of Isfahan and Khuzestan, and the Lur of Zagros), but there were powerful Turkish-speaking confederacies such as the Qashqa'i of Fars province. The tribal mosaic, however, seldom determined lines of political loyalty, especially at times of domestic crisis or war. Before the conscription army of the twentieth century, the tribes were the backbone of Iran's fighting force, and the presence of tribal regiments of different ethnicities in the dynastic armies of the Safavid and post-Safavid periods was the norm. The armies of Nader Shah in the middle of the eighteenth century, for example, included numerous Turkish, Kurdish, Afghan, Turkmen, and Lur contingents.

The "irregular" forces, as these tribal fighters are often identified in Western sources, were almost always mounted, and since the seventeenth century increasingly equipped with firearms, mostly light muskets, the weapon of choice for which the tribesmen of Iran developed an enormous fascination, almost a love affair. The use of firearms decidedly increased the potency and versatility of tribal forces, but it did not essentially change their tactics. The ancient Persian offensive-defensive warfare (*jang va goriz*)—which Xenophon survived to describe in his *Anabasis* from the fourth century BC—still was characteristic of the sorties of the Iranian horsemen in their encounters with modern armies in the early nineteenth century. The required contingents of tribal horsemen summoned by the state were assembled annually to take part in seasonal military expeditions in exchange for partial payment of taxes. Facing modern European armies, though, the Iranian tribesmen no longer had a military edge. By the early part of the twentieth century, they were almost completely subdued by the centralizing state.

PERSIAN CITY AND ITS INHABITANTS

A typical city of the Iranian plateau was an enclosed oasis developed as much by the dictates of the environs as by the necessities of cultivation, trade, and the military, a combination that explained the survival of these cities against many odds, as well as their recovery after natural or human-induced calamities. Connected through a web of caravan routes, they preserved some economic sovereignty, cultural urbanity, political prominence, and ethnic diversity. Surrounded by high walls of thick mud breaks with ramparts, moats, ditches, and other fortifications, the multiple-gated cities controlled not only against illicit traffic but also against hostile forces, be they bandits, marauding nomads, or invading armies. A limited and often crowded space divided into many wards, the city was dominated by two structures at the center: the citadel (*arg*), or the government headquarters and residence, and the bazaar, or the commercial and manufacturing quarter. Complementing the state and the commercial sectors was often the mosque in the center, representing the moral authority of Islam. Numerous other mosques in each neighborhood, moreover, reflected the self-sufficiency of urban wards. Mosques functioned not as mere sacred spaces, but as gathering places to socialize or to stage protests.

Similar to the nomads of the countryside and in villages, patriarchy was the prevailing form of social organization in the cities. Most city quarters consisted of a number of extended families and men of authority, property, and influence, collectively known as notables (*a'yan*), who controlled the city wards. These men wielded influence not only in the affairs of their own wards and in the politics and economy of their city and its environs; they also constituted the backbone of the bureaucracy at the regional level and even in the central government. As in the rest of the Middle East, Iranian urban patricians were of diverse origin and social status, but unlike European nobility, they were not always distinguished from the rest of society by blood and hereditary privileges. They were mostly large landowners of urban or tribal origin, officials in government service, large-scale merchants, and wealthy members of the religious establishment. Conservative in their social outlook and political leanings, the notables viewed themselves as pillars of stability (and when circumstances required, instability) in the city.

Much of the history of urban Iran, especially during periods of unrest and the weakening of the central government, was written from the point of view of the urban notables, their internecine competitions and quarrels, vested interests, political patronage, and control of economic markets. At times, even the rise of one dynasty and the fall of another was not so much the outcome of the overriding might of one powerful tribal leader as it was the support of the patricians for one side against another. The rise of the Qajar dynasty at the end of the eighteenth century is one example. The influence of the notables over the city folks, and especially over the urban vigilantes, known as the *lutis*, occasionally turned city thoroughfares into violent scenes of conflict between neighboring wards.

Fortified by walls at the heart of the city was the citadel (*arg*, originally a fortified military camp in pre-Islamic Iran). The seat of city's government housed
the governor, his ministers and officials, and the army barracks. The citadel
was often located on a hillside or higher grounds overlooking the city, symbolic
of the government's defiant presence and its uneasy dealings with the urban
folk. Yet it could not remain entirely isolated. The *arg* complex was populated
by soldiers, servants, officials, and retainers who had their ties to the city, and
it was served by a string of traders, physicians, artisans, urban officials, village
bailiffs, and tax collectors. The ties to the populace were too numerous to be
easily severed, a fact that explains the government's limitations in enforcing
absolute control. Affairs of the government, at least insofar as involved city notables, were to be settled through negotiation, persuasion, and token punishment rather than sheer force.

The government's interactions with city dwellers were epitomized in the
shape and multifunctional nature of the public square (*maydan*), a vast intermediary space in a typical Persian town that connects the citadel, the market,
the mosque, and the city thoroughfares. An old Persian urban concept with
wide usage throughout the Islamic world and beyond, the *maydan* (lit. "the
space in the middle") was the closest equivalent to the Roman circus and the
English commons. In this public square the government displayed its might
through military parades and playing polo (a game of Persian origin designed
to show the physical fitness and riding skills of the shah and other royalty), as
well as the staging of public performances during national and religious festivals, public executions of rebels, and the flogging of hoarders and profiteers.
For the people the public square was a gathering place to celebrate, protest,
and mourn; to receive and send off caravans; to trade their goods and beasts of
burden; and even to camp (fig. I.4).

The communal function of the *maydan* is evident through its close relationship with another major Persian urban institution, the bazaar. Entering the European vocabulary through the Portuguese language, the word *bazaar* in Old
Persian meant a gathering place (of both humans and for the sale of domestic
animals), comparable to the Greek agora. Located typically on the opposite
end of the citadel, the bazaar served as the commercial, financial, and manufacturing center of the city. A vast network of shops, wholesale trading houses,
caravansaries, storage houses, workshops, and small industries, the bazaar, often
a roofed space, housed guilds and professions in separate clusters along the
arteries and side alleys. Such coexistence in a confined space may not have
engendered entrepreneurial competition, but it did encourage professional
solidarity and, in times of crisis, defiance. Organized in guilds with designated

Figure I.4. A caravan stationed outside the Isfahan city gate.
J. Dieulafoy, "La Perse, la Chaldée et la Susiane," *Le tour du monde* (1881–1882), 180.

leadership, the merchants, traders, and manufacturers of the bazaar constituted one of the most coherent sectors of the society.

The large-scale merchants (*tojjar*) dominated the trade and finances of the bazaar, as well as its political orientation and loyalty. They were an indigenous equivalent of a bourgeoisie with a strong capitalist ethos, but in contrast to their European counterparts, they were often introverted in their private lives and pious in negotiating an Islamic mercantile ethics. Yet in times of crisis they did not hesitate to incite the bazaar to protest, often against government intervention in the market. Because of its economic muscle and its professional cohesion, the bazaar remained an integral part of the political process all through the modern period, demonstrating its power not only through control of the market but also by backing the ulama and other "pressure groups," bribing officials, and staging protests and shutdowns, the latter often being a weapon of great potency.

The caravan (from the Persian term for "army logistics"), the quintessential Persian method of transportation, was the bazaar's long commercial arm extending across the wilderness to markets in other cities. A train of pack animals, usually double-humped Khorasan camels (a sturdy crossbreed between Arabian and Central Asian species), was the most practical and cost-efficient method for the overland movement of goods, operating through caravan routes at a slow but steady pace and relying on a support network of caravansaries throughout the landscape of the Iranian plateau. The crisscrossing caravan network also served as an information network, bringing news from distant lands, a mix of fact and fiction retold by caravanners and pilgrims, which in premodern times was city residents' source of information about a larger community beyond the confines of their own city or village.

CULTURE AND MEMORY

Beyond their indigenous sociopolitical institutions, Iranians shared distinct cultural memories and religious beliefs, which gave them a degree of communal identity long before the arrival of modern ideologies of nationalism. The most evident, perhaps, was the tenacity of the Persian language as an enduring and yet adaptable means of communication, source of literary efflorescence, and repository of collective memories and shared symbols. Belonging to the Indo-Iranian linguistic family (a branch of Indo-European languages), over the course of three millennia Persian evolved from the ancient tongue of Achaemenid times, known as the Old Persian, to the Middle Persian (Pahlavi) of late antiquity, and eventually to "Modern" Persian (*Farsi*) of today's Iran (and with minor variances, Dari of Afghanistan and Tajik of Central Asia). Presumably rooted in the court parlance (*dari*) of the Sasanian period, Modern Persian first developed as a literary medium in the early ninth century CE, only to become, in the following centuries, the lingua franca of the Persianate world, including Iran proper and in use from India to Central Asia.

Remarkable in its development is the Persian language's successful adoption of scripts and borrowing of words and concepts from a variety of linguistic traditions in the rich environment of western Asia and Central Asia. Old Persian not only heavily borrowed words, ideograms, and concepts from Aramaic and other languages of the conquered nations—the Elamites, Babylonians, Assyrians, and Greeks—but its very script was an adaptation of Babylonian cuneiform. Middle Persian, which developed its own Pahlavi script, also borrowed from the Aramaic of Mesopotamia, itself one of the official languages of the Sasanian Empire.

Of even greater impact, Modern Persian of the Islamic period not only adopted the more versatile and more accurate Arabic script, abandoning the confusing Pahlavi script (which itself was an adaptation of Aramaic script), but also came to rely heavily on Arabic vocabulary to widen its literary and conceptual potential. The Qur'an and the *hadith*, in particular, profoundly influenced Persian religious thinking, and Arabic poetics helped shape classical Persian poetry. In later centuries, especially after the Mongol conquest of the thirteenth

century, Persian absorbed a variety of Turkic and Mongolian words and concepts that remained, along with Arabic, inseparable components of today's Persian language and endogenous to Persian culture.

Equally significant on Iran's complex linguistic map is the survival until
very recently of an extraordinary mosaic of regional languages, dialects, and
accents, which functioned side by side with Persian, contributed to it, and borrowed from it. Most notable among these are at least two major dialects of the
Kurdish language in western Iran; the Turkish of Azerbaijan (and other Turkic
variations, such as the Turkmen dialects of northeastern Iran); Baluchi in the
southeast; the Arabic dialects of Khuzestan and the Persian Gulf coasts; a whole
plethora of dialects from the Caspian region and other northern, central, and
southern parts of Iran, many of them relics of the pre-Islamic period; as well as
Armenian, Syriac, and liturgical Pahlavi of the Zoroastrian communities of the
southeast, and the Judeo-Persian of the Jewish communities of Iran.

The diversity of the Iranian linguistic environment and adaptability to both
Arabic and Turkish helped the Persian language to become a vehicle for cultural versatility. Over the course of a millennium, starting in the ninth century
Modern Persian produced a vibrant literary tradition of its own built on epic,
lyrical, and mystical poetry; works of history, ethics, and political didactics;
mystical treatises; popular romance; and in later centuries, passion plays and
religious elegies. As it became more standardized through wider oral and written usage, by the late medieval era Persian was competing with Arabic not only
demographically but also in the production of knowledge. It also competed
with Sanskrit in the Indian subcontinent and held sway over Turkish in Central
Asia (and even in Anatolia) at least up to the seventeenth century.

The cultural content of Persian as a body of oral and written texts took the
language far beyond courtly circles when it first thrived in the early Islamic
period. Even though by the fifteenth century, the Timurid period, large sectors
of the population, especially on the Iranian periphery, conversed in their own
local or ethnic vernacular and produced a body of writings in those languages,
they shared a communal consciousness based on the diverse manifestations of
Persian culture, whether the Sufi liturgy recited in the convents (*khaniqahs*),
stories of the *Shahnameh* (and other variances of pre-Islamic Persian epic poetry and prose) performed by itinerant storytellers, or the sermons and elegies
recited from the pulpits of the mosques.

The *Shahnameh*, and the cultural milieu associated with it, had a lasting
effect on Persian awareness even before Shi'ism became Iran's state creed in
the sixteenth century. Two of Iran's most revered poets and national icons, for
example, the thirteenth-century moralist and lyrical poet Sa'di and the great

fourteenth-century lyricist Hafez, both from Shiraz, were associated with the pulpit, one a preacher of ethical sermons, the other a *hafez* (a person who memorizes the Qur'an by heart and recites it melodically for a living), as his nom de plume indicates. It was in the works of these poets that the genre of lyrical ode (*ghazal*) became the most cherished form of Persian poetry, a genre of amorous odes of longing, often with a mystical subtext, which were amplified in their emotional effect through the medium of Persian music. Remarkably, the life of preaching did not seem to have interfered with the poets' incredibly liberal—indeed, libertine—worldviews as expressed in their nocturnal odes. Their readers, too, were at ease with this seemingly irreconcilable duality.

Poetry occupied a prominent place in the Persian collective memory and perhaps was the most important form of artistic expression in premodern times. Metered and rhymed verse appealed to audiences not only because of the ease of memorization, in a culture still substantially oral, but also because the society praised its bards for employing sophisticated techniques and mastering a language brimming with images and allusions. Lyrical *ghazal* and panegyrics, epics, romances, mystical and religious poetry, as well as satire and metered prose, were widely appreciated in diverse environments ranging from the court to the Sufi convents, mosques, taverns, street corners, and the privacy of one's inner quarters.

While court panegyrics helped solidify a ruler's legitimacy and allowed cultural assimilation of Turkish or Mongolian conquerors, epics and legendary histories, such as the *Shahnameh*, memorialized a national myth. Sufi poetry, with stories, aphorisms, and lyrics, as in the works of the thirteenth-century Jalal al-Din Rumi, offered a mystical discourse with pristine philosophical and psychological dimensions. Praise for his magnum opus, the *Masnavi*, across a wide geographical span, is best captured in a rubric that equated it to "the Qur'an in the Persian language." The liberating space that was Persian poetry thus allowed subversive—indeed, heretical—expressions forbidden in any other media. Skepticism, even about the most sacred beliefs and duties, and sneering at the authorities, religious and political, was tolerated as the fruit of poetic imagination.

A close affiliate of Persian poetry, Persian music, transmitted the messages of lyrics and epics to ordinary people, and as a fluid medium it also was able to incorporate and refashion many of the folk regional melodies and nomadic tunes of Iran and the neighboring lands. The Persian modal system (*dastgah*), with its roots in Sasanian court music, influenced the shaping of musical systems in Anatolia, Egypt, India, Central Asia, and Khotan (Xinjiang). Through forums as diverse as Sufi chants and ecstatic dance, recitations of the Qur'an and the Shi'i elegies and passion plays, court and military music, hymns recited in Zoroastrian temples, the nocturnal melodies of taverns, and means as humble as the chants of itinerant dervishes and vagabond musicians, reed-pipe tunes of shepherd boys, lullabies, and caravanners' calls to their camels, Persian music and its lyrics brought home to the diverse inhabitants of Iran shared experiences and memories. Persian musical instruments, among them the lute-shaped string instruments, also had their share of cultural diffusion. The Persian word *tar* (string) is the name of the long-necked, double-bowled six-string instrument at the core of Persian ensemble, and the word *tar*, signifying "string instruments," influenced a vast geographical array of instruments, from the Spanish guitar to the Indian sitar.

Significantly, these reflective experiences aimed to reconcile contesting sides of Persian, or more broadly, Iranian, culture: the formal with the informal, the mainstream with the subversive, and the inward with the outward. The desire for reconciling opposite trends is evident not only in Persian literature and art but also in Iran's religious modalities, social norms, and political practices, in ways perhaps more pronounced than in cultures of comparable historical experiences. The prevailing duality of the Persian outlook—the private sphere (*baten*, or *nahan*) versus the public (*zaher*, or *ashkar*)—is acknowledged as much in Persian mystical and philosophical discourses as in religious practices, moral dicta, and modes of social etiquette. One can attribute the strong presence of these contrasts, and especially the two-dimensional interior-exterior perspective, to the lasting religio-cultural paradigms and to Iran's complex experience of Islam.

Despite the near predominance of Islam as a socioreligious construct in virtually all aspects of premodern Iranian culture and society, there also persisted an element of subversive irreligiosity—more specifically a non-Islamic, even counter-Islamic, subculture—with equal pervasiveness in most, if not all, areas of Iranian life. Tolerated by most sectors of society as well as by most upholders of authority, this semi-institutionalized "Dionysian" counterreligion often corresponded to the internal, or esoteric, sphere of the Iranian past.

One should note that the Persianate cultural domain was about the only one in the entire Islamic world that over a long period of time preserved and advanced a vibrant and comprehensive musical tradition with an extensive body of lyrical, romance, and epic verse and literature entirely of non-Islamic origin and inspiration. Moreover, it also developed a thriving school of painting and book illustration, with roots traceable to Manichaean and other painting traditions of the pre-Islamic period and with remarkable continuity and artistic creativity. The Iranian world was among the very few cultures, including the Berber (Amaziagh) culture of North Africa, that did not succumb to the predominance of the Arabic language. Nor did it ever entirely abandon its pre-Islamic cultural memories. It preserved not only its endogenous solar calendar along with the Islamic lunar calendar but also its pre-Islamic rites such as the Persian New Year festival of Nowruz at the vernal equinox.

These expressions of identity were preserved over a long period of time despite Islamic disapproval, and even prohibition, and in the face of outcries from the religious establishment. Crystallized into a stern and exclusionist legal tradition, Islamic law emphatically prohibited playing or listening to music for leisure, and reproducing any images of humans and living things in any form; it denounced any preservation and celebration of "pagan" myths and festivals of the pre-Islamic past; and even more intrusively, it banned, at least in theory, social practices such as wine drinking, singing, mixing of the sexes, same-sex affection, recitation of lyrical poetry, and most, if not all, forms of social leisure. Despite political defeat and the relatively swift conversion to Islam, it can be argued that Iran never was fully won over by the predominant culture of normative Islam, perhaps less even than Egypt, the eastern Mediterranean, and Mesopotamia. It converted to Islam at its own pace and on its own terms, and with paradigms and practices it improvised along the way.

Islam as a salvation religion with a distinct notion of prophethood appealed to the endogenous salvation tradition that Iran had inherited from its Zoroastrian past. Though as a religious creed Zoroastrianism suffered steady decline since the rise of Islam (with only a small community surviving in today's Iran, and in India, where they are known as Parsis), the legacy of this Iranian religion had a lasting impact not only on the making of Islamic Iran but also in the shaping of other "Western" religions. In its inception Zoroastrianism upheld a clear notion of a human prophetic agent with inspired scripture, whose mission from Ahura Mazda (the Wise Lord) was to teach his people the wisdom and the agency of choosing between good and evil in this world. The recipients of this wisdom then either are helped by the angels to safeguard their salvation in the hereafter or are misled by Ahriman, the powerful source of all evils, to damnation.

Associated with this sense of prophetic and human choice was the key notion of Paradise (from the Persian *fardis*, from the Pahlavi *pardis*, meaning a walled garden), which later found currency in nearly all religions of the Middle East. This Zoroastrian invention imagined a utopia of consummate blessing in the form of a celestial garden protected from the harms of the wilderness, an idealized Iranshahr surrounded by lofty walls barring outsiders, with lush gardens teeming with game, fruit trees and flowers, domestic animals, and an abundance of water, a world of color and gaiety visualized in Persian garden plans,

Figure I.5. Golshan garden in the oasis of Tabas, in the central
Iranian desert, is typical of Persian walled gardens.
A. von Graefe, *Iran das neue Persien* (Berlin and Zurich: Atlantis-Verlag, 1937), 91.

carpet designs, and miniature paintings (fig. I.5). The Zoroastrian eschatological contribution thus not only lay in the very notions of Paradise, apocalyptic renewal, and millennialism associated with it but also made final salvation conditional on human moral choice between the forces of good and evil.

Inheriting this utopian perspective, either directly or via its Judeo-Christian legacy, Shiʻism also became engrossed with the myth of divine justice and its inevitability. The Shiʻi consciousness found ample grounds for meting out such a vengeful justice in the history of early Islam, especially in the martyrdom of Hosain, the Third Shiʻi Imam, the Prince of the Martyrs, whose tragic fall in the Battle of Karbala in 680 CE stamped in their minds an irrevocable memory. The myth of martyrdom, as represented by Hosain (not unlike at least two Iranian legendary hero-martyrs in the *Shahnameh*), commemorated a heroic but failed attempt to restore to power a legitimate ruler and his deserved community, a paradise lost to the alien forces of oppression and evil. Reversing this could be achieved only through an apocalyptic revolution, whereby the Mahdi, the charismatic savior of Islam, renovates the world, redeems the suffering faithful, and avenges the injustices of the past. The persistence of messianism as a distinctive feature of Iranian religious culture is most evident in the long list of Persian prophetic and crypto-prophetic figures.

The prophetic paradigm stood in contrast to the authority of the religious establishment, which spawned jurisprudence (*fiqh*) and regulated the life of the faithful. The ulama, the men of religious learning, held sway over interpretation of scripture. The jurists (*foqaha*; s. *faqih*), stood at the top of an informal hierarchy in Shiʻi Iran that also included the lower-rank teachers of the madrasa, preachers on the pulpit, reciters of Shiʻi elegies, and even lower, the seminarians, mosque custodians, and presumed descendants of the house of the Prophet.

The jurists were distinct for their legal conservatism, scholastic outlook, and elitist demeanor. These jurists were also known by their judicial status as *mojtaheds* (often inadequately translated as "doctors of law"). They were qualified to issue legal opinions (*fatwas*) to be abided by their "followers" (*moqalleds*). In making their opinions, the mojtaheds exercised limited human reasoning (*ejtehad*; lit. "striving") to utilize the sources of Islamic law. Since the end of the eighteenth century, the concept of following (*taqlid*; lit. "immolation") gave the mojtaheds great legal, moral, and social latitude over the community of believers. What made the ulama especially conscious of themselves as a relatively coherent group was their self-assumed mission to preserve the "kernel of Islam" unmolested against the ever-present threat of heresy. Any sort of nonconformity or innovation contrary to mojtaheds' understanding of the shariʻa was viewed as reprehensible. They were equipped with weapons of denunciation (*takfir*) and censure, which they freely used to mobilized the faithful and to call on the government to come to their aid.

As early as the sixth century CE, Sasanian Iran came up with a dictum that symbolized and sanctified the need for a bond between the state and the religious establishment, above all to combat heresies, which were often labeled "bad religion." Contrary to the modern principle of the separation of church and state, Persian political theorists insisted that the "good government" and the "good religion" were like "twin siblings" who could not survive independent of each other. If either of the two institutions abandoned the other, "bad religion" would prevail and bring about the downfall of both institutions. It was this dictum that for centuries resonated under the domes of the Islamic madrasas and similarly through the corridors of royal power.

Among the authors of the "council to the kings," who prescribed such a symbiosis, was the eleventh-century Abu-ʻAli Hasan Tusi Nezam al-Molk (d. 1092), perhaps the greatest minister and political patron in all of Islamic history. He and other members of the landowning secretarial class were keenly aware of the threat of "subversive" religion because it was prevalent in their time and appealing to the people over whom they ruled. Together with the idea of just rule, symbolized by the aforementioned "circle of equity," concordance between the state and religion was the most pronounced principle in Perso-Islamic political culture. In reality, however, the relationship between the two sources of authority, the quarreling siblings, was guarded at best and antagonistic at worst. In some respects the tension reverberated between them all up to the Islamic Revolution in the late twentieth century.

The fragile accord between the state and the religious establishment, nonetheless, could not be entirely disposed with, because of the crucial function of the jurists as judges and their near monopoly over the judicial system. In contrast to the messianic notion of divine justice to be meted out against evildoers, the mainstream Perso-Islamic political culture viewed justice as a human function that at the macro level was an imperative royal duty bestowed on kings. Justice was the social equilibrium to be maintained by the ruler through acts of reward and punishment and through wisdom and expediency. On a micro level, justice was to be implemented by the jurists through a judicial process that was at best unregulated and at worst haphazard. In practice, however, justice was modified by customary laws and local practices, and by the fact that the shari'a was never codified into a consistent, universal system.

THE SILENCED AND THE UNSEEN

Underneath the prevailing social contract, and the elite who presided over it, there endured a vast sector of the population essentially absent from the public space. If visible at all, they were regulated by binds of the shari'a and by patriarchal mores. It is true, as often noted, that Islamic law was more generous to women than were most premodern orders, including Christian Europe. It recognized women as legal persons and allowed them an economic standing almost equal to that of men. Women received a share of inheritance, albeit less than men did, owned properties, and had the right to accept or reject a marriage proposal and to demand divorce under special circumstances.

The practice of "temporary marriage" (popularly known as *siqeh*), as sanctioned by Shi'i law, gave women some agency through their choice of partner, as well as duration and terms of the marriage. Although open to many abuses, such as prostitution, temporary marriage essentially functioned as an accepted form of cohabitation, which offered some security to women and the right of inheritance to their children. For women of lower classes, such as daughters of peasants in the households of landowning families, temporary marriage with men of higher status served as a form of social mobility.

Yet norms of female inferiority and gender segregation remained strong even as late as the twentieth century under the secularizing Pahlavi rule. The interiors (*andarun*) defined both women's quarters within the carefully segregated

Persian traditional household and a conceptual space as well. Dependency especially in the urban setting on male family members—fathers, husbands, or sons—and displays of loyalty and obedience toward them were accepted norms, as were restrictions on movement and contact with the outside world and limitations on female education and custodianship of their children. Women essentially were recognized, in legal sense, for their reproductive capacity and were valued according to the number of their progeny.

Women, even nonelite women, were nevertheless able to exert a fair amount of agency within the household. A hidden matriarchy below the male-dominated fabric of the elite society, especially in dynasties of tribal origin, had an enormous indirect influence in Iran's political history. Mothers, sisters, and daughters advised the shahs and fought on behalf of the often irresolute or inexperienced heirs to the throne, protecting them against court intrigues and allying themselves with the members of the divan. Outside cities, in village and tribal setting, women were less segregated but more exploited by their male family members to carry out arduous physical duties. In all, Iranian women, as elsewhere in premodern world, experienced a tripartite life cycle: daughterhood, when they were essentially seen as betrothal commodities; wifehood, when they functioned as reproduction units; and motherhood, when they earned power and respect by exerting matriarchal control over their sons.

The history of domestic life in Iran in premodern times, as elsewhere, includes the untold stories of a vast number of women and men who were servants, slaves, concubines, eunuchs, and others—all living under some form of indenture. Repeated raids across Trans-Caucasus in the Safavid and post-Safavid eras, as in the classical Ottoman era, produced a vast number of white female slaves who inhabited the harems of the royalty and the elite and mothered numerous princes of royal families. The purchase of black slaves for domestic service from Abyssinia (Ethiopia), Zanzibar, and the Sudan, imported through the Persian Gulf ports or purchased during the hajj pilgrimage, was also prevalent in affluent households, especially in the Fars province.

The British-enforced ban on the import of the slaves in the middle of the nineteenth century was partially effective but did not prevent slaves from being smuggled through even as late as the turn of the twentieth century. Many descendants of the slaves remained in Persian households, and although it is hard to come by any statistics, their numbers can be safely assumed to exceed two hundred thousand in the early twentieth century, or about 2 percent of the total population. They married other people of black origin and brought up their children within the households of their owners or former owners; children of mixed marriages were not uncommon.

Blacks in Iran were not plantation slaves, as in the New World, but served as house servants, nurses, and trusted attendants. Historical black communities in the Persian Gulf littoral, mostly eking a livelihood through fishing and cultivation, have preserved aspects of their African culture and music. As in Egypt or in Arabia they also mixed with the white population through marriage more freely than they did in the Western world. The slaves did inherit from their owners and could be manumitted in their old age, as recommended by the shari'a. Yet physical punishment and sexual abuses were not rare. In a predominantly white environment, blacks, even if they were not slaves, stood out as anomalies and were treated as such for their accent in Persian, their physique, and their demeanor. Despite inherent racial biases, some blacks nevertheless rose to prominence in the court, where they served as eunuchs, and in the bazaar, where they engaged in trade.

Male slaves were often stereotyped as shrewd and witty, and females as trusted practitioners of white magic. The characterization of black slaves in a genre of popular comedy known as "black acting" (*siyah-bazi*) is a case in point. Here, a black slave lampooned his white master—often a gullible merchant—while he capably attended to his owner's affairs. Role reversals such as this no doubt hinted at the ambivalence with which black people were often perceived by white people. Instances of emotional bonds between the children of the slave owners and their black nannies crossed the boundaries of racial Other.

The religious minorities in Iran's prevailing Muslim society also stood out as an Other and were treated as such, even though communities of Zoroastrians, Jews, and Christians were indigenous to Iranian lands since ancient times. Yet by the early modern times non-Muslims were far fewer in Iran than in the Ottoman Empire or in Hindustan. These communities have further dwindled since the early twentieth century as the result of emigration. The Baha'is, the largest non-Muslim community in Iran, and followers of a religion indigenous to the country, historically were branded as heretics and suffered accordingly. The followers of Ahl-e Haqq (people of the truth), another indigenous religion of Kurdish origin, did not fare substantially better. In the early decades of the twentieth century, the entire non-Muslim population of the country probably did not exceed 5 percent.

The historical place of non-Muslims in the economic and cultural domains nevertheless is significant. Even before the seventh century Armenians of Iran were the core of a vast commercial network that stretched from the Mediterranean to India. The Jewish traders and bankers, too, rendered vital economic functions, even though their social standing steadily diminished since the seventeenth century. As musicians they were important in transmitting classical

Persian music. Though minorities were generally tolerated and the Islamic principle of protecting the "People of the Book" was honored, contingencies of the Shi'i jurisprudence—especially treatment of non-Muslims as ritually polluted (*najes*)—erected insurmountable barriers to the path of social assimilation. A range of discriminatory codes came to define the impoverished Jewish and Zoroastrian communities. They were known as those who were "humbled by Islam" (*moti' al-Islam*). Perceptions of superiority—that Shi'is were the "guided sect" of Islam—expected exclusive salvation for the true believers, an "unfolding destiny" of a sort. The gradual relegation of Sunni communities to the Iranian periphery since the rise of Safavid Shi'ism in the sixteenth century further broadened the sectarian divide. It can be argued that accentuating this sense of internal Otherness—which applied to non-Muslim communities and "heretics" as well—helped reinforce conformity and unanimity among the Shi'i majority in the face of many external perils.

Part One

A Shiʻi Empire

Between the early sixteenth and late eighteenth centuries, the Safavid Empire and its successor states strived to preserve in western Asia an imperial state with a distinct Shiʻi identity. Hostile encounters with Sunni powers on western and eastern frontiers, especially the militarily superior Ottoman Empire, contained the Shiʻi state within the boundaries of Iran proper and peripheral territories. As most of the population converted to Shiʻism in a relatively short period of time, the messianic revolutionary movement of the sixteenth century gradually transformed into a shariʻa-based creed represented by a class of jurists. The Qezilbash Turkish tribal elite who came to power with the Safavids were gradually defanged and replaced with a class of white military slaves. Yet some volatile features of the tribal past persisted.

Despite inherent limits on the economy, the Safavid Empire thrived through trade and found new routes to export its commodities. As the center of the empire gravitated toward the center of the Iranian plateau, the Caucasian provinces, greater Khorasan, and the Persian Gulf were further incorporated into the empire. Commercial and diplomatic contacts with early modern Europe via maritime and overland routes improved, especially after the Portuguese monopoly in the Persian Gulf was brought to an end. Contacts with Europe remained precarious even though they were important for Iran's silk trade. Safavid and post-Safavid Iran never fully overcame the Ottoman commercial block in order to gain secure access to the Mediterranean. Diplomatic contacts with Europe also made the Safavids aware of their geostrategic significance.

The complex set of factors that contributed to the waning of the Safavid Empire and its eventual collapse in the early eighteenth century plunged Iran into periods of nomadic unrest and foreign occupations. It took more than half a century before the problem of succession to the Safavid state was resolved through periodically reignited civil wars along the north-south and Persian-Turkic tribal divides. Economic decline and serious blows to urban life were inevitable outcomes. Nader Shah's expansionist empire proved ephemeral. The Zands, too, only temporarily returned prosperity to southern Iran. The Qajar supremacy in the last decades of the eighteenth century endured in part because of favorable internal and international circumstances, but also because loyalty to Shi'ism contributed to preservation of Iran's socioreligious fabric and the Qajars' reinvented sense of national unity.

SHI'ISM AND THE SAFAVID
REVOLUTION (1501–1588)

In March 1501 Isma'il, a fifteen-year-old descendant from the house of Safavi in the Iranian Azarbaijan, declared himself the "King of Kings" and the founder of a new Shi'i state that came to be known as the Safavid dynasty. Shortly after his accession in Tabriz, the new shah, who entertained wild messianic claims, ordered that all mosques in his realm recite the Shi'i version of the Islamic call to prayer (fig. 1.1). The additional phrase in this version, "I witness that 'Ali is God's friend" (*wali-Allah*), was meant to demonstrate the legitimate authority (*welayat*) of 'Ali, the first Shi'i Imam, and that of his progeny. This was the first time since the eleventh century that a Shi'i call to prayer had been heard from the minarets of an Islamic state. A royal decree issued by Isma'il also required his subjects to publicly curse the Rightly Guided Caliphs of the early Islamic era: "Whoever disobeys, he is to be beheaded."[1]

Isma'il's anti-Sunni audacity was complemented not only by bold practices of the Turkmen warrior clans in his service but also by his patronage of Arab Shi'i jurists who were invited to his kingdom, first from northern Syria and later from southern Iraq and the Arabian Peninsula. The historian Hasan Rumlu, a near contemporary of Isma'il's, notes that at first, "even the basics of the Shi'i law were not known; nor were the rules and rituals of the rightful Twelver Shi'i sect." Until then, to most people in Iran—save for pockets in Khorasan, Gilan, and central Iran—Shi'ism often meant reverence for the House of the Prophet rather than a belief system presided over by Shi'i jurists.

A NEW AXIAL AGE

The rise of the Safavid state and assertion of Shi'ism as religion of the realm at the outset of the sixteenth century (corresponding to the turn of the tenth

Figure 1.1. Isma'il I declaring Shi'ism as the religion of the realm in the
Tabriz Friday Mosque in 1501. The inscription reads: "The king himself
proceeded to the front of the pulpit, unsheathed the sword of the Lord of
Time, may peace be upon him, and stood there like the shining sun."
Anonymous, *History of Shah Isma'il.* © The British Library Board, OR 3248, f. 74.

Islamic century) was a turning point not only for Iran proper but also for the
predominantly Sunni neighboring lands. Since its inception, Shi'ism has been
imbued with a cult of suffering and martyrdom. It also has prompted numerous
messianic movements with crucial roles in the shaping of Islamic history. The
Safavid movement and the brand of Twelver Shi'ism it came to promote were
the end result of one such messianic process. Twelver Shi'ism upheld the belief
that the direct line of succession of twelve Imams from the House of 'Ali is the
sole source of legitimate authority in Islam. The last of these Imams, according
to Twelver Shi'is, is the Mahdi, who is the Lord of the Time. He is currently in
the state of "Occultation" but will return to earth at the End of Time. The Safavid Empire, moreover, came to represent the focal point of a wide geographical
span of Shi'i communities that stretched from tip of the Indian subcontinent to
the eastern shores of the Mediterranean (map 1.1).

Since the middle of the fourteenth century, the Safavid movement had pre-served an embattled enclave in Azarbaijan and eastern Anatolia, despite many military and ideological challenges. Once in power, however, the movement impressed on its subjects a new Shi'i identity and nurtured an imperial state on which Iran's political sovereignty would come to rest. Ruthless and unwavering though Isma'il and his successors were, the Safavids brought (in a relatively short span of time) a degree of conformity to an otherwise disparate mosaic of local dynasties, ethnicities, and cultures that had divided Iran since Timur's time a century earlier. The Safavids thus reconstituted the Guarded Domains of Iran. They patronized a refined Persian material culture and helped articu-late a tradition of Islamic philosophy and theology. They established diplomatic and commercial ties with Europe and facilitated Iran's earliest encounters with Western modernity.

Safavid Iran did not emerge in geographical or political isolation but was very much part of a process that transformed the world, regionally and globally, in early modern times, an age marked by new religious impulses, broadened geo-graphical horizons, shifts in the accumulation of wealth, technological break-throughs, and new thinking about humanity. In the latter part of the fifteenth century, the heartland of Islam, between the Nile and the Oxus (Amu Darya), witnessed the establishment of a new politico-religious system comprising four imperial powers: the Ottoman Empire encompassing Anatolia and the Balkans, and later the eastern Mediterranean and North Africa; the Safavid Empire from Azarbaijan and the Caucasus to the Persian Gulf and greater Khorasan; the Mughal Empire dominating the Indian subcontinent from Sindh and Punjab in the west to Kashmir in the north, Bengal in the east, and Deccan in the south; and the Uzbek confederacy of Central Asia that dominated old centers of Islamic civilization such as Samarkand and Bukhara.

The Gunpowder Empires—as these conquering and quarreling powers were called, because of their increasing use of firearms for conquest and control—were indeed Persianate empires. They were organized around the ancient Perso-Islamic model of government and remained within the parameters of Persian language and culture, at least before the rise of Turkish vernacular in the Ottoman Empire and Urdu and Hindi in the Mughal world (map 1.2).

These imperial systems also shared among themselves, and with the Europe of their time, some rudiments of modernity. Territorially they were tied to rela-tively well-defined boundaries, they sponsored and often enforced a religious creed, their armies enjoyed great firepower, and their agrarian economies be-gan to be affected by a new world system of long-distance trade, overseas and transoceanic contacts, and monetary trends. Changes within these empires

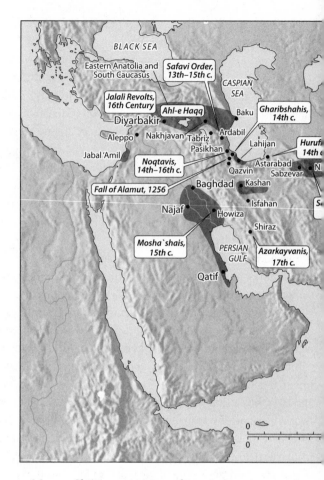

Map 1.1. Shi'i communities and messianic movements in
Iran and neighboring lands, thirteenth
to seventeenth centuries

were in line with revolutionary changes in the world at large. The seventy-year
span between the Ottoman conquest of Constantinople in 1453 and the Mughal
conquest of northern India in 1526 coincided with at least four major global
processes: the "voyages of discovery" and expansion of commercial maritime
empires in both the Eastern and the Western Hemispheres and the coloniza-
tion of the Americas; the shaping of European empire and nation-states with
expansionist ambitions; and the high Renaissance in central and southern Europe, as well as the age of Reformation and Counter-Reformation.

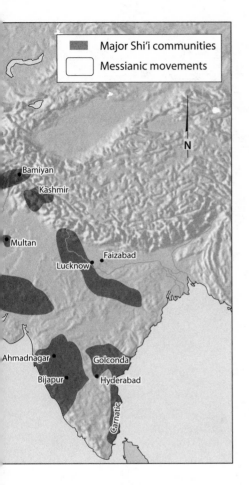

The Muslim empires of this period, similar to the Chinese, Malay, and Japanese societies to the east, were in a transitional stage that combined old patterns of socioeconomic organization and the values of a time-honored culture with new modes of legitimacy and new means of technology. With some degree of historical latitude, the state-sponsored Shi'ism that came about with the rise of the Safavids can be compared to the Reformation in northern and central Europe, and the Sunni reaction to it with the Counter-Reformation. The ensuing schism between the Sunnis and the Shi'is recalls

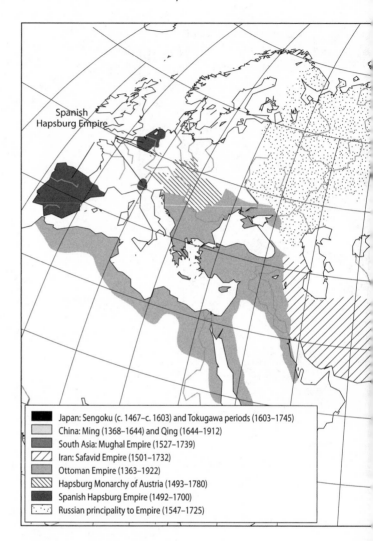

Map 1.2. Early modern empires, 1450–1650

the Protestant-Catholic cleavage that hastened the shaping of the European nation-states (see map 1.2).

The artistic and literary efflorescence that first came about especially in Herat but also in Samarkand and Tabriz was as significant for the Islamic world as the Italian and German Renaissance was for European culture. The military technology that began to change the shape of Muslim domains, from Bosnia to Bengal, was no less palpable than the impact of the same technology in Europe or Japan. Despite such parallels, however, the process of change in Muslim

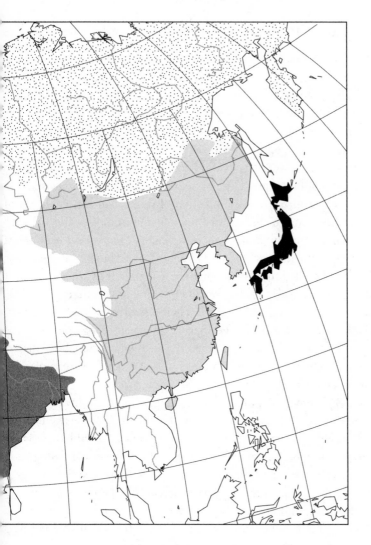

societies did not follow the European pattern and should not be studied as if it did. Though chronologically parallel and equally as revolutionary, and no doubt interconnected, the potential for change in these societies brought about different results. The Safavids' hostile political and ideological relations with the Ottomans, in turn, made Iran's access to the Mediterranean limited and haphazard. Both empires, Safavid and Ottoman, remained essentially introverted and unable to seriously engage with new trends that rapidly were changing Europe of the seventeenth and eighteenth centuries.

FROM A MYSTICAL ORDER TO A MESSIANIC REVOLT

Within Iran, the Safavids' rise to power was the outcome of nearly three centuries of upheavals since the Mongol invasion of the early thirteenth century. More specifically, it was the result of a prolonged period of instability following the demise of the vast Timurid Empire in the second part of the fifteenth century. Despite a short-lived recovery and outburst of cultural brilliance, the Persianate world of the fifteenth century was weakened, at times devastated, and experienced more ethnic divisions than it had before. Politically, it had almost completely fragmented into quarreling principalities and unstable city-states.

Isma'il's rise to power was the culmination of more than two centuries of struggle within the house of Safavi, first for religious authority and then for political power in Azarbaijan and neighboring lands. The Safavid beginnings were rather tragic. Isma'il's grandfather, father, and older brother all met their death on the battlefield fighting crusade-like campaigns in the Caucasus against the Christian population whom they branded as "infidels." These campaigns promised them booty, slaves, and territory. Their enemies saw these leaders of the Safavi Sufi order as nothing more than fanatics with dangerous political ambitions. To their seminomadic Turkmen devotees who gradually gathered around them from neighboring lands, these "Lords of Ardabil" were saints who had been martyred for a divine cause.

The Safavi house originally was among the landowning nobility of Kurdish origin, with affinity to the Ahl-e Haqq in Kurdistan (chart 1). In the twelfth century, the family settled in northeastern Azarbaijan, where Safi al-Din Ardabili (d. 1334), the patriarch of the Safavid house and Isma'il's ancestor dating back six generations, was a revered Sufi leader. He had founded the Safavi suborder, which was still Sunni, composed mystical poetry in the old Azari dialect, amassed great wealth, and enjoyed the respect of rulers and ministers of his time. He lived in an age when Sufi orders enjoyed great popularity because they offered a form of religion more personal and intimate than the shari'a-oriented religion of the jurists and theologians. The Safavi order thrived not only because it attracted peasants and city dwellers around Ardabil and the western Caspian, but also because, under Shaykh Safi's successors, Safavi missionaries in neighboring Anatolia (today's eastern Turkey) and upper Mesopotamia (today's northern Iraq) converted many Turkmen nomads to the order. As early as the mid-fourteenth century, the tomb of Safi al-Din Ardabili was a prominent site of Sufi veneration.

By the fifteenth century the Safavid Sufis, who up to then were moderate Sunnis, had transformed significantly. The order adopted a form of Shi'ism

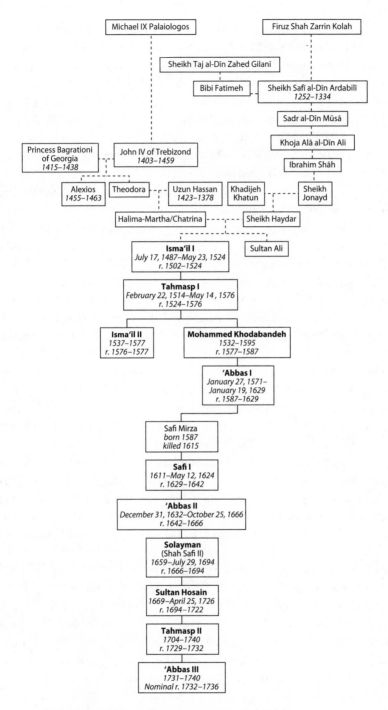

Chart 1. Genealogical chart of the Safavid dynasty

with messianic proclivities and increasingly became a crusading force with
overt political ambitions. The shift was no doubt colored by the "heresies" indigenous to the region, but it also aimed to fill the yawning political vacuum in
western Iran. Economically, the area under the Safavids' fragile control in Azarbaijan was significant because it encompassed trade routes from the Caspian
Sea to Tabriz, and further northwest to the trading centers of the Black Sea and
the eastern Mediterranean. To the political masters of the region, the regular
passage of the caravan trade meant prosperity and power.

To the west of the rising Safavids, who were still a small Sufi enclave, other
mighty powers were in control of the neighboring lands. The Ottoman Turks
were expanding both west and east with a crusading zeal similar to that of the
Safavids. Their exploits were not restricted to Christian lands in the Balkans;
they extended also to the waning principalities of Anatolia. Further toward the
east, the rapidly declining Timurid Empire, with Tabriz as its western capital,
had already fallen to Turkmen dynasties, first the Shi'i Qara Qoyonlu (Black
Sheep, 1380–1468) and then the powerful Sunni Aq Qoyonlu (White Sheep,
1478–1501). Despite their nomadic origins, these Turkmen dynasties upheld a
strong Persian tradition of kingship and court culture, as did most Anatolian
principalities devoured by the Ottomans in the course of the fifteenth century.

The Aq Qoyonlu in particular transmitted much of these Persianate administrative and courtly features to the rising Safavids. To the southwest of the Aq
Qoyonlu were the Burji Mamluks of Egypt and Syria (1382–1517). As the bastion
of Sunni orthodoxy, the Mamluks were in control of the eastern Mediterranean
coasts, but they were unwilling to penetrate deep into the Syrian interiors or
farther north to confront Ottoman military might head-to-head—and probably
incapable of doing so. The temporary political vacuum, lasting for more than
half a century, was ideal for new empire builders in western Iran. A formidable
contender was the founder of the above-mentioned Aq Qoyonlu dynasty, Hasan
Beg, better known as Uzun Hasan ("Tall Hasan," presumably because of his
physique; r. 1453–1478). He managed to reconquer most of the western Timurid
territories and, for a while, return tranquility to the land. He was a prototype,
militarily and politically, for the forthcoming Safavid venture.

The advancing Ottomans were not the only concern of Uzun Hasan. As early
as 1457, mindful of the rising influence of the Safavi order, he exiled the leadership from Ardabil and tried to restrain it both through coercion and through
establishing marital unions. Isma'il's ancestry illustrates how such marital alliances bore fruits beyond Uzun Hasan's intent. Isma'il's grandfather Shaykh
Jonayd, who for years was a hostage in the Aq Qoyonlu court in Tabriz, was
married to Uzun Hasan's sister (see chart 1). Later, Shaykh Haydar, Jonayd's

son and Isma'il's father, married in 1472 Uzun Hasan's daughter Halima, also known by her Christian name Martha. She was born to Uzun Hasan's Greek Orthodox wife, a princess named Theodora Despina Khatun, the daughter of John IV, the penultimate ruler of the Greek house of Megas Komnenos of Trebizond (see chart 1). The Komnenos line was the last of the Byzantine successors (with a history that went back to 1204, when they had fled to the Black Sea port of Trebizond—today's Trabzon—after the Latin Crusaders' conquest of Constantinople). Marriage alliances with Uzun Hasan and with a number of Muslim dynasties, however, did not save Trebizond from the Ottoman advances. By 1461 Mohammad II (Mehmet the Conqueror) had conquered the kingdom, and the last of its rulers—a relative of Isma'il—and his royal family were captured and sent off to Constantinople. Two years later the family was beheaded by order of the Ottoman sultan for their alleged secret communication with Uzun Hasan.

What made the Safavid order especially potent, as Uzun Hasan's successors soon realized, was its combined mystical and military appeal to the Turkmen warriors of the region, who flocked to the Safavi lords of Ardabil once pressure from Ottoman expansion proved unbearable. Organized into a Turkmen confederacy, possibly as early as the 1480s, the Qezilbash (Turkish for "the red heads"), as their enemies first called them, were the backbone of the Safavid fighting force. Organized along tribal lines, both real and invented, their chief function was to launch raids into the interiors of the Caucasus, and most significantly, to Georgia (Gorjestan), to plunder and capture Christian slaves (map 1.3). The twelve-folded cap made of red fabric was a distinct marker of the Qezilbash. It was adopted by Isma'il's father and presumably symbolized devotion to Twelver Shi'ism. In reality, more than anything else, the headgear symbolized devotion to the Safavi leaders, who by the middle of the fifteenth century had begun to refer to themselves with the royal title *shah*.

The beliefs and practices of the Qezilbash were far removed from mainstream Twelver Shi'ism and much closer to the unorthodox beliefs of northwestern Iran and eastern Anatolia. Generally labeled as *ghulat* (religious exaggerators), reverence for 'Ali, the first Shi'i Imam, was at the core of the religion of Ahl-e Haqq prevalent among the Kurdish, Turkmen, Yazidi (originally known as Izadis) and other inhabitants of the region. The diffuse creed of the Qezilbash included non-Islamic folklore ranging from crypto-Zoroastrian beliefs to shamanistic practices, the latter a relic of a distant pagan Turkmen past in their Central Asian homeland. What was remarkable about these nonorthodox trends in the borderlands was a dormant form of messianism, one untouched by the strictures of urban Islam. Notions of divine inspiration and reincarnation

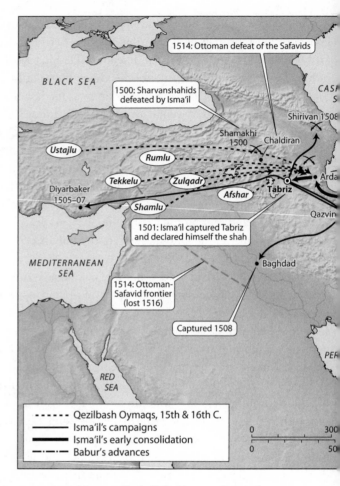

Map 1.3. Early Safavid expansion under
Shah Isma'il I, 1499–1524

were not uncommon, and the Perfect Guide (*morshed-e kamel*), as the Qezil-bash called their Safavid master, was viewed not only as the reincarnation of 'Ali but also as a manifestation of the divine in human form. The potentials for such deep loyalties were immense. As it turned out, the heretical "extremism" of the Safavi order, as its opponents saw it, would successfully channel an amorphous nomadic mass of followers into a powerful military force.

The Qezilbash followers of Isma'il, a mix of nomadic refugees who had lost their pasturelands, and their way of life, to the advancing Ottoman armies, had enigmatic origins. The name of the "tribes" of the Qezilbash confed-

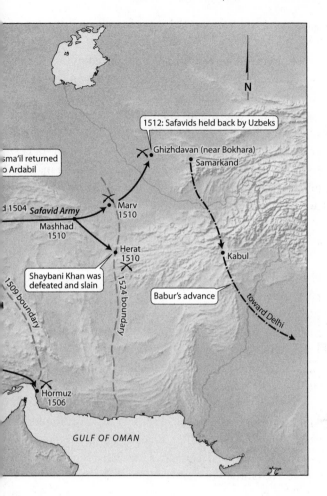

eracy derived from regions they considered to be their homeland. The Rumlu presumably came from Rum (or Anatolia, as Muslims identified the former Byzantine province). The Shamlu from Sham, or Syria; the Takkelu from the Takkeh in the northeast corner of the Mediterranean; the Ostajlu from Ostaj in the southern Caucasus. Others, such as the Qajar and the Afshar, were named after regions in Azarbaijan or after their presumed tribal ancestors. In the early sixteenth century, there were seven major "tribes" of the Qezil-bash, all of whom shared a nomadic or seminomadic lifestyle, the Turkish language, a "messianic" faith, and hatred of the Ottomans. Each tribe was made up of numerous clans and subclans who better reflected the ethnic composition of the Qezilbash.

A charismatic and ambitious young man, Isma'il epitomized the revolutionary process that propelled him into the dual position of a Persian shah and a Sufi master (pl. 1.1). In 1498, when he came out of hiding in the Caspian town of Lahijan to begin his long-awaited revolt, his chances did not seem better than those of his slain predecessors. Yet his capture of Erzenjan in eastern Anatolia, where his grandfather Uzun Hasan had been defeated by the Ottomans in 1473, and soon after his advances in Azarbaijan and the Caucasus against many local contenders, promised something different. Even though he was still in his teens, to his senior followers, who had hosted him while in Lahijan hiding, Isma'il appeared to be a sacred leader who had come to avenge the martyrdom of his forefathers and deliver worldly blessings of land, flocks, and slaves to the Qezilbash.

There was more to Isma'il's claim to power than just his illustrious Sufi ancestry. As a grandson of Uzun Hasan he saw himself as a legitimate heir to his throne and with an agenda to reconquer what had been lost by Hasan's successors. He must have also been aware of his royal Greek descent through his mother, Martha. His ill feelings toward the Ottomans were deepened not only by the memory of Uzun Hasan's decisive defeat at the hand of Mohammad the Conqueror but also by the terrible fate of his maternal grand uncle and other relatives.

To a mix of Turkmen messianism and ancestral claims, Isma'il added a third element of Twelver Shi'ism. While still in hiding in Lahijan, an old Shi'i stronghold in Gilan province, some local dignitaries instructed him in the rudiments of Twelver doctrine. As it turned out, Isma'il himself was not particularly keen on practicing the Twelver (or Ja'fari) law, but it was this brand of Shi'ism that he came to promote with zeal throughout his reign. It could be argued that the sacred kingship he represented, a union between Persian kingship and messianic Shi'ism, could be accomplished only by the promotion of Shi'i shari'a. It is no accident that despite the haphazard beginnings of Safavid rule, Isma'il's Twelver conviction, and its enforcement as the state creed by persuasion and by force, remained an unflinching commitment. Although at first glance it may seem that at the age of fifteen Isma'il was no more than a puppet of the Qezilbash elite (and no doubt they did exert great influence on him), it was apparently his own commitment to Twelver Shi'ism, against the advice of his Qezilbash chiefs, that persuaded him to convert the predominantly Sunni population of his expanding empire.

BUILDING A SHI'I STATE

In the first decade after his accession, between 1501 and 1511, Isma'il conquered nearly all of Uzun Hasan's empire and more. In a series of brilliant campaigns marked by his personal valor and devotion of the Qezilbash irregular forces, he annexed close to seventeen semiautonomous and autonomous principalities, city-states, and local dynasties (see map 1.3). The conquered territory stretched from Diyarbakir in eastern Anatolia, a stronghold for the Qezilbash, to the Shar-vanshah kingdom of the southern Caucasus, and from Azarbaijan and Kurdistan to the western Iranian provinces (known as Persian Iraq). Soon Isfahan, Shiraz, Yazd, Kerman, and Khuzestan in central and southern Iran—even as far south as the shores of the Persian Gulf—were annexed to the nascent empire.

At the outset of his reign, Isma'il adopted distinct strategies to consolidate and to convert. He consciously aimed to create not only a Shi'i state but also a Shi'i society. In waging war against his many rivals both to the east and to the west, his method of conquest involved terror and coercion, perhaps more out of expediency than faith, and promotion of the Shi'i shari'a by appointing clerical representatives to the newly conquered territories. Praising 'Ali, the First Imam, and his House and cursing the first three caliphs of early Islam from the pulpit of the mosques as well as in the streets, Safavid itinerant propagandists, known as the "denouncers," demanded that their terrified audiences respond to their anti-Sunni curses by uttering the words "more upon them and no less." The exercise of "denouncing" complemented by "affirming" loyalty to 'Ali and his House was commonplace. The affirmation also included defaming some of the companions of the Prophet as well as slandering 'Aisha, the Prophet's favorite wife, for her opposition to 'Ali.

Any public resistance met with grave retributions. In Tabriz, where there was initial resistance to the Safavids' forced conversion, thousands of Sunnis, perhaps as many as twenty thousand, were massacred. If this was meant to be a horrifying example for Sunnis in other cities, it was effective, for with very few exceptions, the general public, mostly belonging to the Sunni Shafi'i school, complied once their Sunni religious leadership was sufficiently intimidated or, more often, eliminated. In Isfahan and Shiraz, which both fell to the Safavids in 1503, Isma'il executed a number of resisting Sunni dignitaries, judges, and preachers. In Baghdad, which was conquered by Isma'il in 1508, the members of the local ruling dynasty and their supporting Sunni elite were executed, and the shrine of Abu Hanifa, the eighth-century Sunni jurist and founder of the Hanafi school of law, was desecrated and destroyed. On his way back through Huwiza, on the banks of Shatt al-Arab, Isma'il defeated the house of Musha'sha', a local dynasty with its own messianic claims and massacred the ruling elite.

In at least two mountain fortresses in Mazandaran province, which fell to the Qezilbash army in 1504, Isma'il reportedly ordered the massacre of the entire population, perhaps in vengeance for their stiff resistance. In the same campaign, after the capture of the fortress of Usta in the central Alborz range, where Morad Beg Bayandori, the last of the Aq Qoyonlu princes and a blood relative of Isma'il had taken refuge, the Safavid conqueror ordered his wild Qezilbash devotees to broil the prince alive and devour him. Upon defeating the local Persian dynasty of Shervan in the lower Caucasus, against whom Isma'il's father and grandfather both had fought and died, he massacred the ruling family and exhumed and burned the bodies of their ancestors, a practice he believed would deprive them of final redemption. The Shervanshahids, a local Persian dynasty whose rule dated to the middle of the ninth century, controlled a strategic crossroads in the southeastern Caucasus and prospered from the region's silk trade (see map 1.3).

Isma'il's ferocity and the atrocities committed by his unruly Qezilbash hordes were followed soon after by a systematic and enduring program of Shi'i indoctrination. For this, Isma'il and his advisers found willing allies and ideological commissars among the Shi'i jurists of Jabal 'Amil in southern Lebanon. The Shi'i scholars who long had been persecuted in their homeland by the Mamluk rulers, and later by the Ottomans, found in Isma'il an ideal patron, and in Safavid Iran a refuge for a life of respect and privilege. The enduring symbiosis between the Safavids and the Arab jurists, who began to arrive by the dozens at the court of Isma'il and his successors, was beneficial to both. Unlike the indigenous Shi'i ulama of Iran, or those Sunni jurists and dignitaries who, under duress or to protect their privileges had converted to Shi'ism, the Arab jurists were newcomers to the Iranian scene, had no knowledge of Persian, and the customs and traditions of their host country were alien to them. Thus, they could not easily build a network of local loyalties independent of the Safavid state.

The loyalty of the Jabal 'Amil ulama to the Safavid state also served the Qezilbash chiefs, for they were adapted even less than the Arab jurists to their new Iranian environment. They could barely converse in Persian, if at all, and could scarcely trust or even tolerate the rising Iranian element in the Safavid court and administration, let alone the diverse Iranian public in the remote provinces to which they were assigned as military governors. The Tajiks (from the Persian *tazi*, "alien"), as the invading Qezilbash labeled the indigenous Persian population, posed a serious threat to both the Turkmen and the Arab elements, a competition that affected every aspect of government and society for at least a century.

Isma'il's method of conquest, moreover, allowed the Qezilbash to occupy a position of influence in the newly emerging Safavid state. In the patterns of Turkmen tribes, many settled in the newly conquered territories as a military force and a new landowning class. Yet even at the outset of his reign, the young shah was well aware of the need not only for a centralized state administration but also for a balancing of the major three ethnic groups in his service. He re- lied on the small Qezilbash clique known as the Sufis of Lahijan to hold a num- ber of important high offices. He appointed a regent (*vakil*) to oversee the affairs of the state. Isma'il himself had a noticeable aversion to administrative duties, even though he possessed innate political insights. The *vakil* also occupied a powerful military position as commander in chief of the Safavid army. That this powerful office should first be assigned to Isma'il's Qezilbash childhood tutor from the Lahijan circle was not surprising. Another Qezilbash was also assigned to the sensitive office of *khalifat al-khulafa* (caliph of the caliphs, or chief of the deputies) to oversee maintenance of "spiritual" ties with the shah, their emblematic Perfect Guide, through a network of agents in each Qezilbash division. The post combined ideological oversight at home as well acting as a kind of agent provocateur, especially in the Ottoman territories.

Yet the Qezilbash's unfamiliarity with the state administration (*divan*) soon convinced Isma'il of the need for a division of power. Parallel to the office of the *vakil*, he appointed Shams al-Din from Lahijan, his own Persian teacher, to the office of *sadr* (lit., "heart"), with full authority over the religious affairs of the state. The *sadr* was responsible for all clerical and judicial appointments, chari- table endowments (*awqaf*), and most critically, the conversion of the general public to Twelver Shi'ism. At the same time, Isma'il appointed another former Persian guard of his as *vazir* (vizier) to head, among other tasks, accounting and collection of taxes.

In due course the power of the Qezilbash was further checked, and eventu- ally subdued, as the shah tilted further toward a succession of Persian officials. In 1508 he appointed to the office of *vakil* Najm al-Din Rashti, a goldsmith from Rasht and an old companion of Isma'il. He may have financed Isma'il's early rise to power. The ascendance of Najm gave the office of the *vakil* the kind of authority associated with that of the chief minister in the Persian model of gov- ernment while the religious affairs remained under the *sadr*, another Persian of- ficial. Under Najm's successor, a business-savvy Persian from Isfahan known as Najm II, the office of the *vakil* gained greater prominence. To the dislike of the Qezilbash chiefs, Najm II even led the Safavid forces in military campaigns.

The Turkmen-Tajik tension that flared up periodically during and after Isma'il's reign also involved the jurists from Jabal 'Amil. But no matter how eagerly the Qezilbash chiefs and the Arab ulama resisted the indigenous Persian element's rise to prominence, they could not evade the dictates of a transforming state. The paradigm shift from a messianic crusade to a bureaucratic state appeared inevitable. The shift did not happen overnight, yet Isma'il managed to strike a fragile equilibrium among the restive Qezilbash and their Persian rivals. To be sure, Isma'il felt deeply indebted to the Qezilbash and had to grant them booty and pastureland. He was obliged to assign provincial and district governorships to them as tenured fiefdoms (soyurghal). In these fiefdoms the tent-dwelling Turkmen warriors roamed at the expense of the settled rural and urban populations. Yet the early Safavid drive for territorial conquest and for conversion to Shi'ism also entailed a vision for a Persian imperial state, no matter how haphazardly it would be attained.

FACING THE SUNNI FOES

In the first decade of its creation, Isma'il's nascent state replicated that of the Aq Qoyonlus. Yet his vision of a universal empire emulated Timur's world-conquering ambitions of more than a century earlier. Despite Isma'il's initial hesitation to march on Herat, by 1510 new incentives made him embark on an eastern campaign. The death of Sultan Hosain Bayqara (r. 1470–1506), a celebrated patron of Persian art and culture, whose domain for three decades had remained an island of urbane refinement, exposed the region to new nomadic incursions from further north. By 1500 already a large Uzbek contingent under the leadership of Shayban (or Shaybani) Khan, a descendant of Changiz Khan and founder of the Uzbek seminomadic kingdom, captured Samarkand, the capital of the eastern Timurids. They ravaged much of the region and caused havoc over greater Khorasan as far south as Marv (Merv in today's Turkmenistan) and Mashhad in northeastern Iran. The arrival of the Uzbeks, the latest wave of Turkic-Mongolian incursions into the interiors of Central Asia, posed a grave challenge to the security of the region. Shayban Khan, who saw himself as the legitimate heir to Changiz Khan, eventually managed to capture the prized city of Herat in 1507, putting an end to the last of the Timurid kingdoms.

If Isma'il's needed any further motive to wage a war against Shayban, the capture of the city of Mashhad by the Uzbeks, the looting of the shrine of the Eighth Shi'i Imam of its riches, and declaring the Safavid ruler a dangerous heretic, provided the pretext. In 1510 when he embarked on a campaign against Shayban in Marv, the ground for a Sunni-Shi'i showdown had already been laid. Whether it was an old ploy—luring the enemy into the interior before waging battle or the inferiority of Uzbek forces to those of the Qezilbash, the Uzbeks were routed and Shayban himself was trampled to death on the battle-field (see map 1.3). The defeat of the Uzbeks was an important turning point. The capture of both Marv and Herat set limits on the eastern expansion of Sa-favid Iran, frontiers that remained essentially in place until the mid-nineteenth century, despite many later Uzbek incursions. Isma'il's halfhearted sorties after Herat to conquer Samarkand and beyond, however, proved futile. In contrast to Samarkand and Bukhara, which remained Sunni strongholds, Herat fully incorporated into the Safavid Empire, in part because of its earlier Shi'i-Sufi proclivities, and as the eastern capital of the empire, vastly contributed to the shaping of Safavid culture.

Isma'il celebrated his victory with his typical cruelty. He turned the skull of Shayban Khan, his ideological adversary, into a gold-plated wine cup, witness to his long hours of heavy drinking. Shayban's dismembered right arm was sent off to Prince Zahir al-Din Babur, the future founder of the Mughal Empire, who then was in control of Kabul. It was a symbolic reminder of Safavid reach. The reflective Timurid prince took heed and for a while collaborated with the Safavids against their common Uzbek enemy. He even pretended to be a Shi'i client of Isma'il. Later he headed south to the less formidable tranquility of northern Hindustan. The stuffed skin of Shayban Khan's head also served as an-other carnal dispatch to the Ottoman Sultan Bayazid II (r. 1481–1512). The hei-nous act, though not entirely outside the norms of the time, generated outrage in the Ottoman capital, reaffirming the perceptions of the Safavids as fierce heretics. The rest of Shayban's body was ritualistically devoured by a cannibal clan of the Qezilbash as proof of their devotion to their Perfect Guide.

The Sunni dignitaries of Herat, Marv, and Balkh (who fell under Safavid rule soon after), did not fare any better at the hands of the Qezilbash army, which did not hesitate to massacre the defenseless or coerce them to Shi'ism. The Per-sian (Tajik) officials were no less merciful. Isma'il's chief minister, Najm II, in 1513 after the fall of the Uzbek fortress of Qarshi (on the way to Bukhara), razed the fortress to the ground and reportedly massacred the entire Sunni popula-tion, including children, and their domestic animals. He felt consoled having retaliated for the massacres centuries earlier in his hometown Isfahan by Mon-gol and later by Timurid invaders.

The news of Isma'il's victory over the Uzbeks and consolidation in the east did not sit well with the Ottoman sultan in Istanbul or with the Mamluk sultan of Egypt and Syria. The Safavid movement had become a rallying point for the restive population of Anatolia and upper Mesopotamia whose territories were disputed among three powers. The triumphant prophet of Ardabil thus was a subject of reverence for many of the region's Shi'i Alawite population. Inspired by Safavid missionaries, the Turkmen communities of the Ottoman Empire, as far west as Konya (in today's Turkey), were mobilized into a fervent messianic movement under Shah-Qoli Baba of the Takkelu tribe (on the northeastern Mediterranean coast). Seeking to replicate Isma'il's revolt, they rebelled against the Ottoman state and its provincial agents, perhaps in anticipation of a union with the Safavids. Shah-Qoli was killed in 1511, and the movement halted temporarily, yet even then, the Ottomans' anxiety over losing much of their Asian possessions was not eased. Nor was their hatred for Isma'il diminished, even though he disowned Shah Qoli and apologized to the Ottomans for the atrocities committed during the revolt.

Facing the possibility of a mass Turkmen exodus into the Safavid realm, the Ottoman Sultan Bayazid II opted for conciliation, at least on the surface, and welcomed Isma'il's gestures to establish good neighborly relations. Bayazid, despite a serious revolt from his own son, Salim, who was critical of his father's policy of Safavid appeasement, nevertheless recognized Isma'il as the legitimate ruler of Iran and tried in vain to strike some sense into his fervent head. He even addressed Isma'il in his correspondence as heir to the kingdom of Kaykhos-row—the legendary great king of the *Shahnameh*—and to Dara (Darius) of the ancient Persian Empire. He further advised Isma'il to behave royally, preserve his precious and strategically vital kingdom with justice and equanimity, end forced conversions, and leave in peace with his neighbors.

The situation, however, changed dramatically in 1512. In stark contrast to his father, Salim I (r. 1512–1520), who already had sensed the Safavid danger when he was governor of the Ottoman Black Sea provinces, left no room for compromise. There were many good reasons why Salim, who forced his father to abdicate, was labeled "fierce" (Turkish *yavuz*, rendered in English as Salim the Grim). From the outset he was determined not only to crush the remnant of the Shi'i resistance in Anatolia but also to teach a lesson to, and possibly even eliminate, the reckless heretic Isma'il, who in his view was exporting his Shi'i revolution to Ottoman lands. At the core of Salim's rage was his fear of a Safavid offensive from the east, an old concern of the Ottomans who at the time were making new advances in the Balkans and Eastern Europe. A century earlier, in 1400, Timur's routing of the Ottoman defenses in Bursa and his caging of the Ottoman sultan for public display, was a humiliating memory for a state that was founded on the idea of conquest. That the Ottoman Empire one day succumb to the Shi'i propaganda in its heartland, and even within its own military, was an alarming possibility that was to be avoided at any cost.

Disdainfully labeling Isma'il as the "Sufi kid" and the "Ardabil lad" and addressing him in official correspondence with obnoxious terms, Salim closed all negotiating channels with the Persian shah. While preparing for his anti-Safavid campaign, the first and one of the most crucial of his short but tumultuous reign, he once more wrote to Isma'il. Shortly before reaching the Iranian frontier, Salim called Isma'il "prince" and "the ruler of the Persian kingdom, the owner of the realm of oppression and tyranny, the master of sedition and commander of the rebels, the Darius of his time and the Zahhak of the age, equivalent of Cain." He further accused Isma'il as having

> subjected the pure Mohammedan nation, may peace and greetings upon its
> founder, to his deceptive creed and debunked the foundation of the solemn
> faith [of Islam], hoisted the banners of tyranny by means of coercion . . .
> and encouraged his own wicked Shi'i followers to rape the chaste women
> and freely shed the blood of the dignitaries, . . . destroyed mosques and built
> houses for idol worshiping . . . and called the luminous Qur'an a myth of the
> bygone times.

Referring to the fatwa of the Sunni ulama denouncing Isma'il, the Ottoman sultan went on to say that "since the divine providence and the sacred destiny has placed in our mighty hands the prompt purging of that outright heresy, to abide by that crucial duty, we proceeded toward that land [Iran] . . . so that by the thundering might of our triumphant sward we remove the thorny scrub that has grown in the stream of the lofty shari'a and eradicate and cast away the invasive weeds that has so rapidly spread." He then warned the Safavid ruler to "remove the cotton of neglect from the ear of vigilance, place the shroud on his shoulder and be prepared since . . . by the [Qur'anic] command of 'kill them whenever you encounter them' we are coming to ruin your fortune and leave not [a single person] on that land."

Isma'il's response to this furious declaration of war was dismissive, even cynical, and yet conciliatory. He sarcastically noted that he found his enemy's hostile tone, "driven by courage and audacity," entertaining yet he could not detect the source of hostility since relations with Salim's late father, as Isma'il claimed, was cordial. "The reason I have indeed spared your domain were twofold," he explained. "First, that the majority of the people of that realm are devout followers of my splendid ancestors, may the forgiving God place mercy upon them. Second, my respect for that warrior house [i.e., the Ottomans] is old. We did not wish to impinge on that land a misfortune similar to the time of Timur; indeed, we still don't wish it on you and hence are not offended by such words. Why should we? Animosity among the kings is an old practice." He further intimated that all the "inappropriate words" in the letter should be treated as nothing but the withdrawal symptoms of the "opium-addict secretaries" whose daily doses were delayed. He even sent off along with his "friendly reply" to Salim a golden box of opium bearing the royal seal in order "to bring back soberness" to the royal secretaries, who may have included, as Isma'il's symbolic gift suggested, a number of Persian refugees to the Ottoman court. With an almost fatalistic tone, Isma'il then admitted that though he was busy hunting around Isfahan, he had no choice but to start preparing for war (fig. 1.2). He ended with a well-known motto of Safavid propaganda reflective of his own illusive self-confidence: "For long we tested in this punishing world / Whoever opposed the house of 'Ali, was deposed."

Figure 1.2. A scene of Timur hunting in Hindustan is reminiscent of Isma'il I's frequent hunting expeditions, even on the eve of the Battle of Chaldiran.
Sharaf al-Din 'Ali Yazdi, *Zafar-nameh-e Taymuri*, Golestan Palace Library, Tehran, Ms. No. 708, Tabriz, 935/1528. Attributed to Kamal al-Din Behzad.

Salim's anti-Shi'i campaign began at home. After first preparing a meticulous register of the Turkmens of Anatolia, he carried out a systematic massacre of these presumed Safavid sympathizers throughout the region. The Ottoman forces reportedly killed forty thousand of the local inhabitants. The act of terror also involved atrocities, rape, enslavement of Shi'i women and children, and wholesale banishment of Shi'i villages to other provinces. The Ottoman Sunni jurists considered the massacre legitimate, and even furnished the necessary license for an anti-Safavid campaign. The eternal reward for killing one Shi'i, a fatwa by the mufti of Istanbul declared, was equal to killing seventy Christian infidels.

In the spring campaign of 1514, one of the largest Ottoman armies was assembled under Salim's own gaze in Edirne, the old Ottoman capital on the European side. The Ottoman forces, the most advanced war machine of the time, consisted of 160,000 cavalry and infantry troops, of which 12,000 were the elite Janissary regiments (see map 1.3). The multiethnic Ottoman army brought with it two hundred cannon, one hundred field guns, and well-maintained land and sea logistical lines (via the Black Sea), including eight thousand camels and other beasts of burden. Ottoman military discipline, and Salim's single-mindedness, drove the advancing army to cover more than nine hundred miles—the entire length of Anatolia—in four months, arriving in July 1514 near the plain of Chaldiran in northwestern Azarbaijan, fifty miles northwest of the city of Khoy, where the decisive battle for the future of the region was waged.

Salim, his grand vizier, and his commanders (those, at least, who survived his fits of rage and the many executions) encountered in Chaldiran a meager Safavid cavalry force of less than twenty thousand. The remarkable imbalance should be attributed more to Isma'il's inability to raise a larger force than to his mere miscalculation. The Ottoman campaign came at a time when the Safavids faced a renewed Uzbek incursion in Khorasan, a coordinated effort with the Ottomans, perhaps, to overwhelm the Safavids by forcing them to fight in two fronts. All along, Isma'il was no doubt counting on Salim to change his mind, partly because of the difficult terrain and logistical obstacles on the way to the Iranian frontier, which indeed caused some discontent among the Janissaries. Moreover, in Isma'il's view there were no legitimate grounds for Ottoman belligerence. What was at stake, and what the Safavids' fate depended on it, was predominance in the struggle between the two powers: the imperial Sunni establishment with a vast and disciplined army versus a Shi'i revolutionary movement with a spirit of fatalistic nonchalance.

Isma'il must have harbored mixed feelings about how to respond to the Ottoman advance. His scorched-earth tactics and refusal to give battle were well-tested methods of warfare designed to persuade the enemy to give up and return, a possibility surely enhanced by the inhospitable terrain of northwestern Iran. Yet by late August Isma'il was almost forced to give battle in Chaldiran, for that was the last strategic line of defense before he would dangerously expose his capital, Tabriz, 120 miles to the east. His record of past victories might have made him overly confident about the superiority of the Qezilbash cavalry and its spirit of sacrifice on the battlefield, a fact that explains his lax preparation despite the glaring disparity in troop numbers. As a king-prophet defending the cause of 'Ali and his sacred house, Isma'il could not have doubted that divine providence would prevail.

The fatalist strain running through Isma'il's political life appeared strange even to his own Qezilbash lieutenants. Whether to overcome combat fright or out of sheer self-confidence, he and his Qezilbash chiefs spent the night before the battle drinking until dawn. On the morning of the fateful conflict, August 23, 1514, the drunkard Isma'il began his day hunting quail on the adjacent plain while his vanguard forces suffered heavy blows from Turkish artillery. Even when he joined his loyal Qezilbash troops, his sorties were a mix of valor and vagary rather than studied moves with clear strategic objectives. It is conceivable even that the daring quality of his warfare, which in the past had brought him much success, would have saved Isma'il this time, were it not for the potency of Ottoman firepower, which the Safavids lacked.

Even by 1514 the Safavids did not seem to have appreciated the decisive effectiveness of firepower, even though cannon had been employed in eastern Iran a quarter of a century earlier under the Timurids. Moreover, Isma'il's own maternal grandfather, Uzun Hasan, had been soundly defeated in 1473 by the Ottoman Sultan Mohammad II because he could not access the firearms that had been promised to him by his Venetian allies. The Safavid reluctance to use firearms may have been, as has been often noted, because they considered them unmanly and contrary to the chivalrous code of war (pl. 1.2). Isma'il's Qezilbash devotees, believing they were shielded by the blessing of their prophet, were apparently bothered even less by the thunder of the cannon, at least before they saw them in action. Even when they did see the Ottoman cumbersome muzzle-loading harquebuses, the standard weapon of the Janissaries, and the heavy field guns, with their short range and inaccurate targeting, they did not seem to have been impressed. In fact, the effectiveness of the Ottoman artillery, perhaps the most advanced in the early 1500s, was mostly in siege warfare rather than on the battlefield, which may have encouraged the Safavids to face the enemy on the open plain rather than from within a walled fortress.

At the outset the Safavid hope for victory did not seem wholly misplaced. Under Isma'il's command, the Safavid light cavalry, which was known for its agility and swift maneuvering, embarked on an offensive that almost destroyed the Ottoman left flank. The advances on the right were also impressive—until the Ottoman cannon finally found the chance to fire. By the end of the day, the dual effects of the cannon thunder and shelling, perhaps more the former than the latter, shattered the Safavid defenses. Isma'il barely escaped captivity, but a number of Qezilbash chiefs and Safavid officials fell in the course of the battle or were captured. Also among the captives was Isma'il's influential wife, Tajlu Khanum, who shortly afterward escaped from the Ottoman camp and rejoined her husband. The ancient Persian practice of bringing women to the battle-field, however, cost Isma'il dearly. A favorite woman of his harem, Behruzeh Khanum, was captured and taken to Istanbul. There she was later married off as war booty to Salim's chief military judge. Despite Isma'il's repeated pleas to Salim for her release, Behruzeh remained a hostage even after the chief military judge lost his head by order of the sultan, presumably because he con-summated the marriage, which was to have been only in name. For Isma'il the loss of Behruzeh was a personal humiliation no less than the loss in the battle. Remarkably, a number of women fought on the Iranian side, and a few were among the casualties, a reflection, perhaps, of the revolutionary perspective of the early Safavids that allowed the women to fight alongside the men. A number of Ottoman officials were also killed. The total number of casualties on both sides probably was no more than five thousand, of which more than two-fifths were the Turks.

The capture of Tabriz shortly thereafter completed the humiliation and brought Safavid power to the verge of collapse. The prospect of a Janissary mutiny, however, saved the Safavid capital. Salim was obliged to abandon his original plan to winter in Tabriz, and contrary to earlier Ottoman practice, he departed a week after his arrival in late summer of 1514 without leaving behind a single Ottoman contingent. He nevertheless stayed long enough to allow the city to be looted and then rounded up and took to Istanbul a considerable number of artists, artisans, and merchants from Tabriz and elsewhere in the Safavid domains including more than twelve painters, book illuminators, and calligraphers. They later established in Istanbul a Persian community of artists who would have a lasting influence on Ottoman fine arts.

The consequences of the Battle of Chaldiran were far reaching. The most immediate were a serious downturn in Safavid revolutionary zeal and, along with it, a melancholic bend in Isma'il's personality. The defeat was a se-vere blow to both the myth of his invincibility and the Qezilbash's steadfast adherence to their sacred leader. It is from this point that the charismatic Safavid leadership gradually transformed into a traditional Persian kingship, a process that took several generations of Safavids to be completed. Moreover, the shock of defeat and the extinguishing of the apocalyptic faith laid firmer grounds for the shari'a-orientated creed promoted by the Safavid state and its contingent of jurists. A lurking doubt about the validity of his own mission must have convinced Isma'il to never again take charge personally of any campaign or, later on, to seriously contemplate a counteroffensive against the Ottomans—even though for a while he did make "vengeance" his rallying cry. He even named his young son, born after Chaldiran, Alqas (from the Arabic *qas*, "to retaliate").

The Ottomans continued to consolidate in central and eastern Anatolia. At the obvious expense of the Safavids, they captured the key fortress of Kumakh in central Anatolia in 1514. Isma'il preferred not to risk another confrontation. It is quite possible that the Ottoman sultan, despite his hasty departure from Tabriz, intended to revisit Iran and put an end to the Safavid heresy, perhaps with the ambition to at least partition Iran. In his correspondence with the Uzbek chief and the other archenemy of Isma'il, 'Obaydollah Khan, who was the successor to the slain Shayban Khan, Salim had even proposed Isfahan, at the heart of the Safavid domain, as the rendezvous point for a coordinated pincer movement by the two Sunni armies. Although such an offensive never materialized, the dual Sunni threat on opposite flanks of Iran proper remained in place throughout the Safavid and post-Safavid periods. The exposure of the Guarded Domains of Iran to repeated aggressions on both sides and the stretching limited military resources did not subside before the beginning of the nineteenth century. Ottoman consolidation in Anatolia not only cost the Safavids direct loss of territory but also removed their hopes for unhindered access to the Black Sea through an Anatolian enclave. For at least four centuries the Safavids, and their successors, faced an Ottoman barrier that deprived them of direct political and commercial access to the Mediterranean world.

Equally significant, the victory in Chaldiran stopped the expansion of the Shi'i messianic revolution. Although Alawite communities in Anatolia periodically revolted against the Ottomans during the Jelali revolts of the mid to late sixteenth century, for all intents and purposes the war of 1514 eliminated any potential replication of a Safavid-like revolution there. The Shi'i state was in effect confined to Iran while the Ottoman patronage of Sunni Islam further expanded throughout the Arab Middle East and beyond. Significantly, however, under Salim, and later under his son Suleiman—whose reign marked the zenith of

Ottoman expansion—the Ottomans never succeeded in subordinating their Safavid neighbor. Despite punitive actions, long-term commercial blockages, sectarian belligerence, numerous invasions, and long periods of occupation of the western Iranian provinces, both the Safavids and their brand of Shi'ism persisted. In part this was because of obstacles in maintaining secure logistical lines through Anatolia to Iran, to establish effective control over hostile terrain. The Ottoman troops, especially the Janissaries and the Ikinji light cavalry, moreover, harbored Bektashi Sufi-Shi'i sympathies. Their reluctance to fight inside Iran became evident in a serious mutiny during the siege of Tabriz and later. For the most part, however, it was the religio-political synergy of the Safavids that helped them to resist Ottoman expansion and, in due course, that fashioned Iran into a territorial empire with a distinct identity.

Within the three years after Chaldiran, Salim secured eastern Anatolia and northern Mesopotamia but also successfully shifted the direction of Turkish conquest toward the Mamluk lands. Such an enterprise proved easier to achieve and more materially beneficial. No phenomenon similar to the Safavids barred him from taking Damascus, or even Cairo. By 1517 he had conquered the entire Mamluk territory in the Levantine Mediterranean as well as Egypt and coastal North Africa. Isma'il had little choice but to tread a cautious, even conciliatory, path toward his powerful neighbor who had come to dominate an empire that was far larger than his, as well as materially more prosperous and militarily more advanced.

The Battle of Chaldiran revealed the utter superiority of Ottoman firearms and the organization of a well-equipped slave army over the traditional means and tactics of warfare waged by a tribal army such as the Qezilbash. Although the Safavids were quick to adopt artillery after Chaldiran and use it effectively against the Uzbeks in the east, it took them close to a century before they were able to match the Ottomans' capabilities and later defeat them at their own game. The age of the Gunpowder Empires came to Iran with an experience of defeat even though its memory predictably toned down in the Safavid official narrative.

ISMA'IL'S LEGACY

By the time of his death in 1524, Isma'il was a man of gentler and wiser disposition, but also a heavier drinker with a melancholic mood. In his last years there was a relative relaxing of his forced conversion policy and fewer devastating campaigns. Staying in the confines of his harem or on his hunting grounds, which he traversed throughout his realm with obsessive regularity, he preferred even more than previously to leave affairs of the state to his *vakil*, his *sadr*, and his Qezilbash chiefs. A poet, a compulsive hunter, and an adventurous lover of women and men, he died a premature death at the age of thirty-seven after a bout of severe depression. A curious mix of unbridled prowess, violent tantrum, princely affection, and a streak of genius, Ismaʻil seemed an unlikely candidate to build an empire. Yet he proved an ideal leader for a messianic enterprise that brought together, within his nascent state, a cacophony of erratic Turkmen chiefs, shrewd Persian administrators, and Arab jurists. Although he was heir to several generations of radicalized Sufism and failed political projects, he harnessed the warlike energies of his Turkmen devotees and diverted them remarkably into a state structure with a lasting future. In this respect, his initiative to adopt Twelver Shiʻism as a state creed with legal and institutional capabilities was a conscious policy upon which he intended to build a state and a community of believers. Without him, the Qezilbash—whose enemies called them the "red-headed heretics"—would have remained just that.

Ismaʻil's poetic utterances no doubt helped his devotees to believe in his sanctity. A book of Turkish poetry, by the curious pen name Khata'i (presumably someone from "Cathay," today's China), was most likely composed by Ismaʻil for his Turkmen followers as inspirational literature. Colored by pungent anti-Sunni symbols and prophetic claims common to the cult of venerating ʻAli, the book opens a window into Ismaʻil's mystical world. One poem reads:

> My name is Shah Ismaʻil, I am God's mystery,
> I am the leader of all the warriors [*ghazis*].
> My mother Fatima, my father ʻAli,
> I am the superior (heir?) to the Twelve Imams.
> I have avenged my father's blood from Yazid,
> Be sure! I am of the Haydari essence.
> I am the living Khezr [Arabic *Khidr*; Islamic name for Prophet Elijah] and Jesus, son of Mary,
> I am Alexander of my contemporaries.
> You, Yazid, the polytheist and the accursed, Look!
> I am free from your hypocritical *qibla* [direction of the Islamic prayer].
> Prophethood [*nobowat*] is for me and I am the secret of *welayat* [sacred guardianship].
> I follow the path of Mohammad, the Chosen One.
> I have conquered the world at the point of my sward,
> I am like [the lieutenant] Qanbar to ʻAli, the Elect.
> My sire is Safi, my father Haydar,

To the audacious, I am in the true [devotee of] Ja'far.
I am a Hosainid and I curse Yazid,
I am Khata'i and to that king [i.e., Hosain] I am a servant.[2]

The claim to *welayat*, the sacred succession from the Prophet Mohammad,
more specifically on behalf of 'Ali, and following him Hosain and Ja'far Sadeq
(the Sixth Shi'i Imam and the founder of the Ja'fari creed) clearly illustrated
Isma'il's messianic incarnational beliefs, which also extend to the return of Eli-
jah and Jesus. With pride in his lineage, of both the house of the Prophet and
the house of Safi (i.e., Safi al-Din Ardabili), he intends not only to avenge the
blood of his father, Haydar, but also to wage war against Yazid (the caliph whose
armies killed Imam Hosain in the Battle of Karbala in 680) and the Umayyad
dynasty. The "polytheists" and the "accursed" who pray to the "hypocritical"
qibla thus can be taken as an allusion to his Sunni enemies at home and to the
neighboring Sunni powers whom he conquered.

Yet Isma'il's vision of the state was neither purely messianic nor juristic; it
was primarily based on the Persian model of kingship. The paradigms of royal
power were best reflected in his domestic policy and his self-image as a shah.
In the tradition of the Timurid rulers of Iran and the Turkmen dynasties before him, he was an avid connoisseur of Ferdowsi's *Shahnameh* (*The Book of
Kings*) and other Persian poetic narratives, which helped him portray himself
as the heir to the Persian tradition of kingship. He patronized the production of
great, illustrated copies of these works, especially after the conquest of Herat.
He summoned great painters to his Tabriz court, among them Kamal al-Din
Behzad (1450–1535), arguably the greatest sixteenth-century representative of
the Persian school of miniature painting (fig. 1.2). Fascinated by Persian national legends, Isma'il named three of his four sons after legendary heroes of the
Shahnameh: his oldest, Tahmasp, after the last of the Pishdadid kings; his third
son, Sam, a cultivated prince, after the champion of Manuchehr's court and the
patriarch of the house of Rostam; and his last son, Bahram, after the Sasanian
Vaharm IV, whose romances and hunting exploits, as narrated by the twelfth-
century Persian poet Nezami, accorded with Isma'il's leisurely temperament.

And Isma'il had good incentive to envision himself as a *Shahnameh* king:
perhaps a Kaykhosrow, the prototype of the great Persian king who vanquished
the Turanid king Afrasiyab, the greatest enemy of Iranzamin. Afrasiyab's kingdom, Turan, was routinely associated in the Iranian landscape with the Turks,
and more specifically with the Uzbek kingdom of Central Asia. It was not without reason that Isma'il's victory over the Uzbek Shayban Khan was celebrated in
the Safavid chronicles as a victory over the legendary Turanids. Yet the pervasive

power of the *Shahnameh* over royal memory was not limited to Isma'il and the Safavids. Ironically, both Sultan Salim and Shayban Khan, and later Zahir al-Din Babur Padeshah and his Mughal descendants, viewed their own power in the mytho-historical context of the Persian legends. As it has often been noted, while Isma'il was composing poetry in Turkish, his nemesis Salim I, was composing Persian poetry in the style of the *Shahnameh*. Later Ottoman sultans were avid collectors of illustrated manuscripts of the *Shahnameh* and other classical works of Persian literature. The kingship paradigm to which they all subscribed, from the Ottoman Empire to South Asia and Central Asia, offered a common Persianate political culture despite widening of sectarian divide.

Toward the end of his life Isma'il became more engrossed in book illustration and even worked as an apprentice in the royal workshop. He reportedly collaborated in the production of the celebrated copy of what came to be known as the *Shahnameh* of Shah Tahmasp, one of the greatest examples of Safavid pictorial art. Perhaps filling in the background of a scene depicting one of Kaykhosraw's exploits, one cannot help but wonder whether Isma'il was thinking about the Kayanid king's unhappy end when he renounced his throne and disappeared into the mountains. The Shah Tahmasp manuscript itself witnessed a curious fate. Perhaps preempting another invasion, in 1568 Tahmasp presented it along with numerous other gifts to Sultan Salim II on the occasion of his accession to the Ottoman throne. After nearly four centuries of safe keeping in the Topkapi royal library, the manuscript mysteriously travelled from Istanbul the to the shady world of European art dealers. When it eventually came to the possession of Arthur Houghton, an American patron of art and chairman of the Board of Directors of the Metropolitan Museum of Art, he with the assistance of a renowned Harvard art historian dismembered the manuscript during the 1960s and 1970s and sold off its illustrations in various auctions. Metropolitan Museum, too, received a fair share.

RISE OF JURISTS' AUTHORITY

The empire that Isma'il left to his son and successor, the ten-year-old Tahmasp (r. 1524–1576; see chart 1), had to cope with frequent clashes among the Qezilbash military elite and with Sunni threat on both frontiers. Tahmasp's long reign also proved crucial for consolidation of Shi'ism in Iran. To Tahmasp's credit, the longest-reigning monarch of Islamic Iran was able to harness the colliding forces he had inherited from his father. The Safavid revolutionary zeal was partially channeled into institutions of the state, even though the disruptive ethnic divisions, especially between the Qezilbash and the Tajiks, were never fully resolved. Yet neither internecine quarrels nor external threats nor Tahmasp's own character flaws disrupted economic recuperation, cultural efflorescence, and the relative social calm that would turn Safavid Iran into an empire on par with its Ottoman and Mughal neighbors.

Tahmasp's era is remembered as an age of clerical consolidation, when Shi'i jurists, Arab emigrants, and indigenous Iranians gained prominence in government and in society at large. Their rise as an interest group was due more to the contingencies of Tahmasp's early reign than to a concerted effort by the jurists' themselves. The feud between two Qezilbash factions, the Ostajlu-Shamlu in one camp and the Takkelu-Turkamān in the other, each seeking the regency of the minor Tahmasp, prompted the young shah to engage in an elaborate balancing act that involved the Shi'i jurists. As he grew more independent, the messianic religion of the Qezilbash was played down while the status of the ulama, as trustees of legal Twelver Shi'ism, was augmented. Gradually the incipient Shi'i society of the sixteenth century began to adopt religious rituals and practices that would remain characteristic of Shi'ism for centuries to come. Intricacies of prayer and fasting, ablution, awareness of ritual pollutants and methods of cleanliness, and the assignment of shari'a-validated gender roles are all examples of how Shi'ism defined the private realm. Friday congregational prayers, the creation of charitable endowments, and the promotion of Moharram mourning rituals were among the public aspects.

The career of the prominent jurist 'Ali ibn 'Abd al-'Āli al-Karaki (d. 1534) illustrates the ulama-state bond and the gradual grasp of the jurists over Safavid society. Karaki was a jurist from Jabal 'Amil who had studied in Damascus and Cairo before moving to Najaf, the Shi'i center of learning in southern Iraq. He first came to Iran at Isma'il's behest just after the defeat of the Uzbeks in 1510 to promote "correct" Shi'ism directly from the mouth of its Arab advocate. As Safavid Iran became more shari'a oriented—hence offering greater prestige and affluence to the Shi'i jurists—Karaki returned a second time to become the most prominent religious authority during Tahmasp's era. Through a network of patronage, which included both his Arab and Persian students, as well as beneficiaries of endowments and religious dues, Karaki enhanced the jurists' monopoly as teachers and practitioners of Shi'i law. With a sanctified social standing previously unparalleled, a growing mosque following, and many colleagues with conservative proclivities, a new clerical network began to emerge around the jurists that rivaled, and in due course superseded, the Persian class of landed notables who held sway over the Safavids' religious administration.

With near-autonomous judicial authority, and a self-assigned right to control sources of religious income, the jurists were a force to reckon with. Karaki's acquisition of such titles as "seal of the mojtaheds" and "deputy to the Imam" (na'ib al-imam), revealed the assent of the high clergy. His legal opinions (fatwas) were to be emulated not only by his followers but also by the shah. In a decree issued in July 1533, the young Tahmasp addressed Karaki by his titles and bestowed on him governance over religious affairs of the land, as well as vast estates in Iran and Iraq as charitable endowments:

> We ordained that all the esteemed descendants of the House of the Prophet [sadat], the respected noblemen and notables, the chiefs [of the Qezilbash], the ministers, and all other senior members of the lofty state to consider him [i.e., Karaki] as their guide and leader [pishwa] and in all instances demonstrate their obedience and submission to him. Whatever he commands is to be enforced and whatever prohibits, to be banned. Whoever he wishes to appoint or dismiss from among the officers of the shari'a in the Guarded Domains [of Iran] and among the military [judges] of the victorious army, he can do so without any further approval. And whomever that noble authority dismisses, cannot be reappointed without his approval.[3]

In reality, paying homage to Karaki meant granting him the authority to appoint leaders of congregational prayers (imam-e jom'eh) throughout the Safavid Empire. Congregational Friday prayer in the absence of the Imam of the Age (an honorific for the Mahdi in Shi'ism) was a novel practice in contrast to a prohibition by most Shi'i jurists in the past. The act not only implicitly confirmed the Safavid state as a legitimate Shi'i power but also affirmed the jurists' collective authority as deputies of the Mahdi. Equally important, the royal decree endorsed the practice of emulation (taqlid), whereby Shi'i followers would abide in all aspects of the shari'a by the rulings of a mojtahed of their choice. Unique to Twelver Shi'ism, taqlid became an institution of lasting sway in Iranian history. In exchange, the state earned the legitimacy to collect land taxes in the absence of the Imam of the Age, which up to then was considered legally unattainable. Karaki's free hand in affairs involving shari'a allowed for the demonization of the Sunnis and promoted open cursing of the early Islamic "Rightly Guided Caliphs" while diminishing all forms of nonconformity, at least in the public space. Moreover, autonomy from the office of sadr, implicit in the above decree, in effect foreshadowed the jurists' desire for a semi-independent status in relation to the Safavid state.

Clerical consolidation, however, did not ease internal rivalries, especially ethnic ones, or petty envy among the jurists. All through his career Karaki encountered hostile criticism from other jurists, both Arab and Persian, as well as Safavid officials, for his monopolistic ambitions. He was attacked for his haughtiness and faulty scholarship, including plagiarism. Indeed, much of his work, and works of most jurists of his time, involved tedious commentaries and glosses on works of earlier jurists, on subjects ranging from intricate details of devotional acts to bodily pollutants and ritual acts of cleansing. The only trait of authenticity was in denouncing whatever was different or innovative, or what appeared "heretical"—what Karaki and his colleagues readily labeled as "devious" and "contrary to the glorious shari'a." This included Sufi orders (even the Safavi order), both open Sunnis and crypto-Sunnis, followers of various nonorthodox creeds, and freethinkers. It was not without reason that he composed a treatise on the veracity of Resurrection (ma'ad), an Islamic doctrine that had long troubled many critical minds and raised doubts, particularly in its strict interpretation as a bodily revival of the dead at the Day of Judgment. Other treatises openly and egregiously denounced the Sunni narrative of early Caliphs and other Islamic personalities. Denouncing the Sunni "other" helped reinforcing doctrinal conformity as much as it encouraged a state-sponsored spirit of intolerance. Yet unlike the European Inquisition, Safavid Iran never institutionalized systematic intrusion in the life of individuals.

The urge for greater legitimacy in the face of charges of heresy by Sunni neighbors also persuaded the Safavids to refashion their own ancestry. Although Isma'il, and perhaps his farther, Haydar, did claim to be of the House of 'Ali (āl-e 'Ali), it was from the time of Tahmasp that a thorough holy genealogy traced the ruling house back to 'Ali ibn Musa al-Rida, the Eighth Shi'i Imam, whose shrine in Mashhad was the most venerated site in Safavid Iran. Accredited by contemporary sources (and up to the twentieth century), the association with 'Ali and the House of the Prophet elevated the status of the Safavid dynasty, attaching to it an aura of sanctity evident in many architectural edifices of the period, in public decrees, and in works of scholarship patronized by the Safavid shahs. Ties to the Sufi origins of the dynasty nevertheless remained strong, and symbolic dedication to the shrine of the patriarch of the house reaffirmed the loyalties of the followers of the Safavi order to the person of the shah (pl. 1.3).

Tahmasp himself became an obsessive observer of Shi'i purity laws. Whether out of a desire to serve as a role model for his subjects, or more likely because of a compulsive disorder, in contrast to his father's excessive drinking, Tahmasp in his youth repented and abstained from drinking for the rest of his life. Karaki even wrote, at Tahmasp's request, a tract on the legal implications of obsessive behavior (waswas). One could surmise that the royal's behavior was not entirely unrelated to a surge in works produced on the intricacies of ritual purity, a favorite subject of Shi'i jurists. It stands to reason that the purity-impurity dichotomy, which Shi'i Islam liberally transposes into xenophobic distancing from nonbelievers, was also exacerbated by the threat of Sunni enemies on the Iranian frontiers. Tahmasp's short autobiography, a window onto his moral

world, reveals deep religious convictions, often in the forms of holy dreams—
dreams that served as a guiding light connecting his personal life with a crusading mission in defense of Shi'ism.

RESISTING OTTOMAN HEGEMONY

Tahmasp was a contemporary of the greatest, and perhaps the most belligerent Ottoman sultan, Suleiman I, known as the "lawgiver" (*qanuni*), and to
Europeans as Suleiman the Magnificent (r. 1520–1566). Son of Salim I, Suleiman's reign is synonymous with the peak of Ottoman military power and
its flourishing material culture. For Suleiman's neighbors, however—whether
the Iranians, Armenians, or Georgians in the east, or the Hungarians, Serbs,
Poles, Austrians, or a host of other nations in the west, all of whom sustained
the brunt of Turkish expansionism and devastating Ottoman campaigns—there
was nothing magnificent or lawful about him. In the Iranian case the sustained
threat of Ottoman offensives was evident in three rounds of massive campaigns
undertaken in 1534–1535, 1548–1549, and 1554–1555. The campaigns were stifled
largely because of the same logistical problems that earlier had hindered Salim.
They were launched under the pretext of securing the eastern Ottoman frontiers and presumably aimed to sever Safavid influence over Ottoman subjects in
eastern Anatolia. A low-intensity anti-Ottoman Jelali revolt among Alawite Shi'is
was endemic to the region but was largely independent of the Safavids, and
certainly did not require an extensive military operation into the interior of Iran.

In reality, what motivated Suleiman to undertake these arduous campaigns
of conquest and to move his war machine, larger and more terrifying than that
of his father, was territory. Plunder and slavery, including the capture of both
Shi'is of Iran and Christians of the Caucasus, also served as incentives. The
disloyalty of the Qezilbash chiefs of Azarbaijan and other western provinces
also rendered opportunities for the Ottomans at times of commotion and revolt.
The quarreling Qezilbash, whose privileges were threatened by Tahmasp's balancing act—setting one division against the other—were increasingly restive,
even treasonous. The Safavids' oppressive enforcement of Shi'ism also opened
new doors to Ottoman conquest. In 1535, the population of Baghdad, and the
whole of the Sunni Mesopotamia, who were resentful of Shi'i hegemony, welcomed the Ottomans.

The loss of Mesopotamia made the Safavids' western defenses vulnerable,
enabling the Ottomans to consolidate in eastern Anatolia and to occupy for
decades Safavid provinces in the eastern Caucasus, Azarbaijan, Hamadan and
Kermanshah, Khuzestan, and the Persian Gulf coasts. Yet the Ottoman culture

of conquest could not always effectively produce durable gains in the east as it did in the Balkans and Eastern Europe. The Safavids employed the same scorched-earth tactics that earlier had persuaded Salim's forces to withdraw. Like his father, Suleiman could not hold on to Tabriz for long and was forced to evacuate at the end of the campaign season, resorting to the more fertile, and less hazardous, valleys of the western Caucasus.

The lure of the Caucasus for the Ottomans and Safavids, who fought long and hard for it, was not only its fertile land and green pastures, where their armies could recuperate. For both empires, the Caucasus and the land farther to the north, into the interiors of southern Russia, was a desirable source of white slaves. Under the pretext of "crusade" (*ghaza*), rural Christians of Armenia and Georgians, as well as the "pagan" Circassians, Chechens, Leks, Lezgins, and a host of other tribal peoples from the mountains of the northern Caucasus were prey for Turkish and Persian armies.

On the Iranian side the more organized, and more destructive, campaigns under Tahmasp—four of them between 1540 and 1554—seem to have been modeled on the Ottoman method of conquest and with the idea of creating a system similar to the slave recruitment practice known as *devshirmeh* in the Balkans and other western Ottoman possessions whereby young Christian boys were systematically rounded up as a form of tribute for service in the Ottoman army and administration. For the Safavids the white slaves captured in raids across the Caucasus were valuable for replenishing their diminishing and disloyal old guards from among the Qezilbash. Female slaves from the Caucasus, too, were sought after for both the Safavid and the Ottoman royal harems. A majority of Tahmasp's wives were recognized as "Georgians," a general term for all Caucasian slaves from north of Tiflis (now Tbilisi). Female slaves also populated the harems of the princes and the military elites. During the latter part of Tahmasp's reign, in a single raid to the Georgian interior in 1553, no fewer than thirty thousand Christians were captured and brought back to Safavid territory.

Either through raids or as part of the annual tribute imposed on the newly subdued Caucasian vassals, the population of slave origins significantly increased. The Safavids forced their captives to convert, though not as systematically as the Ottomans did. They were also zealous in destroying the Caucasian symbols of cultural and religious identity, including churches and shrines. In 1551 during the Safavid raid of southern Georgia aimed at the mountain fortress of Vardzia (known as Dezbad in the Safavid sources), west of the Kura River, Tahmasp, "the refuge of Islam," waged a horrific crusade against the Georgian "cursed infidels." The victorious Safavid army gutted the great twelfth-century

Georgian cave monastery inside the fortress and massacred the local population who had taken refuge there. Not a "single breathing soul," declared the
chronicler Rumlu, "from among those infidels could escape unharmed" from
the vengeance of the troops:

> Their wives, households, properties, and belongings were all transferred by
> the law of the shari'a from the killed to the killer. The fair-faced Georgians,
> those fairly-like creatures, each a rarity like a beauty-spot on the face of the
> time, . . . took refuge in high mountains, in deep caves and in neighboring
> fortresses . . . but the courageous army of Islam moved in to rout them out
> with their well-watered swords and their artillery defenses, hence dispatching
> a few thousand of them to the bottom of hell. . . . Like a swarming army of
> bees in front of a beehive, the troops went on plundering and expropriating
> the treasures of the caves, and group after group the terrified fairy-faced slaves
> [gholams] . . . came out in thirst and in fear of their lives.[4]

The impact of the imported slaves, the gholams (Arabic, presumably from
ghol, "collar,"), on the royal household, the army, and entire Safavid system was
immediate and, over the long term, immense. A shift in the concept of gholam,
connoting a young male lover of slave origin, to a white or black slave in military, administrative, or court service happened centuries earlier. By Safavid
times, although the sexual undertones remained in place, the functionality of
the gholams took higher priority from the middle of the sixteenth century as the
number of Christian captives, carried off in the Caucasus raids, substantially
increased. Through the harem and the military, the gholam element amounted
to a third force, a counterbalance to the Qezilbash and the administrators of
the divan. Similar to the Ottoman Janissaries, the introduction of the gholam
recruits injected fresh blood into the Safavid army, with more loyalty to the person of the shah. It can even be argued that the gholam element made it possible
for the Safavids to recapture their lost western provinces.

The impact of Ottoman offensives and unreliability of the Safavid tribal army
had already persuaded Tahmasp to reduce his reliance on the Qezilbash and,
in 1548, to transfer his capital from the militarily insecure Tabriz to Qazvin,
three hundred miles east into the Iranian interior. Although Tabriz maintained
its commercial and cultural prominence at least for another half century, the
decision to move to the Persian-speaking interior and away from the original
Qezilbash base in Azerbaijan was a turning point in the further "Persianization" of the Safavid Empire. Even more important for the political and diplomatic history of Iran was concluding the peace treaty of Amasya in 1555, the first
Safavid-Ottoman diplomatic settlement of their territorial disputes.

The Peace of Amasya (located in today's north-central Turkey) demarcated for the first time the boundaries of the rival empires. While Iraq and almost the whole of Anatolia went to the Ottomans, the treaty restored to Iranian sovereignty Azarbaijan and the rest of the western Iranian provinces from Kurdistan to Kermanshah, Hamadan, Luristan, and Khuzestan, as well as the eastern Caucasus. Although both sides, especially the Ottomans, breached the terms of this treaty repeatedly, it remained in place more or less up to the twentieth century, essentially defining Iran's western frontier. Despite the loss of territory, the treaty was a victory not only because the Safavid defenses endured and Persian armies occasionally even prevailed over the powerful Ottomans—to the point of facilitating peace negotiations—but also because it marked Tahmasp's victory over his unruly chiefs. By the 1550s the quarreling Qezilbash were subdued, the Uzbek offensive in the east had been repelled, and by 1550 the revolt of Tahmasp's brother, Alqas, who ironically had defected to the Ottoman side and furnished Suleiman with a pretext to attack Iran, was crushed.

CULTURAL FLORESCENCE AND CRISES OF SUCCESSION

In the latter part of Tahmasp's reign it seemed that the Safavid state had managed to stabilize despite a sea of Sunni hostility and internal strife. Cities thrived, domestic trade flourished, and the integration of the provinces into a united empire was partially accomplished, at least in the interior. Safavid society recovered from the devastating campaigns of earlier decades, and the worst of the Qezilbash's violence appeared to have come to an end. Even a life of leisure, civility, thinking, and creativity seem to have withstood the stern gaze of Shi'i jurists.

The latter decades of the sixteenth century proved among the most exiting episodes in the history of Persian painting and art of book production. Royal workshops in Safavid Iran produced some of the most exquisite illustrated manuscripts of classical texts. Ferdowsi's *Shahnameh*, stories of Nezami's *Khamseh*, and Sa'di's *Golestan* were among the most favored. Elite women, who commissioned numerous manuscript copies, particularly favored Nezami. In the neighboring Ottoman and Mughal courts, too, a number of Persian artists residing there by choice or by force produced book illustrations and trained Turkish and Mughal artists, who in due course developed indigenous schools of painting.

Relations with Mughal India, already expanding through trade with Kandahar and the Deccan, were complemented by new cultural exchanges. The fifteen-year refuge of emperor Homayun (r. 1531–1540 and 1555–1556) in the court of Tahmasp in Qazvin—after the Afghan warrior, Sher Shah Suri, overran the

Mughal domains—expedited a remarkable era of cultural dialogue between the neighboring empires. Homayun resisted conversion to Shiʻism, but he nurtured a taste for Persian art and culture. When in 1555 Homayun returned to Delhi, he included in his retinue a large number of Persian master painters, craftsmen, and scholars who exerted great influence over Mughal and post-Mughal fine arts and literature. Although Tahmasp remained lukewarm toward the European emissaries who occasionally visited his court, he was keen to welcome friendly relations with his Mughal neighbor, no doubt to balance both the Ottoman and the Uzbek threats (pl. 1.4). In contrast to the Safavids, the Mughal tolerant religious policies, a legacy of Akbar's era, moreover, encouraged an exodus of Persian artists, poets, and religious dissidents to Mughal India that continued well into the eighteenth century.

Despite a fleeting interval of calm and prosperity, the final years of Tahmasp, and the decade following his death (1578–1588), witnessed an unparalleled period of disarray that soon swirled into political chaos. By 1588 the crises were so critical that the very survival of the Safavid state was in doubt. The empire that had been pieced together with Ismaʻil's unremitting energy and held together with Tahmasp's perseverance for more than half a century, was about to disintegrate into fiefdoms of quarreling warlords, many of whom were Qezilbash chiefs of the second and third generations. At the center of this chaotic interlude was the unresolved problem of succession. Yet succession triggered a range of conflicts within the power structure, the most acute of which was quarreling over land among the Qezilbash chiefs and their subsequent ambition to control the Safavid throne. Persian political culture at least informally abided by the rule of primogenitor—the succession of the senior son as heir to the throne. This was the tradition that had brought Tahmasp himself to power. Yet there was the distinct absence of an institutional framework to allow for an orderly succession—and even less so, consensus to implement it. The Qezilbash, to the extent that they were an integrated force, were hardly capable of arriving at a consensus over Tahmasp's successor, given the deep wounds that over the decades had spread through their ranks, some perpetrated by Tahmasp himself.

The uneasy equilibrium achieved during Tahmasp's reign, based on a network of patron-client clans (Turkish *uymaq*), began to crumble. While some of the Qezilbash members were descendants of the older elite, in reality the clans no longer were structured solely along bloodlines. They were more like party factions set up to protect the privileges of their members, to acquire more economic resources, and to monopolize political power. As old group loyalties weakened and the Qezilbash became accustomed to their privileges, their original confederacy showed serious cracks. By the end of the sixteenth century they were no longer a reliable military force. Their vast land assignments in the provinces, generous government pensions, share of war booty, and high status as a class of military nobility made them more prone to factionalism and thirsty for power—a drive satiable only through the elaborate, often foolish, conspiracies that have littered so many pages of Safavid chronicles.

The shah's many sons who were potentially eligible for the throne were desirable targets of Qezilbash ambitions. As the early career of the young 'Abbas I, the ultimate successor to the throne, demonstrates, the Safavid princes were no more than puppets whose only other refuge from their manipulative Qezilbash guardians was their mothers and other female members of the royal household. Although from the early days of the Safavid rule royal women played a distinctive, even decisive, role in the political process, it was in the post-Tahmasp transition era that their presence became more tangible. Though seldom acknowledged, and often in an unfavorable misogynistic light, their agency clearly contested the male-conscious ethos of the Safavid polity.

The implicit matriarchy of the Safavid elite, as in the Ottoman and Mughal courts, became more overt from the late sixteenth century. Known in Ottoman history as the "sultanate of the women," the coincidence of women's influence was probably because all three empires experienced a similar, if not identical, pattern of political transition. Wives of the Safavid rulers were either of Christian slave origin or were party to a marriage of convenience, such as a political union with a subordinate or affiliate power. With the polygamy of the harem, ethnic rivalries were as rampant as clan feuds among the Qezilbash, and mother-son bonds went a long way toward compensating for the lack of affection from the ruling father and the lack of prospects for succession. The rise of powerful royal women, especially in the period of instability, was thus indicative of the breakdown of a dysfunctional male polity, which in effect facilitated women's assertion of authority.

Upon Tahmasp's death in 1578 these strains converged in a minirevolution that stretched beyond the court. Tahmasp's oldest son, Mohammad, who was visually impaired, was passed over in favor of his promising brother, Isma'il Mirza, then in long-term captivity by the order of his father Tahmasp in a remote fortress in Azarbaijan. Isma'il Mirza's succession was made possible thanks to the political exuberance of Isma'il Mirza's half sister, Pari-khan Khanum, a politically astute princess from a Circassian mother (who had been a confidante to Tahmasp). The three-way alliance forged among Pari-khan Khanum with some Qezilbash chiefs and the Circassian *gholams* successfully removed her half brother Haydar Mirza from the succession contest and quashed his Qezilbash and Georgian support.

Ascending the throne in Qazvin as Isma'il II (r. 1576–1578; see chart 1), the new shah, an eccentric opium addict with a temper, had his own agenda. His lethal mix of grudges and paranoia, the product of twenty years' incarceration on charges of "immorality," soon shook the empire. Brushing aside Pari-khan, the new shah ordered a mass execution of nearly all the eligible princes of royal blood, including his own brothers, as well as the opposing chiefs of the Qezil-bash, and the Sufi guards at his court. Though brutal, the carnage was meant to consolidate Isma'il's power, an anxious retraction, no doubt, of his father's delicate balancing act.

Moreover, Isma'il II entertained revisionist views critical of the religious poli-cies of his father. What made his short and bloody reign remarkable was a desire to abandon the Safavids' extreme anti-Sunni propaganda and practice of insult-ing the early Caliphs, and to put an end to forced conversions and other forms of Sunni persecution. He was daring enough to order the removal of anti-Sunni mottos from the walls of mosques and public places. He appointed to govern-ment offices prominent Persian officials with well-known Sunni sympathies, in open defiance of the Arab jurists and their growing followings. Such measures were bound to cause uproar not only within the Qezilbash and among the ju-rists but also at large in a society exposed to decades of anti-Sunni propaganda.

Isma'il II's life soon came to a sudden end, for reasons not entirely unrelated to his radical revisionism. He was found unconscious in his private quarters to-gether with his lover, a young man of humble origins, after a night of nocturnal wandering through the taverns in the capital. Presumably he died of an opium overdose, though his Qezilbash opponents, fearful of their own lives, may have had a hand in his death. The possibility of intrigue aside, the episode tested Iranian society's conversion to Shi'ism and the state's declared commitment to uphold its anti-Sunni stance. Cursing of the Caliphs and other forms of Sunni "othering" were destined to remain the lifeblood of the Safavid ideology. It is possible to imagine that were it not for his mysterious death, Isma'il II and his supporters would have been able to overcome the rabid ideologues and allow for a more inclusive society with lesser harassment of nonconformists, fewer clashes with Sunni neighbors, and perhaps even a decoupling of the state from Shi'ism as its official creed.

Isma'il II's death plunged the Safavid state, and the empire, into a decadelong court intrigue and an ensuing contest for succession, resolved only through a protracted civil war. Lacking any other choice, a council of the Qezilbash chiefs, who temporarily reached a semblance of unanimity after Isma'il II's death, brought to the throne Tahmasp's senior son, Sultan Mohammad (r. 1578–1588), with the throne name Khodabandeh, "God's slave." He proved a mere nominal ruler over a Qezilbash oligarchy. Real power behind the throne emanated from inside the harem, where Khayr al-Nesa, Sultan Mohammad's wife, soon emerged as a serious rival to Pari-khan, who had lost prominence after the death of her brother Isma'il II. Better known as Mahd 'Olya (lit., "the sublime cradle"), Khayr al-Nesa, daughter of a powerful semiautonomous governor of Gilan province, was mother of the then-infant crown prince, the future Shah 'Abbas I.

As Sultan Mohammad's effective regent, Mahd 'Olya quickly arranged for the murder of Pari-khan Khanum and removed her Circassian faction from the court. Yet she could not easily overcome the Qezilbash's desire to hold collective but decentralized sway over her husband. Even hefty payoffs for many years of outstanding salaries could not guarantee their loyalty. On the contrary, a fresh Ottoman invasion of the Safavid Caucasian provinces, furnished the Qezilbash with an excuse to scold Mahd 'Olya for her reluctance to annul the 1555 peace treaty and go to war with the Ottomans. Unwilling to put up with her, in 1579 a group of Qezilbash chiefs broke into the royal harem en masse, pulled Mahd 'Olya from her husband's arms, and cut her to pieces. The trumped-up charge against her was having an illicit affair with a Tartar prince of the Crimean Giray dynasty who was then residing as a refugee in the Qazvin court.

The internal bickering offered the Ottomans a fresh opportunity to march deeper into he Safavid territory. A passage in *'Alamara-e 'Abbasi*, an official Safavid chronicle of the early seventeenth century by Iskandar Beg Monshi, himself a Qezilbash, depicts the complexity of the ongoing power struggle:

> As the shah [Sultan Mohammad] began to give out from the royal treasury with exceeding generosity . . . everyday chest after chest of golden coins was brought in from the treasury and given to the army officers in abundance. . . . Because of hardheaded and self-serving conduct of the Qezilbash their affairs turned into conflict and animosity and duality permeated within military ranks. As the news of contention and lack of discipline among the Qezilbash spread, and as terrible faults began to appear in the state, the enemies among the rulers of the time, who were awaiting such a day, welcomed the opportunity and nursed new ambitions toward the land of Iran from the east and from the west.[5]

Between 1578 and 1590 while the Safavid Empire was at its weakest, the Ottoman Sultan Morad III (r. 1574–1595), in clear breach of the 1555 peace treaty of Amasya, conducted at least four devastating campaigns to capture Azarbaijan and the Caucasus. The 1584 Ottoman campaign, reportedly consisting of three hundred thousand troops and six hundred guns, attacked under the empty pretexts of relieving the Christian Caucasus from Iranian oppression and avenging

the murder of Isma'il II. In the course of several engagements, the Qezilbash defenses crumbled, and the Ottoman forces once more occupied all of the western
Safavid provinces, from Georgia and Armenia to western Azarbaijan, Kurdistan,
Luristan, and Khuzestan. After bloody battles in 1585, Tabriz fell, and this time
the Ottomans were there to stay. They retaliated indiscriminately against the
resistant population, destroyed some of the city's most important wards, built
new fortifications, and for the first time sold the captive Shi'i men, women, and
children to slavery or to indenture in the Ottoman European provinces.

Devastating raids by the Uzbeks into the Safavid Khorasan soon followed.
The periodic occupations of Balkh, Marv, and even Mashhad exposed the Safavids' strategic weaknesses in the face of a two-front offensive and led to the
enslavement of the local Shi'i population, who was carried away and sold in
slave markets of Central Asia. The fatwas of the Sunni muftis in Istanbul and
Bukhara legitimized enslaving the Safavid subjects on the grounds of their heretic Shi'i beliefs. The Safavids retaliated by capturing "Turkmen slaves" (*asir-e
Torkaman*).

'ABBAS MIRZA AS THE CROWN PRINCE

In the midst of civil strife and foreign invasion, the governor of Herat, a Qezilbash chief by the name of 'Ali Qoli Khan Shamlu, had other ideas in mind.
As early as 1581 he declared the ten-year old 'Abbas Mirza, the prince in his
custody, the nominal Safavid shah of Khorasan (see chart 1). The rift between
eastern and western Qezilbash persuaded 'Ali Qoli to unify Khorasan and carve
out a power base for himself independent from Qazvin and the western Qezilbash. 'Abbas Mirza, the third son of Sultan Mohammad and his slain wife,
Mahd 'Olya, had miraculously escaped execution during the 1578 carnage of
Isma'il II. It was clear that 'Ali Qoli and his ally, Morshed Qoli Khan, an ambitious and capable chief of the Ostajlu Qezilbash, were uncertain of the fate of
the government in Qazvin. Fearing occupation of the capital by the invading
Ottomans, they sought in the young 'Abbas Mirza a candidate to form a new
Qezilbash confederacy in the east.

By 1587 the Qezilbash were so divided that even a meager Ostajlu force of
two thousand horsemen under the command of Morshed Qoli was able to
march successfully on Qazvin. Ironically, the Ostajlu chief and the prince in
his charge, 'Abbas Mirza, opted for Qazvin only because they were pushed
out of Khorasan by recurring Uzbek raids. Backed by the people of Qazvin,
utterly disgusted with ten years of civil war, the young 'Abbas Mirza and his
regent were welcomed to the city. By October 1587, Sultan Mohammad had

finally abdicated, and shortly afterward his eighteen-year-old son was enthroned as Shah 'Abbas. Wearing his jewel-encrusted royal crown, the new shah was already entertaining in secret the destruction of the Qezilbash and all they represented. His intent was not much different from Isma'il II's a decade earlier—and his chances of success did not seem to be any better.

Less than a century after its inception, the prospects for the Safavid state seemed ambivalent at best. What Isma'il I and Tahmasp had tried to achieve had been undermined by domestic factionalism and foreign invasion. By 1588 the two most important Safavid cities, Tabriz and Herat, were under occupation, as were vast provinces of the empire's flanks. The Qezilbash had divided the remaining provinces into shaky fiefdoms, and the impoverished population had suffered civil war, oppression, and enslavement. The Safavid central state had sunk to its lowest ebb through machination and incompetence.

Yet there were resilient features that in the face of many calamities distinguished the Safavid enterprise from its ephemeral Turkmen predecessors and even from its powerful neighboring empires. Despite its many failings, Safavid Iran was able to forge a sense of socioreligious conformity bound by territorial constraints. As in few other early modern states—Spain and England, for example—conversion to a state-sponsored creed, in this case Shi'ism, served as the social and moral mortar necessary to hold together the building blocks of a soon rejuvenated empire. Whether by force or by persuasion, the Shi'i creed prevailed and endured. Early Safavid Iran remained vulnerable to the superior firepower of its Ottoman neighbor but less vulnerable to the Ottomans' growing sense of Sunni identity. Although repeated Ottoman invasions and Uzbek sorties were meant to extinguish Isma'il's messianic project, perhaps no other factor contributed more to the very survival of Shi'i Iran and to its gradual conversion to normative Twelver Shi'ism.

Forging a new communal identity within the natural confines of Iran perhaps could not have been achieved without such tumultuous experiences. The Safavids did not initiate an Iranian sense of nationhood, nor did they define Iran as a political entity. The former would emerge, in the modern sense of the term, only centuries later. The latter had been a geopolitical reality for many centuries. What the Safavid state did was help anticipate one and solidify the other. The early Safavid experience demonstrated that southern Mesopotamia, eastern Anatolia, and southern parts of Central Asia could no longer be easily incorporated into Iran proper despite common Persianate cultural, religious, and ethnic ties. Isma'il's world-conquering project was bound to stop at the threshold of Iran's natural frontiers.

2

THE AGE OF 'ABBAS I AND THE SHAPING OF THE SAFAVID EMPIRE (1588–1666)

Few rulers in Iranian history are as idealized in public memory as 'Abbas I, and few epochs as cherished as his reign (1588–1629). He was seen, and with reason, as an empire builder who rose to the challenges of his time, shaping them as much as he was shaped by them. The legend of 'Abbas the Great does not tell us the whole story, of course, but it reflects something of the historical reality. His was a success story that started with dim chances of surviving, let alone retrieving his lost kingdom, but he managed to overcome many domestic and foreign obstacles to build a centralized state of power and prosperity. Perhaps his most enduring legacy is that he helped birth a national community and culture that outlasted him and his dynasty.

The age of 'Abbas endured not only in public buildings and public memory, coinage, and caravansaries but also in the spirit of urban tranquility, artistic and intellectual creativity, and commercial vigor that he patronized. To the Europeans who frequented his realm, the Grand Sophy of Shakespeare's plays was a natural ally and a gracious host, interested in the affairs of their world (fig. 2.1). To modern historians, the contrasts of 'Abbas's complex personality—civil and considerate, yet crafty and cruel; curious and visionary, yet insecure and paranoid—present a formidable case study of Persian kingship.

A man of small but muscular stature with a dark complexion, 'Abbas shaved off his beard entirely but kept droopy mustaches. Dressed in plain clothes in deliberate contrast to his opulent surroundings and the extravagant outfits of his attendants, it was as if he was implying to others his innate majestic qualities in the guise of ordinary man. He wore a self-styled cap, different from the Qezilbash crown of his ancestors. Always wearing his sword, and ready to use it to intimidate or to punish, he impressed many observers, and European visitors in

Figure 2.1. Shah 'Abbas I, by an anonymous Italian artist.
The Land of Kings, ed. R. Traverdi (Tehran, 1971), 48.

particular, as an agile, almost restless warrior, but confident and well informed. The Roman nobleman Pietro Della Valle, who visited 'Abbas in 1618, when the shah was forty-nine years old, describes him as "extremely shrewd, highly alert, and valiant." Bilingual, he conversed in Persian and Azarbaijani Turkish often in a congenial tone.

Though informal and often inclined toward leisure, wine, music, and nocturnal gatherings, he was unpredictable, and at times extremely violent and vindictive. Of 'Abbas's three sons, one was killed in secret at his instigation, and the other two were blinded and imprisoned for life on apparently unfounded suspicions of plotting against their father. 'Abbas had little compunction about executing victims personally, at times in the presence of foreign envoys. He was also a model of a hands-on absolute ruler, distrustful of ministerial power and of his Qezilbash army chiefs. Impressing Della Valle with a panoramic knowledge of European imperial politics, complete with anti-Ottoman sentiment and disillusionment with European powers' disunity, Protestant movements, and re-

ligious wars, he implicitly criticized Philip II's military strategy and the reasons
for Spanish domestic troubles. He went on to say:

> An emperor must himself be a solider and personally lead troops into battle-
> field. . . . A ruler cannot leave the destiny of his country in the hands of his
> ministers and army chiefs. Such a king is bound for misfortune. People are
> often thinking of their own interest and have no other concern but to earn
> wealth and power so as to lead a comfortable and joyful life. They hence fail
> to fully discharge their duties. Rulers should thus be model for all.

Della Valle added that the shah believed a capable ruler either should destroy
the enemy or bring it to submission or himself die on the battlefield.[1]

REBUILDING THE EMPIRE

From the outset of his reign, 'Abbas showed clear signs of independence. His
model of rule was neither the crusading king-prophet of Isma'il I nor the pious
balancing of power of his grandfather Tahmasp. It was as though through the
experience of his father's reign and his own seven years as crown prince in Khorasan with a shaky future, he nurtured deep resentment toward the Qezilbash
hegemony. To survive, he was convinced he had to break the back of the Turkmen aristocracy, a course that had been tried and failed by his predecessors.
Avenging the murders of his mother and his slain brother Hamzeh Mirza, who
earlier had unsuccessfully contested the hegemony of the Qezilbash, 'Abbas
orchestrated a masterful purge that soon eliminated a number of important
Qezilbash chiefs on charges of treason and by fomenting internecine hostilities. By 1589 even his own regent and guardian Morshed Qoli Khan Ostajlu fell
victim of the purge.

How was the power of the Qezilbash crushed with relative ease? The answer
can be found as much in the erosion of Turkmen solidarity as in the dwindling
fighting force they could muster after a ruinous civil war. The career of Morshed Qoli himself illustrates the rise and fall of a new kind of amir, different
from the rustic Sufi crusaders of Isma'il's time. He was the grandson of a camel
driver and son of an Ostajlu soldier. His father rose through the ranks under
Tahmasp to become the commander in chief of Khorasan and guardian of the
then infant 'Abbas Mirza in Herat before being slain during the chaos of Isma'il
II's reign. Despite his personal ambition and abundant energy, however, over
the years Morshed's fighting force dwindled. With numbers at times reaching
as low as a thousand horsemen, the loyalty of the Qezilbash rank and file, which
no longer was entirely based on kinship, shifted rapidly from one adventure to

another. It was the erosion of this fighting power and the breakdown of clan loyalties that enabled the young 'Abbas to arrange, and personally supervise, his own regent's violent murder, as he had done with many other Qezilbash amirs.

'Abbas shrewdly appealed to the Qezilbash rank and file by nurturing a new spirit of loyalty toward the person of the shah. What came to be known as *shahisevan* (love for the shah) rooted in early Safavid memory of allegiance to the person of the king, contrasted solidarity along the tribal ranks. 'Abbas exploited this sense of solidarity not only to undermine the Qezilbash elite but also to uphold it as a principle, a political motto, and even an institution upon which he could rebuild the Safavid army and administration. The *shahisevan* made it possible to break tribal bonds, juxtapose the command structure of Qezilbash contingents, and create new detachments of different ethnic origins, including Tajik Persians, Arabs from southern Iran, and the Daylam of Gilan province, as well as Georgian, Armenian, and Circassian *gholams*. Greater reliance on the slave element, in particular, shifted the balance in favor of the shah. The Qezilbash did not disappear as an identity or as a privileged rank, but it was effectively stripped of its status as a cohesive tribal elite in control of a semiautonomous military force.

'Abbas's defense policy also involved a complex chess game of playing the Turkish tribes within non-Turkish regions off one another. To build a defense barrier against Uzbek incursions, for example, he resettled, similar to the style of the neighboring Ottomans, large divisions of the Qezilbash in northeastern frontiers. By the early seventeenth century as many as 4,500 Afshar families of the Orumiyeh region of Azarbaijan, some thirty thousand families of Belbas Kurds of Erzurum, as well as the Bayats and the Qajars from Iravan, Ganjeh, and Qarabagh (Karabakh) in the southern Caucasus were resettled in strategic locations in northern Khorasan and in Astarabad in the eastern corner of Mazandaran. Massive reallocations such as these helped secure eastern Iran. Yet they also transformed Iran's nomadic patterns and put new strains on the limited pastoral resources. In due course such tensions generated tribal conflicts, well evident in the early eighteenth-century rise of the Afshar and later the Qajar dynasties.

The key to 'Abbas's *shahisevan* solidarity and the cornerstone of his centralizing policy was the effective use of firearms. Although the manufacture and use of cannon and handguns were commonplace from the time of Tahmasp, it was largely due to 'Abbas's initiative that the use of firearms became prevalent in the Safavid army, as instruments of both war against neighboring enemies and domestic security. As it turned out, this new military technology was the first step toward modernity. From around the 1590s until the first quarter of the nineteenth century, cannon became the most effective weapon in the Iranian arsenal, enabling the state, with few exceptions, to achieve eventual victory over domestic contenders and foreign onslaughts. It helped consolidate power in 'Abbas's hands, established a rapport with Europe, and augmented Safavid Iran's image of itself as a victorious power.

Acquiring cannon technology did not prove particularly difficult, given that by the turn of the seventeenth century casting cannon was a relatively uncomplicated and inexpensive operation. Besides possessing an indigenous knowledge from even before Tahmasp's time—especially of casting makeshift siege cannon—there were enough military engagements with the Ottomans and enough renegades from the enemy's army to Iran to furnish the Safavids with their vital needs. Victories over the Ottomans, and later the Portuguese in the Persian Gulf, also provided the Safavids with cannon pieces as spoils of war. The arrival of European soldiers of fortune, moreover, rendered knowledge of modern warfare available to the Safavids. Yet, like Tahmasp before him, 'Abbas was selective in adapting the Ottoman and Western methods of warfare and military organization. The Safavids neither could afford nor were willing to abandon their highly mobile light cavalry, which under capable command continued to prove its worth. Equipped with artillery and reinforced by musketeer corps, for a limited time in the first half of the seventeenth century the Safavid army reached an effective optimal balance between the traditional methods of warfare and the new military technology and tactics.

The artillery could pierce, if not shatter and raze to the ground, the seemingly impenetrable fortresses and strongholds that dotted the Iranian landscape and were even more numerous along the mountainous periphery of the Caucasus, Kurdistan, Luristan, Mazandaran, and eastern Khorasan. 'Abbas aimed not to raze but to capture the semiautonomous strongholds and to subordinate their khans, who had long fallen outside of Safavid control. It took him at least a decade to impose a semblance of tranquility in the Iranian interior. At times he faced the opposition not only of the Qezilbash and other local khans but also of the local populace, city dwellers and peasants, who defied integration primarily because of the heavy taxation imposed on them to finance the state's military campaigns. Repeated uprisings throughout the early 1590s in the cities and countryside of Mazandaran—'Abbas's own maternal homeland and a coveted province because of its natural resources—were but one example of challenges to the centralizing state. Despite regional resistance, however, the new imperial army imposed on the disparate and geographically scattered communities of Iran a new loyalty to the state as guarantor of security, and eventually national identity.

What also gave 'Abbas's career a flavor of the common trends in the empires of the early modern times were a clearer sense of military strategy and political priorities. Far from reacting haphazardly to grave threats to his throne, as he had done at the outset of his reign, he recognized his priorities, planned his action, and waited for the right opportunities. He realized the futility of engaging in a destructive war with the Ottomans when such odds as shattered frontier defenses, trouble at home, traitorous khans, and a demoralized army were clearly against him. In 1590, aware of the hazards of a two-front engagement, he acquiesced to a humiliating peace treaty with the Ottomans that ceded the western Iranian provinces in their entirety to his powerful nemeses. Moreover, the treaty compelled the Safavids to renounce their most inveterate expression of Shi'i militancy, the cursing of the Sunni Caliphs.

The treaty, nonetheless, granted 'Abbas much-needed respite to pacify the interior and, some years later, to start the process that would end Uzbek occupation of the east. By 1598, in a series of campaigns mostly under 'Abbas's own command, Safavid armies recouped their losses throughout Khorasan, including Herat, Mashhad, Balkh, Marv, and Astarabad (map 2.1). The capture of Herat, in particular, was a singular boost to the Safavids' morale, for it restored the Safavid claim to Timurid heritage. Regaining Mashhad further enhanced the shah's stature as protector of Shi'i Islam. For the rest of the seventeenth century all major urban centers of Khorasan remained in Safavid hands, a success that nevertheless proved fragile.

The relative tranquility of Khorasan persuaded 'Abbas to begin the second phase of his strategy to reconquer the Iranian empire, this time from the more formidable Ottoman occupiers. For this he fielded five hundred cannon and a corps of nearly twelve thousand artillerymen and twelve thousand musketeers, which included a mix of Iranians, Caucasian *gholams*, and a reformed *shahisavan* cavalry, now mostly identified by the general name *qurchis* (weapons bearers, or more accurately, "bearer of firearm"). Though numerically far smaller than the Ottoman forces, this was a force to be reckoned with. In a series of brilliant campaigns between 1603 and 1612, 'Abbas routed his Ottoman enemy in Azarbaijan and the eastern Caucasus as much by his tact and creative use of limited resources as by his personal valor and high morale. In this he ranked among the most talented military commanders of early modern times.

Tabriz was recaptured in 1604, after nearly two decades of devastation, repeated changes of hands, and massacres of the local population. A 1612 treaty of Istanbul, moreover, returned to Iran all the territory it had lost since the 1555 Peace of Amasya (map 2.1). Later, the Ottomans' repeated efforts to recoup their losses in western Iran brought even greater humiliation and more injury

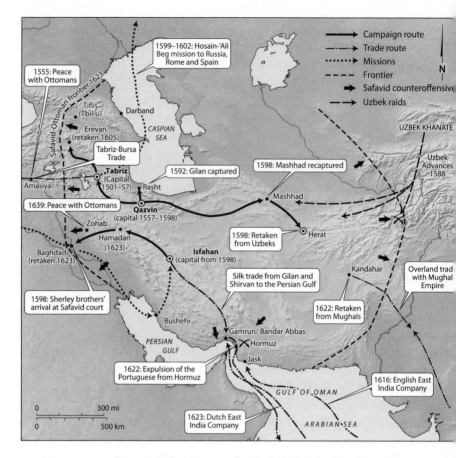

Map 2.1. Safavid Iran under Shah 'Abbas I, 1588–1629

to their military reputation. In the following decade 'Abbas used every opportunity to turn the Ottomans' strategic errors in northern and central Mesopotamia into his own gain, with the aim of pushing into the heartland of the Safavid movement and beyond. By 1623, the recapture of Baghdad and the Shi'i holy cities of Najaf and Karbala, which had been lost to the Safavids in 1535, marked the pinnacle of 'Abbas's career and the reunification of his formerly fractured empire.

ISFAHAN: THE NAVE OF THE SAFAVID UNIVERSE

Coinciding with reconquest of Khorasan in 1598, 'Abbas began to relocate the Safavid capital from Qazvin to Isfahan, in the heart of the Iranian plateau and

Figure 2.2. A seventeenth-century panorama of Isfahan demonstrating the
centrality of Naqsh-e Jahan to the shaping of the Safavid capital.
John Ogilby, *Asia, the First Part, Being an Accurate Description of Persia,*
and the Several Provinces Thereof (London, 1673).

long the seat of power to the Buyid, and later the Saljuqid, empires of the tenth
and eleventh centuries. The shift was significant not only for ethnic, strategic,
and economic reasons, but also because 'Abbas's reconstruction of Isfahan as
his capital gave material expression to the achievements of his reign (fig. 2.2).
The master plan and monumental architecture of the new capital epitomized
power and legitimacy as much as functionality, openness, and leisure—all in an
atmosphere of candor and confidence. Isfahan, this quintessential Persian city,
became even more representative of Safavid Iran under 'Abbas and his successors. As much as they shaped the city, the city and its inhabitants also shaped
them. European visitors of the period, who marveled at Isfahan's greatness and
the mastermind behind its revival, also recorded traits of greater Persian homogeneity among the Safavid political elite.

That 'Abbas opted for Isfahan as his capital even after recapturing Herat, Tabriz, and Baghdad—all three had earlier been recognized as seats of imperial

power—reveals geopolitical common sense. The city's pivotal location was recognized by Saljuq administrators, who apparently were the first to rhyme *Isfahan* with the epithet *nasf-e jahan* (nave of the universe). In 1079 Omar Khayyam
(c. 1048–1141), the celebrated mathematician and astronomer of the Saljuq era
and poet of the *Rubaiyat*, was among the astronomers who positioned Isfahan
as the prime meridian, the *nasf*, of the reformed solar Jalali calendar, the most
pronounced marker of Persian solar time-reckoning and Iran's calendric memory.
The emphasis in rhyme on the centrality of Isfahan should not be taken as mere
glorification of the new capital, as metropolises often are labeled by their proud
rulers and inhabitants. Even today the common phrase *Isfahan, nesf-e Jahan* (Isfahan is half the world) reflects how the misreading of the original epithet, *nesf*
(half), for *nasf* (nave, center), resulted in boosting the greatness of the city.

Geographically, Isfahan was indeed the center of the Safavid Empire. Located equidistant from the former capitals, Tabriz and Herat, it offered an ideal
communicative and administrative advantage. In the face of the Ottomans' virtual trade blockade to the west, Isfahan's proximity to the Persian Gulf also
offered alluring alternative access to European markets. Isfahan also was cen-
trally located on the trade route at the edge of the central Iranian desert that
connected Qazvin and Kashan to Yazd and Kerman and beyond to Kandahar
and northern India. Nearly two decades of war and destruction had reduced
Tabriz's enviable position as the hub of the Eurasian trade, a position that it
would never regain, especially after the rise of Istanbul as the center of trade in
the eastern Mediterranean.

Not yet fully recovered from the ravages of Timurid armies in the late fourteenth century, Isfahan, in contrast, offered abundant natural and human resources. Water from the river Zayandehrud, meaning "birthing river," for its
riverbed springs (or Zendehrud, "the living river"), supplemented by a network
of subterranean qanats on the slopes of central Zagrus range, irrigated the hinterlands of Isfahan. Without the bountiful and reliable food supplies harvested
from the alluvial plains along the Zayandehrud, the only major river in the
interiors of the Iranian plateau, it would have been impossible for any state
to sustain a large urban population, secure a thriving trade and industry, and
maintain a standing army and extensive divan. By the time 'Abbas embarked on
his new cosmopolitan project, his contemporary, the Mughal emperor Akbar
(r. 1556–1605), had already abandoned his newly built capital in Fatehpur in
1586 because of the scarcity of water. The Ottoman capital, Istanbul, however,
offered security, prosperity, and power because of its prime maritime location,
which allowed for the importation of grain from, and easy access to, the Balkans, the Black Sea, and the Mediterranean.

The people of Isfahan provided another incentive for transfer of the capital. Ever since the time of Isma'il, Isfahanis had served in high offices, most notably Najm II, the capable *vakil* who was partially responsible for reassertion of the Persian (Tajik) element in the early Safavid administration. The gradual tilt toward the Iranian center, at the expense of the Azarbaijan-based Qezilbash, signified the triumph of the Persian divan. It was perhaps with the famed and well-chronicled resourcefulness and diligence of the people of the new capital that 'Abbas found the greatest affinity. That they were also labeled shrewd and streetwise, even by native Isfahani authors, conveyed a sense of cosmopolitan confidence vital for the expansion of commerce. The potential for recruitment was not only in the expanding divan but also in the growing trade network and in the famed royal workshops. Isfahan incorporated into its growing economic network industrial centers in its vicinity such as Kashan, Yazd, and Kerman. Artistically, too, Isfahan soon absorbed the traditions of painting and calligraphy from Shiraz as well as Tabriz and Herat, displaying its own distinctive cultural characteristics.

Initially a garrison town—indicated in its original name, *Sipahan* (garrison, barracks)—Isfahan's roots probably went back to a settlement of the Achaemenid period, which later gave rise to a sizable Jewish quarter. Among the oldest inscriptional evidence from the city, dating to the Parthian period, is a dedication tablet from a synagogue in the Jewish quarter. In pre-Safavid times the Jewish quarter, known as Jubareh (Jewish borough), which survives into the present with the same name, may have controlled a sizable volume of trade and financing, important for Isfahan's economic well-being.

The imperial legacy of Isfahan persuaded 'Abbas to bestow his stamp on the face of the city in the form of the new congregational (*jame'*) mosque, a masterwork of Perso-Islamic architecture. In the age of great construction projects around the globe, from Hapsburg Spain to Ming China, the lure of monumentalizing political and military achievements was strong for 'Abbas, especially when the timing was coincidental with the turn of the first Islamic millennium. The years 1591–1592 corresponded to the year 1000 of the Islamic Hijra calendar. It is tantalizing to think that 'Abbas constructed the Isfahan monuments so as to commemorate his millennial stature. Suppressing the millenarian movement of the Noqtavis shortly before moving to his new capital made Abbas's choice of a millennial capital even more plausible.

A century after the rise of Isma'il to power in 1501, corresponding to the Islamic calendar year 906, such a commemoration was even more fitting, for 'Abbas was able to recover once more the full length and breadth of his ancestor's domain while capturing the spirit of his forefather's messianic revolution in the splendor of his own royal monuments. Not without reason, the zodiac sign associated with Isfahan, Sagittarius (Arabic *al-qaws*; Persian *kaman*), also associated with victorious rule in Perso-Islamic astrological culture, adorned the portal of the Qaysariyeh bazaar (from Arabic *Qaysar*, from Latin *Caesar*) in the Naqsh-e Jahan royal square. As with the nomenclature in use in Cairo during the Fatimid era of the tenth and eleventh century, in Isfahan, too, power and glory were associated with the city's investiture as a millennial metropolis.

Between 1598 and 1629, the end of his life, 'Abbas added a new sector to the old city, and all available evidence suggests that its construction was guided by at least a rudimentary master plan he devised himself. The plan consisted of a complex of mosques and madrasas, a massive square, thoroughfares, bazaars, pavilions, and gardens. The buildings were meant to visually display royal grandeur as well as 'Abbas's utilitarian appetite for business and his taste for leisure. Perhaps most symbolic in this emerging urban space was the Maydan Naqsh-e Jahan, first developed in 1590 on the site of a Saljuq garden of the same name. It was a rectangle 512 meters long and 159 meters wide, an expansive multi-functional space, connected through a covered bazaar to the old section of the city and through a network of state buildings and royal gardens to the newly constructed recreational thoroughfare known as the Chahar-Bagh (four-part garden) (pl. 2.1).

The concept of the *maydan* (from the Middle Persian for "empty space in the middle"), as it applied to the Naqsh-e Jahan (*naqsh*, "model" or "pattern," and *jahan*, "the world"), was reminiscent of the city's dual functions as a garrison and a trade center but also of the symbolic representation of the state. The old Maydan in Isfahan was located in front of the original congregational mosque on the other end of the bazaar, which in its own right was a repository of Iran's architectural history. Naqsh-e Jahan, while maintaining these old functions, displayed the royal touch on all sides. Most notable was its accessibility and openness, in contrast to virtually all other royal projects carried out elsewhere in the early modern world (perhaps with the notable exception of Venice's Piazza St. Marco). The new Maydan was not modeled as a citadel (*arg*) with high walls and closed gates barring the public from mingling with the royals and their officials, as so many royal projects were, from the Spanish El Escorial to Istanbul's Topkapi, to Delhi's La'l Qal'a (The Red Fort) and Beijing's Forbidden City, and later Versailles. Naqsh-e Jahan, on the contrary, housed around its perimeter public buildings together with royal pavilions, suggesting to observers a spirit of communal unity. It was as though it were intended to be the pattern for the emerging Safavid world.

This microcosm of the Safavid Guarded Domains was a deliberate mix of sacred and profane. The arched modular arcade around the Maydan consisting of rows of shops was interrupted at four points by monumental edifices. On the southern end was the magnificent royal mosque, symbolic of the enduring presence of Shi'ism, and on the northern end was the picturesque gateway to the bazaar. These public spaces alternated with two royal structures: on the west the Royal State House (Dowlat-khaneh-e Mobarakeh, better known by its Turkish name, 'Āli-qapi, or "the Sublime Threshold") and on the east the royal chapel (better known as the Mosque of Shaykh Lotfallah [al-Maysi], after the scholar of Jabal 'Amil in whose honor apparently the chapel was named). The space in the middle was an expansive ground used for a variety of purposes: the Persian game of polo (and other games), military parades, weekly trade fairs with tents and caravans, and festive gatherings with fireworks, nighttime illumination, musical bands, and entertainers. Not infrequently, 'Abbas himself appeared on the veranda of the Royal State House to view a parade or to observe the Muharram mourning ceremonies, and he mingled freely with the Isfahani public in the Maydan a spirit of pageantry and camaraderie.

Having been advised by an Isfahani merchant-turned-state official on the Maydan project, the shah was mindful of ensuring a return on his invested capital. The first modern commercial development project reflected the empire's new spirit of state mercantilism. Shops in the arcade were rented out at a discounted rate to encourage a different business pattern from that of the occupational clusters of the bazaar. A stone channel ran around the perimeter of the Maydan, serving as a divider between the central arena and a covered walkway around the square. The shaded passageway served the clientele with Persian and European luxury goods, which were becoming increasingly affordable for the prosperous classes, heralding a new age of affluence and consumption. Remarkably, the new Maydan was not divorced from the fabric of the old city; rather, it was a modern extension of it.

The royal congregational mosque—endowed by 'Abbas and named after him: the Masjid Jame' 'Abbasi (or simply known as the Shah Mosque before it was renamed in 1980, in blatant violation of the Islamic requirement to preserve the name of the founder of any charitable endowment, as the Imam Khomeini Mosque)—was designed by the royal architect Badi' al-Zaman Tuni, about whom we know nothing beyond his name. The mosque was built between 1611 and 1638 by a team of architects, engineers, masons, ceramic tile artists, and calligraphers under 'Abbas's close supervision (pl. 2.2). Masterfully integrated into the Maydan complex, the entrance portal was aligned with the Maydan's axis, while the main courtyard, the fifty-two-meter turquoise-colored tile dome, and the rest of the building are turned forty-five degrees to face toward Mecca, a requirement for any mosque. The symbolism could hardly be missed by any observer—from any point in the Maydan, one could appreciate the harmony between the secular space, dominated by the state building and its commercial ventures, and the sacred ambiance of the mosque's interiors. Accessed from the Maydan through a tilted corridor, the contrast between the sacred and profane is further nuanced by the dimmed light in the intermediate space. The harmony between the two spaces is nevertheless accentuated by the resemblance in the design of the polychrome ceramic portals that stand on opposite sides (pl. 2.3).

To complement the mosque, the royal chapel (of Shaykh Lotfallah) on the eastern flank of the Maydan, was a cherished example of Safavid architecture. The ambiance of this building, which lacked a courtyard and featured an off-center dome, was distinct from the traditional design of Persian mosques. It may have been originally planned to serve a function other than a mosque—possibly a madrasa or even a gathering place for the Sufis of the Safavi order, who still maintained a ceremonial position, albeit a much diminished one, at the Safavid court.

The Royal State House on the western side of the square is testament to the greater prominence of the Safavid state. First begun under 'Abbas as a multistory atrium for the complex of royal palaces and gardens behind it, under 'Abbas's successors it evolved into a state house, with new music chambers and banquet halls. An exterior symbol of the state, perhaps comparable in function to the Ottoman Sublime Porte (Bab 'Ali) or Divan 'Amm in Mughal Delhi, the cubic structure and multiple stories of the state house represented a breakthrough in Safavid design and interior decoration. Moreover, perhaps for the first time in Persian architecture, its positioning on one side of the Maydan removed the seat of government from the seclusion of the citadel and placed it squarely in public view. As a state house it was placed in a separate building outside the court and more accessible to the public. Preceding Naqsh-e Jahan, the Doge's Palace in Piazza San Marco in Venice seems to be the only other government building of the time that shared a similar conceptual character and served a similar function.

The innovative design of the Royal State House was in harmony with the new Maydan complex. Not only could the shah's subjects see him on public occasions on the balcony of the state house, but also the government could also be more easily accessed independent of the royal court and the overpowering presence of the monarch. The spatial differentiation between the state and the royal household, in effect between the private and the public functions of the shah, was a tantalizing overture to a modern political division of labor. Yet such a division of private and public in the state's affairs never really materialized under the Safavids or their successors. While the lower floors of the seven-story building housed the headquarters of the two most important officers of the Safavid state: the vizier, as head of the divan, and the *sadr*, as head of the religious administration, the upper floors functioned as reception halls for entertaining royal guests.

From the heavily ornate upper floors with hedonistic wall paintings by the seventeenth-century master painter, Reza 'Abbasi, to the elaborate plasterwork, 'Āli Qapi royal structure seemed to combine the administrative and leisurely faces of the Safavid state. Yet despite its administrative and leisurely functions, the Royal State House could not remain entirely free of religious symbolism. Reportedly, after his 1632 conquest of Baghdad, 'Abbas brought from Najaf one of the gates to 'Ali's shrine and installed it in the entrance portal of government house as a sign of his devotion to the first Shi'i Imam. The shah himself, despite his well-known propensity toward revelry, also had to underscore his humility toward Shi'i foundations of the Safavid state. One of the self-effacing epithets 'Abbas assumed for himself was "the dog of Ali's threshold" (*kalb-e astan-e 'Ali*), which denoted not only devotion to 'Ali but also to the Safavid state's guarding of the legitimate Shi'i state, a concept rivaling perhaps the Ottomans' assumption of custodianship of the sacred shrines of Mecca and Medina.

Beyond the Royal State House were extensive royal gardens, stretching all the way to another of 'Abbas's urban innovations, the avenue of Chahar-Bagh. The idea of *chahar-bagh*, had long been expressed in gardens, as well as in Persian paintings and carpet designs in Iran, in Central Asia, and in Mughal India. The transposition of the celestial ideal in the Chahar-Bagh of Isfahan no doubt reflected the leisurely dimension of the new age of 'Abbas and the material affluence of the Safavid elite, the mercantile classes, and other associated groups. The two-mile-long, 196-foot-wide *khiaban* (a Persian garden pathway with a watercourse, which later evolved into the modern notion of a boulevard) ran the length of the city from north to south in a newly developed sector close to the river, with parallel lines of plane, cypress, and poplar trees and water channels running across it (fig. 2.3). Crossing Zayandehrud via the picturesque bridge of Allah-Verdi Khan (later the Si-o-seh Pol), another edifice of the Safavid era, the upper Chahar-Bagh merged into vast royal parks and gardens in the southern end, which were open to the public.

The Chahar-Bagh quarter as a whole represented a pleasure garden on a large, orderly scale. The shaded and well-irrigated promenade was open to the public, an inviting refuge for strolling. The avenue of Chahar-Bagh crossed the river perpendicularly, crossing Isfahan and its immediate hinterland. Within

Figure 2.3. An early eighteenth-century view of Isfahan's new Chahar-Bagh.
Cornelius Le Bruyn, *Travels into Muscovy, Persia*, 2 vols. (London, 1737), 2:79.

each plot of land that was developed into a symmetrical garden, delicate pavilions were constructed at the cross section, or "eye," of the garden. Having no residential function, the pavilions in the late Safavid era were built for pure visual and sensual pleasure amid the controlled natural environment, recalling the pavilions (*ghorafat*) of Paradise as they were depicted in the Perso-Shi'i eschatological narratives. Under the rule of 'Abbas's successors, the pleasure aspect of the Chahar-Bagh was further emphasized, for instance, in the extant pavilion of Hasht Behesht built at the end of the seventeenth century. The name and design of the building alluded to the pleasures of the eighth and final level of Paradise, and especially to the sensual license available to the saved.

In constructing Chahar-Bagh and the surrounding gardens and parks, 'Abbas and his successor may have been influenced by seventeenth-century European urban planning. The print illustrations of Italy's renaissance gardens and villas, for example, were available in Isfahan through European travelers. The Chahar-Bagh project never neglected the shah's entrepreneurial instincts. 'Abbas acquired vineyards and orchards in the vicinity and developed them into spacious plots to be sold to the nobility and members of the elite. Remarkably,

however, the endeavor did not result only in a residential quarter for the affluent, but rather a horticultural delight for pleasure and for the education of the
senses. As much as 'Abbas and his successors were experimenting with new
modes of commerce and economic development, so were they tasting the pleasures of wine and companionship (pl. 2.4).

A NEW ECONOMY

Financing a well-equipped army and monumental building projects required new monetary and human resources incompatible with the capacity of
an agrarian economy. Relying largely on trickling land revenues from fiefdoms
under the control of the Qezilbash and the provincial nobility, 'Abbas's predecessors had compensated for the gaping shortfall through limited revenue from
overland trade and other urban sources. Whether the cause of the shortfall was
insubordinate fief holders or ailments inherent to fiscal management, the state
had to look for alternative resources. Revenue through booty was of diminishing
returns, upon which the Safavids could never rely as heavily as did the Ottomans during their expansion. Long before 'Abbas's time there was simply little
left for the Safavids to conquer. Losing the eastern half of Anatolia and later
the western Caucasus to the Ottomans was a further blow to the state revenue.

'Abbas resorted to a range of new economic policies aimed not only to reverse the semiautonomous power of the periphery in favor of the center but
also to generate new sources of wealth. His search for new markets, labor, and
monopolies complemented his strategies for better communication and for
long-distance trade. His economic interventionist policies and deliberate mix
of business and government heralded a political economy in tune with the European state mercantilism of his age. Perhaps not as systematic as the English
or Dutch, but surely as determined, by around 1600, when 'Abbas seriously
embarked on building the new capital, he had already laid the foundation for
a new economy.

The cornerstone of his economic reform policy was to shift the landholding pattern from hereditary fiefdoms to state-controlled renewable land tenures
(*tuyul*) assigned as estates to the members of the Persian and *gholam* elite. Still
bestowed as remuneration for their services in place of a cash salary, the recipients of these estates were periodically reassigned to various posts and locations,
making their estates' tax revenue more readily collectible. The vast expansion
of the crown lands (*khassa*), moreover, including the entire silk-producing provinces of Gilan and Mazandaran, which were either conquered by 'Abbas or
were estates expropriated from insubordinate Qezilbash chiefs, increased the

revenue of the crown, which was administered independent of the divan. Unlike the prevailing Ottoman *timar* and the Mughal *suba* landholding practices, whereby the central government received services instead of revenue, the shift to a more centralized landholding regime endowed ʻAbbas with additional income—from both crown and divan—as well as with exchangeable commodities. This in turn allowed for a commercial venture with a profit margin that no other source—neither land nor taxation—could generate.

Silk was the most plausible, perhaps the only, cash commodity at ʻAbbas's disposal in order to compensate for the paucity of other nonagrarian source of wealth. Originally introduced to Iran from China, for more than a millennium silk (*abrisham*, from Old Persian *upa-raishma*, or "the superior thread") was produced in commercial quantities in Iran and was processed, woven, and exported in raw form or as fine fabrics to Europe through ports along the Black Sea and eastern Mediterranean. References in the Sasanian sources of late Antiquity to Perso-Byzantine rivalry over the silk trade, and in Persian poetry and historiography of the early Islamic Middle Ages, confirm the importance of silk as a commodity, as well as its cultural place in the Persian imagination.

By the late sixteenth century, when European consumption was on the rise, disruption of the so-called Silk Road trade lowered the importation of silk overland from China through Central Asia, an ancient trade route that two centuries earlier had attracted Genoese merchants, famously pioneered by Marco Polo and his party, to Iranian silk-producing centers and probably to China. Cultivation of Persian silk, inferior in quality to Chinese silk, nevertheless was given a boost after the Safavid conquest of the Caucasus, especially the silk-producing region of Nakhijevan and Shervan. Both the Iranians and the Ottomans coveted the two regions even before the inception of the Safavid state.

The organization and expansion of the Safavid silk trade, however, had to circumvent a serious barrier. Conscious of Persian competition, for most of the fifteenth century the Ottoman authorities, like their Byzantine predecessors in Sasanian times, imposed strict restrictions on the import of Persian silk to Ottoman silk markets and silk-weaving centers such as Bursa, as well as on its export through their Mediterranean and Black Sea ports. The ongoing religious and political hostilities between the two empires turned such restrictions to a virtual blockade, especially after ʻAbbas's counteroffensive against the Turkish occupation of western Iran. Access to the silkworm-breeding centers of the Caucasus and control of the overland routes was a source of recurring anti-Safavid belligerence and a powerful incentive for repeated Ottoman eastern campaigns.

As resourceful and creative as ʻAbbas was in governing, he simply updated, so to speak, the same callous treatment of the people of the Caucasus as had been done by his predecessors and by his Ottoman neighbors. Congruent with the mercantilist ethics of the early modern empires, he too gave his exploitation of the region's resources a face-saving appearance, one that served his own political and commercial purposes. After more than a century of the Caucasian territories changing hands and scorched-earth warfare conducted by both Turks and Persians, the once thriving silk-breeding centers of the Caucasus greatly suffered and the trade hubs of the Julfa, Tiflis, and Shamakhi were on the verge of collapse. Yet after a series of campaigns leading up to 1604, once 'Abbas had firmly reasserted Safavid control over the eastern Caucasus, his treatment of the Armenian and Georgian communities began to shift from crusading zeal to entrepreneurial circumspection. To him the Armenian communities of the Caucasus, and particularly Julfa (in the present-day autonomous republic of Nakhchivan in the Azerbaijan Republic), a major Armenian center of silk production and commerce even with Europe, served a valuable end. As part of his effort to develop his new capital, and as an overall endeavor to strengthen the center against the periphery, he embarked on a policy of forced migration.

In 1605, retreating from an Ottoman counteroffensive in Kars, as part of the scorched-earth military strategy, the Safavid army razed the city of Julfa to the ground. 'Abbas issued a decree forcing the entire population of the city, some fifteen thousand Armenian families (probably as many as one hundred thousand individuals), out of their homeland and distributing them throughout Azarbaijan, Gilan, and other silk-producing northern provinces. A select population, as many as three thousand families, resettled in the capital, Isfahan, where most were housed in a then-recently-created Armenian quarter, known as New Julfa, on the south bank of Zayandehrud. By a royal decree the new quarter was assigned exclusively to the Armenians, and they were offered funding and materials to develop their new home and build numerous churches and mansions. Some Armenian refugees perished along the way from disease and exhaustion, even though after their arrival they were generally treated well by the Safavid authorities. To the Ottomans, mass exodus (*boyok surgon*) was a familiar practice—rooted in the Mongolian and Timurid culture of treating humans as movable herds—and was often aimed to pacify some newly conquered territory. With an eye on that Ottoman practice, Shah 'Abbas no doubt viewed mass exodus as a canny solution to a century of Perso-Ottoman rivalry over the Caucasus and an effective way to quell repeated anti-Safavid Georgian and Armenian revolts.

The greater incentive, and a novel motive for 'Abbas, was to transplant to his capital Armenian expertise in organizing and operating the Persian silk trade, a move no doubt inspired by the existence of an extensive Armenian trade

network and relative immunity of the Armenian and Jewish merchants in crossing the Perso-Ottoman borders, despite hostilities with rival neighbors. With
the growth of New Julfa and the thriving economy of the Armenian community,
an important piece of 'Abbas's designs for expanding the silk trade fell into
place. By 1615 he was ready to declare silk production and export to be a monopoly of the crown, though earlier he had already commissioned first Jewish,
then Armenian, merchants as his agents and offered them royal protection and
privileges. The Armenian network, extending throughout the Ottoman Empire
and European Mediterranean, was a major asset for the shah's enterprise, functioning almost as an equivalent to the emerging European trading companies,
the English East India Company and the Dutch East India Company, and for
a while successfully competing with them. The nurturing of an Armenian mercantile network was 'Abbas's answer to the Ottoman blockade of what would
potentially be his most profitable commodity.

Despite an increasingly lucrative European silk market, however, Persian
raw silk could not be exported conveniently through Levantine ports, primarily
because of the high tariffs on it imposed by the Ottomans and other obstacles
to overland trade. By the end of the sixteenth century, Persian silk was one of
the most important items exported through Aleppo—then the busiest eastern
Mediterranean entrepôt. The search for an alternative route had already preoccupied 'Abbas and his administration, primarily because the shah's low profit
margins stood in glaring contrast to the high proceeds that the Persian silk trade
generated for the Armenian and Jewish intermediaries and for the Ottoman
treasury. If the advantage of employing Armenian merchants was to access the
European markets directly in hopes of realizing higher profits, the overland silk
route through the Mediterranean did not fully serve that purpose.

To further develop silk production, the shah also experimented with mass
migration of the Armenians and Georgians of the Shamakhi and Tiflis regions
to the Caspian province of Gilan, Iran's largest silkworm-breeding region. The
goal of this venture was to benefit from the new immigrants' expertise in silkworm breeding in a province where high mortality from malaria resulted in
chronic labor shortages. In central Iran, in several villages near Isfahan, 'Abbas also resettled Caucasian Christians to combat population deficiencies, especially where a larger agricultural labor force was needed to boost the new
economy.

As an extension of the older pattern set up under Tahmasp, the Georgians
and Armenians under 'Abbas and his successors not only settled in New Julfa or
in Isfahan itself, or in the countryside; they came to occupy vital posts in the Safavid army and administration. Converting to Islam, Armenian and Georgians

gholams, whether captured or purchased, served in high posts. Most influential among them was Allah-Verdi Khan ("gift of God"), a remarkable Armenian slave-soldier and convert to Islam who rose through the ranks during Abbas's many campaigns to become a commander of the Safavid army and then governor-general of greater Fars that included the coasts and ports of the Persian Gulf. The Christian element in the age of 'Abbas, as merchants, artisans, soldiers, and administrators, had a far greater impact on the state and society proportionate to their population. Under 'Abbas, Armenians rose in status through the army and trade and were the chief beneficiaries of royal favor, far surpassing indigenous Jewish and Zoroastrian minorities. They were viewed as a window to the outside world and a key medium for enticing and sustaining Europe's diplomatic and commercial interests toward Iran.

Material evidence for the tolerant Safavid policy toward the Armenian community is evident not only in New Julfa's public buildings—markets, bathhouses, and bridges—but also in the residences of the affluent Armenian mercantile community. Numerous churches were built throughout the seventeenth century, some of which are among the best examples of Persian religious architecture. By the 1660s, New Julfa had twenty-four Armenian churches as well as several missionary houses and chapels. The best known, Holy Savior Cathedral—popularly known today as the Vank Cathedral—was financed by an affluent Armenian merchant and completed in 1664 (fig. 2.4). Displaying an excellent adaptation of Armenian tradition to the Persian architectural style, the domed structure and the elaborate arched nave replicated the architecture of Persian mosques. What made the cathedral distinct, however, were the interiors, adorned with frescoes executed by a number of local Armenian painters and showing the life of Jesus, the apostles, and the saints of the Armenian Church. The magnificent central panel, which depicts a striking scene of the Resurrection, not only evokes Byzantine and Venetian themes but also the Safavid Shi'i engagement with the themes of Return and the Hereafter (pl. 2.5). Such a conjunction was no coincidence since the Armenians were important partners in the Safavid enterprise of broadening the Persian commercial and cultural horizons.

LOOKING TO THE WEST

Owing either to his political savvy or to his business instincts, 'Abbas came to recognize the power of the new Europe early in his reign, and to value its strategic, commercial, and technological potential. In contrast to his predecessors, and indeed to many of his contemporaries, he could see the advantage of interacting with the West and selectively adopting what it had to offer. If

Figure 2.4. The Vank Cathedral in New Julfa.
Eugène Flandin, *Voyage en Perse de mm. Eugène Flandin, peintre, et Pascal Coste, architecte: Perse moderne* (Paris, 1851–1854). Planches, par Eugène Flandin, vol. 8, fol. 55, pl. 52, Église de Djoulfa. Courtesy of Beinecke Rare Book and Manuscript Library, Yale University.

anything, he was a bit "Westoxicated" (*gharbzadeh*), to borrow the fashionable twentieth-century label anachronistically. Yet he was confident enough in his own cultural identity not to be carried away entirely with Europe's marvels and its artful representatives. That his gaze was directed toward Europe at a time when European commercial imperialism was on the rise, though not yet dominant, was not a sheer coincidence.

Europe's presence was already tangible to the Persians as early as 1507, when a small Portuguese fleet under the command of the adventurous admiral Afonso de Albuquerque raided the strategic island of Hormuz at the head of the Persian Gulf and subordinated the local ruler, a tributary to Iran. The local population repelled him. Late in 1515, Albuquerque, now at the head of a much larger fleet, recaptured Hormuz. This time, he established the Portuguese as the dominant power in the Persian Gulf, which would last for more than a century (fig. 2.5). The island of Bahrain, another Safavid tributary at the opposite end of the Persian Gulf, fell to the Portuguese in 1521. However, attempts to capture the port of Basra, then a fragile Safavid possession, failed. The loss of Hormuz to the Portuguese was Iran's first experience of European imperial expansion.

Figure 2.5. Island of Hormuz in 1572 under Portuguese control.
Georg Braun and Franz Hogenberg, *Civitates Orbis Terrarum* (Cologne, 1572), 1:54.

For more than a century, passage through the Cape of Good Hope and Portuguese control of strongholds throughout the waterways of the Eastern Hemisphere created a web of commercial monopolies, and trade from the Persian Gulf with India, southern China, East Africa, and the western Mediterranean was only one component of this network. The Portuguese monopoly on the lucrative export of Persian silk through the south imposed an almost total control of the customs tariffs and maritime access to and from the Persian Gulf up to the first quarter of the seventeenth century. This was an important competition for Venetians' control of the silk trade of the eastern Mediterranean and their access to the European markets.

Portuguese relations with the Safavid state, however, remained ambivalent at best and brazenly intrusive at worst. Earlier, at the outset of the fifteenth century, Isma'il I, who lacked a navy, could neither evict them nor make them pay the tribute he received from the rulers of Hormuz. After long negotiations, therefore, he was persuaded to enter an anti-Ottoman pact with the Portuguese, which in the aftermath of the disastrous Battle of Chaldiran in 1514 he could hardly afford to implement. Facing the Ottoman blockade in the Mediterranean, the monopoly of the Portuguese was a further impediment to the growth of the Safavids' independent silk export. Reorientation toward the Persian Gulf heralded Iran's reliance on this southern artery to access the markets of Western

Europe. Massive injections of New World gold and silver into the markets of Asia and Africa had given Spain, which from 1580 to 1640 was in union with Portugal, enormous purchasing power and political acumen that could not have gone unnoticed even in remote and hard-to-access Safavid Iran.

The difficulties Iran faced getting access to the Mediterranean or the Persian Gulf were complicated by other geopolitical concerns. From the perspective of the Spanish Hapsburgs, Iran was a natural ally against Ottoman expansion in the Mediterranean and in central Europe, where the Austrian Hapsburgs were under constant Turkish pressure. 'Abbas, who came to realize the advantages of a European alliance early in his reign, wished to complement the anti-Ottoman pact with a viable commercial bond. Yet major problems hindered his liberation from geographical isolation and his ability to nurture relations with European powers beyond the strictly formal. The Turkish barrier made a steady line of communication through the Mediterranean next to impossible since Ottoman provincial governors often arrested and imprisoned emissaries passing through Ottoman territories. Even a simple exchange of correspondence over the land route took months, if not years. Alternative routes through the Cape of Good Hope, or via the Caspian Sea through Russia and the Baltics, proved logistically as hazardous and subject to the whims of either the Portuguese or the Russian Grand Duchy of Muscovy. Yet as early as 1521, the Grand Duchy and Safavid Iran established diplomatic relations. Growth of the Kazan trade in the Caspian through Astrakhan, Baku, and Darband (Derbent); fear of Ottoman expansion in the Caucasus; and the recurring problem of Cossack pirates raiding Caspian shores brought Russian emissaries to 'Abbas's court.

'Abbas's growing fame in Europe as an anti-Turkish champion brought to Iran, especially from the 1590s, a string of soldiers of fortune, missionaries, and merchants with various intents and degrees of sincerity. The poor quality of the missions and the uncharted domain of diplomacy further exacerbated difficult communication. Safavid Iran unavoidably found itself in the midst of intricate European politics, which were divided by sectarian strife, commercial and maritime rivalries, and wars of succession. Toward the end of the sixteenth century, Spain, under Philip II, was at the height of its colonial expansion and interventionist phase. Philip's anti-Protestant zeal, not unlike the Ottoman anti-Shi'i policies, sharpened Europe's sectarian discord. The Ottoman-Hapsburg race for supremacy in the Mediterranean, which reached a climax during the 1571 Battle of Lepanto, also echoed in Safavid Iran and came to influence the nature of its relations with the outside world. Despite a cultural divide and geographical distance, by the late sixteenth century Iran's geopolitical destiny was curiously tied up with Europe's. Safavid rulers' correspondence with European courts often rhetorically questioned the futility of the religious schism that divided Christian Europe while the Turkish threat was at hand. It was as though the reality of the Sunni-Shi'i conflict, of which they were the main party, did not sober them enough to the complexity of European sectarian and imperial rivalries.

In 1598, ten years after the destruction of the Spanish Armada by the English, when the English Sherley (also spelled Shirley) brothers, Anthony and Robert, and their company of about twenty Englishmen arrived in the Safavid court offering their services, they still wished to present 'Abbas with the illusion of a unified European front against the Ottomans (see map 2.1). Previously in the service of Robert Devereux, Second Earl of Essex (partaker in the exploits of Francis Drake and Walter Raleigh), on whose behalf they hoped to develop commercial ties with Safavid Iran, the Sherleys were typical English highborn adventurers in search of fame and fortune. Their claim to have introduced artillery to Safavid Iran and modernized its army can be safely dismissed. In reality, during nearly three decades of dealings with the Safavid monarch, they provided him with much information about Europe and European powers, as well as the possibilities of trade and political alliances, even though much of what they said was likely to have been colored by their proclivities for fame and fortune.

This is particularly true about Anthony Sherley, the older of the two, who in 1599, along with the Persian emissary Hosain 'Ali Beg Bayat, a courtier of Qezilbash origin, was sent on a goodwill mission to the European courts to promote trade and to coordinate a counteroffensive against the Ottomans, a mission that ended most grotesquely. Quarreling with the Persian emissary in Prague, and later in Rome, where they were to deliver the shah's message of friendship to Pope Clement VII, Anthony parted with the bales of silk entrusted to him by the shah to be sold in Europe, apparently to cover travel expenses. He pocketed the proceeds before skipping on to another of his adventures, this time in Italy. He may also have made available to a Turkish agent the contents of the shah's confidential correspondence. The Persian mission nevertheless proceeded, reaching Spain in 1601, but nothing concrete emerged there, as Spain was then rapidly losing ground to Dutch and British commercial contenders in the east.

More embarrassing for the Persian mission, however, was the conversion to Catholicism of a number of Persians in Hosain 'Ali Beg's retinue, of whom Uruch Beg Bayat is the best known. Although other lower-ranking members of the mission had already defected to Catholicism in Rome, it was Uruch Beg's conversion that received attention. Under Philip III's auspices, he was baptized in the Castilian capital, Valladolid, as Don Juan of Persia. His conversion may have been inspired by the splendor of the Spanish court, or perhaps the glitter of the unveiled women, or even the persuasion of the overzealous Jesuits. Don Juan survived to coauthor and publish in 1604 a remarkable account in the Catalan language of the history of Iran, his own life, and the mission that brought him to Spain, perhaps the earliest such chronicle by a living Persian in any European language. Only a year later, however, he was killed in a brawl in Valladolid. His murder was possibly related to the hostilities, prompted by the Spanish Inquisition, that eventually led to the 1609 expulsion of the last of the Moriscos, the former Muslims and crypto-Muslims, from Spanish soil.

The failure of this mission did not discourage 'Abbas from dispatching or receiving other European missions, nor was it the end of the Sherley brothers. Anxious to press further in his objective—trade through the Persian Gulf—and to build on shared anti-Ottoman sentiments, in 1605 'Abbas sent Mahdi-Qoli Beg to the European courts, where he was received by the Polish monarch Sigismund III and later by Emperor Rudolf II of the Holy Roman Empire (fig. 2.6). Later, in 1608, the shah dispatched to the Spanish court yet another mission, this time headed by Robert Sherley. The Hispano-Portuguese influence then waning, the mission was aimed at a new European maritime contender.

Already 'Abbas's recapture of the island of Bahrain from the Portuguese in 1602, and shortly thereafter the port of Gambrun, which overlooked the Strait

Figure 2.6. The Safavid envoy Mahdi-Qoli Beg, dispatched in 1605 by Shah 'Abbas I to the court of the Hapsburg emperor, Rudolph II (r. 1576–1612), in Vienna. Engraving by the Dutch artist Aegidius Sadeler. The Elisha Whittelsey Collection, no. 49.95.2202. Courtesy of the Metropolitan Museum of Art, New York.

of Hormuz, had dimmed his chances of any collaboration with the Iberian power. Instead, the shah was persuaded to turn to the English as an alternative trading and strategic partner. Robert Sherley, dressed as a Qezilbash and bearing the title of khan, which he had earned for his many years of military service to the shah, was something of a sensation when he reached London in 1611 — perhaps the first Persianized exotica to hit fashion-conscious Europe of the time. Although he returned empty-handed, due to resistance by the pro-Ottoman English Levantine Company's lobby, for a while the Persian dress style, perhaps inspired by Sherley, became fashionable in the Stuart court.

'Abbas's diplomacy worked to the extent that it not only opened Iran to European commerce and curiosity but also forged stronger bonds with Mughal India and eventually with the Shaybanid Uzbeks of Central Asia. The primary motives invariably were trade but also security and cultural exchanges, especially with the Mughal court. Despite occasional friction over the control of Kandahar province, which eventually fell to Safavid Iran in the late seventeenth century, Mughal rulers generally felt a strong cultural affinity for Iran. Such cultural integration is evident in a number of allegorical Mughal paintings, which often display 'Abbas, albeit unrealistically, as a junior partner to the Mughal emperor (pl. 2.6).

Moreover, numerous missions from Spain, England, Venice, the Netherlands, and Poland, as well as from Prague, Muscovy, Rome, and later German principalities arrived in Isfahan—though few achieved results as concrete as the English, and shortly thereafter, the Dutch, trading companies (see map 2.1). Although somewhat independent of the English crown, the East India Company conducted business, even at its inception, not entirely unmindful of the English strategic interests. Its first ship reached the Iranian port of Jask on the Gulf of Oman in 1616, only sixteen years after the company's investiture. By the time it arrived in Jask—a port that had long been serving Indo-Persian and East African trade through Muscat (Masqat)—the English company had already won important concessionary privileges from the Safavid court. 'Abbas allowed the Honorable Company, as it was known, to establish a trading factory but did not grant it the right to build strongholds, being well aware of the strategic importance of Portuguese coastal fortresses throughout the hemisphere. He also lifted tariffs on English imports and exports as an incentive to compete against the Portuguese monopoly.

The growth of English trade facilitated Iran's access to European markets, although it did not dislodge the Portuguese altogether. Evident in Safavid correspondence of the time is displeasure with the Portuguese maltreatment of Persian merchants, especially after the expulsion of the Portuguese from Gambrun in 1614, renamed Bandar Abbas in honor of its liberator. Anti-Portuguese senti-ments were backed by Shi'i polemics and fueled by the anti-Jesuit propaganda of the English Reformation. By 1622, the shah felt confident enough to let the powerful governor-general of Fars province, Allah-Verdi Khan, pressure the East India Company into collaborating in a raid against the Portuguese to re-capture Hormuz island, a longtime strategic ambition of the Safavid rulers (see map 2.1). To compensate for the lack of a naval force, a chronic Iranian weak-ness in guarding its southern shores, the Persian troops were transported on board English ships to the island, where they successfully drove away the de-moralized garrison. Portuguese attempts to regain it failed. The loss of Hormuz, a prosperous stronghold, was a serious blow to the Portuguese presence and the beginning of a long and protracted disintegration of their trading empire. Although they persisted up to 1649 in Muscat, on the opposite coast, their trad-ing privileges were lost to the benefit of the English and soon after the Dutch.

That the East India Company was a crucial partner in capturing Hormuz, however, did not result in an automatic export monopoly for the English. Sens-ing the rise of the Dutch seafaring empire as powerful competition for the Eng-lish, 'Abbas and his lieutenants welcomed the market forces and the diplomacy they engendered. Consolidated in 1602, the Dutch East India Company (VOC, for Vereenigde Oost-Indische Compagnie) proved financially stronger and commercially more astute than its English counterpart. To his credit, 'Abbas tried to strike a balance between the English and the Dutch; between southern and northern trade, including the Mediterranean route; and between domes-tic merchants, mostly the Armenians of New Julfa, and the European trading companies.

However, the Safavid reassertion in the Persian Gulf and the return of Gamb-run and Hormuz to Iran did not result in the creation of a Safavid naval force or even a merchant fleet. Adhering to a long Persian tradition of land-bound trade, the Safavids invariably preferred to leave high-seas adventures to the seafaring Europeans. Even the mighty Ottoman naval power in the Mediterranean, and in the early part of the sixteenth century in the Indian Ocean, did not ease Per-sian navigational anxiety. Having been a land power, the Safavids, similar to the Mughals of Hindustan, had difficulty adopting the sea culture of their southern and northern peripheries. After the Portuguese departure, from the 1640s and for more than half a century, the Dutch held a near monopoly on the export of silk, driving English and Armenian competitors out of the market. By the end of the century, the domestic silk exporters, the backbone of the emerging mer-cantile community, no longer benefited from royal protection. Furthermore, the Armenian community of New Julfa and elsewhere did not feel as secure as they did during the time of 'Abbas I, even though they had expanded their international trading network throughout Bengal and Southeast Asia, and to Venice and as far west as England.

The Jews of Iran, especially of Isfahan, fared worse. Although they seem to have played no significant part in the organization of the government silk trade, in their roles as domestic bankers or as exporters of silk from Kashan to the Persian Gulf, they may have been perceived as competition for the state monopoly. It is possible that the eclipse of the Portuguese trade played a part in the further waning of Jews in the Safavid commercial operation, especially in the south. Ironically, the Portuguese, who had expelled the Jews from their lands, relied on the Jewish diaspora, some seemingly of Iberian stock, to conduct their trade in Iranian silk-weaving centers such as Kashan. It is perhaps not sheer coincidence that from the early decades of the seventeenth century, Jews were subjects of discrimination—and later persecution—by the Safavid state, perhaps influenced by the contemporary European, and especially Catholic, anti-Semitism.

The 1622 capture of Hormuz followed a year later by the conquest of the Shi'i holy cities of Iraq and in 1624 by the capture of Baghdad. Remarkably, this highlight of 'Abbas's political career, compensated for the absence of a Persian naval expansion, was an excellent option for the Safavid shah at a time when Ottomans were engaged at their western frontiers. Yet Iran's commercial orientation toward the south continued. Trade through Bandar Abbas and other southern ports was essential for incorporating the Persian Gulf littoral into the Safavid Empire, in much the same way that exporting silk produced in Gilan province through the northern route integrated the Caspian provinces into Safavid Iran and opened trade with Caspian ports of Baku and Astrakhan in the seventeenth and eighteenth centuries (see map 2.1).

Toward the end of 'Abbas's reign, references to the Guarded Domains of Iran were used with greater frequency in the Safavid annals as an alternative for the Sublime Safavid State (*Dowlat-e 'Alliyeh-e Safavieh*). Expelling the Portuguese, repelling the Uzbeks, and retaking the Safavid provinces from the Ottomans engendered in Safavid Iran a spirit of confidence and security. Military success was backed by economic prosperity, at least for a period after 'Abbas's reign. Nearly all European accounts of seventeenth-century Iran confirm a new age of affluence that was facilitated by a more extensive network of domestic and overseas communication, a growing urban population, a nuanced concept of leisure, and a maturing Shi'i intellectual identity.

The appeal of an anti-Ottoman alliance with the Europeans swiftly paled once the Safavids achieved tranquility with their western neighbor. A decade after the death of Shah 'Abbas in 1629, and sixteen years after the Safavids' capture of Iraq, renewed hostilities with the rejuvenated Ottoman Empire under Morad IV (r. 1623–1640) led to the 1639 peace treaty of Zohab (see map 2.1). Under the terms of the treaty, the Safavids relinquished control of all of Iraq, most notably, the Shi'i holy cities, to the Ottomans, recognized Turkish sovereignty over the western Caucasus, and gave the Ottomans a foothold in the Bay of Basra, at the northern tip of the Persian Gulf. In exchange the Ottomans recognized Iranian sovereignty over the eastern Caucasus, consisting of Nakhijevan, Armenia, Qarabagh, the two central and eastern Georgian principalities of Kartli and Kakheti, as well as the whole of Azarbaijan, the western Iranian provinces, and Bahrain. The peace proved enduring, at least for another century, until the end of the Safavid period.

EUROPEAN OBSERVERS

Even before the shift in Perso-European interests, from the anti-Ottoman alliance to commercial competition, Persia had become a space to be experienced by Europeans and non-Europeans through adventure, imagination, and nostalgia. Yet it was only occasionally understood on its own terms. The age of printing generated a new European readership as well as a new popular scholarship, curious to know the world through travel accounts and geographical literature. What Persia offered to the Italian, French, English, Spanish, and German writers and readers—along with the unique marvels of India, China, and Japan, and the might of the Ottoman Empire—was not simply the pomp and circumstance of the Safavid court, its wealth and its trade. Europeans traced the material evidence of Persia's ancient past and its place in the biblical and Greco-Roman experience. Persian literary and historical texts were translated and appreciated, and Persian culture, institutions, and lifestyle observed and sometimes imitated. Some of the earliest Orientalist representations of the East were shaped by images of the Safavid court, culture, and society.

After the removal of the Portuguese from Hormuz, one of the first travelers who returned to Europe through India, in 1623, aboard an English ship, was the Roman nobleman Pietro Della Valle. A talented observer, in a series of long dispatches, he chronicled his six-year stay in Iran, his personal encounters with Shah 'Abbas, and his experiences with the Persian people. Della Valle's letters, published in the following decades and later abridged and translated, provided a wealth of information about Safavid Iran through the eye of an often sympathetic, though occasionally smug, observer—an account interwoven with his own life story of passion and panache. He was a valuable source of information to the shah, and he briefed him about European kings and nobility, alliances and rivalries, social mores and lifestyle. 'Abbas probably relied on sources such as Della Valle to define and readjust his course, although it is hard to see as a whole any specific evidence of European inspiration.

Shortly after 'Abbas's time, a German scholar and Persian interpreter, Adam Olearius, was sent on a mission by Frederick III, Duke of Holstein, to establish commercial relations with Safavid Iran. Olearius arrived in Isfahan in 1637 via the northern route, through Moscovy. The account of his travels to Russia and Persia, first published in 1647, is one of several detailed seventeenth-century narratives that helped introduce Safavid Iran to European audiences beyond the rampant stereotypes of the exotic Orient. His description of Isfahan included useful data on urban life, the court of Shah Safi, 'Abbas's successor, the Armenians and their quarter, the tea- and coffeehouses, gardens, buildings and architecture, and everyday lives of ordinary people. Beyond Isfahan he also made realistic observations of other towns and villages in the Safavid domain. As a man of letters, Olearius's 1654 translation into German of Sa'di's *Golestan* was among the earliest Persian classics to appear in a European language.

A quarter of a century after Olearius, when the French Huguenot merchant of precious stones and luxury goods John Chardin first visited Iran in 1666, the Iranian knowledge of Europe and Europeans was somewhat more accurate. His multivolume account in French, the best known in European languages about seventeenth-century Iran, was first published in London in 1686 and revised several times. Chardin presented the changing Safavid society of the post-'Abbas era as multiethnic and urbane, with an elite culture of serenity and pleasure and languishing socioreligious institutions. Far more than any other account in the vast and diverse travel literature on Safavid Iran, Chardin's was widely read both in his own time and in later years. Almost encyclopedic in approach, he observed, collected, and commented on a variety of topics, from land and ecology to government, religion, literature, history, and everyday life. In due course the representation that he formulated was influential in the eighteenth-century European imagination of Persia.

Montesquieu's *Lettres persanes* relied in part on both Olearius and Chardin and the format of their journals to portray an imaginary Persian observer of French society. In doing so, he wraps his critique of French despotism in a Persian cloak and transposed Louis XIV with an unnamed Persian shah. Voltaire, Rousseau, and Gibbon, among others, read Chardin intentionally and located his Iran in their philosophical and historical discourses, often with grudging respect. Later travelers to Iran, especially in the nineteenth century, dabbled in Chardin's themes and ruminated on his cultural biases often with a stronger sense of cultural superiority. Despite his many factual errors, Chardin was an observer with a degree of understanding of the culture and society he was fascinated with. His knowledge of Safavid domains brought him the reputation of being the prototypical Iran expert who advised, at different times in his career, the English and the Dutch East India Companies.

Whether through travelers or through other means, Shah 'Abbas's European commercial enterprise and political alliances brought mixed results. His hope for an anti-Ottoman pact with Europe never really paid off, for reasons beyond his technological and diplomatic control. Toward the end of 'Abbas's reign, both the Safavids and the Ottomans were realistic enough to appreciate the cautious entente that had emerged between the two powers. Yet contacts with Europe made Iranians realize that they were not alone facing the Ottoman threat. 'Abbas was astute enough to realize that the only way the Ottoman geographical barrier could be successfully crossed was through European diplomacy and trade. To the Iranians, moreover, European visitors offered the earliest encounters with a dynamic and complex Europe, prototypes of the *farangi* "Other" who were curious, resourceful, and shrewd. A corollary to the new European trade, European travelers revealed before the Persian eye a face of modernity that was about to engage, and later threaten, their world.

CONFINES OF THE SAFAVID HORIZON

None of the emissaries of the Safavid era, with the exception of Don Juan of Persia, left behind accounts of his visits to the European courts. The era of 'Abbas I and his immediate successors remained largely insular despite a remarkable florescence in speculative thought and artistic creativity. If there was an awareness of Europe, even among the intellectual elite, so far as we know, it was confined to trade and merchandise, to kingdoms and armies, to a few Jesuit missionaries and Christian monks, and to soldiers of fortune. There were also *farangi*-style caps, matchlocks, and other European or Europeanized paraphernalia in Persian paintings, textiles, and architecture of the period. European-style scenery also appeared in late Safavid paintings. It is hard to believe that in cosmopolitan Isfahan of the time some debate and exchange of information about intellectual and scientific issues would not have taken place among the numerous European visitors, members of trade missions, and missionaries, and the members of the divan or scholars who frequented the Safavid court. 'Abbas's curiosity about everything European, including the Europeans themselves, must have been contagious.

Yet precious little was ever written about Europe by Safavid authors beyond passing geographical references, mostly based on classical Islamic texts rather than on fresh learning and observation. There is little internal evidence in the works of the philosophers and theologians of the period, even the literati and the historians, to suggest a tangible intellectual interplay. Early modern European thinkers and their scientific discoveries remained unknown to the Safavids even as late as early nineteenth century. Despite being produced with renewed vigor, works of Safavid astronomy, mathematics, and sciences ignored crucial questions of modern science, and Iranians seem to be unaware of the European discourses in method and human individuality. If the Safavids were aware, it did not surface in their body of common knowledge. Europeans, despite their notable presence, were infidels so far as the formal scholarship was concerned; their customs and accomplishments could be neither the subject of Muslim curiosity nor imitated. Fear of being branded as heretical, for following the ways of the infidels, dissuaded the curious from traveling abroad or learning European languages; those who did remained anonymous or left no record for posterity. Even imagining Europe seems to have been a perilous venture, since no book of marvel of any significance has yet surfaced from this period. By the seventeenth century the discovery of the New World was known, but to the few who heard about it from the Portuguese and the English, including 'Abbas himself. To them it was no more than a exotic land, rich in gold and silver but also full of "savages," as Native Americans were portrayed in European woodcuts and other representations. Only very late in the eighteenth century a more accurate picture of the Americas began to emerge in the Indo-Persian works of geography produced in early colonial India.

China had largely disappeared from the Safavid horizon, despite the long history of cultural and commercial exchange. Except for precious commodities such as porcelain and spices coming through the Indian Ocean route (and Persian porcelain going to China along the same route), there was little direct contact between the two civilizations on the ancient overland Silk Road. The Chinese-style figures that Persian artists portrayed in their paintings were about the only memory still alive of that rich past. A certain Sayyed 'Ali Akbar Khata'i, an emissary from Bukhara who traveled to northern China and left behind a fascinating account in Persian titled *Khatay-nameh* (The Book of Cathay), was as foreign to the Chinese as they were to him. Perhaps himself a Persian renegade, in 1516 he dedicated his book to the Ottoman Sultan Salim I. It was soon translated to Ottoman Turkish. His description of the Chinese court ceremonies, cities, everyday life, medicine, judicial system, and prisons—he was detained for about a month because a member of his retinue was engaged in a brawl with a group of Tibetans—were presumably all new to his audiences, since his account is devoid of any reference to an earlier body of literature about China.

Eighteenth-century translations in Persian of the life of the famous Jesuit in sixteenth-century China, Matteo Ricci, done by an Iranian exile in the Mughal Empire, remained unknown to the Safavid reader. Likewise, Japan resonated in the mind of the Safavids as nothing more than the distant and exotic islands of Waqwaq, of the classical Islamic books of marvels. Southeast Asia, however, was better known to the Persians, thanks to communities of Indo-Persian merchants who had settled in Indonesia, Burma, and Siam since the fifteenth century. They brought with them to these lands their own brand of eclectic Islam and trade practices.

The secretary to a Safavid embassy to the court of the King Narai (r. 1656–1688) of Siam (or Thailand) in 1685 left behind a fascinating account of the government and the people of that country. *Safineh-ye Solaymani* (The Ship of Solomon), named after the Safavid ruler Shah Solayman (1666–1694), sheds light on the Persian and Japanese merchants, advisers, and mercenaries to the king of Siam, who defied the influence of the native mandarins and European commercial and political rivals. Along the way to Siam, the author Mohammad Ibrahim ibn Mohammad Rabi', who served as secretary of the mission, offered valuable accounts of the English in India and their customs and manners.

Even more than it had in medieval Islamic times, Hindustan loomed large in the Iranian mind as the quintessential exotic place. It was also a profitable trade route, especially since the ships of the English and French East India Companies began to frequent the Persian Gulf with greater regularity. India became more accessible and a place of refuge for those in search of fame and fortune, or an escape from religious and political persecution. Yet before the latter part of the eighteenth century, Persian systematic descriptions of Hindustan were rare.

The scant interest among Shi'i scholars toward the outside world was also obfuscated because of Christian-Muslim controversies. Predictably, among Shi'i scholars there was little interest in nonbelievers and their societies and cultures, and polemical literature of the period conveyed little but doctrinal debates. Likewise, Christian polemics produced by Europeans generally were uninterested in Safavid society and culture. Heeding the shah's request, Zayn al-'Abidin 'Alawi, for instance, a learned jurist descended from a Jabal 'Amil family, wrote a number of Persian refutations in response to Portuguese Jesuit missionaries based in Goa on the western coast of India. 'Alawi's apologias were largely based on classical accounts, although they showed some awareness of the current schisms within Christendom, despite the Jesuits' facade of unanimity. His best-known book, written in 1622, shortly before the Safavids' joint operation with the English East India Company against the Portuguese, conveyed 'Abbas's political agenda. Commissioning 'Alawi to write a refutation was no less transparent than Portuguese support for their missionaries. His wish was no doubt aligned with the duty of the ulama "to preserve the seed of Islam" from disbelief; hence, it appeared only logical to any mainstream scholar of the time to refute and reject Jesuits and their European patrons.

The advantage of the Portuguese Jesuits over their Shi'i respondents of course was more technological than theological. Their Christian literature was the first to be printed in Persian and distributed in India and Iran, while the Muslim responses inscribed in manuscripts never left the royal or elite libraries. The Jesuit print literature in Persian, to which 'Alawi's apologias were directed, was originally produced for Mughal India but also was distributed in Iran, possibly through a network of Catholic missionaries active mostly among the Armenians of Isfahan. In addition to the Jesuits, throughout the seventeenth century, Carmelites, Franciscans, Augustinians, and Capuchins built and maintained monasteries and churches in Isfahan, with the approval of the Safavid government. Relying on 'Abbas's pro-Christian affinities, missionaries nevertheless were no more than benign tokens of European presence. They were unable to convert the Muslim public to their message of faith, let alone spread the secular message of early modern Europe.

One of the earliest books to appear in print in Persian, the *Dastan-e Masih, Historia Christi Persice*, was a bilingual Persian-Latin account of the life of Jesus, compiled by the well-known Jesuit missionary Hieronymo Xavier (fig. 2.7). Xavier offered a single narrative of Christ's story palatable to Muslim readers who were unaccustomed to the notion of four Gospels, in contrast to their own single Qur'an scripture. Despite Xavier's earnest effort, the Persian prose of *Dastan-e Masih* proved somewhat coarse and unreadable, even though he apparently had benefited from the help of Persian-speaking converts in India. As with much missionary literature, this early specimen was not successful in Iran in winning over new converts from among the Muslims. It is not unlikely, however, that it attracted learned readers, for it was offering an alternative narrative of Jesus to that of the familiar Qur'anic and Muslim apocryphal literature. Although Persian readers were familiar with much earlier translations of the Gospels, the printed rendering had a very different effect.

The print revolution gave Europe enormous leverage over non-Western cultures in making available to the literate European public a wide range of material. Such popularization of knowledge and the subsequent breakdown of the

Figure 2.7. Title page of Hieronymo Xavier, *Dastan-e Masih* (Batavia, 1639).
Courtesy of the Sterling Memorial Library, Yale University.

elite's monopoly over texts and learning did not happen in the Middle East before the late eighteenth century. The predominant medium for public knowledge remained in manuscript form and more so in oral form. Knowledge was transmitted through elite channels, and incentives for literacy were limited to a madrasa education and bureaucracy of the divan. Although a small Armenian printing house with Armenian typeface did exist in New Julfa at the time, the idea of printing seems not to have impressed Iranians for a long time.

Disinterest in the printed word, however, was less of a setback with regard to theological disputes. As Imami Shi'i dogma solidified, channels for relaying the state's religious ideology to the public came under greater control of clerical establishment. The state-sponsored propagandists who urged people in the street to recite their rhymed cursing of the early Caliphs now were supplemented in the mosque by melodic readers of the tragedies of Karbala and by preachers who instructed them to implement Shi'i devotional rituals and abide by the teachings of the jurists. Popular associations of the Sufis in their convents as well as the gatherings of the wandering *qalandars* were banned. Likewise the reading of the *Shahnameh* in coffeehouses and in the *zur-khanehs* (houses of strength) was discouraged and generally disapproved by the jurists.

NOQTAVI MILLENNIAL REVIVAL

Practicing Sufi orders were especially the target of persecution, for jurists and the state viewed them as undesirable, if not a dangerous hotbed of non-conformity, and even heresy. Closure of the Safavid frontiers and the hostility of their Sunni neighbors, moreover, restricted the movement of the dervishes who were in the habit of traveling far and wide across the Islamic world. They were an important alternative source of information for ordinary people in towns and villages. The *qalandars*, as they were generally known, were itiner-ant dervishes who wore rags and animal skins; they were tattooed, had piercings and burn marks, exhibited nonconformist behavior, often smoked hashish, and maintained a lax lifestyle. Loosely organized, their convents (known as *langar*), stretching throughout the Persianate world and beyond, from Bukhara to Kash-mir to Baghdad and the Balkans, were home to unconventionalities: sexual, social, political, and at times messianic. Their lifestyle and utterances, which adhered to popularized monism and ideas of reincarnation and transmigration, often in the form of recited poetry, as well as their tales of remote lands and strange people that they narrated to their street audiences, were frowned upon by the ulama, who saw dervishes as competition for preaching in the mosques.

As the Safavid establishment turned against the Sufis, the thrust of the anti-dogmatic policy was first borne by the Noqtavis at the turn of the Islamic mil-lennium (AH 1000, or 1591–1592 CE). The revived Noqtavi (lit. "pointist") movement upheld the memory of Mahmud of Pasikhan (in Gilan province), a Persian prophet who had lived two centuries earlier. His cabalistic creed with a mystic-materialistic bent and an apocalyptic message found new appeal in the Safavid era in reaction to both the Qezilbash hegemony and greater jurist indoctrination of the Safavid public. In its origins, Noqtavism was the most cerebral and systematic manifestation of the greater *qalandari* movement of the late Islamic Middle Ages. The Safavid sources that disparagingly labeled them as "heretics" indeed had a point. For Noqtavis, earth was the most vital of the four elements and was considered the origin of man, whom they identified as the prophet Adam. Humankind's progression in time from one point to the next, they believed, went through successive millennial cycles that had been initiated by the chain of Abrahamic prophets.

The religion of Islam initiated by Mohammad, the prophet of the Arabs, the Noqtavis upheld, was to be abrogated at the end of the Islamic millennium and a new Persian cycle (*dowr-e 'Ajam*) would commence, as foretold by Mahmud of Pasikhan. The Noqtavis' conscious attempt to break away from the dominant religion of the time was a rare phenomenon in Islamic history. The Persian cycle of material progression in the Noqtavis' belief system promised earthly humans freedom from the heavens through a quasi-rationalist cosmology. The point theory, after which the movement was named, viewed the universe as a text consisting of letters, with each letter consisting of points. In its progression through time, the primal point was considered the motivating force behind stages of human perfection. This sense of historical progression stood in contrast to the veneration of the past in normative Islam, especially the prophetic past, so widely celebrated in the study of the theology of the Safavid period and by "traditionalist" scholars whose prime focus was the study of hadith (the reports on the words and the deeds of the Prophet of Islam and the Shi'i Imams).

The alternative convents of the Noqtavis in the Safavid period, so far as the sources inform us, were more about music, wine, appreciation of nature, good food, and intellectual discourse than formalities of the shari'a. A love of Persian literature was combined with aversion toward jurists and what they stood for. These convents were apparently attractive to the general public but also frequented by the urban elite, and later they may have been associated with tea- and coffeehouses as they became prevalent in Isfahan and elsewhere. In his nocturnal outings around Qazvin in disguise, 'Abbas for a while attended the convent of the Noqtavi leader, Darvish Khosraw, who informed the shah about Noqtavi beliefs and educated him in the art of good living, while no doubt warning him about the impending upheaval at the turn of the Islamic millennium.

We may assume that it was the growing popularity of the Noqtavis, and their anti-jurist and even anti-state ideas, which turned the shah against them. The Noqtavis were persecuted under Tahmasp, but it was 'Abbas's millennial anxieties that persuaded him to eradicate the agnostic heretics. Following his astrologer's advice, and under the pretext of avoiding the ominous celestial conjunction in March 1592, corresponding to year 1000 of the Hijra calendar, he temporarily abdicated, placing a Noqtavi dervish on the throne in his stead. This no doubt was a symbolic move, perhaps mimicking a Nowruz ritual of carnival king (mir-e nowruzi), which in effect aimed to bring about the Noqtavi promise of a new era. In a few days, however, once the supposed ominous millennial conjunction was over, the shah promptly ordered the execution of the deceived dervish king. In a concerted move, he subsequently went about destroying the Noqtavi rural and urban network and killing the movement's intellectual and community leaders, on charges of heresy and treason. They had been accused of preparing for a revolutionary overthrow of the Safavid state, and even of collaborating with foreign powers. Their correspondence with Abol-Fazl 'Allami (d. 1602), the celebrated minister to Emperor Akbar (r. 1556–1605), the Mughal ruler of India, reportedly proved the existence of a network and such a plot.

Even if these charges were fabricated to counter the Noqtavis' popularity, by adding an anti-state twist to their proven anticlericalism, there was reality in 'Allami's affinity with the Noqtavis and other Iranian nonconformists. In the following decades Noqtavi sympathizers took refuge in the Mughal Empire, part of an exodus of Sufis, writers, poets, and artists who left behind the suffocating dogmatic world of the late Safavid era for the prosperity and tolerance of the Mughal court. We can detect the Noqtavis' influence in particular on 'Allami's doctrine of Universal Conciliation (*solh-e koll*), perhaps among the greatest intellectual achievements of the Mughal era, and the foundation of Akbar's royal cult, known as the Divine Creed (*din-e elahi*). Contrary to the Ottoman and Safavid sponsorship of the Sunni and Shi'i creeds, Universal Conciliation envisioned the state as the promoter and guarantor of religious diversity. The Mughal millennial king eventually stopped enforcing all predominant symbols of Islam, such as the call to prayer and observation of the fast in Ramadan, in favor of his millennial Divan Creed. The collapse of the Noqtavi movement in Iran, by contrast, signaled the Safavids' favoring of the Shi'i orthodox establishment at the expense of any alternative. The Noqtavi thought thus could have only indirectly influenced the Safavid environment. It is not inconceivable to think that philosophy of the School of Isfahan, and even 'Abbas's patronage of it, or his new perception of urban spaces, with an element of leisure incorporated into it, were inspired by the Noqtavi thought.

Beyond Noqtavis, throughout the seventeenth century other non-shari'a trends, such as the Sufi orders, were systematically banned, forced underground, or driven into exile. Even the Safavi order, the wellspring of the ruling dynasty, was allowed to dry out in all but name, long after the Qezilbash Sufis had bartered their messianic zeal for lucrative state offices. Those who remained associated with the declining order, we are told, served in menial jobs in the Safavid court as the Safavids moved closer to the "correct" Twelver Shi'ism of the jurists. The latter had helped legitimize the state as a sacred institution and proved essential to countering domestic dissent and external influences. The more the Ottoman and Uzbek states turned to Sunni orthodoxy, the more the Safavids became dogmatic Shi'is, and so closing the geopolitical horizons of Iranian territory and society.

WISDOM OF TRANSCENDENCE

The rise of urban piety did not entirely decimate the Safavids' potential for speculative thought. Although similar to the Ottoman post-conquest world, the shift in the Safavid state's ideology allowed conservative jurists to articulate an

ethos of pious legalism through law, ritual, and sacred myth. The Safavid age
also nurtured a new generation of thinkers akin to mystical and philosophical
thought, even at times engaging in proto-modern themes that otherwise were
entertained only by antinomian trends outside the confines of normative Islam.

The founders of the emerging Safavid schools of theology and philosophy
were often men of religious learning. In exchange for state patronage, they generated a politically mute and harmless hybrid of philosophy, theology, and mysticism beneficial to the state's homogenizing agenda. The School of Isfahan,
as it came to be known in modern times, offered an innocuous alternative to
such trends as Noqtavism indigenous to the Iranian environment. This school
of thought's affinity to the Safavid court, and the clerical background of those
who were engaged in it, made the new theosophical interest, at least in the early
stages, a safe enterprise. Yet philosophical discourse, even when disguised as
theosophy, still could not escape the jurists' condemnations; they were labeled
"undesirable" and even "heretical."

The so-called School of Isfahan was heir to a speculative tradition that though
by and large had been abandoned in the rest of the Islamic world, it had survived,
and even thrived, in Iran, Whether in the form of the Peripatetic philosophy
of Ibn Sina (Avicenna), with strong Neoplatonic overtones, or more often the
Illumination School (*Eshraqi*) of Shehab al-Din Sohravardi (d. 1191), Iranians
since the early Islamic era had continued to engage in philosophical discourse.
Shi'ism also utilized the rationalistic premises of the Mu'tazilite movement
of the early Islamic era to buttress its alternative theology. A tamed scholastic
philosophical tradition was thus preserved in the Shi'i curriculum, first among
the Isma'ili thinkers, with emphasis on rationalized religious thought (*kherad*),
and later through works of a towering scholar of the thirteenth century, Nasir
al-Din Tusi. In the same vein, the School of Isfahan never stopped reconciling a rarefied version of Islamic dogma with a crippled rendition of rational
thought, a tedious project, as it turned out, and one of grand scale. Yet such an
undertaking could not entirely abandon such inherent themes in the Iranian
milieu as, for example, Mohammad ibn Zarkariya al-Razi's adherence to the
ancient Iranian idea of eternal time (*dahr*) and Sohravardi's return to a largely
imaginary reconstruction of Zoroastrian wisdom. Residues of Persian agnosti-
cism did survive.

On the surface, Safavid Iran seemed the least favorable climate for the
growth of such speculative thought. Even redefining philosophy (*falsafah*) in
the guise of *hekmat* (gnostic wisdom) did not alleviate the pressure on teachers of theosophy and their small circle of students who displayed every sign of
religious conformity so as to avoid charges of heresy. Yet the growth of specu-

lative thought in the seventeenth century can be viewed as part of a greater assimilation process within Shi'ism. The complexities of urban Persian high culture attracted Arab jurists and Turkish Qezilbash toward such activities as poetry, history, philosophy, and scientific experimentation, while hardly ever inspiring them to learn something about the world beyond their Shi'i domain, except perhaps a cursory interest in Indian thought. One of the most successful figures of the period molded into this Persian cast is the celebrated Baha' al-Din 'Amili (1547–1621), also known by his nom de plume Shaykh Baha'i. A theologian, jurist, mathematician, grammarian, poet, and moralist, his universalistic pursuits might be compared for example to Erasmus of Rotterdam, his near contemporary (fig. 2.8).

An émigré from a family of jurists from Jabal 'Amil, the young Baha' al-Din first learned Persian at the age of ten when he was a novice in a Shiraz madrasa. He perfected it to such a degree that he was able to compose prose and poetry in his acquired language. He rose to prominence at a relatively young age and briefly became the *shaykh al-Islam* of Isfahan, the highest judicial post in the land, in part because of his proper lineage and powerful connections, but also because of his sound scholarship and refined Persian. As an urban designer, Baha'i was credited with devising a master plan for the new city of Isfahan. He reportedly also engineered Zayadehrud's irrigation network for the city and its

Figure 2.8. Baha' al-Din 'Amili (Shaykh Baha'i) smoking a water pipe.
By Mohammad 'Ali Bayg Naqqash-bashi in 1744–1745 (based on a contemporary drawing).
Courtesy of Malek National Museum and Library, Tehran, no. 1393/02/00025.

environs, as well as his own ingenious design for increasing that river's water flow by diverting water from the Bakhtiyari highlands in Kuhrang, in the Zagros mountain range, more than hundred miles northwest of Isfahan. His interest in mathematics, physics, and alchemy generated a number of living legends about him and about the buildings associated with his name.

In greater part, however, Shaykh Baha'i succeeded because he symbolized a compassionate side of Shi'ism, supportive of the jurists but also popular among the laypeople. His *Jame'-e 'Abbasi* (The 'Abbasian Compendium), a manual of the Shi'i jurisprudence in Persian, contained essential Shi'i devotional, contractual, and penal laws and rituals. Commissioned by the shah, as the title suggests, this was the closest Safavid Iran would come to codifying the shari'a with a well-organized, "user-friendly" format and easy style (later to be completed by a student of Shaykh Baha'i). Its vast popularity up to the twentieth century may be explained by its success in rescuing Shi'i law from the tedious elaborations and digressions in jurists' texts and turning it into a usable manual for ordinary people. This and other state-sponsored summaries of Shi'i traditions and devotional acts served to deepen the roots of the state creed in a population still uncertain about its Shi'i loyalty.

Also important for the shaping of a formal creed, Shaykh Baha'i contributed to Shi'i madrasa education through works of law, hadith, and Arabic grammar, as well as his promotion of mathematics and Ptolemaic astronomy. It is difficult to detect much originality in his scholarly output, but he and the ethnically diverse students under him translated, commented on, and popularized Shi'i works of earlier times. At least three of Shaykh Baha'i's own works on the hadith, Arabic syntax, and mathematics remained part of the Shi'i scholastic curriculum up to the twentieth century. His Persian didactic and lyrical poetry, by contrast, promoted individualistic mystical experience. The so-called *'erfani* approach to religion employed Sufi terminology and discourse while also portraying Sufis as deceptive and heretical, presumably because of their emphasis on mystical ecstasy through music and dance. In a didactic fable, *Mush va Gorbeh* (Mouse and Cat, after 'Obaid Zakani's fourteenth-century satire), Shaykh Baha'i lampoons the Sufis, characterized as the shrewd mouse, and sharply attacks their alleged hypocrisy and superstition. The Sufi's opponent, however, is a jurist characterized as a wise and charitable cat who is enlightened by the true path of shari'a. He is often addressed in the story with the royal epithet *shahryar* ("minor king," or "princely ruler"). At the end of a long and dreary dialogue, with many cautionary tales about Sufi trickery, the impatient cat devours the mouse, reflecting the unabashed wish, no doubt, of the jurists to see the Sufis eradicated and for the *faqihs* to acquire their majestic peak.

It is hard not to see why the greatest representative of the School of Isfahan, Sadr al-Din Shirazi, better known as Mulla Sadra (1572–1641), invested so much intellectual energy to make his "theosophy" appear theologically correct. His eclectic philosophy was informed by a remarkably wide range of sources: the Peripatetic and Neoplatonic philosophies, the intuitive philosophy of Sohravardi, and the theoretical mysticism of Ibn al-'Arabi. Yet his synthesis bore the stigma of centuries of arduous adjustments to the demands of Islamic piety, a feature that Mulla Sadra managed to stamp on the future course of philosophical inquiry in Iran and the Persianate world. With its remarkable breadth and complexity, his philosophy could survive the onslaught of the jurists and remain part of the Shi'i madrasa curriculum only if it was wrapped in this pious clothing. Its original and revolutionary potential, however, was lost to the conventionality and conservatism of his students and commentators.

Born to an affluent family of notables from Shiraz, he was not of ethnic Arab descent, as were his teachers, Shaykh Baha'i and Mir Mohammad Baqer Astarabadi, better known as Mir-e Damad (or Mir Damad, d. 1632). He studied theology with the former and philosophy with the latter, but after a while he broke away from the Isfahan circle and settled in Kahak, a village twenty miles south of Qom (which later in the seventeenth century would become the seat of the Nizari Isma'ili Imam). He led a life of solitude and meditation for many years in this village, where his visionary experiences, as he later retold, helped him see the inadequacy of the scholastic reasoning that plagued Islamic philosophy. The existential path that he explored to complement his Avicennian approach to philosophy, however, did not prevent Mulla Sadra from reexamining at length in his numerous works the familiar gamut of arcane philosophical topics: being versus quiddity, substance versus contingence, and preexistence versus accidental.

Reinventing the philosophical wheel, unexciting though it was, seemed necessary in order for Mulla Sadra to lay a "theologically-correct" grounding for his more original contributions. He returned to Shiraz in 1612 from his retreat with the confidence of a philosopher-prophet whose potentially revolutionary thought would never have been tolerated in the ulama-dominated climate of Isfahan. In his hometown he pondered, taught, and wrote relatively unharassed under the protection of the powerful governor of Fars, the aforementioned Allah-Verdi Khan, the Armenian convert from the *gholam* origin. The magnificent madrasa built by Allah-Verdi (today known as Madrasa-e Khan), evidently in honor of Mulla Sadra, showed his enthusiasm for speculative thought.

Mulla Sadra's theory of movement of the substance (*haraka jawhariyya*, often translated as "transubstantiation"), arguably his most significant philosophical contribution, was a novel departure. His theory of substantial movement in part modified the influential Sufi monistic theory of the "unity of being" (*wahdat-e wujod*). The belief in the essential origin of all beings, celestial and terrestrial, and their ultimate union, had long been opposed by conservative jurists and theologians. Mulla Sadra further advanced the idea of "unity of being" by arguing that in the substance of all things created, of which humanity holds the highest rank, there is an innate cosmic dynamism without which all things cease to exist. This elemental movement transforms the quality of all things at all times from one state to another, without their substance ever changing. As the created being separates itself from its divine origin, in its downward journey toward matter it acquires material contingents, making the world as we see and experience it. The same intrinsic dynamism in an upward movement then transforms the substance of material things until ultimately they reach their original celestial state.

Different from similar circular models articulated by Mulla Sadra's predecessors, here progression in time was considered emblematic of the substance of things, rather than a primal initiative of divine origin. In other words, all beings—including humanity—carry the seeds of progression in their journey to perfection. The movement of the human substance, from its original spiritual state to its full realization in this world and then its reverting back to its origin, completes a full circle. Such a journey in Mulla Sadra's view corresponds to the Islamic doctrine of the beginning and the end in the Qur'an and the hadith. In its radical rendition, however, agency was assigned to the very movement of essence in time rather than to the divine initiator; a proto-modern system, perhaps, that aimed to disengage from the divine and focus on the profane.

Mulla Sadra's theory of movement acquired an eschatological dimension as it attempted to answer the dilemma of corporeal resurrection in Islam—that is, that the dead shall rise on the Day of Judgment in their corporal frame. Here we see a reflection, perhaps, of the millennial hopes and anxieties of his time. As a philosopher, who viewed himself as the "guardian" (*wali*) in the center of the universe he posited, Mulla Sadra seemed to view "transcendental wisdom," as he called his philosophy, as a visionary complement to prophetic revelation. In Shi'ism this was during the "absence" (or Occultation) of the Imam of the Age (the Mahdi). The eschatological dimension gave Mulla Sadra's philosophy a sense of temporal urgency, even when safely wrapped in the garb of a theological debate and adorned with Qur'anic verses and Shi'i traditions. The apocalyptic vision of the End, of the rising of the corporeal essence, a chief preoccupation of Mulla Sadra, anticipated a new era for humanity as it began its upward trajectory toward Perfect Intelligence. This stage is the final of the four "journeys" (*asfar*), which he experienced by his own intuition and articulated in a systematic philosophical system in his magnum opus, known as *Asfar al-Arba'a*, completed in 1628. Here the resemblance to the Noqtavi doctrine of mankind as the primal point of progression in time may not be a mere coincidence; nor are Mulla Sadra's four stages in the existential journey toward perfection unlike the four-sided "essential square" in the Noqtavi theory of Mahmud Pasikhani.

Mulla Sadra's eschatological vision, a lifetime preoccupation, which in the first place had caused his excommunication (*takfir*) by the jurists and his subsequent departure from Isfahan, should be viewed as a potential breakthrough from the shari'a-dominated view of his contemporaries. The theory of essential movement, it may be argued, had the potential to transform and innovate Safavid thought. As was his European near contemporary Baruch Spinoza, who lived a generation later and shared remarkable similarities with Mulla Sadra, especially in holding "substance" as a continuity of God in nature, the Persian philosopher experienced much harassment. Like the German philosopher Friedrich Hegel, whom Mulla Sadra preceded by more than a century, the idea of the development of the spirit through time aimed to make human agency the center of the historical unfolding of the absolute.

Yet Mulla Sadra almost never explicitly distanced himself from the cyclical notion of descent and ascent of the soul. His essentially Platonic notion of transcendental wisdom, though evolving with time, still remained loyal to the concept of *welayat*, the sacred agency entrusted by God in humankind. He contemplated the human intellect, both rational and intuitive, in the context of *welayat*, a complex Sufi-Shi'i notion pertaining to guardianship, governance, or authority, and one with legal, mystical, and political connotations.

POWER OF TRADITIONS

By the late seventeenth century the promising intellectual momentum seems to have come to its end. Most evident in this respect was the late Safavid scholars' engagement with the study of hadith (traditions) and *akhabr* (reports) related from the Prophet and the Shi'i Imams, a pedantic preoccupation that clearly contrasted with the speculative thinking of earlier generations. These "traditions," so far as their validity was concerned, enjoyed a degree of sanction second only to the word of the Qur'an. Yet the methodology used among Shi'i scholars to authenticate such reports remained fairly lax. This was especially true among scholars known as Akhbaris, who relied on all traditions as well as copious reports transmitted through a single reporter. In the formative centuries of Shi'ism, this collection of hadith resulted in a huge increase in suspect or fabricated reports being admitted to the hadith corpus, often contrary to the rudiments of authenticating of the hadith.

The range of contradictory and anachronistic reports in the Safavid hadith collections were therefore so wide and so obvious that one cannot but conclude that the growth of Akhbarism as a school was an effort to streamline this corpus. At least initially, Akhbarism functioned as a liberating strategy to sanction social habits and cultural norms, as had been done for many centuries, and to sanctify mystical and esoteric traits present in Iranian Islam. Yet this double-edged sword of reliance on the hadith also could have worked against philosophy, theoretical Sufism, and other nonconformist trends. No better example in this regard can be found than that of Mulla Mohammad Baqer Majlesi (1627–1698), perhaps the most influential religious scholar of Shi'ism before the twentieth century (fig. 2.9). His career as *shaykh al-Islam* and holder of the office *molla-bashi* (chief royal cleric), presiding for more than a decade over all religious affairs of the late Safavid Empire, and his prolific scholarly and popular writings, left its mark on the Shi'i landscape. His conservative brand of scholastic Shi'ism further weakened the remnants of freethinking in the Iranian milieu and contributed to the spirit of social intolerance of the late Safavid era.

Figure 2.9. Mulla Mohammad Baqer Majlesi in Persian attire.
Opaque watercolor on paper by unknown artist. © Freer Gallery of Art and
Arthur M. Sackler Gallery, Smithsonian Institution, Washington, DC: Bequest of Adrienne
Minassian, S1998.16a.

Born to a family of scholars of Arab and Persian descent, Majlesi's father was a student of Mulla Sadra and a noted scholar and mystic. Mohammad Baqer, who had studied philosophy earlier in life, however, focused on the study of hadith. His lifetime preoccupation resulted in an encyclopedic collection in Arabic of Shi'i hadith in twenty-six volumes titled *Bihar al-Anwar* (Oceans of Luminescence). Applying a new arrangement by subject, and presiding over a team of assistants for three decades, he collected and classified Shi'i traditions and commented on them. The topics ranged from creation to manifestation of the Twelfth Imam, eschatology, ethics, and devotional acts. Though himself closer to the Akhbaris, his endeavor laid the foundation for the late eighteenth-century revival of the doctrine of *ejtehad*.

Majlesi's equally influential Persian works, popular renderings of the *Bihar* volumes on subjects such as devotional acts, ethics, and Shi'i sacred history, were instrumental in Iran's becoming a truly Shi'i nation. By writing about the Prophet and the Imams in an easily accessible Persian style, Majlesi, like Shaykh Baha'i before him, offered ordinary people an appealing narrative, rich in emotions, hope, and suffering. Not only the literate public—perhaps no more than 5 percent of the population—could read his works; more effectively, his narratives, such as *Jala' al-'Uyun* (Sparkler of the Eyes, 1697), on the suffering of the Shi'i Imams, recited from the pulpit of the mosques and commemorated through mourning processions during the holy month of Muharram. The manual *Zad al-Ma'ad* (Provisions for the Day of Return), a set of detailed instructions on Shi'i prayers, fasting, and other devotional acts, was commissioned in 1695 by the last of the Safavids, the pious Shah Soltan Hosain (r. 1694–1722). It soon became one of the most widely read Persian religious texts of all time, with at least thirty-two editions printed between 1828 and 1958.

Majlesi's equally popular *Hilyat al-Muttaqin* (The Cloak for the Pious), which elevates Shi'ism to a new ritualistic plane, contains invocations and thaumaturgic instructions for every human activity: clothing, eating, drinking, bathing and personal hygiene, scatology, sexual intercourse, child rearing, education, marital affairs, parental relations, animal husbandry, buying and selling, and commerce. Fetishistic beliefs and the white magic described in this remarkable collection were sanctified on every occasion by sayings of the Shi'i Imams. Even more than mirroring popular practices of the late Safavid society, this book may be seen as an attempt of the ulama to restrain, if not entirely deny, human agency by means of ritualizing individuality at every turn.

The Safavid state was the willing partner in promoting Majlesi's traditionalist doctrine. By the time of Shah Solayman, Majlesi and a network of his protégés exercised great influence in the Safavid administration and on its policies. He himself was pampered as royalty, with tremendous wealth and luxury extending, it was said, to many wives and slave concubines. Repeatedly denouncing the scholarship of his time for deviating toward philosophy at the expense of hadith, he persuaded the Safavid rulers not only to forgo the earlier patronage of philosophy and mysticism but also to suppress signs of religious and social diversity.

Among his many acts of reproof and refutation, Majlesi (following his father's lead) was responsible for active persecution of the Jewish, Zoroastrian, and Hindu communities in Isfahan and elsewhere, as well as for increasing intolerance toward remnants of Sunni communities, especially along the Iranian periphery. His anti-Jewish treatise *Sawa'iq al-Yahud* (Lightning Bolts on the Jews), which called for the imposition of numerous discriminatory measures against Jews, might be seen as natural outcome of sporadic anti-Jewish persecution since the time of 'Abbas I. His call to destroy the image of a Hindu god in a temple in Isfahan belonging to the Indian commercial community, however, was a result of his studied intolerance toward non-Muslims. His anti-Sunni policies, moreover, had some effect on the rise of anti-Shi'i sentiments in the Iranian periphery, as in Kandahar, and on the Safavids' eventual downfall a quarter of a century after Majlesi's death.

The cultural orientation of the Safavid ulama, from Karaki, the leading sixteenth-century jurist from Jabal 'Amil, to Majlesi, had hardly changed even after two centuries of Persianization. The sum total of the anti-intellectual drive, behind a facade of madrasa learning, can be summarized as obsession with the hadith, legal conservatism, ritualization of Shi'ism, rejecting diversity, and popularizing of a tearful myth of suffering of the Imams. Their hostility toward Persian literary and artistic pursuits, and condescending attitude even toward their lay constituency, was typical of their sociocultural orientation. The Iranian public reserved great ambivalence for the ulama, a sort of love-hate relationship, revering them for their hard-to-understand learning and for their sanctified posture, and despising them for their haughtiness, hypocrisy, and greed—all of which is highlighted vividly in Persian literature.

Yet the ulama's inherent conservatism enjoyed the blessing of the Safavid rulers, from Tahmasp to Soltan Hosain, who consistently lavished them with praises and pensions. Vast endowments (*awqaf*) that the Safavids devoted to religious learning, especially under 'Abbas I, made the ulama enormously rich but also further subservient to the wishes of the state. There were occasional quarrels, for instance, about wine drinking and the patronage of such practices prohibited in Islam as music and painting, or about the deviant sexual habits of the royal family, but these were not serious enough to cause a refit between the religious establishment and its royal benefactor.

A handful of jurists, Karaki included, did claim to be the "deputy of the Imam" (na'eb-e imam) and viewed themselves as those who had invested political power in the Safavid ruler. The motives for the Safavids to abide by such pretentions may be traced in part to the religious zeal of rulers such as Tahmasp and Soltan Hosain. Their propensity for hyper-religiosity, served as an incentive for greater acceptance of the ulama and their claim to authority. More so it can be traced to the state's effort to preserve the jurist class as essentially separate from the rest of the society. The more the jurists were alienated from the public, including their inability to converse in proper Persian, the better the ulama could serve the Safavids' wishes. The collaboration proved enduring, following an ancient pattern of interdependence of the "good government" and the "good religion."

The ulama were bound to target the competing "bad religion" of the agnostics, the qalandars, the Sufi orders, the recluse mystics, the philosophers, the Sunnis, Jews, Zoroastrians, Christians, and, soon after, heathen Europeans. Any nonconformity was sinful, and therefore dangerous, particularly if it lapsed into neglect of devotional acts and fetishized practices. Ritual cleansing of the body, obsession with pollutants, and intricate rules of prayer and fasting, which in the jurists' view defined adherence to correct faith, controlled the public. The ulama thus served the state as moral police, defining learning, disciplining leisure, promoting uniformity, and sharpening the divide between the "saved" Shi'i and the "damned" Other.

Very late in the seventeenth century there were converts who also helped reaffirm the Majlesi brand of conservatism. Padre António de Jesus, the Portuguese head of the Augustinian monastery in Isfahan who converted to Shi'ism in 1697 and adopted 'Ali Qoli Jadid al-Islam as his new name, is a case in point. Among his many Persian-language anti-Christian polemics, his Sayf al-Mu'minin wa Qital al-Mushrikin (The Sword of Believers and Slaying of the Polytheists) is a violent attack not only on Christians, Jews, and Sunnis but also on philosophers, Sufis, and antinomians. This all-embracing refutation, rare though it was, epitomized obstacles to cross-cultural exchanges with a secularizing Europe. His appointment as the royal dragoman in the court of Shah Soltan Hosain further confirmed the state's patronage of a prevailing xenophobic tendency.

Until the time of Majlesi, weapons of social control, even when fortified with the sanctity of the hadith, were not fully in place. Leisure and artistic inspirations remained strong, at least strong enough to prompt jurists' lengthy and repeated condemnations of music and dancing, either for pleasure or at Sufi gatherings; wine drinking (which so frequently was portrayed in paintings of the period); women's venturing outside the harem; breaking of the recognized boundaries of sexuality; and above all, public disregard for norms of prescribed religion. Diffuse forms of nonconformity in public persisted, and even thrived, despite the ascendancy of the pious. The tea- and coffeehouses, despite repeated denunciations by the jurists and physical onslaughts by seminarians, continued to be gathering places for poets and artists, and loci of artistic expression. Recitation of the *Shahnameh* by masterful storytellers (*naqqals*) continued to drive many believers away from mosques and from tragic tales of Shi'i suffering to their performances in public places and in coffeehouses. There they could listen to stories of Rostam's exploits in his Seven Trials, his fight with the White Demon on Mount Damavand, or Nezami's romance of the Sasanian King Khosrow and Princess Shirin, the fair Christian ruler of Armenia.

On a different level, the jurists' attack on philosophy and on organized and theoretical Sufism proved more effective. Philosophy, the most vulnerable of all, was banished to small and inconsequential circles at the margins of the madrasa. Even at its best, the energies of the School of Isfahan and Mulla Sadra's theosophy were never translated into a spirit of independent inquiry or any tangible investigation of human individuality so central to the modern self. Instead, the emphasis on the traditions of the Imams, mostly invented by the likes of Majlesi into a nostalgic fantasy of pristine Islam, helped sapping whatever originality could have transpired from the new philosophical interest. The terse language and cryptic content of the philosophy of the School of Isfahan, a legacy of centuries of deliberate ambiguity designed to avoid orthodox criticism, naturally diminished its grasp by all but the closest adept. Later practitioners of Mulla Sadra's philosophy abandoned the most original and innovative in his discourse and clung to the most conventional and pious facets.

Heretics like Mir Sharif Amoli, a Noqtavi thinker of some originality, however, left the persecution of Safavid Iran behind for the relative security of Mughal India. This was the closest intellectual safe haven for many Iranian freethinkers. Mir Sharif thrived for a while in Akbar's court and was an important source of inspiration for aforementioned Abol-Fazl 'Allami. Yet, like many of his Persian counterparts, Mir Sharif eventually ended up in a Sufi convent, leading the life of a mystic, uninterested in the affairs of the world. It was as if the only alternative to the madrasa's scholasticism was a mystic's convent (*khaneqah*), or as Hafez would have recommended, a "tavern" (*maykhaneh*) for the skeptics disillusioned with organized Sufism. Yet both responses, as well as the shari'a-oriented philosophy of the late Safavid era, were unlikely candidates for the advent of any indigenous form of modernity.

Seventeenth-century Iran witnessed territorial consolidation, expansion of economy and communication, and the emergence of an impressive material culture. The state nurtured a class of jurists that advanced the cause of Shi'ism and, to a lesser extent, patronized speculative thought. The Safavid imperial model and its theory of legitimacy proved to endure long after the Safavids' demise. Most of these features were shared with contemporary Mughal India, Qing China, the Ottoman Empire, and Habsburg Spain. Yet despite impressive achievements, in many respects the seventeenth century remained for Iran an age of unfulfilled potential. Neither Shah 'Abbas nor his successors were able to overcome the institutional limitations in the Safavid system. Weakening of the Qezilbash and its replacement with a *gholam* class did not end tribal conflicts, which soon flared up spectacularly. The silk monopoly proved viable, but efforts to create an indigenous trading network competitive with the European trading companies was transient. The Safavids never developed a maritime empire and showed no interest in creating a naval power. Their overland territorial expansion paid off in the southern Caucasus and Persian Gulf, and less so in Iraq, but revenue from these sources was not a long-term remedy for the state's shortfall. Centralization of the agrarian regime raised revenue but over the long term actually weakened Safavid defenses.

3

THE DEMISE OF THE SAFAVID ORDER AND THE UNHAPPY INTERREGNUMS (1666–1797)

On October 23, 1722, after seven months of siege and suffering the horrors of famine and disease, the last of the Safavid rulers, Shah Soltan Hosain (r. 1694–1722), walked out of Isfahan's city gate accompanied by his courtiers and officials, and abdicated in favor of Mahmud Hotaki, the chief of the Ghalzai Afghan invaders. For the previous decade, Mahmud, the Sunni chief of an Afghan tribal force had wrought havoc in the eastern Safavid provinces before reaching the walls of the Safavid capital (map 3.1). The shah personally removed from his Qezilbash cap the bejeweled pin symbolizing his royal authority and secured it onto Mahmud's turban. A few days later the Afghan chief, accompanied by the former Safavid shah, entered Isfahan and was enthroned in the Chehel Sotun ("forty columns") palace as Mahmud Shah. This effectively brought to an end a dynasty that had ruled for 221 years, longer than any dynasty in the history of Islamic Iran. For most people of Isfahan, who observed the events with horror, it was a catastrophe of unequaled magnitude.

The fall of the Safavids resonated in Persian consciousness throughout the eighteenth century. Even though there was a brief Safavid restoration under Soltan Hosain's son Tahmasp II (r. 1732–1736), and despite at least three later attempts to reconstitute, reform, or reshape the shattered empire, in the end only the memory of the fallen dynasty lingered (see chart 1 in chapter 1). Twentieth-century historiography treats the fall of the Safavids as the end of a long period of decline that had politically and militarily weakened Iran and eventually plunged it into political strife and economic decay. The question of decline, in particular, had engaged observers even before the fall of the Safavids. Unlike the neighboring Ottoman and Mughal empires—the former partially modernized and survived up to the twentieth century, and the latter colonized piecemeal and was dismantled in the eighteenth and nineteenth centuries—the dramatic collapse of the Safavids and their surrender to a small tribal army raises questions about the economic and administrative problems of the empire, as well as political legitimacy, Shi'i identity, changes long occurring at the Iranian periphery, and shifting regional patterns across the Eurasian world.

THE UNRAVELING OF THE SAFAVIDS

When 'Abbas I died in 1629, he had not groomed a successor. Of his four sons, one had died, two others were executed at his own order, and one was blinded on feigned charges of treason. His brutal treatment of his own offspring accelerated the internecine killings in the Safavid house and among its successors. 'Abbas I's grandson, a minor, crowned as Shah Safi (r. 1629–1642), shortly after his accession put to death many of the princes of the royal family eligible to ascend the throne, as well as some officials and army officers. Although vicious even by seventeenth-century standards, Safi's actions prevented a war of succession. The weakening of the old elite inadvertently opened the way for a new breed of administrators of non-Qezilbash origin, who for most of the next century would dominate the Safavid state and steer it toward greater centralization. Destruction of the Imam-Qoli Khan, the powerful and accomplished governor-general of Fars province, extended the long arm of the central government to the commercial and agricultural revenue of the southern provinces.

The grand vizier Saru Taqi, a capable minister in office between 1634 and 1645, dominated the divan and the army and effectively ruled on Safi's behalf. Such delegated power, though potentially resulting in separation of the state's administrative arm from the court, did not translate into political security for the grand viziers or into the steady growth of an institutionalized state, free from the shah's meddling. A similar ministerial drive for state building as well as the same royal obstructionism would also occur later, during the tenure of Shaykh 'Ali Khan Zangeneh, grand vizier between 1668 and 1689, and again under Fath 'Ali Khan Daghestani between 1694 and 1721, during the last days of Safavid rule.

A glance at late Safavid administrative charts, such as those found in *Tadhkirat al-Muluk* (memorandum for the rulers) reveals an elaborate state machinery, well staffed and with a relatively sensible division of labor, presiding over a vast system encompassing revenue collection, the judiciary, the court, and the army. Yet the inherent problem of insecurity in high office, especially for the grand viziers, persisted and was aggravated because of the *gholam* origins of

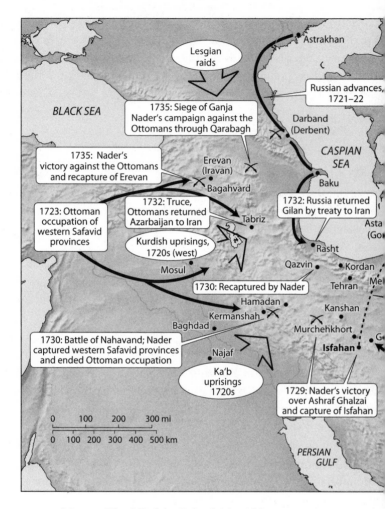

Map 3.1. The fall of the Safavids, the Afghan occupation,
and the rise of Nader Qoli Khan Afshar, 1722–1736

some and the slavelike status of other holders of high office. Safavid ministers
never mustered enough power from the ruler to check the whims of the monarch or harness the wishes of the court. It is worth noting that the symbolic separation of the Ottoman Sublime Porte (Bab-e 'Āli) from the sultan's court in the
middle of the seventeenth century, which over time added to the administrative
power of the grand vizier, never occurred in the Safavid state. Despite their
remarkable attempts to build an administrative base, by the late seventeenth
century the Safavid divan had already been hollowed out by factionalism and
deadly rivalries.

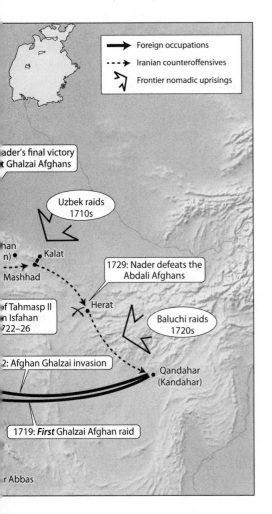

ader's final victory
Ghalzai Afghans

Uzbek raids
1710s

han
n)•   •Kalat
Mashhad

1729: Nader defeats the
Abdali Afghans

Tahmasp II
Isfahan
722–26

Herat

Baluchi raids
1720s

2: Afghan Ghalzai invasion

Qandahar
(Kandahar)

1719: *First* Ghalzai Afghan raid

r Abbas

Foreign occupations
Iranian counteroffensives
Frontier nomadic uprisings

The declining governance of the late Safavid shahs also contributed to the steady weakening of the state. As eligible princes of the royal family, nearly all the late Safavid rulers were brought up in the confinement of the harem. This deliberate isolation was designed to avert rebellious aspirations, a practice similar to the Ottomans' "cage" (*qafas*) policy. Under the supervision of the harem eunuchs, who acted as virtual parents, these princes were largely devoid of public experience and political education before coming to the throne. In the male-dominated public world of court and government, their insecurities translated into impulsive behavior. At times they demonstrated symptoms of paranoia, even insanity, triggered by bad habits. Safi died of alcoholism at the age of thirty; 'Abbas II (r. 1642–1666) apparently of syphilis at the age of thirty-three; and Solayman (r. 1666–1694) of what was diagnosed as gout at the age of forty-seven.

As part of a global pattern, syphilis was raging through Europe. It was introduced to Iran via the Ottoman Empire, reaching almost epidemic proportions by the late seventeenth century. It was known in Iran as *farangi*, or European, disease, among other names. The seventeenth-century French traveler John Chardin claimed that nearly half of the Iranian population had contracted the disease. Even if we treat his opinion with skepticism, it is probable that some members of the royal family suffered from it. Frequent sexual contacts with many partners in and out of the harem no doubt facilitated contracting the disease. References in Safavid sources to royal deaths caused by "excessive sexual intercourse" can be taken as an indication of prevalent venereal diseases. Excessive wine drinking and addiction to a variety of opiates, hashish-based potions, and narcotics in the promiscuous climate of the late Safavid court may also have been remedies for syphilitic pain and suffering. Among the members of the royal house, behavior such as abrupt killings, mutilation, self-inflicted wounds, and utter feebleness might be taken as either withdrawal symptoms or as signs of mental degeneration associated with contracted or congenital syphilis.

Despite all this, degenerate princes and inefficient state machinery were not unique to the Safavids — nor were they by themselves potent enough to bring down a venerable state. Indeed, so far as the subjects of the empire were concerned, the seventeenth century was one of the longest, most prosperous, urbane, and peaceful episodes they had ever witnessed. The reign of 'Abbas II in particular epitomized an age of economic prosperity and social calm. Despite the decay that gradually set in, the late Safavid artistic and intellectual endeavors, refined material culture, and freer contact with the outside world, distinguished this period as one of the most exciting in early modern period. Such prolonged age of tranquility can be viewed as a peace dividend, primarily resulting from the Zohab Treaty of 1639, which immunized Iran against the familiar Ottoman threat for eight decades.

Yet domestically, too, Safavid society had reached a certain cultural maturity well evident in intellectual and artistic expressions of the period. It may be argued that existential questions that engrossed the celebrated Safavid philosopher Mulla Sadra about resurrection of the body or the cultural incentives that motivated the influential theologian Majlesi to write tomes on the intricacies of ritual hygiene were both aspects of a common desire to preserve the body rather than deny it, as classical Sufi doctrine advocated. Likewise, the paintings and poetry of the period, at times daring and expressive, sought to break away from the constraints of Shi'i piety. They came to represent a more realistic picture and in-depth expression of the self. Safavid poetry, though, never returned to the heights it had achieved during the classical age, also presented a new sense of awareness of Safavid surroundings and the poetic self. Sa'eb Tabrizi (1601–1677), a master poet of seventeenth-century Isfahan, who also spent some years at the Mughal court, demonstrated in his poetry technical marvels and aesthetic complexity, along with a novel cosmopolitan outlook reflective of the tranquil spirit of his time.

The originality found in these artistic and literary expressions lay in their greater appeal to the common man. Besides the Safavid poetry produced at the court and under elite patronage in Iran (as in Mughal India), poetry gave voice to the lesser known and amateurs. Merchants, artisans, and ordinary folks were less interested in set themes and tropes of courtly culture and more in earthy pleasures, everyday life, and even unorthodox beliefs—always expressed using allegorical language. Perhaps not technically as sophisticated, the amateur oral poets of the bazaar conveyed the aspirations of the ordinary people better than the panegyrists of the court. As they recited their odes (*ghazals*) in poetic gatherings and at coffeehouses, one cannot fail to detect a joyous inspirations and spirit of skepticism, at times with sexual undertones. Admiring the beauty of youth, often male, became acceptable through the lyrics and paintings of the period (fig. 3.1).

The culture of leisure and pastime was appealing to the urban public. Despite occasional religious sanctions, the number of coffeehouses, taverns, and "pleasure houses," as brothels were known, increased throughout the realm. Consumption of tea and coffee, the former from China (and later from India) and the latter from Arabia and the Levant, made coffeehouses an alternative to taverns. In the mid-seventeenth century we know there were at least six major coffeehouses in Isfahan alone. Poetic competitions (*mosha'ereh*), chess matches, card and board games, music and dancing, and readings of the *Shahnameh* and other "action-packed" Persian epics and romances attracted the male public as well as the royals.

On their nocturnal rounds, 'Abbas I, and later his successors, visited coffeehouses and listened to poetry readings, one of the reasons, no doubt, for these public venues' survival even though they were frowned upon by the ulama. Later on, storytellers of the Safavid coffeehouses incorporated into their repertoire Shi'i stories and performances, such as the popular *Hamza-nameh*, which narrated in accessible language the fantastic exploits of Hamza, the Prophet's uncle. Other epics in praise of 'Ali, the First Imam, were also recited in public by storytellers. The clergy, and at times government authorities, remained

Figure 3.1. The young lovers in this elusive sixteenth-century
drawing are typical of homoerotic references in Safavid art.
Shaykh Mohammad, "Young couple," late sixteenth century. Paper, black ink.
Musée du Louvre, Paris, France. ART520476. © Musée du Louvre, Dist.
RMN-Grand Palais/Art Resource, NY.

suspicious of the coffeehouses' subversive ambiance, of their habitués and their
storytellers. And not without reason. John Chardin informs us that free and
open expressions of beliefs and opinions, presumably religious and political, in
the Isfahan coffeehouses were unique in the world. As part of a global trend,
one cannot fail to note the budding Safavid public space comparable not only
to similar Ottoman and Egyptian establishments, but also to French salons and
English coffeehouses of the period.

Wine drinking also was a popular pastime, with wine consumed, as often
noted, in immoderate quantities. The late Safavid era witnessed successive
anti-drinking campaigns orchestrated by the ulama, under 'Abbas II, Solayman,
and Soltan Hosain. Targeted mostly at the general public, these crusades also
obliged the court to destroy its precious wine cellars, even though prohibition
could not easily change old habits. As part of the drinking culture there were

various establishments for the consumption of narcotics, often highly addictive derivatives of opium, which were also widely used by the public and taxed by the government. Prostitution, both female and male, was also tolerated by society and taxed and regulated by the state, which considered prostitution inevitable, especially during military campaigns.

Although tobacco smoking did not become a national habit in Iran until the early nineteenth century, it was fashionable among the elite of the late Safavid era. Reaching Iran from the New World via Europe and the Ottoman Empire in the early seventeenth century, tobacco quickly found its own place among the courtiers. Although under 'Abbas I there was an initial resistance to smoking, that did not stop the cultivation of tobacco in Iran. A century later, by the late eighteenth century, despite anti-smoking campaigns, the popularity of the Persian pipe (*chopoq*) and water pipe (*qalyan*) superseded opiate and other drugs. These and other leisure activities and social habits presented a very different side of Safavid society from that of the purist pursuits of the jurists. The leisure culture flourished with greater urbanization. Even though one should not exaggerate the grip of either religion or leisure on late Safavid society, it is difficult to ignore the sense of social laxity, even complacency, at least in the urban centers of the empire.

RESURGENCE OF THE PERIPHERY

Despite relative urban calm in the late Safavid era, pressure on the empire's frontiers continued to build. Following the death of 'Abbas I in 1629, Iran experienced yet another Ottoman onslaught, this time under Sultan Morad IV, the last of the great Ottoman conquerors. After nearly three decades of calm, and without any provocation, massive Ottoman armies occupied the western Iranian provinces. Facing resistance in Tabriz and Hamadan, the Ottomans did not hesitate to massacre the population and lay waste to cities. In 1638, Baghdad also fell into Ottoman hands, this time permanently. Despite stiff Iranian resistance, the Safavid state acted circumspectly. The conclusion in 1639 of the Treaty of Zohab once again called for the Ottomans' evacuation of western Iran in exchange for the permanent annexation of southern Iraq. The fragile border between the two empires thus was set roughly along the lines of the previous 1555 Amasiya treaty, even though Iran has to face yet another Ottoman occupation in the early eighteenth century.

On another front, facing the Uzbeks' recurring attacks also obliged the Safavids to act with caution, as the central state began to feel the financial burden of waging war on two fronts. The centralizing policies of 'Abbas I and his successors transformed most semiautonomous provinces (*mamalek*) into crown property. Direct control brought greater revenue, especially in Fars, the Caucasus, and Khorasan, but it also made the empire more vulnerable on the periphery. To remedy such peripheral pressures, 'Abbas has already implemented a complex policy of tribal resettlement. The nomadic defensive walls in the west and east temporarily fended off the external threat while diminishing tribal tensions in the interiors. As many as fifteen thousand Kurdish families resettled in northern Khorasan so as to create a dependable barrier against the Uzbeks' forays. But by the last quarter of the seventeenth century, the Safavid Empire, like its Muslim neighbors to the west and the east, encountered increased threats along its frontiers and trade routes from a variety of nomadic powers.

In the Caucasus, the Lezgian tribes of Dagestan and other semi-nomadic peoples of the Transcaucasus, including the Cossacks, ravaged the prosperous Shirvan region and threatened the overland Caspian trade. To the west, the Kurdish tribes of the Persian and Ottoman frontiers captured Kermanshah and Hamadan, both centers for trade of Mesopotamia and the Levant. In the south, the coastal Arab tribes, often in collaboration with Omani pirates based in and around Muscat, posed a similar threat to the Persian Gulf trade. In Khuzestan the remnants of the Musha'sha autonomous region in the marshlands of Huwiza were in periodic rebellion, and in the southeast, the Baluch tribes of the Makran region began to make raids on the eastern trade with Hindustan. This unrest at the periphery was not uncommon, especially during times of trouble in the center. Yet the simultaneous revolt of so many frontier forces at once was highly unusual (see map 3.1).

The most significant—and fatal—blow came from the revolt of the Ghalzai Afghan tribes of Kandahar province, in today's southern Afghanistan. A coveted Safavid southeastern stronghold and frontier trade center, the possession of Kandahar was long disputed by the Mughal Empire. Though by 1653 the Safavids had managed to make Kandahar their own, their reassertion of city control bred much anti-Persian sentiment. As early as 1701, after several petitions to the Safavid court, Mir Vays Hotaki, the mayor (*kalantar*) of Kandahar, who resented the anti-Sunni policies of the Safavid state, rose in rebellion and murdered the Safavid governor-general of the province who was a Georgian of *gholam* origin. Mir Vays was supported by his Ghalzai kinsmen in the vicinity of the city and backed by the Mughal emperor Aurangzeb (r. 1658–1707). Aurangzeb's policy toward the Safavids was guided not only by Mughal territorial claim over Kandahar but also by a new spirit of Sunni reassertion. The Kandahar rebellion, also blessed by the anti-Shi'i fatwas of the Meccan jurists, successfully resisted the Safavids' reprisal. Less than two decades later, Mir Vays's son Mahmud, in collusion with subordinate Afghan and Baluch tribes, felt confident enough to raid the Iranian interior and go as far as attempting to lay siege to the cities of Kerman and Yazd, albeit unsuccessfully. These would be rehearsals for what came in 1722, when Mahmud Hotaki laid siege to Isfahan, a city virtually intact and long unaccustomed to nomadic incursions.

Shah Soltan Hosain proved utterly helpless in his handling of the Afghan crisis. He was the quintessential product of a confined upbringing in the harem. Even if we allow for some exaggeration in the European and Ottoman eyewitness accounts of the Safavid capital, they convincingly portray a government on the verge of collapse, with rebellions and insurrections in the making, an army unprepared to fight, statesmen and army chiefs in the throes of ethnic and factional disputes, and an indecisive shah incapable of controlling his quarreling courtiers, many wives, eunuchs, clerical dignitaries, and corrupt officials. Shortly before the attack by the Afghans, the elimination Fath Ali Khan Daghestani, the grand vizier and decimation of his allies in the Safavid army on charges of Sunni proclivities shook not only the administrative and financial stability of the empire but also its defenses. The downfall of the shrewd Lezgian minister, who earlier had established his power base in Georgia, was one example of how the spread of Shi'ism in the Safavid realms gradually eroded tribal support for the empire on the Sunni periphery.

The air of complacency that had set in at the Isfahan court after decades of trouble-free lives of both luxury and laxity as well as zealous religious policies was to be rudely interrupted by the arrival of a half-starving, ragged band of nomads. At the Battle of Golnabad on the outskirts of Isfahan in May 1722, the more numerous and better-equipped Safavid forces were defeated by no more than twenty thousand Afghans who forced the Safavids to retreat behind the city walls. Somewhat surprised by the ease with which they had routed the imperial army, the Afghan forces laid siege to the capital and waited for the starved and terrified population of the city to surrender. Empty coffers and sheer incompetence of the shah and his administration deprived Isfahan even of the backing of the Georgian mercenaries who had been summoned to the capital.

During the seven-month siege, vital links with the outside were severed and the supply of provisions was blocked. Once the city dwellers had consumed the cats and dogs, they devoured rats, and reports of eating corpses became rampant—then the diseased-ravaged city caved and defenses crumbled. Once inside the walls of Isfahan, Mahmud and his troops rode though the deserted streets and bazaars before arriving at the Chehel Sotun palace. There the Ghalzai khan unceremoniously enthroned himself as Mahmud Shah. He detained the royal family and divided up the Safavid household and the harem as booty for himself and his chiefs. It did not take long before he found himself presiding over an empire riddled with rebellion and chaos. What interested the Afghan invaders, however, was not the running of a broken empire but the wealth of the capital and the glitter of royal edifices such as Chehel Sotun, which whetted the invaders' appetite for plunder (pl. 3.1 and pl. 3.2).

At the outset Mahmud tried to act graciously toward the people of Isfahan and, to some degree, even to remedy the war-ravaged and starving capital. By the end of the Isfahan siege, nearly eighty thousand inhabitants had perished. He also enjoyed the support of Jews and Zoroastrians of Isfahan, and elsewhere in the empire, who had long been felt the discrimination of the Safavids' religious policies. Yet soon his attitude began to change as he sensed persistent loyalty to the Safavids within the divan and among the population at large. Insecure and paranoid, he quickly resorted to violence. He executed nearly all of Soltan Hosain's sons and relatives. The shah himself was spared, only to later die at the hand of Ashraf, Mahmud's nephew and successor. A vast number of the ranking officials who ran the Safavid divan also fell victim to repeated massacres that were motivated by the Afghans' fear of mass uprising. Even the Armenians, considered the Safavids' favored minority, did not fare any better. The city quarter of New Julfa was plundered, houses and churches destroyed, and women and children enslaved.

The occupation of Isfahan and the collapse of the Safavids sent signals to the former empire's western neighbors. Almost immediately a new Ottoman campaign was launched by the pasha of Baghdad under the pretext of restoring the former Safavid shah to the throne. In response, in 1726 Ashraf Hotaki, whose survival on the Iranian throne was at the stake, executed Soltan Hosain and sent his head to the Ottoman pasha as proof of the Safavids' demise. Even if the last of the Safavid shahs could have repelled the Afghans, it is debatable whether the demise of the dynasty could have been averted.

CLIMATE, INSOLVENCY, AND INVASION

Whatever the shortcomings of late Safavid rule and the defects of its administration and army, the surprise Afghan invasion and the sudden fall of the Safavid state deserves further explanation. The expulsion of the Afghan occupiers less than a decade after the fall of Isfahan did not bring back peace and tranquility to Iran. The failed attempt to restore Safavid rule under Tahmasp II, and the consequent rise to power of the tribal strongman Nader Shah Afshar (r. 1736–1747) instead ushered in a period of extraordinary turmoil. With the exception of short-lived interludes, material destruction, urban, agricultural, and commercial decline, continued almost to the end of the eighteenth century (see map 3.1).

One underlying factor of this decline may be the tribal resurgence, which was possibly caused by climate change that was taking place over the whole of the Eurasian landmass. The impact of this climate change, the so-called Little Ice Age, has primarily been studied in the context of seventeenth-century Europe, but western Asia also was affected by these changes. The late decades of the seventeenth century and early decades of the eighteenth century seem to have witnessed a period of dryer and colder air with longer and harsher winters and less rainfall in the spring. In western Asia, the sudden outbreak of nomadic unrest, and the perennial pattern of peripheral resurgence, affected not only Iran but also the far more populated and wealthier Mughal and Ottoman Empires.

On the Iranian plateau, the shaping of new Afghan warring confederacies, both the Ghalzai takeover of Kandahar and the occupation of Herat by the rival Abdali tribes, may be attributed to the same climatic changes. It is likely that the nomadic and seminomadic pastoral Afghans in the highlands of the Hindu Kush, who decades earlier had descended to the adjacent plains, could no longer sustain a growing population because of colder weather and scarce pastureland. The simultaneous rise of the Baluch tribes in the Makran, the Kurdish tribes in northwestern Iran, and the Cossacks and Lezgians in the Transcaucasus, all soon followed by unrest among the Afsharids and other tribes of Khorasan, the Kurdish tribes of the northern and eastern Iranian periphery, and the confederacy of frontier Turkmens in the northeast, may also be contributed to the same phenomenon. From the middle of the seventeenth century not only the periphery but also the Safavid heartlands suffered hardship due to intemperate weather. Contemporary European reports about Safavid Iran observe that within a short span of two decades, from the 1650s to the 1670s, agricultural production fell drastically, perhaps by as much as half. Repeated crop failures and recurring droughts coincided with the shrinking of the agricultural hinterlands, decline of trade in Persian Gulf and Mediterranean ports, and the depopulation of the cities. The impacts were so evident that in 1666 the royal astrologer, fearing an ominous celestial conjunction, advised the Safavid ruler to abdicate his throne, only nominally, so as to avoid ongoing calamities. He was then reinstated to the throne with the freshly assumed name Shah Solayman. The investiture, though, did not change the empire's fortunes. When John Chardin visited Iran for the second time in the 1670s, he encountered a country weakened by natural and manmade calamities, a fact that other visitors of the time also attested to.

The Afghan invasion was not the last of the tribal insurgencies that ravaged the Iranian countryside and damaged cities throughout the eighteenth century. The nomadic inroads were marked by violence and by the nomads' mass-scale decimation, mutilation, and displacement of people. Increased access to firearms, in particular, greatly enhanced tribal capabilities. It is quite likely that the dissipation of Safavid armies and concurrent dispersal of the state arsenals offered the restive tribes of the frontier, and soon after the nomads of the interior, an unprecedented firepower. Throughout the eighteenth century, Iranian cities suffered from recurring occupations by competing tribes, the destruction of residential quarters, the collapse of the bazaar economy, and insecurities that seriously disrupted travel and trade.

Administrative malfunction and domestic turbulence hastened the collapse of the already-troubled Safavid silk trade. The Arab privateers of the Oman coasts who had successfully evicted the Portuguese from Muscat and created a maritime power in the Persian Gulf were the latest in a series of threats to Iranian trade. Earlier, the near monopoly of the silk trade by the Dutch had weakened Portuguese and British competition and helped undermine the state-backed Armenian commercial enterprises and network. The Safavid state welcomed the commercial overtures from the French in the final decades of the seventeenth century. The Safavids' failure to persuade the Portuguese, still lingering on the horizon, to fight back against the threat of Omani pirates made French intervention desirable. But the French, too, proved unwilling to venture into the hazardous waters of the Persian Gulf while they were also fighting against English supremacy south of the Indian subcontinent. French representatives engaged in Safavid court intrigues and in the missionary politics of Isfahan without offering any substantive alternative to other maritime powers in the region. Nor were the Safavids able to benefit from their French connection to compete effectively through the alternative Levantine route.

The attacks by the Baluch tribes on Bandar Abbas in 1721 and the pillaging of the Dutch and English factory houses there was an ominous prelude of the troubles still to come. They soon wiped out much of the long-distance trade in the south. Not until the beginning of the nineteenth century did trade in the Persian Gulf recover, and even then it did not reach the heights of the Safavid period. The decline of the silk-producing centers of Gilan and the Shirvan was further hastened by the Afghan occupation. The nascent commercial bourgeoisie of the Safavid cities never mustered the financial resources or the political prestige to be able to avert this course of events.

The empire's fundamentally agrarian economy, based on centuries-old practices of sharecropping, became more susceptible to bureaucratic abuse in the late Safavid period. The gradual shift from the Qezilbash-held land tenure to crown land and the appropriation of the old fiefdoms granted by the state as private property only added to the peasantry's burden. The diminishing revenue from booty, trade and crown lands—the latter due to mismanagement and corruption—demanded heavier taxation on private land at a time when income from properties was dwindling because of agricultural shortfalls and depopulation of the countryside.

The tax burden and inflationary pressures, even before the fall of the Safavids, became intolerable enough under Solayman and Soltan Hosain that the peasants and nomads had to be forcefully kept on the land and prevented from fleeing. This policy of near serfdom, previously alien to the Islamic world, may help explain the explosion of restlessness among the nomadic and seminomadic tribes once the central state had largely collapsed. The relocation policy of warring nomads by the Safavid government from one place to another, and their reallocation from one tribe to another, which was the routine practice under Tahmasp I and 'Abbas I, had created a highly volatile pattern of displacement, with the potential to ultimately lead to breakup once the state no longer possessed the military resources for surveillance and coercion.

Safavid Iran had a far smaller and more vulnerable economy than that of its imperial neighbors. Whereas the population of Safavid Iran probably never grew beyond ten million, by the early eighteenth century the neighboring Mughal Empire ruled over a population of over one hundred million, and the Ottomans over more than twenty-two million. The Safavids, even at the best of their time, could not exact from their landed population the gigantic revenues available to their competitors. That Iran's agrarian economy historically was susceptible to nomadic pressure, and to state mismanagement, may offer further explanation for Safavid agrarian decline.

By the last decades of the seventeenth century, Safavid Iran had fully suffered the consequences of a global inflationary crisis that since the sixteenth century had affected the fortunes of eastern empires. The large volumes of New World gold and silver injected into Western European economies gave those economies enormous purchasing power vis-à-vis the agrarian economies of Asia. This resulted in the devaluation of the silver-based currencies of the Ottoman Empire and Iran. Inflationary pressures in the form of depreciating currency, as well as higher costs of overland trade and prices for agricultural products, not only weakened the once-prosperous Safavid mercantile class but also reduced the empire's ability to defend itself. A shortage of currency, hoarding by state authorities and the privileged classes, drainage of currency, and overall weakening of the agrarian base intensified the empire's fiscal crisis.

In particular, the siphoning off of Persian silver by the Dutch and English trading companies to Europe and by Indian traders (*banyans*) to the subcontinent had a long-term negative impact. This was a lucrative trade that went on for more than a century hand in hand with the silk trade. Despite the apparent abundance of New World silver in European markets, it was still beneficial to the trading companies to smuggle Iranian silver in the form of bullion for a handsome profit. Despite repeated Safavid measures to stop the drainage of currency, between 1642 and 1660, the Dutch East India Company smuggled the equivalent of more than nine million guilders from Iran, a gigantic drainage of spices profoundly contributive to the Safavid insolvency. In a similar manner, the Dutch remained in their Persian Gulf factories even at the darkest hours of the early eighteenth century when there was little to gain from the declining silk export. The cycle of trade from Europe through the Ottoman Empire, Iran, and to Mughal India generated three to four fold profit for European trading companies at the expense of impoverishing the empires of the east.

Even if the Safavids could have withstood nomadic pressures and embraced domestic challenges, they stood little chance against a fresh wave of foreign inroads. News of the Afghan invasion and the siege of Isfahan set in motion an intense race to annex Iran's northern and western provinces between the Ottomans and the fast-expanding Russian Empire (see map 3.1). Counting on Iranian military vulnerability, in 1721–1722, the Russians dispatched a huge army first into the northern Caucasian provinces of Darband and Dagestan, under Safavid suzerainty, and then southward to Gilan. Before the occupation, Peter the Great (r. 1682–1721) was encouraged by reports from Isfahan that painted the northern Iranian provinces as ripe for conquest and annexation. The thirteen-year occupation of the greater part of the Caucasus, Gilan, Mazandaran, and Astarabad, though in cahoots with the Ottomans, proved disastrous not only to Iran but also to Russia. The ravages of malaria were one of several reasons for the hasty Russian withdrawal. This was the first Russian sortie along the Caspian shores, presaging a course of expansionism that for the next 270 years placed Russia at the center of Iran's foreign policy.

In 1723, the Ottomans capitalized on the waning of their traditional enemy and crossed Iran's western border to attack the Safavid Caucasus without any provocation. This was the fourth wave of Ottoman expansion since 1514. A contest thus began between the Russians and the Ottomans to partition the northern Safavid provinces. As in earlier instances, the Ottomans aimed to recoup territory in the east while retreating in the Balkans to the Austrian Habsburgs. By 1725, successive Ottoman campaigns resulted in the loss of a vast swath of

Iranian territory stretching from Georgia and Armenia to the western provinces of Ardabil, Tabriz, Kermanshah, Hamadan, and southwestern Iran. Earlier in 1722 the Ottomans supported the Afghan invasion and even sent a contingent to Mahmud's aid. However, they later changed their position under Ashraf, Mahmud's nephew and successor, in favor of restoring Safavid rule presumably because the Afghan regime in Isfahan was willing to go to war and recapture the Iranian provinces lost to the Ottomans.

In 1725, Ashraf Hotaki (r. 1725–1729) assassinated his mad uncle, Mahmud Ghalzai, ascended the throne and began to mobilize his forces against the Ottoman invaders. Despite relative success on the battlefield, Ashraf had a weakness: both the Ottomans and the Russians preferred to negotiate with Tahmasp II, Soltan Hosain's surviving son and the powerless claimant to the Safavid throne. Escaping the Afghans' ever-shrinking circle, the wandering Tahmasp's only recourse was to comply with the territorial demands of his neighbors in the vain hope of being recognized as the legitimate ruler of Iran and eventually restoring the Safavid throne. For the same reason, Ashraf agreed to the humiliating treaties that ceded vast parts of Iran to the occupying Ottomans and the Russians. His stance was further impaired when in 1726 he decided to execute the incarcerated Shah Soltan Hosain so as to remove any possibility of Safavid restoration in Isfahan.

By 1727 Safavid Iran had nearly ceased to exist as an empire. The Afghans, their rule harsh and alien to the Shi'i Iranians, held only a semblance of control over what was left of Iran. Within a few short years not only the most prosperous northern and western provinces were snatched away; cities and countryside throughout the empire were depleted, nomadic forces on the periphery were in rebellion, and confidence in the culture and social order was at its lowest ebb. Even the extensive Safavid state archives in Isfahan were completely destroyed by the invading Afghans, obliterating more than two centuries of dynastic and administrative records.

In the meantime Tahmasp was blundering his way through northern Iran. He settled briefly in Qazvin, then Ardabil, and next in Tehran, which marked the first time this small leafy town on the outskirts of the Alborz range would become a seat of power. He finally arrived in Astarabad, a northwestern hub where the khan of the Qajar tribe, a member of the Qezilbash confederacy, was his host. Virtually a puppet in the hands of his many ministers, Tahmasp found in Fath 'Ali Khan Qajar a protector and a determined kingmaker. Yet the Qajars were destined to lose the contest for control of the Safavid shah and restoration of the empire to a more potent contender, Nader-Qoli, the future Nader Shah

Afshar, whose appearance on the stormy political horizon raised hopes for Safavid restoration.

NADER-QOLI AS THE LIBERATOR

Few leaders in recent Iranian history have provoked such conflicting sentiments as Nader Shah Afshar (r. 1736–1747), a military genius who emerged out of the post-Safavid interregnum to put an end to foreign occupations and soon to the Safavid dynasty itself (maps 3.1 and 3.2). His countrymen viewed him first as a restorer of the empire and a savior but later a tyrant and a maniac. For his contemporary Europeans he was a thundering conqueror whose Indian campaign paved the way for British colonial domination.

To the incoming Qajar dynasty, he was a despicable usurper, yet in the Pahlavi era he was glorified as a hero and a forerunner of national unity, a prototype of a sort for Reza Shah, who admired him for his discipline and resolve. Today he is still part of Iran's nationalist narrative, appealing to pan-Iranian sentiments of some and anticlerical aspirations of others. Beyond the constructs of the later centuries, however, Nader looms large as a unique phenomenon, in some ways reasserting tribal identity of the Iranian periphery and in other ways as a prototype anticipating the nationalist trends of later centuries.

Born around 1698 to a poor herding family among the Turkmen nomads of northern Khorasan, Nader-Qoli belonged to the Qereqlu subdivision of the Afshar tribe, one of the original members of the Qezilbash. The Qereqlu had been resettled in the hinterlands of Mashhad under 'Abbas I primarily to repel frequent incursions by the Uzbeks, who pillaged widely and enslaved the Shi'i residents of towns and villages. As a youth he apparently was taken captive by the Uzbeks, living as a hostage-slave for four years before escaping captivity and leading a life of banditry.

Soon after, Nader-Qoli joined Malek Mahmud Sistani, a self-styled claimant to the legendary Kayanid dynasty of the *Shahnameh*. In the years following the collapse of the Safavid state he had carved out territory for himself that stretched from northern Khorasan to Sistan, with his capital in Mashhad. Relying on a loose tribal and urban coalition, Malek Mahmud soon viewed Nader, then a local warlord, and his band of nomadic horsemen as a threat to his aspirations. It is not unlikely that his claim to kingship of the legendary dynasty, complete with an invented Kayanid crown and regal symbolism, inspired Nader's image of himself as champion of a unified Iran, a concept of authority different from the Safavids' claim to Shi'i sacred kingship.

Nader nevertheless lost out to Malek Mahmud in the struggle for control of Mashhad. He returned to the life of a benevolent bandit, as his largesse helped at times to swell the ranks of his supporters. By 1725 when he offered his services to Tahmasp II, he probably mustered no more than two thousand horsemen with shaky loyalty and no artillery or other heavy weapons. What he really offered to Tahmasp, who was helplessly vacillating among several tribal contenders, was an instinctive ability to lead, military talent, and tactful strategizing. Soon he elevated himself to become Tahmasp's regent after successfully masterminding the slaying of his Qajar rival. This was the first step in a willful struggle that eventually brought him to the throne of Iran.

Adopting the title Tahmasp-Qoli (slave of Tahmasp), within a year he was able to secure his base in Khorasan and sack Mashhad, removing Malek Mahmud. Soon after, in a series of successful campaigns, in 1727 he first subdued the restive Abdali Afghans in Herat and prepared to march against the occupying Ghalzai Afghans in Isfahan. Routing Ashraf's forces in two battles, first near Damghan and then in Murchehkhort in the vicinity of Isfahan, in December 1729 he triumphantly entered the Safavid capital in the company of Tahmasp II (see map 3.1). Restoring the Safavid shah to his throne added to Nader's prestige, although the pillage and killing of Isfahan's population by the "liberation" army was an ominous sign of what was to come. Marching to Fars he pushed the demoralized Afghan forces southeast. Ashraf and a few of his companions were killed on their way to Kandahar, but the remnant of troops who survived the battle conveniently joined Nader's forces. In an ever-growing enterprise for conquest, he soon turned his attention toward the provinces under Ottoman and Russian occupation.

Key to Nader's early successes and his meteoric rise was a talent for organizing disjointed tribal groups into an army. These included Kurdish tribes of Khorasan, some of the Qajars and their Turkmen allies, the Baluch and other tribes of the southeast, the Abdali and Ghalzai Afghans, and even the Uzbeks. He often took command of these desperate nomadic forces by enticing their chiefs to join him, only to eliminate them at an opportune moment. What made his enterprise different from familiar Turko-Mongolian tribal ventures of the past was that the multiethnic character of Nader's army also incorporated a contingent of peasants displaced from the interior. Perhaps for the first time in Iranian history—and possibly in the history of empires in the region—his crude method of drafting able-bodied men from remote villages and towns, often without serious resistance, set the precedent for a new conscription army.

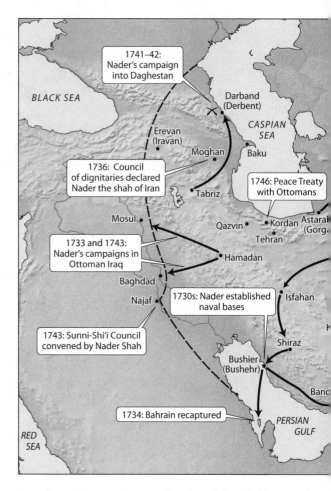

Map 3.2. Major campaigns of Nader Shah Afshar, 1736–1747

Comparable to similar European armies of his time, Nader's drive for a disciplined military force increasingly entailed an element of protonational integration. Long campaigns, under unified command and with the reward of shared booty, instilled a sense of unanimity and emphasized pronounced elements of shared identity, such as standardized insignia in campaigns, the use of *Shahnameh* legendary motifs, and later the creation of a new royal crown for himself instead of the Safavid Qezilbash cap. The effective use of firearms, matchlocks and light artillery, with which he quickly equipped his army once he got hold of the Safavid arsenal in big cities, also proved crucial in giving Nader's troops mobility and tactical advantage, and in boosting their morale and semblance of a modern military discipline. Nader himself became a champion of national

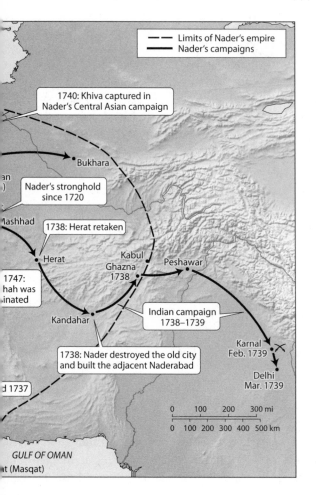

assertiveness, distinct from the late Safavids' public image of debauchery on the one hand and excessive religiosity on the other.

Even before taking Isfahan, Nader was adamant that he would repulse the Ottoman occupation—with force if necessary. But unlike campaigns of the Safavid era, Nader did not rely on the Shi'i identity to garner support. Rather, he was campaigning against Ottomans almost purely on territorial grounds. It was as though prevailing over the Afghan enemy sublimated, at least momentarily, Nader's personal ambitions into a patriotic objective tied to defending the Guarded Domains and preserving Iran's territorial integrity. As it turned out, this was a project different from carving out a tribal kingdom for himself with no specific geographical boundary and no ties to its subjects.

Beginning in 1730, Nader, now acting as the Safavid regent, reclaimed most western provinces in a series of brilliant campaigns (see maps 3.1 and 3.2). Despite Ottoman reinforcements to fight the unexpected rise of the new contender, the resounding defeat of the Turkish army generated a serious crisis in Istanbul and contributed to the abdication of Sultan Ahmad III (r. 1703–1730). Nader's military pressure to recapture the province of Baghdad and the Shi'i holy cities, however, met stiff Ottoman resistance. The loss of Baghdad would have been a serious blow to Ottoman prestige and its strategic and commercial interests. With his troops stranded at the western front, Nader sensed a greater need for Shi'i solidarity.

To display his Shi'i loyalty, he repaired and gilded Shi'i shrines in Mashhad and Shiraz. Although he frowned on the demoralized clerical establishment, he still acted with loyalty to the Safavid sovereign. But this lasted for only a short while. Tahmasp's failure to repulse a renewed Ottoman offensive in the west and the subsequent loss of nearly all the territory Nader had temporarily secured, gave the latter the long-awaited excuse to remove Tahmasp. In 1732, in a carefully staged scene in an Isfahan palace, designed to display Tahmasp's nocturnal debauchery, Nader persuaded the state notables and chiefs of the army to depose the shah and replace him on the throne with his eight-month-old son, 'Abbas III, for whom Nader was regent.

As the de facto ruler of the country some seven years after his emergence, Nader could act with greater facility in making new administrative and military appointments in his favor. He levied heavy taxes to finance a series of campaigns that, between 1732 and 1736, restored all of the western and northwestern Iranian provinces occupied by the Ottomans, including Georgia, Armenia, and the economically rich Shamakhi, and even established footholds in Ottoman Iraq. Nader's forces crushed the Lezgian revolt in the Caucasus, defeated the restive Ghalzai Afghans and forced them back to Kandahar, recaptured Herat, restrained the Turkmens of northern Khorasan, forced the Russians to fully evacuate the Caspian provinces, and reasserted control over the Persian Gulf (see map 3.1). It seemed as though Safavid rule, nominal though it was, had finally restored stability and calm to the empire.

FROM MOGHAN TO HINDUSTAN

The long shadow of the "son of the sword," as Nader often referred to his own lineage, had already been cast over the Guarded Domains. In the winter of 1736, he summoned to the plain of Moghan on the bank of the Aras River in northern Azarbaijan a great assembly of khans and notables to consider the future of the Iranian state. It was an open secret that the ambitious "slave of Tahmasp" was ready to abolish Safavid rule altogether and make the Persian throne his own (pl. 3.3).

Of the nearly twenty thousand dignitaries who were present in the Moghan assembly, reportedly only a single *shaykh al-Islam* (the chief clerical authority) of the last Safavid sovereign dared to express, in private, the Iranian people's sympathy for the Safavid house. Overheard by informants, he was brought into Nader's presence and duly executed, setting a clear example for other potential voices of dissent still loyal to the Safavids. The large gathering of patricians, urban officials, religious leaders (including the patriarch of the Armenian Church), state officials, and army chiefs from all over the country—albeit a "rubber stamp" assembly—was meant to signify the consent of the country's elite. Perhaps inspired by the Mongolian tribal gatherings of the Ilkhanid era, the Moghan assembly was the first time that the notion of representation was introduced to the Iranian milieu. Moreover, Nader justified deposing the Safavid monarchy, and his own "reluctance" to carry the burden of kingship, on the grounds of restoring Iranian sovereignty when the Safavids were no longer fit to rule the country.

The greatest divergence from the Safavid concept of authority, however, was Nader's extraordinary—and as it turned out, quite impolitic—call to relinquish Shi'ism as the religious creed of Iran, at least in the way it was practiced under the Safavids. This was one of three conditions he set forth in Moghan for his acceptance of the crown of Iran. His declaration also called for total loyalty to himself and the abandoning of any sympathy for the house of the Safavids and hope for their future restoration. Instead of the Safavids' Twelver Shi'ism, which in his view had long been divisive internally and offensive to Iran's Sunni neighbors, Nader proposed the relatively improvised Ja'fari creed (after the Sixth Shi'i Imam, Ja'far Sadeq, who died in 765).

Devoid of anti-Sunni exclusivity, messianic longing, and juristic tradition, Nader's Ja'fari brand seemed to be a diluted form of the Safavids' state-dominated creed. More than two centuries of religious conflict, which had facilitated the Afghan invasion, must have persuaded Nader, whose own career, oddly enough, had been built on expelling Sunni invaders, to see the ills of an exclusionist form of Shi'ism. He hoped that declaring the Ja'fari creed would persuade the Ottomans to comply with the terms of his peace proposal, which called for the establishment in Mecca for the Shi'i pilgrims of a fifth platform around the Ka'ba (lit. *rokn*, "pillar"), adjacent to that of the Hanafis, which was to be taken as recognition of Shi'ism as a legitimate Islamic creed.

Yet there were other implicit motives behind Nader's conciliatory move. His army included among its ranks a growing number of Afghans, Uzbeks, and other

Sunni mercenaries whose loyalty to Shi'i rule for the cause of a Shi'i empire was in doubt. On a deeper level, Nader, who earlier in his life seemed to have adhered to Sunnism, realized that minimizing Sunni-Shi'i differences would enhance his chances for conquering Sunni lands. Annexing southern Iraq, eastern Anatolia, and perhaps beyond seemed within his reach, given the visible signs of the Ottomans' disarray. Here, perhaps for the first time in a political context, the notion of a pan-Islamic solidarity (*ettehad-e Islam*) found expression in Nader's conciliatory proposal, which, though it never materialized, denoted a shift away from the creed-based Ottoman and Safavid Muslim empires. As it turned out, Nader's proposal was unacceptable to both sides. To the Shi'is of Iran, being an inconsequential subsidiary of the Sunni Hanafis was a humiliating reversal of their Shi'i identity despite all the Sunni hostilities. To the Ottoman authorities, who for two centuries were angered by the rude anti-Sunni propaganda of Safavid Iran, even partial recognition of Shi'ism was an anathema.

Imagining himself as a new Timur, or even an Isma'il, Nader's first major move after the Moghan assembly was to conquer Kandahar, the homeland of the Ghalzai Afghans (see map 3.2). Rather than claiming vengeance or even reclaiming the plundered Safavid riches or recruiting a larger number of Afghan mercenaries to his expanding army, Nader's main goal was to capture the strategic gateway to Mughal India. The rise of a new sectarian conscience in the eighteenth-century Islamic world, as evident in renewed Afghan and Ottoman Sunni aggressions against the Safavids, coincided with a rapid decline of the Ottoman and Mughal empires on both Iran's eastern and western borders. Yet militarily the Ottomans were effective enough to slow Nader's western advances, which in turn persuaded the Iranian conqueror, desperate for funds, to abandon his anti-Ottoman campaigns and look eastward once it became clear that his pan-Islamic project would not render the desired benefit.

At the most basic level, Nader's ambition was to access the Mughal Empire at its most vulnerable time, to plunder its riches, and to use these exploits to defeat his Ottoman nemesis. The urge to conquer Hindustan, as the Indian subcontinent was known, became irresistible when he realized that the impoverished people of Iran could no longer sustain the cost of his territorial ambitions. By contrast Mughal India was a longtime repository of circulated precious metals of the Old World, which had accumulated over centuries. Even though as early as the sixteenth century the European trading companies had drained off substantial quantities of Indian gold and silver, there was enough left to entice Nader and his army chiefs.

Success on the battlefield, despite some Mughal resistance, proved the worth of Nader's Indian campaign. Having first secured the walled city of Kandahar in

1738 and razed it to the ground, he used the last of the Ghalzai stronghold to build adjacent to the old city the new city of Naderabad named in his own honor. He then moved on to capture with relative ease the major urban centers of Peshawar, Kabul, and Lahore (see map 3.2). His eastward expansion into northern India was beyond anything a northern power had ever explored since the Afghan conquest of Sher Shah Suri two centuries earlier. Yet the agonizing breakup of the Mughal Empire during the first half of the eighteenth century had turned it into an easy target for Nader's invasion, and soon after for colonial exploits.

Nader routed the lackadaisical Indian armies in Karnal north of Delhi in February 1739. In the course of the battle he defeated the numerically superior Mughal army and triumphantly entered Delhi (pl. 3.4). That he almost immediately agreed to reinstate to the throne the desperate Naser al-Din Mohammad Shah (r. 1719–1748), reaffirmed Nader's predatory intent: the unfortunate emperor reportedly surrendered his entire royal treasure, consisting of ancestral jewels, precious metals, and other objects of value. In addition, the conquering army levied a hefty toll on Delhi notables. Nader's total take reportedly amounted to seven hundred million rupees, one of the largest booties ever extracted in early modern history. Among many dazzling items that would later adorn the Persian (and the British) royalty were the two great diamonds, Kuh-e Nur (or Koh-i Noor, mountain of light) and Darya-e Nur (or Daria-i Noor; sea of light), and the legendary Peacock Throne (Takh-e Tavus) built by the Mughal emperor Shah Jahan. Nader's avarice did not spare the resisting population of Delhi. His troops, drunk and fierce, rampaged through the city, raping and plundering. A popular revolt in response cost the lives of three thousand of Nader's mercenaries. In retaliation, Nader ordered a massacre of the city population, which within few hours reportedly took the lives of as many as twenty thousand civilians.

COLLAPSE OF A FRAGILE EMPIRE

After returning from his Indian campaign, Nader amassed his Indian spoils in the impenetrable fortress of Kalat-e Naderi near his birthplace in northern Khorasan. Hoarding at such massive scale was meant to finance his world-conquering project, whereas his merciless acts of violence were meant to instill fear in his impoverishing subjects. The darkening image of Nader, despite the awe he inspired in the European press of the time, did not bring prosperity or stability to his empire. On the contrary, military success whetted his appetite to extort with cruelty matched only by his historical role models. Some contemporary authors eulogized him for "reviving the Changizian rites," while others depicted horrifying scenes of atrocities committed against defenseless towns and villages. Marauding across the land from Mesopotamia and the Transcaucasus to Central Asia, the Persian Gulf, and the interiors of Hindustan, and fighting destructive wars, led to the image of short-lived empire devoid of a center of gravity or a sustainable imperial vision. With Iran's resources stretched to their limits, he left behind a ruined agrarian economy, little trade and manufacture, and decimated administrative infrastructure. It was as if Nader and his army represented a nomadic revenge of the periphery against Iran's urban centers.

During the following eight years of his reign, Nader's ceaseless campaigns to recapture Iraq and Anatolia, with the aim of accessing the Black Sea, brought mixed results. He seriously threatened the stability of the Ottoman eastern provinces. It seemed as though he would prevail. Yet long campaigns and even longer sieges did not deliver Iraq to Nader's empire. The frequency of rebellions of the Baluch, who were allied with tribes of the interiors of Fars province, and the Afghans and Kurds of northern Khorasan, compelled him to rush back to the east. Predictably, the Sublime Porte also rejected his proposal for recognition of the Ja'fari creed. Likewise, his punitive action against Daghestani mountain people in hopes of stabilizing the Iranian Caucasus and his repeated campaigns against the Turkmens of the northeast and the Lur confederacy in the Iranian interior proved ephemeral.

Nader's unrelenting campaigning and the movement of large armies across the country devastated what was left of the prosperity of the Iranian cities and the countryside. His forced relocation of the nomadic populations was as disruptive as his appointment of Afghan, Turkmen, Kurd, and other Sunni tribal commanders to military governorships of the Persian provinces. His confiscation of private property and the appropriation of vast Safavid charitable endowments, though aimed to stop rampant corruption and raise more revenue, actually added to fiscal confusion. Heavy taxation weakened the peasants and the landowning elite alike. Forced conscription alienated the rural population and at the city gates tall conical structures made of his victims' skulls were a gruesome reminder of Nader's frenzied rage.

What eventually cost Nader his life, however, was not the dismal treatment he inflicted on his subjects but his evident inability to strike a balance in his multiethnic army. His progressive insanity, which erupted in bursts of violence, fueled the fire of ethno-religious tension among his officers and troops. Relying heavily on Uzbek and Afghan mercenaries, he had planned to eliminate the growing opposition among his Persian officers and troops. Yet before he could put his coup into action, he was assassinated in June 1747 in his camp in northern Khorasan while attempting to quell yet another rebellion among the Kurds of the region (fig. 3.2).

Figure 3.2. Nader's assassination in this contemporary English
engraving is consistent with the attention he received in Europe as
a mighty conqueror, especially after his Indian campaign.
Thomas Bankes, Edward Blake, and Alexander Cook, *New System of Geography*
(London: J. Cook, 1787). Author's collection.

A group of Afshar and other Iranian military chiefs attacked him while he was
sleeping in the royal tent. Despite his desperate resistance, they managed to kill
him. They dispatched his severed head to his nephew Herat, who collaborated
in the plot, as an invitation to succeed his uncle on the throne. The mostly Shi'i
Iranian faction among his troops, who had now regrouped under the title of
Qezilbash, had felt threatened by Nader's ominous drift toward his Afghan and
Uzbek mercenaries. The latter under the command of Ahmad Khan Abdali,
later known as Ahmad Shah Durrani (r. 1747–1773), posed a serious challenge.
In the Iranian faction's emphasis on the Qezilbash identity, more a memory
than an institutional reality, one may trace a desire not only to check the Afghan
presence but also to restore some form of Safavid rule.

Nader's failure to put an end to post-Safavid tribal turmoil cost Iran dearly.
Though he aimed to create a stable imperial model distinct from the Safavids,

he essentially remained a tribal chief in control of a formidable war machine devoted to conquest. His capital, as he was quoted as saying, was on the back of his horse, and his disgust for the machinery of government was evident in his consistent crushing of the old Safavid bureaucracy and haphazard replacement of it with a military elite. His policy of deemphasizing Shiʻism and disengaging from its clerical core never led to a tolerant alternative. It became apparent that the people of Iran, at least of the Persian-speaking urban centers, no longer would abandon Shiʻism. It is therefore not surprising that shortly after his accession, the Persian urban public of the interiors viewed him as a usurper of the Safavid throne.

Soon, a string of pretenders to the Safavid throne raised among the populace with messianic hopes for restoration of the demised dynasty. An obscure dervish from Rafsanjan, one of several who claimed to be Safi Mirza, the younger son of Shah Soltan Hosain, rebelled against Nader during his siege of Mosul in 1744. He was first given refuge in Istanbul in 1729 in the hopes that he could advance the Ottoman objective in the power scramble in progress in Iran. As Shah Safi II, he was encouraged to rise against Nader, but his enterprise came to no fruitful end. Once he had proved useless, the Ottomans sent him off to the exile on the island of Rhodes, where he died in obscurity some years later. Other pretenders were no more successful.

REGENCY OF KARIM KHAN ZAND

With Nader's death, his short-lived empire, stretching from Marv and Herat to Georgia and Dagestan, and on to Bahrain and the shores of the Persian Gulf, plunged into turmoil. The mosaic of nomadic and seminomadic people took part in a pandemonium that took at least another decade before a semblance of tranquility would emerge under Karim Khan Zand (r. 1751–1779). Despite three attempts by Nader's successors to try to stabilize his amorphous empire, the Afsharid base in Khorasan proved too fragile to allow for an orderly transition. Besides jealously guarding the remnants of Nader's hoarded treasures in Kalat, which came to be a curse rather than a blessing, his successors could barely subordinate Nader's unruly army, no matter how generously and hurriedly they squandered his legendary wealth in exchange for loyalties. Nor were they able to hold together from Mashhad or from Isfahan the disjointed provinces of his empire.

The ensuing struggle for power plunged Iran into another civil war that lasted a whole decade. By 1757 the rise of Karim Khan Zand in the south was the only positive outcome. His regency was the most benign and durable of any attempt since 1722 to revive a nominal Safavid rule and govern in the shadow of its memory. Contrary to Nader's diabolical temper, Karim's personality combined political sagacity and soldierly valor with beneficence, acumen, and conviviality—a rare combination especially when compared to his cohorts. His rule of more than two decades marks one of the most tranquil in Iran's early modern history, a remarkable example of how the ruler's personal qualities, rather than the institutional framework within which he operated, determined political stability, the well-being of subjects, and cultural florescence. Under favorable conditions fostered by the Zand dynasty (founded by Karim Khan), Shiraz and the whole of the Fars province, which had terribly suffered under Nader, quickly bounced back.

Brought up in exile in northern Khorasan, Karim belonged to the Lak, a subtribe of the Zands and part of the lesser division of Lurs of western Iran. They were banished by Nader to the northeastern frontier presumably to guard against the Uzbeks. Karim had fought in the Afsharid campaigns, involuntarily perhaps, even though Nader had eliminated all senior members of his tribe. After Nader's assassination, Karim led the return of the Zand contingent back to their ancestral homeland in the Malayer region in Luristan. From there, over the course of ensuing civil war he eventually became the master of Fars province, with Shiraz as his base. Zand victory in effect reaffirmed the ascendancy of the southern Iranian interior, albeit Lur and still tribal, over the mostly northern Turkic periphery, an ascendancy tied to a new sense of Persian awareness.

Karim Khan's reluctance to assume royal authority independent of nominal Safavid sovereignty gave his rule a distinctive character. He learned from Nader's mistakes. He was realistic enough to acknowledge the place of Shi'i faith and wise enough to respect devotion to the Safavid memory. Karim's choice to remain *vakil al-dowleh* (deputy of the state), however, was a subtle shift from acting as mere regent of an obscure Safavid prince, a nonentity. By allowing reference to himself as the "deputy of the subjects" (*vakil al-ro'aya*), moreover, he seemed to have implicitly shifted his own mandate to that of deputizing people rather than mere Safavid kingship (pl. 3.5). The subtle shift corresponded to Karim's popularity with his subjects, especially the urban population. Distancing himself from the tormenting experience of the recent past, he further relied on the legends of Iranian of kingship closely associated with Fars province. Though the extent of such Persian awareness should not be exaggerated, it is evidenced in the literary and material culture of the period. Tracing the Zand revival back to Fars as the cradle of Persian culture and its rich poetic tradition was one example. Wider use of the term *Iran*, as an alternative to the Guarded Domains of Iran, is another.

Interest in rebuilding cities under Karim Khan went along with revitalization of the Persian Gulf trade and development of Shiraz as its hub. Consolidation of the Zands soon gravitated the political center, at least temporarily, toward the south and away from the perils surrounding Isfahan, Qazvin, Tabriz, and Mashhad. Similar to 'Abbas I, Karim Khan created an urban complex commemorating his political achievements. His reconstruction projects complemented, and at times replaced, Safavid public buildings and palaces. Most notable among Karim Khan's grand edifices were the new bazaar, the mosque, and a new citadel (*arg*), together forming the core of a new urban development (fig. 3.3).

The Zand material heritage, while incomparable in grandiosity to Isfahan of the Safavid era, was remarkable for what it accomplished in a short period of time. It was also notable for its innovations. The design features of the Vakil mosque, a vast space of more than ninety thousand square feet built between 1751 and 1773, for example, served to reaffirm a new political agenda. The absence of any domed structure, in particular, may be seen as a break from the glorification of Safavid royal patronage. The use of forty-eight single-piece marble columns throughout the mosque's vast prayer hall, the well-proportioned courtyards, and high *ivans* (arched portals)—two instead of the usual four—shows artistic confidence (fig. 3.4).

EVERYDAY LIFE IN SHIRAZ

Beyond the political history of the period, we know something of everyday life in the Zand period. A remarkable narrative, *Rostam al-Tawarikh*, provides details about the minimum wage and the price of goods and commodities. An average laborer in Zand Shiraz earned as much as nine tumans per year, enough, the author reckons, to feed and clothe a family of seven, the average size of an Iranian household at the time. One tuman, consisting of ten thousand dinars, would have bought roughly all the commodities needed annually for such a family: 950 pounds of wheat, 220 pounds of various grains, 115 pounds of rice, 220 pounds of red meat, 25 chickens, and 150 eggs. Another tuman or two would have bought spices and condiments, cooking oil, salt, sugar, coffee, tobacco, soap, wood, charcoal, burning oil, vegetables and fruits, and other necessities. Clothing, mostly cotton, but also woolen and silk for special items, constituted a hefty figure, perhaps as much as two tumans. A quality woolen carpet of about 130 square feet was worth about a tuman and a half, but a kilim of the same size was half that price. In contrast, an average urban house cost no more than ten tumans.

Figure 3.3. The Vakil bazaar, vital to the trade of the south, was at the
center of Zand urban development and part of a network of bazaars,
caravansaries, trading houses, workshops, and retail stores.
J. Dieulafoy, "La Perse, la Chaldée et la Susiane," *Le tour du monde* (Paris, 1881–1882), 120.

Figure 3.4. Columned prayer hall (*shabestan*) of the Vakil mosque, Shiraz.
© Pawel Opaska/Dreamstime.com.

Land was relatively cheap as well. One *jarib* (nearly two and a half acres) went for only a quarter of tuman, compared to one tuman for a *jarib* of orchard. The most prized items, however, were horses. A pedigreed horse could cost as much as twenty tumans and even a well-bred mule was no less than ten tumans. Yet an average urbanite could afford riding a very good donkey for one tuman while a peasant could buy a plowing cow for the same price and a working donkey for one third of that. Though raging inflation, our source informs us, had led Karim Khan to introduce some measure of price controls, still the standard of living seems well within an affordable range.

Rostam al-Tawarikh nostalgically recalls the life of prosperity and leisure under the great Vakil. The author praises Karim Khan for combating crime and restoring calm to Shiraz, well known for its harassing urban brigands (*lutis*). Among other measures he instituted a liberal policy of establishing taverns and brothel districts for the troops and for the city folk, presumably to forestall the raping and abduction of women and children, an endemic problem under the Afsharid regime. The author also offers a long list of well-known female entertainers of Shiraz, whom he praises for their sophistication and taste.

The charming Mulla Fatemeh, no doubt an educated female entertainer, was praised for her "pleasant conversation." She was "good natured, tender, and mannerly; never acted presumptuously, always compassionate to the prince and the pauper alike. . . . She knew by heart about twenty thousand select verses from classic and contemporary poets, and could recite them appropriately in every assembly accompanied with tambourine, drum, reed pipe, harp, lute and *kamancheh*."[1] She was also credited for her intelligent critiques of clerical bigotry and misogyny, as well as for being an advocate of the weak and disadvantaged. According to the *Rostam al-Tawarikh*, on one occasion quoting the poet Sa'di, she cautioned Karim Khan about the transitory nature of his power and the egalitarian tyranny of death. The Shiraz environment was liberal enough for Fatemeh not only to utter such sentiments but also to express them in public through poetry and music. At the crossroads of the Vakil bazaar she and her band reportedly performed for the public, no doubt in the face of the ulama's objection.

The portrayal of female entertainers became popular in the Zand paintings, and later was inherited by the artists of the early Qajar period. Large-scale oil painting on canvas celebrating court life of leisure and merrymaking was a late Safavid development, possibly inspired by Italian and Dutch portraitures. Yet it was in the Zand era that the inner life of the harem became the prominent subject of a school of painting distinct for its depiction of women, wine, and music. Portraitures of the Zand and Qajar periods showed unveiled women in private settings off-limits to the public eye, an indication no doubt of the concern of the patrons of these works not to transgress shari'a sanctions and face criticism of the ulama.

REORIENTING TOWARD THE PERSIAN GULF

Public space remained primarily a male domain. The Vakil bazaar and the adjacent caravansaries were not constructed merely to augment the ruler's image or to please the growing out-of-town visitors. They served as the main outlet for the emerging mercantile classes and as a new market for the Persian Gulf trade being conducted through the port of Bushehr (Bushier), the main entrepôt for Fars province. The piracy common in the lower Persian Gulf, French naval attacks on English ships in the area, and the growing maritime ambitions of the Imam of Muscat and his Omani privateers undermined most of the trade of the lower Persian coast. By the mid-eighteenth century, Bandar Abbas gradually ceased to function as Iran's chief port of entry. The British East India Company and Dutch commercial firms searched for safe harbor along the upper shores of the Persian Gulf. They first settled in Bushehr and Kharg Island and soon after in the rival port of Basra, which was the outlet of Ottoman Iraq to the Persian Gulf.

Despite Iran's desire to safeguard its southern shores and its foreign trade, its greatest weakness in establishing a secure presence in the Persian Gulf was its lack of either a naval or a commercial fleet. Nader's effort to build a naval force was a notable exception. By 1745 he had gathered a fleet of more than twenty boats of different sizes, purchased from the Portuguese or constructed in India. Portuguese officers and Indian sailors largely manned his navy. He also built a dockyard in Bushehr, and at great expense, and with much difficulty he imported timber from Mazandaran for the construction of warships. The major objective was to quell privateers along the Iranian coasts and revive maritime trade, although it is conceivable that he had maritime ambitions in the Indian Ocean. Nader also used the expertise of an Englishman to build a fleet in the Caspian Sea with the similar objective of securing the Iranian coast from Turkmen and Cossack piracy. He also appointed for the first time an admiral (*daryabayg*) to organize Iranian defenses in the Persian Gulf. Yet after Nader's assassination, the Omanis resumed their raids of the Iranian coasts, even carrying off the ships of his navy.

By the time of Karim Khan, the ruler of Muscat and the Qasimi privateers, who were operating from the southern coast of the Persian Gulf, were capable of barring Iran from effective control of its own coast. Any effort to establish a naval presence in the upper Persian Gulf, moreover, was bound to face heavy competition from the semi-autonomous Mamluks of Iraq. While keeping their Ottoman suzerain at bay, the Mamluks were eager to host the lucrative trade of the East India Company. This offered the English unprecedented freedom to dictate terms and win greater concessions by playing the Iraqi Mamluks against the Zands. Even a joint military operation in 1768 by the Iranians, the Mamluks, and the East India Company intended to crush the Ka'b tribes on the banks of the Shatt al-'Arab waterway, did not result in further commercial cooperation.

It did, however, whet Karim Khan's appetite for expansion not only in the Persian Gulf but also across the frontiers of Ottoman Iraq. Counting on the weakness of the Mamluks of Iraq and the Sublime Porte's sluggish response, Karim Khan lent substantive support to the chiefs of Iraqi Kurdistan, who sought autonomy from their Turkish masters. But it was above all the vigorous English backing of the Ottomans in disputes with the Iranian state that in 1774 persuaded Karim Khan to send a force under the command of his brother Sadeq Khan, to capture Basra, the valuable strategic and commercial lifeline of Mesopotamian trade. This was the first time since Nader's overland sorties into the Ottoman territory that Iranian advances had paid off in Iraq, albeit momentarily.

The fragile five-year Zand occupation of Basra, which ended with Karim Khan's death in 1779, proved a failure (map 3.3). It interrupted the export of Persian silk and pearls from Bahrain to Europe, and it discouraged profitable trade with Mughal India, now largely fragmented into regional princely states and progressively prey of French and the British colonial gains. Moreover, it demonstrated the difficulty Iran faced in securing an important commercial outlet to the Indian Ocean, not only to compete with expanding European trade but also to outmaneuver Ottoman Iraq. As an alternative to the Persian Gulf, Karim Khan also followed Nader's steps in developing the northern Caspian trade with Russia, which was largely conducted from Astrakhan, on the Caspian's northern shore. The chief beneficiaries of that trade, however, were not the Zands but the northern-based Qajars, who soon after Karim Khan's death emerged as the chief contenders for control of Iran. Russian commercial and diplomatic presence along the southern and western shores of the Caspian, which included Armenian and Muslim traders' relations with Baku, Anzali, and Astarabad, anticipated Russia's territorial advances in the early decades of the nineteenth century.

RISE OF THE QAJARS

Karim Khan died in 1779 an old man, a rare phenomenon in an era of great political turmoil. With him perished his fragile balance of tribal alliances, built

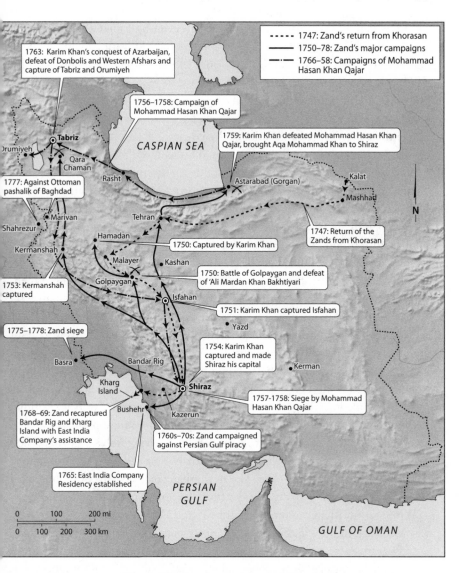

Map 3.3. Rise of Karim Khan and consolidation of the Zands, 1747–1778

by means of consent and coercion. After his death, as Iran experienced another round of civil war, the third since the fall of the Safavids, the problem of political legitimacy resurfaced once more to haunt the many contenders. Not for another two decades, until the last year of Aqa Mohammad Khan Qajar (r. 1789–1797), the prevailing leader of the Qajars of Astarabad, did a solution to the question of political authority emerge.

The collapse of the Zand dynasty, if it can even be called a dynasty, was a dismal affair. The tribal truce that was the outcome of Karim Khan's political acumen withered rapidly after his passing. In the thirteen years between his death and the capture of Shiraz by the Qajars, in 1792, which put an effective end to Zand rule, no fewer than eight contenders successively vied for the shaky Zand seat of power. All but one, who died of acute alcoholism, were murdered in a climate of treachery and violence. In a dynastic free-for-all, brothers fought against brothers and fathers against sons. The seed of the Zands' rapid downfall are to be found first and foremost in the self-destructive behavior of Karim Khan's successors and the internecine tensions that long had simmered while he was alive. The small Zand tribe, moreover, had to rely on an assortment of other tribal forces, whose loyalties were up for sale to the highest bidder. The haphazard southern alliance of Greater Lurs of Fars province in the south, of which Zand was a member, had to face the Tangestani and Dashtestani warriors of the Warm Country, the Arab tribes of the Persian Gulf littoral, the Bakhtiyaris of the southwest, and the Kurds of the Kermanshah region (see map 3.3).

Two decades of urban calm had hardly tamed the nomadic culture of perpetual warfare among this quarreling bunch in the south. Karim Khan's wisdom and foresight had clearly failed to instill values of stability and collaboration, let alone a Fars-based sense of shared identity or a commitment to a centralized state. It was as if the Persian urban centers were destined to endure another round of nomadic strife, both north and south. Yet contrary to Nader's time, the cities, and Shiraz in particular, did not remain entirely passive. Tired of internecine Zand bickering, there emerged a new civic resolve, one that relied on a tacit alliance of landowning urban notables (*a'yan*), city administrators, and members of the ulama class. The new urban voice became even more pronounced once a new Qajar contender from the north appeared on the horizon.

While Karim Khan was on his deathbed, Aqa Mohammad Khan Qajar, who was a hostage in the Zand court in Shiraz, escaped the Zand capital and galloped toward Astarabad, his tribal base in northeastern corner of Mazandaran. After his rebellious father had been killed in war with Karim Khan, the ambitious Qajar heir was captured and exiled to Shiraz, where he spent fifteen years in the Zand court under Karim Khan's watchful eye (see chart 2 in chapter 4). Karim Khan viewed the Qajars as his most formidable adversary. For three generations, since the last days of the Safavid dynasty, the Qajar khans' bid for power had been rudely interrupted. Tahmasp II's original regent, Fath 'Ali Khan Qajar, had fallen victim to the more ambitious Nader-Qoli. Even though as a member of the Qezilbash the Qajar khan was committed to a Safavid nominal sovereignty, he was no less fervent than his Afshar rival in a contest for power.

A decade later, Fath ʿAli Khan's son, Mohammad Hasan Khan, renewed the family's claim to power, this time against the Zands. After a series of inconclusive sorties that at one point even brought the city of Isfahan under the Qajar control, he was contained in Astarabad, where he eventually perished. Some years later, Fath ʿAli Khan's grandson Hosain-Qoli (Aqa Mohammad Khan's younger brother), an audacious brute with the self-proclaimed title "Inflamer of the World" (*jahansuz*), rebelled against Karim Khan. He, too, was killed in action, ironically at the hands of the Turkmen horsemen who made up his fighting force. It is noteworthy that the Qajar contender relied on the Turkmen tribes of the northeast frontier, as had the early Safavids on the Qezilbash Turkmens of Azarbaijan three centuries earlier.

It therefore seemed inevitable that Aqa Mohammad Khan would take up the family feud, even though he himself was its hapless victim. An Afsharid pretender to Nader's throne had castrated Aqa Mohammad at a very young age to disqualify him from any future claim to the throne. In the tribal culture of the period the removal of testicles, similar to blinding, was a common form of body mutilation. The assumption was that only able-bodied men were entitled to rule. Yet the success of Aqa Mohammad Khan in establishing the new Qajar dynasty proved the opposite. The eighteenth century might be labeled the "golden age of mutilation," since no ruler or pretender of the period from a tribal background shied away from the brutal practice. Acts of bodily mutilation also included cutting off the victim's tongue, and more commonly, the partial or complete removal of the nose and the ear. Aqa Mohammad Khan was not just the victim of such punishments; he was their ultimate practitioner.

Aqa Mohammad Khan's complex personality was no doubt affected by his bloody family history, the bodily mutilation he sustained, and years of confinement in the land of his paternal enemy. His ruthless discipline, his grudges toward family and tribal enemies, his love for booty—especially gems—and his deliberate acts of violence resembled Nader Shah's. Yet Aqa Mohammad Khan can be credited for his great success in reunifying Iran, an enterprise in which Nader Shah and Karim Khan both failed. In military discipline and determination, the Qajar khan was reminiscent of Nader. For his political foresight and desire to rebuild the state as a social contract rather than a tribal war machine, he was indebted to Karim Khan and the Zand administration. He evidently valued continuity more than Karim Khan's own successors did.

Contrary to Nader's enmity toward the Safavid divan, he partially rehabilitated the existing Zand bureaucrats, who themselves often had their roots in divan families of the late Safavid era. He also learned from Nader's error not to alienate the Shiʿi clerical establishment. The rise of the Usuli legal school, represented by a new class of Shiʻi jurists, created an important source of support for the nascent Qajar state. Above all, Aqa Mohammad Khan assiduously avoided the destructive free-for-all contest for succession, which twice he had witnessed ruin the Afsharid and Zand states. By the time he was assassinated in 1797, he had eliminated nearly all potential pretenders to the Qajar throne. One of the most important political figures of modern Iranian history, he founded a dynasty that survived for more than a century despite many odds. Only a man devoid of private life, who spent more time in the saddle and under the tent than on the throne or in the harem, was destined to bring Iran out of its long period of turmoil.

The Qajar success nevertheless depended on more factors than the character and resolve of the dynasty's founder. An important feature of the rise of Aqa Mohammad Khan was a shift in Iran's center of political gravity away from the provinces of Fars and Isfahan. On one level, the rise of the Qajars was indicative of the Turkic tribal periphery in the north reclaiming power from the Persian south, except this time the Qajars replaced the Afshars. Aqa Mohammad Khan was attempting to reconstruct the same Qezilbash-like alliance that Nader had earlier assembled, and his objectives for political unification were almost identical to those of his predecessor.

ON THE THRONE IN TEHRAN

By Nowruz of AH 1200/March 1786 CE, when Aqa Mohammad Khan declared Tehran his capital, it was as if Iran was about to witness another contest for Safavid succession. Earlier on, Aqa Mohammad Khan was still loyal enough to the memory of the demised dynasty to issue new coins on behalf of yet another obscure Safavid prince, but with his own name included. The date for choosing the new capital, however, carried a centennial significance: as if the beginning of the thirteenth Islamic century marked the end of the Safavid era and the start of a new imperial fortune. That he now issued coins into circulation, this time in the name of the Mahdi, the Twelfth Shiʻi Imam, was not accidental. Most likely it pointed at his presumption that his rise to power was a prelude to a new imperial era, not dissimilar to the rise of Ismaʻil I at the beginning of the tenth Islamic century. Likewise, as Isfahan was a millennial city for ʻAbbas I, so was Tehran a centennial capital for the Qajars. He was no longer a regional contender but an autonomous ruler who, utilizing the revenues of the Caspian trade and on the backs of his Turkmen, Kurdish, and Afghan mercenaries, secured northern and central Iran, and even held a shaky grip over Isfahan (see map 3.3).

The choice of Tehran, a leafy town in the southern foothills of the central Alborz range, over Isfahan proved to have lasting consequences. The locale offered an ideal strategic advantage, for it was a gateway to the Iranian interior and provided easy access to Astarabad and other Qajar strongholds in the north. Moreover, being devoid of a sizable urban population, Tehran was free from Isfahan's pro-Safavid and Shiraz's pro-Zand sentiments. The Alborz range immediately north of the city provided a natural wall of defense, and its many ravines and gorges afforded great hunting grounds with an abundance of game.

These features were attractive to the Qajars, as they had been earlier to the Safavid rulers who had erected a wall around the town and constructed a citadel, and to Karim Khan, who built a small residence where the Qajars later built the Golestan Palace complex. On its southern edge were the ancient ruins of Rhages, a city of biblical fame, and later the city of Ray in the early Islamic era. Not far from the edge of the central Iranian desert, Tehran was blessed with another natural defense against southern sorties. The new capital under the Qajars thus came to represent the rising north versus the weakening south (fig. 3.5). Its geopolitical polarity was to be affirmed in the decades to come by the arrival of European powers on the opposite side of the Iranian plateau, the Russians on Iran's northern frontiers and British India on its south. Not before the twentieth century, however, would Tehran supersede Tabriz or Isfahan in size or significance.

As a first step after declaring the new capital, Aqa Mohammad Khan aimed to capture the south from the Zands. Since 1786, his repeated attempts had faced stiff resistance, most recently from the last and the most charismatic of Karim Khan's successors, Lotf-'Ali Khan Zand (fig. 3.6). The young heir to the waning Zands had repelled the Qajar army three times, once driving it out of Isfahan. He spent his entire fragile reign (1789–1794) on campaigns, most of them against the Qajars in attempts to hold the Zand stronghold in the south. Yet the disruptive effects of his campaigns were all the more evident to the war-exhausted people of Fars, and especially to the landowning nobility of Shiraz who were asked to finance his campaigns.

After more than a decade of conflict and economic disruption, some had come to accept the reality of the Zands' eclipse. Among them was the chief administrator of the province of Fars, Haji Ibrahim Shirazi (1745–1801), better known as Kalantar (mayor), a shrewd statesman with influence throughout the south. Haji Ibrahim Kalantar apparently found nothing more redeeming in Lotf-'Ali Khan than in any of the seven Zand claimants before him. In 1792, while the prince was out campaigning, Haji Ibrahim conducted secret negotiations with Aqa Mohammad Khan. In return for his own security and ability to

The City of Teheran from the Ispahan Road.

Published by Longman, Hurst, Rees, Orme & Brown, Paternoster Row, 1821.

Figure 3.5. "The City of Teheran from the Ispahan Road." Even
in 1819 Tehran looked like an agricultural town at the foothills of
the central Alborz and not at all like Iran's former capitals.
J. Clark, after Robert Ker Porter (1777–1842), from *Travels in Georgia, Persia, Armenia,
Ancient Babylonia* (London: Longman, Hurst, Rees, Orme, and Brown, 1821), 1:312. Courtesy of
Yale Center for British Art, Paul Mellon Collection.

retain his property, and those of his relatives and cohorts, and perhaps with an
eye toward the safety of the people of the city, he promised to deliver Shiraz to
the Qajar khan.

Upon Lotf-'Ali's return, Haji Ibrahim ordered the city gates shut and denied
him entry into his capital. Through bargaining and stratagems the mayor then
bought off some of the prince's tribal chiefs and imprisoned others while encouraging the rest of the Zand forces around Shiraz to disperse. The desperate
Lotf-'Ali had no choice but to take refuge in Kerman in the hopes of mustering
enough pro-Zand recruits to recapture Shiraz. By switching sides, Haji Ibrahim
opened the gates of Shiraz to the eventual Qajar supremacy. Although later in
the Pahlavi era he would become a target of anti-Qajar narratives, painted as
a harbinger of the Qajar "calamity," in reality he was a savvy notable who garnered urban influence and economic power to safeguard his city, and his own

Figure 3.6. Lotf 'Ali Khan, the last of the Zands, after a wall mural
in the Shiraz citadel. Though popular throughout the south, he
lacked the military means to resist the Qajar advances. His tragic end
turned him into a hero-martyr commemorated in folk songs.
P. M. Sykes, *A History of Persia*, 2 vols. (London, 1915), vol. 2, opp. 380.

land and property. He was a partner with Aqa Mohammad Khan in making
Qajar Iran a more stable and enduring state (fig. 3.7).

In July 1792 Aqa Mohammad Khan took over Shiraz, he spared the ordinary
people from his usual retribution; however, he enslaved a number of Zand
women and children as war booty and sent them to his new capital to be dispersed in the royal harem and among the Qajar chiefs. To keep his side of the
bargain, he reaffirmed Haji Ibrahim as the governor of Fars and gave him the
title of khan, a rare honor for an urbanite. Suspicious of potential pro-Zand
sentiments in his next seasonal campaign, he also ordered the fortified city walls
and the fortification around the citadel to be leveled. The purpose of destroying
Karim Khan's edifices was to deny the city notables the advantage that earlier
they had used against the Zand prince. He further carried off the marble columns and doors of Karim Khan's palace in Shiraz to be reinstalled in Golestan Palace in Tehran. Vengefully, he even ordered Karim Khan's bones to be
exhumed and reburied beneath the threshold of Golestan Palace's reception
hall, reportedly along with the remains of Nader Shah, where he could step
over them every day. He thus callously repaid Karim Khan for saving him from
certain death and keeping him as a guest in his court for fifteen years.

Two years later, on his next visit to Shiraz, he appointed Haji Ibrahim as his *sadr-e aʻzam* (chief minister), the first time in recent memory that such rank had been recognized in the Iranian divan. His successor, Fath ʻAli Shah, also bestowed on him the title of *Eʻtemad al-Dowleh* (trustee of the state), reserved in the past for the Safavid chief ministers, thus anticipating the revival of an elaborate system of titles and honorifics in the Qajar period. He also recruited a number of trusted Zand officials to his nascent divan, which until then had relied on northern bureaucrats from Mazandaran. The southerners soon formed a powerful faction in the divan and were largely responsible for setting the tone of the bureaucratic culture of the Qajar era.

The main thrust of Aqa Mohammad Khan's ferocity was reserved for Lotf-ʻAli Khan and for the people of Kerman. In 1794 he eventually reached Kerman at a time that the city was riddled by sectarian divisions. A majority of the population supported the Zands, while a minority backed the Qajars. Lotf-ʻAli Khan's escape before the Qajar forces but his taking refuge in the besieged city enraged Aqa Mohammad Khan to such an extreme that he ordered the city to be looted and thousands of its civilians, including women and children, to be killed, raped, and enslaved. Reportedly, he also ordered the gouging out of twenty thousand pairs of eyes of the city's residents. Whether this is historically accurate or not, there is no doubt about the level of cruelty displayed by his troops. Even the Qajar historians of the time witnessed and recorded the "Mongolian-like" atrocities of the Qajar army and the ferocity of the mostly Sunni Turkmen troops against the Shiʻi inhabitants (pl. 3.6).

When Lotf-ʻAli Khan was finally captured, the Qajar khan ordered his eyes to be gouged out and his troops to rape him before sending him to Tehran for execution. His tragic end is recorded in Persian memory, especially in folk songs of the Fars countryside. In the popular memory, his image of valor, virtue, and heroism stood in contrast to Aqa Mohammad Khan's vengeful conduct and unhealthy physique, whose deep facial wrinkles, high-pitched voice, and small stature had long been subjects of contempt and ridicule, imperfections that theoretically should have disqualified him for kingship.

BUILDING AN EMPIRE ANEW

As with disinterring Karim Khan's corpse, the destruction of his handsome rival was meant to reaffirm Aqa Mohammad Khan's still-fragile legitimacy. Soon after he routed the Zands and conquered the south, he moved on to the Iranian periphery in pursuit of reconstructing his empire on the Safavid model. For the rest of his years, and to some degree for his successors, the urge to recover Iran's lost provinces remained the chief objective. In the northwest, the Caucasian provinces, including Georgia and eastern Armenia, were at stake. In the northeast, Marv and its vicinity on the Turkmen frontier and Herat and its environs further to the east were the priority. In the south, Bahrain and the Persian Gulf shores, and in the west much of Kurdistan and even the Baghdad province, were not excluded from this program of reconquest. Recovering the Caucasus was of special importance. The revenue from silk and other products and the perpetual urge for booty motivated early Qajar campaigns. Fighting a crusade (*ghaza*) provided the justification.

The new Qajar ruler of Iran had to pacify Azarbaijan. Once the northwestern tribes were subordinated with relative ease, the size of the Qajar army soared to as many as forty thousand cavalrymen. In the Caucasus, however, Aqa Mohammad Khan faced formidable challenges. The autonomous khans, who after Nader's demise had entrenched themselves in their seemingly impenetrable fortresses—such as Iravan (Yerevan or Erevan, today's capital of the Republic of Armenia) and Ganjeh (in today's Republic of Azerbaijan)—succumbed to the Qajar army after some resistance. Further north, the joint principality of Kartli-Kakheti of central Georgia, an Iranian vassal state since at least the sixteenth century, showed greater resistance. King Irakli (Heraclius) II (r. 1762–1798), who since the fall of Nader had ruled free of Persian suzerainty, entered into a treaty of protection with Russia in 1783 in an effort to withstand the reimposition of Persian rule. To the Qajar khan, such a shift in loyalty was no less than an act of treason worthy of punishment, especially because it anticipated Russian advances in the Caucasus under Catherine the Great and her successors. Irakli miscalculated both Aqa Mohammad Khan's resolve and the level of Russian support. More than a decade after Irakli's alliance with Russia, Aqa Mohammad was ready to move in and teach Irakli a lesson. After the Battle of Krtsanisi in September 1795, in which the Georgians were outnumbered and soundly defeated, the besieged city of Tiflis finally fell.

The Qajar army systematically sacked the city and thousands of civilians were put to death, and raped and pillaged. Georgian priests, the core of the resistance, were thrown into the river; churches were looted and razed to the ground. As many as fifteen thousand men, women, and children were taken captive and deported to Iran, where they were dispersed to Qajar households as concubines, eunuchs, and page boys. Not surprisingly, a vast number of Qajar princes of the following generation were born to Georgian and Armenian mothers, as they were in the neighboring Ottoman Empire, where several princes of the royal family were also born to Caucasian mothers. The sacking of Tiflis marked another shameful episode in Qajar annals. It also marked the beginning of Iran's permanent loss of the Caucasus. While in purely political terms this was a temporary setback for Russia, in the long term it further justified Russian southern expansion, allowing it to capitalize on resentment toward Iranians among the Christian population of the region.

Returning from the Georgian campaign, in 1796 Aqa Mohammad Khan wintered on the plain of Moghan, on the very same site of Nader's coronation six decades earlier. There he was crowned Aqa Mohammad Shah Qajar. He reluctantly accepted the title of shah at the pleading of Haji Ibrahim Khan Kalantar, his chief minister, an indication of the latter's desire to turn an essentially tribal khan into a Persian monarch. It was in the same spirit that the ceremonial sword of Isma'il I, kept in the shrine in Ardabil of the Safavid patriarch Shaykh Safi al-Din, was brought in and wrapped around the waist of the Qajar king.

Aqa Mohammad's self-styled Kayanid crown, named after the mythical dynasty of the *Shahnameh* was inspired by the new shah's keen interest in Iran's ancient legends. Perhaps the outcome of his years in Shiraz at the Zand court, he listened frequently and avidly to Persian epics that were read to him while he was resting. The new Kayanid crown was a dome-shaped structure inspired by the Qezilbash cap, albeit of gold-plated copper built by a humble craftsman from Mazandaran (fig. 3.7). Its style was distinct from Nader Shah's feathered

Figure 3.7. (*Left*) Aqa Mohammad Khan Qajar and Haji Ibrahim Khan Kalantar Shirazi around 1792. The image of the shah and his chief minister was a new development in the paintings of the period, representing the complementing institutions of kingship and the divan. (*Right*) Aqa Mohammad Shah Qajar, based on a portrait by an anonymous Persian artist. In its original simplicity, his crown symbolized the Qajars' unifying sovereignty. (*Left*) Nineteenth century lacquer binding, BL ms. Add. 24903. Courtesy of the British Library Board. (*Right*) J. Malcolm, *A History of Persia*, 2 vols. (London, 1815), vol. 2, opp. 262.

cap. He also wore two armlets with the legendary diamonds Darya-e Nur and Taj-i Mah, both booties from Nader's Indian campaign (the other piece, the Kuh-e Nur, which was captured by Ahmad Shah Durrani, ended up in the British crown jewels). Lotf-'Ali Khan had earlier failed to sell the stones to an English merchant, Harford Jones, at a bargain price to finance the war with the Qajars. Aqa Mohammad Shah snatched them away.

The assemblage of the Safavid and Afsharid regalia, complete with the dynastic rubric of "Safavid Qajar" (*Safavi-e Qajar*) that the court chronicles soon coined for Aqa Mohammad Shah and his successor aimed to put an end to a seventy-five-year crisis of royal authority. But he was not naive, nor was his grand vizier, to believe that Qajar sovereignty could be achieved through the feat of a coronation ceremony. He seems to have reflected on his place in the Persian kingship tradition and his designs for rebuilding an empire when he warned that if he assumed the title of shah, he intended to be one of the greatest.

Beyond the Caucasus, which remained partially insubordinate, Aqa Mohammad Shah had to quell an assortment of eastern tribes before moving to Mashhad, the last Afsharid stronghold under Shahrokh, the aging grandson of Nader. With familiar cruelty, in 1796 he deposed the blind Shahrokh, extracting the remaining of Nader's treasures. Before departing from Khorasan, he wrote the emirs of Afghanistan demanding the return of the ancient cities of Balkh (near today's Mazar-e Sharif) and Herat, Iran's eastern capital of the Safavid Empire. From the Uzbek khan of Bukhara he demanded the return of the old city of Marv, the recognized Iranian frontier with the then-fragmented Uzbek state. He also demanded the repatriation of thousands of Iranian captives who had been carried off to Bukhara during renewed Uzbek and Turkmen raids, a recurring calamity that would haunt the Qajars in the years to come. The piecing together of the Safavid Empire, now under Qajar rule, evidently shaped Aqa Mohammad Khan's imperial project.

Back in the Caucasus, Aqa Mohammad Shah's last campaign came to a fatal end. He reinstated control over Iravan, the old Safavid stronghold, and captured the fortress of Shushi (Susi) in Qarabagh, two hundred miles to the east. For a moment, the Qajar repossession of the Caucasus seemed feasible, in part because of a brief lull in Russia's southern expansion after Catherine the Great's death. Yet the situation dramatically shifted when in June 1797 Aqa Mohammad Shah was assassinated at his camp outside Shushi. He was murdered at the hands of two of his private servants, one of them a Georgian, presumably a survivor of the Tiflis campaign. The assassination apparently was a preemptive act by the servants, who had been condemned to die the following day on seemingly innocuous charges; they had quarreled behind the royal tent. It is difficult, however, to ignore the involvement of one of his ambitious generals,

Sadeq Khan Shaqaqi (chief of the Shekak tribe), who could have exploited the servants' resentment to his own unseemly ends. Immediately after the assassination, he robbed the royal tent and carried off Aqa Mohammad's beloved treasures, including the Kayanid crown, then he headed to his tribal base in western Azarbaijan, taking with him the two culprits.

In a scene reminiscent of Nader's assassination, the Qajar camp almost instantly dispersed and the allied tribes returned home. The "death of the king" (*shah-margi*) nearly always led to a period of chaos and a struggle for succession. Haji Ibrahim and the Fars troops loyal to him and the Mazandaran regiment under a Qajar chief, however, quickly returned to Tehran. Surely no one shed tears over the dead Qajar khan; but even beyond the grave, his vision for an enduring dynasty seemed to have held more firmly than Nader's or Karim Khan's. The ruthless warrior did not leave the fate of his heir to chance or to a free-for-all contest. His nephew and designated successor, Baba Khan, who ascended the throne as Fath 'Ali Shah (r. 1797–1834), still had to earn his crown, literally, but at least he did not have to fight for it against his many powerful uncles. His predecessor had eliminated all but one of them. That Fath 'Ali Shah managed to remove the last one without a hassle promised a more orderly succession. This was a great credit to the founder of the Qajar dynasty, who was ferocious but not fickle.

The order established at the dynasty's inception was in no small part due to the state officials of the divan, who became partners in the Qajar enterprise. Headed by the grand vizier, they began early on to stamp their image of governance on the emerging Qajar state. At stake were their own survival, as well as the stability of urban life and the agrarian economy. To achieve this, they had to ensure dynastic continuity and structured growth of the bureaucracy. The officials and their affiliates, among them the Shi'i jurists and other urban notables, amounted to an influential group willing to avert another round of tribal resurgence.

REFLECTIONS ON A GLOOMY CENTURY

The eighteenth century, with the exception of the Zand interlude, ranked Iran quite poorly. Even compared to the Ottoman Empire, and its Tulip Era, the once-thriving Persian garden appeared dreary and dry. Yet eighteenth-century Iran was not devoid of cultural agility or intellectual inquiry. Liberated from the strictures of the late Safavid Shi'i dogma, one might argue, writers, poets, and artists benefited from the Safavids' cultural repository. Reflecting on the political climate of their own time, they expressed, predictably, a sense of gloom but not helplessness, even in exile or in captivity.

One early example was Shaykh Mohammad 'Ali Hazin (1691–1766), a representative of the Persian scholarly and literary elite of the period. A prodigy from Isfahan brought up in the universalistic tradition of Safavid education, he witnessed the agonies of the Afghan occupation and the rise of Nader before immigrating to Hindustan in 1734. In a "brain drain" that continued throughout the eighteenth century, thousands of scholars, artists, artisans, poets, writers, merchants, bureaucrats, and religious dissidents took refuge in India. Some escaped the Shi'i conservatism that had set in; others wanted to avoid the political insecurity that ensued after the Safavids' fall. The Mughal court and, later, the Muslim and Hindu successor princely states were generous patrons and promoters of Persian culture, whether statecraft, historiography, poetry, music, art, cuisine, or court culture. Despite French and English colonial inroads, there was still an appetite for culture and plenty of material wealth in local kingdoms, from Kashmir and Bengal to Golconda, Awadh, Deccan, and Mysore, just to name a few, all of which patronized Persian newcomers. Employed as secretaries (*munshis*), advisers, poets, and religious scholars, as well as architects, painters, and calligraphers, Persians (i.e., Iranians who represented the Persian culture, regardless of their ethnicity) were often treated as a sort of status symbol.

The poet Hazin, who had lost revenue from his estate in Lahijan in Gilan province, could no longer finance his expensive peripatetic habit except by seeking patronage abroad. In 1742, after many years of travel and eight years residing in India, mostly homesick, he penned the greater part of his autobiography in just two days. Interlaced with vivid accounts of the events of the period, his memoirs begin with his childhood and end with Nader's Indian campaign. Different from his nearly two hundred Arabic and Persian literary and scholarly writings, Hazin's memoirs are written in simple and direct style and in the first-person singular, allowing him to be unhindered in expressing emotions and impressions. The nostalgia for his homeland, which Hazin praises in his memoirs and his poetry, did not stop him from lamenting the destruction of cities, mass killings, famine, and cholera, and from criticizing Nader's regime for imposing ruinous taxes and extracting them by force, for his oppression and cruelty toward peasants and the urban populace alike, and above all for destroying the Safavid dynasty.

He is particularly reproachful of the declining quality of political leadership throughout the Muslim world, an insight that must have been sharpened after many interviews with the rulers of his time. "Of the requisites of heavens in this age," he writes,

> One is that there is no leader qualified for leadership. As I pondered the con-
> dition of each of the kings and leaders and commanders on the horizon, I
> found them more inferior and repulsive than most, if not all, their subjects,
> except some of the rulers of the countries of Europe [*Farang*] who are firm in
> enforcing laws [*qawanin*] and in [keeping] means of livelihood and in taking
> care of their own affairs. Yet because of complete incompatibility, they are not
> beneficial to the people of other lands and climates.[2]

Hazin's first acquaintance with the Europeans of Bandar Abbas and later with those in India was likely the source of this praise, even though he underscored incompatibility with Muslim ways. Attraction to *Farang* was not quite enough to persuade Hazin to take the advice of an English sea captain to immigrate to Europe rather than to India, a decision he later regretted.

Hazin nevertheless was open to new ideas and enthusiastic to learn about other cultures. While still in Isfahan, he had conversed with Christian missionaries and read the Gospels and other Christian theological works. He also discussed Judaism with Isfahan's rabbis and Zoroastrianism with Yazd priests (*mobads*), though neither impressed him, for what he suspected was their shortsightedness and bias. Hazin also spoke of his youthful love affair, without specifying the gender of his affections; his protracted illnesses, which repeatedly caused him to be bedridden; and his extensive travels, which included at least sixty-two cities from Baghdad to Banaras. Furthermore, he crafted a careful list of his teachers, colleagues, and friends, as well as men of learning among his contemporaries and his own extensive writings. He wrote not only on the conventional learning of his time, including Aristotelian and Neoplatonic philosophies, mysticism, and jurisprudence but also grappled with mathematics, physics, and astronomy. Though within the constellation of traditional Islamic learning, he demonstrates in his memoirs a rare sense of human agency, a voice of self-awareness and belief in historical causality.

In his poetry, too, Hazin (his pen name means "the sorrowful") demonstrated a sense of protonationalism, no doubt edified by living in the Indian diaspora. "The land of Iran is the sublime paradise," he exhorted in a nostalgic poem.

> May its domain be under the ring of Solomon-like kings.
> May the sublime paradise be homeland [*vatan*] of our souls
> May not that ring fall into the hand of the demon."

Aspiring for a Solomon-like king to rule over his homeland instead of the demons that had possessed the ring of power, he invokes powerful cultural memories.

These are complemented by other cultural references to Iran as the kingdom of Fereydun, the founder of the Kayanid legendary dynasty of the *Shahnameh*; the throne of Jamshid (*takhtgah-e Jam*), the Persian name for Persepolis; the remains of the arch of Kasra (Khosrow), the Sasanian palace in Ctesiphon (or Mada'in, north of Baghdad); and to Behistun, a double reference to the famous Achaemenid inscription near Kermanshah and to the nearby Sasanian site. "The Rum and the Rus were shivering, the day Kavus beat the drums of war"[3]—it is as though Hazin wishfully was calling for a warrior-king to end the Afghan occupation and repulse the Ottoman and Russian invasions. That may have already come through with the rise of Nader, whose "patriotic" yet destructive conduct resembled that of the *Shahnameh*'s Kay Kavus.

Through disaster and defeat, one can detect flickers of a new national awareness, one no longer tied to Safavid sovereignty but to the sorrowful memory of a glorious past, one that repeatedly would be invoked in the later Iranian experience. The same melancholic awareness of the self and of Iran, narrated through an autobiographical account, can also be detected a generation later in the remarkable memoirs of Mirza Mohammad Kalantar, the longtime mayor of Shiraz under the Zands. Heir to an old landowning family of Shiraz clergy and administrators, he was born during the last years of Safavid rule and lived long enough to write his memoirs around 1785 in the captivity of Aqa Mohammad Khan in Tehran. Between his birth and incarceration, he witnessed the coming of the Afghan invaders, the horrors of Nader's army, the ruination of Fars following a prolonged struggle among competing warlords, a fluctuating family fortune, and finally the wars of succession that, much to his displeasure, made the Qajars masters of his land. Only a decade or two of the tranquility of the Karim Khan era lightened his litany of misfortunes.

In his memoirs, Mirza Mohammad Kalantar is as relentless as he is acerbic, full of wry humor, as he frequently showers obscenities upon his power-hungry enemies, be they uncouth tribal chiefs or corrupt members of divan. Brimming with references embedded in Persian poetry and folk culture, he writes in direct, almost conversational, Persian, and with the frankness of an old political player at the end of his rope. In captivity in Tehran he was almost deaf, which he attributed to a venereal disease he contracted from a prostitute in Shiraz. He had lost most, if not all, of his substantial estate, and he was disillusioned about his own prospects as well as the future of his city and his country.

Nowhere better than in Kalantar's account do we see the complex maneuvering of the landowning notables to preserve their wealth and influence against tribal intruders from outside and popular insurgency from within. In tackling this complex task, Kalantar, like his protégé and successor in office, Haji Ibrahim Shirazi, and like other Iranian urban officials, relied on his administrative and accounting skills as well as on his connections with merchants and the ulama. He fostered rivalries between competing tribal leaders, raised his own private army from the peasants in his estate, and played the neighborhood brigands (*lutis*) against one another. Kalantar's acute sense of Shirazi citizenship, however, was not always altruistic or instructive. He had to face the revolt of the urban poor, represented often by the same *lutis*, and the insurgent peasantry in the vicinity of the city who viewed Kalantar, and urban officials in general, as self-serving allies of the strongest bidder for power.

The growth of the urban notables and their control of the cities, against all odds, is a remarkable feature of the eighteenth century in Iran as in the Ottoman world. Here we can detect the seeds of an indigenous communal awareness made sharper by the loss of influence and wealth in the south to a new dynastic power from the north. Contrary to Haji Ibrahim, who sided with the Qajars, Mirza Mohammad ended his days regretting his many political errors and reflecting on the causes of his country's misfortunes:

> May dust be on the grave of the people of Iran; may dust be on the grave of Iranians for this scarcity of capable men. I wish a woman had come to power that would have been competent, like the one in Russia [Catherine II]. Central Iran has been destroyed half by this bastard [Aqa Mohammad Khan] and half by that rascal [Jaʻfar Khan, the penultimate Zand ruler], two faithless, two tyrants, two damned souls.

Kalantar's complaint then takes the form of a desperate supplication:

> O God, the pure and the omnipotent! Have you created the people of Iran for these two unmanly [cowards]? You are not impotent; you are omnipotent. Now for the sake of your saints and in honor of your favored, send us a king who at least in appearance looks like a human being; what is wrong with Europeans, the Zoroastrians, and the infidels. . . . Now two demon-faced evildoers who are servants of their [evil] nature have come to dominate us. Do not allow it to happen and do not leave your country leaderless.

Hinting at an awareness of historical causality Kalantar then cites a verse by Rumi:

> The world is a mountain and our deeds voices,
> The voices have echoes, to us they will return.

He follows with the word of another great Persian poet, his own co-citizen, Hafez:

It is our frail and crooked body that we should blame,
Otherwise your robe of honor is not short on anyone's frame.[4]

On this sober note Kalantar concludes his memoirs, which he dedicated to his wife and cousin, to whom he also left his estate. He died in Isfahan the same year.

Hazin and Kalantar represented a broader spectrum of Iranian urbanites acutely conscious of their country as a troubled political entity rather than an empire. The failed project of reconstructing the Safavid Empire through military conquest, a common answer to the post-Safavid crisis of legitimacy, made such awareness more palpable. Not before the early nineteenth century did a lasting model of the Persian state reemerge. The sacred Safavid kingship and the presumed descent of its shahs from the House of the Prophet was a lineage that could not have been easily replaced. Nader's initiation of a new kingship and Karim Khan's *vakil* status both proved impermanent. The divan officials who were inherited by the Qajar state proved crucial for the stability of the new dynasty. The post-Safavid experience made this class of landowning notables more conscious of their urban identity and increasingly aware of Iran as a broader national entity.

Succumbing to the Qajars as a political necessity came with the realization that urban welfare, and the prosperity of the landowning classes, especially in the south, could not be maintained without a unifying power. The Qajars themselves structured their authority not only according to tribal loyalties but also on the basis of coopting the divan class of the Zand era and the emerging class of jurists, known as Usulis, who came back to Iran at the end of the eighteenth century from southern Iraq, where their ancestors had taken refuge after the fall of the Safavids. The Qajar rulers relied not only on the claim of legitimate heredity that went back to their membership in the Qezilbash of the Safavid era; they claimed for themselves the memory of the legendary kings and dynasties of the Persian past, kings who defended the land of Iran against its Rum and Turan neighbors, identified with the Ottomans and the Turkic nomads of the northeast in modern times. Likewise, the Qajar cultural and artistic expressions remained indebted to the southern spirit of leisure, music, and the good life, a continuity of the late Safavid and Zand eras. What remained largely unnoticed by Iranian observers at the dawn of the Qajar era was the consequential emergence of two European powers on Iran's horizons: the expansionist Russian Empire in the north and the colonial British Empire in the south.

Plate I.1. "Court of Solomon" is typical of Persian presentation
of the kingship's symmetrical structure. In Persian popular narratives Solomon often
was associated with Jamshid.
Attributed to Isma'il Naqqash-bashi, Isfahan, c. 1870s. Author's collection.

Plate 1.1. Shah Isma'il I, by an unknown Venetian artist.
Original rendering in Uffizi Gallery, Florence, Italy.

Plate 1.2. Battle of Chaldiran in 1514 as depicted by Moʻin Massaver in 1687 from Isfahan. Ismaʻil *(center)* and his Qezilbash forces are charging against the Ottoman artillery while Sultan Salim I *(top left)* views the battlefield from a distance. *History of Shah Ismaʻil.* © The David Collection, Copenhagen. Ms. 27/1986.

Plate 1.3. Completed in AH 946/1539–1540 CE, probably in Tabriz, the "Ardabil Carpet" was one of a pair dedicated by Tahmasp to the shrine of his ancestor Safi al-Din Ardabili. Below Hafez's famous verse, the master weaver Maqsud Kashani signed and dated the work. The design presumably echoes the plan of the prayer hall where Safavi Sufis performed ritual incantations.

No. 272-1893. Courtesy of Victoria and Albert Museum, London.

Plate 1.4. Mural in the Palace of Chehel-Sutun in Isfahan depicting Tahmasp's banquet in honor of Homayun Padshah, produced in the latter half of the seventeenth century. The artistic trope of the king and his guest flanked by the Qezilbash chiefs conveyed a message of Mughal-Safavid symbiosis in a festive environment that included female dancers and wine drinking.
Photograph by author, March 2002.

Plate 2.1. Naqsh-e Jahan Square showing in the foreground the diagonal layout of the 'Abbasi (Shah) Mosque. At right is the Lotfallah Mosque. Behind the Government House (Dowlat-khaneh or 'Āli Qapi) are the remnants of the Chahar-Bagh complex.
© Bruno Barbey photographer/Magnum Photos, 1976.

Plate 2.2. The commemorative panel of the portal of the 'Abbasi (Shah)
Mosque in Isfahan. The blue ceramic reads: "The father of victory, 'Abbas of the
Hosaini-Musawi descent of the House of Safavi."
Photograph by author, March 2002.

Plate 2.3. Main courtyard of the 'Abbasi (Shah) Mosque.
Architectural drawing by Pascal Coste, 1841. "Place Royale et mosquée Masjid-i-Shah, Vue de la
cour," *Monuments modernes de la Perse mesurés, dessinés et décrit* (Paris, 1867).

Plate 2.4. 'Abbas I and his page boy depicted in a tranquil pose.
The couplet reads: "May the world fulfill your wishes from three lips / Lips of the beloved,
lips of the stream and lips of the cup."
Musée du Louvre, MAO 494. © RMN-Grand Palais/Art Resource, NY.

Plate 2.5. Vank Cathedral, central panel of the nave, New Julfa, Isfahan.
© Antonella 865/Dreamstime.com.

Plate 2.6. Mughal emperor Jahangir (*left*) entertains Shah 'Abbas I. The imaginary scene presumably commemorated the embassy of Khan 'Alam (*standing to 'Abbas's left*) to the Safavid court. Verses underscore fraternal bonds; the panel above traces the Mughal lineage back to Timur. In his own hand Jahangir added, "Image of my brother Shah 'Abbas." By the Mughal painter Bishandas. © Freer Gallery of Art and Arthur M. Sackler Gallery, Smithsonian Institution, Washington, DC: Purchase-Charles Lang Freer Endowment, F1942.16a.

Plate 3.1. Chehel Sotun reception hall was an example of mid-seventeenth-century Safavid architecture. The frescoes of the interior, narrating scenes of the Safavid war and peace, highlighted a century and a half of dynastic continuity. P. Coste, "Jardin et pavillion Chehel Sotoun (1840)," *Monuments modernes de la Perse mesurés, dessinés et décrits* (Paris, 1867).

Plate 3.2. The interior doors from the Chehel-Sotun reception hall
are typical of decorative art of the late Safavid era.
Courtesy of the Yale University Art Gallery.

Plate 3.3. Nader Shah's coronation on the plain of Moghan in March 8, 1736.
Wearing his improvised Naderi cap, Nader is flanked by his three sons and
surrounded by chiefs of the army and representatives from his empire. Cannon in the
background announce the auspicious hour.
From a 1757 illustrated manuscript by Mohammad Mahdi Astarabadi,
Jahangushay-e Naderi (Tehran: Sorush/Negar, 1370/1991), illustration no. 8 by unknown artists.

Plate 3.4. Nader in an equestrian pose against the background of burning
Delhi while the Battle of Carnal is still raging.
Probably by the Indo-Persian artist Mohammad 'Ali Jobbahdar. © Francis Bartlett Donation of 1912 and
Picture Fund, Museum of Fine Arts, Boston, access no. 14.646.

Plate 3.5. Karim Khan Zand with the Ottoman envoy Vehbi Effendi, who visited
Shiraz in 1775 to apologize for the ill treatment of Iranian pilgrims by the Ottoman
governor of Iraq. He is suitably obsequious, having arrived at a time when the Zand
forces had captured Basra. Attributed to Abol-Hasan Mostowfi, the
patriarch of the celebrated Ghaffari family.
Courtesy of the David Collection, Copenhagen. Inv. no. 21/1999.

Plate 3.6. Aqa Mohammad Shah Qajar's massacre of people of Kerman in 1794. Most
adult males of the city were killed or blinded for their pro-Zand sympathies, and nearly
twenty thousand women and children were given as captives to the Qajar troops.
Illustrated copy of Fath 'Ali Khan Saba, *Shahanshah-nameh*. © The British Library Board.
IO, Islamic, 3442, f. 235r.

Plate 4.1. Gowhar-Taj Bani-'Abbasi dancing with a parrot on her hand. Her dazzling
appearance is typical of female entertainers of the period.
Unknown artist, oil on canvas, S'adabad Museum of Fine Arts (formerly Negarestan Museum), Tehran.
Published in *Qajar Paintings: A Catalogue of 18th and 19th Century Paintings* (Tehran, 1971), pl. 18.

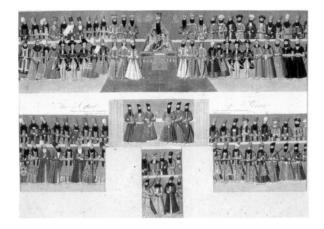

Plate 4.2. Court of Fath 'Ali Shah as depicted in wall panels from 1812 in the audience hall of Negarestan Palace in Tehran. The "King of Kings" on the Sun Throne is surrounded by senior prince-governors, chief statesmen, and military officers and flanked by court functionaries, Qajar khans, civilian dignitaries, and neighboring Afghan, Kurdish, Georgian, and Turkmen princes (who took refuge in the Persian court), Ottoman, English, and French envoys, and representatives of Tipu Sultan of Mysore, the Wahhabi Emirate of Central Arabia, and the princely state of Sind. The rival British and French missions conveyed a message of imperial counterbalance; the Qajars' Russian nemesis is absent.
Color engraving after 'Abdollah Khan Naqqash-bashi's 1815 murals by an unknown European artist, opaque watercolor, reproduced in *Royal Persian Paintings: The Qajar Epoch, 1785–1925*, ed. Layla Diba and Maryam Ekhtiar (London: I. B. Tauris, 1999).

Plate 4.3. Fath 'Ali Shah slaying a Russian commander during the first round of the Russo-Persian War (1805–1813).
Fath 'Ali Khan Saba, *Shahanshah-nameh*. © The British Library Board.
IO, Islamic, 3442, 1225/1810, f. 354r.

Plate 4.4. These scenes of Shi'i tragedies of Karbala in the *pardeh* style of the Qajar era are based on a late nineteenth-century mosaic fresco in the Moshir al-Molk *takkiyeh* in Shiraz. Presented in a wider context of the Last Judgment, such popular paintings served as visual aids to itinerant storytellers.
Painting by 'Abbas Bolukifar, 1975. Courtesy of Fereshteh Kowssar.

Plate 5.1. The Badgir (wind tower) pavilion in the Golestan complex of the Tehran citadel, reconstructed by Naser al-Din Shah, is an example of Qajar royal architecture.
By Mahmud Khan Kashani, oil on canvas, Golestan Palace Museum and Library, Tehran.

Plate 5.2. Shams al-'Emareh and its clock tower, seen from the
interior of the Golestan complex.
By Mahmud Khan Kashani, oil on canvas, dated 1285/1868.
Golestan Palace Museum and Library, Tehran.

Plate 5.3. The 'Abd al-Azim gateway to Tehran.
H. Brugsch, *Reise der K. Preussischen Gesandtschaft nach Persein, 1860 und 1861*, 2 vols.
(Leipzig, 1862–1863), vol. 2, frontispiece.

Plate 5.4. Bab-e Homayun Avenue, Tehran, in 1871. One of the
first thoroughfares in the European style, this avenue was adjacent to the royal citadel
and equipped with lampposts, sidewalks, and modern shops.
By Mahmud Khan Kashani, oil on canvas, dated 1288/1871. Golestan Palace Museum and Library,
Tehran.

Plate 5.5. Wedding of Nazhat al-Zaman from the *Thousand and One Nights*. The
Qajar setting depicts scenes of women dancers and a mixed musical group,
illuminated streets, and the newlywed couple's lovemaking.
Golestan Palace Museum and Library, Ms. 2240, vol. 1.

Plate 5.6. A brawl in Tabriz, where the saber-rattling Caucasians
terrified the chief of police and panicked the crowd.
Abol-Hasan Sani' al-Molk, watercolor, dated 1268/1852, by order of Naser al-Din Shah.
Golestan Palace Museum and Library, no. 2706.

Plate 5.7. A young Qajar prince and his retinue. The cartoonish characters are a
commentary on the complex master-servant power relationships among Qajar nobility.
Abol-Hasan Sani' al-Molk, watercolor, dated 1260/1844, by order of Naser al-Din Shah.
Golestan Palace Museum and Library, no. 8671.

Plate 5.8. The 1858 painting *Estensakh* (Copying) represents
Mahmud Khan Kashani's avant-garde experimentation with light and shadow and
with new subjects. The portrayal of an author and his scribe in a humble setting was
a refreshing departure from royal scenes.
Oil on canvas, Golestan Palace Museum and Library.

Plate 5.9. The royal ensemble of the Naseri era led by Sorur al-Molk playing the *santur*
(Persian dulcimer). It included celebrated musicians of the time, as well as vocalists and
dancers. Among them is the *tar* virtuoso Mirza 'Ali Akbar Farahani (*center*), whose
family's musical contribution was crucial to the classification of Persian traditional
music, and Musa Khan Kashani (*front row, second from left*), a master of *kamancheh*.
By Mohammad Ghaffari Kamal al-Molk, Golestan Palace Museum and Library.

Plate 6.1. Deputies of the first Majles in late 1906 (before the arrival of provincial deputies) with the premier and a few ranking officials in front of the Tehran military academy, which served as the Majles's venue before it moved to the Baharestan mansion. Contemporary postcard, Tehran, c. 1909. Author's collection.

Plate 6.2. A preliminary session of the first Majles as imagined in a French weekly. *La croix illustrée*, no. 315, January 6, 1907, p. 1.

La cour du château de l'assemblée nationale à Téhéran, lorsqu'un orateur (Baha-al-vaezine) parle pour les assistants.

عکس مجلس مقدس شورای ملی ایران

Plate 6.3. Supporters of the Constitution outside the Majles listening to Baha' al-Wa'ezin, one of several preachers who echoed views of the *anjomans*.
Contemporary postcard, Tehran, c. 1909. Author's collection.

ATTENTAT CONTRE LE SHAH DE PERSE

Plate 6.4. Assassination attempt against Mohammad 'Ali Shah as portrayed in a French weekly.
Le Petit Journal, Supplément Littéraire Illustré, no. 997, March 15, 1908, p. 88.

Les soldats nationaux de Téhéran.

Plate 6.5. Nationalist fighters from Tabriz (*right*), Bakhtiyari (*center*),
and Rasht (*left*). The slogan reads, "Long last the National Consultative Assembly;
long live national soldiers."
Contemporary postcard, Tehran, 1909. Author's collection.

Plate 7.1. With the rise of Pahlavi nationalism, images of Nader Shah—the savior of Iran and the presumed forerunner of Reza Khan—replaced the familiar portrayals of Qajar rulers. Responding to market demand, the designer (or weaver) of this pictorial rug replaced Fath 'Ali Shah's head with that of Nader Shah, leaving the king's torso and surroundings untouched. The omnipresent chief minister nevertheless appears in his customary pose. Although Nader brought the legendary Peacock Throne of the Mughal Empire back from his 1739 Indian campaign, the throne he occupies in this scene was commissioned by Fath 'Ali Shah a good half century after the original was destroyed after Nader's assassination.

Pictorial rug, Ravar (Kerman), c. 1928. Author's collection.

Plate 8.1. Galubandak intersection near the Tehran bazaar in 1938, reflecting changes in the capital as shown in the style of architecture and means of communication. To the right is the newly constructed Buzarjomehri Avenue. By Isma'il Ashtiyani, 1317/1938, *Iran dar Negare-ha: Tehran* (Tehran: Negar Books, 1989), n.p.

Plate 9.1. Commemorative stamp series issued in 1949 in recognition of Iran's efforts during the war. The stamps show the Persian corridor (*top right* and *bottom middle*), the port of Khorramshahr (*bottom right*), and the Veresk railroad bridge (*bottom left*). Author's collection.

Plate 9.2. Based on a well-known legend of the *Shahnameh*, here in these Allied propaganda leaflets, produced in the style of the Persian miniature paintings, Hitler is portrayed as the tyrant Zahhak (*left*) with serpents on his shoulders representing Mussolini and Tojo, the Japanese premier. Goebbels is his satanic cook with a blood-dripping saber. Kaveh, the blacksmith, came to Zahhak's court demanding the return of his sons, who were captured to provide food for the serpents. The caption above the picture reads: "He cried out and protested of the shah's conduct: 'Ye the shah! I am the justice-seeking Kaveh. Oppression may be moderate or may be extreme, but your oppression is a pretext [to destroy].'" The Allied leaders (*right*)— Roosevelt, Stalin, and Churchill—are represented as "three warriors from the palace of the King of Kings," who came to the aid of Kaveh, who became the leader of the anti-tyranny revolution. He carries the Kaviyani standard, the symbol of Iranian independence, which is his blacksmith leader apron. These leaflets served as visual aids to the coffeehouse storytellers (*naqqals*) to convey an anti-Nazi message.

آرایش داد و زینت کرد ز ا   ملت که چهل سال به پروردنرا   ...م﮲ﺸﺮ و طه غان﮲م ...
آخر به چه صورتی در آورد نرا   سرپنجه سلمانی خواب آ لوده

Plate 9.3. The constitution, here portrayed as Ms. Mashruteh (Constitution), is disfigured by the government of Premier Mohammad Sa'ed (1881–1973) during the fifteenth Majles (1947–1949). After the assassination attempt against the shah, the Majles passed emergency legislation granting the government powers to declare martial law, censor the press, and arrest political dissidents. The 1949 Constituent Assembly also gave the sovereign new prerogatives. The cartoon in the satirical *Towfiq* branded Sa'ed, the hairdresser in the Baharstan salon, as a British creature and held him responsible for turning civil liberties into repression, allowing poverty and starvation, and promoting "imperialism." On the wall are portraits of celebrated constitutionalists Jahangir Sur Esrafil and Malek al-Motekallemin. The flame on the barber's bench is labeled "BP" (British Petroleum), alluding to the AIOC's part in disfiguring Ms. Constitution, who finally has been cast onto the floor of the salon.
By Hasan Towfiq, *Towfiq*, no. 1, 20 Mordad 1328/August 12, 1949.
Courtesy of Mohamad Tavakoli-Targhi.

Plate 9.4. "In the nocturnal revelry of the world-devouring Sultan Naft-'Ali Shah." With an eye on Mosaddeq's Qajar ancestry and his negotiation for an American loan, the scandalous cartoon in the pro-Tudeh *Chalangar* draws on Fath 'Ali Shah's hedonistic court to accuse Mosaddeq of dancing for the pleasure of the United States and Britain. Members of the National Front are depicted as entertainers and courtesans.
Chalangar, no. 1, 17 Esfand 1329/March 8, 1951. Courtesy of Mohamad Tavakoli-Targhi.

Plate 10.1. The shah meeting with President Kennedy and Secretary of Defense Robert McNamara in the White House, April 1962. The Cold War considerations persuaded Kennedy, despite his qualms, to accept the shah as the sole master of the country, in charge of land reform and other modernizing initiatives.
JFKWHP-1962-04-13-A. Courtesy of the John F. Kennedy Presidential Library and Museum, Boston, MA.

Plate 10.2. Literacy Corps' open-air schools represented the state's resolve
to rapidly transform the rural and tribal countryside.
The Land of Kings, ed. R. Tarverdi (Tehran, 1971), 129.

Plate 10.3. The annual celebration of the White Revolution in front of the
Iranian Senate was a staged exercise of loyalty to the Pahlavi project. By 1968 there were
2,800 women volunteers recruited into the Literacy Corps. Placards announce
slogans of the White Revolution.
The Land of Kings, ed. R. Tarverdi (Tehran, 1971), 172.

Plate 12.1. Replica of the Achaemenid siege tower, Persepolis parade, 2,500-year
celebration of the Persian Empire, October 1971.
Spiro T. Agnew Papers, box 48. Courtesy of Special Collections, University of Maryland Libraries.

Plate 12.2. A poster for the 1970 Shiraz Arts Festival, inspired by reliefs of Persepolis.
Designed by Qobad Shiva. Courtesy of Vali Mahlouji.

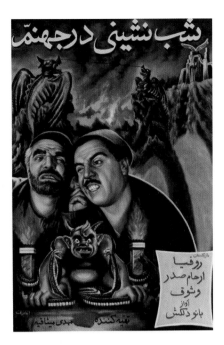

Plate 12.3. Poster for the popular 1957 movie *Shabneshini dar Jahanam* (Banquet in hell), a Persianized take on Dickens's *A Christmas Carol*.
M. Mehrabi, *Sadd va Panj Sal E'lan va Pster-e Film dar Iran* (Tehran: Nazar Publishers, 1393/2014), 68.

Plate 13.1. At Neauphle-le-Château near Paris in October 1979, Khomeini is surrounded by eager listeners.
Tasvir-e Aftab (Tehran: Sorush Publishers, 1989).

Plate 13.2 and Plate 13.3. Popular posters offered a triumphant narrative of the revolution. Depicting Khomeini as an Abraham-like prophet and the martyrs of the revolution as the faceless "heart of history," they vilified the shah and the Pahlavi elite as traitors. While revolution is in progress (*left*) and the shah is fleeing with $165 trillion in his bags, his ministers, labeled "corruptors of the earth," face the firing squad. Persepolis serves as the backdrop to a ruined monarchy, clad in Anglo-American flags (*right*), and the severed heads of the Pahlavi statesmen, which are about to be devoured by the dragon of the inferno.

(*Left*) By Hasan Isma'ilzadeh c. 1979. Middle Eastern Posters. Collection, Box 1, Poster no. 11, Special Collections Research Center, University of Chicago Library. (*Right*) *Honar-e Enqlab, 57 Poster az Enqelab-e 57*, ed. Rasul Ja'farian (Tehran: Kitabkhaneh, Muzeh va Markaz-e Asnad-e Majles-i Shura-ye Islami, 1390/2011).

Plate 14.1. Fayziyeh madrasa, rebuilt in the Qajar era, is in front of the shrine of Ma'sumeh (*background*) and the Grand Mosque (*right*), completed in 1958.
Mehr News, Tehran, Iran. http://www.mehrnews.com/news/3578630.

Plate 15.1. "To salvage the ship of the revolution, throw off all heavy stuff that you can reach." As early as July 1979 the left-leaning *Ahangar* mocked the Islamist monopoly on power. Freedom of the press, workers, Kurds, Arabs, and air force cadets are victims.
Year 1, no. 13, 26 Tir 1358/18 July 1979. Courtesy of Siavush Ranjbar-Daemi.

Plate 16.1. Mourners see off a martyr headed for the heavens on angelic wings.
Middle Eastern Posters. Collection, Box 3, Poster no. 107, Special Collections Research Center, University of Chicago Library.

Plate 16.2. A propaganda poster renders the familiar portrayal of the war as a reenactment of the Battle of Karbala on 'Ashura with Imam Hosain as the patron saint of the martyrs.
Middle Eastern Posters. Collection, Box 3, Poster no. 96, Special Collections Research Center, University of Chicago Library.

Plate 16.3. Imam Hosain and the headless martyrs of Karbala witness a blindfolded
Revolutionary Guard being shot by an Iraqi firing squad.
Middle Eastern Posters. Collection, Box 4, Poster no. 197, Special Collections Research Center,
University of Chicago Library.

Plate 17.1. "Musighi dar Khafa" (Clandestine music), a painting by Iman Maleki
depicting Mohammad Reza Lotfi and Mohammad Reza Shajarian (*in the back,
second and third from right*) and their group rehearsing revolutionary songs in the fall
of 1978 in the basement of Lotfi's house in Tehran.
Courtesy of Iman Maleki.

Plate 17.2. The fraudulent presidential election brought hundreds of thousands of protesters to a mass rally in Tehran's Azadi Square on June 15, 2009.
© Ben Curtis, Associated Press.

Part Two

RESHAPING OF THE GUARDED DOMAINS

Consolidation of the Qajar dynasty set the stage for Iran's gradual transformation through the long nineteenth century. New strategic and economic realities, particularly the rise of two European empires on the northern and southern frontiers, turned Iran into a buffer state, a mixed blessing with important consequences. Despite the loss of territory and depleted economic resources, Qajar Iran preserved its political sovereignty and reinvented the Persian institution of kingship. Stronger bonds with the urban elite included the revived clerical establishment, sustained the state's otherwise fragile sway over the tribal periphery, and brought about a period of recovery.

The growing volume of foreign imports from industrialized Europe and the export of cash crops, such as tobacco and opium, tilted the economic balance in favor of big merchants, large landowners, and European firms. Less privileged sectors of society, such as guilds, retailers, and peasants, bore the brunt of the changing economy. Chronic visitations of famine and pandemics worsened their lot. Popular grievances against the Qajar state and the Shi'i clerical establishment in the middle decade of the century triggered the millennial Babi movement. A pivotal event in the anti-shari'a trends in the Iranian milieu, the movement, charged with Shi'i messianic aspirations, gave voice to anticlerical and socioeconomic grievances. Despite its military defeat, the clandestine Babi loyalties remained the vehicle of popular dissent throughout the Qajar period. By contrast, the discourse of reform that was articulated by modernist intellectuals enjoyed a far smaller audience.

In the second half of the nineteenth century, selective projects of modernization, particularly the creation of a telegraphic network and the introduction of modern banking, anticipated the rise of a national market. Though primarily beneficial to foreign interests, these networks allowed the Qajar state to further centralize and more effectively govern the provinces. By the close of the nine-teenth century, modern communications also allowed for voices of protest to be widely heard during the Tobacco Protest. By the turn of the twentieth cen-tury, mass protests that came to shape the Constitutional Revolution fused older demands for social justice and national salvation with modern notions of the constitution, rule of law, popular representation, material development, and awareness of modern nationalism. The revolution brought together for the first time dissident intellectual, merchants, members of the high-ranking clergy, and reformist elements within the nobility. Against many domestic and for-eign odds, the Constitutional Revolution proved a transformative experience with multiple facets. Beyond its sociopolitical discourse, the revolution piqued a period of rich cultural and artistic fluorescence, and the Qajar period found its distinct voice in poetry, painting, calligraphy, book production, architecture, music, photography, journalism, and performing arts. In what might be called a process of Persianization, aspects of Western art and literature were incorpo-rated with an air of cultural confidence.

4

THE MAKING OF THE QAJAR ERA (1797–1852)

During the first half of the nineteenth century, Qajar Iran partially recovered from the material losses of the previous decades. The slowing of nomadic incursions from the periphery allowed a degree of stability, and the Persian model of government they had adopted brought a semblance of control over most of Iran proper. Agriculture recuperated and regional and international trade revitalized. Urban populations began to grow and the hinterlands were recouped. Yet by the end of Fath ʿAli Shah's reign (1798–1834), Iran's population still barely exceeded four million.

Facing European powers on its borders, both Russia and Britain, Qajar Iran appeared unprepared. It began to sense the magnitude of challenges to its empire in war and diplomacy while still recovering from ravages of the past. European powers defeated Iran in war, seized portions of its prized territory, put pressure on the state through diplomacy and trade, and at times even threatened its very sovereignty. At the outset of the nineteenth century, the east-west two-frontier Iran of the Safavid and post-Safavid eras was substantially changed to a new north-south two-frontier reality. Qajar Iran's self-image as an empire at the center of its own universe also changed into one of a vulnerable nation in the throes of Christian powers. Yet despite its inherent disadvantages, Qajar Iran escaped domination by colonial powers in part because of the dictates of its geography but also because of a degree of resistance displayed by the Qajar state and its subjects. Iran endured within its shrunken borders while many countries in the non-Western world gradually succumbed to colonial rule. The Iranian state and society also began to adopt, in their own terms, selective aspects of Europe's material and intellectual cultures. The mixed experience of contention and adoption helped shape Iran's perceptions of modernity throughout the Qajar period.

The early Qajar period also witnessed the emergence of a potent Shi'i clerical establishment. It was conservative in outlook and at times defiant toward
the state, suspicious of its modernizing measures. To maintain its network of
privileges and social influence, the jurist establishment of the Usuli school articulated a legal theory that promoted believers' close following (*taqlid*) of the
mojtaheds in all intricate matters of religious life. Grounded in Safavid learning, the Usuli school regulated not only the believers' behavior but also society's moral and legal conduct through an elaborate set of rules and rituals. The
Qajar state's desire to preserve the status quo helped sustain the Shi'i jurists as
a formidable force. Yet the symbiosis of the state and the ulama establishment
acted as a barrier against innovative thinking and wider cultural adaptation.

These themes have provoked contesting viewpoints about the Qajar period.
Much historiography of the twentieth century, influenced by condescending
European attitude, viewed the Qajar period as an age of defeat and decadence.
Such an outlook belittles, if not discredits, the important achievements of the
Qajar period, not only its survival as a sovereign state but also its cultural agility.
The early nineteenth century witnessed a literary and artistic revival of lasting
influence. Shi'i legal scholarship scored great gains. Despite their scholastic
rigidity, Shi'i jurists of the period articulated a complex discourse of methodology of law, better known as the "Principles of Jurisprudence" (*usul al-fiqh*), after
which the Usuli school is named.

The revival of the Aristotelian philosophy of the School of Isfahan also encouraged new approaches and produced new commentaries. The revival of
the Shi'i Sufi orders, a legacy of the Zand period, counterbalanced the ulama
in the cities at all levels and generated new theosophical and mystical works.
The Qajar era also witnessed the rise of new socioreligious movements that
espoused indigenous reforms embedded in Perso-Shi'i environment rather than
being wholesale imports from the outside. The Babi movement was the culmination of a process of dissent within Shi'ism with a message of religious and
social renewal rooted in Iran's messianic experiences of the past. Later in the
century reformists of all shades—freethinkers, revolutionaries, state officials,
and dissidents—addressed moral and material decline, critiqued the social and
cultural norms of their time, and offered either indigenous or Western-inspired
syntheses.

Qajar Iran displayed remarkable artistic and literary vitality in painting, calligraphy, bookmaking, music, and architecture, as well as in poetry and prose.
Traditional industries and crafts, especially textiles, reached a new level of refinement, and Western techniques and technologies including the telegraph,
photography, and book printing gained popularity. These landmarks stand in

contrast to the backdrop of depravity and misfortune with which the Qajar era has often been associated.

RECLAIMING IMPERIAL AUTHORITY

Even before encountering the European powers on his doorsteps, Fath 'Ali Shah had to quell half a dozen rebellions throughout Iran, first in Azarbaijan and Isfahan, where he faced a pro-Zand resurgence, and later in Luristan, Khorasan, Yazd, and the Caucasus, where a variety of tribal chiefs shunned the notion of loyalty to the Qajars (map 4.1). Even though Aqa Mohammad Khan believed that he had "raised a royal palace and cemented it with blood"—the blood of actual and potential contenders to the Qajar throne—there were still claims to the Qajar crown, and not just allegorical ones. Sadeq Khan Shaqaqi, the ambitious Kurdish chief in Aqa Mohammad Khan's army and possibly the brains behind his assassination, had snatched away the newly constructed Kayanid crown and the royal jewels and marched back to his tribal estate in northern Azarbaijan. In 1798 Fath 'Ali Shah had to wage a war to recover Azarbaijan and regain his symbols of royal power, which he could do only piecemeal. The rebellion of the Shaqaqi chief more importantly demonstrated a palpable desire by the Kurdish tribes to rule over a region stretching from Sulaymaniyah (in today's Iraqi Kurdistan) to the southern Caspian coasts and on to northern Khorasan. Sadeq's defeat and destruction—by the shah's order his prison cell was bricked up and he was left to die—put an end to the Kurdish defiance. By 1800 the Qajars took the last stronghold of the Afsharids in Khorasan after several expensive campaigns.

The Qajar shah, nevertheless, was mindful of his Qajar chiefs and their whimsical loyalty. Some of them covertly backed the shah's younger brother in his bid for the Qajar throne. With great difficulty Fath 'Ali Shah eventually succeeded in removing his adventurous brother but not before destroying his influential grand vizier, Haji Ibrahim Kalantar, who was accused of treason, presumably for colluding with the shah's rebellious brother. The chief minister was put to death along with most members of his extended family. His execution was the first of a number of executions of viziers in the Qajar era, as a sign of the monarch's consolidation of personal power. The practice once more displayed the fundamental vulnerability of the divan with respect to the shah's authoritarian rule. The struggle between the minister and the monarch for control of the government hindered the divan's autonomy and its greater institutionalization. Haji Ibrahim has often been harshly judged by posterity, seldom credited for his motivations to cure Iran of tribalism and civil war. The British

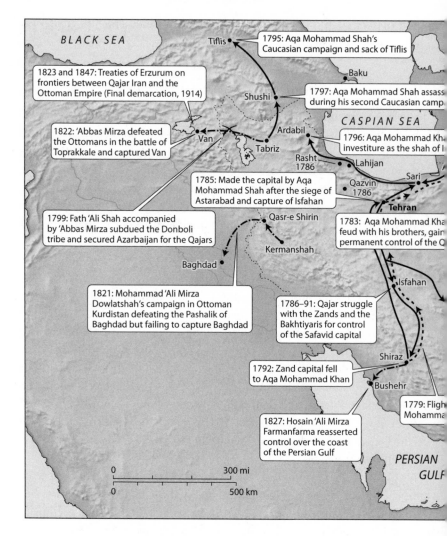

BLACK SEA

Tiflis — 1795: Aqa Mohammad Shah's Caucasian campaign and sack of Tiflis

1823 and 1847: Treaties of Erzurum on frontiers between Qajar Iran and the Ottoman Empire (Final demarcation, 1914)

Baku

Shushi — 1797: Aqa Mohammad Shah assass during his second Caucasian camp

CASPIAN SEA

1822: 'Abbas Mirza defeated the Ottomans in the battle of Toprakkale and captured Van

Van

Ardabil

1796: Aqa Mohammad Kha investiture as the shah of I

Tabriz

Rasht 1786

Lahijan

Sari

1785: Made the capital by Aqa Mohammad Shah after the siege of Astarabad and capture of Isfahan

Qazvin 1786

Tehran

1799: Fath 'Ali Shah accompanied by 'Abbas Mirza subdued the Donboli tribe and secured Azarbaijan for the Qajars

Qasr-e Shirin

Kermanshah

1783: Aqa Mohammad Kha feud with his brothers, gain permanent control of the Q

Baghdad

Isfahan

1821: Mohammad 'Ali Mirza Dowlatshah's campaign in Ottoman Kurdistan defeating the Pashalik of Baghdad but failing to capture Baghdad

1786–91: Qajar struggle with the Zands and the Bakhtiyaris for control of the Safavid capital

Shiraz

1792: Zand capital fell to Aqa Mohammad Khan

Bushehr

1779: Fligh Mohamma

1827: Hosain 'Ali Mirza Farmanfarma reasserted control over the coast of the Persian Gulf

PERSIAN GULF

0 ——— 300 mi

0 ——— 500 km

Map 4.1. The rise of Aqa Mohammad Shah Qajar
and early Qajar consolidation, 1779–1835

representative of the East India Company, Capitan John Malcolm, who met Haji Ibrahim shortly before the grand vizier's downfall, advised him to respond with a better temper to the shah's "occasional fit of ill-humor and violence." In response, the vizier restated his yearning for a united country under a strong government. "I could easily save myself but Persia again be plunged in warfare. My objective has been to give my country one king; I cared not whether he was

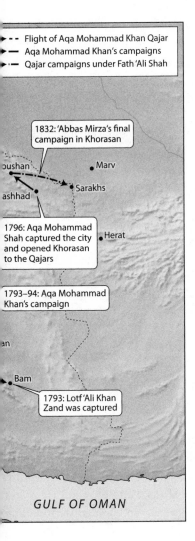

- - - Flight of Aqa Mohammad Khan Qajar
►— Aqa Mohammad Khan's campaigns
►·— Qajar campaigns under Fath 'Ali Shah

1832: 'Abbas Mirza's final campaign in Khorasan

oushan • Marv

• Sarakhs

ashhad

1796: Aqa Mohammad Shah captured the city and opened Khorasan to the Qajars

• Herat

1793–94: Aqa Mohammad Khan's campaign

an

• Bam

1793: Lotf 'Ali Khan Zand was captured

GULF OF OMAN

a Zand or a Kajir (Qajar), so that there was an end of internal destruction. I have seen enough of these scenes of blood; I will be concerned in no more of them."[1]

After Haji Ibrahim, some members of the Fars bureaucratic faction who were suspected of collaborating with the fallen minister returned to royal favor and gained high office within the divan's multiregional structure. They were the counterforce to the northern party, the officials who were from Mazandaran, especially the Nur region, who early under Aqa Mohammad Khan came to the service of the Qajar. The influence of both factions was curtailed by a third party from the central provinces, mostly from Farahan and its vicinity, a region of high literacy with a culture of statecraft. Even more than the southern and the northern parties, the Farahan faction secured its own continuity in the state administration. Having earlier served under the late Safavids and the Zands, Farahan produced capable statesmen, including the Qa'em-Maqam family and their client Mirza Taqi Khan Amir Kabir. The Qajar rulers played off the competing factions and manipulated rivalries to their own advantage.

Subduing provincial revolts, the Qajar khans and divan went hand in hand with a new spirit of grandiosity in Fath 'Ali Shah's court. Elaborate protocol, ceremony-laden public and private audiences (*salam*), an ostentatious show of wealth, and large numbers of court attendants, page boys, servants, guards, musicians, and dancers, as well as ornate dresses, sumptuous dishes, a lavish lifestyle, numerous royal palaces, gardens, hunting grounds and royal cavalcades—all became symbols of Qajar power. A large number of life-size portrayals of female musicians, singers, and dancers, no doubt many of whom were employed in the sprawling courts of Fath 'Ali Shah and his sons, exhibited an epicurean culture of leisure and revelry (pl. 4.1).

Fath 'Ali Shah was as much the center of this glittering universe as his uncle Aqa Mohammad Khan had been the master of the military camp, of long horse rides, incessant campaigning, and military discipline. Even Fath 'Ali Shah's personal appearance epitomized this stark contrast. Unlike Aqa Mohammad Khan's slight physique and wrinkled, beardless face, Fath 'Ali's long, black, bushy beard and his attractive, though rather effeminate, countenance was meant to announce to all his majestic dignity and sexual potency. In contrast to the rough and ready tent-dwelling warrior khans, Fath 'Ali was a calm and colorful king of kings, well established in the secure and opulent surrounding of the royal palaces (pl. 4.2; fig. 4.1).

This surely was the image the court painters of the period were commissioned to present in their numerous life-size portrayals of the shah. He often was shown sitting on his new Sun Throne (*Takht-e Khorshid*, later known as the Peacock Throne, or *Takht-e Tavus*) wearing his reconstructed Kayanid crown, which was distinct from Aqa Mohammad Khan's. The shah dressed in the most exquisite silk robes, wore the legendary armlets with the Darya-e Nur and Taj-i Mah encrusted on two armlets, and was surrounded by the implements of his sovereignty: sword, shield, mace, and royal scepter. All these were meant to convey symbolically a sense of continuity and control, particularly to the neighboring European empires. The new Kayanid crown, which replaced the

Figure 4.1. The open veranda of Golestan Palace in the Tehran citadel functioned as the public facade of the Qajar court, where public levies (*salam*) were held. The supporting columns were removed from a Zand palace in Shiraz and reinstalled here by order of Aqa Mohammad Shah. The Marble Throne, a creation of the early Fath 'Ali Shah era, recalled the magical thrones of Persian legend. E. Flandin and P. Coste, *Voyage en Perse*, vol. 8, *Perse moderne* (Paris, 1851–1854).

turbanlike cap of the Zand period, advertised the recapture of the royal jewels, spectacular trophies bundled together in a cylindrical structure symbolic of the political power gathered in the office of the King of Kings.

The Qajar kingship drew attention to the memory of the ancient Iranian past, as narrated in the *Shahnameh* and visible in the rock reliefs and ancient ruins of the Achaemenid and Sasanian periods. Fath 'Ali Shah, who was brought up in the Zand court and served as governor of Fars under his uncle, assimilated these imperial symbols to underscore centralization of his rule and to forge an alternative source of legitimacy. These perceptions of Iranian kingship were revived and maintained alongside Timurid ties to a tribal past, which the Qajars had a difficult time abandoning entirely. These perceived sources of authority, of course, went hand in hand with a Qajar claim to temporal leadership of the Shi'i community and defense of Shi'i Islam, a Safavid legacy. It can be argued that the Qajars' multiple layers of political authority tied the image of the King of Kings more closely to Iran.

The royal image that was put on display—through the media of stone sculptures in rock reliefs, large-scale paintings, epic poetry, and dynastic histories—was meant to be seen by both the elite and the general public, and by the Europeans. As early as the 1810s the Qajar rock reliefs and other pictorial presentations were being carved in the Achaemenid and Sasanian styles, some adjacent to ancient sites. Even acts of archeological vandalism, such as the rock relief commissioned by one of the shah's sons, Mohammad 'Ali Mirza Dowlatshah, carved over a corner of the famous seventh-century Sasanian relief in Taq-e Bostan in Kermanshah province, were meant to remind viewers of the return of ancient royal splendor. Another rock relief that depicted a courtly scene, near the ancient ruins of Ray, south of Tehran, was a clear breach of the general Islamic ban on depicting the human image (fig. 4.2).

Efforts to demonstrate historical continuity are also evident in the literature of the period, notably in the revival of the classical Khorasan school of epic poetry. A clear break from Safavid metaphorical formalism, such a conscious return to the style of the classical masters of the tenth and eleventh centuries is well evident in the *Shahanshah-nameh* (book of the King of Kings) by the poet Fath 'Ali Khan Saba. Like many figures in the literary "royal society" (*anjoman-e khaqan*) patronized by the shah, Saba came from the Zand cultural milieu. Modeled on Ferdowsi's *Shahnameh*, Saba's long poem recounted Fath 'Ali

Figure 4.2. Fath 'Ali Shah hunting a lion. The rock reliefs of Cheshmeh 'Ali, near the ruins of the ancient city of Ray (Rhages), south of Tehran, conveyed the revival of Persian royal tradition. Hunting lions, which are still extant in Fars province, was a symbol of regal valor.
E. Flandin and P. Coste, *Voyage en Perse*, vol. 8, *Perse moderne* (Paris, 1851–1854).

Shah's epic deeds (pl. 4.3). With generous poetic license, it imagined the exploits of the Qajar ruler in battle and on the hunting grounds. The triumphant spirit in the poem nevertheless militated against the reality of heavy setbacks in the war with Russia.

ROYAL PROGENY AND THE DILEMMA OF SUCCESSION

To further strengthen royal authority, Fath 'Ali Shah also embarked on a long-term policy of ridding the throne of the troublesome Qajar chiefs, largely by installing in their place members of his own immediate family, especially a new generation of royal princes who soon were to come of age (chart 2). In an incredible feat of reproduction, more than one hundred sons and daughters were born to the shah in less than fifty years, the outcome of maintaining a large harem with hundreds of wives and concubines. Fath 'Ali's conscious effort to compensate for the childlessness of his castrated uncle has been the subject of much criticism and ridicule by later observers. Though certainly he was not free from sensual indulgence and narcissistic extravagance, as evident from the reports of the period, having a large harem and many children was not without a political rationale.

The senior princes of the royal family liberated the shah from the yoke of the rancorous Qajar khans and provided him with more reliable tools of governance. Political marriages, whether his own or those of his sons and daughters, fostered family ties with khans of Qajar and other tribes, military officers, and urban dignitaries. Multitudes of royal offspring, moreover, were progeny of captive Zand, Afshar, Kurd, and Lur wives. Others were born to Georgian and Armenian women captured during earlier campaigns in the Caucasus, or to Jewish young women taken by consent or by force from communities throughout Iran. The shah's sons also created their own large households, in the image of their father. By the 1860s, some three decades after Fath 'Ali's death, the highly procreative Qajar princely class numbered about ten thousand.

In reclaiming imperial authority, Fath 'Ali Shah introduced a semi-autonomous system of princely governments under the umbrella of the central state. A legacy of the Safavid era, and before that the Saljuq period, this feature gave new meaning to the official title of the country as the Guarded Domain of Iran. Senior princes mostly served as provincial governors in Tabriz, Shiraz, Kermanshah, Isfahan, and Mashhad or as high officials in the expanding Qajar court and military. Younger princes were sent to smaller governments. Creating regional governments was a realistic solution to the center-periphery tension embedded in the geopolitical setup of Qajar Iran. There was a limited degree

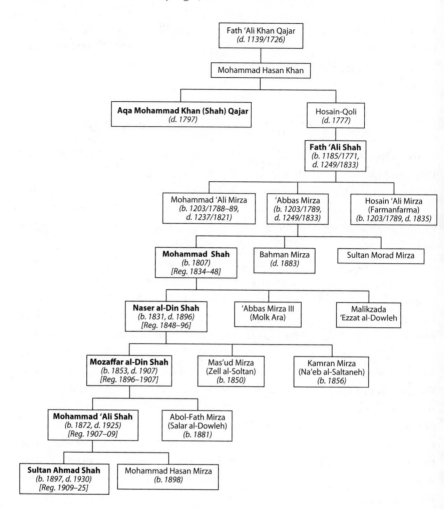

Chart 2. Genealogical chart of the Qajar dynasty

of interference from the capital, but the prince-governors often acquiesced to the shah's oversight. They were accompanied by their tutors, often high-ranking members of the Qajar nobility, and by senior bureaucrats who served as acting governors. Both officers reported directly to Tehran.

'Abbas Mirza (1789–1833), the crown prince and most celebrated of the shah's sons, was sent off to Tabriz in 1799 with the title of viceroy (*na'eb al-saltaneh*), the highest of the princely ranks. His minister Mirza 'Isa (Mirza Bozurg) Qa'em-Maqam was a former Zand official of the Farahani faction and one of the most capable statesmen of the early Qajar period. 'Abbas Mirza came to Tabriz at a time when the city was recovering its position as a gateway to the Caucasus and beyond. It also became the center for a flourishing trade with Europe, through the Ottoman Black Sea port of Trabzon, and it maintained its overall prominence for the rest of the century as the most prosperous and most populated city in the realm. It was through Tabriz in the first quarter of the century that the earliest manifestations of modern European military arrived: regimentation, new weaponry, drill officers, uniforms, and military education. Also through Azarbaijan came European and American missionaries, the press and publications, the earliest foreign newspapers, luxury goods, machine-manufactured fabrics, gadgets of all sorts, and the much-admired Sheffield penknives.

The Tabriz administration was given significant latitude by the central government to conduct diplomacy and trade, and if necessary, war, in the northwest. 'Abbas Mirza's diplomatic engagements with both Russia and Britain gave Qajar Iran its first taste of European empires. During the two rounds of war with Russia, Tabriz served as the hub of diplomacy and the headquarters for conducting military operations. As the "abode of sovereignty" (Dar al-Saltaneh), the official title of the city, Tabriz held control over its own army, finances, and regional affairs. 'Abbas Mirza himself not only held the title of viceroy but also was frequently addressed by the title of *shah*, in contrast to Fath 'Ali Shah's title, *shahanshah*. Only toward the end of his father's reign was 'Abbas Mirza officially recognized as crown prince (*wali-'ahd*; lit. "the guardian of the [royal] covenant"). Tehran's official name, Dar al-Khilafa (the abode of the caliphate)—an odd title for a Shi'i capital, which possibly claimed in competition with Istanbul as the capital of the Ottoman caliphate—pointed to the multipolar nature of Qajar sovereignty. The eastern Safavid capital, Herat, which also was referred to as Dar al-Saltaneh, never acquired by the Qajars, despite several attempts.

Azarbaijan's regional autonomy was offset by at least three other powerful princely seats in the south, the west, and the east, and by several less prominent seats in Kerman, Isfahan, and Kurdistan. After ousting his rebellious brother, Fath 'Ali Shah assigned Fars and the Persian Gulf provinces to another of his senior sons, Hosain-'Ali Mirza. The same age as 'Abbas Mirza, but of a non-Qajar mother—his official title being *farmanfarma* (lit. "enforcer of royal decrees")—Hosain-'Ali Mirza maintained regional autonomy in the south. And as did 'Abbas Mirza, he survived in his post for more than three decades. Similarly, a vast domain in western Iran was assigned to the shah's oldest son, Mohammad 'Ali Mirza, a bold and ambitious prince born to a Georgian mother whose title, *dowlatshah* (lit. "the shah's political fortune") implied that he, too, was shah of his own domain. He remained in office until his death in 1821 (see map 4.1).

Long-term tenure entrenched the princes in their provinces and fostered the all-too-familiar rivalry among the shah's sons. Yet the balancing act in the Qajar princely system proved successful insofar as it recognized the reality of Iran's regional diversity and helped the country's economic recovery. The manner of succession, however, despite efforts to regulate it, remained a contentious issue in early Qajar politics, and it had domestic and foreign implications. Competition for the succession, which had not been fully decided, began very early. To prove their worth, the princes were encouraged not only to rebuild the economy and secure calm in their domains but also to resume territorial expansion along Iran's frontiers. The shah gave his implicit consent for such campaigns, often carried out to deflect attention from internal strife. He even played a part in fostering some fraternal rivalry. 'Abbas Mirza's investiture as heir apparent in 1828 was not fully supported by all his ambitious brothers. Later, from the 1830s on, the struggle for succession further entangled the Qajar throne in a web of European imperial politics.

WELCOMING THE ENGLISH

The domestic equilibrium that was achieved under Fath 'Ali Shah was put to the test of European power politics from the very beginning of the nineteenth century. This was a mixed blessing for Iran, which had emerged from its eighteenth-century isolation only to encounter Europe at the outset of Napoleonic era. On the one hand, the presence of European powers helped stabilize the Iranian frontiers and consolidate the Qajar state. On the other hand, European strategic, territorial, and commercial ambitions turned Iran into an arena of intense—and at times highly disruptive—rivalries. Europe's territorial gains and diplomatic pressures came with interventions in Iran's domestic affairs and with a race to acquire commercial and other advantages, capitulatory rights, and, later, economic concessions. Europe's condescending attitude, gradually setting in as Iran's weaknesses on the battlefield became more apparent, served as a cultural backdrop.

In the north, Iran was taken by surprise at the territorial ambitions of its northern neighbor and soon bore the brunt of Russian expansion in the Caucasus and then Central Asia. To Iran's south and southeast, somewhat more distant but still threatening, was the expanding British India, with its concerns for the security of its most precious colonial possession. Concern with Afghan principalities in the northwest, and soon after fear of French and then Russian advances toward the Persian Gulf and the Indian subcontinent, largely determined the British strategy toward Qajar Iran. Russia and Britain's mutual fears and suspicion of each other in effect sealed the fate of Iran's geopolitics for the entire Qajar period. Increasingly, Iran became a buffer between two ambitious empires, neither of which was particularly mindful of its wishes or its plight (maps 4.1 and 4.2).

The arrival in 1800 of the East India Company's mission, headed by Captain John Malcolm, opened a new chapter in Anglo-Iranian relations. Perhaps the most influential envoy of the Fath 'Ali Shah period, Malcolm sought an alliance to persuade Iran to move against Zaman Shah, the Afghan ruler of Kabul who posed a threat to Punjab, then in the midst of a complex power struggle.

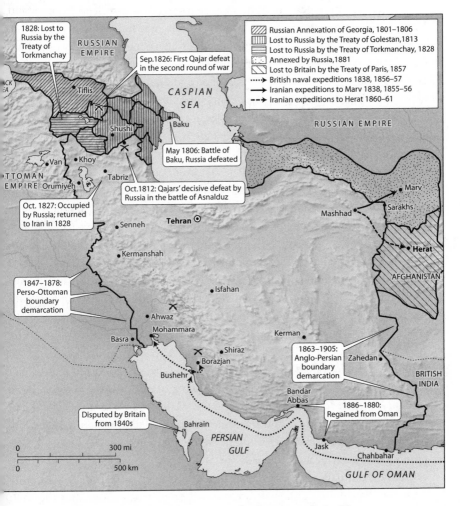

Map 4.2. Iran's loss of territory in the Qajar era, 1806–1881

He also announced the East India Company's victory in 1799 over Tipu Sultan, the ruler of Mysore. Shortly before Malcolm, Tipu Sultan had sent a mission to the Persian court proposing a grand anti-British alliance to Fath 'Ali Shah, as well as to Zaman Shah in Kabul and the sultan of Masqat. Malcolm, who played a pivotal role in the conquest of Mysore, and later as the private secretary of Marquess Wellesley, the chief architect of British colonial hegemony, viewed Iran as an important party to the security of Hindustan, a policy that remained in effect for the entire Qajar period.

After the lapse of a century, the Qajar government welcomed diplomatic and commercial relations with Britain. Yet before granting Malcolm and his retinue a royal audience, the state officials were anxious to learn more about English advances in India. As early as the victory over the French at the Battle of Pondicherry in 1759, and later the English advances in Bengal in the final decades of the eighteenth century, the Zands—and later the Qajars—viewed British colonial successes with a mix of awe and anxiety. The arrival of a sizable English mission at the Qajar court therefore had symbolic implications insofar as it allowed the Qajars to register equality with the British crown. The state officials thus were careful to negotiate with Malcolm the details of court etiquette. English officers' caps and boots particularly became a major issue. The court agreed that caps could be removed, as it was the British custom, and the boots to be wrapped in makeshift covers, to observe Persian custom of taking off shoes in interior spaces. Permission to sit in the presence of the shah, however, was denied. The audience with Fath 'Ali Shah went amicably. There was every reason for each side to impress the other with displays of wealth and might, but also of knowledge. Malcolm amused the shah and amazed his court officials with his knowledge of the Qajar tribe and its history. Fath 'Ali Shah impressed Malcolm, and later other English envoys, with his awareness not only of the East India Company's advances in India but also of the loss of the American colonies and the rise of a modern republic in the New World.

Other examples of cultural exchanges highlighted the contrasting goals that each hoped to achieve. Offering and receiving of gifts was but one symbolic language employed in this new diplomacy. Malcolm's presents of jewels and luxury goods for the shah and his ministers and officials, which had cost the East India Company a small fortune, were meant to impress the Persian court, purchase their favor, and persuade the shah to act against the Afghan threat, which he eventually did. The English had long been accustomed to offering gifts to Indian princely states in exchange for colonial treaties. But the shah preferred to receive the presents and view the company's overtures in a different light. He did not see the gifts as an incentive to facilitate his cooperation; rather, he received the gifts as a tribute brought to his throne as proof of his imperial might. The pomp and circumstance of Fath 'Ali Shah's court, his opulence and elaborate protocol, may well be viewed as a necessary display of political power to impress his domestic and neighboring contenders having been aware of the English naval might and commercial power.

It perhaps took two decades before the Qajar ruler and his government fully absorbed the complexity of European colonial enterprise and what it meant for Iran. At the outset of the Russo-Persian conflict in 1800 (the same year as Malcolm's arrival in Tehran) over the vassalage of Georgia, it would have been highly impolitic of the shah to turn down Malcolm's offer of friendship and the prospects of concluding a treaty of cooperation and commerce—one that took thirteen more years to be ratified, in 1814, at the close of the Napoleonic Wars. In contrast to the Russians, whom the Qajars considered as brute aggressors, the English were perceived as shrewd, disciplined, and foresighted. They were admired for their negotiating skills, stratagems, and measured use of military force.

Malcolm epitomized the enterprising spirit of the British colonial expansion in its most flourishing era. A colonial strategist, soldier, diplomat, and scholar, he defined British policy toward Iran and promulgated the British attitude toward Iranians. His *History of Persia: From the Most Early Period to the Present Time*, first published in 1815, featured Iran as a nation with geopolitical integrity and historical continuity stretching back to ancient times—a nation whose best days, in his portrayal, had already passed. Based on European and Persian sources, in every respect his *History* displayed the spirit of the English Orientalist enterprise: curious and disciplined and with a desire to collect, systematize, represent, and ultimately dominate. He portrayed a Persian state that was alert and even awe inspiring, and a society that was fascinating and complex. Yet he pointed to decadence and despotism everywhere.

Malcolm's was among a host of early nineteenth-century European accounts published on Iran as the country and new state became a focus of European strategic interests. Travelogues, histories, geographical descriptions, and archeological discoveries, many of them illustrated, became a source of fascination for European readers. These accounts, not as extensive as the literature produced on Hindustan or Egypt, nevertheless were influential in shaping perceptions of Iran. Like other travel literature of the colonial period, they were often taken by readers as reassuring evidence of European, and especially British, material and cultural superiority. By contrast, Persian knowledge of Europe and colonial India remained scant and anecdotal. By the time Malcolm's mission arrived, the Qajar state knew little about modern Europe and its geography, history, society, and politics, and even less about the New World. A few Persian accounts of contemporary Europe had been compiled, mostly by members of the Persian secretarial class residing in Hindustan and in contact with the British colonizers. They translated brief passages from European almanacs about the history and geography of Europe and the New World.

One such example, *Tuhfat al-'Alam* (Gift of the world), by Mir 'Abd al-Latif Shushtari (with an addendum completed in 1805), in addition to praiseful review of Western scientific innovations and contempt for such upheavals as the French Revolution, offered a view on the systematic pathology of British colonial expansion. Annexing Indian princely states, he observed, invariably began with early trade relations and the signing of treaties of friendship, then continued in the next stage with the offer of military assistance and political advice to what Shushtari viewed as lethargic and hedonistic rulers, eventually leading to full takeover by means of persuasion or coercion. Shushtari ended his account with a hopeful note, wishing for the Iranian state to not go down the Indian path, to remain alert and withstand the imminent threats to its sovereignty through insight and good government. His word of caution, however, was heard by his compatriots only years later, when *Tuhfat al-'Alam* was finally published in 1847, and then only in Hyderabad. By then Iran has already lost to Russia its prized possessions in the north.

RUSSIAN MENACE AND EUROPEAN RIVALRIES

For Qajar Iran the strategic value of an alliance with England was primarily the ability to withstand the Russian threat. By 1801 Tsar Alexander I (r. 1801–1825) reaffirmed his predecessor's seizure of Georgia over the objection of a few of his advisers (see map 4.2). What made the southern drive appealing to the tsars was in part a desire to place Russia on an equal footing with other European powers in the race for colonial gains. Alexander and his like-minded advocates of Russian expansion relied on sympathizers in the Georgian royal family and in the Armenian Church who viewed Russian annexation of the eastern Caucasus as the only way to lift the yoke of Persian rule. Memories were still fresh of Aqa Mohammad Khan's Tiflis massacre and abduction of Christian woman and children remained.

Yet Persian rule generally had been favorable to the people of the Caucasus, allowing them communal autonomy and lenient taxation. Armenian landowners (*maleks*), in particular, were content with Persian rule, although their voices were lost to the self-serving enthusiasm of wealthy Armenian merchants abroad and their ecclesiastical allies at home. Similarly, a faction of the Georgian ruling elite viewed decentralized Iranian suzerainty as a blessing, while another faction was lured by the idea of Russian protection. By 1803, Russia claimed sovereignty not only over Georgia but also over all other Iranian possessions east of the river Kora, provinces coveted for their silk production (see map 4.2).

In response, the government of Tabriz, under 'Abbas Mirza, began to exert greater control over the remaining provinces of the Caucasus. But even the Qajar governor of Iravan, who had already anticipated Russian intervention, was not willing to yield. The first round of the Russo-Persian wars, which began in 1805 with sporadic raids by Iranian irregulars into the interiors of the Caucasus were aimed to reassert Qajar authority. The Russians ominously retaliated in campaigns organized from Tiflis. For seven years thereafter, the two parties, Russia and Iran, engaged in campaigns for control of the region north of the river Aras. During the early phases of the war, the Iranians often emerged victorious. By 1807, they had been able to repulse the Russian onslaught, slaying the Russian governor-general of Tiflis in a move much celebrated for its symbolism and recapturing nearly all the Caucasian provinces except for Georgia (see map 4.2). Despite the arrival of Russian reinforcements, in 1810 a Qajar general defending Iravan managed to repel the Russian offensives and capture a substantial number of prisoners of war. The new Russian commander in chief was obliged to ask for a peace treaty.

Yet the Persian gains remained unconsolidated, and in a matter of just three years the fortunes of war were reversed. In October 1812 at the Battle of Aslanduz on the banks of the Aras River, some 120 miles north of Ardabil, the Russians, despite their numerical disadvantage, struck a heavy blow to Persian forces. Qajar methods of irregular warfare were incompatible with modern Russian tactics. Reforms of the Qajar army along the European model were too little to have any effect, and then there was the questionable loyalty of local vassals in the Caucasus, some of them of Qajar blood. They were as defiant of Qajar rule as they were resistant to Russian control. By October 1812 Napoleon's disastrous invasion of Russia had reached its final stages, making the victorious Russians, now more confident, capable of striking a heavy blow to their southern nemesis.

The Treaty of Golestan, concluded with British mediation in October 1813, granted Russia nearly all of the eastern Caucasus north of the river Aras, and Russia annexed the whole of Georgia and southern Caucasian provinces of Baku, Shirvan, Qarabagh, Darband (Derbent), and Ganja. Only Iravan and Nakhijevan remained in Iranian hands. The treaty also gave exclusive rights to Russia to maintain a naval force in the Caspian Sea, in effect exposing northern Iranian provinces to future Russian exploits. By the way of conciliation, the tsar recognized, albeit ambiguously, 'Abbas Mirza's claim as the rightful heir to the

Qajar throne while promising, at the same time, not to interfere in any potential succession disputes over the Persian throne.

The Treaty of Golestan was a turning point in modern Iranian history, for it epitomized the gravity of the Russian threat for the remainder of the Qajar era. Golestan, however, was not the final word on the question of the Caucasus. Russia had left several articles of the treaty deliberately ambiguous as a pretext for making further territorial and concessional demands. It took another round of war before the Russo-Persian border was permanently settled along the Aras. War with Russia also brought Qajar Iran to the realization that its northern neighbor was a world power with an advanced army and military capabilities that could repel a massive French invasion on its European front while checking, and eventually defeating, both the Qajars and the Ottomans on its southern front.

What also became evident, almost immediately after the start of the conflict, was Iran's entanglement in European politics. In search of security and potent allies against Russian aggression, the Qajar state intermittently negotiated with both Britain and Napoleonic France. Already in 1801, in the draft treaty negotiated by Malcolm, Iranians had been promised British military and monetary incentives to move against Zaman Shah of Afghanistan and soon after to pre-empt a potential Franco-Iranian alliance. In the aftermath of Napoleon's 1797 occupation of Egypt, British authorities were fearful of a potential overland French campaign against colonial India via the Ottoman Empire and Iran. Napoleon's sortie into the Levant, though unsuccessful, added to British anxieties. To the British, this was a tangible sign of the French using Iran as a gateway to India. Although such a prospect was highly unrealistic, it made the Qajar shah and his advisers more conscious of their own strategic position. Playing off the warring British and French, they hoped to muster support for their own objective of containing Russia.

British hesitation to ratify the 1801 draft treaty and to honor articles pertaining to monetary support for Iran in the event of foreign aggression disappointed Fath 'Ali Shah and his advisers. By contrast, he was encouraged by French diplomatic overtures. Early in 1805, an emissary, Amédée Jaubert, arrived in Tehran, proposing an alliance with Napoleon. Having already terrified both Russia and Britain on the battlefield, in 1805 Napoleon appeared to the Iranians a brilliant warrior and a natural ally. The French overture was irresistible, even though the shah had a difficult time accepting Napoleon as the product of a popular revolution that had executed the French monarch. More so, he found it implausible that the French army could ever cross Ottoman territory and overland reach Iran.

The May 1807 Franco-Persian Treaty of Finckenstein, nevertheless, was assuring enough for the shah to give it his seal of approval. The treaty not only
promised French support for the return of Georgia to Iran, presumably upon
the defeat of Russia in the war with France, but also, and more realistically,
offered training and modernization of the Iranian army by French officers and
military engineers. With Iran an ally of France, the treaty demanded that Iran
expel the British from Iran and declare war on England at a time when Iran was
already engaged in war with Russia. Moreover, it obliged Iran to persuade its
Afghan subjects in Herat and Kandahar, still considered Iranian vassalages, to
attack British possessions in India. In the event that Napoleon started an Indian
campaign, a scheme he contemplated when he could not defeat England at
sea, Iran would be required to provide overland passage to the French army as
well as to make available its ports along the coast of the Persian Gulf.

The French military mission in Iran, under General Charles-Matthieu Gardane, an aide-de-camp to Napoleon, began training Qajar forces, building
foundries, and surveying the land. Under the competent general, the French
drill officers and engineers worked with revolutionary zeal. It seemed there
might be a chance for the Qajar state to modernize its army and withstand
Russian pressure. Soon, however, Gardane was obliged to abort his mission
and return to France. In July 1807, two months after the Treaty of Finckenstein,
Napoleon concluded another peace treaty, this time with the Russian tsar. The
Treaty of Tilsit with Russia, one of the many short-lived alliances concluded by
the French emperor, betrayed Napoleon's erratic war policy. To Fath 'Ali Shah,
however, the treaty was at odds with, if not detrimental to, the French obligations laid out in his own treaty with the French conqueror.

Napoleon's fickle opportunism offered the English an excellent chance. Although in 1808 the shah, still hopeful about the French initiative, had rebuffed
Malcolm on his second mission to Iran, in early 1809 he was ready to welcome
to his court another envoy of the British crown, Sir Harford Jones Bydges. He
was accompanied by the secretary of the mission, James Morier, the future
author of the Oriental satire *The Adventures of Haji Baba of Ispahan*. Jones,
in his earlier career as a merchant of precious stones and English council in
Basra, was aware of the Iranian affairs at a turbulent juncture, when political
power was acquired by the Qajars. He even had once dissuaded the desperate
Lotf-'Ali Khan Zand to sell off Nader Shah's jewels, the same jewels that now
adorned Fath 'Ali Shah. As a diplomat, Jones hoped to gain Iranian favor for
an anti-French alliance to the tune of £120,000, a backhanded payoff in place
of the subsidy that had earlier been promised to Iran but later denied. This
was in addition to a large diamond that Jones presented to the shah on behalf

of George III (r. 1760–1820). Negotiations with 'Abbas Mirza and his team in Tabriz were followed shortly afterward by further negotiations with John Malcolm, on his third mission, representing the East India Company. The rivalry between the two envoys, Jones and Malcolm, reflected conflicting British priorities for acquiring Iran's friendship.

London's chief objective was Britain's security in Europe through an anti-French coalition, one that must include Russia. For the government of British India, the chief objective was to sustain Iran as a buffer against French threat and against possible Russian expansion toward the Persian Gulf and India. The two objectives finally were reconciled during the 1811 mission under Sir Gore Ouseley, the British crown's special envoy to Iran, who managed to exert greater influence over the shah and the court. 'Abbas Mirza's administration had already welcomed the British officers who accompanied Malcolm from India as partial fulfillment of the earlier British commitment to support Iran. By 1810, they were serving on the Caucasian front along with the Iranians and training soldiers in the art of European warfare.

The British government refused, however, to pay the monetary assistance it had promised. Article 4 of the Anglo-Persian Definitive Treaty of Defensive Alliance, renegotiated in 1808 by Jones and finally ratified in November 1814 by Britain, stipulated:

> In case of any European nation invading Persia, should the Persian government require the assistance of the English, the Governor General of India, on the part of the Great Britain, shall comply with the wish of the Persian Government by sending from India the force required, with the officers, ammunition, and warlike stores, or, in lieu thereof, the English government shall pay an annual subsidy . . . it is hereby provided that the amount of the said subsidy shall be two hundred thousand (200,000) tomans annually. It is further agreed that the said subsidy shall not be paid in case the war with such European nation shall have been produced by the aggression on the part of Persia.[2]

The British government rather artfully interpreted Iranian war in the Caucasus as an offensive rather than a defensive measure. Hence, there was little hope that it would support funding Iran with a subsidy or military support. Instead, Ouseley persuaded the shah and his ministers to accept defeat and enter into peace negotiations with Russia, with himself acting as the mediator and ultimately as peace broker.

By 1814, Iran received far less than what it had initially bargained for. Not only had it lost the greater part of its Caucasian provinces; its prestige had been ransomed to conflicting foreign demands. With France defeated and Napoleon in exile, the shah and the Qajar elite came to the conclusion that if Iran were to survive Russia's onslaught, it had to rely on British support and bravely accommodate that power's whims and wishes. The silver lining for the Qajar state, if there was one, was that Iran served usefully as a buffer between them, even if both Britain and Russia wished to parcel out its valuable pieces. For Qajar statesmen such as 'Abbas Mirza and his minister, who were the first line of defense, there was still hope for them to regain what had been so painfully lost. As in Egypt, and shortly after in the Ottoman Empire, Muslim modernizing regimes in the early nineteenth century eagerly sought to make military reforms, not only to resist European advances but also, and more urgently, to accelerate the power of the centralized state against the periphery at a time when external defeat incited domestic subversion.

The "New Army" (*nezam-e jadid*, lit. the "new [military] order") of Azarbaijan was the first of several attempts to create a modern force capable of waging modern warfare, if not always effectively against foreign enemies, at least against rebels at home. Clad in Western-style uniforms with red jacket, blue pant, and long boot, and equipped with fixed-bayonet musket, the soldier of the New Army, named *sarbaz* (lit. "he who sacrifices himself"), was a novelty on the Qajar landscape. The conservative ulama initially disapproved of the new uniform for being made in the image of the infidels and as a breach of Islamic dress. Yet they were persuaded by the state officials to accept it as necessary for the defense of Muslim lands. In 1838, a firman by the Qajar monarch Mohammad Shah praised the new military uniform, made of Iranian fabric, as the most honorable attire not only because it was durable, simple, and practical, as compared to the old military uniform, but also because it distinguished the defender of the nation, including the shah, from the rest of the population, just as soldiers appeared on the carvings of the ancient palace of Persepolis.

The New Army of Azarbaijan successfully adapted itself to the training and tactics of a modern army. Throughout the late 1810s and early 1820s it put on an impressive show of discipline and endurance, and the Iranian soldiery was viewed favorably by European observers for its battle hardiness (fig. 4.3). The New Army certainly helped 'Abbas Mirza remain atop the princely hierarchy, and in later decades it served as a potent agent of the state, eventually facilitating the rise of the reformist premier Mirza Taqi Khan Amir Kabir in 1848.

THE AGE OF THE USULI MOJTAHEDS

War with Russia left a lasting impression on the Iranians and on the shaping of their responses to the outside world. Though in their collective mem-

Figure 4.3. Shah Square in the capital in the early 1840s (leading to the
Tehran citadel), with soldiers drilling in modern uniforms. The cannon at the
center, manufactured in 1818, later became an object of urban legend.
E. Flandin and P. Coste, *Voyage en Perse*, vol. 8, *Perse moderne* (Paris, 1851–1854).

ory there were many foreign invasions, this was the first loss of territory to a
Christian power since the rise of Islam. The last land war with a Christian
power was in 1071 at the Battle of Manzikert in eastern Anatolia, between
the Saljuq Empire of Iran and the Byzantine Empire, which ended in the
former's decisive victory. The only significant Iranian defeat by Christians
occurred in 627, when the Byzantine emperor Heraclius defeated the Sasanian Empire in the Battle of Nineveh in northern Mesopotamia, 285 miles
north of Ctesiphon.

    Defeat in the hands of the Russians were significant since it made early
Qajar Iran more conscious of its Shi'i identity, independent of the sphere of
the state but related to it performance in the war. The high-ranking Shi'i jurists, the mojtaheds, controlled a growing religious domain that included the
judiciary, the mosque, the madrasa, and religious public endowments. These
institutions gave them considerable social status and political leverage, which
they began to exploit at times to their own advantage, often at the expense
of mystical or other non-shari'a interpretations of Islam. The closer involvement of the Shi'i mojtaheds in the affairs of the community, and eventually
the conduct of the state, especially after calling for jihad against Russia after
defeat in the first round of the war, could not have come about without a key
doctrinal component.

By the middle of the eighteenth century, the Shi'i ulama had to reinvent themselves to regain the ground they had lost since the fall of the Safavids. They were no longer functionaries of the state, nor were they bookish scholars in the secluded seminaries of Isfahan and Najaf endlessly debating the minute details of Shi'i hadith and brandishing hefty glosses and commentaries on the works of earlier jurists. The Usuli Shi'i mojtaheds' answer to the crisis of the post-Safavid era was to come up with a new legal approach to shari'a that stressed the methodology of jurisprudence (or roots of jurisprudence, *usul al-fiqh*) as the key to a broader legal application of the principle of *ejtehad*. The sole authority to exercise *ejtehad*, or legal judgment based on sources of Islamic law and through limited use of deductive analogy, distinguished the Shi'i ulama, and more distinctly the Usuli mojtaheds, from their contemporary Sunni counterparts.

For mojtaheds, the study of jurisprudence (*fiqh*) was the most authentic articulation of Islamic shari'a, and they, as jurists, were the only experts qualified to interpret Islamic law. The Usuli jurisprudence in effect equipped the mojtaheds with claims for collective representation on behalf of the Hidden Imam. The Hidden Imam, or the Lord of the Age, was the Shi'a reference to the Islamic Mahdi, whose advent from the world of invisible according to the Shi'is was expected to trigger the End of the Time. Such self-assumed authority offered doctrinal grounds for the mojtaheds to demand that their followers, or more specifically, their "emulators," seek their legal and moral opinion and follow their expert advice in all matters of shari'a. The doctrine of emulation (*taqlid*) obliged Shi'i believers to follow an individual mojtahed of their choice in all issues of Islamic law. Any qualified Shi'i mojtahed could issue independent legal opinions (fatwas). More important, given their social implications, these opinions were to exert, at least in theory, an unprecedented degree of control over the beliefs and practices of followers

Progressively over the course of the nineteenth century, the binary of *ejtehad-taqlid* became axial to the mojtaheds' legal authority and at times key to their social and economic power. Emulation involved a wide range of duties, as benign as saying prayers behind a mojtahed during "congregational" Friday prayer, and as critical as conducting jihad, even though the latter duty was not always seen within the mojtaheds' jurisdiction. Even the permissibility of holding Friday prayer long was disputed among the Shi'i jurists. Earlier in the Safavid era, the followers of the declining Akhbari school had rejected Friday prayers on the basis that in absence of the Hidden Imam, no authority has the legitimacy to lead public prayers. By the late eighteenth century, however, the Usulis came to accept congregational prayer, utilizing it as a powerful tool to expand their authority and display their personal acumen.

The dynamics of the mojtaheds' interaction with their followers, however, was a complex one. Shi'ism never set objective standards for *ejtehad* beyond unspecified years of studying various subjects in the madrasas colloquium and acquiring some kind of informal accreditations from their teachers. The ulama's greater autonomy from the state in the post-Safavid era made the latter practice more prevalent. The success of the mojtaheds thus largely hinged on their followers. To attract more followers and create a larger constituency, so to speak, a mojtahed had to listen to his followers, comply to a certain extent with their wishes, and even sometimes succumb to demagogy and crowd pleasing. The intricate interplay between the mojtaheds and their followers was further complicated because of the so-called one-fifth of the expendable income (known as *khoms*) and other religious dues disbursable to the mojtaheds by their followers. Collecting the one-fifth, at times referred to as the "share of the Imam," became the major source of income for the Usuli mojtaheds in the Qajar era as they began to assume greater authority over the affairs of the community.

The inefficacy of the literalist Akhbari approach to shari'a became more apparent with the rise to power of the Qajars and the return of some degree of urban tranquility. It is not a coincidence that Usuli mojtaheds grew in number and influence during the same period. Contrary to Nader Shah, who wished to emasculate, or even destroy, the ulama establishment of the Safavid period, Aqa Mohammad Khan and then Fath 'Ali Shah appeased the mojtaheds and sought their blessing in order to buttress their lack of sacred descent. The mojtaheds yielded to the Qajars' wishes from a position of relative strength, not merely as clients of the state. At the close of the eighteenth century many mojtaheds returned from the Shi'i cities of southern Iraq, where some of the ulama had taken refuge after the fall of the Safavids. Soon the new class of the Usuli mojtaheds began to build an urban network while the Qajars were still consolidating their power over the country. The new dynasty, and Fath 'Ali Shah in particular, could hardly afford to lose support of this influential class of the urban elite.

For most of the nineteenth century, however, the mojtaheds remained partners in power with the Qajar state. They did so by remaining within the self-defined boundaries of their legal mandate, what they called "authority to adjudicate" (*welayat-e qada*), and by leaving the political affairs of the realm to the state. While shari'a was the domain of the mojtaheds, the customary law ('*orf*), or more broadly, the political affairs, was more or less left to the government and its agents. The Usuli ulama, despite their legal activism, never really abandoned the Shi'i idea of avoiding the temporal government, a relic of piety-minded tendencies in early Islam. In theory, they considered any government authority in the absence of the Imam of the Age unjust and tyrannical, a presumption that required their distance from political affairs and from holders of political power.

That in the post-Safavid era the chief center for Shiʻi learning remained in Ottoman Iraq, and therefore outside the jurisdiction of the Qajar state, created a new power dynamics, one that persisted throughout the nineteenth and the twentieth centuries. Fath ʻAli Shah's numerous gifts to the ulama of Najaf and Karbala, who were mostly of Iranian origin, as well as his lavishing of enormous sums in cash, gold, and jewels for the restoration and beautification of Shiʻi holy shrines of southern Iraq helped elevate him, and later his successors, to the position of patrons of Shiʻi scholarship and protectors of the Shiʻi community of Iraq. Despite Fath ʻAli Shah's patronage of Iranian mojtaheds and the revival of teaching centers in Isfahan, Qom, Kashan, and elsewhere, Najaf maintained its standing as the center of scholarship and produced important texts in jurisprudence while also training mojtaheds at an advanced level of their education.

Najaf scholars were known for their conservative approach on issues of jurisprudence, and they were universally recognized as authorities by generations of mojtaheds throughout the Shiʻi realms. The works of Shaykh Mohammad Hasan Najafi, a jurist of Iranian origin who specialized on rules and rituals (*furu'*), exemplified the high receptivity of Najaf scholarship. His major work, *Jawahir al-Kalam fi Sharh Sharayiʻ al-Islam* (The jewels of the words in explication of religious laws of Islam), was a forty-four-volume compendium of Shiʻi religious rules and rituals based on the work of the well-known thirteenth-century jurist Muhaqqiq Hilli. Completed in 1846, a high point for Najaf scholarship, it went through twenty-four printed editions between 1846 and 1957, and many editions still later (its 1981 Beirut edition amounts to more than eighteen thousand pages).

Widely used as a comprehensive manual, *Jawahir* glaringly revealed the insularity of the Shiʻi legal scholarship. Loyal to the antiquated organization of the Shiʻi law, it was divided into four major categories of devotional acts, contracts, individual obligations and religious commands. In all, about 46 percent of the work was devoted to purification rites (*taharat*) and devotional acts (*'ebadat*). Within this category, a hefty 26 percent was on pollutants and rules of purity, 40 percent on prayer, and the remaining 44 percent on fasting, Hajj, and religious dues. Placing great emphasis on the issues of purity and pollutants, perhaps a relic of the deep memory of the Zoroastrian rituals of the pre-Islamic past, *Jawahir* discussed with fetishistic precision the minutiae of pollutants and methods of purification. Scatological cleansing in particular, including ritual purging of traces of urine and excretion, as well as menstrual discharge and other "tainting" bodily fluids,

sexual intercourse, corpses, and pollutant animals received overzealous treatment. Other polluting situations, such as coming into contact with the religiously
impure, including infidels, were also discussed at length.

Beyond cleansing and devotional acts, some 24 percent of *Jawahir* discussed
the laws of contract (*'oqud*), to include marriage and trade, and 21 percent, individual obligations (*iqa'at*), such as methods and rules governing inheritance
and divorce. By contrast, only 9 percent of the compendium was devoted to
the commands (*ahkam*), of which the most significant was enforcement of the
penal code. Operating on the Islamic principal of "enforcing the good and prohibiting the evil," harsh penalties (*hadds*) and laws of retribution (*qesas*) were
prescribed, including lashing, stoning, and beheading, for such breaches as
drinking, playing music, gambling, homosexual relationships, out-of-wedlock
intercourse, and prostitution.

What was most remarkable about Najafi's comprehensive treatment was the
preoccupation with individual behavior and the means of controlling and policing it. This ritualistic aspect, more than civil or public conduct, interested the
Shi'i jurists over the centuries with little, if any, deviation. What determined the
shari'a primarily and predominantly were rituals and individual conduct, not
the modern sense of law. Remarkably, despite jurists' great emphasis throughout the Qajar period on the methodology of law, as is evident in the field of
usul al-fiqh, the traditional division of legal categories remained firmly in place.
Inaccuracies in defining contract versus individual obligations versus religious
commands remained unresolved, and the two categories of "approbated" (*mos-
tahab*) and reprehensible (*makruh*), the gray areas of the law, so to speak, were
preserved. Most striking, Shi'i legal concern never extended to the areas of public law or attempted to define the social rights and obligations of the individual
in the modern sense. Nor did it made the faintest attempts to define the boundaries of state power. Instead, it adamantly adhered to the rituals and rules that
regulated the life of the individual.

Even then it remained notoriously bookish and out of touch with the realities of the society it was supposed to serve. A vast number of intricate cases
discussed in *Jawahir*, as in all compendiums on *fiqh*, were purely academic and
had little, if any, practical implications. More than anything, they represented
their authors' legalistic obsessions and the scholastic acrobatics of the madrasa
environment in which they were produced. *Jawahir* was rife with hypothetical
cases devoid of any practical application: implausible, even bizarre, situations
of bodily defilement and remote and highly improbable annulment of ritualistic ablution, daily prayers, fasting, and correct practice of Hajj rituals. Like most
scholastic and exclusive teaching environments, it was as if these elaborations

were to impress jurist counterparts and rivals in the madrasa rather than having any useful purpose even for jurists' own students and training as mojtaheds.

Yet despite rising rivalries and bickering among the jurists, at moments of crisis, the ulama felt their duty to defend the survival of the shari'a, what they called the "kernel of Islam" (*bayzeh-ye Islam*), even at the cost of contesting the state. Such interventions, however, were far less common and far more anecdotal than some modern apologists for the authority of the ulama versus the Qajar state would like us to believe. Contrary to popular images of the ulama as champions of the weak, most mojtaheds were supplicating subjects of the shah and admirers of Qajar rule. At no time before the end of the nineteenth century did any Shi'i mojtahed of significance question the legitimacy of the temporal rulers of their time. The few who did protest the government's action, such as during the Regie Protest in 1891 and 1892 against the concession granted by the Qajar state to a British company, did so at the urging of political activists and only briefly and on specific issues.

The early incubation of the Usuli school took place in the seminaries of Najaf, in Ottoman lands. Though safely distant from the seat of the Persian shah, they were more dependent on their Qajar patrons to protect them from the Sunni Mamluks of Iraq and later, in the early Tanzimat era, from the Ottomans. The first generation of Usuli jurists, mostly teachers rather than judges, overcame their Akhbari opponents in Najaf under the leadership of Aqa Mohammad Baqer Behbahani (1706–1791), the recognized initiator of the Usuli school in modern times, who is often esteemed by his students as the "unique one" (*vahid*) and the "renovator" (*mojadded*) of the thirteenth Islamic century.

A descendant of Mohammad Baqer Majlesi, the prominent theologian of the late Safavid era, and himself a refugee of the Afghan invasion and reign of Nader Shah, Behbahani succeeded in establishing the Usul school in Najaf not just by triumphing in debates with his mostly Arab Akhbari opponents or by producing legal works on *usul al-fiqh*. His greater success was building a network of patronage and a growing body of mostly Persian students who studied with him and with other senior Usuli cohorts in Najaf, with the intention of returning to Qajar Iran to occupy judicial positions. By the turn of the nineteenth century, the Usuli network was firmly in place in most Iranian cities, patronized by the state and the urban elite, and well assimilated into the religious affairs of its communities.

Contrary to a number of "aristocratic" ulama families, both Arabs and Iranians, who dominated the teaching circles of Najaf and Karbala (known as the 'Atabat, or "the thresholds"), the mojtaheds who returned to Iran were often of humble origins. Typically they were village boys who had gone through arduous years of education in dire poverty and then returned home, equipped with one or several "certificates" (sing. *ejazeh*) from their Najaf teachers. Home often was a newly revived trading center such as Isfahan, Yazd, Qazvin, and Tabriz, a place where they could gradually build their constituency, "prohibit the evil deeds" (*nahy 'an al-munkar*), compete with one another for prestige and influence, and often amass fortunes.

Perhaps the foremost example of an early nineteenth-century Usuli is the celebrated Sayyed Mohammad Baqer Shafti (1767–1844), a powerful mojtahed in Isfahan whose career highlights all facets of the ulama's power and privilege. Before the twentieth-century days of prolific use of honorifics among the clergy, Shafti was the sole Shi'i figure referred to as *Hojjat al-Islam* (lit. "the proof of Islam"), a title normally reserved in Shi'ism for the Imam of the Age, which implied that Shafti was solid evidence of Islam's steadfastness. He was a poor boy from Shaft (fifteen miles south of Rasht) who had gone through long stretches of madrasa education in Iran and attended the "right" teaching circles of Najaf while still living in dire poverty, subsisting on stale bread and rotten melons, as he reminisced in conversation with his students

In Isfahan, which was gradually regaining its status as the most important religious center in Iran, Shafti steadily rose in the clerical hierarchy despite the fact that he was not a native of the city. He built his base by, among other things, issuing harsh legal opinions, lashing moral offenders, smashing wine cellars, crushing musical instruments, banishing prostitutes from the city, fining drunkards, and — if we trust his biographer — personally executing some of the seventy individuals he had sentenced to capital punishment. In one case, he beheaded an offender charged with pederasty and afterward said prayers at his burial. He held a popular teaching circle, appropriated the trusteeship of unclaimed or disputed pious endowments (*awqaf*), and acquired vast private properties that included shopping alleys, villages, and agricultural estates.

Isfahan at the time was just beginning to recuperate from many decades of decline and depopulation. Shafti engaged in trade and acquired property in collaboration with a merchant from Gilan, enriching himself through astute investments and even moneylending, in violation of the Islamic ban on usury. A key to his success was the immediate confiscation of collateral upon default, which in due course provided him with vast estates in and around Isfahan, as well as in Shiraz and Yazd. According to one source, by the 1830s his wealth included forty caravansaries, a thousand shops, and a vast number of villages in the fertile district of Borujerd and in Yazd. Though perhaps exaggerated, such figures reflected the awe he inspired among the ordinary people of his time.

Amassing such wealth was often associated with high-ranking officials or tribal khans, and seldom with members of the clergy, who normally held a reputation for frugality.

Shafti was a bibliophile with a substantive private collection and a keen observer of domestic and regional affairs. On his Hajj pilgrimage, he took the Persian Gulf route, reportedly accompanied by two thousand followers. He corresponded with Mohammad 'Ali Pasha of Egypt, then in control of the Hejaz, and reportedly persuaded him to endow the income from the famous Fadak hamlet, claimed by Fatima, daughter of prophet Mohammad, to the *sayyeds* of Medina. Shafti's response in 1839 to the British envoy Sir John McNeill on the question of Iranian claims over Herat reveals political astuteness and maturity, some knowledge of the British parliamentary system, and recognition of the legitimate authority of the Qajar state in matters of defense, governance, and diplomacy. Shafti, nevertheless, regularly made demands on the Qajar state that were more for his own interest, rather than the public. His bickering with the government in his latter years tarnished his image even in the eyes of his followers as he resorted to violence and demagogy. Finally, it was left to the powerful governor of Isfahan, Manuchehr Khan Mo'tamad al-Dowleh, a Georgian convert to Islam, to put an end to Shafti's rule. A shrewd state official, Manuchehr Khan had risen from being a eunuch in Fath 'Ali Shah's inner circle to the shah's confidant, and then to one of the most powerful statesmen of the era of Mohammad Shah (r. 1834–1848). In Isfahan he crushed the city's brigands (*lutis*) and restrained Shafti's control of the market and the judicial affairs.

Fath 'Ali Shah generally condoned the mojtaheds' growing power, granting them tax exemptions and reaffirming tenure over their properties. Royal patronage, however, was not the only grounds for the mojtaheds' success. They were astute maneuverers who negotiated with big landowners, merchants, and city officials. Haji Mohammad Hosain Isfahani, the future *sadr 'azam* of Fath 'Ali Shah, for example, sought Shafti's legal sanction to reconfirm his own hold on land and property. The mutual collaboration between mojtaheds and members of the landed class did not exclude the Qajar state at the local and central levels, so long as the mojtaheds were rewarded with lands and gifts from the shah and his administration.

The mojtaheds were able to broaden their base through the madrasa, the mosque, and the bazaar. Their constituency included the lower clerical ranks, multitudes of students of the madrasa (*talabeh*), preachers and reciters of Muharram tragedies, and custodians of mosques and shrines. Their large and often chaotic teaching circles, where textual instruction was interlaced with the practical adjudication of legal cases, offered hands-on education on how to become a mojtahed. Big merchants as well as smaller retailers and shopkeepers were also among the mojtaheds' followers. Placing themselves in the clerical pecking order, some urban mojtaheds controlled the *luti* brigands and, if necessary, incited a mob. It was not uncommon for the influential mojtaheds to settle differences between the provincial governors or officials and other urban elite by inciting riots. Despite the *lutis'* popular image as protector of the weak, some terrorized neighborhoods, living a life of violence and heavy drinking, extortion and racketeering, and even sexually violations of young boys and women. Such crimes were often condoned by their patrons. At the lower echelon of the ulama hierarchy, the village mullahs offered religious instructors to the headmen and peasants and often served as a nominal shield from the excesses of the government tax collectors and other sources of coercion.

Fath 'Ali Shah's willingness to caress the mojtaheds' egos or assign to them monetary gifts and land tenure was not entirely out of love of shari'a. He must have been tempted to wash away the significant public evidence of his greed and lust with a good dose of religiosity. What was at stake, however, was the very credibility of Qajar rule, both domestically and in the face of menacing neighbors. The shah had to keep the ulama content to acquire their approval, especially in dealing with the Europeans. Powerful mojtaheds were aware of the Qajars' weakness and willing to exploit it.

In 1811, while Sir Gore Ouseley was in Tehran, the English Evangelical missionary Henry Martyn visited Iran to spread the message of Christ and find some converts among the Shi'i Iranians. Fiery but naive, he entered into theological disputation with a Shiraz mojtahed in which Martyn was declared, rather unjustly, to be the winner. The clerical establishment all over the country was up in arms to prove that the mojtaheds were the true saviors of Iran's Shi'i soul. In his treaties, young Martyn challenged the veracity of Islam and the authenticity of the prophet of Islam. In his private notes, he dreamed of Christianizing Iran and the rest of the Muslim world. The Shi'i mojtaheds, by contrast, came across in their responses as more tolerant and open minded, even if their approach to Martyn's challenge was outmoded and decidedly oblivious to its colonial subtext. They were alert and consistent but insular and intellectually unprepared. Martyn did not win any converts, although his translation of the New Testament into Persian, published in 1815 in St. Petersburg by Ouseley's support, and in 1816 in Calcutta by the Church Missionary Society, went through several editions. It was one of the earliest printed books to be widely distributed in Iran and have some impact on the Persian readership. Ouseley's support for Martyn and sponsorship for his translation of the

Gospels—Ouseley even presented a manuscript copy to Fath 'Ali Shah—may be seen as part of the English desire in the early decades of the nineteenth century to spread Christianity in Iran and India. Shi'i Iran offered even less fertile ground for conversion than India did.

If the Martyn episode demonstrated clerical vigilance in encountering a theological challenge, such wariness proved inadequate in the face of modern military threat. During the first round of wars with Russia, the ulama backed the state as the defender of Islam waging jihad against infidel intruders. To save face, the Qajar state had to portray the 1813 defeat in war with Russia a temporary setback, not the final word. Subsequently, the Tabriz administration under Mirza Bozorg Farahani had to approach the prominent mojtaheds of Iraq and Iran to seek their approval for another jihad against the Russia aggressor. The exercise also aimed to buttress 'Abbas Mirza's succession in the eyes of the public, as he faced new challenges from his ambitious brothers.

The mojtaheds' responses, particularly a cogent one by Sayyed 'Ali Tabataba'i, a respected teacher of *usul al-fiqh* in Najaf, served as the basis for the 1819 publication of a small volume titled *Jihadiyah* (On jihad), the first publication to be produced by the newly founded government-run press in Tabriz. This exercise to seek public support by publishing a collection of fatwas far exceeded government expectations. As representatives of the Imam of the Age, the ranking mojtaheds willingly accepted the Qajar state's initiative. They called for jihad on the grounds that defense of Muslim lands against outside aggression was an inalienable "individual duty" of all qualified believers. The mojtaheds' assertions of their role as leaders of the community and their widening jihad to include all able-bodied civilians had important implications. On the one hand, it allowed mass mobilization to wage a successful war, while on the other hand, it took the initiative out of the hands of the state in favor of the ulama.

A few years later a collection of fatwas by Mohammad Baqer Shafti in the form of a catechism (written before 1826 but published in Tabriz in 1831) echoed the outmoded attitude of the mojtaheds in dealing with the Russian challenge. It included a section on jihad and the believer's individual duty. Reinstating an arcane Islamic injunction, Shafti declared in one instance that all captives of war with infidels, no doubt a reference to the Russians, Armenians, and Georgians captured during the war in the Caucasus, were to be killed except for the children, the old, and the women, who were to be enslaved. Oddly enough the Russian captives, in practice, were welcomed and treated well, many preferring life in Muslim Iran over the arduous and inhumane lifetime of military service in the tsar's army. Shafti's ruling, and similar opinions by other mojtaheds, also showed the limits on the jurists' impact on the relaxed and often nonconforming Iranian public. The mojtaheds were revered for their zeal and learnedness, but they were not always followed. Coming out of the madrasa and into the social arena, they sought status, wealth, and legal influence, and while not disappointed, they were unable to fully dictate the course of state policy or dominate the minds and hearts of most of their followers. The equilibrium between the state and the clerical establishment, though, would soon be put to a new test.

DEFEAT IN THE WAR AND TORKAMANCHAY TREATY

Among the reasons for renewed hostility were disagreements over implementation of the Treaty of Golestan, demarcation disputes, and anti-Russian resistance among the Muslim population of the annexed territories. At least some ranking Russian generals were determined to consolidate Russian gains as far south as the river Aras, which they considered the natural Russo-Persian border. Furthermore, for the majority of ulama and Iranian statesmen, the loss of the Caucasian provinces had not yet been fully absorbed. These anxieties became more transparent during the second round of wars with Russia between 1826 and 1827. ʿAbbas Mirza was convinced that the price for his eventual confirmation as heir apparent would be a successful Persian offensive in the Caucasus. Only a small antiwar party at the Qajar court and administration were realistic about Iran's vulnerabilities and its prospect of defeat should it engage in another war with Russia.

What seemed to have tipped the balance against the antiwar minority, however, was the call for jihad by prominent members of the ulama. Distraught by the fate of the Shiʿi in the Caucasus under Russian occupation, who lived in fear of mass deportation, in July 1826 a group of mojtaheds marched to Fath ʿAli Shah's military camp near Soltaniyeh (today's Arak, some 180 miles southwest of Tehran). They were led by, among others, Sayyed Mohammad Tabataba'i, son of the above-mentioned ʿAli Tabataba'i, who came to be known as Mojahed (crusader), as well as by Mohammad Baqer Shafti. They pressed the war council, convened by the shah, to opt for war with Russia. They also pressured the shah and his officials to abandon negotiations with the enemy and ask the Russian envoy, General Alexey Yermolov, to leave the camp. The state had little choice but to comply. It was as if a spirit of defiance enwrapped the Qajar elite, which was patriotic and religiously galvanizing but essentially untenable.

Despite early advances by the New Army into the interior of the Caucasus and the valiant resistance mounted by a handful of Qajar commanders—for instance, in the defense of the fortress of Abbasabad near Iravan—the Iranian forces were soon routed in a few short campaigns. The troops of General Ivan

Fyodrovich Paskevich, the commander of the Russian army, secured control over the entire region north of the Aras, crossed the river, and marched in the direction of Tabriz. The celebrated general, a member of the Ukrainian Cossack gentry, epitomized the thrust of Russian imperialist ambitions. He had earlier distinguished himself during the Napoleonic Wars and also defeated the Ottomans in 1814, which made him a hero of the conquest of the Caucasus but hated by the Iranians. Later, he would be equally despised by the Poles for his victory in the 1831 Battle of Warsaw during Polish-Russian War. He also served as the commander of the tsar's army that crushed the Hungarian Revolution of 1848.

The demoralized Iranian camp was dispersed, most of the artillery deserted behind enemy lines, and Iravan and Nakhijevan, the last of the Iranian strongholds, fell into Russian hands. The expected uprising by the populations of Shirvan, Baku, Ganja, and Tiflis never occurred, and the ulama, who had relied on mass resistance could not persuade the people of Azarbaijan to organize a vigilante force or to put up a meaningful defense against the advancing Russian army. Some of the ulama of Tabriz did not even bother to pretend that there was a call for jihad; they were busy preparing speeches to welcome the Russian generals to the seat of the Qajar viceroy. Fleeing before the Russian army, 'Abbas Mirza himself, accompanied by his small entourage, had taken refuge in his summer resident in Khoy on the Ottoman border. Betrayed and disillusioned, he hoped at least to retrieve his capital through negotiation. The English envoy John Macdonald Kinneir—summoned to help him—was obliged to lend the crown prince some cash for his subsistence. This was probably the lowest ebb of 'Abbas Mirza's career (fig. 4.4). Residing near Chaldiran, the scene of the decisive defeat in 1514, 'Abbas Mirza must have wondered how similar was his misfortune to that of Isma'il I.

The peace treaty of Torkamanchay, concluded in February 1828 between the victorious Russian army, then in control of the entire Caucasus and Azarbaijan and even threatening to march on Tehran, and the demoralized Qajar officials, could not have been negotiated in a gloomier climate or with greater disadvantage for the vanquished party. Torkamanchay has often been deemed the most disastrous treaty in modern Iranian history, even though territorial Iran came out of the ordeal relatively intact (see map 4.2). Perhaps it was the perseverance of the Iranian negotiators, with the assistance they received from the British, or the Russians' desire to conclude the peace because the prospect of another war with the Ottomans was looming large, which saved Iran from further humiliation and subservience, and perhaps even from the loss of all of Azarbaijan or even Iran's descent into some kind of Russian vassalage.

Figure 4.4. 'Abbas Mirza receiving the victorious general Ivan Paskevich and his officers in November 1827 in Dehkhvareqan, south of Tabriz. Behind 'Abbas Mirza is his young son Khosrow Mirza, later sent as special envoy to St. Petersburg to convey the apologies of the Persian court for the assassination of Alexander Griboedov (*fifth from right among Russian delegates*) and members of his mission in 1829. Contemporary engraving based on a painting by Vladimir Ivanovich Moshkov, *Batailles de la glorieuse campagne du Comte Paskevitch-Arivansky, dans l'Asie mineure en 1828–1829* (St. Petersburg–Paris, 1836). © «Государственный литературный музей» (State Literary Museum), T. 47–48, S. 221, Sm. ill.

The final loss of seventeen khanates of the Caucasus, consisting of the eastern part of today's Republic of Georgia, as well as the Republics of Armenia and Azerbaijan, amounted to more than 10 percent of Iran's territory at the time and more than 10 percent of its population of about five million. The Caucasian provinces were highly prized for their agriculture, silk production, trade, and manufacturing. The loss of revenue from the khanates, therefore, was substantial — perhaps as high as 20 percent of the Iranian government's total income of about three million tumans ($3,560,000). Politically, the loss of the Caucasian provinces was even greater, for it compromised the very prestige of the Qajar state as protector of Iran's Guarded Domains. The Qajars' tarnished image further cast a shadow on their ability to govern, as the postwar period witnessed insurgencies throughout the remaining years of Fath 'Ali Shah, especially in Khorasan.

Figure 4.5. Qajar officials disbursing in gold the first installment of the five-million-tuman war reparations (twenty million silver rubles in 1828 currency) as stipulated in article 6 of the Torkamanchay Treaty. The war booty is weighed with a huge scale hanging from the ceiling and packed by Russian officers to be sent to St. Petersburg. Contemporary engraving based on a painting by Vladimir Ivanovich Moshkov in *Batailles de la glorieuse campagne du Comte Paskevitch-Arivansky, dans l'Asie mineure en 1828–1829* (St. Petersburg–Paris, 1836) © «Государственный литературный музей» (State Literary Museum), T. 47–48, S. 221, Sm. ill.

The war indemnity imposed by Russia, no less than five million tumans in gold (about US$6 million, or twenty million Russian silver rubles), was nearly twice the size of Iranian state's annual income. Of the four million tumans collected immediately, a huge sum by any standard, a smaller part was drawn from the royal treasury, but the greatest portion was raised through extra taxation (fig. 4.5). Disbursing the indemnity brought the Qajar state to virtual bankruptcy. In addition, the victorious army carried away from occupied Ardabil vast possessions, including manuscripts and artifacts, from the shrine of Shaykh Safi al-Din Ardabili, the patriarch of the house of Safavi. In Tabriz, too, the defeated Qajar ruler was forced to make more gifts of great value to the tsar in the hopes of lubricating peace negotiations. On his return to St. Petersburg, Paskevich received, in addition to a promotion and new title, a reward of a million rubles from the tsar, which no doubt contributed to the construction of his vast estate and palace in Belarus.

It was not only the Qajar state but also the high-ranking mojtaheds who also lost face. The hollow exhortation to wage jihad stood in sharp contrast to the realities of defeat. The transfer of the Shi'i population of the Caucasus, the so-called emigrants (*mohajerin*), mostly to Iranian Azarbaijan, was a stigma and humiliation visible to ordinary Iranians. The Shi'i Muslims constituted the majority of the population of the most provinces of southern Caucasus, and their grievances had been a major reason for the outbreak of the war. In the khanate of Iravan they constituted as much as 80 percent of the total population. Although a majority remained in their homeland, the Russian government insisted on a population exchange, no doubt aimed to enhance the Christian identity of the annexed provinces. Over the course of the population exchange, a substantial segment of the Armenians, mostly from Iranian Azarbaijan, left their homeland to settle in Iravan province under the Russian aegis, while some of the Shi'i population of the Caucasian provinces immigrated to Iran. As late as the 1850s the Iranian government was paying a hefty sum for the upkeep of the émigrés from the Caucasus. Much higher amounts, however, were paid over the years in installments to disburse the Russian war indemnity.

Torkamanchay also reaffirmed Russia's commitment to 'Abbas Mirza as heir to the Persian throne, the only favorable term the devastated and ailing crown prince could procure during the treaty negotiations (see chart 2). The defeat had emboldened other senior sons of the shah to challenge the crown prince, which in turn encouraged him to seek the tsar's blessing. The end result was that the Tabriz administration accepted the harsh terms of the treaty to buttress 'Abbas Mirza's shaky stance. As far as the Russians were concerned, this was nothing short of 'Abbas's admission of his virtual vassalage status. Upon his death in 1833, the Russians, along with the British, imposed on Fath 'Ali Shah a purposeful reading of the article of the Treaty of Torkamanchay according to which Abbas's son would succeed to the throne, which would remain hereditary in his house. For the rest of the Qajar period the rule of primogenitor was observed in the house of 'Abbas Mirza, and with the blessings of the neighboring powers. Although the new rule of succession did not prevent a mini–civil war after the death of Fath 'Ali Shah, the new order of succession was an important departure from the customary contest between sons of the deceased king, which often bore ruinous results for the state and society.

The treaty also defined the Iranian northwestern frontier as it still appears today. The Iranians had exchanged peace treaties and settled frontier boundaries with their foes as early as 450 BCE, in the aftermath of the Greco-Persian wars. This was the first time, however, that Iran's boundaries with its neighbor Russia were defined by meticulous demarcations. This in effect initiated a process throughout the nineteenth century of defining Iranian boundaries vis-à-vis British India and the Ottoman Empire. Shaping an integrated Iran proper thus came at the expense of losing the periphery to the neighboring powers. Russia's exclusive rights to navigate both naval and commercial vessels in the Caspian Sea, reaffirmed in the Treaty of Torkamanchay, also deprived Iran of whatever control it had once held beyond the Caspian shores.

The supplementary commercial treaty attached to Torkamanchay imposed on Iran equally important articles with long-term consequences. Russia acquired not only the right, long resisted by Iran, to open consulates in Iranian cities but also the capitulatory rights of the so-called Most Favored Nations, for Russian diplomatic representatives to preside over disputes between Russian and Iranian subjects. In due course, the denial of both the state's and the mojtaheds' legal jurisdictions set a precedent for granting similar capitulatory privileges to other European nations, most notably to Britain, which concluded a new commercial treaty with Iran in 1841. Likewise, the supplementary commercial treaty granted Russian traders, and later other Europeans, fixed customs duties and other commercial advantages over their Iranian competitors, with negative results for Iran's balance of trade. The effect of the capitulatory rights was not in commerce alone; European powers routinely included these privileges for their own Iranian employees and clients. In the following decades, these protégés of the foreign legations frequently posed challenges to the authority of the Qajar state.

GRIBOEDOV AFFAIR AND THE AFTERMATH OF DEFEAT

Not surprisingly, Iran's image degraded after 1828 in the eyes of foreign observers, becoming a weak state with vulnerable frontiers. The image of decline is visible most intensely in literary works by such writers as James Morier and James Baillie Fraser. The prejudices in these works aside, there was some substance to this shift in attitude toward Iranians as the Qajars' weakening grip over the country became apparent immediately after the defeat by the Russians. In addition to a number of provincial uprisings, the notorious Griboedov affair in the capital demonstrated not only the intensity of public anger toward the triumphant Russians but also the ulama's gaining ground at the expense of the demoralized state.

In 1829 a large Russian embassy had arrived in Tehran under Alexander Griboedov (1795–1829), the celebrated Russian poet and writer. Implementing the terms of the treaty, the envoy Griboedov displayed the condescending zeal of a conqueror toward the "natives." At the instigation of an Armenian eunuch, himself a captive from earlier Qajar raids into the Caucasus, Griboedov demanded the release into his custody of Georgian concubines who were kept in the harems of the Qajar nobility, including that of Allahyar Khan Asaf al-Dowleh, a Qajar khan who formerly served as grand vizier. He was an advocate of war with Russia. Relying on a provision in the Treaty of Torkamanchay calling for the exchange of prisoners of war, Griboedov sent out his Armenian and Georgian aides to bring the women to the Russian legation. Such an act was bound to be seen as a violation of great symbolic weight, threatening the authority of the state and Shi'i religious mores. Allahyar Khan, who was known for his pro-British sentiments, pleaded with the Tehran mojtahed, Mirza Masih Tehrani. In turn, the mojtahed called upon the people of the capital to rise up and rescue the concubines, now presumably converted to Islam, and return them to their Muslim households. The ensuing clashes with the Russian guards led to the deaths of three of the demonstrators. Following a fatwa by Mirza Masih, the angry mob then attacked and massacred Griboedov and the entire Russian embassy staff of seventy, except for one.

Griboedov had largely fallen victim to his own indiscretion, although one cannot entirely dismiss provocations from other quarters, including the British envoy in Tehran or the crown prince's many rivals. The episode came across as much as a sign of public discontent as one of government inability to handle the angry crowd. Though it did not substantially change the European power's future attitude toward Iranians, it did draw a line as to how far Europeans could meddle with Iran's mores and religious sanctions. The shah and 'Abbas Mirza rightfully feared a Russian military reprisal, or at least imposition of new monetary retribution. Yet circumstances helped Iran escape any harsh consequences. At the time, Russia was at war with the Ottoman Empire and did not wish to renew hostilities with Iran. Furthermore, Griboedov was not a popular figure at the court of the new Tsar Nicholas II, for he had been accused of collaborating with the Decembrist reform movement.

To apologize for the incident, 'Abbas Mirza dispatched one of his young sons, Khosrow Mirza, to St. Petersburg, along with a large retinue. Anxious to reaffirm his own shaky position, he even spread rumors that if his brothers were to actively oppose his succession, he might go as far as defecting to the Russian side to seek the support of the tsar. The Persian mission was cordially received by the tsar and the young Khosrow and his retinue for a short while were the focus of the curious Russian elite. The only retribution requested was that Mirza Masih Tehrani be exiled to Ottoman Iraq.

Relying on heavier taxation in the provinces to finance the war and to pay the indemnity, the Qajar state faced renewed resistance from tribal khans, the clergy, and ordinary folks. In Yazd, a major commercial and industrial center in the south, there was a popularly backed uprising by the local governor. In Fars, the prince-governor, 'Abbas Mirza's chief rival, was at odds with the shah for not being able to raise the hefty dues requested by Tehran. In Khorasan there were insurgencies by the eastern Kurdish tribes of the region and renewed raids by the frontier Turkmen and Afghan tribes. Clearly besieged by the sudden change of political climate, the shah called on 'Abbas Mirza and his Azarbaijan New Army to quell the insurgencies, a campaign that gave the crown prince a chance to rebuild his tarnished reputation, boost his officers' morale, and ingratiate him with his father.

The New Army's greatest success was a campaign against the Tekeh and Akhal Turkmen of the northeastern frontier (see map 4.1). These semi-nomadic camel and horse breeders of the desert steppes of Karakum, around Marv and Sarakhs, were nominally subordinate to the khanate of Marv (in today's Turkmenistan), an ancient Iranian vassalage which in it heyday controlled the large-scale export of horses from Central Asia. Increasingly restive since the late Safavid period, and an endless source of vexation to Nader and his successors, the Turkmens were early allies of the Qajars in their bid for power but after Aqa Mohammad Khan's consolidation were soon left out. Pressured by the khanates of Khiva and Bukhara to their north, the Tekeh Turkmen had for some time engaged in banditry, raiding, and pillage (*chapu*) of cities and villages of Iranian Khorasan. Blessed by fatwas of the Sunni jurists of Bukhara that declared the Shi'is of Iran infidels, their plunder and abduction of the peasant and urban population stretched all the way into the Iranian interior.

Riding durable horses, Turkmens carried out night raids on the caravans and settlements and carried thousands of defenseless Iranians first to their desolate nomadic settlements and then across the Central Asian desert to the slave markets of Khiva and Bukhara. Alternatively, they held their captives in yurts in their nomadic camps until a ransom was paid for their release. For the Qajars, the Turkmen raids were a serious nuisance and a source of embarrassment. According to one estimate given by the crown prince's minister Mirza Abol-Qasem Qa'em-Maqam, during the 1832 Sarakhs campaign on the northeastern frontier, the Qajar forces were able to free more than twenty thousand Iranian captives from the Turkmen camps. The Turkmen casualties were heavy, and so were the ravages to the countryside along the trail of the New Army.

The Khorasan campaign was celebrated by the Qajar state as a great, and badly needed, victory, and 'Abbas Mirza and his sons as its champions. Yet the Turkmen threat to the northeast remained throughout the nineteenth century and was a source of horror to the sedentary population. The Kurdish and other tribal populations of northern and central Khorasan, who had barely succumbed to Qajar domination, posed an additional problem. Powerful tribal coalitions put up stiff resistance to the Qajar state before Khorasan was fully incorporated into the Guarded Domains after the 1850s. The anti-Shiʻi overtones of the Turkmen raids, especially those conducted against Mashhad, a city that held a special place in Shiʻi sacred memory, sharpened the Shiʻi awareness of its historical vulnerability. Like the Muslims of Azarbaijan, in Khorasan, too, the sense of insecurity fostered distrust toward the Qajar state and triggered disillusionment with the ulama establishment. The Qajar tribe itself was not free from internecine conflict and insurrection.

In 1833 ʻAbbas Mirza returned to Mashhad and died at the young age of forty-four, remembered, like his Safavid namesake, as a champion of Shiʻi liberation. Although his military record carried more defeats than victory, the memory of ʻAbbas Mirza has remained unblemished. More than any member of the Qajar royal family, he embodied a new national awareness and understanding of modernity. Despite his strong tribal and family loyalties and his traditional notion of royal power, and despite yielding to Russian wishes in his final years, he viewed Iran not merely as a disparate conglomerate of peoples and territories but a country in need of modern defenses and new technological and industrial advances from Europe. Thanks to his small corps of advisers who schooled him in Persian history and literature, he entertained a sense of indigenous state-centered identity.

ʻAbbas Mirza's reform measures, mostly military modernization and ancillary expertise such as European medicine, engineering, and uniforms, were meant to strengthen the state, much in line with the policies of his contemporaries, Mohammad ʻAli Pasha of Egypt and Mahmud II of the Ottoman Empire. His model was to be adopted later by Qajar statesmen trained in the Azarbaijan administration, most notably fifteen years later by the premier Amir Kabir. Students who were dispatched by ʻAbbas Mirza to Europe to study medicine, engineering, glassmaking and tool making, however, proved less influential in shaping Qajar Iran than did homegrown officials such as Amir Kabir, men who came to know about Europe indirectly, and often through experiences in the New Army. A generous prince with an inquiring mind, ʻAbbas had resided in Tabriz since he was ten. There he came to learn about Europe and European powers through merchants, diplomats, and missionaries, as well as through newspapers and other Western and Turkish publications. Much in the style of Peter the Great of Russia, ʻAbbas Mirza was inclined to invite Europeans as agents of reform to settle in Azarbaijan, and he went as far as placing advertisements to that effect in the *Times of London*. After him, his vision of modernity was inherited, to an extent, by a few of his many sons, including the following crown price and future ruler Mohammad Shah.

Fath 'Ali Shah died in Isfahan in October 1834, while on a campaign to collect taxes in arrears from his own son, the governor of Fars. The dictum appearing on the royal emblem—"Thus rested the seal of kingship by the eternal might, in the hand of the king of the time, Fath-'Ali"—reflected some of the achievements of his reign. He was able to transform largely Turkic and tribal rule into a centralized and stable monarchy based on the old imperial model. He offered Iran a period of relative calm and prosperity, secured a symbiosis of state and ulama, laid down rudiments of the Qajar divan, and fostered a period of cultural and artistic revival that has remained the hallmark of the Qajar era. Traditional Persian industries also received a new lease on life after a half-century hiatus. Demand for refined woolen shawls of Kerman, the silk fabrics and delicate rugs of Kashan and Isfahan, and other luxury goods substantially increased as the royal court, the Qajar harems, and the urban elite became accustomed to a lavish lifestyle. Exports of Persian silk also were revived. Raw silk and refined fabrics were exported to neighboring Russia and the Ottoman Empire. As far northeast as Kashmir, where a community of Persian craftsmen and merchants from Hamadan was established as early as the fourteenth century, both the patterns and the technique of Persian textiles, especially shawls, were used in the production of cashmere and pashminas of the Ladakh region, even as late as the nineteenth century. Cotton fabrics of all kinds for the domestic market also increased in volume once the rising population, especially in the larger cities, acquired greater purchasing power.

The vast building project commissioned or patronized by Fath 'Ali Shah, the prince-governors, and the divan officials, including numerous palaces, mosques, madrasas, caravansaries, and designed gardens, left distinct marks on the Iranian architectural landscape. Although Qajar architecture remained loyal to the Safavid style, there were also evident signs of innovation. The mosque and madrasa of Aqa Bozorg in Kashan, built in honor of the chief mojtahed of the city, Mulla Mahdi Naraqi (known as Aqa Bozorg), is an excellent example of sustainable architecture. The novel design of multistory garden structures in Tehran and Shiraz, perhaps influenced by the garden design of the Zand era, is another (fig. 4.6).

Under Fath 'Ali Shah, the Qajar state successfully incorporated the Persian tradition of statecraft and imperial authority. It established a system that weathered for a century despite external and internal pressures. Yet his complacency, rooted in a culture of conquest, was never distant enough from tribal norms

Figure 4.6. The multistoried garden palace, Takht-e Qajar (Qajar throne), in Shiraz commemorated the capture of the Zand capital. Unlike the Persian garden design, it may have been inspired by the raised platform in nearby Persepolis. L. Dubeux, *La Perse* (Paris, 1841), pl. 48.

and familial mores. With few exceptions, the budding of a modern state, on par even with his Ottoman and Egyptian contemporaries, was stifled. At the outset of his reign, the shah still stood a fair chance to slow down, if not repel completely, European military expansion that had begun to affect his country. By the end of his reign, his compounding financial troubles and military and technological disadvantages brought about a serious crisis hastened by an ensuing war of succession.

PANDEMICS AND UNDOING OF THE OLD ECONOMY

The full effects of the defeat and unraveling of the imperial order became apparent under Fath 'Ali Shah's grandson and successor, Mohammad Shah. Though transition to the new rule did not result in a protracted civil war, the transformational effects of European influence and the domestic dynamics that ensued, were significant. The accession of the new shah marked a departure from earlier imperial culture, and especially the state-ulama equilibrium that it had sponsored. The new shah's swift victory over a pretender to the throne—his own uncle, the prince-governor of Fars—and rounding up of half a dozen suspect brothers and uncles promised a strong start to his rule. The power of the Azarbaijan army became instantly apparent when regiments of the New Army (Nezam Jadid) brought a relatively quick end to the claims of succession. The understanding between the European powers became an enduring feature of Qajar succession. This was the first tangible recognition of Iran as a "buffer" state, as a calmer Iran served both powers well and kept the space between them unperturbed.

The premier, Abol-Qasem Qa'em-Maqam, a major statesman of the Tabriz school and a figure belonging to the literary revival of the early Qajar era, dominated the new administration almost to the exclusion of the young shah. By 1835, however, the premier had lost most of his allies in the court as well as his master's trust. His secret murder at the order of Mohammad Shah, recalled the ugly tradition of murdering the vizier, which had last been practiced by his predecessor a quarter of a century earlier. Above all, Qa'em-Maqam's fall can be attributed to the young shah's fear that his premier was conspiring to remove him from the throne in favor of one of his senior uncles from among the princes of Fath 'Ali Shah's house, an anxiety rooted more in his insecurities than in Qa'em-Maqam's intent. At a deeper level it was a tangible departure from the governing style of Fath 'Ali Shah era and the class of powerful officialdom of whom Qa'em-Maqam was a representative.

Mohammad Shah's new premier was his own tutor and mystical guide, Mulla 'Abbas Iravani, better known as Haji Mirza Aqasi, an émigré from Iravan with some religious and Sufi training. Aqasi's self-deprecating personality appeared to some of his contemporaries, and to later historians, to be a sign of his weak and eccentric character. He exerted influence on the young, and soon ailing, shah, who he had converted to some modified interpretation of Ne'matollahi Sufism, the most prominent Sufi-Shi'i order in Iran of the nineteenth century. The shah's serious gout, which incapacitated him toward the end of his reign, further cleared the way for Aqasi's escalating control. During his thirteen-year term of office, Aqasi transformed the Qajar state in two distinct ways. First, he removed most, if not all, of his real and potential competitors from among the Qajar aristocracy of the Fath 'Ali Shah era. His critics labeled him "destroyer of the nobles" (*hadem al-anjab*). Second, he tried with some success to place a degree of state control over the powerful mojtahed establishment, reminiscent of the Safavid practice.

Undoubtedly there was a spirit of modernity in Aqasi's restructuring of the Qajar state (which incidentally was a source of inspiration for his successor in office, Mirza Taqi Khan Amir Kabir). Yet Aqasi was an outsider, untrained in the state bureaucratic tradition. He never mastered the ins and outs of the government's revenue collection, court etiquette, troop recruitment and maneuvers, or conventions of diplomacy. In a few short years state revenue dropped, payments and salaries were delayed, troops could no longer be sufficiently maintained, communications were stifled, disputes with foreign legations had increased, and signs of discontent had become more visible throughout all sectors of society. The changes that came about with the Industrial Revolution as well as with greater Anglo-Russian diplomatic and commercial presence in the 1830s and 1840s contributed to Iran's economic and political setbacks.

The first obstacle the new premier faced was the entrenched Qajar nobility. Having successfully kept Mohammad Shah under his thumb, the new premier, who called himself "First Person" instead of the customary *sadr-e a'zam*, presumably to avoid the sad fate of his predecessors, had to rely on the support of émigrés from Iravan and officers of the Azarbaijan New Army. He appointed many of them to military posts in the provinces to counterbalance the provincial governors chosen from among 'Abbas Mirza's numerous sons. In due course a few of Mohammad Shah's uncles were replaced by a handful of the new shah's brothers. Some of this latter group, the third generation of Qajar princes and their descendants governed the provinces for the following half century. But they often governed either nominally or with shorter terms of office than was customary under Fath 'Ali Shah. The new arrangement was applied haphazardly, however, and was seen as a sign of the state's weakness.

Numerous urban uprisings throughout the 1840s in Tabriz, Mashhad, Yazd, Isfahan, Shiraz, and Kerman characterized the state's loosening grip over the provinces. One frequent cause of these uprisings was clashes between the local population and the government troops stationed in the cities whose members were of different ethnic and geographical backgrounds. Often badly paid and near starvation, the unruly troops harassed the population; plundered city neighborhoods; engaged in brawls, theft, and extortion; and abducted women and children from the very cities they were dispatched to protect. Adding to the conflicts was the discord between the governors and the military chiefs, echoed in a host of local factional, as well as sectarian and personal, rivalries. The mojtaheds were not the only urban provocateurs; landowning tribal khans residing in the cities, municipal officials in control of urban wards, and members of the older Qajar nobility frequently had their fair share of the action. The *lutis*, hired guns serving the highest bidders, were active as well.

Not all troubles were because of urban unrest or the government's lack of resources. Far more disruptive were outbreaks of cholera, plague, and smallpox. The growth of foreign trade throughout the nineteenth century, especially with India and with Russia, both overland and through sea routes, opened new conduits for the transmission of cholera. Pandemics often spread through Iran to neighboring provinces of the Ottoman Empire and Russia, though at times Iran also was on the receiving end of diseases transmitted in reverse direction. The high mortality rate from cholera in the cities and in the countryside was a major cause of depopulation, which in turn resulted in a reduction in the workforce, lower economic output, and routine occurrences of famine. From the 1820s to the 1840s, tens of thousands died of cholera in the big cities at a time when there were no effective sanitary measures or medical treatment.

Although accurate statistics are difficult to come by, it is quite plausible that in one early outbreak of cholera in 1820–1821, within four weeks some three-quarters of Shiraz's total population of forty thousand was ravaged. By the time cholera reached the capital, the casualties throughout the country exceeded one hundred thousand. A decade later, an outbreak of plague in the northern Iranian provinces of Azarbaijan, Kurdistan, Gilan, Mazandaran, and eventually Tehran, reportedly killed two hundred thousand people. About the same number of casualties is given for the cholera outbreak of 1831–1832 in neighboring Iraq, with the highest number of casualties in Baghdad and the shrine cities of Karbala and Najaf. In the years between the 1840s and 1890s, cholera, now an endemic malady throughout the country, flared up at least six more times, each time in short intervals of four to eight weeks in each locale. Although by the 1870s the rudiments of a public health network were in place, including frontier quarantines, the rate of casualties barely subsided.

A conservative estimate of the total population losses to pandemics stands as high as a million, a staggering figure given that the average population of the country did not exceed eight million by the end of the nineteenth century. As in Europe, before the discovery of germ theory, contagious epidemics in Iran were associated with noxious air. They were accepted as horrifying facts of life and feared as acts of divine punishment. One significant feature of divine favor, however, was social class. The Qajar elite and more affluent sectors of the urban population soon learned that once the pandemic was at its peak, taking refuge in their less populated and more isolated estates in the countryside was safer than staying in the cities. The ordinary urban populations, however, were easy prey. The declining economic output caused by these outbreaks brought major decreases in agricultural production, at least during the middle decades of the nineteenth century, which in turn triggered starvation in most provinces and periodic famines, at times countrywide.

Beyond damage from pandemics and famine, Iran's agrarian economy faced other setbacks in the middle decades of the nineteenth century. The revenue loss from Caucasian raw silk after 1813 was compounded by the decline in silk production in Gilan province. From the 1860s, the Caspian provinces experienced the virulent phylloxera pest, originally from North America, which ravaged European grapevine and silkworm production as far as west Asia. Once

Figure 4.7. As late as the 1870s, silkworm breeding in Gilan province was a
viable local industry, though at a smaller scale than in the Safavid era.
"Silk and Silk Culture," *Frank Leslie's Popular Monthly* (New York: Frank Leslie's Publishing
House), vol. 8, no. 6 (December 1879), 661–669.

it reached Iran, it caused irreparable damage to an industry that had endured
since medieval times and brought revenue to the state. It took a while, as long
as a few decades, before the loss of the Persian silk market was compensated
for by other major exports, such as cash crops and the expanded Persian carpet
industry (fig. 4.7).

Cultivation of the new crops such as opium and tobacco, though already a
nascent industry, only picked from the 1870s, bringing much-needed income to
Iran's otherwise subsistence and localized agriculture. The long-distance merchants of Tabriz, Shiraz, Yazd, and Mashhad became, over time, the driving
force behind the cultivation and processing of these new crops for domestic
consumption and, importantly, for export to Europe and China. The merchants had a major stake in security on the road and in the marketplace, and
they suffered from the state's inability to offer either.

Land ownership had been transformed since the rise of the Qajars, although
the rules governing the agrarian economy remained essentially unchanged.
Most of the land used for agriculture, usually consisting of a village, its orchards,
and the surrounding arable land, theoretically was recognized as crown land.
Throughout the century, however, more and more land came under private
control. The mostly absentee landlords consisted of tribal khans, urban nobility, ranking bureaucrats, and—from the 1830s onward—wealthy merchants and

the mojtaheds. Some estates were assigned by the shah as fiefs (*toyul*) to Qajar princes, officials, and the ulama, and these often became hereditary among their descendants. Vast religious endowments, in contrast, were controlled, and at times appropriated, by the ulama. If privately created, the endowments remained in the hands of the trustees, mostly the descendants of the founders of the endowment.

As the century progressed and private landowning became more prevalent, the sharecropping regime became less favorable to peasants. Land taxes ranging from 10 percent to 20 percent of total income, depending on region and prevailing customs, were to be paid proportionately by the landlord and peasants in cash or in kind. Yet in reality a large part was extracted from the peasant's meager share, which reduced his actual share to as little as one-tenth of total income in exchange for a year of labor. Even though the Qajar tax collection system became increasingly inefficient, peasants could barely subsist given the extortion of bailiffs acting on behalf of the landlords and harassment from tax collectors. It was not unusual for an entire village to flee to the surrounding hills and plains at the first sight of the dreaded tax collector and his accompanying troops. Nevertheless, the Iranian peasantry was not bound to the land by any form of serfdom. Families, even a whole community, could migrate and settle on a different estate and enter into sharecropping pact with a new landlord.

The harshness of village life, the insecurities it involved and varying agricultural production, did not go entirely unnoticed. One measure undertaken by Aqasi was to repossess the misappropriated *toyul* and their development as property of the divan. This had the dual objective of increasing agricultural production, especially around the capital, and increasing government revenue. For the first part, to increase agricultural output, the government dug numerous subterranean *qanat* irrigation systems around Tehran and built a water canal from the Karaj River in order to improve the city's water shortage. Similar irrigation projects in Shiraz and elsewhere were initiated to increase wheat and grain production, as well as to introduce new plants, fruits, and flowers. By the end of his premiership, Aqasi had appropriated, purchased, or revived nearly ten thousand estates. He transferred all land ownership to the shah, out of desperation perhaps, though he seems to have intended to use the revenue to boost the state's income. The scale of Aqasi's operation, however, was negligible in comparison to the size of the problem.

The most visible change during the middle decades of the century was growth in the trade sector, most significantly foreign trade. After a lull of nearly a century, Iran began to become reincorporated into the world economy, and not only through contacts with Europe. In the decades after 1828, the revival after a long lapse of Persian Gulf trade via Bandar Abbas and Bushehr to Muscat, the western coast of the Indian subcontinent and Europe was a major breakthrough in trade for the south. The Yazd-Kandahar overland route to India also became more active. The opening of the northern Trabzon-Tabriz route through the Ottoman interior and the Black Sea port, as well as Caspian trade with the Caucasus and southern Russia, and Khorasan trade with Central Asia and Herat, revitalized the markets of Tabriz, Qazvin, Anzali, Barforush, Mashhad, and other commercial towns in the north. Despite growing insecurity foreign trade expanded out of an already-brisk domestic network of caravans crisscrossing the Iranian interior. This network connected agricultural suppliers in smaller towns with merchants and wholesalers in larger cities, as well as weaving and tool-producing workshops and other local manufacturers of glass, pottery, metals, and carpets with growing consumer markets (see map 5.1).

The merchants often supplied raw material to manufacturers and distributed their final products domestically or to foreign markets. Their social standing and financial means, but also their reputation for honesty, frugality, prudence, and piety, made them natural leaders of the bazaar community. Most merchants were thriving in the nineteenth century and the community grew in size and operations, acting also as bankers and moneylenders. Their operations grew within Iranian cities and beyond to Mumbai, Calcutta, Srinagar, Muscat, Baghdad, Basra, Istanbul, Beirut, Alexandria, and Cairo, then later to Shanghai, Ceylon, and Rangoon (Yangon). Trade was a family business, and though it was not always hereditary, there was a natural tendency to preserve capital within the family network. In the early nineteenth century most long-distance merchants, as well as most local merchants and distributors, were Muslim. This was in contrast to the neighboring Ottoman Empire and Egypt, where Christian and Jewish merchants dominated trade. There were merchant families from non-Muslim communities in Iran: Armenians in Isfahan and Tabriz; Zoroastrians in Yazd and Kerman; Jews in Kashan, Isfahan, and Mashhad; and Hindus in Yazd. However, these became more prominent toward the end of the century.

By the early 1840s the Iranian merchants faced new challenges, largely as a result of growing foreign trade. The commercial treaties with Russia in 1828 and with England in 1841, both imposed on Iran, greatly facilitated imports by European firms and their agents. Machine-made cotton cloth at affordable prices, the miracle of the European Industrial Revolution, was the first to have an impact on the Iranian markets. Manchester chintz, calicoes, and other print cloths soon captured a large share of the market at the expense of local textile manufacturers, whose manual looms could not compete with factory products. The local manufacturers were not entirely ruined, as they were, for instance, in some parts of British India, but serious disruptions did occur in the old weaving centers such as Yazd, Kashan, Isfahan, and Kerman.

In 1845, Keith Abbott, then the British consul in Tabriz, could observe that British manufacturers

> appear to have found their way into the remotest parts of the country and they are continually superseding those of Persia. Their present very low prices, owing partly to the influx of too great a quantity of goods this year (1845) will probably lead to their becoming still better known and there is yet abundant scope for increased consumption, for at present our manufactures are little used by, and indeed little known to, a great number of the rude Tribes in this country.[3]

Two years later Abbott reported that Persian manufacturers had "declined for some time past in consequence of the trade with Europe, which has gradually extended into every part of the [Persian] Kingdom to the detriment or ruin of many branches of native industry."[4] By 1850, of the total eight thousand silk looms at work in Kashan, only eight hundred had survived; in Isfahan, only two hundred.

The import trade required fewer merchants as agents and offered a smaller profit margin. The Persian merchants lost business to European firms that sold directly to the Iranian market, often through Armenian, Assyrian, Jewish, and later Zoroastrian agents or through a handful of foreign nationals such as Greeks, Georgians, and Hindus who, as protégés of the European powers, controlled near monopolies. In Tabriz alone, between 1839 and 1845, there was a 45 percent increase in the volume of European trade. Of the total of £1,547,050 ($7,735,000) in foreign imports to Tabriz in 1845, cotton and wool manufacturers accounted for 94 percent of that, and 80 percent were from England. In the south, the total imports through the Persian Gulf ports were about £900,000 ($4,500,000), and the greatest part was British textile goods.

The terms of the treaties with the so-called Most Favored Nations, among other privileges, required that their merchants pay a fixed tariff of 5 percent of the value of imported merchandise (known as ad valorem), which was well below the rates charged to Iranian merchants. The unfair competition consequently resulted in financial loss for Iranian merchants and an increase in the number of bankruptcies. Their numerous petitions to the Iranian government, particularly during the 1840s, complaining of unfair trade practices and economic hardship had little effect. Even the Qajar state's periodic campaigns to encourage the consumption of Persian goods, and in particular Mohammad Shah's insistence on wearing Persian fabrics and encouraging others to do so, bore only limited results. The local manufacturers could not compete with the lower prices and wider variety of European cloth, which was less durable but within the reach of the poorer classes. It cost considerably less to make an over-coat in Tehran from German woolens than it did to make a Khorasan *barak* or a Kerman shawl. The average woman in Tabriz and even Isfahan would pay less for Manchester chintz or calicoes than for the local products, even though some of the local products themselves were woven with English yarn.

The high volume of imports only intensified Iran's monetary problems. The chronic drainage out of the country of Iran's precious metals, mostly silver, which had endured since the Safavid era, now also included payments for the widening trade deficit. The depletion of gold and silver to foreign export, as well as actual export of Iranian species in the form of bullion, were chief cause of the Iranian currency's fall in value throughout the nineteenth century and its drastic depreciation. Between 1817 and 1823, for instance, the total of £1,533,194 (about $7,665,000) of Iranian bullion, specie, and pearls were exported from the Persian Gulf ports to India and Arabia, mostly by British and Banyan traders.

As the century progressed, the volume of these exports swelled. At the begin-ning of the nineteenth century, one Iranian tuman (of ten *qaran*) was equal to one English pound sterling (about US$5). By 1845, the tuman had depreciated by half, and by the end of the century it was one-fifth of its original value. The tuman's loss of purchasing power brought major inflationary pressures to Iran's economy, most visible in the foreign-trade sector. The impact of currency de-preciation and the ensuing inflation, moreover, was compounded by a visible shortage of funds on the Iranian market and a higher cost of borrowing. Exorbi-tant rates of interest, as high as 25 percent annually, were not uncommon. The shortage of funds encouraged not only usury, against all Islamic prohibitions, but also a culture of the middleman, indicative of the high rate of hidden un-employment. Goods changed hands several times between the manufacturer and the consumer, which added to the price while providing a meager income for a host of intermediaries. Shortage of funds and high rates of interest in turn encouraged commercial defaults and the prevalence of buyers' reneging (*dab-beh*) after the transaction was complete.

By the middle of the century, the gap between the incomes of Iranian aver-age urbanites and elites had become glaring. Throughout the first half of the century, the Qajar princely class, the court, the high-ranking state officials, the landowning khans, and the wealthy mojtaheds, as well as a sector of the mer-cantile community (those who had succeeded in warding off the ravages of the economy by affiliating themselves with the European import trade) all accu-mulated wealth. The state officials' income from informal proceeds, known as *madakhel,* particularly became rampant, serving as a substitute for inadequate and irregular fixed salaries. From ministers and governors all the way down to state accountants and tax collectors, *madakhel* was condoned as an institutional form of corruption. The government's failure to redress the economic injustices of the market and protect the domestic workforce from intrusions and social insecurity plunged Qajar society into even greater crisis.

SEARCHING FOR ALTERNATIVE SHI'ISM

The state's endemic flaws and the country's economic plight barely concerned the ulama establishment. Mojtaheds were increasingly seen as part of the power structure, if not always in cahoots with the state. They held sway over the madrasas, including their curricula and the stipends of students. They also distributed funds to their network of followers and could excommunicate at will dissidents, critics, or rivals. There were influential jurists who were accused of bribery and of acting for the benefit of a party that was offering them greater largesse.

In 1826 the call for war with Russia further tarnished their image. With the prevalence of Usuli legalism, the rival Akhbari tendency virtually disappeared, except for brief instances of last-ditch resistance. Most significant among such resistance was a scholar of Indian origin, Mirza Mohammad Akhbari, whose anti-Usuli pronouncements were the first of several calling for an end to the mojtahed's power and control. His pleas to Fath 'Ali Shah, however, remained unheeded. He also entertained protomessianic ideas and esoteric interpretations of Shi'ism. His virtual isolation demonstrated the waning of alternative voices within the ulama community.

The mojtaheds also faced competition from Sufi orders that had made a successful comeback after an absence of more than a century from the Iranian landscape. Most notably, the Ne'matollahi order, named after the influential fourteenth-century mystic Shah Ne'matollah Wali, emerged from obscurity and made remarkable gains throughout the Zand period, first in collaboration with the newly revived Isma'ili Shi'i community in Kerman and later in other Iranian cities. Under the leadership of a Perso-Indian mystic, with the Sufi title of Ma'sum 'Ali Shah (d. 1798), the Ne'matollahi order recruited from among artisans, madrasa seminarians, merchants, princes and officials of the Qajar court—especially in Tabriz—and women of the nobility. In the initial stage of its revival in the late eighteenth century, the Ne'matollahi order was virtually identical with Isma'ili Shi'ism, which itself made a comeback in Kerman after a hiatus of more than a century. Soon the two trends diverged, but a degree of affinity survived between them.

The Sufi message provided relief from the tedious world of the madrasa and the stern loftiness of its jurists. It was one attuned to music, poetry, and painting, as well as love for God and for fellow men and women, adoration of beauty—both in nature and human—nocturnal gatherings, and a community of brotherhood. Through mortification, prayers, fasting, and devotion the Sufis sought the "truth," which among most Shi'i orders, if not all of them, still corresponded to a modified form of unitarian pantheism. The so-called unity of being (vahdat-e vojud) had been cherished in Persian Sufism for many centuries. God was perceived not as a terrifying transcendental lord of vengeance but as an all-encompassing emanation in all beings. For the Sufis, whether in their speculative writings—mostly commentaries on the Qur'an and mystical poems—or in their popular exhortations, the divide between human and divine was not unbridgeable. Persian Sufism of the nineteenth century was distinct from the unyielding Sunni "neo-Sufi" revival in India and North Africa, which often led to puritanical and revivalist interpretations of Islam.

To the mojtaheds, the threat of the Sufis was not only confined to what they labeled as heretical beliefs and corrupt practices. More important, the Sufis' mostly implicit claim to the status of walayat (friendship) rivaled the mojtaheds' religious claim of welayat (guardianship) as legitimate leaders of the community. The living Sufi "guide" aimed to liberate believers from stifling rituals and obligations of the shari'a and steer them instead to the path of inner purity. The poetry of the celebrated Ne'matollahi leader Nur 'Ali Shah (d. 1801), for instance, urged seekers to surpass the superficiality of the shari'a and find the truth in the unfolding mandate of the Sufi saint, a claim that brought them close to the idea of moral representation on behalf of the Hidden Imam.

The Ne'matollahis were part of a wider Sufi revival that swept through Iran during the early nineteenth century. The mendicant dervishes of the Khaksar order, with their curious demeanor and unusual outfits, were familiar sights in the Persian popular landscape. Their chants in praise of 'Ali, the patron saint of all Shi'i Sufis, were heard in the streets, bazaars, the "houses of strength" (zurkhaneh), and the Sufi convents (khaneqah). Use of drugs, commonly hemp and opium, was accompanied by the recitation of lyrical odes and musical instruments. Their alternative lifestyle and unorthodox pronouncements, some relics of a waning Noqtavi past with clear antinomian messages, were not mere curiosity but markers of their persistent nonconformity.

The dervishes' widespread network—stretching from Sufi convents in northern India to Central Asia, Anatolia, Iran, Kurdistan, and beyond to the shrine cities of Najaf and Karbala and to Mecca and Medina—allowed for frequent encounters with urban and rural communities in their path. Their street performances and storytelling in the coffeehouses offered ordinary people an outlet to learn about distant lands and peoples, events beyond their limited surroundings, and marvels of the past sacred history. Later in the century some itinerant dervishes equipped with large portable paintings (*pardeh*), which they sequentially unrolled to narrate the Shi'i tragedies of Karbala and events of the Day of Judgment in multiple iconic scenes, presented believers with a poignant audiovisual narrative that echoed the stories in the murals in the Armenian churches, such as those in New Julfa. They functioned as compact versions of the *ta'ziyeh* passion plays (pl. 4.4).

To the mojtaheds, however, the unconventional beliefs and lifestyle of the Sufis and their dervishes were worrying signs of moral corruption and ploys to deceive their followers. They assumed the task of defending public morality under the rubric of "commanding the good and forbidding the evil," which required that they combat Sufis not only through numerous polemics produced in the Qajar period but also by issuing and enforcing fatwas on apostasy. Several leaders of the early Ne'matollahi revival fell victim to the mojtaheds' anti-Sufi campaign. Ma'sum 'Ali Shah and a few of his followers were executed in 1798 in Kermanshah by a fatwa of the powerful Usuli mojtahed Mohammad 'Ali Behbahani, popularly known as the "Sufi killer" (*sufi-kosh*). He was the son of Mohammad Baqer Behbahani, founder of the neo-Usuli school who earlier challenged the Akhbaris.

Ma'sum 'Ali's favorite pupil, the poet Nur 'Ali Shah, also died three years later under suspicious circumstances. An icon of popular art in the Qajar period, images of Nur 'Ali Shah as a youthful saint of serene innocence and handsome look were depicted in pictorial rugs, the covers of pen cases, and in metalwork. The endurance of these images mirrored silent praise for the Sufi saint among the artisans and the ordinary folks in defiance of the jurists and their exhortations. The talented Ne'matollahi poet and master musician Mohammad Moshtaq 'Ali Shah, who is credited with adding a fourth resonator to the three-stringed Persian *setar* instrument, was killed in 1791 by a mob incited by an Usuli mojtahed of Kerman. He was condemned for blasphemy, for reciting the Qur'an with musical accompaniment by his *setar*. The mojtaheds' anti-Sufi campaign enjoyed the blessing of Fath 'Ali Shah, whose unfavorable attitude toward the Ne'matollahis dated to their support for the Zands, as in Kerman in 1792.

Even though the mojtaheds' campaign under Fath 'Ali Shah succeeded in containing the growth of Sufi orders, it could not stop them altogether, and least of all within the elite circles. Under Mohammad Shah, himself a Sufi, the Ne'matollahis benefited from royal patronage and for a while were shielded against further persecution. Haji Mirza Aqasi even appointed fellow Sufis to positions of power, including assigning a Ne'matollahi scholar to the newly revived office of *sadr* to oversee the religious affairs of the kingdom, a move no doubt aimed to harness jurist hegemony. This gesture was not received kindly by the conservative mojtaheds, who by the middle of the century had become even less tolerant of nonorthodox trends.

Even traits of mystical philosophy within the madrasa curriculum did not escape charges of heresy. The students of philosophy, almost always followers of Sadr al-Din Shirazi, were harassed and forced into isolation. Those who endured had to cover their discourse in a garb of shari'a so thick that nothing remained but dreary regurgitation of philosophized acrobatics, devoid of any creativity. To the ulama's chagrin, in 1815 a celebrated Ne'matollahi scholar produced the most comprehensive exposition in reply to Henry Martyn's polemics. His version was adopted as the Qajar state's official response. Another Ne'matollahi scholar, Zayn al-'Abdin Shirvani (from Shirvan, in today's Republic of Azerbaijan), who traveled the length and breadth of the Islamic lands produced some of the best geographical travel narratives of the Qajar era. Yet despite its scholarly grounding and support in high circles, Ne'matollahi Sufism was not match for Usulism and the mojtaheds' grip on Iranian society.

A greater challenge to the ulama's supremacy, however, came from within the clerical milieu in the form of the Shaykhi theological school. Named after Shaykh Ahmad Ahsa'i (1753–1826), a peripatetic scholar from the Shi'i province of al-Ahsa' on the northeastern coast of the Arabian Peninsula (map 4.3), the Shaykhi school appealed to a younger generation of seminarians in search of something more than sheer study of jurisprudence. In the early decades of the nineteenth century, Ahsa'i held a reputation as an accomplished scholar of theology and jurisprudence. Above all, he was a practitioner of mystical philosophy (*hekmat*) with roots going back to Mulla Sadra (who, ironically, he denounced as a heretic) and even farther to the familiar older trends of Perso-Islamic Sufism, Neoplatonism, and the "Illumination" (*eshraq*) philosophy.

Ahsa'i's popularity among madrasa students especially in Karbala, and later with a growing body of followers in Iran, was primarily because his eclectic approach to Shi'ism, which offered a third alternative to the shari'a of the mojtaheds' and the mysticism of the Sufis. He was well versed in scholastic tradition but posited a moral-mystical alternative that went beyond the strict legalism of the jurists. His piety—a quality that for centuries marked the behavior of reluctant ascetics in the Shi'i-Iranian world—was particularly appealing to some among the merchant classes and other members of the nonelite.

Ahsa'i utilized the rich apocalyptic tradition in Iranian milieu to answer to an essential question in Shi'i theology, namely the extra-corporeal exis-

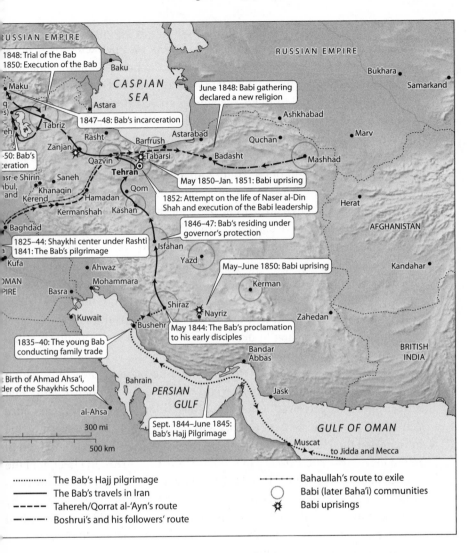

Map 4.3. The Babi movement, 1844–1852

tence of the Hidden Imam in the invisible world, the means of recognizing him, and the time and circumstances of his advent. Ahsa'i sought salvation for humankind not through sheer religious obligations but through an intuitive experience of the sacred in a space he called *horqalya*, an intermediary world between the earthly existence and the heavenly world. In the imaginary world of *horqalya*, a concept he borrowed from the twelfth-century Iranian philosopher Shehab al-Din Sohravardi, the Hidden Imam was invisible to humankind, as were all the souls of the believers as prototypes awaiting the Day of Resurrection. In this world, the believers who perfected their intellectual and moral potential could meditate on the presence of the Imam of the Age and experience his "manifestation" in this world. For Ahsa'i, the "Perfect Shi'a" thus referred to the one who had arrived at this state of visionary perfection and could guide others along the same path. This notion was a reworking of the familiar idea of the "Perfect Man" (*ensan-e kamel*) that had long been contemplated in speculative Sufism. He thus proposed an answer to the troubling question of the Hidden Imam's thousand-year longevity in a non-physical state by assuming the existence of his celestial prototype in the *horqalya* sphere. Though in his often cryptic works Ahsa'i never explicitly stated it, he allowed for the conclusion that the Hidden Imam would manifest himself in a new earthly body at the End of the Time.

Such a rendition was a radical departure from conventional Shi'i belief on the subject of the return of the Hidden Imam. The Imam's celestial existence not only facilitated visionary encounters with the Imam of the Age but also enabled his eventual return to the world of matter not as the son of the Eleventh Imam, who according to mainstream Shi'i belief had gone to Occultation a thousand years earlier, but in a new metaphorical human cast. Ahsa'i and his successor also reinterpreted the fantastic Signs of the Hour, which were a precondition for the apocalyptic return of the Hidden Imam. The Perfect Shi'a was perceived as a status reserved for Ahsa'i himself, and after him by his successor, Sayyed Kazem Rashti (1793–1843), as the person most conscious of the Hidden Imam and who would prepare the preliminary steps before his return. The Perfect Shi'a, and not the mojtaheds, in effect held the true mandate (*welayat*) on behalf of the Hidden Imam. Human perfection in the Shaykhi school, moreover, required the historical progression in the course of time and called for the eventual return of the Hidden Imam, when time is mature for him to reveal himself from the implicit world of prototypes into the explicit world of reality.

The millennial markers in the Shi'i calendar no doubt added to the Shaykhis' messianic preoccupation and its appeal. The approach of a millennium after the presumed Occultation of the Twelfth Imam in AH 260 (873–874 CE) corresponded to the year AH 1260 (1844 CE). The latter date played prominently in the Shi'i imagination, invoking messianic speculations. By the 1840s the Shaykhi school, under Rashti's leadership, had grown into a network distinct from that of the Usulis and in competition with it. Shaykhis consisted mostly of younger madrasa students and new mojtaheds trained under Ahsa'i and Rashti. They were critical of the Usuli jurists for their archaic madrasa education, their futile study of *usul al-fiqh* at the expense of moral and mystical dimensions of religion, and their corruption and excesses.

Ritual symbolism also played a remarkable part in dividing the two communities, especially the visitation of the sacred tombs and shrines. The Shaykhis performed the rite of visitation (*ziyarat*, in Imam Hosain's shrine in Karbala) by staying at the foot of the tomb, as a sign of respect, and by performing visitation in utter humility. The belief in the prototypical existence of the Imams made the ritual of visiting their tombs an existential experience. This contrasted the usual Shi'i practice of standing at the head of the tomb, embracing the shrine's outer case (*zarih*), tying rags and padlocks to it to make wishes, and reciting the visitation tablet rather routinely. In the eye of the Shaykhis, these acts were symbols of utter irreverence toward the Imam; hence the Shaykhi label of "head standers" (*balasari*) for the Usulis.

Shaykhi adepts were often of village or small-town backgrounds and accustomed to the austere life of the countryside, which was at odds with the lifestyle of some of the established mojtaheds in Iran. The associated Shaykhi merchants and artisans, to the extent we know about them, shared with Rashti and his students the ideals of material detachment and ethical rectitude, characteristics they no longer identified with the ulama establishment. The Usuli denunciation of Ahsa'i and attempts to excommunicate Rashti outraged the Shaykhi and further sharpened their aspirations for a messianic breakthrough. Rashti, whose inner circle recognized him as the "gate" (*bāb*) to the Imam of the Age, even foresaw a messianic revolt in the face of his Usuli harassers. Surely, the bloody Karbala rebellion against the Ottoman authorities hastened such expectations.

In 1842, the new governor of Baghdad province, Mohammad Jajib Pasha (d. 1851), harshly reacted to Shi'i defiance of the Ottoman authorities, which included establishing Sunni state courts in Shi'i cities. The gang leaders of the revolt in Karbala, and the Usuli mojtaheds who blessed it, heeded Rashti's attempts at mediation and resisted the pasha's warnings. The result was the Ottoman massacre of close to nine thousand Shi'i civilians, nearly half the population of the city of Karbala. The Shaykhi leader's willingness to cooperate with the Ottomans saved some lives. Those who showed allegiance to Rashti were spared, and Rashti himself emerged as a voice of moderation, presumably favoring the Ottoman judicial and administrative reforms. The heavy-handed assault, endorsed by the Sublime Porte, nevertheless was in brazen contrast to what the Tanzimat era of reforms was supposed to usher in: greater latitude toward minorities. In reality, it reasserted Istanbul's full control in place of the pro-Shi'i Mamluk rulers of Iraq.

To the Shi'i victims, the Turkish atrocity was another sign of Shi'i disempowerment in the face of Sunni oppressors. Only four decades earlier, in 1802, the Shi'is of Karbala and Najaf had witnessed a horrifying assault, that time by the marauding Wahhabi warriors of the Najd in the Arabian Peninsula who considered it their religious duty to massacre nearly five thousand Shi'i civilians and plunder and destroy Shi'i holy shrines. In both instances the killing of innocents and the defiling of the shrine of Imam Hosain distressed the Iranian public, and both times the upheavals demonstrated the Qajar state's inability to defend the Shi'is of Iraq or alleviate their suffering. It was against this complex sectarian backdrop that the Babi movement found its first adherents.

THE BABI MOVEMENT AND DOCTRINE OF RENEWAL

As a significant consequence of the Shaykhi teaching, the Babi movement echoed the ongoing crisis both in Shi'i Iraq and in Qajar Iran. In 1844, a young merchant from Shiraz called Sayyed 'Ali Mohammad (1819–1850) proclaimed to a small group of young Shaykhi mullahs who had come from Karbala to pay their allegiance to him that he was the "gate" (*bāb*) to the Truth. This was interpreted not only as a claim of Rashti's succession but also a representation on behalf of the Hidden Imam. The Bab, as he came to be known, called upon all believers to denounce the mojtaheds' authority in favor of his proclamation, for which he offered as proof verses composed in the style of the Qur'an. His messianic call for the imminent coming of the Mahdi attracted young converts across Iran and Shi'i Iraq among mullahs, seminarians, merchants and small-time bazaar retailers, artisans, urban and later village women, divan functionaries, small landowners, and soon villagers and landless laborers.

The loose network of the early Babi converts conveyed the new message to an eager public and to Shi'i authorities, calling on them to recognize the Advent (*zohur*) of the Bab as the only sacred source of authority, or else await dire consequences at the Mahdi's impending advent. The spread of the new movement stirred some enthusiasm in Shiraz, but soon the Bab and his followers were denounced heretics and became targets of growing harassment. Even the Shaykhis, loyal to the old school, turned against them. At the instigation of the mojtaheds, who feared the movement's rapid growth, government authorities intervened especially after the Bab claimed that he was the awaited Mahdi himself, and soon afterward when he further asserted that he was not only the Mahdi of Shi'i faith but also the initiator of a new prophetic cycle. His new religion, he claimed, had brought an end to the Islamic prophetic cycle and had initiated a new order in which Islamic shari'a and its representatives were no longer legitimate. Predictably, any claim to the imminent advent of the Mahdi, who was safely relegated to theological limbo, was bound to be treated as blasphemous.

In the coming years, Babi efforts to engage the ranking jurists in peaceful debate were dismissed offhandedly as ludicrous and heretical. Facing more persecution, the radicalized Babis called for more drastic action against their opponents, especially the ulama, whom they criticized for their illicit material gains, conservatism, and insolence toward the new prophet. Between 1848 and 1851 the Babis were forced to take up arms against the government. The move proved detrimental. By 1852, the movement had been suppressed and its leadership killed, exiled, or driven underground, only to reemerge as a clandestine religion of protest in the following decade. Eventually the prevailing faction within the movement, which denounced violence in favor of peaceful moral reconstruction, prophetic continuity, and interfaith tolerance, emerged as the Baha'i faith in the final decades of the nineteenth century (see map 4.3).

The young Bab, who was born to a family of petty merchants and clothiers with a clerical connection, had gained some business training in his family's outlet in Bushehr. When he first made his claims public, he was engaged in local trade in the south, importing tea and other items from India and exporting them along with dried fruits and other local products of the Fars province to the Iranian interior. The young Shaykhis who had given their allegiance to him were mostly from the villages and small towns of Khorasan and Azarbaijan. The Bab's proclamation in May 1844 marked a turning point in the evolution of the Shaykhi inner circle to an open movement with a public following. Shaykhi teachings, complemented with memories of sectarian tensions in Karbala, charged these eager followers. Their adherence to a young merchant from Shiraz with a reputation for sanctity and devotion but no clerical credentials was highly unconventional. It no doubt denoted a search for a charismatic leader from outside the sphere of the madrasa. Thanks to the energetic Mulla Hosain Boshru'i, the Bab's first convert and a key figure in shaping the movement, by 1848 there were Babi cells in most cities in Iran and in the Shi'i shrine cities of Iraq.

Almost from his first public proclamation in his hometown of Shiraz, the Bab was labeled a heretic and soon after put under house arrest (fig. 4.8). Even though for a while he took refuge with Isfahan's governor, Manuchehr Khan Mo'tamad al-Dowleh, who took a serious interest in him and his message, he was soon deprived of his protector. While still in hiding in Isfahan, sheltered by

Figure 4.8. The House of the Bab in Shiraz was typical of the merchants'
residences in southern Iran. The two-story structure is where the Bab
first proclaimed his mission and later was kept under house arrest.
Drawing by Houshang Sayhun, November 1976. Private collection.

the governor, at his request the Bab wrote a treatise on the validity of Mohammad's prophetic mission, an indication no doubt of Manuchehr's ambivalence
about Islam as a divine religion. That the Bab penned the treaties to convince
his patron also confirmed his belief in the cyclical recurrence of prophetic revelations, of which he considered himself the latest. However, upon the death
of the Isfahan governor, perhaps foul play devised by Haji Mirza Aqasi, the
Bab lost a powerful protector, and with him any realistic chance to successfully
expand his mission.

In 1846, unable to meet with Mohammad Shah, who had initially invited
him to the capital to hear his call, the Bab was rerouted halfway to Tehran by
the order of the premier, then sent off to the fortress of Maku in Azarbaijan,
a safe Aqasi territory at the northwestern corner of the Russian and Ottoman
borders (see map 4.3). It was in the seclusion of the remote fortress that he
articulated the Babi doctrine in his most systematic work, *Bayan* (lit. "explication" [i.e., of divine secrets]). Composed in the style of the Qur'an but with
heavy esoteric undertones, the *Bayan* offered a mélange of occult Shi'i beliefs,
elements of modern social ideas, and kernels of a cyclical view of history that
consciously strived to break away from Islam.

The Bab envisioned his mission as the most recent among prophetic cycles
that were divinely inspired and progressively renewed toward the gradual

perfection of humankind—what came to be known in Babi thought (and later for the Baha'is) as "progression" of the divine "megacycle." Messianic Shi'ism, whether in its Isma'ili era or during other trends in the Iranian world, long had adopted the idea of prophetic cycles, a notion shared with ancient Zoroastrian belief in Renewal (*farashkart*) at the end of consecutive millennial cycles. The Qur'an also accepted the idea of a chain of divine revelations that went back to Abraham and through the biblical line to Adam, the first human and the first prophet. Such concepts of religious reification seem to have had their origins in the Manichaean religion of the second century CE, which was widespread throughout the Iranian world. The Islamic orthodoxy considered Mohammad, the prophet of Islam, as the Seal of the Prophets (*khatam al-nabi'in*) and his religion as the most perfect and the final one until the End of Time. The idea of perfection through time cycles, however, was never abandoned in heterodox circles or in the speculative mysticism of medieval Islam. Though the theory of cycles was often reconciled with the idea of Islam's perfection, the idea of the advent of the Mahdi at the End of Time, especially in Shi'ism, remained the major conduit for survival of the idea of cyclical revelation.

The Babi doctrine interpreted Resurrection not as an apocalyptic destruction of the material world but as the eclipse of one revelatory cycle and the dawn of the next. Relying on a long history of millennial speculations, the Bab utilized the familiar metaphor of seasonal changes to explain the nature of cyclical progression. The "tree of prophethood," as he called it, blossoms in the spring, gains strength in the summer, bears fruit in the fall, and dies in winter, only to be reborn in the next seasonal cycle. It is the same tree and yet it is different every year as it grows with time. The sense of historical relativism embedded in this notion of prophetic renewal acknowledged historical change. It allowed for the potential for human innovation and promoted a forward-looking perspective, concepts that defied the essentially regressive worldview of the Shi'i orthodoxy.

The human potential for moral and intellectual growth through these cycles was immense. Echoing the Neoplatonic thought widely appreciated in the Persian mystical milieu, *Bayan* implied that humankind not only can climb to a prophetic status but in fact can surpass that status by mirroring the light of the divine sun in its entirety. The Babi intention was to make this reality explicit and final. The Babi endeavor, it can be argued, was striving to build in its own esoteric language an indigenous concept of modernity that relied on historical progression rather than the sanctity of the past. Likewise, it called implicitly for human agency rather than prophetic finality. In this light, the Babi message should be seen as the fulfillment of more than a millennium of Shi'i apocalyptic yearnings to break with shari'a, and more specifically with the shari'a that had been set in place with the rise of the Safavid Empire.

A MESSIANIC COMMUNITY IN REVOLT

The making of the Babi community in a way resonated an important social momentum. As a grassroots movement, it brought together, perhaps for the first time, converts from all over Iran, from different occupations and social groups, to share a new objective based on their own individual convictions rather than their traditional loyalties, geographies, or ethnicities. A national community in the making, it was independent of both the state and the ulama establishment, and it eventually opposed both of them. It was a network patterned more on the needs of the bazaar than of the madrasa, and therefore was symptomatic of mercantile and artisan aspirations and deprivations as well as those of other marginalized and underprivileged groups.

Its inconsistencies aside, and there were many, and its destructive preoccupation with fulfilling Shi'i messianic prophesies, the nascent Babi faith carried with it the kernel of a new national identity. The Bab wrote some of his works, including the *Bayan*, in Persian, which he considered a sacred language, like Arabic. Babi theology was encoded with scores of familiar Persian theosophical and mystical terms and notions. He designated his birthplace, the ancient Fars province, as the sacred land of the Bayan and the house in Shiraz, where he first declared his mission, the direction of the Babis' daily prayers. He adopted a "novel" (*badi'*) solar calendar consisting of nineteen months, with each month consisting of nineteen days. The start of the year was the Persian Nowruz celebration at the vernal equinox. The new calendar, with its first year being the start of his mission in AH 1260/1844 CE, was to replace the lunar Islamic Hijra calendar. A drastic change of calendar conveyed more than the sheer computation of time; it symbolically denoted the advent of a new era.

While still a junior merchant in the Persian Gulf port of Bushehr, the Bab had witnessed some display of Europe's industrial power and naval force. His "Letters of the Gospel" (*horuf-e enjil*), as he often identified the Europeans, were threatening and yet appealing—both characteristics that anticipated the Iranian ambivalence—and more generally that of the non-Western world—toward the West. In his writings he applauded European manufacturing and allowed for trade with Europeans within certain limits. He prohibited their commercial penetration into the land of Bayan unless they could bring useful trade and occupations. He considered their gifts ritually pure and acceptable. He praised their material advances, their cleanliness, and their outward dignity. He was impressed by their legible handwriting, efficient postal communication, and press and publications. Despite these approbations, however, the Bab believed that as long as Europeans denied the veracity of the prophet of Islam, they could not be saved on the Day of Judgment. He expressed hopes that in future they would welcome his true message and be included among the "letter of light."

Despite its novel potentials, the Bayani religion remained entrapped in the heterodox milieu in which it was rooted. The Bab viewed his own mission and those of his early followers as the fulfillment of the Shi'i Islamic prophecies. The Shi'i tragic narrative of martyrdom became even more tangible as he and his followers faced persecution and death. He saw his own mission not only as a Mahdi and a new prophet who brought a divine creed but also as the "return" of Imam Hosain, the paradigm of Shi'i martyrdom, an image of himself that anticipated his tragic end.

The Bab's growing following, with little direct supervision from their detained leader, continued in Khorasan, Mazandaran, and elsewhere. Concerned with the rapid growth of the new movement, the ulama persuaded the reluctant government of Haji Mirza Aqasi to act. A tribunal was held in the presence of the young crown prince Naser al-Din Mirza (1831–1896) in Tabriz in 1847 to examine the Bab's claims. There the Bab unequivocally declared himself none other than the Mahdi whom the Shi'is had been expecting for a whole millennium. The Bab's audacious claim had a number of important implications. For the first time in recent Islamic history, at least since the fifteenth-century Noqtavi movement, a conscious break from Islam came at a time when Iran was experiencing a period of socioeconomic inertia and foreign intrusion.

The Babi uprising that later began in 1848 was in some respects the fulfillment of the apocalyptic prophecies anticipated by the Bab and his early followers. While most mullahs among the Babis opted for a jihad scenario as perceived in the Shi'i literature, others began to articulate the meaning of the interregnum after the abrogation of Islamic shari'a and the coming of a new age. Perhaps the most pivotal figure among the Babi leadership, with no less influence in shaping the movement than the Bab himself, was a young woman—the poet, scholar, and revolutionary protofeminist Fatemeh Zarrin-Taj Baraghani, better known as Qurrat al-'Ayn (the apple of the eye) and by her Babi title, Tahereh (the pure). A remarkable figure in modern Iranian history, Tahereh is unique not only because she stood in contrast to the persistent misogynistic norms and attitudes of a patriarchal society but also because she represented a break from the prevailing shari'a limitations, which were palpable to women of her background.

Born to an influential and affluent family of Usuli mojtaheds in Qazvin, Ta-hereh shared with her mother, her aunt, and her sisters a rarely known example of women with literary and scholarly interests. Despite her family's predomi-nantly anti-Shaykhi stance—her senior uncle denounced Ahsa'i—she studied in Karbala under Rashti and acquired proficiency, a rare achievement for a women of her time. She accepted the Bab's claim in absentia and the Bab in return included her among his "Letters of the Living," a radical break from the gender barriers of the time. The Bab also defended her against the criticism of conservative Babis who were shocked by the young women's uninhibited demeanor.

An independent woman with a growing following, both female and male, Tahereh eloquently defended herself in Arabic before the mufti of Baghdad while under house arrest by Ottoman authorities on a charge of inciting anti-Shi'i sentiments. Married and with four children, but estranged from her hus-band, who was her first cousin, she was forced by family pressure to return from Karbala to Qazvin. Soon after her arrival, however, in 1847 she escaped house arrest when her uncle and father-in-law, the prominent Imam Jome'h of Qazvin, was assassinated by radical Babis. The assassination was the first violent Babi reaction to the rising tide of persecution.

Shortly after her flight, and while in hiding, Tahereh attended a crucial gath-ering of the Babis in the village of Badasht in northern Iran in June and July 1848. The meeting was convened to discuss the future of the movement and the fate of the Bab, who was incarcerated in another remote castle in Chehriq in western Azerbaijan, near the Ottoman border. In the course of deliberations Tahereh emerged as the leader of the radical faction, which was seeking not only a break with Islam but also open defiance of the Shi'i ulama.

Tahereh's public appearance at the Badasht gathering without a facial veil (*neqab*) during her public speech from a pulpit shocked her fellow Babis as a symbolic breach of one of the most sacred Islamic mores. This was probably the first instance in the history of Islamic Iran that an urban Muslim woman had intentionally removed her facial veil in public, an act that remained unre-peated for at least another half a century. Echoing the Bab, she argued that the Babi movement was an independent revelation that abrogated the Islamic cycle and that in the post-shari'a interregnum, religious obligations were no longer binding. In contrast, the charismatic leader of the opposing faction, the young Mulla Mohammad 'Ali Mazandarani, better known by his Babi name Qoddus, rejected a complete break with the Islamic past and viewed the Bab's mission only as fulfillment of Shi'i prophecies.

The Badasht debate brought to the surface a major dilemma. While Ta-hereh's position—that the Babi faith was independent of Islam—prevailed, the opposing camp succeeded in impressing on the gathering a need for a messianic jihad, a course of action fashioned by the Shi'i scenario of the advent of the Mahdi. Given the growing hostility the Babis were experiencing mostly from the ulama's corner, and the bleak prospects of any sympathies, let alone protection, from the Qajar state, the Babis could hardly have opted for a more disastrous course.

The fateful armed resistance in the fortress of Tabarsi in central Mazanda-ran during 1848 and 1849 embodied both of these tendencies (see map 4.3). Emboldened by prospects of a millennial victory and encouraged by the political unrest after the death of Mohammad Shah, a band of Babis from Khorasan headed by Boshru'i marched toward Azarbaijan to liberate the Bab from captivity. The armed Babi contingent, no more than two hundred in number, poorly equipped and poorly armed, faced harassment from the local government militia in the city of Barforush (today's Babol), where they were temporarily stationed. Fearing for their lives, the Babi contingent moved out of town and eventually took temporary refuge inside a small structure over the shrine of Tabarsi in the thick of the forest, some twenty-five miles south of Barforush. Fellow Babis, among them Qoddus, were soon joined by other Babis from all over Iran, as well as new converts from among the smaller landowners and peasants in the vicinity.

Loyal to their messianic vision, the besieged Babi party engaged the government forces for several months in bloody partisan warfare. Despite early successes, soon starvation, casualties, and low morale brought them to an ignominious surrender, which was followed by the execution of nearly all remaining fighters. As in many messianic movements of the same nature, the Tabarsi community, while still hopeful, lived an austere camp life with communistic ideals (fig. 4.9). Most significant, the leadership of the movement during the Tabarsi resistance evolved. Since the incarcerated Bab could not assume the movement's active leadership, both Boshru'i and Qoddus were identified as "risers" (*qa'em*), another name for the Mahdi that previously had been applied only to the Bab. The diffuse Babi leadership and democratization of the notion of the Mahdi were not entirely alien to the collective vision of its founder, as evident in the concept of the eighteen Letters of the Living and the utopian community modeled on the unity of nineteen. Deeply preoccupied with numerology and numerical value inherent in letters of the alphabet, the Bab held the number nineteen as the organizational cornerstone

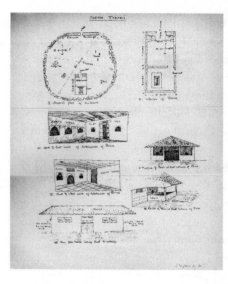

Figure 4.9. This drawing of Shaykh Tabarsi in 1888 by the young scholar
Edward Granville Browne is probably the oldest visual record of the Babi
stronghold. The humble size of the site and even smaller covered interiors of
the shrine reveal the trying conditions inside the makeshift fortification.
Edward Granville Browne, trans. and ed., *The New History of Mirza 'Ali Muhammad the Bab*
(Cambridge, 1893), opp. 56.

of his emerging community. Within this community the role of the Mahdi
could be shared among the "Letters of Living," a feature symbolic of the egalitarian traits inherent in the movement.

The failure of the Tabarsi community and the loss of more than four hundred
lives left a lasting mark on Babi morale. Other insurrections in Zanjan in northern Iran, in Nayriz in Fars province, and elsewhere lacked Tabarsi's revolutionary flair, even though they were as intense and as bloody as the Tabarsi affair. In
Zanjan, where the Babis briefly controlled some quarters inside the walled city,
there were more than five thousand Babi casualties in the factional fighting and
in clashes with government forces. The Nayriz uprising, in contrast, was fueled
by the peasants' revolt against landowners and tax collectors.

In all instances, the Babi message motivated dissent and gave the people a
sense of agency and hope for their eventual triumph. The Qajar state under
the new premier Mirza Taqi Khan Amir Kabir had to invest a great deal of its
military and financial resources to extinguish Babi insurrections. In 1850 when
the Bab himself was brought to Tabriz to be executed by firing squad, he stood

his ground to the end despite great pressure to recant and gain his freedom. His public execution in the courtyard of a military barracks, was the first in Iran to be conducted in the European military style. It was aimed not only at crushing the revolt and intimidating its sympathizers but also at displaying the restored power of the Qajar government under the new chief minister.

Two years after the execution of the Bab an unsuccessful assassination plot against the new ruler, Naser al-Din Shah (r. 1848–1896) cost the lives of the movement's remaining prominent leaders. In a frenzy of torture and killing orchestrated by the government, Qajar princes, the clergy, merchants, and bureaucrats took part in a gruesome mass execution. A short while after, Tahereh, who had been held in detention by the governor of Tehran, was brought before two mojtaheds who, after long and inquisitive debate, issued a death sentence on charges of blasphemy. One late night, in secret, a drunkard *gholam*, on the orders of the commander in chief of the army, killed Tahereh, suffocating her by stuffing a scarf in her throat. Her body was dumped in a shallow ditch at the edge of a garden outside the capital. At the time she was thirty-eight.

Tahereh's death signified the end of the first phase of the movement. Eight years into its inception, the Babi call had gained popularity despite widespread persecution of its followers. The movement's political defeat signified a chance to articulate a new, though sketchy, version of religious reform inspired by the inner dynamics of Shi'i Islam. This was at a critical juncture when Iranian society had become more conscious of its own national identity, more aware of external military and economic challenges, and more critical of the shortcomings of its own state and religious institutions. In this sense, the Babi movement was a messianic answer to the millennium-long unresolved question of temporal versus sacred authority. The concept of divine progression and renewed cycles, though not new in Iranian Shi'i thought, found a new resonance in Babi teaching. That the movement emerged just before Iran's full exposure to imported models of modernity in the second half of the nineteenth century adds to its significance.

Despite its many shortcomings, the Babi movement anticipated the alliance of small-time merchants, artisans, low-ranking clergy, and other voiceless and marginalized groups a half a century later during the Constitutional Revolution. The suppression of the Babi movement under Amir Kabir, a modernizer with Western notions of state-enforced reforms, in effect exemplified the clash between two visions of change. The state's actions did not eradicate the movement but forced it underground and banished abroad any remnants of its leadership. That the Babi project could not succeed in its original phase was in part because of its inability to disengage from its Shiʻi past. The Bab's language of prophecy and perception of change did carry the important kernel of renewal; however, it was often imbued with mystical and metaphorical language unable to create a cohesive program of rational modernity. In later decades, the division of the majority Baha'is versus the minority Azalis would reflect more than a succession dispute; it highlighted competing visions. Whereas the Azalis remained mostly committed to political dissent, the Baha'is eventually aimed for a universalistic vision of moral renewal.

During the leadership of Baha'ullah (1817–1892), the Babi movement—in a period of more than half a century, between the upheavals of 1852 and the virtual end to Ottoman exile in Palestine in 1909—adopted an ecumenical message of universal reconciliation and socio-moral modernity. Most of the Babis of Iran, first simply known as "People of Baha'," paid their allogeneic to the new prophet. Born to a family of affluent landowning officials of the Qajar divan, Mirza Hosain ʻAli Nuri—later known by his Babi title, *Baha'* (radiant glory) and afterward *Baha'ullah*, throughout the period of his exile in Baghdad (1853–1864) and later in the old Ottoman capital, Edirne, and eventually from 1869 to 1892 in the Ottoman penal colony of ʻAkka in Palestine—rendered a novel mystico-moral message. This was mostly a non-shariʻa rethinking of "divine command" (*amr*) that, unlike nearly all Islamic modernist trends of the time, tried to fuse the Perso-Islamic Sufi heritage of Iran (such as Sohravardi's Illumination philosophy) with European modern humanist and universalist endeavors. Moving beyond the then-prevalent paradigm of territorial nationalism, Baha'ullah did not remain impartial to some ideals propagated by some leaders of the Young Ottomans—his co-prisoners—and to the reforms of the Tanzimat era. His approach to such social notions as universal peace, racial and gender equality, economic justice, and the rudiments of a democratic model, were groundbreaking though mostly inspirational. As a step beyond Babi millennialism, the Baha'i message was fused with familiar Sufi imagery of the "sun of truth" projecting on the mirror of the human heart. Maturation of "human status" (*maqam-e ensan*), Baha'ullah argued, calls for human agency to define the world almost independent from the biblical and Qur'anic notions of divine intervention. The new rendering of the doctrine of the "Unity of Being" (*vahdat-e vojud*) appealed to the post-apocalyptic Babi community of Iran, which absorbed the evolutionary, rather than the revolutionary, message coming from ʻAkka and proselytized it through the nascent Babi network in the Iranian, and eventually non-Iranian, environments.

5

NASER AL-DIN SHAH AND MAINTAINING
A FRAGILE BALANCE (1848–1896)

In the second half of the nineteenth century, Qajar Iran survived as a sovereign state in the face of growing foreign pressures and domestic tensions. It did not break up and was not taken over by a colonial power. The Naseri era, as it came to be known, was dominated by Naser al-Din Shah (r. 1848–1896), who ruled over the country for nearly half a century. It was an era of gradual state consolidation, appeasement of the religious establishment, adjustment to European diplomatic and economic realities, and limited success with domestic reforms. Facing a host of economic problems, the era was marked by sporadic urban riots and popular protests. It also witnessed further material and cultural influences from abroad. A new generation of dissidents came to nurture a sense of despair about the future of their country but also a resistance to intervention by European powers. A stronger sense of national resolve began to emerge.

The government's modernization projects, starting with Amir Kabir's reform program at the outset of Naser al-Din Shah's reign, continued piecemeal, although the conservative Qajar elite resisted any substantial changes; there are similarities with what had come about in Meiji Japan or even in Khedivate Egypt or the Ottoman Tanzimat era. No modern industry of any substance emerged, except perhaps workshops established with European capital to export handwoven Persian carpets to Europe and America. Roads and communication remained underdeveloped. The modern educated sector constituted a small and largely ineffective part of the elite, and the political structure of the Qajar state remained more or less intact.

For the Iranian people, the Naseri period entailed some changes in their lifestyle. New technologies such as steamships and the telegraph emerged, and the consumption of commodities such as tea, tobacco, and sugar, as well as the purchase of European fabrics, became more common (map 5.1). Iranians came to learn more about the world beyond their familiar frontiers. The railroad, that great benchmark of the nineteenth-century economic progress, however, remained an unfulfilled dream, primarily because of Anglo-Russian imperial rivalries, but also because of insufficient capital. The lack of a modern rail and road network, whether a curse or a blessing, left Iran far less open than the rest of the Middle East, such as Egypt, to European capital and colonial projects.

The late nineteenth century also generated new intellectual syntheses and fresh artistic creativity in painting and architecture. Contact with Europe invigorated Iran's artistic and literary potential without, in most cases, undermining its cultural confidence. The Persian artistic imagination and exquisite craftsmanship survived without being entirely enamored of or bedazzled by the West. On the darker side, the Naseri era was marked by calamities—earthquakes and drought, devastating outbreaks of cholera and plague, and periods of famine— often beyond the capacity of the government's meager resources. Abject poverty and chronic starvation, in part because of changes in the pattern of agricultural production, and hoarding and interference in the flow of essential food items, became common in the cities and in the countryside.

The greater tranquility of a small but powerful landowning elite seldom trickled down to benefit the majority. Rather, wealth discrepancies sharpened social divisions and added to popular discontent. If the first half of the nineteenth century reconstituted the Guarded Domains of Iran under the Qajars, the second half was an age of national consolidation through common bonds of deprivation, and later, popular protest. So often such frustrations manifested in petitions to the shah, in taking refuge in shrines and royal palaces, and in spontaneous food riots. The final demarcation of Iran's geographic boundaries further distanced Iran from its neighboring ethnic Sunni communities and hence reinforced Iran's Shi'i identity. At the turn of the twentieth century, an average inhabitant of Iran, *ahl-e Iran*, as he or she was likely to be identified, was more conscious of a collective Iranian identity than a subject of the Qajar empire under Fath 'Ali Shah, even though he or she had not yet been exposed to the modern ideology of nationalism.

THE AGE OF AMIR KABIR

Few figures of the Qajar era have left their mark on Iranian historical awareness as did Mirza Taqi Khan Farahani (1807–1852), better known by his military title, Amir Nezam and, briefly, as Amir Kabir. He has often been celebrated as the champion of national sovereignty and his age as one of the missed

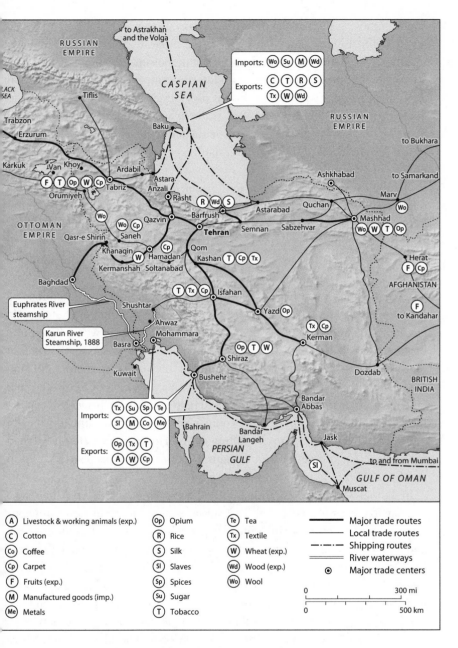

Imports: Wo Su M Wd
Exports: C T R S
Tx W Wd

RUSSIAN
EMPIRE

CASPIAN
SEA

to Astrakhan
and the Volga

to Bukhara

Tiflis

BLACK
SEA

Trabzon

Erzurum

Baku

RUSSIAN
EMPIRE

Ashkhabad

to Samarkand

Marv

Karkuk   Van Khoy
F T Op W Cp
Orumiyeh   Tabriz

Ardabil
Astara
Anzali

Rasht R Wd S

Quchan

Wo

Wo

Qazvin

Barfrush

Astarabad

Mashhad
Wo W T Op

OTTOMAN
EMPIRE   Qasr-e Shirin

Wo Cp
Saneh

Tehran

Semnan   Sabzehvar

Herat
F Cp

Khanaqin   Cp
W Hamadan
Kermanshah Soltanabad

Qom
Kashan T Cp Tx

AFGHANISTAN

Baghdad

T Tx Cp Isfahan

F
to Kandahar

Euphrates River
steamship

Shushtar

Yazd Op

Tx Cp
Kerman

Karun River
Steamship, 1888

Ahwaz
Mohammara
Basra

Op T W
Shiraz

Dozdab

BRITISH
INDIA

Kuwait

Bushehr

Imports: Tx Su Sp Te
Sl M Co Me

Bahrain

Bandar
Abbas

Bandar
Langeh

Jask

Exports: Op Tx T
A W Cp

PERSIAN
GULF

Sl

to and from Mumbai

GULF OF OMAN
Muscat

A Livestock & working animals (exp.)
C Cotton
Co Coffee
Cp Carpet
F Fruits (exp.)
M Manufactured goods (imp.)
Me Metals

Op Opium
R Rice
S Silk
Sl Slaves
Sp Spices
Su Sugar
T Tobacco

Te Tea
Tx Textile
W Wheat (exp.)
Wd Wood (exp.)
Wo Wool

——— Major trade routes
——— Local trade routes
—·—·— Shipping routes
=== River waterways
⊙ Major trade centers

0   300 mi
0   500 km

Map 5.1. Trade and trade routes in Qajar Iran

opportunities on the path of progress. He was portrayed as a martyr who had fallen victim to the court's intrigues, vested interests of the nobility, foreign machinations, and a deep-seated culture of despotism. The heroic aura aside, the reality of Amir Kabir's career is no less illustrative of the domestic and foreign obstacles on the way to the serious program of state modernization. During his brief term of office (1848–1851) as the first chief minister of Naser al-Din Shah, he strove to instill a new governmental order (*nazm*), one rooted as much in the Persian ideals of "good government" as informed by nineteenth-century notions of reforming the state.

As a middle-ranking bureaucrat in the Tabriz administration, Amir Kabir first made a name for himself in the mid-1840s as Iran's chief negotiator in the Perso-Ottoman boundary commission, where he negotiated the second Treaty of Erzurum. Eventually concluded in 1847, it placed Perso-Ottoman relations and especially agreement on pilgrimage traffic between the two countries on firmer footing. He later served as the secretary of the all-powerful Azarbaijan New Army and helped incorporate it into Iran's traditional forces. In his training as a state comptroller and in his reformist perspective, he was a product of the 'Abbas Mirza era and a protégé of the Qa'em-Maqam family, to whose household his father served as the chief cook. He shared with Haji Mirza Aqasi, to whom he was indebted for patronage and promotion, his humble background. Coming from a village in the Farahan region, Amir Kabir was snubbed by the Qajar elite no less than they had despised Aqasi. His aversion to the parasitic Qajar nobility and his desire to win over the young crown prince Naser al-Din Mirza in Tabriz also followed after Aqasi's path to power. He was more determined than his predecessor to hold the orderly reins of power and in his plans for reform and his foresight in implementing them.

In Tabriz, Mirza Taqi Khan first gained access to Naser al-Din Mirza, who was serving as prince-governor. The young prince was child of an unhappy arranged union between Mohammad Shah, who held little affection for him, and a powerful and protective mother, Jahan Khanum (later Mahd 'Olya), of the Qovanlu branch of the Qajars (see chart 2 in chapter 4). She had heavily invested in her son's accession to the throne, although Naser al-Din's childhood was one of parental neglect. He was viewed as feeble, unimpressive, and unworthy of the Qajar crown. A capable uncle of his, backed by the Russians, seriously disputed his right to the throne. After Mohammad Shah's death, Mirza Taqi Khan proved indispensible in bringing the young crown prince to the capital and help consolidate his royal power. He was like a father to Naser al-Din and a tutor, teaching his pupil how to act as a king, conduct the affairs of the state, and resist demands of his family members and court attendants. He intended to hammer out of the young shah a modern ruler: assertive, educated, and disciplined, perhaps having in mind 'Abbas I, three centuries earlier. To Naser al-Din Shah's credit, he opted for Amir Kabir and was prepared, to an extent, to listen and learn.

Typical of his age, Amir Kabir saw the military as the way to reorganize the government. His vision of overhauling the state was informed by such state reformers as Peter the Great, who had subdued the all-powerful but unruly Russian nobility, and the Ottoman Mahmud II, who had destroyed the remnants of the Janissary corps as a prelude to the Ottoman military and administrative reforms. Amir Kabir, who three times visited Russia and the Ottoman Empire, witnessed the fruits of these reforms. While in Tabriz he was also close to the British commercial consul, and as early as 1838 he had shared some of his aspirations for political power with the consul. His idea of ministerial control may well have been patterned after the famed Persian viziers of the past.

Amir Kabir's appointment in 1848, at the beginning of Naser al-Din's reign, to the triple office of *sadr-e a'zam* (chief minister), commander in chief of the army (*amir-e kabir*), and guardian (*atabak*) to the young shah came across as an unusual monopoly of power. It was visibly comparable to that of the celebrated Persian minister Abu-'Ali Hasan Tusi Nezam al-Molk, whose example may have been in Amir Kabir's mind. The young shah was obliged to grant him emergency powers while the country was in a state of political transition. His control of the Azarbaijan army and the orderly investiture of Naser al-Din to the throne made such a choice almost inevitable. By 1848, the Babi movement had reached revolutionary momentum. At the same time, a serious secessionist revolt in Khorasan, led by Mohammad Khan Salar, of the rival Davalu wing of the Qajar tribe, also loomed large. Salar was backed by Turkmen and Kurdish tribes of the northeast who resisted both the Qajar state's control over Khorasan and virtual exclusion of the Davalu Qajars from positions of power. To restore order, the premier relied on the New Army of Azarbaijan. In the three years that followed, he further reorganized the Qajars' mostly tribal military resources along the lines of the Azarbaijan corps. By 1851, the army had crushed both the Babi uprisings and the Khorasan insurrections.

Amir Kabir was also aware of the need for steady revenue to pay and equip a modern army. This required a sound fiscal policy and the creation of supporting institutions. The polytechnic academy that came to be known as Dar al-Fonun (abode of skills), the first Western-style educational institution, was in reality a cadet school designed to meet the army's needs for engineering, medical, and artillery officers as well as interpreters. Late in 1851, shortly after the downfall of its founder, Dar al-Fonun started to operate with a handful of

European instructors and some one hundred pupils handpicked mostly from among the sons of middle-ranking military and bureaucratic officials. The instructors consisted of a mix of Austrian, Italian, and French infantry, artillery, and cavalry junior officers, as well as a capable surgeon, a mine engineer, and a military surveyor, and language instructors in French, English, and Russian. Instructors communicated with their students through mostly Iranian Armenian teaching assistants, who later became part of the teaching staff. The college's building was an early example of Perso-European style, inspired by the design of the British Woolwich military academy and improvised by an Iranian engineer who studied there (fig. 5.1 and fig. 5.2).

The launching of a government gazette under the new premier was also a step toward modernization. The *Vaqaye'-e Ettefaqiyeh* (A chronicle of events) was meant to educate the public about Western advances and to enable the state to communicate with its subjects, especially provincial elites, in accessible and concise language. Here, Amir Kabir's initiative followed in the footsteps of 'Abbas Mirza's administration and the publication of the first newspaper in Tehran in 1837 under the editorship of Mirza Saleh Shirazi, later a protégé of Amir Kabir. Nearly two decades earlier a press in Tabriz, sponsored by Manuchehr Khan Mo'tamed al-Dowleh, the Georgian confidant of Fath 'Ali Shah, used

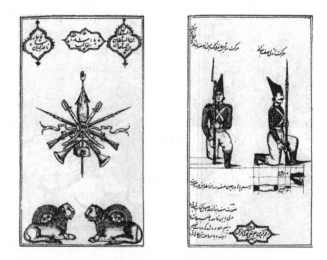

Figure 5.1 and Figure 5.2. Pages from the booklet *Qanun-e Nezam* (Military drill book) commissioned by Amir Kabir. The title page (*left*) bears Naser al-Din Shah's name and the lion and sun emblem of the Iranian state. Drill posture (*right*) is described with geometric precision. By 'Ali-qoli Kho'i (signed at the bottom of the right page). Courtesy of Ulrich Marzolph.

Persian movable type of the *naskh* style as early as 1819 to print a host of books, including a history of the Qajar dynasty and popular works by Mohammad Baqer Majlesi. By the 1830s other presses in Tehran and elsewhere had begun to produce lithographic publications.

Under Amir Kabir, and for more than a decade after him, the *Vaqaye'-e Ette-faqiyeh* reported government appointments and decrees, court and provincial news, and public announcements. It also offered foreign news, both Western and regional, and printed some of the earliest commercial advertisements. Emphasis on world geography and politics, including the earliest public information on the American continent and the United States government and people, new geographical explorations, and technological inventions and engineering feats, opened up a new vista for the Iranian readership. The United States was presented as a young nation successfully liberated from the yoke of English colonialism. In the following decades Qajar Iran witnessed, if not a printing revolution, at least a steady growth of private printing houses (fig. 5.3).

A considerable number of Persian books published in the Naseri era included religious texts, works of Shi'i elegy, ethics, poetry, popular tales, and some translations of European novels (fig. 5.4 and fig. 5.5). Before the turn of the twentieth

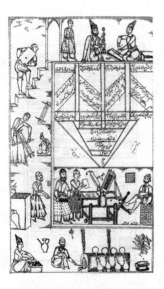

Figure 5.3. The process of lithographic printing, as shown by master illustrator 'Ali-qoli Kho'i, consists of seven stages of preparing the slates, calligraphy, and lithographic press. From the closing page of an 1847 edition of Nezami's *Khamseh*.
Courtesy of Ulrich Marzolph.

Figure 5.4. Head of Imam Hosain paraded by the enemies
(*ashqiya*) on the day of 'Ashura. Illustrated books of elegy such as
this amplified emotional effects of the Karbala tragedies.
Isma'il Khan Sarbaz Borujerdi, *Asrar al-Shahada* (Mysteries of martyrdom),
illustrated by 'Ali-qoli Kho'i (Tehran?, 1268/1851). Courtesy of Ulrich Marzolph.

Figure 5.5. Akvan carries away Rostam in sleep. The transvestite
demon (*div*) was a staple of popular illustrations of the period.
Shahnameh illustrated by Ostad Sattar (Tabriz, 1275/1858). Courtesy of Ulrich Marzolph.

century, newspaper publications inside Iran remained a listless endeavor firmly controlled by the state.

Beyond education and the press, Amir Kabir's modernizing strategy relied on harnessing the influence of foreign powers in the country's internal affairs. This is evident, for instance, in his resistance to British intervention in the Khorasan revolt or to Russian demands for a greater say in the affairs of Azarbaijan. His earlier affinity in Tabriz with Colonel James Farrant, who later became the British chargé d'affaires in Tehran in 1848, and with Colonel Justin Sheil, the British envoy who succeeded Farrant (both were British officers of the Indian Army who had been given diplomatic posts) facilitated British support and financing of Naser al-Din's march to the capital and accession to the throne.

Once in office as the premier, Amir Kabir did not hesitate to assert his independence. Like his predecessors, he viewed the British as a necessary ally and counterweight to the growing Russian threat. Yet he was careful to reserve Iran's authority over a range of issues, including trade regulations, protégé status for Iranian subjects, sovereignty over the Persian Gulf coasts, and the behavior of foreign diplomats at the Persian court. The dignity and sovereignty of the Persian state, he insisted, required that European representatives respect the Qajar crown but deal exclusively with the premier in all affairs of the state. Reversing Iran's growing trade deficit, export of precious metals under the pretext of trade, and shortage of cash required the enforcement of a strict monetary policy, an option that was not at Amir Kabir's disposal. Boosting the domestic manufacturing base was a realistic alternative. Expansion of the Tehran bazaar, including a spacious thoroughfare, the magnificent caravansary Saray-e Amir, and a complex known as Dar al-Sanaye' (abode of fine arts) devoted to the revival of fine arts and traditional crafts signaled the premier's interest in reinforcing domestic trade and manufacturing (fig. 5.6).

Finance remained Amir Kabir's greatest concern as he grappled with losses in state revenue, the legacy of the Aqasi era, and the rise in expenditures. In addition were the heavy cost of military campaigns, court expenses, pensions for the Qajar nobility, and reform projects, including new building construction. His experience as an army accountant no doubt helped with collecting taxes in arrears and reducing expenditures. Given the near bankruptcy of the state in 1848, a balanced budget proved daunting. Enforcing an austerity regime that cut all salaries and pensions in half across the board was daring but contentious. Reducing the young shah's "pocket money" brought constant nagging, and slashing the pensions of the court and divan officials bred serious grudge. With the accession of Naser al-Din Shah, a host of his maternal relatives gained prominence. Some of the paternal uncles of the shah served as governors and

Figure 5.6. "Weighing merchandise in a caravansary at Tehran" is
a realistic portrayal of everyday trade in Saray-e Amir in the Tehran
bazaar. The caravansary was founded around 1849 by Amir Kabir.
S. G. W. Benjamin, *Persia and the Persians* (London, 1887), 75.

army commanders, but few of his maternal relatives who were given provincial
offices rendered useful services.

Government accountants (*mostowfis*) resisted centralizing measures that limited their monopoly over finances and threatened their hereditary offices. Qajar
Iran's decentralized state accounting and the many abuses associated with such
a system worked against any modernizing initiative, and Amir Kabir's new appointments only partially strengthened his hand. Bringing some measure of discipline to the divan was a step forward. Likewise, the creation of a new agency,
the Government Bureau of Justice (*divan-khaneh 'adalat*) aimed to bring discipline to the otherwise muddled division between the mojtaheds' civil courts
and the government's control of customary law (*'orf*), which was responsible for
the adjudication of criminal cases.

The new agency also heard some cases involving foreign nationals and addressed other cases related to religious minorities. Frequent petitions from Jewish, Christian, or Zoroastrian families involved cases in which one of the heirs
to a deceased person momentarily converted to Islam and appropriated the
share of other survivors. Contrary to the shari'a courts, which routinely ruled in
favor of the convert, the Bureau of Justice aimed to prevent such abuses, in part
because some non-Muslims subjects involved in foreign trade were affiliated

with European embassies. The de facto division of state versus religious courts nevertheless continued to plague the Qajar system after Amir Kabir. The mutual reluctance of the ulama and the government to create a uniform code, such as the Ottoman civil code known as Majilla Ahkam 'Adliya, compiled during the Tanzimat era, served as a major obstacle to judicial reform.

That Amir Kabir relied on the shah's goodwill to implement his reform measures ignited, almost from the start, the enmity of the Qajar elite. They viewed him as haughty and monopolizing, and considered his draconian measures an unfair breach of their entitled privileges. His marriage at the age of forty-two to the thirteen-year-old sister of the shah, which he reluctantly complied at the shah's behest, generated further envy. In particular Mahd 'Olya (1805–1873) loathed Amir Kabir not only because the premier limited her access to the shah but also because of his effort to rein in the Qajar nobility. His anti-corruption measures to abolish the practice of *madakhel* as well as bribery and extortion by government agents, and his ban on the practice of taking sanctuary (*bast*) in holy shrines and in other safe locations by suspects or culprits of crimes, made him even more enemies. Barring many idles and busybodies from access to the shah and reducing the salaries and privileges begrudged many attendants and court functionaries. Close supervision of the shah's everyday affairs and his whereabouts, even cautioning him against engaging too much pleasure rather than discharging his royal duties, also had a cumulative effect of cooling Naser al-Din's affection and eventually his support for the chief minister.

Treading a narrow noncommittal path toward either of the two neighboring empires also caused trouble. Amir Kabir's diplomatic conduct was proper and considerate, but he did not hesitate to assert his independence and, if necessary, voice his opposition. He nurtured a controlled sense of resentment for European emissaries' unjustified interference in Iran's domestic affairs. Without idealizing him beyond his reality—as many nationalist narratives of the twentieth century have done—Amir Kabir can be seen as an anti-imperialist with a proto-nationalist vision. He resented the obsessive nitpicking of foreign envoys, who at every turn tried to check him and his policies even if they were not remotely threatening to the vested interests of their countries.

During the Aqasi era, when the full effects of the Treaty of Torkamanchay became evident, the neighboring powers missed no opportunity to embarrass and humiliate the chief minister, the shah, and the government, and to employ whatever was in their means to display their imperial superiority. Amir Kabir was adamant that he would not budge in the face of the kind of demands and pressures that were sustained by his predecessor. Yet he had to give in to their reasonable demands. He agreed, for instance, at least nominally, to the British request to ban torture. After much resistance he gave his implicit consent to ban the slave trade in the Persian Gulf as well. Contrary to Aqasi's time, seldom under Amir Kabir were there diplomatic crises caused by the Russian or British envoy demanding official satisfaction from the Iranian government for trivial cases.

It is undeniable that Amir Kabir had come to power with the British diplomats' financial and moral support. In response, he remained, for a while at least, indebted to them. His dismissal of the French military officers in the Iranian service and the subsequent break in relations with France, in order to please the British, was one obvious error of judgment. Aqasi had nurtured relations with France, despite the condescending attitude of the French representative, so as to balance the pressures from the British side. Friendly gestures toward Britain, although limited, had the additional cost of incensing the Russians. Although after assuming power Amir Kabir sufficiently distanced himself from the British, and in due course developed genuine differences with them on a range of issues, the Russian envoy in Tehran refused to label him anything other than pro-British.

By late 1851, Amir Kabir's growing isolation and diminishing power base became more apparent. The young shah, under pressure from his mother and her allies in the conspiring court and among ranking officials, turned increasingly fearful of his chief minister and guardian. He dismissed Amir Kabir from office in December 1851, a decision that proved to have grave consequences. Fearing for his life, a fate similar to Qa'em-Maqam's fifteen years earlier, Amir Kabir first sought some form of security from the shah and, later, when disappointed, from other quarters. Yet neither his plea for protection from the British envoy in Tehran, which was quietly denied, nor an offer of protection from the Russian legation in Tehran proved effective. Diplomatic involvement only added to the shah's suspicions and gave Amir Kabir's enemies a perfect excuse to conspire for his destruction. He subsequently was banished to Kashan, where he briefly stayed under house arrest in the nearby royal garden in Fin. Soon after, in January 1852, the shah dispatched a court confidant to Kashan with the secret mission of murdering Amir Kabir. While he was in a bathhouse in the Fin Garden, the executioners arrived. They cut his wrists open and let him bleed to death.

As some observers noted even in his own time, Amir Kabir was an exceptionally capable though autocratic statesman in the mold of the nineteenth-century modernizers. His vision of reform was top down, functional, and clearly designed to create a disciplined and orderly regime. He was inspired by the European ideas of material progress, by industrialization under the shield of a militarized state. Naturally such a vision could not tolerate an indigenous movement of religious reform such as that of the Babis, which was rooted in messianic aspirations and seeking finality to the unresolved Shi'i problem of authority. Clashes between the two visions were inevitable. Yet as it turned out, they both succumbed to the conservative Qajar rule that soon prevailed and endured in one way or another until the end of the nineteenth century.

OBSTACLES TO REFORM

The fall of Amir Kabir illustrated many obstacles in the way of state modernization. Above all, there was a clear shortage of financial and human resources. The state-enforced initiative envisioned by Amir Kabir lacked an independent base of power. His anticorruption agenda and his resolute conduct also deprived him of a network of allies and exposed him to the onslaughts of the Qajar nobility. It was another painful demonstration of the divan's inherent inability to free itself of the hegemony of the shah and his court. The Qajar establishment viewed Amir Kabir as a necessary tool and tolerated him insofar as he could return security to the land, prevail over the Babis and the Salar revolt in Khorasan, and bring about a semblance of order. Once these tasks were reasonably accomplished, the Qajar elite was ready to remove him from office, as in the past they had eliminated other "slaves of the sublime Shadow of God."

The formidable task Amir Kabir faced can best be measured by the state's income and expenditures. Iran's total revenue for the tax year 1851–1852, at the end of Amir Kabir's era, was no more than 3,177,000 tumans (US$7,731,000), of which 84 percent was in cash and the rest in grains and other agricultural products. In the late 1840s Iran's total revenue stood at 2,991,000 tumans ($7,475,000), of which some 60 percent came from four provinces: Azarbaijan, 20 percent; Tehran and adjacent provinces of central Iran, 16 percent; Fars, 13 percent; and Isfahan, 11 percent. The remaining 40 percent was raised from nine other provinces of the realm. This explains how the four major centers of political power in Qajar Iran—Tehran, Tabriz, Isfahan, and Shiraz—could maintain a certain degree of autonomy by relying on their own resources.

Even after Amir Kabir's financial overhaul, a quarter of the state income, almost 800,000 tumans ($2,000,000), was still spent on salaries, pensions, and divan expenditures, of which 67 percent was devoted to the ranking officials and to the royal household. Of this latter figure, one-third (i.e., 8 percent of state revenue) went to salaries of the shah and the royal family; 15 percent to Qajar khans and nobles; at least 20 percent to the court attendants, servants, royal guards, and the royal stable; and about 5 percent to the chief minister and his office and household. Of the remaining 33.5 percent, only 3.25 percent went to the officials and secretaries of the _divan-khaneh_ and 2.85 percent to poets, physicians, interpreters, and the ulama. The huge discrepancy between the Qajar establishment, which received 66.5 percent of the salaries, and the divan, which took only 3.25 percent, demonstrates the power and privilege of the ruling elite versus the rank and file of the central bureaucracy.

In the same tax year of 1851–1852, the total of 2,656,601 tumans ($6,640,000) of the state's annual cash revenue, some 12 percent went to such general expenses as gift giving, construction, the postal service, and other limited public works, and only 10.9 percent went to provincial expenses. A staggering 45 percent, however, went toward upkeep of the military. In early 1852 Iran's armed forces stood at least on paper at 137,248 strong, which included 94,570 infantry in fifty regiments, 23,419 cavalry in twelve regiments, 9,927 riflemen, 6,349 artillerymen (working with one thousand pieces of artillery), and 2,733 rural police. By comparison, in 1849, at the outset of Amir Kabir's term, the Iranian army was 92,724 strong. Sixty-seven percent growth in the size of the military in three years presumably was in response to the challenges the Qajar state faced, but also it is indicative of Amir Kabir's desire to build up Iran's defenses. The cavalry and most of the infantry were recruited from among the tribes. In the 1850s, of Iran's total population of nearly five million, no less than 50 percent were nomadic or seminomadic, 30 percent were villagers, and some 20 percent (about eight hundred thousand) were urbanites.

The tribal population scattered throughout the country made up more than 343,000 tents (the nomads were tallied by number of tents), consisting of eighteen tribes and subtribes in Azarbaijan (20 percent of the tribal population), nineteen in Fars (16 percent), twenty-seven in Khorasan (24 percent), and the remaining 40 percent in other provinces. There were at least nine major tribal groups: the Turkish-speaking tribes of Azarbaijan and elsewhere, the Kurds, the Lurs, the Bakhtiyaris, the Qashqa'is, the Arabs, the Baluch, and the Turkmens, as well as tribes throughout Gilan, Mazandaran, and Astarabad. These four divisions all together comprised at least 188 subtribes and clans of different sizes, languages, and ethnicities. They were vastly different in their habitats and often barely accessible to central or provincial authorities. Their extraordinary diversity made collection of taxes from them an arduous task, let alone any attempt toward greater centralization. Nevertheless, some form of capitation was collected from the tribes, which applied not only to women and children but also to animals. The tribal leadership was also obliged to render a seasonal tribute in the form of fighting men in addition to or in place of the taxes. That tribes honored even such a degree of compliance was a credit to the Qajar state.

Taxes on the urban population were set figures, about 10 percent in most cases, collectible through the bazaar guilds, to whose coffers individual members contributed according to the size of their business. There was also up to a 20 percent tax on rental properties. The greater burden of the taxes, however, was on the most accessible and the most vulnerable agrarian sector, which made up no more than 30 percent of the population. Invariably, government tax collectors were responsible for collecting the peasants' share of the taxes directly from them on the location and often in kind. The rates differed from province to province and ranged between 10 percent and 20 percent. The lack of a consistent and updated tax register and the diverse and complex system of land tenure and sharecropping allowed for a range of abuses, often taken for granted.

Amir Kabir's short term of office did not allow him to complete his intended reassessment and update of the land survey that had originally been made at the time of Karim Khan Zand, some eighty years earlier. His efforts to repossess some of the land tenures (*toyul*) and the crown lands that were misappropriated by the high officials in earlier decades barely contributed to the government's revenue growth. The vast number of estates around the capital, as many as ten thousand, that were appropriated under Aqasi and eventually brought into the possession of the divan, seems to have been returned to their owners. Yet even an increase in land taxes by as much as 10 percent angered the landed nobility. By the time Amir Kabir was deposed, the Qajar establishment was ready to return to the familiar pattern of governance.[1]

OLD WAYS AND NEW AMBITIONS

The appointment of a new chief minister (*sadr-e a'zam*), Mirza Aqa Khan Nuri (1807–1865), was a return to the traditional governance of the Fath 'Ali Shah era. It had every sign of a conservative "palace coup" aiming to benefit the Qajar nobility and affiliated bureaucratic elite. Beyond the influential Mahd 'Olya who was in cahoots with Nuri, the appointment of the new premier also enjoyed the active approval of the British envoy, Colonel Justin Sheil. At the time, Sheil shared with the young and insecure Naser al-Din Shah his suspicions of Amir Kabir's Russian leanings. Both sides, therefore, viewed the Anglophile Nuri as the way to block the possibility of Amir Kabir's return to power with Russia's blessing. The course of events further proved the intensity of the European powers' rivalry. Not only did it contribute to Amir Kabir's murder; it also plunged the shah and his new chief minister into a serious quagmire, most visibly in the disputed province of Herat, which the Qajars had long claimed as an inseparable part of Iranian Khorasan.

Nuri was a statesman of some complexity. A great tactician, though lacking strategic foresight and scruples, he was a persuasive negotiator and a skilled maneuverer. His gift was in the art of compromise, and he was seasoned by many years of the divan's scheming. His political conduct was conditioned by a mix of self-preservation—hence earlier acquiring the British status of protégé—and his advocacy of the old Qajar values was untouched by the modernizing outlook of his predecessor. His very appearance—he wore a long beard and a longer sheepskin hat, an embroidered silk gown, and loose trousers—was reminiscent of the style of Fath 'Ali Shah's era. His wit and comforting demeanor made him a new fatherly figure to the young shah, far gentler than Amir Kabir. Yet the tragic fate of his predecessor, a fate for which Nuri was partially responsible, persuaded him not to lose sight of the royal wishes and fickleness. To assert his maturity and independence, the young shah's *rite de passage* necessitated not only the destruction of Amir Kabir, his old tutor and guardian, but also reverting to the Qajar dream of territorial conquest and military glory.

Capturing Herat province was an obvious objective, even though it was bound to run counter to British wishes. The policy of keeping Afghanistan as a virtual protectorate, a costly Great Game enterprise, had already taken many British lives. Fearful of Russian advances through Central Asia, the Russophobes in Calcutta and London saw it as a move toward the Persian Gulf and the Indian subcontinent. Lord Palmerston (1784–1865), the British Foreign Secretary and conservative architect of British colonial policy in the early Victorian era, viewed Iran as a weak link, vulnerable to Russian pressure and an obstacle to the British grand strategy to unify Afghanistan. The 1853 agreement between Iran and Britain was an undeniable success for Nuri, who negotiated it with great diplomatic skill. It allowed Iran to interfere in Herat if Britain, or its adventurous Afghan ally, Dost Mohammad Khan, infringed on that province's neutrality. The young Naser al-Din Shah saw this diplomatic advantage as a prelude to securing Iranian suzerainty over Herat, what his father and, before him, his grandfather, 'Abbas Mirza, had failed to accomplish. London, however, began to have qualms about the agreement and his rapport with the Qajar government began to deteriorate.

The Crimean War (1853–1856) offered the shah and his premier a chance to strike a secret deal with Russia, at war with Britain and its allies, to secure support for the capture of Herat while British attention was diverted to other quarters. Suspicious of Iran's secret deal, London sent a new envoy, Charles Murray, to Tehran to underscore its annoyance with the Iranian government's desire to reassert control over Herat. But the quarrelsome British representative, who from the start was determined to teach the shah and his minister a lesson, soon found himself in the midst of an scandal caused as much by his own foolhardy conduct as by Nuri's scheme.

An utter scandal by diplomatic standards of the Victorian era, Murray was accused not only of having an illicit relationship with a sister-in-law of the shah but also of harboring her and her husband, enemies of the premier, inside the British legation. The envoy's hard-to-satisfy gentlemanly honor, so closely tied up with the British colonial ethos and prestige, was injured. The resulting break in diplomatic relations between the two countries came as a golden opportunity to the shah, who almost immediately dispatched troops to Herat. Over the protests of the British authorities and at the expense of draining the treasury, the Iranian troops captured the city in October 1856 after many months of laying siege against Herat and the seemingly impenetrable walls of its citadel. The conquering prince commander Morad Mirza Hosam al-Saltaneh, a valiant uncle of the shah, even struck a victory coin and ordered the Shi'i call to prayers to be announced from the minarets and the name of the shah to be included in the Friday sermon in Herat's mosques.

Qajar sovereignty over Herat did not last long. Soon the British Indian fleet appeared at Bushehr with as many as fifteen thousand British troops and sepoys. By January 1857, British forces had penetrated deep into Fars province. Although the tribal militia of Tangestan and Dashtestan in southern Fars put up a stiff resistance and inflicted some casualties on the advancing British, the regular Iranian forces were slaughtered by the enemy in the battle of Khushab. Fearing further territorial loss, the demoralized Qajar government hastily withdrew from Herat with no visible accomplishment in exchange for the cessation of all hostilities with Britain and the resumption of protracted peace negotiations. Yet British punitive actions did not end even after a peace treaty was negotiated in March 1857 in Paris. Under General Outram, a commander with many colonial credits under his belt—including humbling the rebellious people of Afghanistan and Sindh, the British fleet reached the head of the Persian Gulf and in late March heavily bombarded the Iranian port of Mohammara (today's Khorramshahr) (fig. 5.7). At the end of the 1857 Paris peace treaty, mediated by the French emperor Napoleon III, Iran was obligated to renounce any territorial claims over Herat or any other part of Afghanistan.

The Paris peace treaty represented a turning point in Iran's relations with Britain just as the 1828 Torkamanchay Treaty did with Russia. The Herat affair made clear to the Qajar state the grave consequences of militarily engaging a European colonial power. The shah and his government realized that negotiation, brinksmanship, and the politics of balancing the two empires on Iran's opposite borders were the only realistic alternative. In the age of empires, it

Figure 5.7. British Indian Navy bombarding Mohammara in 1857.
G. H. Hunt, *Outram and Havelock's Persian Campaign* (London, 1858), frontispiece.

became painfully apparent that Iran would have to accept the loss of territory on its periphery for the sake of preserving its center. The loss of Herat, like the Caucasian provinces earlier, demonstrated the limits of sovereignty over regions that historically and culturally were parts of greater Iran but could no longer remain provinces of the Guarded Domains.

Four years later, another loss of a nominal vassalage, the city of Marv and the surrounding province of Iran's northeast, further proved the inevitability of abandoning the difficult-to-control frontier lands. The continued Turkmen raids in northern Khorasan and the abduction of thousands of Iranian captives further blemished the image of the Qajar crown. In 1861, a campaign against the Tekkeh confederacy was poorly organized and badly executed, ending disastrously with many casualties and troops falling into Turkmen captivity. By 1862, it was reported, the price of Persian slaves in the Bukhara market dropped to as low as five English shillings.

DISCONTENT AND HALFHEARTED REMEDIES

By the early 1860s Iran began to experience new forms of popular unrest. Recurring famine and devastating outbreaks of cholera, which continued well into the twentieth century, became familiar features of the Iranian social landscape.

The state's failure to effectively deal with these calamities lowered its prestige among its subjects, as did shifts in the economy. Riots in the capital and in the provinces, and a string of real or suspected assassination attempts, resulted in the government's repeated punitive actions but to no avail.

Violence toward urban and rural subjects visibly increased, putting the government on the defensive. Cruel practices, such as bodily mutilation, subsided in number except in the case of such heretics as the Babis and later the Baha'is. Yet there were enough punitive actions still in place to intimidate the public. The widely used *dagh va derafsh* (branding and piercing), carried out by the court's chief discipliner (*nasaqchi-bashi*), was a reminder of the centrality of punishment to the Qajar system. It ranged from the most popular bastinado (*falak*) to more violent modes of torture, imprisonment, and execution. That even the ranking state officials were not entirely immune from bastinado, at times by instantaneous order of the shah or a prince-governor, pointed to the egalitarian nature of the practice—a symbolic display of royal control over the fate of servants and subjects at large.

Bread riots were a common feature of urban life with greater regularity from the mid-1850s onward. They were in part caused by the landowners and government officials who hoarded their grain to bring about a price hike, and so maximize their profits. Poor interprovincial communication was another cause. Moving toward a market economy and the production of cash crops, such as tobacco and opium, also affected grain production (see map 5.1). Occasional tax relief lightened the burden of the peasants in famine-stricken regions, but taxes were often recouped by a heavy-handed collection in the following year. In the long term, concentration of wealth in the hands of a tiny elite, including the landowning notables, Qajar princes, high-ranking officials, and tribal khans, meant the impoverishment of the multitudes. The house of Qavam (the family of Mirza Ibrahim Kalantar Shirazi, the fateful first premier of the Qajar era) is but one example of urban elites' ability to endure throughout the Zand, Qajar, and early Pahlavi periods thanks to large landholdings, control over urban offices, and the administration of tribal confederacies in their provinces.

Nuri's regime itself was grounded in amassing wealth. His network of relatives and subordinates drew enormous salaries from the state's coffers. By the late 1850s his annual salary alone topped sixty-five thousand tumans. It was not without reason that he remained suspicious of, if not entirely opposed to, measures that could improve the government's performance and increase revenue. Contrary to Amir Kabir, he kept the shah at bay and indulged him with nighttime feasts, hunting, leisure, and a barrage of gifts and flattery. Even the shah's favorite wife, Jayran Khanum, a dancer of humble origins whose meteoric rise inside the royal harem caused much envy, fell short of derailing Nuri. Yet the premier's old-school politicking was bound to run aground as the shah, then more financially astute, came to realize the enormous cost of Nuri's administration. The Nizamiyeh mansion Nuri had built for his family was the most ostentatious symbol of his wealth. By 1858, after seven years serving as *sadr-e a'zam*, the Nuri era came to an abrupt end. Not unlike Amir Kabir, he was dismissed and exiled to the Iranian interior, from which he never returned. Humiliated and broke, in 1865 he died under suspicious circumstances, clearly arranged by his enemies and with the shah's consent.

Nuri's dismissal brought to an end the prime ministerial epoch that had been in place since the 1800s. Even if chief ministers were frequently dismissed, and occasionally destroyed, the office itself survived apart from the court. Direct rule—the shah's taking on of government responsibilities—removed even partial ministerial autonomy, at least for the time being. It also promised a more efficient government, a desperate move, no doubt, to break through the chief ministers' monopoly. In the long term, direct rule resulted in a haphazard system of petty bickering between the conservative and reformist factions of the government. It also ransomed off the government to the whims of a capricious but shrewd ruler. He organized new ministries and created a cabinet of ministers under his direct supervision. Shortly afterward, he also convened a consultative council, whose members were mostly from among the officials and elites, with a few progressives in their midst. Yet once the council embarked on even minor municipal reforms, these were sufficient to raise the shah's innate suspicion toward delegation of power. Within a year the council became almost defunct—the same pattern would repeat itself many times in later years.

In introducing reform measures, the shah for a while was inspired by the French model under Napoleon III and his project of reconstituting an authoritarian imperial regime. Among Iranian advocates of reforms was the celebrated Mirza Malkom Khan (1833–1908), a young French-educated diplomat, teacher, and political essayist who was close to the shah. An Armenian from New Julfa who converted to Islam, he had witnessed the 1848 revolution and the Paris Commune. After his return to Iran, he was discovered by Nuri and included in the Iranian mission to the Paris peace negotiations. His political essays, written in simple Persian prose and mostly circulated anonymously and in manuscript form, sought a model of state reform compliant with the Qajar establishment's conservative view of government. His "Essay from the Invisible" (*ketabcheh-ye ghaybi*), written circa 1858, promoted a model of government not dissimilar from that of the Ottoman Tanzimat (which had been reaffirmed by the sultan's 1856 Imperial Rescript) but also inspired by Russian constitutional absolutism and the French Second Republic. His "orderly absolute monarchy" called for a constitutional government based on enforcement of the law (*qanun*) and a legislative council (*majles*) whose members were to be appointed by the shah. Most of Malkom's proposed constitution concerned administrative and state affairs and steered clear of the domain of the shari'a. The shah was recognized as the ultimate source of all decisions, but the legislative task of the council was clearly distinguished from the executive power of the cabinet. The latter consisted of ministers appointed by the shah for education, justice, war, foreign affairs, and other departments.

Malkom's call for the urgent undertaking of state reforms was closely tied in his essay to the danger of Europe's colonial expansion and how Iran should withstand it. In a dramatic tone, he urged the "chief minister" to whom he addressed his essay:

> Put the map of Asia in front of yourself and read the history of the past one hundred years and examine carefully the course of the two bursting deluges that were propelled in the direction of Iran from Calcutta [the first administrative capital of British India] and St. Petersburg and see how these two streams which in the beginning were not noticeable in a short time became so great. . . . [You can then] see two deluges that from one side reached Tabriz and Astarabad and from the other side entered Herat and Sistan. Then you can tell how many minutes remain in the life of this state.[2]

Malkom's cautionary words were among the earliest conceptual expressions in Persian political literature of Europe's imperial threat. It is doubtful that the newly appointed council ever considered such a caution or took into account Malkom's recommendations, let alone implement them.

Shortly after Malkom Khan produced his early treatises, he also formed a semi-clandestine society around 1861 in Tehran to further his reformist agenda. The Faramush-khaneh (house of oblivion), presumably modeled after Masonic lodges (and vocally sounded like the word *Freemasonry*), was the earliest modern political association independent of the state. As in his "Essay from the Invisible," here, too, Malkom relied on the familiar Persian notion of secret society to further his political agenda. The society was headed by the progressive prince Jalal al-Din Mirza, a son of Fath 'Ali Shah, and later the author of the first modern history textbook in a "pure" Persian prose devoid of Arabic words and with a nationalist overtone. The society included a handful of literary figures, poets, historians, liberal clergy, and a number of Babi affiliates and freethinkers. Though little is known about the society's activities, thanks to the Qajar state's effective eradication of most evidence, it must have been significant enough to draw the hostility of conservative elements within the court who managed to invoke the shah's gravest suspicions.

As quickly as Naser al-Din Shah forgot about the council, he also lost interest in Malkom and his initiative to create a semblance of a political party. Retracting his earlier reform measures, in what could only be called a military coup, in 1864 the shah appointed a conservative Qajar army officer, the head of the royal guards, as commander in chief of the army and granted him extensive civilian responsibilities. Soon a royal decree banning the Faramush-khaneh was followed by raids on the society's headquarters, arresting some, intimidating others, and driving into exile the most vociferous among the members. Some may also have been murdered. Malkom himself, along with his father, Y'aqub Khan, who served as Persian secretary of the Russian mission in Tehran, was allowed to take refuge in the Ottoman capital. Alleged subversive activities were the official cause for the clampdown, even though the society's debates, insofar as we know, barely went beyond Malkom's proposed program of orderly constitutionalism. Even debating such issues as civil liberties was sufficiently threatening to the shah and the conservative elite to bring about the closure of the clandestine Faramush-khaneh, let alone an alleged call for republicanism.

With its closure, all hopes for political reforms were dashed for at least another decade. The conservative camp, whose advocates viewed any measure of political modernization as a conspiracy to destroy their vested interests, prevailed, and in the coming years the shah and his government opted for minimum, and mostly cosmetic, changes in the organization of the state.

ECONOMY IN DISARRAY

Fiscal and monetary reforms that had been earlier contemplated, even on a limited scale, also were met with laxity and nonchalance. The powerful class of government accountants (the *mostowfis*) jealously guarded their trade secrets and resisted a centralized revenue and expenditure regime. The Ministry of Finance (*maliyeh*), created in the early 1860s on the Ottoman model, proved largely window dressing, with minimal operational control over the *mostowfis*. It was neither capable of implementing an efficient fiscal policy nor able to put an end to bickering between the rival factions. By the very end of the Naseri period, the Qajar statesmen still could not clearly or permanently differentiate the government treasury from the shah's own private purse, the latter normally administered by some trusted wife of the shah—one of the many whom he kept busy with a variety of semiofficial tasks. Even basic measures introduced by Amir Kabir were left to wither.

The practice of annually auctioning off provincial posts to the highest bidder was more damaging than beneficial for efficient governance of the provinces. From the late 1860s, the shah pursued the sale of offices with greater vigor once his senior uncles were no longer in full control of provincial posts. The sale of provincial posts were intended to maximize revenue rather than bar governors from laying roots in provincial seats, a policy leading to increased abuse over the decades. Often irrespective of the suitability of the appointee or the methods of tax collection, and to the detriment of the peasants who ultimately bore the burden, the shah and his ministers received in advance a fixed sum in exchange for approving a candidate to office. The appointees to these revolving-door governorships came from a small clique of princes of the royal family, ranking bureaucrats, and court hangers-on. They bid for these offices in the expectation of regaining their investment plus a handsome profit, which was essentially the royally approved form of extortion.

Even if the appointees were experienced and merciful souls, often the unrealistically high monetary commitments that they made to the central treasury left little room but for them to pressure the district governors and their menacing tax collectors. They were responsible for extracting taxes from the peasantry, at times up to their last penny or the last bag of fodder for their donkeys. The landowners, who were mostly local nobility and tribal chiefs, often bore little or no responsibility for honoring their share of taxes and offered little, if any, shelter to their peasants from the state's tax collectors. Once the landlords took their share from the harvest, based on a sharecropping arrangement, the field was open for government agents to collect, and by means of physical punishment if necessary. Crop failure because of droughts, locusts, or other natural disasters occasionally exempted villagers, but not always. It was not uncommon that villagers would evade the tax collectors by taking refuge in the mountains or hiding in underground shelters, even at the expense of losing their crops and livestock, their livelihood.

Yet despite all the harsh measures, the voracious governors not infrequently ended their annual term with a loss, collecting less than they paid the state's treasury. Although from the 1860s, improved security and reduced troop movements—which often relied on villagers for provisions—brought greater prosperity, they did not substantially improve the peasants' lot. The shift in the patterns of landownership—most significantly, the transfer from crown lands to private ownership—reduced the state's direct control over properties that for generations had been assigned as *toyuls* to government servants and beneficiaries. Other incentives, especially the production and export of cash crops, did not substantially increase the state's revenue from the agricultural sector.

Like most non-Western societies of the time, Iran simply did not generate a substantial volume of wealth comparable to that of the industrial world. Beyond cash crops that could be marketed abroad to earn currency and the foreign trade that enriched a handful of Iranian merchants, but mostly European firms and their subsidiaries in the import-export trade, no other sector promised a major source of income (see map 5.1). The bazaar chronically suffered from decline in traditional manufacturing and loss of market share to European imports, especially for textiles, metals, and luxury goods. Foreign trade was brisk and merchants engaged in it were the chief beneficiaries. In the second half of the nineteenth century, opium and tobacco increasingly came to dominate the export market and helped maintain Iran's fragile balance of foreign trade. Only from the 1870s did the Persian carpet industry offer a viable export alternative to agricultural commodities. The export of Persian carpets to the United States, Europe, and Russia remained mostly in the hands of English and Italian firms or Greek and Armenian subjects of the Ottoman Empire.

To the elite of the Naseri period, however, any concerted effort to industrialize appeared untenable. A program of introducing modern industries, even remotely comparable to that of Meiji Japan or the Khedivate period in Egypt, was perceived as unrealistic. Naser al-Din Shah simply could not see the advantage—and there were good reasons for his technophobia. Lack of capital, either in the private or the public sector, was the most obvious. The urge to industrialize was absent from the Qajars' reform agenda since most reform-minded statesmen of the period continued to advocate for reorganization of the machinery of the state rather than expanding the country's economic base. The few efforts under Amir Kabir, and later under Moshir al-Dowleh, to establish small-scale industries, such as candle making, glassworks, and sugar refineries, were short lived. Inept management and inadequate capital played a role, but so did the absence of an industrial infrastructure. A trade-oriented market economy, as opposed to an industrial economy, was traditionally held as the accepted, even revered, norm. Private capital was perceived as being far better invested in foreign and domestic trade than in industry. Even the surplus capital from trade, which was substantial, was reinvested in agriculture or moneylending rather than in the risky business of factory-based industries. The merchant capital that financed much of the small-scale local industries in and around the bazaar, such as textile looms, never grew into larger industrial concerns.

The high interest rates common in the market, as high as 20 percent or 25 percent annually, absorbed much of the merchants' surplus capital. Despite Islam's strict prohibition on usury, merchants borrowed from or acted as moneylenders through such religiously sanctioned practices as the interest-bearing agricultural and commercial loans. Before the establishment of European-style banking in Iran, the Muslim merchants competed with the small-scale Jewish and Zoroastrian moneylenders in one of the few areas that minorities could excel. The chronic paucity of funds, which was in part due to monetary disorders caused by the European export of Iranian precious metals, further added to the sky-high interest rates and in turn the shift of excess capital to moneylending. Before the turn of the twentieth century, there was a near consensus that Western industries were supreme, and any competition with them would be fierce and insurmountable. And surely British trade policies of the Victorian era knew no bounds in undermining their competition overseas, least of all in a fragile economy such as Iran's.

At no time over the course of the Qajar period did European powers encourage the import of new technologies and industries or allow Iran to adopt policies to protect domestic manufacturing. As far as they were concerned, Iran was a limited but promising export market for European manufactured goods. To reduce the yawning gap in its balance of payments, all Iran could hope for was to export raw materials in exchange for European imports, which in reality meant only a few agricultural commodities, carpets, and livestock (especially horses and mules) to British India. The shah and his advisers were content that Iran was a partner, albeit a minor one, in the world economy (fig. 5.8). Even the construction of railroad, the backbone of a modern infrastructure, was largely seen as a means of expanding trade rather than creating an industrial base.

As demand for market commodities such as cotton, opium, and tobacco grew in the international and domestic markets, so did the merchants' direct investments, especially in Fars, Isfahan, and Azarbaijan (see map 5.1). Streamlining all stages, from production to processing to wholesale and export, promised a higher rate of return. When it came to the profitable opium trade, Iranian exporters were willing to dodge the British maritime regime and compete with the British opium monopoly in the Chinese market (fig. 5.9).

An enormous increase in the domestic consumption of tobacco also offered new investment opportunities. Increasingly, landowners, among them merchants and mojtaheds who purchased crown lands directly from the government or indirectly from fief holders, turned into cash crops, notably because the production of raw silk had been nearly wiped out by diseases. The shift in commodities was one contributing factor to the horrible famine that ravaged Iran between 1869 and 1871, claiming, according to some estimates, more than a million lives, or about one-sixth of Iran's population. This was perhaps the greatest calamity to strike Iran in the nineteenth century.

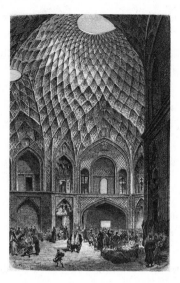

Figure 5.8. Amin al-Molk's caravansary, created with a charitable endowment in Kashan, is an architectural masterpiece of the early Naseri era. It is one of many multifunctional trading establishments in the Iranian bazaars and a venue for domestic and export trade.
J. Dieulafoy, "La Perse, la Chaldée, et la Susiane," *Le tour de monde* (1881–1882), fascicule xi, 99.

Figure 5.9. A Frenchman supervises preparation of pharmaceutical opium in Isfahan in 1881. British and European firms initiated export of the Iranian opium, but Iranian merchants soon began to participate in the production and export of this lucrative commodity.
J. Dieulafoy, "La Perse, la Chaldée et la Susiane," *Le tour du monde* (1881–1882), fascicule xiii, p.125.

Food shortages during the 1871 famine were compounded by consecutive bad harvests as a result of exceptionally harsh winters. Export of grains to neighboring countries for higher prices also contributed to the shortage. Bread riots and disturbances across the country became more common in response to the mischief of those landowners, prince-governors, wealthy clergy, and the high-ranking officials who hoarded their grain supplies in the pitiless expectation of higher prices. The starving crowds, often with women at the forefront, gathered in the mosques in protest and in front of government houses, cursing the Qajars, the mojtaheds, and the landlords alike and even attacking and plundering the grain silos.

As the famine intensified and food supplies further dwindled, people were forced to eat grass, tree bark, stray dogs and cats, beasts of burden, rodents, crows, and the entrails and blood of slaughtered animals. There were plausible reports, as in Qom, of eating corpses and abduction of young children—mostly orphans—as well as widows and homeless strangers. Even though the starving population mostly viewed recurring famine and ravaging epidemics as acts of divine punishment and fateful calamities, there was also growing resentment toward the state authorities for their indifference and for collaborating with the hoarders. The famine further revealed to the people the government's inability, if not incompetence, to remedy in a meaningful way the misfortunes that had befallen them. The means of relief available to the government were limited. The shah's decree (*farman*) banning the export to Russia of grain produced in the north was largely ignored, and at any rate it would have little impact on the central and southern provinces, where the famine was worst. With the famine compounded by raging cholera and banditry, it became almost impossible for the government to transport large quantities of grain on the backs of camels and mules.

THE AGE OF MOSHIR AL-DOWLEH

The dire situation helped in the appointment in early 1870 of Mirza Hosain Khan Moshir al-Dowleh (1828–1881) as *sadr-e a'zam*. A seasoned diplomat, one who for many years had served as ambassador to the Ottoman court, his rise to power signaled the shah's periodic return to the idea of reform. First serving as minister of justice in 1870 and soon after as *sadr-e a'zam* (1871–1873), Moshir al-Dowleh later intermittently, or concomitantly, depending on the shah's fickle mood or his fear of a conservative revolt, served as foreign minister and war minister. In reality, his wide range of responsibilities turned him into the leading statesman for the rest of the 1870s.

Frequent vacillation in Moshir al-Dowleh's posts no doubt was because of the shah's ambivalence to revert to the office of *sadr-e a'zam* after a hiatus of seven years. Hosain Khan Moshir al-Dowleh, who would later receive the title *sepah-salar* (commander in chief of the army), brought new hopes for the stranded program of institutional reforms but also posed the danger of monopolizing power. Having served many years in Tiflis, Mumbai, and Istanbul, Moshir al-Dowleh's vision was largely shaped by a centralizing model of state governance through a diplomatic prism. He was a keen observer of the Tanzimat and a close friend of the Ottoman statesmen who presided over it. He was sharp, amicable, and politically skilled, and also corrupt, willing to amass massive wealth at the expense of his professional integrity.

By the beginning of the 1870s there was a new concern, fueled by the British, that Iran and Afghanistan would eventually fall victim to Russian expansionism and become vassalages of the tsar. As an astute statesman, Moshir al-Dowleh hoped to capitalize on these anxieties. By presenting Iran as a viable buffer state on the road to modernization, he also hoped to overcome the shah's earlier ambivalence toward reforms and to make gains against the conservative camp. By appointing Mirza Malkom Khan as the Persian minister plenipotentiary to London, he anticipated making a fresh diplomatic start with London. Malkom's return from exile was followed by the appointment of a number of other reform-minded statesmen and, to some degree, the opening of the public sphere. All the same, he proved vulnerable to the wishes of the shah and unable to ward off the conservatives in the divan and among the nobility, who eventually outmaneuvered him just as they had his predecessors.

Expanding and streamlining the institutions of the state were the primary objectives of Moshir al-Dowleh's administration, most significantly in the ministerial divisions, but he also aimed to create a centralized judiciary, a unified fiscal policy, and an efficient army. His efforts to remedy the chaotic divisions between the jurisdiction of the mojtaheds' civil law courts and the divan's haphazard enforcement of an unwritten customary penal code encountered antagonism from both sides. The ulama opposed even modest measures such as transparency in boundaries of clerical jurisdiction or the creation of an administrative sorting house to allot litigation to the appropriate court. The local governors and their judicial officers, especially such powerful prince-governors as Mas'ud Mirza Zell al-Soltan in Isfahan, however, viewed centralized supervision as irksome meddling in their prestige and authority.

Modernizing Iran's military, to the extent of maintaining a viable force for the purpose of domestic security, also ran into trouble. Despite the Qajars' inflated pride in their military culture and their pretense of power, military reforms ever since 'Abbas Mirza's New Army had been plagued by a host of problems. Old tribal recruitment practices, the haphazard adoption of European military organization and tactics, and discrepancies between the assumed and real strength of the forces were all chronic maladies. Frequent reshuffling and reorganization of the regiments, insufficient training of the troops, old methods of managing the logistics, and misappropriation of military funds by ranking officers compounded to further plague the system. Bickering among Qajar officials, the sale of military posts to unqualified nobility and favorites of the court, and the shah's inconsistent attention to military affairs also undermined reform.

Since the first decade of the nineteenth century, as the Qajar army lost confidence in its own methods of warfare, the state had placed undue faith in the presumed miracle of European training. Through the course of the century Qajar Iran employed at least three French, two British, two Austrian, and one Italian mission to train its army, not to mention miscellaneous Polish, Prussian, and Italian officers in the Iranian service. Increases in the number of European drill officers, some with questionable skills, encouraged more parades and other illusory exhibitions of military prowess. Condescending attitudes toward Iranian subordinates and undue proximity of some of these hired officers to various European missions in Iran, as well as profiteering through lucrative arms deals, were not uncommon.

To be sure, Iran's military rank and file were kept large enough to preserve a semblance of peace and border security. Reasserting Iran's sovereignty over Bandar Abbas in 1868, once the tenancy agreement with the Sultanate of Muscat came to a close, was but one example. The Qajar military also quelled Shaykh 'Obaydollah's rebellion in northern Kurdistan in 1881. But the cost to maintain an army far exceeded its benefits. Naser al-Din Shah and the Ministry of War, first established in the 1858, no doubt kept up appearances of supervision and efficiency. Handguns and ammunitions were manufactured in military workshops in Tehran, Tabriz, and elsewhere. European arms consignments, such as a vast number of Austrian Werndl rifles, were purchased at high prices. Barracks and garrisons, even in remote parts of the country, were maintained and their operations monitored. With all the problems that riddled the Qajar army, it was evident that the costly upkeep of a large force served purposes other than sheer domestic security. Beyond serving as a conduit for embezzlement, the sheer prestige and appearance of power helped perpetuate the military.

The creation of a small Cossack cavalry regiment (later brigade) in 1879 on the Russian imperial model, manned by a Russian commander, was one of Naser al-Din Shah's later military enterprises. Favorably impressed by the Cossacks in the imperial army during his second Russian tour in 1878, the shah may have intended to counter Moshir al-Dowleh's tilt toward the British. The Iranian Cossack force, which by the end of the century included no more than 1,500 personnel, was primarily manned by the Muslim émigrés from the Caucasus and their children. That the commander of the force remained almost entirely loyal to Russia, and often in cahoots with the Russian embassy, raises a question as to the raison d'être of this force. At best, one can attribute it to Naser al-Din's policy of keeping the tsar on his side by offering him an affordable token of friendship. At worst, it was an impulsive blunder that for decades to come would help protect the throne while exposing Iranian subjects to the overbearing conduct of the Cossack commanders and their troops.

Beyond the military, Moshir al-Dowleh's intention was to expose the shah and the Qajar elite to advances in science and industry. He also sought to attract European capital and technology, build up a viable infrastructure, and facilitate development of Iran's yet unexplored minerals and other natural resources. The most symbolic development, of course, was the construction of a railroad, which was key to the nineteenth-century notion of progress. The project had remained unfulfilled largely because of the neighboring powers' paranoid wrangling over the strategic repercussions of constructing a trans-Iranian railroad linking the Persian Gulf to the Caspian shore. There was a new air of optimism, though, that the astute and well-connected premier would overcome obstacles standing in the way of Iran's technological progress and facilitate catching up with European "civilization." Naser al-Din Shah welcomed Moshir al-Dowleh's overture primarily because he had been anxious to visit Europe since his youth. He viewed Moshir al-Dowleh as one statesman capable of negotiating Iran's case internationally and containing the resistance domestically to his travel abroad.

ROYAL TOURS ON BEHALF OF THE SUBJECTS

To test the waters, the new premier negotiated the shah's visit to the Shi'i holy cities of Iraq with the Ottoman Sublime Porte. Accompanied by a huge retinue, the shah's pilgrimage in 1871 was the first time in recent history that any Iranian ruler had left his domain in peacetime. On the Ottoman side the authorities were apprehensive that a royal visit to the predominantly Shi'i province might cause a flare-up of anti-Ottoman sentiments at the time of great tension. In practice, however, the amicable reception of the royal guest by the capable Ottoman governor, Midhat Pasha (1822–1884), a friend of Moshir al-Dowleh with a comparably modernist outlook, demonstrated the advantages of implementing reforms in a neglected Arab province of the Ottoman Empire.

The Tanzimat under Midhat had weakened the Shi'i mojtaheds' grip over the civil courts and public life. Although it had added to communal tensions and caused recurring Shi'i unrest, it also had the benefit of undercutting the ulama's hold on the community. There was a lesson to be learned by the shah. The royal pilgrimage elevated Naser al-Din's religious devotion beyond a blemish in the public eye. The shah's account of his pilgrimage published in the same year was no doubt meant to communicate this image to his subjects. As the guest of the Ottoman sultan, he was revered and respected not only by local authorities but also by the ulama and the population at large.

Throughout his tour Naser al-Din was received as the shah of Iran and as a king, with an extraterritorial aura and symbolic authority over the Shi'is of Iraq, as when he visited the shrine of 'Ali, the first Shi'i Imam, in Najaf. The treasury of the shrine that had been walled up since the time of the Wahhabi attack on Shi'i Iraq in 1802 was reopened in his honor. In the shah's presence, the shrine's treasures, mostly of the Safavid era, were reassessed and listed in a register before the treasury was sealed off again by royal Qajar and Ottoman seals. Standing before the shrine's casket (*zarih*), he then offered his own diamond hatpin to be placed atop the shrine as a sign of his humility and devotion. The royal pilgrimage went on while the famine of 1870 and 1871 was at its peak. On his way back to Iran, the royal cavalcade camped at the outskirts of the city of Qom, where the shah witnessed the extent of the human disaster. Upon his departure two days later he ordered four hundred *kharvar* (equal to 120 tons) of grain stored in government silos to be distributed among the city's poor.

Naser al-Din Shah's subsequent royal European tour in 1873 began at a time when the worst of the famine was over. This and the two ensuing royal European tours in 1878 and 1889 captured much attention at home and abroad and broke a major taboo. That a Persian ruler, with pivotal place in the symbolic stability of his kingdom, could travel abroad despite a religious ban on entering lands of nonbelievers, was a novelty even in the late nineteenth century. The visit proved to be a successful public relations exercise, consolidating Iran's image abroad as a sovereign state and reasserting its independence during the age of colonial expansion. His royal counterparts in European capitals respectfully received the "Shah of Persia" as the heir to an ancient civilization that, though possibly diminished in its prowess, still carried some weight. The shah conveyed an image of grandeur equal to that of his European hosts, capable of holding his own as a wise and independent ruler—weaker and more vulnerable, perhaps, but one who could converse, negotiate, and stand his ground. His success in this endeavor, especially during the 1873 tour, contrasted with earlier setbacks and reminded the Western powers that Iran was not up for grabs in the imperial game, at least not for the time being. The royal trip attracted more attention than the royal visits by Sultan 'Abd al-Aziz (r. 1861–1876) of the Ottoman Empire and the Egyptian Khedive Isma'il (r. 1863–1879), which took place about the same time (fig. 5.10).

For Europe's elites and its public, Persia called to mind the biblical Persian Empire of Cyrus the Great and Ahasuerus (presumably Xerxes I of the Achaemenid Empire). It also recalled the land of Zarathustra, the rediscovered wise prophet of the Enlightenment. It invoked the romantic memory of the Persian Empire that once had fought a decisive war with the ancient Greeks and later was a formidable rival to the Roman Empire. This was an empire of which they could see its many archeological remains displayed in the newly founded museums. This was the shah whom they knew from classical accounts and modern travel literature.

An air of fanfare was attached to such distant memories, as if the shah and his retinue had turned into a spectacle to be gazed at, teased and even

Figure 5.10. Naser al-Din Shah during his 1873 European tour. He is seated in the royal carriage, entering Balmoral Castle in the Scottish Highlands, together with the premier Mirza Hosain Khan Moshir al-Dowleh and Prince Leopold, the youngest son of Queen Victoria. Standing next to the carriage appears to be Mirza Malkom Khan, then Iranian envoy in London.
Period photograph. Author's collection.

condescendingly looked upon. Proud Europe was eager to see how this ruler of a distant land, once their formidable nemesis, had adapted to the ways of their civilization; how he followed European mannerisms and etiquette; and how he was astounded by the magnificence of its technological, architectural, military, and communications advances. The shah was yet another showcase for displaying imperial power, similar to the artifacts and mummies of ancient Egypt and Mesopotamia on display in European and American museums, in the world exhibitions of London, Vienna, Paris, and Chicago. He was a living testimony, complementing the statues and memorials that glorified the heroes of colonial exploits.

Sailing through the Caspian Sea to the port of Astrakhan, the royal company visited Moscow and St. Petersburg, the first major stops on a long journey that between April and September 1873 included Prussia, the Rhine Valley, Belgium, Britain (mostly London and Manchester), France, Switzerland, Italy, and Austria, then via Istanbul and Georgia back to the Caspian port of Anzali. The shah's busy schedule throughout his visit included burdensome welcome and farewell ceremonies, military parades, elaborate balls and banquets, as well as visits to barracks, cannon foundries, and ammunition factories. There was enough time, however, to also stroll in parks, go to concert halls and opera houses, visit museums, see London's Crystal Palace and the Vienna World Exhibition, and tour hunting grounds.

Fire engine drills, fireworks, rides on trains and carriages, and horseback excursions all proved amusing, and throughout the shah maintained his royal comportment with dignity. Customs and appearances of nobility and such novelties as electrical lighting, steamships, railroad stations, hotels with hot and cold water, circuses, concert halls, and brass bands fascinated him. He was as majestic in calling upon Tsar Alexander II, Queen Victoria, and Emperor Franz Joseph as he was astute in negotiating with English, Russian, and French statesmen. In Berlin he attended the coronation of Wilhelm I (as first emperor of the united Germany) and had two long conversations with the architect of the new empire, Otto von Bismarck, the substance of which remained unknown to the readers of the shah's published diary. He marveled at the chancellor's political skill in piloting a divided Germany into a united empire of great power.

What emerged from the European visit was not exactly what Moshir al-Dowleh had in mind. Naser al-Din and the princes, ranking statesmen, and senior court officials who were accompanying him could appreciate the advantages of a strong state over the revolutionary alternative that was then in progress. Beyond Russia, the shah could see the advancements and military glory of autocratic Prussia becoming the German Empire, as opposed to defeated and revolutionary-stricken France. In July 1873 the shah described in his diary the ruinous outcome of the Franco-German war; the melancholic mood of the people; divisions within the Paris Commune, including the "red republicans"; and the material destruction that turned palaces and government buildings into rubble.

His observations of England did not persuade the shah to substantially transform his own country's political order. He witnessed English democracy in action with its bicameral parliament, judicial independence, government accountability, and above all, limitations on the monarchy. He was an avid reader of history and knew about the English Civil War and the fate of Charles I. Yet he preferred to focus on those aspects of government that were in harmony with his own vision. In effect, he and many of his contemporaries among the Qajar elite self-servingly internalized an assumption that the gap in political culture with Europe was unbridgeable. Europe, unlike Iran, so the shah believed, did not have restive tribes on its periphery, nor did it have an intransigent clergy wielding its power over the state with the weapon of shari'a.

Upon his July 1873 visit to the Palace of Westminster, the shah's description of the House of Commons was brief and devoid of any apparent interest in parliamentary deliberation, at least in the printed version of his diary:

> Lord Gladstone, Disraeli, and the other Ministers, Whig and Tory, were present. The Whigs were (seated) on one side (of the house), the Tories on the other side. . . . They brought forward a question, on which there was a difference of opinion. The President (Speaker) of the House adjudged according to the "majority," i.e. the greater number, the lesser number being called the "minority." The whole of the members went forth, to be counted outside; the (place of) assembly remained vacant, no one being left except the President. After a minute or so they came (back); the Whigs were the victorious party, who now hold office. Then Lord Gladstone—the Premier, came up to us, and we had a little conversation.[3]

It is difficult to see how much the shah was impressed with the display of the British parliamentary debate, but whatever his opinion, the orderly fashion in which the Whigs and the Tories abided by the vote of the majority could not have escaped his notice. Perhaps it wasn't sheer coincidence that after his return to Iran, the dividing line between conservative and reformist factions in the shah's government became more pronounced. It was as if he had recognized even more clearly the need to strike some form of balance between the two factions. Yet at no time did he go so far as granting any of the "government consultative councils" that he periodically convened, and then dissolved, the authority to conduct affairs of the state free of his personal control.

Likewise, while the shah was impressed with Europe's material culture, he hardly was convinced to build an industrial base in his own country, at least not along the lines that reformists of his time wished would happen instantaneously. An imported modernity seemed to the shah, and to like-minded Iranian elites, untenable. Who, after all, would wish to re-create, so the shah must have reckoned, the suffocating, polluted, poverty-stricken, regimented, revolution-ripe, smokestack-filled urban environment of the kind he saw in places like industrial Yorkshire or the Ruhr Valley? He surely did not wish to add to the existing problems of his country a set of new ones by creating manufacturing plants for which he did not have, or remotely hope to have, capital or know-how.

And imperial Europe of the late nineteenth century was not generous in sharing its jealously guarded knowledge with others, nor would it abandon its long-nurtured export markets. The lure of Europe's material culture, though, knew no bounds. The more the shah and his company traveled, the more they were charmed by urban spaces, royal gardens, palaces, and public buildings, as well as by European modes and manners, especially timekeeping, dress, and appearance, as well as the ease of travel and communication, the variety of foods and produce, and of course the presence of women in public life.

The latter created a moral crisis of sorts for the shah and his retinue. Not accustomed to encountering unveiled women outside their own harems, here members of the royal party were obliged to mingle happily not only with women of royalty and nobility, who conversed with them intelligently and freely, but also with female opera singers, ballerinas, popular performers, circus girls, and prostitutes, as well as ordinary women in the streets and parks. The presence of women in the public space was in sharp contrast to the limitations on Iranian women of all classes.

An incident involving a senior wife of the shah is a case in point. Fatemeh-Soltan Khanum Lavasani, better known by her title Anis al-Dowleh (companion of the state), an influential and astute favorite of the shah from humble origins who had risen in the harem to become his chief wife and adviser, a de facto queen to the shah, persuaded Naser al-Din to include her in the 1873 European tour. Surrounded by her female attendants, Anis al-Dowleh, who was receptive to European ways and most likely prepared to adopt to them, reached as far as Moscow, all along covered with a facial veil and segregated from the men. However, once in the Russian capital, it became apparent that the shah's wife could no longer stay out of sight, for the tsar and tsarina insisted that she be present and unveiled at official functions.

Facing the dilemma of Russian court protocol there was little alternative to the shah but to send Anis al-Dowleh home. She complied, but with bitter dismay, holding Moshir al-Dowleh responsible for the disgraceful termination of her visit. It is not difficult to imagine, however, the dire consequences of the ulama's disapproval back home should a royal wife be unveiled in the land of Farang. Back in Tehran, Anis al-Dowleh retaliated by participating in a palace coup involving Qajar princes and Tehran mojtaheds, which upon the shah's return led to the temporary dismissal of Moshir al-Dowleh. Saving the royal honor that was safely protected back home did not stop the shah from indulging in the world of carnal pleasure. Among other escapades he purchased a Circassian (or possibly Chechen) slave girl as a portable pleasure companion. Her disguise as a page boy in the shah's retinue became an open secret and something of an embarrassment.

In his 1878 private tour and his official state visit in 1889, Naser al-Din Shah met more statesmen, royalty, concessionaires, and celebrities. He visited more palaces, manors, arms factories and barracks, parks and hunting grounds, operas and music halls, museums, and zoos. He attended both the 1878 and 1889 Paris World Expositions (fig. 5.11).

Figure 5.11. Iran's pavilion at the 1878 Paris Exposition Universelle, designed and built by Hosain 'Ali Ma'mar Isfahani. Persian handicrafts and specialty fabrics and carpets displayed in the mirror hall and on the upper floor drew public attention. Contemporary postcard. Author's collection.

The shah's published diaries, especially that of the 1873 visit, no doubt were intended to remind his subjects of the esteem and attention he received, especially in Russia and Britain. They were part of a public relations exercise to buttress the royal image at home and abroad. The diaries also narrated to his subjects the spectacular Farang the king had observed on their behalf. The shah's simple and unencumbered Persian, brought to life, almost like a camera, the momentous and the mundane. As much as the shah's journals were masterful in describing novelties, they were devoid of depth, let alone critical reflection, as if meant to see but not observe. A sense of envious inaccessibility, moreover, is most evident in the journals in their descriptions of voluptuous fair ladies, powdered, bejeweled, fragranced, and revealing. In contrast to the aesthetic values and mores he was accustomed to, the Western women he met conversed, smiled, danced, and even courted in public. Fascination with Farang permeated even through the controlled tone of the closely edited published version of the diaries.

THE REUTER FIASCO

Even before his forthcoming European tour of 1873, the shah and Moshir al-Dowleh hoped to accelerate modernization projects by attracting European capital. The outcome, the granting and then repeal of the Reuter Concession (1871–1873), proved a bizarre episode, driven as much by the Qajar shah and his statesmen's naïveté and bewilderment in their first direct experience of Europe as by their greed. It also displayed a brazen example of European profiteering in the early age of capital venture and acquiring unbridled concessions. Only through massive investment by European private capital, Iran's chief minister argued, would Iran ever be able to leap forward to be counted among the world's advanced nations. He, and his chief collaborator, Mirza Malkom Khan, focused on an investment proposal that was tabled by a well-known communications magnate of his time, Baron Julius de Reuter.

Reuter was a shrewd and persuasive German-born immigrant to England who made his fortune in the early days of telegraphic telecommunication and had bought his title from a duke of a defunct minor German principality. In 1851 Reuters, one of the first modern news agencies (and one of the most enduring) began to transmit stock market quotes between London and Paris. By the early 1870s, Reuter had expanded his operation worldwide while fortifying his connections to men of money and influence in his adopted country. His appetite for investing in Iran seems to have been whetted by the successful operation of the British owned Indo-European Telegraph Department. He understood

Iran's strategic potential as a railroad link between India and Europe, but he also sensed the shah's rush to secure a purchasable piece of European progress. He saw profit in both opportunities. The 1869 completion of the Suez Canal was hailed worldwide as a major engineering marvel made possible through private financing.

By July 1872, when the Reuter Concession, a monopoly on construction of a railway line and other development projects in Iran, was finally signed after a remarkably short span of secret negotiations, the level of fascination with Europe's technological advances and its financial power easily overrode any skepticism in and outside of Iranian government circles. With virtually no chance for debate, even within elite circles, the royal advisory council, consisting of mostly pro-reform statesmen, ratified the unbelievably generous concession. It was taken for granted that Iranians could neither raise the capital nor master the technology to undertake a project of such a scale. Beyond the inferiority complex of the Iranian negotiators, however, there were important ulterior motives. A few, including the premier and Malkom Khan, had received substantial bribes from Julius de Reuter, who had spent £200,000 ($1,100,000) in advance to lubricate the granting of the concession.

The sweeping terms granted a seventy-year concession to the person of Reuter for the construction of a single-track trans-Iranian railroad with its direction still to be decided, possibly from the port of Bushehr in the Persian Gulf to the port of Anzali at the Caspian Sea. In exchange, the government of Iran agreed to offer enormous facilities to Reuter unconditionally, including all the public and privately owned land and property required, as well as labor and security free of any taxes, customs, or other dues. Moreover, the Qajar state granted to Reuter what amounted to exploitation of all of Iran's natural resources and its future economic and financial potential for the duration of the concession. This included a monopoly on the exploration and development of all of Iran's mines and minerals, forests, underground and surface water resources, and all future industrial and infrastructural developments such as the telegraph, urban transportation, steelworks, textile mills, and other industries as well as a monopoly commission on all of Iran's customs for twenty-five years.

It further allowed the concessionaire to establish modern banks, including issuing Iranian banknotes and the right to change at some future time the base of Iran's metal-backed currency from silver to gold. Reuter reserved all rights to transfer, sell, or let to whomever and whatever entity he wished all or part of the above monopolies. He would pay 20 percent annually of the net railroad income and 15 percent on all other monopolies. And of course Reuter would provide the shah with a loan for his forthcoming European visit. The only redeeming feature was that the concessionaire was obliged to start construction within fifteen months of the signing of the concession or risk its cancellation. The whole enterprise sounded nothing short of an outrageous swindle. Reuter had yet to raise any of the £6,000,000 in capital on the volatile European stock markets that he was obligated to provide by issuing public shares. No one in his right mind would purchase such shares, except of course for the Iranian government, who had agreed to pay a minimum of 7 percent interest and principal on Reuter's capital. Besides, since Reuter's company had virtually no technical expertise in any of the areas of the concession, he was bound to subcontract or otherwise auction off or rent out nearly all of his monopolies, a fact that cast further doubt on the success of the operation. The British Foreign Office and most of the English establishment were the least convinced. Only concession hunters across Europe, who had already managed to bring Egypt, the Ottoman Empire, and Tunisia to the verge of bankruptcy, and the African-coast safari slave hunters of earlier times who bartered copper wire and looking glasses for slaves, must have marveled at Reuter's scheme and laughed at Naser al-Din Shah, his modernizing premier, and the eight high-ranking ministers and dignitaries who put their seals of approval on the concession.

What blinded these otherwise seasoned officials and led them to believe they had struck a good deal was complex. In part, it was their sycophantic desire to give the shah what he wanted, namely the necessary funds for his European tour, which also included many of them in the retinue. They had let themselves, moreover, be bamboozled by Reuter's negotiator and the argument that because Iran could not afford the necessary security to guarantee the railroad project, the only alternative was to pay it through monopolies. Not before reaching St. Petersburg, however, did the shah realize the gravity of his blunder. The Russian authorities, including Tsar Alexander II himself, in no uncertain terms confidentially warned the shah that the concession was diametrically opposed to Russian interests, not least because it gave the British access to the Caspian and thus to Russian frontiers. By the time he reached London, the shah had serious second thoughts. Snubbing Reuter was an early sign of what was to come.

On the shah's return home in September 1873, resistance to the concession among the Qajar princes, his favorite wife Anis al-Dowleh, elements in the palace, and some of the Tehran ulama was so vehement that upon arriving at the port of Anzali, the shah had to immediately dismiss Moshir al-Dowleh. To preempt further trouble, Moshir al-Dowleh was temporarily appointed governor of Gilan and instructed to stay there. Once the immediate threat of a palace revolt subsided, the shah summoned back Moshir al-Dowleh, reappointed him as minister of foreign affairs, and instructed him to immediately repeal the concession. The shah's concern with the conservative faction required circumspection at first and a balancing act afterward. The sum total of counterbalancing the conservatives and the progressives meant a loss of momentum for Moshir al-Dowleh and a tangible slowdown for the reform measures.

A master negotiator and a flatterer toward his royal master, Moshir al-Dowleh argued long and hard with Reuter's representatives that since they had not started the railroad construction project within the first fifteen months, the concession was automatically canceled. To the British Foreign Office, lukewarm in its support of Reuter, he justified the repeal by recalling the usual ghost of Russian reprisal. By 1874, it seemed that at least for the time being, Reuter no longer had a case. Yet he was a man of perseverance who patiently awaited opportunities and doggedly nurtured the support of the British authorities. Naser al-Din, who anxiously asked for and received the original copy of the Reuter concession to strike it out with his own hand as null and void, must have realized that long after Moshir al-Dowleh, he again would have to face the claims of the shrewd concessionaire, this time under British pressure. After sixteen years had passed Reuter eventually succeeded in securing a new concession on the grounds of the original for the creation of the Imperial Bank of Persia to issue banknotes on behalf of the Iranian government. Reuter's company also again received the monopoly to develop all of Iran's unused mine and mineral resources.

Iran's first experience with large-scale Western capital bore all the marks of unreserved exploitation. One redeeming point, however, was the degree of resistance to the concession. Even if the shah and most of his pro-reform advisers were intimidated by the material power and glamour of the West, there were some who voiced criticism and persuaded the shah to change course. The motives of princes of the royal family and their associates during the palace revolt were mostly hostility toward Moshir al-Dowleh, in part because of his open homosexual orientation but also his modernizing scheme. They shared grievances with a handful of high-ranking ulama who felt that a railroad and such Western-style developments would open the way to the *Farangis* and corrupt the faith of the Iranians. Yet their argument was not based entirely on the demerits of imitating Westerners. Chief among them, Mulla 'Ali Kani, the influential mojtahed of the capital, in a reproachful letter to the shah, criticized the Reuter concession not because it robbed Iran of its economic sovereignty but for the provisions in the concession that violated private ownership contrary to Islamic law. The ulama's defiance of Europe's economic intrusion had to wait for another two decades before it would flare up during the Tobacco Protest.

By the late 1870s Moshir al-Dowleh's high hopes for transforming Iran had run aground. The state bureaucracy and diplomatic corps grew in size, but despite the introduction of Western-style ministries and attempts to rationalize the government machinery, such measures did not greatly improve efficiency or accountability. Finance, military, and the judiciary remained almost unchanged; the old elite's inertia effectively offset any serious overhaul. Efforts to introduce modern education and a relatively free press and publication proved short lived.

That a skilled statesman with twenty years of experience abroad should have made a blunder as evident as Reuter concession—which tarnished Moshir al-Dowleh's image even in his own time—remains a mystery. Tilting toward the British as a counter to an impending Russian threat may be one motive. One cannot rule out his wide-eyed rush for a wholesale purchase of modernity either, not unusual to many modernizers of his period, intoxicated with the myth of European progress. Yet Moshir al-Dowleh may have also been driven by greed, and other instances of graft marred his career. In this respect he was not an exception to the rule, as many Qajar statesmen used their high offices to acquire wealth as a security against their many occupational hazards.

By November 1881, when he died in Mashhad at the age of fifty-three, he was serving as trustee of the shrine of the Eighth Imam in Mashhad. His death under suspicious circumstances may well have been carried out by administration of the venomous "Qajar coffee" (*qahveh-e qajar*), which was a swift and quiet method preferred by Naser al-Din to rid unwanted officials who had fallen victim to his suspicion or grudge. Afterward, there was little appreciation for him and his services from the Qajar establishment, and nothing but apathy from the shah, not unlike what had happened with Amir Kabir three decades earlier.

Upon hearing the news of Moshir al-Dowleh's death, Mohammad Hasan Khan E'temad al-Saltaneh, the shah's astute confidant and dragoman, observed in his secret diaries on November 15, 1881:

> Despite all his deplorable habits, he [Moshir al-Dowleh] was wise and shrewd and aware of political stratagem [*politik*] and European customs. If the shah hadn't turned him mad with undue promotion, he would have been the best servant of the government. But within one year the shah first made him the justice minister, then the war minster, and then the chief minister; and [the latter] with such an autonomy as if the very [office of] kingship was delegated to him. That is what made him mad and arrogant. Today the shah was saying: "He offended me much. . . . This man had reached a stage that there was no way out for him but to die. He put us into much trouble. He almost behaved like Midhat Pasha." What [the shah] meant was treason toward his [royal] benefactor.[4]

The reference to Midhat Pasha was not mere coincidence. Only a few months earlier, in April 1881, Sultan 'Abd al-Hamid had arrested the celebrated reformer and architect of the 1876 Ottoman constitution, put him on trial, and condemned him to death on the unproven charge of the murder of Sultan 'Abd al-Aziz. Less than three years later Midhat was executed. Naser al-Din Shah, who was well aware of the friendship of the two statesmen, must have feared a similar fate at the hand of his former chief minister. The doomed Moshir al-Dowleh was the fourth chief minister to fall victim to the shah's paranoid fears.

As it was the royal practice, the shah soon appropriated all of Moshir al-Dowleh's possession, including his Baharestan mansion, designed in 1880 by a French-educated Iranian architect in grand Baroque style. It was adjacent to the still incomplete Naseri complex, the trusteeship of which Moshir al-Dowleh had offered to Naser al-Din Shah out of a mix of fear and devotion. The shah granted the use of the mansion to his own favorite page boy, Malijak (which in Kurdish means "little sparrow"—he was also known as Aziz al-Soltan, "the favorite of the king"), an ultimate affront to the deceased minister. The Baharestan mansion later became the seat of the Majles, the Iranian parliament, during the Constitutional Revolution and after.

Moshir al-Dowleh's decadelong era marked the third and final attempt of Naser al-Din Shah to undertake reform in a serious and systematic fashion. The limited success once more revealed the structural barriers in the way of transforming the state and the economy of the country. While the vacillating shah saw his own survival in playing off factions within the Qajar polity, the entrenched conservative nobility and ulama class remained deeply suspicious of European-style reforms.

REFASHIONING THE CAPITAL

If the shah consciously stayed away from the import of major state institutions and political culture, far more than his Ottoman and Egyptian counterparts had, he was eager to absorb and adopt symbols of Europe's material culture. Unlike technology and industrialization, which were hard to import, material culture and luxury commodities traveled well. And it was these, rather than Europe's industrial and political achievements, that first left their mark on Iran's urban life, culture, and artistic expressions. They served as physical projections of Qajar power and its quest for grandeur, pleasing changes that could elevate the image of the shah as a progressive, on par with his Ottoman and European counterparts.

The Qajars were always good builders, as evident in the numerous palaces, gardens, and public buildings constructed under Fath 'Ali Shah and later. In the same vein, the Naseri era, from the late 1860s on, witnessed an unprecedented urban revival, partly under Moshir al-Dowleh. Princes and statesmen, as well as tribal khans, wealthy merchants, and mojtaheds, built sizable residences and private gardens and created charitable endowments, including mosques, madrasas, caravansaries, bazaars, *qanats*, bridges, bathhouses, and water reservoirs. Examples of Naseri-age construction that survived ravages of later Pahlavi modernity are examples of great architectural endeavors that express serenity and delicateness.

As may be expected, the first changes in style appeared in the architecture and decoration of Golestan Palace. The great Reception Hall (Talar-e Salam), perhaps the most significant interior court architecture of the late Qajar period, was in part inspired by the Hermitage in St. Petersburg (which it shared with Dolmabahce Palace in Istanbul) but built at a smaller scale and with an exquisite taste, indicative of the technical and architectural abilities of Qajar master builders (fig. 5.12). The adjacent Mirror Hall obviously alluded to Versailles but was decorated with elaborate Persian mirror tile-work. As part of his construction program, Naser al-Din restored or reconstructed earlier royal buildings in the Golestan complex as well (pl. 5.1).

Even before the shah's European tour in 1873, the new Perso-European style had appeared in the five-story Shams al-'Emareh (sun of the palaces) in the Golestan complex, with a view of the capital's panorama. Completed in 1867 possibly with the Safavid 'Ali Qapu in mind, construction was supervised by the chief of royal palaces, Dust-'Ali Khan Mo'ayyer al-Mamalek, a descendant of a family of masters of the royal mint with roots in the Safavid era. It was built by 'Ali Mohammad Kashani, a master builder who, presumably for the first time in Iran, used a steel frame in a multistory building. The design was meant to evoke a house of amusement reminiscent of the stories of the "Seven Domes" (Haft Gonbad), a well-known romance by the twelfth-century Persian poet Nezami Ganjavi. Atop the building was a clock tower housing a massive two-faced clock, a gift from Queen Victoria, which invited the people of the capital to keep time accurately (pl. 5.2). Poor maintenance and complaints from the women of the harem, though, soon brought the clock to a standstill, a sign the Qajar era was more accustomed to its own dawn-to-dusk timekeeping than the disciplined timekeeping of the state.

In addition to the Golestan complex, the late Naseri age witnessed the building of at least eight other palaces and numerous royal gardens in and around the capital. The palace of 'Eshratabad (lit. "abode of indulgence") on the

Figure 5.12. Reception Hall of Golestan Palace. The enclosure has
a typical Persian architectural ambiance, though decorative patterns
and much of the ornamentation reveal the Europeanization of Qajar
taste, especially after Naser al-Din Shah's 1873 European tour.
S. G. W. Benjamin, *Persia and the Persians* (London, 1887), 79.

eastern side of the capital was Naser al-Din Shah's version of *jardin d'amour*.
The Saltanatabad summer palace, first built in 1850 to the north of the capital,
was lavishly restored and rededicated in 1878 as Sahebqarniyeh, to celebrate
the thirtieth anniversary of Naser al-Din's reign. The palace of Shahrestanak
(now demolished) was built high in the Alborz, overlooking Tehran and the
Farahabad garden palace on the eastern outskirts of the capital (known as Qasr-
e Firuzeh), an expanded version of the royal hunting lodge.

The remarkable Takkiyeh-e Dowlat, the state hall designed to perform the
mourning ceremonies of Muharram, was another landmark of the Naseri age
(fig. 5.13). Commissioned by the shah in 1868, its building was supervised by
Mo'ayyer al-Mamalek, and its design, in the style of European opera houses,
benefited from the advice of the Frenchman Jules Richard, once a French
teacher to Naser al-Din and later a teacher at Dar al-Fonun and an antique
dealer. The design of Takkiyeh—with its massive hall, steel-framed semi-
permanent dome, arched private balconies, several lower-levels seats for city

Figure 5.13. Takkiyeh-e Dowlat in Tehran was the focal point
of the royal homage to the Moharram ceremonies.
S. G. W. Benjamin, *Persia and the Persians* (London, 1887), 373.

Figure 5.14 Humble *ta'ziyeh* settings, such as this one in Qazvin, revealed
grassroots devotion to the visual representation of Karbala tragedies.
J. Dieulafoy, "La Perse, la Chaldée et la Susiane," *Le tour du monde* (1881–1882), 57.

folk, and circular center stage—was particularly designed for the performance of Shi'i passion plays known as *ta'ziyeh*. The royal edifice was in sharp contrast to the modest sites where *ta'ziyeh* was usually performed in towns and villages throughout the country (fig. 5.14).

In this state-owned takkiyeh, too, under one roof the Qajar elite gathered along with ordinary men and women of the city to witness, for free, not only the most elaborate *ta'ziyeh* in town but also the shah in person, to marvel at his state's great symbol of devotion to Shi'i martyrs. Greatly appreciated by the Qajar public and by the elite, the staging of the tragedies of Karbala was an old tradition that went back at least to the tenth century. The art of *ta'ziyeh* involved the melodic recitation of rhymed set verses, both by protagonists and by antagonists, use of wind and percussion instruments, costumes in the Arab style of the seventh century, horses and camels, and a great deal of dramatic—often bloody—action. No doubt the performative aspect of the *ta'ziyeh* was a motivation for the construction of an elaborate state takkiyeh. Not only members of the diplomatic corps in the Qajar court were invited to attend the performance; the *ta'ziyeh* of the Qajar era also included in the cast an imaginary delegation from the land of Farang, which toward the end of the performance offered its support and sympathies for the anguished Imam Hosain. There was, however, an entertaining aspect of the performance, and to lighten the mood of religious tragedies at times the court clowns performed comedies in the state takkiyeh.

Through the medium of architecture Qajar Iran borrowed and internalized occidental concepts and technologies while preserving Persian character and function. Beside constructions in the citadel (*arg*) and other royal complexes, the most significant development was the expansion of the capital, including the construction of new city walls, modern thoroughfares, European-style stores, and, a decade later, a horse-driven tramway with three lines and many stops. By the 1870s the four and half miles of Tehran's old city walls—first built by the Safavid Shah Tahmasp in the sixteenth century and reinforced by Fath 'Ali Shah—could no longer house the city's growing population, which had reached more than 150,000 (pl. 5.3). By 1900 Tehran's population had reached about two hundred thousand. The old Tehran consisted of four wards (*mahalleh*), a royal citadel, and six city grates, but the new city walls, which took ten years to complete, encompassed twelve miles surrounding five wards, each of which had numerous quarters (*patoq*). No fewer than twelve city gates had handsome designs and Persian tile work with designs invoking the signs of zodiac and in honor of the twelve Shi'i Imams.

According to a survey of the capital completed in 1853, there were 7,872 houses and 4,220 shops and businesses in Tehran. By 1867 the total population of 147,256 resided in 9,581 houses: 68 percent owned their house, and 32 percent were tenants. By 1900 the number of houses had grown to 16,275, with 9,420 shops and businesses, a growth of roughly 45 percent from 1853. The 1853 survey also identified that 2,580 of the houses, or 32 percent of them, belonged to government employees. Twenty of these were large complexes consisting of four or more units, which housed the extended families of senior officials. Of the 5,844 houses belonging to civilians, some 95 percent were Shi'i Muslims; 96 houses belonged to 180 Armenian households and 129 houses to 134 Jewish families. By 1867 there were some 130 European families residing in the capital.

A typical house of the Naseri era sheltered an extended family of three or more generations. But even smaller houses belonging to the urban middle classes improved in quality and size. An affluent Qajar household included a sizable number of domestic workers, cooks, and gardeners, as well as male and female slaves, often from Zanzibar or Abyssinia, who had been in Iran for generations and had their own families. According to 1867 statistics, more than seventeen thousand people, or 11.5 percent, of the total population of Tehran belonged to the servant (*nowkar*) class, attached to 9,581 houses—and among them, 10,568 were servants, 3,802 were domestic workers, and 3,014 were slaves. These servants and slaves almost entirely were attached to or resided in households of the nobility, ranking officials, large landowners, merchants, and affluent ulama. Yet outside the small but very prosperous urban elite, discrepancies in wealth among the rest of the population were not that extreme, even including the immigrant population of the city. In 1867, even before the physical expansion of the capital, immigrants from the provinces—mostly Azarbaijan, Isfahan, and Kashan—constituted 71 percent of Tehran's population.

The statistics on public spaces is also noticeable. The survey of Tehran in 1867 counted 47 mosques, 35 madrasas, and 34 takkiyehs, as well as 190 public bathhouses, 130 caravansaries, and 20 ice makers (*yakhchal*). By 1900 there were 80 mosques and madrasas, 43 takkiyehs, 182 public bathhouses, 184 caravansaries, and 24 ice makers. The 1900 statistics also identified seven churches, two synagogues, seven barracks, two hospitals, two government schools, and 215 gardens and orchards in and around the city. Almost in all areas, perhaps with the exception of mosques and madrasas, Tehran witnessed steady urban growth, indicative of its political centrality, even though provincial centers such as Tabriz, Mashhad and Yazd still held an economic and demographic edge over the capital. Such a diversity of functions, which remained in place until the early decades of the twentieth century, was a hallmark of the decentralized Qajar system.

Yet as part of Tehran's urban development, municipal services began to emerge in the latter part of the nineteenth century. Naser al-Din Shah created a small sanitation department responsible for removal of unsightly rubbish from street corners. The leaders of the city wards continued to serve under the city mayor but were overshadowed by the capital's office of governor under Kamran Mirza, Naser al-Din Shah's younger son. The newly created post of chief of police, held by an Italian officer with a dubious claim to nobility, overlooked a growing force that came to replace the old policing style in the wards and the bazaar. With the Italian police chief arrived new police administration and new methods of surveillance and control. Wary of anti-Qajar dissent in the final decades of the nineteenth century, the police force, under the supervision of Kamran Mirza, created a rudimentary secret police responsible for rounding up dissidents among officials, intellectuals, and the Babis.

Overall, Tehran's modernization project was extensive, but not as much as that of Cairo, the so-called Paris on the Nile under the Khedive Isma'il, or of Istanbul under Sultan 'Abd al-Majid and his successors. Nor was it as Western-ized as those cities in style and construction. Much of old Tehran remained intact up until the 1920s and 1930s, as was the case for other Iranian cities, perhaps with the exception of a handful of Western-style structures such as missionary schools and hospitals that were built in Tabriz and Isfahan. The old streets and alleys, forming a network that crisscrossed through the city wards and meandered between houses and gardens, were seldom paved or laid with stone; instead, passersby had to negotiate their way through the mud and dirt of the narrow streets. It would still be another half century, though, before the Western notion of the urban grid would ruin the fabric of the old city.

A few modern avenues built in the Naseri era, as early as the 1860s, cut through the old wards but seldom disturbed the coherence of the city's original space (pl. 5.4). Most visible among the new developments was Naseri Avenue, north of the bazaar and west of the citadel complex—both sides of the wide thoroughfare were lined with shops offering goods and commodities not available inside the bazaar. Further north, Lalehzar Avenue, connected the Arg through Maydan-e Mashq (Drill Square) in the older part of the city to the newly developed Dowlat ward and the northern outskirts of the city. It was the first for-profit housing and shopping project developed by Naser al-Din Shah himself. As a shortage of empty land within the city walls raised prices, the shah saw an opportunity to turn Lalehzar (meaning "tulip field"), a delightful royal garden built by Fath 'Ali Shah, into a moneymaker for his ever-hungry royal purse. It remained the most fashionable sector of the capital well into the twentieth century. The 1853 survey identified 113 trades and professions in Tehran;

almost all were traditional wholesale and retail occupations based either in the central bazaar or in neighborhood shopping alleys. A similar pattern was also in place in major provincial centers. Only in the latter decades of the century, though, did shops and businesses offering Western luxury goods gradually appear in the newly developed streets of the capital. Although European woolen and cotton fabrics and some metalwares were popular since the 1840s, the number and variety of Western goods—such as china, glassware, and women's toiletries—were negligible even at the turn of the twentieth century.

Moshir al-Dowleh's construction of the massive Naseri mosque and madrasa complex east of the capital soon became a landmark. Built in the "seven dome" (*haft kaseh*) style, between 1878 and 1883, it was a testimony to the achievements of late Qajar architecture. Aimed to introduce a reformed curriculum and teaching method to Shi'i madrasa education, the Naseri madrasa held one of the richest libraries of Islamic manuscripts in Iran, including rare scientific and geographical texts. Many private collections belonging to the Qajar nobility were closed to the public, and numerous libraries in the shrines and madrasas, such as the valuable collection in the shrine of Imam Reza in Mashhad, were limited to teachers and students. And because the Royal Library at Golestan Palace, with a rich manuscript collection going back to the thirteenth century, was for the shah's private use, and the small library of Dar al-Fonun was largely for teaching purposes, the Naseri library was the closest concept to a public library in the Naseri era.

Trading centers all over Iran also witnessed a degree of expansion and improvement. Mansions built in innovative styles housed members of the provincial elite. In Kashan, Yazd, and Isfahan, merchants and landowners built numerous grand houses with revenue from the tobacco, opium, and textile trades (see map 5.1). Kashan merchant families in particular thrived in the latter decades of the century and, in addition to their mansions, built new alleys and bazaars, caravansaries, mosques, and water reservoirs.

NARRATING EUROPE: REAL AND IMAGINARY

The "Persianizing" of European styles was also evident in other areas of material culture throughout the latter part of the nineteenth century. A sense of confidence in freely adopting and adapting is notable in painting and the decorative arts, popular stories, music and performance, the introduction of new foods, dress and cosmetics, urban planning and beautification, garden designs and new plants and flowers. Arguably, the most Persian of all cultural expressions, poetry, also began to experience new form and content. These cultural adaptations did not imply bowing to Europe's imperial power. Contrary to what purists often claim, art and architecture of the Qajar period were neither decadent nor bastardized replicas of European archetypes. Rather, they emerged out of a period of cultural florescence, which displayed a distinct Persian taste.

The works of Abol-Hasan Ghaffari, with the title of Sani' al-Molk, the great painter and graphic artist of the period, is but one example. Born in 1814 to an old family of great artists and statesmen from Kashan, he was trained in the Isfahan school of portraiture before developing his own technique and perspective. He visited Italy in the mid-1840s to be trained in the European style and returned a few years later with a nuanced view of Western art, more socially contextualized than any other Iranian artist of his time. After he visited Italy, his choice of subject matter diversified, without being overwhelmed by the European masters (although he did copy a few works for practice and for teaching purposes). Upon his return to Iran in 1851, just after Amir Kabir's downfall, and as part of the former premier's patronage of Persian arts and crafts, Abol-Hasan established the first modern studio in the newly founded Dar al-Sanaye' (house of crafts) complex in the Tehran bazaar. Besides promoting painting, Dar al-Sanaye' was a notable attempt, possibly inspired by Safavid royal workshops, to preserve and promote Persian handicrafts and small industries such as textiles, carpet weaving, lacquerwork, bookbinding, mosaics, and silver works as well as modern crafts, such as manufacturing horse carriages.

In his studio Sani' al-Molk displayed his copies of the European masters Raphael, Michelangelo, and Titian, as well as classical Greek torsos. He admitted apprentices to work in the new style and every Friday invited the public to view the new artwork. He gave instruction not only in drawing and painting but also in graphic arts, the printing press, and lithography, and he accepted orders for lithographic reproductions. Illustrating the famous *One Thousand and One Nights* (*Hezar o Yek-shab*), a collection of Indo-Persian and Arabian stories (sometimes known in the West as the *Arabian Nights*), was one early achievement. In 1851 he was commissioned by Naser al-Din Shah, under the patronage of Mo'ayyer al-Mamalek, to illustrate a royal copy of the text, which a talented writer and a poet jointly had translated from Arabic into Persian around the same time. This was perhaps the greatest artistic project of the post-Safavid period and one of the most notable in the nineteenth-century Muslim world. Supervising thirty-four assistants and apprentices in his workshop (not including calligraphers, bookbinders, and illuminators) for a period of three years, Sani' al-Molk created a six-volume manuscript consisting of 3,600 watercolor illustrations on 1,134 pages. He was paid the hefty sum of 6,580 tumans (almost $65,000) for the commission.

Sani' al-Molk's artistic creativity is evident in his realist style, which had been unknown to the Persian tradition of illuminated books. He placed the scenes of *One Thousand and One Nights* not in an imaginary era of the Baghdad caliphate but in his own time and surroundings. He used the ancient tale to comment on Qajar society and politics, making subtle allusions to contemporary personalities and events. Everyday life in the bazaar and the street, dress, food, musical instruments, transportation, and, of course, Europeans were the subjects of many of the illustrations. He highlighted the private life of women, servants, slaves, and eunuchs, as well as leisure, entertainment, dancing, and drinking, and he presented daring illustrations of love and sexuality. To make the narratives more accessible and relevant, he used bright colors and dynamic designs, almost bordering on caricature. The illustrated manuscript preserved in the library of Golestan Palace was only viewable by the shah and his courtiers and was never published—a sad fate of artistic works with royal patronage even in the age of printing (pl. 5.5).

The same spirit of acerbic humor is evident in a number of Sani' al-Molk's watercolors with social themes. The complex scene of a brawl in Tabriz involving *lutis* (pl. 5.6), or an odd bunch of court attendants surrounding a dandy Qajar prince (pl. 5.7), or a group of ludicrous court hangers-on—these were critical commentaries on violence, greed, and the absurdity of the Qajar court, all wrapped up with a fresh wit. As the editor of the government gazette, Sani' al-Molk introduced for the first time sketches and cartoons of daily crime scenes and urban unrest, as well as royal parades, horse races, and hunts, often with subtle references to social undercurrents of the time. It is probable that his critical eye caused a fallout with the Qajar establishment shortly before his mysterious death in 1866 at the age of fifty-four, perhaps another victim of the notorious Qajar coffee.

Later painters of the Naseri period continued in the Perso-European hybrid style, with great innovations. The works of Mahmud Khan Kashani Malek al-Sho'ara not only captured the delicacy of the royal architecture of his time but also arrived at a novel expressionist style (pl. 5.8). Works of Mohammad Ghaffari Kashani, better known as Kamal al-Molk (1859–1940), a relative of Sani' al-Molk, in contrast, was directly inspired by European realism of his time. His scenery and portrayal work, much admired by Naser al-Din Shah, proved more influential in the development of Persian painting in the early twentieth century. By the time of the Constitutional Revolution, there was a visible shift toward European realism and away from the artistic innocence of the earlier period. Pictorial traits characteristic of Persian cultural identity nevertheless remained strong. Likewise, the music of the Naseri period mostly under court patronage, paved the way for the efflorescence of the Persian classical *radif* system around the time of the Constitutional Revolution (pl. 5.9).

The Persian popular imagination also explored Farang and its exotic delights. The humorous romance of *Amir Arsalan Rumi*, a popular adventure yarn bridging old Persian folktales with the modern novel, reflected an ambivalence toward Europe between seduction and violence. Narrated by Mohammad 'Ali Naqib al-Mamalek, the chief storyteller (*naqqal*) of the court, to Naser al-Din Shah as his bedtime entertainment, the adventurous story evidently appealed to women of the royal harem. Tuman Agha Fakhr al-Dowleh, a gifted daughter of the shah, who transcribed the story while being narrated by the storyteller, apparently also illustrated it. Once the printed editions came out, as early as 1898, the novel not only appealed to the literate public but also became part of the *naqqals'* repertoire.

In the story, Amir Arsalan is an orphaned prince whose father was slain and whose Rum kingdom (the Ottoman Empire) was attacked and occupied by forces of the powerful Petros Shah, a king of Farang, perhaps an allusion to Peter the Great of Russia. In revenge, Amir Arsalan, who had been brought up in Egypt, recaptures Rum and ascends to the throne. In the bloody campaign of cleansing Istanbul of all Christian churches and priests, he discovers a portrait of Farrokh Laqa (blessed countenance), the dazzling daughter of Petros Shah, and immediately falls in love with her. A handsome, hotheaded youth with a taste for Christian blood, Amir Arsalan abandons his kingdom in search of his beloved to arrive incognito in the perilous land of Farang. There, with the help of secret Muslim converts in high offices, he eventually meets Farrokh Laqa, who also had seen Amir Arsalan's picture and fallen in love with him. Working as a bartender in the theater, Amir Arsalan, who fluently speaks several languages of the land of Farang, becomes involved in a series of escapades that lands him in a magical world of demons and fairies, where after many adventures he eventually rescues his beloved and returns with her to the land of Farang. Impressed with Amir Arsalan's valor and devotion, Petros Shah is obliged to allow the couple to get married. Amir Arsalan returns to his seat of power, Farrokh Laqa is duly transferred to the harem, and peace is restored between the two kingdoms (fig. 5.15).

While drenched in mindless violence, the story is also colored with hilarious dialogue, sentimental romance, and childish antics. Such material was meant to entertain the shah (and later on readers and the coffeehouse audiences) and to satisfy their curiosity about Europe. Such fanciful Persianizing of Europe as a hostile yet seductive realm may be read as symptomatic of Iran's conflicting aspirations; a Layli and Majnun (or English Romeo and Juliet) paradigm of

Figure 5.15. Amir Arsalan serves incognito as a bartender (here conveniently
modified to teahouse waiter) in his quest for Farrokh Laqa in the land of Farang.
Naqib al-Mamalek, *Dastan-e Amir Arsalan-e Rumi* (Tehran, 1317/1900).
Illustrated by Hosain 'Ali. Courtesy of Ulrich Marzolph.

the amorous hero falling in love with the chaste beauty from a hostile land.
Yet contrary to the languishing Majnun of medieval romance, Amir Arsalan
embodies all Iranian aspirations for power, virility, and success (even though he
is an Ottoman prince born in Egypt).

Another fictional character of the period displayed the other side of the dilemma of incorporating Western modernity. *Ibrahim Bag's Travelogue* is a realistic novel by Zayn al-'Abedin Maraghehi, an Iranian émigré merchant who
spent most of his life in the Caucasus, Russia and the Ottoman Empire. Based
on the author's own experiences, the novel narrates the story of a young and
idealistic merchant of Azarbaijani origin whose glorified perception of Iran is
rudely shattered once he visits his ancestral homeland. Ibrahim Bag is a prosperous, widely traveled, and educated man with lofty moral values and wholesome
Shi'i faith. He is deeply pained by the decay, corruption, and backwardness his
country suffers from and aspires to bring to it material progress, social justice,
and moral reconstruction. Yet at every turn he faces intransigence.

Maraghehi's account, an excellent example of the simple prose of the late
Naseri period, is a passionate litany on the flaws of the Iranian state and society
as voiced by a Babi sympathizer. Unlike Naser al-Din's rather nonchalant attitude, Ibrahim Bag's encounter with the West makes him see the weaknesses of

his own society, state, and culture. He further observes Iran's economic stagnation and lack of investments, as well as the poverty of the majority in contrast to the wealth of a few, recurring famines and starvation, and diseases. He comments on the growth of petty crimes and an unproductive culture of peddling and usury. In particular, he notices a lack of public hygiene in bathhouses, the scarcity of modern medication, and an absence of modern hospitals. The financial chaos and mismanagement, the scarcity of money in the market, and nonexistence of modern financial institutions such as banks all incense the author. He is also troubled with lack of modern industries and modern road communication, disinterest in exploring Iran's rich mineral resources, the tragic destruction of Iran's forests, unemployment, mass migration to neighboring countries in search of menial jobs, lack of planning and statistics, and absence of standardized weights and measures.

Like most non-Western reform-minded writers of the late nineteenth century, he laments the lack of modern education and Western-style schools and secular curricula, for which he blames the conservative clerical establishment. He held the Qajar elite, along with the ulama, responsible for Iran's chronic weaknesses and its curse of being subordinate to superior powers. Domestic culprits aside, there was little blame on the Western powers' territorial and economic exploits. Typically, he does not foresee a chance of the West respecting Iran's sovereignty or caring for its well-being, so long as the state and the people are in their "deep slumber" and do not wake to care for themselves. Ibrahim Bag's critical outlook is of course complemented by a conscious sense of patriotism and a love for his homeland, for its glorious past and a desire to reconstruct it again—a viewpoint no doubt idealized by the author's long years residing abroad. Here we see the crux of an Iranian bourgeois ethos aspiring to reconcile adopted modernity with Perso-Shi'i identity, a trait that was to be sharpened with the Constitutional Revolution. Not surprisingly, in the wake of the Constitutional Revolution Ibrahim Bag's imaginary travels were widely appreciated in the prerevolutionary secret societies of the time.

THE IMPERIAL BANK OF PERSIA

Even by the 1880s the Reuter Concession entanglement had still not gone away. The persistent financier pushed the British Foreign Office and pulled strings at home in the hope of being compensated for his canceled concession. For fifteen years, his pleas to the British government had only served to block Iran from granting concessions to any other agent for the construction of railroads or other projects. This was a mixed blessing, for although it discouraged economic and financial dependence on European interests, as for example, happened in Egypt and the neighboring Ottoman Empire, it also hindered capital investment and slowed Iran's economic and human development. Yet it is important to note that the construction of railroads, despite the high hopes in this enterprise, failed to play a key role in the industrialization of the Middle East. It did, however, increase the mobility of the population, as well as of foreign goods and the export of cash crops. Even in the Pahlavi era, construction of the trans-Iranian railroad did not result in any industrial miracle.

If no major railroad project was ever undertaken in Iran before 1928, there was discussion, negotiation, and preliminary schemes throughout the 1880s and beyond. The building of a railway, the favorite pastime topic of discussion of the shah and his advisers, was often aborted by concerns over rival European powers and lack of capital. And although there was no railroad, Qajar Iran did have a five-and-a-half-mile narrow-gauge tramway built by a Belgian firm to ease Tehran's pilgrimage traffic to the nearby Shah 'Abd al-'Azim shrine south of the capital. Opened in 1887, this pride of Qajar modernity, called Chemins de Fer, but soon to be known by the public as *mashin dudi* (smoke machine), remained in service until 1961, a relic of the Qajar desire for progress and a sad remark on the dictates of geopolitics.

In 1888, the appointment of the flamboyant English envoy Sir Henry Drummond Wolff dramatically shifted the situation in favor of greater British economic involvement in Iran. Wolff was the son of an eccentric convert to Protestantism, Josef Wolff, who in the 1820s had traveled to Iran and Central Asia as a missionary, in search of the lost tribes of Israel. Before coming to Iran, Henry Drummond Wolff had served as a diplomat in Egypt and later as a British member of Parliament. He nurtured strong ties with the London financial community, including the Rothschilds, the Sassoons, and Julius Reuter. He was a vocal advocate of British economic investment abroad and of the use of capital finance to leverage British imperial supremacy. A friend of Lord Randolph Churchill and Arthur Balfour and a founding member of the influential conservative Primrose League, with its quasi-Masonic hierarchy, Wolff shared his vision of economic expansionism with Lord Salisbury and, in many respects, foreshadowed George Curzon. He listened to Julius Reuter and found in his repealed concession the potential for opening Iran to British venture capital as an arm of imperial diplomacy.

Already in 1887, after a decade of hard negotiation, Naser al-Din Shah had been pressured by the British Foreign Office to open up the Karun River, Iran's only navigable waterway, to international shipping between the Persian Gulf and to Shushtar, in central Khuzestan, and from there over a new carriage road through Bakhtiari land to Isfahan. Learning his lesson from the Reuter episode, Naser al-Din and his government were cautious in drafting the terms of this concession so as to avoid a British monopoly. They strictly regulated the shipping companies in doing business, purchasing property, and collaborating with their Iranian counterparts. Having in mind the fate of the Suez Canal and the British occupation of Egypt some six years earlier, the shah was adamant that he would not be remembered as the prey of British capitalism.

In the following decade, the Karun navigation thrived as British and Iranian shipping companies competed for cargo and passengers, hence supporting the local labor market (see map 5.1). The privately owned English company, Lynch Brothers, with years of operation along the Tigris and Euphrates, was engaged in healthy competition with a number of European and Iranian companies, of which the most successful, the Naseri Navigation company, was run by the Iranian government. The volume of trade in the Karun region increased nearly seventeen-fold between 1891 and 1902, and the building of the Bakhtiari road anticipated even larger economic advances after the first production of Khuzestan oil in 1908.

Wolff brought with him a number of proposals, plans, and potential concessions for development. Chief among them, and as it turned out the most successful, was renegotiating the Reuter concession, now a valuable instrument of British diplomacy. If a railroad was not strategically feasible, there were other projects to pursue. Establishing a modern bank seemed the most tangible and more in line with the spirit of European capital investment. The Imperial Bank of Persia (Bank-e Shahi-e Iran), established in 1889, took over the operations of the existing Oriental Bank, which had been active since 1885. The concession allowed for the first time branches to be established all over the country and to engage in all aspects of modern banking and finances, except mortgage loans for the purchase of property. Most remarkably, the government of Iran granted the bank the exclusive right to issue currency banknotes—a new development in Iran, as until then, currency had been exclusively coins. For the remainder of the Reuter concession, the Imperial Bank in effect gained control not only over the volume of the money in the Iranian market but also over Iran's finances and monetary policy. It also reserved once again the right to exploit Iran's unexplored mineral resources, as collateral for the success of the bank operation.

The Imperial Bank relied on a cadre of colonial bankers and employees brought from Egypt and elsewhere to quickly start operations, first in Tehran and soon after in major commercial centers in Iran and abroad. The issue of public shares on the London Stock Exchange raised the initial capital of £6,000,000 ($29,210,000). This hefty sum by Iranian standards dwarfed the volume of funds available to the private bankers in the bazaar (*sarrafs*) and posed immediate challenges to the usurers. As the bank began lending, the outrageous interest rates in the bazaar dropped sharply and the bank's modern operations soon supplanted the arcane practices of local competitors in many areas. Most notably, the long-distance transfer of money for domestic and foreign trade and other financial transactions was substantially eased, as bank transfers and commercial credit gradually replaced the old *barat* money orders.

The bank's greatest advantage was its monopoly on issuing banknotes, which, despite some initial resistance, was quickly accepted as the preferred medium of transaction, over the cumbersome and unreliable silver and copper coins that had long plagued the Iranian economy. The issue of banknotes of various values was a clear sign of a centralizing monetary system. While the shah's government had a limited say in the volume and issue of the new currency, the appearance of the shah's portrait on the banknotes was a symbol of his sovereignty (fig. 5.16). This proved a mixed blessing for the Iranian government, which in the following years was associated even more closely with financial downturns. The reversals of fortune were not limited to the merchants who declared bankruptcy because of mismanagement or vacillations in the worldwide markets or the bank's manipulations. The state and the Imperial Bank were blamed for market fluctuations.

Figure 5.16. Even in 1910, nine years into the Constitutional Revolution, Naser al-Din Shah's portrait still appeared on banknotes issued by the Imperial Bank of Persia. The five-tuman note was payable only in Yazd. World Banknotes and Coins (http://www.worldbanknotescoins.com/2014/12/iran-5–tomans -banknote-1910–imperial-bank-of-persia-naser-al-din-shah.html).

In 1895, for instance, the British legation's "news writer" in Shiraz reported that a leading merchant in the city in the opium export trade, Mirza Aqa Shirazi, declared bankruptcy, with debts amounting to 400,000 tumans (about $1,000,000) of which about 90,000 tumans were owed to the Imperial Bank of Persia. He wished to pay back his debts provided that the amount of 80,000 tumans that he had already paid to the bank as interest be deducted. Reaching a deadlock, the merchant subsequently took sanctuary (*bast*) in Shiraz's New Mosque. Even a visit by the bank's vice director and pressure from the provincial government, which had cut off the supply of water and food to the mosque, did not persuade him to come out. Eventually under the prime minister's direct instruction, Mirza Aqa accepted the arbitration of the Imam Jum'eh, the chief religious officer of Shiraz and a prestigious mojtahed of the city. Not only did Mirza Aqa have to plea to the Imam Jum'eh for arbitration, but also to the powerful chief of the Qashqa'i tribe of Fars, who was indebted to the bank to the tune of 73,000 tumans. To pay off his debt on a seven-year arrangement, the khan settled by mortgaging a number of his villages in the Qashqa'i land to the bank.

By the 1890s a mortgage bank funded by Russian capital and backed by the Russian legation in Tehran, cornered another financial market, making loans to the Iranian elite for their purchase of properties and other oft-unsuccessful enterprises. The riches of many of the nobility were lost to this bank, squandered on luxury goods, ostentatious mansions, horses, carriages, and travel abroad. Yet the Russian bank never came close to the breadth of the Imperial Bank's activities. As the sphere of activities of these foreign banks grew, so did the dependency of the merchants and notables on these institutions. Banks operated within a regulated framework very different from the flexible bazaar finances to which the Iranian merchants were accustomed. As the high-ranking mojtaheds became more involved in economic affairs of the community, they became more critical of the government and its foreign associates.

THE TOBACCO PROTEST AND RISE
OF CLERICAL INFLUENCE

By the late 1880s the Qajar state began to experience fresh financial pressures caused by worldwide inflation and the collapse of silver-based currencies. The growth of the state and the increasing royal and ministerial appetite for luxury and good living also demanded new sources of income, which could not be secured through agrarian and other traditional taxation. Even the increasing sale of crown lands to private ownership, mostly to influential merchants and the wealthy ulama, and farming out of the customhouses to domestic agents, could not meet the state's needs. To Naser al-Din Shah and his advisers, the sale of concessions seemed the easiest and most efficient option. And imposing a monopoly on tobacco seemed the most promising.

The politics of the late Naseri era also paved the way for greater foreign presence. Coinciding with the Karun River concession, in 1888 the British government bestowed the highly coveted decoration of the Star of India on the pro-British prince Mas'ud Mirza Zell al-Soltan (1849–1922), the Shah's powerful senior son and the semiautonomous governor of Isfahan and a number of central and western provinces of Iran. The decoration was in return for the prince's friendship to the British government, and especially his services toward the conclusion of the Karun concession and in hopes of further concessions and greater British influence in the south. Whether a premeditated move or out of fear for Zell al-Soltan's pro-British bent, the shah almost immediately dismissed the prince from all his posts except the governorship of Isfahan. The move orchestrated by the shah's shrewd new premier, 'Ali Asghar Khan Amin al-Soltan (1858–1907), was meant to curb Zell al-Soltan's unchecked ambition and to direct Britain's attention solely to Tehran.

Amin al-Soltan, son of the shah's butler who was of Georgian slave origin, started his service as a page boy in the shah's private quarters (*khalvat*) and moved his way up, first to the court and then to the divan. After the demise of Moshir al-Dowleh, he emerged as a partner in power with the chief government accountant Mirza Yusef Ashtiyani—better known as Mostawfi al-Mamalek (chief state accountant of the empire)—the shrewd leader of the government's conservative camp and a man who had served in his hereditary post since the mid-1840s. Known merely as "His Excellency" (*Jenab-e Aqa*), Mostawfi had enough skeletons in his closet to make even the shah deferential toward him and mindful of his intrigues. His death in 1890, however, opened the way for Amin al-Soltan, as the new *sadr-e a'zam*, to push for greater accession to foreign capital and expertise. A cunning confidant of the shah and a master of realpolitik—more in the style of Aqasi and Nuri than Amir Kabir and Moshir al-Dowleh—he symbolized the eventual triumph of the Naseri courtiers over the divan class. With no grand vision for overhauling the divan and no illusions of steering an independent course in foreign policy, he had vacillated between the Russian and the British embassies in search of the best deal for his royal master and himself. Struggling for survival in the age of empires, he came to share with the shah a progressively cynical attitude toward government. With the prime ministerial landscape littered with dead and disgraced predecessors, to what else could he aspire other than pleasing the shah and persuading him to comply with his schemes? The relationship between the shah and his last premier turned increasingly complex and mutually exploitative.

The shah and Amin al-Soltan, who had earlier decided against a plan to impose a state monopoly on the production of tobacco, later entered into negotiations with a British concessionaire. By 1889, during the royal visit to Europe as a guest of the British government, the shah finalized the granting of a monopoly on Iranian tobacco to a certain Major G. F. Talbot. Then probably the largest grower and exporter of tobacco in the Middle East, Iran exported largely to the Ottoman Empire and supplied its own growing domestic market (see map 5.1). The Regie monopoly, as the company came to be known, after an earlier tobacco monopoly granted to it by the Ottomans, was given a fifty-year concession for the purchase, distribution, sale, and export of all tobacco products throughout Iran. As a major income-earning commodity, tobacco was also a vital to Iranian daily life. By the 1890s as many as two and a half million people, a good 25 percent of the Iranian population, both men and women, were regular smokers, mostly in the form of water pipes (*qaliyan*, better known today in the West as *hookah*). Peasants and the poorer classes used long pipes (*chopoq*) and consumed inferior-quality tobacco. No other commodity, except perhaps tea, held such sway over the public. Since its introduction in the late sixteenth century, the production of Iranian tobacco increased all over the country, especially in the provinces of Azarbaijan, Khorasan, Isfahan, and Fars.

It is remarkable to note how imprudently the shah had once again fallen victim to a foreign concession, and for a commodity vital to a large sector of Iranian producers and consumers. It was as though the memories of the ill-fated Reuter concession had all but faded. No doubt, the glamour of the English surroundings, the subtle hints of his British host, and the not-so-subtle persuasions of his chief minister convinced the shah to go ahead with the concession at the time the ruling elite was ever more oblivious to the public's growing anti-Qajar sentiment. The shah's hopes for short-term gain had no bounds, even at the expense of the growers and merchants whose sustenance was crucial to the national economy. If the merchants could pocket a substantial profit from the tobacco trade, the shah must have reasoned, why not him? The royal gain, of course, came at the expense of a large sector of Iranian exporters, wholesalers, distributors—perhaps as many as five thousand—and a much larger body of medium- and small-scale tobacco growers.

Yet even the hope for a hefty profit was illusory. The Regie concession allocated to the Iranian state no more than a meager royalty of £15,000 ($75,000) and one-quarter of annual net profits, after deducting expenses. By early 1890, the Regie monopoly had begun to establish a network of provincial offices throughout Iran, manned mostly by colonial bureaucrats, and had started to purchase tobacco from the Iranian growers soon found, to their dismay, that they had no choice but to sell to the Regie at uncompetitive fixed prices. Yet the main opposition came from the tobacco merchants and their associates. Contrary to the hopes of the shah and the Regie, eliminating the Iranian middleman and breaking the exporting merchants' hold on the market did not pass uneventfully.

Standing to lose their livelihoods, they began to mobilize whatever popular and clerical support they could muster to oppose the monopoly and persuade the state to repeal it. A movement of mass protests between late 1890 and early 1892 successfully challenged both the foreign monopoly and the authority of the Qajar state. This was the first nationwide protest movement, at least since the collapse of the Babi resistance in the 1850s, with popular participation and a pronounced anti-imperialist agenda, a rebellion that anticipated and in some ways paved the way for the Constitutional Revolution some fifteen years later. The Tobacco Protest was the first time that the merchants of the bazaar, a number of high-ranking clergy, and a handful of dissidents found common ground to mobilize the public nationwide and challenge the authority of the shah.

Sporadic protests in the cities began in Shiraz in late 1890 and continued over the course of the next year in Isfahan, Tabriz, Mashhad, and other tobacco-growing centers (map 5.2). In nearly all instances, it was the merchants who pleaded with local mojtaheds to render their support and voice the merchants' grievances. Public gatherings in the mosques denounced the *Farangis* for their intrusion into the affairs of the Muslims and, more urgently, for ritually polluting the handling of tobacco. Condemnations such as these were familiar staples of anti-European rhetoric in the Qajar period. Yet the mojtaheds of influence and wealth were generally reluctant to sever their traditional ties with the state and openly criticize the shah's initiative, for fear they would make themselves targets of government retaliation. They nevertheless soon realized that they had no choice but to side with the merchants and large-scale growers. The slowing of the flow of religious taxes and dues originating in the bazaar brought the message home. By the beginning of 1891, the mojtaheds, especially in Isfahan, with the Najafi family at the helm, came to occupy a prominent place in the protest movement.

It was Tabriz, however, that witnessed the most serious protests against the monopoly by ordinary men and women. To be sure, there are traces of anti-Regie provocation by the Russians in the Tabriz bazaar. Iran's powerful northern neighbor viewed the Regie as a British operation designed to infiltrate Azarbaijan, a province Russia traditionally considered its own backyard. But

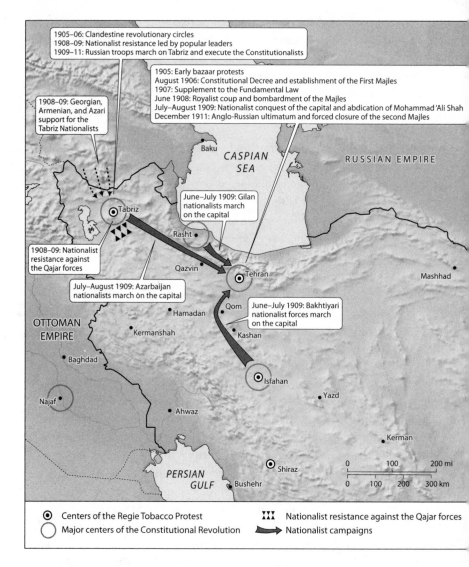

Map 5.2. The Tobacco Protest and the Constitutional Revolution, 1891–1911

the thrust of opposition again came from exporting merchants whose very livelihood had been jeopardized. Facing the angry crowd and Russian objections, the crown prince Mozaffar al-Din Mirza (1853–1907) and his provincial minister alerted Tehran that unless something was done, they could not guarantee the safety of the province or the Regie agents against the gathering revolutionary storm. In response, the Regie company, in consultation with the shah, decided to temporarily cease operations in Azarbaijan. This obvious setback was the first victory for the growing opposition. That a protest movement that had started in the south of the country was fully embraced in the northern commercial center signified a shared economy that surpassed Iran's typical regional polarity.

The final act of the anti-Regie revolt, however, played out in a dramatic boycott that involved more than the merchants and their allies. In November 1892, a fatwa attributed to Mirza Hasan Shirazi was widely distributed throughout Iran; it called for a ban on smoking tobacco so long as its distribution remained in the hands of the infidels. Even though as early as 1891, rumors of the ban on smoking were in circulation in Shiraz, it was the name of the chief mojtahed in the 'Atabat (the shrine cities of southern Iraq) that gave the legal opinion the necessary weight. "Smoking under such circumstances," the fatwa declared, "is tantamount to combating the Imam of the Age, may God hasten his return." That the fatwa was rumored to be fabricated by the head of Tehran's merchant guild, Haji Mohammad Kazem Malek al-Tojjar, and his associates in the name of Shirazi proved of secondary importance. The ranking mojtaheds in Isfahan and Tehran—who were in contact via telegraph with Shirazi in the town of Samarra in southern Iraq—made sure that he would approve the fatwa issued in his name (fig. 5.17).

By early 1890s Shirazi was recognized and referred to as the *marja'-e taqlid* (the source of [universal] emulation) throughout the Shi'i world, a position for which he was at least in part indebted to the celebrated advocate of pan-Islamism, Sayyed Jamal al-Din Asadabadi (better known as Afghani). In a widely circulated letter to Shirazi in 1891, Afghani praised his clerical compatriot as the leader of the Shi'i world and called on him to oppose Naser al-Din Shah's despotism, corruption, and selling out to foreign interests. Aside from the Babi anti-Qajar opposition, some four decades earlier, this was the first open call in modern Iranian history for the overthrow of the shah, even though it did not call for the fall of the Qajar dynasty or the monarchy as a whole. Afghani, who earlier had been invited back to his homeland by the shah shortly before the Regie crisis to serve as an adviser to the state, soon came under suspicion for his implicit criticism of the shah. He received the cold shoulder from the shah and shortly thereafter, coinciding with the beginning of the Regie protest, was disgracefully dragged out of the shrine of 'Abd al-'Azim, where he had taken sanctuary (*bast*), and escorted to the Iraqi border.

A renowned dissident, who appeared all his mature life in the guise of a Sunni Afghan, and chief advocate of pan-Islamism, Afghani stirred anti-British sentiments from British India to Afghanistan to Istanbul to Egypt. Born in 1839 in the village of Asadabad, 32 miles east of Hamadan in western Iran, a region known for its heterodox Ahl-e Haqq community, Afghani received some standard

Figure 5.17. The Regie Protest further raised Mirza Hasan Shirazi's standing
as the undisputed *marja'-e taqlid*. The multitudes sitting for the Friday
prayer behind the leader of prayer here, identified as Shirazi, presumably in
the town of Samarra in southern Iraq, is a testament to his popularity.
Postcard c. 1910. Author's collection.

Islamic philosophical training before moving to the Shiʻi cities of southern Iraq, where as a seminarian he was exposed to Shaykhi and Babi ideas. By the 1880s his magnetic presence had earned him a few devotees in Iran, including Malek al-Tojjar, and a few Naseri courtiers and statesmen. Yet contrary to his popularity in Egypt and India, and admirers such as the celebrated Shaykh Muhammad ʻAbdu, Afghani never earned great support in Iran in his own time. The complexity of his personality, his peripatetic lifestyle, his political versatility, and above all concealing his Shiʻi identity under a Sunni façade could allow his message to be heard only through insidious channels. Having been humiliated in Iran in 1891, Afghani nursed a deep grudge against the shah, a resentment that no doubt contributed some years later to Naser al-Din Shah's assassination. His collaboration with former Babis, such as the celebrated writer and intellectual Mirza Aqa Khan Kermani, may have influenced Afghani's emphasis on the shah's illegitimate rule. His plea to Shirazi as the "head" (*ra'is*) and supreme exemplar (*marja'-e taqlid*) of the Shiʻi community served to propel Shirazi to the forefront of the political struggle.

Whether it was Afghani's provocation or the emerging consensus among dissidents and discontent merchants, the Tobacco Protest had widened the gap between the state and the ulama, and displayed the latter's compliance with the grievances of their mercantile clients. Popular involvement was an unexpected outcome of a protest rooted in deeper economic problems. In Iran men and women complied with Shirazi's fatwa in public and in private. Water pipes were broken and thrown into the streets, or otherwise stored in backrooms and out of sight. Tobacco retailers shut their businesses, and banners were brought out to demonstrate public solidarity. To the shah's great annoyance, apparently even women of his own harem refrained from smoking on the grounds that they followed the *marja'-e taqlid* on religious issues, not the shah. The public ban, perhaps aggravated by tobacco withdrawal symptoms, demonstrated the power of mass protest and persuaded people to take even bolder steps. Negotiations with Amin al-Soltan, exchanges of telegrams between the shah and the ulama, and between the mojtaheds in the capital and in the provincial centers, added to the sense of urgency. The rebellion was no longer localized or confined to one economic sector but increasingly gave voice to popular frustrations on a national scale.

The prerevolutionary scene—complete with vigilante enforcement of the smoking ban, appearance of clandestine posters and leaflets known as "night-letters," and declaring a curfew in the capital—reached its climax in January 1892. The government's threat to expel from the capital the chief mojtahed of Tehran, Mirza Hasan Ashtiyani, if he continued to provoke the public and refrain from breaking the smoking ban, backfired. He refused to accept the terms offered by the government. The violent demonstration soon after, following the closure of the bazaar, brought a huge crowd to the Arg square in front of the royal citadel calling not only for the repeal of the tobacco monopoly but also for an end to government corruption and the shah's despotic rule. The crowd showered insults not only on Kamran Mirza, who served as governor of the capital and minister of war, but also on the premier Amin al-Soltan and on the person of the shah. This was followed by an attempt to break through the gates of the citadel. The armed confrontation with the royal guards and the elite troops who were brought in to defend the royal compound, ended in the deaths of ten demonstrators, with many more injured.

The open revolt and clandestine propaganda denouncing the shah for despotism and corruption but also chastising the mojtaheds for compromise and inaction, were sufficient that both the shah and the ulama recognize the greater danger—an imminent uprising that threatened the very survival of both institutions. Immediately following the demonstration, the shah announced the complete repeal of the Regie monopoly in the domestic market and for the export of tobacco. The latter issue nevertheless remained a matter of dispute with Regie for a long time afterward. The shah also made sure that the mojtaheds who threatened mass migration to Iraq in sympathy with Ashtiyani were financially rewarded in the capital and in the provinces.

Despite his initial hesitation, Mirza Hasan Shirazi consented to lifting the tobacco ban. Once the shah was assured of British support, he went along with the terms of the repeal, including payment to the Regie of a cancellation penalty. To do so, the Iranian government was forced for the first time to borrow the necessary sum from the British-controlled Imperial Bank of Persia—a half million pounds sterling ($2,500,000), with an interest rate of six percent over a forty-year period. Foreign borrowing was a road well trodden by the Egyptian khedive and the Ottoman sultan, and in both cases it led to bankruptcy. The shah and his government, perhaps the Qajar establishment as a whole, however, had a more urgent issue than bankruptcy to worry about.

The Tobacco Protest was able to destabilize the hard-won order of the Naseri era and ignite a popular protest led by a fragile coalition of merchants, the ulama, and dissidents. In the months and years after the Regie, Iran more frequently witnessed expressions of turmoil in the provinces, often with mojtaheds at the helm. In Isfahan, a center of Shi'i activism, the notorious Aqa Najafi, the doyen of a wealthy and powerful clerical family (who for years had fought a dirty war with Zell al-Soltan, prince-governor of the city), even declared the advent of an "Islamic government" on the heels of a declining monarchy. It was as though faith in the shah as an icon of stability had been shattered. Some four years after the end of Regie, on May 1, 1896, Naser al-Din Shah was assassinated on the eve of a jubilee celebrating his fiftieth lunar year on the Qajar throne (AH 1264–1313). He had gone to the 'Abd al-'Azim shrine to pay homage to the Shi'i saint and give thanks for his long rule, which had been the longest since the Safavid Tahmasp I. After saying his prayers, he walked freely among the pilgrims, who, contrary to the normal practice of royal visits, were allowed to stay inside the shrine. There he was shot point-blank by Mirza Reza Kermani, a devotee of Jamal al-Din Afghani. Kermani was an eccentric itinerant dealer in luxury goods and expensive fabrics, who harbored a grudge against the shah's son, Kamran Mirza, for torturing him and subjecting him to years of imprisonment.

The bullet that killed the shah heralded the end of an era, a half a century of relative constancy. The veneer of modernization that covered the Qajar state was just that. The reformist measures by statesmen such as Amir Kabir and Moshir al-Dowleh never truly transformed Qajar society. Some features of European material culture came to shape urban space, art and architecture, dress, food, and music. The foundations of the state, however, remained largely unchanged. The old Qajar elite were being gradually replaced by a new class of court appointees who were more dependent on the person of the shah, yet the general conduct of the court and divan remained essentially the same.

Naser al-Din's private life, and the life of the royal harem, also remained unchanged, except that his numerous wives, sisters, and concubines became more languid and, with few exceptions, more vain. With age, the shah's inner court acquired a prurient ambiance, well evident in many entries in the secret diaries of E'temad al-Saltaneh. With a sarcastic eye, he observed changes in the shah's conduct, the degrading quality of his companions and favorites, his endless daily sorties to the outskirts of the capital to visit royal resorts, pleasure gardens, and mountain retreats, and his camping out with a huge retinue around Tehran and elsewhere. He quietly recorded the childish pleasures that punctuated the hideous routine of the court. Among his recurring topics were the shah's obsessive affection for his favorite page boy Malijak, trivial envies and enmities in the harem and inner court, the shah's curious taste in dress and appearance, and above all his patronizing strategies of favor and fury (see fig. 5.17).

After the failure of Herat during the first decade of his rule, Naser al-Din's relations with European powers also remained constant, if not entirely uneventful. The shah's success in keeping the imperial neighbors at arm's length is one of his notable achievements. European intrusion into economic and commercial spheres seemed inevitable, as had happened with the Reuter concession, the Imperial Bank of Persia, the Karun River concession, concession for a large scale export of Caspian lumber to a Russian private concern in 1883, and the Regie monopoly. Yet Naser al-Din had been far more successful than his contemporaries—Sultan 'Abd al-Hamid, the khedives of Egypt, Central Asian khanates, the amir of Afghanistan, and the subjugated rajas of the Indian princely states—in preserving his country's political sovereignty and territorial integrity in the age of colonial expansion. He learned how to turn the terms of the European presumption of Iran as a buffer state to his favor, and how to play the Russian territorial threat in the north against British ambitions in the south and in the Persian Gulf. The 1857 loss of Herat province, a major territorial setback, comparable to the loss of the Caucasus, and minor border compromises to peacefully settle Iran's eastern boundaries, did not minimize the achievements of the Naseri era.

The state's relations with social groups also remained largely unchanged until the last decade of the nineteenth century and especially after the Tobacco Protest when the tacit state-ulama relationship went through a momentary crisis. The merchants and artisans also began to voice their discontent as their economic livelihood was further exposed to vacillations in world markets, foreign trade, and foreign concessions. More than ever before, people held the state responsible for its inability to shield the country against such vulnerabilities, for the lack of security in their everyday life, and for weak economic infrastructure. Greater contact with the neighboring world—Russian-annexed Caucasian and Central Asian provinces, the Ottoman capital and Ottoman provinces such as Iraq and Syria, Egypt under British occupation, and British India—made many émigré Iranians aware of their country's relative underdevelopment, economic disadvantages, and the Iranian government's failure to deal with mounting poverty, health, and social problems. By the last decade of the nineteenth century more than quarter of a million Iranians had emigrated in search of work and a better life to neighboring cities and regions, especially Baku, Tiflis, Ashkhabad, Istanbul, Cairo, Alexandria, Mumbai, and the pilgrimage cities of southern Iraq.

The Tobacco Protest, and later the assassination of the shah, were symptoms of deeper discontent that first surfaced in makeshift jellygraph posters denouncing the shah and his government, in the exile newspapers such as *Qanun* published in London by Malkom Khan and smuggled to Iran to clandestine reading groups and discussion circles. Dissent found wider and more organized public expression in the coming years as the Naseri age gave way to a more relaxed decade under Mozaffar al-Din Shah (r. 1896–1906). Broader access to the printed word through newspapers and books broadened the intellectual horizons. The nascent press was hardly allowed to criticize the Qajar state and its local agents, but newspapers and translations of Western popular knowledge brought greater awareness of scientific and technological advances, world geography and history, institutions of a modern state, discovery of new lands, and Western colonial advances and economic penetration. The Constitutional Revolution of 1905–1911 signified the rise of a new national community conscious of itself and its deprivations largely through press and telegraph communication inside Iran and with the outside world.

6

THE CONSTITUTIONAL REVOLUTION: ROAD TO A PLURAL MODERNITY (1905–1911)

On December 12, 1905, following closure of the bazaar, a huge crowd gathered at Tehran's Friday mosque to protest the mistreatment of the city's sugar merchants by the governor of the capital and to demand that the mojtaheds of the city come out in their defense. The crowd listened to Jamal al-Din Isfahani, a middle-ranking popular preacher and a crypto-Babi, who rebuked the governor for his cruelty, warned that the Iranian nation under the aegis of the deserved justice and public security, and called for the lifting of the state's draconian price controls. Further, he declared that both the common law, as enforced by the state, and the Islamic law, as practiced by the mojtaheds, must comply with "the law" (*qanun*), a notion new to Iranian audiences that implied the Constitution. If the shah is a true Muslim, he stressed, he too must comply with the people's wishes. The demands epitomized the predicament of a revolution that his sermon served to inaugurate.

These bold claims were bound to agitate the pro-state ulama. In the midst of Jamal al-Din's sermon, the government-appointed Imam of the Tehran Friday Mosque, outraged by the preacher's outspokenness, ordered him forcefully pulled from the pulpit and expelled. Subsequently, the club-wielding government guards rushed into the mosque and drove out the protesting crowd. The next day, some of the ulama who had been present at the gathering and were offended by the government's overreaction left the city in symbolic protest and took sanctuary (*bast*) in the local shrine of 'Abd al-'Azim south of the capital. The shrine soon became the center of protest, and the population of Tehran came in droves to sympathize with the protesters.

The incident marked the beginning of a popular movement that eventually came to be recognized as the Constitutional Revolution (Enqelab-e Mashruteh), a transformational experience with major consequences for twentieth-century Iran. The previously described episode highlights most, if not all, of the elements that would shape the revolution: merchants and artisans resentful of an inefficient and intrusive state; the lower- and middle-ranking mullahs of various shades calling on the mojtaheds to come out in support of the people; the Qajar state's desperate reactions to demands for popular participation and eventually for a constitution; and finally, the urban population in large numbers (fig. 6.1). To these groups were added in due course the Western-educated elite, who joined the indigenous radical elements and helped shape the parliament (Majles) and frame the modern constitution.

The emerging constitutional movement, with its distinctive pluralistic features that allowed for diverse social and political groups to participate, however, soon ran counter to a royalist front that, backed by imperial Russia, aimed to reassert the power of an autocratic Qajar shah in power and preserve the privileges of the ruling elite. The revolution also contested the privileges of the very

Sabzi Meïdan - Téhéran.

Figure 6.1. The multitudes gathered in Sabzeh Maydan (in front of the Tehran bazaar) to commemorate the day of 'Ashura signified a new urban force that was soon to propel the Constitutional Revolution.
Postcard, c. 1900s. Author's collection.

clerical class that first came to its support but soon changed course as the constitution and the Majles imposed limits on the mojtaheds' sphere of authority and defined the boundaries of the shari'a. The outcome was a multifaceted struggle that helped define Iran's modern national identity, emerging first in the civil war of 1908–1909 and continuing in the two decades before the rise of Reza Shah and the establishment of the Pahlavi order in 1925.

In these respects, the Constitutional Revolution was unrivaled in the history of the modern Middle East. Neither the Young Turks Revolution of 1908 nor the anticolonial movements in Egypt in 1919, and elsewhere in the Arab world after World War I, shared the extent of the Constitutional Revolution's grassroots base. During the five decades of Pahlavi rule, many of the political achievements of the Constitutional Revolution would be compromised by the arbitrary conduct of the state. Later, the Islamic Revolution of 1979 abrogated the Constitution of 1906 altogether. Yet the Constitutional Revolution remained a turning point in the history of Iran above all because it marked a step forward on the path to sociopolitical modernity. Under the veneer of Western liberalism and constitutional order, the revolution tried to offer indigenous answers to a distinctly Perso-Shi'i problem of social justice that had long been present in the milieu of Iranian dissent. In effect, the revolution sought to secularize Shi'i millenarian aspirations by incorporating such modern concepts as nationalism, the rule of law, limits to state power, individual rights, and people's representation. The revolution juxtaposed these principles with the ancient vestiges of kingship and the clerical establishment. The civil war of 1908–1909 between the constitutionalists and the royalists was the climax of a revolutionary struggle, for it weakened Qajar rule and relegated, at least temporarily, the conservative clergy to the political wilderness. The turmoil caused by the revolution, however, was compounded by the European threat of military occupation before and during World War I, which brought an abrupt end to the constitutional experiment and dampened revolutionary aspirations.

NEW VOICES OF DISSENT

Internal dissent on the eve of the Constitutional Revolution drew on popular discontent from the pulpit of the mosques and through the nascent press and modern schools, but it still relied on voices of protest abroad to articulate its message. Greater exposure to the outside world through education, press, and travel for some Iranian observers augmented Western material advances and in turn bolstered the discourse of decline and renewal, as well as the urgency to adopt what they called modern civilization.

Polemical tracts reached the Iranian public less in print form and more through handwritten copies that circulated in dissident circles and influenced the rhetoric and the substance of revolutionary preaching. Based mostly in Istanbul but also in Cairo, Beirut, Calcutta, Mumbai, and in the Caucasus, the works of this small circle were barely known to the general public, and even the educated elite did not engage in their reformist discourse throughout the Naseri era. Only by the turn of the twentieth century did the reform literature enjoy greater exposure among semiclandestine circles inside Iran. In particular, despair over Iran's material plight and moral degeneration, and denouncements of the corrupt establishment and the intransigent, found new audiences. The small circle of Iranians abroad consisted mostly of those of heterodox or minority backgrounds who were often in contact with one another and reading one another's works—a "republic of letters" of a sort. Their improvised ideas of reform included critiques of the conservative officialdom but seldom the mojtahed establishment. The alternative models they suggested were often based on facile readings of the French Enlightenment or inspired by ideals of benevolent rule, as seen through the prism of Russian authoritarianism. Overall, they were naively praiseful of Europe, though often inconsistent in their quest for modernity.

An important area of dialogue centered on education. Reformist literature of the late Qajar era and the Constitutional Revolution lamented illiteracy and the absence of modern educational institutions and was critical of the madrasa curriculum and its deficiencies. It also called for a change in the Persian script, one instance of a broader preoccupation shared by reformers in many non-Western societies. The Persian highly stylized *shekasteh* handwriting common in the Qajar era, though undeniably an art form, was viewed as cumbersome for the demands of public education. The lack of modern sanitation and modern medicine, malnutrition, and the absence of an effective public health system to combat outbreaks such as cholera and to control diseases such as smallpox and trachoma were other sources of grievance. Glaring scientific and industrial shortcomings in comparison with "civilized" countries was the cause of profound concern. Images of decay and deprivation in Iran were contrasted not only to idealized notions of Western material advances but also to an idealized vision of Iran's ancient past. Only on the model of Western powers, it was argued, and the modern rule of law and constitution, could Iran overcome its rampant maladies. The reformist literature of the nineteenth century was generally oblivious to Europe's colonial ambitions, and when it wasn't, it often implied that falling under Western imperial might was an inevitable fate of the weaker nations.

One notable anomaly with reference to the impending colonial threat was the celebrated statesman Mirza Malkom Khan (1833–1909). His critique not only showed some awareness of the European threat but also aspired to adapt to the realities of the Iranian environment and to Islamic mores and values. A man of complex personality, Malkom's creative mind nevertheless left a lacuna between his high-minded positivist perspective and his self-serving financial interests. His influence on the Constitutional Revolution nevertheless went beyond a mere proposal for the state's reorganization. He considered the reform of the Persian script as key to the transmission of knowledge to the masses. To demonstrate his point, in 1884 he even published in London Sa'di's *Golestan* in his improvised alphabet.

Malkom's eclectic "Humanity" creed (Adamiyat), inspired by August Comte's positivist Religion of Humanity, was an extension of his quasi-masonic Faramush-khaneh of earlier years. Rising above organized religion, it aspired to the universal values of scientific progress, human rights, and tolerance. He even persuaded Naser al-Din Shah to issue a decree similar to the Ottoman 1856 Imperial Rescript of the Tanzimat period, to recognize for the first time the security of all the subjects' basic rights to their lives and properties. Yet it was the disregard for such measures rebuked in the pages of the periodical *Qanun* that began to reach Iranian readers through clandestine channels.

In publishing *Qanun*, Malkom joined forces with Sayyed Jamal al-Din Afghani, and his cohorts. Expelled from Iran in 1891 at the outset of the Regie Protest, Afghani became a vociferous critic of the Qajar state. As much as Malkom was a prophet of secular modernity, Afghani was a pioneer of political Islam, albeit in the garb of Ottoman-backed pan-Islamic activism, an ideology with little popular support among Shi'i Iranians. What did appeal to Afghani's Iranian audiences, to whom he spoke in Persian, his mother tongue, was a politicized reading of Islam not merely as a set of beliefs and practices, or the tedious works of the Shi'i jurists, but as a community of resistance, a force of unanimity that had already proved effective during the Tobacco Protest. The message of defying Europe's imperial powers through religio-national solidarity resonated in the Iranian milieu through wide distribution of his famous letter to Shirazi. The clandestine "nocturnal letters" (*shabnameh*) jellygraphs in Iran also circulated dissident views and were even posted on the mosques' gates and other public buildings. After the assassination of Naser al-Din Shah, Afghani acquired greater fame in Iranian dissident circles for instigating the removal of a tyrant who had arrested the course of Iran's progress. That Afghani and some of his devotees were paid agents of another tyrant, Sultan 'Abd al-Hamid, and that he himself wished to be a "sword" in the hand of any power that could hire his services (perhaps with the exception of the British), did not seem to tarnish his image even at the end of his life—he died of cancer in 1897 while under house arrest in Istanbul. For the "philosopher of the East," as Afghani liked to portray himself, a nostalgic reading of the Islamic past was complemented by a call for religious renewal, for an Islamic Reformation, as he called it, that could rescue Muslims not only from the yoke of Christian colonialism but also from their tyrannical rulers.

The odd union of Malkom and Afghani, prophets of Western modernity and pan-Islamism, anticipated the ideological tension that later riddled the Constitutional Revolution. The ideological link between these figures and a new generation of Iranian activists at the turn of the twentieth century was maintained through the likes of Mirza Aqa Khan Kermani (1854–1897). An original thinker with some zest, he indigenized Malkom's positivist reformism and borrowed from Afghani his anti-imperialist stance. What he contributed to this admixture of nineteenth-century Iranian dissent was an ideology of conscious nationalism rooted in the idealized narrative of the ancient Iranian past and set against the gloomy realities of its present. Kermani's nationalism, with its anti-Arab and even anti-Islamic outbursts, underscored a collective destiny and called for the overhaul of Iran's waning moral resolve and cultural orientation. His writings, mostly unpublished, nevertheless came to be an important feature of the constitutional and the post-constitutional intellectual landscape. Kermani's personal makeup contributed to the fluidity of his ideas, but also to his many flaws and his vacillating political orientation. Born in 1856 to an old but impoverished Sufi family with Zoroastrian ties in the religiously diverse city of Kerman, in the remote heart of southeastern Iran, he was an early example of a modern intellectual dissident. His birthplace, a venue of Sufi Ne'matollahi, Shaykhi, Usuli, Zoroastrian, Babi, and Baha'i loyalties, not only helped shape Kermani but also produced numerous dissidents in the constitutional period. Kermani gravitated toward Babi thought through his philosophy teacher, who also taught him the rudiments of Mulla Sadra's philosophy. His short career as a tax collector came to an abrupt end following a quarrel with the provincial governor, who forced him into exile.

The young Kermani eventually landed in Istanbul, where he worked the rest of his short life as a freelance journalist, translator, political activist, and private tutor. Writing for a while under a pseudonym for the Persian popular weekly *Akhtar*, published out of Istanbul, Kermani's articles addressed current affairs, economy, politics, education, and culture from a critical perspective but in a veiled language acceptable to the newspaper's readership. By underscoring Iran's sociopolitical ills, he hoped to reach wider audiences. Displaying symptoms typical of an angry intellectual in exile grappling with an identity crisis, he conceived of a national identity enthralled with the glories of the ancient past, which he had discovered mostly through the *Shahnameh* but also through Greek and Roman texts available in French and the emerging European scholarship on the subject. In contrast, in his later years he portrayed Arabo-Islamic influence as alien, backward, and responsible for Iran's presumed degeneration and decline. Only by casting aside this dark legacy of prejudice and pollution, Kermani argued, could the Iranians recover their lost purity and once more rejuvenate their country.

Drastic critique of the Islamic past, it can be argued, could have occurred only in a milieu impregnated with heterodoxy. Kermani was not a conventional Babi loyal to the messianic precepts and its proto-shari'a system devised by the Bab in his *Bayan*, even though for a while he did remain loyal to the Azali activist brand of Babism and a passionate supporter of the Azali sectarian battles against the Baha'is. Yet the Babi past served Kermani as an intellectual springboard to come to terms with European modernity. His intellectual profile included not only the European Enlightenment but also a complex amalgam of materialist philosophy, socialist political programs, and nationalism with a chauvinist bent. It was the renewed subversion against the Qajar state, however, that in 1896 cost Kermani his life, when he and two of his cohorts were arrested and detained by order of the Sultan 'Abd al-Hamid, who seems to have been alerted of an anti-Qajar conspiracy in the making. After the assassination of Naser al-Din Shah, they were duly extradited to Iran as accomplices and executed in Tabriz by the order of then crown prince Mohammad 'Ali Mirza (1872–1925). Whatever Kermani's role, it was his memory as an anti-Qajar dissident that elevated him to the status of a martyr in the narrative of the Constitutional Revolution.

Despite his curious support for pan-Islamism, Kermani shared anti-Islamic sentiments with another intellectual exile of his time, Mirza Fath 'Ali Akhundzadeh (1812–1878), an Azarbaijani playwright and ardent social commentator who had spent most of his adult life in the Russian civil service in Tiflis. An unabashed critic of all organized religions, and especially Islam, he advocated a rationalistic view of civilization that was the closest a nineteenth-century Iranian expatriate could come to the Deist ideas of the French Enlightenment (albeit via Russian literature). The chief vehicle for this social and moral critique was modern European theater, a medium new to the Iranian (and Azarbaijani) audience. Even though Akhundzadeh's plays were published abroad and enjoyed a sizable readership in their original Turkish and later in Persian translation, they were hardly ever performed. A major theme in Akhundzadeh's works, inspired by the simplicity of Molière's plays, was the contrast between the hold of old beliefs and practices, the "superstitions," in Muslim societies and the potency of modern civilizational forces, especially the modern sciences and medicine.

More so in his unpublished polemics, Akhundzadeh internalized the positivist critique of Islam and its incompatibility with the demands of the modern world. In fictional correspondence dated 1863 between Kamal al-Dowleh, an Iranian skeptic writing from Tabriz, and his interlocutor, an Indian Shi'i prince residing in the holy cities of southern Iraq, Akhundzadeh offered a daring criticism of Shi'i beliefs and institutions. He held Islam, its scripture and doctrine, and more pointedly, the Shi'i beliefs and teachings responsible for Iran's current state of affairs and the root cause of the decline of the Persian civilization. In Voltairean fashion he ridiculed the idea of divine inspiration, the tales in the Qur'an, and the force of bigotry and unreason that the Islamic religion and the disastrous Arab conquest of Iran had unleashed on his countrymen. Like Kermani, he also lamented the loss of the great civilization of pre-Islamic Iran. Drawing historical and sociological comparisons with his own time, he chastised Islam for its antirational and unenlightened principals, including the ignorance, arrogance, and superstitions of the religious authorities and for their condoning of slavery, torture, and the mistreatment of women. With lesser intensity he also held the Qajar state responsible for corruption and mismanagement, and he attacked the undeserved privileges of the elite.

Yet in his discourse of decline, Akhundzadeh, who was a great admirer of Russian high culture, barely ever held the European powers accountable for their part. For him, as for Malkom and most other reformers of the nineteenth century, the major sources of evil were domestic rather than geopolitical. European imperial rivalry barely drew his attention, and he had little to say about colonial ambitions all over the globe. One can almost read between the lines a cold reality that echoed the message of the old Persian "mirror" literature: might is right. If Iran was disempowered and subdued by the West, it was not the West's fault; instead, Iranians, and Muslims in general, had failed to cast aside their threadbare cultural and religious values and embrace Western civilization. Movements of indigenous reform within Shi'ism, too, were denounced by Akhundzadeh. Although he condemned the persecution of the Babis, still fresh in his mind, as barbaric, he treated the message of the Babis and the Shaykhis as merely a reiteration of Shi'i superstitions and yet another obstacle to the march toward civilization.

Like Akhundzadeh, the Qajar prince Jalal al-Din Mirza, another ardent nationalist with whom Akhundzadeh corresponded, viewed the Arab conquest of Iran, and its cultural and political legacy, as a historical catastrophe that pummeled the superior Iranian civilization under its hoof. Jalal al-Din Mirza, the former honorary head of Malkom's Faramush-khaneh, had produced a rudimentary history textbook, presumably for elementary teaching in the Dar al-Fonun. The *Nameh-ye Khosravan* (Book of the kings), though mostly a facile list of Iranian dynasties, was written in "pure Persian," in a simple style and devoid of Perso-Arabic words. Illustrated with imagined portraits of the Persian mythological and Sasanian kings, his was a conscious effort to narrate Iranian history from its legendary origins to the Islamic period. To demonstrate continuity in the Iranian past, there was no significant reference to Islam or the Arab conquest, which, like the Mongol conquests, was portrayed as a dark aberration.

Themes of civilization and reform, the need for constitutional recourse, the heritage of the ancient past versus decline in the present, and the critique of conservatives' obstacles to modernity all laid the foundations of the constitutional discourse. They simply had been woken from their dormancy when the economic crisis at the turn of the twentieth century needed a language of protest.

ECONOMIC DOWNTURN AND MERCHANTS' GRIEVANCES

The assassination of Naser al-Din Shah put an end to Iran's political isolation, to which it was subjected by the canny monarch. The accession of the new ruler, Mozaffar al-Din Shah, almost inadvertently broadened Iran's cultural horizons (see chart 2 in chapter 4). He possessed neither his father's panache nor his political skills to pull strings at the court and the divan, or to play the competing European powers off one another to his own advantage. He was a man of gentle disposition, with an earnest desire to open up the country to social and educational reforms. His naïveté aside, he tried to break away from the web of Machiavellian politics of earlier years. Yet to maintain some continuity, he briefly reinstated his father's chief minister, 'Ali Asghar Khan Amin al-Soltan, who was given the additional title of Atabak, or "guardian tutor," even though the new shah was well into his fifties. Atabak, the sole chief minster of the Naseri period to escape elimination at the hand of his former royal master, had orchestrated a bloodless transfer of power. Yet he proved helpless in the face of mounting economic pressures, the intrigues of the greedy inner court circle that came with the new shah from Tabriz, and rising popular discontent. His weapon of realpolitik was no match for the new challenges that loomed large after Naser al-Din's death, and he was dismissed later in 1896.

The new premier, 'Ali Khan Amin al-Dowleh, who had long been hailed as a champion of reforms, did not last in office for more than a year either. His program of fiscal, administrative, and educational reforms was the closest a Qajar statesman could come to the lofty ideals contemplated by people like Malkom Khan. Yet Amin al-Dowleh's dream of reconstructing what he dubbed "ruined Iran" (*Iran-e viran*) ran counter to the three-headed dragon of foreign interests, court intrigue, and economic downturn, not to mention clerical conservatism. The budding modern schools, inspired mostly by the Ottoman *Roshdiyeh* system, were the test case. Advocated by a dissident educator of the Babi leaning, Mirza Hasan Tabrizi (better known as Roshdiyeh), who had spent years in Beirut and Istanbul, the new schools soon were to meet the clergy's open antagonism. Such mojtaheds as Shaykh Mohammad Taqi Najafi, better known as Aqa Najafi, the powerful jurist of Isfahan, were at the forefront of opposition. The teaching of European languages in particular was branded as mimicking the ways of the infidels. Modern sciences, geography, and even a new classroom arrangement, with chairs, desks, and chalkboards, did not fare any better. Droves of madrasa students under the Najafi's thumb ransacked elementary schools and drove teachers out, even forcing them into exile. Even Amin al-Dowleh's largesse paid to the clerical authorities, a courteous bribe to keep them on his side, did not fully work.

Severe financial pressures on the economy, aggravated by sharp fluctuations in the international currency market, further dimmed Amin al-Dowleh's chances. The secondary impact of the Panic of 1893, the first major US economic depression, which had global consequences by contributing to the collapse in the price of silver worldwide, had a serious impact on the Iranian silver-based currency. Between 1892 and 1893 the value of the Iranian tuman dropped 28 percent, a staggering fall by any standard. Moreover, the predominance of modern banking and international capital, though less tangible in Iran than in Egypt or the Ottoman Empire, created new obligations for the state and the business community. Yet access to international finance lured the Iranian state to borrow hefty loans in order to pay for court expenditures, the shah's two royal tours to Europe between 1900 and 1905 in the extravagant style of his father, the expanding bureaucracy, and government-funded projects. The state had to borrow either directly from European powers or from foreign-owned banks, often by farming out the revenue of much of the country's custom houses as collateral, a practice that temporarily helped the cash-starved government coffers.

Earlier in 1892, under Naser al-Din Shah, the income from Iranian customs was assigned to the Imperial Bank of Persia to service a loan of £500,000 (US$2,500,000) that was secured to pay off the indemnity for the repeal of the tobacco concession to the Regie company. After much back and forth, Amin al-Dowleh had managed to negotiate a new loan from the Imperial Bank in exchange for the provincial tax receipts. The terms of this loan further obligated the government to ransom its meager resources over the long term. As expected, much of the loan was squandered on state bureaucracy and the shah's European tours. By 1898 Amin al-Dowleh's reformist agenda had effectively reached a dead end. He was left with no choice but to resign and retire to his estate in Gilan province, where in 1904 he died a disillusioned man. In a broader context Amin al-Dowleh's dismissal marked the end of ministerial reforms from above, which at least since the middle of the nineteenth century had preoccupied such statesmen as Amir Kabir and Moshir al-Dowleh. The alternative, a movement of dissent from below, which was long in gestation, soon evolved into a popular revolution.

Upon Amin al-Dowleh's dismissal, the shah and his courtiers reverted back to the old ways by calling on Amin al-Soltan to return to office, primarily to secure yet another loan, this time from Russia. The nearly bankrupt Iranian treasury secured a loan of £2,400,000 ($12,000,000) from the Russian Mortgage Bank of Persia to pay off previous British loans, but at the heavy price of farming out nearly all the remaining Iranian customs revenue. A team of Belgian officials who initially had been employed to supervise the administration of Iranian customs gravitated toward the Russian authorities. Although they introduced new regulations, revised practices, and increased state revenue through the imposition of stricter tariffs, they were more loyal to the Russian creditors than to the Iranian government. The Iranian merchant community was already resentful of the ad valorum tax imposed on Iranians at a higher rate than the tariffs for European trading houses, a disadvantage rooted in the Torkamanchay commercial treaty. The doubling of customs duties under the Belgian administration only generated further discontent, but higher customs duties were only part of the problem. The greater part was a shift in trade patterns. In the last quarter of the nineteenth century, Iran's foreign imports, mostly commodities such as tea and sugar as well as manufactured goods including cotton and woolen fabrics, increased substantially.

By 1900 Iran's population had reached ten million—twice the size of the population a century earlier—and nearly 25 percent lived in cities. In the first decade of the twentieth century cotton fabrics, sugar, and tea constituted 61 percent of Iran's total imports. Sugar from Russia, France, and Austria amounted to 26 percent of all imports, with a value of $6,250,000. In the mid-1890s Iran's estimated volume of foreign trade stood at $25 million, while total state revenue for the same period was no more than $12,500,000. The increase in the volume of imports was in contrast to a steady drop in the value of exports. Compared to the middle of the nineteenth century, by 1910 the value of Iran's three traditional export commodities—silk, opium, and cotton fabrics—had dropped in proportion to total trade by a massive 74 percent. The exports of raw cotton and carpets, however, had increased in value, but only by 26 percent. By 1910 Iran exported about $20 million and imported $25 million annually, causing a cumulative 20 percent deficit in the balance of its foreign trade. This imbalance contributed to a steady fall in the value of Iranian currency. Between 1875 and 1900 the tuman depreciated 100 percent against the British pound, which triggered a rise in the price of imported goods in the domestic market and more vulnerability to international fluctuations.

EARLY SIGNS OF DISCONTENT

By 1905, an increasing number of clandestine publications and makeshift posters on the gates of mosques and the walls of government buildings held the shah and his government responsible for a deteriorating economy, rising prices, and mistreatment of the people of Iran. In response, the government of the Qajar prince 'Ayn al-Dowleh, who came to power to restore order and stabilize prices, resorted to draconian measures. As a symbolic gesture, the governor of Tehran ordered the arrest and bastinado of four merchants on the charge of cornering the sugar market and hiking prices. The public humiliation of reputable merchants had the adverse effect of bringing crowds to the Friday Mosque in sympathy with the leaders of the bazaar.

Yet there was still visible change from the time of the Tobacco Protest. The voices of dissent were more articulate in their critique of the state and, to a limited extent, in their vision for change. Already in 1900, Jamal al-Din Isfahani had published a tract in Shiraz titled *Libas al-Taqwa* (An attire of virtue), calling on the Iranian public to wear domestic clothing and avoid imported European fabrics. He pleaded with Iranian merchants to join forces against European competition by consolidating their capital in commercial companies and urged them to manufacture fabrics domestically. Engaging in such activities, rather than entering into war with guns and rifles, was the true jihad and citizens' patriotic duty. Earlier Jamal al-Din, in collaboration with his Babi associates in Isfahan, had organized the Progress Society (Anjoman-i Tarraqi), one of the earliest prerevolutionary secret circles. The society was instrumental in persuading Isfahani merchants to establish a public company, known as the Islamic Company (Sherekat-e Eslamiyeh), to issue stocks, and to raise the necessary resources to set up mills and manufacture clothing for domestic consumption. Creation of commercial companies (known as *kompani* and later *sherekat*) with shareholders was a novel concept that was accepted only gradually at the turn of the twentieth century. Traditionally Islamic law recognized only individuals, not shared entities, as legitimate legal personalities. The formation of new companies and the higher volume of investment in them no doubt added to merchants' economic power, but it also exposed more of them to the vagaries of the market, commitment to larger loans from modern banks, and vacillations in international trade. In due course this budding commercial bourgeoisie placed new demands on the state and contributed to the growing public discontent.

Later, Jamal al-Din directed his criticism toward both the Qajar elite and the clerical establishments, whom he held to be exploitative, corrupt, and tyrannical masters of the country. In 1903 he and Nasrollah Beheshti, better known as Malek al-Motekallemin, another crypto-Babi cleric in the Isfahan circle and later a celebrated preacher of the Constitutional Revolution, anonymously published the tract *Roya-ye Sadeqeh* (A truthful dream), a satirical reproof of the mojtaheds of Isfahan, especially Aqa Najafi, as well as the powerful prince-governor of Isfahan, Zell al-Soltan. Here, the mojtaheds of the city were depicted as a bunch of greedy, arrogant, and poorly trained mullahs who swindled people's land and property to accumulate enormous wealth for themselves and their families, and who accepted bribes and favors from the rich and the powerful to issue partial, even conflicting, rulings. He accused them of collaborating with the oppressive and violent government to squash the weak and suppress alternative voices by wielding their weapon of *takfir* (excommunication) to kill, plunder, and appropriate property.

The self-aggrandizing and self-indulgent mojtaheds of Isfahan, the tract claimed, were hoarding grain in their silos, hiking prices, and committing racketeering—all the while starving people were dying in the streets. It further characterized the mojtaheds as reactionaries and accused them of opposing any social change as non-Islamic, including modern education, the learning of foreign languages, and contact with non-Shiʿis, let alone with non-Muslims, whom they considered ritually unclean. All reforms that potentially affected the individual or communal privileges of the clergy, the authors declared, were branded by these pseudoscholars as evil, and they called for their punishment. The clergy were blamed for their demagogic grip on their ignorant following, whom the mojtaheds exhorted to zealotry and violence. Throngs of seminarians (*talabeh*) and urban brigands (*lutis*) served as their vigilantes.

Writing in the familiar genre of the dream narrative, Jamal al-Din employed a theatrical dialogue to scandalize the mojtaheds' deceit and hypocrisy. Even on the Day of Judgment, which is the stage on which Jamal al-Din's narrative is played out, Najafi employs his crafty rhetorical skills, all in colloquial Isfahani accent, to bargain with God his own salvation during the Final Reckoning. Such lampooning of the clergy was not entirely new in Persian literature, yet here, for the first time, the semiclandestine publication brought criticism out into the open and made it available to a wider public in poignant and accessible language. Though the print run of the earliest edition of *Roya-ye Sadeqeh* was no more than mere eighty copies, it had an impact on the Iranian audience.

In their later sermons Jamal al-Din and his fellow preachers were more respectful of the "good" mojtaheds. They praised the two progressive clerical leaders of the Constitutional Revolution, Sayyed Mohammad Tabataba'i and Sayyed 'Abdollah Behbahani, for upholding the nation, protecting the interests of the motherland, and defending the constitution. Instead, the thrust of Jamal al-Din Isfahani's later criticism, at the outset of the revolution, was shifted toward the state and the conservative Qajar elite and their allies. From 1907 until his murder after the coup of 1908, a newspaper named after him, *al-Jamal*, published his sermons in Tehran to be distributed to a wider audience throughout the country. This was a clear example of how the press and mass communication transformed clandestine dissent into a revolutionary discourse.

The most progressive preachers, journalists, and activists shared their criticism of the conservative Qajar aristocracy and the high clergy, though seldom by name, favoring instead the pro-constitutional and the enlightened members of the state elite. Earlier critics like Malkom, Afghani, and Kermani, and the moderate Yusef Khan Mostashar al-Dowleh, considered such a course a tactical necessity. The latter was the author of the critical tract *Yak Kalameh* (A single word), among the earliest in this genre published in 1871. It advocated the constitution as the remedy to the country's ailments. Aiming to reconcile the preamble to the French constitution with Islamic principles, Mostashar al-Dowleh offered a very liberal reading of Islamic theology and law in defense of the rule of law, human and civil rights, and limits on the state's power. His comparative approach found little following at the time, but no doubt it later influenced the framers of the Iranian Constitution. Mostashar al-Dowleh's facility pairing articles of the French constitution with Qur'anic verses and the Islamic hadith may not have always met the jurists' seal of approval, but is was sufficient to later persuade the Iranian constitutionalists, many of them laymen, not to leave the task of interpreting shari'a entirely to the jurists.

By the time of the Constitutional Revolution a trend within the Iranian opposition indeed articulated an Islamic discourse similar to that of Mostashar al-Dowleh. Preachers and activists, some with a latent Babi-Azali affiliation, were ready to offer their support to moderate mojtaheds such as Sayyed Mohammad Tabataba'i (1842–1920) and Sayyed 'Abdollah Behbahani (1840–1910) as a realistic way to rock the weakling Qajar state. The shift within the Babi-Azali camp, which had become radical since the 1880s after Yahya Sobh-e Azal endorsed call for an anti-Qajar revolt, allowed for the concealment of past Babi affinities—an act of "disguise" (*taqiyyeh*) in a moment of danger that is fully endorsed by the Shi'i legal tradition and, by implication, by the Babi-Azalis. Fifty years of persecution at the hands of the ulama and the state convinced them that a dual challenge to the Qajar state and the Shi'i establishment was untenable. They were, however, receptive to the notions of democracy, representation, and even republicanism, which they felt were in harmony with the essence of the Babi beliefs. And they were eager to share their invigorated political dissent with sympathetic Shi'i authorities.

In contrast, the Baha'is, who accounted for the majority of those stigmatized under the general rubric of the Babi heresy, remained largely uninvolved and often resolved to disclose their religious identity, a conviction that resulted in tragic bouts of severe persecution. The sporadic mob brutalities committed against the Baha'is in the late nineteenth and early twentieth centuries were frequently provoked by ambitious mojtaheds and carried out by their followers. The growth of these anti-Baha'i campaigns may be attributed to the mojtaheds' losing ground to more liberal voices outside and within the religious community. They viewed conversion to the new faith, an avenue to religious modernity for many laypeople and for members of the clerical class critical of the Shi'i establishment, with great anxiety. The atrocities were often condoned by the Qajar government and its local agents, who were either helpless to stop them or perhaps more often saw a chance to enhance their public image as disseminators of heresy and as upholders of the true Islamic faith.

Such hysteria took place in the city of Yazd in 1902–1903, when a frantic mob led by *lutis* and equipped with fatwas of the local mojtaheds from over a period of months attacked and looted Baha'i households and businesses, and arrested and executed as many as a hundred Baha'is. These acts were committed in public and in the most gruesome fashion. The victims, mostly artisans and small-scale tradesmen, but also a few affluent merchants, paid not only with their lives but also with the lives of their wives and children. Some Baha'i women were forced to convert back to Islam and were duly married off to their Muslim tormenters. Those who resisted were raped and chased out of the city. Children were enslaved or abandoned, and helpless families died of thirst and starvation on remote back roads hundreds of miles from their homes. Mohammad 'Ali Jamalzadeh (1892–1997), a renowned Iranian writer of the twentieth century and son of the aforementioned Sayyed Jamal al-Din Isfahani, recalled a haunting sight of the Baha'i refugees from Yazd dying of hunger at the outskirts of a village near Kashan. Together with his mother, the young Jamalzadeh was himself fleeing a vicious anti-Babi campaign in Isfahan.

The ferocity of the Yazd persecution, one of several at the time, only confirmed the Babi-Azali incentive for *taqiyyeh*, if for no other reason than security. As a result of concealing their identity, many Azalis inevitably were assimilated into the majority Muslim population at the expense of the gradual fading away of their Babi identity. Yet assimilation in many cases did not soften their anti-Qajar agenda. As the popular constitutional movement gradually gained momentum, Babi sympathizers among the lower clerical ranks gravitated toward political activism, which was wrapped safely in the guise of Islamic conformity.

FROM THE HOUSE OF JUSTICE TO THE NATIONAL ASSEMBLY

The dissidents in exile had only an indirect impact on the course of the constitutional movement, and this was mostly through domestic activists. Enjoying the blessing of two high-ranking mojtaheds, Behbahani and Tabataba'i, the activists among middle- and lower-ranking mullahs made more demands on the state. This helped turn an initially limited protest movement with mundane aims into a national outcry for a constitution, popular representation, and civil rights. These ideas, adopted by a handful of advocates from such sources as Malkom Khan's *Qanun* and the fictional travelogue of Ibrahim Beg by Maragheh'i, were communicated to high-ranking clerical leaders and then passed down to the general public. Sayyed Mohammad Tabataba'i's support for constitutionalism, rooted in his admirably liberal predilections, was atypical among the jurists of the period. His ally, Sayyed 'Abdollah Behbahani, however, seemed to have been driven as much by ambitions of leadership and alleged monetary concerns as by aspirations for democracy. Both leaders belonged to families who had enjoyed social distinction for more than a century. At the outset they relied heavily on their better-informed subordinates for their knowledge of such notions as civil rights, legislation, and national sovereignty, but their courage and prestige made them enormously popular with the public. Tabataba'i in particular was endowed with a genuine urge to establish a pluralistic society based on rule of law and individual freedoms, concepts that he himself acknowledged as inconsistent with the best interests of the mojtahed class.

The early absence of a coherent political agenda among the protesters is evident, for instance, in the set of demands set forth in December 1905 during the *bast* (sanctuary) that was organized in response to the government's treatment of sugar merchants. The most significant demand was a call to establish a "house of justice" (*'adalat-khaneh*), which would be compatible with shari'a and would protect subjects from the state's arbitrary measures, especially in collecting taxes. Yet the list of demands also included such seemingly mundane items as dismissal of a notorious carriage driver who monopolized the route between Tehran and the nearby shrine of Shah 'Abd al-'Azim, and whose uncouth conduct generated many complaints from the pilgrims. No mention, however, was made of the *qanun* (law or constitution), division of powers, or creation of a legislative assembly. Even the concept of the "house of justice" was not particularly favored by many, for it implied a potential departure from the decentralized judicial courts that the ulama had long cherished. The notion of the house of justice, which eventually transformed into a call for a national assembly, had its roots in the writings of the Bab and the messianic aspiration to establish a house of justice (*bayt al-'adl*) under the Imam of the Age.

That the beginning of the constitutional movement in AH 1323/1905 CE was only six years before the millennial anniversary of the "Greater Occultation" (*ghaybat-e kobra*) of the Hidden Imam, who was presumed to have gone into Occultation in AH 329/941 CE, added to the messianic spirit of the moment and to anticipation of the "return" of the Mahdi. This was evident in many statements, names of a number of newspapers, and the sermons of the pro-constitutional preachers. In effect, the "awakening" (*bidari*) of the people, often referred to in the literature of the period, and their demand for the establishment of a just order, implied some form of modernization, or more specifically, democratization, of a messianic paradigm and its utopian ideals that were indigenous to the Iranian environment.

Dispensing justice (*'adl* and *'adalat*) in the world to redress wrongs and remove tyranny, one of the precepts of Shi'i Islam with a millenarian connotation, was soon adopted by a new generation of European-educated state elites and complemented by European notions of the rule of law and limits on the despotic power of the state. Domesticating these Western notions in the Shi'i political space enabled the growth and early success of the constitutional movement. Yet from the start, it also injected into the process inherent ambiguity, even some resistance to divulging the true secular agenda of the constitutionalists. By somewhat naively trying to dress many articles of the emerging constitution in Islamic garb—not dissimilar to Mostashar al-Dowleh's *Yak Kalameh*—the constitutional activists hoped to appease the conservative and escape labels of heresy and religious innovation. As such, they introduced a troubling feature to the Iranian experience of democracy, one that would remain inherent for decades, if not for a whole century thereafter.

The Joseph Naus affair offered a pretext for expressing indignation at and discontent with foreign presence. As the Belgian director of Iranian customs under Mozaffar al-Din Shah, since 1897, Naus had restructured Iranian customs and raised state revenue through higher tariffs and the rigorous collection of duties. Yet public discontent with his regime was expressed in Islamic ethical terms. He had appeared at a European costume ball in Tehran in Persian traditional attire, remotely resembling that of the ulama. The widely distributed photograph of him in costume, smoking the Persian water pipe, became a source of outrage, and his dismissal one of the demands of the protesters in Qom.

The protest was fueled, and possibly financed, by Iranian merchants resentful of Naus's discriminatory practices, which favored Russian firms. His partiality to Russia was reciprocated by Russia's extending near-protégé status to Belgians and threatening the Iranian government with retaliation for any action taken against Naus's practices or against his amassing of personal wealth. Yet even after his departure in May 1907, the outcome of public protest, the Belgians' grip on customs remained firm.

In July 1906, a renewed call for the government to convene a "shari'a-bound assembly (*majles*) of the house of justice" regained momentum. In support of the Majles, the restive Tehran population gathered in Tupkhaneh Square (Maydan-e Tupkhaneh), adjacent to the citadel complex, and staged one of the earliest public demonstrations that had occurred outside the mosque or the shrine setting. The clampdown on demonstrators by government troops resulted in the death of a young religious student, offering a pretext to a group of pro-constitutionalist ulama headed by Tabataba'i to leave the capital and reside in Qom. The ulama's departure in protest was always treated with anxiety by the Qajar government, especially in times of crisis. Simultaneously, the merchants of the Tehran bazaar rallied behind Behbahani (who had ties with the British legation in Tehran), playing a crucial role in the burgeoning protest movement. Fearing government retaliation, the Tehran merchants managed to organize a vast sanctuary (*bast*) in support of the Qom protesters in the safety of the British legation in Tehran.

Taking sanctuary in the grounds of a European power was an unprecedented, even sacrilegious, move. More so because it was in the British legation that the protestors openly demanded for the first time the establishment of a constitutional (*mashruteh*) order. The *bast* attracted a crowd from all walks of life, particularly from the bazaar guilds, small merchants, and artisans. Altogether there were about five hundred tents representing trades and professions, as humble as cobblers, porcelain menders, and fresh walnut vendors. On the final day as

Figure 6.2. Members of the clothiers guild in the July 1906
sanctuary (*bast*) in the British legation in Tehran.
Contemporary postcard published in Tehran, c. 1910. Author's collection.

many as fourteen thousand individuals participated (fig. 6.2). The atmosphere
was joyous but orderly, and the mood congenial and optimistic. The chief merchants of the bazaar sustained the cost of the tents and food for the public for
the full two weeks of the *bast*. Massive copper cauldrons were brought from
the mosques and the takkiyehs and placed on makeshift hearths in a common
kitchen to prepare huge quantities of rice, stew, and Persian *ash*, which were
delivered on trays to the tents, whose banners identified guilds and other organizations. There were also frequent sermons and speeches highlighting the evils
of tyranny and the benefits of a constitution (fig. 6.3).

The protest was novel, above all, because of the central role of the merchants. They took the lead from constitutional activists in persuading the ranking mojtaheds to comply with the idea of the constitution. Even more than
the Tobacco Protest fifteen years earlier, the merchant class was the engine
behind the protesters and the voicing of their grievances. Moreover, the *bast*
enjoyed the tacit support of some middle-ranking British diplomats in Tehran.
Facing the protesters' enthusiasm and their growing numbers, British diplomats
could do little but allow the *bast* to proceed unhindered. The British blessing,
momentary though it was, hinted toward a shift in the British Foreign Office's
policy in Iran under Sir Edward Gray—a subtle response to Russia's increasing
commercial and political influence in Iran and to the Qajar court's tilt toward
its northern neighbor. As far as the constitutionalists were concerned, the *bast*

Figure 6.3. Feeding protesters who sought sanctuary in the British legation in
Tehran in July 1906. Haji Mohammad Taqi Bonakdar (*standing at left center*),
who offered his services, was a textile wholesaler in the Tehran bazaar.
Contemporary postcard. Author's collection.

in the legation offered not only immunity against the government and the blessing of a European power, but also a secular space, one outside the mosque and
religious sanctuaries. The relative freedom in the new space allowed Western-
educated intellectuals and graduates of the Dar al-Fonun to help refashion the
idea of the "house of justice" into a demand for a European-style constitution.

The coinage *mashruteh* in fact meant "conditional," denoting the setting of
conditions on the power of the sovereign. Borrowed from the neighboring Ottoman Empire's first constitutional regime of 1876, which was aborted in 1878
by Sultan 'Abd al-Hamid, *meshrutiyet* (as it pronounced in Ottoman Turkish)
represented for the Iranians more than just the new conditional system; it represented the entire constitutional experience and political order it entailed. The
term *mashruteh*, moreover, implies a familiar chapter on "conditions" (*shorut*)
in Islamic law, which in turn gave it a certain Islamic acceptability and in the
eyes of the ulama and the public put it at a safe distance from such alien notions
as constitution and constitutionalism.

Public debate and publications further gave the term *mashruteh* and associated buzzwords a greater currency. The growing telegraphic communications
throughout Iran's major cities made it possible for protesters in the capital to
transmit the constitutional message of the movement and to coordinate their
efforts with cohorts in Tabriz, the true center of radical activism, and elsewhere.

Figure 6.4. Protesters in Shiraz taking sanctuary in the telegraph house.
Communicating with the capital via telegraph was a common feature of the
constitutional era. Many demands and petitions flooded the young Majles.
By Hasan 'Akkas-bashi, c. 1908. M. Sane' *Paydayesh-e 'Akkasi dar Shiraz* (Tehran, 1369/1990), 100.

Thus, the movement was no longer seen as a quarrel between the ulama and
the Qajar state; it had acquired a nationwide constituency that was increasingly
becoming conscious of its message and its national identity. "Long live Iran!" —
a rallying cry of the constitutionalists from the earliest days — touched on such
patriotic sentiments.

As has often been noted, only a small number of the elite understood the idea
of the constitution and the liberal values associated with it. Yet the Iranian public was quick to employ the term to air its resentment of their destitution, material decline, and the insecurities they faced in everyday life. For these ills, the
people held the ruling establishment responsible. If notions of constitutional
rights and democratic representation were new to them, poverty, decline, and
state arbitrary rule were familiar. It is rather naive to blame the ordinary people,
as critics of the Constitutional Revolution often have, for their unfamiliarity

with the lofty liberal ideals of Jean-Jacques Rousseau, Montesquieu, or John Stuart Mill. It is even more condescending to expect that all revolutions would have a standard interpretation of modernity.

The sanctuary in Qom, protests in Tehran, and mediation between the *mashruteh* seekers and the royal court by moderate statesmen obligated the weary Qajar shah and his court officials to dismiss the unpopular premier, 'Ayn al-Dowleh, whose draconian measures triggered the earliest protests. He was the third member of the Qajar tribe in a century to serve as premier and stir a crisis. Later, in 1908, his part in quashing the revolutionary resistance in Tabriz further blackened his image as a staunch reactionary. Shortly thereafter, the protesting ulama who had taken refuge in Qom returned after the shah only implicitly accepted their demands. Yet on August 10, 1906, under increased public pressure, he could see no other way but to issue a rescript that came to be known as the Constitutional Decree (Farman-e Mashrutiyat). Addressed to the new premier, Nasrollah Khan Moshir al-Dowleh, the receipt called for the establishment of a "national consultative assembly [*majles-e showra-ye melli*] . . . to carry out the requisite deliberations and investigations on all necessary subjects connected with important affairs of the state and empire and the public interests; and shall render the necessary help and assistance to our cabinet and ministers in such reforms as are designed to promote the happiness and well-being of Iran."[1]

Although ironically the word *mashruteh* was carefully avoided in the rescript, the text did speak, albeit vaguely, of "legislative reforms" and further endorsed that the Majles, the first with any representation beyond the elite, be elected from among seven classes: the princes of the Qajar family, the ulama, the notables (*a'yan*), the nobles (*ashraf*), the landowners, the merchants, and the guilds. The Electoral Law Committee appointed to draw up election bylaws consisted of mostly young Western-educated bureaucrats. Among them were Mahdi-Qoli Hedayat and Hasan Moshir al-Molk (later Moshir al-Dowleh Pirniya), liberal moderates with family histories of divan service over several generations. The latter was a graduate of the Russian military academy and a student of law who had founded the School of Diplomacy (Madreseh-e Siyasi) in Tehran in 1899. Perhaps inspired by the model of the Estates-General during the French Revolution, the committee opted for a representational system that surprisingly gave the greatest number of "deputies" (*vakils*) to the guilds and the merchants. Of the 168 deputies, Tehran was designated sixty seats, four of which were to go to the Qajar princes and nobles, four to the ulama and students (*tollab*), ten to the khans and landowners, ten to merchants, and one each to the thirty-two guilds. Azarbaijan and Fars were to receive twelve seats each, and the remaining ten provinces, eighty-two seats. By September the electoral law was ratified and the designated deputies began to convene in the capital (pl. 6.1).

The inauguration of the Majles in October 1906 aimed to frame the "Fundamental Law" (*qanun-e asasi*). Remarkably, the issuance of the Constitutional Decree and the convening of the Majles closely followed developments during the 1905 Russian Revolution and the establishment of the short-lived Duma in April 1906. Adopting the term "Fundamental Law" also seems to have been inspired by the Fundamental Laws issued by Tsar Nicholas II, according to which the Duma was granted limited legislative powers but only with the ultimate endorsement of the tsar, who called himself the "supreme autocrat." Similar tension between the Majles and the monarch was soon to emerge with the Iranian Constitutional Revolution.

The members of the Electoral Law Committee adopted the term *Fundamental Law* in place of the French *constitution* so as to avoid conservatives' accusations that they were adopting an alien institution contrary to Islamic shari'a and the tradition of monarchy in Iran. Yet the secularizing agenda of the constitutionalists, boosted by dissident preachers and the burgeoning liberal press outside the Majles, was clear enough not to be missed by opponents, even though a handful of radical deputies led by likes of Hasan Taqizadeh, the celebrated deputy from Tabriz, did their best to camouflage their antiroyalist and anticlerical views. Fearing their opponents in the court and among conservative ulama, the Majles deputies soon realized that to avoid the fate of the Russian Duma—which was dissolved in July 1906 by order of the tsar—they had only a brief window of opportunity. The Majles thus hastily drew up a document to be signed by the shah on December 30, 1906, on his deathbed. The Fundamental Law recognized the separation of three powers—with the Majles as the legislative body—far more than earlier demands for it to have a mere judicial function, and with the shah as the head of the executive. The news of the revolution stirred some interest not only nationally but in the European press as well (pl. 6.2). The shah died of kidney failure on January 3, 1907, and was immediately succeeded on the throne by his son, Mohammad 'Ali Shah (r. 1907–1909), a man of decidedly different temperament and political orientation from his father.

FRAMING THE CONSTITUTION

It was remarkable enough that Iran had convened a parliament against all the odds. It was even more significant that the Majles not only framed a constitution

but soon after, in October 1907, ratified a substantial document, the Supplement to the Fundamental Law. The latter document guaranteed basic liberties
and laid the foundation for a constitutional system. This was achieved in an
environment of growing tension with the court of Mohammad 'Ali Shah and
open hostility from the anticonstitutional clerical camp under Shaykh Fazlollah Nuri (1843–1909), who was allied with conservatives at the court.

Despite his early support for the constitutional movement, Nuri soon parted
ways, posing a potent challenge to the Majles and the cause of constitutionalism. He coined the term *mashru'eh*, obviously mimicking *mashruteh*, to imply
that the *shar'* (i.e., shari'a), and not the *shart* (condition), ought to be the foundation of the new constitutional order. Though a prominent Usuli jurist, he
did not articulate the meaning of *mashru'eh* beyond generalities. Perhaps aware
of the past Shi'i jurists' aversion to engaging in issues of political governance
(which in the absence of the Imam of the Age considered any other form of
worldly government to be categorically oppressive), Nuri remained in essence
loyal to the theory of state-religion dual authority. Yet facing the reality of a
modern legislature, he strove to find a role for the jurists, with himself at the
helm. Not merely a judicial one but a role to enforce the shari'a far beyond
its accepted limits. He viewed the nascent Majles and its constitution as no
more than a conspiracy hatched by heretics, Babis, and atheists, and he called
on his clerical cohorts to oppose them. In his "rescripts" (*lawayeh*), periodically published from Shah 'Abd al-'Azim, where he had taken sanctuary, he attacked as non-Islamic such precepts as freedom of speech and equality before
the law. Once the appeasing gestures by the Majles, including the inclusion in
the constitution of a five-member mojtahed supervisory committee, appeared
to be mere lip service to the ulama, Nuri quietly abandoned the idea of the
mashur'eh and became a royalist supporting Mohammad 'Ali Shah.

Beyond Nuri and his supporters, the infant constitutional regime had to face
the consequences of a new alliance between its European neighbors. In August
1907, Russia and Britain concluded an agreement that recognized two zones of
influence for the powers in northern and southern Iran, with the middle region
declared neutral. This was the first time such an agreement had replaced the
old power rivalries. The agreement reaffirmed the powers' traditional guarantees for the Qajar throne without acknowledging the Majles or the new constitutional process. This generated new anxieties and, as it turned out, contributed
to the precarious nature of the emerging order and, a year later, to the coup of
June 1908 that destroyed the Majles and suspended the constitution. The events
that unfolded then gave the Iranians little comfort in the European powers'

assurances that they would respect Iran's political sovereignty and territorial integrity.

The first Majles was composed of deputies with little legislative experience and misperceptions about how the Majles—and indeed the entire constitutional system—was to function. Among the deputies, those of the Azarbaijan contingent were the most influential members. From the outset a few deputies, most significantly, Hasan Taqizadeh (1878–1970), a young charismatic orator from Tabriz with a radical agenda, came to dominate the debates. Born in Nakhijevan, the southern autonomous region in today's Republic of Azerbaijan near the Iranian border) to a family of Shi'i local clergy, Taqizadeh started as a seminarian in Tabriz but, soon becoming critical of traditional madrasa schooling, turned toward modern sciences and Western political thought. With the help of his cohorts he established a small lending library in Tabriz, a means of self-education also aimed to enlighten his fellow citizens. He later left for Beirut and Cairo, where, still in clerical attire, he was further exposed to current trends of secular thought and nationalism. He also perfected his Arabic and learned some English and French. He returned to Tabriz at the beginning of the constitutional era and was designated a deputy from Azarbaijan.

The Azarbaijan contingent was in part backed by the semi-clandestine socialist circle in Tabriz and by the Iranian émigré community in the Caucasus. Many were dislocated peasants from Iranian Azarbaijan, but there were also enthusiastic Iranian merchants and wealthy industrialists who offered their moral and financial support. Other deputies from the provinces, including Isfahan, Kerman, Fars, and Gilan, added to the Majles' credibility as the first nationwide legislative body created by the will of the people. The two constitutionalist mojtaheds, referred to as the "two glowing starts" (*nurayn-e nayyerain*), attended the Majles session not only as representatives of the ulama class but also as surrogates for the so-called recognized religious minorities. Only in the second Majles, after 1909, was a Zoroastrian dignitary elected to represent the long-persecuted followers of Iran's indigenous religion. The Jewish and Christian communities also appointed representatives, but the Babi Azalis or Baha'is were never elevated beyond the label of "despicable heresy." Neither were women considered worthy of standing as deputies or even being part of the electorate.

The Supplement to the Fundamental Law was inspired by the French, Belgian, and Bulgarian constitutions but in substance was adopted to the requirements of the Iranian environment and the precepts of Shi'ism. It reflected contingencies and contradictions inherent in the Iranian system that were hard to overcome. Yet every article of the constitution was genuinely argued and heatedly debated in open sessions and before enthusiastic audiences. One of the most remarkable aspects of the Majles was indeed its openness, even though at times the deputies of the guild and mercantile backgrounds were intimidated by the oratorical skills of such leading figures as Taqizadeh.

The Fundamental Law and the Supplement to the Fundamental Law declared a division of powers into three branches. The shah was acknowledged as the head of the executive, whose divine grace was bestowed on him by the will of the people. This was the first time in the long history of Persian kingship that a document subordinated, albeit partially, the king's authority to the people's institutional mandate—an assertion over which a bloody civil war would soon be fought. The constitution also regarded the Majles as the legislative body in charge of making laws but also delegated to it supervisory powers over the affairs of the government including consent in appointing the premier and his ministers as well as the prerogative to dismiss them.

To appease detractors within the ulama camp, the constitution stipulated that all laws (*qanun*) legislated by the Majles was to remain within the bounds of political order, and thus outside the sphere of the shari'a. In reality, however, it subverted the accepted universality of the shari'a in some key provisions. In contrast to Islamic law that discriminated between Muslims and non-Muslims, the constitution recognized equal rights for all citizens. It further secured freedom of the press and publication, and freedom of association, so long as they were not against principles of Islam. Freedom of expression in particular was seen by the opposing ulama not only as a clear breach of restraints that Islam placed on individuals but also as sanctioning the spread of un-Islamic ideas and heresies.

Article 1 of the 1907 Supplement to the Fundamental Law specifically declared Twelver Shi'i Islam as the official religion of Iran, and article 2 specified:

> At no time must any legal enactment of the Sacred National Consultative Assembly [Majles Moqaddas Showra-ye Melli], established by the Imam of the Age and His Majesty the *shahanshah* of Islam and the whole people of the Iranian nation, be at variance with the sacred principles of Islam or the laws established by His Holiness the Best of Mankind [i.e., Prophet Mohammad].[2]

This, of course, was not merely a lip service; it reflected the framers' serious dilemma of how to reconcile the will of "the people of Iranian nation" as a source of the constitution's legitimacy with the ancient pillars of authority: Shi'i Islam and Iranian kingship. After much bickering over the language, to appease Nuri and the *mashru'eh* opposition who were battering the constitutionalists from their sanctuary near Tehran, the Majles approved, after several drafts, that a committee of five mojtaheds and experts of Islamic law would oversee the compatibility of legislation with preconditions laid out in the shari'a. Though in reality the committee never convened and was forgotten after 1910, compatibility with the shari'a remained an issue that would reemerge seven decades later during the Islamic Revolution of 1979.

Other articles of the constitution betrayed the same undercurrent of obsequiousness in fear of being labeled "irreligious." Article 8 of the same document granted all the people of Iran "equal rights" before the law, a milestone for Iran's political culture. The equal rights were spelled out in the following articles in specific terms, including the safeguarding of lives, properties, homes, and honor from "every kind of interference," and prohibited arbitrary or extrajudicial arrest, detainment, and punishment all citizens, as well as infringement in their private dwellings and confiscation of their properties. Beyond basic rights to life and property, article 18 declared freedom of "the study of all sciences, arts and crafts," unless forbidden by the law of Islam, and article 19 demanded that the government establish public schools and supervise public education. More significant, article 20 allowed all publications, "except heretical books and matters hurtful to the perspicuous religion [of Islam]," and exempted them from any censorship. In the same spirit, article 21 sanctioned freedom of "all societies and associations," provided that they were not "productive to mischief to religion and state, and are not injurious to good order."

The Majles was also under great pressure to limit the sovereign's power. The division of powers, a cornerstone of any modern constitution, had to be maneuvered against anticonstitutional Mohammad 'Ali Shah and his dubious ambitions. The constitution's crucial article 27, which assigned legislative, judicial, and executive powers to three branches of the government, granted nominal power to the shah. The king's executive power—known as the laws of ordinance—were to be "carried out by the ministers and state officials in the august name of his Imperial Majesty in such manner as the law defines." Moreover, article 44 exempted the shah from any political responsibility for the affairs of the state, instead holding the ministers of the state responsible to the legislative branch. Under enormous pressure from the court, however, the framers of the constitution were obliged to assert in article 35 that "the sovereignty is a trust confided as a divine gift by the people to the person of the king." It is reported that Mohammad 'Ali Shah only agreed to sign the Supplement to the Fundamental Law in October 1907 after inserting in his own hand the phrase "as a divine gift," rendering the article obsolete.

MAJLES VERSUS THE MONARCH

Conferring the "divine gift" to the shah in the constitution reflected the constraints and trepidation of the Majles, just as the provision to convene the committee of the mojtaheds to oversee legislation did. However, it would be an error of historical judgment to assume that the Fundamental Law and its Supplement were merely loose translations of European constitutions. The Iranian Constitution was shaped article by article after hours, days, and months of fierce debate in and out of the nascent parliament, and the proceedings of the Majles is witness to the heated exchanges between deputies as well as the sincere optimism with which they engaged in debates. All the more remarkable, this was a document produced by a Majles unaccustomed to the traditions of the Magna Carta, the Long Parliament, the civil and constitutional refinements of John Locke, Montesquieu, and John Stuart Mill and the tradition of legal procedure and secular humanism that had engendered the 1787 Constitution of the United States, the 1789 French Declaration of the Rights of Man, and the 1791 ratification of the American Bill of Rights.

The deputies of the Majles and the people who elected them to office soon realized (as did the English, French, and Americans) that a constitution and constitutionalism did not come easily or cheaply. The *mashruteh* and implementation of the Fundamental Law resulted in much bloodshed, political conflict, and the chaos of a civil war before being acknowledged as a "revolution" (*enqelab*). The term in Persian originally denoted a seasonal climatic change or a sudden shift in human medical condition (of the same root as the Arabic verb *qalaba*, "to turn"). Only in the late nineteenth century, and more clearly during the 1908–1909 civil war, *enqelab* acquired its modern political meaning and gradually came to replace constitutional "movement" (*nahzat*) in the revolutionary discourse. However, as early as 1907 the shift in and out of the Majles toward greater radicalization anticipated nothing less than a full-scale revolution.

Between May 1907 and July 1909, the Majles at every turn faced enormous threats to its very survival (see map 5.2). A range of issues contributed to the instability of the nascent constitutional regime. Chief among them were disagreement on limits of the legislative authority, growing tensions with the shah and his court, and a constant barrage of defamatory propaganda from Nuri and advocates of the *mashru'eh*. Unrest in the provinces provoked by the court and by the powerful tribal khans and the local ulama, as well as serious skirmishes and sectarian fighting on the Ottoman borders, further challenged the young order. By mid-1907, Azarbaijan was being harassed by the royalist Shahseven tribe in the vicinity of Ardabil, who, provoked by the Qajar shah, pillaged towns and villages in the name of securing the crown. Further to the west, in the Oru-miyeh region, Kurdish irregulars backed by Ottoman troops repeatedly crossed the border and attacked Assyrian and Armenian villagers in Iranian territory. In Fars, Isfahan, Zanjan, and Kashan urban unrest, sectarian clashes, and banditry were on the rise. Na'eb Hosain, a former member of the Qajar rural police turned bandit, together with his gang, since the late 1890s organized repeated raids on the city of Kashan and villages in its vicinity stretching as far east as the central Iranian desert. Posing himself as a friend of the poor and the underprivi-leged, in reality he was no more than a ruthless plunderer and killer of innocent people whose reign of terror lasted for more than two decades. Failure to quash the Na'ebis, as they came to be known, epitomized the weakening of the central government during the revolution and its aftermath.

Under these circumstances, it became painfully evident to the Majles and its radicalized supporters among the revolutionary societies (*anjomans*) that no peaceful solution was in sight. The return of Amin al-Soltan, the shrewd pre-mier of the Naseri and Mozaffari eras, to the post of prime minister in April 1907 provoked various reactions from the constitutionalists. Some viewed the reinstatement as Mohammad 'Ali Shah's design to forge an anti-Majles front consisting of the court, the conservative mojtaheds (headed by Nuri), the tribal chiefs, and the patronage of the Russian legation, with which the new premier was reputed to be on excellent terms. Amin al-Soltan's claim to mediate peace between the Majles and the shah won him few supporters among moderates in the Majles, but it also angered the radicals, especially once it became evi-dent that the he was financing Nuri's anti-Majles operation in the sanctuary of Shah 'Abd al-'Azim. His assassination in front of the Majles in August 1907, at the hand of a young devotee affiliated with a socialist revolutionary cell with connections to the Iranian émigré community in the Caucasus, was a shock-ing development. The act, perpetrated by a small-time moneylender originally from Tabriz, was justified in the eyes of the plotters because of fear of the return to power of the crafty pro-Russian statesman would soon result in the closure of the Majles and destruction of the revolution.

Weeks before Amin al-Soltan's assassination, the prorevolutionary orators in Tehran had called for the premier's removal as the opening act of an inevi-table revolution—a term with a peculiarly fresh ring to Iranian ears. The person presumed to be behind the clandestine cell was Haydar Khan, later known as 'Amu-Ughlu but also known as Bombi (bomb maker), an Azarbaijani émigré trained as electrical engineer in Tiflis. He was employed by Tehran municipal-ity to run the capital's first tiny electrical power plant. A Marxist revolution-ary motivated by the Baku oil workers' labor movement and radicalized by the botched Russian Revolution of 1905, Haydar Khan, a handsome and charismatic man of persuasive character, would come to play a distinct, and arguably destructive, part in Iran's dissident politics over the following decade.

The assassination of the premier on August 31, 1907, coincided with the signing in St. Petersburg of the 1907 convention recognizing two "zones of influence," clearly drawn diagonally across Iran's map. The agreement, part of a larger understanding between the two powers, also included Afghanistan and Tibet. With an ironic ring to its curious wording, the agreement was only a step short of occupation, at least on paper. Although the two powers had the temerity to announce it to the Iranian government a month later, the press abroad and at home had already drawn public attention to its ominous consequences. Most evident was Russia's free hand to force its wishes on the Iranian government in every way possible, including military intervention, especially in the adjacent provinces of Azarbaijan and Gilan. Even before the conclusion of the agreement, Russia repeatedly threatened to dispatch troops to Tabriz under the pretext of protecting the interests of its citizens and protégés in the face of revolutionary chaos. The agreement only made such threats more real and, as far as the powers were concerned, blatantly legitimate. Iranian constitutionalists were dumbfounded.

Facing Russia's hostility, Iranian constitutionalists in and out of the Majles hoped for British support. Yet the combined effect of Amin al-Soltan's assassination and the conclusion of the Anglo-Russian agreement dissuaded Britain from lending its support to the Iranian cause. New geopolitical realities, above all the rise of Imperial Germany, were the chief motive behind the 1907 agreement. One outcome so far as Iran's domestic politics was concerned was a greater polarization of Iran's revolutionary politics, which less than a year later led to open confrontation with the Qajar shah and a civil war. The anti-constitutional camp consolidated once influential courtiers joined hands with the *mashru'eh* supporters. There was also strong regional support for anti-constitutionalists. The Russian tsar Nicholas II (r. 1894–1918), alarmed by the revival of the 1905 revolutionary spirit at Russia's southern borders, threw his moral weight and military support behind the Qajar throne. And so did Sultan 'Abd al-Hamid II having been equally terrified of the mounting discontent among his officer corps at the very outset of the Young Turk Revolution. That he dispatched troops to the Iranian frontier to back the marauding Kurdish irregulars who looted and killed Azarbaijani and Assyrian Christian villagers may be viewed as token enmity toward the Iranian constitutionalists.

The constitutionalist camp, though nominally abiding by the Majles, was increasingly disillusioned with its slow course of action and the compromising attitude of its many deputies. The radicals among the deputies and outside the Majles were supported by the revolutionary societies known as *anjomans*. Members of the *anjomans*, some of them armed with small weapons, assumed the task of guarding the Majles, but also acted as a pressure group, dictating their wishes to the legislature. Whether former Babis, nationalists, or socialists, the *anjomans'* leadership came to play a decisive role in the political process (pl. 6.3). By mid-1908, there were at least seventy *anjomans* in Tehran alone, with an estimated five thousand armed fighters. Best known among them, Anjoman-e Azarbaijan, acted as a political party and a paramilitary force, and was the political agent for the influential provincial council in Tabriz known as Anjoman Ayalati Azarbaijan.

The mouthpiece of the constitutionalists and their supporting *anjomans* was the budding press, which had multiplied since 1905. They made explicit demands of the Majles, attacked the *mashru'eh* camp and the court, and criticized the shah for not complying with his constitutional duties. By 1908, more than eighteen newspapers were in circulation all over Iran, as well as a vast number of tracts and clandestine posters. The journalists were of varying quality; some, like Mirza Jahangir Khan Shirazi (1870–1908), an intellectual from a Babi family, created the influential weekly *Sur-e Esrafil* (Seraphim's trumpet) and set the tone for liberal constitutional debate with intelligent editorials (fig. 6.5). The columns by a gifted satirist, Mirza 'Ali Akbar Qazvini, with the pen name Dehkhoda (1879–1956), offered a vivid portrayal of revolutionary politics and current affairs through the eye of a witty Qazvini village headman. Other papers, particularly *Habl al-Matin* (Strong cord), published in Calcutta since 1893 under the editorship of Jalal al-Din Mo'ayyed al-Islam Kashani (1863–1930) and his daughter Fakhr al-Soltan (and during the constitutional period in Tehran and Rasht) placed Iranian constitutionalism in a broader regional context and amplified its international significance.

The thrust of most newspapers, however, focused on political education and advocacy of secular modernity, invariably tied up with emphasis on Iran's window of opportunity to liberate itself from the slumber of centuries of ignorance and oppression by authoritarian institutions. The subtext was more drastic; it was as though between the lines they were calling for the removal of the old institutions: the Qajar kingship and the Shi'i establishment and even a secular republican order. The passage of a press law in early 1908 that allowed for greater freedom of expression in turn brought more direct attacks on the shah and the royalists.

Beyond the press, the *anjomans* were successful in mobilizing not only the guilds and merchants of the bazaars but also a new class of government

Figure 6.5. *Sur-e Esrafil's* logo captures the spirit of the Constitutional Revolution as an apocalyptic moment of national awakening. The Qur'anic verses about the Day of Resurrection, a seraph trumpeting, and the dead rising confirm the association. At left in the background Mount Damavand is erupting. The journal has lunar Islamic as well as solar Sasanian and Gregorian calendar equivalents. No. 3, page 1 (June 13, 1907). Courtesy of Sterling Memorial Library, Yale University.

bureaucrats and even telegraph, post, and Tehran's transportation workers. The state employees were willing to go on strike in support of the Majles. Remarkably, the Persian telegraph system, manned primarily by sympathizers of the constitutionalists, created under the government's nose a semiclandestine communication network. The telegraphic network connected constitutionalists and their *anjomans* all over the country, thus allowing for the rapid exchange of ideas and decisions, calling on the Majles deputies to act quickly, and admonishing them for compromise and indecision. It reinforced a sense of national accord all over Iran from Tabriz and Rasht to Isfahan, Kerman, Shiraz, and Kermanshah (see map 5.2).

The virtual national community created by telegraphy was already in place during the 1891–1892 Tobacco Protest. Thousands of telegrams were exchanged in the relatively short revolutionary years, often instantaneously and with the sense of empowerment that the new technology offered. A huge volume of messages exchanged in all directions: between constitutionalists in the provinces, the ulama in Iran and Iraq, the government and the provincial authorities, the shah and his officers, the foreign representatives and European capitals, the Majles deputies and the *anjomans*, the leaders of the bazaar, the Caucasian revolutionaries and socialists of Tabriz. Likewise, a vast number of complaints, petitions, and messages of both support and protest were transmitted from the ordinary people in remote towns and villages throughout Iran who had found a new voice through telegraphic communication.

The press and the telegraph, both modern means of communication in the public space, elevated the Majles in the eyes of the people to a sacred institution, as the epithet: "sacred" (*moqaddas*), attached to the full name of Consultative National Assembly, denoted. The Majles became the embodiment of lofty goals of the constitution, expected, quite unrealistically, to dispense social justice; to ensure peace, prosperity, and security; and to defend the country against foreign intrusions—all goals far beyond the frugal means of the Majles and the competence of most its deputies. Yet despite inexperience and inefficiency, the Majles' record was still impressive enough to alarm its opponents and ensure continued animosity.

Beyond the drafting of the Fundamental Law and its Supplement, the Majles had tried, with some success, to tackle the urgent overhaul of the state's frail finances and arcane practices. By 1907, Iran's total state revenue was about 7,700,000 tumans (about $20,000,000), whereas annual expenditure for that year was projected at 10,700,000 tumans ($27,500,000), a deficit of 37 percent. The foreign debts that had accumulated since the 1890s only added to the burden. By 1909, it amounted to a colossal $30,000,000, with cumulative interest to be serviced by acquiring new loans. Greater dependency on imports added to global inflation and increased trade deficits. As much as the Majles tried, it shaved a mere 400,000 tumans ($1,000,000) from state expenditure. It abolished the ancient land tenure (*toyul*) system, an important move that nevertheless in practice proved largely symbolic. Most tenured lands were already incorporated as private estates during the Naseri and Mozaffari periods and were soon to be ratified, in 1910, by the legislation of the second Majles. The pensions of the Qajar princes and hereditary bureaucratic elite were also reduced or terminated altogether, an act of greater consequence for the decline of a sector of the nobility that was devoid of private estates. The court budget too was cut to a mere 75,000 tumans, an act viewed by the shah as a deliberate offense against the monarchy and its public image. Yet he and his weakling court could do nothing but wait. For the time being, the climate was not in their favor. Popular support was for the Majles.

On other items of the reform agenda, the Majles' record was less impressive. Efforts to create a national bank and national army faltered. Ending the monopoly of the British-controlled Imperial Bank of Persia over the issuance of Iranian paper currency and its grip on Iranian finances (only to be rivaled by the Russian-controlled Mortgage Bank of Persia) had long been a national aspiration. The Majles' hesitation to establish a national bank was motivated less by insufficient capital, lack of expertise and misuse of the funds, pretexts under which the measure was eventually abandoned, and more by fear of injuring British financial interests at a time when the Majles needed that great power's unsparing support. The creation of a uniform national army seemed even less of a tenable proposition given the other imperial power's vested interest in the Russian-trained and Russian-backed Cossack Brigade, the most effective of the forces in the Qajar army. The coup d'état of July 1908 reaffirmed Russia's use of the Brigade as an instrument of violent repression to sustain Qajar rule (see map 5.2).

THE COUP AND THE DESTRUCTION OF THE MAJLES

In February 1908 two bombs were thrown at Mohammad 'Ali Shah's cavalcade. At least four were killed, and the royal automobile, one of the earliest in Iran, was damaged, but the shah escaped unharmed (pl. 6.4). The failed assassination, apparently masterminded by Haydar Khan and carried out by Azarbaijani émigrés from Baku, made the shah even less secure about his survival on the throne. His suspicions were aggravated as rumors circulated in Tehran of the candidacy to the throne of his uncle, Prince Zell al-Soltan, whose raw ambitions for the Qajar throne were long the subject of popular speculation. It was starkly clear that the Qajar nobility, afraid for their own survival, were no longer unanimously behind the shah. As early as mid-1907 radical constitutionalists, especially in Tabriz, called on the Majles and the public to remove Mohammad 'Ali Shah from power. The revolutionary newspapers and preachers were no less shy. By early 1908, it appeared that an armed confrontation between the parties was inevitable.

In fear of the revolutionaries, armed with light weapons, especially in Azarbaijan, the shah was encouraged by his Iranian generals and his former Russian tutor, by then his adviser, to react. More decisively, the Russian commander of the Cossack Brigade, Colonel Vladimir Liakhov, was able to persuade the shah that destruction of the Majles and the *mashruteh* was the only way out. Liakhov, a career officer who epitomized the brute autocracy of the tsarist era, with a particular taste for violence, seemed to have been motivated by the January 1905 Bloody Sunday clampdown on the revolutionary movement in Russia. As the commander of the Cossacks, he was in a position to coordinate the shah's intent with the wishes of the Russian authorities in Tiflis and St. Petersburg, perhaps even the approval of Tsar Nicholas II himself. Russian authorities were anxious to wipe out a revolutionary movement that could reignite unrest in the Caucasus. To them, the fall of Mohammad 'Ali Shah seemed a dear loss not only because the Iranian radicals and the Baku revolutionaries would have gained the upper hand, but also because it could potentially strengthen the chances of the pro-British Zell al-Soltan.

Once the shah stormed out of Golestan Palace in protest and began to fortify himself in the Bagh-e Shah royal compound to the northwest of the capital, it became evident to all but a few reconciling deputies of the Majles that the royalists were preparing for a violent showdown with the Majles, the *anjomans*, and the advocates of republicanism. The shah was surrounded by the Cossack elites and regular troops, who were anxious to move against the Majles. In response, the armed supporters of the *anjomans* who identified themselves as Mojaheds (crusaders), took positions on the roof and minarets of the grand Naseri Mosque (later known as Sepahsalar Mosque), adjacent to the Majles. As a consolatory gesture, some Majles deputies still hopeful of reconciling with the shah managed to persuade most of the fighters to abandon their posts, hence inadvertently exposing the Majles to an artillery assault.

On the June 23, 1908, Cossack forces—as many as two thousand cavalry and infantrymen carrying four pieces of artillery—surrounded the Majles and the roads leading to Baharestan Square. The remaining Mojahedin fighters were ready to engage, even though they were reluctant to aim at the Russian officers out of fear of graver consequences. Yet once fighting started, they offered a fierce resistance that last four hours and cost at least forty lives, mostly on the Cossack side. In response, Liakhov ordered the bombardment of the Majles and surrounding buildings. The Majles building, a handsome early example of Perso-European architecture, was severely damaged. Having demolished the symbol of the constitutional regime, the troops swarmed in and looted whatever they could, as they also did with the surrounding buildings occupied by the *anjomans* and their fighters. To intimidate the general public, the troops then embarked on a bloody campaign of rape, pillage, and killing in the neighborhoods adjacent to the Majles. The Qajar cities were not foreign to government troops' harassment and ransacking neighborhoods, yet the show of force by the Russian Cossacks was novel, the first to bear the ominous signs of a modern military coup. Taking advantage of the coup in Tehran, royalists coordinated efforts in Tabriz, Shiraz, Zanjan, Isfahan, Kerman, and Rasht by clamping down on the constitutionalists.

A handful of deputies were trapped in the Majles, as well as the two mojtaheds—Sayyed Mohammad Tabataba'i and Sayyed 'Abdollah Behbahani, who had come to give their moral support and prevent the bloodshed.

The journalist Jahangir Shirazi and the revolutionary preacher Malek al-Motekallemin, fearing arrest outside, had taken sanctuary in the Majles. To escape, they cut a hole in the back wall and rushed to take shelter in the surrounding houses, only to be swiftly betrayed and rounded up, battered, and arrested by the Cossack detachments. At least thirty of the most vocal revolutionaries were arrested and detained in the Bagh-e Shah compound, where they were further beaten, interrogated, tortured, and detained. The few who were alerted in advance of the ensuing coup, including Taqizadeh, took refuge in the British and French legations and a handful managed to escape the capital and leave the country. The remaining deputies stayed home, unharmed.

Two among the Bagh-e Shah detainees, the revolutionary preacher Malek al-Motekallemin and the journalist Jahangir Khan Shirazi, topped the shah's blacklist. They were unceremoniously executed by strangling shortly after their arrival in Bagh-e Shah. Suspected of Babi affiliation (even though they most likely were both agnostics), they were easy and legitimate prey, used to instill terror in the hearts of the public. The other revolutionary preacher, Jamal al-Din Isfahani, another Babi suspect who had fled the capital, was captured in the western town of Borujerd and swiftly put to death by the governor of the province with the shah's approval. Two other journalists were murdered in prison. The rest of the detainees, including the two mojtaheds, were gradually released and sent into exile, and a few were employed by the shah as go-betweens to the remnants of the Majles deputies (fig. 6.6). The newspapers were all closed down and the *anjomans* were declared illegal. Two royal announcements proclaimed that, with the removal of the heretics and agitators, the shah intended to restore the "correct" constitutional regime within three months.

The royalist coup, the bombardment of the Majles, and the executions had the effect of terrorizing the public into silence, at least in the capital. People began to go about their business again, and the Tehran bazaar reopened with a sense of relief. With Nuri and his growing contingency of clergy fully integrated into the royalist camp and having abandoned for the most part their *mashru'eh* objective in favor of Qajar absolutism, there were hopes that Mohammad 'Ali Shah would consolidate his reign. Some sycophants among the Majles' deputies began to ingratiate themselves with the shah, who liked to believe, at least for the sake of appearances, that he favored the constitutional regime. He declared, in conformity with Nuri's propaganda, that he was against the prevalence of the radicals, heretics, and anarchists.

The royalists needed such rhetoric for domestic consumption but also to improve their tarnished image abroad. Although the coup was welcomed in

Figure 6.6. A group of twenty-two revolutionaries enchained in Bagh-e Shah during the June 1908 coup. The verse reads: "If you wish, your justice breaks up a hundred chains of injustice / Welcome the suffering and endure the chains of tyranny." W. M. Shuster, *The Strangling of Persia* (New York, 1912), 265.

St. Petersburg's conservative circles, it was frowned upon in London and elsewhere. Save a handful of liberals in the Persia Committee—formed in October 1908 in support of the Iranian Constitutionalists—the European public was prepared to forget about Iran and its revolution. Most significantly, the great scholar and supporter of Iranian revolution Edward Granville Browne, protested the brutal clampdown in numerous pamphlets and newspaper articles. If it were not for the popular resistance that soon reignited in Tabriz and thereafter in Rasht and Isfahan, constitutionalism seemed to have lost.

There was also a sense of relief among the public, who hoped to see an end to chaos and a return to the relative calm and security of earlier decades. Growing harassment in towns and villages by plundering tribal horsemen and armed bandits, and encroaching Kurdish irregulars and Russian frontier guards in the northern provinces killed thousands and ravished the countryside. The Majles' failure to deliver remedies to the country's economic and social needs was an added source of public frustration. By the time of the coup, it was as though the whole mystique of the *mashruteh* had been spoiled, if not lost altogether.

MINOR TYRANNY AND THE CIVIL WAR

Even though the Tehran parliamentary experiment had collapsed, there was still a flicker of hope in the provinces. In the following months a prolonged, and at times bloody, urban war was waged between the revolutionary fighters and a combination of local royalists, mostly of the Anjoman-e Islamiyeh (Islamic *anjoman*), belonging to the Usuli neighborhoods of Tabriz, who collaborated with the government troops. During the latter half of 1908 and early 1909, even before the fall of the Majles, the Tabriz militia put up an armed struggle that shifted the fortunes of the Constitutional Revolution, making it even more populist, nationalist, and secular. Once it had grown into a national movement, the civil war consolidated Iran's national community perhaps more than any other single event in the twentieth century before the oil nationalization movement of the 1950s.

Tabriz was the predictable stage for such a struggle. Like any former capital, there existed a sense of pride and power there, reinforced by the strength of the Tabriz economy, the growth of its population, and its relative openness to the Western presence and practices. As Iran's largest and most prosperous city, with a population of more than two hundred thousand, it was the hub of northern trade connecting the Anatolian and Caucasian overland routes to the Black Sea and to the Russian Railway across the Caucasian border, and thus the Russian, Ottoman, and European markets. Importing manufactured goods, fabrics, and consumer commodities, the Tabriz merchants competed with the European commercial agents in the city despite unequal customs duties and other disadvantages. The export market of Tabriz, including various cash crops and a magnificent handmade carpet industry that by the turn of the century had surpassed those of Kashan and Isfahan, brought significant income to the city. The Tabriz merchant class financed the constitutional movement and the eventual civil revolt, while the poor and disadvantaged local labor, mostly peasants who intended to benefit from the urban economy, provided the manpower.

Foreign connections brought modern schools and hospitals, including those established by American Presbyterian missionaries. By the turn of the century, city and provincial telephone lines were established. Road and railroad connections to the Caucasian cities and beyond carried Azarbaijani migrant workers to the Baku oil fields, where they constituted the largest ethnic group, and to other Russian cities in search of work. They came back from Baku and Tiflis, then hotbeds of revolutionary socialism, with new radical ideas. Azarbaijani merchant capitalists who made their fortunes in Baku, Tiflis, and Istanbul also viewed with pride and sympathy the growth of the constitutional movement in their homeland. The city's large and industrious Armenian community also served as an important conduit for technology and business, as well as for revolutionary ideas.

Yet despite tokens of modernity, Tabriz was a traditional city with strong loyalties to religion and geography. Still tied to Shi'i rituals and shrines, the political maneuvering of influential mojtaheds and old sectarian conflicts divided the city. While some of the largest of the twelve city wards (*mahalleh*) were identified as Shaykhi, for following mojtaheds from that school, since the early decades of the nineteenth century (possibly replacing the older sectarian loyalties), other important wards were identified as *Motesharre'* (shari'a-orientated), for their loyalty to the Usuli mojtaheds. As in most other Iranian cities, urban wards served not only as units of municipal administration and a source of communal loyalty but also as bases of operation for the neighborhood vigilantes—generally identified as *lutis*, with their often precarious life of extortion, violence, and acting as hired daggers for the city notables. As much as there were "bad" *lutis* known for their dangerous conduct, there were also "good" *lutis* credited with protecting the neighborhood and extending charity to the poor. With their own code of honor, demeanor, lingo, hierarchy, and appearance, the *lutis* were feared but also admired.

The two most prominent popular leaders of the Tabriz resistance—Sattar Khan and Baqer Khan, who later were elevated to the status of national heroes—were *luti* leaders, as were many of their fellow fighters. They were associated with the Shaykhi wards of Amirkhiz and Khayaban, respectively, both of which played a pivotal role in the success of the Tabriz resistance (fig. 6.7). It was primarily the two leaders' sectarian rivalry with *lutis* of the opposite league that shaped the conflict and ensured its resilience. But contrary to earlier instances of urban strife, the two leaders were operating largely as free agents. This gave the resistance a popular character somewhat distinct from the politics of the elites that had so far characterized the Constitutional Revolution. Over the course of the fighting in 1908 and 1909, neighborhood loyalties transcended their immediate surroundings to include Tabriz and eventually the whole of the country. The accelerating revolutionary process clearly set "supporters of the constitution" (*mashruteh-khvahan*) against the royalist camp, who invariably labeled them "supporters of the tyranny" (*mostabeddin*).

That the Shaykhi quarters opposed the royalist cause was not accidental. Nor was the backing of the Usuli quarters for Mohammad 'Ali Shah and for Nuri's *mashru'eh*. The Shaykhis had a natural propensity for new ideas and

Figure 6.7. Leaders of the 1908–1909 Tabriz resistance, Sattar Khan (*wearing white*)
and Baqer Khan (*to his left*), with their fighters brandishing their rifles in
a gesture of defiance.
Contemporary postcard. Author's collection.

institutions, which can be attributed at least in part to their theology of reconciling the shari'a with ideas of historical progression, but also to their place in
society as upholders of an alternative creed. In contrast, the anti-constitutional
Islamic Anjoman of Tabriz operating out of the Dovechi ward was subsidized
by the shah's court to prop up local support for the government onslaught.

Activism in Tabriz, though, was based on more than neighborhood politics.
The so-called Markaz-e Ghaybi (the invisible center), an early clandestine revolutionary cell founded by a certain 'Ali Monsieur perhaps on the model of the
secret societies of the French Revolution, motivated by socialist ideas in vogue
in the Caucasus during and after the 1905 Russian Revolution. It was instrumental in organizing the Tabriz neighborhood militias into an effective fighting
force. A large numbers of émigrés revolutionaries from among the Muslims,
Armenians and Georgians of Baku and Tiflis also joined the resistance. The
Baku Social Democratic Party, which included Iranian émigrés, and Russian
Social Democrats also supported Tabriz with manpower, money, weapons, and
tactical advice.

Sattar Khan (1866–1914), a former horse trader and reformed *luti*, was a
natural leader whose gift for urban warfare complemented his habit of extorting "contributions" for the national cause. Access to the government arsenal
inside the Tabriz citadel allowed the fighters, who had adopted the general

Figure 6.8. Sattar Khan's street barricade in the Amirkhiz ward in Tabriz in 1909.
Contemporary postcard. Author's collection.

name Fada'i (devotee), to indulge in a cache of weapons, ammunitions, and field guns (fig. 6.8). Using local expertise, and often improvising, they fortified barricades, gates, and other strategic locations around constitutionalist wards. Beginning with a handful of devotees, Sattar endured not only enemy fire but also defection from his own ranks. Motivated by neighborhood rivalry, personal gain, and a code of honor, he did not easily accept defeat. Though at the outset the Fada'is were primarily motivated by neighborhood loyalties, over time they cultivated greater appreciation for value of constitutionalism.

For the Tehran coup to succeed, subduing the Tabriz rebels seemed essential, and the shah mustered all the forces he had to achieve this objective. At the outset, and at an enormous cost, he mobilized several regiments from Azarbaijan and elsewhere and sent off to Tabriz the Shahseven irregular cavalry. Later, Cossack reinforcements were dispatched. He financed and gave his blessings to the Tabriz Islamic Anjoman and its affiliated Usuli ulama in the royalist wards. Under the pretext of protecting foreign nationals, the Russian consulate in the city also collaborated with the shah.

The government forces almost succeeded in their objective to isolate Sattar, Baqer, and a handful of their cohorts. But as time passed, fortunes changed once the Fada'is learned how to conduct urban warfare. Government troops in and around the city relentlessly pounded their positions and engaged in pitched battles in narrow streets and in orchards and adjacent villages. Casualties were heavy on both sides, throughout the eleven months amounting to at least five thousand dead and many more injured and displaced. Parts of Tabriz were ruined and villages at the outskirts and along the trade routes in every direction suffered. Innocent citizens were plundered and killed, and merchandise in the Tabriz bazaar and in a new shopping arcade was looted or destroyed by the troops, armed brigands, and by the constitutionalist partisans.

At first, looting and extortion were about the only means of survival for the starving Qajar army and the revolutionary fighters. Later, however, the revolutionary leadership enforced greater discipline among their troops and gradually improvised a chain of command, including fighting units with regular shifts, detachments for special tasks, logistics, a camp kitchen, medical aids (including a camp hospital), makeshift communication and intelligence, a minimum wage, and even a uniform Fada'i karakul cap. These improvements allowed the Tabriz fighters to defend their ground, but they barely made any physical advances between July and October 1908. What was at stake, however, was a symbolic resistance against the Tehran regime that neither the shah nor his Russian backers could afford to ignore. When a new round of fighting began in March 1909 after a three-month lull, the Tabriz fighters enjoyed better finances thanks to a donation committee that had been established to persuade affluent citizens to contribute. They acquired superior weapons, and above all, there was growing moral support within Iran and beyond in the Caucasus and the Ottoman Empire. The Young Turk Revolution that had removed Sultan 'Abd al-Hamid from power in April 1908 was welcomed by the fighters in Tabriz as much as it was despised by Mohammad 'Ali Shah in Tehran.

High morale is evident in numerous group photographs that have survived. Tabriz fighters proudly pose for the camera with their rifles, rounds of ammunition, and cannon. The palpable allure of firearms in the photographs of the time signified a new mood of defiance, as if weapons empowered ordinary citizens to resist the coercive state and its agents. The photographs, and especially portrayals of the two leaders of the resistance, widely circulated in the form of postcards. They were meant to build up confidence among the people of Azarbaijan and the rest of the country, and soon after to celebrate their victory. And in that, images of the photogenic Sattar proved particularly effective.

The sense of camaraderie was also evident in the way that Georgian and Armenian as well as Baku Muslim volunteers were incorporated into the Tabriz resistance. Recruited by the Baku Social Democratic Party and other radical organizations, these militia forces brought with them superior techniques of urban warfare and a new revolutionary spirit, which helped transform the Tabriz resistance into a national struggle. The Georgian detachment of one hundred volunteers was skilled in urban warfare and the use of explosives, whereas the

Armenian Dashnaktsutyun nationalists were experienced in tactical warfare. Baku socialists, in contrast, were crucial in supplying ammunition and new weaponry, and in transferring funds and crossing government lines, at great risk and loss of life.

Of the handful of Westerners who observed the Tabriz resistance, one decided to join in. Howard Baskerville, a twenty-four year-old Nebraskan and recent graduate of Princeton who was serving as a teacher of English and science at the American Presbyterian Memorial Boys School in Tabriz, was a passionate volunteer. Moved by the courage and sacrifice of the Tabriz fighters, and especially the assassination of one of his Iranian colleagues, and despite the wishes of the American consulate, he resigned from his post and embarked on training an elite force. At one time, the group totaled nearly 150 volunteers from among the city's affluent youth. Relying on his own rudimentary military training, Baskerville and his "rescue squad" hoped to break the government siege of the Fada'i neighborhoods by a surprise attack on the Cossack contingent that was camping at the edge of the city. Despite Sattar's reluctance, and lacking the support of his own volunteers, Baskerville decided to charge, only to be shot point-blank. His grand funeral was a tribute more to his heroism than his good judgment. It was also the height of an ecumenical camaraderie that broke through ethnicity, religion, and nationality.

Baskerville's death occurred at the height of the Tabriz resistance, in April 1909. Mustering all its forces, the Tehran government eventually and with great difficulty blockaded all supply routes to Tabriz in hopes of starving the city into surrender. The grievous siege of Tabriz between January and April, which caused widespread shortages, had the potential to break the resisting constitutionalists (see map 5.2). Although fighting forces in Rasht and Isfahan, by then called the nationalists (*melliyun*), were acting in greater accord with Tabriz, and although the Tehran regime appeared pliant—issuing a royal decree that promised restoration of the constitutional regime—the Russian legation in Tehran, conveying St. Petersburg's wishes, was not willing to compromise. The loss of Tabriz would be a serious blow to Russian prestige, not only because the tsarist government was heavily invested in Mohammad 'Ali Shah's survival but also because a constitutionalist victory could rekindle a revolutionary spirit in the Caucasus. All the more, even the liberal press in St. Petersburg praised the Tabriz fighters and was critical of Tehran's callous despotism.

Securing the safety of Russian nationals offered the needed pretext for Russian troops to intervene in accordance with the Anglo-Russian agreement of 1907 and with the tacit approval of London. They crossed the Iranian border and by the end of April 1909 marched into Tabriz. Their arrival, the first since the 1827 occupation of the city after Iran's defeat in the war with Russia, aroused mixed feelings among the inhabitants. It opened the supply lines, relieving starvation, and facilitated the resumption of trade. The de facto cease-fire brought calm and security, which had been missing since the start of the fighting nearly a year before. Yet occupation was seen as a major setback for the national struggle. Though government troops lifted the siege, retreated to their camps, or withdrew completely from around the city, the prospects of the Russian military presence were ominous enough for Mohammad 'Ali Shah.

Seldom in Iran's history had an urban uprising succeeded in repelling government troops. But even less typical was the support of a tribal power for a popular urban cause. The Bakhtiyaris of central and southwestern Iran, arguably the largest confederacy in the country, were an odd candidate to support Tabriz, since a few detachments of Bakhtiyari horsemen were among the government troops fighting in Tabriz. Yet a rival faction in the Bakhtiyari leadership turned in favor of the constitutionalists. It was headed by 'Ali-Qoli Khan Sardar As'ad (1856–1917), a cultivated khan with nationalist predilections whose interest in Iranian history, and that of his own tribe, along with his previous residence in Europe, had converted him into a liberal nationalist of some valor. Beginning early in 1909, the Bakhtiyari horsemen under his command, well equipped by standards of the time, were a formidable force in the south of the country. Unlike the constitutionalist fighters in the Tabriz wards, they enjoyed the freedom of the steppes and nomadic mobility, which allowed them to capture Isfahan with relative ease. Sardar As'ad was successful in forging a semblance of unity among the khans of his tribe's major league. That the Bakhtiyari lands happened to be where oil was first discovered in Iran, as early as 1908, was not entirely irrelevant to the future prominence of this tribe in national politics. In 1909, however, the issue of oil and British dealings with the Bakhtiyaris were not yet a factor.

The call for a concerted march to Tehran first came from the fighters in Rasht, where an assortment of Caucasian social democrats and Armenian volunteers, arriving in Russian vessels via the Caspian, joined hands with the Rasht fighters for control of the provincial center. They came to be known as Melliyun (nationalists). As with the Bakhtiyaris, here, too, a major local dignitary, Gholam-Hosain Khan Tonekaboni, later known as Sepahdar, and some of his allies among the landowning classes of prosperous Gilan province, shifted their loyalties from Tehran to the nationalists' side. Sepahdar, who earlier had fought with his troops against the Tabriz resistance, reappeared in a new nationalist guise. His rise to prominence denoted the dawn of a provincial landowning class that would come to play a major role in the politics of the postrevolutionary era.

Despite the despair and uncertainty of the moment, there was an air of optimism for constitutional restoration, and even though radical elements vowed to remove Mohammad 'Ali Shah, there was a fair amount of support for compromise as well. This virtual telegraphic community in Iran, for they primarily communicated through telegraphic messages, was defiant toward elements within the Tehran court, and in that they found themselves in a surprising accord with the two neighboring powers. In April 1909 a strongly worded Anglo-Russian memorandum warned the shah that unless he restored the constitution and removed its enemies from his court, he stood to lose the two powers' already-sinking confidence in him—a warning that appeared to the shah's opposition as a green light to capture Tehran. In reality, it was meant to encourage the shah to restore some semblance of a constitutional regime in order to stop the constitutionalists' advances.

RESTORATION OF THE CONSTITUTION

On July 13, 1909, the nationalist forces, as they collectively came to be known, headed jointly by Sardar As'ad and Sepahdar, finally entered the capital. The skirmishes south of Tehran with the demoralized Cossack regiments headed by Russian officers and regular government troops were indecisive. Despite months of repeated Russian and British warnings that jointly and individually demanded that the nationalists stay away from the capital, a force of nearly three thousand Bakhtiyari and Gilan fighters engaged for two days in a mopping up operations inside the capital. Colonel Liakhov and his troops surrendered, only to be commissioned, ironically, back into service by the nationalists even though they momentarily faded out of the revolutionary limelight. Mohammad 'Ali Shah himself and an entourage of five hundred, including his hated army chief, Hosain Pasha Amir Bahador Jang, negotiated his way to the Russian legation, where he took refuge under the joint protection of the two powers. Conscious of European sensitivities, the nationalists quickly secured diplomatic missions and assured the safety of foreign residents, even before marching to the ruins of the Majles building, where on July 15 they officially announced the abdication of Mohammad 'Ali Shah from the Qajar throne.

With a discipline that impressed even the mostly hostile European press corps, the Bakhtiyari tribesmen and a contingent of the Armenian fighters from Gilan restored order in the capital, set up a rudimentary headquarters, and soon declared Mohammad 'Ali Shah's minor son, Sultan Ahmad (1898–1930), as the new shah. The elder of the Qajar tribe, 'Ali Reza 'Azod al-Molk (1847–1910), became his regent. By any account, the success of the nationalist forces was impressive. There was no looting, revenge killing, or retaliation. Even more remarkable was the level of cooperation between the heterogeneous rank and file of Gilani and Bakhtiyari fighters, who could barely communicate with one another in Persian.

The conquest of Tehran was an ephemeral, but defining, moment in Iran's modern history. Soon after the arrival of the Tabriz fighters and their heroes — Sattar Khan, now celebrated as *Sardar Melli* (national commander) and his colleague Baqer Khan as *Salar Milli* (national chief) — instilled a spirit of optimism in the hearts of many Iranians. Deposing Mohammad 'Ali Shah and his *mashru'eh* ally, despite Russia's unabashed backing of the royalists, was a rare triumph in the age of high imperialism. For a moment, it seemed as if the desire to create a liberal democratic order had overcome not only the impediments of arbitrary rule and reactionary ulama, but also brutish European imperial ambitions. It was as though through a national struggle, and its narrative of salvation, the beast of misrule and misery had been subdued and a new road to prosperity paved (pl. 6.5). The new Ahmad Shah was hailed as a constitutional monarch, despite some talk of republicanism in the radical circles.

The nationalists' maneuvering to power, and the level of independence their leaders displayed, took the representatives of Russia and Britain by surprise and generated much dismay. Russia had only complied with restoration of the constitution and abdication of the former shah with grudges, and Britain was not far behind. By the time Tehran was taken by the nationalists, at least three thousand Russian troops had already crossed the border and occupied northern Iran, stretching from Azarbaijan to Gilan and northern Khorasan and advancing as far south as Qazvin, only ninety-five miles from the capital. The audacity with which imperial Russia trampled Iran's sovereignty, contrary to the terms of the Anglo-Russian agreement ensuring the opposite, apparently required not even a diplomatic fig leaf. No longer shackled by a British counteraction, the Russian move had already cast its shadow over the newly restored but fragile regime. It also heightened anti-Russian sentiments that had been boiling up since the turn of the twentieth century. Iranians admired Japan's victory in the Russo-Japanese War of 1904 and saw it as a promising sign that a European expansionist empire could be defied, if not defeated (fig. 6.9) Earlier defeats of the British colonial army in the Second Anglo-Boer War, in 1902, stirred similar sentiments.

Even worse than Russian intervention, now masked as preserving its "interests," were the Russians' profound cultural biases. The condescension of diplomatic communiqués about the nationalists' advances and their eventual victory was outdone only by the hostile reporting of newspapers such as the *Times of*

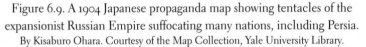

Figure 6.9. A 1904 Japanese propaganda map showing tentacles of the expansionist Russian Empire suffocating many nations, including Persia. By Kisaburo Ohara. Courtesy of the Map Collection, Yale University Library.

London and echoed by the *New York Times*, among others. That the Iranians could resist, fight back, and defeat a regime militarily backed and financially buttressed by European imperial powers was something that could not be easily accepted or forgiven. Evoking familiar Orientalist paradigms, there was an obsessive anxiety that the "safety" of the European residents in Tehran would be violated by hordes of nomadic invaders and socialist radicals. Their expressed disbelief that the capital could be captured without bloodshed was even more telling while at the same time conveniently ignored the arrival of the Russian invaders in the north. Reading between the lines, one can see in the begrudging expressions of approval for the nationalists' success a skeptical dismissal that the constitutional project could never succeed, as if a scheme to destroy this delicate chance already lurking in the back of diplomats' minds.

The coverage of the Tabriz resistance, the recapture of Tehran, and the downfall of Mohammad 'Ali Shah inaugurated Iran's first major exposure in the international press, making front-page headlines. A handful of correspondents from English, Russian, and French dailies and freelance observers with diverse viewpoints brought to Western audiences the unfolding of a struggle that contradicted stereotypes of indolence and deceit meticulously crafted over centuries and even admitted by Iranians in their own narratives of decline. Now there was a new revolutionary resolve apparent even in the midst of the civil war. Awaiting the final assault on Tehran in his camp outside the capital, Sardar As'ad, the French-educated Bakhtiyari khan, daringly replied to the English and Russian representatives who were warning him of the dire consequences of storming the capital in one sentence: "on se verra à Téhéran" (see you in Tehran).

Contrary to the cynicism of most European observers, and contrary to perceptions of failure in later historiography, the Emergency Committee, formed just after the conquest of the capital, mustered an impressive list of accomplishments. To restore calm and security to the terrorized capital, the committee put Yeprem Khan (1868–1912), an Armenian revolutionary commander originally from the Ganjeh province (today in the Republic of Azerbaijan) in charge of Tehran's police department. With his aides among the Rasht fighters, he quickly ended the looting and terrorizing by government troops, by irregulars disbanded after the collapse of the old regime, and by the newly arrived revolutionary forces. The committee, or Supreme Council, as it came to be known, consisted of the two nationalist leaders and a number of ministers from among the younger bureaucratic elite. Soon to be dominated by Taqizadeh, who had returned from his exile, the committee came to play a major part in the days after the restoration of the constitution. It allocated ministries to its members but avoided appointing a prime minister, and it successfully negotiated the terms for the exile of the deposed shah. Through the mediation of the two powers, the committee granted the deposed shah a hefty salary and saw that he would be deported along with his entourage. Once a revolutionary cabinet was formed with Sepahdar as premier, the electoral law was swiftly revised, replacing the seven classes of deputies of the first Majles with direct representation. A nationwide election was held, and by November 1909 the second Majles was in session.

More symbolic, and more daring, were the trials held shortly after the nationalists' victory. To the Supreme Council's credit, a national amnesty was declared, and there were hardly any vengeful killings. Only a handful of reactionaries were arrested and tried. Of the five who were executed by order of a special tribunal on specific charges of murdering constitutionalist protesters in the sanctuary of 'Abd al-'Azim during the final days of the old regime, the most prominent was Shaykh Fazlollah Nuri, the relentless opponent of the constitutionalists. The tribunal held as proof of its verdict Nuri's fatwa to the effect that killing the protesters in the sanctuary was lawful. It hence underscored the new regime's wishes not to punish anyone for ideological orientation. In the final months of the so-called Minor Tyranny, as the period of the civil war came to be known, Nuri had abandoned his earlier call for *mashru'eh* in favor of the old absolutist order and avowed support for Mohammad 'Ali Shah's suppression of the constitutionalists. With peculiar zeal he orchestrated clerical petitions from the growing number of clergy in Tehran and elsewhere expressing loyalty to the Qajar regime and warning the shah of any compromise that might result in restoration of the constitution. Hanged by the gallows in Tup Khaneh Square in front of a dazed public witnessing the unprecedented execution of a mojtahed, one of the most prominent Shi'i jurists of his time, the execution was emblematic of changing times. It seemed as though the kingship and the clergy, the two pillars of the ancient Iranian order, were cracked, if not shattered, by contingencies of a modern revolutionary movement.

Another encouraging sign of change was the diversity of voices in the public sphere. The growth of the press and publications, the emergence of parliamentary factions and political parties, the first audible pleas of women protesting society's misogynistic norms, and a greater sophistication in cultural and political discourse were evident and seemingly irreversible. By the end of 1909 there were half dozen dailies and a growing number of book titles catering to a larger readership. In the following months and years, despite major upheavals, the number of newspapers multiplied, and although many of them were short lived, they demonstrated not only a new relish in the freedom of expression—even freedom to slander—but also the potency of the press in fashioning the country's nascent public opinion.

Among the most articulate was the daily *Iran-e Naw* (New Iran), edited by the formidable Azerbaijani socialist, Mohammad Amin Rasulzadeh (1884–1955), who later was a founding father of the Azerbaijan Socialist Republic. *Iran-e Naw* offered domestic and international coverage, acute political analysis, and debates on poverty, corruption, elitist polity, conservative Islam, and women's rights. Yet there was a limit to how far the burgeoning press could challenge the time-honored sanctions. Already in late 1909, largely to counterbalance the effects of Nuri's execution and to exonerate itself as the guardian of Islam, the revolutionary regime convicted a leading journalist of the time, Hasan Mo'ayyed al-Islam Kashani, editor of the celebrated *Habl al-Matin*, of blasphemy. He was sentenced to three years' imprisonment for alleging in a rhetorical piece that the religion of the seventh-century Arabs and subsequent primacy of Islamic conservatism were at the root of Iran's backwardness and steady decline. Whatever its historical accuracy, such claims (ironically made by a man whose title meant "confirmer of Islam") heralded the agnostic, even anti-Islamic, propensity among modernists of the period. Idealizing the ancient Iranian past as an alternative to its recent Islamic legacy was to become a pillar of Iranian conscious nationalism in the postconstitutional period. More immediately, however, the episode foreshadowed the clashes in the political arena between conservatives and progressives.

OBSTACLES TO THE DEMOCRATIC PROCESS

The very convening of the second Majles, though a victory for the nationalists, was riddled with factionalism, ideological rifts, and foreign intimidation. These pressures brought the Majles to a temporary halt by December 1911 and resulted in suspension of the constitution. The period between 1909 and 1911, and in a broader sense between 1905 and 1921, proved an unequal experiment in Iranian history. Remarkable though it was, however, it ended in tragic setbacks for it was unable not only to keep European intrusion at bay but also bar the old landed elite from return to power.

Two broad political tendencies emerged in the second Majles, each with its own support from among activists and the press, even though the revolutionary *anjomans* of the first Majles failed to transform fully into political parties and even to effective interest groups. The Moderates (*E'tedaliun*), as they came to be known, were the largest block consisting of landowning magnates and tribal leaders among the nationalists, the younger generation of the Qajar officialdom, remnants of the Qajar elite who adjusted to the new realities, and the leaders of the Tabriz resistance, including Sattar Khan and Baqer Khan. The Social Democrats (*Ejtema'iun 'Ammiun*), or simply Democrats, as the progressives came to be known, were mostly intellectuals inspired by European liberal thought, by the Caucasian and Russian socialists, and by the Young Turks who had recently came to power in the Ottoman Empire.

In contrast to the Moderates' gradualist approach, the Social Democrats intended to carry out a comprehensive program of reforms, the rudiments of which were already laid out in the debates of the first Majles and articulated in exile during the Minor Tyranny. Best known among the democrats was Taqizadeh, who allied with progressive elements ranging from members of the nobility with a socialist bent, Sardar As'ad, and liberal ulama of the younger generation to some revolutionary fighters and influential journalists. The Democrats' most urgent demands included basic land reform, the elimination of hereditary privileges, public education, use of the state apparatus for social reform, and even a call for the inclusion of women in the public arena. They shared with their moderate colleagues (with varying degrees of sincerity) calls for the unification of Iran's armed forces and an urgent need to restore security and peace in the provinces, centralize finances, and increase state revenue through efficient taxation and the establishment of a national bank. Put simply, the party had to address the dire needs of a nearly bankrupt government that had grown in size over the previous decade.

A comprehensive program such as this was bound to encounter obstacles, especially in the area of security and finances. Most glaring, yet predictable, was a sharpening divide among the constitutionalists, which soon led to political assassinations and factional clashes. The most notable victim of political unrest was Sayyed 'Abdollah Behbahani, a clerical icon of the constitutional struggle. In June 1910, he was assassinated by a Caucasian terrorist cell associated with Haydar Khan 'Amu-Ughlu, who apparently had taken his cue from Taqizadeh and his radical supporters. Behbahani's fall displayed a resistance among the Democrats toward the presence of the clerical dignitaries on the political stage. This surely contributed to demoralizing the ulama, and even the diminishing pro-constitutional wing of the Shi'i leadership in Iran and in Iraq.

Mulla Mohammad Kazem Khorasani (1839–1911), a leading pro-constitutional jurist and a *marja'* in Najaf and his anti-constitutionalist rival, found themselves united in denouncing Taqizadeh as a heretic and calling for the exile and punishment of his cohorts. The other clerical father of the Constitutional Revolution, Sayyed Mohammad Tabataba'i, had wisely retired from politics; he later died in Tehran in near obscurity. The clerical element did not abandon the revolutionary stage altogether, but never again would it occupy the prominent position it had maintained since the Tobacco Protest of 1891. The incident also demonstrated the disruptive role of the radical left in the politics of the period. Three major assassination attempts since 1907, all orchestrated by Haydar Khan and his cohorts, helped polarize the climate. In the decade after 1911 more political violence justified further draconian measures.

A more extensive clash between rival revolutionary factions occurred shortly afterward in August 1910. Most Tabriz fighters headed by Sattar Khan backed the moderates. Yet they acted as free agents, causing huge problems of law and order in the capital. Their street clashes with the equally rowdy, and superior in number, Bakhtiyari fighters from the province of Isfahan, were seen by the Supreme Council as a precursor to another civil war. The Tabriz Fada'is' grievances revolved around their inability to financially support themselves, which in turn made some resort to extorting the rich. Their exclusion from the newly reorganized police force under Yeprem Khan was another source of discontent. Accused of insubordination, the Azarbaijani fighters who were clustered in the Atabak Park, the confiscated residence of the assassinated premier Amin al-Soltan, engaged in a random shootout with government troops. The combined forces of Cossack regiments, serving under the revolutionary government; the regular troops; and the Bakhtiyari riflemen routed the Fada'is' resistance. Sattar Khan, who unsuccessfully tried to mediate a cease-fire, was shot in the ankle and removed from Atabak Park in disgrace. The Tabriz fighters were disarmed, and some of the most radical elements among them, mostly Caucasians, were forced to return to their homelands.

The incident was a clear victory for the government and the Majles, which had long called for the disarming of the revolutionary factions. Sattar's downfall epitomized the end to street resistance in favor of the provincial landed elite, that came to substitute for the old Qajar nobility, and the new generation of the officials, mostly sons of high bureaucrats of the Naseri period who had been brought up in wealth and privilege. The latter formed the backbone of a new class of officialdom. Mostly educated in Europe or exposed to Western ways, the air of respectability of these ministers and officials came to define the emerging polity of the period and the conduct of its agents. The large landowners who were their natural allies were distant from the mass constituency of the revolution who had put them in office. Yet patriotism, devotion to the constitution, and belief in reform and progress were still powerful motives among the members of the new elite, often outweighing personal and group interests.

What was missing was a common vision to nurture an indigenous mode of democracy that had been first made tangible in its early days of the revolution. The new elite simulated this goal more in form than in substance. What remained a characteristic of the postrevolutionary period, for instance, was the mutual distrust between the Majles and the executive branch, manned by the political elite. Between March 1907 and November 1911 there were eleven changes of prime ministers and additional reshuffling of the cabinets. The widespread problem of a rapid succession of weak and irresolute governments, each holding power for a few months, recalled musical chairs, with characters from the old and new elite routinely occupying various posts to a monotonous tune of timidity and indecision. The ministers were often backed by the Moderates in the Majles, who viewed the ministers' inefficiency as an opportunity to protect their own privileges against threats from the Democrats' quarter. Both tendencies, however, shared the misperception that the Majles' function did not end with legislation but also included close monitoring of the day-to-day affairs of the executive branch—a notion understood by many in the parliament as an abiding principal of constitutionalism.

Even if such confusion in the division of powers can be excused in a nascent democratic experiment, the obvious increase in foreign influences cannot. In the following years, leading up to the rise of Reza Khan Pahlavi in 1921, Russia and Britain brazenly pressured the government and the Majles, persuading its members through intimidation or favors. The Russians in particular acted with a vengeance, having felt discredited after the fall of Mohammad 'Ali Shah. Even more than the Qajar officials of the past decades, some members of the new elite feared the European powers and their intrigues or felt helplessly inferior, if not entirely submissive, to them. The haughty conduct of the two powers, especially during the 1911 Shuster episode, fostered feelings of desperation and disillusionment among Iranian statesmen and the public.

THE SHUSTER EPISODE

Following an initiative in the Majles to reform the country's finances and the urgency for an efficient revenue collection, the Iranian legation in Washington, DC, asked the US State Department to recommend an American financial adviser to serve as treasurer general of Iran. William Morgan Shuster, a banker who had also served in the US government with integrity and candor, was recommended at a time when Iranian finances were suffering from diminishing income, the obligation to service foreign loans, and growing expenses. The Iranian public finance, fiscal policy, and tax collection, though partially improved by greater centralization, still suffered from the arcane practices of the state accountants. Employing an American expert was thought to be prudent because it would have saved Iran from pressures exerted by the neighboring powers. Shuster's arrival stirred excitement among nationalists while causing anxiety to representatives of both powers and their Iranian associates.

A man of frank demeanor and daring initiatives, Shuster and his American team represented the first serious involvement of the United States in Iran, albeit as a purely private initiative. Before then the US presence in Iran had been limited to a few nongovernmental areas, including American Presbyterian missionaries who had been active in northwestern Iran among the Nestorian Christians since the 1830s. Later in the nineteenth and early twentieth centuries, modern American missionary schools in Orumiyeh, Tabriz, Hamadan, and Tehran educated non-Muslims and eventually Muslim girls and boys. Though negotiations to establish diplomatic relations went back to an unratified treaty of commerce and navigation from 1856, it was only in 1883 that formal relations between the United States and Iran materialized. Even then, despite Iran's repeated attempts under Naser al-Din Shah to engage the United States in trade, finance, and security—even offering the right to a naval presence in the Persian Gulf to counter British predominance—there was a serious reluctance on the side of the Americans to cross into the traditionally recognized Anglo-Russian zones of influence. Recommending Shuster, even though he was first cleared with the British embassy, indicated a cautious change in American attitudes toward the emerging democratic regime in Iran.

From the start, Shuster rebuked Iran's chaotic finances, political vacillation, and infirmity of the government and the Majles. He was outspoken in his critiques of the imperial powers and their discriminatory practices. In his 1912 *The Strangling of Persia*, published just after his forced departure from Iran, he gave a vivid portrayal of the Iranian plight in the face of European aggression. He dedicated his book to the Persian people, who by "their unwavering belief, under difficult and forbidding circumstances," employed him to help with the task of the "reorganization of their nation." In the foreword to the book, he expressed deep disappointment at "being forcibly deprived of the opportunity to finish [this] intensely interesting task in that ancient land," where "two powerful and presumably enlightened Christian countries played fast and loose with truth, honor, decency, and law, one at least, hesitating not even at the most barbarous cruelties to accomplish its political designs and to put Persia beyond hope of self reorganization." In a passionate plea to his American readers, he then stated: "The Constitutionalists of Modern Persia will not have lived, struggled, and in many instances, died entirely in vain, if the destruction of Persian sovereignty shall have sharpened somewhat the civilized world's realization of the spirit of international brigandage which is marked the *welt-politik* of the year 1911."[3]

The lightly veiled reference to Britain and Russia, and especially the latter's hostility toward Iran's constitutional regime, reflects not only Shuster's anti-imperialist sentiments but also the nature of troubles that he and his American colleagues faced the moment they set foot on Persian soil. Even before he began the financial reorganization, most of his time and energy during his stay—from May 1911 to January 1912—was wasted resisting greedy high officials and the intrigue of the two powers. Preying on the bankrupt treasury, the old elite hoped to secure even more loans, this time £4,000,000 ($20,000,000) from a private English financier. Moreover, Shuster's effort to organize a new gendarmerie force under the treasury led to an acute crisis that threatened the very survival of the constitutional regime.

Shortly after Shuster's arrival, a counterrevolutionary movement reached its peak in July 1911, when the deposed Mohammad 'Ali Shah, who had resided in Odessa in the Ukraine since his abdication, arrived in the small Caspian port of Gomish Tappeh in northeastern Iran, near Astarabad, aboard a Russian steamship. Aided by a few thousand Turkmen tribesmen, he marched toward Tehran. At the same time his brother, Abol-Fath Mirza Salar al-Dowleh (1881–1961), mobilizing the Kurdish tribes of the northwest, occupied the western city of Kermanshah and advanced toward Tabriz and Hamadan. The initiative to restore Mohammad 'Ali or his brother to the Qajar throne enjoyed more than an implicit blessing from St. Petersburg. Predictably, the news of these advances plunged Tehran into panic. The revolutionary government feared the vim of a Russian reprisal more than the vigor of Turkmen and Kurdish horsemen. Moreover, it could not secure from the representatives of the two powers even verbal condemnation of the pincer assault on the constitutional government, despite their commitments to bar the deposed shah from ever returning to Iran. The government in Tehran, surrounded by remnants of old Qajar loyalists in the capital, in desperation mobilized an assortment of Bakhtiyari horsemen fresh from Isfahan, police detachments under Yeprem Khan, and Armenian volunteers from the Caucasus to march against the counterrevolutionary hordes, who were less than thirty miles from the capital.

Persuaded by Shuster, Tehran also issued a public warrant for Mohammad 'Ali Shah dead or alive, setting a prize of 100,000 tumans ($237,000). In a brief engagement the commander of Mohammad 'Ali Shah's forces was captured and shot. Even before his retreating horsemen arrived back to their base north of Astarabad on the Russian side of the frontier, the deposed shah boarded the same steamship and fled back to Russia, then Europe. He died in 1925 in exile in San Remo, Italy. Soon after his retreat, Salar al-Dowleh was defeated south of Tehran and fled abroad. The deployment of a Maxim gun operated by a German artillery instructor who was serving with Yeprem's troops inflicted swift military defeat on Salar al-Dowleh's forces. A major blow to the constitutionalists, however, was the loss of Yeprem Khan, who in May 1912 was killed in the course of engagement. By October 1912 all aspirations for restoring the ancien régime had dissipated.

ULTIMATUMS AND MILITARY OCCUPATION

The failure to restore the former shah to the Qajar throne further infuriated Russian authorities and added to their hostility toward Iran's constitutional government. Seeking another pretext to humiliate, and eventually eliminate, the parliamentary regime, in October 1911 the Russian minister in Tehran served an "ultimatum," demanding that the Iranian government formally apologize for the "insult" committed against the Russian consul general or face immediate military consequences. The apology sought from the Iranian government was in response to the Majles' authorization of the Treasurer General Shuster to confiscate the properties of the treasonous Salar al-Dowleh and his brother Sho'a' al-Saltaneh, the chief perpetrators of the counterrevolutionary plot. Under the pretext that the latter prince had secured a loan from the Russian Mortgage Bank the Russian consul general subsequently ordered the Cossack officers to occupy the prince's residence as collateral and force out Shuster's agents who had come to appropriate the residence. The vengeful consul offered an equally fictitious claim that the prince was a Russian protégé and therefore subject to capitulatory rights extended to Russian subjects.

Fearful of dire consequences, the Iranian government succumbed to the threat of brute force. To appease St. Petersburg, the Iranian minister of foreign affairs arrived in person to the Russian legation and offered a formal apology on behalf of his government. Yet there was no end to the demands of the two powers or their shared desire to dismantle Iran's young democracy. Almost immediately after the so-called satisfaction was given, on November 29 the Russian government served a second ultimatum to Iran, this time openly backed by Britain.

In a rare expression of international bullying, the second ultimatum required Iran to immediately fulfill three conditions or else face Russian military occupation, and in effect an end to its national sovereignty. It demanded that Morgan Shuster be dismissed from his post of treasurer general together with his American colleagues. It also demanded that in the future, the Iranian government not engage the service of foreign nationals without the consent of the two powers. Most outrageous of all, the ultimatum demanded that the Iranian government pay "indemnity" for the "expense of the present dispatch of troops" to Iran, the amount and manner of which was to be determined later. This demand was made at a time when Russia had landed more troops in Gilan and Azarbaijan provinces to reinforce its so-called zone of influence. The two powers in effect blatantly required that Iran reimburse the cost of the violation of its own sovereignty to an aggressor who, as it turned out, went on a rampage of massacres and maltreatment of defenseless Iranians.

The second ultimatum, even more than the first, raised a storm inside and outside the Majles, leading to a nationwide movement of outrage, speeches in mosques and the Majles in support of Shuster, and telegraph messages of

Figure 6.10. Imam Jom'eh of Shiraz preaching to the women.
Despite segregation, women's presence in mosques and mourning
rituals allowed for their participation in the social sphere.
By Hasan 'Akkas-bashi, c. 1901. M. Sane' *Paydayesh-e 'Akkasi dar Shiraz* (Tehran, 1369/1990), 78.

solidarity from the provinces. The Shi'i clerical condemnations of the Europeans' nefarious designs on the constitutional regime and the oppressed Iranian nation were headed by Mohammad Kazem Khorasani and his colleagues in Najaf. They called for the boycott of Russian and English goods in the bazaar, the revival of armed revolutionary *anjomans*, and the elimination of the royalists.

A rare voice of protest was also raised by women, who for the first time in public acted on their own—not merely beside their male relatives—to call for a struggle against the nation's foreign and domestic enemies and support for the constitutional government and adoption of modern social and ethical values (fig. 6.10). It was as if the spirit of *mashruteh* had been resurrected. Except this time it became painfully evident that the primary terminator of Iranian aspirations was not the Qajar regime and its clerical allies, but the dictates of European grand strategy—this even before a drop of Iranian oil had reached Europe's Great War.

The seventy deputies of the Majles, encouraged by calls to defy the Russian threat, including a women's demonstration along Lalehzar Avenue, voted against the government's recommendation to accept the ultimatum just minutes before the forty-eight-hour deadline the Russians had set. The Bakhtiyari-dominated cabinet nevertheless succumbed to pressure and dismissed Shuster.

Driven by realistic fears of Russian onslaught, the Bakhtiyari oligarchs were also willing to comply with Russian wishes, because at the time they were negotiating with British authorities over land rights in the newly discovered oil field of Masjed Soleiman in Khuzestan province. The prospects in their tribal territory were too lucrative to be jeopardized by offending Russia, now the ally of Britain.

The Majles, however, stood firm until the end. Even the disheartening news of the sudden death on December 13 of Mohammad Kazem Khorasani in Najaf did not deter the deputies. Dying under suspicious circumstances while on his way to Tehran, Khorasani was apparently contemplating declaring jihad against Russia. Rumors in Tehran held Russian agents responsible for his death even though tacit British blessing was not ruled out. Even if these were sheer speculations, they were enough to demoralize the public and erode support for the Majles.

The Russians had no intention of coming to terms with the Majles. Since December 1, Russian troops had reoccupied Tabriz and gone on a rampage of plunder, rape, abduction, and killing of innocent people. The Tabriz urban militia, the remnants of the Fada'is remobilized under the acting city council, put up a stiff resistance during three weeks of street battles with a Russian force of five thousand. Yet despite nearly eight hundred Russian casualties, the Tabrizi snipers were eventually outnumbered by Russian reinforcements of royalist Shahseven tribes. Together they inflicted heavy casualties on the population and destroyed some of the city's most remarkable monuments, including Arg 'Ali-Shah, the formidable thirteenth-century Ilkhanid citadel. Even more vicious, on the day of 'Ashura (September 13, 1912), the occupying Russian forces publicly hanged eight leaders of the Tabriz resistance, including the enlightened constitutionalist Shaykhi mojtahed of the city, 'Ali Aqa Seqat al-Islam Tabrizi (1861–1911). Their bodies remained on the gallows for days after. In due course, thirty-six other nationalists were hanged on bogus charges of resisting foreign occupation.

By early 1912 the Russian army, then twenty thousand strong, had occupied the entirety of Iran's northern provinces, from Khoy in western Azarbaijan to Sarakhs in the extreme northeastern Khorasan. Facing resistance from the population of Mashhad, who had taken refuge in the shrine of Musa al-Rida, the Eighth Shi'i Imam, the holiest site in Iran, Russian field guns battered to ruin the shrine's golden dome while invading troops looted the shrine's treasury. For the following five years through terror and violence, the occupying Russian army kept a tenuous hold on the northern half of the country. Small wonder that Iranians welcomed the news of the 1917 Bolshevik Revolution.

Not to fall behind, Britain also brought in more troops to the south. Under the pretext of securing British interests against tribal unrest, the sepoy detachments of the Indian Army moved up from the Persian Gulf port of Bushehr to Shiraz and Isfahan, where they faced open hostility. In both cities bazaars were closed in protest, the ulama boycotted British products, and a ban was observed on the sale of goods and provisions to the invading troops. The nationwide spirit of resentment of the foreign occupation went beyond the cities and into the countryside, where southern tribes, most significantly the Qashqa'i and the Khamseh of Fars, staged a revolt against the pro-British Bakhtiyari khans in Tehran. Yet the tribal resistance soon fizzled out in internecine rivalry and disarray.

In Tehran, twice rejecting the ultimatum, the Majles in effect gave a vote of no confidence to the premier Najaf-Qoli Khan Samsam al-Saltaneh (1846–1930), the pro-British Bakhtiyari khan, who came to dominate the political stage. Irrespective of the vote, he stayed in office throughout the crisis. Earlier, on December 24, 1911, under enormous Russian and British pressure, and after some twelve thousand Russian troops had amassed in the Caspian port of Anzali, ready to march on Tehran, the Bakhtiyari premier, aided by Yeprem Khan, had ordered the newly formed Homayun regiment to occupy the Majles, expel all the deputies from the premises, and close the gates. The deputies were threatened with death if they attempted to meet in the parliament or elsewhere.

The cabinet had already secured the support of Abol-Qasem Nāser al-Molk (1826–1927), the second person to occupy the office of regent to the minor Ahmad Shah. A well-versed, Oxford-educated aristocrat of the powerful and wealthy Qaragozlu family of Hamadan, and a friend of both Edward Gray and George Curzon, he proved to be a learned man but a timid statesman when it came to leading the country at a critical juncture. Fearing Russian occupation of the capital, he declared the end of the second Majles and suspension of the constitution under extraordinary circumstances. A committee of five ministers thereby accepted the Russian ultimatum and abided by its terms, with minor modifications. Soon after, in January 1912, Morgan Shuster and his party of American associates resigned and left Iran, traveling in motorcars less than a year after they had arrived in horse carriages (fig. 6.11).

On the eve of his forced departure, demonstrations were held in the Baharestan Square in front of the Majles, and schoolchildren shouted, "Independence or death!" Witnessing this scene, the great bard of the Constitutional Revolution, Abol-Qasem 'Aref Qazvini (1882–1934), composed a song for which only the lyrics have survived:

Figure 6.11. Morgan Shuster and his family leaving Tehran in January 1912
after the second Anglo-Russian ultimatum required his departure.
W. M. Shuster, *The Strangling of Persia* (New York, 1912), 228.

Shame on the house that let the guest leave the table,
Renounce life and let not the guest depart!
If Shuster leaves the country, Iran will be lost,
O youth of the country, let not Iran be lost! . . .
The cup of our patience brimmed,
For the thief wishes to rub our house with impunity.
Our story will be the shame of the world history,
If we allow Shuster to leave Iran.[4]

In his heart-wrenching account of the suspension of the *mashruteh*, Shuster himself called the destruction of the democratic experience in Iran "a sordid ending to a gallant struggle for liberty and enlightenment." Reflecting on his short experience he further wrote:

That the Persians were unskillful in the practical politics and in the technique of representative constitutional government no one could deny; but that they had the full right to develop along particular lines of their customs, character, temperament and tendencies, is equally obvious. Five years is nothing in the life of a nation; it is not even long as a period for individual reform; yet after a bare five years of effort, during which the Persian people, with all their difficulties and harassed by the so-called friendly powers, succeeded in thwarting a despot's well-planned effort to wrest from them their hard-earned liberties, the world is told by two European nations that these men were unfit, danger-ous and incapable of producing a stable and orderly form of government.[5]

This was the judgment of an American in 1912, just before the disasters that befell Iran during World War I—before the British attempt to turn Iran into a semi-protectorate in 1919, and years before the Allied occupation of Iran during World War II, before the brazen Soviet attempt to snatch away Iran's territory and subvert its government, and before Shuster's own country conspired in 1953 with Britain to deprive Iran of economic sovereignty over its natural resources and its democratic aspirations. It sounds almost prophetic that he concluded that Iran "was the hapless victim of the wretched game of cards which a few European powers, with the skill of centuries of practice, still play with weaker nations as the stake, and the lives, honor and progress of whole races as the forfeit."[6]

Shuster's was not the only voice outside Iran that supported the Constitu-tional Revolution. The most courageous and consistent, perhaps, was that of the celebrated English scholar of Iran Edward Granville Browne (1862–1926). From the outset of the movement, Browne lent his moral support through cor-respondence with major constitutionalist players and sympathetic British dip-lomats in Iran. He also organized the Iran Committee in the United Kingdom in support of the revolution, sought out other voices of support in the West, responded to vicious attacks on the constitutionalists in the British press, and provided an updated narrative of the revolution in Iran as it unfolded. Browne's *The Persian Revolution of 1905–1909*, published in 1910 was a remarkable work of contemporary history based on his published pamphlets and tracts, his cor-respondence, and his investigative scholarship. It offered the English reader an inside view of the revolution, distinct for its direct conveyance of the ideas and feelings of the Iranians, the dilemmas and obstacles they were facing, and the prospects of their revolution, as was visible by the middle of 1909.

Almost an instantaneous classic, Browne's account questioned not only the imperialist biases of his own time but also the validity of the all-embracing cri-tiques of Orientalism and the common assumption that Orientalists invariably were pioneers of imperial hegemony. Though Browne, like most scholars of his generation, was enamored of a romantic vision of the East, his *Persian Revo-lution* was an anti-imperialist project that helped define the *mashruteh* as an authentic voice of protest against domestic oppression and foreign intrusion. That on the cover of his book was embossed the Persian phrase "Long live the Iranian Constitutional Revolution" (*payandeh-bad mashruteh-e Iran*) dis-played the author's sympathies for the Iranian cause. It also denoted his role in "representing," free of a nefarious motive, the Iranian voice against crimes committed by the great powers in Iran, even though he, and a small group of like-minded liberals, failed to change the course of British foreign policy. Yet his *Persian Revolution* was an enduring narrative for the Iranian revolution, one that for decades defined its forerunners, heroes, and villains.

POETS OF DISSENT AND DESPAIR

'Aref's song about Shuster was part of the poetry of dissent that found expression during the Constitutional Revolution. In what might be called the poetic space, Iranians often questioned the prevailing political and religious values of their society and condemned hypocrisy, greed, and violence. With the coming of the Constitutional Revolution, the press and publications offered a new generation of poets and intellectuals a chance to free themselves from the patronage of the Qajar court and nobility and compose work in a language accessible to ordinary people. Using classical Persian forms and images, the host of poets of the period went beyond political discourse to appeal to their audiences not only through press and publications but also through musical concerts, performances, and especially the medium of popular songs (*tasnif*).

The message of the new poetry engaged with the revolutionary aspirations and agonies. While still loyal to such themes of classical poetry as pantheistic gazing at nature, longing for the beloved, expressing nostalgia for bygone times, and despairing over the loss of youth, the poets of the period also bemoaned the ruination of the motherland and its loss to hostile and covetous foreign powers. The glorious days of Iran's ancient past versus the cruel tyranny of its present, the grip of the greedy and corrupt elite on the people, the ignorance and bigotry of clerical leaders, the destitution and starvation, and the dark destiny that awaited Iran's immediate future were also common themes. Aspirations for progress, prosperity, and social justice were also present; they were goals that were achievable, it was thought, through mass education, modern sciences, technology, hard work, and the abandonment of past biases. Over time such hopes turned to despair as postrevolutionary Iran plunged further into political disorder and was subjected to foreign occupation. Visitation of deadly disease outbreaks, mass famine, and destitution of the multitudes were other reasons to mourn the fate of the nation. By the end of World War I, the Iranian intelligentsia, among them a few modernist poets, wished that a savior would appear to rescue Iran and accomplish the objectives of the revolution, even at the expense of forgoing the luxury of constitutional democracy.

Of seven major poets of the period, the most distinguished in poetic excellence and clarity of social message is perhaps Mohammad Taqi Bahar (1884–
1951), who was then at the beginning of a long and eventful political, journalistic,
and scholarly career. Born in Mashhad to a literary family, he inherited from
his father the title of the poet laureate (*malek al-sho'ara*) of the shrine of the
Eighth Imam. He soon turned to journalism and revolutionary poetry in his
hometown, before moving to Tehran in 1912. In a famous poem in the *mostazad*
style titled "It Is From Us What Befalls Us" (*Az mast keh bar mast*), composed in
the same year, Bahar makes a dramatic call for self-criticism, a call that touches
on issues typical of the intellectuals of the period:

> The black smoke that arises from the roof of the motherland,
> It is from us what befalls us.
> The burning flames that flare from left and right,
> It is from us what befalls us.
> Even if we are at our last gasp, we should not complain of the stranger,
> We shan't quarrel with the other.
> But complain of ourselves, this is the core of the matter.
> It is from us what befalls us. . . .
> We are that old plane tree who does not complain of the storm,
> But grows on the soil.
> What can we do? Our fire is in our belly,
> It is from us what befalls us. . . .
> Ten years were wasted in disputation in the madrasa,
> While staying awake all night.
> Today we see that all was a riddle.
> It is from us what befalls us.
> We claim we are awake now, what an illusion!
> What is our wakefulness,
> But that of an infant who needs a lullaby?
> It is from us what befalls us.
> We detest history, geography, and chemistry.
> We are alien to philosophy.
> But every madrasa is clamoring with "he said" and "I say."
> They say Bahar is enamored of the West, body and soul,
> Or he is a crusading infidel.
> We do not dispute, for it is self-evident from this point:
> It is from us what befalls us.[7]

At a time when the Majles closed under the Russian ultimatum and the constitution was suspended for the second time since its inception, Bahar evidently

held the Iranian political left and the right, not the aggressive European powers, responsible for Iran's plight. Typical of his time he represents the seemingly awakened Iranian nation as an infant who listens to childish lullabies rather than maturing with the study of humanities and sciences.

One of 'Aref's well-known *tasnifs*, composed on the occasion of the capture of Tehran by the nationalists and dedicated to Haydar Khan, reveals similar mournful pessimism even at the moment of victory. Two of many stanzas of this song, composed in the *Dashti* mode (one of the most sorrowful in the Persian *dastgah* musical system, often adopted from Iran's pastoral melodies) are embedded in the Persian past but enriched by motifs of European romanticism in mournful memory of the fallen:

> Of the blood of the youth of the motherland tulips bloomed.
> Mourning their erect heights, cypresses bowed.
> Under the shadow of the rosebush the nightingale crept.
> Like me, the flower ripped apart in grief its shirt.
> How cruel are the heavens, how deceitful, how vengeful.
> The [Majles] deputies are asleep, the ministers corrupt.
> All the gold and silver of Iran was robbed.
> O God! Take the poor's revenge from the powerful.
> How cruel are the heavens, how deceitful, how vengeful.[8]

At about the same time, his disappointment with infighting among the Majles and its parties prompted 'Aref to write an ode (*ghazal*) reflective of the suffocating anguish for the future of the revolutionary movement:

> The cry of the captive bird is all for the motherland.
> The conduct of the bird in the cage is like mine. . . .
> Think of a remedy to save your liberty, O my compatriots,
> For if you don't, you are a captive like me.
> A house that is to become prosperous in the hands of the aliens,
> Sink that house in tears, for that is a house built on grief. . . .
> It is better to put on women's garb if the aliens arrive,
> For there is no one more deprived in this country than women. . . .[9]

'Aref's own end was no less mournful than his poetry. At the time of his death in 1934, his passionate tone and often unrealistic, if not naive, aspirations for instantaneous democracy and freedom in his homeland had turned into an opiate melancholy. The orderly but autocratic Pahlavi rule no longer cared for him.

At a more popular level, the message of despair was blended with satire and put in a language more accessible to the people of the street. This is particularly evident in the poetry of Ashraf al-Din Qazvini (1870–1934), better known by his pen name and the title of his satirical journal, *Nasim-e Shomal* (Northern breeze). As the title implies, many of the themes in his poems, as well as style and subject matter, were inspired by journalistic trends from the Caucasus, and especially by the celebrated satirical journal *Molla Nasr al-Din*, published in Azarbaijani Turkish in Baku starting in 1906. *Nasim-e Shomal* successfully reinterpreted this satirical spirit for Persian tastes. In the thirty-five years of its irregular appearance since 1907, the modest but highly popular weekly, printed out of a small Jewish press in Tehran, reiterated in a lower register songs of nostalgia for Iran's great past, lamenting its current ruination, ignorance, and poverty. Edward Browne's rhymed rendering of the *Nasim-e Shomal* piece attacking Mohammad 'Ali Shah just before the 1908 coup is one example:

Vainly our lives to hardship we expose,
While in each heart the fire of hatred glows:
For while the nation doth the shah oppose,
And while the shah supports the nation's foes,
    And while reaction dominates the state,
    Needs must our caravan be lame and late!
We say that now at last the press is free,
That Persia shall regain prosperity,
That firmly based is now our liberty,
That colleges abound increasingly,
    Bottles and stone best typify our state!
    Needs must our caravan be lame and late!
An ass becomes our arbiter supreme,
A dog controls each project and each scheme,
A fox the object of respect doth seem,
Shapshal [the shah's Russian tutor] a trusty treasurer we deem:
    What pawn can move to save the king from mate?
    Needs must our caravan be lame and late![10]

The prose satire of the period was no less forgiving of Iran's failings. The most remarkable, the column "Charad Parand" (Charivari) in *Sur-e Esrafil*, written by the aforementioned Dehkhoda, produced a penetrating and stylistically sophisticated scrutiny of the values and practices of society at this eventful time. Born in Qazvin to a family of small landowners, Dehkhoda's agrarian background, early madrasa education, and short diplomatic career in the Balkans turned him into one of the best critics of his generation. With an alternative satirical pen name Dakhow ("headman," in the Qazvini dialect), Dehkhoda's intimate tone and simple but piercing logic, published in thirty-two issues of the journal be-tween May 1907 and July 1908, lampooned the conservative and sneered at the court and corrupt nobility while highlighting the suffering of ordinary people and the misfortunes of the downtrodden: hungry peasants, broken artisans, op-pressed women, and a host of imagined character types who appeared as the author's alter ego. It was partly because of Dehkhoda's contribution that *Sur-e Esrafil* reached its widest circulation of twenty-four thousand in 1908.

In the first issue, the author employs an ingenious cure for the acute prob-lem of opium addiction in Iran to remedy problems of adulterated bread flour and health care for the poor. Browne's excellent translation of a short passage displays the novelty of style and content:

> After several years traveling in India, seeing the invisible saints and acquir-ing skills in Alchemy, Talismans, and Necromancy, thank God, I have suc-ceeded in a great experiment; no less than a method for curing the opium habit. . . . To all my zealous, opium addict Muslim brethren I now proclaim the possibility of breaking the opium habit thus: first, they must be firmly determined and resolved on abandoning it. Second, one who, for example, eats two *methqals* [nine grams] of opium daily should every day diminish this dose by a grain and add two grains of morphine in its stead. One who smokes ten *methqals* of opium should daily reduce the amount by one grain adding instead two grains of hashish. Thus they should persevere until such time as the two *methqals* of opium which he eats are replaced by four *methqals* of morphine.

By the same logic he then proposes to Iran's statesmen that, since "people are poor and cannot eat wheaten bread, and that the peasant must spend all his life in cultivating wheat yet must himself remain hungry," they should consider the following:

> On the first day of the year they bake the bread with pure wheat flour. On the second day in every hundredweight they put a mound of bitter apricot stones, barley, fennel flower, sawdust, lucerne, sand—I put it shortly as an illustration—clods, brickbats, and bullets of eight *mithqals*. It is evident that in hundredweight of corn, which is a hundred mound, one mound of these things will not be noticed. On the second day two mounds, on the third three, and after a hundredth day . . . in such fashion no one will notice it, while the wheat breads habit has entirely passed out of men's minds.[11]

After the coup of 1908 and the execution of Jahangir Khan Shirazi, the edi-tor of *Sur-e Esrafil*, Dehkhoda escaped to Switzerland but returned after the constitutional restoration to begin a scholarly career as Iran's greatest modern lexicographer. Like Bahar, he preferred to stay out of politics and alternatively to pursue language and literature as expressions of Iranian national identity.

PONDERING THE SECULAR MODERNITY

Poetry, satire, music, journalism, and later literary studies and lexicography, remarkable though they were in defining the national culture of the period, could not fill the visible lacuna in the theoretical grounding of the constitutional order. Throughout, there was precious little articulation of political thought: democratic rule versus despotism, civil and human rights versus power of the state, legislated human law versus the primacy of divine law, and secular values of the emerging society versus requirements of the shari'a. The paucity is all the more puzzling given Iran's tradition of Islamic philosophy and its grounding in Platonic and Aristotelian thought (to the extent they were selectively known through classical Arabic translations). Moreover, Iranians had long produced in the genre of "mirrors," advising rulers on the theory and practice of government. Most cursory references to such theoretical concerns, often by political activists, were to be found in musing of such writers as Malkom Khan and 'Abd al-Rahim Talibov Tabrizi (1834–1911), works that even at the time of the Constitutional Revolution were not widely available in print.

In part, such disinterest toward modern political philosophy can be attributed to the petrified scholastic tradition, which had prevailed since the late seventeenth century, especially in Isfahan, where students of Mulla Sadra abandoned the pursuit of political philosophy and hindered any potential for an indigenous alternative thought such as the one that flickered on the speculative horizon of their teacher. In trembling fear of jurists' censure, most philosophers of the Qajar period and the constitutional era avoided engaging, even on their own terms, with notions conducive to individual rights, toleration, and social contracts. Nor were there the forum or the patronage to translate, articulate, and indigenize such notions from European sources. Constitutionalism and its corollaries thus were seen as commodities to be imported and implemented, often regardless of their theoretical underpinnings.

Even before the raging debate over the legitimacy of constitutionalism, its protagonists were anxious to define it as a notion that concerned only the sphere of government and the restriction of the authority of the ruler, while in reality the adopted constitution reached beyond the political sphere into areas that traditionally were claimed by shari'a. Constitutionalists insisted that reforms to the institutions of the state would in no way interfere with Islamic principals and the requirements of the shari'a, and they repeatedly claimed that *mashruteh* was concomitant with the teachings of Islam and its true spirit. They dismissed anticonstitutional attacks of jurists like Shaykh Fazlollah Nuri as merely shortsighted and based on intraclerical rivalries.

Whatever the sincerity of such interpretations and its necessity so as to ward off the clerical cudgel of heresy, there was little effort in earnest to articulate theoretical boundaries of liberal democracy. In other words, Islam as a comprehensive divine order with claims over the individual, the government, and the community was never seriously dealt with in the constitutional period, nor was an effort made to spell out a workable compromise. At the time, constitutionalists did not see any urgency for speculative debates, nor could they see a paradox in complying with Islam as a comprehensive social order on the one hand and advocating secular modernity on the other.

A notable exception, however, was Mohammad Hosain Na'ini (1860–1936), a high-ranking jurist then residing in Najaf. During 1908, while the civil war was raging in his homeland, Na'ini argued in his book *Tanbih al-Umma wa Tanzih al-Milla* (Alerting the community and purifying the nation)—which was written in relatively accessible Persian, a rarity among jurists at the time—that constitutionalism is compatible with the teachings of Shi'i Islam. He argued that in the absence of the just and equitable rule of the Imam of the Age, constitutionalism is the lesser of the evils and the most viable alternative to autocratic rule, despite its shortcomings. The deputies of the Majles, he proposed, collectively represented an institution that in the absence of the Imam could attend to "public affairs" so long as they acted under the supervision of the mojtaheds.

Despite this notable point of departure, largely in response to Nuri and opponents of the Majles, neither Na'ini or anyone else was willing to acknowledge such issues as inequalities of Muslims and non-Muslims, limitations on freedom of speech and association, gender inequality, slavery, torture, and intolerance toward nonbelievers. These stood in contrast to requisites for developing a tolerant, pluralistic, and inclusive society. Nor was there even the desire to articulate against the largely nonhistorical assumption that the shari'a held comprehensive sway over all affairs of society and the state. Ironically, with the relative growth of secular society in Iran after 1909, even Na'ini retracted his earlier assertions and attempted to remove his published work from circulation. Like most mojtaheds, he retreated back to the traditional jurist's niche, recognizing, at times explicitly, monarchical autocracy as a necessary evil that was complementary to the jurists' supervision of the shari'a sphere. This, in essence, was what Nuri advocated, at least toward the end of his anticonstitutional struggle.

Translations and adaptations of Western works of political philosophy, published in Persian before and during the Constitutional Revolution, came to substitute for the paucity of a robust theoretical discourse and helped shape the ideology and rhetoric of the revolution. One example was the translation of 'Abd al-Rahman Kawakebi's *Tiba'i' al-istibdad wa masarih al-istib'ad* (Modes of despotism and stages of exclusion), an Arabic rendering of a Turkish translation of Vittorio Alfieri's *Della tirannide* published in 1800, which itself was a summary of Montesquieu's *De l'esprit des lois*. Translated into Persian under the same title by the liberal Qajar prince 'Abd-al-Hosain Mirza and published in Tehran in 1908, it was instrumental in defining despotism and articulating the claims of constitutionalism.

LEGACY OF THE CONSTITUTIONAL REVOLUTION

It is perhaps in this inadequate theoretical grounding of constitutional ideals that we should seek at least a partial answer to the Constitutional Revolution's political setbacks. Despite staging an earnest liberal movement with urban support, the Iranian constitutionalists never really succeeded in defining the relationship between the religious and the political spheres. Nor did the geopolitical contingencies of European powers allow for the natural growth and fruition of this experience. From the outset, the Constitutional Revolution faced not only opposition from the Qajar regime and the affiliated clerical conservatives but also the growing hostility of the great powers, which together eventually brought the movement to a standstill. The predominance of the Qajar nobility, though shaken, by no means was purged. Domestic unrest, the inertia of the landowning elite who controlled the institutions of the state, and mere inexperience also bear a share of the blame (fig. 6.12). The all-embracing assault of these hostile forces demonstrates why the experience of modernity in Iran, and the rest of the Middle East, proved lopsided and inconsistent, and why Iran would witness two other major political upheavals in the course of the twentieth century.

Yet it is wrong to view the Constitutional Revolution as an outright failure, as some do. Iran in 1914 was fundamentally different from Iran of 1905. In less than a decade not only were the two pillars of the old order, the Qajar monarchy and the mojtahed establishment, weakened; the revolution had also managed to remove important barriers to social and cultural change. The modernizing project of the early Pahlavi era was the legacy of the Constitutional Revolution. State centralization; an integrated army; reforms in finances, civil and penal codes, and modern public education; and road and rail communication all

Figure 6.12. The Qajar establishment weathering the revolution. Just after the
July 1909 constitutionalist victory, the Qajar regent, 'Azod al-Molk, together
with officials, prince-governors, landowners, and a chief of the Bakhtiyari
tribe posed for the camera. Prince 'Ayn al-Dowleh (*second from right*)
commanded the Qajar forces that fought against the Tabriz revolutionaries.
Contemporary photograph, Tehran, Iran, c. 1911. Institute for Iranian Contemporary
Historical Studies, Photo Gallery.

grew out of the debates of the constitutional period and lingered in the aims
and aspirations of that era. Despite undeniable abuses of political power during
the Pahlavi era, especially involving the royal court and its affiliates, notions of
law and order and due process remained in place and shaped the everyday life
of ordinary citizens.

The ideology of Iranian nationalism and its historical narrative, moreover,
was nurtured during the constitutional period. Notions of patriotism and love
for the motherland (*mihan*) were incorporated into the discourse of the revolution, and especially after 1909 frequent usage of *national* (*melli*) and nationalists
(*melliyn*) anticipated the nationalist ideology of the Pahlavi era. Most statesmen who saw through the reforms of the postconstitutional era, including Reza
Shah himself, were shaped by the experience of the revolution and burned by
its political setbacks. Indeed, it was the wholesale adoption of the nonpolitical
objectives of the *mashruteh*, while also renouncing its liberal ideals, that bound
these men together and gave them a sense of purpose. They saw their mission
as the reconstruction of a new Iran through the alternative route of a strong
state. In their view, this was the only way to save Iran from imperial hegemony,

political chaos, and factional bickering, and the best strategy to project a vision of stability, prosperity, and power.

By no means, however, did all involved share this vision of progress. The journey from the tumultuous liberal experience of the constitutional period to the positivist but rough-and-ready autocracy of the Pahlavi era had to travel a rugged path that took Iran through even darker days of more foreign occupation, regional rebellion, starvation, disease, and loss of life during and after World War I. War had raised Iranian nationalists' hopes but also left bitter memories in the hearts and minds of many who felt robbed of the true constitutional legacy or of the true values of Islam. They saw themselves as victims not only of the onslaught of foreign powers but also of the betrayal of the constitutionalists, and later of the brute power of Reza Khan. He was seen as a usurper who had come to power on the backs of British occupiers and with the help of a privileged elite. It was these memories that were to haunt many generations of Iranians, both secular and religious, for decades to come. For some, the experience of the Constitutional Revolution proved that Western powers would not allow the establishment of a free and democratic regime and that domestic political players were incapable of maintaining it. For others, the *mashruteh* liberal democracy was an imported commodity, even an "ailment" devoid of imagined "authenticity."

The memory of the Constitutional Revolution, lingering in journals and memoirs of participants and eyewitnesses, later was reconstructed as a narrative of national resistance. In the 1940s and 1950s the Allied forces' occupation of Iran and subsequently the oil nationalization movement persuaded Iranian political players and observers to view their own national aspirations and the foreign intrusions as continuation of the constitutional struggle. The parallels were indeed striking, even if the agents and players were not all the same. Mohammad Mosaddeq, the champion of oil nationalization, was a member of the late Qajar elite whose worldview and ideals were largely shaped by the Constitutional Revolution and its prescribed parliamentary process. Nearly a quarter of a century later, Ruhollah Khomeini's doctrine of Islamic government under the "Guardianship of the Jurist" was a clear rejection of the secular liberalism of the constitutional period, and more along the lines first preached by Fazlollah Nuri and supporters of the *mashru'eh*. Attempts to materialize this alternative vision transformed Iran in directions strikingly different from the constitutional experience, yet it still left Iranians grappling with issues of democracy, national identity, and geopolitics as during the Constitutional Revolution.

Part Three

A NATION RECAST

In the seven decades following the Constitutional Revolution, the Pahlavi era (1921–1979) transformed the politics, society, and economy of Iran. In the aftermath of World War I and the upheavals of the postwar period, Reza Shah's authoritarian rule, boosted by oil revenue and a consolidated military, helped centralize the country, create modern administrative and educational institutions, co-opt the old elite, nurture a nationalist ideology, and conduct a relatively independent course of foreign policy. These were achieved at the expense of democratic aspirations and individual and political freedoms that were at the core of the constitutional experience. Westernization also deepened the rift between the Pahlavi state and the retreating clerical establishment.

In the aftermath of World War II hopes for an open society and for greater economic sovereignty reignited during the short and volatile era of party politics and the oil nationalization movement under Mohammad Mosaddeq. The bitter end of that episode left a lasting impact on the Iranian intelligentsia, who remained weary of foreign intrigue and arbitrary rule. The quarter of a century after the 1953 coup offered Mohammad Reza Shah Pahlavi a chance to augment his father's project of state modernization. A program of land reform in the 1960s and rapid growth of oil revenue in the 1970s boosted the shah's political ambitions, his self-image as a savior of Iran, and his repressive rule. A submissive technocracy and a dreaded security apparatus enhanced his illusion of stability and sense of confidence. Yet as early as the 1960s, opposition to the shah and the Pahlavi order brought radical Islamic trends to the political stage. Ayatollah Khomeini's criticism of the shah demonstrated a serious rift between the Westernizing state and the radicalized clergy. Other voices of opposition, including the radical left, showed symptoms of greater crisis to come. The changing political horizons were well evident in the literary and artistic expressions of the period. Greater urbanization, growth of education, the presence of women in public spaces, greater prosperity, and the adoption of modern values and lifestyles in turn engendered both new anxieties about the loss of authenticity and a call for return to traditional values. It was as if the Iranian intelligentsia yearned for an alternative to the Pahlavi promises of glory.

7

THE GREAT WAR AND THE RISE
OF REZA KHAN (1914–1925)

On the morning of February 21, 1921, the people of Tehran woke up to the news of a military coup that in the early hours of the day had brought to power a new government. It was headed by a fiery journalist and backed by Reza Khan, a brigadier general in Iran's Cossack Division. The nine-article communiqué posted on public thoroughfares announcing the new regime carried an unprecedented authoritarian tone. It began with the ominous phrase "I command!" (*hokm mikonam*) and called upon the people of Tehran to be "quiet and obedient to military commands." It warned that martial law was in effect; that all press and publications were banned, pending permits from the future government; that public gatherings were illegal; that taverns, theaters, cinemas, and gambling clubs were closed; and that all government departments and communications were suspended. "Whoever fails to obey the above orders," it sternly concluded, "will be brought before the military tribunal and receive the harshest penalty." The proclamation was signed, "Reza, Chief of His Majesty's Cossack Division and Military Commander of Tehran."[1]

Reza Khan, an ambitious forty-three-year-old officer soon came to be recognized as a "strongman" who promised to save Iran from perpetual crisis and desperation. His meteoric rise to power and eventual establishment of the Pahlavi dynasty in 1925 was as much the outcome of the frustrations and setbacks experienced after the Constitutional Revolution as it was the outcome of a decade-long foreign occupation and imperial ambitions. He was able to rapidly consolidate because of his shrewdness and personal qualities, but also because he operated in a setting in which other options for Iran's political survival seemed to be exhausted. By 1921, the opportunity for a sovereign and functioning constitutional regime was nearly lost, leading to what Shuster had labeled a decade earlier as the "strangling of Persia." It was a feat of fortune, perhaps, but also an engaging historical question as to why Iran eventually managed to escape disintegration and remain a sovereign state.

At the outset of World War I, most Iranian nationalists were hopeful that imperial Germany's challenge to the great powers would liberate Iran from Anglo-Russian hegemony. In reality, however, further misfortunes, prompted by the war, brought the Iranian government to a standstill and the country to further disarray and misery. Iran was not even a party to a war that was fought violently over Europe's imperial ambitions, pride, and power games. And if the Young Turk regime in the neighboring Ottoman Empire was reckless to side with one power against another, the weakling Iranian government was sober enough to declare neutrality, at least on the surface. It seemed entirely unwise for Iranians to join either of the warring parties, given the high level of resentment toward Russia and Britain at home but also the uncertain gains if Iran officially sided with the Central Powers.

Despite repeated pleas to the fighting parties—Russian, British, Ottoman, and German—Iranian territory was overrun by the first three almost from the start of the war, the country's sovereignty was undermined, and its people were subjected to starvation and disease directly or indirectly resulting from the military operations. At no time since the civil wars of the eighteenth century had Iran faced a darker political moment than the period between 1915 and 1921. War and occupation coincided with the eclipse of nationalist hopes and the rise of secessionist movements. The rippling effects of the Bolshevik Revolution and Iran's ill-fated 1919 treaty with Britain further complicated the quagmire.

Long before the outbreak of World War I, the emergence of imperial Germany on Middle Eastern horizons impressed the Iranian nationalists, who viewed it as a dynamic but relatively benign world power. The appeal of Germany, however, went beyond its role as a diplomatic counterbalance. German nationalism as a unifying ideology, one that made possible industrial development and created an efficient state with a powerful military, was an intriguing model for Iranians, as it was for the neighboring Young Turks. Ever since the 1870s, Iranians had admired Bismarck for unifying Germany through war and diplomacy. In 1903, German success in finalizing the agreement with the Ottomans for the construction of the Istanbul-Baghdad railway was viewed internationally as a major strategic breakthrough. It brought Germany, for the first time, close to the shores of the Persian Gulf, a body of water the British considered essential to the security of British India. Further plans to connect Tehran to the Baghdad railway through a line across western Iran equally alarmed the Russians, who saw it an intrusion into their zone of influence (fig. 7.1).

Figure 7.1. Even during the constitutional era the Iranian press
portrayed Britain retreating in the face of Russian and German
aggression and dragging along enchained Asian nations.
DR: *Kashkul*, 1:37 (Tehran, 13 Rabiʻ I 1326/April 14, 1908). Courtesy of Mohamad Tavakoli-Targhi.

DISCOVERY OF OIL IN KHUZESTAN

The rise of Germany on the Iranian horizon coincided with the discovery of oil in Iran by a British concessionaire in the southwestern province of Khuzestan. As the site of the first oil exploration in the Middle East, the Khuzestan field proved a vital strategic resource for Britain throughout the war and after. Beyond the 1907 Anglo-Russian Agreement, the discovery of oil further tied Iran's fate to the fortunes of the Great War. After the war, and throughout the twentieth century and beyond, no other resource came to play as crucial a role as oil in shaping Iranian politics and economy.

In 1900 a British financier, William Knox D'Arcy, who met the head of Iranian customs at the Paris world exhibition, was persuaded to acquire a concession from the Qajar government for the discovery, production, and export of the vaguely identified oil fields of southern Iran. The sixty-year monopoly, granted tax-free to D'Arcy, offered remarkable advantages to the concessionaire in exchange for only a £20,000 ($100,000) advance, another £20,000 worth of stocks, and 16 percent of the net profit from the revenue of all the companies that were to be incorporated under the concession. In 1901, Mozaffar al-Din Shah ratified the concession, following a successful campaign led by the British envoy in Tehran and D'Arcy's representative, who once worked for Julius Reuter and was recommended to D'Arcy by Henry Drummond Wolff. It was as if D'Arcy was to compensate for the failures of the previous Reuter and Regie concessions.

After several years of fruitless explorations, in May 1908 D'Arcy's British engineers struck a massive oil reserve in the Masjed Soleiman oil field in central Khuzestan, inside Bakhtiyari territory (map 7.1). Soon, the construction of a 140-mile pipeline to the refinery and port facilities in the island of Abadan on the westernmost Iranian shores of the Persian Gulf made possible the overseas export of an increasing volume of oil. As early as 1909, the British Admiralty, with its eye on utilizing D'Arcy's concession, conceded to forming the Anglo-Persian Oil Company (APOC) as a private enterprise. In due course, the huge volume of Khuzestan oil offered an incentive to the British government to switch, following the German navy, from coal to oil, eventually for the entire Royal Navy fleet. Despite much resistance from conservatives, by 1914 the British government had acquired the majority of APOC stocks, allowing the government full control over exploration, production, and export. In his role as the First Lord of the Admiralty, Winston Churchill was the driving force behind the purchase, an accomplishment he later hailed as one of the greatest in his long career (fig. 7.2). APOC's purchase, a rare acquisition by the British government, set Iran not against a private concessionaire, but the British Empire.

The popularity of automobiles and greater reliance of all industries on oil revealed the British dependency on the Iranian resource throughout the war and beyond as an alternative to California oil, Russian-owned Baku oil, and the other oil fields explored in Burma and elsewhere. Subsequently, the security of the Khuzestan oil fields and installations became a major concern of the British, concern not only in their dealings with the Iranian central government but also in their dealings with the Bakhtiyari khans and the Arab sheikhs of the Banu Ka'b confederacy, who had a virtual control over the Iranian port of Mohammara (later Khorramshahr) and its vicinity. As early as 1907, Major Percy Cox, then the British political resident in the port of Bushehr, arranged for the arrival of a detachment of Indian sepoys to boost the security of the installations and pipelines. By 1916 this detachment had been upgraded to a full military force, called the South Persian Rifles, based in Bandar Abbas. Despite stiff resistance from the Iranian nationalists, the South Persia Rifles soon was in control of the entire British zone of influence in southern Iran (fig. 7.3).

COMMITTEE FOR NATIONAL DEFENSE

Not long after the first shots were exchanged on the European fronts, and ironically, soon after Iran declared its neutrality, as early as October 1914 both

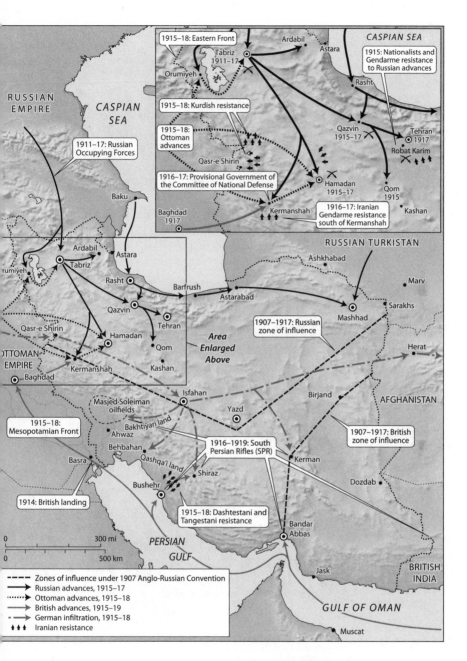

Map 7.1. Iran during World War I, 1914–1918

Figure 7.2. A section of casing for the Anglo-Persian Oil Company's
pipeline being transported near Masjed Soleiman.
Illustrated London News, June 27, 1914.

Figure 7.3. The British-led Bengal Cavaliers and Russian-led Cossack forces parading
in Naqsh Jahan Square in Isfahan in September 1916. In the foreground are the
Cossack commandant and Brigadier General Sir Percy Sykes. The 1907 Anglo-
Russian agreement made Isfahan the meeting point of the two zones of influence.
British Ministry of Information, First World War Official Collection, catalog no. Q 15925.
© Imperial War Museum, London.

the northwestern and southern Iranian provinces became battlefields for the warring parties (see map 7.1). Devoid of an effective force to defend them, the Iranian people witnessed repeated offensives from the Russians and Ottomans along the Eastern Front, where they marched in and out of the provinces of Azarbaijan, Kermanshah, and Hamadan. Between the winter of 1914 and the spring of 1917, parts of these provinces changed hands at least eight times between the Russian and Turkish forces, at an enormous humanitarian and economic cost to the civilian population.

Both the Ottoman Turks and the tsarist Russians committed repeated atrocities toward urban and rural inhabitants; houses were looted, women raped, children abducted, fields burned, and their provisions confiscated. The Young Turk operations in neighboring Ottoman Anatolia forced the dislocation of a million and a half of Armenians from their ancestral homeland on a massive, genocidal scale. Tens of thousands of refugees fleeing the Ottoman army and the collaborating Kurdish irregulars, crossed the border to nearby Iranian towns and villages. Tabriz and Hamadan, in particular, bore the brunt of the occupations, which caused, among other things, a typhus epidemic and widespread starvation. British advances on the Mesopotamian front between 1915 and 1917 cut off the western supply route that connected the Persian Gulf to the markets of central Iran through Basra, Baghdad, Kermanshah, and Hamadan (see map 7.1). This further aggravated the depressed state of the Iranian economy and wreaked havoc on the price of commodities.

Tehran could view this state of affairs only with a mix of horror and resignation as the warring armies moved closer to the capital. In December 1914, after a hiatus of two years, the third Majles was convened. Even though the provinces were not fully represented, the very survival of the parliamentary order provided only fleeting solace to Iran's embattled nationalists. New faces represented the Democrats and Moderates. Most visible among the Moderates was Hasan Modarres (c. 1870–1937), a man of austere lifestyle and forthright demeanor. He was a middle-ranking cleric from Isfahan with oratorical talent and parliamentary skills. Solayman Mirza, the Qajar nobleman who led the Democrats, would be among a handful of socialists to survive exile and assassination in the coming years. In the absence of Taqizadeh, who had fled first to Istanbul, and then Berlin, he would play a significant role in the postwar era. Yet regardless of political orientation, both factions in the Majles soon found themselves facing domestic and international crises beyond the capacity of the feeble parliament and constant government turnover. Between 1914 and 1918, there were no fewer than twelve changes of government, nearly all headed by elite statesmen and manned by a combination of the Qajar nobility and figures who had risen to

prominence during the constitutional era. Brazen intervention by the representatives of the two neighboring powers left a limited role for the Majles over the
rise and fall of these cabinets.

By 1915, the zones of influence agreed to in 1907 were no longer limited to the
northern and southern provinces (see map 7.1). There was a tacit understanding
between the two powers that the entire country was fair game, so long as the
accepted zones of influence were still honored and, equally vital, Germany and
the Ottoman Empire were barred from operating in the two zones at all costs.
In November 1915, Russians occupied Qazvin with the intention of marching
on Tehran, and soon after an advanced detachment reached Karaj, only thirty
miles west of the capital. The pretext was to preempt a pro-German "coup" in
the capital. The upheaval brought about the closure of the third Majles.

Iranian nationalists were sympathetic toward imperial Germany, as they were
toward the Young Turks and their pan-Islamic advocacy. Before sufficiently becoming disillusioned with the Young Turks' haughty conduct or outraged by
their pan-Turkist (occasionally pan-Turanist) territorial ambitions over Iranian
Azarbaijan, they saw collaboration with the German-Turkish axis as a viable
counter to Anglo-Russian occupation. Ottoman connections, nevertheless,
were always hampering the German efforts in Iran, and Iranians never really
warmed up to the idea of pan-Islamism. Backed by the energetic German envoy
in Tehran and his staff, members of the nationalist bloc—a coalition of politicians, mostly Democrats, as well as veterans of the 1909 civil war and a number
of intellectuals and journalists—created the Committee for National Defense
and began to withdraw toward Qom. They were supported by a negligible force
from among the constitutionalist fighters of earlier years and some gendarme
units led by Swedish officers.

Facing the Russian advancing army, the committee intended to transfer the
capital to Isfahan and hoped to persuade the young Ahmad Shah, who at the
age of fifteen has just been invested as the new Qajar monarch, to join them
there. Once a mismanaged coup, organized by the German military attaché
Count Kanitz, failed to move to Qom the government of premier Hasan Mostowfi al-Mamalek (c. 1871–1932), the young shah, under pressure from the British and Russian representatives, abandoned the idea at the last hour. He was
vaguely assured by the two powers that his capital would not be overrun and
that he would survive on the Qajar throne. With the departure to western Iran
of the so-called Mohajerin (immigrants) as the supporters of the Committee for
National Defense came to be known, the capital fell even more firmly under
the spell of Anglo-Russian influence and their demands for greater compliance
(see map 7.1).

The breakdown of Iran's fragile resistance after brief engagements with Russian forces in the vicinity of Qom and Hamadan forced them to withdraw further west to Kermanshah and beyond toward the Ottoman border once the Young Turks had prevailed over the British army in Kut, in the summer of 1916. There, under the Turkish shield and with the backing of the German agents who were assigned to help the Iranian nationalists, the Committee for National Defense formed a provisional government in exile. There the provisional government maintained a precarious presence until the winter of 1917, when a new Russian offensive drove the Turks—and with them, most of the Mohajerin—out of Iran. With an odd mix of Majles deputies, elderly statesmen, political activists, clerical leaders, soldiers, and intellectuals, the provisional government aimed to organize a resistance movement through a network of urban and tribal supporters. It further concluded an agreement that obligated Iran support the Central Powers in exchange for German and Turkish efforts to wipe out the Allied presence in Iran and restore the nationalist government in Tehran. With the Russian defeat of the Ottomans in Kermanshah in April 1916, however, most of the Mohajerin were forced to retreat further to Anatolia, Kurdistan, and southern Iraq, where they awaited an uncertain future. Disillusioned and out of funds, the struggling resistance quickly fizzled; some trickled back to Iran, and others wandered in Iraq and Syria, gravitating toward Istanbul and beyond.

The provisional government was the peak of German efforts to build an anti-Allied coalition of nationalists and tribal forces in Iran. By the middle of 1915, German agents, playing on Iranian resentment toward the Allies, successfully penetrated the southern and central provinces. Through propaganda, agitation, the supply of firearms, and financial reward (or the promise of it), tireless German agents and operatives in Hamadan, Isfahan, Shiraz, Yazd, and Kerman were able to create a network that stretched from the Kurdish tribes of the Kermanshah to the Qashqa'is and Tangestani in Fars and to the Banu Ka'b Arab tribes of southern Khuzestan (see map 7.1).

Most famous among these, Wilhelm Wassmuss, a free agent of the sort operating in Fars province who coordinated his efforts with the German Intelligence Bureau of the Orient (responsible for covert operations in the east) was able to mobilize, along with other German officers, the Qashqa'is of the Fars province and smaller tribes of southern Fars. They fielded a sustained insurgency against the British and their Khamseh tribal allies. Von Kardroff, taking refuge with the Bakhtiyari and protected by Bibi Maryam, the influential sister of Sardar As'ad, the chief of the tribe, fostered a momentary pro-German pact among the Bakhtiyari. Rudolf Nadolny, the chief of the Intelligence Bureau, helped mobilize the Sanjabis and other Kurds of Kermanshah into an effective force.

Oskar von Niedermayer, a senior German agent, was active in Afghanistan even though Iran proved more fertile ground for German war efforts.

The German agents represented a new brand of covert operation that relied on dedication, knowledge of the terrain, military savvy, and the promise of large monetary reward. To facilitate war efforts in western Iran, the German treasury even distributed German marks with equivalents in Persian *qeran* printed on the banknotes. The proxy war fought in Iran relied on resources of modern German armaments that were crucial for the spread of firearms throughout the Iranian countryside. German gold—which was promised and at times spent lavishly—bought the notoriously shifting tribal loyalties only to an extent (fig. 7.4).

The war operation in Iran, Afghanistan, and the Persian Gulf gave the German agents an aura of heroism that contradicted the unfulfilled financial promises made to the khans of the collaborating tribes. A number of Iranian Germanophiles among intellectuals and poets of the period, including Mohammad Taqi Bahar, composed popular poems in support of Germany and Perso-German symbiosis. They even employed wandering dervishes to recite these poems in the mosques and bazaars of Isfahan and elsewhere. Sayyed Ahmad Adib Pishavari, a reclusive scholar and poet originally from Peshawar, who nursed a deep grudge against British colonialism, composed numerous panegyrics in praise of Kaiser Wilhelm II. He also composed *Qaysar-nameh* (Book of kaiser), an epic poem of about five thousand verses in honor of the German

Figure 7.4. To advance its war efforts in 1916 and 1917, the German Treasury issued a tuman and mark banknote, including this twenty-five-*qeran* (ten marks) note, for circulation in the German sphere of influence in western and central Iran. Courtesy of the National Numismatic Collection, National Museum of American History.

emperor, in the style of the *Shahnameh*. By 1918, however, hopes for a German victory over the Allies fizzled, and with it the prospects of ending the Anglo-Russian hold over Iran. Later during the interwar period, German cultural symbiosis with Iran, underscored by archeological excavations and philological studies of shared Aryan roots, held powerful sway over the Iranian imagination.

The short-lived provisional government in exile, barely lasting until 1917, revealed all the flaws of the nationalist resistance since the days of the Constitutional Revolution. It brought to the fore factional bickering between the Democrats' leadership and their Moderate rivals, the generational gap between the elder statesmen and younger firebrands, and petty rivalries and flickering loyalties. The episode also heightened romantic cries for the plight of the beloved country among such poets of national fame as Bahar, 'Aref, and Mirzadeh 'Eshqi (1893–1924). Chiefs of the western frontier from the Sanjabi tribe of the Kermanshah region, who closely collaborated with the Mohajerin, also paid heavily for their loyalties. The ancient tactics of nomadic warfare proved inadequate in the face of European superior firepower when in 1918 they were heavily defeated by the assault of the advancing British forces of the Mesopotamian front at the very end of the war (see map 7.1).

RESISTING THE SOUTH PERSIAN RIFLES

In the Fars province, the Germans allied with Qashqa'i khans and further south in the "warm" country (*garmsir*) with tribes of the Persian Gulf region among them the Tangestanis north of Bushehr, and the adjacent partisans from the Dashtestan region. The chief of Tangestan, Rais-'Ali Delvari, who put up a stiff resistance, was killed in clashes with Indo-British forces, and his positions were pounded by British battleships. The German infiltration, and prospects for a combined urban and tribal armed resistance in western and southern Iran, was a legitimate pretext in the eyes of the British authorities for them to undertake, as early as 1915, similar countermeasures. The arrival of Brigadier General Percy Sykes and his British and Indian officers in March 1916, and the creation of the South Persian Rifles (SPR), secured the southern oil fields but also countered, and eventually supplanted, the Iranian gendarme units in the south (see map 7.1).

First initiated by Morgan Shuster in 1911 under Swedish officers, the Iranian Gendarmerie had turned into an effective arm of the state in the countryside, replacing the older Qajar rural police. By the time of the war, a number of Iranian officers in the Gendarme ranks openly sympathized with the nationalist cause during the "immigration" and effectively fought against the Russians in Kermanshah. Their Swedish counterparts, though first supervised by British officers, also gravitated to the German side and openly sympathized with the Tangestani and Dashtestani tribal partisans, as they did in the north with the Lur and the Kurdish fighters. They served as a counterforce not only to the SPR but also to the Russian-led Cossack Division, which until 1917 had held strong ties to imperial Russia.

Relying in part on local recruits, the SPR force of up to eleven thousand, under a British officer corps and Indian petty officers, operated throughout the region, stretching from the Baluchistan border with British India to Kerman, Fars, Khuzestan, and Bakhtiyari lands, linking in the southwest with British forces in Basra and across the Mesopotamian front. Control over the shores of the Persian Gulf and the Iranian interiors proved a formidable task even for Sykes, a diplomat, historian of Iran, and experienced colonial officer who traveled widely inside Iran and wrote about it. By the time he took over the new post, he had produced his two-volume *History of Persia*, the most extensive in the English language, nearly a century after John Malcolm's and predictably from a colonial British perspective.

By the end of the war, the fate of the SPR had become another complex issue in the already-strained relationship between Britain and Iran. Responding to repeated objections from Tehran, the British authorities, who earlier had given their tacit agreement to hand over command of the force to Iran, made the transfer conditional on implementing the terms of the more comprehensive 1919 agreement. Specifically, the transfer was tied to the creation of a national army under British supervision. It took the coup of 1921 and the rise of Reza Khan for the British authorities to terminate the SPR in favor of a centralized state with a national army.

THE IMPACT OF THE BOLSHEVIK REVOLUTION

By the middle of 1917, it seemed that the British and the Russian forces and their proxies had been able to strike heavy, perhaps fatal, blows to the fragile Iranian resistance in western, central, and southern Iran. German capabilities to offer meaningful support to any sustained insurgency also diminished. The eventual defeat of the Ottomans on the Mesopotamian front and the British capture of Baghdad in January 1917 shattered the nationalists' hopes for recovery on the western Iranian front. To many it appeared as if their country would never recover from the bouts of political chaos and foreign intervention.

Yet the Bolshevik Revolution of October 1917 rekindled Iranian aspirations at a time when Germany and its Turkish ally were rapidly losing their strategic gains—and with it their credibility. With the exception of the Great War itself, perhaps no other international event left as lasting an effect on Iran's early twentieth-century history. The collapse of tsarist Russia, then in control of nearly two-thirds of Iranian territory, both terrified and exhilarated Iran. Fear of the Bolshevik regime and its communist ideology heightened among the elite as the Red Army moved closer to the Caucasus and the Iranian border. On the one hand, as became apparent in early 1918, the collapse of imperial Russia promised an end not only to Russian occupation but also to more than a century of its hegemonic ambition. That Iran could escape what had appeared to be almost certain disintegration—the north annexed by Russia and the south by Britain—could hardly be considered anything less than a miracle.

As early as December 1917, the vulnerable Bolshevik regime, searching for regional allies, denounced the 1907 Anglo-Russian Agreement as a ploy of Western imperialism and called on the world to allow Iran to decide its own destiny. By June 1919 Moscow not only rescinded all of Iran's loan commitments due to Russia but also repealed all the public and private concessions acquired by the tsarist regime as early as the capitulatory privileges of the 1828 Treaty of Torkamanchy. Moreover, it handed over to Iran most of the Russian port facilities on the Persian side of the Caspian and the sector of the Julfa railroad on Iranian soil, and it gave Iran control of the Russian Mortgage Bank. Nullification of these concessions was finalized in the 1921 Soviet-Iranian Treaty of Friendship, which was skillfully negotiated by Iranian diplomats in the face of British obstruction.

Despite these friendly gestures, the appeal of communist ideology to many Iranian nationalists was by no means imminent. Many Democrats who entertained a homegrown socialist ideology admired the Bolshevik revolution and the new Soviet model, but not slavishly. Democrats in Shiraz, for instance, well equipped and in good morale, welcomed the Russian Revolution as a lifesaving breakthrough that could unravel the SPR's hold over the south (fig. 7.5). The conservative statesmen in Tehran were mostly accustomed to the Anglo-Russian rivalry or, worse, subservient to Britain and its hostility to the Bolsheviks. Nevertheless, by 1918 the premier Samsam al-Saltaneh took advantage of the new regime's friendly gestures and, much to the anger of the British, unilaterally denounced the 1907 agreement and canceled all privileges for any foreign powers in Iran.

The instability of successive short-lived governments in Tehran, however, did not allow for more serious engagement with the Bolsheviks. Yet, despite the cool reception at the capital, soon the majority of the Iranian polity began to feel the Soviet ideological and military presence. As early as the end of 1919,

Figure 7.5. Local militia supporting Democrats in Shiraz in 1917. Fars province
was the hotbed of pro-German resistance against British occupation.
Fathollah Chehrehnegar, M. Sane', *Paydayesh-e 'Akkasi dar Shiraz* (Tehran, 1369/1990), 112.

Bolshevik partisans landed in the Caspian port of Anzali, with the apparent intent to recapture the Russian fleet and dislodge the loyalist detachments of the
Russian counterrevolutionary White Army from northern Iran. They advanced
as far south as the vicinity of Qazvin before being pushed back by Iranian regular forces and units of the Cossack brigade.

This happened at a critical juncture, when the newly created North Persian
Force (Norperforce), under British command, had come to the rescue of the
White Army (map 7.2). Earlier, in late 1917, immediately after the Russian withdrawal from World War I, the British Norperforce had consolidated its gains
in northern Iran by occupying Hamadan, Kermanshah, and Qazvin and had
moved toward the Caspian shores, where it joined forces with the White Russian detachments. The default occupation of northern Iran as far as northern
Khorasan, which was outside the traditional scope of British interest, was a remarkable gain but also a huge liability. As it turned out, the British move had
important consequences for Iran's political future.

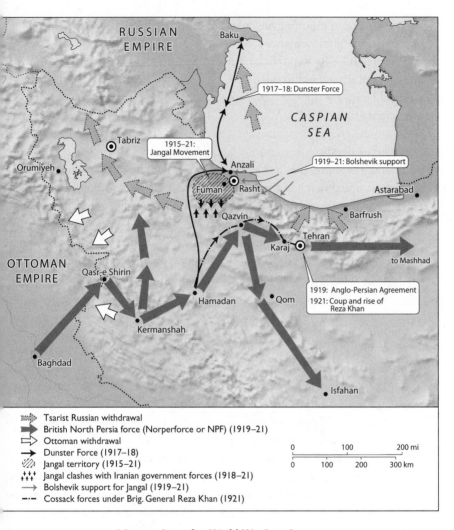

RUSSIAN
EMPIRE

Baku

1917–18: Dunster Force

CASPIAN
SEA

Tabriz
1915–21:
Jangal Movement

Orumiyeh

Anzali

1919–21: Bolshevik support

Fuman Rasht

Astarabad

Qazvin

Barfrush

Tehran

Karaj

to Mashhad

OTTOMAN
EMPIRE

Qasr-e Shirin

1919: Anglo-Persian Agreement
1921: Coup and rise of
      Reza Khan

Hamadan

Qom

Kermanshah

Baghdad

Isfahan

- ⇢ Tsarist Russian withdrawal
- ▶ British North Persia force (Norperforce or NPF) (1919–21)
- ⇨ Ottoman withdrawal
- → Dunster Force (1917–18)
- ⧄ Jangal territory (1915–21)
- ↑↑↑ Jangal clashes with Iranian government forces (1918–21)
- → Bolshevik support for Jangal (1919–21)
- –·– Cossack forces under Brig. General Reza Khan (1921)

0   100   200 mi
0   100   200   300 km

Map 7.2. Iran after World War I, 1918–1921

By the spring of 1920, the Soviet Red Army replaced bands of Caucasian Bolshevik partisans in an operation aimed not only to remove the remnants of the White Russian detachments and the local Caucasian nationalists in Baku and Tiflis but also to aid the Iranian nationalist Jangal movement in Gilan (see map 7.2). The chief aim of Russian revolutionaries, such as the war commissar Leon Trotsky, in landing troops in Iran was to frighten the British and hamper their support for the White Army. They held the view that Iran was not ripe for a Bolshevik-style revolution, while others, mostly communists from the Caucasus, firmly believed in exporting revolution by covert or overt assistance to the indigenous nationalist movements.

As in neighboring Republic of Turkey, the lure of Bolshevism grew stronger among Iranian nationalists once the Great War came to an end and the Iranian political landscape appeared ever more bleak. In 1918 hope for the Paris Peace Conference and President Woodrow Wilson's doctrine of self-determination to address Iran's grievances soon evaporated. This was at a time when British forces occupied nearly the entire country, and the Jangal movement was divided and distraught. It was as if Iran had gotten a worse deal than it had when tsarist Russia had occupied much of the country. Nationalists were further disillusioned and disarmed as the weakling central government struggled to remain relevant. On the more positive side, the Bolshevik invasion of the north provided a justification for Iran to be accepted into the League of Nations. Soon after, by March 1920, to counter growing British influence, the Iranian government reached out to Moscow in the hope of stabilizing the situation in the north.

THE ANGLO-PERSIAN AGREEMENT

The Anglo-Persian Agreement of 1919 was a clear indication of how Iran was about to be shepherded into a semiprotectorate status. This was in contrast to the buffer status that had defined its geopolitics for more than a century. The controversial agreement was the brainchild of two men and their evolving visions for the British imperial presence in the region: George Curzon, then the British acting foreign secretary and a longtime observer of Iranian affairs, and Percy Cox, then the British envoy in Tehran and, as it turned out, one of the most influential players in the shaping of the Arab Middle East. Earlier in his career Curzon visited Iran, in 1891, as the *Times of London*'s special correspondent, and produced the voluminous *Persia and the Persian Question* — an overview of everything Iranian, with unmistakably imperial overtones. He viewed Iran's material development under the benevolent aegis of the British as key for securing long-term British interests. Cox, educated in colonial India, shared with his superior the view that the agreement would grant Iran an undeclared British protectorate status under the guise of financial and military cooperation.

On the surface, the 1919 agreement indeed promised in benign terms collaboration between the two sovereign states. Britain consented to provide Iran with financial, technical, and military assistance in exchange for Iran's exclusive reliance on Britain for such matters as defense and foreign advisers. The preamble to the agreement reaffirmed the "ties of friendship" between the two countries and promoted "progress and prosperity" of Persia, while article 1 reiterated "in the most categorical manner . . . the independence and integrity of Persia." Other articles stipulated the appointment of British financial and military advisers at Iran's expense, promised a long-term British loan to finance military and economic development for which government revenues and customs were sought as security. The agreement also recognized the need for growth in trade and for development projects such as the railway. A supplementary loan agreement set the amount of the loan at £2,000,000 ($9,580,000), with 7 percent interest, and subordinated it to the servicing of an earlier loan due to be paid to Britain.[2]

Yet below the veneer of diplomatic platitude lurked an agenda. The British motives for entering into the 1919 agreement sprang primarily from Curzon's desire to create a chain of mandatory states and protectorates to guarantee a secure overland connection throughout the empire. He had long argued that only through active engagement in the Iranian economy, and with the control of its government apparatus and reconstruction of its army, could Britain expect a secure and stable Iran. The arrangement served not only as a bulwark against the threat of Bolshevism but also as a sure way to include Iran, a vital but weak link, in a *pax britannica* that stretched from India and the Persian Gulf to Iraq, Palestine, and Egypt. The grand strategy that Curzon prescribed appealed to like-minded politicians such as Winston Churchill, who in 1919, as secretary of state for war, underscored the importance of the security of the Iranian oil fields to British postwar supremacy.

From the perspective of Iranian statesmen, most notably the premier Hasan Vosuq al-Dowleh (1868–1951) and chief members of his cabinet, the agreement carried the promise of saving Iran from domestic disarray and Bolshevik threat. The agreement, moreover, provided the state with much-needed funds and technical expertise. By the second decade of the twentieth century, it appeared to Iranian statesmen, such as Vosuq al-Dowleh, that with the collapse of imperial Russia, Iran's role as a buffer state had come to an end and that its sovereignty and territorial integrity could be guaranteed only through the backing of British Empire, the winner of the war and the new master of the Middle East. In an exchange of letters between Cox and Vosuq al-Dowleh, Britain reassured Iran of its support for war reparations in the Paris Peace Conference and favorable renegotiation of all Anglo-Persian treaties.

Yet behind the seemingly benign terms of the agreement, most Iranians detected the ghost of British hegemony. If any proof was needed, it was furnished, after the collapse of Vosuq al-Dowleh's government in June 1920, in large monetary gifts paid by Cox to the premier and two of his chief ministers to lubricate the ratification of the agreement. The rumor-ridden political circles of Tehran opposed the agreement, and the nationalist press, with few exceptions, portrayed it as compromising Iran's sovereignty. In this regard, the efforts of Vosuq al-Dowleh to present the agreement as the best Iran could afford under the circumstances did not succeed. A capable and cultured statesman of great erudition, who once served as the speaker of the first Majles, Vosuq hoped to leverage the agreement to bring political stability and economic reform.

Vosuq al-Dowleh, and his energetic foreign minister Firuz Mirza Nosrat al-Dowleh, were unfairly labeled in nationalist circles as traitors to the Iranian cause. Almost unanimous opposition to the agreement—which had yet to be ratified by the then suspended Majles—expressed by the burgeoning, though often naively sentimental, press. After a decade of national struggle, compliance with the spirit of the 1919 agreement discredited the Qajar nobility and its associated bureaucratic elite in the eyes of the urban intelligentsia.

Iranian public opinion was further buoyed by international condemnation of the British desire to unceremoniously devour Iran as yet another client state. The Woodrow Wilson administration in particular was incensed by the disingenuous methods the British employed in the Paris Peace Conference to keep Iran from presenting its grievances, even though it is quite possible that earlier the United States had condoned the agreement. In contrast to the Egyptian Wafd Party, whose presence at the conference highlighted the Egyptian nationalist struggle for independence, the Iranian delegation was barred from even bringing to the table its demands for mere recognition, let alone compensation, of the foreign occupation and economic and human losses that Iran had sustained during the war.

The British delegation, overruling the Americans, argued that the Iranian case could not be heard in the conference since Iran was not a party to the war and thus did not have a place in the postwar settlement. Informally, Curzon assured the American and French delegations that Britain respected Iran's sovereignty and would help rectify its grievances. With the prospects of Britain as the mandatory power in Palestine and Iraq, the implementation of both to be presided over by Percy Cox, such assurances about Iran appeared highly suspicious. The 1919 agreement was thus seen by Wilson administration as a backdoor method to greater British colonial expansion. The French had their own ax to grind. They were evidently unhappy with the 1919 agreement because the implementation of the 1916 Sykes-Picot Agreement had left Palestine out of the French Syrian mandate and under British control.

Domestic and international uproar cast a shadow over the ratification of the Anglo-Persian Agreement, although this did not stop its advocates from trying to implement some of its terms. The Vosuq al-Dowleh government began employing British civilian and military advisers, who practically were to run government ministries, reform the country's finances, and try to realize the long-standing aspirations for a uniform Iranian army. With British financial backing—essentially resuming the monetary payments negotiated during the war—the Iranian government managed to score a few successes, primarily in quelling unrest in the provinces. The persistent Jangal rebellion, sustained heavy blows from the joint operations of the Iranian regular army and the Iranian Cossack and Gendarme regiments. Since the end of the war, they had both enjoyed the logistical backing of British forces. In Kashan, too, the highly disruptive Na'eb Hosain, a bandit whose raids terrorized the entire region, was captured and hanged. Most of his men were disbanded as well.

Yet the possibility of Bolshevik advances toward Tehran, however remote, never dissipated. Nor were the Iranian nationalists or the young Ahmad Shah ever convinced of British sincerity. In a rare display of courage in his otherwise unhappy career as the last Qajar monarch, Ahmad Shah showed evident signs of dismay over the conclusion of the agreement during his official visit to Britain in September 1919. It is likely, however, that his hesitation was motivated by his exclusion from receiving a share of the British commission for the conclusion of the agreement surreptitiously paid to his minsters. Having lost backing from Britain, in June 1920, the Vosuq al-Dowleh government was dismissed by the shah. With domestic and international pressure, the chances of the agreement ever being ratified by the prospective fourth Majles had faded. By early 1920, it became evident even to Curzon, and his critics in the British parliament, that the Anglo-Persian Agreement was essentially dead. In Iran no one celebrated the demise of the agreement, not even the vociferous nationalist press. Most people recognized that as long as Britain maintained a military presence, held sway over the political elite, and controlled the southern oil fields, it was unlikely to give up its interests in Iran.

MIRZA KUCHAK KHAN AND THE JANGAL MOVEMENT

If one individual can characterize all the hopes and despair of nonelite Iranians of the postwar period, that individual most likely is Mirza Kuchak Khan (1880–1921). Likewise, if one movement epitomizes the tragic ideological drifting and factional conflicts of postconstitutional Iran, that movement is the Jangal movement. Together Kuchak Khan and his Jangal resistance would become part of the martyr narrative that permeates Iran's mythical memory and marks its historical landscape.

Born to a family of petty landowners in the provincial capital of Rasht, Kuchak Khan was a student in the local seminary when he first heard and was moved by the message of the Constitutional Revolution. Following flocks of Iranians to the oil rich-city of Baku and later to the Georgian capital of Tiflis, he was exposed to the revolutionary trends among the Azarbaijanis and Armenians in the Caucasus, and to the émigré merchants, home-brewed revolutionaries, and drifters. On his return to Iran, he joined the Gilan constitutionalists during the civil war of 1908–1909, but in Tehran the euphoria of the 1909 victory quickly gave way to disillusionment as Kuchak Khan witnessed the return to power of the old elites joined by wealthy provincial landowners.

By the time he volunteered in July 1911 to fight against the deposed Mohammad 'Ali Shah in the battle of Gomish Tappeh north of Astarabad, where he was wounded and captured by Russians, he seemed to have lost hope in the success of the parliamentary process. Upon his release from detention, distraught and penniless, he returned to Rasht, where his anti-Russian activities forced him into hiding from the Russian occupying force. A devout and austere Muslim, at the outset of the Great War he seems to have been sufficiently enamored of the message of pan-Islamism, which at the time was heavily promoted by the Young Turks regime, to contact the Ottoman and German legations in Tehran. He entertained the idea of organizing a partisan war in the thick forests of his homeland in the province of Gilan.

With little logistical support and even less local backing, Kuchak and a handful of like-minded local supporters managed to mobilize a small guerilla force. By 1914 they had consolidated in and around the village of Pasikhan near Rasht, the birthplace of the fourteenth-century founder of the Noqtavi movement (see map 7.2). Soon after he was joined by local peasants, artisans, shopkeepers, and petty landowners, but also by journalists, intellectuals, and former revolutionaries. Handsome, charismatic, and witty, yet also easily irritable and fatalistic, the thirty-three-year-old Kuchak Khan founded what is perhaps the twentieth century's first guerilla movement, with its revolutionary ideology and a semblance of partisan organization (fig. 7.6).

He may also be considered a crucial link between romantic nationalism with a socialist flavor and new interpretations of Islam as an anti-imperialist force. He was dressed in an iconic local outfit of the Galesh peasant of Gilan: a round felt cap, coarse leather shoes, and the thick sleeveless felt jacket worn by the shepherds of the Fuman region. With wild, uncut hair and a massive black beard, the sight of Kuchak and the Jangali fighters was utterly and deliberately divorced from the urbane world from which most of their leaders had come. Posing proudly for cameras, often with their rifles held diagonally across their

Figure 7.6. Kuchak Khan (*center*) meets with Bolshevik emissaries
in Anzali, c. 1919. Present were his Caucasian, Iranian, and
German supporters and Kuchak Khan's Kurdish allies.
Ibrahim Fakhra'i, *Sardar-e Jangal* (Tehran, 1376/1997), 242.

chest and with bulky rounds of ammunition strapped to their torso, they embodied patriotism and a love affair with firearms. Towering high over his disciples, Kuchak Khan loomed as a prophet in the wilderness, defying occupation and corrupt authorities and seeking to make right all the wrongs his nation had sustained. That he chose a forest (*jangal*) to launch a partisan war may in part be because of his familiarity with his native terrain but also because of the symbolism that the forest invoked as the birthplace of a salvation movement.

Before 1917 the small band of Jangalis was little more than a nuisance to the Russian occupiers and the provincial authorities who collaborated with them. They occasionally ambushed Russian troops, looted their arsenals, and extorted revolutionary levies from local landowners and merchants under the pretext of protecting peasants against their oppressive landlords. In collaboration with the Committee for Islamic Unity in Rasht, itself motivated by the Young Turks Pan-Islamist propaganda, Kuchak Khan organized a Jangal committee of local dignitaries from the towns and villages of Gilan to expand his grassroots network beyond his base in the forests of Fuman. He even published a newspaper, *Jangal*, as an organ of the movement and issued a stamp.

Government and military attempts to defeat the Jangalis failed, even with Russian help. Repeated emissaries sent to negotiate a peaceful surrender bore little result. Nor, though, did the Jangalis achieve a breakthrough in its first objective to control Gilan and therefrom to launch a liberation movement and capture the capital. Several skirmishes with the Iranian and Russian detachments resulted in casualties on both sides, but there was no strategic or popular victory on either side. In mid-1917 it seemed as though the Jangal movement had been contained to the level of a native rebellion. It had lost much of its steam and stood little chance of ever coming out of the woods.

The Bolshevik revolution and the subsequent withdrawal of Russian troops from Gilan, however, helped transform the Jangal movement. The October Revolution, as it turned out, also hastened the collapse of the Jangal resistance. By 1918, the demise of the Young Turks had resulted in the loss of logistical support for the Jangalis. The withdrawal of Turkish officers, who provided military support to the movement, also prompted an ideological shift. Kuchak Khan and his followers deemphasized pan-Islamism and instead highlighted revolutionary socialism. They nonetheless strived to remain loyal to their anti-imperialist ideals while preserving their Islamic identity. With Bolshevism in the air so close to the Jangal base, a greater tilt toward socialism in the movement seemed unavoidable. British military advances toward Gilan, as well as government troops and the prospect of implementing the 1919 agreement, served as other incentives.

With the collapse of the White Russian resistance under General Anton Denikin along the Caspian coast, the Russian fleet that had taken shelter in the port of Anzali fell to the Bolsheviks (see map 7.2). Declaring their support for the Jangalis, the Bolsheviks and their supporters from the Caucasus soon took the initiative away from Kuchak Khan. Backed by the Red Army, they aimed to use the Jangal movement as a springboard to incite a socialist revolution on the Russian model. Most important among the newcomers from the socialist Adalat Party of Baku was Ehsanollah Khan, an Iranian, French-educated native of Azarbaijan who came from a Baha'i background. He was previously an active member of a revolutionary cell in Tehran known as Komiteh-e Mojazat (the punishment committee) that plotted the assassination of a number of government employees and conservative clergy. As much as Kuchak was a nationalist with Islamic sentiments, Ehsanollah and his band were unabashed secularists with a Marxist program. Relying on Bolshevik support in June 1920, Ehsanollah and his supporters declared the short-lived Soviet Socialist Republic of Iran, better known as Gilan Socialist Republic, with Ehsanollah himself the first president. Kuchak Khan was left with no choice but to give his consent. He was bestowed with the largely ceremonious title of president of the Council of People's Commissars.

Backed by a Bolshevik commissar and an assortment of Russian partisans and other revolutionaries anxious to establish a socialist regime in Iran, the Jangalis managed to capture Rasht in June 1920. They not only defeated the local gendarme detachment but pushed back British troops to Manjil, forty-five miles south of Rasht on the way to Tehran. The assault inflicted great damage on the mercantile community of the city, destroyed the bazaar, and resulted in the Bolsheviks' looting of merchandise. The affluent merchants and landowners were terrorized and their properties confiscated. Although Kuchak Khan left Rasht in protest, the socialist wing of the Jangal movement hailed the capture of the provincial capital as a great victory and the first step toward installing of a Soviet-style republic.

Labeled by Tehran as "intruders" (*motejaserin*), the Bolsheviks and their Jangali allies were declared a national threat, especially after having quashed the Iranian Cossack regiment that Tehran had dispatched from Qazvin to counter their advances (see map 7.2). Among the Cossack officers taking part in the operation was Reza Khan who would later remind his officers and troops of the humiliating defeat as the lowest point of his military career and single it out as a motive for the February 1921 coup. Moreover, the poorly equipped and starving Cossack regiment was not helped by friendly fire from the British Royal Air Force, which mistakenly bombed the central government's positions in the thick of the Caspian forest.

These advances put the Jangal movement on Iran's political map as a revolutionary counterpoint to the weakling Tehran establishment and the doomed 1919 agreement. The chances of the Jangal-Bolshevik forces breaking through British defense lines in Qazvin and marching on Tehran caused great anxiety. Surprisingly, despite visible signs of a rift, the Tehran government proved incapable of exploiting the ideological divisions within the Jangal movement. In July, subject to an internal coup, the marginalized Kuchak Khan found himself at an unwelcome impasse. Retreating to the forest, he was unable to stop the movement's bent toward revolutionary socialism or enter into a reliable alliance with the rejuvenated Democrats in Tehran.

STARVATION, PANDEMICS, AND A RUINED ECONOMY

The bleakness of the Iranian situation went beyond occupation, political disarray, banditry, troop movements, skirmishes, and domestic strife. Even more, human and material losses came to haunt the people of Iran. By the close of the Great War, a famine ravaged Iran, claiming a vast number of lives. It was primarily a result of successive droughts, which in turn caused repeated crop failures and disruptions to the agricultural cycle. Excessive production of cash crops at the expense of foodstuffs also contributed to shortages, and a lack of efficient road and communication networks barred the transport of relief to remote towns and villages. Not since 1869–1871 had Iran experienced such widespread starvation, and in some instances towns and villages in the central provinces experienced massive depopulation. Along with Armenia, greater Syria and Greece, the Iranian plight drew Western public attention, especially in the United States, and encouraged charity collections and an organized relief operation (fig. 7.7).

The casualties from the famine were further exacerbated by an outbreak of cholera, endemic to the region, and the more deadly Spanish influenza pandemic of 1918–1919, whose virulent worldwide spread was facilitated by troop movements. Unlike in Europe and the United States, where the spread of in-

Figure 7.7. Famine in the Near East and Persia motivated the American
Committee for Relief in the Near East, the oldest US nonreligious
relief organization, to set an ambitious fund-raising goal.
Poster designed by W. T. Benda, 1918.

fluenza was partially checked by preventive measures, in Iran there was next to no prevention or even recognition of the disease known as "European common cold" (*zokam-e farangi*). The casualties from influenza are difficult to assess, but a conservative estimate of loss of life in Iran due to famine and disease exceeded one million. This was an enormous loss for a country with a total population of no more than nine million, that did not field a single soldier in the war, and was not allowed to bring its grievances to the table after the war.

Foreign occupation no doubt also intensified the Iranian famine. Large consignments of grain and foodstuffs were both purchased and confiscated by Russian and British armies for consumption by their troops. The starving population in the countryside had no choice but to move to towns and cites in search of food. The growing population in urban centers not only overwhelmed the miniscule relief operations but also increased the spread of disease (fig. 7.8). Some popular historians claim that the famine was a result of deliberate and sinister starvation policies of the British, but such claims are not substantiated.

Figure 7.8. Poorhouse in Shiraz in 1918 established by the governor of Fars province, 'Abd al-Hosain Mirza Farmanfarma. The famine-stricken in this picture exemplify the widespread starvation throughout the country at the time.
F. Chehrehnegar, M. Sane', *Paydayesh 'Akkasi dar Shiraz* (Tehran, 1369/1990), 116.

For those Iranians who survived, the future was no more promising. World-wide inflation at the end of the war sharply raised the prices of imports, and the export of traditional commodities declined. War increased Iran's dependency on European markets at a time when the economy of its major partner, Russia, had come to a complete standstill because of the revolution there. The German economy was in recession, and Ottoman markets were depressed because of the defeat in the Great War and the ensuing civil war. Britain remained the only viable partner, and trade thrived along the newly revived Basra-Kermanshah-Hamadan route. Yet even the British economy was in the grips of hyperinflation, with a labor revolt both at home and in British India. As a result, Iranian export commodities such as wool, carpets, cotton, tobacco, and opium became less marketable.

The Iranian countryside was more volatile than it had been since perhaps the eighteenth century, largely because of the volume of firearms dispersed by German and British agents during the war among the Qashqa'i, the Bakhtiyari, the Lurs, the Kurds and the tribes of the southern Fars or looted after 1917 from Russian armories. The effects of gunrunning and increased tribal unrest were twofold: they reduced the economic productivity of nomadic regions and made the trade routes through those regions insecure. Aside from tribal rebellions, by the close of the Great War there were at least fifteen groups of bandits wreaking havoc in smaller cities and ravaging the countryside. No doubt the war economy did create its own profiteers, smugglers, and suppliers of provisions to the occupying armies. This class of traders and merchants gradually came to compete with, though not supplant, established merchants in large cities.

Throughout the 1910s, political unrest and economic downturn weakened the enterprising spirit of the mercantile bourgeoisie that had emerged from the Constitutional Revolution. Enthusiasm sapped for new industrial initiatives such as cotton mills, textile factories, sugar refineries, and banking establishments. By the end of the war, the merchant class that a decade earlier had acted as the engine behind the revolution in Tabriz, Baku, Isfahan, Kerman, and Tehran had run out of steam. Even in the province of Gilan, where the merchants of Rasht and Anzali first collaborated with Kuchak Khan in hopes of maintaining a semblance of stability, soon came to be terrorized by the excesses of Jangal radicals. The pro-Bolshevik faction of the Jangal movement adapted a hostile attitude toward large landowners and merchants of the province. Their Russian Bolshevik counterparts had already ruined the affluent merchant community of Baku across the Caspian, a community once supportive of the Iranian constitutionalists.

On a broader scale, starvation and abject poverty became familiar features of the Iranian landscape. Memoirs, reports, and photographs from the end of the war reveal multitudes of beggars in rags; malnourished children clinging to their parents searching for food; day laborers with sunken eyes weakly searching through the rubble; and crowds of angry women gathering in front of government offices to protest food shortages, the deteriorating quality of bread, and swindlers. The sight of strangers dying of hunger or disease on street corners was not uncommon. Even more common were starving people hunting stray dogs and cats, and rats in basements and water holes. Rumors of young children being snatched and eaten circulated with the same rapidity as reports of the Bolsheviks breaching Tehran's walls.

For the Iranians, it was as if the entire world around them were crumbling. Looking beyond their borders, they saw how the neighboring Ottoman Empire, in its death throes, had birthed competing nationalist entities. That Arab nationalist regimes were first nursed by European powers and then exploited by them under the guise of the "mandate" regimes, so as to advance the British and the French colonial ambitions, was a fact not entirely missed by the Iranian intelligentsia. The Russian Empire was no more, and there was no imperial Germany to counter the unnerving pressures of the British Empire. Britain appeared to be the victorious party throughout Palestine, Mesopotamia, and the Persian Gulf, and even in the newly emerging Wahhabi-dominated central Arabia. For Iranians with historical ties to the Shi'i lands of southern Mesopotamia, the 1920 Shi'i revolt against British occupation aroused much sympathy if for no other reason than the fact that the revolt included in its leadership several activist Iranian ulama. By October 1920 the British crushed the revolt, a disheartening message especially for a sector of the Iranian population in contact with the large community of *mojaverin* (those who took residence in the Shi'i shrine cities of Iraq) or followed the *marja's* in Najaf. Shortly after the creation of Mandatory Iraq, assigned to Britain by the League of Nations in 1921, was an even more striking development: the Mandate almost instantaneously patched together a new country from three heterogeneous and ethnically and religiously diverse provinces of the defunct Ottoman Empire. The emergence of the Republic of Turkey from the ruins of the Young Turks' military adventures, in contrast, was a success story for neighboring countries. The carving up of the Ottoman lands nevertheless generated more despair and resentment than optimism in the Iranian press (fig. 7.9).

THE RISE OF COLONEL REZA KHAN

On the surface it seemed that sheer luck had saved Iran from being broken up or otherwise subordinated to a British regional scheme. Yet a complex set of political and cultural factors made possible the coup of February 1921 and the

Figure 7.9. "A spectacle of a country of donkey-camel-cow-leopard, and its moral standing among its neighbors." This curious drawing of unknown origin seems to be a satirical commentary on post–World War I Iran. A mullah carrying the club of excommunication in one hand and a book of superstition in the other rides the animal that is Iran. He is led by colonial Britain, whose feet are India and Egypt, and whose arms are the Hashimite Amir Faisal and British agents in Iran. The nosebag is the Imperial Bank of Persia, tied to the mullah's annuity via the government and Majles. The hammer and sickle threaten the commerce and politics of the country, and the press dangles like a cowbell. Political parties are its testicles. The angels of honor and Islamic civilization are kicked out while the angel of nationhood has fallen under the creature's hoof. Iranian contemporary postcard, Tehran, c. 1919. Institute for Iranian Contemporary Historical Studies, Photo Gallery.

subsequent rise of Reza Khan. There were as many rumors about an imminent takeover of the capital and partition of Iran into a Bolshevik north and a British south as there were yearnings in nationalist circles for the rise of a leader who could offer a viable alternative to the bleak state of affairs.

The coup of 1921 would prove this point, though with a curious twist. The process that brought to power Sayyed Zia al-Din Tabataba'i, with Reza Khan as the military leader of the new regime, was an alternative to the 1919 Anglo-Persian Agreement—a backdoor solution to the troubling political impasse that Iran faced at that time. The solution was brewed at least in part by British diplomats and senior army officers and manned by ambitious Iranian upstarts. The astute British minister in Tehran, Herman Norman, sensed the futility in adhering to the disempowered Qajar elite while in the wake of postwar demobilization there was an urgent call to evacuate the British troops stationed in Iran. With socialist aspirations on the rise, Democrats returning to the Tehran political stage, and the threat of the Gilan Socialist Republic on the horizon, it stood to reason that the British minister search for an alternative ally. An Anglophile distant from the Qajar elite who could resonate with larger sectors of the Iranian public and at the same time appear sufficiently distant from the British.

Sayyed Zia al-Din Tabataba'i (1888–1969), a young fiery political activist known for his pro-British sentiments, was about the only Iranian journalist who consistently advocated the ratification of the 1919 agreement and its benefits for Iran in his newspaper *Ra'd* ("thunder"). Contrary to the maligned image of him as a British proxy in later Iranian historiography, Sayyed Zia may well have proposed the idea of the coup to the British legation in Tehran rather than being a mere catalyst for the coup. A madrasa novice-turned-journalist with a dramatic style and sensational rhetoric, Sayyed Zia was a product of the post-constitutional era. Though still in clerical garb, he epitomized a new breed of political activists at a time when religious training was no longer valued and the dent in clerical prestige was substantial.

Known for his sensational attacks on the old Tehran political guard, he allegedly used his newspaper as an extortion tool. Initially mentored by the premier Vosuq al-Dowleh to counter criticism of the 1919 agreement and raise the alarm of the threat of Bolshevism, he was dispatched in 1919 to Baku to sign a friendship treaty with the anti-Bolshevik nationalist regime, in the illusive hopes of forging a new confederation between Iran and Azerbaijan. The mission was aborted over disagreement with the premier on the terms of the treaty. After the collapse of Vosuq's government, Sayyed Zia remained in contact with the British legation. With the change in the political climate and the surge in antielite propaganda in the Persian press, Sayyed Zia became a more viable choice to head the semiclandestine Iron Committee, a quasi-revolutionary party financed by the British legation to foster popular anti-Bolshevik sentiments.

In December 1920, the political impasse reached a point of crisis. After the resignation of Moshir al-Dowleh (1872–1935), a respected statesman with a far-reaching program of reform who headed a short-lived coalition, no one among the Tehran statesmen seemed to be capable of forming a government or even volunteering to undertake such a task. Fath 'Ali Khan Sepahdar Rashti (1878–1947), a large landowner from Gilan with no political talent to speak of, also gave up, after twice tinkering with creating a cabinet. The fourth Majles, which was elected in the long shadow of the 1919 agreement, was incapable of even convening its inaugural session, lest it face the prospect of ratifying the hated agreement. The Bolshevik-Jangali threat loomed large in Gilan and in the provinces of Azarbaijan and Khorasan new revolts were in gestation. The south was almost in the hands of the Qashqa'is, and most of the other tribal powers of greater Fars, Isfahan, and Luristan were restive.

The "constitutional monarch," Ahmad Shah, was a timid procrastinator who regarded his constitutionality as one of cynical nonaction. He was genuinely frightened by the prospect of British military withdrawal from Iran and baffled by the consequences of such an event for the survival of his throne. Major figures of the constitutional era, on the other hand, were invariably disillusioned and divided. Some lost credibility or went into exile; others were retired from politics or killed in action. The most distinguished among the exiles, Hasan Taqizadeh, the ranking member of the first Majles, had resided in Berlin since 1915. He was invited there by the German government to organize a resistance circle of Iranian nationalists, intellectuals, and activists to be dispatched back to Iran as agent provocateurs. Taking advantage of the occasion, together with a group of talented writers and intellectuals, he founded the influential periodical *Kaveh*. By 1920, the Berlin circle was nearly at its end, but Taqizadeh was still uncertain of a political prospect in Tehran. Closely identified with the vanquished party in the war, he lingered there.

It was in such a climate that the British envoy Norman endorsed Sayyed Zia's plan to stage a coup and subsequently form a national government. He did so perhaps without the Foreign Office's prior knowledge and full support. By the last months of 1920, more than two years after World War I ended, the British forces stationed in northern Iran were ready to leave. With Mandatory commitments in Iraq and Palestine straining British finances, the budget for the upkeep of British forces faced serious opposition in the House of Commons. These considerations made any plan for a successful coup dependent on a viable military partner that could stand as a substitute for the departing British forces. The search for such an alternative had preoccupied for some time the British command in Qazvin, the headquarters of the Norperforce (see map 7.2). Major General Edmund Ironside (1880–1959), the commander of the Norperforce, his second-in-command Lieutenant Colonel Henry Smyth, and a few other middle-ranking officers were saddled with the task of reorganizing the Cossack Brigade, which they ultimately hoped to incorporate into a uniform Iranian army—an objective of the 1919 agreement.

After 1917, the Cossack Brigade, deprived of moral and material support from imperial Russia, found itself underbudgeted, poorly equipped, demoralized, and devoid of a strong command; it was a shadow of what it had been only a few years earlier. Defeated by the Jangal forces and their Bolshevik allies in Gilan, it became clear that Russian senior officers, even if unsympathetic to the Bolsheviks, could no longer reliably command the entirely Iranian rank and file, given the Russian officers' deep hostility toward the British and their Iranian supporters. Ironside was anxious to find a capable Iranian senior officer with combat experience and anti-Bolshevik credentials to lead the force.

Colonel Reza Khan, recommended by another Iranian senior Cossack officer, seemed to be the desirable person to match such a job description. Tall, dark, broad shouldered and charismatic, with piercing eyes, Reza Khan's rugged military demeanor and management skills, as it turned out, were ideal for the task. As a Cossack officer he had demonstrated leadership and savvy but also severity and ruthlessness, qualities that had allowed him to rise through the Cossack ranks from his humble beginnings as a stableboy at the age of fifteen to senior officer in the Hamadan Cossack regiment at the age of forty-three.

Born around 1877 to a soldiering family from the Palani clan in the remote village of Alasht in the mountainous Savadkuh district of the Caspian province of Mazandaran, Reza Khan's father and grandfather had served in the Qajar army. His mother was the daughter of a Muslim émigré (*mohajer*) from Iravan who had settled in Tehran after the population exchange at the conclusion of the Russo-Persian War of 1826–1828. Reza's father died while he was still an infant, so his destitute mother took her son to Tehran, where she lived with her brothers, one of them a soldier in the newly established Cossack Division. Reza had lost his mother at the age of six, and his childhood and early youth were filled with forlorn neglect and virtually no education.

The first available record of Reza Khan's service dates to 1911, when as a petty officer he fought in the northwest against the counterrevolutionary prince Salar al-Dowleh. By 1918, when the Cossack Brigade, now renamed Cossack Division, repelled the Na'ebi rebellion in Kashan, Reza was promoted to the rank of colonel. Involved in the inner politics of the Cossack Division, he took an active part in the removal of a commanding Russian officer because of his alleged Bolshevik proclivities. As he sensed an opportunity for power, he further gravitated toward the British officers in their headquarters at Qazvin. With the changing political climate, which put the British officers in control of all resources, promotions, and the very existence of the Cossack Division, it is difficult to imagine how a shrewd and ambitious officer like Reza Khan could have done otherwise.

It is also hard to believe that Reza Khan's involvement in the coup in the making could have been organized without at least tacit British knowledge. Without subscribing to the wild speculations common at the time, or the later hypotheses that the British hatched the coup, reliable evidence points to some British effort to facilitate collaboration between the civilian wing of the coup and its military counterpart. The Cossack force of about four thousand under Reza Khan's command was partially reequipped and financed in Qazvin by officers of the Norperforce. They may even have encouraged Reza Khan to march on the capital to block perceived Bolshevik advances. However, it was only in the vicinity of Tehran that Reza Khan came to know Sayyed Zia. Even at this stage, the latter did not have a clear idea of the practicalities and logistics of the coup. Yet if Colonel Reza Khan had collaborated with British officers, or was even handpicked by them, he was by no means their poppet or even willing to succumb to their wishes.

THE COUP AND CONTROL OF THE CAPITAL

The Cossack regiment, which arrived at Tehran walls three days earlier, entered the capital on February 21, 1921, without resistance (see map 7.2). The ranking Iranian Gendarme officers were willing participants, and the Tehran police force, led by a Swedish chief, immediately surrendered. The Cossack troops were stationed in Maydan-e Mashq (Drill Square), and in the early morning hours of the same day, they began to round up high-ranking Qajar statesmen and notables. Soon, similar arrests were followed in the provinces. By the end of Sayyed Zia's government some three months later, nearly five hundred officials were in government custody.

The detentions and house arrests, a joint initiative of Sayyed Zia and Reza Khan, were meant to emphasize the revolutionary character of the coup, presumably to counter the socialist propaganda of the Jangalis, but also to scare the ruling elite and perhaps even extort from them the assets they were accused of amassing through corruption and nepotism. All telegraph, telephone, and road communications with the provinces were temporarily cut off, and key government offices taken over. Three days later, the vexed Ahmad Shah, sufficiently intimidated by the coup organizers and persuaded by the British minister as well as by his own advisers and courtiers, issued a decree appointing Sayyed Zia prime minister with full authority. His appointment registered a significant shift, for it was the first made from outside the circles of the Qajar elite, anticipating a new era of middle-class politics.

In Reza Khan's second communiqué two days later, possibly penned by Sayyed Zia, Reza Khan assumed the title of commander in chief of the armed forces. There he made it abundantly clear that he entertained ambitions beyond mere leadership of the Cossack Division. The tone was indignant, underscoring the Cossack forces' suffering and highlighting the troops' wounded honor and depravity, but there was nothing that amounted to a program of reform, just an early taste of an autocrat in the making. The reform program came through, however, in Sayyed Zia's first communiqué, on February 26. It was a manifesto of sorts, aiming to justify the coup as a last resort to save the country from corrupt and inept statesmen who for the previous fifteen years had betrayed the Constitutional Revolution and the sacrifices made by the people. Yet it made no reference to the fourth Majles, which at the time was yet to be convened.

Instead, Sayyed Zia called for the downfall of the landowning and aristocratic elite who long sapped the nation of its riches. "Destiny called on me," he declared, to save the country and the monarchy from these predators by relying on the loyal armed forces to shoulder his sacred duty and end misery and insecurity. The communiqué further called for measures to stop corruption and bureaucratic inefficiency, to promote reliance on domestic income in order to improve national security and the standard of living of working people, and to overhaul the dysfunctional judiciary. He also highlighted the need for greater social justice through land reform and distribution to the peasants the crown and state lands, and called for an end to the chaos in the government's finances. He further called for the promotion of a spirit of patriotism and national pride, and promised modern schools for children of all classes, growth of trade and industry, a campaign against high inflation and racketeering, a better communication network, urban amenities and the beautification of the capital.

On the sensitive question of foreign policy, Sayyed Zia promised peace and coexistence with all neighbors but called for an end to the capitulatory rights of the so-called most favored nations—the discriminatory extraterritorial privileges extended to foreign subjects as early as the 1828 Treaty of Torkmanchay. Shortly thereafter, in another statement, he renounced the 1919 Anglo-Persian Agreement, although for all intents and purposes it was already dead. Praise for British assistance in Iran over the past century, as well as for the Iranians' loyalty toward Britain, were other predictable features of the communiqué, as was Zia's hope that revoking the 1919 Agreement would remedy the misunderstanding between the two nations.

With minor variations, Sayyed Zia's program following a course already set out by the governments of Vosuq al-Dowleh and later Moshir al-Dowleh, and it served as a blueprint for the forthcoming Pahlavi reforms. As an important counterbalance, the new regime also announced the conclusion of a friendship treaty with the newly established Soviet Union. Although in 1918 Iran was among the first countries to recognize the Bolshevik regime, the signing of the treaty in Moscow actually took place on February 26, 1921, five days after the coup in Tehran. As early as 1919, Vosuq al-Dowleh and his successors in office—and the insightful foreign minister 'Ali-Qoli Ansari Moshaver al-Mamalek, who had negotiated the treaty—realized the value of normalizing relations with the Soviets. Like the abrogation of the 1919 agreement, the signing of the 1921 agreement with the Soviet Union further vindicated a return to Iran's traditional "buffer" position.

The twenty-six-article treaty, which remained in effect until the early days of the Islamic Republic, reaffirmed the Soviets' renunciation of Russian imperial concessions, economic interests, and unpaid loans. It recognized Iran's full sovereignty, called for nonintervention in internal affairs, recognized existing boundaries, and called for resolving border disputes through negotiation. In return, the treaty stipulated a unique concession to Soviet Union: the right to intervene militarily in Iran in the case Iran was threatened by a third party, in effect reaffirming the conduct of tsarist Russia since 1909. In a reference to Britain and its anti-Bolshevik policy, article 6 stipulated the following:

> If a third party should attempt to carry out a policy of usurpation by means of armed intervention in Persia, or if such power should desire to use Persian territory as a base of operation against Russia, . . . and if the Persian Government should not be able to put a stop to such menace . . . Russia shall have the right to advance her troops into the Persian interior for the purpose of carrying out the military operation necessary for its defiance.[3]

Moscow's further clarification in December 1921 defining the contingencies for any military intervention and confirming the Bolsheviks' evacuation from Gilan persuaded Iran to ratify the treaty. The initiative demonstrated a certain degree of agency on the Iranian side even at a time of great turmoil and uncertainty. Whether the conclusion of the treaty was also a motivation for British support for the coup is a matter of debate. What is clear, however, and important for future the of Iran, was that by the end of 1920—what we might call Iran's "Wilsonian moment"—a new equilibrium between the two powers began to emerge that allowed Iran to join the League of Nations and enjoy a period of relative freedom in its foreign affairs.

Sayyed Zia's critics almost instantaneously labeled his government as "divorcer" (mohallel) and the "black cabinet." Its hundred-day term, nevertheless, was a major shift, for it relied on a coup by a populist British proxy and a Cossack officer to implement a course very different from Curzon's vision to incorporate Iran into the British colonial sphere. The move cost Norman his career. The seasoned diplomat who knew Arabic and Turkish and earlier had served in Cairo and Istanbul and then at the Paris Peace Conference grasped the depth of Iranian resentment toward British designs better than his superior. Curzon, who called him back from Tehran after only sixteen months, refused to meet with him and soon after Norman was forced to retired at the age of fifty-two.

REZA KHAN AS THE COMMANDER IN CHIEF

If Sayyed Zia's time would soon come to pass, Reza Khan's would not. His rise between 1921 and 1925, culminating in his ascent to the throne and the founding of the Pahlavi dynasty, brought to power a new military elite, co-opted some Qajar notables but marginalized the rest, crushed the Jangal movement and other centers of autonomy and secession, bulldozed through a state-sponsored program of secular reforms, and pacified the countryside with ruthless efficiency. It was as if a surgical knife had lanced an infested cyst that had long troubled Iran's body politic. At the outset, the measures implemented by the new strongman of Iran were welcomed by nationalists and left-leaning Democrats alike, but once the autocratic nature of his regime became more apparent, support began to evaporate. Reza Khan and his close circle showed little hesitation to force into silence these independent political and religious voices as long as they could secure the backing of the growing class of professionals, modernist intellectuals, and even a generation of mullahs who exchanged their clerical garb and turban in exchange for European attire. These new sectors laid the foundation for the secular middle class that would form the backbone of Pahlavi Iran.

Resolute and calculative, Reza Khan—by then known by his new military title, *sardar sepah* (chief of the army)—proved a quick study and a shrewd maneuverer. Giving the cold shoulder to Sayyed Zia from the start, even though at times they appeared to be in the same camp, within a year he consolidated his hold over the Cossack Division and its officer corps, some of whom were senior to him, and merged it with the Iranian Gendarmerie, the police, and Iran's regular troops. Two months after the coup, when he assumed the position of minister of war, he was widely recognized as Iran's savior, and treated accordingly. Reza Khan was a figure reminiscent of Nader in 1732, when he elevated himself to the position of Safavid regent. Ahmad Shah was not yet completely ostracized, nor was Reza Khan the absolute master of the political stage, but the grounds were well prepared for the rise of a new autocracy (fig. 7.10).

Sayyed Zia's political fall happened as fast as his meteoric rise. Once he had aroused enough resentment among the Qajar elite and lost both the confidence of the British and his usefulness to Reza Khan, he was forced into exile in Palestine under British mandate, where he would remain for two decades. Iran's new

Figure 7.10. Ahmad Shah and Reza Khan, c. 1922, while Reza Khan
served as minister of war.
Contemporary photograph, Tehran, c. 1922. Institute for
Iranian Contemporary Historical Studies, Photo Gallery.

master soon realized that collaboration with select members of the Qajar elite
and landed aristocracy was more advantageous than working with a rabble-rousing journalist tarnished by his close association with the British. Soon he began
to see the merits of having on his side the likes of Ahmad Qavam al-Saltaneh
(later Ahmad Qavam, 1873–1955), Vosuq al-Dowleh's younger brother, Hasan
Moshir al-Dowleh and Hasan Mostowfi al-Mamalek, members of the old guard
who were popular with the intelligentsia.

The situation on the ground also helped lift Reza Khan's stature. The withdrawal of the British Norperforce in May 1921 coincided with Bolshevik disengagement from the Jangal movement and the subsequent withdrawal of the
Red Army from Gilan. The rapid end to military occupation, three years after
the end of the war, in turn created a power vacuum. For one, the British envoy
in Tehran and his superiors acknowledged that Britain no longer wielded the
kind of military presence that could dictate its wishes to the rising Reza Khan,
whom Norman had characterized as a "peasant" upstart. It seemed as though
overnight British prestige had suffered a setback.

Yet Reza Khan's ascendancy was not achieved without serious domestic challenges. A senior Gendarme officer in Khorasan, Colonel Mohammad Taqi
Khan, better known as Pesian (1891–1921), staged what eventually turned into a
full-scale revolt against Tehran. A Germanophile romantic, Pesian had earlier
served as Kermanshah military commander during the provisional government

in exile before escaping to Berlin. After his return, as military commander of Khorasan in February 1921, he was instrumental in the arrest of Qavam al-Saltaneh, which brought him the blessing of a handful of Mashhad notables and the loyalty of subordinate gendarme officers. Wary of Reza Khan's rapid rise, he chose to resist a merger with the Cossack Division and, upon Qavam's appointment to premiership, the colonel, resentful of a return to elite politics, resisted disarmament. In October 1921 he died in clashes with government forces, and the Khorasan rebellion collapsed soon thereafter.

Throughout mid-1921, Reza Khan and his troops also scored a final victory against the Jangal movement, the greatest challenge to the Tehran government. After the withdrawal of Soviet forces, the divided Jangal movement rapidly disintegrated. Even mediation by the legendary revolutionary Haydar Khan 'Amu-Ughlu, could not heal the ideological and personal divisions. After his exile from Iran in 1910, Haydar Khan had spent several years in Europe, including Germany, and during the war years he organized a socialist brigade to fight the Allies alongside the Young Turks in northern Iraq. The Bolshevik revolution boosted Haydar's morale. Close to Russian revolutionaries and known to Lenin, he was dispatched by the Bolsheviks first to Central Asia to fight against the Russian Whites. In the mid-1920s, during the famous Baku Congress, he won the leadership of the Iranian-dominated Adalat Party that had been initiated in 1916.

In mid-1921, after the coup in Tehran, he moved from Baku to Gilan to mediate between Jangal's rival factions. Ehsanollah Khan and his fighters from the Caucasus opted to first fight it out against government forces, but under pressure from the newly appointed Soviet representative in Tehran, Theodor Rothstein, who was anxious to normalize relations with the Iranian central government, they later were forced to leave for Baku with the evacuating Bolsheviks. In Ehsanollah's absence, Haydar Khan saw an opportunity to fill the gap, possibly with Rothstein's support. He persuaded Kuchak Khan in August 1921 to appoint him as commisar of foreign affairs for the Gilan Soviet Republic. Soon after, however, Kuchak Khan's supporters assassinated Haydar Khan in October 1921 because of suspicions that he favored Soviet conciliation toward Tehran. From his beginnings as a socialist agitator in 1907 to a mediator in the forests of Gilan, Haydar Khan left behind a legacy of violent radicalism and often futile agitation that has since been glamorized by generations of Iranians on the left. Ehsanollah's end was no less tragic. He spent the rest of his life in Baku, where he reportedly was arrested in 1937 and killed in one of Stalin's purges.

Haydar's fall anticipated the final collapse of the Jangal movement. With Reza Khan himself leading the troops to recapture Rasht, Kuchak Khan retreated back into the forests. Once his war commissar, leader of a Kurdish affiliate of the Jangal movement, surrendered to Reza Khan, Kuchak and a small band of his loyal disciples took to the high mountains of the Khalkhal region west of the Caspian. In October 1921 Kuchak Khan and a German junior officer and friend who had remained loyal to him through the years, died of exposure, perhaps trying to reach Russian Azerbaijan.

The defeat of the Jangal movement signified the end of a socialist anti-imperialist tendency in Iran. Rooted in the Constitutional Revolution, the Jangal movement thrived in its aftermath but lost out to a centralizing state that relied on a superior military aimed to implement a secular state-building project. In January 1922, when another Gendarme officer, Abol-Qasem Lahuti (1887–1957), a socialist revolutionary and poet, rose in the rebellion and briefly captured Tabriz, he was quickly besieged and forced to defect to the Soviet Union. Lahuti's attempt was fueled by secessionist tendencies in Iranian Azarbaijan. Less than two years earlier, an urban uprising led by a clergyman Mohammad Khiabani (1880–1920), another Azarbaijani nationalist with socialist leanings, had been put down by the governor-general Mahdi-Qoli Khan Hedayat Mokhber al-Saltaneh. Khiabani also died under suspicious circumstances.

Contrary to Azarbaijan's Iran-centered nationalism throughout the constitutional period, and despite the fact that Azarbaijanis acted as the engine for that revolution, both the Khiabani and Lahuti revolts pointed at an emerging ethnic resentment, which would pan out in a generation during the post–World War II Azarbaijan secessionist crisis. There was no question that Azarbaijan had a distinct ethnolinguistic identity, and the Persian-centric nationalism dictated from Tehran did not go over well with Azarbaijanis or other Turkish-speaking populations, who constituted perhaps a quarter of Iran's population. Yet one cannot ignore such ideological threads that tied these sentiments to the pan-Turkism of the Young Turks era and later to the Bolshevik-inspired propaganda of Soviet Azerbaijan.

Reza Khan's military not only curtailed the Jangal movement and wiped out the nationalist-Islamic idealism embedded in it but also crushed nearly all sources of tribal resistance to the centralizing state (map 7.3). There were repeated crackdowns between 1921 and 1931 on the Kurds in the northwest, Boyer Ahmad and other Mamasani tribes of Luristan province, the Shahseven of Azarbaijan, the Qashqa'is of Fars, and the Bakhtiyaris of Isfahan. Employing heavy weaponry as well as air bombardment, the notorious Western Division of the reorganized Iranian army, headed by Reza Khan's senior officers, pummeled the lightly armed tribal forces.

Soon after victory over Jangal, the Iranian army raided the rebellious chief of the Kurdish Shakak tribe, Isma'il Aqa Simku (Semitqu), who had long wreaked

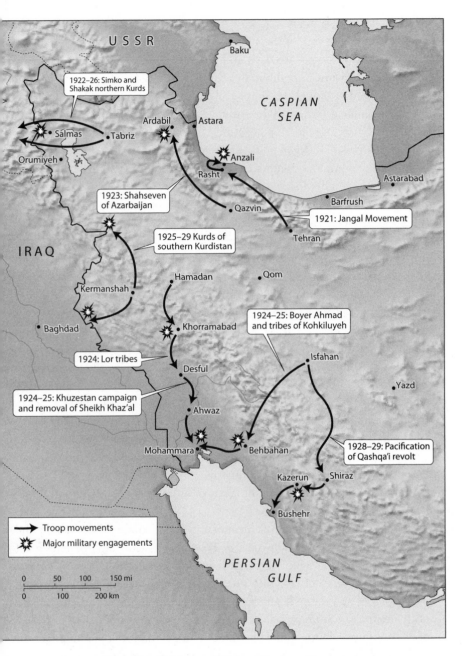

Map 7.3. Reza Khan Pahlavi and the pacification of Iran, 1921–1929

havoc in western Azarbaijan, looting Christian villages and killing the inhabitants. With the blessing of the retreating Ottoman army, in 1918 Simku massacred several hundred Assyrians and committed other atrocities. He wished to unite into a Kurdish republic the Kurdish tribes on both sides of the Iran-Ottoman border, though he never truly succeed crossing over the line from bandit to political leader. In the summer of 1922, Iranian forces drove Simku across the Ottoman border and captured his fortress in Chehriq in the Salmas region. The pro–Reza Khan press celebrated the defeat of the Shakak as a major victory, although it took another eight years of clashes before Simku would die in skirmishes with the Iranian army.

Insurrections aside, major sources of resistance in tribal regions were against the state's relentless tax collection and various forms of extortion by army officers. Moreover, the weakening of Iran's political center, especially since the start of World War I, had encouraged regional autonomy along the periphery, which at times benefited from real or potential economic opportunities. Later on, the state's policy to make nomadic communities sedentary—profoundly disruptive to the nomadic way of life—triggered revolts. For Tehran, as for any modern centralizing state, nomads were a potential threat, for they constituted a population difficult to control, especially if armed and in command of their terrain.

The amalgamated armed forces, further consolidated by the merger of the South Persian Rifles in September 1921, were reorganized into four divisions, with central command firmly in Reza Khan's hand. Taking advantage of the prolonged martial law that had been in place since the beginning of the coup, a small group of army officers, perhaps no more than two dozen, became masters of the country, ruling with impunity as military governors over provinces and cities. In their new uniforms—shiny riding boots, rimmed caps, and fancy accoutrements—they instilled in the heart of ordinary Iranians fear and hatred, but also admiration.

For many officers, a violent demeanor and disdain toward the general public were considered natural and necessary. Peasants, nomads, and urbanites had to pay tribute to officers with flattery, cash, and gifts—or else face grave repercussions. Appropriation of land and property, summary executions, cruel public punishments, and severe beatings of civilians and troops were accepted norms of this military culture. A facade of discipline and efficiency held by officers of all ranks was complemented by military pride and loyalty to the new commander in chief. The military became a new moneyed class with an appetite for luxury, leisure, and promiscuity.

The funds for military modernization, recruitment, and campaigns were secured by appropriating indirect taxes and state income from the crown lands.

Reza Khan attached both departments to the Ministry of War. Soon, a large chunk of the back payments from the country's share of the Anglo-Persian Oil Company, nearly £1 million (US$5 million), negotiated earlier by Vosuq al-Dowleh, was also appropriated. This shot in the arm made military expenditures the largest item in the budget and a burden for still-ailing state finances. Attempts by statesmen like Mohammad Mosaddeq al-Saltaneh, then minister of finance in Qavam al-Saltaneh's first cabinet, to negotiate a fair budgetary deal with Reza Khan ended in frustrating deadlocks, and Mosaddeq resigned in protest in January 1922. It was apparent that the Qajar statesmen had lost to the military upstart.

COERCION AND THE CALL FOR A REPUBLIC

By October 1922, a bread shortage in the capital resulting from the army's misuse of the state's wheat monopoly brought the public to Baharestan Square in front of the Majles, which had been in session since July 1921. With women at the forefront protesting the shortages, this act of public discontent ended in a violent showdown with security forces. The opposition newspapers and a handful of deputies of the Majles, notably Hasan Modarres, criticized Reza Khan and his military machine for mishandling the demonstration and misappropriating funds. Gradually, a unified opposition, timid though it appeared at first, began to take shape.

The parliamentary minority was backed outside the Majles by a handful of journalists and intellectuals, middle-ranking clergy in Tehran and elsewhere, a few tribal chiefs, discontented merchants of the bazaar, and elements of the Qajar court and aristocracy buoyed by the prince regent Mohammad Hasan Mirza (1899–1943). After Ahmad Shah departed for Europe—an exile from which he never returned—the shah's younger brother became the focus of Qajar solidarity. As the prince regent, he symbolized the last bastion of resistance against Reza Khan and all that he and his supporters stood for. By autumn 1922 the anti–Reza Khan coalition was able to put a temporary halt to the otherwise irrepressible rise of the commander in chief. Reza Khan was unprepared for a showdown, and politically did not feel confident enough to oust the old regime. Reza Khan's performance as a military commander and a political operator nevertheless earned grudging praise not only from the new British minister Percy Lorraine but also from the Soviet minister Theodore Rothstein, who after his arrival comfortably slipped into the role of a Russian diplomatic counterweight to the British minister. Both sides were impressed with Reza Khan's discipline and resolve, as well as his detachment from everyday politics and his display of political astuteness. No longer did his "peasant" and "humble" origins bother the class-conscious British diplomats who were accustomed to hobnobbing with refined members of Iranian nobility. The Soviet comrades, too, forgot that he had crushed the Jangal movement as soon as they discovered Reza Khan's proletariat origins and later the redeeming qualities of the national bourgeoisie.

In what appeared to be a shrewd maneuver, Reza Khan resigned from the War Ministry only to be invited back by the Majles. He reconciled with Modarres, the prince regent, and the willing nobility, and even with the leader of the Majles's ever-shrinking socialist faction, Solayman Mirza. Martial law was suspended, the army budget was regulated, and momentarily there was hope for greater freedom of the press—yet this would prove to be only an interval. The one-year respite gave Reza Khan the chance to learn more, to consolidate his base, and to gather around him a capable cadre of civilians with vision. By October 1923, when Reza Khan formed his first government, with himself as the prime minister, he extended his power base beyond the military and presented a program of reforms. He was backed by a public prepared to see him not as the rough and ready military commander, but as a national savior who had pacified the country, secured its sovereignty, boosted national confidence, and pledged to fulfill Iran's long-awaited dreams of structural reforms.

After three years of an effective presence on the political stage, it seemed almost inevitable that Reza Khan would entertain higher ambitions. There was very little, it appeared, that could stop him from claiming total control as the head of a republican state. After Ahmad Shah's departure for Europe, the fate of the Qajar monarchy was virtually sealed. The fourth Majles had come to its end and the election of the fifth Majles, at least in part, was manipulated in such way as to favor Reza Khan's ambitions, though it was still not clear in which fashion. With very few exceptions, the Iranian notables were willing collaborators, and large segments of the public were ready to accept a change in regime. In 1907, radicals among the constitutionalists advocated republicanism as an alternative to the Qajar dynastic rule, though soon they were marginalized by a conservative landowning elite and a clerical establishment that preferred monarchy, even a new Pahlavi monarchy, over a republic.

By November 1923, the declaration of the Republic of Turkey, with Mustafa Kemal as its first president, deeply impressed the Iranian political milieu. The story of Kemal's departure from Istanbul in May 1919 to embark on an endeavor that eventually resulted in the creation of the new republic appealed to Reza Khan and his supporters, but also to the Iranian intelligentsia. Kemal Pasha was also an army officer—albeit trained in a military academy—a war hero, and a strong-willed leader with nationalist zeal who stood firmly against occupying armies and crushed secessionist tendencies. The parallel with Reza Khan was unmistakable. Not surprisingly, the first calls for the creation of an Iranian republic appeared in an Istanbul newspaper. Less than three months later, the abolition of the Qajar monarchy and the establishment of a republic was the first order on the agenda of the fifth Majles. Thousands of telegrams encouraged by pro–Reza Khan army commanders were sent from the provinces urging the Majles to act without delay. Indeed, in the days leading up to Nowruz festival, coinciding with March 21, 1924, the change in regime seemed likely to be ratified by the Majles. And yet the campaign eventually failed, causing Reza Khan a great loss of prestige.

A grand coalition of pro-Qajar elements led by Hasan Modarres and supported by remnants of the Qajar aristocracy loyal to the Crown, the conservative preachers of the mosques, and liberal journalists afraid of Reza Khan's dictatorship managed to kill off the "republican commotion," as it came to be known. Fear of Reza Khan's dictatorial ambitions affected liberal intellectuals such as the poet Mirzadeh 'Eshqi, the editor of the fiery newspaper *Qarn-e Bistom* (Twentieth century), who eventually paid with his own life for mocking the republican campaign as a charade. In one of his popular song (*tasnif*) he wrote:

To ruin the land of the Persians, the agents of the aliens
Spread the word, put it in people's mouths:
"Republicanism is sweet, like the Indian sugarcane."
But a voice from the invisible duly cautioned:
"Republicanism is [nothing but] a sugarcoated sheep dropping,
"It is beautiful, it is attractive . . ."
"But what appears in republican clothing
Is bigotry and tyranny . . ."
Of this ugly clamor the motherland trembles,
For it brought conflict and vengeance between the nation and the state.
The chaste child of liberty is aborted at birth,
And we forgot [even] the name of unity.[4]

Yet what brought the Tehran public to the streets, via mosques, was in greater part the clergy's deep fears of Reza Khan's secularizing agenda. They reckoned that like Mustafa Kemal in Turkey, Reza Khan's republicanism would establish a laic order hostile to the precepts of Islam and the Qur'an, allowing the atheists, the Baha'is, and other anti-Islamic elements to gain primacy.

Manifold displays of "irreligion" in the public space terrified the mosque-going public and vindicated local preachers and their pleas to defend the shari'a against open displays of profanity: makeshift movie theaters, the earliest in Iran, screening *farangi* silent one-reelers, taverns offering opium and home-brewed '*araq*, musicians and dancers and storytellers narrating in coffeehouses the legends of the *Shahnameh* and the romances of Nezami's "Seven Domes." Promiscuity and prostitution were available for the affluent, and popular painters depicted erotica from *One Thousand and One Nights*. More men were appearing in European attire with beardless faces, and there were more mustachioed dandies wearing white shirts with detachable collars. Even daring women were appearing in lighter and less suffocating facial hijab.

The greater visibility of the junior army officers in uniform, younger officials, and professionals educated in secular schools were also unwelcomed by the conservatives. They witnessed the young generation abandoning madrasa training, leaving behind clocks and turbans, shaving their beards, and putting on ties and Western-style suits to be government employees, defense lawyers, judges, tax collectors, journalists, or officials in registry offices. These were members of a new urban middle class who, though small in number, were distancing themselves from the old elite and their constituency. The landed notables, mojtaheds, petty merchants, artisans, and shopkeepers of the bazaar formed the backbone of the conservative sector. The multitudes of the poor, unemployed, and downtrodden were their foot soldiers, often frequenting mosques and pilgrimage sites and eking out a living at the margins of society with handouts from the mojtaheds.

On March 22, 1924, nearly five thousand demonstrators gathered in Baharestan Square. The protestors were mostly bazaar merchants and members of the poor urban classes who came to demonstrate against heathen republicanism and its advocates and to show support for the constitutional monarchy. They clashed with the Tehran police and the auxiliary troops, and the subsequent shots fired over the crowd injured dozens and added to public fury. Reza Khan, who appeared in person to boost the morale of the security forces, was booed and missiles thrown at his carriage. Inside the Majles, the speaker confronted him and—in a rare show of courage—rebuked him for breaching the parliamentary sanctuary. Shortly afterward, Modarres, who was slapped in the face by a prorepublic deputy on the floor of the Majles, was able to capitalize on Reza Khan's haughtiness and his own aggrieved demeanor to carry a majority and defeat the proposed bill calling for establishment of the republican regime. Reza Khan, dejected and furious, left the Majles and, as a sign of his disapproval, left the capital for a village nearby. But soon thereafter he reassessed his options and sought an alternative route.

Modarres was a savvy maneuverer who had built for himself a reputation for honesty and frugality, a "man of the people" who lived simply, voiced the plight of the weak, and challenged excesses of the power. A master of persuasion, his commonsense parliamentary debates, in an unadulterated Isfahani accent, won him many admirers. He first rose to significance as a representative of the Najaf mojtaheds in the third Majles but soon transformed himself into a consummate politician guided more by realpolitik than by the dictates of Najaf. His rise typified a new kind of public figure who did not belong to the nobility, a man propelled to power by the Constitutional Revolution and kept there because of his public appeal.

If Modarres's opposition to establishing a republican regime was based on the best intentions—that he sensed the coming of a military dictatorship and moved against it—in the end his recourse only helped monarchical autocracy to endure. It is questionable whether Modarres's campaign to stop Reza Khan was entirely altruistic or merely a power grab, for there is little doubt that he held an alliance with reactionary mullahs in the city, the *lutis* of Tehran's city quarters, the Qajar prince regent Mohammad Hasan Mirza, and the defeated Qajar nobility who were anxious to preserve their privileges.

What eventually allowed the opponent of republicanism to prevail, however, was Mustafa Kemal's abolition of the Islamic caliphate in neighboring Turkey. Between the demise of the Ottoman sultanate in October 1923 and the end of the caliphate on March 3, 1924, Kemal utilized his symbolic office to consolidate power over the republic. After the Great War Shi'i Iranians paid even less attention to the Sunni caliphate yet the fact that the new president of the Turkish Republic—a devout secularist—was able to abolish the much-augmented caliphate may have suggested to the Shi'i mojtaheds that the same fate would await the clerical establishment should Reza Khan succeed in turning Iran into a republic. The uncanny parallel between Turkey and Iran scared the high-ranking mojtaheds in Najaf and in Iran.

The strategy to rein in Reza Khan and defeat republicanism paid off at a time when public sentiments were high and the lethargic Qajar monarchy was still lingering. For a moment, it seemed as if Modarres had succeeded in forcing Reza Khan to bow to the authority of the Majles. But as it turned out, he underestimated Reza Khan's resilience and overestimated his own popularity. Four days after the demonstration of March 22, Reza Khan made a pilgrimage to the shrine city of Qom, where he met with three grand ayatollahs of Najaf who were temporarily residing there after having been deported from Iraq by the British Mandatory authorities in the aftermath of the 1920 Shi'i revolt. Thankful to Reza Khan for negotiating with the British authorities for their safe return, they were willing to mediate a solution. After a closed-door meeting with the three *marja's*, Reza Khan issued a public statement renouncing republicanism as unsuitable for Iran and assuring the public that he would focus on promoting "Islam's prominence," "Iran's sovereignty," and a "nationalist government."

Shortly thereafter, the three ayatollahs also issued a statement to all religious authorities, elites, merchants, guilds, and the rest of the Iranian nation reiterating the undesirability of establishing a republic:

> Since there have been some utterances about establishing a republican regime that was not acquiesced to by the majority (of the people) and was incongruent with circumstances in this country, at the time when his Excellency the Prime Minister, may he be forever prominent, was visiting Qom, the Abode of Faith, to say farewell (to us), we requested and he (graciously) accepted that this issue be obliterated and such debates abandoned and an announcement (to that effect) be sent to all provinces. God willing, everyone would appreciate the value of such a blessing and remain fully grateful for this benevolence.[5]

The three signatories were 'Abol-Hasan Isfahani (1860–1946), a *marja'* with a large following; Mohammad Hasan Na'ini, the mojtahed who had previously produced the treatise on the compatibility of a constitutional regime with Shi'i idea of government, and 'Abd al-Karim Ha'eri (1859–1937), who was instrumental in developing Qom as a major center for study of jurisprudence. Ha'eri would later be Ayatollah Khomeini's teacher and mentor.

Despite all the negative publicity surrounding the republican initiative then and later—that it was a backdoor to Reza Khan's dictatorship, contrary to Iranian political tradition and against Islam—its defeat proved a major loss for Iran's political future. It could be argued that Reza Khan's opting for a dynastic monarchy as an alternative to the republic only a year later perpetuated a long tradition of dynastic rule. It undermined the Majles and crushed all sources of opposition, including Modarres. Moreover, the Pahlavi hereditary succession in and of itself would be a major obstacle to long-term political change even after the fall of Reza Shah in 1941. Adopting a monarchy allowed the Pahlavi regime to bank on the historical tradition of Iranian kingship and earn for itself political legitimacy far beyond what a president of a republic, even a dictatorial one, could have done.

In the course of the sixteen months leading up to the abolition of the Qajar dynasty and the investiture of Reza Shah Pahlavi in December 1925, the political climate noticeably shifted in favor of Reza Khan and his drive toward the

Persian throne. In July 1924 the minority in the Majles, headed by Modarres and supported by, among others, the poet and Majles deputy Mohammad-Taqi Bahar, held a vote of no confidence in the government on the grounds of the unconstitutionality of Reza Khan's conduct in office, disrespect for the Majles, mistreatment of citizens, and financial misappropriation.

Yet their maneuver was defeated by a vast margin. In a short period, the climate had dramatically changed against Modarres and his supporters. Fearing intimidation, physical attacks, and threats to their life from agents of Reza Khan's police and their hired thugs, members of the dwindling minority did not feel safe even taking their seats in the Majles.

Bahar, who earlier had welcomed the rise of Reza Khan but soon became one of his eloquent critics, expressed the mixed feelings that intellectuals of the period reserved for the emerging dictator. In one of his masterpieces, *Damavandiyeh* (on Damavand; also known as enchained white demon), composed in 1922, he calls on the highest summit of the Alborz range, Mount Damavand, overlooking Tehran, to burst open on the Iranian capital and destroy its sinful inhabitants. Once an active volcano, Damavand is the center of Iran's mythological geography in the *Shahnameh*. Bahar writes:

O, Damavand! the enchained white demon,
The dome of the world! . . .
You, the heavy fist of the Time,
Untouched by the passage of Time.
Rise to the heavens!
And blow on the land of Ray a few times . . .
From the fire of the oppressed,
And flame of divine punishment,
Send clouds over the land of Ray,
Rain fear, war and terror . . .
Like fire and brimstone,
That blow Sodom to oblivion,
Like the city of Pompeii,
That Vulcan brought to instant death.
Destroy the pillars of this deceit,
Tore apart this race and this kinship. . .
Take the revenge of the wise,
From these ignoble idiots.[6]

Calling on the enchained white demon is an obvious double entendre, for it is an allusion not only to the volcano's white cap but also to the white demon killed by Rostam in the Seven Trials he undertook in Mazandaran. The white demon can be taken as an allusion to the Jangal movement and the Bolshevik support for it that was eventually brought to an end by Reza Khan. That is all the more plausible since the mythical Damavand also holds inside the tyrant Zahhak of the *Shahnameh*, who usurped Jamshid's throne and ruled over Iran for a millennium before the hero-savior Fereydun eternally chained him on Mount Damavand. It is as though here Bahar were making a second reference to Reza Khan, who has turned into a tyrant. Moreover, in Bahar's poem, Damavand is portrayed as the dome of the Giti, the Iranian mythological goddess of the fast-revolving terrestrial universe with fatalistic potency. She nurtures then destroys humans and civilizations. The reincarnated Zahhak, therefore, is destined by the fortune of the Giti to make his climb to absolute power before an inevitable fall. The volcanic task that the poet thus invites Damavand to perform is to destroy the old Qajar order and whatever is associated with it, just as Zahhak was invited to overthrow Jamshid's once-glorious but fast-decaying kingdom. Despite its apparent pessimism, Bahar's complex imagery makes sense only if the unleashed Zahhak of Damavand is to be seen as the lesser of the two evils, but one that is also destined for eventual destruction.

Later, in October 1925, on the eve of the abolition of the Qajar dynasty, Bahar's criticism of Reza Khan almost cost him his life. In a case of mistaken identity, the plainclothes henchmen of the new regime assassinated in front of the Majles an unfortunate person who resembled Bahar. The other deputies got the message. Landing in Reza Shah's jail a few years later, Bahar got the message. He gave up politics and became a renowned professor of Persian literature in Tehran University. One of the twentieth century's greatest students of Persian culture, he was far from the revolutionary fire of his youth, though not devoid of the modern values that shaped his generation.

THE IMBRIE AFFAIR AND THE DISPLAY OF RELIGIOSITY

What would come to be known as the Imbrie Affair (or *saqqa-khaneh* incident), embarrassing as it was for the Iranian government, greatly contributed to the atmosphere of fear and intimidation and may have struck the final blow to Reza Khan's opposition. In July 1924, Tehran was abuzz with reports of a miracle in a water fountain (*saqqa-khaneh*) where the sick would be cured and wishes granted. This would have been a familiar occurrence in Shi'i Iran, had it not been for the fact that it fit too well with the struggles between Reza Khan and his opponents to be seen merely as a coincidence. It was rumored that a Baha'i who had refused to pay a customary donation to the sacred fountain had instantaneously gone blind, but once he repented his heretical beliefs and paid the tribute, he was immediately cured.

The story of the blessed fountain had its political beneficiaries and was likely orchestrated from Reza Khan's quarters. Greater social freedoms since 1921 no doubt had given the Baha'i a degree of visibility, and Reza Khan was accused of favoring them. Now that the crypto-Azali radicals of the constitutional era were no more, the Baha'is briefly came to offer a moderate path to modernity, one in tune with the emerging Pahlavi order. A long history of anti-Baha'i campaigns made such a design plausible, though not perhaps its unintended results. Reza Khan's agents probably hoped for a short and manageable uproar to display his loyalty to Shi'ism, dispel the rumors of his anti-Islamic project of reforms, and possibly even set the stage for reinstating martial law. Yet the episode brought about serious consequences.

Among the growing number of onlookers who visited the now-sacred fountain was the acting consul of the US legation in Tehran, Robert Imbrie, who also freelanced as a journalist for the National Geographical Society. Imbrie was not a professional diplomat but a special agent, a maverick with a strong anti-Bolshevik credentials. An Indiana Jones of sorts, he was a graduate of the 1906 Yale Law School and a protégé of Allen Dulles, the future head of the US Central Intelligence Agency in the 1950s. Imbrie was dispatched to Iran by the US State Department to facilitate the implementation of an ongoing oil concession between an American company and the Iranian government. Sinclair Oil, the first American attempt to explore oil in Iran's Caspian shores, had faced serious opposition from the Anglo-Persian Oil Company, which considered the Iranian oil as it exclusive tenure.

Hoping to make an illustrated report out of miracle-making water fountain, a piece of Oriental exotica no doubt appealing to the readers of the *National Geographic*, Imbrie set up his camera near the site. But he soon faced angry bystanders' objections to an infidel's photographing what had become a sacred site. Mayhem broke out, in the course of which Imbrie and his associate were deliberately beaten and bruised. With the help of some bystanders they managed to reach the carriage that had brought them to the scene and headed for the hospital. But quite inexplicably, the carriage was stopped by a police officer on duty. Later, when they were brought to the government hospital for treatment, Imbrie was followed by a group of thugs who soon entered the operating room and resumed beating and stabbing him, in the presence of policemen. He died shortly after.

The ugly incident generated an outcry. Several arrests were made, presumably the culprits were later executed, and the Iranian government accepted making monetary compensation, but it never became clear if the incident was a fantastic mob outburst perpetrated against the American diplomat, or against the Baha'is, or more likely a maneuver orchestrated by Reza Khan's agents that had gotten out of hand. Whatever the case, the incident allowed Reza Khan to declare martial law and round up more of his critics. They had become vocal especially after the assassination of the dissident poet and journalist Mirzadeh 'Eshqi, whose assassination was also traceable to Reza Khan's police. With martial law again in place, opponents were arrested or silenced. The Imbrie Affair also allowed Reza Khan to outmaneuver Arthur Millspaugh, the American financial adviser to the Iranian government, who was soon forced to resign. Millspaugh had resisted allocating all the revenue that the Iranian government earned from APOC concessions to the Iranian armed forces. By doing so, he outraged Reza Khan, who relied heavily on that revenue to reorganize the army and consolidate his hold over the political establishment and the country.

The Imbrie Affair served to cast off the stigma of irreligion from Reza Khan. Not long before the night of 'Ashura mourning ceremonies during Muharram 1343 (August 1924), Reza Khan, accompanied by some senior officers, joined the procession of the "night of the bereaved" (*sham-e ghariban*). Clad in black, candles in hand, and beating his chest, he recited along with the mourners tragic verses about the martyrdom of Imam Hosain and his family. In another show of devotion, then premier Reza Khan received from the shrine of 'Ali in Najaf a medallion portrait of the First Imam. It was offered as a token of gratitude on behalf of the two ayatollahs upon their safe arrival in Najaf. The medallion, a nineteenth-century rendering, was presented to Reza Khan with pomp and circumstance, in a ceremony reminiscent of Naser al-Din Shah's investiture of an 'Ali decoration seventy years earlier on the occasion of his ephemeral victory in Herat. It was as if Reza Khan were toying with the idea of kingship.

IN SEARCH OF LEGITIMACY

Having learned his lesson from the republican campaign, Reza Khan acted with greater circumspection. In an effort to acquire public confidence and greater legitimacy during his second term in office, he even acquiesced to the minority in the Majles. He and his cohorts, civilian and military alike, not only displayed Islamic sentiments but also began to borrow from historical memory and Persian nationalist icons that were prevalent during and after the Constitutional Revolution.

Persian legendary and historical memories were powerful tools for augmenting the Pahlavi image. By 1924, the pro–Reza Khan press routinely depicted their hero as a second Nader Shah—a savior who emerged at Iran's darkest hour, drove out the foreign intruders, pacified rebellions, reunited the country, and successfully pursued a program of reform. Like Nader, Reza Khan was of humble origins, and his determination, military gifts, and sharp mind outshone the weaknesses of his enemies and allowed him to outmaneuver restive khans, bandits, and rebels. It did not take long before new pre-Islamic royal figures complemented Reza Khan's heroic image. References to the Achaemenid Cyrus the Great and Darius (Dara in Persian sources of the period), also prevalent in the postconstitutional literature, accompanied references to Reza Khan in newspaper articles and books. His public statements also relied on the revived memories of the rulers of the fifth century BC to augment his new age of revival.

Crafting his own image after these glorious narratives of Iran's distant past—a notable feature of the emergent Pahlavi era—made Reza Khan and his modernist project appear wholly distinct from the ethos of the Qajar era. The Constitutional Revolution had already turned the Qajar monarchy and its Turkic-Mongolian roots into a liability, an image of alien rule, despotism, and weakness (pl. 7.1). The new Pahlavi power, in contrast, invoked the ancient Iranian past. A gradual shift from myth to history, from legends of the *Shahnameh* to the modern description of the Achaemenid and Sasanian empires, was grounded in archeological discoveries and greater knowledge of ancient Greek texts, which boosted public awareness and national pride. As early as 1914, a decade before the rise of Pahlavi dynasty, Iranian postal stamps—a public marker of nationalist sentiment—showed Darius I on his throne under the Zoroastrian *Faravahar* insignia (fig. 7.11). Another scene of Persepolis showed Tachara, the residential palace of the Achaemenid kings (fig. 7.12).

Such publications as the Berlin-based periodical *Kaveh*, edited by Hasan Taqizadeh and his associate—the gifted short-story writer Mohammad 'Ali Jamalzadeh—contributed to Iran's budding cultural nationalism. With centralization at its core, the nationalist awareness promoted by the Berlin circle anticipated the rise of a strong state. Hasan Moshir al-Dowleh's 1927 *Iran-e Bastani* (Ancient Iran), the first of several versions of his canonical history of Iran's pre-Islamic past, is a notable example of a metamorphosis from legendary kings of the Kayanid dynasty in the *Shahnameh* to the Persian Empire of Herodotus and the Achaemenid dynasty of the archeological digs. The new Pahlavi potentate strived to be the apex of this reconstructed historical pyramid.

The Majles passed a new bill in 1925 abolishing all Qajar titles and in favor of adopting family names through a national registry, a novel idea for Iranians and the first of several measures that augmented the state's power over its own citizenry. First and last names fixed citizens with a clear personal identity that was only implicitly, if at all, connected with their paternalistic lineage. New family names were meant to be short and simple. For the nobility, they were often much shorter versions of their Qajar titles. Others identified themselves

Figure 7.11 and Figure 7.12. As early as 1914, images of Persepolis appeared on Iranian stamps. The Zoroastrian image of Faravahar (*left*), above Darius's throne, symbolized pre-Islamic sentiment in the postconstitutional era.
Author's collection.

by their ethnic, tribal, clan, or family identity. And others by their father's first name, their town or village origin, their profession, a chosen virtue, or by nationalist, religious, or other real or imagined affiliations. The abolition of titles was a further blow to the old class system, for it removed symbols of proximity to power, giving the appearance of a more egalitarian society.

Reza Khan himself adopted the family name *Pahlavi*, presumably a variation of *Palani*, the name of his subtribe in the Savadkuh region. As a family name, however, *Palani* had an unfortunate association with *palan*, a cargo saddle for beasts of burden, especially donkeys, whereas *Pahlavi* clearly resonated with a pre-Islamic past—specifically, an aristocratic clan of the Sasanian period. Even more edifying, Pahlavi was a general reference to the Middle Persian of the Sasanian period and the written culture in that language. Mentioned in the *Shahnameh*, the word *Pahlavi* evoked historical continuity particularly since Pahlavi was still in use as the liturgy language of Zoroastrians of Iran and their Parsi coreligionists in India. Modern scholarship of pre-Islamic Iranian languages in Europe largely recovered Pahlavi texts and resolved their many ambiguities. A glorious, though vague, association with the Iranian past, *Pahlavi* became the name of the new dynasty.

Beyond hearsay and from the newspapers on his payroll, Reza Khan came to learn more about Iran's past, its history and culture in the months before his accession to the throne. For a while, a group of erudite Majles deputies were invited to meet with him on a regular basis to discuss the idea and practice of constitutionalism, political and international affairs, and programs of reform, as well as to allow Reza Khan to absorb more of Iran's long history and geography. Among them was the aforementioned Hasan Moshir al-Dowleh, now with the family name Pirniya, who had wisely given up on politics for scholarship. Others included Yahya Dowlatabadi (1862–1940), a leading constitutionalist of prominent Azali background and later a gifted memoirist, and Mohammad Mosaddeq (1882–1967), a Swiss-educated lawyer and member of the Qajar nobility.

For a while, the advisory group met with Reza Khan in the spirit of mutual understanding. While the participants hoped to nurture in him a commitment to constitutional principals, he evidently aimed to appease the Majles's liberal opposition, if not co-opt it. The informal advisory group, however, failed to instill in the ambitious Reza Khan a lasting love for democracy or much respect for the constitution. Efforts to educate him succeeded only in allowing Iran's strongman to articulate a nationalist vision of his own of territorial integrity, centralized and effective state power, independent foreign policy, and a program of cultural reconstruction. Once they were dismissed as a group, and then individually snubbed into isolation, they began to recognize, along with a vast majority of constitutionalists, that the Pahlavi path to absolute power was at the point of no return. Most resigned to this inevitability and hoped for its benevolence while only a few resisted.

RECLAIMING KHUZESTAN

One outcome of the Pahlavi show of patriotic resolve was the Khuzestan campaign in the fall of 1924 (fig. 7.13). It boosted Reza Khan's prestige and reasserted control over this oil-rich but otherwise isolated and impoverished province. Also known as 'Arabestan, in the Qajar era, Khuzestan was a sparsely populated land with few urban centers, virtually no major agriculture except for palm groves, and a large minority population that spoke an Arabic dialect common to the northwestern coasts of the Persian Gulf. Organized into a tribal system, the Banu Ka'b and Banu Tarf were the most powerful Arab confederacies in Khuzestan. At least since the eighteenth century, they had been active as a political player in the region. The interior highlands were the Bakhtiyari winter resort and a vital asset for the confederacy's pastoral economy.

In between the quarreling chiefs of Banu Tarf and Banu Ka'b and the competing branches of the Bakhtiyari, there was limited space for Tehran's presence in cities such as the ancient Shushtar, Dezful, and Ahvaz. Most initiatives to

Figure 7.13. Units of the Southern Division (Lashgar-e Jonub) in 1924 leaving
Shiraz for Khuzestan province. The four divisions of the newly amalgamated
armed forces played a crucial part in Reza Khan's consolidation.
Fathollah Chehrehnegar, M. Saneʿ, *Paydayesh-e ʿAkkasi dar Shiraz* (Tehran, 1369/1990), 137.

penetrate Khuzestan since the eighteenth century and attempts to develop it
since the nineteenth century had failed because of a scarcity of resources and
technology. The port of Naseriyeh south of Ahvaz, later named Bandar-e Shah-
pur under Pahlavi rule (and Bandar-e Khomeini under the Islamic Republic),
was one exception. It had been developed under Naser al-Din Shah as an alternative to the strategically vulnerable port of Mohammara and to compete with
the Ottoman port of Basra. Naseriyeh was also the home port for *Persepolis*,
Iran's only battleship in the Qajar era.

Since the 1880s, the interiors of Khuzestan were somewhat revived as a result of the British-operated Lynch Navigation Company, which operated a
steamboat service on the river Karun, Iran's only navigable river, from Mohammara some 140 miles north to Shushtar. From there, construction of Shushtar-
Isfahan commercial road through Bakhtiyari lands opened up the hard-
to-access Iranian countryside to the southwest of Isfahan for the first time. The

Anglo-Persian oil exploration, moreover, proved a major factor in changing the province's economic and political landscape. The Masjed Soleiman oil fields were in Bakhtiyari territory, whereas the newly built Abadan refinery—which by the 1930s would be the largest in the world—fell within the Banu Ka'b territory on the eastern shore of Shatt al-Arab.

Tehran's campaign to reclaim Khuzestan, under the initial pretext of collecting taxes in arrears, naturally alarmed the British, APOC, and chiefs of the Banu Ka'b. London felt that Tehran's ambition to administer Khuzestan directly would spoil its careful arrangements with the Bakhtiyari and Bani Ka'b, who had been granted minuscule shares of the oil revenue in exchange for land use, security, and labor. Bakhtiyari tribesmen were employed at the oil rigs with negligible wages as oil workers or as guards, and they were treated with little mercy. The growing influence and wealth of Shaykh Khaz'al of Āl-e Mahsin, the chief of the Banu Ka'b, was but one example of the transformation of tribal chiefs of the Shatt al-Arab and Mohammara regions under British auspices. A shrewd maneuverer, Khaz'al colluded with APOC, along with some Bakhtiyari and Lur chiefs, in the hopes of finding a common front against Tehran's advances.

By November 1924, the cavalry and armored columns of the Iranian army ventured toward Khuzestan in a pincer movement through Luristan and Isfahan, which already were pacified. With great speed, the government forces managed to occupy Ahvaz, remove Khaz'al, and capture the entire province. Once their mediatory efforts failed, the British bowed to Tehran's daring measure. They were assured that British hold over the oil fields and the oil industry, then one of the most profitable oil operations in the world, was secure. The assurances were confirmed by Reza Khan's action. Khaz'al's efforts to coordinate with Reza Khan's opposition in Tehran, through Modarres, among other channels, also failed, and Khaz'al was forced to take back his bold disowning of Reza Khan and his claims that he was a usurper who undermined the country's constitution and illegally seized power. Khaz'al was sent off to Tehran, and soon his wealth and property were confiscated.

Reclaiming Khuzestan marked the last stage of moving away from the concept of the Guarded Domains of Iran toward the centralizing "Sublime State of Iran" (*dowlat 'alliyeh Iran*). That the British condoned the Pahlavi centralization program is astonishing, given their enormous diplomatic and military presence only four years earlier. The change of heart was understandable, given that the British inadvertently discovered in the new regime some fulfillment of the 1919 agreement, at least insofar as it created a centralized military capable of securing Britain's investment and strategic interests, albeit in the hands of a nationalist modernizer. Reza Khan was not entirely of their making, but he was not entirely opposed to their vested interests either. In the months following Curzon's departure, the Foreign Office quickly condoned a utilitarian policy of accommodating the new Iranian regime. Even when Reza Khan postured to capture the Persian crown, the British bowed to his ambition. They abandoned their pledge since 1828 to keep the Qajar house on the throne. They complied not only because Reza Khan's rise proved irresistible, and because he dislodged within the Iranian polity most agents of British influence, the so-called Anglophiles, but also because he offered a reliable bulwark against the Soviet threat.

Even before the fall of the Jangal movement, Reza Khan had managed to establish friendly relations with the Soviet legation. Later, during the campaign for republicanism he even instructed some of his trusted military and civilian supporters to surreptitiously hoist a few red flags in the style of the Bolsheviks. Yet his anticommunist credentials were intact, and that is what mattered most for British interests at a time when there seemed to be no viable Russian party with whom the British could negotiate Iran's status as a buffer state.

THE GREAT WAR IN RETROSPECT

More than at any time in its modern history, during World War I and its aftermath, Iran was affected by the military, economic, and human repercussions of a global conflict. Iran was incorporated deep enough into a geopolitical system not to be able to ignore threats to its neutrality or to weather conflicting imperial pressures on its borders. Despite such threats, however, the Iranian state survived heavy blows to its sovereignty. This was all the more remarkable because the decade-long upheavals between 1911 and 1921 not only revealed serious rifts in the ruling elite but also brought about the Qajar monarchy's eventual demise. The war also brought into light political players, intellectuals, and military officers who were the product of the Constitutional Revolution. It was to the credit of this mix of the old and new classes, rather than the goodwill of the occupying powers, that Iran barely avoided partition along the lines set in the 1907 Anglo-Russian agreement. Despite obvious limits to its authority and its effectiveness, and despite all its failings, the Iranian state managed to navigate the stormy waters of the war period and its aftermath through diplomacy and political maneuvering. If there was a single event beyond its borders that saved Iran, it was the destruction of the Russian Empire.

Remarkably, before 1921 none of the nationalist-inspired movements that hoped to liberate Iran from foreign occupation and from the declining Qajar elite succeeded in their task. The government in exile of the Committee for National Defense, German covert operations inside Iran and the Berlin resistance circle, and subsequently the Jangal movement in Gilan and the nationalist rebellions in Khorasan and Azarbaijan failed, while the center continued to hold a degree of legitimacy and political agency. The Iranian state employed its meager financial resources, including revenue from the Anglo-Persian Oil Company, and its limited military capabilities, such as the Cossack Division and the Gendarmerie after 1918, to withstand secessionist challenges. In despair, the ruling elite also subscribed to a halfhearted British effort to resuscitate the Qajar state. Yet the nationalist polity took advantage of the international uproar to successfully resist the semiprotectorate status that the 1919 Anglo-Persian Agreement offered. Its failure paved the way for the rise of a rough and ready strongman in the person of Reza Khan. He and the Cossack Division under his command came to the rescue of the central state by systematically quashing the rebellious periphery. The implicit blessing of the British representatives and shortly after the consent of the Bolsheviks upheld the new regime in its drive for state building. In retrospect, Reza Khan's consolidation between 1921 and 1925 appeared as an unavoidable outcome of World War I; a price that Iran had to pay to conclude two decades of political revolution, economic vacillation, and sociocultural change.

8

REZA SHAH AND THE PAHLAVI
ORDER (1925–1941)

By the fall of 1925 all that was needed to remove the Qajars and establish the new Pahlavi dynasty seemed to be in place. Ahmad Shah had long been in voluntary exile, with no serious intentions to return. His brother and regent, Mohammad Hasan Mirza, was isolated in Golestan Palace, and the Qajar loyalists were intimidated and silenced, or else had been co-opted, as were the leading Shi'i mojtaheds of the time, together with their associates and cohorts. Even Modarres was enticed to collaborate. The tribal rebellions had been largely quashed, and the most defiant khans exiled or destroyed. The rest walked the line prescribed by the state, at least for the time being.

Content with the semblance of order made possible under Pahlavi, the public was willing to endure army officers' abuses of power. Quelling the political opposition by the boisterous police force also was condoned. The public was no longer willing to come out to the streets, except to see the victory arches erected to honor Reza Khan's campaigns. The last pro-Qajar call to demonstration in October 1925 was answered by a heavy show of force, machine guns, and counterdemonstrations in favor of Reza Pahlavi. Women protested on both sides, and a few pro-Pahlavi women demonstrators dared to appear without veiling their faces, condemning the "reactionary" mullahs and the "rotten aristocrats" as obstacles to Iran's road to progress.

PILLARS OF THE PAHLAVI THRONE

On October 31, 1925, with an overwhelming majority—and without any substantive debate—the fifth Majles passed a bill that abolished the Qajar dynasty and appointed Reza Khan as His Royal Excellency in charge of the provisional government. Abolishing the Qajar dynasty was a clear overture to Reza Khan's accession to the throne. Amending several articles of the 1906–1907 constitution, the Majles dissolved itself and announced the convening of a constituent assembly to determine the country's political future.

Before the final vote on abolishing the Qajar dynasty, Modarres, in his characteristically disparaging manner, left the chamber in protest, shouting, "Not even one hundred thousand votes will make it right!" Four independent deputies stayed to speak against the bill, however, though all praised Reza Khan's service to the nation. Hasan Taqizadeh, hero of the constitutional period, questioned the constitutionality of the bill and proposed an expedient way out. The English-educated moderate, Hosain 'Ala, raised similar concerns. Mohammad Mosaddeq, the most articulate in the group, argued rather shrewdly that elevating Reza Pahlavi to the status of a constitutional king would only deprive the nation of an effective prime minister and reformer. Yahya Dowlatabadi, the most daring of the four spoke—if we trust his memoirs—of the ongoing threats and intimidation by Reza Khan's agents to deliver votes in favor of the bill. Though appreciative of Pahlavi's service, he nevertheless aired his displeasure with the hereditary monarchy—perhaps the only regret expressed, and implicitly at that, over abandoning the republican option. Fearing personal harm, each speaker immediately left the chamber after his speech. They all knew that their opposition to the bill was merely symbolic; it was as if they were delivering a eulogy for the Constitutional Revolution just two decades after its birth.

On December 12, 1925, the newly convened constituent assembly unanimously voted for the new Pahlavi hereditary monarchy, and three days later Reza Khan was sworn in as the new shah. The coronation ceremony, in late April 1926, was staged as a joyful celebration, very different from the solemnity of the Shi'i public culture—it was an event meant to announce clearly the advent of a "modern" era, with street decorations, banners, electrical lights and lanterns, stamp issues, victory arches, and, of course, lengthy homilies glorifying the new reign. Yet the very act of coronation helped to reaffirm, and in the process reinvent, the same monarchical tradition that the Pahlavi regime was replacing, albeit with a touch of borrowed European style, typical of the period. The shah sat on an armchair atop the Marble Throne in the open veranda of Golestan Palace, and donning a royal robe over his military uniform, he received people in the palace courtyard as Fath 'Ali Shah and Naser al-Din Shah had before him, but without wearing the Kayanid crown of the Qajars. The new Pahlavi crown, crafted for the occasion, was inspired by the Achaemenid scaling up motifs as appeared on the ramparts of Persepolis. The Islamic side of the coronation ceremony was scaled down accordingly.

Long before the coronation, remnants of the Qajar house were cleared out of Golestan Palace and other royal properties. A few days before the detrimental Majles vote, the new regime replaced the palace guards with regular troops. Immediately afterward, the prince regent Mohammad Hasan Mirza and his small entourage left for exile. To humiliate the last icon of Qajar sovereignty, Reza Shah paid the prince regent for his travel expenses in the smallest denomination of silver coins, which were delivered in leather purses by a ranking general of the Pahlavi army who had headed the palace guards. The troops drove the prince and his attendants to the border and unceremoniously dumped them at the Iraqi customhouse in Khaniqain. To symbolically right the wrongs of the founder of the Qajar dynasty, one of Reza Shah's earliest acts was to order that the remains of Karim Khan Zand be exhumed from the *ivan* of Golestan Palace and reinterred in Shiraz.

This was the end of 150 years of rule by the Qajars, a dynasty that had survived as only a shadow of itself since the Constitutional Revolution. But if the Qajar dynasty came to an end, its legacy endured not so much in the institutions of the government as in the blood of the Iranian elite, who had long intermarried with the vast Qajar progeny. The Pahlavi regime co-opted this old elite, some to serve in the bureaucracy and the rest to hold on to their land and property. Many were impoverished and eventually lost out to the new classes, but a few survived, and even thrived, for another generation or two. During the first decade in power, Reza Shah and his military and civilian supporters were poised for a massive leap forward. They felt supremely confident that they would be able to fulfill the long-awaited national aspirations for sovereignty and material progress, and that they could successfully recast Iran as a modern nation and Iranians as refashioned citizens of such a nation.

The mixed experiments with constitutional democracy over the previous two decades, foreign interventions, a self-serving political elite, and the inevitable disarray that came first with the Constitutional Revolution and then with World War I, had convinced most urban Iranians of the necessity of the alternative offered by Reza Shah. In Turkey, Italy, the Soviet Union, and soon Germany, many viewed the authoritarian state model as the only solution to postwar maladies. In 1925 and 1926 hundreds of flattering telegrams poured in from the provinces to congratulate the new monarchy. They were manufactured with a good deal of persuasion from army officers, yet they were not entirely empty of genuine sentiments. It was as if the whole nation were ready to make a new start. If the agenda for the new regime was essentially scripted in the constitutional period and set in motion in the postconstitutional era, then Reza Shah was the real agent who brought it to fruition. To do so, he relied heavily on a handful of loyal statesmen on whose vision and efficiency the Pahlavi order was built.

As early as 1924 a group of four officials formed an informal alliance that placed them above the old Qajar cabal of the earlier decades. They aimed to harness Reza Khan's power toward creating a more institutionalized order and transform the regime's image from that of a mere military dictatorship. Yet it is wrong to assume that Reza Shah was just an overseer or a puppet in the hands of his chief ministers. To the contrary, reminiscent of Naser al-Din Shah's court, the shah controlled his ministers and officers with persuasion, rivalry, and outright coercion while increasingly falling into an entangling web of mistrust and fear. On the more positive side, the shah was receptive to initiatives his ministers and advisers proposed and saw them through with tenacity. As long as the blend of ministerial initiative and dictatorial drive worked, there was a visible change in the affairs of state, at least in a material sense.

The four civilian ministers soon dominated the new government and initiated many of the reform projects during the first decade of Pahlavi rule. They were from a younger generation of notables of the postconstitutional period who had gained power, or preserved their privileges, primarily because of their Western education. 'Abd al-Hosain Teymurtash (1883–1933), son of a provincial Khorasan landowning notable, was a dashing young graduate of St. Petersburg Military Academy when at the age of twenty-nine he was elected to the second Majles. Later, as governor of the province of Gilan, he left behind a record of cruelty, including the execution of Dr. Heshmat, a medical doctor and revolutionary intellectual who had joined the Jangal movement but later was tricked into surrendering himself to the authorities. In 1922 as an influential deputy in the fifth Majles, he was instrumental in the rise of Pahlavi dynasty and soon was rewarded as the shah's confidante and powerful court minister.

Perhaps more than any other statesman, Teymurtash helped shaping Reza Khan's public image. He regulated the shah's access to the public, nurtured his taste for all things modern, dignified and even glamorized the Pahlavi court, and above all helped restore equilibrium to Iran's foreign policy. Though Russian-educated and for a while an Anglophile, under Reza Shah he steered a steady course in tune with Iran's nationalist ethos. He was articulate and persuasive, flattering toward his master, and patronizing to his subordinates. His gambling, womanizing, and reckless drinking—reminiscent of the tsarist army officers' lifestyle to which he had been exposed—was emblematic of the modern hedonism that came with breakdown of the traditional moral order. Reza Shah, who once considered him almost as his alter ego, at first rewarded his services

handsomely before turning against him with a vengeance. Dismissed and accused of the groundless charge of spying for the Soviets, in 1933 Teymurtash was
arrested and tried on a propped-up charge of bribery. Sentenced to three years'
imprisonment, he was murdered in prison by the shah's dreaded police chief.

An ally of Teymurtash in high office, Firuz Mirza Nosrat al-Dowleh (1889–
1937), was a savvy statesman of impeccable Qajar lineage and the promising senior son of the influential 'Abd al-Hosain Mirza Farmanfarma (1857–1939), the
scion of a powerful family. Having studied first in Beirut and then law in Paris,
he was a deputy of the third and fourth Majles, and in 1919, while still young,
he had joined Vosuq al-Dowleh's government as minister of justice and later of
foreign affairs. Yet the failure of the Anglo-Persian Agreement did not entirely
destroy his career. Despite his apparent ambition for staging a coup in 1921,
which was delayed because he was stranded on his way to the capital, he later
welcomed Reza Khan's rise to power and, like Teymurtash, was instrumental
in consolidating the new dynasty. In 1925 he joined the cabinet as minister of
finance and later minister of justice, and in collaboration with Teymurtash, he
carried through the earliest reform measures of the Pahlavi era. As the first of
the four ranking aides to Reza Shah, however, in 1929 Firuz was dismissed on
a fabricated charge of embezzlement and put on trial. After his conviction, he
was barred from government posts. In 1936 he was again arrested and sent into
exile on no apparent charge, then murdered two years later. Well informed,
shrewd, and diplomatic, Firuz Mirza was an asset to the new shah, strengthen-
ing the regime's ties with the old nobility and adding to Iran's international
reputation. As an early victim of Reza Shah's paranoia, Firuz Mirza was viewed
as a potential risk to the throne for his alleged proximity to the British.

The third in the group, 'Ali Akbar Davar (1885–1937), who came from a
middle-ranking bureaucratic family, was most instrumental in overhauling the
government administration. A Swiss-educated lawyer, he began as a left-leaning
journalist and politician, and was a founder of the Radical Party. In 1922 he
formed a powerful block in the fourth and fifth Majles supporting Reza Khan.
A kingmaker, in the true sense of the word, he was the one who put forward
the bill to abolish the Qajar dynasty, and he energetically defended the transfer
of power to Pahlavi. As minister of public works in 1925, and minister of justice
between 1926 and 1932, and thereafter minister of finance, he was responsible
for implementing the most radical reforms under Reza Shah: restructuring the
judicial system and introducing modern civil and penal codes, as well as consolidating the framework for public finances that had first emerged under Shuster
and later under British and American advisers.

Davar was different in character and lifestyle from Teymurtash and distinct from Firuz Mirza in his mild temperament and lack of snobbishness; he was also ambitious and yet prudent and single minded, serving perhaps as the most capable public administrator of the Pahlavi era, with a rare gift for fostering younger talents and transforming Iran's entire divan culture. As the high priest of the Pahlavi etatism, more than anyone else in high office he promoted the cult of state intervention, which in the long run deteriorated into a malignancy. State hegemony, overreliance on government services, and the waning of civil and private initiatives were predictable outcomes. In February 1937, in his early fifties, Davar committed suicide, apparently for fear of the paranoid Reza Shah and his perceptions of Davar's misconduct. He had already witnessed the downfall of his colleagues with the same imagined faults.

Ja'far-Qoli As'ad Bakhtiyari, son of the Constitutional Revolution leader Sardar As'ad Bakhtiyari, was the least political of the group. He was an important agent of stability in the early Pahlavi era, for contrary to his aristocratic and civilian colleagues, As'ad descended from the leadership of Iran's largest tribal confederacy, which a decade earlier had established a political base in the capital and even stood a chance of constituting a Bakhtiyari dynasty. His multiple appointments as minister of war in early Pahlavi governments were meant to symbolize the compliance of the Bakhtiyaris with the emerging Pahlavi order—a fragile compliance no doubt, but effective enough to keep him in the shah's favor as an advocate of the policies of pacifying the tribes and making them sedentary. Like his colleagues, however, he too would eventually fall victim to Reza Shah's suspicion. He was poisoned in prison, and then murdered in March 1934.

That all four victims fell to Reza Shah's regime denoted something more than Reza Shah's paranoiac state of mind or sense of inferiority toward men of higher class and superior education—men whom, despite their genuine show of loyalty to him, the new shah still viewed as a liability and potential threat. He utilized them to his own ends before destroying them, just as Naser al-Din Shah did many decades earlier. The Pahlavi ministers, a modern equivalent of the old divan, were exposed even more than their Qajar predecessors to the whims and wishes of the Pahlavi shah. One can attribute this remarkable continuity to the tenacity of a political culture that persisted even after the Constitutional Revolution, even after a mass movement that primarily aimed to contain and regulate the arbitrary power of the monarch and managed against all odds to oust the despotic Mohammad 'Ali Shah.

Predictably, from the early 1930s, a number of officials and military officers came to occupy positions of power. Some were of the old families who adjusted themselves to Pahlavi rule; others were members of the new middle classes. They proved less resolute and imaginative, more pliant to the shah's wishes, and increasingly corrupt. Ironically, the fate of the four ministers proved almost identical to that of many intellectuals and political activists, tribal leaders, and elder Qajar statesmen who were spied on, kept under house arrest, sent into exile, put on trial, imprisoned on false charges or quietly eliminated.

RAILROAD AND MODERN INFRASTRUCTURE

The efforts of the new state elite bore material results. For many Iranians the construction of a railroad was the ultimate symbol of empowerment, and it was small wonder that the Pahlavi elite make railroad a priority. In 1925 the sixth Majles passed the railway bill. Immediately the Pahlavi state negotiated with British, German, and Danish firms over the planning and construction of the trans-Iranian railroad, which was to extend from the southwestern oil-producing province of Khuzestan on the Persian Gulf to Mazandaran on the northeastern shores of the Caspian (map 8.1).

The north-south axis aimed to open the Iranian markets on both ends to the ports of the Persian Gulf and Caspian Sea, a strategy reminiscent of the Safavids' export of Gilan silk through the Persian Gulf, and later the British initiative to open the Karun-Bakhtiyari link to Isfahan. Yet the Iranian railroad, as it turned out, functioned more as a means of hauling imports into the interior rather than exporting Iranian goods abroad or facilitating the domestic economy. By the mid-1920s early signs of a rejuvenated Soviet economy built upon the ruins of industries of imperial Russia raised Iranian hopes for a renewal of the old trade partnership with Russia, even though the world was at the outset of a global depression. In the south, the port of Khorramshahr (the old Mohammara) seemed a logical terminus for the railroad, given the growing domestic consumption of Khuzestan refined oil as well as the vital need for modern port facilities for international shipping. Although economic and geopolitical realities later revealed the strategic vulnerabilities of the Iranian railroad, at the time it seemed a perfectly sound infrastructural project. True, the planners failed to design a national system to connect the major commercial cities of the interior—a northwest-to-southeast line seemed more viable for connecting Azarbaijan to Tehran and Isfahan and through Yazd and Kerman to Bandar Abbas on the Persian Gulf, and from Tehran to the northeast to Mashhad.

Yet one should be wary of conspiratorial myths common after World War II that accused Reza Shah of constructing the railroad to advance British strategic interests. The Khuzestan line, it can be argued, helped incorporate the oil-rich

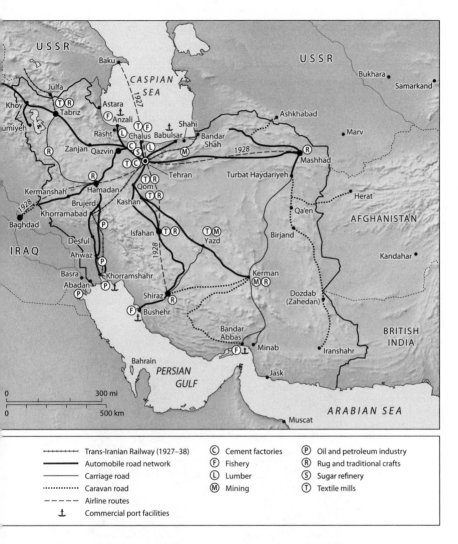

Map 8.1. Communication and industrial development in early Pahlavi era, 1924–1941

province into the state system and enforced Iranian sovereignty in the south despite British vested interests in the oil fields and the British alliance with the Banu Ka'b and the Bakhtiyari khans. Maintaining control of Khuzestan was crucial for the Pahlavi state, not only to boost its nationalist credentials but also to facilitate Reza Shah's desire to claim a bigger share of the oil fields and their enormous revenue. In the long run, Khorramshahr became Iran's largest commercial harbor, facilitating the massive growth of trade with Europe, and later with Japan and the United States, and catering to domestic demands for imported manufactured goods and raw materials.

Financing the Tehran-Khuzestan line in 1927 with revenue from the state's sugar monopoly—one of several monopolies on consumer goods introduced during this period—the southern line became operational by 1929. By 1930 with the construction of the Karun Bridge, two-thirds of a mile long, then the longest steel bridge in the Middle East, the railroad reached the Persian Gulf. By 1936 the eighty-two-mile stretch of picturesque mountainous railroad from the capital to the newly constructed Caspian port of Bandar-e Shah (now Bandar-e Torkaman) became operational. A project of considerable complexity, the trans-Iranian railroad negotiated steep gradations of the Alborz and Zagros ranges through numerous tunnels, bridges, and passes. When in 1938 it officially opened, the total cost of the trans-Iranian railroad was estimated at 10.1 billion rials (US$500 million), making it the most expensive and most extensive project ever in modern Iranian history (except perhaps for the British-owned oil industry and refinery installations) (fig. 8.1).

Figure 8.1. Ascending the Alborz terrain to build the trans-
Iranian railroad was an engineering feat.
Gaduk on the northern sector. A. von Graefe, *Iran das neue Persien* (Berlin and Zurich, 1937), 41.

The rail system was the cornerstone of the infrastructure revolution under the early Pahlavids, even though it was never fully incorporated into the country's traditional commerce or into the new network of roads that linked the capital to the provinces. Centralization required easy access to the provinces, and a growing number of motorcars offered new roads as an alternative to rail. Already by 1921 there was a network of dirt roads navigable by cars. These were either improved Qajar carriage roads, such as the Tehran-Rasht and Tehran-Qom roads, or were roads inherited from the Allied armies that connected northern and western cities to the capital, or the ports of the Persian Gulf to Shiraz, or cities like Isfahan and Mashhad to their surroundings (see map 8.1). The Pahlavi reliance on motorized logistics to quell the Jangal movement and tribal uprisings in the provinces, especially in Fars and Luristan, soon demonstrated the relatively low cost of road transportation compared to the railroad for moving troops, and soon after the movement of peoples and goods (fig. 8.2).

In 1926 the new Firuzkuh road connected the capital through the Alborz range to Reza Shah's birthplace in Savadkuh. It was followed in 1928 by the opening of the Luristan road across the Zagros range. The former facilitated the development of the north, and the latter signified a desire to pacify the south. In 1933 the new hundred-mile "special" (*makhsus*) road was completed; this third access to the Caspian through the central Alborz was a feat of civil engineering, for it negotiated the high Chalus Pass through tunnels and bridges, halving the

Figure 8.2. In 1916 an omnibus operating between Tabriz and Julfa, on the Russian frontier, was the only means of access to the trans-Russian railroad.
W. Warfield, *The Gate of Asia: A Journey from the Persian Gulf to the Black Sea* (New York and London, 1916), opp. 127.

travel time to the newly developed tourist resorts along the Caspian. For ordinary Iranians who were accustomed to the hardships and slow pace of caravan
travel, such triumphs over the rugged Iranian terrain earned the Pahlavi state
awesome prestige (see map 8.1).

By the end of 1930s, the road network of fourteen thousand miles—and along
with it the culture of motorcars, trucks, and buses—had already began to transform the face of Iranian cities and facilitate the demise of the provinces' isolation. For the rugged terrain of the Iranian plateau, roads and motor vehicles
proved as much an agent of change as they were in industrial Europe and the
United States, and despite incredible obstacles. At first, it was mostly Iranian
Armenians and Assyrians or foreign nationals from Russia, Azerbaijan, and Turkey who chauffeured expensive cars for the wealthy, Ford Model Ts, passenger
station wagons of the 1930s, and British-manufactured Leyland trucks. In 1928
Tehran registered 1,099 rental and taxicabs and 490 private cars, in comparison
to 459 horse carriages. All these vehicles were to abide by a traffic code introduced the same year.

Less than two decades after the introduction of mass-produced cars in the
United States—which was manufacturing 80 percent of motorcars in the
world—Iranians, like people across Asia and the Middle East, adopted cars,
created makeshift city and intercity transportation services, and hauled agricultural and semi-industrial goods to urban markets. With motor vehicles there
emerged a homegrown industry of repair and the manufacture of spare parts,
dominated by the technologically savvy Armenians. As in the Safavid and Qajar periods, the Armenians of the postconstitutional and early Pahlavi periods,
some of whom had emigrated from the Caucasus or eastern Turkey, contributed more than any other community to Iran's material modernization and
technological culture.

Rapid change was also visible in aviation. As early as 1916, British airplanes
appeared over Iranian skies, first for reconnaissance, and then in 1918, to bomb
remnants of the Kurdish resistance in western Iran. By 1928 the German Junk-
ers had established regular air service in Iran and neighboring lands. By the
early 1930s Iran had developed a viable air force of its own (fig. 8.3).

URBAN DEMOLITION AND CONSTRUCTION

No other modern invention changed the face of Iranian cities as the motor-
car did. This was the most visible impact of American mass culture on Iran's
traditional cities. As early as 1921, the Pahlavi municipalities accelerated the
overhaul of the late Qajar-era city administration, improving urban sanitation

Figure 8.3. An advertisement in the first tourist guidebook on
Iran identifies ten destinations.
Guide Book on Persia, ed. Gh. H. Ebtehaj (Tehran, 1933), endpaper.

and establishing regular garbage collection, centralized telephone and electricity networks, street lighting, and police precincts. By the early 1930s the most visible impact was the new thoroughfares for motor vehicle traffic, first along the newly developed northern edge of the capital and then right through the heart of the old neighborhoods.

Rebuilding and beautifying the capital and improving its sanitation were major priorities for the Pahlavi state, as well as a material projection of its power. Beyond functionality, which in the main meant removal of heaps of garbage and eliminating neighborhood *luti* street gangs, orderliness imbued a sense of power and confidence, which was conspicuously tied up with displays of Western-style progress. Urban advancement, often thinly concealing a sense of inferiority toward the West, was dressed up with broad avenues and the ever-present statue of the shah in public squares. It was no surprise, therefore, that for most of the Reza Shah era, the replication of European city planning and street grids was presided over by a senior army officer and Reza Shah's former Cossack colleague, Karim Aqa Buzarjomehri. As mayor of Tehran, Buzarjomehri lumped together military-style doggedness with a crude version of Baron Haussmann city planning, so as to implant in the capital, or impose upon it, an image of Pahlavi grandeur.

With vengeance he unleashed throughout the neighborhoods of old Tehran an army of immigrant laborers, superimposing on the centuries-old slow and undisciplined Qajar urban growth a grid of parallel avenues and streets. In the process he destroyed the old fabric of city neighborhoods, demolished their urban symbols, and forever ruined Tehran's delicate character of a walled city surrounded by gardens and green spaces at the southern slopes of the Alborz range. According to one count at the turn of the twentieth century, there were at least twenty-four major Persian gardens in and around Tehran, nearly all of which fell victim to urban growth and construction booms over a period of half a century.

As the novelist Bozorg 'Alavi put it, it was as if Pahlavi modernity could not be brought into the capital without first destroying all twelve city gates built in the Naseri era. The bazaar neighborhood was cut through with a characterless broad street, bisecting the old business and economic center. It was appropriately named after the mayor himself. The adjacent Sangelaj neighborhood, important as a center of activity during the Constitutional Revolution, was emptied of its inhabitants and completely razed to ground to provide space for a Western-style city park. As European-style residential and commercial buildings went up in northern Tehran, often replacing the grand old houses in Persian or Perso-European style or replacing barren land, old gardens, and agricultural plots, the older neighborhoods fell into disrepair and eventually housed the urban poor and new immigrants. In the short period between 1921 and 1941, the face of Tehran substantially changed: avenues and cars replaced narrow alleys and horse carriages; new neighborhoods of modern houses were constructed, often in the Western style but built with traditional Persian construction materials.

From the late 1920s, Tehran witnessed the construction of a number of grand public buildings. Among the earliest was Rolleston Hall of the Alborz American Presbyterian College, completed in 1927, and the Tehran central post office, completed in 1934, both designed by the Georgian architect Nikolai Markov (1882–1957) and inspired by Persian architecture of the Islamic era. The Iran Bastan Museum and the National Library of Iran, both completed in 1937, were designed by André Godard (1881–1965)—a French architect and director of Iran's Archeological Service under Reza Shah—in a tasteful style inspired by Sasanian architecture. From 1934 to 1941 a mixed group of European and Iranian architects oversaw the construction of the campus of Tehran University. Yet other public buildings, such as national police headquarters, completed in 1935, and the National Bank of Iran, completed in 1938, were examples of an architectural archaism then in vogue. These buildings were inspired by the ancient Persian colonnade style of Persepolis and employing the Zoroastrian symbol of Ahura Mazda atop Achaemenid-style columns (fig. 8.4).

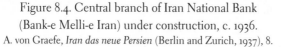

Figure 8.4. Central branch of Iran National Bank
(Bank-e Melli-e Iran) under construction, c. 1936.
A. von Graefe, *Iran das neue Persien* (Berlin and Zurich, 1937), 8.

Most of these public buildings, as well as a chain of luxury hotels on the Caspian's shores, public schools in major Iranian cities, and royal palaces, were designed and constructed under Reza Shah's supervision. He was well aware of the importance of public buildings as physical projections of state authority, just as his Safavid and Qajar predecessors were. The presence of many European and European-educated architects engaging in public projects, though, transformed Iran's architectural style. Plans for most of these public building complied with requisites of modern functional architecture, but they were often clad in a thin veneer of Persian architectural references.

Even the old royal citadel (the Arg) that had developed over a century under the previous dynasty was not spared from the new construction boom. Major buildings of the Qajar complex, including the royal residential quarters, were razed to make room for the Ministry of Justice and later on the Ministry of Finance, and for other government departments. These new structures represented the growth of the state's sprawling bureaucracy. Symbolically and physically they were built in place of the Qajar royal palaces and divan buildings, as if the new regime were anxious to erase traces of the previous dynasty's physical manifestations of kingship and statecraft.

Soon thereafter, and increasingly in the 1940s and 1950s, most provincial centers were also subjected to the forces of Europeanized modernity and with mixed outcomes. Nearly in all towns and cities the walls and city gates were the earliest victims of urban growth. Thereafter the old neighborhoods were gradually demolished or badly segmented by the introduction of the Western grid; many instantly turned into slums. With the coming of Western-style architecture, the existing swirling pathways and gated alleys, local shopping rows, subterranean irrigation network of *qanats*, public reservoirs, ice-making structures, bathhouses, madrasas, takkiyehs, and "houses of strength" (*zurkhanehs*)—where young and old in the neighborhood exercised and fraternized—either demolished or left to become dilapidated. Many old houses with magnificent cooling towers, outer and inner quarters, quadrangles with a refreshing mix of symmetrical gardens surrounding a fresh water pool, fell to disrepair. Many were divided and sold, often replaced by cheap and ugly residential quarters that were shabby imitations of Western modern architecture. Some of the most egregious demolitions of old quarters and historical edifices took place without the slightest alarm in Shiraz, Isfahan, Kashan, and Kerman, wiping out some Safavid, Zand, and Qajar residents.

Yet in Tehran and in the provinces, urban amenities improved in the prosperous neighborhoods, streets and avenues were paved, and rows of trees appeared along the newly constructed avenues. New shops and small shopping centers offering Western imports served the more affluent middle classes, and European-style hotels and restaurants popped up. An inevitable Pahlavi Avenue in every major city, a symbol of order, cleanliness, and security, was a contrast in the eyes of citizens with the crooked, dark, and unsafe alleys of the old neighborhoods (pl. 8.1).

ECONOMY AND INDUSTRY

The centralizing economy of the early Pahlavi era was characterized by the state's intervention in finance, modern banking, trade, and industrialization. Some of the state's initiatives echoed aspirations of the constitutional period, and others in the 1920s and 1930s were modeled on the economic policies of the neighboring Soviet Union and the Republic of Turkey. Thanks to the growing population, urbanization, greater consumption, and new sources of revenue—including royalties from the Anglo-Persian Oil Company—the economy grew in size and diversified. The overhauling of state finances and the state's investments in infrastructure and industry were in contrast to the noninterventionist, and chronically bankrupt, economy of the Qajar state.

The population growth was particularly remarkable. In 1921 the population of Iran was estimated to be slightly above 11 million, with less than 1 percent annual growth; by 1941 the first official census placed the total population at 14,760,000. The annual population increase of about 1.5 percent for the two decades of Reza Shah's rule resulted in part from lower infant mortality but also from fewer outbreaks of cholera and typhus. Urban growth was particularly notable, with the population of Tehran in 1941 for the first time exceeding 500,000; Isfahan, 200,000; and Shiraz, less than 130,000. Between 1929 and 1941, the state budget also grew more than eleven-fold, from 31 million tumans income and 34 million tumans expenditure to more than 361 million tumans income and 432 million tumans projected expenditure.

Old patterns persisted especially in the countryside. The economy remained essentially agrarian, with no major changes in landownership or mechanization, while the pastoral nomadic economy remained at a standstill or took a turn for the worse. The bazaar began to lose its age-old grip on commerce and manufacturing, resulting in the decline of the traditional mercantile sector, and this in turn hindered the growth of a capitalist bourgeoisie in the bazaar. The global economic depression and collapse of the financial markets in the United States, and subsequently in Europe, also had dire repercussions in Iran, as in the rest of the world, leading to rampant bankruptcies in the 1920s and 1930s among the cash-strapped and credit-laden bazaar merchants. Unemployment rates also rose in the traditional sectors that relied on workshop weaving and carpet industries and on small-scale imports and exports. The slow recovery of the Soviet economy also contributed to Iran's recession, as much of the Iranian network in Baku, Tiflis, Ashgabat, and Tashkent had perished during the Stalin era due to confiscation, forced repatriation, and economic hardship.

The arrested growth of the private sector, the widening gap between living standards in the city versus the countryside, and the rise of the state's reliance on independent income through monopolies on commodities and oil revenue were the most significant legacies of the first Pahlavi era. While the state became less dependent on its citizens and the meager revenue it could extract through taxation, it sped up military and police spending to safeguard the increasingly unpopular regime. To maintain its presence in nearly all economic sectors meant that the state should become the largest employer in the country by far. These patterns persisted through the whole of the Pahlavi era and beyond, with few exceptions—a curse on the modern Iranian political economy that continues to the present. Like other state-run economies, the early Pahlavi period also proved increasingly inefficient, another legacy handed down through the decades.

Centralizing and modernizing state finances was the Pahlavi regime's first priority. The Shuster mission in the constitutional period and later British and other European administrators employed by the Iranian government had partially reformed the state's financial machinery and helped increase public revenue despite domestic and foreign opposition. In 1922 the Iranian government employed Dr. Arthur Millspaugh (1883–1955), a former adviser to the US State Department's Office of Foreign Trade, and his team of American financial experts to update Iran's finances and generate greater state revenue, especially through taxation of the tribal territories. Employing Millspaugh was a gesture of defiance in the face of the bitter memory of the 1911 ultimatum and Shuster's forced departure. Over the course of nearly five years as treasurer general, Millspaugh tried with some success to apply the American model of internal revenue collection while the British war subsidy was being phased out, as well as to rationalize fiscal policies, produce detailed annual budgets with set goals for incomes and expenditures, and reduce inefficiency and influence peddling.

The relative success of the Millspaugh mission helped consolidate the Pahlavi state at a critical juncture. The still-minuscule 16 percent royalties from production and export of Iranian oil that began to trickle in—after a great deal of postwar altercations and in the face of Anglo-Persian Oil Company's disingenuous accounting practices—was a vital shot in the arm, but it was not sufficient. Even though Millspaugh contemplated increasing income through monopolies, he resisted direct state intervention in the market. Yet a greater challenge for Millspaugh was Reza Shah and his ministers' desire to increase military expenditures through, among other ways, exclusive allocation of the oil royalties, which the American adviser resisted. Under pressure from the shah, in June 1927 Millspaugh resigned, giving way to swift implementation of a series of measures that reshaped Iran's economic future.

By 1928 the oil revenue reserve had reached six million tumans (US$3,518,000), a hefty sum that was meant to be devoted to economic development but was instead appropriated by the state to consolidate the military and pay for the growing bureaucracy. The sugar monopoly was imposed in 1927 to pay for the construction of the railroad, followed in 1929 by a monopoly on the sale and export of opium, and thereafter on tobacco and other commodities. As a sign of the changing times, control of the commercial markets faced no resistance from the bazaar, in stark contrast to the Tobacco Protest of 1891–1892 or the protests against government price controls on the eve of the Constitutional Revolution. This was another cause of the bazaar's reluctance to abandon the small-scale patterns of patronage and networking in favor of investment in modern financial and industrial sectors. A weakened bazaar and the relative worsening of the affairs of the bazaar merchants meant that the middle and lower ranks of traders and guilds suffered. The ensuing growth of conservatism in the bazaar surfaced in a firmer alliance with the conservative clergy, the other losing sector in Pahlavi society.

The new banking network further strengthened the state's hold over the market at the expense of the bazaar. By the end of the Reza Shah era, at least four major Iranian banks were operating: the National Bank, the Pahlavi Bank for army veterans (Bank Sepah), the Mortgage Bank, and the Agricultural Bank. They partially replaced not only the old moneylending institutions of the bazaar and their system of promissory notes and pledges, but also the small-scale financial networks that had been in operation since the late Qajar era, such as the Armenian Tumanian Brothers, who had branches in Iranian cities and partners in European capitals, and the Zoroastrian banking houses. Fulfilling one of the earliest demands of the constitutional period, in 1928 the National Bank of Iran (Bank Melli Iran) was established, with initial capital of two million tumans (approximately $1,172,000) that only partially was paid. It was envisioned in the Banking Act of 1927 as an institution to promote commerce, agriculture, and industry; in practice, it functioned more as the central bank.

Employing German expertise, the National Bank soon replaced the British-owned Imperial Bank of Persia in the issuing of Iranian currency. For the first time since the 1880s the portrait of Naser al-Din Shah on the banknotes was replaced with a portrait of Reza Shah, ending nearly half a century of the Imperial Bank's monopoly. This was followed in 1932 by a change in the name of the unit of currency from the old *qeran* and tuman of the Qajar era to the new rial, mostly a symbolic move to reflect the nationalist resolve to break with the Qajar memory.

Banking became an integral part of Iran's modern commerce, mostly conducted with European countries. Britain, Russia, and increasingly Germany were main partners in state-dominated trade. Between 1928 and 1939 the total volume of Iranian imports grew more than 250 percent, whereas the volume of non-oil exports remained stagnant, an indication of Iran's growing dependency on foreign imports. The widening deficit in Iran's balance sheets had to be paid off by a steady increase in oil exports, of which only a fraction reached the state's coffers. During the same period, the volume of oil exports nearly doubled. The Iranian royalties from oil production constituted about 25 percent of the state's annual revenue during the same period. By 1940, they amounted to $19,150,000. Reliance on royalties thus anticipated a long-term pattern in

Iranian finances as the state became addicted to oil revenue to finance its needs and less accountable to its citizens.

The Pahlavi initiative to pioneer large-scale industrialization was another outgrowth of the state's centralizing mission (see map 8.1). The textile mills, part of any early industrializing project, developed especially in Mazandaran province on or near Reza Shah's vast private estate. His estate almost entirely was appropriated by force from large landholders and petty sharecroppers. He also allocated plots of appropriated land to senior army officers and officials whom he favored. Several state-run textile mills in Shahi, Tabriz, Isfahan, and Tehran produced a variety of consumer and specialized fabrics to meet domestic demands. These had been preceded by privately owned mills earlier in the century in Isfahan and Qom, but they were crucial for training a skilled workforce. The cement factories, sugar refineries, and power plants were other sectors of Iran's infant modern industries. Aspiring to revive Iran's traditional textile industry and handicrafts, the early Pahlavi state aimed for self-sufficiency. A textile mill in Chalus in Mazandaran used local silk to produce fine silk clothes. It harkened back to the Safavid memory of silk production in Gilan, even though like other state-run projects, soon after Reza Shah, it fell on bad times and closed down.

Carpet production also received a new lease of life in the early Pahlavi era. As an important item of export and representative of Iran's handicraft industry, the promotion of carpets became a source of national pride. Production of Persian handmade rugs and carpets reached a semi-industrial level as early as the 1870s, when Iranian merchants as well as European and American firms began to invest in the production and export of Persian carpets to Western Europe, Russia, the Ottoman Empire, and the United States, where demands were on the rise. Carpet workshops of different capacities, some having tens of carpet looms and employing up to a hundred weavers, began to appear in Tabriz, Kerman, Kashan, Sultanabad, Isfahan, and Hamadan (see map 8.1). As early as 1874 in some 150 villages around Sultanabad (today's Arak), for example, at least five thousand looms were manufacturing carpets and employing as many as ten thousand weavers.

By the turn of the twentieth century, firms such as Ziegler, Oriental Carpet Manufacturers, and Castelli Brothers independently, or in collaboration with Iranian carpet manufacturers and exporters, developed new designs and color schemes suitable to the Western market. By 1914 Ziegler and Oriental Carpet had invested at least £400,000 ($1,755,000) in Iran's carpet industry. The high volume of exports boosted Iran's status as the biggest and finest supplier of handmade carpets throughout the world. The highly appreciated Persian carpet became a requisite luxury item during the Gilded Age in America and was part of the opulent home decor during the Belle Époque when Persian carpets became Iran's most closely identified artifact. By 1914 the total exports of Persian carpets had risen to about £1 million ($4,930,000), and exported via Tabriz-Trabzon or through Persian Gulf ports.

Growth of the carpet industry transformed the Iranian textile industry and quickly replaced the declining silk and cotton handlooms. Some of the carpet designs were reminiscent of carpets manufactured in the Safavid royal workshops. Most, however, were designs indigenous to various urban, rural, and tribal regions; others were inspired by designs of shawls and other silk fabrics, the production of which were no longer economically viable. Patterns of the Kerman shawl, in particular, were adopted for the high-quality Kerman carpets, even though traces of European tapestry designs, such as millefleur, were not rare. With remarkable versatility, master designers in Kerman, Tabriz, Kashan, and elsewhere came up with novel ways to meet the demands of the export and domestic markets while at the same time trying to preserve the integrity of authentic patterns and color schemes.

Transformative though carpet production was for the Iranian economy, it barely propelled the country forward into an industrial age. More tribal and semitribal regions were incorporated into the production processes. High-quality wool and natural dyes were essential items supplied by nomadic herders from around the carpet-producing centers. The workforce largely consisted of women and young children, whose small hands were suitable for producing very fine carpets with a high number of knots and complex designs.

The early Pahlavi era witnessed a greater awareness of the carpet as a national heritage worthy of protection and improvement. The state-owned Iran Carpet Company aimed to improve carpet design and quality and to introduce standardization. Yet throughout the 1920s and 1930s carpet production continued to follow the demands of the international and domestic markets rather than complying with government standards. Even the working conditions for most of the workforce did not substantially improve. Child labor, dark and dusty workshops, exploitative wages, and long hours continued to undermine the industry up to the end of the twentieth century (fig. 8.5). The quality, too, was later compromised. The shift to affordable synthetic dyes, inferior wool, designs reproduced en masse, and bastardized techniques plagued commercial carpet production. Yet throughout the latter half of the twentieth century, still a considerable number of high-quality pieces were manufactured all over Iran. Despite a gradual change in consumer taste, especially in the American market, solid demand for Persian carpets continued to make it the second-largest export, after oil, all through the period and a major employer in Iran.

Figure 8.5. Carpet manufacturing workshop in Tabriz.
A. von Graefe, *Iran das neue Persien* (Berlin and Zurich, 1937), 47.

Workers in industrial sectors, together with workers in the carpet industry, the oil fields, and the service industries, would form the core of the working class. In the postwar era this workforce began to organize itself into unions. Often in close partnership with the Tudeh Party these unions called for higher wages and better working conditions. In the private sector, except for a few textile mills, there was little large-scale industrial investment, which in turn meant that most of the industrial workers up to the 1940s were state employees. The early Pahlavi administration offered housing and other benefits to workers and their families, even though it kept wages low and discouraged unionization. The high inflation of the postwar era wiped out much of the workers' job security, adding to the discontent and radicalization of labor.

PUBLIC EDUCATION AND THE RISE
OF A PROFESSIONAL CLASS

More than the army, economy, or infrastructure, the growth of public education shaped Pahlavi society and its nationalist culture. Between 1921 and 1941 state-run public schools grew by more than fifty times, and the budget for education increased by nearly two hundred times. In 1901 there were only 17 all-male modern primary schools and a single high school; by 1924 there were 638 and 86, respectively, and by 1940, there were 2,331 and 321. Although the literacy rate increased only meagerly from an estimated 5 percent in the 1900s to nearly 15 percent in the 1940s—a malady only partially remedied in the postwar era—the growth was tangible among the urban population, laying the foundation for a middle class that would staff the army and bureaucracy and create the core of Iran's professional sector for the coming decades.

The state's emphasis on education, evident from the outset of Pahlavi rule, was the outcome of the modernizing project of the late Qajar period and the constitutional era. Like the Ottomans and Egyptians, but at a somewhat slower pace, the Iranians adopted a primarily French model that stressed public education as key to the state's social engineering and mission to shape its citizens' outlooks and mores. Primary schools first established in 1887 in Tabriz by Mirza Hasan Tabrizi, better known as Roshdiyeh (1851–1944), the aforementioned educator who prior to coming to Tabriz had taught in Iravan. He produced the earliest modern pedagogical tract in Azarbaijani Turkish. These schools grew in the late 1890s under the aegis of 'Ali Khan Amin al-Dowleh and were prototypes for primary schools of the constitutional period (fig. 8.6). As early as the early 1900s, the reform-minded Yahya Dowlatabadi also established a modern school for girls of the sayyed lineage. Though from the middle decades of the nineteenth century missionary schools were active in the capital and provinces, among them American Presbyterian schools in Oromiyeh and Tehran, and soon after the Alliance Israélite Universelle, it was only after the Constitutional Revolution that they were allowed to admit Muslim pupils. The American Alborz College in Tehran, established in the 1870s, came to be an institution of higher education that during the long tenure of Samuel M. Jordan (1871–1952), from 1899 to 1940, strived to adopt the American liberal arts model (with a Presbyterian bent) to the Iranian environment. As in the rest of the Middle East, the missionary schools in Iran for boys and girls not only contributed to the education of the new elite but also provided an organizational and curricular model for private community schools.

In the aftermath of the Constitutional Revolution, the Baha'i schools in Tehran and the provinces also offered rigorous curricula for pupils of all religions, ethnicities, and classes. Adopting a mix of Persian and American methods, the flagship Tarbiyat School in Tehran—and others in cities with sizable Baha'i communities—tried to forge an Iranian identity through the study of Persian literature and history. They were open to Western innovations while avoiding

Figure 8.6. Roshdiyeh boys' school celebrating its second year. The message on the
blackboard complains of the eleven-thousand-tuman school fund being squandered.
Postcard, c. 1898. Private collection.

both the cultural alienation of missionary schools and the conservatism typical
of madrasa education. Even before the missionary and community schools, the
Baha'i schools were the first victims of the government's nationalization of education. Their closure in the late 1930s at least in part was tainted with growing
anti-Baha'i propaganda.

From the mid-1920s, with the growth of state-run schools, a standardized
curriculum, and a highly regimented pedagogical outlook came to dominate
Iranian public education. The state system bore stigmas of Pahlavi authoritarianism: a cumbersome bureaucracy, inadequate funding, unimaginative pedagogy, and cruel punishments. Introducing reading, writing and arithmetic at
the primary level and sciences at the high school level, modern schools operated on an entirely different plane from that of the customary *maktabs* (often
rendered in English rather inaccurately as "Koranic schools") and madrasas.
The new program of study at regular hours during an academic calendar, a
twelve-grade system with a set curriculum, class periods, textbooks, uniforms, a
grading system, and examinations—all were governed by a hierarchy of teachers, school principals, and centralized administrators. It was a new system with
many shortcomings that had to adapt to the realities of a changing society with
a short period of two decades.

The schoolchildren who learned geography, history, and Persian literature as well as modern sciences internalized a different perspective of the world from that of their parents, one that gave prominence to secular knowledge and material progress. Yet the shift from instructing elites to a system of public education, part of a trend that revolutionized literacy worldwide, often reinforced uncritical learning. It rewarded uniformity and obedience and punished imagination and diversity. The prevailing pedagogical culture, to the extent perceived by its framers, militated against the body of knowledge in the sciences and humanities that was supposed to open intellectual horizons and change worldviews. Modern sciences in particular augmented Western achievements and were considered key to future material success both individually and collectively. Humanities, in contrast, instilled a spirit of Iranian nationalism that glorified the distant past, especially the pre-Islamic imperial past, at the expense of the more relevant recent past, which often was labeled "decadent" and "corrupt." It promoted a canonized body of Persian high literature and a standardized Persian language that significantly improved average students' language skills but played down Iran's regional and ethnic diversity. The study of geography, too, emphasized national harmony, homogeneity, and territorial integrity. The subtext for the entire design of modern education thus was to promote the place of a powerful state as the embodiment of an awakened nation, a new positivist spirit that called to duty the new generation of educated Iranians as soldiers for reconstructing a modern and secular Iran. Conspicuously left out of this nation-building project, except for the bare minimum, was Iran's Islamic, and more specifically its Shi'i, identity.

Yet pedagogical blind spots aside, public education under Reza Shah made impressive gains. Its system of primary schools, high schools, and vocational schools helped train a new workforce. Despite its relatively humble beginnings, these institutions served as the engine of economic progress and were the marker of social status and political advancement. Most students in the schools' early years were children of government employees, army officers, landowners, small and large business owners, proprietors of new street businesses and members of traditional middle classes, including bazaar merchants and even the upper-ranking ulama. For a disproportionate number of students from religious minorities—Baha'is, Zoroastrians, Jews, Armenians, and Assyrians—modern education served as a social ladder to improve their economic lot and social status. For children of tribal chiefs and provincial notables, too, education served as a threshold of access to the centralized state and a means of stabilizing their otherwise diminishing local influence.

Established in 1934, Tehran University was the pinnacle of Pahlavi higher education. Incorporating a number of professional state schools, it educated generations of lawyers, medical doctors (and other medical professions), engineers, and scientists, as well as scholars of humanities, architecture, fine arts, and social sciences. In the postwar era it also became a hotbed of political dissent and a core for antiregime protests and rallies. All shades of political opposition, from Marxist to nationalist to Islamic, were present among the students and the faculty. Higher education became inseparable from the Iranian political dissent.

Typical of the reforms of the Pahlavi era, the rise of Tehran University became synonymous with the mindless ruination of Dar al-Fonun, which was established eighty-three years earlier. Even before receiving its deathblow at the hands of Reza Shah's educational bureaucrats, in the postconstitutional era, Dar al-Fonun had already fallen by the wayside. As with other symbols of Qajar material culture, Dar al-Fonun was also deemed unfit by the artless Pahlavi modernists. By the early 1920s having been starved of funds and fallen into disrepair, it was demoted to a high school. Some of its old buildings were demolished to give way to the ugly architecture of Ministry of Post and Telegraph. Some of the teaching staff was reassigned to Tehran University, and the remainder were sent off to teach in high schools.

The demise of Dar al-Fonun was also hastened by new educational possibilities abroad. By the turn of the twentieth century, when the informal ban on travel aboard enforced during the Naseri period was lifted, an increasing number of students of the elite, and occasionally the nonelite, found their ways to schools, colleges, and universities in Lebanon (the American University of Beirut a favorite destination), then increasingly to France, Switzerland, imperial Russia, and later Germany. Far fewer opted for England or the United States. By the mid-1920s a state-run program selected the cream of the crop among Iranian high school graduates and dispatched them mostly to French and later to German universities and polytechnics. Upon their return, they were employed as faculty of Tehran University or held high government posts.

'Ali Akbar Siyasi (1896–1990), a Sorbonne-educated professor of psychology whose 1930 dissertation on the theme of Iranian cultural contacts with Europe won him an award from the French Academy, was a notable example. A year after his return to Iran, he founded the Iran-e Javan (Young Iran) club, a cultural society favored by many of the Pahlavi educational elite and cultural reforms who found it a venue at a safe distance from state intervention. He was also a central figure in the framing of Tehran University's charter and was for many years the university's rector. His administrative skills and academic rigor characterized many of his French-educated cohorts among the first generation of Iranian students abroad. Whereas most French graduates who came to dominate Iranian higher education remained loyal to the post–World War II nationalist cause, the Iranian graduates of the German system often tilted toward the left and were influential in shaping of the Tudeh Party and other independent socialist tendencies.

By the mid-1930s the Pahlavi administration had gained enough confidence, though barely operational sophistication, to take over most private-run missionary schools and try to further regulate the educational system—a move concurrent with the introduction of a new dress code, restrictions on religious madrasas, and a ban on some Shi'i mourning rituals. With high demand for graduates in government offices, the military, industries, and the private sector, there were new incentives for the lower middle classes—shopkeepers, the bazaar middlemen, urban émigrés, seminarians who abandoned the madrasa, and even motivated village boys—to enter public schools. In 1941 the 3.3 million urban Iranians—22 percent of the total population of nearly 15 million—received close to 90 percent of the educational budget of 155 million rials. They were mostly boys. Only in the capital and in larger cities, and among the upper middle classes, was there a desire to educate girls. These represented meager strides that state modernization had made in a still firmly patriarchal society.

The old *maktab* system was no match for public schooling and thus was doomed to disappear in the larger cities. Everything worked against it: the informal surroundings, haphazard attendance, almost no curriculum, and arcane textbooks, if any. The teachers often were low-rank mullahs with rudimentary training but a reputation for ferocity. Memories of former pupils who later became Pahlavi-style modernists described frequent caning, thrashing, and bastinado as the norm. As elsewhere, including Europe, corporal punishment in the *maktab* was seen as a character-building exercise. The historian Ahmad Kasravi, who like many of his contemporaries started at the *maktab*, recounts in his memoirs a *maktab* teacher who would hit the heads of innocent pupils with long canes of weeping-willow branches for no apparent reason. No other memoirist of the period reserved any cherished memories of the *maktab*.

The hierarchy of harassment that was thus implanted in the hearts and minds of *maktab* pupils became lifelong baggage that could not easily be cast aside. The state public schools successfully blended the legacy of *maktab* cruelty with the accepted severity of European pedagogy the same way they adopted the *maktab* memorization practices into uncritical adaption of the Western curriculum. Yet despite the obvious inadequacies of the *maktab* and the madrasa, the inclusion of such texts as Sa'di's *Golestan*, passages from the Qur'an, the utterly impenetrable *Sarf-e Mir* in Arabic grammar and syntax, and *Jami' al-Muqaddimat*, a compendium of rudimentary logic, did nurture a level of Perso-Arabic erudition that was largely missing from modern schools.

Such texts as the thirteenth-century *Nisab al-Sibyan* (children's handbook), a long poem of two hundred verses to be memorized by young schoolchildren (even as late as the 1930s), probably was among the most influential in the Persian language. Essentially an Arabic-Persian vocabulary list in verse, this incredibly dull and impenetrable text instructed schoolchildren in the rudiments of both languages as well as in complex poetic meter; names of Prophet Mohammad, his offspring, and his wives; names of the Shi'i Imams; chapters of the Qur'an; calendrics and basic astronomy; names of musical modes; names of animals and properties of horses, camels, and sheep; names of various metals; as well as recipes for ink making and details on how to select a reed pen. Such a mélange of medieval erudition must have perplexed even educated adults in thirteenth-century Herat, where it was composed, let alone young pupils in the twentieth-century Iranian *maktab*.

In contrast, the modern school curriculum entailed a paradigmatic shift from an overtly Shi'i identity expressed in Arabic to a rarefied Iranian cultural identity manifest in Persian. In addition to elevating standardized Persian to a superior status, the new education oversaw the establishment of a Persian literary canon and a historical narrative. Emphasis on the luminous Persian heritage in the textbooks, as in higher education, public media, and state propaganda, as well as celebrating memories of classical poets, and attempts to "purify" the language of its past "pollutants," were all part of a cultural project with parallels in the neighboring lands.

REFASHIONING A CULTURAL IDENTITY

By the turn of the twentieth century the Persian language and Persianate culture, which had once spread as far as Bengal in the easternmost corner of the Indian subcontinent to the outer edges of Central Asia, and was an important part of the high culture of both the Mughal and the Ottoman worlds, became largely confined to Iran's geographical boundaries. In Afghanistan, where it was known as Dari, and in Tajikistan, where it was called Tajik, the Persian language faced new and debilitating challenges. By the late 1940s Persianate culture in the rest of the region had been orphaned, if not entirely lost, in the collective memory, often the victim of exclusive cultural nationalisms and their accompanying educational apparatus.

Cultural nationalism was the order of the day as much outside Iran as it was inside. The state sponsorship of Persian high culture, inevitable though it may have seemed since the time of the Constitutional Revolution, came at the cost of ignoring, or actively suppressing, a plethora of languages and dialects throughout Iran, along with their associated regional cultures and folklores. Equally prevalent was an obsession with "purifying" Persian of its foreign words—from Arabic, Turkish, and Mongolian—as relics of what was considered an alien and embarrassing past. In both respects, the Pahlavi state and its cultural officialdom held a vital stake in standardizing Persian and pushing for purification of the language. Elevating Persian to Iran's national language, often at the expense of the regional languages of the periphery, served to homogenize the Iranian population through education, press, and the media.

In the early twentieth century speakers of Azerbaijani Turkish, about 20 percent of the total population, and Kurdish (the three dialects of Kormanji, Sorani, and Gorani), about 10 percent of the population, accounted for nearly one-third of the people of Iran. Speakers of Gilaki and Mazandarani dialects, Luri dialects of Western Iran, Baluchi of the southeast, the Arabic dialect of Khuzestan, Turkic of eastern Iran, and other dialects together accounted for another 20 percent of the population. Although they dominated the geographical periphery, these languages and dialects were in the main within the family of Iranian languages and coexisted with Persian as language of state and high literature. This was a powerful tool in the hand of the Persian-speaking cultural elite not to encourage regional vernaculars. From Tehran's standpoint, the inclusion of vernaculars in the school curriculum was tantamount to acceding to demands for political autonomy or even secession. The centralizing project of the state and its pacification policies also revealed such fears.

Highlighting the resilience of Persian against historical odds—and its roots in the pre-Islamic Pahlavi language of the Sasanian period and the ancient Persian of the Achaemenid Empire—was another tool of the Pahlavi state. After all, the very name of the new dynasty implied—and in the mind of Reza Shah, himself a Mazandarani, affirmed—an ancient connection ethnically as well as linguistically. This tracing of Persian to ancient times went hand in hand with renewed interest in Zoroastrianism as the indigenous religion of an "authentic" past, and archeology further buttressed such claims (fig. 8.7).

In particular, works of the acclaimed German archaeologist and philologist Ernst Emil Herzfeld (1879–1948) greatly contributed to a better understanding of pre-Islamic Iran in the broader context of Middle Eastern civilizations of the period. One of the greatest archeologists of his time, Herzfeld, throughout the 1920s and up to 1934, excavated the first Achaemenid capital, Pazargadae, and later Persepolis, as well as Sasanian Ctesiphon in Iraq. Although the rise of Nazi Germany seriously disrupted Herzfeld's academic career—he was forced

Figure 8.7. French archaeological excavation in Shush, site of the
ancient city of Susa in upper Khuzestan. Excavating Iran's
pre-Islamic past contributed to the nationalist narrative.
A. von Graefe, *Iran das neue Persien* (Berlin and Zurich, 1937), 60.

to retire from his prestigious post for being of Jewish descent—he was able to
continue writing on Zoroastrianism and on aspects of Iranian past while taking residence in the United States. In his many years of residence in Iran, he
was instrumental in raising awareness about Iran's pre-Islamic heritage among
officials in charge of cultural affairs and scholars alike. Despite rivalries with
French archeological mission, which held a monopoly over excavation in
Persepolis and Shush, and quarrels with André Godard, the director of the Iranian archeological service, Herzfeld influence loomed large, comparable only
to Edward Browne a generation earlier.

Iranian cultural archaism and the coining of "pure" Persian words, in part
a legacy of archaeology, were never as severe as critics often alleged. Very few
of the linguistic atrocities that ravaged Turkish, Hindi, or even Tajik (the latter
adopted the Cyrillic alphabet thanks to Soviet cultural hegemony), succeeded
in taking root even at the height of Reza Shah. The measured reforms introduced by an influential cultural circle tangibly improved the quality of written
and spoken Persian and its adaptability to new education, press and media, and
scientific needs. Discouraging the use of quaint Persian words; coining new
terminology for foreign terms, ideas, institutions, and new technologies; and

standardizing Persian grammar and syntax proved essential for modern education and for society's emerging needs.

The Farhangestan-e Iran (Iran Abode of Culture), founded in 1935, similar to the Académie Française, helped supervise the development and reform of the Persian language. It promised a balanced approach to language reform and a consistent response to the "crisis" of neologisms. In addition, the new institution was mandated with regulating methods of teaching Persian and with standardizing grammar, facilitating the production of dictionaries and other reference works, collecting the folklore of Iran, enlightening the public about the true meaning of literature, and encouraging new literary talents. The twenty-four members, including distinguished cultural figures of the time, were led by one of the most influential figures of the Pahlavi era, Mohammad 'Ali Forughi. Over the course of six years, Farhangestan proposed Persian equivalents to Arabic, Turkish, and French terms that found public acceptance and became part of everyday language of Iranians. Prudently, however, it avoided the sensitive debate about reforming the script, which Farhangestan's constitution had called for.

Concurrent with language reforms was a movement of literary and lexicographical production. Influenced in part by European Orientalist scholarship and in part by traditional Persian biographic dictionaries and lexicographical works, numerous critical editions of classical texts, encyclopedic lexicons, literary histories, and textual commentaries were published throughout the 1920s and 1930s. Close paleographic and bibliographic research unearthed forgotten texts and laid the foundation for a Persian literary canon. In turn, a new cultural and linguistic style was made current through textbooks, the press, literary journals, and later radio broadcasts. Pioneered by intellectuals of the constitutional period, found in scholarship an escape from the suffocating political milieu of the time. Editing a classical text while in exile or while sequestered at home was far safer than venturing into public office and ending in the dungeons of the Pahlavi regime. For people like Forughi, being relegated to the political wilderness at least had the unintended consequence of laying the foundation of modern Persian literary and historical identity.

The aforementioned Mohammad 'Ali Forughi (1877–1942) was typical of this circle of the literati. Coming from a cultural family in the Qajar service, he presided over translation projects, editing, and historical publications even before serving as the first prime minister of Reza Shah (and as it turned out, the last one, who in 1941 negotiated the shah's abdication). He produced, between 1931 and 1941, the first general history of Western philosophy in Persian, a seminal text not only in offering the Iranian reader an insightful treatment of Greek and

Western thought but also in pioneering a technical prose that would become the hallmark of modern Persian scholarship for decades to come. In 1937 he also translated from Arabic into Persian part of a major work by Ibn Sina (Avicenna) dealing with the philosophy of natural sciences. As much as his history of European philosophy accentuated the desirability of understanding in one's mother tongue the West's rich intellectual tradition—in contrast to the often impenetrable Arabic prose of Islamic philosophy—his translation of the section on natural sciences from the Arabic text reflected a positivist perspective that at the same time strove to incorporate the Persian Ibn Sina into the narrative of modern Iranian nationalism. Such a balancing act may also have had in earnest other objectives for it came at a time when the regimented nationalism of the Pahlavi state threatened to undermine Iran's Islamic intellectual heritage. Moreover, Forughi's translation came at a time when the identity of Ibn Sina was being heatedly contested by neighboring nationalisms in Turkey, Central Asia, and the Arab world.

Not surprisingly, for a man as well versed in European and Islamic cultures as in Persian culture, Forughi also produced during his years in the political wilderness a standard edition of the works of the thirteenth-century Sa'di of Shiraz, one of the four "greats" of Persian classical literature. His editing project can be viewed as another cultural statement that aimed to highlight the centrality of Sa'di's prose and poetry to Iran's intellectual reawakening. Sa'di's didactic works, *Golestan* and *Bustan*, could in effect offer a conceptual framework toward a socially tolerant and politically open society. His lyrical odes, along with those of Hafez, promised a liberating worldview very different from the strictures of legalistic Shi'ism. It was as if through the medium of Sa'di's *Divan* or his history of Western philosophy, Forughi intended to promote a blueprint for an Iranian national identity, one that was free of the conservatism of the Shi'i jurists and of oppressive rulers and their blind Westernism.

Preserving Persian at the core of cultural identity is also evident in the lexicographic production of 'Ali Akbar Dehkhoda, who became an avid scholar of the language and popular culture. His ambitious compilation of a multivolume encyclopedic dictionary was not the first in Persian. For centuries, scholars in India, Iran, and elsewhere (including since the eighteenth century in Europe) had produced massive Persian dictionaries. Yet Dehkhoda's effort stood out to his Iranian contemporaries as a monumental attempt to preserve a literary tradition, beyond mere words and expressions. Completed posthumously, the *Loghat-nameh* of Dehkhoda is the closest work in Persian to a historical dictionary for it contains extensive poetic and prose citations from classical sources. That in 1946 the fourteenth Majles passed a special bill sponsoring the completion and publication of the *Loghat-nameh* reveals a desire to establish Persian as a component of national sovereignty. Earlier, Dehkhoda's four-volume dictionary of Persian proverbs and aphorisms, *Amsal va Hekam*, an impetus for his dictionary project, was a response to the national desire to preserve people's language and folklore in fast-changing times, something that tied Dakho of the *Sur-e Esrafil* era to the Dehkhoda of *Loghat-nameh*.

Mohammad Taqi Bahar who was of the same generation as Dehkhoda and bore the brunt of Reza Shah's repression, also loomed large on the cultural landscape. His *Sabk-shenasi* (A study of stylistics), published in 1942, was a systematic study of Persian prose over a millennium, tracing its roots to the pre-Islamic Pahlavi and Avestan languages. As professor of Persian literature in the Faculty of Letters and Human Sciences of the newly founded Tehran University, Bahar wrote this study for the doctoral program to stress the versatility of evolving Persian prose in the face of religious encroachment and nomadic invasions. As Iranian intellectuals of Bahar's generation became more familiar with textual studies, philology, and critical methodology of the European Iranists, their awareness of the link between pre-Islamic and Islamic Iran served as the impetus to form a Persian canon. Along with the historian Ahmad Kasravi and a few other Iranian intellectuals, Bahar studied ancient Iranian languages with Ernest Herzfeld.

During World War I and through the early 1920s, the Berlin circle of Iranian intellectuals in exile had already sown the seeds of cultural nationalism. Influenced by cultural trends of the Weimar Republic, Hasan Taqizadeh, who founded the circle, and his cohorts (including the pioneering short-story writer Mohammad 'Ali Jamalzadeh, renewed scholar Mohammad Qazvini, and Ibrahim Purdavud, a specialist in Zoroastrianism and ancient Iranian texts), who mostly were former activists of the constitutional period, experimented with new literary genres and historical interpretations. Witnessing the German defeat and the crises of postwar Germany, Taqizadeh and his colleagues shifted their attention to cultural issues. The Berlin circle's mark on Iran's nationalist culture of the period is well evident in the periodical *Kaveh*, named after the *Shahnameh's* legendary blacksmith who rebelled against the tyranny of Zahhak, hinting, no doubt, at powers who had occupied Iran during World War I. Published between 1916 and 1922 in two series, the biweekly journal gave voice to Iranian anxieties and indignation under occupation. Its barrage of anti-Russian and anti-British articles, some of the most poignant the Iranian readership had seen up to that time, were complemented by in-depth analyses of Iran's geopolitical perils and its economic difficulties, its troubled history of relations with the two powers, and the humiliation of living under occupation.

At the end of the war, *Kaveh* noticeably turned to Persian history, especially European scholarship on ancient Iran, Persian art, calendar and time reckoning — a favorite of Taqizadeh — as well as philology and Persian prose and poetry. A series of articles on the *Shahnameh* and its historical sources by Taqizadeh, among the earliest modern Persian scholarship on the seminal epic, was typical of the journal's focus on Iranian identity and its historical roots and mythical memories. The earliest short stories in the Persian language, authored by Jamalzadeh were first read to the Berlin circle, and some were published in *Kaveh*.

An enduring collections of Persian short stories, Jamalzadeh's *Yaki Bud Yaki Nabud* (once upon a time), first published in 1922, masterfully employed street language, folk expressions and proverbs, and nuances of regional, class, and ethnic parlance to poignantly depict life in the postwar era. In his "Farsi shakar ast" (Persian is sweet), a plain-speaking peasant finds himself in the Anzali customshouse (on the Caspian coast) in a detention cell together with both a Westernized Iranian fresh from Farang whose faulty Persian can barely be understood, and a mullah in traditional garb whose Arabicized Persian is utterly incoherent to others. The terrified peasant, a symbol of average Iranians, cannot understand either of his compatriots' utterances. In desperation he takes refuge with the narrator, another detainee in the jail who is able to communicate with the peasant and share his fears and anxieties. The cultural gulf between the three types in Jamalzadeh's story, and himself as the observer, is an early depiction of the sharpening class differences that were about to emerge in the Pahlavi era.

In another story in the same collection, *Dusti-ye khaleh kherseh* (With friends like that), inspired by Jamalzadeh's own experience during World War I, a humble coffeehouse waiter on his way to Kermanshah rescues a wounded Russian Cossack on the side of the road despite the advice of his fellow travelers, who are suspicious of the wounded solider. Only later, when the travelers reach their destination, the kindhearted waiter falls victim to the treachery of the Cossack, who had eyed his humble savings. Perhaps the most compelling story in the collection, the story of the waiter and the Cossack, symbolized the tragedy of the occupation.

In 1922 when publication of *Kaveh* was coming to an end, Taqizadeh also published in Berlin a number of Persian literary and historical classics, including works of Naser Khosrow, the great eleventh-century Persian Isma'ili dissident poet, traveler, and philosopher. It was as though Naser Khosrow's travelogue was a statement about Taqizadeh's own "turbulent life" (as he later named his memoirs), a life in exile that took him from Berlin to Tehran and back to Europe with many ups and downs. After having served in sensitive ministerial posts under Reza Shah, Taqizadeh was eventually forced into exile in

England, where out of desperation he became an instructor of Persian language at the School of Oriental and African Studies in London. After World War II he returned to Iran to become a deputy in the fifteenth Majles and later the president of the Iranian Senate. In the 1930s, Taqizadeh oversaw the publication in Iran of another series of Persian classical texts, the production of which he assigned to literary figures such as Mohammad Qazvini, an old friend and colleague. Published by Iran's Ministry of Education on the model of European classical text series, they allowed greater access to a rich repository of classical works of history and literature and in turn fostered a tradition of critical Persian editions.

FROM MADRASA TO MODERN ERUDITION

As were with a whole host of figures among Iran's cultural elite of the period, Mohammad Qazvini (1877–1949) was a hybrid scholar between traditional madrasa education and modern Orientalist scholarship. A literary expert, bibliographer, and editor of classical texts, Qazvini held sway over a generation of Iranian literary scholars. He started out as a young seminarian, with a remarkable command of Arabic and a meticulous literary taste for classical Persian. Later he developed an aptitude for the kind of Orientalist discipline that had fascinated him over the thirty-five years he spent in European libraries and manuscript collections. He viewed the mission of Iranian scholars as one of textual studies, critical editing, and a Renaissance-like unearthing of Iranian heritage. Among many works, he coedited with Qasem Ghani the *Divan* of Hafez, which helped reaffirm the poet's place in the Persian literary canon as a favorite bard of nearly all Iranians.

The greatest methodological influence on Qazvini—and a host of his cohorts—was the English Orientalist Edward Granville Browne. Contrary to the stereotypical image of an Orientalist, Browne was an exceptional blend of nineteenth-century romanticism, literary and historical scholarship, and anti-imperialist advocacy. His four-volume *The Literary History of Persia*—written between 1902 and 1924—chronicled a millennium of Persian literature with vigor and originality, setting the field against a panorama of political and cultural developments. His editing and publications, which included important Persian classics, were complemented by his encouragement and support for the likes of Qazvini and Mohammad Iqbal Lahori (1877–1938). It is wrong to assume, however, that the discourse of Orientalism was one-way. The movement to publish texts spearheaded by Browne owed much to a complex interplay between the Orientalist, who was equipped with tools of modern methodology and print culture, and learned scholars from Iran, Hindustan, and elsewhere who had mastered bibliographic and paleographic skills.

Beyond the work of Browne, the narrative of Persian cultural endurance against hostile forces of nomadic invasions and an imposed religion is also evident in new readings of Iran's pre-Islamic past. This Orientalist scholarship and the state's support for new archeological expeditions emphasized the Achaemenid Empire of the sixth to fourth century BCE as Iran's moment of civilizational inception and the Zoroastrianism revival of the Sassanian era in late antiquity as a moment of rebirth. Such reorientation in Iran's historical narrative from traditional historiography in the nineteenth century to modern incorporation of the pre-Islamic past was slow and complex. Beginning in the Qajar era, early accounts such as Jalal al-Din Mirza's *Nameh-e Khosravan* and later Aqa Khan Kermani's *A'ineh-e Sekandari* (Alexandrian mirror), a history of ancient Iran, struggled to bridge the ancient past to the Islamic past by reconciling the *Shahnameh* legends with modern archeology, Greek and Latin texts, and Western scholarship. The Constitutional Revolution and its aftermath further inspired intellectuals to seek a soothing alternative not only in classical Persian literature but also in attention to ancient Iranian past.

Hasan Pirnya's reissued history of ancient Iran, completed in 1933, proved a boost to the Pahlavi state's legitimacy and its claim to the ancient Persian past. Beyond the traditional Persian sources, Iranians for the first time were learning about the might of the Persian empire, its expanse and its conquests, its administrative and civil organizations, and its commercial and cultural exchanges with Greek and Roman worlds through archeology, as well as through ancient Greek, Roman, and Byzantine sources and modern Western scholarship. The vital link that Iran created for more than a millennium between civilizations of the east—China and South Asia in particular and the Mediterranean world— through trade, economy, administration, and culture, and contributions of Zoroastrianism, Manichaeism, and Iranian languages, were reassuring signs of endurance and hope for renewal. The 1934 millennial celebration of Ferdowsi's *Shahnameh*, which brought to Iran scholars from around the world, and the completion of Ferdowsi's mausoleum by Iranian architect Karim Taherzadeh Behzad, which had started in 1928, proved important markers on Iran's map of cultural history.

Public display of cultural symbols and the commemoration of Iranian literary and intellectual icons such as Ferdowsi (and later Ibn Sina), made the Iranian nationalist narrative to gradually trickle down to the level of general public. Even men and women outside the immediate reaches of the state—clerical classes in the mosques and the madrasas, the merchants of the bazaar, and villagers and nomads in remote parts the country—began to adjust to the standard-ized Persian language and the Persian cultural symbols and historical narrative even though some consciously resisted the state's monopoly over what consti-tuted "Iranian" and the homogenizing policies employed to implement it.

Ibrahim Purdavud (1885–1968) can be regarded as a key scholar responsible for incorporating ancient Iranians languages and texts into the Pahlavi nation-alism. Another product of the madrasa, in Rasht, his eventful life took him during the 1910s and 1920s to Lebanon, Paris, Berlin, and Mumbai. His stud-ies over three decades ranged from Shi'i jurisprudence, Arabic grammar, and traditional medicine to the study of law in France and Germany and learn-ing a host of European languages. During World War I he joined the Berlin circle and returned to Kermanshah as an agent provocateur. There he coedited with Jamalzadeh the antioccupation journal *Rastakhiz* (Resurrection). On his return to Berlin, and as part of the nationalist discourse of the Berlin circle during the Weimar years, he was involved in the study of Zoroastrianism and ancient Iranian languages and came to know a number of important German and later French, English, and American Iranists. The experience profoundly transformed Purdavud. He later moved to India, where he collaborated with Parsi scholars to translate *Avesta* from original Avestan into Persian. On his re-turn to Iran in 1937, he was appointed as professor of ancient Iranian languages at Tehran University. In his life and his scholarship, during which he trained generations of students in Tehran University, Purdavud, like Bahar and Ahmad Kasravi, clearly displayed the shift from the activism of the constitutional era to Iranian nationalist discourse of the Pahlavi period.

UNRAVELING AN ANCIENT PACT

Awareness of Zoroastrianism and revival of the ancient Iranian memories incited a challenge to the whole project of Pahlavi secularism on the side of the Shi'i clerical establishment. Even though in the earlier years of Pahlavi rule relations with the ulama classes were relatively amicable and mutually benefi-cial, by the late 1920s and throughout the 1930s a widening rift had begun to occur, with lasting consequences. Even before the rise of Reza Khan, a marked decline was evident in clerical prestige, symbolized by the 1909 execution of Shaykh Fazlollah Nuri. By 1939, a generation later, the introduction of new dress codes and mandatory unveiling culminated the state's success in under-mining the conservative mores and values of the clerical establishment and its loyal following. The secularizing agenda, conceived and enforced largely by the Pahlavi cultural elite and overseen by the shah himself, further eroded an ancient social accord that tied, at least in theory, the "good government" with the "good religion," the "inseparable twins" as they were known to classical authors. This was a principle that had been in operation in one form or another since the Sasanian era, and since the Safavid times had defined sociopolitical norms. The unraveling of this pact, an inevitable outcome of the state's secularizing policies, proved more potent than subduing the tribal countryside or keeping at bay European imperial ambitions. In due course the experiences of the Reza Shah era transformed the Shi'i clerical establishment into a force of political dissent.

Earlier signs of a widening gap between the Pahlavi regime and the clerical class had appeared in 1927, with the compulsory military service for all males, including students of the madrasa. The ulama of Isfahan, who feared that the godless Pahlavi military was brainwashing Muslim youth, called for resistance but rallied little popular support; their appeal quickly withered. Likewise, other reform measures carried out by the state, such as introducing a Westernized dress code for men, deemphasizing and eventually eliminating religious education from schools' curricula, and even the government's greater control over charitable endowments, did not result in mass support in favor of the clergy. The real test, however, came in the 1935 protest in various cities against the compulsory unveiling of women. In Mashhad popular demonstrations led to a bloody scene in the Gowharshad Mosque, adjacent to the shrine of the Eighth Imam, where provocations of Shaykh Mohammad Taqi Bohlul (c. 1900–2005), a low-ranking, rabble-rousing preacher, led to the mob lynching of a government official. In response, security forces indiscriminately opened fire on protesters, killing more than a dozen and injuring a few hundred more. The ominous incident signaled not only the state's audacity in violating the sanctuary of an important mosque but also the ulama's futile objections.

Reza Shah and the Pahlavi elite categorically regarded the clerical establishment and what it stood for as an impediment to progress and sought to reduce it in size and substantially emasculate its influence among the conservative bazaar sector. To further weaken opposition voices among the ulama, the Pahlavi government also adopted a conciliatory course toward moderates. Despite restrictions on preaching in the mosques and donning clerical attire, the state never dismantled the clerical hierarchy or the institution of the madrasa, the *waqf*, and other means of revenue. Remarkably, in the early Pahlavi era although the number of madrasas decreased, Qom acquired greater visibility as a clerical center.

A majority of moderate ulama succumbed to the diminishing status of their class with a mix of resignation and remorse (the latter for not fighting hard enough for Qajar survival). They viewed Reza Shah and Pahlavi modernizing as an inevitable, even a necessary, evil so long as the residue of their clerical power remained in place. Unlike the Sunni clerical institutions in other Muslim lands, which for centuries were under the aegis of the Ottoman state, the Shi'i Iranian ulama had maintained their institutional independence even after the demise of the Qajars. Even if they lost Pahlavi patronage, and the unwritten contract with the state was about to be abrogated, their group solidarity was not entirely lost. As it turned out, the immediate hardships imposed on them added to overall clerical resilience and their rebound after Reza Shah.

Many members of the cultural elite—the influential culture minister 'Ali Asghar Hekmat (1893–1980), the nationalist historian Ahmad Kasravi, and the polemical journalist 'Ali Dashti (1896–1982), for instance—themselves were products of the madrasa and felt a certain affinity with their educational past, especially when faced with the brutish Pahlavi army officers or with the hedonistic conduct of such powerful statesmen as Teymurtash. Yet the Westernizing Pahlavi culture could not help but mock the arcane mentality and demeanor of the clergy. The nationalist narrative, moreover, marginalized, and even belittled, the experience of Iranian Shi'ism as an unfortunate historical aberration, an affliction. To the extent that Shi'ism was incorporated into this national narrative—in school textbooks or state propaganda—the potent Shi'i story was diluted into a facile history of the Imams. Even the role of Shi'ism in the rise of Safavids and as an important element of national identity was downplayed. It was valued, and thus tolerated, for being part of the Iranian identity that set it apart from the Arab and Turkish Sunnis. In this setting, the story of Hosain and Karbala, and the rituals of Moharram, were seen through a modernist prism as embarrassing symptoms of superstitious religiosity.

Most displays of collective rituals were banned: Moharram processions with banners, flags, and other symbols; the recitation of mourning liturgy; performance of *ta'ziyeh* passion plays; the self-punishing acts of chest biting, chain biting, wearing shrouds, inflicting wounds on one's forehead with a saber (*ghameh-zani*), and piercing one's body with spikes and padlocks. Characteristic of its cultural hostility, the Pahlavi state even went on to demolish the magnificent Tekkiyeh-e Dowlat, a visible example of the Qajar tribute to Shi'ism. The destruction of this remarkable structure in the 1930s was replaced, tellingly, with a branch of the Iran National Bank built in a faux Persian style on the aforementioned Bozarjomehri Avenue—a rude reminder, no doubt, to the religiously minded bazaar merchants that the days of ritual Shi'ism were over.

The quiet renouncing of the clergy on the charge of obscurantism further helped debase their public standing. And from the modernist perspective, there was plenty to be critical of: the clergy's outmoded demeanor, their pseudo-Arabicized accent denoting their pride in long years of study in Najaf, their obsession with ritual purity and pollution, and above all their aversion to all things Western. These offered opportunities to the modernist detractors to disparage at least the middle and lower clerical ranks as ignorant, flea-infested, starved mullahs raving for a handout or a session of *rawzeh-khwani*.

More damaging to their public image, however, was a brain drain that sapped the clerical ranks, pulling many into the government bureaucracy and state institutions. The new avenues to prestige, even if they meant a meager but regular source of income, were enticing. A desk job in a government bureaucracy had gained a certain mystique because of the association with government, even though it was often as tedious as cramming the intricate rules of Arabic syntax in the madrasa. Becoming a civil servant, and hence being included in the machinery of government, meant success. Earning degrees in engineering or modern medicine, and engaging in business or teaching in modern schools, also attracted the younger generation, including the children of the ranking clergy, who saw little future for themselves in donning clerical garb when sources of clerical incomes were drying up. Journalism, practicing law, and even politics, and especially opportunities in the reformed judiciary as judges and advocates were all alternatives for the best and the brightest. Above all, however, it was running the government-approved registry offices that provided a safe job: conducting state-regulated marriage and divorce; drawing up official documents, deeds, and contracts; and serving as public notary.

The judicial reforms under Davar, beginning in the winter of 1927 with the temporary dismantling of the existing Ministry of Justice and continuing throughout the Reza Shah era, introduced codified statutes and monitored judicial appointments. These measures diminished the clergy's reach in the judicial sphere and deprived the study of Islamic jurisprudence (*fiqh*) of nearly all its practical applications. The elaborate, though bookish and cumbersome, Shi'i law of contracts (*mo'amelat*) was no longer considered valid, even though the authors of the new statuary laws made ample use of it to adjust the French civil code to Shi'i contingencies. Nor were Shi'i "roots of jurisprudence," a system at the core of the clerical profession, considered the sole source for civil or penal law. More important, interpretation of law and its enforcement were now squarely in the hands of state courts and thus outside the traditional domain of the jurists.

What was left unregulated, however, was the devotional and obligational aspect of the shari'a dealing with purity and pollutants, as well as rules on prayers, fasting, pilgrimage, alms, and other devotional acts. Such aspects, predictably, became the chief preoccupation of the ulama and received ample attention in a new genre of legal manuals known as *tawzih al-masa'el* (explication of legal problems) being catechisms and fatwas in response to real or hypothetical queries. These treatises in due course would become mandatory for leading ayatollahs who were recognized by the community, or who wished to be recognized, as a "source of emulation" (*marja'-e taqlid*).

The judicial reforms under Davar put the final touch on a process that had begun with the Constitutional Revolution. Since the early Qajar era, the rise of the mojtaheds as a powerful interest group effectively barred any codification or universal enforcement of law through regulated courts. In contrast to the Ottoman Empire and Khedivate Egypt, especially after 1882, and Muslim law in colonial India, state intervention in the Qajar period was minimal and ineffective. Despite the impressive conceptual development of Shi'i jurisprudence and legal methodology and despite halfhearted attempts by reformist administrations, the notion of a universal code applicable to all remained largely foreign to Iranians. The practice of law within a regulated judicial framework was held ransom by the ambiguities of the shari'a, contradictory interpretations of the mojtaheds, the vagaries of their verdicts, arbitrary court procedures, and the jurists' notorious propensity for corruption and bribe taking. The postconstitutional judicial reforms of various administrations set the stage for statutory legislation but also helped complicate the situation by creating a parallel legal framework.

The new Pahlavi legal reforms, primarily based on the Napoleonic Code, adopted the French system to reasonable dictates of the Shi'i shari'a, and did this perhaps more effectively than many other Muslim countries in the twentieth century. Under Davar's supervision, a council of legal experts, consisting of middle-ranking mojtaheds and state administrators of madrasa background who were familiar with European law, reviewed the French codes in a relatively short period of time, refashioning them according to Islamic contingencies. The 1927 Penal Code and the subsequent 1931 Civil Code replaced, in stages, the mojtahed-run shari'a courts. The new codes featured all the deficiencies of a state-dominated bureaucratic system, yet the Islamic provisions in the system proved vital for the state's legitimacy.

The new statutory codes rooted in the 1906–1907 Constitution aimed to protect the rights of citizens, due process, and equality before the law. Yet the arbitrary rule of the Pahlavis, the passivity of a rubber-stamp legislature, the lack of public scrutiny, and the residue of the traditional legal culture posed serious obstacles. Family law—particularly issues of marriage, divorce, and custodianship—remained firmly congruent with the dictates of Islamic law and its patriarchal underpinnings, as did the laws of inheritance and, to a lesser extent, penalties for sexual offenses and domestic violence. The law allowed for polygamy, though subordinated it to some conditions, and in general granted little protection to women beyond being wives and mothers in the traditional framework of Islamic law. Women's lives were ransomed to a variety of traditional deprivations and insecurities, with few incentives for legal, financial, or professional independence. The striking disregard for women's legal rights was often blamed by the Pahlavi reformers on the society's conservative values and fear of the ulama's opposition. Yet the Pahlavi modernizers were not devoid of a patriarchal mentality and were tainted by the European culture of male superiority of their time.

The new reforms, moreover, obligated most upper and middle ranks of the clergy to be content with meager incomes through registry bureaus, the fast-diminishing income of the charitable endowments (*waqfs*), and the generosity of bazaar merchants. Their loss of income was further exacerbated by the bleak economy of the Depression era, which hit Iranian trade and agriculture, and by the mismanagement and corruption that had long beset the institution of *waqf*. Between 1927 and 1933 the passage of new laws gave the state custodianship of all public endowments—most significantly the extensive endowments of the shrine of Imam Reza in Mashhad and control of the private *waqfs* presumed abandoned or with unknown trustees.

State intervention also struck a blow to the incentives for creating new *waqfs*. Whereas in the past creating a charitable foundation was a safe way to preserve control over family fortunes and avert state intrusion while performing an esteemed religious duty that was beneficial to the public, in the Pahlavi era it came to be considered an outmoded, cumbersome institution of little significance. Bureaucratization of the *waqf* and failure to enforce effective supervision led to decay or the expropriation of many endowed *qanats*, bathhouses, water reservoirs, takkiyehs, bridges, and libraries. Many villages, farms, and bazaar shops, which provided support for the upkeep of these public institutions, were also misappropriated or their potential diminished. Yet the clergy did not entirely lose their control. The government appointed many as custodians and set up pensions for others that were sufficient to let them carry on with their duties.

DRESS CODE, UNVEILING, AND
THE CLERICAL PREDICAMENT

Even as the state's intervention into the judicial, educational, and economic domains was considerable, intrusion into citizens' private lives was the most glaring. The dress code of December 1928 required all male citizens from school age onward to dress in a European-style jacket and trousers and a short, cylindrical rimmed hat, known as the Pahlavi hat, similar to the French kepi. By the turn of the twentieth century selective Westernization had made a wide range of European clothing fashionable among the urban elites. Yet Iranian society was still conscious of attire as a powerful social marker that determined social status, region, profession, communal loyalty, and even sexual orientation. The introduction of dress uniformity, with its militaristic undertones, was a radical departure from this landscape of apparel diversity whereby mullahs, merchants, craftsmen, government functionaries, khans, peasants, dervishes, and *lutis*, as well as women of various social classes, the nomadic men and women of Iran's vast network of tribes and ethnicities, and religious minorities were all identified not only by their dialect but also by their distinctive appearance.

Like the ideologies obsessed with uniforms in Europe and in neighboring Turkey, the Pahlavi dress code was a powerful tool to transform Iranian society into a bland and featureless mass, amnesic of its diversity and ready to be recast in a Westernized mold. Reza Khan, a Savadkuh peasant who was transformed in the Cossack barracks into the "man of destiny" was the prototype. Dressed in a plain military uniform, short cape in the style of Mussolini, and knee-high leather boots, he exuded power. Ordinary Iranian citizens, however, appeared frightened and awkward in their new ill-fitting outfits. Even so, the swift currents of change were all-embracing.

For the ulama the mandatory dress code was anathema even though they were partially exempted from it. They resented the Pahlavi outfit primarily because Westernized uniformity was a symbolic statement against what they stood for. Besides fear that the rimmed hat was a deliberate move by the godless state to make it impossible for believers to prostrate during daily prayers, they considered the Western trousers and short jacket as scandalously revealing. Moreover, the indignity of being subjected to the state's qualifying criteria, which also included a written examination on the madrasa curriculum—made the clergy feel degraded and resentful. Losing the privilege to put on clerical attire, particularly from the mid-1930s as new restrictions began to take effect, meant that many could no longer be recognized outright as holy, as they had for centuries, solely by wearing a turban: black for the presumed descendants of the House of the Prophet (a disproportionately high number among the clergy) and white for others. The turban, at times a domelike structure made of layers of twisted cloth, was complemented by a robe (*'aba*), slippers—preferably yellow—and a loose cloak known as *rada*, items of clothing with a sacred lineage in the biographies of the Prophet and the Imams. A long, dyed beard, the scent of rosewater, green rosary beads, and at times a white or green shawl around the waist were essential vestments that clashed with the prevailing exigencies of the profane state. Having been excluded from the mandatory dress code, the clergy stood out as a historical anomaly and were looked upon by the modernizing middle classes with condescension, if not disdain.

More provocative than any other reform measure under Reza Shah, however, was the unveiling of women, the removal of both the facial hijab and the all-body chador—first in selective venues such as public gatherings organized by the government, and from 1934 as a mandatory, state-enforced policy. What was at stake did not concern the ulama only but touched on a core issue of the society's mores and patriarchal identity. Women's cover, and their social exclusion, had been practiced since ancient times, and assiduously since the early Qajar era in the male-controlled urban setting. Women's cover was seen as a symbol of male honor (Persian *namus*, from the Greek *nomos*, "universal law"), family virtue, and female sexual and moral chastity—considered building blocks of the social universe and its strict maintenance through rules of reproduction, lineage, and gender boundaries. It was this order that was challenged.

Yet it is naive to assume that unveiling was a Pahlavi invention ex nihilo. Besides the Babi legacy and memories of Tahereh Qurrat al-'Ayn, some seventy years earlier, the progressive constitutionalist press and poets of the period—'Aref Qazvini and Iraj Mirza (1874–1926), among others—and a handful of women's journals after 1910 called for women's inclusion in the Iranian national discourse through education, control over their own lives, combating legal discrimination, and emancipation from social depravities. 'Aref called upon "regiments of women combatants" to fight along with the poet against superstition and tyranny. In a famous piece from the late 1910s, Iraj masterfully satirized the bigotry of his clerical contemporaries. Once a female image was carved on the portal of a caravansary (presumably in Mashhad), the news soon reached the "masters of turbans," who rushed to the scene. Worried that the unveiled image would instantaneously wipe out the believers' faith, the seminarians (*tollab*) soon imposed on the image a makeshift veil. "The honor [*namus*] that was about to be weathered thus was saved with a handful of dirt." Now the ulama could rest assured, Iraj sneered, that female seduction no longer could sink the public "into an ocean of sin" and the undisturbed *nomos* barred all hell from breaking loose. "With such [zealous] ulama," he concluded, "why are our people still gloomy about progress in our kingdom?"[1]

In the aftermath of Reza Khan's rise to power, and especially during the debate over republicanism, support for unveiling grew as women's groups organized and demonstrated, casting off their veils and clashing with opponents. But it was after 1927 that sporadic voluntary unveiling was visible among

Tehran's elite. By 1932 unveiling was encouraged for schoolgirls and for wives and daughters of military officers and civil servants. By 1934, in the aftermath of Reza Shah's official visit to Turkey—the only foreign visit he ever made—the new government decree required nationwide mandatory unveiling among all classes. The rigorous enforcement of the new policy, which continued up to the end of the Reza Shah era, meant that women belonging even to the most conservative families were to remove their veils and chador (fig. 8.8). Carefully monitored by the shah himself, the universal enforcing of unveiling was not free of social tension. Ugly scenes of the police forcefully removing women's chadors in the streets, reprimands and sacking of military and civilian officials who were reluctant to abide by the new policy, and general disregard for conservative sentiments against unveiling cast a shadow over the whole episode.

Yet contrary to a common perception that mandatory unveiling was unpopular and oppressive, its liberating effects were undeniable. A large sector of the female population, especially younger women, welcomed unveiling with the same enthusiasm as they welcomed modern education, participation in public

Figure 8.8. First public gathering in Shiraz attended by government employees and city notables and their unveiled wives (c. 1935). The mandatory event was to enforce the lifting of the facial veil.
M. Sane', *Paydayesh-e 'Akkasi dar Shiraz* (Tehran, 1369/1990), 149.

Figure 8.9. Learning to work with Singer sewing machines. As early as 1921
Azizeh-Jahan Chehrenegar (*standing*) held such classes in Shiraz.
M. Sane', *Paydayesh-e 'Akkasi dar Shiraz* (Tehran, 1369/1990).

life, and greater control over their lives. It is telling that after 1941, when mandatory enforcement was quickly abandoned, only a fraction of urban women—
mostly in smaller cities and among the more religious classes—took up chador
again, and almost none, even wives and daughters of the clergy, readopted the
facial veil (*neqab*). This was in clear contrast to the universal use of facial covering for women before 1927, as imposed invariably in all Muslim societies of the
time (fig. 8.9).

The generational divide also played a part. Older women, who in compliance with the requirement of the shari'a had seldom, if ever, ventured out from
the inner quarter (*andarun*) of their houses, opted to stay inside for good, out
of fear of the dishonor that casting off of their *neqab* and chador might bring to
them; the younger generations, however, were far more willing to cast aside the
suffocating traditional mold (fig. 8.10). Violent enforcement aside, the unveiling was simultaneously a credit to Reza Shah's secularization program and a
loss to the clergy's prestige.

Intimidated and unsure, the clergy had little choice but to accept the reality
in silence; no major fatwa against unveiling was issued at the time, though in
later years there was ample resentment toward enforcement of the hijab. Even
families of modest means soon began to adapt to the unveiled appearance and
acquire sentiments that were unmistakably modern.

Figure 8.10. This image of a woman in chador with her facial veil lifted and her young child in Western dress was symbolic of the changing times. Behind them is an old Persian poster of the 1927 German silent movie *Der letzte Walzer* (The Last Waltz). A. von Graefe, *Iran das neue Persien* (Berlin and Zurich, 1937), 10.

Opposition to unveiling was symptomatic of the clerical failure to forge an alternative to the Pahlavi model. The jurist establishment conceivably could have addressed, but never did, the predicaments of the shari'a, the arcane teaching methods, the textbooks and the curriculum, and the conservative worldview associated with them. It was as if the ulama within the madrasa walls remained unperturbed and in a state of denial, despite a revolution that had shaken their very social foundations. The shrinking of the clerical horizons had begun long ago, when they rebuffed alternative modes of thinking—even something as benign as Islamic philosophy—and rejected innovation (*bed'at*) as heretical even within the well-guarded bounds of jurisprudence, instead augmenting the fundamentals of their legal corpus as sacred and thus unchallengeable. Even such mild revisionist traits emerging on the margins of the clerical community—as in the views of Mohammad Hasan Shari'at Sangelaji (1892–1944), were roundly condemned by the mainstream as sacrilegious.

Himself a mojtahed, Sangelaji proposed, to the dismay of his detractors, a rational approach to shari'a that aimed to accommodate some measure of modernity in theology and law compatible with the legal reforms of the Pahlavi era. He called for an unambiguous reading of the Qur'an as a window to a new jurisprudence that was not obfuscated by the dubious hadith, scholastic convolution, and popular superstition. His rationalistic approach, blended with elements of Salafism and messianism, brought Sangelaji to the point of reject-ing the literal Shiʻi narrative of the Hidden Imam's violent and vengeful *Kho-ruj* (apocalyptic return). He opted instead for a gradual transformation of the community—a view that brought him somewhat close to the Baha'i idea of moral reconstruction. The proximity may explain his antagonism toward the Baha'is and his anxiety over increasing numbers of conversion to the new faith. The ulama remained equally unmoved by lay critics such as Ahmad Kasravi (1890–1946), the influential journalist and prophet of moral reconstruction in the 1930s and 1940s. Blissfully proud of their heritage, they brushed off cri-tiques of their theology and jurisprudence, in the same way they reacted to the Baha'i missionaries (*moballeghs*)—whom they viewed as their gravest doctrinal enemies—and later to socialists and to Islamic modernists.

Such predicaments of Islamic law and theology as denying equal rights to all citizens regardless of gender and creed; intolerance toward non-Muslims, non-Shiʻis, and religious dissenters; institutional and legal discrimination of women; sanctioning of such punishments as stoning, vengeance killing (*qesas*), blood retribution, punishment of homosexuality, and execution of sexual offenders and heretics; denial of freedom of speech and the press; obstinate anti-intellec-tualism; and the assumption of an elevated status for the clerical elite—all these remained unresolved.

The shrinking social domain of the Shiʻi clerical class was undeniable, and so was the greater cleavage between the modern and traditional sectors of Iranian society. The clerical community who survived doctrinal challenges, the state's secularizing policies, and counter-incentives of the economic market became more conscious of itself as a deprived and persecuted community. Qom, more than older theological centers such as Isfahan and Mashhad, from the late 1920s came to represent this ethos of isolation, most starkly evident in the impover-ished life of the students of the madrasa. For the most part they were dependent on pensions from the *marjaʻs*, handouts from "mourning societies" to recite eulogies at the *rawzeh* sessions during Moharram and Ramadan, and alms dis-tributed by pilgrims to the Shiʻi shrines in Iran and southern Iraq.

The clergy also lost ground in the public forum against the media and enter-tainment. The establishment of a small government radio station in 1927, later to be expanded to a more powerful broadcast as Radio Iran in 1940, and the growing number of theaters and cinemas in the capital and later in the prov-inces through 1930s and 1940s, were competition for sessions of *rawzeh-khawni* and preaching in the mosques. Hollywood movies, early Persian films produced in Mumbai, and the introduction of gramophones and recordings of Persian classical and popular music opened new avenues for leisure, though roundly condemned as blasphemous by the ulama.

From the early twentieth century, the growing production of discography for the Iranian market made various genres of Persian music, classical and popular, accessible to an eager public. They gave Persian music and musicians a new public forum, different from parties in nobility's houses and revelry in the lowly taverns on city outskirts. By the late 1930s there were at least three Western recording companies, and their Iranian subsidiaries, producing in London, Istanbul, Baku, Tashkent, and later in Tehran recordings that captured the best of the Persian musical ensembles and vocal performances, both male and female. The Iranian public came to admire such composers and virtuosos as Darvish Khan (1872–1926), who recorded the Persian *dastgah* system on *tar*—and the celebrated female singer Qamar al-Moluk Vaziri (1905–1959). These lent to Persian music a new aura of prestige and respectability. Patriotic anthems and popular songs, comical parodies, and popular comedies were also released.

Western films introduced dashing male movie stars in exotic costumes, glamorous actresses, spectacular epics, slapstick, Westerns, and Hollywood melodramas, with growing appeal to the younger public. Cafés and restaurants, a novelty for the upper classes in the capital, also offered a secular ambiance. For ordinary Iranians the traditional coffeehouses, now almost exclusively serving tea and inexpensive bazaar dishes, remained a venue for listening to storytellers (*naqqals*) narrating tales of the *Shahnameh* and other classical and popular texts. With the growth of modern entertainment, storytelling in coffeehouses and by wandering dervishes, who displayed large-scale paintings as visual aids for their narratives of the Shi'i tragedies and the *Shahnameh* stories, gradually disappeared. The Shi'i ulama no longer objected to or approved of these forms of public entertainment, as they had in the seventeenth century. They had other displays of heathen leisure to worry about. Many among the ulama and their conservative followers avoided radio broadcasts altogether, and did not even own a receiver, on the grounds that possessing a medium that broadcasts music is religiously unlawful.

THE END OF REZA SHAH'S REGIME

By the mid-1930s Reza Shah's regime had turned increasingly oppressive and unpredictable. The old elite had been cowed into submission and in time was replaced by a new generation of technocrats; the army generals were subdued to the shah's whims and wishes; the clergy were demoralized and in retreat; the Majles was reduced to a nonentity; the tribes by and large were pacified and their leadership eliminated or exiled; and a police apparatus—including a vast number of secret agents—became a vicious tool of the shah's paranoiac fears. Despite the appearance of absolute power, however, the popular base for the Pahlavi order had been eroded and its legitimacy questioned. World War II made these cracks more obvious, and the foreign policy quagmire in which Iran found itself unfathomable. In August 1941 Reza Shah was forced to abdicate, and Iran was occupied by Britain and Russia for the second time in twenty-five years. The irony of this was borne out by the Iranian people with a mix of cynicism and despair.

At the outset of World War II in August 1939, Iran declared neutrality, as it had done in 1915, but as it turned out with no effect. Suspicious of Reza Shah's true intentions, and concerned with the sizable German presence in Iran, as early as January 1940 Britain began mobilizing a British-Indian force with the intention of occupying the oil fields of Khuzestan. Given the vitality of Iranian oil for the British economy and war efforts, Reza Shah's 1933 renegotiation of the oil concession made British authorities even more suspicious, especially after Winston Churchill's ascendancy in May 1940 as prime minister of Britain. His unabashed hegemonic sentiments took on a new patriotic ring and resonated through the British diplomatic ranks. The British minister in Tehran, Reader Bullard, a diplomat with profound colonial biases, qualified his condescension toward Iranians with concerns for Reza Shah's collaboration with the Nazis and thereby the threat of German infiltration in Iran.

Even before 1933 and rise of the National Socialist Party to power in Germany, Iran relied on German technical and financial expertise for building new industries, railroad construction, the banking system, and training the workforce at a German-run technical school. German industrial ascendancy from the early 1930s made that country an attractive choice for Iran's trade and industry and a willing partner. Hoping to be on the side of the winner and reap the potential benefits, in August 1939, at the outset of the war, the shah appointed as the new premier the French-educated Ahmad Matin-Daftari (1891–1971), who was known for his Germanophile tendencies.

The memories of German support in World War I for the Iranian nationalists were reinforced by Nazi propaganda highlighting the presumed common Aryan origins of the Germanic and Iranian peoples. The change of the country's official name in European languages in 1935 from Persia to Iran was a gesture of nationalist assertion implying Iran's "rebirth." In the Persian language the country's name always was Iran (at least since the third century CE), yet the Pahlavi decision to use a new nomenclature abroad may have been influenced by the etymological association between *Iran* and *Aryan*. Undermining two and a half millennia of historical and cultural memories associated with the name *Persia*, the ultranationalist officials and military officers in the Pahlavi service argued that the old nomenclature projected an image of weakness and subservience abroad. In reality such an argument was grounded less in a desire to pay homage to Iran's ethnic and regional diversity than in raw nationalist sentiments.

The fear of British retaliation over ties with Germany, however, soon persuaded Reza Shah to change course and even propose to the British a secret defense pact and proposal for military assistance, primarily to withstand what seemed an imminent incursion by the Soviet Union, then an ally of Germany, into the Iranian territory. London turned down both proposals. Mindful of the impending British occupation of the southern oil fields, in June 1940 in the midst of uncertainty about the fate of the war, out of desperation the shah even sacked and arrested his premier Matin-Daftari and replaced him with an Anglophile, 'Ali Mansur (1886–1974), a move that unleashed the wrath of Nazi Germany and its sympathizers. Though a group of German residents, numbering a thousand, were working in Iran, Radio Berlin's Persian broadcast, the first of foreign broadcasts beamed to Iran, began to attack Reza Shah as a British stooge and anticipate his forthcoming downfall. The forecast, which enjoyed a wide listening audience, gave further credence to the popular fear of a pro-German coup while diminishing the shah's stature in the public eye.

A rapid sequence of events, almost fatefully, terminated Reza Shah's effort to balance the two powers and sealed his political fate. Early in 1941 the pro-German coup led by Rashid 'Āli Gailani was staged in neighboring Iraq. Its subsequent collapse in late May, once British forces captured Basra and Baghdad, underscored the possibility of a similar hazard being perpetrated against Iran's fragile sovereignty. Gailani and his cohorts fled to Iran in early June presumably on their way to Germany, a move that added to the British suspicion of Reza Shah's pro-Axis sentiments. The invasion of Syria and Lebanon, too, by a joint operation of the British and the Free French forces further drove home the message of an impending thereat to Iran. Yet what ended for good Reza Shah's time on the throne was the grand Anglo-Soviet alliance after Hitler's decision to invade Russia, his former ally, in June 1941. The Grand Alliance — backed by American support under the Atlantic Charter — was reminiscent of the World War I Anglo-Russian alliance. Likewise, the survival of both powers in war against their nemesis once more was destined to wreck Iran's political and social stability.

Even though Britain and Russia gave assurances that they would respect Iran's territorial integrity, in what seemed a predetermined course, both powers in July 1941 submitted an ultimatum demanding the immediate expulsion of all German nationals in the service of the Iranian government. Although earlier Iran had reasserted its neutrality in this new phase of the conflict—as did Turkey—and promised to ask all nonessential German civilians to leave, and even though Berlin intensified its attacks on Reza Shah on the airwaves, the signs of open Anglo-Soviet hostility were not abating. The Red Army began to amass troops along Iran's northern border while the British Broadcasting Corporation began to heighten its criticism of Reza Shah's tyranny and his amassing of a huge fortune through misappropriation of land, especially in Mazandaran province. That the BBC championed the liberal and constitutional cause in Iran was a surprise shift from its earlier condoning of many years of the shah's autocratic rule—no doubt with a clear goal of inciting anti-Pahlavi sentiments. The skeptical Iranian public interpreted the change in tone as proof that Reza Shah was no longer in control, even as a presumption that he was no longer a useful puppet in the hand of his British masters. Resentful of British machinations—real and imagined—some openly sympathized with the Axis and their advances on the Russian front. Bewildered and demoralized, the shah, too, felt that he was caught in the middle of a deadly conflict with no certain end.

The end game came in a crushing order that started with the Allied ultimatum and Iranian appeasement in July 1941 and ended in a checkmate that removed Reza Shah less than two months later. Demanding expulsion of all Germans from Iran and abdication of Reza Shah, both obvious ploys to facilitate the joint invasion of Iran, the Allies appeared uncompromising from the outset. The Iranian government tried in vain to satisfy the Allies' demands not only to expel all German nationals but also to provide full access to the Iranian road and railroad network to transport cargo, military hardware, and supplies across Iranian territory and through the Caspian and the Caucasus to the besieged Red Army in Stalingrad and on other fronts. In a faint hope of saving Iran from another invasion, the government of 'Ali Mansur, barely free of Reza Shah's iron fist, agreed to most of the terms. The two powers were to benefit free and unconditional access of the same rail network that they—Britain and Russia—had prevented Iran from constructing for more than half a century. They were about to depose the person who built it and occupy a nation that paid for the railroad through taxes on sugar and tea.

Before negotiations could come to any conclusion, on August 25, 1941, the coordinated Allied armies marched into Iran through its northern and southern borders (map 8.2). The two powers did not even declare war or serve any other notice to the Iranian government; a sheer display of force tinged with a dose of colonial conceit was meant to deliver the message. It also implied that

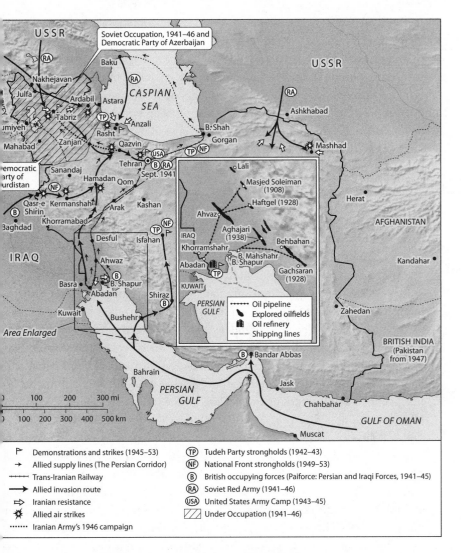

Map 8.2. Iran during World War II, 1941–1946

occupation was not an act of aggression but a wartime contingency. Facing the overwhelming superiority of the Allied forces, the demoralized and ill-prepared Iranian army soon caved and, shortly after, almost completely dissipated. The Red Army took over the whole of Azarbaijan and the Caspian provinces and rallied toward Tehran, while the British-Indian forces crossing the frontiers in southern Iraq and entering through the Persian Gulf ports rushed in the same direction.

Allied air forces began bombing civilian and military targets in major cities, causing havoc and undermining civilian confidence, while leaflets dropped from the air spoke of the occupiers' benevolence, friendship toward the Iranian people, and desire to leave Iranian territory at the close of the war. The small Iranian navy in the Persian Gulf offered a heroic resistance, only to be soundly crushed; the sizable army, on the other hand, abandoned the lines of defense or surrendered. An effort to organize the defense of the capital failed, and even senior officers deserted, leaving thousands of starving conscripts to slowly head home to their towns and villages. Since the turn of the nineteenth century, this was the seventh time the frontiers of Iran had been violated by one or both of the European powers.

On the same day of the invasion, in an audience at dawn with Reza Shah requested by the British and Soviet envoys, they repeated demands for the expulsion of all Germans and for unconditional access to Iranian railroads and roads. The shah had no choice but to comply with a fait accompli. The envoys' real intent, however, came in a subsequent communiqué demanding the immediate abdication of Reza Pahlavi, with the assurance that his son Mohammad Reza would replace him. Under Allied pressure, a new government was formed by the elderly statesman, Mohammad 'Ali Forughi, who was brought out of retirement to undertake a formidable task. In the midst of panic and confusion, Forughi in a public announcement assured the public that the Allied occupation was transient and declared the cessation of hostilities, which in effect put the final touch on the dismantling of the Iranian armed forces. The shah's abdication seemed inevitable.

It is startling how quickly the forces of chaos set in. The ensuing tribal unrest, economic havoc, and public panic caused by food shortages and fears of starvation were compounded by the uncouth conduct of the Indian Army's sepoys and the Red Army's *tavarishes*, as well as by the prospects of the Allied march on the capital. The shah's plea telegraphed to President Franklin Roosevelt proved to be of no avail. Yet the shah's customary wrath had not diminished completely. In the last meeting with his army command he showered invectives on all for destroying an army he had built up for over two decades and physically beat up the chief of staff for cowardly conduct. He ordered the army commanders to be detained on the charge of treason and to stand a military trial, which in the end was never held.

On September 3, 1941, while the people of Iran were hearing on the newly established Radio Iran the still unbelievable news that Reza Shah had abdicated, he was on his way to Isfahan, where he was to be united with his family. On September 16, after formally abdicating the throne, the shah and his family departed from the port of Bandar Abbas aboard a British postal ship to an undisclosed destination. The most that Reza Shah could secure from the Allies, through the good offices of Forughi, was the promise of his elder son's succession, an issue briefly debated by the British in favor of a Qajar prince, but then quietly set aside. On September 26 while the Allied forces were establishing their headquarters on the outskirts of the Iranian capital, the twenty-two-year-old crown prince Mohammad Reza Pahlavi (1919–1980) was sworn in as Iran's new constitutional monarch. In less than three months the reign of the once invulnerable Reza Shah came to an ignominious end.

After a brief stay on the Indian Ocean island of Mauritius, then a British possession, Reza Shah and his family were transferred to Johannesburg in the British colony of Southern Africa, where they lived a life of seclusion destined for many former foes of the empire. Two years later, on July 26, 1944, Reza Shah died at the age of sixty-seven of a heart ailment. In his last photographs he is in a civilian suit—a notable contrast to his lifelong public appearances in military uniform—a broken man, humiliated and visibly aged. His coffin was sent to Cairo, where it was temporarily buried in the crypt of the Rifa'i Mosque and later brought back to Iran in May 1950 to be buried in an impressive mausoleum built near the shrine of 'Abd al-'Azim in southern Tehran.

A CAREER IN THE BALANCE

The downfall of Reza Shah came at the end of a career of contested legacies. Perhaps the most influential ruler in Iranian history since Isma'il I in the early sixteenth century, he was instrumental in carrying out massive changes that transformed Iranian society, culture, and economy. He has been remembered as a man of vision and resolve but also as autocratic, avaricious, and increasingly paranoid. With the benefit of hindsight, he may be seen as the most realistic option for Iran in the post–World War I era, a leader who reasserted sovereignty and carried out nearly all the nonpolitical objectives of the Constitutional Revolution. He and his cohorts created a centralized state with modern institutions, infrastructure, education, and improved health, new industries, and modern finances. The Pahlavi order engendered an optimistic sense of national identity that revolved around cultural heritage, collective memory, and national symbols. It put an end to the political impasse in the center and pacified Iran—albeit with brute force—and helped the rise of a new middle class. It increased government revenue and efficiency and restrained foreign influences in domestic affairs. It curbed the power of tribal leaders, checked the conservative clergy, and lessened—if not demolished—the long-held monopoly of the Qajar ruling elite.

Reza Shah's successes came at a high price. Despite his emphasis on institutional modernization—as in finances, judiciary, and education—and despite a semblance of cultural modernity, the reforms of the Pahlavi period remained decidedly lopsided. The agrarian economy—still the largest economic sector—remained essentially intact and the landowning culture of exploitation was reinforced by Reza Shah's own greed. He built a vast estate through brazen appropriation of the lands belonging to Mazandaran's small and large landowners. The industrialization and trade policies relied heavily on government monopolies and state ownership, at the expense of fostering an expansive industrial bourgeoisie. The hasty introduction of new secularized institutions, with few exceptions, was marked by uncritical borrowing of Western models and misconceived positivist values, and it was often combined with contempt for Iran's indigenous traditions and cultural mores.

The nationalist ideology of the Pahlavi era, too, tended to undermine Iran's ethnic and linguistic diversity and to accommodate Iran's long and complex Shi'i past. Yet the budding aspirations of the constitutional period for democracy and popular representation were not completely crushed. Iranians received the news of Reza Shah's ouster with a mix of indignation, for it came with yet another foreign intrusion, and with relief, ending an era of political repression. Soon after his death, however, ordinary people remembered Reza Shah more for his transforming reforms than his police apparatus.

Yet Pahlavi absolutism was far less loyal to the checks and balances that under the rubric of the "circle of equity" had for centuries kept the Persian kingship in a functional relationship with the society over which it ruled. The two arms of the traditional state—the executive consisting of the divan and the army—no longer were kept at bay, and the judiciary, consisting of the clerical establishment, had no place in the structure of power. One can attribute the rise of the new culture of unbridled autocracy under Reza Shah above all to the environment of frustration and insecurity that thrived in the postconstitutional era. This spirit of militarism was reinforced after the virtual collapse of the Qajar social contract and during World War I. Reza Shah in effect stood at the pinnacle of a power pyramid that with shrewd maneuvering had incorporated an assortment of the existing military forces and glued them together by appropriating a large chunk of Iran's oil revenue. The military culture that came to dominate the new Pahlavi armed forces was the despotic ethos of the Russian Cossack barracks in which Reza Khan and his senior officers had been trained. The nationalistic ideals of a few Gendarmerie officers who joined the Pahlavi army and the more familiar rough-and-ready conduct of the officers of the regular Iranian armed forces who also were incorporated both had their part in the shaping of the Pahlavi military elite. Even some of the civilians in Reza Shah's service, such as Teymurtash, were graduates of European military academies. The German and Turkish officers who in the course of the World War I came into contact with their Iranian counterparts, mostly the Iranian gendarmes, also conveyed a much-admired spirit of Prussian military.

That such an authoritarian model prevailed in Europe after World War I and brought to power fascist regimes resonated with the Pahlavi regime. As in Italy, Germany, and the Soviet Union, and to some degree in the early Turkish Republic, in Iran too, the new ethos quickly overcame the democratic ideals of constitution, division of powers, popular representation, rule of law, and individual rights. In Iran, arguably, there were even more causes for this shift of paradigm, given all that was experienced by Iranians in the period between 1907 and 1921, with disarray in Majles and incapacitated postconstitutional governments, persistence of the old elite and their feeble governance, foreign occupation, and the economic and human prices that society endured.

It was from this milieu that emerged a culture of empowerment well reflected in military uniforms, shiny riding boots, ready-to-use riding crops, rough tone of speech, and harsh treatment of inferiors. The sense of superiority that the ranking officer under Reza Shah came to display and the proud esprit de corps that held them together as a new privileged class, proved more potent than shaky political parties, daring journalism, moving poems, and fiery speeches from the pulpit of the mosques and the podium of the Majles.

9

CHAOTIC DEMOCRACY, OIL NATIONALIZATION, AND DENIED HOPES (1941–1953)

The Allied occupation of Iran in September 1941 was a rude shock to most Iranians. Facing the soldiers of the Red Army, the British Indian Army, and soon after American military personnel seemed almost a surreal reversal of two decades of Pahlavi assurances of Iran's reclaimed sovereignty and the might of the Iran's Imperial Armed Forces. The shock was transient, but the consequences were not. The occupation triggered one of the most eventful episodes in Iran's modern history and revealed persistent themes in the country's recent past: the struggle for democracy, foreign intervention, and grave tensions within the polity and between the center and the periphery. Disruption of the economy, political instability, tribal rebellions, secessionist movements, frequent imposition of martial law, and growing hatred toward foreign powers were the darker outcomes. On the other hand, a national movement for nationalizing Iran's oil industry, the opening up of the political space, greater freedom of the press, parliamentary politics, and a nascent labor movement were promising developments. Despite many political failures, the following twelve years witnessed the resumption of a process that was first started with the Constitutional Revolution but interrupted by the rise of Reza Shah.

The opening of the public space came with new ideologies, ranging from Marxist-Leninist to ultranationalist and Islamic extremist. A dose of demagogy, covert and overt foreign influences, proxy politics, and the reemergence after a brief interlude of the royal court and the army in the political arena all led to an atmosphere of distrust and conspiracy. The new era of political openness also allowed members of the old elite and nonelite to return from the political wilderness, often clothed in a new garb. Chief among them were the Qajar aristocrat and seasoned statesman Ahmad Qavam; the journalist and partner in the 1921 coup Sayyed Zia al-Din Tabataba'i; and Mohammad Mosaddeq, the Swiss-educated lawyer from an old family of high divan officials. The younger generation of the middle-class intellectuals, professionals, and journalists were partners in the new polity motivated by Marxism or by secular nationalist vigor. The bazaar community and the urban lower middle classes, however, more often tilted toward Islamic activism.

Ironically, the new era of political pluralism facilitated under the aegis of the same occupying powers that had helped shut down Iran's democratic process three decades earlier. Changes in the political and economic spheres too were conditioned by the geopolitical ambitions and vested interests of those powers. The Soviet Union wished to expand its sphere of influence through friendly enclaves in Iran's northern provinces and by sponsoring pro-Soviet brand of communism. The British government held not only sway over a sector of the Iranian polity but also unyielding claims over the oil fields in the south, claims that came with some measures of intervention and intrigue. And the Cold War strategic concerns of the United States transformed its relations with Iran—as elsewhere in the Middle East, South East Asia, and Latin America—from an anti-Imperialist and a bystander of goodwill to a member of the hegemonic club.

In response to the domestic turmoil and foreign ambitions in the 1940s and early 1950s, a potent nationalist response seemed unavoidable. The rise and fall of Mohammad Mosaddeq characterized the successes and failures of the period, revealed first through legislation and parliamentary maneuvers, then through nationalization of the Iranian oil industry, and finally during Mosaddeq's turbulent term as prime minister. Ending with the coup of August 1953, his story is an unhealed wound in the Iranian persecution narrative and a well-known chapter in the history of covert Anglo-American interventions. Iran's return to arbitrary Pahlavi rule after 1953 put a premature end to Iran's perilous experiment with participatory politics.

OLD MALADIES REVISITED

A striking feature of the Allied occupation was the breakdown of the Iranian economy, triggered by soaring inflation, scarce provisions, hoarding, and even starvation. These were indirect outcomes of a series of measures dictated by the Allies, and despite their assurances to the contrary, that Allied forces would refrain from meddling in Iran's internal affairs. Their war aims and needs of their troops proved otherwise. The occupying armies camped out in the north and south as well as on the outskirts of the capital needed food and provisions far beyond the surplus output of the Iranian economy, which already had been disrupted by insecurity in the countryside and limited road communications.

The Allies' decision to float Iran's currency from the unrealistically low official rate of exchange under Reza Shah substantially increased the Allies' purchasing power to acquire provisions at a lower cost. The new measures triggered, almost instantaneously, a rise in prices and high inflation that lasted to the end of the war and beyond. Iranian consumers, most of whom had meager incomes and fixed salaries, viewed with resentment the foreign troops' buying power. Poverty was at the root of the riots and earliest civil unrest that broke out in larger cities and was an incentive to join the pro-Soviet Tudeh Party, with its promises of greater social justice. The convulsive price increases shook public confidence in other ways. The export trade, mostly to Germany and Britain via the Persian Gulf, suffered a sharp decline as a result of the hostilities. Likewise, the import of manufactured goods such as small machinery, consumer goods, and pharmaceuticals noticeably declined. Lacking spare parts and other imported material in turn affected nascent industries such as textiles, sugar refineries, and cement factories that had been established under Reza Shah.

To serve the war effort, the Allies took control of the Iranian rail and road networks (see map 8.2). The massive logistical convoy organized by the Allies' Middle East Supply Center hauled through the "Persian corridor" to the Soviet Union millions of tons of mostly American war matériel provided under the Lend-Lease Act passed by the US Congress in March 1941 (fig. 9.1). Military hardware, provisions, fuel, and machinery were transported from the Persian Gulf ports of Khorramshahr and Bandar Abbas across the Iranian plateau to the Caucasus or through the Caspian ports to the Russian eastern front. The supplies, amounting to at least 70 percent of Soviet military needs in the crucial years of 1941 and 1942, included 648,000 vehicles assembled in a plant set up by American personnel and manned by the local Iranians in Khuzestan province to assemble military vehicles and aircrafts (fig. 9.2). After the war Iran was praised as the "Bridge to Victory," in recognition of its strategic location and contribution to the war efforts, and memorial stamps were issued (pl. 9.1). Yet only meager compensation was paid for the services and the hardware, and that only after many appeals by the Iranian government to the former Allies. The Americans duly paid their share, the British procrastinated for years, and the Soviets ignored the appeals altogether.

With military convoys, the Allied camps, and their personnel also came political influence and intervention in internal affairs. To its credit, the Iranian government, despite many short-lived cabinets, numerous reshufflings, and appointments and dismissals, managed to preserve a semblance of control. The

Figure 9.1. US convoy on the Persian corridor. A village boy is putting
snow chains on a truck carrying supplies to the Soviet Union.
LC-USW3–028452–E [P&P]. Courtesy of the Library of Congress.

Figure 9.2. US military planes stand ready for pickup at Abadan
airfield. As part of the Lend-Lease Program, five types of aircraft
were delivered to the Soviet Union via the Persian corridor.
Courtesy of the National Museum of the United States Air Force.

agreement reached with the Allies by the Forughi government and ratified in 1942 after months of tough negotiations, guaranteed on paper Iran's sovereignty and territorial integrity while defining the Allied presence not as an occupation but as temporary logistical access. It required the Allied forces to evacuate Iran within six months of the end of hostilities. Yet Forughi's famous pronouncement in response to public anxiety—"They come, they go, and they don't bother us" (*Miayand va miravand; kari be kar ma nadarand*)—proved a gigantic understatement.

Although the agreement obliged the Allies to collaborate with the government in matters of internal security and to contribute to Iran's economic recovery, it also allowed for as many troops as the Allies wished to bring in. It granted the Allies full access throughout the country to all means of communication, including railroads, roads, rivers, airports, ports, pipelines, oil installations, telephone, telegraphs, and radio. What was not mentioned in the treaty, but assumed, was Britain's free hand to hunt German agents, collaborators, and sympathizers, which became a factor adding to anti-British and anti-Russian feelings among the Iranian public. For some pro-German elements, even as late as 1943, there was a hope that the Wehrmacht's advances over the Soviets in the Caucasus would eventually liberate Iran from the throes of Allied occupation. The Allied propaganda in Iran targeted such Germanophile tendencies, which had persisted since World War I (pl. 9.2). A declaration issued jointly at the Tehran Conference by Roosevelt, Stalin, and Churchill in December 1943 thanked the Iranian government for its assistance in the war against Germany, promised to provide it with economic assistance both during and after the war, and expressed the desire for Iran to maintain independence, sovereignty, and territorial integrity. Yet Iran's future was not a priority for the Allies. Nor did the declaration resonate much with the Iranian public (fig. 9.3).

To the detriment of the Iranian government, a number of insurrections in the tribal regions complicated the occupation. They challenged the authority of the Iranian government first in Kurdistan, then among the Bakhtiyari and the Mamasani of central and southwest Iran, and soon thereafter among the Qashqa'is of Fars province. Tribal rebellions were in greater part a response to years of harsh treatment under Reza Shah and to his pacification campaigns. For the tribal khans who were released from government detention after Reza Shah's departure engaging in customary infighting was a way of reasserting after many years of exile their place within the tribal hierarchy. The new climate also encouraged chief of powerful tribes, the Qashqa'i and the Bakhtiyari in particular, to take part in the political process even though they were susceptible to their own raw ambitions and at times to manipulations by foreign powers and

Figure 9.3. Marshal Voroshilov shows the Stalingrad sword to Franklin
Roosevelt during the Tehran conference on November 28, 1943.
Winston Churchill and Joseph Stalin look on. No Iranian official
attended the conference, held at the Soviet embassy in Tehran.
© Imperial War Museum, London.

their proxies. Confrontation with armed forces, especially after 1945, disrupted
tribal economies and life in rural populations in the vicinity.

The central government's answer to these mounting problems was at best
conciliatory, occasionally draconian, and often ineffective. The ministerial
posts were given to ranking bureaucrats, landowners, and secular professionals educated in the Reza Shah era, whereas premiership often went to notable
members of the old divan families. Short-lived and lacking a viable constituency, the governments in the postwar era were caught between the conflicting
demands of a revitalized Majles, which soon turned into an arena of personal
and ideological rivalries, the whims and wishes of the court, and the real or
assumed influence of the occupying powers. In the twelve years between 1941
and 1953 there were fifteen governments in office and many more instances of
reshuffling.

With economic problems looming large, the situation called for new sources
of revenue beyond taxation and the meager oil income. The agrarian tax base
was small, the village population impoverished, and the state endemically
lacked the means of collecting taxes. In the 1943 fiscal year the deficit ran close

to 90 percent of the total government revenue. By 1947 it was reduced to 45 percent, thanks in part to reform measures introduced by Arthur Millspaugh and his team of American financial advisers who had been employed for a second time between 1942 and 1945 to overhaul taxation and fiscal policies. Yet a chronic shortage of funds for development was serious enough to persuade successive governments to seek foreign aid, primarily from the United States, the only member of the Allied forces capable of helping Iran. Financial assistance, however, came with strings attached, mostly in the form of military assistance and advisory missions as a counter to growing Soviet influence. An increase in Iran's oil revenue, with the goal of complete nationalization of Iran's oil industry, thus seemed a viable alternative. As early as 1946 such demands were audible, even though almost from the start they ran up against the jealously guarded British interests of the shrinking British Empire.

Fragile governments, tribal insurrections, and expansion of the pro-Soviet network of sympathizers and activists in turn contributed to the growth of the armed forces as the guarantor of internal security. After the fiasco of dismantling the Iranian army in mid-1941, the armed forces were reorganized in early 1942 and after the war with the partial assistance of US advisers and the purchase of surplus US military hardware. Anxious to display its might and recoup its sinking prestige, the Iranian military command, schooled in the brutish discipline of the Reza Shah era, reacted severely to public protests. In December 1942 a Tudeh-inspired crowd attacking the Majles and looted public buildings demanding the removal of the prime minister Ahmad Qavam and his government on the charge of pro-American sympathies. The Qavam government, declaring martial law, allowed the military to send troops into the streets to quell disturbances in a bloody show of force, the first of several to come.

The emergence of the army as a political instrument and the arrival of the American advisory corps to rebuild the armed forces was hardly a coincidence. Nor were the efforts of the young Mohammad Reza Shah at the outset of his reign to woo the army as a natural ally and a reliable support base. A series of public trials revealing the heinous crimes of the high-ranking police officers and henchmen of Reza Shah's time soiled the Pahlavi image. The young shah's fear of the old notables, many with Qajar ties, and some with real or perceived foreign connections, added to his sense of insecurity. Army officers, on the other hand, were entangled in their own power struggles, and some, like the chief of staff, Haj 'Ali Razmara (1901–1951), entertained political ambitions. Others were sympathetic to the nationalist cause, and a few in the lower ranks were loyal to the Tudeh Party. Yet most army officers sought more than a figurehead in the person of the young shah; they sought a refuge and a chance to regain their lost privileges and repair their tarnished image. The Azarbaijan crisis of 1946 provided the army with the chance to act as a counterforce to the growing Soviet influence and appear as a savior of the nation.

EMERGENCE OF THE TUDEH PARTY

As in Europe and elsewhere, Soviet membership in the Allies' grand coalition offered the left an indispensable chance to reorganize, and soon thrive, as a major force in postwar politics. As early as September 1941, Iranian communists and socialists from previous years began to organize themselves into a broad coalition under the rubric of the Tudeh Party, the "party of the masses," which was chosen to camouflage the party's overt communist identity. Some had been released from Reza Shah's prison. Others had arrived fresh from Europe or from exile in the Soviet Union. A coalition dominated by Marxists educated mostly in Weimar Germany and a few old hands trained in the Soviet Union, the Tudeh quickly developed into a disciplined and doctrinaire political machine with growing membership among the intellectuals and urban middle classes and some industrial workers, and with almost complete loyalty to Moscow (see map 8.2). In the following years, Tudeh affiliates, including some trade unions, the Society of Friends of Peace, and youth, women, and university organizations, also helped spread the socialist message.

Modern socialist ideologies were not entirely alien, having been part of the Iranian environment since the turn of the twentieth century. In a land that as early as the sixth century CE nurtured Mazdakism—perhaps the first protocommunist movement in the world—such ideals had lingered for centuries and occasionally had been rekindled, such as in the early ninth-century Khorramdinan movements, in the fifteenth- and sixteenth-century Noqtavi movement, and even during the 1849 Babi resistance in Mazandaran. During the Constitutional Revolution modern socialist ideologies, a spillover from the 1905 Russian revolution, reached Tabriz through the Caucasus, mostly via Azerbaijani émigré workers in the oil fields of Baku. A few managed to gain prominence on the Iranian political stage after 1909, and Iranian socialists joined the Adalat Party after 1916. Among them, Avates Mikailian, known as Habib Soltanzadeh (1889–1938), a theoretician of some sophistication and later a critic of the Soviets' heavy-handed indoctrination, was the chief counterweight to Haydar Khan 'Amu-Ughlu and Ehsanollah Khan. He met a predictable fate, falling victim to one of Stalin's purges.

Among nonrevolutionary socialists, Solayman Mirza Eskandari (1863–1944), a Qajar aristocrat and veteran leader of the Democrat coalition in the second

Majles, emerged as a political leader of the moderate Ajtema'iun Party with socialist proclivities. He had maintained an ambivalent attitude toward Reza Khan, and even briefly served as a minister under him. A cultured man, Solayman Mirza represented the last of the generation who viewed socialism primarily as an anticolonial force in a constitutional framework. The consolidation of Pahlavi rule, however, wiped out any such chance for the Iranian left. Loyalty to the Soviet leadership over world communism reduced most socialists in the eyes of authorities to dangerous agitators, if not traitors. The Pahlavi secret police quelled any form of left-leaning labor protest and trade union activities, and from 1931 on, new legislation declared illegal any communist (*eshteraki*) organization. Recruiting among Iranian students abroad remained the only alternative for die-hard veterans, and interwar Germany, with an active communist movement, proved fertile ground. Many Iranians studied in Germany on government scholarships.

The career of Taqi Arani (1903–1940), a forerunner of the Tudeh Party, and his gradual conversion from nationalism to Marxism, is a case in point. A product of the postconstitutional environment, he started as an ardent nationalist (as his adopted surname *Arani*—meaning "Aryan" but also "someone from Aran," the ancient name for Azarbaijan—suggested). His later education as a student on government scholarship in Berlin in the tumultuous years of the Weimar Republic gradually turned him into a socialist with a penchant for dialectic materialism and the scientific theory of relativity. Upon his return to Iran in 1931, when he had earned a doctorate in chemistry and accepted a teaching post at Tehran Technical College, founded by the Germans, Arani's circle of Marxist-leaning intellectuals still operated on the idea of gradually transforming Iranian society toward greater social justice and improving the lot of the poor and deprived. His publication of *Donya*, a journal of social and scientific debate, also was meant to reflect a spirit of evolutionary rather than revolutionary progress through education and raising social awareness. The highbrow articles ranged from causality, scientific reality, and dialectical materialism to sophisticated criticisms of the then-fashionable Bergsonian spiritualism, which he compared to the Persian counterrationalist legacy of Persian Sufism, obstacles, in his view, to scientific progress.

His arrest, subsequent trial, and ten-year sentence as the alleged ringleader of a communist circle, which came after a student protest at Tehran University in 1938, ruined the young Arani. He joined a few other Marxists of various persuasions in the dreaded dungeons of Reza Shah. That Arani perished in February 1940 at the age of thirty-seven, after eighteen months of solitary confinement, is a sober statement on the fate of the intellectual left, who potentially could have articulated a different reading of Marxism at least partially free of the shackles of Stalinism. Whether he died of typhoid, as prison authorities claimed, or was murdered in jail—as happened to many of Reza Shah's real or perceived opponents—he was destined to become a martyr of the left.

In the years that followed, prominent figures among the Group of Fifty-Three (*panjah o seh nafar*)—as the Marxist convicts in Reza Shah's jail came to be known (thanks to the author Bozorg Alavi, whose memoirs of his confinement appeared under the same title)—gravitated toward Marxism-Leninism, often with unabashed loyalty to Soviet Union. An early show of the Tudeh's true colors came during the 1943 "northern oil" affair, when the Soviet Union pressed the Iranian government to acquire an oil concession in northern Iran. The Tudeh leadership advocated granting the concession in the Caspian littoral to counter, as it argued, British control of Iran's southern oil fields. By 1945, at the end of the war, while insisting on the northern concession, which Tudeh described as "positive equilibrium," it also closed ranks behind Stalin's decision to continue the Red Army's occupation of Azarbaijan.

The Tudeh was largely influential among schoolteachers, university students, and some faculty, low-ranking civil servants, intellectuals and some labor organizers, activists in the northern centers such as Rasht and Tabriz, industrial workers in Isfahan, and oil-field workers in the south. Organized and disciplined, at least among its rank and file, the strength of the Tudeh was in its frequent street demonstrations, labor protests, and engaging of the public through its numerous publications and "dialectical" debates. The strike in the southern oil field in March 1946 over low wages, appalling living conditions, and the overall exploitation of workers by the Anglo-Iranian Oil Company (AIOC, as the Anglo-Persian Oil Company came to be known after 1938) demonstrated Tudeh's popular base and political muscle (see map 8.2).

The image of the strength the Tudeh projected was enhanced by the fact that other political tendencies failed to present a viable program or a solid party structure. The Tudeh's domestic program called for better wages and working conditions, land reform and an end to agrarian exploitation, mass literacy, and workers' profit sharing. These were objectives later adopted with some modifications by the liberal nationalists and, in due course, in the 1960s by the shah's White Revolution. Yet despite common grounds, the Tudeh did not hesitate to label liberal nationalists as tools of American imperialism, a conspiratorial worldview shared by most communist parties of the time as well as by others in the Iranian political arena.

THE AZARBAIJAN CRISIS

The end of the war ironically added to Iran's political strife. By 1945, as post-war discord solidified in the Cold War, it complicated Iran's domestic politics almost instantaneously. This was nowhere more palpable than in the auton-omy-seeking movement led by the pro-Soviet Democratic Party of Azarbaijan, an episode short in duration but with important consequences for Iran's domes-tic and foreign policies. The Azarbaijan crisis was the first clear contest between the Western bloc and the Soviet Union during the Cold War.

As the time for evacuation of the Allied troops drew near, the British and American forces withdrew before the end of the six-month grace period that was stipulated in the 1942 treaty. The Soviets procrastinated, however, under the pretext of security concerns for the Baku oil fields and the possibility of sabotage from the Iranian side. The prospect of the Red Army's prolonged oc-cupation of Azarbaijan not only alarmed the Western powers, their Iranian sym-pathizers, the shah, and the army but also increasingly the nationalist circles. The memories of Russian occupations during the Constitutional Revolution and World War I came back to haunt Iranians once it became evident that the Red Army had no intention of evacuating the "liberated" territories under its control. More worrisome was the steep shift in the Azarbaijan Democratic Party's rhetoric on secession, which appeared to many observers in Tehran as an ominous prelude to Iran's disintegration. That the Democratic Party of Kurdis-tan was seeking autonomy in cahoots with its Azarbaijani counterpart added to these worries (see map 8.2).

The leader of the Democratic Party of Azarbaijan, Sayyed Ja'far Pishehvari (1893–1947), was a revolutionary veteran of the Jangal movement who also partici-pated in the short-lived autonomy-seeking movement in 1920 of Mohammad Kh-iabani in Azarbaijan (which Khiabani labeled as Azādestan, "the liberated land"). Earlier as an émigré to the Russian Caucasus, young Pishehvari was among the first to join the Adalat Party of Baku and take part in the 1917 Russian Revolution. He was deeply impressed with Lenin and the Bolsheviks' message of social justice and equality for all ethnicities and religions. After spending ten years in Reza Shah's jail on charges of communist activities, upon his release in 1941 Pishehvari became one of the founding members of the Tudeh Party. Soon, however, he parted with the Tehran Marxist intellectuals and resumed his activities under direct Soviet supervision. A vocal advocate in his Tehran newspaper of the Soviet positions, he was a communist in action but an ethnic nationalist at heart.

Pishehvari returned to Tabriz enraged after he was disqualified as a deputy from Azarbaijan to the fourteenth Majles on the grounds that he had tampered with the votes with the blessing of the Soviet occupiers. Arriving in Tabriz he was joined by a clique of émigrés from the Soviet Republic of Azarbaijan and by a handful of local Azarbaijani radicals. Together they formed the central cadre of the Democratic Party. Almost simultaneously in Mahabad the Kurdish nationalist Qazi Mohammad (1893–1947), the head of the Democratic Party of Kurdistan, declared autonomy and at the behest of the Soviets soon declared support for the Azarbaijan movement.

The program of the Azarbaijan Democrats was impressive, at least on paper, and in some ways reflective of resentment toward the Tehran government. The Pahlavis' centralization policies and particularly the mandatory study of Persian in schools at the expense of Azarbaijani Turkish—treating the latter as somewhat an alien language—was a source of justifiable outrage. Beyond the issue of language, the belief that Azarbaijan had not received its fair share of political representation or economic and infrastructural priorities added to animosities toward Iran's Persian-speaking majority. Also emphasized in the Democrats' program of action were autonomy in all provincial affairs including creation of a militia force to maintain security and implement provincial policies; primary education in Turkish, Turkish-language press, broadcast, and cultural activities; establishing a university in Tabriz; proportional representation in the Majles; overhaul of the taxation policies; and earmarking provincial revenue for development of Azarbaijan's road building, communications, urban amenities, and infrastructural improvement. Moreover, they sought administrative reforms and purging of the hated gendarmerie of the Pahlavi government and end to abusive practices against the villagers, redistribution of the state lands, and appropriation of estates belonging to large landowners who had fled the province.

In achieving these objectives—potentially an experiment in federalism—the Democrats relied on a small group of communist old-timers and émigrés, left-leaning middle-class activists, a number of middle- and lower-ranking army officers, and a small peasant militia armed by the Red Army. Capitalizing on the legacy of the Constitutional Revolution, the Tabriz resistance of 1908–1909, the Khiabani movement, and drawing on the neighboring Turkish Republic's 1920 National Pact, the Azarbaijani Democrats envisioned their role, at least early on, as saviors of all of Iran. Yet during its short life, the autonomous government sharpened its secessionist rhetoric; leaned more toward the Soviet Union; quarreled with the central government; disarmed the Iranian army in their Azarbaijan barracks, the police, and the gendarmerie; dismissed non-Azarbaijani officials; suppressed voices of opposition; and promised to defend itself "to the last drop" against Tehran's attempts to reintegrate the province. To make the

Tabriz government more secure, it also drove out big landowners and distributed the state lands. It paved roads, built schools, and fought hoarding and price
hikes. Moreover, it advanced for the first time universal suffrage and appointed
women to the party's governing body. Adopting the Soviet model but under the
guise of the Iranian Constitution, it even created regional and urban councils.

Subservience to the Soviets aside, the successes of the autonomous government were impressive even in the eyes of critics. No Pahlavi provincial authority had made such gains in a short period. That the Azarbaijan regime was
self-conscious of its "Turkish" ethnicity to the point of secession clearly contrasted with Azarbaijan's role four decades earlier during the constitutional period, when, devoid of ethnic sentiments, the province served as the powerhouse
of a nationwide Iranian revolution. The tangible change in tone was primarily
ideological. As Tehran under Pahlavi rule swung more toward a Perso-centric
nationalism, so did the Democrats toward an Azarbaijani identity. That there
was a Soviet Republic of Azarbaijan on the other side of the border helped all
the more to manipulate a sense of Turkish solidarity. From Moscow's perspective the autonomous movement was a long shot in unifying the two Azarbai-
jans. There were other immediate objectives, too.

QAVAM'S QUEST FOR "GOOD FAITH"

The belligerent gestures of the Democratic Party raised anxieties in Tehran.
The land reforms implemented by the Democrats had forced large-scale landlords from Azarbaijan and appropriated their estates. The shah and ranking
army officers, moreover, were convinced that Azarbaijan's secession is a prelude to Iran's breakup. The Red Army's candid support for the autonomous
regime, and especially barring Tehran's military reinforcements from reaching
Tabriz, reaffirmed such anxieties. These also resonated with the British and
the American concerns for the imminent creation of Soviet satellites in Iranian
Azarbaijan and neighboring Kurdistan. Yet neither the Iranian political lineup
nor the still-courteous relations among the Allies expedited any drastic action.
Negotiating with the Democrats seemed the only plausible way. The coming
to office of the seasoned statesman Ahmad Qavam as prime minister in 1946, at
the head of a broad coalition, was intended to achieve this objective, which had
brought down earlier governments.

Born to a family of divan nobility who for four generations were in the service
of the Qajar state, Ahmad Qavam was always proud that he had prepared in
1906 the final draft of the royal rescript known as the Constitutional Decree. As

Qavam al-Saltaneh ("foundation of the monarchy")—the Qajar title of which he was highly proud and fiercely protective—he learned his time-honored political skills in the Qajar court. His vast hereditary estates in Azarbaijan and Mazandaran also contributed to his financial resilience. Shrewd, lofty, and yet pragmatic, he was more successful—or luckier—than his older brother, Hasan Vosuq al-Dowleh. Always ready to take calculated risks, Qavam's career was punctuated with many ups and downs. Fearing Reza Shah in his final years, Qavam wisely spent his time in internal exile and like many notables of similar stature, in 1941 returned to the political limelight. He nursed a subtle grudge toward the Pahlavi crown while maintaining a working relationship with a wide range of players on the political stage.

His premiership between January 1946 and December 1947—the second since his rehabilitation—was a renewed chance to engage in a balancing act typical of the Qajar elite but with some important innovations. By juggling at one time the shah, the army, the Azarbaijan Democrats, the Tudeh Party and its Soviet patron, the British and the Anglophile clique (and later the pro-British southern tribes), the American diplomats and the US military mission, as well as the old elites and ambitious members of the middle class, he managed to gain impressive results, though only briefly. His policy of "positive equilibrium" resembled Naser al-Din Shah's treatment of his powerful neighbors, and his advocacy of negotiation in "good faith" (*hosn-e niyyat*) with his many political adversaries was rooted in shrewd pragmatism.

Most urgent were three interrelated issues: persuading Stalin to evacuate Azarbaijan, finding a solution to Soviet demand for an oil concession, and finding a way out of the Azarbaijan autonomy crisis. Soon after his appointment, he flew to Moscow along with his left-leaning deputy Mozaffar Firuz (1906–1988), a political enabler from the powerful Farmanfarma family. The son of Firuz Mirza Nosrat al-Dowleh, Mozaffar at the time was Iran's ambassador to the Soviet Union. Direct negotiations with Stalin led to a surprisingly favorable accord signed in March 1946 that committed the Red Army to a swift withdrawal from all Iranian territories. A Soviet-Iranian joint oil company was also to be formed to explore granting a concession in the northern Iranian provinces, but with a crucial caveat. Any such concession was conditional on the ratification of the forthcoming fifteenth Majles. This was essential, as Qavam argued, since the fourteenth Majles, thanks to Mohammad Mosaddeq, then the leader of the opposition in the Majles, and his allies, banned Iranian government from negotiating any oil concession with a foreign government without the approval of the legislature. The April 1946 Qavam-Sadchikov Accord, as it came to be know, also recognized that the Azarbaijan crisis was purely an Iranian internal affair and hoped that it would be peacefully resolved within the existing constitutional framework and in a spirit of good faith.

Keeping the momentum, Qavam quickly invited to Tehran representatives of the Azarbaijan Democrats and negotiated a fifteen-article agreement from a position of strength. It conceded to them genuine grievances and their proposed reforms while modifying their claim of autonomy by defining the Democrats' elected assembly as a provincial council (*anjoman-e ayalati*) endorsed by the Iranian constitution but long neglected. To further nurture the new accord with the Soviet Union, and as a gesture of goodwill toward the Iranian left, in a government reshuffle Qavam brought into his cabinet four ministers from the Tudeh Party, an unprecedented move that earned him the praise in the Soviet press as the "greatest politician of the East." He complemented his balancing act by appointing centrist ministers to meet the liberal nationalist constituency as well as appointees close to the royal court and the army.

To further consolidate his government, and his domestic program of reform, in May 1946 Qavam created his own Democratic Party of Iran, a wide coalition that included younger socialist and liberal politicians, mostly of middle-class backgrounds; elites and conservatives of older generations; supporters of the shah; supporters of the army; and representatives of the powerful tribes—all bundled together under one shaky political tent. By mid-1946 it seemed that his government had overcome multiple challenges and was about to remedy the country's chronic aliments. He formed for the first time a supreme council for devising a planned economy, overhauling labor laws, and reforming the much-abused election laws; he established a state-owned investment bank for industrial and mining developments; and he began to distribute state-owned agricultural lands to small landowners. His program appeared to be closer to an American capitalist model than the familiar state-based notions of development.

Yet Qavam evidently underestimated the forces of opposition, both domestic and foreign, and their ability to close ranks against his politics of reconciliation. A group of powerful khans from the central and southern tribes hastily colluded under the banner of Nahzat-e Jonub (Southern Movement) seeking autonomy and demanding countermeasures to stop communist infiltration in the south. They enjoyed the full support of the Anglophile party of Sayyed Zia al-Din Tabataba'i, the tacit support of the shah (and probably his financial backing) and blessing of the British consuls in Fars and Khuzestan. Employing their tribal riflemen, the Qashqa'i and the Khamseh of Fars, the Dashtestani and other tribes of southern Fars, branches of the Bakhtiyari confederacy of Isfahan and Khuzestan, and the Mamasani and Boyer Ahmad of Luristan raised havoc with the population of the neighboring towns and villages, raiding gendarmerie and police posts and disarming the demoralized government troops. Their chief targets, however, were the oil workers of the Anglo-Iranian Oil Company and their Tudeh-affiliated trade union, which had gone on strike over pay and better working conditions. The Arabic-speaking communities of Ahvaz and around the Abadan refinery had joined in seeking recognition for Khuzestan as part of the grater Arab nation. They even sent a delegation to Baghdad to seek support. To many nationalists and to centrists in Tehran, this was further sign of an impending disintegration of the country.

The prospect of a civil war involving the autonomy-seeking movements in Azarbaijan and Kurdistan and the threat of the rebellion of the southern tribes were too great for Qavam. Even before the start of the fifteenth Majles, he was already facing tensions within his own party and from the parliamentary opposition led by Mosaddeq and from the conservative quarters. No more merciful were the press, which painted him as a corrupt and arrogant aristocrat and a leftover from the rotten Qajar elite. To lessen the pressure, Qavam had to disown the Azarbaijan regime for its secessionist ambitions, dismiss the Tudeh ministers from his cabinet after only seventy-five days of their being in office, appoint more pro-shah ministers, bring back the centrist General Razmara as the army chief of staff, and reaffirm the American military advisory mission headed by Colonel Herbert Norman Schwarzkopf (1895–1958, the earlier chief of the New Jersey police and a Roosevelt appointee). Moreover, at the urging of the United States and Britain, Qavam affirmed Iran's complaint against the Soviet Union in the newly established UN Security Council and eventually allowed for preparation for the long-overdue election of the fifteenth Majles, which was made conditional to the Allies' withdrawal.

To outside observers, the sudden shift in Qavam orientation seemed opportunistic and thus a sign of weakness, even though by moving away from the left and embracing the center-right, Qavam was making the most out of a difficult situation. Though like his Qajar predecessor he did not fully adhere to either of the two camps, his realpolitik no doubt was succumbing to pressure from the shah, and from the United States, especially on the question of Azarbaijan. Under the pretext of safeguarding a fair election in Azarbaijan for the fifteenth Majles, the Qavam government thus felt confident enough to dispatch troops to the bordering Zanjan region, then controlled by the Azarbaijan Democrats. After a brief pause and a bloody confrontation on December 12, 1946, the Iranian army swiftly marched to Azarbaijan, crushing local resistance along the way and soon took control of the province.

The advance of the army after months of negotiations and reneging on both sides was not unexpected, even by the Tabriz leadership. Pishehvari and most of his staunch supporters, despite their reassurances to the contrary, quickly fled across the border to Soviet Azerbaijan, leaving behind some apparatchiks and exposing their rural militia to vengeful troops and the whims of large landlords and their henchmen. In reclaiming their lost estates, landowners proved even more oppressive than the indoctrinated Democrats. Some lower-ranking party members were captured and sentenced to long prison terms, others were retaliated against, and yet others went into hiding. The army officers who had defected to the Democrats' side were promptly tried and executed. In a short time the whole of Azerbaijan, and soon after Kurdistan province, returned to government control, putting an inglorious end to what was soon to be labeled the Azarbaijan "rebellion," and its perpetrators, alien "aggressors."

As it turned out, the real winner of the "heroic" return of Azarbaijan to the motherland was not Qavam but the twenty-seven-year-old Mohammad Reza Shah and generals of his army, who were anxious to score a victory to reverse the bad memories of the 1941 fiasco and years of imposing unpopular martial law over the Iranian public. The United States, the chief sponsor of the rejuvenated Iranian armed forces, also scored an early success in the escalating Cold War, at least on the Middle East front. The crisis had placed the shah and most of the Iranian senior military in the American camp. The shah, who flew to Azarbaijan piloting a small military aircraft, was basking in a glory that was not really his for he hadn't played a major part in the operation's planning or execution. In later years he made sure that repatriation of Azarbaijan was commemorated annually with military parades, radio broadcasts of jingoistic slogans and military music, and the naming of streets after the felicitous event. It was the first of many acts the shah used to exalt his own image.

The collapse of the Azarbaijan autonomy movement reaffirmed the power of the political center over the geographical periphery. Soviet ambition aside, the Azarbaijan movement was a reaction to the intense centralization of the Reza Shah era and his imposition of a cultural homogenization policy over diverse ethnicities. It in effect sealed the position of the Iranian state as a centralized power and demonstrated that ethnicity—and in the Azarbaijan case the emphasis on language as the core of ethnic identity—had little chance to win out when territorial nationalism as the dominant ideology of the state complemented geopolitical factors.

Qavam, however, was not entirely out of the picture. The final act of the Azarbaijan drama had yet to play out on the floor of the fifteenth Majles, and chiefly through the actions of Qavam's rival and relative Mohammad

Mosaddeq. After the withdrawal of the Red Army and demise of Azarbaijan autonomy, the fate of the northern oil concession was to be decided. Rigging the election with the help of the royal court and the army, Qavam hoped to control the majority in the legislature even though a small minority headed by Mosaddeq, who was highly critical of Qavam, were reelected. In October 1947 when the bill to establish a joint Soviet-Iranian oil venture in northern Iran was proposed by Qavam's government, it was declared dead on arrival. Mosaddeq and his nationalist allies, some still members of Qavam's Democratic Party, vigorously campaigned against granting any oil concession to foreign powers, a crucial move that set the stage for the nationalization of Iran's oil industry two years later.

Soon after the vote, Qavam's government, the longest serving in the postwar years, began to crumble. Massive strikes and frequent demonstrations orchestrated by the Tudeh Party and affiliated labor unions, which had become Qavam's sworn enemies, paralyzed his government. Ministers who even a few weeks earlier were loyal to him resigned, some because he appeared to be sticking to his end of the agreement with the Soviets, and others because he appeared to be reneging it. Rabble-rousers in the Majles such as Hosain Makki (1911–1999) and Mozaffar Baqa'i (1912–1987), who earlier supported Qavam, resigned and joined Mosaddèq's parliamentary faction. The press, too, labeled him the "old fox" of Iranian politics. Having no choice, he resigned in desperation in December 1947 and quickly left for medical treatment in Europe. Yet despite this apparent defeat, whether out of good faith or through sheer maneuvering, he had achieved the immediate goals he had set for his government, something that no other premier during the tumultuous postwar years could claim. He had ended the secessionist crises, had brought together the left and the center (at least briefly), had opened new avenues for middle-class mobility, and had initiated a planned economy for the country.

IN PURSUIT OF OIL NATIONALIZATION

The annulment of the northern oil concession, Qavam's unforeseen political Achilles' heel, immediately rekindled both in and out of the Majles the long-standing demand to renegotiate the oil concession that had been granted to the Anglo-Iranian Oil Company (AIOC). The failure of Reza Shah's government to improve the terms of the original D'Arcy oil concession of 1901 had left a lasting scar. The 1933 concession extended for another sixty years AIOC's full control over the huge oil fields of Khuzestan as well as over production levels, distribution, pricing, bookkeeping, taxation, and ownership of installations and equipment at Abadan refinery. The AIOC, which was owned by the British government, was not only a vital source for replenishing the postwar British economy but also a source of steady income, having extended operations beyond Iran into neighboring Iraq; Kuwait; and the British-controlled emirates of the Persian Gulf, the so-called Trucial States stretching from Abu Dhabi to the border of Oman (the future United Arab Emirates).

The Iranian share, a meager royalty on the production of Iranian crude, amounted as late as 1951 to barely 16 percent of the total. In a clever ploy, moreover, the Iranian share was subject to income taxes paid to the British treasury not only on the oil extracted from Iranian fields but also on AIOC production in the whole region. In 1947 AIOC's after-tax profits exceeded £40 million (US$161 million), which entitled Iran to just £7 million ($34 million), or 17.5 percent royalties, from its own production, and this only after preliminary efforts to increase the Iranian share. There were other flagrantly unfair AIOC practices in determining Iranian royalties and other revenues, to which the Iranians had long objected. Discriminatory treatment toward Iranian technicians, engineers, and managers was another source of grievance. The AIOC—the forerunner of today's British Petroleum (BP)—ran the Iranian oil industry not unlike a colonial plantation, exerting the hierarchy of class-conscious English society and preserving a culture of colonial privilege. Iran's other major contribution to the workforce was cheap labor, mostly Bakhtiyari herdsmen and the Arabic-speaking population of Khuzestan working under harsh conditions and with exploitative wages and poor living standards. On the oil workers' living conditions in Abadan one observer wrote:

> Wages were 50 cents a day. There was no vacation pay, no sick leave, no disability compensation. The workers lived in a shantytown called Kaghazabad, or Paper City, without running water or electricity. . . . In winter the earth flooded and became a flat, perspiring lake. The mud in town was knee-deep, and . . . when the rains subsided, clouds of nipping, small-winged flies rose from the stagnant water to fill the nostrils. . . . Summer was worse. . . . The heat was torrid . . . sticky and unrelenting—while the wind and sandstorms shipped off the desert hot as a blower. The dwellings of Kaghazabad, cobbled from rusted oil drums hammered flat, turned into sweltering ovens. . . . In every crevice hung the foul, sulfurous stench of burning oil. . . . [I]n Kaghazabad there was nothing—not a tea shop, not a bath, not a single tree. The tiled reflecting pool and shaded central square that were part of every Iranian town . . . were missing here. The unpaved alleyways were emporiums for rats.[1]

The cancellation of the northern oil concession thus offered to nationalists in the Iranian Majles a golden opportunity to demand renegotiation of the AIOC concession and eventually a call for nationalization of the Iranian oil industry. The policy of negative equilibrium set forth as early as 1946 was favored by Mosaddeq, his close colleague Hosain Makki and their cohorts, as well as by the Tudeh, which nevertheless was furious over the cancellation of the northern oil concession. With negative equilibrium, the nationalists aimed to cancel unfair privileges of both powers and to preserve Iran's precarious balance in an increasingly polarizing world. Stalin's gradual abandonment of the idea of an Iranian oil concession (apparently because of new prospects in western Siberian oil reserves) further helped Iranian nationalists in their quest.

Demands for better terms, and eventually for nationalization, also coincided with the decolonization of the postwar era, and no doubt were boosted by it. The end to nearly two centuries of British colonial presence in India and the eventual victory of the Indian nationalist movement was cherished by the Iranians, who for long had been mindful of the British power to the east. Yet Indian independence in July 1947 came with the painful experience of partition and the rise of the adversarial nations of India and Pakistan, an event coinciding in November 1947 with the partition of Mandatory Palestine and the emergence of the state of Israel despite Arab Palestinian protests.

Receiving wide coverage in the Iranian press, these events added to the already-tense relations with AIOC and mounting resentment toward the "old lion" of the British Empire, or as the Iranian press portrayed it, the "old fox." Partitions in Palestine and India were seen as British ploys to divide and prolong colonial rule in a new disguise, in the same way that AIOC was exploiting the fractured Iranian polity for its own benefits. Suspicion and distrust toward Britain thus bordered on open hostility. From the 1930s onwards, oil was no longer seen by the majority of Iranians just as a thick black material extracted from the underground by *farangis* in the midst of the remote southern Bakhtiyari mountains and then exported through the distant shores of the Persian Gulf. Now the Iranian oil was something connected to Iranians' everyday lives from the kerosene they put into their lamps to the gasoline that was needed for buses and trucks. Now they felt intensely that their national wealth was being excessively pumped out from under their feet at frivolous prices and shipped away to distant lands in order to secure the prosperity and well-being of powerful nations at the expense of their poverty and disempowerment.

Besides being an issue of Iran's moral right over its own resources, the demand for higher oil income became an urgent national cause given the fall in other sources of state revenue. Income from direct and indirect taxation, and customs and excise taxes, all diminished because of the postwar economic downturn. Over a quarter of a century the Iranian state—and to an increasing degree the Iranian economy—became heavily reliant on oil revenue for reorganizing its armed forces and later for financing its growing bureaucracy and public works. Even more so this was the case after World War II. US military aid after 1943 only partially helped the growing deficit, and US loans promised in the late 1940s and early 1950s did not materialize until after 1953. Enamored of the then-popular idea of the state as agent of economic development, Iranian nationalists considered oil revenue the only key to industrial and infrastructural transformation. The left hoped to replicate the Soviet planned economy, whereas the pro-Western tendencies relied on the American model of development, as articulated by the Roosevelt administration. The Iranian state sought an almost complete monopoly over oil income as a pragmatic means to achieve these objectives.

The increase in oil revenue since the 1920s, though impressive at first glance, was deceiving. While Iran's crude production increased nearly fivefold to thirty-one thousand long tons daily (equal to 252,500 barrels) between 1941 and 1950, its fixed royalties of 16 percent, a paltry one-sixth of the total AIOC income of £100 million (about $400 million), was canceled by near hyperinflation of the postwar years. The Iranians naturally felt the British government was not negotiating in good faith for better terms for Iran. The British public, in contrast, demanded that its government, then led by the Labour Party under Clement Attlee, compensate them for their sacrifices and hardships during the war and uphold the overseas interests crucial to the recovery of their nation. This was in clear contrast to demands for Iranian nationalization as in 1956 the British public opinion was diametrically opposed to Egypt's demand for nationalization of the Suez Canal. Even though the Labour government at the time was nationalizing major British industries including coal and the railroad, the rationale for nationalization was barely extended to investments abroad. Even Labour's leniency toward Iran at the outset of negotiations was countered by AIOC's rigidity, even hostility, toward Iranian demands, which remained unresolved.

POWER SCRAMBLES AND MISSED CHANCES

The oil negotiations only deepened Iran's political divide, which by now was conditioned by Cold War rivalries. Whether directly or by proxy, a multiparty scramble between 1949 and 1951 involved ambitious army generals, Mohammad Reza Shah and the royal court, conservative statesmen, the Tudeh Party and its sympathizers, the politicized clergy who were returning to the political stage, their affiliated Islamist organizations, and liberal nationalist and their diverse allies who were organized under the umbrella of the National Front (Jebheh-ye Melli).

In January 1949 a renewed call in the Majles for the nationalization of Iran's oil industry added fresh momentum to the anti-British sentiments. Though not entirely unprecedented, the Majles debate energized the minority deputies led by Mohammad Mosaddeq, pressing the government to negotiate a new deal with AIOC. Less than a month later, in a tense environment of polarized politics and short-lived alliances, an unsuccessful assassination attempt was carried out against the shah by a presumed Tudeh sympathizer. The shah, who was attending a public event at Tehran University, escaped major injuries, but the incident offered a chance for forces supporting the shah to declare the Tudeh Party illegal, arrest its leadership—some of its members appeared to be involved in the plot—and start a nationwide crackdown on the left.

Soon after, the shah, who exploited the incident to gain a greater say in domestic affairs and presumably to defuse maverick factionalism in the Majles, demanded the revision of the constitution so as to provide him with a new royal prerogative. In July 1949 a hastily convened Constituent Assembly amended article 48 of the 1906–1907 constitution thus granting new constitutional powers to the shah to dissolve the Majles at his discretion but on the condition that a new election be held within the following six months. This victory for Mohammad Reza Shah was doubtless achieved with some level of support from the populace, tired of political skirmishes and skullduggery in and out of the Majles (pl. 9.3).

If the amendment to the constitution was clearly in the shah's favor, the rapidly changing political climate was not. With frequent street demonstrations becoming an effective tool of the Tudeh, and with pro-Mosaddeq advocates taking the upper hand in the press and behind the podium, the election of the sixteenth Majles was bound to become the focal point of nationalist opposition to the status quo. Protesting the rigged election—which favored conservative candidates mostly of the landowning classes—a coalition of nationalist deputies headed by Mosaddeq took advantage of the new constitutional amendment and demanded that the shah cancel the old election and order a new one. At the outset this proved a futile maneuver, even after Mosaddeq and his allies took a prolonged sanctuary (*bast*) in the royal palace. Yet a few months later, the shah succumbed to public pressure and ordered a new election only in the capital. In January 1950 when the Tehran electorate went to the polls, Mosaddeq and candidates of the National Front gained the highest number of votes, a starting point for a process that eventually brought Mosaddeq to the office of prime minister. The tacit alignment of the shah with the National Front, however, was ephemeral and largely a reaction to both the growth of Tudeh and the rise of General Razmara as the new strongman of the armed forces.

General Haj 'Ali Razmara's premiership in June 1950 came in the wake of many months of political turmoil and changes or reshuffling in the weak cabinets. A rising star of the Iranian army, Razmara was a French-educated field officer who served throughout Iran in various capacities in the military and was popular among the lower ranks. He was the key officer in recapturing Azarbaijan in 1946, and at the age of forty-seven he had become Iran's youngest chief of staff. Ambitious, disciplined, and politically astute, he had married up in the nobility.

While reaching an understanding with the Tudeh Party, Razmara nurtured some support among conservatives, which allowed him to keep the shah at bay for a while and try to rein in the National Front on the crucial issue of oil negotiations with AIOC. He had the blessing of the United States, which saw him as a bulwark against both communism and the reactionaries and had promised him much-needed financial aid. He had the confidence of Britain in settling the oil crisis, at least at the outset, and was on good terms with the Soviet Union, which was heartened by his soft handling of the Tudeh. For a moment it seemed that he had mastered the most volatile stage four years after Qavam's coalition government had brought a semblance of political stability to the country.

Siding with the moderates, Razmara backed the Supplemental Agreement, a proposal negotiated earlier with the Anglo-Iranian Oil Company and was before the Majles since July 1949. It offered Iran better terms but fell far short of the demands set forth by the Iranian nationalists and backed by the popular press. He soon realized that the Supplemental Agreement had no chance in the face of fierce opposition from the National Front. Nor were the AIOC's negotiators willing to offer better terms. Loyal to the colonial mentality of the time, the AIOC executives—and the British civil servants who backed them in London— came up with the ingenious ides of holding the Iranian government in breach of the 1933 agreement, a concession that the British government had earlier almost imposed on Reza Shah and his minister of finance, Hasan Taqizadeh.

Furthermore, the AIOC condescendingly viewed Iranian subordinates in its employment as incapable of holding managerial posts and unable to grasp the company's bookkeeping—which the Iranians viewed as shady and full of dishonest accounting practices. It moreover brazenly defended its treatment of the Iranian workforce. Stubborn and shortsighted–almost cynical—it turned a deaf ear to Razmara's repeated pleas and to the United States' mediation efforts behind the scene. The US interest in the negotiations was perceived by AIOC as likely to allow Americans an eventual foothold in the Iranian oil industry. American oil companies—themselves not models of fairness and integrity—

had negotiated new contracts with the government of Venezuela on a fifty-fifty profit sharing basis, and in 1950 they were about to do the same with Saudi Arabia, where ARAMCO, a conglomerate of giant American oil companies, had been operating since 1933. ARAMCO had received, in exchange for the fifty-fifty deal with Saudi Arabia, a 50 percent tax break from US Congress (known as the "golden gimmick"). The AIOC refused to consider any of that and quietly urged the Americans to keep the Saudi deal a secret until the Iranians agreed to their far less favorable terms.

By November 1950, when the Majles finally rejected the Supplemental Agreement, the reluctant AIOC began to entertain similar terms of fifty-fifty profit sharing, which, as it turned out, was too late. Despite signs of earlier moderation, the Majles' Oil Committee—chaired by Mohammad Mosaddeq—was no longer interested in anything short of full ownership of Iran's oil industry. Razmara recognized the eventuality of nationalization and the potentials of public enthusiasm aroused by months of debates in and out of the Majles. He argued that Iran was technically and financially unprepared to take over the giant oil industry and instead suggested that it was more realistic to adopt a gradualist approach toward nationalization. Yet the firebrands within the National Front, and Mosaddeq himself, were in no mood to back down from the rhetoric and give Razmara a chance. They accused him instead of financial corruption, hounding the press, and being a "British lackey" and a traitor who deserved to be eliminated.

Razmara's proposed decentralization program also met with disapproval from the National Front, even though the Constitution envisaged the popularly elected provincial councils as the basis for a less centralized political arrangement. His plan was labeled by his opponents as a "conspiracy" to partition Iran. Razmara's anticorruption campaign, to rid the country of the inept officialdom—and more important, his proposed land reform—faced resistance from the landowning deputies in the Majles. Curbing the influence of the royal court functionaries equally angered the shah. The press moreover damaged his moral standing by hinting at his secret liaisons. The Tudeh Party, too, whose leadership had escaped prison and fled to exile in the Soviet Union—allegedly with the help of Razmara's pro-Tudeh officers—were no kinder to the premier and even branded him an agent of American imperialism. In reality, Razmara's foreign policy parted ways with the Americans' patronizing support and even went so far as to end the US military aid program and abort reconnaissance flights over the Soviet border.

In March 1951, still at the political helm and determined to resolve the oil dispute, Razmara was assassinated by Khalil Tahmasbi, a member of the

Fada'iyan-e Islam (those who sacrifice themselves for Islam) terrorist organization when he was attending a memorial in a Tehran mosque. The assassin was loyal to the speaker of the Majles, Ayatollah Abul-Qasem Kashani (1877–1962), and to the maverick politician Mozaffar Baqa'i, a Majles deputy and ranking member of the National Front who had a checkered past. Other members of the National Front were also accused of involvement. Whether the assassination was the work of a deranged mind or, more likely, triggered by Razmara's personal feud with Kashani—who was bitter over having been temporarily exiled by Razmara after the attempt against the shah's life—remains a matter of speculation. The Iranian narrative often downplayed Razmara's assassination, for if he was not demonized as a foreign agent, he was considered a potential dictator in the model of Reza Khan. His removal benefited both the shah—who was afraid of his energetic general—and the National Front at a time when quarrels over oil nationalization had reached a new height.

Two weeks after Razmara's assassination, on the eve of the Nowruz celebration (March 20, 1951), the oil nationalization bill passed the Majles after more than two years of heated debate. Vast popular support for Mosaddeq in rallies and in the press was a sign of a clear public mandate. The absence of a balancing force, such as Razmara, also triggered a massive anti-AIOC strike throughout the oil industry, organized by the Tudeh Party. It turned violent and cost many lives. Both events promised more conflicts domestically and internationally.

The rise to prominence of Ayatollah Kashani as an ally of the National Front and speaker of the Majles registered a turning point, for it signaled the end of clergy's political isolation under Reza Shah. As an activist leader he should be seen as the historical link between Modarres, a generation earlier, and Ayatollah Khomeini, a generation later. After returning from exile in Beirut at the shah's personal urging, Kashani not only had gained a new accolade but also had added a new element of Islamic radicalism to the public space. As a result, the Fada'iyan-e Islam, his implicit allies, acquired greater acceptance in the political fold. Abul-Qasem Kashani, a mojtahed trained in Najaf in the late 1910s, had earned his prestige by his politics rather than his scholarly record. Witness to the British occupation of southern Iraq during World War I, in 1919 he was sentenced to death in absentia by the British mandatory authorities for his part in the Iraqi Shi'i revolt. Fleeing to Iran, he became a protégé of Hasan Modarres and stood with him against Reza Khan's 1924 proposed republic. Shortly afterward, however, when he was elected to the Constituent Assembly that abolished the Qajar dynasty, he voted in favor of Pahlavi rule and remained on amiable terms with Reza Shah.

During World War II he was arrested by the British occupying forces in Iran on charges of harboring pro-Nazi sentiments and was sent into exile. Soon after his return a few years later, he rose to prominence, first by organizing a contingent of Iranian volunteers to the Arab-Israeli War in 1948 and afterward as the patron of the Fada'iyan-e Islam. Naming Razmara an infidel whose blood was to be shed, his pronouncement acted as a virtual fatwa emboldening the Fada'iyan to murder the premier. As an influential cleric, Kashani appealed to the National Front for he mustered large crowds of the lower-middle classes and the bazaar merchants in support of the nationalist cause. Later as the speaker of the Majles he proved only partially committed to the National Front's program and soon after became something of a liability for Mosaddeq. By 1953 he had abandoned the National Front altogether and implicitly defected to the shah's camp, a glaring shift of loyalty to be followed by most members of the clergy. Rumored to be colluding with the AIOC representatives, his turnaround was a major blow to the nationalist cause.

As tactical allies of Kashani, the Fada'iyan-e Islam a small but effective semi-clandestine militant group, routinely resorted to terror, intimidation, and assassination of the "enemies of Islam." Their utopian Islamic order was disciplined by a strict reading of the shari'a, and they shared characteristics with advocates of Salafism. The Fada'iyan's founder and leader, who chose the nostalgic pseudonym Navvab Safavi, or "prince of the Safavid house," was a maladapted seminarian in Qom who once was an AIOC employee in Abadan. He was no doubt inspired by Ikhwan al-Muslimin (Society of Muslim Brothers) in Egypt and like that group's founder, Hasan al-Banna, nursed anticolonial sentiments after having worked in a British-controlled environment. Like the Ikhwan, the Iranian Fada'iyan tried to build a hierarchical network of devotees. Their use of the term *fada'i* (one who sacrifices his life for a cause) may have been inspired by memories of the twelfth-century Isma'ilis of the Alamut and legend of the Assassins, but in practice it was modeled after the Ikhwan's hierarchy.

A disturbing development of the postwar era, the Fada'iyan—nearly all laymen with backgrounds in the bazaar—were intolerant of both secular society and critics of Islamic shari'a as interpreted by mainstream clergy. In 1946 they assassinated Ahmad Kasravi for his disparaging remarks about Shi'ism. In 1949 they killed the minister of the royal court 'Abd al-Hosain Hazhir (1902–1949), a capable statesman and ally of the shah, presumably on charges of irreligious conduct and selling out to foreign interests. To achieve their ultimate goal of establishing an Islamic government, however, the Fada'iyan were willing to form tactical alliances even with members of the National Front or the Pahlavi court. Their radical convictions led to their eventual destruction however when in 1955 Navvab Safavi and two of his lieutenants were executed after a failed assassination attempt against the prime minister Hosain 'Ala (1884–1964), a statesman of some integrity from the Qajar nobility who was viewed as an Anglophile. Their memory lingered and inspired others in later generations and especially among the activists of the 1979 Islamic Revolution.

MOSADDEQ AND POLITICS OF PROTEST

After an interregnum of an interim government and weeks of negotiations with the shah, on April 28, 1951, Mohammad Mosaddeq was appointed the new prime minister. He had received seventy-nine votes of confidence out of the total of ninety-one Majles deputies present on the voting day. The leader of the National Front and one of the most eminent deputies in the whole life of the Majles, Mosaddeq was hailed as the defender of national sovereignty, constitutional rights, free and fair elections, and above all a champion of the oil nationalization campaign. His long career of more than half a century distinguished him as an ardent liberal, a seasoned parliamentarian, and a charismatic orator. His political savvy as a premier proved less immaculate, as he struggled to maneuver a bankrupt government through a tumultuous period of internal and external crisis.

Physically frail and melancholy in character, Mosaddeq was something of a hypochondriac, a condition not uncommon among members of the Qajar nobility. Mocking references in the Western press to the "crying" prime minister and his eccentricities, though thoroughly biased, may well be attributed to an anxiety disorder that made him susceptible to nervous collapse and bouts of depression. Frequently bedridden, he embarked on his national crusade from under a blanket, as if it might shield him from a hostile world. His informal manner of conducting government affairs from his bed, complete with pajamas and a white robe de chambre, became the subject of unfair ridicule. In formal attire, however, his abiding by rules of Persian etiquette and old-school courtesy made him a charming man of verve and character. Yet it was his public image of frailty and poor health that prevailed. As he once observed in conversation with Dean Acheson, the American secretary of state, his poor health reflected the condition of his nation, which had long been battered and bruised (fig. 9.4). It is no wonder that he was destined to be written into modern Iranian history—and modern Iranian psyche—as a fallen hero, a virtual martyr, and a personification of his nation, which was in cosmic battle with adversarial forces.

A principled and at times stubborn man, he was approaching seventy years of age when he accepted the office of premier. Like his relative Ahmad Qavam,

Figure 9.4. US Secretary of State Dean Acheson confers with
Prime Minister Mohammed Mosaddeq at Walter Reed Army
Medical Center in Washington, DC, October 1951.
Department of State, Courtesy of Harry S. Truman Library.

he belonged to Iran's bureaucratic and landowning nobility and had old family
ties to the Qajar house. His Qajar title was Mosaddeq al-Saltaneh ("validator of
the kingdom"). Having lost his father at a young age, he was brought up by his
mother, a matriarch who proved deeply influential to his personality and the
shaping of his public career. A pageboy in Naser al-Din Shah's court and later a
state accountant (*mostowfi*)—a hereditary office in his family—he rose through
the ranks to hold various high offices in the postconstitutional era. He observed
the Constitutional Revolution with a mix of respect and reservation, as any
nobleman of his standing would, before heading to France in 1910, followed by
three years of studying law at Neuchâtel University in Switzerland.

The experience of studying law in a modern European setting seemed to
have made him a lifetime convert to constitutionalism and the rule of law. Yet
unlike many Europeanized modernists of his time, he remained truly engaged
with his own culture and society. Having married into the family of the Imam
Jom'eh of Tehran—one of the oldest clerical families of Iran, with roots in the
Safavid era—Mosaddeq's somewhat unusual union seems to have helped give
him a new perspective on the place of Shi'i Islam in Iranian society and traditions. It also offered him a subject for his Swiss doctoral dissertation on will and
testaments and inheritance in Islamic law, a subject novel for a dissertation at
the time and for a man of his background. Examining subtleties of the Shi'i

legal system through the lens of modern European law helped him recognize impediments in enforcing these in a modern context. Upon his return in 1914, on the eve of World War I, he began a career of teaching and administration while publishing in Persian on such topics as capitulatory rights of imperial powers and national sovereignty. These were themes instructive in shaping his political vision.

By February 1921 and the rise of Reza Khan to power, Mosaddeq, like many of his cohorts, probably viewed the coup as a foreign plot in the wake of the aborted 1919 agreement (to which Mosaddeq had been adamantly opposed while he was still in Europe). Fearing arrest, he took refuge in Bakhtiyari territory in central Fars, a move that was seen by Tehran as prelude to a rebellion. Yet soon after the restoration of the Qajar notables, he returned to Tehran to serve in various sub-ministerial and ministerial posts. He came to accept Reza Khan as a necessary evil, though he did so with an air of condescension. He even joined a small group of like-minded statesmen and cultural figures who, in 1921, briefly took it upon themselves to educate the culturally uncouth Cossack officer. In 1922 Mosaddeq briefly served as finance minister under Qavam and in early 1923 as foreign minister under Hasan Moshir al-Dowleh Pirniya, though in both posts he performed as a conscientious but reluctant statesman. In every post he found a perfectly convincing reason to resign, a favorite resort in the face of resistance—or perceived resistance—to his moral high ground. Aside from the vagaries of the politics of the time and undeniable causes for frustration, one cannot help but sense in Mosaddeq a certain moral gratification in his ingenious ways of opting out of the system.

Yet peculiarities aside, soon Mosaddeq found himself out of the government loop. Even after his courageous speech in 1925 in the fifth Majles against abolishing the Qajar dynasty, Mosaddeq survived as a deputy in the next two sessions of the Majles and on a number of occasions opposed the government's reform program. He opposed for instance the north-south axis of the proposed trans-Iranian railroad on strategic and financial grounds. Instead, he favored a cheaper road network and a northwest-to-southeast railroad to connect the European network through Turkey to South Asia. Though he seems to have been oblivious to the importance of the Persian Gulf's sea access, he was correct in realizing the possibilities for expanding cross-border trade. On judicial reforms he was not in favor of Davar's drastic overhaul of the judiciary. He questioned the hurried and harmful urbanization process, and especially the mindless destruction of the city quarters, which he correctly thought injurious to the Persian urban fabric and architectural monuments. In nearly all cases his objections were ignored, adding to his frustration with the Pahlavi Westernizing process—and to Reza Shah's suspicion of the outspoken deputy.

Mosaddeq's stance relegated him to political exile. From 1928 to 1943 for fifteen years he lived the life of a recluse, sequestered in his private estate near Tehran farming his land and fighting various illnesses. Yet seclusion did not save him from arrest and imprisonment when in 1940, during the last phase of Reza Shah's vengeful purge of the old elite, he was detained in a remote fortress in Birjand in southern Khorasan for his alleged pro-German sentiments. This was after his pro-German son-in-law, Ahmad Matin Daftari, who served as the penultimate prime minister of Reza Shah, was dismissed from office and arrested. Mosaddeq's physical elimination would be almost certain were it not for the crown prince Mohammad Reza's intercession with his father. By 1943 when Mosaddeq was elected to the fourteenth Majles as a first deputy from Tehran, he was recognized as a leading voice against the mistakes and atrocities of Reza Shah's time. His was also an audible voice against undue British influence in Iranian affairs and intrigue through proxies. He objected to the failings of the postwar governments and flagrant irregularities in the Majles election.

Motivated and reenergized by new political horizons, he came to view the politics of the notables as no longer viable and essentially bankrupt. Even more than Qavam and Razmara, both of whom he opposed, he was willing to align himself with the growing middle classes, who shared his high aspirations. He was quick to learn the populist politics of the postwar era and quicker to grasp and indigenize its anti-imperialist message as it circulated throughout the non-Western milieu, from China, India, and Southeast Asia to Africa and Latin America. In this and other respects, Mosaddeq represented a new face of postcolonial leadership pioneered by the likes of Mahatma Gandhi and later by Sukarno in Indonesia and Jamal Abdel Nasser in Egypt. Yet in contrast to most postcolonial leaders, Mosaddeq was an anomaly: he neither rose from the underprivileged classes or the bourgeoisie, nor did he entertain revolutionary views at the outset of his career.

OIL CRISIS AND POLITICAL REFORM

From the start of his premiership in April 1951, Mosaddeq's agenda was set with an almost heroic fervor. He had come to office to implement the oil nationalization as his prime objective—an aspiration that, despite a popular mandate, was soon to face opposition from many quarters: from Britain, which was fundamentally against it; from the Tudeh, which still advocated a northern oil concession to the Soviet Union; and soon from the shah and conservatives and eventually from Mosaddeq's own allies in the Majles and the National Front. Soon after he officially declared the nationalization in May 1951, in a public address from Radio Iran in June, he summed up the motives behind the decision:

> Long years of negotiations with foreign countries have thus far yielded no results. With the oil revenue we can meet our entire budget and combat poverty, disease, and backwardness among our people. . . . By eliminating the power of the British company [i.e., AIOC], we would also eliminate corruption and intrigue, by means of which the internal affairs of our country have been influenced. Once this tutelage has ceased, Iran will achieve its economic and political independence.[2]

High hopes for oil nationalization as key to economic sovereignty, prosperity, material development, and an end to foreign intervention remained at the core of Mosaddeq's agenda throughout his term in office. In the same address he restated the need for compensation—which the nationalization law passed by the Majles had set at 25 percent of Iran's net profits from oil production in order to cover AIOC's legitimate claims and ownership of the oil installations. Mosaddeq also denied any intention to expel the British technical staff employed in the oil industry.

To achieve this, he had to cross a treacherous course. His first cabinet, chosen hastily, consisted of a mix of conservative generals, devout nationalists, and old-hand bureaucrats, no doubt to balance the diverse constituencies whose support he hoped to muster. During the twenty-six months he was in power, he repeatedly reshuffled his cabinet (five changes of ministers of the interior in the first ten months), a record even for Iran's turbulent politics of the time. His noncabinet appointments were no more stable. Within the Majles, support for his program and its implementation also dwindled. Even if such instability was in part the outcome of the semirevolutionary climate Mosaddeq inherited or intrigue from domestic and foreign quarters, he also contributed to it. Despite lofty objectives, his managerial flaws—aggravated by illness, anxieties, and obstinacy—never allowed him to fully grasp the reins of power. Instead, these paved the way for his eventual downfall, which he anticipated himself with an air of fatalism almost from the start. Yet he seemed to thrive in the environment of confrontation, as if political idealism brought out the best of his public performances.

At the outset, nationalization went ahead with an overwhelming public mandate and with the Majles' support. Mosaddeq emerged as the hero of "dispossession" (khal'-e yadd), as the takeover of the oil industry from British control came to be known. After an angry exchange of notes with the AIOC, soon an Iranian team was dispatched to the heart of the British oil operation in Abadan to hoist the Iranian flag over the oil refinery. To AIOC's surprise, Iranian technicians and a few engineers who were assigned to Khuzestan were able to manage the oil industry's day-to-day operations. Yet with limited experience in oil exploration and refining, it soon became apparent that they needed time and cooperation to master the managerial skills and the technical knowhow that were jealously guarded by the British company. Despite Mosaddeq's public assurances, AIOC quickly withdrew its entire staff and the Iranian government's call for British employees to resume work in the nationalized industry remained unheeded. Under the shadow of British warships harbored at Abadan, the British government soon evacuated nearly all its nationals. It also put Royal Air Force squadrons in Cyprus on full alert to support the anticipated naval takeover of the oil installations.

Outraged by Iranian action, the British government also lodged complaints with the International Court of Justice at The Hague, demanding that Iranian oil nationalization be declared illegal and thus void under international law. In response, Iran lodged its own counterclaims and sent representatives to defend its case. The Iranian oil nationalization thus rapidly developed into an international crisis, with important security and strategic repercussions that soon invited US intervention. At the time, Iran supplied more than 20 percent of the world's total oil production and the imminent cutoff of such a vital source threatened to disrupt the Western economies that were coming out of the postwar recession. Yet the American mediation, headed by President Harry Truman's emissary Averell Harriman (1891–1986), proved ineffective. Wary of British sincerity, Mosaddeq's government turned down the proposal for a fifty-fifty profit sharing proposed by the Americans. Mosaddeq and his advisers were legitimately concerned with many provisions and hidden clauses that such a proposal had made in favor of the British company. Torn between loyalty toward Britain, its most important ally, and support for a country long abused by European powers, the Truman administration seemingly was not prepared to press its case any further. Public demonstrations organized by the Tudeh Party against the American "goodwill" mission and the ensuing clashes with the mounted police in front of the Majles resulted in ten fatalities and many injured.

By September 1951, as Anglo-Iranian relations further deteriorated, the British government took its case to the UN Security Council. To contest the British claim, Mosaddeq was prompted to travel to New York as the head of a large delegation, a move designed not only to press Iran's case but also to draw support in the United States and from the international community. A warm reception by the American public was promising even before Mosaddeq's passionate speech at the Security Council reiterated Iran's position that the dispute with AIOC was an internal affair and outside the jurisdiction of both the Security Council and the International Court of Justice. Mosaddeq's speech was coached in a proficient legal language.

To further pressure Iran, in September 1951 the British government imposed a full maritime embargo on the export of Iranian oil. A few customers who were willing to purchase Iranian oil were quickly scared off and with equal rapidity the shortage in demand was filled by increased production of the Iraq Petroleum Company, a subsidiary of AIOC, and of other Persian Gulf oil fields in Kuwait and Dubai. Initial impact aside, the long-term effect of the embargo on the British market was minimal. Yet its effect on the Iranian economy was substantial throughout Mosaddeq's premiership. Issuing national government bonds to compensate for the loss of income could barely avert a financial crisis. A later increase in the volume of currency issued by the Mosaddeq government only intensified the inflationary trend. It became apparent that nationalization, though a brave move expressive of national sentiments, was a formidable task, if not an untenable one. By early 1952, oil production had come to a complete standstill—for the first time since 1909—threatening with bankruptcy the government that aimed to liberate Iran from the yoke of economic hegemony.

In the coming months more battles were to be fought in the streets, in the Majles, at negotiating tables with AIOC and with American negotiators, in international forums, with the shah and army, and even within the ranks of the National Front. Riding on Mosaddeq's popularity and feeding on Iranians' bitter memories of foreign intervention, the National Movement (Nahzat-e Melli)—as the oil nationalization campaign came to be known—appeared triumphant. Mosaddeq was a national hero the likes of whom Iran had rarely seen: a civilian rather than a military man, an articulate member of the nobility but also a fatherly figure with genuine compassion for ordinary folks, and though physically weak, determined and morally upright. Evidently willing to settle the oil issue in a reasonable fashion, he nevertheless was committed to restore the "rights of the nation," a quandary that was not eased by the AIOC's highly vindictive attitude, the British government's resolve to destroy Mosaddeq almost from the start, the vagaries of the Cold War, and the treacheries of Iran's domestic politics.

By early 1952 his opponents began to close ranks. On the left, the Tudeh Party portrayed him as a landowning aristocrat and an American agent and demagogue, while labeling the nationalization of oil as a backdoor entry for American economic imperialism (fig. 9.5). Even though a socialist splinter,

Figure 9.5. Portrayed by a pro-Tudeh satirical journal as a baboon, Mosaddeq
is dancing to the tune of his master, Uncle Sam. Baqa'i plays the tune.
Chalangar, no. 2, Ordibehesht 3, 1331/25 April 1952. Courtesy of Mohamad Tavakoli-Targhi.

which seceded from the Tudeh Party in 1948 and later came to be known as
Niru-ye Sevvom (Third Force), joined the National Front and supported Mosaddeq, the Tudeh leadership and its press, loyal to the Soviet party line, did
not. Through its frequent rallies in the capital and provinces, Tudeh presented
itself as the party of the oppressed and underprivileged; it was not only against
the monarchy and Western interests but also against Mosaddeq's crumbling
"bourgeois liberalism" (pl. 9.4).

Counterdemonstrations by supporters of the National Front, as well as by
the members of the Sumka (the Persian acronym for National Socialist Party of
Workers of Iran) and supporters of Fada'iyan-e Islam, often resulted in bloody
clashes and crackdowns by the police and the armed forces. Sumka was a small
but openly fascist party that in every respect fashioned itself after the defunct
German National Socialist Party. It advocated "Aryan" supremacy, engaged in
thuggish street battles, and thrived on appearing militaristic (black-shirt uniforms in particular), and invented racist rituals. Officially founded in 1951 by
a group of Iranian Nazi sympathizers headed by Davud Monshizadeh (1915–
1989), a SS collaborator during the war and later a professor of Iranian philology in Munich, Sumka treated the Tudeh and the National Front as perfect
targets of vocal and physical violence, much in the spirit of the Nazis. Sumka's
agitations were frowned upon by the pro-shah security forces but tolerated as

a counterforce to the Tudeh. Mosaddeq's government and is police force were too feeble to take meaningful action.

The security forces were themselves a source of trouble. During Mosaddeq's first term, which ended in July 1952, there were at least ten serious cases of police crackdowns on street demonstrations, resulting in injuries and deaths. Pro-shah officers ambivalent about Mosaddeq's abilities and critical of his alleged leniency toward the left often headed up the police force. Social unrest and violent rallies tarnished Mosaddeq's image as a well-intentioned leader inundated by enmity and intrigue. Serious fractures within Mosaddeq's own ranks heightened doubts of his political survival. At its inception, the National Front, a coalition of diverse and at times opposing political groups (few could be called parties) and independent politicians, espoused oil nationalization as its chief objective. On the left there was Hezb-e Zahmatkeshan-e Iran (Party of the Toilers of Iran)—itself a merger of nationalists of the left, headed by Mozaffar Baqa'i, and the socialist Niru-ye Sevvom, headed by Khalil Maleki (1903–1969), a German-educated academic, an articulate theoretician of socialism and a man of political integrity. The Third Force included a number of intellectuals and activists of the younger generation who were disillusioned with the Tudeh subservience and dogmatic line and by its totalitarian structure. Among them was Jalal Al-e Ahmad (1923–1969), later an influential author and social critic. At the center was the Iran Party, dominated by liberal nationalists including Allahyar Saleh, Karim Sanjabi, Gholam-Hosain Sadiqi, and Hosain Fatemi. They were Mosaddeq's close allies and shared his vision of liberal nationalism.

Hosain Fatemi (1917–1954), a close adviser to Mosaddeq and one of the founders of the National Front, was a firebrand editor of the influential newspaper *Bakhtar-e Emruz* (Today's West), the unofficial organ of the National Front. Later as minister of foreign affairs and spokesman in Mosaddeq's last cabinet, he was among the harshest critics of the shah and the royal court and a supporter of republicanism. His stance against Fada'iyan-e Islam's intrusion into the political realm, which nearly cost him his life, did not deter him from steering Mosaddeq's political course toward greater radicalism, much to the disgust of British and the American diplomats and negotiators. Adding to the volatile mix was Fada'iyan-e Islam, which soon concluded that, contrary to their earlier wishes, Mosaddeq was not their man and had no intention of enforcing the shari'a as law of the land, let alone laying the ground for an Islamic government. Navvab Safavi, who openly aspired to establish the Caliphate, soon found himself in prison during most of Mosaddeq's premiership.

As the oil dispute heated up and the stakes got higher, other allies of Mosaddeq, such as Baqa'i and Makki, gradually abandoned him; some switched to the shah's camp, others abstained from taking sides, and others openly criticized the premier on the issues of oil negotiation, its disastrous outcome, and what appeared to be his increasingly authoritarian conduct. His critics viewed Mosaddeq's struggle in the face of foreign and domestic opposition as quixotic, but few could propose a way out of his political quagmire. By mid-1952 it was as if he had exhausted most of his options and was ready for an honorable exit. Yet the oil dispute was one issue that kept the premier going in his arduous crusade. As he repeatedly confessed to his allies and foes, full implementation of oil nationalization at any price was the single most important mission—perhaps the only mission—of his premiership.

In addition to legal claims lodged with the International Court of Justice, the British threatened military intervention in the Persian Gulf. The United States came to realize sooner than Britain that, given Mosaddeq's popularity, any direct confrontation with his government was unwise, illegal, and would most likely fail. Thinking within a Cold War frame of reference, the Americans advised that if Mosaddeq was to be removed from power, there was a chance that Iran would fall into the hands of the communists. The British opted to procrastinate in the hope that the transient nature of Iranian politics would soon put Mosaddeq out of office and open the way for a more pliant successor, such as the Anglophile Zia al-Din Tabataba'i.

The shah, sensing that political climate was in favor of Mosaddeq and oil nationalization, was not yet prepared to take part in an overt move against his premier. Simmering for sometime, however, were deep disagreements between them that were bound to boil over soon. He nursed a suspicion that Mosaddeq, a member of Qajar nobility and a longtime critic of his father's rule, was contemplating an end to the Pahlavi monarchy in favor of a republic. Anxieties translated into frequent clashes—while still maintaining proper etiquette—not only over military and ministerial appointments but also over where Mosaddeq's government was heading. The shah viewed his premier as a political maverick, and his personality as bold but unbalanced. Confrontation with Britain and engaging in street politics, the shah believed, is bound to result in economic ruination and possibly even a communist takeover. A majority of the old elite, the higher ranks of the army, majority of the senior ulama, and businessmen who suffered from economic stagnation shared his perspective. Mosaddeq's political independence and his subtle patronizing attitude toward the shah, despite expressions of utter loyalty, did not help to ameliorate the shah's fears.

Mosaddeq harbored his own misgivings. In earlier years he had not disfavored the young shah as a constitutional monarch even though he remained apprehensive toward most members of the royal family, especially the shah's twin sister, Ashraf Pahlavi (1919–2016), whom he viewed, perhaps with an air of misogyny, as the source of intrigue and conspiracy. By 1949, however, the shah's newly acquired power to dissolve the Majles at will alarmed Mosaddeq. With the army's higher ranks mostly loyal to the shah, especially after Razmara, and with the conservatives closing ranks behind him, the shah appeared to Mosaddeq and his allies as a serious obstacle to the democratic process and even more to the successful fruition of the nationalization campaign. The shah received the attention—if not the confidence—of the Americans and maintained his ties with the British both through diplomatic channels and by means of informal contacts. As differences hardened over policy and over appointments, Mosaddeq began to point fingers at the shah not only for meddling in the affairs of the government and for sabotage in the Majles but also for fraternizing with his foreign foes.

A REVOLUTION IN THE MAKING

By the time of the election of the seventeenth Majles in January 1952, Mosaddeq's government had begun to experience major obstacles on all fronts. Oil negotiations reached a deadlock, largely because the British were procrastinating in hopes of a favorable vote of the International Court of Justice. The Iranian public loyal to Mosaddeq anticipated a rapid victory even though the deputies of the Majles had increased their attacks on the government's performance. A victim of his own rhetoric, Mosaddeq could hardly comply with any settlement short of full control of the oil industry while Britain, concerned with its own imperial prestige, was in no mood to recognize nationalization as a sovereign right of the Iranian nation. Any compromise on Mosaddeq's side would have prompted the swelling ranks of his opponents to accuse him of betrayal or, worse, of being an agent of the foreign powers, a charge that Mosaddeq had leveled at many of his own detractors.

The election of the seventeenth Majles was in shambles. In Tehran the electorate of about 140,000 returned to the Majles all twelve candidates of the National Front, a victory that inevitably raised the suspicion of Mosaddeq's opponents such that they accused him of fixing the results. In other pro–National Front constituencies outside Tehran favorable candidates were also elected. Yet having realized that not all provincial results would be favorable to him—and would therefore relegate the National Front to a minority—Mosaddeq simply suspended the election and allowed the seventeenth Majles to be convened with a mere 85 deputies out of the total of 136. The pretext that if elections were held in anti–National Front constituencies they would be rigged by his opponents could be interpreted only as political maneuvering and, in fact, went down on Mosaddeq's record as his first constitutional breach. In due course, even the eighty-five-member chamber proved increasingly critical of Mosaddeq.

In mid-July 1952 Mosaddeq was still popular enough to receive a vote of confidence from the Majles—sixty-five voted for him and nineteen abstained. Armed with parliamentary support, in a private audience with the shah ten days later he demanded for himself a full delegation of defense responsibilities, including control of all promotions, retirements, and appointments in the armed forces. The shah adamantly resisted on the grounds that he, not the premier, was head of the executive branch and responsible for army appointments. The crisis was rooted in contested readings of the Constitution and its ambiguous definition of the monarch's power. Was the premier a mere enforcer of the monarch's wishes or, as head of the government, designated by the legislature, was he responsible for all affairs of the state—this was a question unresolved in the text of the 1906–1907 Constitution. Deeper down, the dispute reflected the ancient tension between the royal court (*dargah*) and the divan, which for centuries upset the Iranian state.

When the shah refused to comply, Mosaddeq submitted his resignation and returned home. For a moment it seemed as if his term of office were over, along with his hopes for oil nationalization. The shah instantly appointed in his stead Ahmad Qavam, who had returned to the political arena after an absence of five years. The shah's many grievances against the shrewd aristocrat aside, the appointment aimed to lessen political unrest and help resolve the oil crises. Qavam's record as a skilled maneuverer persuaded the shah, the British and the Americans, and the conservative establishment to opt for the veteran statesman who now promised to resolve the oil crisis and restore law and order. Yet two independent developments completely changed the climate against Qavam and in favor of Mosaddeq, a turning point that shifted Iran's politics toward a more radical course. The news of victory at the International Court at Hague came four days after Qavam's appointment on July 17 as the new premier.

Though on July 19 the Majles gave its vote of confidence for the new premier, Qavam's premiership met with spontaneous mass resistance. His promise that he would take a series of draconian measures to quell unrest, end the undue intervention of the clergy in politics (especially of Kashani), and bring the oil crisis to a conclusion, outraged a wide-ranging sector of the public still supportive of Mosaddeq. Street rallies in the capital and provinces on July 21, 1952 (which came to be known as *si-e tir*, or "thirtieth of the month of Tir 1331" of the Persian solar calendar)—perhaps the largest Iran had ever witnessed at the time—soon turned violent. Clashes with the police resulted in dozens of deaths and hundreds of injuries. The troops and tanks stationed in sensitive locations throughout the capital fired at the angry crowd. Even in Baharestan Square, in front of the Majles, despite protests by deputies of the National Front, the troops continued aiming at demonstrators. The riots made strange bedfellows. Members of the Tudeh Party, together with Sumka and the Fada'iyan-e-e Islam, attacked government buildings and beat troops and police officers. The call for the return of Mosaddeq to power displayed overt support for him and was a clear setback both for the seventy-seven-year-old Qavam, who immediately resigned on July 22, and for the shah, who quickly reappointed Mosaddeq to office. The shah also succumbed, resentfully, to Mosaddeq's demand for control over the military.

The street slogan "We sacrificed our lives, we write with our blood: either death or Mosaddeq," voiced by ordinary people, saw in Mosaddeq not merely a political leader but a savior of the Iranian nation. Mosaddeq's victory was a serious blow to British and American hopes to see a compromising premier in his place. Both powers had actively sought out Qavam and backed him as an alternative to a coup or direct military action. Moreover, the July 21 uprising displayed the power of the urban lower and middle classes as a counterforce to the politics of the elite; this was a victory for Mosaddeq, who mustered such sentiments despite the Tudeh Party's long-standing claims to be the party of the masses. Though Tudeh leadership still criticized Mosaddeq, during the uprising its rank and file embraced the National Movement en masse with Mosaddeq as their leader.

If a further providential sign was needed, it came with the news of Iran's victory at The Hague on the same day: July 21, 1952. The ICJ agreed with Iran that the court lacked jurisdiction in the Iranian oil dispute since AIOC was a nonstate entity operating under an Iranian license; therefore, the court could not hear the case, as the British government had urged. This was the position initiated by Karim Sanjabi (1904–1995), a French-educated lawyer and a loyal member of Mosaddeq's inner circle, who was a member of the delegation representing Iran in the court. The chief lawyer hired by Mosaddeq's government, the Belgian Henri Rollin, skillfully argued Iran's case. In June 1952 Mosaddeq himself attended the final court sessions to personally present Iran's case and offer moral support to the defense team. The vote was perhaps the most constructive international victory for Mosaddeq and his allies, having reversed the International Court of Justice's earlier injunction and vindicated the position Iran had taken all along.

With a public mandate and the vote of the International Court of Justice, Mosaddeq stood to gain an unprecedented advantage, and he was quick to exploit that in hopes of implementing his reform agenda beyond oil nationalization. Despite stiff resistance in the Majles, including from his own National Front allies, he push through legislation that delegated to him an unprecedented six months of full legislative power, amounting to rule by decree. Even before the end of the six-month period on August 11, 1952, Mosaddeq had succeeded in extending the delegation of power for another year, a move that was possible only through backdoor deals and reliance on street support. The virtual suspension of the legislature by a man who had built his career on defending the Constitution and legislative independence not only was ironic but also contentious, if not entirely unconstitutional.

Resort to rule by decree, however, seemed unavoidable, at least at the juncture where Mosaddeq found himself after July 21, when he became increasingly concerned with the mischief of the royal court and even the possibility of an army coup. Moreover, the Majles during most of its recent sessions had proved a quarrelling and rambunctious body with scores of demagogic and fraudulent deputies. It was a body with wide-ranging powers over the executive, and it often abused those powers with impunity. In the polarized climate of the time, if any government aimed at serious reforms, it would have found it a daunting task to pass legislation through the Majles. Yet Mosaddeq, when he was a Majles deputy, vehemently denied any outright delegation of power to the executive branch. Most recently in the case of Razmara, when he asked for far less delegation of power to renegotiate the oil concession, Mosaddeq and his allies called him a traitor, an agent of British and American imperialism, and as a generalissimo entertaining dictatorial aspirations in the style of Reza Khan.

To his credit, Mosaddeq employed his extraordinary powers to carry out a series of urgent reform measures, which he had promised in the program of his second government and mostly arose from the oil crisis. These included purging the army and the administration of corrupt elements (what amounted to eradicating Mosaddeq's opponents), balancing the budget through higher taxation, and reforming election laws. Yet in reality, the sum total of Mosaddeq's second government included measures that could least be justified by Mosaddeq's own moral standards and legal principles. In November 1952 the law of social security (*amniyat-e ejtema'i*) vastly extended the power of the state to detain and prosecute individuals and organizations at the expense of the most basic civil rights. On pain of exile and threat of imprisonment, dismissal, and financial penalties, the law banned most forms of civil disobedience, demonstrations, strikes, and expressions of political dissent. The enforcement of martial law throughout nearly all of Mosaddeq's second term further tarnished the image of a man who had been hailed as defender of constitutional liberties.

No less problematic was reform of the press laws. It goes without saying that the behavior of the press all through the period was often egregiously reckless, if not criminal, with frequent cases of calumny and personal vendettas, absence of journalistic ethics, and plenty of ideological bias and outright lies. Yet imperfect as the press was, it still was the most influential forum for political debate and expression of dissent, especially since the airwaves were fully controlled by the state. Criticizing all sources of power and influence—the ministers, Majles deputies, the royal court and the shah, and the proxies of foreign powers—it was a thorn in the side of all governments of the period. The new regulations, however, made such functions ever more formidable, if not practically impossible. The new press bill before the Majles for ratification faced harsh criticism not only from newspaper editors and publishers who took sanctuary (*bast*) inside the Majles but also from among some of the most ardent former supporters of Mosaddeq.

With little hesitation, Mosaddeq's government, with himself occupying the post of minster of defense, undertook a widespread purge of army officers suspected of hostility toward the National Movement. By September 1952 more than 150 senior officers were forced to retire, thus adding fuel to the rampant fires of discontent among the military ranks. Angered by attacks in the press and in the Majles, more and more officers turned against Mosaddeq. The officers supportive of the National Front were too few and too hesitant to counter the restive officer corps. Likewise, purges in the judiciary created serious discontent. Relying on delegated power, Mosaddeq's judiciary reform commission, presided over by a zealous minister of justice, dismissed without any set procedure close to two hundred sitting judges, state attorneys, and higher-ranking officials on charges of corruption and ineptitude, despite resistance from members of the reform commission. The en masse dismissal of the judges of Iran's Supreme Court under the pretext of eradicating corrupt elements from the court and giving it a more "Islamic" face, further frightened the judicial establishment, which was largely the product of reforms under 'Ali Akbar Davar, the celebrated minster of the early Reza Shah era.

Mosaddeq's more successful measures in the area of finance, labor laws, rural development, and housing—to the extent they ever were implemented—projected the image of a welfare state committed to the improvement of the standard of living and well-being of ordinary citizens. Yet here, too, a bureaucratic reform agenda—in the same vein as many state-run reform programs elsewhere—aimed to centralize services and strengthen the government's hold over the public domain. Land reform, an idea contemplated since the constitutional period, was left aside by the Mosaddeq government until such time that the oil dispute was resolved. As a member of the landed nobility, Mosaddeq could not have fully dissociated himself from a worldview that still considered Iran an agrarian society, governed by ancient landlord-peasant covenants.

Added to the tensions caused by Mosaddeq's restructuring, there was a growing level of discord with the shah and the royal court. Mosaddeq had closed down the offices of the shah's brothers and sisters, banished Princess Ashraf to Europe on charges of conspiracy, and after July 21, 1952, had tried to rein in the shah by strictly treating him as a constitutional monarch. As early as February 1952 the shah appeared politically disarmed and isolated—ready to leave the country on a journey that appeared to be a prelude to his abdication or, as some viewed it, a shrewd move to outmaneuver his premier. In either case, it did not help Mosaddeq's image that he was an old Qajar aristocrat facilitating the departure of a seemingly innocuous monarch who, though ambitious and even scheming, was constitutionally the head of state. On February 28, when Mosaddeq went to the royal palace to see the shah off, he encountered a small but angry pro-shah crowd—some of them the very same knife-wielding thugs (*chaqukesh*) who five months later, on July 21, were hired in pro-Mosaddeq rallies to set up barricades and attack the police. Fearing for his life, the premier fled the royal palace and took refuge in his own house nearby, which by then was functioning as his headquarters.

Relying more on a handful of his radical ministers and advisers such as Fatemi, and all the while fearful of his own violent removal, Mosaddeq tilted even more toward a political chasm. Even his former National Front colleagues were attacking him as an extremist while being repudiated, on and off, by Kashani and his allies. Viewed as the presumed "spiritual leader" of the National Movement, in reality Kashani relied not only on Fada'iyan-e Islam and on street toughs but also on the royal court, which he viewed as a counter to Mosaddeq's excesses.

Earlier during Mosaddeq's first tenure as premier and while Kashani was serving as the speaker, the Majles passed a bill with the utmost urgency releasing Khalil Tahmasbi, the assassin of the former prime minister Razmara—a clear interference in the conduct of the judiciary condoned by Mosaddeq's government. The assassin was hailed by the Fada'iyan as a hero and a "master" and was received by Kashani at his home. Equally appalling was the passage of a bill initiated by Mosaddeq's supporters that labeled Ahmad Qavam a "corruptor on the earth" (*mosfsed-e fi'l arz*), a charge in Islamic law punishable by death, and that called for the expropriation (*mosadereh*) of his properties. As a measure of duplicity of the speaker of the Majles, and his rapid shift in loyalty, on the morning of July 21, while rioters were denouncing Qavam on the streets of the capital, Radio Iran was broadcasting Kashani's message congratulating Qavam for his premiership. In the meantime the angry crowd led by thugs looted Qavam's house for the second time in a decade. He took refuge in Qom and in late July fled the country in fear of his life. The confiscated Qavam's estate save for a portion that is to be allocated as pension to his family, was set aside for compensation to the martyrs of the July 21 uprising.

When the newly established Iranian senate, the second chamber of the Iranian legislature envisaged in the Constitution and convened in August 1951, refused to ratify either of the above two bills, Mosaddeq's supporters, with his consent, first reduced the term of the senate from four year to two and then unceremoniously dissolved the senate altogether. The speaker of the senate and other senators, including Hasan Taqizadeh, declared the dissolution unconstitutional, but in the intimidating climate of the time, they seemingly had no choice but to abide. Mosaddeq's supporters in the Majles accused senators of being reactionaries who were either appointees of the shah or large landowners who bought their way past the ballot box to guard the status quo and their own vested interests.

THE END GAME

Mosaddeq's domestic reforms, especially in the areas of administration and economy, were meant to answer to public unhappiness with the inconclusive nationalization campaign and the hardships caused by the absence of oil revenue, as well as the "oil-free" economy that he was courageous enough to advocate for. Yet by early 1953 he seemed to be at an impasse with dangerous options before him. Mosaddeq's earlier conciliatory tone welcoming an amicable end to the oil crises during his first term had reached fever pitch by the second term. In October 1952 the defiant premier broke diplomatic relations with the newly elected Conservative government after the Iranian oil embargo went into effect. This provided a further pretext for the Tories to convince the United States of the need to force Mosaddeq out of office. With Winston Churchill as premier and Anthony Eden as foreign secretary and the most influential voice in the cabinet, the British government was in no mood to compromise. The British establishment and the conservative press routinely portrayed the Iranian premier as a dangerous xenophobe, an erratic rabble-rouser, and—after July 1952—a dictator. Eden, who had studied Persian at Christ Church and earned his degree in Oriental studies, viewed the world through the all-too-familiar Orientalist prism and was unwilling to accept the painful prospects of a postcolonial Britain at a time when Egyptian nationalism was on the rise.

The Egyptian Free Officers, with Colonel Abdel Nasser as the force behind the coup, came to power on July 23, 1952, two days after the uprising in Iran. The British authorities could hardly have missed such a coincidence.

To them, as to many in the British establishment (and the British public at large), clinging to AIOC not only seemed vital for the postwar recovery but also symbolically crucial to project abroad an image of power and prestige, despite the realities of a waning empire. The British government thus chose to procrastinate while awaiting the outcome of the American presidential election in November 1952. The election of Dwight Eisenhower was indeed a turning point, for, among other things, it allowed the new secretary of the state, John Foster Dulles (1888–1959), to articulate a more aggressive foreign policy to assert the US presence in the world. Eden and Dulles, the two grand strategists, thus flanked Churchill and Eisenhower, the two wartime heroes, who strived to solidify the two powers' Cold War alliance.

From the British perspective, the only feasible option in the oil dispute with Iran after the defeat of Ahmad Qavam was to bring about the downfall of Mosaddeq, rather than to opt for leniency or wait for Mosaddeq's government to fall under the weight of its own difficulties. By February 1953, a joint declaration prepared by Truman and Churchill—the last in a series of back-and-forth proposals and counterproposals between Iran and Britain conducted through the intermediary of the United States—put forward three options to settle the oil dispute. The Iranian government found the terms highly burdensome and turned them down. In particular, the British demand for massive compensation, which amounted to Iranian economic indenture for many decades, could not have been condoned by any sovereign state, least of all by a nationalist government in the midst of a revolution. It was as if the terms were designed to be rejected, paving the way for an aggressive course.

Mosaddeq, sensing the changing international climate, offered a conciliatory counterproposal. In exchange for the British government complying, at least in public, with the principle of nationalization, he consented to arbitration by the International Court of Justice on the amount of compensation to be paid for the AIOC's installations and other investments, but not for future losses of oil revenue. He further offered AIOC partnership with Iran—but not a monopoly—in the production and distribution of Iranian oil, at a percentage negotiable by the two sides. Under normal circumstances, this Iranian counterproposal would have provided viable grounds for an amicable agreement, but this was not to be the case, for the two Western powers obviously were not negotiating in good faith.

By March 1953 the new Eisenhower administration was convinced that the only plausible course for the United States was to remove Mosaddeq by means of a military coup. John Foster Dulles and his brother, Allen Dulles (1893–1969), the director of the newly organized Central Intelligence Agency, were architects of a foreign policy that came to be known as the Eisenhower doctrine. It was designed primarily to contain what seemed to Americans as the impending communist threat. Among countries neighboring the Soviet Union, Iran proved particularly crucial because of its long borders with its northern neighbor, its massive oil reserves, access to the oil-rich Persian Gulf, and its powerful Tudeh Party. The climate of communist phobia in the United States marked by the Red Scare and the hearings of the House Un-American Activities Committee further vindicated in the Americans' eyes the undertaking of preemptive measures in a contentious case such as Iran.

Such concerns were not divorced from the growing American business interests in the postwar Middle East. Besides the oil fields of Saudi Arabia—which had been developed by the American conglomerate ARAMCO since the 1930s and reached full production in the early 1950s—Iranian reserves were highly promising. The US giants, among them Standard Oil of California, required new fields of operation overseas to fulfill the growing demand for oil, and Iran offered an excellent opportunity, except for the ongoing political turmoil in the country. The Iranian nationalization had put an end to the British monopoly, yet the remaining obstacle appeared to be the unpredictable political climate presided over, as John Foster Dulles put it, by that "madman" Mosaddeq.

This was a clear shift from earlier US approach to Iranian crisis. As early as 1949 the Truman administration was anxious to bring about a peaceful settlement in accordance with the initial postwar policy of supporting nationalist and anticolonial movements all over the world as a bulwark against communism. Mosaddeq and his colleagues, too, viewed the United States as Iran's natural ally and a key to a peaceful solution to the dispute, as a young superpower whose global interests were not in line with the exploitations of the European colonial powers such as Great Britain or ideological expansionists like the Soviet Union. The earlier stages of US mediation bore out such impressions of good faith. Yet in practice—even before Eisenhower's administration—the United States shifted gears, backing the British claims on the 1933 AIOC concession and pressuring Iran to honor its terms.

The new US administration warned Iran, rather condescendingly, to preserve its neutrality in the face of pressure from the Soviet Union. It also expressed anxiety over the Tudeh Party's increased anti-American activities. The US efforts were effective enough to persuade the British to accept nationalization—in concept, if not detail—in exchange for agreeable compensation. To strengthen his position, Mosaddeq had earlier juggled between the communist and the Western blocs, yet the United States' lukewarm support for him did not encourage an overt anticommunist stance. When, for instance, in October 1951 Mosaddeq visited the United States on the occasion of the UN Security Council's debate on the Iranian crisis, his reception by the Truman administration was mixed. Though he was welcomed in some liberal quarters as an anti-imperialist champion, in other more conservative circles he was considered an eccentric troublemaker.

While Mosaddeq was in the US capital, William O. Douglas (1898–1980), the longest-serving justice of the US Supreme Court at the time, rendered his support to Mosaddeq and the Iranian nationalization campaign. He was a best-selling author, public commentator, faculty of the Yale Law School, and a widely traveled mountaineer who by 1952 had extensively traveled three times throughout Iran, climbed the summit of Mount Damavand, and for years observed Iranian politics and society. Hosting Mosaddeq's daylong visit to the Supreme Court, Douglas called on Truman to value leaders like Mosaddeq and Jawaharlal Nehru as statesmen withstanding communist penetration. He later criticized the Eisenhower administration for abandoning Iran's just cause in favor of covetous British colonial interests. On the occasion of Mosaddeq's departure, he also wrote to the Iranian premier offering his moral support and consoling him for vicious attacks against him in the American press. He added: "I think the great body of the American sentiment will grow and grow in favor of you and your wonderful people . . . as the ugly and greedy British policy under Churchill's management becomes as plain to everyone as it is to you and to me."[3]

Time magazine declared Mosaddeq "Man of the Year" in 1951, overlaying on his cover portrait the caption: "He oiled the wheels of chaos." The accompanying article conveyed a similar massage: Mosaddeq is an inevitable voice of the developing world's national aspirations who nevertheless is a hazard to the West's economic and strategic concerns. This captured the ambivalence of much of the American press, which followed, somewhat slavishly, the British line. Encountering a sophisticated man and a tough negotiator who did not fit their stereotype of a Middle Eastern weakling or a lascivious desert sheikh, the Washington polity was at loss. Mosaddeq was accompanied and aided by men capable of successfully putting forward their case in international forums and speaking out about decades-old Iranian grievances against European powers. Mosaddeq's repeated exhortations that his "oppressed and poor" country was resolved not to carry the burden of exploitation was well symbolized in the confident, resolute message that emanated from his own trembling frame. The press, however, still nicknamed him "Old Mossy."

By early 1953 the image of the United States as a benevolent savior of the weak had fully evaporated in the heat of the oil dispute. The myth of the common destiny of the "English-speaking peoples" advocated by Churchill during World War II still resonated with influential Anglo-Americans such as Dulles, who were brought up with a WASP missionary mind-set and were unsettled by their Cold War anxieties. Mosaddeq's resolve outraged Americans who had difficulty appreciating his domestic hurdles. Increasingly, men such as Loy Henderson (1892–1986), the American ambassador to Iran, began to see him as a huge liability for the United States in its anticommunist crusade. Henderson was a seasoned diplomat, a Soviet specialist who served in the Soviet Union and then as the head of the Bureau of Near Eastern Affairs in the State Department before being appointed as ambassador in 1942 and again in 1951.

Armed with a superpower worldview that clearly clashed with Mosaddeq's dogged logic and hard reasoning, by early 1953 Henderson concluded that the premier's character flaws and contrarian combativeness would soon take him to a political abyss from which there would be no return. Not only had he antagonized the British and alienated the shah and the army, Henderson observed, but he had also angered his own former allies in the Majles and in the press. As a result, he believed, Mosaddeq will sooner rather than later turn his back on the United States and rely heavily on left-leaning street politics. With his popular support diminishing and his enthusiasm for the US curbed, Henderson predicted that Mosaddeq would have no choice but to welcome the Tudeh Party (fig. 9.6). Taking full advantage of the situation, the Tudeh would eventually topple Mosaddeq's shaky government and in the absence of an effective US presence would establish a pro-Soviet enclave in Iran. Such a perceived scenario was not acceptable at any price to the US ambassador and his superiors in Washington. Invariably Henderson and his seniors gravitated toward the long-standing British option of removing Mosaddeq from office.

The CIA plot, inspired and assisted by British intelligence, was simple and yet somewhat brutish. To start, legitimate grounds had to be laid by persuading the reluctant Iranian monarch to give his consent and use his constitutional, though disputed, prerogative to sack the premier and appoint in his stead their handpicked candidate, General Fazlollah Zahedi (1897–1963). Zahedi was a long-serving and ambitious, though adventurous, senior officer who fought against the Jangal movement in 1920, survived Reza Shah's purges and haphazard dismissals, was arrested during World War II, and exiled by the British for his role in the German-instigated rebellion in Isfahan. After his release, he was later rehabilitated and returned to the political stage. He had been appointed as minister of war in Mosaddeq's first government in 1951.

Figure 9.6. The first anniversary of the July 21, 1952, uprising gave the Tudeh Party a chance to show its muscle. It was one of several parties in the hundred-thousand-strong demonstration in front of the Majles denouncing the United States and Great Britain. The textile worker in the cartoon poster is kicking Uncle Sam and John Bull out into the Persian Gulf. The Persian slogan reads: "Yankee go home!"
© Bettmann/Corbis/AP Images.

Despite the joint American and British pressure, and the behind-the-scenes selection of Zahedi as a viable replacement, the shah was not willing to dismiss Mosaddeq outright. Having in mind the horrific experience of July 1952 uprising, the shah argued behind closed doors that the premier should be allowed to exhaust all his options in the oil dispute. If dismissed midway through the negotiations, the shah felt the monarchy would be seen by his people as having betrayed the National Movement and as serving as an agent of foreign powers, a charge he and his father had long fought to disprove.

In late spring 1953 Mosaddeq's premiership took a grave turn, inadvertently unifying his domestic and foreign opponents and furnishing the necessary pretext for the staging of a military coup. In July 1953 a motion of no confidence was brought to the table against the government in the Majles over the torture of some detainees who were accused of the murder of the Tehran chief of police General Mahmud Afshartus (1908–1953)—a supporter of the National Front. In April 1952 Afshartus was kidnapped, tortured, and murdered by a group of conspirators who evidently included Mozaffar Baqa'i, the former member of the National Front, and a disgruntled group of army officers whom Mosaddeq had forced into retirement. His killing, the news of which terrified the public, was the first step in the staging of an anti-Mosaddeq military coup.

Mosaddeq, who sensed defeat in the Majles, urged all his allies to collectively resign their seats, thus effectively ending the quorum and dissolving the seventeenth Majles. He realized that once the Majles was not in session, he was in jeopardy, since the Constitution allowed the shah under the circumstances to appoint a new premier without the customary vote of approval from the Majles. To prevent this—since Zahedi's appointment seemed certain, especially after he had taken sanctuary in the Majles under Kashani's protection—Mosaddeq resorted to a new maneuver. Shortly before the first anniversary of the July 21 uprising, he took the daring—and arguably most controversial—decision of his public life: he called for a public referendum to ratify his decision to dissolve the Majles, amend the election laws, and rule by decree. More broadly, it was a call for a popular mandate against his many enemies. He still appeared strong on the surface but was becoming deeply vulnerable beneath.

The referendum, carried out in mid-July 1953 haphazardly and without any serious debate, was unprecedented and clearly damaging to Mosaddeq's image as a man of principle. Referenda not only were not envisioned in the Iranian Constitution; this referendum was designed to grant the premier authority to dissolve the Majles at will, a power that the 1949 amendment to the Constitution had reserved, no doubt unjustifiably, for the shah. It was as if he were relying on the will of the people against the monopoly of power in the hands of the Pahlavi monarch and the Majles, which had become subservient to the shah.

Yet opposition to the referendum was broad. Mosaddeq's opponents accused him of visibly gravitating toward dictatorship and called the referendum a demagogic tool to extend his rule by decree. Kashani, who earlier had resigned as speaker of the Majles and allied himself with the shah, issued a fatwa against the referendum and labeled Mosaddeq the "incarcerator of freedom." Even Mosaddeq's close allies in the National Front—or what was left of it—advised him against the move. At the time the government was already under attack for the unauthorized increase in the volume of the Iranian currency (to combat the loss of state revenue). Moreover, the Mosaddeq government was accused of laying the ground for the shah's forced abdication, a charge that the premier vehemently denied.

Mosaddeq took the political risk while the United States had stopped its mediation efforts and denied Iran the long-promised loan of $100 million under the Point Four Program. The oil dispute had reached total deadlock despite Mosaddeq's conciliatory pleas, and he had alienated the shah and most ranking army officers. As his politics gravitated toward the left, he appeared more susceptible to the Tudeh exploits. In such a climate, some form of a military coup was not implausible. Short of quitting, appealing to the people on the streets and mobilizing the public remained the only available path to Mosaddeq. Yet he appeared more like a tragic hero ready to fight to the end, which was coming.

THE COUP OF AUGUST 1953

In late June 1953 in a meeting in the office of John Foster Dulles—attended, among others, by Allen Dulles and Loy Henderson—the plan for a CIA-led covert operation to remove Mosaddeq was finalized. Operation Ajax, as it was named, was to be carried out in collaboration with British intelligence. The operation's leader Kermit (Kim) Roosevelt Jr. (1916–2000), a grandson of Theodore Roosevelt and a senior CIA operative, was aided by a number of figures, including the quintessential Oxford don Robert Zaehner (1913–1974), then a lecturer in Persian and specialist in Zoroastrianism who served as a wartime counterintelligence officer of the British embassy in Tehran; Donald Wilber (1907–1997), an archaeologist of Iran at Princeton and the link to Iranian agents and officers; and Colonel Herbert Norman Schwarzkopf Sr., formerly an American military liaison in Iran who helped rebuild the Iranian gendarmerie in the postwar period and who knew the shah well. As if it were a working draft of Graham Greene's 1955 *Quiet American*, Operation Ajax had all the drama of a spy thriller and all the drawbacks. The difference was that it was real, a blatant intervention in the affairs of another country.

Back in Tehran, Roosevelt and Schwarzkopf, after tough negotiations that lasted for days, managed to overcome the shah's reservations about staging a coup. He was persuaded to sign in secret two royal decrees, one dismissing Mosaddeq and the other appointing Zahedi as prime minister. The new appointment had to be officially approved by the Majles, which had not yet been dissolved but was no longer functional. The issuance of Mosaddeq's dismissal was a sheer formality. On August 9 the shah and his wife, Queen Soraya (1932–2001), left for the Caspian resort of Ramsar, anxiously awaiting the course of events.

The attempt to force Mosaddeq from office failed miserably on the first try, when in the early hours of August 16 the chief of the royal guard, Colonel

Ne'matollah Nasiri (1911–1979), a staunch royalist removed from his post during Mosaddeq's military purge, carried the dismissal decree to Mosaddeq's headquarters. Nasiri was arrested on the spot and his troops disarmed by the prime minister's guard. Once the news reached the shah in the Caspian resort, he and the queen flew to Baghdad on his private plane. There they were received briefly by the Hashemite King Faisal II before leaving for Rome, where they remained, perhaps preparing for abdication and permanent exile, reportedly in the United States, where the shah entertained the idea of buying a large ranch.

The news of the failed coup had a great radicalizing effect on Mosaddeq's supporters. On the same day Mosaddeq officially dissolved the Majles and in a public rally openly attacked the shah and the royalist officers involved in the coup. His foreign minister Hosain Fatemi openly called for the shah's abdication and an end to the Pahlavi monarchy. The idea of creating a republic, which had been in the air for some time and lately advocated by the Tudeh Party, was never endorsed by Mosaddeq, at least openly. The Tudeh, now lending its support to Mosaddeq, in the course of the following three days quickly rephrased the call for a republic to one of a "democratic republic." To many, even among Mosaddeq's supporters, this was ominous, a euphemism for a Tudeh-dominated pro-Soviet regime. The next day in the main city squares, statues of Reza Shah and Mohammad Reza Shah—edifices of self-glorification that had survived the postwar years—were brought down and in some instances red flags hoisted on the pedestals. The Tudeh sympathizers presumably hoisted them, though the provocative act could have been the work of pro-coup elements hoping to stir the already-murky waters.

Whether responding to the demands mostly from Tudeh quarters for a change in monarchical regime, or perhaps on his own, on August 18 Mosaddeq ordered yet another referendum, this time on the fate of the Pahlavi monarchy (or as he later claimed, to convene the royal council to act in the shah's absence); this was another hurried move that met the resistance of some of Mosaddeq's close supporters, including Gholam-Hosain Sadiqi and Karim Sanjabi. It also alarmed Henderson, who hurriedly returned to Tehran to witness the CIA coup as it unraveled. The ambassador had the audacity to go to Mosaddeq's home and forewarn him of the imminent danger of his downfall, not from a CIA-sponsored coup but as a result of a Tudeh takeover. Mosaddeq, who no doubt was aware of American support for the royalist officers, if not of US sponsorship of the botched coup, nevertheless listened to the ambassador, who also assured him that General Zahedi was not hiding out in the American embassy. He was technically correct, since Kim Roosevelt had arranged for Zahedi to hide in the house of a staff member of the American embassy.

It is plausible that Mosaddeq, while benefiting from Tudeh support, feared the potentially grave consequences. He did not wish to be seen as the Alexander Kerensky of the Iranian revolution. Nor did he wish to go down in the pages of Iranian history as a frightened leader overwhelmed by the enormity of events or as a confused leader pressed between two competing superpowers whose agents, foreign and domestic, were busy plotting his overthrow. He must have had in mind the fate of his own relative, Ahmad Qavam, and preferred to stay and face the torment rather than make a humiliating exit. When on August 18 he declared martial law and banned further street demonstrations, it was still in the hopes of proving to his people, and to the Americans, that he was on a sound constitutional course. It became clear, though, that he was barely in touch with the rapidly changing realities, and his sense of confidence soon proved all but an illusion.

The Iranian plotters and their American and British counterparts were disappointed with the outcome of the first attempt, but they had not given up. It was apparently at the behest of Zahedi and his military and police cohorts that the plan for a second attempt was set. He was aided and encouraged primarily by Iranian agents on the British payroll, such as the Rashidi brothers, and a number of journalists unimpressed with Mosaddeq's ability to withstand a Tudeh takeover. Although Kim Roosevelt's role had somewhat paled after the failure of the first coup, and he himself was lukewarm about the success of the second one, he was still seen by the plotters as a source of moral, and if need be, financial, support.

Next day, August 19 (28 Mordad 1332 in the Persian solar calendar, as the date is engraved in Iranian memory), Mosaddeq's ban on demonstrations, though by no means fully enforced, may have inadvertently kept many of his supporters off the streets and at home. The Tudeh, too, stayed away, perhaps thinking that they stood to benefit from any attempt by the military to oust Mosaddeq. From the Tudeh perspective, in the absence of the shah and with "bourgeois liberalism" having already run its course, the future would surely be theirs without having to resort to a bloody struggle. The Tudeh's dormancy may also have been rooted in ignorance. At the time, the CIA involvement was unknown to all but a handful of officers around Zahedi and the Iranians agents working for the British and Americans. Even though Mosaddeq recognized the potential threat from the American side, he apparently could not bring himself to believe that the United States would go as far as bringing about his violent downfall, especially after his encounter with Henderson a day earlier.

With astounding speed, in a matter of hours Mosaddeq's political fortunes changed. It was as if agitators—some from the poor neighborhoods south of the capital who were angered by the prolonged economic hardship of the Mosaddeq years—and cash that Schwarzkopf had used to buy an anti-Mosaddeq crowd were sufficient to trigger a series of small, effective, demonstrations in key locations in the capital. No more than seventy thousand dollars were spent, indicative of the tinderbox waiting to flare up. The hired guns, which included the knife-wilding *lutis* of Tehran's poorer neighborhoods and Tehran's wholesale produce market, their associated gangs centered in certain *zurkhanehs* (houses of strength) and, allegedly, prostitutes from the poverty-stricken red-light district known as Shahr-e Now, were assigned with carrying the shah's portrait and shouting pro-Pahlavi slogans. An angry crowd swarmed the streets from Sepah Square, north of the bazaar, attacking some government buildings on their way and taking control of sensitive installations before moving toward Mosaddeq's house, near the royal palace. More effective than the crowd were the police and army units under the control of the officers loyal to Zahedi and his cohorts, who were evidently defiant of the shaky chain of command that Mosaddeq had tried to establish but could barely control. Tanks and troops were brought into the streets, quickly silencing a brave resistance set up by the prime ministerial guards—a loyal detachment of officers and soldiers whom Mosaddeq had handpicked to safeguard his office. The pro-shah units then began shelling the premier's house. The casualties were at least seventy-five dead and hundreds injured.

All the while Mosaddeq stayed in his office surrounded by a core of his loyal advisers. To the extent the reports of this episode illustrate, he could not be persuaded to resign or to face the perilous reality in which he had found himself so unexpectedly. The demonstrations appeared spontaneous, even though they may have been planned in advance, and the attack on the premier's house was so sudden that it took him and his ministers by complete surprise. Mosaddeq's assumed "national esteem" (*vejahat-e melli*), a source of pride and confidence, had given him an illusion of invincibility. A glaring lack of government intelligence to gauge public empathy or the imminent conspiracy deepened his misperceptions.

Once Mosaddeq realized that the troops would not be countered by a popular uprising in his favor, as had happened in July 1952, he opted to resist to the last, as he had admitted to the American ambassador a day earlier: "I will stay here no matter what happens; let them come and kill me." Lying in bed clad in his pajamas and surrounded by a number of bewildered ministers, advisers, and staff, it was as if he were welcoming his tragic fate—not resignation, but martyrdom. He was persuaded, only for the sake of saving other people's lives, to declare a truce.

Under intense pressure, with his house nearly ruined by shells, he sent a loyal guardsman to hoist from the roof of his house a makeshift white flag, made from his bed linen. Presumably his legal convictions made him believe that by declaring truce, his house would be immune from further assault. Once that gesture was ignored and shelling continued, another bed linen was hoisted, but to no avail. The tragic situation eventually came to an end when he and a handful of his loyal colleagues including Gholam-Hosain Sadiqi (1905–1992), a French-educated professor of sociology at Tehran University and Mosaddeq's minister of interior, fled over the wall of his house to a neighboring garden, where they spent a restless evening under threat of arrest. From the window of his temporary shelter, later Sadiqi recalled, Mosaddeq could see his house in smoldering flames.

The next day, the mob looted what was left of the premier's half-burned house—including all the furniture, carpets, bedding, even the window sashes and goldfish in the courtyard pond. Mosaddeq himself came out of his hideout and voluntarily turned himself over to the military authorities, along with two of his close advisers. The new premier and leader of the coup, General Zahedi, and his staff received them personally in the Tehran Officers' Club. He was first treated with respect and while staying in the club could contact his family and his aides. Concurrently, the pro-shah crowd attacked the National Front affiliates and began to arrest Mosaddeq's chief aides, ministers, and supporters who had not yet gone underground (fig. 9.7).

Once the military authorities solidified their ground, Mosaddeq was transferred to police headquarters and charged with treason and insubordination. The military prosecutor asked for the death sentence, but during the military tribunal held two months later, where he put up a dogged and systematic defense of his political conduct as the premier, he received three years of solitary confinement, which apparently had been determined by the shah from the outset. This was to be followed by a lifetime in exile in Ahmadabad, his estate near Tehran.

It took three more years of Mosaddeq's life while imprisoned to unsuccessfully go through the deliberately prolonged appeal process, whereby he tirelessly defended himself and his political career. By the time his appeal reached a futile end, he was transferred to his estate, where he lived his final years modestly and in relative seclusion. Though he was only to be visited by members of his family, he kept some contacts with the outside despite security surveillance and occasionally exchanged rigorous correspondence with opposition forces at home and abroad, especially in the early 1960s. He died on March 5, 1967, at the age of eighty-five (fig. 9.8). In his will he requested a simple funeral, to be

Figure 9.7. A club-wielding crowd tears down the Iran Party's
sign from its headquarters in Tehran, August 19, 1953.
© Bettmann/Corbis/AP Images.

Figure 9.8. Mosaddeq in Ahmadabad, 1962.
Ahmadabad near Tehran, photo by Ahmad Mosaddeq, 1962. Courtesy of Farhad Diba.

attended only by close members of his family, and he wished to be buried next to the July 21 martyrs. That his remains were interred in his own estate—in a modest grave under the floor of the living room in his humble dwelling—was a testament to his years of struggle that ended in a hapless captivity.

The effects of the 1953 coup were widespread and transformative. Martial law was declared throughout the country, which continued until 1957. Many of Mosaddeq's close colleagues and ministers were given prison terms or sent into exile, though with a few exceptions they were soon released. They were allowed to continue with their academic, administrative, and professional careers so long as they would not entertain political ambitions or express oppositional views. Others went into hiding and reemerged only gradually. One of the most vociferous, Hosain Fatemi, was executed in 1954 on charges of conspiracy and treason. Mosaddeq's appointees were sacked, and in due course the eighteenth Majles nullified all prime ministerial decrees during Mosaddeq's extraordinary powers. With greater vigor his military appointments were purged, and some officers loyal to Mosaddeq were given light sentences. The officers loyal to the shah were restored in rank and promoted. They created the backbone of Zahedi's regime and later the shah's power base.

Three days after the coup, the shah returned from Rome, though to no fanfare. Zahedi was the man of the day and the one who claimed all the credit for ousting Mosaddeq. He was also the United States' trusted man, for a while at least, and the main channel for exerting influence. Though something of a maverick, Zahedi was an effective military leader but also—as often was the case with the American-backed military officers in the 1950s—a general with a reputation for corruption. He demanded and received from the Americans $2 million for his part in the coup, and he was not shy in helping himself and his cohorts to large commissions from the American aid program that poured into Iran in the following years. His major task, demanded no doubt in exchange for US favor, remained the systematic eradication of the Tudeh Party organizations and cadres.

Over the course of the following five years Tudeh suffered most as a result of purges, trials, and executions. Although most of the top leadership fled to the Soviet Union and spent long years of exile in the countries of the eastern bloc, their rank and file were easy prey for the newly founded security apparatus, which later became Savak. The Zahedi regime and the subsequent governments announced with much publicity the discovery of several covert Tudeh organizations, arms caches, and clandestine presses. Especially hard hit was the Tudeh Party's military organization, consisting of a group of middle- and lower-ranking officers with determined Marxist-Leninist orientations. More than twenty were arrested, tortured, put on trial, and executed over the following sixteen months.

MOSADDEQ'S LEGACY AND MYTH

The downfall of Mosaddeq brought to an end the eventful postwar era, a revolution of sorts that was aborted by familiar forces of conservative opposition and foreign intervention, but also by errors of judgment that proved destructive. In this and other respects, the Mosaddeq era resembled the Constitutional Revolution. In many respects, it was a follow-up to that unfinished revolution, resurfacing a generation later. Mosaddeq's dilemma, and his tragedy, was that in the outset he tried to fulfill national aspirations while remaining committed to the principles of constitutionalism and democracy. Yet his disturbing display of autocratic conduct toward the end of his premiership may be seen as a conundrum, a vacillation between two modes of constitutional liberalism and radical populism. Mosaddeq and his colleagues also exhibited another dichotomy familiar to the constitutional period: they paid homage to Islam as a source of Iranian identity and courted religious authorities while also hoping to preserve the ideals of a secular society, freedom of the press, and equality before the law—notions that were in contrast to the conservative outlook of the Shi'i establishment and its radical allies. Mosaddeq's vision and frame of reference were in part the Shi'i tradition of Iran. For the greater part, however, he was a man with a secular mind-set that he and his cohorts hailed as a necessary framework for individual rights, division of powers, and liberation from economic hegemony and foreign intrigue. This was a difficult balance to maintain.

The forces that brought the National Movement to a bitter end, however, were more complex. Above all, the political volatility of the postwar era and the presence of many players created an environment of perpetual turmoil. The combination of an insecure monarch with memories of his father's downfall, a royal court susceptible to intrigue, a reinvigorated officer corps in search of power and privilege, an old elite clinging to its privileges, corrupt deputies in the volatile Majles, the comings and goings of impermanent governments, the presence of a well-organized and ideological Tudeh Party, and extremist Islamic tendencies—all these made designing any workable consensus highly formidable, if not impossible. Before Mosaddeq, both Qavam and Razmara had failed to master the treacherous political terrain. The widening political chasm aside, the forces at play in any particular moment could forge odd and opportunistic alliances while others were willing change course or even to act as foreign proxies, a situation that called into question the loyalties of many politicians of the period.

The security contingencies arising from the Cold War, as Western powers viewed them, and deep anxieties about rising Soviet influence across the globe left little room, and respect, in the minds of most Western strategists, for non-Western national leaders and their aspirations. In countries like Iran, caught in the midst of the Cold War, Western economic interests and hopes for new energy exploits further justified interventionism. A potent combination of security and energy dimmed the chances of nationalist movements at the outset of the postcolonial age and made inevitable violent clashes of interests.

Mosaddeq's own behavior in office did not help alleviate his differences with many domestic and foreign nemeses. In essence, he took for himself two powerful and simultaneous challenges. On the external front the oil nationalization campaign and on the domestic front rectifying the entrenched ills of authoritarianism, conservatism, and corruption. Relying on a level of public mandate unprecedented in modern Iranian history, he believed he could prevail by taking to task the shah and the royalists, a vast sector of the army, most of the Majles deputies, the landed elite, and most of the religious establishment—in other words, all those who controlled traditional sources of power and influence. This was a potent mix for any government and at any given time, even if it could rely on popular support. With the benefit of hindsight, one might envision a more circumspect and more realistic Mosaddeq prioritizing his objectives. But it is debatable if at the time he could have even exercised any order of priority in picking his fights, given how closely the oil dispute and domestic unrest were intertwined.

Mosaddeq may also be seen as a captive of his own rhetoric. As a Majles deputy and later during the first year of his premiership, he raised public expectations too high. He frequently accused other statesmen, like Razmara and Qavam, of compromise, conspiracy, and even treason. Such hyperbole made any compromise virtually impossible for fear that his friends and foes also label him a traitor. Yet it should be noted that AIOC and the British government never really offered any plausible deal to Mosaddeq for a viable compromise. Instead, the British preferred his demise, and as early as 1951 by military force, which hung like the Sword of Damocles over Mosaddeq's head. Nor could US mediation substantially change the British resolve, even though some elements within the Truman administration were willing to give their support to Iran's legitimate demands.

Before any politician of his time—especially from the class of landed notables—Mosaddeq had discovered mass politics, rallies, and public protests.

Such wide national appeal, as has often been noted, proved an obstacle to the emergence of a solid and well-organized political organization. The National Front throughout its five-year existence remained a fluid coalition of an odd bunch of individuals, political tendencies, and embryonic parties. The lack of organized political support with a coherent program contributed to the volatility of Mosaddeq's power base and his government.

Arguably even as late as early 1953, Mosaddeq could still safely maneuver on the back of a popular mandate that allowed him to challenge the interests of foreign powers and counter their schemes, and those of the shah and the Majles. Yet up to the very end he barely sensed the limitations of resorting to street politics. The general public, hard hit by rising inflation and unemployment, was ready to leave behind a decade of political turmoil, demonstrations, and much disillusionment. Despite earlier support for the oil nationalization campaign, by August 1953 the climate of indifference was palpable. Once triggered by anxieties over the shah's departure and a perception of a Tudeh takeover, public support for Mosaddeq evaporated. The Tudeh's eleventh-hour support for him only heightened fears among his liberal supporters afraid of communist manipulation.

All the above must have shaken the foundation of Mosaddeq's pact and perhaps were sufficient to bring down his government. If he were not overthrown, at some stage he would have been compelled to resign under the weight of the obstacles and deadlocks he faced. Yet the prospect of foreign involvement in the form of a conspiracy to oust a nationally mandated leader—almost a prophetic figure—profoundly changed the political climate and brought about a paradigm shift. It also helped create a mythical personality out of Mosaddeq. The coup of 1953 put an end to an era of political engagement, no matter how imperfect, and launched a second era of Pahlavi autocratic rule that by and large excluded the public from the political process. Under the aegis of the shah, and backed by the United States and its allies, Iran's chances for a plural society were further diminished.

In the following years as the CIA's covert involvement became more apparent, the fall of Mosaddeq came to be seen by most Iranians as a flagrant intrusion by Western powers into Iran's sovereignty and economic destiny. The shah's authoritarian rule, evident shortly after the coup, further convinced his opponents of the United States' malicious designs to impose on Iran a dictator subservient to its strategic interests. The fall of Mosaddeq turned into a traumatic memory that in the coming decades produced a narrative of victimization. It reinforced not only xenophobic suspicions but also pushed the Pahlavi opposition forces toward an anti-Western—more specifically, anti-American—discourse. There

was plenty of evidence of Western imperial interventions to support a historical narrative in which the coup of 1953 was the climax, starting with the 1813
and 1828 treaties with tsarist Russia and ending with the 1941 Allied occupation
of Iran. These were painful memories that once arranged in a cohesive narrative could deeply traumatize any national culture. If collective memories of a
national community can be called "deep history," the experience of the Mosaddeq era and its tragic end constructed such a history for generations to come.

10

THE WHITE REVOLUTION AND ITS OPPONENTS (1953–1963)

The gradual return to autocratic practices after 1953 put an undue end to Iran's perilous experiment with participatory politics. Instead, an era of stability, albeit politically repressive, began to set in, and with the exception of a brief interlude in the early 1960s, it remained essentially unchanged until the Islamic Revolution in 1979 and the collapse of the Pahlavi order.

The period between 1953 and 1979 was an era of relative prosperity for the urban middle classes of both the secular and the bazaar sectors, even though economic improvement over the long term did not always translate into political capital for the regime. The quality of life of the rural population, which in the early 1960s still accounted for more than 65 percent of Iran's total population, also improved, especially with the implementation of land reform (*eslahat-e arzi*), better education, and better health care—although, as elsewhere in the developing world, changes in the countryside did not reduce migration to cities and only marginally improved agricultural output. It also caused discontent among rural migrants, both the first and the second generations, who resented the privileged classes and began to take solace in the message of the radicalized clergy, who often came from a similar background.

The second Pahlavi era was marked by royal politics of self-aggrandizement, especially in the 1970s, and this image was enhanced by the growth of oil revenue, the rise of a subservient technocrat class, and the unprecedented expansion of security forces and the secret police apparatus. Iran's visibility as a regional power friendly to the United States and the Western world, and episodes of choreographed populism, also contributed. Mohammad Reza Shah's White Revolution of the early 1960s in reality came to fruition in the mid-1970s with greater industrial growth, infrastructure development, institution building, implementation of a planned economy, greater professional expertise, and educational and legal advances for women.

These crucial transformations also triggered contesting visions of modernity. The shah's image of progress, patterned on a Westernizing model similar to his father's, was questioned by a small but influential circle of secular dissidents and intellectuals—many with roots in the Tudeh and the National Movement of the postwar era. They began to question wholesale subservience to the West and the regime's positivistic ideas of progress. With the uprising of June 1963, a turning point in Iran's shift to Islamic activism, this laymen's critique of repression, nepotism, and the perceived "moral decline" of society increasingly took on an Islamic veneer. Not only young radical clergy but also revolutionary Marxists and Islamist guerrilla organizations critical of the predominant Westernism began calling for resistance to the Pahlavi regime and eventually to its violent overthrow. Islamic militants, mostly under the aegis of Ayatollah Khomeini, were the ultimate beneficiaries of anti-Pahlavi discourse. They succeeded in incorporating the semantics of the nationalists, the anti-Westernists, and the radical Marxists into their own rhetoric of "pristine Islam."

IRAN AS A US ALLY

The rise of the shah after 1953 as Iran's new political master was gradual but predictable, given the nearly unanimous support of the Iranian armed forces and the blessing of the United States. In a matter of months the government formed under General Zahedi, the key agent of the coup that overtook Mosaddeq and returned the shah to power, silenced nearly all forces of dissent. Under the American aegis, a new agreement was also reached on the oil question. On paper Iran's nationalization of its oil industry was recognized, and in 1954 the National Iranian Oil Company (NIOC), which had been formed under Mosaddeq, became the partner in a fifty-fifty profit-sharing agreement with a new holding company, Iranian Oil Participants Limited (IOP), which consisted of eight major American, British, and European oil companies. These partners replaced the Anglo-Iranian Oil Company's monopoly. The pattern roughly resembled the ARAMCO consortium of Saudi Arabia, with a similar sharing arrangement. Although the new agreement was a far cry from the objectives of the Nationalization Movement, and was unpopular with the general public, it was a face-saving measure for the shah and for the United States.

Known as the "seven sisters," these oil companies held 60 percent of the newly formed consortium. They were Standard Oil of California (later Chevron), Standard Oil of New Jersey (later Exxon), Standard Oil of New York (later

Mobil), Texaco (later Chevron) and Gulf Oil (later Chevron), each holding an 8 percent stake; Royal Dutch Shell, with 14 percent; and Compagnie Française des Pétroles (later Total), with 6 percent. Taking over from AIOC, the newly renamed British Petroleum (BP) held the remaining 40 percent of the consortium's shares. The consortium was responsible for the exploration, production, and international distribution of Iranian oil and controlled production levels and the pricing structure. Admittedly operating within a smaller area under concession in Khuzestan than had the former AIOC monopoly, Iran nevertheless remained on the receiving end of the production process, with the National Iranian Oil Company in charge of domestic distribution and overall supervision of the operation, a position that proved mostly a formality, at least in the earlier years. IOP held full control over all operations, did not open books to outsiders, did not allow any AIOC representation on its board, and kept a low political profile while maximizing profits. This was a victory for the big oil companies in tightening their monopoly not only over Iranian oil but also over more than 80 percent of world oil production.

The amended twenty-five-year concession granted in 1954 to IOP was a further departure from the objectives of the National Movement. At least until the early 1973, when the shah managed to negotiate better terms for production and pricing—and eventually in 1975 declared another "nationalization" of the oil industry (the third such announcements since 1933)—IOP reigned supreme. With the Americans holding the upper hand, the issue was not so much the AIOC's colonial culture, which was gradually disappearing, but a new corporate mentality that allowed the oil companies to manipulate prices and production levels for the Middle East oil market, which, in addition to Iranian oil, included Saudi and Iraqi supply, and soon after those of Kuwaiti and other Persian Gulf producers.

Oil production came to occupy an increasingly vital place in the Iranian economy, in turn empowering the state. Whereas in 1950, the height of AIOC's operation, annual Iranian oil production stood at 221 million barrels, by 1969 it had reached 1.064 billion barrels, a nearly fivefold increase. In 1950 Iran's direct revenue from oil production was slightly more than US$45 million but by 1969, in less than two decades, it increased by more than twenty times, to $905 million. Allowing for an average rate of inflation of 2.5 percent in the period between 1959 and 1969, the overall revenue of the state in absolute terms was no less than eighteen-fold. In terms of contribution to the country's total revenue, there was also a significant increase. Whereas between 1949 and 1956 oil income constituted 37 percent of Iran's revenue, by 1965 it had risen to 67 percent, steadily increasing thereafter until 1980. As oil consumption grew worldwide, Iranian oil revenue steadily increased throughout the 1970s, in part because of the shah's success in persuading the reluctant IOP to increase production levels.

Oil revenue thus became a crucial factor in the stability of the Pahlavi state. The massive injection of US financial support in the 1950s and early 1960s, as well as military assistance, training, and advising, further boosted the Pahlavi prestige. Up to the mid-1960s tens of millions of US dollars—originally promised but never delivered to Mosaddeq's cash-strapped government—poured into Iranian coffers as nonobligatory aide, or were funneled through the Point Four Program's health and agricultural development projects, or through the purchase of military hardware, infrastructure development loans for building dams and a power grid, direct investment in Iranian industry, and major construction projects won by American firms.

The US government's aid program in reality was a fraction of what US oil companies collected from investing in Iranian oil and a negligible expense compared to the benefit of keeping Iran as a strategic ally in the Cold War. This may well explain the United States' reluctance to enforce stringent measures against rampant corruption in high offices and the army. From the American perspective, Iranian collaboration had to be preserved at any price so as to eradicate any remnants of the Iranian Tudeh and other real or potential sources of dissent after the Mosaddeq era. The United States' greater involvement also coincided with a gradual eclipse of British influence in Iranian affairs, especially after the 1956 Suez debacle and British disengagement east of the Suez.

The shah was yet to display the ambitions that made him in the 1970s a regional leader and an international figure of some weight. Beyond systematic eradication of all levels of the Tudeh, in the months after the coup a few serious protest movements in the bazaar and in the Tehran University were also crushed. On one occasion confrontation with the bazaar merchants in October 1953 led not only to mass arrests but also, in effect, to the demolition of the Tehran bazaar's historic entry archway, apparently a punitive measure against merchants. On December 8, 1953, in Tehran University, the armed forces opened fire indiscriminately on students who were protesting the visit of US Vice President Richard Nixon, aimed to consolidate US-Iranian ties. Organized by the left, which resented the arrival of the well-known American "Cold Warrior," the demonstrations saw at least three students killed and many more injured, thus marking the event as the "student day" of protests in the Iranian dissent calendar. Though the shah tried to commiserate with the victims, and even issued his regrets, the giving of an honorary degree to Nixon a few days later on the campus of Tehran University added insult to injury. One of the shah's close

American friends and staunch advocates, Nixon also benefited in later years from the royal largesse during his presidential campaigns.

The unrest displayed the unpopularity of the new regime among the bazaar merchants, the intellectuals of the left, and university students. The shah, quickly taking center stage, was able to convince the Americans to abandon General Zahedi, in his own favor. Under Zahedi's watch, much had allegedly been embezzled. The shah also argued that the Pahlavi regime, without Zahedi at the helm, would enjoy greater legitimacy and popular acceptance from the bazaar and the clergy. Zahedi was ambitious and independent, and frictions with the shah over control of the army and government affairs were unavoidable. By April 1955 General Zahedi resigned and left the country to serve as Iran's ambassador to Rome, the same city where the shah had taken refuge less than two years earlier. The virtual exile, from which Zahedi never returned, removed a powerful contestant but also exposed the shah, in due course, to greater public scrutiny and made him a target of domestic and international criticism.

THE ANTI-BAHA'I CAMPAIGN

The recurring suppression of sporadic protests in the wake of the 1954 oil agreement, the systematic arrests of Tudeh members, the long sentences handed down in military courts, and several rounds of merciless executions of Tudeh members all tarnished the shah's image. The purging of pro-Mosaddeq elements was less severe and often conducted on case-by-case basis, in accordance with the shah's degree of dislike for one or the other individual. The United States could barely disguise its blessing for these purges, a demeanor that militated against its efforts to buttress the shah's regime as popular and democratic.

To seek rapprochement with the high-ranking clergy in Qom and elsewhere, the shah capitalized on the common dislike for Mosaddeq and a joint desire to eliminate the Tudeh. Despite all the lip service to Islam, the Tudeh remained second only to the Baha'is in posing a doctrinal challenge to clerical establishment. A few months earlier, in the fall of 1954, the impending execution of Mosaddeq's foreign minister Hosain Fatemi, who entertained some Islamic sentiments, caused uproar among the clergy. Their earlier petition to commute his death sentence was ignored. By early 1955 the shah thus was looking for an occasion to mend fences. He was also anxious to secure the clergy's blessing to join the 1955 Baghdad Pact, a defense treaty that included Iran's neighbors Iraq, Turkey, and Pakistan, as well as Britain and the United States as observer members (after Iraq's withdrawal from the treaty in 1958, it became the Central Treaty Organization, or CENTO). A Cold War strategic alliance complementing the North Atlantic Treaty Organization (NATO), the pact was inspired as much by the Eisenhower doctrine as it was orchestrated by Britain out of anxiety over the Suez Canal and the increasingly anti-British posture of Egypt's president Jamal Abdel Nasser. The shah's insistence on being included in the pact sprang more from his own insecurities than from persuasion by the observer members. With the growth of pro-Nasser sentiments, even in Iran, support of the clergy seemed essential to the shah.

The shah's approach to Ayatollah Sayyed Hosain Borujerdi (1875–1961), a senior mojtahed who had emerged in the late 1940s as the sole *marja'* (supreme exemplar) with a wide acceptance in the Shi'i world, would have been a clever move had it not been for its unexpected consequences (fig. 10.1). Mostly through a network of students, agents, and followers in the bazaar, Borujerdi had created a power base unmatched by any *marja'* at least since the time of Mirza Hasan Shirazi some fifty years earlier. Coming from a middle-ranking clerical family in Borujerd, he was a product of Isfahan and Najaf Shi'i training. A student of Najaf's pro-constitutional Mohammad Kazem Khorasani, Borujerdi gained prominence after he moved to Qom in 1945 and helped build it up as a Shi'i clerical center that, if not on par with Najaf, was at least the most important such center inside Iran. He indeed was the first *marja'* to emerge inside Iran,

Figure 10.1. The young shah visits Ayatollah Borujerdi
in Firuzabadi Hospital in Tehran in 1944.
Mohammad Baqer Najafi, *Shahanshahi va Dindari* (Tehran: NRTV, 1355/1976), n.p.

and more than earlier *marja's* in Iraq, he had to adjust to Iran's political realities and build up his standing with his Iranian constituency. The renewal of the ancient fellowship of the "good religion" and "good government," especially after a cooling off under Reza Shah, required the public disowning of a "heretical" Other. Now that Tudeh and Mosaddeq were out of the picture, both Borujerdi and the shah wished to consolidate their grounds by no more viable a target than an anti-Baha'i campaign.

The eclipse after 1953 of Ayatollah Abul-Qasem Kashani, the controversial clerical leader of the National Movement era, and his absence from the public arena, further contributed to Borujerdi's rise and his restoration of the old state-clergy pact. Shrewd, pragmatic, and resolute, Borujerdi was willing to negotiate with the shah, giving his implicit blessing to the monarch in exchange for a freer hand in quashing presumed threats to Islam and Muslims. Above all, he demanded a thorough purge of the Baha'is at all levels within and outside the government. Among the Shi'i authorities, animosity toward the Baha'is was deep, in part because of doctrinal reasons but also, in the twentieth century, because of a paranoiac fear of Baha'i infiltration of government and society and of their presumed success in converting Muslims over to their "deviant path." Through intermediaries Borujerdi demanded that because the clergy, with himself at the helm, supported Tudeh purges, in return the shah should repay them by eradicating the Baha'i menace.

In April 1955 at the outset of Ramadan, a relatively obscure preacher, Mohammad Taqi Falsafi (1908–1998), whose fiery oratorical style compensated for his checkered past, began an orchestrated anti-Baha'i campaign that lasted through the month of fasting. The lunchtime sermons from the government-controlled Masjed-e Shah at the entrance to the Tehran bazaar were broadcast live on government-controlled Radio Iran, an unprecedented favor that denoted the state's endorsement of the campaign. With Borujerdi's personal blessing, Falsafi attacked Baha'i beliefs as heretical and anti-Islamic and accused them of betrayal of the nation, of conspiracy and moral corruption, and of being a major threat to the preservation of Islamic Iran. He demanded the government not only ban all Baha'i communal events and administrative bodies but also expropriate all Baha'i communal and personal property and remove Baha'is from all government posts and private enterprises, and he even went as far as calling for their mass banishment from the country. The Baha'is were the largest religious minority in Iran, and by the mid-1950s they constituted a population of at least three hundred thousand, widely spread throughout the towns and villages of Iran.

Falsafi's campaign found resonance among the clergy and their conservative following, resuscitating a sense of unanimity, especially in the aftermath of

Mosaddeq era. They were happy to find a sympathetic partner in the Pahlavi state. Since as early as the Babi persecutions in the Qajar period, Baha'is had been routinely demonized as enemies of Islam. With the new campaign against them, however, the nature of the accusations shifted to a higher level: they were accused not only of doctrinal enmity to Islam but also of being politically disloyal to the country. These set the ground, starting in the 1960s, of accusing the Baha'is of being agents of British colonialism, and soon after of being agents of American imperialism and international Zionism, charges that after the 1979 Islamic Revolution had serious repercussions for the Baha'i community in Iran.

The anti-Baha'i campaign soon led to discrimination against the Baha'is and acts of violence, especially against smaller urban communities and those in rural areas. In Najafabad, then a small town 180 miles west of Isfahan known for its conservative Shiʻi loyalties, the large Baha'i community was ostracized through an economic boycott. In Ardestan, another old, semi-agricultural community, the Baha'i were to be evacuated overnight for fear of a massacre. In Yazd, when some Baha'is were killed by a mob, the members of the Baha'i assembly—the elected local governing body—were held responsible for alleged crimes and sentenced to long prison terms. A climate of fear and intimidation soon overcame Baha'is everywhere. Advocating the message of the radical preacher and his powerful backer, some deputies in the Majles—fast becoming pliant to the shah's wishes—proposed a bill designed to expropriate all Baha'i properties and expel them from Iran.

Even though the bill was eventually withdrawn, this did not stop other drastic measures. A crowd of supporters buoyed by Falsafi's hate campaign organized a vigilante takeover of the Baha'i center in Tehran. In Shiraz the mob attacked the house of the Bab, the holiest site for the Baha'i and Azali in Iran, and all but destroyed it. As a sign of the government's solidarity with the anti-Baha'i campaign, but in reality a weak attempt to control the situation, in May 1955 General Nader Batmanqlij, chief of staff of the Iranian armed forces, dispatched troops to occupy the Baha'i center in Tehran. The general personally climbed to the roof to strike the first symbolic blow, demolishing the center's dome (fig. 10.2).

Under pressure from Western governments and facing international criticism (and from Baha'i communities worldwide), the shah began to back off, having sensed the looming repercussions of the campaign getting out of hand. By the end of Ramadan, the most egregious persecutions had subsided. Yet the ban on Baha'i communal activities remained in force. They continued to be banned from government employment, at least officially, and the Baha'i center in Tehran was converted into the headquarters of the Tehran military command and

Figure 10.2. General Batmanqlij and General Timur Bakhtiar, military governor
of Tehran, attend the seemingly joyous occasion on the roof of the Baha'i center
in May 1955. The Iranian correspondent of the Reuters News Agency urges the
generals to strike the first blow to the dome structure, for the sake of the cameras.
Private collection. Courtesy of Fereydun Vahman.

army counterintelligence, the nucleus of what later became the Organization
for Security and Intelligence, or the Savak. Yet the plight of the Baha'is could
have been far worse. The anti-Baha'i campaign, as it turned out, was not as severe as, for example, the mistreatment of the Jewish community of Turkey during World War II; it was also incomparable to anti-Jewish campaigns in Egypt
in 1956 and 1957 in the aftermath of the Suez crisis and in Iraq during the war
and more systematically from the 1950s onward.

For the Shi'i leadership, the anti-Baha'i campaign nevertheless reasserted
Borujerdi's leadership at the expense of Islamic activists and Fada'iyan-e Islam.
For years to come, the low-intensity anti-Baha'i posture gave to the Shi'i leadership weight and panache. Such fatwas as banning Pepsi-Cola on the grounds
that it was bottled in Iran under a concession granted to a Baha'i entrepreneur,
Habib Sabet (1903–1990), was one such example. The anti-Baha'i smear moreover facilitated the launch of other initiatives by Borujerdi, including the building of Masjed-e A'zam (the grand mosque) next to the shrine of Ma'sumeh in
Qom, the expansion and further centralization of the *howzeh* (a conglomerate

of seminaries) in Qom, and the sponsorship of anti-Baha'i publications, such as a new Persian translation of the thirteenth volume of Mohammad Baqer Majlesi's encyclopedic *Bihar al-Anwar.* An earlier translation of this volume, which was exclusively devoted to the Shi'i hadith on the return of the Mahdi and apocalyptic events at the End of Times, had stirred much polemical debate among Baha'i preachers because of inconsistencies in the Shi'i narrative. The new translation, commissioned by Borujerdi in the last year of his life and carried out by the Shi'i scholar 'Ali Davani (1929–2007), streamlined *Bihar's* inconsistencies by omitting some reports and rendering others in such a way as to offer a congruent version useful for anti-Baha'i debates. The thrust of Islamic energies during the 1950s and 1960s indeed included anti-Baha'i actions (mostly polemical debates on the issue of prophecies) by such organizations as the Hojjatiyeh Society, a network of lay and clerical activists around Shaykh Mahmud Halabi (1900–1998). Yet rapprochement between the shah and the pro-regime clergy did not stop Shi'i radicalism altogether.

CONSOLIDATION OF ROYAL POWER

By the late 1950s the rapid expansion of the Security and Intelligence Organization (known by the Persian acronym Savak) proved crucial in suppressing all forms of opposition. It also proved a successful tool in intimidating the general public. Rooted in the Tehran military command under the charismatic, though ruthless, General Teymur Bakhtiar, the new organization, under the Americans' watch, was designed to uproot communism within the armed forces, government, and society at large (similar to the demands of the United States for most of its authoritarian allies in the developing world). Relying on the law of national security, first initiated by Mosaddeq and revived after him, in 1957 Savak was mandated to operate under the prime minister's office. Teymur Bakhtiar (1914–1970), son of a Bakhtiyari tribal chief, was educated in Beirut and Paris, where he attended Saint-Cyr. He quickly rose to prominence under General Zahedi, and as head of the military command, he had a major part in hunting Tudeh activists and other political dissidents.

When the last of the Tudeh cells had been cracked and operatives such as Khosrow Ruzbeh (1915–1958), a radical Marxist-Leninist theoretician and core organizer of a secret communist officers' cell, were captured and executed, Savak began to search for other dissidents. Ruzbeh, who for some years before his capture in 1957 had lived a clandestine life marked by armed clashes with security forces, failed to rekindle a meaningful resistance even within his own small circle of sympathizers. After his execution, however, he gained legendary, almost romantic standing as a martyr of the left and a symbol of resistance. His advocacy of armed resistance may well be considered an inspiration for the Marxist urban guerrilla movement of the late 1960s.

By the early 1960s Savak, under the shah's sponsorship, had begun to earn a reputation for efficiency and discipline, but also for fear mongering and ruthlessness, purposefully cultivating an image even darker than its reality. Among Savak's new targets were independent political figures, the younger generation of intellectuals, members of the former National Front, leaders of student demonstrations, and outspoken clergy. When the shah ousted Teymur Bakhtiar in 1961, Savak was brought even more tightly under his direct control. Accused of conspiring against the Pahlavi regime in the outset of a new episode of anti-Pahlavi resistance, the general was forced into exile in Geneva, where he began organizing an anti-Pahlavi front together with an exiled Tudeh leader and Ayatollah Khomeini, the emerging de facto leader of the antiregime clergy in Qom. Bakhtiar consequently fled to Lebanon, and then to Iraq, where a Savak agent assassinated him in August 1970. The ouster of Bakhtiar was the last significant military hurdle in the shah's path to absolute power. He was also the first of the top brass to fall victim to the shah.

Throughout the 1960s the forced retirement of a number of high-ranking generals and the sacking of career officers revealed the shah's desire for greater control, in the style of his father. The dismissed officers were accused of real or propped-up charges of financial misappropriation, ineptitude, and even spying for the Soviet Union. Nearly all the chiefs of staff during the 1960s and early 1970s were dismissed with disgrace or put on trial and imprisoned, or they were sent into exile. Like the civilian technocrats, the top military soon learned to sing the glories of their imperial master. The shah's ever-growing thirst for the latest military hardware and his buildup of the armed forces into a megamachine further cultivated a spirit of blind submission to the wishes of the King of Kings, the "grand commander of the armed forces" (*bozorg arteshtaran*) and even the "godhead" (*khodaygan*)—epithets by which the shah was exalted in the pure Persian adopted by the armed forces. The figurehead of limited means of the 1940s had transformed into a man of great ego with a complex personality and a burgeoning sense of mission.

Born in 1919, when his father was still a middle-ranking officer of the Cossack Brigade, Mohammad Reza was brought up in the early Pahlavi era under the watchful eye of a demanding father who had an overpowering personality. He remained closer to his caring mother than to his father, and he bonded with his twin sister, Ashraf Pahlavi, a great influence on him. As the senior son of a growing family, Mohammad Reza was nominated to be crown prince at the age of six, and he was educated accordingly in the newly established Pahlavi court by a number of private tutors. Later in the 1920s, he briefly attended the Tarbiyat Baha'i School, then a progressive institution in Tehran. In 1931 he was sent off to Switzerland to the elite Le Rosey boarding school, and he returned in 1936 proficient in French and English. He was interested more in sports, especially soccer, than in international affairs or intellectual pursuits. In the Iranian military academy, which he attended to fulfill his father's wishes, he reached the rank of lieutenant, shadowing his father in most public events during the final years of his rule. His arranged marriage with Princess Fawziya (1921–2013), a sister of King Farouk of Egypt, at the age of twenty was more to buttress a political alliance and gain prestige for the Pahlavi court than being his own personal choice. It turned out to be an unhappy union.

The shy and mild-mannered young Mohammad Reza, brought up under the stern shadow of his disciplined father, at the age of twenty-two faced the first test of his political career when he inherited a shaky throne with questionable legitimacy. Largely ignored by the leaders of the occupying Allies during World War II—with the exception of Joseph Stalin, who paid him a visit during the 1943 Tehran Conference—and separated from his family, who remained in exile in Johannesburg until his father's death, the new shah seemed unprepared for the political turmoil of the postwar era. He was suspicious of elder statesmen and wary of the freer political climate that had emerged virtually overnight. With a barrage of attacks in the press and from the public against his father's misdeeds and crimes, he had little choice but to express his regrets and promise the return of confiscated properties to their original owners, as well as compensation for past abuses. In the court of law his father was condemned for expropriating villages and estates—more than five thousand of them—and for accumulating substantial illicit wealth in personal bank accounts.

In the face of numerous political challenges to the Pahlavi throne from the Tudeh and other contenders, the young shah could do little but to nurture the loyalty of the statesmen and army officers who had served his father. At the same time he was trying to remain a monarch loyal to the constitutional process, a role he soon began to reconsider when faced with enormous political challenges to his office. He was compelled to play a more proactive role. The success of the 1946 Azarbaijan campaign was a turning point. He was recognized not merely as the nominal head of the armed forces but also as an active participant in the campaign. The Azarbaijan crisis, moreover, was the beginning of long-term reliance on advice and moral support from the United States.

An attempt against his life in 1949, from which he miraculously escaped, and soon afterward the arduous course that ended with the coup of 1953, transformed the young shah from a reactive maneuverer into a shrewd, even devious, manipulator. Especially after the tumultuous Mosaddeq years he learned to dominate the political stage at the expense of any independent voice within or outside his immediate reach. The bitter experience of the Mosaddeq years washed away whatever faith he might have had in the democratic process or in what his more liberal-minded advisers urged him to adopt. The experience made him suspicious of popular participation at any level and of genuine debate on any political issue.

Although he offered his early support for the oil nationalization campaign, after July 1952 he found himself marginalized and unwanted. From his perspective, Mosaddeq's course not only aimed to overthrow him and eliminate the monarchy but also would bring the country to the brink of chaos and eventually the throes of communism. His flight to Baghdad and then to Rome in August 1953 after the failure of the first coup to oust Mosaddeq, and his return under the shadow of a second coup staged with active help from American and British agents, was a tormenting memory, even though he presented it to his people as a patriotic victory over unspecified enemies. In later years, the annual anniversary of the coup of the twenty-eighth of Mordad (August 28, 1953) was an exercise in hollow slogans bellowed across the radio waves, military music, and flag-waving rallies. Underneath the annual ritual there was an unsettled royal psyche that wished to convince people of the shah's troubled legitimacy.

The shah's attitude toward foreign powers was no less problematic. He remained generally suspicious of their intrigues and entertained conspiratorial fantasies, especially toward the British. The forced abdication of his father taught him to remain distrustful of Britain's real or presumed mischief, and his Cold War mentality—darkened by the Tudeh experience—made him, even more than the British, fearful of Russian-backed plots, which also had been a fear of all of his predecessors since the early nineteenth century. The United States appeared to be a natural ally and a moral refuge for the shah: a superpower willing to lionize him and ingratiate itself to his wishes. The United States, to the shah, was the innocent abroad: powerful and well intentioned but naive.

For all practical purposes the shah's ties to the US appeared to be a perfect match, offering him security and support in exchange for America's strategic concerns and energy needs. The American policy makers, with few exceptions, viewed the shah's authoritarian rule as simply an unpleasant fact of life, about which they could do little, if anything. Such an attitude partially changed in the early 1960s when the Kennedy administration came to office. But once the shah's White Revolution had reached a certain momentum, he managed to persuade the United States, and the Western world, to view him not only as the only viable choice for Iran but also as a bulwark against rising anti-American sentiments in the region. Policing the strategically vital Persian Gulf against Egypt and Iraq was a mission he undertook primarily of his own volition. He viewed his regime, at least for the sake of the captivated Western media, as heir to the ancient Persian Empire and a potent alternative to what he conceitedly viewed as the waning of Western democratic institutions.

The early 1960s witnessed a major shift in the country's agrarian structure but also in the rise of literacy, urbanization, and living standards—all with lasting consequences. The series of state-sponsored reforms that came to be known as the White Revolution (Enqelab-e Sefid), largely implemented between 1961 and 1965, produced a sizable population surplus in the countryside, which poured from the villages into towns and cities, unleashing a popular force that, though first backing the Pahlavi reforms, eventually shifted away from the state toward other alternatives.

Even as early as the 1950s, new cracks were visible on the surface. Corruption and mismanagement within the civilian administration and military took a turn for the worse, especially with the influx of US aid and growing income from oil. Oddly enough, at the same time, the budget deficit, particularly its foreign exchange reserves, grew to such an extent that the government was brought to the brink of bankruptcy. The token show trials and purging of army officers and civil servants on charges of corruption and embezzlement did little to win over a public suspicious of the state's sincerity, the role of the foreign powers, and the shah's goodwill.

The trial of general Mohammad Vali Qarani (Gharani), the head of the military counterintelligence, who was arrested in 1958 and tried along with his accomplices on the charge of contemplating a military coup with the backing of the US Central Intelligence Agency, was one example. He was convicted and served a prison term, but the shah's anxiety hardly subsided. He viewed the planned coup as a symptom of the Americans' uncertain loyalties toward him and, even worse, as providing the potential for American, British, and even Soviet manipulation and mischief within Iranian armed forces. Qarani's case, in effect, was an early sign of American displeasure with Iran's unstable state of affairs.

To remedy growing public mistrust, and fearing a revival of the opposition forces from the Mosaddeq era, the shah briefly toyed with the idea of a two-party system to allow for a semblance of popular participation. In reality, the two parties: the Melliun Party (the party of the nationalists) and the Mardom Party (the party of the people), were presided over by two of the shah's most trusted aides, known for their subservience to the royal's wishes. The result was nothing short of a puppet show, cynically staged to enhance the shah's public image at home and abroad. By the time the election of the twentieth Majles was under way in August 1960, there was enough fraud and vote rigging that even the shah could no longer put his seal of approval on the sitting premier Manuchehr Eqbal, the leader of the Melliun Party. Eqbal (1909–1977), a French-educated medical doctor and former health minister in Ahmad Qavam's Democrat Party, had served as premier since 1957. An early example of the kind of technocrat who later manned the Pahlavi administration, Eqbal was a capable manager with a facade of sincerity, but he was nevertheless fully obedient to the wishes of his master, even after his removal from office.

Yet neither forcing Eqbal to resign nor annulling the election results in the fall of 1960 could persuade the Iranian public of the shah's democratic intentions. The next government formed under Ja'far Sharif-Emami (1910–1998), another of the shah's cronies, further aggravated general malcontent. Born to a family with old clerical ties, he was trained as an engineer in Germany in the interwar period. His appointment was largely the result of the shah's concern over the restive clergy. Most likely, he viewed Sharif-Emami's appointment as a conciliatory gesture toward the clerical moderates, especially in the face of Khomeini's gradual rise to prominence. The new premier's brief term, ending in May 1961, more than a month after Borujerdi's death in March 30, was riddled by corruption scandals.

With the American presidential election campaign under way, and viable prospects for a Democratic victory, there was growing concern in Tehran about what the implications of John F. Kennedy's presidency would be for the Pahlavi regime. Kennedy was openly critical of the Republicans' foreign policy in the developing world, and he questioned outright military aid to oppressive regimes that ignored economic development and democracy. He considered economic and political reforms as alternative means of saving non-Western societies from the lure of socialist-inspired revolutions. The collapse in Cuba of the US-backed dictator Fulgencio Batista in early 1959 and Fidel Castro's rapid shift from a nationalist revolutionary to a committed Marxist made his points all the more glaring. At the time, perhaps no other country besides Iran fit Kennedy's disapproval of the US granting of unconditional military largesse and moral support. It was therefore quite plausible that beyond Latin America Iran would become a priority for the new administration.

Changes in the American attitude aside, by 1960 the Iranian economy was in crisis. Poor monetary management, aggravated by meager economic performance and imperial grandeur, stirred popular resentment. A handful of elite figures, veterans of the National Front, and clerical critics of the shah were buoyed by the prospects of a shift in US policy toward Iran. The appointment of 'Ali Amini (1905–1992) as prime minister was seen as a fresh start, as he aimed to implement long-awaited reforms to Iran's agrarian economy and, as Amini used to say, "tighten the belts." Disliked by the shah because of his American connections and the fact that he was personally acquainted with Kennedy, Amini was expected to liberate Iranian politics from the yoke of autocracy and represent a wider political spectrum.

During his fourteen-month term of office (May 1961–July 1962) Amini barely managed to deliver what was expected of him, given the enormity of the problems he had to grapple with and his own managerial limitations. Born into a Qajar aristocratic lineage, he was a grandson of the reformist statesman 'Ali Khan Amin al-Dowleh. Having received two French doctorates in law and economics, Amini's political career displayed encouraging signs of independence and pragmatism but also compromise and resignation. He had been a protégé of Davar in the Reza Shah years, and later an associate of Ahmad Qavam, but he also served under Mosaddeq as minister of education, and after the coup under Zahedi he was instrumental in concluding the 1954 oil concession with the IOP consortium. In the late 1950s, as Iranian ambassador to Washington, his credentials as a middle-of-the-road statesman appealed to the Americans. For a brief period at the outset of his premiership he also enjoyed some popularity among the Iranian public as a clean and progressive statesman.

The Amini government was a mix of the old elite and new faces, even radical veterans from the Mosaddeq era. The most visible, and most effective, was Hasan Arsanjani (1922–1969), minister of agriculture and the architect of the land reform campaign. A fiery journalist and lawyer who once had belonged to the radical wing of Qavam's Democrat Party, Arsanjani long entertained land reform as the key to dismantling the landowning elite (including Amini's own family). His rapid land distribution program aimed not only to parcel out the state-owned arable land (*khaleseh*) to peasants already working on it but also to redistribute private estates controlled by a small but powerful class of landowners (*mallakin*).

LAND REFORM AND THE CHANGING VILLAGE

Even by the 1960s agriculture was the largest sector of the Iranian economy outside of government-controlled revenue from the oil industry, and it employed the largest number of people as tillers of the land, providing subsidiary and secondary jobs as well, and sustaining the landowners. Made up mostly of absentee landlords residing in the cities, the large landowning sector consisted of bureaucratic nobility and their offspring, tribal khans and their urbanized offspring, provincial elite, and bazaar merchants, who altogether owned more than 70 percent of the country's arable land. The remaining 30 percent was held by small landowners, independent farmers (mostly in the northern provinces), and religious endowments. Operating on an ancient agrarian sharecropping arrangement known as *boneh*, the five-part means of production—land, water, seed, ox, and labor—determined the respective portions of income for landlord (*arbab*) and peasant (*ra'iyyat*), with some local variances. While the landlords controlled the first three (and occasionally the fourth as well) and reaped shares accordingly, the peasants could provide only labor and the ox, while often paying a larger portion of taxes to the state at harvest time. The system was marked by extra burden for the peasant, who had to deal with bailiffs, government agents, and gendarmerie, as well as conditions that at best offered a life only at the subsistence level and at worst sheer destitution for as much as half of the country's population. Scattered across the vast span of the Iranian plateau and the slopes and ravines that punctuated it, Iranian villages typically consisted of adobe-like mud structures that, though scenic from afar, close up displayed the extent of rural deprivation. The houses, more often clusters of primitive huts, made of unbaked mud bricks with few windows, little ventilation, and unstable wooden roof beams, contrasted with the better built and better maintained landlord's mansion. For villagers there was no running water—even though there was frequently access to a clean communal source such as a spring well or a *qanat*—and no modern amenities (including electricity) or access to modern medical facilities or modern schools.

Ironically, the end of the Qajar land tenure system and sanctioning of the right to private landownership in the Iranian Constitution and in the subsequent register of land titles had only reasserted control of the private landowning sector over the haphazard agrarian system. Organized around sedentary or seminomadic economies, the village tied the subsistence agrarian economy to animal husbandry. Although the landlord, or the bailiff on the landlord's behalf, oversaw the operation of the village with a certain autonomy and along a patriarchal model, the system did allow peasants some freedoms of mobility, such as negotiating the terms of the sharecropping contract, and encouraged some level of village communal solidarity.

Yet the village economy was barely able to withstand drastic changes such as those introduced by the land reforms of the 1960s. The substitution of the landlord by a government-run agency—first the Ministry of Agriculture and then the Ministry of Land Reform—added layers of bureaucratic complexity to the system and with unexpected outcomes. The small parcels of land distributed to each peasant often were not economically viable. The "liberated farmers," as the state-run media dubbed them, did not have access to sufficient capital and lacked experience in running modern farming machinery, and had to rely on traditional methods. Despite widespread state publicity to the contrary, soon inefficiency, a relative decline in agricultural production, and the glaring failure of agricultural cooperatives (set up to address these problems) became apparent. Haphazard mechanization, and soon migration to the cities, further hindered a successful transition to the new system.

Already in the 1950s some of the estates and smaller plots expropriated by Reza Shah, mostly in the Caspian provinces, had been returned to their original owners or redistributed to small landowners. First through litigation in the courts, which after the fall of Reza Shah handed down judgments in favor of the original owners, and then voluntarily by the shah, most, if not all, confiscated lands were returned. The Pahlavi Foundation, both a charity and a holding company for the Pahlavi family, was in charge of early land distribution. Yet much remained in dispute with the Pahlavi family members and with some of the army officers from the Reza Shah era, who had forcefully expropriated lands and refused to return them.

The Land Reform Law of 1960 (amended in 1962) allowed the Amini government in 1961 to start the first stage of distribution of the large estates, some consisting of tens of villages belonging to a single owner or an extended family. First in Azarbaijan province and soon after in other provinces, a new survey of the large estates was followed by the parceling out small plots to resident tenants and, later, some seasonal workers. The compensation made to landowners and the methods of recovering over the long term the price of the land from villagers, though generally judicious, proved hard to implement. The law allowed landlords to retain the title for one village under their own name, but a notorious loophole made it possible for the landlord's immediate family members to secure villages under their names as well.

By 1966 the end of the first phase of the land reforms, four years after the fall of Amini's government, nearly fourteen thousand villages, some 30 percent of the estimated total number of Iranian villages, were wholly or partially distributed to more than half a million families, a population that roughly corresponded to about 30 percent of Iran's rural population. Often, the plots of land allocated to farmers were not sufficient for a profitable operation, even by preindustrial standards, in a country with limited water resources, routine fallowing practices, and low crop return. The second and third phases of land reform implemented between 1965 and 1969 were more conservative, for they

allowed landlords to retain much larger arable plots. The state apparatus, moreover, often failed to provide sufficient credit and machinery for the newly created agricultural cooperatives that were replace the landlord's function. By the
end of 1968, more than 8,500 rural cooperatives were in place throughout Iran,
although far fewer than that were economically competitive.

Poor living and working conditions in villages also contributed to the slow
progress of land reforms. Even by 1966 fewer than 4 percent of rural households
had electricity, and less than 1 percent benefited from piped water. By 1966
still some 85 percent of the rural population was illiterate. In terms of income,
the rural population, which accounted for more than 60 percent of the total
population, earned only 30 percent of the national income. The culture of
maintaining agricultural machinery was weak, and modern agricultural methods, fertilization, and disease prevention were inadequate or unsuitable to the
local climate.

Encountering throughout the 1960s disparities between investment returns
in the agricultural sector versus the urban sector, and a parochial village culture
resistant to mechanization, the government first resorted to handing out small
agricultural loans and sending assistance in the form of technicians and Literacy Corps (Sepah-e Danesh) workers. Later on, similar to the Soviet kolkhozy,
the regional agricultural cooperatives were established, relying, somewhat unrealistically, on farmers' collaborative capabilities. Soon it became apparent
that the cooperatives could not replace the villages in their role as the time-
honored units of production. Despite the regime's optimistic wish to create a
rural utopia, villages stubbornly preserved some of their traditional customs and
production methods, even though as the backbone of the agrarian economy
they were visibly weakened.

An emerging class of landowners—among them landlords and moneyed intermediaries—began to purchase smaller plots from villagers and turn them
into enterprises, often independent of the traditional village economy. By
the 1970s villages were rapidly becoming a liability for the state rather than
functioning as productive agricultural units, as they had been for centuries.
Thousands of small, self-sustaining, often isolated villages and hamlets, with
populations as large as a few thousand or as small as a few families, started
a slow decline. The villagers soon turned into consumers of subsidized commodities, even foodstuffs provided by government agencies, while sending off
their young labor force to the cities to earn the much-needed subsidy income
for the family. Villages near cities were all but absorbed into urban sprawl, and
larger ones far from urban centers proudly declared themselves towns and cities, though with diminishing agricultural production. By the mid-1970s Iran,

with its rising population and changing demography, became for the first time a net importer of grain, and then later of other foodstuffs as well.

It is difficult not to feel nostalgic about a rural economy that had persisted for millennia across the Iranian plateau. Some villages retained names from Sasanian and pre-Sasanian times, and many were scattered across remote corners of the country, at high elevations, on the mountain slopes, on riverfronts, deep inside forests, and on the edges or in the midst of the central and eastern deserts. These were the only viable oases for a human presence, often with limited but renewable water resources furnished by the long trails of *qanat* canals stretching from the mountain slopes to fertile plains, irrigating small and hard-worked fields along with smaller fruit and vegetable gardens. The houses in the village were close together, leading to a village commons where the *qanat* water poured into a common cistern. There were a few stores, and the walled garden of the landlord's manor house was nearby.

The tightly knit village community predominantly practiced endogamy, preserved a clear kin lineage, and a patriarchal seniority represented by the village headman. Among a host of lasting issues dividing neighboring villages from one another were disputes over water rights putting the so-called upstreamers against the downstreamers. Villagers often distrusted urbanites, especially the bailiffs and government gendarmes. Most lived in relative poverty, though compared to Egyptian *fallahin* and Indian *kisanas* they enjoyed a better standard of living. Although it is difficult to generalize, one can compare Iranian peasants' quality of life as favorable to that of most other peasants in regions of the Middle East, perhaps with the exception of the Levant and the Aegean coast.

The land reform slowly transformed that communal life and with it the village. Modern brick houses with better lighting and sanitation, but often clumsily built and climatically unsuitable, appeared on the landscape. With new roads came pickup trucks, deep-well technology, and power generators. Donkeys, mules, and camels gradually lost their function as beasts of burden and diminished greatly in numbers. Western clothing replaced customary village dress and headgear; radios, and later television, tainted regional accents; and modern household goods and appliances changed living and even eating habits, as well as modes of leisure. The inevitable process of change had the unintended consequence of liberating the majority of the population from the land and, in due course, profoundly changing Iran's socioeconomic and cultural composition.

The 1969 film *Gaav* (The cow) by the gifted director Dariush Mehrjui (b. 1939) and based on a short story by Gholam-Hosain Sa'edi (1936–1985; inspired probably by a children's rhyme), offers a piercing metaphor for the metamorphosis of Iranian villages. Mashdi Hasan's pregnant cow, the only one in the village, dies of mysterious causes. The villagers, aware of the owner's attachment to his animal, try to cover it up. Once Mashdi Hasan learns of the death, he falls into a deep depression and begins to see himself as his beloved cow, a mental condition that leads to his total estrangement. Though one may detect a certain romanticizing of idyllic rural life, the film carried a poignant message of the impact of modernity on rural routines. With the cow as the symbol of life, and as the only asset of the peasant (besides his labor) in the agrarian system that came with the land reform, it is as if the cow's death alludes not only to the loss of the peasant's means of production but also to a melancholy demise of the traditional village life and, in a broader context, the cultural alienation of the country as a whole.

AMINI'S TROUBLED TENURE

Aside from the land reform, which was soon to face stiff resistance from tribal khans and a some ranking clergy, the focus of Amini's government was mostly fiscal—he had served in the Ministry of Finance—and utilized austerity measures, an anticorruption campaign, and a large loan negotiated with the United States to pay off the budget deficit. The dissolution of the twentieth Majles was meant to assist Amini in carrying out his reform program. The mandate to uproot corruption brought Amini momentary popularity, which he proved unable to convert into a solid base of support. An avid centrist, he quickly became a spoof for the satirical press. The weekly *Towfiq*, which relished taking cheap shots at Amini and his cabinet, took advantage of the opening political climate to mock the premier for being hopelessly ineffectual. Dailies were no less cynical about Amini and his promised reforms.

The global recession of the early 1960s, moreover, hit the Iranian economy hard. The country's increasing dependence on Western markets because of oil exports and foreign imports had become painfully apparent. The psychological impact of the recession reached a crisis level once Amini declared the government virtually bankrupt, which he attributed to mismanagement and fraud. The credit market collapsed, and imports and exports came to a standstill, causing a chain reaction of bankruptcies in the bazaar at a time when the land reform program had begun to deprive many big merchants of supplementary revenue.

Amini's hesitancy to hold yet another election to convene the Majles brought him head to head with the revived second National Front. They were mostly statesmen of the Mosaddeq era, including Allahyar Saleh, Karim Sanjabi,

Gholam-Hosain Sadiqi, and Shapur Bakhtiar, with recognition among university students, civil servants, the secular middle classes, and some bazaar businesses, though they also enjoyed some grassroots support. As was the case with the first National Front, their style of leadership favored rule of law, free and fair elections, and public deliberation. These were at variance with Amini's calls for quick economic measures and rule by decree. Amini evidently feared that another round of elections might return to the Majles reactionary landlords and their agents, who no doubt would block land reforms and other programs. Relying on popular support, the National Front rejected Amini's argument having been convinced that the premier, in collusion with the shah, was determined to bar members of the opposition from entering the Majles.

Despite an impressive show of immediate support in street demonstrations and university protests, the second National Front generally did not make any political headway. The shah, the army, and the conservative clergy, not to mention Amini, were suspicious, especially of the younger generation of left-leaning activists under the umbrella of the National Front. Tehran University, a center of National Front activism (which included the remaining Tudeh loyalists), witnessed a series of demonstrations against the regime. They met with riot police, intimidation, and detention by the Savak, which predictably further radicalized the already-tense climate of confrontation. Loyal to the constitution's principles, the leaders of the National Front neither could fully embrace the aspirations of the younger generations of activists nor were they able, or willing, to collaborate with the Amini government. That Mosaddeq from his exile in Ahmadabad increasingly rendered his blessings to the younger and more radical elements on the fringes of the National Front further disheartened the leadership. Hoping for a breakthrough, they waited for a ripe moment, which never came. They were instead harassed, arrested, and eventually banned from political activity by the shah. Amini, trying to keep the Americans on his side, lost a crucial chance to check the shah's unwieldy ambitions.

Isolated after only fourteen months in office, Amini's government showed signs of weariness when it faced its final challenge over the allocation of the budget. Hoping to cut the military budget as an austerity measure, Amini met the shah's stiff resistance. The shah was well aware of the Americans' strategic desire to build up Iranian armed forces, as he was mindful of his own support within the military. That the United States denied a $250 million loan promised to the Amini government made it clear where the superpower's priorities lay, hence precipitating the government's downfall. Amini resigned and left the country, leaving the stage clear for the shah, who, during his visit to the United States in April, had prepared the ground for the forthcoming change.

By June 24, 1962, Julius Holms, the American ambassador to Tehran, considered Amini a "spent force."

THE WHITE REVOLUTION

The shah's return to center stage, to the displeasure of the opposition, began a new era of a more determined imperial rule that lasted until the end of the shah's reign. In this new guise he was to be the savior of exploited peasants and workers, an almost revolutionary pose that aimed to replace his earlier image as a malleable pawn of the Western powers. The new initiative, the White Revolution, primarily hinged on a government-enforced reform program that incorporated the land redistribution but soon continued to add other features. It was meant to convey a sense of peaceful and bloodless but drastic change. In this scheme of things the losers were supposed to be the landowning elite and their associates, and the chief winner the shah and "the people." Hence the "Revolution of the Shah and the People" (*enqlab-e shah va mardom*) underscored a new mandate that bypassed the old structure of power, in effect eliminating the intermediaries who stood between ruler and ruled.

The shah's visit to the United States in April 1962 at the invitation of President Kennedy offered the moral support for the shah to take over the reform agenda of the Amini government and expand on it (pl. 10.1). By August 1962 President Kennedy's letter, though guarded in tone, gave the shah the necessary assurances that Iran will receive the military hardware and economic assistance the shah had insisted upon for some time:

> The United States greatly appreciates the highly important strategic location of Iran and your steadfastness in remaining vigilant against the pressures of international communism. In deciding what we both can do to strengthen Iran's national security, however, it is also necessary that your urgent social and economic programs and the resources available to carry them out be taken into account.[1]

To implement the reforms, in July 1962 the shah had already appointed, in place of Amini, his longtime confidante Asadollah 'Alam (1919–1978), a shrewd enabler and a scion of a landowning family from central Khorasan. 'Alam was once the leader of the all-too-loyal-opposition Mardom Party. He proved himself a trusted agent who was ready to implement the shah's "royal wishes." Retaining Arsanjani for a few more years as agriculture minister, the shah accelerated the land reforms despite serious opposition, which had begun to build even before Amini's dismissal.

In February 1963 a stage-managed referendum on the six points of the White Revolution brought out six million voters, for the first time including women. With no meaningful debate put forward and with heavy propaganda in the state media, the approval rate was a predictable 91.6 percent. The referendum, though devoid of any constitutional legitimacy, furnished the much-needed nominal mandate for the shah's six-point revolution. The much abused term *enqelab* clearly was appropriated from the left, and the "white" attribute had a double meaning, implying a mass movement distinct from the "red traitors" and the "black reactionaries" (*erteja'-e siyah*), labels the shah appended to the Tudeh opposition and vociferous clerical critics, respectively. As early as 1959, it is noteworthy, the shah's government had threatened Ayatollah Borujerdi with implementing a "white coup" if the latter failed to comply with the legislation on land reform before the Majles. Although the measure did not win immediate approval among the deputies, it soon offered the shah a chance to reiterate his demand in the form of the White Revolution.

Aside from land reform, the most effective article in what came to be known as the "six points" of the revolution was the Literacy Corps, inspired as much by Kennedy's Peace Corps as by the Soviet, North Vietnamese, and Chinese regimented literacy campaigns. The program drafted thousands of urban high school male (and later female) graduates to be sent off, as part of their two-year military service, to villages throughout the country. They were given rudimentary training on how to run a rural elementary school and carry out a literacy program for both children and adults (pl. 10.2 and pl. 10.3).

Often being the sole teacher and administrator in their remote posts, these corps members enjoyed a privileged status in the village community. Aside from their teaching function, draftees into the Literacy Corps represented the secularizing culture of the cities. They stood apart from the landlords and their bailiffs (now mostly gone), headmen, village elders, village mullahs, and the rural gendarmes. Their teaching method, educational material, and school space, too, stood apart from the humble village *maktabs* run by female tutors (fig. 10.3).

The outcome, at least in the earlier years, was impressive by the standards of the time. Hundreds of thousands of young villagers, boys and girls, were educated in often mixed single-room schools with bare facilities, and some went on to continue their secondary education in district schools or nearby towns. Within five years of the start of the program in 1963, more than 500,000 boys and about 130,000 girls were enrolled in Literacy Corps schools; by 1970, 3,000 such schools had been built throughout Iran. By 1977 enrollment in these schools had grown nearly sevenfold in fifteen years. Yet the education they received often served as an additional incentive for rural migration.

Figure 10.3. Qur'anic school (*maktab*) in the village of Gelian in northern Khorasan. It was still operational in 1969 while a Literacy Corps school was in place in the village.
Photographed by the author, March 1969.

A degree of social alienation was prevalent among the young Literacy Corps teachers. Few observers believed in the effectiveness of the campaign, despite its remarkable efforts to reach remote villages, far from provincial towns and accessible only by mule over nearly impassable mountain tracks. Some recruits remained cynical of their "wasted" time in the isolation of remote villages and acted condescendingly, if not hostilely, toward villagers. Others were struck by the abject poverty and deprivation, and the experience soon converted some to radical causes. Despite many drawbacks, the Literacy Corps, perhaps more than its subsequently introduced campaigns, the Health Corps and Development Corps, was effective in breaking through the barriers between city and village.

Some modern amenities followed the trail of the Literacy Corps: rural health clinics with local paramedics, dirt roads with motorbike or van service, electricity generators, fertilizers, vaccination, agricultural machinery, household goods, and telephone communication. Yet opening to the outside also brought vices and tensions, ranging from opium addiction among young recruits (illegally but inexpensively available in many villages) to involvement of inexperienced corps members in local feuds, inappropriate advances toward young village girls and embarrassing sexual escapades, and violation of local ethnic and religious traditions.

One achievement of lasting consequences was the steady rise of literacy throughout the 1960s and 1970s, which reached nearly 75 percent by the end of the Pahlavi era (at least on paper). This success was offset by the uncritical nature of state-sponsored education in the cities as well as in the countryside. The lopsided school curriculum favored an approach to education that glorified the state and demanded conformity and compliance. The widening gap in the 1970s between the deafening state propaganda on the success of the White Revolution and the grim realities of everyday life was glaring. For the vast majority of educated and semieducated youth with growing demands, education thus contributed to their fascination with the alternative ideologies that would soon shake the Pahlavi regime to its core.

KHOMEINI AND THE JUNE 1963 RIOT

The White Revolution, and in particular the land reforms and women's greater visibility in public life, were bound to raise grave concerns among conservative sectors of Iranian society. The land reform had already triggered a revolt among tribal khans and large landowners who were discontent with the prospects of losing their easily earned livelihood. As for the clergy, as early as the 1950s some tensions were detectable between the Pahlavi state and the Qom establishment. Yet despite the differences, there existed a guarded rapport. The Shi'i upper ranks viewed the shah as an imperfect but viable partner, and in the course of the 1953 coup most of the upper and middle ranks, Khomeini included, had sided with Kashani and Borujerdi in their tacit support for the shah, being fearful of the Tudeh takeover. With the introduction of the shah's reform program, however, that view began to change. The up-and-coming clerics with radical views and their students in Qom clearly were disgruntled with the Pahlavi state on ideological as well as material grounds.

As early as September 1962 signs of public discontent were visible to foreign observers. A US intelligence report warned:

The growing political unrest of the urban middle class was being manifested increasingly openly, and we estimated that profound political and social change was virtually inevitable. We added that such change would most likely be revolutionary in nature. . . .

In reasserting his own exclusive dominance, the Shah has acted in accordance with his longstanding belief that Iran is far from ready for a true parliamentary government and that the country can be ruled effectively only by a strong man like himself who understands Iran's problems. . . . He will be reluctant to share power with anyone . . . [and] will not consent to any such permanent impairment of his authority as would be implied in a meaningful compromise with the nationalists [a reference to the second National Front]. His preoccupation with military matters and his relative indifference to administrative and fiscal improvement will almost certainly persist. Under these circumstances, Iran's political structure will continue to be extremely fragile. Over the longer term, profound political and social change appears virtually inevitable.[2]

Though not yet clear to American observers, militancy within the clerical community greatly accelerated this state of influx. Borujerdi's death in March 1961 triggered a leadership contest that brought to the surface tensions between the moderate camp and the radicals, forever transforming clerical politics. As the most prominent representative of the radical leaning, Ayatollah Ruhollah Khomeini (1902–1989) seriously clashed with the Pahlavi state not only over the course of the reforms but also on issues of foreign policy. By 1963 he mobilized against the shah a sizable sector of the population, mostly associated with the bazaar and the urban lower-middle classes—a rehearsal, perhaps, for the Islamic Revolution that would flare up seventeen years later.

Khomeini's life and thoughts may offer clues to this fundamental shift toward militancy and to the challenges the Shiʻi clergy faced throughout the early part of the twentieth century. He was born to a provincial landowning clerical family in Khomein, a small agricultural town in the well-watered valleys of the ʻIraq-e ʻAjam region of central Iran, 220 miles south of Tehran and halfway between Isfahan and the emerging clerical center of Qom. His extended family of middle-sized landowners led a relatively affluent life in a climate of violence and insecurity that characterized the early life of Ruhollah, the youngest of six children. Clashes among feudal landlords and local bandits were one sign of the breakdown of the Qajar order in the years just after the Constitutional Revolution. His father—a third-generation Shiʻi cleric who migrated first from Kashmir in northern India to Najaf, settled in Khomein in the 1840s. He himself was victim of violent local skirmishes when, acting as a public advocate for the local merchants and landlords, he was gunned down by rival gangs.

The young Ruhollah (Ruh-Allah means "the Spirit of God," a Qurʼanic title for Jesus and a relatively rare first name for the children of Shiʻi clergy) was brought up by his mother, and after his mother's premature death, by his paternal aunt, a woman of strong character who left her footprint on the young boy.

He received a typical elementary *maktab* education in Khomein from female and male instructors, including his older brother, but not modern schooling. In the years following the Constitutional Revolution, Khomein, like most small towns, was untouched by modern education, even though the young Ruhollah may have learned rudiments of arithmetic, calligraphy, and some Persian poetry.

In his early years Ruhollah witnessed armed bandits harassing the local population and warlords feuding among themselves, an occurrence so common that even his own family house, built as a small fortress, had to be defended against frequent sorties. At times, members of his household were engaged in shootouts from the ramparts; at other times the family rented out the humble but strategic tower to rival bands. The family defended itself with guns, available in greater abundance in the aftermath of the Constitutional Revolution, at a time when the lines between banditry and self-defense were blurred.

In 1918, at the end of World War I, cholera visited the region, killing Ruhollah's mother. This loss may have weakened the boy's ties with his hometown. Two years later, as a young seminarian, he moved to the town of Arak (old Soltanabad), then a bustling mercantile center with vast agricultural estates, an important carpet industry, and an active madrasa network. He studied under, among others, 'Abd al-Karim Ha'eri, the reputed jurisprudence teacher and *marja'* who served as his mentor. A year later, in 1921, he followed Ha'eri to Qom, a pilgrimage town that would soon transform itself under Ha'eri, and later Borujerdi, into the foremost teaching center (*howzeh*) in Iran. Perhaps faintly inspired by the idea of the university, the *howzeh* consisted of a number of madrasas and smaller teaching circles affiliated in an informal network; it offered a somewhat systematic approach to Shi'i education and clerical training.

The move to Qom coincided with the ascendency of Reza Khan, whose rise to power and secularizing program left an indelible impression on the young Khomeini and his worldview. His deep hostility toward Reza Khan, as Khomeini invariably referred to Pahlavi ruler, was at the core of his opposition to the new regime. Yet, ironically, in 1924 in Qom he must have witnessed his admired teacher and mentor orchestrating a grand reconciliation between the Shi'i *marja*'s—some more senior than Ha'eri himself—and Reza Khan.

In Qom, while following his education in Islamic law, a discipline quickly losing all its societal relevance in Pahlavi Iran, Khomeini did not shy away from speculative mysticism (*'erfan*) and Islamic philosophy. Such fields, even when innocuously termed *hekmat* (wisdom, gnosis) rather than philosophy (*falsafeh*), continued to be denounced by the insular jurists of Qom as heretical, dangerous, and essentially antithetical to the teachings of Islam. Yet contrary to Najaf, the study of 'erfan and hekmat, with a strong Neoplatonic bent, was not entirely absent in Qom teaching circles. His teacher of mysticism, Mohammad 'Ali Shahabadi (1872–1949), seems to have played an important role in Khomeini's mystical and philosophical orientation and understanding of Islam not simply as mundane teachings of fiqh but as deeper moral values and self-discovery for personal and social improvement.

A blend of Shi'i jurisprudence, speculative mysticism (as opposed to mysticism of the Sufis and the Sufi orders), and Islamic ethical and revivalist awareness thus characterized Khomeini's training. Yet despite his interest in speculative mysticism, he remained loyal to the jurist tradition that carried a certain element of clerical entitlement especially among high-ranking mojtaheds. He not only inherited this conservative, pedantic, text-oriented legacy but also shared a sense of communal loyalty to fellow jurists that was reinforced by isolation under the Pahlavi rule. Sensitivity toward the wishes of their constituency (the moqalleds), a perpetually frown and aloof demeanor, and a display of apparent independence from sources of temporal power were his other hallmarks. He was heir to a closely knit madrasa environment with a strong patron-client relationship between teachers and students, as well as a culture of austerity among students, honed by years of communal living, often in a state of abject poverty.

Crucial though legal training and madrasa culture were for Khomeini, they did not seem to satisfy his questioning mind. He remained troubled by the predicaments of his time and what he considered the fading of Islam as society's moral standard. In practice these boiled down to such anxieties as how to avoid the mandatory dress codes under Reza Shah that forced many of his cohorts, and even members of his family, to don Western suits and wear the rimmed Pahlavi hat. The very resistance to state-enforced conformity helped fashion a new ethos of dissent. Typical of many Muslim reformists of clerical origin who were wary of studying jurisprudence in the madrasa curriculum, Khomeini searched in speculative mysticism for a deeper understanding of Islam's message and its relevance to his time. The study of philosophy—mostly Avicenna's selective reworking of the Greek masters—had never been abandoned in Shi'i learning. Mainly through the seventeenth-century school of Isfahan and by taking on the eclectic approach of Mulla Sadra, the Shi'i students of philosophy were able to engage even the mystical discourse of such defining figures as the twelfth-century Andalusian mystic Ibn al-Arabi. Most conservative jurists, though, denounced Ibn al-'Arabi and even Mulla Sadra as heretics and condemned the study of their works as unconscionable.

Such speculative preoccupations brought Khomeini in the 1940s and early 1950s to the limits of madrasa tolerance. Fearing charges of heresy, and even denunciation by the Qom jurists, he was persuaded to abandon the teaching of philosophy—at least in public—and return to the jurists' fold. He even produced a "practical treatise" (*resaleh-ye 'amaliyeh*) on the intricate points of Shi'i rituals and civil law, mostly based on the fatwas he had issued over the years on such issues as ablution and ritual pollutants, nullifiers of prayer and fasting, perverted sexual behavior, and relations with nonbelievers. Adopting the guise of a conventional mojtahed and publishing his *resaleh* helped qualify Khomeini as a grand ayatollah. His political activism, which soon erupted in open defiance of the Pahlavi state, would not have had the desired effect had it not been for his recognition as one of the four highest-ranking jurists in Iran to emerge after Borujerdi.

Yet what turned him into a revolutionary prophet anxious to save the "wronged Islam" from threats of a secular world came essentially from his mystico-philosophical bent. Ibn al-Arabi's claim to be the "seal of the saints" (*khatam al-awliya'*) may well have contributed to Khomeini's later articulation of the doctrine of the "authority of the jurist" (*welayat-e faqih*). In effect, by returning to the jurists' fold, Khomeini "reinvented" jurisprudence. No longer was it a mere obsession with pollution and intricate points of ritual cleansing, the rudiments of Shi'i jurisprudence; rather, it aimed at cleansing the polluting politics and morals of secular modernity.

Khomeini's engagement with the sufferings of the Shi'i Imams and their agonies, a sacred narrative of endurance to Shi'is of all backgrounds, formed the third dimension in his multilayered outlook. In his mind, the Shi'i "friends," essentially followers of the clerical establishment, were differentiated from the Pahlavi "foes" and their "heathen" allies, in the same cosmic scheme that separated the friends of Hosain ibn 'Ali in Karbala from his foes. This was a universe inhabited by many saints of the past and many demons of the present. In this universe of anger and defiance, his communal brethren, mostly the clergy and their lay followers, constituted the "self" while the alien other, the secularizing state and its domestic and foreign allies, were to be kept at a safe distance. In Khomeini's worldview, if this alien other and its intrusive pollutants were not defied and denounced in their entirety, they were bound to destroy the very essence of pristine but vulnerable Islam.

Through an act of remembrance (*rawzeh-khani*), the narrative of martyrdom in Shi'i sacred history, recited in a melodramatic tone from the pulpit of the mosques, was a powerful means of mass mobilization. Khomeini was fully aware of its power and skillful in employing it at crucial moments. The Moharram ceremonies, mourning processions, weeping, and self-flagellation became conduits for connecting with the popular culture of ordinary believers. In this respect Khomeini utilized features of Shi'i culture, complete with intonation, figures of speech, and a firm loyalty to the popular myths of rituals of suffering and martyrdom.

His small-town upbringing (and later his stay in Najaf) were not entirely alien to the world outside the Shi'i madrasa, or the pulpit of the mosque, or the Moharram ceremonies. Though before 1979 he never lived in a large city, in his own terms he absorbed selected elements of modernity in defiance of state-sponsored secularism. As early as 1944, in an open letter he called on Iranians to rise up against the "injustices" that the "despicable" Reza Khan imposed on them, and he held advocates of Pahlavi secularism responsible for degrading the clergy, removing the veil from chaste women, having a corrupting influence on the press, and sending "bogus deputies" to the Majles. The absence of communal solidarity, he lamented, was what brought defenseless Islam to an abyss into which it had now fallen, making it an easy target for the onslaught of heathen modernists and enemies of Islam. In a prophetic tone he went on to caution:

> It is because of sheer selfishness and neglect to stage an uprising for the sake of God that we are doomed to such a dark fate that the whole world has prevailed over us and the Islamic nations were brought under the domination of [alien] others. It is the selfish interests that has suffocated the spirit of unity and brotherhood within the Islamic nation. . . . O, the spiritual leaders of Islam! You, the ulama of God! Today is the day that the breeze of divine spirituality is blowing on us and it is the best of times to start a reformative uprising. If you miss this opportunity, and don't rise up in the path of God and don't restore religious rites, tomorrow yet another lustful licentious bunch will prevail over you and make all your faith and honor subject to their false malevolence. Today what excuse do you have before God the creator?

Remarkably, he then went on to contrast the lack of solidarity among Muslims to the Baha'i' sense of camaraderie: "Even if in a small village a slightest affront would have directed toward [Baha'i] religion, all coreligionists would have risen in one spirit and with a single objective."[3]

In this declaration, as in other writings, Khomeini also responded in the postwar era to critics of clerical Shi'ism, including Ahmad Kasravi, the well-known journalist and scholar who, in the 1930s and 1940s, initiated a modernist religious movement of unitarian character, free of what he called "superstitions" and "fallacies." In his influential essays—and later in his 1944 pamphlet titled *Shi'a-gari* (Shi'ism)—Kasravi depicted Shi'i Islam as nothing more than a jumble of myths, rituals, and fables manufactured by demagogic mullahs and designed to preserve their vested interests and control over the ignorant masses. Kasravi's prophet-like call for a moral revival and his campaign against the Shi'i clerical establishment, as well as against the Sufis, the Baha'i, and the cultural establishment of the Pahlavi era, brought him few devotees and many sworn enemies. In his *Kashf-e Asrar* (Unveiling mysteries) Khomeini systematically tried to retract such charges brought by, among others, Kasravi. In his judgment, attacks on Shi'i beliefs and rituals were comparable to the attacks the Wahhabi "savages of Arabia" had long leveled against Shi'ism. Holding nothing back, he was among the first to call upon believers to physically eliminate Kasravi for his blasphemy; it was not mere coincidence that members of Fada'iyan-e Islam assassinated Kasravi in March 1945 shortly after the publication of Khomeini's book.

Critics of Shi'ism aside, the defiance in Khomeini's early writings was also directed at the Shi'i clerical establishment, which he viewed as timid and compromising. The modern intelligentsia, too, he depicts as disloyal to Islam and captivated by the West. The Muslim people—in Iran and elsewhere—were also portrayed as victims of tyranny at home, foreign powers, and a general lack of awareness of Islam. The decadence and decrepitude he sensed in Islam's waning power was typical of most Islamic activists, at least since the middle of the nineteenth century. Yet what set Khomeini apart from other resentful Islamic advocates was his loyalty to the conservative Islam of the jurists and the clerical establishment, whom he wished, even in the early years of his activism, would become natural leaders of the community, at the forefront of the war against satanic forces that threatened Muslim integrity.

CONFRONTING THE SHAH

The opening of the political climate under Amini made Khomeini's anti-Pahlavi presence more pronounced on the political stage. This was something of a shift in his position, for it was not a secret that Khomeini disliked Mosaddeq for not complying with Islamic principles. He even criticized Kashani for presumed abandoning the Fada'iyan-e Islam in favor of Mosaddeq. In the late 1940s he had met with the shah a number of times as Borujerdi's emissary, expressing concern over the threat of the Tudeh and the role the Fada'iyan could play as a counterweight to the left. In the late 1950s, however, Khomeini's relationship with Borujerdi turned sour not only over control of the Qom *howzeh* but also because of Borujerdi's occasional compliance with the government's wishes. Khomeini generally disapproved of the nonpolitical mojtaheds' for their compromising stance toward the state and reluctance to speak out unanimously. His criticism was reciprocated by the politically conservative clergy. They distrusted Khomeini all the more because of his popularity among the younger generation of seminarians who were attracted to his teaching circle.

In the late 1950s and early 1960s Khomeini began to question a number of issues of domestic and foreign policy. Starting with marginal issues—such as the mingling of Boy Scouts and Girl Scouts and the performing of dances—he soon moved on to more substantive concerns such as the passing of the first land reform legislation in 1959 and the opening of informal diplomatic relations with Israel and economic collaboration with the Jewish state. In 1962, when the government tried to introduce the elected provincial councils sanctioned by the 1906–1907 Constitution, mostly the shah's window-dressing to compensate for closing other political channels, Khomeini was at the forefront of clerical opposition, objecting even to the hint of women's right to vote. He argued that the voting regulations failed to specify the male gender—and hence exclude women—from the electorate. Along with other ayatollahs in Qom, he also objected to dropping the oath of allegiance to the Qur'an for the provincial councils' delegates, an omission seen in Qom as a concession to the Baha'is and their election to the councils rather than as a symbolic delinking of religion and politics. In his telegram to the premier Asadollah 'Alam in October 1962, Khomeini further threatened that on these and other issues contrary to shari'a, he would not remain silent and that, in response, the government would face severe clerical opposition.

Under pressure, the 'Alam government caved, abandoning, at least temporarily, the idea of provincial councils. This only helped bolster Khomeini's opposition to issues ranging from the six points of the White Revolution to the regime's corruption and mismanagement, its subservience to the United States, and its friendly relations with Israel. Now elevated to the lead opposition figure, at the expense of the second National Front and other secular voices, Khomeini went as far as boycotting the proposed referendum of February 1963. His grounds for objection predictably were women's right to vote and the illegitimacy under Islamic law of the land reforms and other reform measures. His radical stance gained some support in Qom, which went through unrest and bloody clashes with security forces. Beyond Qom, a sector of the landowning classes, as well as some bazaar merchants, both large and petty, was unhappy with the economy growing outside their reach, and so backed Khomeini.

In the following months a showdown between Khomeini's supporters and the security forces seemed inevitable. A serious tribal uprising in Fars province among the Qashqa'i and other affiliated tribes against the land reform program persuaded the shah to assume that there was a grand alliance between Khomeini and his supporters, the tribal khans, and their allies. Even though the shah had tried to work out with the Qom establishment a peaceful understanding of their differences, he was anxious not to convey an image of weakness when his entire political enterprise was at stake.

The demonstrations in Qom against the regime and in support of Khomeini soon triggered a violent reaction from the government. An unprovoked attack by the security forces on the prayer congregation in the Fayziyeh mosque and madrasa, the core of Qom activism, in March 1963 resulted in multiple deaths and injuries, as well as property damage. The "fortieth" memorial (arba'in) of the Fayziyeh crackdown in early June 1963 coincided with Moharram observances, always a time of great emotional upsurge. In his speech on the tenth of Moharram, the 'Ashura, the most sacred day in the Shi'i calendar, Khomeini, on the pulpit of Fayziyeh and before thousands of Moharram mourners, openly condemned the government in a highly emotional tone (fig. 10.4).

Comparing the Fayziyeh incident in March to the wrongs inflicted by the Umayyads on the Third Shi'i Imam, he held the shah responsible for the atrocities and further denounced Israel, and its presumed domestic collaborators, for aiming to destroy the very foundations of Islam. The emphasis on Israel was particularly effective. He accused the shah of selling out Iran to the Israelis, who, he claimed, intended to destroy Iran's agriculture and take over its economy. He denounced the shah's referendum on the White Revolution as a fraud and accused the Pahlavi state of corruption, misappropriation of public funds, and accumulation of illegitimate wealth. He contrasted these excesses of the regime with the frugal and selfless clergy of Qom. He "advised" the shah, as he put it, in the strongest terms to abandon Israel, to listen to the marja's, and do not deviate from the path of Islam so as to avoid the sad fate of his father, whose abdication brought joy to Iranian hearts.

Touching upon such sensitive themes in an emotionally charged environment, Khomeini's speech was repeatedly interrupted by the loud weeping of the mournful audience. For the first time a copy of the recorded tape of his speech soon traveled across Iran and resonated with the people in the bazaars and streets of the poorer neighborhoods. The powerful call for defiance quickly bore results, leading to a bloody uprising in the capital and some provincial cities. In the early hours of June 5, two days after his Fayziyeh speech, Khomeini

Figure 10.4. Khomeini at the pulpit of the Fayziyeh Mosque in Qom, June 3, 1963.
Tasvir-e Aftab (Tehran: Sorush Publishers, 1989).

was arrested by security forces and brought to Tehran, detained in the Officers'
Club, where Mosaddeq had been detained, before being sent off to jail. On
the same day, June 5, as the news of Khomeini's arrest reached the public,
Iranian cities witnessed a violent uprising. As if the crowd had anticipated the
arrest, tens of thousands of protesters holding makeshift placards of Khomeini's
portrait and shouting slogans against the shah poured into the streets near the
bazaar and other neighborhoods of Tehran, smashing shop windows, burning
down banks and cinemas, and attacking bus stations, police stations, and government buildings. Among other places, the Pepsi bottling facility, the Iran-US
cultural center, and Iranian broadcasting services were attacked and burned
down. The crowd, aroused by devout supporters of Khomeini from among the
gang leaders (*lutis*) of Tehran's wholesale vegetable market, armed with sticks
and knives, began to move in the direction of the Marmar royal palace in central Tehran, where the shah's office was located.

Facing a mass rebellion destabilizing the shah's regime, the security forces
moved in with trucks, tanks, heavy machine guns, and thousands of troops. Declaring martial law, the Tehran military command began a systematic clamp-

down in the center and on the edges of the capital. Surrounding the main entrance to the Tehran bazaar with a half circle of menacing M35 (REO) troop carriers, M103 heavy tanks, and fire engines, all with their headlights on, the troops first aimed high-pressure water cannons at the crowd trapped at the bazaar entrance. Shortly afterward, machine guns began to shoot, first intermittently and then indiscriminately. Once the first round of the assault downed protesters at the entrance, squads of riot police moved into the bazaar's main thoroughfare, pummeling the fleeing crowd with their batons.

At least 125 people were killed (though some estimates put the figure as high as 400), and many more were injured in two days of bloody confrontations in the capital and provincial centers. Hundreds more were detained before relative calm could be returned to the cities. Bodies of victims, it was rumored, were buried in unmarked mass graves outside the capital, and those who had fallen in Qom were dumped in the salty swamp deep into the Qom desert. In Fars province a simultaneous uprising among the Boyer Ahmad Lur tribes was put down, and the Qashqa'i and other tribes of the region were contained and disarmed. Since the start of land reforms, a series of revolts had been pacified, marking perhaps the last of the tribal unrest Iran was to witness over the nearly 250 years since the fall of the Safavids. With the end of what came to be labeled the "Fars Uprising," never again did the Iranian tribes—or what was left of their nomadic lifestyle—play a significant role in shaping Iran's political history. Chiefs of the Qashqa'i and other affiliated tribes, deprived of their tribal titles, were detained and sent into internal exile—a few charged with armed rebellion were also sent before the firing squad. The government declared the tribe itself as "officially terminated," and by then they had mostly settled in and around Firuzabad, seventy miles south of Shiraz.

Khomeini was held in an army barracks in Tehran for nearly two months before being put under house arrest for another eight months. A handful of mojtaheds in major cities, many Khomeini's supporters and students, were temporarily detained. The gang leaders responsible for the Tehran uprising were tried and hanged, and all physical signs of destruction in Tehran were quickly removed or restored. Yet the psychological wounds inflicted by the revolt remained unhealed. Khomeini, seemingly unrepentant and untarnished, returned to Qom in March 1964. He was spared the death sentence and released from detention after the other *marja*'s in Qom, including Ayatollah Shari'atmadari, pleaded with the shah, cautioning him of the dire consequences of executing a major figure like Khomeini. There was no love lost between Khomeini and the other ayatollahs in Qom. What was at stake, however, was clerical prestige and their glaring display of ineffectiveness before the state were one of their cohort to be detained or eliminated, an unprecedented event, save for the 1909 revolution-ary trial and execution of Shaykh Fazlollah Nuri.

In March 1964 the coming to office of a more appeasing government under Hasan-'Ali Mansur (Mansour, 1923–1965) was instrumental in Khomeini's re-lease. His appointment generated further hope for reconciliation. Khomeini, relying on his growing popular support in and out of the bazaar, was deter-mined to carry on his crusade even if, as he stated, it were to cost him his life. As if retreating from the Fada'iyan-e Islam agenda of the 1950s (whose supporters no doubt were crucial in the June uprising), Qom, under the spell of Khomeini, demanded implementation of Islamic laws and abolition of the White Revolu-tion's anti-Islamic decrees, which in reality meant reversing the land reform program, and especially returning *waqf* properties to their trustees. Honoring the demands of the Shi'i clergy also meant annulling women's right to vote, the possible enforcement of hijab, and allowance of *ta'ziyeh* passion plays and other mourning ceremonies that the regime had deemed superstitious and bar-baric. In a speech in Qom a few days after Khomeini's arrival, he also called for dissolution of the Majles and the Senate, accused the Pahlavi state of being in cahoots with Israel and "the agents of Zionism," and called for an end to corruption. More vociferously than on earlier occasions, he also accused the Baha'is of perceived charges of occupying positions of power and collaborating with Israel. Most important, the declaration called for the implementation of article 2 of the 1907 Supplement to the Iranian Constitution, which stipulated the creation of a five-member mojtahed body to oversee the legislation of the Majles. The Pahlavi state and its projected reform program could not remotely honor any such demands.[4]

Six months later Khomeini found a new occasion to renew his vitriolic attack on the shah and the Mansur government, this time objecting to the judicial immunity granted to American military personnel (and their dependents) who served as advisers to the Iranian armed forces. In a speech delivered in Octo-ber 26, 1964, he attacked the concession as a renewal of the hated capitulatory "most favored nations" rights of the Qajar era. His criticism stemmed from a clause in the 1961 Vienna Convention on Diplomatic Relations, to which Iran had become a signatory, whereby the host country had the option of relinquish-ing jurisdiction over foreign diplomats and their associates by granting them im-munity from prosecution in the host country. Passed after some heated debate in the Majles, the issue was quickly picked up by opposition circles.

Ayatollah Khomeini, now fully recognized as a *marja'* and decidedly tilting the clerical balance toward political opposition, made the most of the state's new diplomatic concession. In a passionate speech delivered in Fayziyeh before a huge crowd (coinciding with the lavish celebration of the shah's birth-day on October 26), Khomeini skillfully played on the bitter memories of the nineteenth-century capitulatory rights first granted to Russia in 1828 and then to other countries. In light of Reza Shah's 1927 abolition of the capitulation, hailed at the time as a major Pahlavi victory in reclaiming Iran's judicial sover-eignty, the concession extended to the US advisory mission seemed exception-ally bold, even foolhardy. From the Iranian perspective, as voiced by Khomeini, this was yet another sign of Pahlavi subservience to the superpower and a slap in the face of Iran's Islamic pride.

The clause was included in the treaty at the request of the United States to allow for the ratification of a long-negotiated loan of $200 million to build up the Iranian military. A stronger military was a point of confluence between the US Cold War strategic concerns and the shah's insatiable appetite for the latest military hardware. Within the higher echelons of the US government, more-over, there existed a sense of moral entitlement that disbursing such a hefty loan, and the advisory military expertise that would accompany it, could not be done without firm immunity for the US personnel in a country like Iran, which by the Americans' judgment was facing religious discord and anti-American sentiments.

To Khomeini, and to the majority of the Iranians, this was nothing short of neocolonial indenture. "If a servant or a cook of an American citizen kills or pummels under his feet your *marja'-e taqlid* in the middle of the bazaar," Khomeini contended, "the Iranian police cannot arrest him; the Iranian courts would have no jurisdiction. His file is to be forwarded to the United States so as to be adjudicated by the masters there." In a mix of hyperbole and combative-ness, heightened after his release from detention, Khomeini then leveled a lit-any of charges against the shah and his government, including selling off Iran's sovereignty, being subservient to the Americans, facilitating Israel's economic influence, pandering to the Americans for a huge loan with a scandalously high interest rate, convening a fraudulent Majles, guarding animosity toward religious authorities, attempting in vain to create divisions among the ayatol-lahs, causing the decline of agriculture, and forwarding the White Revolution as a mere propaganda scheme.

He further condemned the mingling of boys and girls, especially in mixed schools; attacked as distorted the history textbooks portraying the clergy as det-rimental to the prosperity of the country; and above all, called on the clergy, the armed forces, statesmen, and the businessmen of Iran to beware of the impending decline and loss of Islam. Calling on the Najaf Shi'i ayatollahs and heads of Islamic nations, including the shah, he warned: "Since we are a weak nation and don't have dollars, does it mean that we should be pummeled under the American boots? America is worse than Britain and Britain is worse than America and the Soviet Union is worse than both of them; each is worse than the other and each more evil than the other. Yet today we are faced with America." The focus of this vitriolic attack was the US president Lyndon B. Johnson, whom Khomeini believed to be "the most spiteful toward our nation than any human being because of the wrongs he inflicted on the Islamic nation. The Qur'an is his enemy; the people of Iran are his enemy. The government of the United States should know that in Iran he has been debased and scandalized."[5]

This fuming rhetoric left little room for compromise. A week later, coinciding with the ratification in the Majles of the American loan, the Iranian special forces surrounded Khomeini's house in Qom. He was whisked out of the city directly to Tehran airport and put on an airplane that took him to Turkey, where he spent a year in exile in the city of Bursa, known for its Islamic loyalties. Accompanied by his son, Mostafa, and clad in civilian clothing, he visited mosques and shrines in the ancient city (fig. 10.5). Later on, moving to Najaf, he kept a distance from the city's clerical politics, although he was by no means iso-

Figure 10.5. Ayatollah Khomeini and his son Mostafa in exile, Bursa, Turkey, 1964.
Hamid Ruhani, *Barrasi va Tahlili az Nahzat-e Imam Khomeini*, 2 vols.
(Tehran, 1364/1985), vol. 2, n.p.

Figure 10.6. "Khomeini, the Deputy-Imam" appears on an Islamic new year's
greeting card (c. 1963). With a copy of the Qur'an in hand, he is surrounded
by the slogan "fraternity, truth, justice, and liberty." The standard carries a
Qur'anic verse promising the parting of evil and the arrival of the good.
Hamid Ruhani, *Barrasi va Tahlili az Nahzat-e Imam Khomeini*, 2 vols. (Tehran, 1364/1985), vol. 1.

lated. He remained in exile for the following thirteen years, writing and teaching but also preserving his network of supporters and followers throughout Iran.
Through his devout students and bazaar contacts he collected religious dues
and redistributed funds among his former and current students and for other
religious causes (fig. 10.6).

With Khomeini's departure the four-year-old campaign of the Islamic militants lost momentum even though it did not come to a halt before taking the
life of Hasan-'Ali Mansur who ironically aimed to mend fences with Khomeini.
In January 1965, ten weeks into Khomeini's exile, the Fada'iyan-e Islam assassins
gunned down the premier in front of the Majles. The assassins almost all were
veterans of the Fada'iyan cadre, with connections to Khomeini's circle. Inspired
by his diatribe, the assassins viewed Mansur as a pro-American "agent." They no
doubt were active in organizing the June 1963 protests to recruit a private army
that included *lutis* and lower ranks of the bazaar.

With the effective removal of the liberal and nationalist option of the Mosaddeq era, the Pahlavi royal autocracy and the Qom clerical militancy stood
face-to-face, each prescribing a very different vision of the future. Both adhered
to the nationalist narrative, but commonality ended there. The Pahlavi grip
on power, implementing a reformist agenda from above, enabled an alliance

with the West, adherence to a modernizing program, and an oil-dependent economy. It relied on loyal statesmen and apolitical technocrats, often children of the earlier generation of military, landed bureaucratic classes and the educated middle classes. Even if they were from religiously observant families or the old elite, they received a secular education, and often had some experience in the West. Their demeanor, lifestyle, and outlook—at least in public—were largely in tune with the Pahlavi project. Like the shah, they aspired to a secular Iran modeled on the West and relying, at times slavishly, on Western expertise, know-how, and advice. Yet the milieu in which the Pahlavi elite used to operate often nurtured a degree of cynicism and hypocrisy injurious to the very loyalties on which the Pahlavi order was first erected.

The world of Qom in the post–Reza Shah era, in contrast, turned more insular, radical, and anti-Western. As the Pahlavi state recruited from among the turbaned classes and turned them into stiff, tie- and-fedora-wearing civil servants, a new class of seminarians from among the peasants, small landowners, and urban lower classes gradually replaced them. They built a new clerical community predominantly hostile to the Pahlavi approach. Inspired by radical trends beyond Iran, from Salafi Islam of the Arab world to the leftist propaganda of Radio Cairo and Radio Moscow, many among this generation of the clergy developed a new perspective loyal to conventional readings of the shari'a—parochial in its worldview and radical in its politics. They were against women's presence in public life; coeducation and mixing of genders; such leisurely expressions such as cinema, music, tourism, and fashion; and sexual liberties and homosexuality. As much as they were hostile to these "foreign" trends, they were also at war with the indigenous voices critical of clerical insularity from the Baha'i and the Sufi to various intellectual critics such as Kasravi and his message of moral reform. After the June 1963 uprising, the Khomeini brand of clerical radicalism retreated but was not defeated. Returning to the madrasa, they began to solidify their ground over the following decade and would reemerge fifteen years later, better equipped and with access to a larger audience.

NEW POETRY AND NEW ANXIETIES

Even if the Pahlavi state momentarily basked in its successful crushing of Islamic activism and implementation of its own vision of reform, the intellectual critiques of the state, especially after 1953, revealed a sharply different perspective. Most Iranian writers, poets, and social critics of the postwar era, impressed with the discourse of the left—often through the Tudeh Party—moved away from the Persian classical norms and modes of expression, which they shunned as arcane and elitist. They gravitated instead toward new literary forms, prose and poetry, and new schools of thought, mostly products of the twentieth-century Western European milieu. They found such media more effective in portraying the plight of the ordinary people, which they considered their "social mission." Realism with a Marxist overtones and Existentialist *engagé* literature of the period were appealing to a small but influential clique of Iranian intellectuals who engaged in these trends so as to express the anxieties of their time and portray their political disillusionment, moral predicaments, and sense of alienation.

A quest for authenticity, a predictable reaction to the positivist modernity of the Pahlavi state, further shaped Iranian cultural production between the 1940s and 1960s, questioning the wholesale acceptance of Western values and their hegemony over non-Western societies—what came to be known in the intellectual vernacular of the time as *gharbzadehgi* (meaning "struck by the West," "Westoxication," or "plague of the West"). The debate over the evils of Westernizing gradually shifted the intellectual horizons from a typical wariness toward anything Islamic—calling it superstitious—to an idealized interpretation of Islam as remedy against Westernism and a means of resisting the Pahlavi regime. After 1953 both the discourse of alienation and the quest for cultural authenticity gradually transformed the Marxist-Stalinist orientation of the postwar era and moved it in new directions.

Ahead of themselves many of the literary voices could see only prolonged gloom, a dawnless night, which became a recurring image in the literature of the period. The ancillary to this was an almost messianic hope for a savior of sorts who would end the status quo, more by revolution than by political process. No matter how secular, these intellectuals did not seem to have liberated themselves from the legacy of Iranian messianism, both in motif and in aspiration, or the cult of revering the failed hero. Their secular, often leftist, frame of reference could hardly conceive of a revolution of the shape and magnitude that would occur less than two decade later. They could hardly foresee a prophetic figure like Khomeini, even though the June 1963 uprising seemed like a rehearsal for what was in the offing.

An early critic of the moral universe of Shiʻi Islam and European cultural intrusion was the aforementioned Ahmad Kasravi (1890–1946). His vision was an uneasy marriage of nationalism and prophetic inspiration. A former seminarian from Tabriz who witnessed the last phase of the Constitutional Revolution in his hometown and was shaped by that experience, Kasravi, in his secular attire, represented a brand of nationalist positivism of the early Pahlavi era. His history of the Constitutional Revolution, a widely read narrative, defined the revolution as a national liberation movement pioneered by the enlightened mojtaheds and brought to fruition by ordinary folks. Kasravi also employed "pure language" (*zaban-e pak*) devoid of Arabic and other "foreign" words to narrate his story. More than his historical work or his use of pure Persian, however, as a social critic his iconoclastic attack on the masters of Persian classical poetry gained Kasravi notoriety. His portrayal of classical poetry as decadent and morally corrupting—for it promoted homosexual love and a hedonistic lifestyle—angered the literary establishment of the time.

Kasravi's critique of religion and culture was part of a mission to promote a form of deistic monotheism. He called his crusade for a "rational" religion Pakdini (the pure religion), a path to counter what he considered the superstitious, worthless, and harmful teachings of established religions. It was a new creed to combat all the deviations that corrupted the pristine kernel of prophetic endeavors, deviations he alleged were introduced by deceitful and misguided followers of these religions. He denounced "false myths" (including Greek mythology), Christian and Muslim cults of saints, and any form of religious symbolism and ritual. His critique of Shi'ism, in particular, aimed at the ulama's demagogy. Generating deep antipathy among his Muslim opponents reflected a critical cleavage between the secularized and the traditional sectors of the society of his time. That flicker of antinomian rationalism, however, died out with Kasravi's assassination.

Dissecting the arcane Islamic tradition, and especially Shi'i orthodoxy, also produced works of remarkable complexity and penetrating satire by Sadeq Hedayat (1903–1950), arguably the greatest literary figure of twentieth-century Persian literature. He was operating in a sphere smaller even than Kasravi's, though perhaps with greater influence on the intellectual trends of the next generation (fig. 10.7). Born to a family of bureaucratic nobility of the Qajar period, Hedayat's French education and home tutoring provided him equal facility in European literature as in Persian high and folk cultures. Struggling with depression most of his life—which ended in his suicide in Paris—he was a pacifist by nature and a man of penetrating wit. As he was attracted during his residence in interwar France to the expressionist and surreal literature then in vogue, Kafka in particular left a lasting influence on him. He was equally well versed in Persian culture but critiqued it from a perspective very different from Kasravi's positivistic stance.

Hedayat transformed his exposure to Western literature into a Persian setting both in substance and in style. Mostly writing short stories and novellas, his characters were set in the fast-disappearing world of an idealized past. His skeptical worldview and poignant, soul-searching quest nevertheless kept Hedayat away from ideological indoctrination or prophetic visions. His *Buf-e Kur*

Figure 10.7. Sadeq Hedayat (*left, sitting with papers in hand*) and his cohorts in
Tehran in the house of the literary scholar Mojtaba Minovi (*second from right,
standing*), c. 1934. Hedayat, Monovi, and the writer Bozorg 'Alavi (*leaning on piano*)
were members of the Rob'ah (Quartet) literary circle. Jan Rypka (*first standing at
right*) was a Czech historian of Persian literature. André Sevruguin (*sitting to Hedayat's
left*) was the miniaturist artist of Russian origin who used the pen name Darvish. He
illustrated the 1934 *Shahnameh* edition by Solayman Hayyem published in Tehran.
J. Hedayat, *Hasrati, Negahi va Ahi* (Tehran: Did Publisher, 1379/2000), 78.

(Blind Owl, 1937), recognized as his literary masterpiece, is a surreal depiction
of the author's fictional multifaceted self and his complex interplay with many
Others. Here in the novel, Hedayat manifests himself in multiple characters.
The reclusive opium addict who narrates the story imbues a sense hopelessness
and despair, and a lustful old man conveys the author's inner contempt for his
cultural baggage, his class and family legacy, and political authority. Hedayat's
idealized notions of love, and his homosexual anxieties, are portrayed by a two-
sided female character who appears alternately as an ethereal woman and a
promiscuous hag. They all reflect a preoccupation with decay and death, and
yet they all seem to be fellow travelers in a mystical journey in search of something unattainable, an awareness of a layered inner world, a world of subjectivity. Unique in the context of Persian modern literature—and to a great degree
indebted to the worldview in Khayyam's poems—this was the voice of a cultural outcast who defied the world of banal modernity built on a ramshackle of
state authority. The title of the novel, "blind owl," alludes to a popular Persian

expression (the owl is a bird of ominous presence in Persian folk belief) implying a dazed onlooker who no longer can see through the darkness of the night.
Written at the height of Reza Shah's absolute power, and while Hedayat was residing in India (where he studied the Pahlavi language with Parsis of Mumbai),
the blind owl represented a dysfunctional member of the old elite who could
not see a place for himself in the superficial world of Pahlavi modernity.

A far less veiled criticism of religion and politics, of Iran's experience of
modernity and its encounters with European hegemony, appears in Hedayat's
1949 *Tup-e Morvari* (Cannon of Good Omen), a piercing and profane satire of
great intricacy with a loosely structured narrative reminiscent of James Joyce's
stream of consciousness. Here, Islamic scripture, beliefs, and rituals (and those
of other monotheistic religions) are mocked with singular insight. It is small
wonder that the book, written under a pseudonym, was published only clandestinely more than three decades after its creation. In it, in the institutions of
Islam and the conduct of the clerical class—especially Shi'i clergy—Hedayat
sees a legacy of cruelty, institutionalized violence, and obsessive ritualism. He
also detected as much brute military force and blind Westernism in the follies
of the Reza Shah era and the strictures imposed by that regime. Likewise in
European colonial expansion, characterized by a comical take on the sixteenth-
century Portuguese maritime control of the Persian Gulf, he detected ruthless
greed, aggression, and carnage. To this he added a sarcastic critique of a culture of pettiness, fear, inferiority complex, pandering, animal cruelty, filth, and
disease (despite the Shi'i obsession with scatological purification). This was a
culture of decadence that he felt had accumulated over centuries and was the
origin of his own inescapable lot: an unending night of gloom.

Hedayat's bitter sarcasm and fatalistic disdain for anything Islamic came with
a nostalgic allure for the pre-Islamic past and pain over Iran's loss of its pristine
language, culture, and identity to the Arab conquest of the seventh century—
a sentiment he shared with Kasravi and a host of other Iranian intellectuals,
poets, historians, and scholars of his time. His lifelong collecting and publishing of Iranian folklore and popular culture, studies in Middle Persian (Pahlavi)
texts, his historical plays on the tragic fall of the Sasanian Empire and crushing
of the Iranian resistance movements by the Islamic Caliphate—all pointed to
a cultural nationalism that sought glory in the past but denied renewal ahead.

Hedayat's piercing skepticism aside, perhaps the most iconoclastic literary
figure of the 1940s and 1950s was the poet Nima Yushij (1896–1960). His break
with the conventions of rhyme and classical meter, which had been observed
for centuries and viewed as almost sacred by the Persian literary establishment,
distinguished him as a literary revolutionary. His poetic themes, moreover,

Figure 10.8. Nima and three poets of the "new poetry" movement,
c. 1952: (*from right*) Houshang Ebtehaj (Sayeh), Siyavush Kasra'i, Nima Yushij,
and Ahmad Shamlu together with literary figure and Tudeh activist Mortaza Kayvan.
In nocturnal gatherings the left-leaning poets debated politics and
poetry with a sense of social mission.
Hushang Ebtehaj, *Pir-e Parniyan-andish*, ed. M. 'Azimi and 'A. Tayyeh, 2 vols.
(Tehran, 1391/2012), 2:1340.

were not free of expressions of romantic despair, inspired by the pastoral motifs
of his Mazandaran homeland, experiences of his solitary life, and his deep feel-
ing for society's ills. Informed as much by the modern French poetry of his time
as by his Tudeh affinity, these were equally important for Nima's endurance as
a literary icon.

Born to a landowning family from Yush (in the Nur region 160 miles north
of Tehran), he was brought up in the country, before receiving a French education in a missionary school in Tehran, an education he shared with his friend
Hedayat. The literary war over the "new poetry" (*she'r-e naw*), waged for decades in the press, literary circles, and academia, had a subtext of political orientation (fig. 10.8). Nima's poetry reflected the simplicity of pastoral life and its
pristine beauty, but also a social mission to give voice to suffering, hardship, and
political suffocation. His famous 1948 ode, "Mahtab" (moonlight)—composed
at the height of his political involvement—reflected the poet's failing hopes for
a mass awakening while a faint desire for a dawn or renewal is still alive:

The moonlight gleams.
The glowworm glows.

Not a moment of broken sleep in anyone's eyes.
Yet,
Agony over this slumbering lot,
Shatters sleep from my tearful eyes.
Anxious beside me, stands the dawn,
Morning urges me to break the news of its blessed breath,
To this soulless lot, . . .
I wring my hands in worry,
To open a door.
I wait in vain,
For one to come to the door.
But their derelict windows and walls,
Crumble on my head. . . .
Tired, with blistered feet from a long journey,
Before the village gate,
Stands a lonesome man.
His bundle on his back,
His hand on the knocker, he whispers to himself:
"Agony over this slumbering lot,
Shatters sleep from my tearful eyes."[6]

The glowworm in moonlight no doubt symbolizes the poet in a liminal environment of insecurity and doubt. His faint throbbing light, promising the daybreak, is set against the indifference of the slumbering village who closed its doors on him and his message. Tired and tearful, he is about to be crushed under the caving of a derelict house, which no doubt is an allusion to the legacy of his country's past.

Another poet of the younger generation, Mahdi Akhavan Sales (1928–1990), expressed similar sentiments. He lamented not only the demise of the National Movement and the return of Pahlavi coercion but also the futility of the experience of the left and the ideological betrayal it sustained. Akhavan, better known by his pen name "Omid" (meaning "hope"), resorted to the memories of Iran's pre-Islamic past, the purity of the Zoroastrian religion, and the egalitarian memory of Mazdakism to highlight the grim decay of his own time.

Born in Mashhad, and proud of the literary heritage of Khorasan, Akhavan remained loyal more than any other modernist poet to classical masters. He rendered a subtle mix of classical and modern with a powerful message of cultural nationalism, an undertone of social commitment, and—predictably—a sense of defiant despair. The last theme is evident in his 1956 masterpiece, *Kaveh ya Eskandar* (Kaveh or Alexander), composed while in prison on charges of pro-

Tudeh activism. It portrays the suffocating calm that pervaded the aftermath of the 1953 coup. Conveying a message of betrayed hopes and futile resistance, he skillfully uses Persian expressions, proverbs, and allegories to break from artistic isolation and speak with ordinary folks:

> The waves have calmed, quiet and subdued.
> The drum of the storm has fallen silent.
> Springs of smoldering flames have now dried up.
> All the waters have run their course.
> In the tombstone land of this pulse-less city,
> Not even the call of an owl can be heard. . . .
> The gallows were removed, the blood washed away.
> In place of flowers of agony, fury and revolt,
> Now the evil weeds have taken their sprawling root. . . .
> It is night here, indeed, a nightmarish dark.
> Yet beyond the hill there was no daylight either. . . .
> Whoever came over, grabbed his loot and moved on.
> Again miserable, humiliated and deprived we remained.
> Of that what did we reap but lies and lies?
> Of this what did we reap but deceit and deceit?
> Then again they say: "Another day,
> Wait for another to come."
> No Kaveh will ever be found, O Omid!
> I wish an Alexander would be found.[7]

The powerful ending, lamenting the absence of Kaveh, the ironsmith revolutionary of the *Shahnameh* legend who rose against the tyrant Zahhak, is most likely a reference to Mosaddeq and an unlikely future struggle against the regime. Omid's shattered hopes could seek only the return of an alien Alexander, the archvillain of Zoroastrian memory who destroyed the ancient Persian Empire.

In his 1957 *Akher-e Shahnameh* (meaning "*Shahnameh's* ending," alluding to the ironic Persian proverb "*Shahnameh* has a happy ending"), he further contrasts the dream of the epic past—wiped out by Alexander, here no doubt an allegory for the damning forces of the West—with the sad fate of his own country, depreciated and decayed:

> This out-of-tune broken harp,
> Tamed in the hand of that frenzied old bard,
> As if at times it dreams,
> Sees itself in the glittering presence of the sun,
> That unique vista of the happy countenance of Zarathustra.

Here the poet wishfully imagines his nation, confident and righteous, challenging the hegemonic demons and conquering their arrogant land of nothingness:

> We
> Conquerors of castles of historical pride,
> Witnesses to glorious cities of every era,
> We
> Memorials to forlorn innocence of epochs past,
> Narrators of sweet and happy tales.

Yet the reality of his people is tragically different from the impossible dreams of the poet's harp. The new tune is nothing but the tragic lament at the end of the legendary part of the *Shahnameh*, where Rostam, son of Dastan, the greatest of the *Shahnameh*'s heroes, is dying at the bottom of a pit, having been set up by no less an enemy than his own traitorous half-brother. The poet plays on the tragedy of two Rostams—the other is Rostam, the son of Farrokhzad, the commander in chief of the Sasanian army. His defeat and capture in the battle of Qadesiya in 636 at the hands of the invading Arab armies brings the narrative of the *Shahnameh* to its tragic end. The poet, rebuking his broken harp, comes to his mournful finale, a famous passages in modern Persian poetry:

> O you miserable babbler, change your tune!
> Never again will the Son of Dastan emerge from his half-brother's pit,
> Died, died, he died!
> Now recite the story of the son of Farrokhzad.
> One whose laments come as if from the depth of a yawning well,
> He cries and laments,
> Laments and says:
> "Alas, we now appear,
> Like hunchbacked old conquerors,
> Aboard ships of waves with sails of foam
> Hearts set on glorious lambs grazing in fields of hollow times,
> Our blades rusty, ancient and blunt,
> Our drums eternally silent,
> Our arrows broken-winged.
> We
> Conquerors of cities gone with the wind,
> With a voice so faint it can never escape our lungs,
> Narrators of long-forgotten tales.
> Not a soul will take our coins for anything, even an old penny.
> As if they're an alien king's,

Or a prince's whose dynasty has vanished long ago.
From time to time we wake from this charmed slumber,
Like that deep sleep of the Companions of the Cave,
Rubbing our eyes, we cry: "Behold, that unique golden castle of sweet
   morning light!"
But alas the tyrant never dies.[8]

Here the "tyrant," the Daqyanus of the Islamic legend who claimed to be divine (evidently based on the third-century Roman emperor Decius [r. 249–251] and the persecution of early Christians) probably is an allusion to Reza Shah. The seven Companions of the Cave (*ashab-e kahf*)—who fearing Daqyanus's persecution took refuge in a cave and fell into a deep sleep, from which they awoke centuries later—however, makes reference to the fate of the Iranian people. Fearing their tyrannical rulers, they too fell into a deep sleep, from which they awakened to a brief moment of hope, which was only to be followed by another cycle of tyranny. The poet's last assertion, "But alas the tyrant never dies," has an ominous ring, given what would come to pass in the quarter century after the poem's composition.

Against a background of shattered hopes, a yearning for a rebirth, a nostalgic longing for a world of natural purity, began to emerge in the poetry of Forugh Farrokhzad (1935–1967). A poet of tormented love and sensibilities, she explored a feminine self keenly aware of her social surroundings. Born in Tehran to a middle-class military family, Forugh questioned religious conventions, sexual stigma, and patriarchal tyranny. Gender awareness is evident in her earlier collections, but it is in her *Tavallodi Digar* (A rebirth) from 1964 that she transcended to a new plane of almost mystical awareness, achieved after a journey of self-discovery (fig. 10.9). As a critic of women's marginality, religious dogma, and social deprivation, Forugh has already reacted to the clerical establishment that stigmatized her as rebellious and profane.

By questioning in the fashion of Khayyam the very notions of divinity and religious faith, in her "Bandegi" (Servitude), a long poem in the form of dialogue with the Creator, composed circa 1956 in the genre of Sufi monologues and dream narratives, she states:

On my lips a shadow of a mysterious question,
In my heart a pain, restless and burning my soul.
The secret of this rebellious, wandering spirit,
I now wish to share with you. . . .
Does my lament ever reach you,
So that you may crush your cup of self-adoration,

Figure 10.9. Forugh on the cover of her *Tvallodi-e Digar*.
Tvallodi-e Digar, 5th ed. (Tehran: Morvarid Publishers, 1350/1971).

And sit with me, the earthy one, for a moment,
And drink the pain of existence from the lips of my poetry?

This existential questioning brings Forugh to an agnostic portrayal of a God who is tyrannical, self-engrossed, and exploitative — an unusually candid expression for poets of the period, most of whom were engaged with earthly rather than with divine tyranny. She goes on:

You cast a shadow upon the End and in your hand,
A rope on the other end of which were necks.
Dragging people on the pathway of life,
Their eyes bedazzled by the image of the Hereafter. . . .
So long as we, the wretched ones, call you just,
You cover your countenance in a silky mask of compassion.
And turn Paradise into a mysterious myth,
Offering it as credit in exchange for the cash of people's lives.[9]

Forugh's personal soul-searching later increasingly turned into social themes. In her poem "Ey marz-e por-gohar" (O bejeweled fatherland), a parody pub-

lished in 1963 on the title of Iran's banned national anthem, she sneers at clichés of Pahlavi patriotism and bureaucratic fixing of individual identities. She
mocks bogus surroundings, suffused with jingoism, a culture of sycophancy,
cheap ambitions, the even cheaper material culture of Western imports, and of
course imperial vainglory:

> I am victorious!
> I managed to register myself.
> I managed to adorn myself with a name on an identity card,
> And my existence is now marked by a number.
> So, long live 678, issued in district 5, Resident of Tehran.
> Now I can rest assured that everything is in order:
> The bosom of the caring motherland,
> The pacifier of prideful historical heritage,
> The lullaby of civilization and culture,
> And the rattling of the rattles of the law.
> Now I can rest assured that everything is in order.
> So elated was I,
> That I rushed to the window and with ecstasy inhaled down into my lungs
>   six hundred seventy eight times the air infused with dung,
> And dust and the odor of trash and urine.
> And signed at the bottom of six hundred seventy eight IOUs,
> And wrote atop six hundred seventy eight job applications: Forugh
>   Farrokhzad.
> In the land of poetry, of the "flower and nightingale,"
> Living is a blessing, particularly
> When after many, many years your existence is acknowledged. . . .
> I have come to existence among such productive masses,
> Who, despite having no bread to eat,
> Have an open and far-reaching field of vision,
> With geographical boundaries that currently span
> In the north to the lush and sweet-smelling Firing Range,
> In the south to the ancient Gallows Square,
> And in the heavily-populated areas reach the Artillery Square. . . .
> I am victorious, yes, I am victorious!
> Long live 678, issued in district 5, Resident of Tehran,
> Who relying on her perseverance and resolve,
> Has reached such a high station that she stood on the frame of her window,
> That is six hundred seventy eight meters above the ground,
> And has the great honor,
> From that very opening, not through the staircase,
> Of throwing herself, madly, headlong onto the lap of the caring motherland.

And her last wish would be,
That for a gift of six hundred seventy eight gold coins,
His Excellency the poet laureate Abraham Sahba,
Would, as a tribute to her life, conjure a mournful ode rhyming with
    gobbledygook.[10]

That in her last poems, published posthumously in 1973, she finds a messianic vision not unlike that of other members of her literary cohort, is a corollary
to the bleak humor of the above-mentioned poem. A revolutionary upheaval
comes to transform her unlivable surroundings. In her poem "Kasi keh mesl-e
hichkas nist" (The one who is not like anyone else), the poet sees a revolutionary future through the eyes of a working-class child from the poor neighborhoods of southern Tehran:

I dreamed that someone is coming,
I dreamed of a red star . . .
[Someone] who can do something [so spectacular] that the Allah (neon) lamp,
That was green; green like the light of the dawn,
Will be lit up again over the neighborhood mosque . . .
He who is with us in his heart, with us in his breath, with us in his voice,
He whose coming can not be arrested, handcuffed and thrown into jail . . .
The one who comes down from the sky of Artillery Square in a night of
    fireworks,
Who spreads the tablecloth and divides up the bread,
And divides up the Pepsi,
And divides up the public park,
And divides up the whooping-cough syrup,
And divides up school registration day,
And divides up the hospital waiting numbers,
And divides up the rubber boots,
And divides up the Fardin movies,
And divides up the clothing of Sayyid Javad's daughter,
And divides up every unsold jumble,
And gives us our share too,
I had a dream.[11]

The ending especially is remarkable coming in the aftermath of the June 1963
uprising and containing tantalizing allusions to a socialist revolution with clear
Islamic undertones. That the poet of "joyful sin"—whose poems once were
publicly denounced on the pulpit—was now dreaming the descent of a savior,
was a telling example of how the mystique of a forthcoming revolution began to
take root among the intellectuals of the period.

Ahmad Shamlu (1925–2000), also the son of a military officer, perhaps was the most avant-garde in his coining of complex poetic imagery and rich symbolic language. He, too, engaged with melancholic disillusionments and delved into the discourse of messianic aspirations, but with the image of a savior who preached not only a worldly reality devoid of hereafter but also peace and nonviolence. In his 1965 "Lawh" (The tablet), inspired by the imagery of the Hebrew Bible and the narrative of the Gospels, his messiah, no doubt the poet himself, brings a "clay tablet" with a message of compassion to a public as incredulous and inattentive as those in Nima's "Mahtab":

Then I raised the clay tablet,
To the end of my arm.
And cried out to the crowd:
"Whatever all there is,
Is this, and beyond there is nothing else.
It's an old tablet, worn out, this here, behold!
Though soiled with filth and the blood of many wounds,
It speaks of compassion, friendship, and purity."
But people's ears and hearts were not with me,
As if from expectation, one could surmise,
They got profit and pleasure.
I shouted:
"If you were true to yourself,
You'd know that you're waiting in vain.
The last message is all here!"
I cried out:
"The time of lamenting your crucified messiah has passed.
For now every woman is Mary,
And every Mary has Jesus on the cross,
With no crown of thorns, cross or Golgotha,
Without Pilate, judges or trial.
Messiahs all of a common destiny,
Identical Messiahs,
In identical uniforms,
With identical boots and gaiters, all the same
And equal rations of bread and broth,
(Yes, equality is the precious heritage of mankind.)
And if there is no crown of thorns, there is a helmet to put on,
And if no cross to carry on the shoulder,
There is a rifle.
(The means of greatness now is all ready!)

And every supper may very well be the Last Supper,
And every gaze the gaze of a Judas.
But don't waste time to find a garden,
For you will encounter the tree on the cross,
When the dream of humanity and compassion,
Like a fog, soft and light-footed, will dissipate. . . .
And, alas, the path of the cross,
Is no longer the path of ascent to heaven,
But a path toward Hell and eternal wandering of the soul."
I was crying out in the depth of my fever,
But people's ears and hearts were not with me.
I knew they were awaiting not a clay tablet but a book,
And a sword, . . .
Alas, these people seek the truth only in legends,
Or else know the truth as nothing but legend.
And my fire did not alight within them,
For I had spoken the last word about heaven,
Without ever bringing heaven to my tongue.[12]

Shamlu's "last word" about heaven and on the messianic return was a fitting end to the postwar antinomian discourse. His counter-messianic hero aimed for a faith akin to the Iranian experience. Yet the message of this humanist messiah, as the poet laments, was bound to be rejected by a public enamored of militarism, war, and violence. These, too, were experiences known to the people of his generation. The elaborate imagery and complex message of the "new poetry," masterful and penetrating though they were, hardly ever reached beyond an intellectual elite, as Shamlu's poem admits.

Ironically, much of this gloom in the poetry of the period was expressed at a time when Iran of the 1960s experienced tangible material progress, relative prosperity among the secular middle classes, and a level of general stability. Perhaps this was also the best decade of the twentieth century in terms of artistic ingenuity and poetic symbolism, even though the poets and intellectuals of the period were essentially at odds with the Pahlavi regime. This was a respite for them to pause and ponder the naive idealism of earlier years and come up with a reflective reading of themselves, their society, and the baggage of their past. Though with hindsight they were removed from the harsh realities of their time, there was something remarkably novel in their production. Perhaps despite their wishes, their anguished vision paved the way for an alternative route to authenticity—a discourse with far-reaching consequences and, ironically, a very different kind of revolution.

11

DEVELOPMENT, DISARRAY, AND DISCONTENT (1963–1977)

The exile of Ayatollah Khomeini and the shah's success, at least for a while, in silencing the forces of opposition generated a sense of royal self-confidence with an almost prophetic mission. The decade of 1963 to 1973 represented, with all its shortcomings, the best of the shah's years: an age of economic development, success in foreign policy, and relative popularity at home. Despite repression and movements of radical dissent, for a moment the shah seemed to have cast away the shadow of dependency on the West. Yet the sobering message of the June 1963 uprising remained largely unheard by the new ruling elite. And when it was heard, they dismissed it as the last gasp of the "black reactionaries," as the shah had labeled the clerical opposition.

EXPANDING ECONOMY

Between 1965 and 1975 Iran's population grew by 40 percent, from more than twenty-four million to more than thirty-four million; growth was facilitated by lower infant mortality, longer life expectancy, and greater access to medical care. Rural migrants continued to move to larger cities in search of higher-paying jobs and a better standard of living. In 1971 Tehran's population exceeded three million, and by 1975 it bordered on four million. In 1972 there were an estimated five hundred thousand cars on the streets of the capital, a number that by 1979 had doubled mostly thanks to the domestic production of an affordable sedan, the Paykan, a brand assembled since 1967 under license from a soon-to-be-defunct British car manufacturer. Not only the capital but also all provincial centers began to experience the unavoidable forays of the proud owners of private cars congesting urban thoroughfares. By the late 1970s cars, vans, buses, and trucks, whether domestic or foreign in manufacture, new or old, private or public, had conquered every corner of the country's rural and urban roadways, realizing the worst of Al-e Ahmad's "Westoxication" nightmare. Polluting the air—especially in Tehran, where the Alborz range created a barrier that trapped the smog over the city—vehicles became one of the greatest hazards to life and safety, with escalating road accidents and fatalities. For the haves and the have-nots, cars became not only a status symbol but also a monster demanding that all roads, even sidewalks, and all public spaces to be sacrificed at its altar. The slogan of a TV commercial on the Iranian network, "In the hope that every Iranian can have a Paykan," summed up the consumer culture that began to take shape in the 1970s and would continue after the 1979 revolution.

The state's industrialization initiative was not limited to car manufacturing and consumer goods, and often was not as present in the public mind. Throughout the 1960s and 1970s during the third and fourth development plans—implemented by the Planning and Budget Organization—Iran expanded its infrastructure. It constructed new roads and railroads and improved existing ones; built massive dams to cultivate more lands and generate more electricity; installed a countrywide electrical grid and communication networks, water purification plants, and irrigation projects; and built heavy industry, petrochemical, cement, and sugar plants, as well as port facilities and new oil and natural gas pipelines. The private sector also contributed by expanding the capacity of spinning mills and textile plants, consumer and household goods, foodstuffs, packaging and bottling industries, motor vehicles, and even the steel industry. By the mid-1970s Iran had developed a substantial domestic market for cars and related industries, household goods, clothing, food and drinks, furniture, and construction material, and the balance of the public and private sectors promised a viable mixed economy for a developing nation that still was heavily relying on oil revenue for its public investment.

The critics of the intellectual left and later the extreme left, some still carrying the incurable Tudeh bug, belittled much of Iran's industrialization as a mere "assembly" (*montage*) of useless products that had been imposed by Western consumer culture and were for the benefit of a "dependent bourgeoisie." Often looking up to the smoke-belching, inefficient, labor-intensive, centralized Soviet and Eastern European industrialization model, such criticism later was picked up by the Islamic radicals and became part of the rhetoric of the 1979 revolution. Yet it is fair to say that in later years, the state industrialization program became overambitious and out of control, leading to waste, corruption, and nepotism—at times it was devoid of any meaningful relation to the state's preconceived master plan.

The growth of the industrial sector barely satisfied the domestic markets' growing demand for goods and services. Imports of all sorts from Europe, the United States, and Japan flooded Iran's markets, mostly at the expense of the bazaar sector and associated small-scale manufactures and wholesalers. As the larger import-export and industrial businesses gradually moved out of the bazaar district into more fashionable areas, the bazaar's demographics began to change, especially in Tehran but also in larger provincial centers. In due course the bazaar came to house mostly small merchants, distributors, wholesales, and retailers of small industries catering to the poorer and more traditional sectors of the population. The change in its function was not necessarily detrimental to the bazaar, despite the government's unfavorable attitude toward the bazaar merchants for harboring antiregime, and particularly pro-Khomeini, sentiments. Undeniably, demographic changes turned these old centers of commerce not merely into bastions of conservatism but also into important components, financially and otherwise, of the fomenting Islamic activism.

The evolving bazaar moreover presented a physical and geographical anomaly in the midst of the modernist image of the Pahlavi economy. The jewelers, goldsmiths, watchmakers, fabric stores, shoe stores, perfumeries, draperies, china shops, and kitchen stores—side by side with wholesale carpet merchants, import-export businessmen, bankers, moneylenders, and haberdasheries, hardware wholesalers, apothecaries, and thousands of small workshops producing a variety of goods in the sprawling neighborhood, often in the oldest part of major cities—were still vibrant enclaves. And given their size, they were engaged in brisk business. Yet the bazaar's prosperity and what it offered, at least economically, was no longer essential to Iran's economy.

The changes evident in the Iranian economy were well demonstrated by the rising oil prices and their effects on the government budget. Between 1965 and 1972 Iran's annual budget grew rapidly from nearly US$1 billion to $8 billion, a sizable increase that resulted from incessant wrangling with the Iranian Oil Participants Limited (IOP), better known as the Consortium of Iranian Oil over production levels and higher prices. The rise of the Organization of Petroleum-Exporting Countries (OPEC) in the 1960s—with its first secretary-general being Fo'ad Rouhani (1907–2004), an adviser to Mosaddeq and a historian of Iran's oil nationalization—gave the shah another tool to persuade the consortium. By the mid-1960s Iran had limited the consortium's operations to a smaller territory in Khuzestan and had signed more favorable agreements than the 1954 concession with French and other oil companies to develop Iran's offshore oil in the Persian Gulf and inland. This compelled the consortium to increase both the production level and Iran's share of the income. By 1966 there was an annual increase of 17 percent in Iran's income from oil, exceeding for the first time $1 billion, and constituting nearly 50 percent of Iran's annual budget for that year.

By 1969 Iran's annual production passed one billion barrels, and in the following year its share of income substantially shifted from the burden of the fifty-fifty agreement in 1954 to the new 61 percent of Iran's share versus the consortium's 39 percent. At the time, although oil prices worldwide were extremely low—an outcome of giant oil companies' many decades of deliberate exploitation of oil-producing countries—the Iranian success appeared to be a triumph for the shah and allowed him to come out from the shadows of the oil nationalization campaign of the 1950s. The massive oil price rises in the following years, however, proved to be not entirely a blessing, as it appeared at first glance, for they shook the Iranian economy and helped in due course to unsettle Iran's sociopolitical balances.

The oil crisis from October 1973 to March 1974 and the multiple price increases that came in its wake was a turning point, perhaps an inevitable one, not only for Western economies and the global inflation that it triggered but also for the economies of the Middle East, and especially oil-exporting countries that relied on oil income to develop their infrastructure and raise standards of living. What was earned from oil income, as it happened, at least in part purchased affluence for these countries' privileged classes, or alternatively was squandered on vainglorious projects. Iran stood at the very top of the oil-producing countries of the Middle East, bearing the brunt of the overflowing revenues that came into its coffers. This was not merely because it was economically more developed than its neighbors, and therefore more vulnerable, or because it was the most populated of the OPEC members in the Middle East; it was because of the choices made by those in power, headed by the shah and a small group of technocrats at his service; choices that were enthusiastically endorsed by his foreign friends and allies but that eventually helped undermine the very survival of the Pahlavi regime.

Between 1971 and 1977 Iran's annual budget further grew sixfold from $8 billon to $48 billion, an upsurge substantially due to direct and indirect oil receipts. Shortly before the October 1973 war between Egypt and Israel that led to the Arab Oil Producing Exporting Countries' oil embargo and triggered a rapid rise in oil prices, a barrel of Persian Gulf light crude traded at the exploitatively low price of $1.95, a price that was the outcome of many negotiations in previous years. Soon after the October war, however, the price jump stunned even the oil producers; by 1975 it had reached nearly $11 per barrel in the European spot market and even higher prices in the United States. By not taking part in the Arab embargo against the United States, Iran stood to benefit not only financially but also politically. In contrast to the unfavorable image of Arab oil producers in Western media, which stereotyped the Arab sheiks as greedy plunderers with undeserving riches, Iran was seen, at least by those who could differentiate Iran from its Arab neighbors, as something of a friend—still greedy and unfair, no doubt, but not hostile and uncompromising.

Yet since 1972, even before the oil crisis, Iran was at the forefront of an OPEC campaign for increased prices. Initially, it was the loss of revenue due to depreciation of the US dollar that unified OPEC members in their demand for higher prices (after the United States decided in 1971 to terminate the Bretton Woods Agreement that ended the convertibility of the American currency to gold). In later years Iran increasingly justified its price hikes by pointing at rising inflation, which hiked the prices of imported goods and domestic manufactures. It also argued that oil, a finite commodity that deserved to be conserved and fairly priced, had long been extracted to the advantage of the too-powerful oil companies to supply Western economies with cheap oil.

In early 1973 the situation had shifted in favor of the oil producers to the extent that the shah, long discontent with Iran's production levels, announced that his country would not renew its operation agreement with the consortium that was due to expire in 1979. His threat found a new momentum given the long-term guarantees that the consortium required to plan its exploration and production. Concurring with the nationalization of oil industries initiated by other OPEC countries such as Iraq, the shah felt confident enough to nullify the 1954 agreement two years earlier than it was due to expire. For domestic purposes, the move was portrayed as "nationalization"—the third one after 1933 and 1949—and a new laurel for the glory-hungry monarch. In April 1975 he flew back to his capital to be received by the crowds that had been bused in to Aryamehr sport stadium to express their "gratitude" (*sepas*). Yet the exercise in imperial adulation was not without its repercussions, for the "gratitude" ritual took place in an atmosphere of public sarcasm and at a time when the Marxist and Islamist urban guerilla organizations projected a very different picture of heavy handed Pahlavi rule.

The impact of increased oil income on all aspects of the Iranian economy and society cannot be exaggerated. Already in 1973 Iran was experiencing an official inflation rate of 11 percent, setting a pattern that was precipitated in coming years both because massive funds were injected into a domestic economy with limited capacity and because there was a huge inflationary trend worldwide. Although by 1973 Iranian per capita income had risen to $566, the impressive increase was diminished, if not entirely eroded, by a higher cost of living. By the late 1970s inflation stood at as much as 25 percent annually. At the time, Iran's growing income from oil, as the shah and his government were eager to point out, appeared highly beneficiary to Iran: more oil income meant a larger allocation of funds to development projects, greater affluence for all sectors of the population, stronger defenses, and a greater international prestige. These were all essential ingredients for the shah's dream of recapturing what he called the "Great Civilization" (*tammadon-e bozorg*), a catchphrase meant to recapture the glories of the ancient Iranian past. The arrival at the threshold of this Great Civilization, however, was imminent only to the person of the shah and his sycophants. It was as if the rise in Iran's oil fortune, and the shah's active campaign to capture what had been denied to his deposed premier, Mosaddeq, had made him see an inspired vision for reshaping his country. *Mission for My Country* was indeed the title he had chosen for his memoirs first published in 1961, a mission that over the years took the shape of a prophetic call.

A NEW TECHNOCRATIC ELITE

It is untenable to treat the shah's evolving self-image in isolation, and especially as distinct from the new technocratic elite that came to serve the monarch and populate his government after the mid-1960s. With the appointment in 1965 of Amir 'Abbas Hovayda (1919–1979) as prime minister—after the assassination of Mansur, in whose government Hovayda had served as minister of finance—the role of the new technocratic class became more obvious. Often younger professionals—Hovayda was forty-five when appointed prime minister—were mostly the fruits of a generational shift that came about in the later years of Pahlavi rule. Educated in modern schools and often holding a graduate degree from Western universities or having some experience in the Europe or in the United States, they had mostly built careers after 1953, some through the bureaucratic ranks and others through family and other connections. In contrast to the landowning notables of the postconstitutional period who endured the Reza Shah era, the new class, though affluent, was not bound to large hereditary estates, particularly after land reforms. Unlike the liberal nationalists of the postwar years who supported Mosaddeq, and more like the military elite of the Reza Shah era, the new class of officials was essentially nonideological, and they seldom possessed any political agency. Though a few were from notable families or families of wealth and influence, the new generation of ministers, diplomats, and high officials relied on their education and expertise, but also on the Pahlavi patronage network, their proximity to circles of power, and obedience to the higher echelons of government.

Amir 'Abbas Hovayda was a case in point. Born to a family of middle-ranking notables of the late Qajar period, his father became a diplomat under Reza Shah (and abandoned his own father's, Hovayda's grandfather's, devotion to the Baha'i faith). He was brought up a secular Muslim, educated in a French lycée in Beirut and later earned a political science degree from a Belgian university before entering the Iranian diplomatic corps. Fascinated with French literature, and an admirer of André Gide, he frequented intellectual circles in Paris and Tehran and befriended the likes of Sadeq Hedayat, to whom he would send the latest works of European and American literature. An enigmatic personality, Hovayda later joined an Iranian Freemasonry lodge, and presumably through that patronage network, he was appointed a member of the board of directors of the Iran National Oil Company. A cofounder of a circle of young progressives, which later became the nucleus for the Iran Novin (Modern Iran) Party, Hovayda was appointed finance minister to Mansur's cabinet.

Though first serving in a caretaker role as prime minister, Hovayda's personality evidently appealed to the shah, who retained him in office for the following thirteen years (1965–1977), a term of office equaled in duration only by that of Hajji Mirza Aqasi (who served as Mohammad Shah Qajar's premier between 1835 and 1848). Though not as influential as Aqasi when it came to controlling the shah, or as paternal, Hovayda's interplay with the Pahlavi monarch despite his complexities were mutually beneficial to both sides. The shah viewed Hovayda as unthreatening and subservient, as a humble executive who acted on behalf of the powerful ruler, a role with a long history in Iran's ministerial past. Hovayda was prepared to play such a part while quietly expanding his network and advancing his agenda. Fearful of a prime ministerial monopoly, the shah favored his understated style and sycophantic passivity while playing the premier against other senior officials, notably his powerful court minister Asadollah 'Alam. Hovayda, however, fully submitted to the reality of royal power, especially in the areas of security, military, and foreign affairs. He was a soldier in the service of his beloved monarch, as he often asserted.

That Hovayda remained relatively unblemished by deals and wills, nepotism, and the excesses of the last years of the Pahlavi rule was in part because of his personal integrity and lack of appetite for material gains—a characteristic shared by only a few of his subordinates. This largely was because he carried a lesser burden of governance than what was expected constitutionally of the prime minister. It is fair to say that more than anyone, he was responsible for the culture of ministerial passivity that prevailed through his tenure as prime minister. With few exceptions, a generation of officials who came to occupy high offices was perhaps best characterized by subservience to royal will, obsequious timidity, and lack of moral spine—even more so lack of political vision. The culture of statecraft that emerged in these years accepted the shah's ultimate authority in all affairs at the expense of critical thinking, much less voicing criticism of royal policies and practices. The atmosphere of fear and compliance spread a certain numbness throughout the system and decreased the chances of promoting independent views. A veneer of optimism about the dawning of a glorious vista opening up under the shah's wise leadership concealed undercurrents of cynicism or opportunism.

The lack of any stance independent of the shah further weakened political agency among statesmen of the late Pahlavi era. The censorship and coercion imposed by Savak, the closure of even the pro-regime political parties such as Iran Novin and Mardom in favor of the all-embracing Rastakhiz (Resurrection) Party in 1975, and the absence of any alternative political forum effectively eliminated all chances of building up a civil society outside the bounds of the state and untouched by royal wishes and whims. Although patronage networks did exist and high officials exerted a great deal of favoritism toward their partners and protégés, there was a palpable dearth of creative thinking and even less room for political action. Despite the creation of the Rastakhiz Party, meant to boost popular participation, the gap between state actors and the general public widened throughout the 1970s. State actors operated in a sanitized bureaucratic cocoon, divorced from the realities of the society they claimed to represent. Ministerial posts became channels for doling out contracts or buying influence, the Majles turned into an assembly of faceless nonentities rubberstamping legislation, and—after many rounds of dismissals—the emasculated military fell even further under the shah's spell.

The small network of well-connected and compliant technocrats thus came to control and use up, if not squander, the massive oil revenues that began to pour in after 1973. In addition to Hovayda and his cabinet members, who were routinely reshuffled, there were other networks of power and influence that included 'Alam and his cohorts, the entourage of Empress Farah, who received the title *Shahbanu* (lady shah) in 1967, and other members of the royal family, among whom Ashraf Pahlavi was the most visible. To varying degrees the shah presided over these networks of influence and favoritism, at times rebuking some for moral and financial excesses and at other times promoting some for their merits or their loyalty. Counterbalancing rival factions proved a formidable task, one that could be achieved by allowing huge quantities of funds to lubricate the channels of power and for smooth operations of the state and its affiliated bodies and institutions.

In pursuit of his earlier intellectual interests, Hovayda also tried with moderate success to arrive at a rapprochement with discontented intellectuals, hoping to lure them into collaboration. This was meant to soften the regime's image by means of employing the unemployed and underemployed poets, writers, artists, critics, and former activists, making them less contentious toward the regime and more dependent on its largesse. He funded cultural institutions, patronized artistic activities, and listened to moderate voices of reform. He was of the belief, at least in the earlier years of his premiership, that with a powerful leader like the shah at the helm—a necessity in his view, given the painful experience of democracy in earlier years—Iran could be transformed into a prosperous society with material and cultural advancements; his was a positivist view of social progress that paid homage to secular modernism while echoing the shah's rhetoric. Yet this view did not give any priority to pluralism, popular representation, or respect for individual freedoms. Though Hovayda was sold on the royal rationale of progressive autocracy, he exerted a modifying influence over the system through push and pull, and through persuasion. His self-deprecating demeanor, in contrast to the elite culture of indulgence and arrogance that flourished in the period, was refreshing but not altogether convincing to the regime's critics or even to intellectuals and activists co-opted by the Pahlavi state.

A more significant player of the period was Empress Farah and her fledgling clique of intellectuals and artists who came to dominate the cultural stage in the late 1960s and 1970s. She had a moderating influence on the otherwise monolithic Pahlavi course and its bland cultural perspective. A French-educated student of architecture in Paris when she married the shah in 1959 at the age of twenty-one, Farah Diba came from an affluent military family with ties to old nobility in Azarbaijan. A woman of intelligence, with diverse cultural interests and a flair for the recovery of lost Iranian heritage, she was a refreshing voice of refinement in the royal court and beyond. As mother of crown prince Reza Pahlavi, who was born in 1960, and later as a woman with a taste independent of her husband, Farah Pahlavi earned a stature beyond what was usually permitted or expected of the women of the court. Having influence over the shah, especially in matters of culture and education, she was also audible, through direct and indirect channels, in the deeply male-dominated political sphere. Having been brought up more as a commoner, she was less alienated from the life of ordinary folks, even though over time she seemed to have been discouraged by the prospects for any major reform of the system. Like Hovayda, and at times in cahoots with him, the empress offered a fresh style, even though she remained essentially complicit in the Pahlavi power rationale.

By the late 1960s the four major branches of power and influence were almost entirely subservient to the shah. The civilian branch consisted of the court circle under the court minister Asadollah 'Alam, who also loosely supervised the networks around the member of the royal family, facilitated much of the shah's relations with the diplomatic corps, and enabled the shah's private life. The machinery of government and its many enclaves were supervised by the prime minister Amir 'Abbas Hovayda and his ministers and allies. The circle around Empress Farah was smaller in number and limited in its power but exercised some influence over the broadcasting network. The extensive military branch consisting of the personnel of the Iranian armed forces was even more tightly under the shah's direct control than the civilian branch. He made all the senior military appointments, decided on purchase of military hardware and weapon systems, and monitored the conduct of the ranking officers.

Also under the shah's surveillance, though officially being departments of the government, were the Savak, the National Iranian Oil Company, the Planning Organization, and the Pahlavi Foundation, a "charity" that held, developed and operated many of the properties appropriated under Reza Shah (including a hotel chain) as well as managing the shah's many private investments. Likewise, he personally presided over the most sensitive aspects of foreign policy, meetings with the heads of states and appointing ambassadors to major world capitals. All important, and in many respects not-so-important, affairs of the state were to be brought before the shah and received his seal of approval. A category of state affairs that were to "receive the royal honor" (*sharaf-e 'arzi*) was the ultimate stage of decision-making in the Pahlavi hierarchy of power.

Beyond the structure of the state and its bureaucracy, which constituted the public sector, those organs of the private and semi-private sectors which were in routine interaction with the government, including major foreign investments, had to report their economic policies and development priorities to the shah for his approval. They included most banks, major industries, and universities. In all, the shah was the supreme source of authority in a power hierarchy that was largely devoid of agency and critical perspective. It was above all a system driven by loyalty and obedience to the shah and fear of him. It is wrong to believe that such a structure under the shah's thumb was merely for his financial benefit and material pleasure, even though his private life was brimmed with sexual escapades. It is true that like many autocratic leaders of the developing world, he amassed a substantial wealth for himself and owned numerous private investments and development projects. He also allowed many of his aides, members of his family, court cronies, and ministers to accumulate illicit and undeserved wealth. A powerful clique of businessmen, industrialists, financiers and developers also benefited from their close ties to the shah and the Pahlavi elite. There were few major economic projects in the country that could successfully operate without some form of partnership with members of the ruling elite or paying kickbacks in the form of bribes, commissions, and shares in new ventures. By the mid 1970s some scandalous deals acquired a level of notoriety even intolerable by the shah. Yet Iran under Mohammad Reza Shah was not a mere kleptocracy.

Far more crucial incentives for enforcing royal control however were the two interconnected personal traits in the shah's personality: a sense of political insecurity and a drive for prestige and glory. He invested a major part of his time and energy to personally supervise, and in most instances micro-manage, the affairs of the state rather than delegating power to his subordinates through constitutional channels. As if he had to prove his worth above all to the ever-present ghost of his father and to ghosts of his nemeses that no doubt included Mosaddeq. Prestige, especially on the international stage, equaled in the shah's mind with Iran's military might, political and diplomatic presence and projecting unrealistic images of royal confidence and Iran's power and material progress. Such an arrangement endured for more than a decade, especially on the international stage, though increasingly it was corroded from within and challenged by overt and covert forces of opposition to which the shah, and his lieutenants, remained insensitive if not being in a state of denial. A narrative of ancient glories, and the hurried rush to recapture it, was so blinding that it could not allow any ray of reality to seep through.

FOREIGN POLICY AND REGIONAL POLITICS

If there was limited room for other state players in the conduct of the domestic policy, foreign policy basically was the sole domain of the shah. Relations with superpowers and regional powers were too vital to be left to ministers, advisers, or the diplomats of the Ministry of Foreign Affairs. In the 1960s and 1970s Iran's foreign policy aimed to secure Iran's regional interest, especially in the Persian Gulf, while augmenting the shah's international stature. He remained a staunch ally of the United States and generally a friend of the Western Bloc while improving relations with the Soviet Union, the Eastern Bloc, and the People's Republic of China. At every turn he had to prove his loyalty to the West, whether through engaging with the Central Treaty Organization (CENTO) defense alliance, making massive purchases of arms, facilitating US investments in Iranian oil and other sectors, and, whenever needed, acting on behalf of the United States and its allies in the region. Over the years, however, he displayed greater independence, even the desire to balance superpowers with his improving negotiating skills. He was also capable of furthering his wishes with the United States and other Western allies—at times even dictating to them—a reality very different from his perceived image in his own country as a docile subordinate of the Americans.

In return, successive US administrations from Johnson to Ford, and especially during the Nixon years, maintained close ties with Iran in matters of security, defense, energy, and investment. Despite voices of dissent—for instance, George Ball (1901–1994), US undersecretary of state in the Kennedy administration, who criticized the shah's autocratic rule in a number of occasions—the US polity and public opinion overwhelmingly viewed Iran as America's indispensable ally in the Middle East and the shah as a modernizing agent for his people. Friendly relations with Israel also contributed to Americans' favorable attitude toward the shah, especially after 1973. The shah's affinity with Israel was primarily grounded in common geopolitical and strategic concerns, but undeniably it helped ingratiate the shah to his American allies.

Iran enjoyed an edge over Israel or Saudi Arabia, the other two US allies in the region. Even after the 1967 war, that greatly augmented Israel's place in American public opinion—from the perspective of US policy makers, Israel was more a costly commitment than a sustained regional power. In the same period, US ties with Saudi Arabia were considered vital almost entirely because of the Saudis' huge oil reserves, in which the United States had heavily invested for a long time. Even by the 1960s, however, the kingdom's limited demographic and economic potential, and its tribal power structure, made it an odd ally of the United States—the United States could hardly rely on Saudi Arabia's commercial and military capabilities.

Iran offered a different prospect. Its long border with the Soviet Union made it an indispensable first line of defense against the United States' Cold War nemesis. Iran was the only other US ally besides Turkey with a common, and longer, border with the Soviet Union (Finland was considered neutral). Iranian oil and gas reserves were among the largest in the world. In the aftermath of the 1973 October War, the shah proved himself a trusted ally unmoved by Arab solidarity. Iran's political stability, though at the expense of repression at home, with a pro-Western leader at the helm who was capable of speaking the political language of the West, was an important incentive to the Americans and to the British. In contrast to the political flux in most of the Arab world, and gravitation of vital Arab regimes toward the Soviet Union, Iran's geographical span, growing middle class, and expanding economy constituted the third consideration for the United States. With British withdrawal from the Persian

Gulf in the early 1970s, Iran earned even greater ascendancy as the guarantor of security in the Gulf, providing free Western access to its oil resources. Policing the Persian Gulf, which was eagerly embraced by the shah, became a bone of contention with the newly emerging United Arab Emirates and its supporters in the Arab world.

Successive US administrations almost invariably lionized the shah, both in public and in private, as a capable and sagacious leader and often paid homage to his international bearing and regional prominence. Even though he was occasionally criticized in the press for his overblown rhetoric and sneered at in private for his military ambitions and his autocratic grip, the prevailing US position was to support his domestic reforms. His buildup of the Iranian armed forces, and his opening up of the country to foreign, and especially American, investment was another motive. The implicit US approval of Savak's firm hand in dealing with dissidents was further confirmed after urban guerrillas made several assassination attempts in mid-1970s against the American advisory officers who served in the Iranian military.

Despite growing publicity in the American press about violations of human rights, Iranian political prisoners, allegations of torture, military tribunals, and press censorship, American envoys to Iran and high-ranking politicians in Washington were, by and large, willing to turn a blind eye to such unpleasant realities. At most, they treated such issues as an unavoidable evil to be tolerated from a loyal and dependable friend. Even if objections were occasionally raised in private to trusted officials, such as the court minister Asadollah 'Alam, or to the shah himself, they were often on specific issues that directly concerned the United States rather than any cautionary advice about the nature of the shah's autocratic rule, the excesses of the secret police, the absence of credible elected bodies, press censorship, and the evident disarray in economic policies. These were seen by US administrations as issues related to the internal affairs of a sovereign nation, and hence outside the diplomatic mandate.

The shah and his small circle of key advisers were undeterred in their quest for regional primacy. Even before 1971, when growing oil revenues opened doors of informal diplomacy and influence peddling, the shah had been able to throw his political weight around in ways that made it difficult for the US administration to downgrade him as a mere despot. In the mid-1960s he had gained enough confidence to engage in complex international diplomacy involving many players, including the Soviet Union and the Eastern Bloc, the People's Republic of China, and the countries of the Non-Aligned Movement. Neither the United States nor Britain could hold sway over his conduct. During Nikita Khrushchev's years, and continuing under Leonid Brezhnev, despite several spells of intense propaganda wars between Moscow's Persian radio broadcast and Radio Iran, the shah managed to mend fences with his northern neighbor and its satellites mostly through trade and manufacturing contracts. Wary of being portrayed as an American puppet and anxious to display his political agency, the shah in 1965 visited the Soviet Union, the first visit by any Iranian monarch, to reciprocate Brezhnev's visit to Iran three years earlier. He dispatched diplomatic and trade missions, signed numerous deals, often negotiated barter agreements, and established joint development projects with the Soviets and the energy-hungry countries of the Eastern Bloc.

The shah's crowning achievement in 1965 was an agreement to build a massive steel mill complex in Isfahan. Though Russian know-how was relatively backward and hard to fit to Iran's predominantly Western technical expertise, the project was a success. That the acquired Soviet technology was outmoded and polluting did not stop the government from hailing the plant as key to Iran's industrial development, a national aspiration that had remained unfulfilled since a German-assisted initiative to produce steel was abandoned in 1941. In later years other steel plants with more updated designs were built, as well as a tractor manufacturing plant. Warmer relations with Nicolae Ceausescu's Romania and Josip Broz Tito's Yugoslavia, as well as with Pakistan, India, and China, were also meant to emphasize the shah's desire to accommodate the Non-Aligned nations through economic incentives and friendly gestures.

In a geopolitical setting still dominated by two contending superpowers, rapprochement with the communist bloc not only helped diminish Soviet pressure, often conducted through the Tudeh network abroad, but also counterbalanced the United States' primacy and in due course helped Iran in acquiring coveted sophisticated weapons from the United States. The increasing Pahlavi power in the 1970s ironically reduced Iran's dependency on the United States at a time when Iranian public perceived US influence to be at its maximum. The issue of arms sales to Iran, especially after 1973, when Iran enjoyed greater purchasing power thanks to growing oil revenue, from time to time was a source of tension not so much with the Pentagon or the White House as with US Congress. A number of senators raised questions about the sale to Iran of the latest military equipment, such as F-14 and F-15 fighter jets, on the grounds that it might disturb the balance of power in the region at a time when the shah demonstrated appetite for policing the Persian Gulf.

Iran-US relations, especially resolving their differences, were conducted through informal diplomacy and the shah's effective lobbying of key policy makers and influential Washington mediators. The Iranian ambassador in Washington between 1973 and 1979, crucial years in US-Iranian relations, was Ardeshir

Zahedi. Born in 1928, he was son of General Fazollah Zahedi and a former son-in-law of the shah who had served for five years as Iran's minister of foreign affairs. A high-flying player skilled in cultivating personal ties, he acquired the reputation as one of the most effective diplomats in the US capital. Most of the embassy's business carried through private channels, hobnobbing with Washington power elite and with the rich and the famous, including Hollywood stars. He threw extravagant parties in the opulent Iranian embassy, lavished expensive gifts (Iranian caviar was a favorite) on influential deal makers, and offered other favors to lubricate the wheels of power. His confirmed talents made him indispensable to the Iranian regime and to the Washington establishment. High-level diplomacy in Tehran was no less effective, involving frequent meetings between the US and British ambassadors and the court minister 'Alam and the shah himself. Frequent visits to Iran of Western heads of states, prime ministers, and foreign ministers were above all to sweeten various trade and economic deals while quenching the monarch's thirst for prestige and recognition.

During the Kissinger years, with his shuttle diplomacy, direct channels of communication with the shah were important for both parties on such breakthrough issues as the Egypt-Israel peace process and the security of the Persian Gulf. Whatever his deeper convictions were, Kissinger's attitude toward the shah was evidently complimentary, even deferential. His praise of the Pahlavi monarch as a wise, experienced leader with an acute grasp of the complexities of Middle East affairs was based on frequent conversations with him and his ministers, an attitude shared by both presidents he served, Richard Nixon and Gerald Ford (fig. 11.1). That the shah established all but full diplomatic relations with Israel, collaborating on economic projects and sharing intelligence, added to the Americans' wish to include Iran as a party to the Egypt-Israel peace process, and later to the flourishing of Iran's close ties with Egyptian president Anwar al-Sadat.

Nixon had known the Iranian monarch since the early 1950s and visited Iran as Eisenhower's vice president in December 1953. He backed the shah as a stalwart Cold War ally and a friend of the Republican Party. In 1960 the shah had made an illicit contribution to Nixon's presidential campaign, which raised some controversy, and later during Watergate he had commiserated in private with the embattled president. Throughout the difficult years of the Vietnam War, which coincided with the shah's growing stature as an international statesman, he continued to reap the benefits of being a reliable US ally, defying radical Arab states, helping open up China, and playing a major part in bringing about a breakthrough in the Egypt-Israel peace process. Even though the US public image suffered badly in the eyes of the Iranians (and most people of the

Figure 11.1. Henry Kissinger and Amir 'Abbas Hovayda enjoying
a post-banquet gathering in Tehran in May 1972. Minister of
Foreign Affairs Amir Arsalan Khal'atbari is at the far left.
Henry A. Kissinger Papers, May 1972. Manuscripts and Archives, Sterling Memorial Library.
Courtesy of Yale University Library.

region) during the civil rights movement, and even more so because of the Vietnam War and thereafter the Watergate scandal, the shah's overall standing was not seriously tarnished by taking sides with the US Republican establishment.

It was not without reason that on the day of his inauguration on August 9, 1974, President Gerald Ford wrote to the shah "with the full support and participation of Secretary Kissinger," pledging his full commitment to the shah. He added:

> In particular, I want you to know of the extremely high importance I attach to maintaining, expanding and strengthening the very close ties and cooperation between our own two countries. The special relationship between us has been built up through many trials over more than a generation. It has not only stood the test of time but has grown stronger from year to year. I shall do everything in my power to foster the friendship between Iran and the United States.[1]

All in all, despite the domestic disadvantages of appearing to be a junior partner in the Middle East to the West and despite the Iranian opposition's sour memories of the US role in reinstating the shah in 1953 and sustaining him for decades in power as an arbitrary ruler, he navigated his difficult course with some success. This task became even more arduous as Iran confronted the potent challenge of the Arab states in the region on strategic and ideological grounds.

FACING DETRACTORS IN THE ARAB WORLD

Relations with the United States, and Iran's foreign policy trajectory more broadly under the shah, hinged not only on Cold War geopolitics but also on Iran's evolving role in the region as the West's chief ally against the Arab regimes in the contest for supremacy over the Persian Gulf. The shah's growing confidence and his ambition to be viewed as an international player are well evident in, for example, his conversation in October 1975 with a CIA emissary in Tehran. Responding to the American press's criticism, he defiantly argued that Iran's rising oil prices contributed only minimally, as little as 0.4 percent, to inflation in the United States. His prime concern was the leftist rise, especially in Europe and the Arab world, which he claimed he intended to combat with money and troops. He moreover criticized the United States in unambiguous terms for not leading the anti-communist campaign worldwide and in the Arab world. Reviewing a range of issues from Sino-Soviet relations and China's rise as a world player, Egyptian ambitions in the Arabian Peninsula, and security of the Persian Gulf, the shah readily defended his positions on protecting Iran's strategic interests and the survival of moderate Arab regimes and US interests in the region. Through diplomacy, financial support, and military action, which included support for the Barzani Kurdish rebellion against Ba'athist Iraq and military support for the kingdom of Oman in combatting the Dhofar rebellion, the shah's proactive course was convincing enough for the CIA operative to conclude the following:

> In summary, thanks to the Shah himself and oil resources, Iran is well on its way to playing a leading role in the Mid East with a modernized elite, large economic resources and strong forces. Succession is always a question in an authoritarian regime, even a benevolent one, but each year reinforces the social and political momentum in the direction the Shah has set. I believe the U.S. can keep close to and benefit from this process and even influence Iran toward a positive regional and world role rather than a bid for area hegemony or other adventurism.[2]

Whether it was hegemony or adventurism, Iran's often strained relations with neighboring Iraq after the 1958 Iraqi revolution and with Nasser's Egypt throughout the 1960s carried heavy ideological and ethnocentric undertones. Competing Arab and Iranian nationalist ideologies manifested in border disputes with Iraq and regional rivalries with Egypt brought these differences into sharper focus.

Almost inevitably, the question of Palestine and relations with Israel came to play a part in Arab-Iranian discord, and both countries came to view their tacit alliance as a natural defense against a common nemesis. What may be called the Arab-Iranian "cold war" in the 1960s, which continued in various ways into the 1970s, was largely waged by the states rather then by their citizens. Nevertheless, shared ethnic memories and cultural stereotypes rooted in the distant past reemerged on both sides with vehemence, helping to fuel new ideological and strategic tensions. The shah followed in his father's footsteps to promote a brand of Iranian cultural nationalism that held "Arabs" as the ultimate "Other." Closely tied to the narrative of glories of ancient Iran and the Pahlavi's revival of "modern Iran," portrayal of the "Arabs" as backward Bedouins hostile to "authentic" Iranian culture was firmly incorporated into popular Iranian nationalist narrative and generally accepted by majority of Iranians.

As a founding member of the United Nations in 1947, Iran had voted against the partition of Palestine and in favor of a federal system whereby both the rights of the Arab Palestinians and Jewish settlers were to be guaranteed. A year later Iran also voted against the creation of the Jewish state. Yet by 1950, during a volatile period of national politics, Iran offered Israel de facto recognition, largely as a result of the new Jewish state's efforts to win over non-Arab friends in the region. This was at a time when the newly born Israel still projected the image of a victimized small nation that was building a modern society in a hostile environment.

The Jewish Iranian community—one of the oldest in the world, with roots going back to biblical times—supported the initiative, having gradually adopted Zionism since the mid-twentieth century as a defining ideology and in hopes for a better future. A population exceeding one hundred thousand scattered throughout urban Iran. The Iranian Jews were economically impoverished and had long been exposed to bouts of persecution in the Safavid and Qajar eras. Instances of extortion by government agents and clerical authorities, the looting of Jewish neighborhoods, the abduction of young women, allegations of blood libel and other illicit acts, harassment and humiliation in public spaces, and forced conversion to Islam were not rare. Added to these were modern expressions of anti-Semitism in the interwar period, mostly sponsored by Nazi propaganda, that were rolled over into the postwar era. Yet the Pahlavi state and most secularized middle-class Iranians entertained a more favorable attitude toward the Jewish community than their counterparts in the neighboring Iraq or in other Arab countries in the region.

In the postconstitutional era and throughout the Pahlavi period, the economic condition of the Iranian Jews noticeably improved. Many earned higher economic status through education, business, and professional life, though glaring examples of abject poverty also persisted, especially in the depopulated

Jewish quarters in larger cities. A distinct accent—sometimes a remnant of Middle Persian dialects of Iran, strict adherence to rabbinic teachings, and a sense of cultural isolation imposed on the non-Muslims by the majority population—impeded assimilation. Zionism, an ideology foreign to most non-European Jews, was increasingly embraced by Iranian Jews as an alternative to social isolation or to national assimilation. In the early decades of the twentieth century, conversion, especially to the Baha'i faith, offered an accessible channel to religious and social modernity and in turn facilitated cultural assimilation. From the late nineteenth century a large number of Jews of Kashan, Shiraz, and elsewhere converted to the new faith—a non-traumatic break from the strictures of the old religion and from the segregated life of the ghetto. The Baha'i universalist perspective appealed to the Jews as fulfillment of their messianic prophecies.

Yet in contrast to conversion to the Baha'i faith, which meant even more discrimination and persecution in the Muslim environment, even in the Pahlavi era, Zionism promised empowerment by essentially transplanting the Jews, landing them in a Jewish homeland elsewhere, and giving them a new Jewish identity. Throughout the 1950s and early 1960s, hosts of underprivileged Iranian Jews immigrated to Israel and settled there, though many hopes for a brighter life were dashed in the face of harsher realities of life in the new Jewish state. The Ashkenazi elite in Israel looked upon the "Oriental Jews" as second-class citizens, and the notion of kibbutzim was alien to urban Iranian Jews. Some returned, but the majority stayed and eventually assimilated.

Yet in so far as the Iranian-Israeli relations were concerned, the Iranian Jewish community whether at home or in Israel played a negligible role. Several factors contributed to the growth of Iranian-Israeli diplomatic and economic relations. Most crucial was Iran's search for security in the face of its Arab adversaries. Iran's membership in the British- and American-sponsored 1955 Baghdad Pact along with Hashemite Iraq, Pakistan, and Turkey was a search for regional alliance not only against the presumed communist threat but also against the tide of Arab nationalism, and especially Nasser's pan-Arab ambitions. Egypt's gravitation toward the Soviet Union and Nasser's anti-Iran propaganda alarmed the shah and his government. During the 1956 Suez Crisis, although Iran officially condemned British, French, and Israeli aggression, it supported the canal's control by an international regime, a proposition doomed from the outset. The crisis, moreover, caused dormant pro-Palestinian sentiments to flare up among the Iranian public. In the aftermath of the 1953 coup in Iran, many dissidents in Iran, including Islamists, admired the Young Officers in Egypt and especially Nasser's anti-imperialist stance. For the shah, who once was married to Princess Fawzia, the sister of King Farouk (r. 1936–1952), the fall of monarchy in Egypt was treated with alarm.

Two years after the Suez Crisis, in 1958, the creation of the United Arab Republic through the union of Egypt and Syria—which later proved a dismal failure—at the time was seen by many outside the Arab world as a prelude to the greater dream of pan-Arabism, and so a potential threat for non-Arab leaders like the shah. The success of the Iraqi Revolution in the same year, with palpable pro-Nasserite sentiments, and the brutal execution of the Hashemite King Faisal II (r. 1939–1958), a personal friend of the shah, brought the message closer to home. The Algerian Revolution, in contrast, which gained momentum during 1958 against French colonial rule, also received positive coverage in the Iranian media and aroused sympathies among the Iranian population. The still-inchoate Islamic radical circles in Iran viewed the Algerian Islamists as an admirable model.

By the mid-1960s Israel's cultivation of friendly relations with Iran sharpened Nasser's attack on the Pahlavi regime. Through trade and development projects, as well as the sharing of regional intelligence and defense ties, Iran became a partner with Israel. The regular supply of Iranian oil to Israel starting in the late 1950s and expanding after 1967, and the joint investment in a pipeline through the port of Eilat on the Mediterranean, further consolidated bonds. The agro-industrial Qazvin Plain Development Project started in 1962 by an Israeli private firm was the largest undertaken by Israelis outside their own country. It covered two hundred villages around Qazvin, ninety-five miles northwest of Tehran, and aimed to introduce large-scale drip irrigation methods and conduct other agricultural experimentations.

As Egypt further gravitated toward the Soviets—especially after the Eisenhower administration's failure to collaborate on the Aswan High Dam project—Egypt's sensitivity toward Pahlavi Iran as an ally of the US and Israel substantially increased. The Cairo-based Sawt al-'Arab (Voice of the Arabs) radio, the mouthpiece of Nasser's regime, was quick to launch a sustained propaganda war against Iran once the shah admitted his country's ties with Israel in 1960, even though Israel's diplomatic mission to Iran remained semiclandestine and was never officially recognized. This led to a decade-long break in diplomatic relations between Iran and Egypt. In turn, the shah had no compunction over accusing Nasser of being an agent of Soviet imperialism and a flighty Pharaoh conspiring against his country, harboring Iranian terrorists, and stretching his long arm of Arab radicalism to the Persian Gulf.

Growing oil exports in the early 1960s from the Persian Gulf increased Iran's anxiety over the Egyptian and other radical Arab influences in the region. Britain's gradual disengagement as overlord of the former Trucial States—a confederacy of shaykhdoms on the southern shores of the Persian Gulf (now the United Arab Emirates and Qatar)—added to Iran's security concern. Once Kuwait, a British protectorate since 1899, gained independence in 1961, Nasser began to capitalize on his pan-Arab popularity to bring the newly liberated state under his wing. He viewed Kuwait a source of cheap oil for his energy needs and as a foothold for enhancing his anti-Iranian stance. Pan-Arabism, even after the collapse of the union with Syria, still carried enough ideological weight to make the shah deeply anxious about Nasser's ambitions, and this anxiety would become a lifetime fixation. Nasser's propaganda machine was hard at work renaming the Persian Gulf as the Arabian Gulf, a bogus nomenclature popularized in the face of undeniable historical evidence to the contrary. This was clearly in defiance of Iran's geopolitical interests. The British and American ambivalence toward Nasser, especially in the early 1960s, further agitated the shah. Nearly all Iranian oil exports were passing through the Strait of Hormuz; thus, the very financial security of the Pahlavi regime depended on keeping Nasser away from the Persian Gulf.

Dispute over the Persian Gulf's nomenclature also carried emotional undertones that went beyond the shah's detestation of Nasser and came to affect most Iranians. Since ancient times the term *Khalij-e Fars* (Persian Gulf) had applied to the body of water adjacent to the ancient province of Fars. Sinus Persicus in Greek geographical sources, and later Bahr al-Fars in Arabic texts, carried no ideological weight; they simply identified an association with the Persians who lived and navigated the gulf for more than two millennia. The shift to Arabian Gulf, however, first appeared in the mid 1940s among overzealous British popular commentators. The British were keeping the oil shaykhdoms acquiescent while also tapping to their massive oil fields. Hatred of Mosaddeq and the Iranian oil nationalization may also have played a part in the curious use of a term with no historical precedence.

At the other end of the political spectrum in the 1930s and 1940s, the activities of the Society of the Muslim Brothers in Egypt offered an influential model for Islamic militants in Iran, first for Fada'iyan-e Islam and later for the young clerics in Khomeini's circle. Sayyid 'Ali Khamenei, the future Supreme Leader of the Islamic Republic, was a great admirer of Sayyid Qutb (1906–1966), the radical theoretician of the Muslim Brothers, and had translated some of Qutb's works into Persian. Yet even in the years after the execution of Sayyid Qutb in 1966, despite his long incarceration by the Egyptian regime, the Iranian Islamist opposition praised Nasser's populism, his defiance of Western powers, and his anti-Pahlavi stance. Nasser's campaign, despite its periodic intensity,

Figure 11.2. The shah during the 1968 'umra pilgrimage
to Mecca performing the rite of sa'y (effort).
Mohammad Baqer Najafi, *Shahanshahi va Dindari* (Tehran: NRTV, 1355/1976), n.p.

nevertheless proved to have some positive impact on the shah's policies. There
was an extra urgency, for instance, to the Pahlavi regime's land distribution and
other reform measures throughout the 1960s, to compete with revolutionary
land reform in Egypt and Iraq.

Facing domestic and regional challenges, both secular and Islamic, it was
not unreasonable for the shah to display greater signs of religiosity. In 1968 he
made a well-publicized pilgrimage to Mecca, where he performed all the Hajj
rituals with great humility (fig. 11.2). A year later he attended a conference of the
Islamic heads of states in Rabat, where he played a crucial part in founding the
Organization of Islamic Cooperation (fig. 11.3).

BA'ATHIST IRAQ AND POLICING THE PERSIAN GULF

Greater ideological and territorial challenges were found closer to home in
neighboring Iraq. These started with the 1958 Iraqi Revolution and continued
for most of the volatile decade with military coups and political instability fol-

Figure 11.3. The 1969 meeting in Rabat of the heads of the Islamic states endorsing the charter of the Organization of the Islamic Cooperation. The shah stands next to the host, King Hasan II of Morocco, surrounded by other leaders, including King Faisal of Saudi Arabia, King Hussein of Jordan, and General Boumédiène of Algeria.
Mohammad Baqer Najafi, *Shahanshahi va Dindari* (Tehran: NRTV, 1355/1976), n.p.

lowing the fall of the Hashemite dynasty. After the 1967 coup that brought to power the Ba'ath Party (party of resurrection), the two countries engaged in border disputes almost continuously, especially over the shared waterway Shatt al-Arab (or Arvand Rud as the Iranians began to call it, remembering its historical Persian name). Intermittent frontier skirmishes along the Zagros mountain range stretching from Khuzestan to Kurdistan, propaganda wars over radio waves and in the press, and retaliatory actions further troubled Iraq's relations with Iran. The Shi'i population in southern Iraq and the Iraqi Kurds in the north badly suffered at the hands of the Ba'athist regime, which primarily drew support from the Sunni Arab population. For the most part, before the 1990s the West turned a blind eye to Ba'athist atrocities, primarily because of the vast Iraqi oil exports, which rivaled Iranian production, but also the lucrative military and economic contracts that Western firms had begun to secure in Iraq.

By 1971 with the rapid rise to power of Saddam Hussein (1937–2006) and his menacing grip over Iraqi state and society, confrontations with Iran took a turn for worse. The death in 1970 of Nasser, defeated and demoralized, offered President Saddam Hussein an opportunity to emerge as the new strongman of the Arab world. He championed the Palestinian cause, challenged conservative Arab regimes, and offered a bold match to the shah of Iran, at least for those on the international stage who were loath to see the shah as the unrivaled master of the Persian Gulf. Relying on Iraq's oil revenues, which multiplied after the 1973 oil crisis, and his pan-Arab politics, Saddam seemed to have been successful at tilting the balance in the historic rivalry between Cairo and Baghdad in favor of the latter, especially after President Anwar al-Sadat's 1975 expulsion of Soviet military advisers and his overtures of peace to Israel. The threat of Saddam's Iraq in turn persuaded the shah to move closer to the United States and purchase more arms for his sizable arsenal, whereas Iraq acquired almost client status with the Soviet Union, becoming its most important Arab ally after signing a treaty of friendship and cooperation in 1975.

Ba'athist hostility toward Iran was rooted in historical tensions that frequently flared up along the countries' common border. It was based on the assumption that since ancient times Iran had always entertained territorial ambitions over Iraq. The Sasanian Empire, named after a dynasty that originated in the Iranian plateau, had expanded its domains to Mesopotamia, where its capital, Ctesiphon, was located on the banks of the Tigris River. As breadbasket for an expansionist empire, Sasanian Mesopotamia was an ethno-cultural and religious melting pot whose indelible mark survived for centuries, even beyond the Islamic high caliphate. As the birthplace of Shi'ism, and home to the holiest Shi'i shrines and centers for Shi'i learning, it had additional appeal to Shi'i Iran. It was not mere coincidence that twice under the Safavids Baghdad was conquered by Shi'i Iran and afterward in the eighteenth and nineteenth centuries Iran made deep sorties into the Iraqi territory.

The border dispute between powers on two sides of the Zagros dated back centuries, perhaps one of the oldest in the history of the world. Iran's western border was the oldest natural boundary—perhaps the only one—in the whole of the Middle East, dividing the Mesopotamian lowlands from the Iranian plateau. In the highlands of Kurdistan, the population on both sides of the border maintained close cultural, tribal, and linguistic ties and preserved a degree of autonomy. With the rise of Turkish, Arab, and Iranian nationalisms, the Kurds also developed their own nationalist identity and since World War I intermittently dreamed of a united Kurdistan. Ethnic and linguistic differences with the Kurds of Turkey, moreover, made unification more elusive, if not untenable. Yet the Kurds on the Iranian side were somewhat more integrated, in part because of their ethno-linguistic affinity with Iran.

There were strong ethno-cultural underpinnings to the frontier tensions with Arabic Sunni Iraq, however. The young country of Iraq, charged with a sense of Arab pride and laying claim to the legacy of the Abbasid caliphate of Baghdad, as well as the ancient Babylonian civilization and the Assyrian Empire, had developed a brand of national identity under the Ba'athist regime that was existentially antagonistic to the realities of its own diverse population. It was at odds with its own Arab neighbors as well, let alone non-Arab Iran. The nation-building project of the British Mandate in the post–World War I era succeeded only nominally in integrating the ethnically and geographically diverse populations into a nation of shared values and shared destiny. Even less than Turkish and Iranian nationalism, Ba'athist Arabism hardly ever tried in earnest to integrate, or tolerate, other identities within its borders.

The autonomy-seeking movement of Iraqi Kurdistan was a source of deep anxiety to the Baghdad government and frequently the victim of its atrocities. It also was a source of hostility vis-à-vis Iran. Under the leadership of Mulla Mustafa Barzani (1903–1979), a veteran of the earlier short-lived Mahabad Republic of 1945–1946, the Iraqi Kurds from the late 1950s intermittently fought against Baghdad and negotiated with it in a bitter struggle for autonomy. With the hardening of the Ba'athist positions under Saddam Hussein, in 1974 a major Kurdish revolt brought the Iraqi government head-to-head with the Iranians who had supplied arms and provisions to the Kurds over the years and later sheltered as many as two hundred thousand refugees and Peshmerga guerrilla fighters in border camps and in the Iranian interior.

The Iranian support for the Kurdish revolt was primarily political—over the years Pahlavi Iran had adamantly resisted similar autonomy-seeking aspirations, even cultural ones, among its own Kurds. The shah's action was part of a broader pattern of retaliation against the Iraqi regime that, at least since 1968, had dampened relations between the two countries. Saddam's hostile move against its Shi'i population—especially against a community of Iranian descent who had long resided in the Shi'i holy cities of Iraq as early as the thirteenth century. Between 1968 and 1974 the Iraqi government drove out more than sixty thousand people of Iranian descent and dumped them on the Iranian side of the border. The arrival of these returnees injured Iranian sentiments and brought the conflict with Iraq to a boil.

Iran had maintained a religious, political, and cultural presence in the Iraqi south for at least five centuries. At least since the thirteenth-century Ilkhanid period, Iran had laid a moral claim over the Shi'i shrines of Karbala and Najaf and drew on the loyalties of the Iraqi Shi'is in the south. Nearly all the Shi'i shrines and other religious sites had been built, restored, and funded by Persian rulers and dignitaries, and there were extensive pious endowments devoted to the upkeep of these shrines. The steady stream of Iranian pilgrims was a major contributor to the Iraqi economy of the south, and most religious seminaries were populated by Iranian teachers and students, with a vast network of custodians and other beneficiaries of the mojtaheds' distribution of alms and other religious funds. Many of the cemeteries of Najaf and Karbala, and whatever space was left in and around the Shiʻi shrines in these cities, were filled with bodies of pious Iranians who were brought to southern Iraq as late as the twentieth century. Vast sums of alms and other religious dues were also donated by the Iranian faithful to the coffers of the Shiʻi *marjaʻs* in Najaf. Saddam's regime despised the Iranian Shiʻi connection and found it against its project of Arab homogenization. Typical of any dictatorial regime with a constructed identity, Saddam determined to wipe out the Persian malady.

The arrival of the Kurdish refugees and the Shiʻi returnees coincided with heightened border clashes, which had taken place on and off along the common border since 1968. These were in part because of demarcation disputes that stemmed from numerous border commissions since the middle of the nineteenth century. Iran was dissatisfied with the 1937 Saʻdabad nonaggression treaty involving Iran, Iraq, Turkey, and Afghanistan concluded under the aegis of the British. The treaty assigned to landlocked Iraq full control over the Shatt al-Arab waterway, so as to offer a reliable outlet for its oil exports and access to the open seas via the port of Basra. Insisting on its historic rights, however, in 1969 Iran declared the treaty null and void on the grounds that it was a British colonial legacy that deprived Iran's free shipping along the waterway to the Persian Gulf. Access to the port of Khorramshahr, Iran's most important commercial entrepôt, and further south to Abadan, the site of Iran's most extensive refinery, was at stake. What Iran demanded was a shared control of the waterway and full shipping rights along its maiden baseline. From the Iraqi perspective, this was a breach of its sovereignty; from the Iranian perspective, it was a restoration of its territorial rights under international law.

The Baʻathist narrative embraced by the Iraqis viewed the Iranian claim as a repeat of the old Persian hegemony and an ominous sign of the shah's growing ambitions. Iraq's repeated sorties against Iranian border guards were disruptive, though not wholly effective. By 1974 the Baʻathist regime, clearly on the defensive, was anxious to reach some face-saving settlement with Iran. Mindful of internal dissent among the Kurds in the north and the Shiʻis in the south, as well as in his own Baʻathist ranks, Saddam became uncharacteristically conciliatory toward his neighbors. Following a meeting between the shah and Saddam arranged by the Algerian president in March 1975, during the annual meeting of OPEC leaders in Algiers, the two sides signed a preliminary agreement addressing three crucial issues in dispute. The Algiers Accord, as it came to be known, served as the basis for bilateral treaties later that year, calling for the delineation of common boundaries based on the 1913 Constantinople Protocol; delimitation of the water boundaries of Shatt al-Arab/Arvand Rud, based on the thalweg line; and joint monitoring of the boundaries to guarantee the security of both sides.

The remarkable concessions ceded by Saddam were a clear victory for the shah in his long and acrimonious dealings with Iraq and a new zenith in his Persian Gulf policy. Yet the concessions came at a dear cost to the Kurdish rebels, who, having heavily relied on Iranian support against Baghdad, viewed the agreement as a betrayal of their cause. Mustafa Barzani, who had taken refuge in Iran and as a guest of the Iranian government was housed, along with his top commanders, outside Tehran, remained there until his death in 1979. Ironically, in 1946 he was driven out of Mahabad by the Iranian government and treated ever after as a persona non grata. Most refugees returned to Iraqi Kurdistan having been assured by Baghdad of amnesty and guaranteed safe passage. Unaware of the tragic fate that awaited them, and the hundreds of thousands of their fellow Kurdish citizens in the towns and villages of Kurdistan, they succumbed to the abrupt end to the Iraq-Iran conflict—at least for the time being.

The successful settlement of the conflict with Iraq, though ephemeral, boosted Iran's involvement in the Persian Gulf beyond anything it had experienced at least since the heyday of Shah 'Abbas I in the early seventeenth century. Already the occupation in November 1971 of three small and largely uninhabited but strategically important islands in the middle of the Persian Gulf—and in the wake of British withdrawal—raised angry protests from the newly established United Arab Emirates and other neighbors. The Arab world viewed the annexation as a breach of UAE sovereignty, and Iran considered the occupation merely the reassertion of its inalienable territorial rights. Coming in the wake of Bahrain's independence, which was declared after Iran, under British pressure, gave up its historical claims to the island—Iranian annexation of the three islands seemed almost inevitable.

As early as Sasanian times, Iran claimed sovereignty over Bahrain and its environs, which continued intermittently through the Islamic medieval period. In the early Safavid era, Isma'il's ambition to recapture the island from a local Arab shaykhdom was frustrated by the arrival of the Portuguese, who in 1521 established their strategic base at the head of the Persian Gulf. It was another seventy years before Shah 'Abbas I could expel the Portuguese, in 1602, and establish Shi'i rule on the island as part of its supremacy over the Persian Gulf shores, in competition with Ottoman control of Basra at the head of the gulf. Persian suzerainty, often through local dynasties, lasted for two centuries. Only British naval supremacy over the Persian Gulf from the beginning of the nineteenth century, along with its long-standing colonial policy that often backed regional enclaves vis-à-vis the Iranian center, allowed the shaykhs of Al-e Khalifa, a minor clan from Kuwait, to thrive in Bahrain under the British colonial gaze. Repeated protests by the emasculated Qajar state throughout the nineteenth century were dismissed. As an important naval base and hub of local trade, Bahrain, like nearby Qatar and Kuwait, was a British protectorate conforming to the so-called Trucial States. It was important not only for its bustling trade conducted by a cosmopolitan trade community but also for combating piracy at the head of the Persian Gulf and along its southern coasts, as well as deterring the Omani and Wahhabi threats. Oil exploration from the 1930s only offered further incentives for continued British colonial protection.

Already in 1970 the United Nations had held a plebiscite that established the Bahraini desire for independence. The eventual settling of the Bahrain question obliged Iran to renounce its claim of sovereignty over the island. A fair amount of nationalist uproar at home for what was viewed as bowing to British pressure persuaded the shah to remain adamant about the Iranian claim to the three islands in the middle of the Persian Gulf, despite vehement objections by UAE members and other Arab states. Iran's geopolitical ambitions beyond the Persian Gulf and into the Arabian Sea (and Gulf of Oman) and Indian Ocean, further agitated radical Arab regimes from Libya to South Yemen.

Beginning in 1973, Iranian military involvement on behalf of the Sultanate of Oman in a war waged against the Popular Front for the Liberation of the Occupied Arabian Gulf, a communist South Yemen–backed guerilla movement in the Dhofar region, on the eastern coast of the Arabian Peninsula, revealed the shah's anxiety over communist penetration of the region. Inheriting a conflict from British times, a small battalion of Iranian special forces backed by the Iranian air force fought a costly war with the Omani troops. The rebellion was crushed by 1975.

Border disputes with Iraq, the war of words with Nasser, annexation of the three islands, and the Dhofar intervention did not seriously dent the shah's overall success in his regional policy throughout the 1960s and early 1970s. Aiming for friendship with moderate Arab regimes, he befriended King Hussein of Jordan (r. 1952–1999), who often was a recipient of the shah's largesse and moral support against the king's many enemies. Anwar al-Sadat (1918–1981), whom the shah fully backed and advised throughout the Egyptian-Israeli peace process, was another important friend. Both the Lebanese Shi'i and the Maronite leaders were his tactical allies, including Musa Sadr (1928–1978?), the Iranian-born leader of the Shi'i Amal Movement in Lebanon. On Iran's eastern borders, Pakistan, under Zulfiqar 'Ali Bhutto (1928–1979), relied heavily on Iran's economic aid, moral support, and diplomatic backing, as did Mohammad Daoud Khan (1909–1978), the first president of Afghanistan, after he deposed Mohammad Zahir Shah (r. 1933–1973) in a bloodless coup in 1973. Daoud benefited from Iranian aid to counter the growing Soviet influence in his country, as did the deposed Mohammad Zahir in exile. Daoud also appealed to Iran to settle border disputes with Pakistan, a reflection of the shah's rising regional stance.

By the mid-1970s the shah had been able to carve out a strategic niche in the midst of a superpower divide on which the stability of the Persian Gulf and neighboring countries depended. Contrary to the conventional narrative articulated by his domestic and Western critics, and despite his many blind spots, the shah came to be seen by the two superpowers and by European powers as an experienced statesman and a crucial ally who built up a popular base at home, carried out domestic reforms, averted conservative opposition, thwarted his radical Arab neighbors, and worked toward stability and peace in the region.

From the shah's perspective, his compliance with US foreign policy objectives not only was inevitable, given his country's perilous geopolitics, but also was beneficial to Iran's stability and prosperity. Though always anxious to prove his loyalty to the West, he was skillful in appeasing his Soviet neighbor, too, often to his advantage. It could be argued that the shah's latter years were the most stable in Iran's foreign policy, considering Iran's fateful geopolitics since the turn of the nineteenth century. In retrospect the shah's stabilizing effect may be gauged by the aftershocks that the region witnessed after the collapse of the Pahlavi order and the revolution of 1979: Soviet invasion of Afghanistan, destabilization of Pakistani politics, the rise of Saddam Hussein and the Ba'athists as a regional menace, the emergence of Saudi Arabia as a petroleum empire, and subsequent Wahhabi-Salafi militancy.

EVOLVING IMAGE OF THE UNITED STATES

By the mid-1970s repression at home and shortfalls in economic spheres cast a long shadow over the Pahlavi state, beyond even the reality—an image further blemished by perceptions of compliance with Western interests. The United States, in particular, came to be seen by the Iranian public—even beyond a cluster of liberal and leftist trends and clerical dissidents—as a selfish superpower that exploited Iran's natural resources, kept the shah in power, and perpetuated repression. The bourgeoning anti-Americanism of the 1940s and

1950s was later internalized by a wide spectrum of Iranian dissenters. The image of the United States as a hegemonic superpower was further blemished during the Vietnam War, which received extensive coverage in the Iranian press. That the massive US armed forces were relentlessly carpet-bombing and dropping napalm and Agent Orange on the Vietcong struck average Iranians—as average people elsewhere around the world—as brutal and unfair. Sympathy for the suffering Vietnamese often meant hatred for the Yankee aggressor.

Before President Jimmy Carter's human rights policy in 1977 raised implicit concerns over the Iranian situation, US administrations had barely made any visible public criticism of the shah's conduct. Nor did any major voice within the US intelligence community, to the extent that is known, or other circles close to Washington, seriously assess the consequences of his arbitrary rule. His stronghold over Iranian society was taken for granted by American statesmen, with a mix of condescension and forced respectability. It was not unlike nineteenth-century colonial administrators' honoring of local chiefs' tyrannical hold over their tribe. When there was criticism, it often concerned Iran's economic performance and drawbacks to its development, often with an eye toward US vested interests or anxieties over the fate of private American investments.

Such negative perceptions slowly submerged the memory of the contributions made over the years by the US government and its citizens. Iranians of the 1970s could barely recall, if at all, America's contribution to Iran's modern education, agriculture, urban improvement, and heath. Ever since the nineteenth century, through the establishment of missionary schools for boys and girls, Americans had helped train a generation of the Iranian elite. Even after these schools were appropriated in the Reza Shah era, along with other missionary or community-run schools, they continued to produce generations of educated Iranians in such institutions as Alborz High School, originally a Presbyterian liberal arts college that expanded under the dedicated leadership of Samuel Jordan in the 1920s and 1930s, and the Nurbakhsh School for Girls (later Reza Shah Kabir), the earliest in Iran. As early as 1835 the first American Presbyterian physicians arrived in Orumiyeh, and later in the nineteenth century, American hospitals in Tabriz, Tehran, and elsewhere introduced new advances in the treatment of endemic maladies. The first female physician practicing in Iran in the late nineteenth century was an American missionary.

The US Point Four Program, initiated in 1949 to aid countries like Iran, also proved crucial for development projects in the early 1950s. These included new rural schools, improved agricultural and animal husbandry methods, irrigation techniques and seed improvement, rural health clinics, and urban amenities such as a water treatment master plan for Tehran and water delivery systems. In collaboration with the Iranian Water Authority, which had been active since 1942, the Point Four Program helped install Tehran's water treatment plant and complete the urban clean water distribution network, a major improvement in health and sanitation for the Iranian capital. American technical and financial support further had contributed to the construction of the Karaj Dam (later Amir Kabir), the first modern dam project undertaken in Iran. Completed in 1961 northwest of the capital, it proved a crucial water source for water-deficient Tehran.

In the area of culture, perhaps no American initiative was as influential as Franklin Publication House, a conduit for the translation and publication of important works of American literature, academic texts, and inexpensive paperback publications that in due course became a model for other Iranian publishers. In the post-1953 era, Franklin Publishing House (financed by the nonprofit Franklin Publications of New York) aimed to nurture a liberal cultural climate. It attracted Iranian talent, often intellectuals disillusioned with the left or unemployed because of past Tudeh and other political affinities on the left. Franklin gave them a chance to translate, edit, and produce in an environment relatively free of state intrusion scores of new titles, often in collaboration with Iranian publishers or through Franklin's own subsidiary. Among other American authors Herman Melville, Jack London, Ernest Hemingway, and John Steinbeck were introduced to a Persian readership. Franklin also collaborated with the Iranian government to produce school textbooks and a series of supplementary textbooks for universities that used new pedagogical methods in a format superior to the authority-oriented, tedious texts that had been produced by the Ministry of Education since the early decades of the century.

Also influential for cultivating a favorable picture of the United States as supporter of art and culture was the Iran-America Society and its cultural centers. First established in the 1950s in the United States as a quasi-governmental institution—and up to the eve of the 1979 revolution—the society's cultural centers in Tehran, Isfahan, Shiraz, and Mashhad offered courses in English language, maintained lending libraries, and published books and journals. They also served as forums for cultural activities: art exhibitions, film series, avant-garde plays, storytelling, musical concerts, and poetry readings by dissident poets. For many Iranian intellectuals and university students tired of cheap entertainment and monotony of government-controlled media, the centers were refreshing venues relatively free of state surveillance. With a larger budget and better facilities, including an impressive cultural center in Tehran, the Iran America Society successfully competed with other foreign cultural institutions active in Iran during the 1960s and 1970s. Besides the American cultural centers, the British Council, the French Institutes, the Soviet-Iranian Friendship Society, the German Goethe Institute, and the Iranian-Italian Cultural Society also served as forums for intellectual dissent, such as the left-leaning Iranian poets and writers.

Ever since the creation of the US Peace Corps in 1961, Iran ranked among the first countries to be enlisted for an educational mission. Between 1962 and 1976, some 1,748 male and female American volunteers served in towns and villages of Iran at all levels ranging from village schools to universities teaching English and sciences. Many Iranians who came into contact with Peace Corps volunteers, attended their classes, or took part in other instructional activities, were impressed by the US humanitarian mission and its commitment to improving the lot of many underprivileged communities in Iran and elsewhere. For volunteers, too, working with ordinary young Iranians in smaller towns and villages was a valuable experience, which many cherished and developed great attachment to it. It is likely that Iran's Literacy Corps, first established in 1963 as an important part of the shah's White Revolution, was inspired by the positive experience with the American Peace Corps volunteers.

Yet aside from the favorable ambiance created by the US cultural and educational commitments, the closer US association with Iranian security and military exposed ordinary Iranians to another aspect of American presence. By the mid-1970s there were tens of thousands of Americans working in Iran, including in substantial number in the service of the government as military advisers, contractors, technicians, and skilled labor. Some were former military personnel of the post-Vietnam era who, in pursuit of handsomely paid jobs, moved to Iran. They were attracted to the country's bourgeoning military industry, such as the US-franchised Bell Helicopter plant in Isfahan operational by 1975. Others were employees of big corporations involved in large-scale construction, oil, communication, and technology projects. As far as the Pahlavi state was concerned, the American and European pool of expertise was a natural resource with which Iran could address the shortages in the skilled and technical labor during the boom years of the Iranian economy.

A majority of these military personnel and civilians serving in Iran were employed at far higher salaries than their Iranian counterparts who had mastered comparable skills and had similar experience. In turn, they enjoyed a standard of living higher than their Iranians counterparts. The economic disparity became a source of disgruntlement, soon to be compounded by notions of Americans' cultural insensitivities. Instances of Americans' condescending attitude toward Iranians in the workplace and in the street were amplified beyond proportion. Examples of rowdy, heavy-drinking, unrestrained young American

men in particular publicized the imprudent Yankee stereotype in such traditional settings as in the city of Isfahan.

Even less complimentary for average Iranians was the mere perception of the
American military and security personnel as training, supplying, and monitoring the Iranian security forces and supervising the Savak. In a society devoid of
free and diverse media, rumors and anecdotes, mostly unsubstantiated, went a
long way toward confirming negative perceptions of the United States. They
brought out xenophobic feelings embedded in Iran's recent history while most
Iranians were welcoming Americans (and other foreign nationals) with warmth
and hospitality. The image of the innocent American abroad nevertheless was
seriously compromised. Predictably, Iranians began to perceive two faces of
America, almost independent of each other: a benevolent America and a superpower America. The first was the one to which Iranians dispatched their children in increasing numbers for higher education, purchased US manufactured
goods such as cars and home appliances, watched Hollywood movies and other
cultural productions, and admired technological and scientific advances such
as the US space program. The ugly America, in contrast, conspired and staged
coups against legitimate governments abroad, fought hegemonic wars, and supported unpopular leaders in power through financial aid and military support.
The two faces persisted even after the rhetoric of the Great Satan became part
and parcel of the Islamic Revolution.

INSTRUMENTS OF CONTROL: SAVAK AND RASTAKHIZ

As the shah's international standing grew, he was exposed to greater criticism
for his human rights record and repression at home. With Iran's greater wealth
and power, especially after 1973, came a greater exercise of arbitrary rule and
royal self-indulgence. Complacency and a disconnection from the realities of
Iranian society slowly eroded the foundations of the Pahlavi order. The shah's
all-embracing royal power began to be hollowed, first and foremost, because of
his aversion to meaningful modes of pluralism and public participation. The
memories of the pre-1953 years seem to have convinced him, as he declared
even in public, that in Iran democracy could generate only discord and chaos.
His resolve, his vision, and his people's loyalty and compliance, he insisted,
were viable assets for Iran's progress toward "Great Civilization." Such a vision,
if it was to be believed, served as a potent excuse for applying all means of political control, without respect for contesting views that challenged his positivist
vision and the arbitrary means of materialize it.

By the middle of the 1960s, a few years after the June 1963 uprising, the Pahlavi regime had managed to dismantle nearly all semblance of independent political organization. The second National Front was quickly demolished and its leaders detained before being allowed to return to their nonpolitical careers. The Islamist Nahzat-e Azadi (Freedom Movement) had no better luck. An offshoot of the second National Front founded in 1961, it was led by Mahdi Bazargan (1907–1995), a professor of thermodynamics at Tehran University. Though it remained active for a number of years and recruited from among Islamically "committed" professionals, especially engineers, it was barred from any public engagement.

The remnant of the Niru-ye Sevvom (the third force), a small coalition of independent socialists all but disappeared. In March 1966 Khalil Maleki (1903–1969), a professor of chemistry and a theoretician of the independent left who presided over the party, was put on trial in a military tribunal and convicted to serve three years' imprisonment on preposterous charges. The regime also silenced virtually all independent voices of dissent, including the intellectual left, most of the activist clergy, and university students. Accommodating Maleki and his trait of socialist thought probably was the best chance the regime would have had to stop the frustrated younger generation drifting toward the radical left.

By the early 1970s, the shah's intolerance extended even to those loyal to him who dared to uphold even moderately diverse views to his lofty dreams. Since the 1965 ouster of Teymur Bakhtiar, the powerful military governor of Tehran in the post-1953 era and the first director of the Savak, until 1963, who entertained his own political ambitions, the shah seldom allowed any official with independent standing, military or civilian, to emerge on the national stage. Holding views contrary to the official narrative of the White Revolution or benign criticism of the state's economic policies and development plans was subject to censorship. More than the shah's actual distaste for genuine criticism was fear of the consequences, which helped nurture a climate of mediocrity and distrust. Shows of subservience were routinely staged to convince the public of the shah's unquestionable power (fig. 11.4). Yet beneath the tedium of monolithic technocracy and sycophantic praise was a reservoir of cynicism that could slip through only in private conversations and political jokes in intimate circles.

With the Savak under the shah's direct control, and headed since 1965 by his loyal henchman General Ne'matollah Nasiri, a man of little education or political wit, what was meant to be the government's security and intelligence apparatus for the most part became a vast, network of control and coercion, arrests and torture, spying on all critics of the regime or presumed suspects, excessive surveillance, and secret files. Far more than its actual capabilities, not

Figure 11.4. Clergy paying homage to the shah during the 1971 feast of Mab'ath.
Mohammad Baqer Najafi, *Shahanshahi va Dindari* (Tehran: NRTV, 1355/1976), n.p.

to mention its official mission, Savak operated on perceptions of terror, of the ability to infiltrate dissident circles, and of horrifying interrogation methods and torture cells.

Presenting a public face, Parviz Sabeti, known as the "security official" (*maqam amniyati*), Savak aimed to win over the Iranian public with a demonstration of its agility and intelligence skills. At stake was a proud demonstration of success in a covert war against the remnant of the Tudeh and followers of the recently emerged young Marxists and Islamist organizations, or indeed any other dissident. The television broadcasts in the late 1960s and early 1970s, mocked by the public as the "Savak Show," only added to the rampant cynicism and fear of the organization's long arm of intrusion and terror. Contrary to Nasiri's image of a rough and ready general insensitive to realities of the Iranian society, Sabeti, the deputy director for intelligence, wished to portray himself as a reforming professional. Even if this were the case, a dubious proposition, Savak's image hardly ever softened.

By the mid-1970s Savak had a staff of five thousand and a budget of $100 million, and it was regarded as among the most efficient organizations in the country. Its staff consisted of aged army officers, civilians with a blind sense of obedience, and a large number of field officers, intelligence specialists, and interrogators (in most cases a euphemism for torturers). The organization also maintained an extensive network of informants, moles, and minders in all ministries, government organizations, universities, radio and television organizations, presses and publications, large to midsize factories and businesses, labor and guild organizations, among the clergy, in intellectual gatherings, in the bazaar, and in all other public and private institutions and workplaces of any significance. Savak informers had infiltrated guerrilla organizations and clandestine political events, mosques and religious gatherings, Iranian delegations abroad, dissident student organizations in Europe and the United States, and foreign embassies in Iran and Iranian embassies abroad.

With ties to and regular arrangements for exchanges of intelligence with the CIA and other American intelligence agencies, the British MI5, and the Israeli Mossad, Savak appeared well equipped, well informed, and fully in charge. Having been barred by the shah from foreign intelligence gathering, it primarily focused on domestic security rather than international espionage. Instilling awe even among the top echelons of the Pahlavi state, it vetted government appointments, even relatively minor posts, and kept extensive files, going back to the prewar era, not only on dissidents and those critical of the state, including former Tudeh supporters, liberal nationalists, clergy, religious activists, and intellectuals, but also on all those who had repented and returned to the Pahlavi fold. The organization used its information and interrogative resources, as well as its reputation for efficiency and brutality, to leverage its control over the society and the state.

Savak nevertheless suffered from disastrous flaws. Following directives of its master, it was suspicious of any initiative independent of the shah, and it was an agency devoted to silencing not only Marxist guerrillas and other activists on the left, but anyone who publically criticized government policies and the regime's corruption and failures, or the conduct of the shah and royal family. It did so more through an impression of omnipresence than interrogation and detention. Moreover, even those who were considered the brains behind Savak suffered from myopia and misperceptions. Savak was as paranoid as the shah and his top statesmen, subscribing to conspiratorial theories involving imagined foreign hands, superpowers, and former superpowers in Iran's domestic troubles, ranging from guerrilla movements to provisions shortages and economic gridlock.

Even among ministers and top civil servants Savak suspected foreign moles and sympathizers, oddly enough more British and American than Soviet. The

Savak shared this paranoid perspective with the shah and most members of the Pahlavi elite. Bureaucratic and inflexible, Savak proved utterly incapable of detecting the root causes of radical challenges and growing popular discontent. It also proved inept in forecasting the 1979 revolution, and when it arrived, its ability to handle it was miserably paralyzed. For its entire history Savak was more in the business of coercion and abuse than inquiry and analysis. In many respects it lived and died by the failings of its royal master.

The dismantling of even moderate voices of dissent was followed by a reckless attempt to manufacture an all-embracing political party. By the mid-1970s the semblance of a two-party scheme was no longer viable even by the shah. In 1964 the Iran Novin Party headed by a younger generation of mostly upper-class technocrats under Hasan-'Ali Mansur, and after his assassination under Amir 'Abbas Hovayda, tried to steer a moderately independent course but was quickly persuaded to comply with royal wishes. Despite maintaining a parliamentary caucus and occasionally engaging in heated discord with the Mardom Party, both parties seldom were seen as anything but incredulous outfits designed to lend the image of constitutionality to the royal autocracy.

Added to the failure of the two-party model, the country's mounting problems of inefficiency, nepotism, and corruption persuaded the shah to opt for a one-party political model, and with a hasty arbitrariness reminiscent of Naser al-Din Shah and his frequent government restructuring. There was no public debate and few devised plans. Motivated by the Soviet and Chinese models perhaps, or the Ba'ath Party in neighboring Iraq, the royal decision in March 1975 to launch the Rastakhiz Party was a turning point in the shah's desire to engage his people at a deeper level. Inherently autocratic, the party was hailed by the regime's propaganda machine as the magic solution to political bickering, going beyond the politics of the elite, and a way to mobilize ordinary Iranians over common goals of the "Revolution of the Shah and the People." As a monopoly over the political process, Rastakhiz aimed, ominously, to include all Iranians among its membership.

To the extent that any program was articulated for the new party, it was to encourage popular participation in the affairs of their community and their workplace. Political engagement, however, was carefully avoided and everyone—leaders and the rank and file—understood from the outset that serious political discourse was not in the agenda. Party participation aimed to generate new dynamics to combat deficiencies and economic shortfalls and to open new channels for social and economic development. Anyone who refused to join the party, declared the shah in a remarkably blunt statement, evidently was not a patriot and might as well resign his or her citizenship and leave the country for permanent exile. The mandatory party membership was a prelude to harsher measures to come: overhaul of the social order, education, labor relations, bureaucracy, and economy.

Yet compromises quickly unmade the Rastakhiz Party's lofty goals. In a fashion befitting any autocratic regime incapable of reforming itself, the two wings of the party, the "Progressive" and "Constructive Liberal," were led by two of the most faithful technocrats of the regime. They were powerful ministers in Hovayda's government and long had enjoyed regime favors and all the privileges of the Pahlavi elite. Despite their predictable professional credentials, as it turned out they were devoid of any vision or program, much less a mission. It soon became clear that so far as the hierarchy of power was concerned, it was business as usual. The shah and his advisers, if the best of intentions were to be attributed to them, were naive to believe that most Iranians—teachers, workers, villagers, bazaar merchants, students, low- and middle-ranking civil servants, and homemakers (not to mention intellectuals and skeptics)—would genuinely believe in such lackluster gimmickry. The lofty slogans routinely spewed from state-controlled media and the vast financial resources at the party's disposal resulted in superficial extensive grassroots mobilization in the villages, factories, neighborhoods, schools, and government offices and for a moment created some stir.

The Rastakhiz solution to glaring lack of democratic process, however, soon began to unravel. Even the most ardent supporters of the regime quickly turned into skeptics. By 1977, only two years after it was first launched, the party's performance appeared dismal even to the shah, who tried to reshuffle the top leadership so as avoid a political fiasco. The new party leaders, also picked from the small reserves of Pahlavi male elite, were no more imaginative or effective in the task of building a reliable popular base while Iranian society was fast rushing toward full-scale revolution. A year later the last-ditch effort to reinvent Rastakhiz also failed, even as the shah tried under public pressure to liberalize the party. Under the weight of popular protests, the Rastakhiz Party was the first of the Pahlavi enterprises to crumble. Unrelenting in adulation for the shah and lacking a political spine, it never offered a forum for critically examining the many urgent defects of the regime, let alone providing a genuine vehicle for public participation.

INFLATION AND PRICE CONTROL

Coinciding with the years of Rastakhiz Party, and as part of its populist plan of action, the government started a campaign to "stabilize prices," an initiative to harness raging inflation. It intended to remedy the problem primarily by fixing consumer prices at the retail level, a measure resembling the Persian proverbial punishment of the neighborhood backers for the rising wheat prices. The campaign resulted in a wave of business closures, massive penalties, state takeover of private industries, and detention of industrialists and wholesalers for alleged hoarding and price hiking. The high inflation, by some accounts nearly 25 percent annually by the late 1970s, was triggered mainly by the undue injection of oil income into the Iranian economy. With all the new revenue entering the economy, the government, too, was persuaded to go on a shopping spree of unprecedented scale: new development projects, massive imports, military hardware, high-level services, and a whole range of investments in cities. Rapid growth of the construction industry and a subsequent shortage of skilled and unskilled labor force would soon follow. Symptoms such as these were to be expected in most, if not all, developing economies. Less common, however, and probably avoidable, were the remedies adopted by the Pahlavi state.

Undermining domestic markets, the newly earned revenue favored importers but worked against other sectors of the economy, especially manufacturers and their suppliers. Rising prices, moreover, concerned the regime because they exposed weaknesses in planning and policy making, where the public had little say in the direction of the market or in economic decision making. To remedy the situation, however artificially, the state effectively retaliated against the industrial and retail sectors, the backbone of its consumer economy. Some manufacturers were forced to lower quality to stay within price ranges, while others lowered volume, causing shortages of vital consumer goods and agricultural products, hence creating new incentives for foreign imports and hoarding.

With the growth of the population and the rise in the standard of living, demand for food and consumer goods noticeably went up. As early as the mid-1960s, because of urban migration, an unintended consequence of the land reform, Iran's agricultural output could not keep up with growing demand. Beginning in the early 1970s, Iran, having long relied on its own domestic production, became a net food importer, bringing in products ranging from meat from New Zealand and Australia to grains, sugar, and dairy products from Europe, Russia, Canada, and the United States. Since the beginning of the Pahlavi era, moreover, the Iranian population had improved in every generation physically, hygienically and medically, from the frail, malnourished, and diseased population at the turn of the twentieth century—visible in many photographs of the period—to a relatively healthy, sanitary, and better-nourished people in the last quarter of the century. The need for greater quantities and greater varieties of food, home appliances, electronics, and cars thus was bound to become a burden for a government anxious to keep its population economically content.

Particularly striking were shortages in utilities—especially electricity—and agricultural produce, an embarrassment to the state's projected image of power and prosperity. The hollow promises smacked of a shortage of essentials, from onions, potatoes, and rice to propane gas. These were compounded by arbitrary restrictions on urban zoning and a construction moratorium. Traffic congestion in Tehran and other provincial centers, compounded by air pollution, only added to discontent among a public not yet fully accustomed to economic bottlenecks.

The state's anticorruption campaigns, periodically making the headlines, had limited effect. Embezzlement, nepotism, and illicit deals were not rare. The state had neither the serious desire to stop nor the means of stopping the corrupt practices in which many of its own ministers, high officials, and members of the royal family had a stake. In October 1975 a series of corruption trials put behind bars a few generals and high-ranking officials for taking illicit commissions for the purchase of arms abroad, commissions that seemingly had been approved, at least in the eyes of ordinary people, by the shah and the government. In February 1976 another scandal concerning the $28 million purchase of F-14 fighter jets from the US corporation Grumman also resulted in dismissals and imprisonments. A purchase of $40 million of sugar on the open market, also in 1976, resulted in the conviction and imprisonment of officials. In their trials the defendants argued that in such deals they were aided by high officials whose names and positions they could not reveal. Yet in the booming economy of the 1970s the temptations to make a quick fortune were too great and the restraints too relaxed to allow any widespread anticorruption campaign to take root.

URBAN GUERRILLAS AND THE LURE OF ARMED STRUGGLE

In the absence of viable alternatives to secular dissent, and with Pahlavi absolutism firmly in place, the rise of guerrilla movements in Iran in the late 1960s appeared to many younger dissidents an alluring alternative. With party politics long dismantled, except for the sham Rastakhiz Party, the liberal nationalist veterans and moderate socialists were silenced or voluntarily went into exile. With them went the once-appealing call to restore the constitutional monarchy. In the absence of the Tudeh Party, which had once been a grassroots political organization, the hard-line alternatives were narrowed down to two: Islamic militants, who advanced a double message of anti-Pahlavi and antisecular opposition, and guerrilla armed struggle to overthrow the Pahlavi regime. While the former essentially appealed to the mosque-going lower-middle classes in the bazaar and poorer neighborhoods, the latter recruited from the younger middle classes, mostly university students. Marxist insurgency appealed to children of families with Tudeh or other leftist tendencies. Islamist ideology, such as that of the Mojahedin-e Khalq, however, attracted the children of pious families. Their numbers were small but their impact tangible.

Predictably, guerrilla struggle in Iran came about in the 1960s when Marxist-inspired movements abounded around the world. The radical left everywhere fell captive to the aura of such revolutionaries as Fidel Castro and his comrades-in-arms in the 1959 Cuban Revolution. As elsewhere, in Iran, too, the bearded image of the handsome and charismatic Che Guevara (before being commercialized on posters and T-shirts) greatly appealed to the left. In the Vietnam War years, the Vietcong's unyielding resistance against the Americans also struck chords of sympathy among the Iranians. These replaced the steely image of the mustachioed Comrade Stalin who had long fascinated Tudeh members and sympathizers. The equally steely image of Mao Zedong survived in the Iranian revolutionary pantheon even after the crimes of the Cultural Revolution became better known. Moreover, the left was moved by the intensity of the Palestinian struggle and its revolutionary voice during the heydays of the Palestinian Liberation Organization. It was seen by many as the closest, and the most pertinent, cause in the face of Pahlavi rapprochement with Israel. The rise of the new European left, manifest in the 1968 Paris uprising, was another source of inspiration. The Algerian independence movement also served as shining example. The Iranian guerrilla organizations viewed themselves as one such vanguard in a grand struggle against Western hegemony and its agents, and the shah in their eyes was a prime candidate.

As with most movements of the time, the Iranian guerrillas were disillusioned with the Soviet Union and its modified Stalinist ideology under Brezhnev and his colleagues. The crushing of the Prague Spring and the Soviet occupation of Czechoslovakia in August 1968 came as a shock to the left and its intellectual affiliates. In addition to Mao Zedong, Ho Chi Minh, and Che Guevara, all praised for their armed struggles, and Patrice Lumumba, for being a martyr of African struggle, there were Iranian heroes. They ranged from the sixth-century Persian prophet Mazdak, the founder of probably the earliest communist-style movements in world history, to Mirza Kuchak Khan. The likes of Taqi Arani and Khosrow Ruzbeh were held in awe. Mosaddeq, however, held an ambivalent place in their ideological landscape, as did socialist intellectuals such as Khalil Maleki. As a liberal nationalist coming from an aristocratic background, Mosaddeq was admired for his anti-imperialist stance but was also seen as a transitory figure whose struggle was bound to lead to the revolution of the masses.

Over the years the movement itself generated its own martyrs and upheld them as role models for the new recruits. That there were too many of them fallen in clashes with security forces added to the movements' appeal.

The ideology of the Iranian left brought together classic Marxism-Leninism, often from a Maoist perspective, with nationalist traits inspired by Latin American movements. To a lesser extent, the experience of the Iranian left since the Constitutional Revolution informed the new radical trends. Though the left distrusted the Tudeh as subservient to the Soviet Union and deluded by Stalinist ideology in its strict application of class struggle, it was not free of Stalinist legacy. Nor did it budge from the Tudeh ideal of dismantling the Pahlavi "bourgeoisie comprador" — seen as an agent of Western capitalism — and creating a dictatorship of the proletariat. Armed struggle spearheaded by the urban guerrillas, it was believed, was soon to be backed by the "masses": the working classes, the urban poor, and the rural population. The greatest threat, it was agreed, was US hegemony and the US support for police states, which, the militants contended, could not have survived without active American backing.

Almost exclusively made up of young men and woman in their twenties and early thirties, the clandestine Guerrilla Organization of the Fada'iyan-e Khalq (Sazman-e Cheriki-e Fada'iyan-e Khalq; literally, "the organization of the devotees who sacrifice themselves for the people") was founded in 1966 through a merger of several smaller radical Marxist groups. One of its influential affiliates, Bizhan Jazani (1937–1975), a doctoral candidate in philosophy at Tehran University and a theoretician of the movement, came from a family of Tudeh activists. While Bizhan was a young boy, his father, a junior army officer, had joined the Azarbaijan Democrats and in 1946 defected to the Soviet Union. Bizhan himself was a dissident in Tudeh circles and an affiliate of the second National Front. Though repeatedly detained and imprisoned by the Savak, he managed to disseminate his revolutionary message in and out of prison even after 1969, when he and a number of his cohorts received long prison terms from military tribunals on common charges of membership in an illegal Marxist organization and conspiracy to overthrow the Pahlavi regime. His tragic end, along with eight other cohorts, added to his aura as a martyr for the cause of the left. They were cold-bloodedly executed in secret in the vicinity of the Evin prison in April 1975, apparently in reprisal for the upsurge of guerrilla warfare and a wave of assassination of Savak agents. Executions were masked as outcome of an escape attempt.

Jazani's pamphleteering was not devoid of a historical perspective. It was primarily informed by class analysis, deeply critical of US hegemony and Pahlavi dictatorship. Yet in comparison with his comrades, he suffered less the

Fada'iyan's typical naïveté and their almost messianic call to spearhead an impending socialist revolution. He was critical of the Tudeh past, its subservice to the Soviets, and its rebuff of Mosaddeq. Having returned after a lapse to Tehran University, he wrote a dissertation supervised by Gholam-Hosain Sadiqi on the forces and objectives of the Constitutional Revolution. Familiarity with the Iranian constitutional struggle and the complexity of Iranian historical experience set him apart from the hotheads who came to dominate the organization. Over the years, however, Jazani's intellectual journey did not lead him to a liberal socialist perspective, but rather to a Maoist "rural" revolutionary model in Iran in place of the Bolshevik model.

Most of the Fada'iyan envisioned themselves as forerunners of a revolutionary process that would eventually awaken the "peoples" (*khalq-ha*) of Iran and erect a utopian society of liberated workers and peasants (fig. 11.5). The movement nevertheless was rife with internal rivalries and ideological splits, which was as effective as Savak in rendering the movement dysfunctional. Their advocacy of autonomy for Iran's ethnicities—mostly in the realm of imagination—was theoretically luring but politically dangerous, giving an ominous green light to Kurdish, Azarbaijani, Turkmen, Arab, and other dormant cessation tendencies. There was a sincere desire to recognize Iran's ethnic patchwork of diverse cultural identities, and the left invariably paid homage to such diversity. Yet it was oblivious, or ideologically blind, to the hazards that threatened Iran's integrity in the 1920s and then again in the 1940s. Despite its blind spots, the Fada'iyan movement can be credited with sensing the rise of social discontent in Iran of the 1960s, even though its prescribed class struggle proved misplaced, at least according to its definition of class.

The Fada'iyan-e Khalq shared its indoctrination with the Mojahedin-e Khalq (People's Crusaders) guerrilla organization that emerged in the same time period. Founded in 1965, it was a movement with firmer grass roots bridging Marxism and political Islam. Rooted in Islamic trends of the postwar era, and in due course the revolutionary romanticism of 'Ali Shari'ati and solidarity with the "third world," then in vogue, the Mojahedin movement was a rough Islamic equivalent of Latin American liberation theology, but with an appetite for armed warfare. Gleaning selectively from the Qur'anic verses, mostly prescribing violence and warning of vengeance, and investing in politicized Shi'i paradigms of sacrifice and martyrdom, the Mojahedin sought in Islam more than devotional acts or a sense of community. They criticized, for the same reason, the passive compliance of most members of the clerical class and their conservative readings of Islamic values. Masses were to be liberated through the exemplar of Shi'i Imam 'Ali and his son Imam Hosain to create a classless

Figure 11.5. "Without true participation of women no revolutionary movement would ever triumph." Makeshift poster of the Fada'iyan Khalq, c. 1980.
Ken Lawrence collection, 1940–2010, HCLA 6312. Courtesy of Special Collections Library, University Libraries, Pennsylvania State University.

society, not by the forces of historical materialism but by means of egalitarian Islam and collective sacrifice on the model of Karbala.

The Mojahedin's culture of armed struggle resembled that of the Marxist Fada'iyan but wrapped in a garb of Islamic symbolism. It was no surprise, then, that some of the Mojahedin, while in the shah's prison, could dispose of their diluted Islamic Marxism in favor of a Marxist offshoot that rivaled both Fada'iyan and the Mojahedin. Almost religiously puritanical, later it was renamed Paykar (warfare) on the eve of the 1979 revolution, appealing to younger recruits, who joined its ranks in droves. Even more than other Marxist movements, Paykar members were the target of street clashes as well as arrest and execution by the Islamic Republic's newly organized Revolutionary Guards.

In more than one way the guerrilla movements in the late 1960s and 1970s left their mark on Iran's radical politics. In the decade and a half before the 1979 revolution, most immediate was their unsettling effect on the public space, tarnishing the otherwise ultraconfident Pahlavi image at the height of its seemingly imperturbable power. Street clashes with Savak and the security forces, which resulted in the death of legendary guerrilla leaders like Hamid Ashraf (1946–1976), attacks on gendarmerie outposts, reports in the press with pictures of men and women killed or captured, television appearances whereby the "security authority" boasted about Savak's successes in eliminating the "saboteurs" (*kharab-karan*), and even television broadcasts of the military courts sentencing young guerrilla detainees to long-term imprisonment or execution—all had a disquieting impact on the Iranian public. The unintended consequence of the state's publicity, along with refuting the damning reports of Amnesty International and other human rights organizations that highlighted oppression and torture in Iran, marred, if not entirely discredited, the state's image of success and grandeur that it was keen to display internationally.

The most striking at outset of the guerrilla armed struggle was the Siahkal episode. In February 1971 twelve members of Fada'iyan who intended to ignite an uprising in Siahkal, a scenic rural town deep in the forests of Gilan province 220 miles north of Tehran, attacked a gendarmerie outpost to release one of their comrades. After a fatal exchange of fire, several were killed and ten captured and subsequently tried and executed in March of that year. The botched incident proved the naïveté of the Fada'iyan and its wishful reliance on the support of villagers, which never materialized. The state's attempt to amplify Siahkal beyond what it was, even after eliminating the armed guerrillas, also revealed the depth of the regime's anxiety. The incident acquired an iconic place in the narrative of the left, and a few allusions in songs and films celebrated the incident as a heroic challenge to the power of the state.

Intensified clashes with the security forces after 1971, coinciding with the celebration of 2,500 years of the Iranian monarchy, though never remotely reaching the level of urban warfare, resulted in several assassinations of military prosecutors, police chiefs, Savak agents, and state officials, and at least four instances of assassinations of American military advisers to the Iranian armed forces between 1972 and 1976. It was the Mojahedin who mostly carried out these attacks.

At the height of the guerrilla movement came the arrest and trial of the Fada'iyan activist and poet Khosrow Golesorkhi (1944–1974), who was sentenced in a public trial in the military court in January 1974 and executed along with his cohorts. Charged with subversion to overthrow the Pahlavi regime, he was seen as a martyr of the left for his valiant defense (fig. 11.6). Even for those who did not sympathize with his ideology, Golesorkhi's execution epitomized all that was wrong with the Pahlavi regime. Even though the revolutionary left, whether Marxist or Marxist Islamic, was more a symptom than an agent of

Figure 11.6. Khosrow Golesorkhi (*first row, fourth from right*) and his
comrades and their court-appointed lawyers during the 1974 military tribunal
that condemned him and another member of the group to death.
Contemporary Iranian photograph, Arshiv-e Asnad-e Opozision-e Iran (http://www.iran-archive
.com/start/323).

instantaneous change, their struggle anticipated the mass appeal of the Islamic
Revolution that arrived in their wake shortly afterward.

By 1978 the era of urban guerrilla struggle was almost at its end. Yet a number
of men and women who lost their lives in bloody street clashes or in safe houses,
or who died in front of firing squads, were harbingers of still more ominous
times awaiting these guerrilla organizations. According to one estimate in the
eight years between 1970 and 1978, Fada'iyan-e Khalq lost the total of 198 of
their fighters of whom 169 were men and 29 women. The 15 percent rate for
woman participation was remarkable since very rarely did women take active
part in earlier resistance movements in Iran. By contrast, the number of Mojahedin casualties between 1971 and 1976 was no more than fifteen of which only
one was a woman. The significant discrepancy may well be attributed to the
strength of the Marxist ideology as opposed to Islamic-Marxism. Only during
and after the Islamic Revolution, and coinciding with the ascendency of radical
Islamic rhetoric, greater appeal for Islamic Marxism shifted the balance in favor
of the Mojahedin-e Khalq. In the first decade after the revolution, both organizations suffered horrendous losses far higher than in prerevolutionary years.

12

CULTURES OF AUTHORITY AND CULTURES OF DISSENT

Iran in the 1960s and 1970s witnessed an era of cultural florescence, a period remarkable for artistic creativity, the rise of new talents, and greater international exposure but also greater state sponsorship. Expressions of artistic and intellectual dissent, often transmitted through a language of symbols, emerged in cinema, poetry, and popular music. Such efforts were tolerated by the state and even patronized by the state-controlled media and by governmental and semigovernmental cultural institutions. They were treated as outlets for intellectual dissent and deemed necessary as cultural safety valves. The period also witnessed a new drive for glorification of Pahlavi rule and for the shah's vision of imperial greatness. Curiously, the two currents—cultural subversion, operating underneath a calm surface, and glorification of the monarchic cult—lived side by side and even nurtured each other. As the author and cultural critic Jalal Al-e Ahmad once commented, the state successfully managed to bring all intellectual dissidents into its cultural stable. This complex dialogue bore important consequences during and after the 1979 revolution.

SUNLIGHT OF THE ARYANS

In April 1965, when the shah closely escaped another assassination attempt by a soldier of his royal guards in the Marmar Palace, he became even more convinced that he was providentially protected. A small cell of intellectuals with Maoist leanings had masterminded the assassination attempt. They were tried and sentenced to death but later pardoned. Perhaps it was not a coincidence that in the same year the shah also assumed the title of Aryamehr, or "Sunlight of the Aryans." The Majles bestowed it on him, no doubt at his own instigation. Coined by a professor of ancient Iranian studies in Tehran University, the title was a nod to the Persian notion of "royal glory" (*farr*) and in recognition of all the benefits the shah had offered to the Aryan nation of Iran, so it was declared, through the "Revolution of the Shah and the People," which was accomplished under his aegis.

The magnitude of imperial self-glorification became more evident two years later when, in 1967, after twenty-six years on the throne, the shah decided to officially celebrate his coronation—and that of Queen Farah—in an elaborate ceremony. Driving through glittering decorations of the Tehran streets in a carriage reminiscent of the British royal household, the shah and the queen arrived at the Golestan Palace (fig. 12.1). There, in full royal regalia and with much heavier accoutrements than his father's coronation outfit, he first placed on his own head the Pahlavi crown and held the royal scepter. He then placed a newly made crown, designed by the New York jeweler Harry Winston, on the head of his queen. Despite its fairy-tale extravagance, the event was not treated as a farce, at least not by most Iranians, who probably enjoyed watching the fanfare on television and were content to see their shah having his moment in the sun.

Yet his thirst for celebrations grew, almost addictively, to fantastic dimensions when in 1971 the shah celebrated 2,500 years of the Iranian monarchy in a more extravagant style. It was an event aimed, even more than the coronation, to place the Pahlavi monarchy and the reign of the shah in particular within an imperial narrative that stretched back to the ancient Achaemenid Empire. The idea, first proposed by European Iranists in the 1950s, was escalated in scale by the mid-1960s to a huge event of loftier consequence. It was to commemorate

Figure 12.1. Royal cavalcade during coronation ceremonies, October 1967.
The Land of Kings, ed. R. Traverdi (Tehran, 1971), 4.

not merely the founding of the Persian Empire (presumably calculated from the death of Cyrus in 530 BC rather than the conquest of Babylon in 539 BC) but also the very continuity of Iranian imperial history that had culminated in the Pahlavi era and the return of Iran's might and glory.

The subtext was unmistakable; Iran's "immortality," as the propaganda for celebrations reminded many foreign guests, in reality meant to script the image of a prophet-king, a latter-day Cyrus, into an Iranian metahistory. It was not without reason, therefore, that at the beginning of the commemoration ceremonies, the Sunlight of the Aryans stood before Cyrus's mausoleum in Pazargad, near Persepolis (in Fars province) and as an homage to the founder of the Persian Empire solemnly declared: "Cyrus the Great! Rest in peace; we are awake" (*Kurosh-e bozorg! Asudeh bekhab, ma bidarim*). These were words that a generation would be destined to sound so sobering and yet ironic, given the velocity of the revolutionary process that destroyed the Pahlavi regime—and seemingly forever ended monarchy in Iran—less than a decade later.

The festivities left in many minds, Iranian and foreign, a curious impression. It became the staple of many reports about contemporary Iran to view the extravagance and the ludicrous expenses lavished on foreign invitees as demonstration of the excesses that eventually brought down the Pahlavi regime. In October 1971 some six hundred foreign royals, heads of state and other dignitaries, and their entourages were brought to Shiraz to be housed in a 160-acre luxurious tent city that had been set up on the reforested plain of Marvdasht, opposite the colossal ruins of Persepolis. They dined in a marquee for the banquet that was two hundred feet long and served on Limogès dinnerware manufactured for the occasion, sat around opulent tables decorated with fifty roasted peacocks with their tail feathers set in foie gras, ate Caspian golden caviar and other delicacies catered by Maxim's and flown in from Paris, and drank such rare wines as a 1945 Château Lafite Rothschild. A visual show with fireworks followed the nearly six hours of formal dinner, accompanied by Iannis Xenakis's musical piece *Persepolis* that had been commissioned for the evening. It all went down in the Guinness Book of World Records as the most lavish official banquet in modern times, a very dubious distinction for the host country, given the enormous cost and breezy arrogance displayed by host and guests alike.

The next day, below the stairway of Persepolis, foreign guests witnessed a parade through the ages of Iranian imperial armies, from Achaemenid to Pahlavid, with performers in colorful period costumes, complete with gear and military equipment. Even a full-scale model of a navy vessel and a siege tower from the Achaemenid period were rolled through—all choreographed no less spectacularly than a Hollywood epic and with taste and expertise drawn from Hollywood studios (pl. 12.1 and fig. 12.2). Yet from nearly all these festivities, even the march

Figure 12.2. Qajar regiment of the Nezam Jadid, Persepolis parade,
2,500-year celebration of the Persian Empire, October 1971.
Spiro T. Agnew Papers, box 48. Courtesy of Special Collections, University of Maryland Libraries.

of colorful imperial armies, the Iranian general public was excluded as if the events were merely to impress foreign guests and satisfy an outsized royal ego that had been long injured by a sense of inferiority. The shah had to prove that he was no less majestic than his European counterparts.

There were also security issues and fear of popular protests or armed attacks on the shah and his guests. Queen Elizabeth and President Richard Nixon both declined their invitations, apparently for security concerns, dispatching others instead. It is small wonder that as many as 250 red Mercedes-Benz limousines were assigned to transport guests through the massive security that radiated beyond Persepolis to cover nearly all of the country. In a carefully designed operation, the Savak rounded up hundreds of political dissidents, blocked roads, monitored airports, and cordoned off neighborhoods.

Of at least $21 million spent on the event, no doubt the most enduring aspect of it was the commemorative monument, Shahyad Aryamehr, built at Tehran's gateway in a novel style that incorporated Persian architectural traditions. Designed by Hossein Amanat (b. 1941), a graduate from Tehran University, the vast square and monument at its center display Iran's cultural continuity while at the same time conveying a message of revival. The four massive columns rising to make the two complementing arches of the Sasanian and Islamic epochs are intertwined in an hyperbolic latticework of stone and mosaic beneath an observation tower reminiscent of the Toghrel Tower of the Saljuqid era. A 148-foot concrete structure encased in crafted blocks of white stone from Jowsheqan marble—with its complex geometry, modernist contours, and advanced construction techniques—espoused not only a conceptual departure but also an optimistic sense of permanency beyond its immediate function (fig. 12.3).

In the following decades, Shahyad endured the test of time throughout the fiercely antimonarchical revolution of 1979, hosting under its arch some of the most memorable rallies, which were attended by millions carrying revolutionary banners. Renamed Borj-e Azadi (freedom tower) in the aftermath of the revolution, in the following decades it transcended both its monarchical and revolutionary past to become perhaps Iran's most popular icon. No longer a state symbol, it was adopted by most Iranians as a national emblem and as late as June 2009 as a memorial site for the Green Movement's mass rallies.

In the following years the shah was ever more convinced of his prophetic mission and ready to drag Iran across the threshold into his Great Civilization. In February 1971 his court minister Asadollah 'Alam recorded in his secret diary a private conversation with that shah:

> His Majesty mentioned strange things about his belief in divine support for him. "I have noticed that whoever opposed me, he has been eliminated,

Figure 12.3. Shahyad was dedicated in 1971 and renamed Azadi Tower in 1979.
Private collection.

whether domestic or foreign." He gave the example of Kennedy Brothers. The [US] president and two of his brothers, who were senators, and disliked the shah. "John Kennedy was assassinated. Robert, the senator, was assassinated. And the last of them, Edward, because of a strange affair over the death of a girl, was scandalized and now his star is fading. Nasser, the Egyptian president, was also eliminated." Khrushchev, the Soviet premier, who also disapproved of His Majesty, was eliminated. In Iran, too, whoever opposed the shah was deposed, for example Mosaddeq and to some extent Qavam al-Saltaneh. Razmara, I am sure, held ominous designs for the shah and he, too, was assassinated. "Mansur, who was an obvious American poppet, a man of unbridled ambitions, was also assassinated."[1]

Also well evident from the pages of 'Alam's secret diaries, and the shah's own public statements, for him Iran increasingly turned into a utopian object to be desired, a mechanical contraption to be assembled, and an edifice to be embellished rather than a complex society—often in disarray, deprived of a voice, and deeply skeptical of his enterprise. If the best of intentions were to be assigned to him, the shah demanded obedience and gratitude in exchange for an imagined fairy-tale land that he believed was within his grasp. However, self-aggrandizement, coupled by a profound conspiratorial perspective in international and domestic politics, misplaced pride, and overconfidence in his judgment, blurred the royal's vision and prevented him from seeing trouble on the horizon. Virtually in every international event of consequence the shah saw the hidden hands of the great powers. From the Vietnam War to the Arab-Israeli conflict to political upheavals in neighboring Iraq, Saudi Arabia, Afghanistan, and Pakistan he saw British or American or Soviet covert involvement. Domestically, too, he attributed any criticism of his policies or any independent trend to some behind-the-curtain foreign force, a reflection perhaps of his own insecurities. Nor did the shah sense the climate of cynicism and indifference that gradually set in during the last decade of his reign, despite efforts to rein in or whip out forces of opposition.

STATE SPONSORSHIP AND CULTURAL REVIVAL

By the middle of the 1960s cultural patronage came to occupy a greater place in the Pahlavi search for imperial legitimacy and for appeal to a larger spectrum of Iranian population. Empress Farah and her coterie were instrumental in projecting a softer, more refined image of the Pahlavi state through media, music, architecture, literature, and visual arts. Dissident intellectuals and artists of earlier years, and potential dissidents among the younger middle classes, found the more relaxed cultural climate appealing. So long as the boundaries of political dissent were not crossed, artists and intellectuals could explore new, even implicitly subversive, themes through television production, cinema, theater, painting, and music. Though not completely free of harassment by the Savak, vast numbers found employment in the well-funded state media and cultural institutions. Farah Pahlavi's frequent travel to remote towns and villages of Iran also presented a new image of a caring queen willing to learn about the country and help improve the lot of ordinary folks (fig. 12.4).

The shift in cultural policy relied on tangible changes in Iranian society. Beyond the circles of power, Iranian society of the 1960s and 1970s underwent sociocultural and demographic integration, which in turn revealed new sociocultural demands. Although regional identities, ethnicity, religion, and class remained indelible parts of the landscape, public education, growth of a national market, and growth of media and entertainment boosted a greater sense of homogeneity. Public media, particularly radio and television, though completely under

Figure 12.4. In Kish in 1977 Queen Farah listens to children on a Persian Gulf island. African Iranians are descendants of the slave trade of earlier centuries.
Farah Pahlavi, *Safarnameh-e Shahbanu*, ed. M. Pirniya (n.p., 1371/1992), 64.

government control, were able to patronize Iranian art, music, and cinema that contrasted with the positivist Westernizing obsessions of earlier decades. Some members of the clergy, and their followers, avoided the new media on the grounds that it disseminates deviant pleasures such as music, but most Iranians welcomed radio and television, and increasingly foreign and domestic motion pictures. By the 1960s the introduction of battery-powered transistor radio sets and the expansion of the provincial radio broadcasting network increased audiences in towns and villages. Television, too, quickly replaced traditional storytelling in the coffeehouses. The prominent display of a television set installed high up on a makeshift shelf on the wall of the neighborhood coffeehouses, with patrons watching a low-budget Hollywood production, symbolized the state's new means of dominating the public at the expenses of local voices and local dialects.

An earlier example of the state's patronage of high-quality programing, with the aim of offering a more sophisticated take on Persian musical heritage that was more palatable to the middle classes, was the celebrated *Golha* (Flowers) program produced by Radio Iran. Started in the mid-1950s, it was a natural outcome of earlier efforts by 'Ali-Naqi Vaziri (1887–1979) and his music academy, established in 1923. In its mix of orchestral, vocal, and solo performances, *Golha* interspersed Western instruments such as piano, violin, and clarinet with Persian *tar*, *nay* (reed pipe), *tunbak*, and *santur* (Persian dulcimer) to produce an elegant Persianized music loyal to the *radif* system but culturally confident enough to employ Western composition and orchestration with a romantic undertone—all while preserving Persian taste and texture. This was a genre greatly appealing to Iran's bourgeois sensibilities. Vaziri was highly influential in this reincarnation of Persian music.

Born to a father who was a Cossack officer and a celebrated feminist mother, Bibi-khanum Astarabadi (1859–1921), young Vaziri, a German-educated military officer was a product of the constitutional era and no doubt deeply influenced by the modernizing trends of that period. He established the first academy of music in 1924 and soon after Iran's first national orchestra, and he was among the first to commit Persian music to Western notation. In his musical academy he taught composition, orchestration, and theory, as well as training some of the best musical talents of the generation and himself composing new pieces for Persian instruments and developing new performing techniques for *tar*. Although occasionally criticized for trying to discipline the probably undisciplinable Persian quartertone (*rob'-e pardeh*), Vaziri's contributions were crucial not only for the development of technique and for adapting the *radif* to orchestral demands but also for presenting Persian classical music as a "respectable" tradition on par with Western tradition, and for including music in the school curriculum.

The *Golha* program was the brainchild of Davud Pirnia, descendant of an important Qajar family of the cultural elite, who also attracted descendants of other cultural families to the program as well as new talents. Among them was Abol-Hasan Saba (1902–1957), an influential composer and music teacher who belonged to a family of poets and painters from Kashan whose origin went back to the eighteenth century. He was a master violinist in the Persian style and a composer for the Persian *radif*. His students mastered Persian style and dominated the musical stage. Gholam-Hosain Banan (1911–1986), a vocalist of great ingenuity, also came from a Qajar family. Of the latter group Mortaza Mahjubi (1900–1965), a piano virtuoso with his own distinct Persian style, demonstrated how European instruments could be employed in a completely different genre. Marziyeh (1924–2010), a stage name for a young and talented female *tasnif* singer with a powerful range and nuanced voice, was of humble origins. Singing old *tasnifs* of the Qajar era, she was a product of the *Golha*. The most influential, however, was Ruhollah Khaleqi (1906–1965), a gifted composer and musical director of the Golha Orchestra who, as a student of Vaziri and admirer of Saba, emerged as the musical force behind *Golha*'s success and in his short life composed many memorable pieces in the 1950s and early 1960s. By all accounts the *Golha* project rescued Persian music from the formulaic tedium and barren repetition to which it had fallen for decades.

As early as 1944, during the Allied occupation of Iran, Khaleqi had become well known for his composition of a patriotic song "Ey Iran" (Thou Iran!), which was based on a folk song from Gilan (known as "Zard-malicheh," which means "Yellow sparrow"). Performed in the Dashti mode, the playful melody was first picked up by Saba but later, in Khaleqi's hand, turned into a vivid and moving piece (fig. 12.5).

The lyrics by Hosein Golgolab (1895–1984) reflected Iranians' injured sentiments under occupation, praising Iran as a "bejeweled land" and "wellspring of human gifts" and wished it to "endure for ever, immune from evil designs." The patriotic song, first performed in a public concert by Banan in the same year, soon came to be adopted as Iran's true national anthem and a song of resistance, in clear defiance of the imperial (*shahanshai*) anthem commissioned by Reza Shah in 1933. As much as the official anthem glorified the shah and the imperial power, "*Ey Iran*" highlighted the land and people of Iran without any reference to the shah or state. All through the Pahlavi era and later under the Islamic Republic, "Ey Iran" reflected such dissenting sentiments. As late as 2009 during the Green Movement (Jonbesh-e Sabz), the youth would sing it among other places in street rallies and while riding Tehran's subway cars.

Figure 12.5. Persian National Music Society Orchestra, conducted by Khaleqi,
performing in the 1948 Persian movie *Tufan-e Zendegi* (Life's tempest). The
orchestra's principal singer, Gholam-Hosain Banan, was accompanied by
the first violinist Abol-Hasan Saba and Mortaza Mahjubi on piano. The
Westernized style and the predominance of Western instruments reflect
the hybrid musical culture of the time. In later years, as the Orchestra
of the Golha Program, it came to include Persian instruments.
Still from the 1948 Iranian movie *Tufan-e Zendegi*. Jamal Omid, *Tarikh-e Sinema-ye Iran*,
1279–1357 (Tehran, 1374/1995). Courtesy of Jane Lewisohn.

The creation of the National Iranian Radio and Television (NIRT) in 1967,
funded and controlled by the state, incorporated—almost coercively—not only
the nationwide radio network that had been in operation since 1928 and other
local radio stations under the state umbrella, but also the privately owned National Iranian Television, established in 1958 by the entrepreneur Habib Sabet,
which chiefly served the capital with coverage of about two million viewers and
limited domestic production, later expanded to Abadan. By 1971, NIRT rapidly
increased its coverage several-fold, and by 1976, thanks to generous government
funding, especially support from Queen Farah and under the energetic directorship of Reza Qotbi, it offered complete nationwide radio coverage and nearly
70 percent television coverage, amounting to more than twenty million viewers.
    The significant growth of NIRT provided the Pahlavi state with a powerful
monopoly to relay not only its overt political message but also a subtle agenda
of secular nationalism. Television sets became an essential household good,

first for the affluent middle classes in larger cities and soon in smaller towns and many villages, with a growing viewership from all ages. Domestically manufactured sets made television more affordable, and multichannel broadcasts—including an international channel in English that in 1972 replaced the US Army broadcast of earlier years—and regional stations with folk music and some production in local dialects, helped expand the appeal of the new media to one of the most effective arms of the state.

The growth of state media absorbed intellectuals and discontented university graduates, with artistic and literary talents, and others with technical and media expertise into a growing organization with an institutional culture different from the state bureaucracy. An effective means of diverting dissent into exciting yet politically benign activity, NIRT reserved relative independence in its production and internal policies so long as it paid effusive homage to the shah. The state's monopoly on broadcasting nevertheless meant sketching a bright future for the nation in a sanitized narrative devoid of meaningful criticism. It also meant a barrage of pro-Pahlavi propaganda suffused with images of the beloved Aryamehr extemporizing, inaugurating, hobnobbing with world leaders, or promoting his liberating White Revolution. From time to time it also had to stage Savak-sponsored "shows" or even allowing the public to witness trials of Marxist intellectuals in military tribunals.

Yet beyond the propaganda function, NIRT also conveyed a message that inadvertently contrasted the regime's glossy narrative. Through serials, music, variety shows, and documentaries television soon became the most influential media and a source of information and entertainment. Replacing imported American serials—*Peyton Place* was exceptionally popular—Iranian television audiences began to learn through domestic productions about their own country, its social problems, and its ordinary people and their subsistent struggles. Though sanitized and made politically harmless, often the comic serials of life in poor neighborhoods, housing problems, overcrowded rental quarters, struggling itinerant handymen, the changing face of villages as they were devoured by cities, increasing urban crime and problems of law and order, the pretentious irrelevance of the old elite and their xenophobia fostered a certain level of social awareness.

The mini-series *Da'i-jan Napoleon* (Dear uncle Napoleon), directed by Nasser Taghvai, was a highly successful production aired by NIRT in 1976. Based on a satirical novel by Iraj Pezeshgzad, it narrated the coming of age of a young boy during the World War II Allied occupation of Iran. The central character, a retired Cossack officer, is the patriarch of a "Qajaresque" extended family whose internal feuds shape the hilarious plot and many subplots. Dear Uncle's paranoid fears of British mischief and his imagined victories in bygone battles no doubt were a parody of the conspiratorial anxieties of the old elite.

The cultural sponsorship of NIRT was complemented by other sources of patronage linked to Farah Pahlavi's cultural office. Persian music, modern painting, new museums, cultural centers, art festivals, cinema and theater, children literature, and innovative television productions were among them. Her interest in architecture allowed for experimentations in modern style far subtler than the rude imported modernism of the 1960s, and with a Persian component. The art and architecture projects primarily monumentalized the Pahlavi era, albeit with more sophistication. Yet their effect on the outlook and training of artists, performers, filmmakers, and architects cannot be underestimated. A whole generation of artists, filmmakers, and actors who later became representative of Iran's independent cultural flourishing in the post-1979 era first learned their trade in the Pahlavi institutions and with some form of state support.

The Shiraz Arts Festival (Jashn-e Honar) was one obvious example of injecting enthusiasm and interest within both the Western and the Iranian art communities. Initiated by a pioneering filmmaker, Farrokh Ghaffari (1921–2006), heir to another remarkable artistic family of the Qajar era, it was meant to be an artistic bridge between diverse traditions from Europe and the Americas to Japan and Southeast Asia. It was also a conscious effort to recapture authenticity in Persian music and performance arts and put them on stage unapologetically and away from the positivist anxieties of earlier decades. Established in 1967, the festival invited a long list of celebrities ranging from Arthur Rubinstein, Ravi Shankar, and Yehudi Menuhin to playwright August Wilson and theater director Peter Brook. Their dazzling performances and avant-garde productions, interspersed with performances by Iranian master musicians such as *tar* virtuoso Jalil Shahnaz (1921–2013) and great *tubak* percussionist Hosain Tehrani (1912–1974). The candlelit performances, accompanied by the odes of Hafez recited on the very site of the poet's tomb (a Persianized "temple of love" designed in the 1930s by the French architect André Godard) in the midst of a Persian garden, offered a novel experience (pl. 12.2).

After a decade during which it was annually held and at great expense, the festival left behind a mixed legacy. Above all, it helped promote traditional Persian music, boosting its preservation and development for decades to come. It was here that the great vocalist Mohammad Reza Shajarian first found a live audience more eager and more demanding than that of his mainstream radio programs. With an amazing vocal range, musical texture, technical knowledge, and artistic consistency, he worked his way through the Shiraz Arts Festival to

become one of the greatest artists Iran produced in the latter half of the twentieth century. Parisa (Fatemeh Va'ezi), another vocalist of quality and grace, who
sang Persian *radif* in the festival with the same ease as she did Qajar and early
Pahlavi *tasnifs*, was the representative of a generation of performers and composers who made there debut at the Shiraz Arts Festival. The Western music
and theater, classic or avant-garde, and other ethnic performances in the festival
left only little lasting impact.

CITY OF TALES

Theater in particular became a conduit for an ambiguous message of dissident that was barely tolerable by the state's security in any other venue. As
early as the latter half of the nineteenth century modern theater began to take
roots in the Persian cultural environment primarily as means of educating the
public and social awareness. Outside Iran playwrights Fath 'Ali Akhundzadeh
and Zain al-'Abedin Maragheh'i produced plays critical of the decaying social
mores, superstitions, and moral ills. The masterful verse rendering by Mirza
Habib Isfahani (1835–1893) of Molière's famous play *Misanthrope*, published in
Istanbul in 1875 as *Mardom-goriz*, was a literary breakthrough even though this
play, and others produced abroad, only received a limited readership and was
never staged for larger audiences. Nevertheless, like imaginary travel accounts,
novellas, and other reform literature of the late nineteenth century, this body
of early plays had some echo in the Constitutional Revolution's sociocultural
setting.

From the mid-1920s on, theater gained wider reception among the Iranian
urban middle classes, especially in the capital. With the growth of leisure time,
a number of modern playhouses were built in Tehran and in the provincial
centers, and new theatrical troops routinely performed, mostly adaptations of
French plays. They met the entertainment needs of a secularizing intelligentsia
but also conformed to the Pahlavi modernizing project. The moralistic messages in plays such as those staged by Sayyed 'Ali Nasr (1891–1959) were unmistakable, stressing family values versus decrepitude and such ills as drinking
and addiction, reason versus superstition, and of course patriotism and sacrifice
for the fatherland. With some trepidation, women, first Russian émigrés or Armenian and Assyrian semiprofessional actors, appeared on the stage. Not unlike European nineteenth-century drama, themes of honor and shame received
ample attention. There was even a touch of social naturalism.

By the 1940s and early 1950s the ascendency of the left in Iranian artistic milieu also found its place in dramatic productions, often with a mild sociopolitical

message. A number of talented Tudeh directors, actors, and actresses staged Western dramas distinct from the moralistic plays of earlier years. Yet original Persian plays of substance were seldom staged. One of the few in the 1950s was Sadeq Hedayat's *Mohallel* (a temporary husband needed under Shi'i law to allow for a special kind of marriage annulment so that the original parties can resume their earlier union). It was a predictable commentary by a sharp critic of Islamic shari'a on the outdated practices of Shi'i law and its grip on Iranian society. The post-1953 climate of censorship and intimidation brought this interlude in Iranian theater, thriving and hopeful though it was, to an abrupt end. Cinema, mostly Hollywood movies, and a growing number of movie theaters successfully competed with the stage and by the early 1960s largely sapped the entertaining appeal of the theater.

A new lease on life for Persian theater came in the late 1960s, this time voicing a more refined critique of the prevailing social order. Allegorical and increasingly in tune with the European "committed" theater, as the theater of the Jean-Paul Sartre era came to be known, and even with the theater of absurd, it found a smaller but more engaged audience. Playwrights such as Gholam-Hosain Sa'edi staged new productions in a playhouse built by the Pahlavi state and ironically named 25th of Shahrivar — ironic not only because the playhouse was built and named in honor of the shah's coronation in 1967 but also in that it was patronized by Queen Farah, who called for a more open cultural space at times at odds with the pressures of censorship and the Savak. Despite their innocuous surface, the new plays predominantly cast a skeptic, at times surrealistic, shadow on the boasted "glories" of the Pahlavi state and its White Revolution with subtle hints to the suffocating political climate.

A remarkable example was the 1968 *Shahr-e Qesseh* (City of tales) by Bizhan Mofid (1935–1984), a musical play with rhymed prose that employed Persian animal fables and children folktales to convey a semi-satirical commentary on the Pahlavi state, society and identity. At home with the working-class culture of his home city, Tehran, Mofid used street lingo and popular proverbs along with Persian music to depict a richly allegorical tableau. Pantomime, animal masks, and a mix of satirical and sardonic dialogue created an ambiance of childlike innocence but also mockery of the realities of modern Iran. The "fabulous City of Tales" resembles the "city of Farang" (*shahr-e Farang*), a reference to the fast-changing face of the Iranian urban landscape and its artless mimicking of the West (fig. 12.6).

The cast of characters, inhabitants of the city, included a crafty mullah in the guise of a fox, a lecherous fortune-teller in the guise of a bear, a sycophantic poet-parrot, and a cynical intellectual in the guise of a monkey. While the

Figure 12.6. *Shahr-e Qesseh* (The city of tales) was first
performed at the Shiraz Arts Festival in 1968.
Courtesy of Vali Mahlouji.

first two satirized the clerical establishment and the folk religion of the poorer
classes, the parrot hinted at the literary establishment and its adulation of the
Pahlavi regime, and the monkey sneered at the intellectuals' marginality. A *luti*
in the guise of a donkey represented the working classes. By profession he was a
turner, a maker of wooden household implements, a craft that had been ruined
by the invasion of plastics. In a moving monologue, unmasked, he shared with
the audience his nostalgia for bygone times and the depth of alienation felt by ordinary Iranians. The elephant, another character from Persian children rhymes,
was a curious newcomer to the glittering city. At the outset of the play he slips and
breaks his tusk. In pain, he appeals to the inhabitants for help, but unschooled in
the complexities of the city, he receives nothing but mockery and tricks. In the
end he comes to a bitter realization that not only has he lost his tusks, the most
precious symbol of his identity, but he also has morphed into a miserable composite, a mirror image of the ramshackle place that is the City of Tales.

Welcomed by audiences first at the Shiraz Arts Festival and later in the 25th
Shahrivar Playhouse, *Shahr-e Qesseh* was the longest running play in history of
serious theater in Iran. It succeeded in reaching wider audiences beyond the
Tehran intelligentsia because its rhythmic narrative and the characters were

entertaining without being banal, and its poignant message was not lost even on the nonelite. What Al-e Ahmad articulated in his *Gharbzadehgi* (translated as "Westoxication") some years earlier with a defiant tilt, here is conveyed by Mofid in a metaphorical language attuned to the Persian era. He nevertheless shared the disenchantment typical of the dissent culture of his generation. The play was a noted example of how the subtle messages of dissent were conveyed through theater, cinema, and television to a wider audience—an inadvertent, and possibly inevitable, outcome of Pahlavi efforts to widen their popular appeal and coopt actual or potential dissidents. The coded language of allegories and allusions went a long way, even through the state-controlled media, to increase cynicism toward the state and its privileged elite.

NEW ARTISTIC DEPARTURES

Aside from Mofid, only a handful of artistic personalities of the period were able to transcend political disenchantment that dominated the culture of the late Pahlavi era. Sohrab Sepehri (1928–1980), whose minimalistic style of paintings and poetry offered a new mystical reading of nature, is one such exception. He was a poet of water, of trees and birds, of solitude and serenity, an artist in pain about a fast-disappearing space that was about to be conquered by the forces of modernity. In the poem "Water" from his 1967 collection *Hajm-e Sabz* (The expanse of green) he wrote:

> Let us not muddy the water,
> Downstream, maybe a dove is drinking,
> Or on the woods afar, a finch preening its feathers,
> Or in a hamlet, an earthen jug is being filled to the brim.
> Let's not muddy the water,
> Perhaps the stream is on its way to a poplar tree,
> To quench a heart, heavy with sorrow.
> Perhaps a pauper has his hand immersed, dipping his stale bread. . . .
> Upstream, people understand water,
> They did not muddy the water,
> We too
> Should not.[2]

The simple imagery drew Sepehri's readers to his reflective space, a world detached from trivial realities of his surroundings. His deep interest in Buddhism no doubt shaped Sepehri's worldview and references in his poetry. Yet here, too,

Figure 12.7. Installed in the Niavaran Palace in 1972, Parviz Tanavoli's
Heech (now in the Niavaran Palace Museum, Tehran) may be
an acerbic statement on the ephemeral nature of power.
P. Tanavoli, *Heech* (Tehran: Bongah Publishers, 2011), 35.

references to breeze, dawn, and light, among others, can be read as elusive symbols calling for a moment of deliverance. Much of his appeal to the younger generation of Iranians lied not only in his poetic simplicity but also in his desire to experience an authentic self.

On a different plane, but with a similar urge to break the conventions of his time and seek artistic authenticity, was Parviz Tanavoli (b. 1937), a sculptor known for his artistic perseverance stretching over six decades. Even more than Sepehri he moved away from the committed art of the 1960s to experiment with new concepts and media. As one of the founders of the *saqqa khaneh* (water fountain) artistic genre, Tanavoli sought in Shiʻi popular symbols and rituals raw material for his abstract sculptures. His journey through mourning emblems and shrine symbolism and his recasting of Farhad, the tragic hero of the Persian romance, as his artistic alter ego, eventually led him to an existential quest. A series of sculptures on the theme of nothingness conveys a seemingly perplexing message. One may see in his sculpting the word *heech* (nothing) in numerous variants a skeptical view of the cultural milieu within which he was operating (fig. 12.7). Similar to Sepehri, Tanavoli's artistic message was novel insofar as it was free of ideology and distant from the prevailing discourse of political dissent. Yet the existential anxiety, along with aesthetic quality and masterful craftsmanship, proved lasting. His *Heechs* remained confident and uncompromised, as if in their glossy surface the words mirrored the transience of their surroundings.

POPULAR CULTURE AND ITS ICONS

To complement social commentary, television also offered light entertainment and, significantly, Persian contemporary music, popular with audiences across class barriers. Perhaps the best-known diva was the gifted singer and actress Googoosh (Faegheh Atashin, b. 1950), who since the late 1950s had appeared first as a prodigy child entertainer and later as a successful pop singer. Her melodramatic voice complemented her melodramatic private life, which was followed by the press at every turn. A victim of the male-dominated entertainment industry, most of her successful songs bore sad melodies and gloomy lyrics. They narrated her personal story as much as the mood of her audiences, and with a growing touch of dissent. Her 1971 "Qesseh-ye Do Mahi" (Tale of the two fish) recounts the tragic end of two fish in a murky sea, intimate and in love and oblivious to the perils ahead (fig. 12.8).

Figure 12.8. Googoosh on the cover of the 1971 album
Qesseh-ye Do Mahi (Tale of the two fish).
Album cover, SARE-1009, Ahang-e Ruz record company, Tehran, 1971.

When a kingfisher takes one fish, the other mourns the loss and waits for its own fatal end. This was evidently a reference to the young guerillas fighting and dying in the street battles against the security forces of the kingfisher:

> We nipped at big bubbles,
> Until a kingfisher killed my pair.
> May be he damned, that wrecker of the nests,
> Now is my turn, its shadow cast over the water.
> After us, it'll be the turn of other pairs,
> Days are ahead for other hearts to be cruelly wrecked.
> No longer I wish to be a fish in the sea,
> But wish to endure in tales.

The subliminal message of suffocation and despair came through with dramatic undertones in the songs of another well-known pop singer, Dariush (Eqbali, b. 1951). His highly popular 1971 "Bu-ye Khosh-e Gandom" (Fresh scent of wheat) with lyrics by Shahryar Ghanbari and composed by the gifted Iranian Armenian Varoujan Hakhbandian (1936–1977), voiced the fate of the dispossessed, who, having lost all their belongings to the powerful, only wished to preserve a patch of land on which they could survive. These are people, as the lyrics went, whose skin is the color of the night. They are coming from the city of prayers with golden domes and are longing for the scent of the wheat. The song calls on the people of power and affluence whose skin is made of velvet of the dawn; they are travelers from the city of Farang and their goal is to build a forest of steel and skyscrapers. But "what is the use of moaning the loss?" so asks the song. The dispossessed, the blood in the veins of the land, will cry out this time, demanding not only the fresh scent of the wheat but also their harvest and land, an obvious message of protest directed at the ruling elite.

> For me the scent of the wheat,
> For you whatever I have.
> For me a patch of land,
> For you whatever I reap.
> I am from this plague-ridden eastern clan,
> You are the glassy traveler of the land of Farang.
> My skin is of the color of the night, yours of the red velvet,
> My wound is of blisters, your robe of leopard skin. . . .
> You are thinking of forests of steel and skyscrapers,
> I think of a room big enough for you to rest.
> My body made of the soil; yours made of wheat stalks,

Our bodies are thirstier than ever for a drop of water.
Your land is the land of Farang, its people clad in embroidered silk,
Mine is a city of prayer with golden domes.
Your body is like an ax; mine a dying root,
Carved on the tree trunk a heart still throbs. . . .
Enough lamenting for the soil of my body,
You are a passerby; I am the blood in the veins of this land.
My body doesn't wish to be injured in your hand,
And I cry out laud, whether there is someone out there or not:
"For me the scent of the fields,
For me whatever I have.
For me a patch of land,
For me whatever I reap."

The lyrics not only alluded to the outcome of the land reform and fate of the displaced peasants but also reflected the brooding public mood and dream of repossessing a lost cultural legacy. The familiar imagery of the night, code for all-embracing political suppression, had traveled from highbrow new poetry of the earlier years to popular songs, and with wider popular appeal. Most striking, though, was the reference to the city of prayers with golden domes. Like Forugh's messianic allusions in her later poems, here too the imagery had come out of a purely secular milieu. The veiled call for a return to Islam and Shi'ism was reminiscent of Al-e Ahmad, and reclaiming the land for the dispossessed at the end of the song reflected the growing aspirations for revolt. Not surprisingly, the singer, the lyricist, and the composer ended up in Savak's brief detention.

The most overtly activist, however, was Farhad Mehrad (1944–2002), who voiced the same sense of despair but with a more discernable revolutionary vigor. He too was detained by Savak. His 1971 "Jom'eh" (Friday, lyrics by Shahyar Ghanbari and music by Esfandiyar Monfaredzadeh, b. 1941), the day of rest in the weekly calendar, represents not only the boredom often associated with Friday but also doom and gloom. Monfaredzadeh, a gifted composer, made this song as an implicit commemoration of the Siahkal incident:

Through the soaking frame of my window,
I see the picture of a bleak Friday.
How dark is the black of her mourning dress,
In her eyes, I see, black clouds thickening. . . .
Blood drips from those black dark clouds,
Fridays, blood comes down instead of raindrops. . . .
Friday's age is nearly a thousand years,
On Fridays grief takes its toll,

Bored with oneself,
One cries out with the mouth shut. . . .
"Friday is the time for departure, the season for breaking away."
But he who is my fellow traveler,
Stabbed a dagger in my back.

Black (*siah*) is a clear wordplay with the word *Siahkal*, with mourning and blood allusions to how the incident went awry and collapsed into disaster. "Stabbing in the back," a reference to betrayal by a fellow guerrilla fighter, perfected the modern martyrdom narrative bemoaned by a generation of sympathizers. The "Siahkal genre," as it came to be known, was plain and accessible, with a message effectively released through record singles, then popular with middle class youth. It romanticized for a generation an armed revolt that idealized revolution as the only way ahead. During the thousand-year-old barren Fridays of repression, as Farhad reminded his audience, one can only "cr[y] out with mouth shut," a paradox of silent protest that defined the spirit of the age.

FILMFARSI AND RECLAIMING INJURED HONOR

In the same vein, though at a lower register and emitting a subversive message at a slower pace, the Iranian popular film industry in the 1960s and 1970s churned out a huge number of low-rate productions essentially for the working-class market and provincial tastes. Despite the primarily entertaining function of these movies, some carried a message of social injustice and class divisions. They were labeled by highbrow film critics as "hodgepodge stew" films, in reference to the frequent portrayals of a poor family eking out a difficult but honorable existence, often symbolized by gathering around a bowl of Persian stew (*abgusht*). Starting in the late 1930s, Iranian popular cinema, labeled *filmfarsi*, like their Indian and Egyptian counterparts, often follow a simple plot: a righteous man of meager means (though seldom a woman) from a poor urban or village background who, having been exposed to the temptations of large city, money, sex, and bad company, sinks low into a dangerous or hapless lifestyle. He is saved only by a moral awakening of some sort that leads to a happy ending, often in the form of union with a chaste woman. Scenes of singing and dancing, often in a lowbrow nightclub, were associated with the evils of drinking and inevitable café fights (borrowed from Western saloons). The reformed hero, in contrast, upholds virtues of sacrifice, generosity, care for his parents, and, of course, manly honor. Though the affluent classes were not always demonized, there were plenty of villainous capitalists, land speculators, and money grabbers (pl. 12.3).

With captivated viewers who packed movie theaters throughout the country, *filmfarsi* competed with foreign imports, both Hollywood and Indian productions, in offering entertainment and moral messages customized for Iranian popular tastes. Such films as *Ganj-e Qarun* (Qarun's treasure, 1965) and *Soltan-e Qalbha* (King of hearts, 1968) starred Mohammad 'Ali Fardin (1931–2000), a freestyle-wrestling Olympic silver medalist who became a movie star. Dashing and athletic, his lead character often championed the cause of the poor and deprived, lived modestly but honorably, and upheld the bonds of friendship while remaining cheerful, adventurous, and entertaining. This was all in the garb of a down-and-out modern *luti* who was always ready for a good fight. Fardin's physique, singing, dancing, and rascality that made him appealing in the film to rich and beautiful girls and opened the doors of privilege and wealth nevertheless could not divert the hero from his modest roots, a message particularly congenial to his viewers, who held the affable hero as one of their own.

In the best-known song in the 1965 *Ganj-e Qarun*—dubbed by Iraj (Hosain Khwajeh-Amiri, b. 1933), a professional singer of *luti* intonation—the penniless hero renounces the legendary treasure of Qarun (originally the biblical-Qur'anic Korah) along with other symbols of affluence and power in favor of a frugal but tranquil existence. As he sings, life is too short and not worth the trouble of amassing wealth, a message long embedded in the *luti* ethos. At the end, however, once the hero has defeated the rich villains, thanks to his chivalry, congeniality, and street smarts, he not only gets the girl but also the riches of Mr. Qarun, his own repentant father. More than just a predictable cliché, presumably a creation of Ahmad Shamlu, the happy ending reflected something of the aspirations of the working people, who were hoping to preserve values of modesty and honor while amicably sharing with the affluent their prosperity and pleasure. In 1965 more than two million viewers saw the movie and it brought in more than 53 million rial (about $7.5 million), remarkable numbers for any screening in Iranian film history.

In the 1969 drama *Qaysar* (meaning "Caesar" in Arabic and Persian), directed by Mas'ud Kimia'i, the theme of working-class morality took a very different turn. With a more professional directorship and sophisticated plot, the motivating force in the story is not a happy ending but vengeance for soiled family honor. The central character is not a rascal but an angry *luti* in modern guise, furious but committed to his chivalrous code of conduct. He has been left with no choice but to resort to violence against vicious enemies who dishonored his sister and killed his older brother. The fateful struggle ends with the family honor restored not only by the spilling of the blood of the villains but also by the hero's tragic end. The highly successful film, a hybrid of popular and artistic genres, did not employ singing and dancing or resort to a happy ending, as if reflecting a changing mood among its viewers. As later films by the same director made more explicit, *Qaysar* was a call to traditional values closely intertwined with religious symbolism. To save society from the onslaughts of its villains, there should be blood sacrifices, a message that not unsubtly denounced the Pahlavi vision of modernity and anticipated violence ahead.

A less idealized image of the changing code of chivalry than what was portrayed in *Qaysar* appeared in Dariush Mehrjui's 1975 *Dayereh-ye Mina* (Enameled Circle; *Cycle* in its English release), a piercing critique of the health profession in Iran written by the foremost playwright of the time, Gholam-Hosain Sa'edi. A psychiatrist by profession, Sa'edi had long explored in his plays and short stories a subversive and yet surreal Beckett-like world of the Iranian underclasses: haunted villagers, forgotten fishing communities, pimps and old prostitutes, beggars. A prolific writer, his Tudeh activism of the earlier years was transformed in the 1960s and early 1970s into an imaginative, at times disturbing, body of literary works with covert symbolism. The horrific world of the professional blood seller is one such setting.

The film is a study of mostly poor drug addicts in the neighborhoods of southern Tehran who sold blood for a living and the Mafia-like network that monopolized the trade. This is the world of 'Ali, a teenager coming of age in a big city. His metamorphosis turns him from an innocuous émigré into a ruthless agent of tainted blood, an antihero who in the process sells himself out, abandons his fatally ill father, and loses all his virtues in the ruthless pursuit of money and pleasure. The naked symbolism of the blood network, a commentary no doubt on the cruel forces that had infected Iranian society, especially its youth, was too naked to be missed. It was banned at the outset when the Iranian Medical Association protested the film's portrayal of hospital administration and later by censors who found it to be a negative portrayal of Iranian society.

Despite the growing Persian film and television industry, both popular and artistic foreign films and serials, especially Hollywood productions, continued to dominate the Iranian *écran* throughout the 1960s and 1970s. Entertainment value aside, in these films Hollywood in many ways visualized for ordinary Iranians images of Western societies, lifestyles, and gender roles, and in the process reinforced potent stereotypes. It was essentially through film that Iranians perceived America as an exciting land of opportunity, though not free from violence. The images of cowboys in the Wild West, the Mafia fighting in the streets of big cities, and plenty of racism, militarism, and promiscuity all complemented in the eyes of the non-Western viewers the realities of the Vietnam War, the civil rights movement, and political assassinations.

Biblical epics predictably were favorites of all classes, for they portrayed familiar stories of ancient prophets in a novel context. Starting with such high-budget productions as *Quo Vadis?* (1951) and *The Robe* (1953), the stream of movies with biblical content culminated with Cecil B. DeMille's 1956 remake of *The Ten Commandments*, William Wilder's 1959 *Ben-Hur*, and finally the 1961 *King of Kings* (released in Iran as *Forugh-e Bi-payan*, or "unending glory," presumably to avoid implying the Pahlavi royal title *shahanshah*, or "the king of kings"). For Iranian filmgoers, especially in larger cities, these moralistic narratives of the origins of Judaism and Christianity were complementary to the Islamic portrayal of Moses and Jesus, and yet different in many ways. Qur'anic narratives (*qisas*) aside, for centuries the prophets of the Hebrew Bible, especially Joseph and Moses, and the story of Jesus and Mary, had been revered in Persian literature. Hollywood also displayed images of America not only as promoter of biblical narrative or liberating force that saved the world from Nazi Germany and later stood against Soviet aggression but also as a land of prosperity and industrial and technological advances. The high-budget epics, as well as

Figure 12.9. This Persian poster of the 1950 *King Solomon's Mines* was typical of the publicity for Hollywood's blockbuster adventures.
M. Mehrabi, *Sadd va Panj Sal E'lan va Pster-e Film dar Iran* (Tehran: Nazar Publishers, 1393/2014), 480.

adventure movies, slapsticks in early days and light comedies later, thrillers, and gangster movies each in their own way enamored viewers by their scale, glitter, technical marvel, and acting skills (fig. 12.9).

Movie stars were household names and beside American presidents just about the only American personalities known to the general public. Glamour, physical appeal, and daring stunts captivated younger viewers. For some, mostly the urban secular middle class, the films served as prototypes of fashion and outfit; for others—mostly males of puritanical religious persuasion— they were demonstrations of sinful outrage. As more movie theaters opened in smaller cities across Iran in the 1960s and 1970s, often screening second- and third-rate Iranian and foreign movies, the magic of cinema fascinated more Iranians not merely as a form of entertainment but also as a point of reference to measure the realities of their own society and culture and those of the others—a world of imagination that could be admired or despised, sought after or avoided, and many times mixed feelings of desire and rejection were intertwined. It is not without reason that from the mid-1970s movie theaters became chief targets of militant Islamist attacks, who burned them down especially in smaller and more religious cities as symbols of an alien malady.

TAKHTI, PEOPLE'S CHAMPION

The cinema and its popular heroes and antiheros had a strong competitor in the world of sports, an alternative arena in which the Iranian working classes could engage and occasionally excel. Of all the Iranian sports, traditional wrestling (*koshti*) made the most successful transition to modern sports to become what is today freestyle wrestling. Part of the workout in *zurkhaneh*, wrestling was the physical test for a *pahlavan* (champion), placing him within the ritualistic setting of the *zurkhaneh* above any other role model. The *zurkhaneh*, probably the most accessible venue for the underprivileged, with an exclusively male membership, were magnificent sports houses rooted in the Persian culture of chivalry (*javanmardi*), often affiliated in distant past with popular Sufi orders. In reality, they were often venues for neighborhood *lutis* and their rookies. Before their decline in the Pahlavi era, they could be found in most neighborhoods—a domed structure with modest appearance, a sunken arena in the middle, a *morshed* (trainer) in his elevated bench conducting the collective workouts with the exhilarating rhythm of an enormous Persian drum, reminiscent of kettledrums, and melodic recitations from the *Shahnameh* and from Shi'i-Sufi poetry repertoire.

As the Pahlavi state began to encourage and sponsor modern sports through schools, factories, and modern gyms, much of the *zurkhaneh*'s talent and energy was diverted to new sports stages. Freestyle wrestling, along with weightlifting and soon soccer, became popular sports. Iranian teams made their appearance as early as the 1948 London Olympic Games, and by the 1952 Olympic Games in Helsinki they were earning medals. For the Iranian public, success in the Olympics was a source of excitement and pride coming at the time of Iran's oil nationalization campaign.

The most luminous of all Iranian sportsmen in modern times, on both the national and the international stage, no doubt is Gholam-Reza Takhti (1930–1968), a hero of undiminished popularity whose tragic end elevated him in the public esteem to the pantheon of modern Iranian icons. A great wrestler with a magnificent physique who won medals in three Olympics—silver in 1952 in Helsinki, gold in 1956 in Melbourne, and another silver in 1960 in Rome—he managed to stay in form for as long as twelve years, during the golden years of Iranian wrestling when the national team twice was world champion. He was loved, however, beyond his sporting successes for his amiable personality, his shy and unassuming demeanor, and in later years, his independent political views. A stalwart supporter of Mosaddeq and a member of the second National Front, he personified in truth a modern *luti* in his most upright manifestation: someone who in the public eye revived the chivalrous tradition of the *zurkhaneh* and upheld its values. It was not without reason that in winning the traditional wrestling championship he earned the title of world champion (*jahan pahlavan*), bestowed on him by the shah, who personally fastened on Takhti's arm the traditional armlet (fig. 12.10).

When he committed suicide in 1968 in a hotel room in Tehran, probably in a bout of severe depression, it was rumored that his death was foul play perpetrated by the Savak, just one of several untimely deaths of opposition figures (including Jalal Al-e Ahmad in 1969 and Ali Shari'ati in 1977) attributed to the security services but without any credible evidence whatsoever. The symbolism of Takhti's death was evident. He appeared to his admirers as a victim of the shah's regime; he was a tragic hero reminiscent of the virtuous Dash Akol, the chief character of Sadeq Hedayat's 1932 short story, who died fighting a wicked contender to save his honor. After 1979 Takhti was among the few popular heroes who survived the revolution. His name was conferred on many sport stadiums across the country so that it has become almost generic.

With the growing popularity of soccer through the 1960s and 1970s, and its regular media broadcast, wrestling and weightlifting took second place in favor of a team sport. Like societies of Latin America, Eastern Europe, and Africa, Ira-

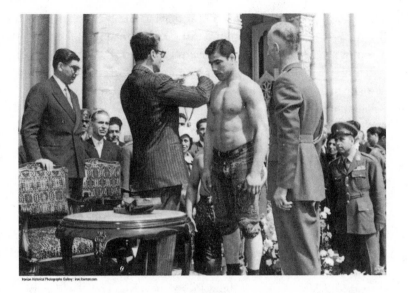

Figure 12.10. As a champion of traditional Persian wrestling, Takhti
receives a medal of honor from the shah, Tehran, c. early 1960s.
Contemporary Iranian photograph, https://www.tumblr.com/search/gholamreza%20takhti.

nian football soon emerged as an alternative public space reflecting collective
aspirations, often in the absence of meaningful political venues. The gathering
of large crowds in stadiums and the excitement of the match, particularly if
played against foreign teams, carried a nationalistic weight. For the vast majority of Iranian fans attending the matches or watching them on the nationwide
television broadcast, this was a shared experience of national solidarity. In the
case of the 1968 match-up of Iran and Israel during the Asian Cup in Tehran,
even though the Iranian team was victorious, afterward the Tehran crowd took
to the streets in a mix of jubilation and an instantaneous anti-Israeli—and by
implication, antiregime—protest. Fearing future such occurrences, the government introduced stringent security measures. A restive crowd displaying an
ideological motive was an early indication of the popular defiance that would
erupt a decade later in a popular revolution.

PLAGUE OF THE WEST AND SEARCH FOR AUTHENTICITY

Signs of dissent in music, cinema, and sports complemented a conceptual
rethinking of Iranian culture, and eventually a reassessment of religious myths
and values. At the heart of this revisionist trend, beyond the familiar mood of

frustration and despair in poetry and music that had been characteristic of Iran's intellectual production ever since the 1950s (not to mention the postconstitutional era) was reassessment of such tokens as modernization and Westernization. To this end, Jalal Al-e Ahmad's 1962 *Gharbzadehgi* was hugely influential in setting a nativist discourse of a return to the "authentic" culture and, by extension, to the authentic self. In the pungent days of the 1970s Al-e Ahmad's discourse of cultural authenticity evolved into a journey of rediscovery for "true Islam." A powerful motif before and during the 1979 revolution, *Gharbzadehgi* later rendered a rhetorical tool in the service of the Islamic Republic and its polemicists.

By all appearances Al-e Ahmad (1923–1969) was an implausible candidate for the Islamic hall of virtual martyrs to which he was elevated after his premature death. He was a beret-wearing, cigarette-smoking, heavy-drinking *intellectualle de gauche*, loyal to the demeanor of that type. Handsome and witty, with a critical outlook and a sharp tongue, he held court in fashionable cafés in Tehran, where he discussed the latest highbrow French novels and remarked on works of his protégés with an air of subtle sarcasm worthy of an *engagé* intellectual. After visiting the United States in 1965—he was a fellow in the Harvard program for foreign intellectuals run by Henry Kissinger—he also became a jeans-wearing jazz buff. He had married an American-educated professor of art history, Simin Daneshvar, who became a celebrated novelist in her own right and arguably superior to Al-e Ahmad (fig. 12.11). He was a translator of Gide, Camus, and Sartre, he read Steinbeck and Faulkner (in French or Persian translation), and he was influenced most visibly in his unique prose style by the French writer Ferdinand Céline. He was a literary critic, reviewing novels and plays as well as painting exhibitions; an ethnographer of sorts with a true nostalgia for the old world of the Iranian countryside and its dying culture; and a travel writer who visited the Soviet Union, the United States, and Israel, among other places, and wrote with his typical mix of biased sarcasm and skewed self-righteousness.

Yet there was more to Al-e Ahmad's story. He was the son of a village mullah from the Taleqan region. His father immigrated to Tehran in the 1920s. In his teens young Jalal was a part-time apprentice in the Tehran bazaar while preparing to enter a seminary and become a mullah. His father's hopes were dashed when Jalal abandoned the life of the Shi'i clergy for a modern education and eventually became a high school teacher of Persian literature. Like most of the young and educated in the postwar era, he joined the Tudeh Party in its early days but soon became disillusioned with its Soviet-style communism after witnessing the duplicity of the Tudeh leadership and their subservience to Soviet ambitions during the Azarbaijan crisis and the botched Caspian oil concession.

Figure 12.11. Simin Daneshvar with her husband, Jalal Al-e Ahmad, Tehran, 1955.
Private collection.

Reading André Gide's 1937 *Return from the USSR* (which he translated from French to Persian) only confirmed his aversion to Stalinism, although it did not erode his faith in socialism. He split from Tudeh in 1948 along with his mentor, Khalil Maleki, and in 1952 he cofounded Niru-ye Sevvom (Third Force), the Iranian version of the French Troisième Force, as an affiliate of the National Front. In 1960 the Third Force, under the new title Society of the Socialists of the National Movement, attracted a host of independent socialists, intellectuals, and younger activists. Despite internal tensions, even between Maleki and Al-e Ahmad, the society survived for another decade, having been barely tolerated by the regime.

The nagging ghost of the Islamic clerical past never fully deserted Al-e Ahmad. As if he never came out from under his father's clerical robe, he discovered in the Shiʻi clerical space an "authentic" quality. In this he found a bastion against the onslaught of what seemed to him an alien, hegemonic "West" that metamorphosed non-Western societies into Westernized fakes that are gratefully subservient to their almighty hegemon. This was an outlook not in variance with the discourse of alienation in neo-Marxism of the 1950s and 1960s and its permutation among the French existentialist thinkers, and in line with the fashionable debate of *machinisme*, all of course with an Islamicized cultural twist.

Al-e Ahmad's serious pitfall, however, was to take this accidental café talk on *Gharbzadehgi* a step further into a grand cultural theory that he hurriedly, and carelessly, pieced together. Its aim was to place blame for the cultural, political, and social ailments of non-Western societies, such as Iran, squarely on the shoulders of Western modernity, and more so on the faulty experiences of Westernism in the twentieth century. In this respect *Gharbzadehgi* turned out to be—independent of the author's intention, perhaps—an ill-defined and self-righteous nativist theory. Such a discourse fit well into the grand narrative of Shi'i persecution, for it laid all the blame on the shoulder of the villainous Other. Oblivious of the blind conservatism of the clerical elite, Ale-e Ahmad shepherded the hapless intellectuals of the post-1953 generation to go back to their origins by seeking salvation in Shi'i culture of resistance, not in Marxism.

Al-e Ahmad's *Gharbzadehgi* was, needless to say, an obvious reaction to the mindless positivism of the Europeanized (*mostafrang*) type that dominated the stage in the postconstitutional era and even more assertively during the Pahlavi epoch, a generation with a built-in inferiority complex over all things Western. These worshippers in the temple of Western "civilization" built the post–World War I Middle East from Turkey to the Arab World and South Asia. For them, even Europe's mad militarism, genocide, slavery, colonialism, and litany of other evils that darkened Europe's and America's histories were not all visible, or at best were rationalized by the all-too-familiar rationale of "might is right."

First inspired through reading other Iranian critiques of Westernism (such as Kasravi), a greater conceptual influence upon Al-e Ahmad came from Ahmad Fardid (1909–1994), who had coined the term *gharbzadehgi*. Fardid was a professor of Continental philosophy in Tehran University and for a while had become the focus of Al-e Ahmad's attention and the core of his cultural orientation. As was Al-e Ahmad, Fardid was a reinvented intellectual who came from a madrasa background. A Heideggerian of sorts, or so he believed, with sporadic knowledge of Islamic philosophy and mysticism, Fardid had spent some years in postwar Germany, France, and Switzerland, where he immersed himself, unsystematically, in German idealist philosophy and was deeply influenced by the anti-Semitic and anti-modernist traits still strong in post-Nazi European milieu. Returning to Iran in 1955, he was exposed to a discourse of Iranian Shi'i philosophy advanced by Henry Corbin (1903–1978), the French scholar and head of the Institut Français in Tehran. Also a former Heideggerian, Corbin's keen interest in the philosophy of light (*maktab-e eshraq*) and the so-called theosophist school of Isfahan influenced a number of Iranian students of philosophy and intellectuals of his time. Corbin also belonged to a European circle of anti-modernist intellectuals who, concurrent with Heidegger's teachings, thrived in the early part of the twentieth century in France and Germany.

Contentious and eccentric, Fardid had a paranoid view of Iranian modernity, which was inherited by Al-e Ahmad. Fardid's ahistorical vision of the Islamic intellectual past made him argue that the course of Islamic philosophy had long been influenced—indeed, adulterated—by the Greek post-Socratic, and especially Aristotelian, philosophy; he first labeled this the "Greek-malady" (*Yunan-zadehgi*) and then *gharbzadehgi*. Having Heidegger's notion of reorientation in mind, as well as the German philosopher's preoccupation with pre-Socratic sages, Fardid prescribed a "return" to a new understanding of Persian mysticism and mystical poetry and to Islamic philosophy as a way of transcending the prevailing "reality" of the West.

Al-e Ahmad tendentiously borrowed Fardid's *gharbzadehgi* and popularized it by injecting a heavy dose of third worldism. He also adopted Fardid's anti-modernist stance, especially his critique of Iranian modernity of the twentieth century, from the Constitutional Revolution to the Pahlavi era, in nearly all its aspects. This was a revolt against the kind of modernity of which Fardid and Al-e Ahmad both were undeniable byproducts. "Westernism," in Al-e Ahmad's scheme, had become a pervasive affliction, like cholera or the plague, affecting all aspects of society and culture in Iran as in all non-Western societies. Such a malaise, he argued, affected all aspects of education, culture, lifestyle, economic development, and social relations. These are "symptoms that are devoid of any traditions to rely upon, any historical continuity, and any means of measuring change; they are only the gift of the machine." The phenomenon of the *gharbzadehgi*, Al-e Ahmad believed, "is characteristic of an era in our history when we have not yet mastered the machine and are unaware of its structure and knowhow." In other words an era when "we are not yet fully acquainted with [modern] science and technology."[3] Pahlavi modernism, he thus implied, was subservient to Western economic and geopolitical interests and the chief reason for Iran's dependence and for Iranian alienation. Al-e Ahmad's critique acquired him a growing readership, even though the censors had banned the book's official release.

The weakest aspect of *Gharbzadehgi* was its often erroneous, and highly tendentious, reading of the Iranian past. His careless and ideologically colored assertions and his overall contemptuous view of Iran's political legacy came to influence generations of eager but naive readers. In this respect *Gharbzadehgi* may be counted among the most damaging Persian texts produced in the twentieth century. Clandestinely available to all who wished to read it, in the climate of the 1960s and 1970s, when all other avenues of open and dispassionate political debate, even social criticism, were effectively closed, Al-e Ahmad's pamphleteering offered a fresh alternative. *Gharbzadehgi*'s conspiratorial view of history blamed the West for everything that went wrong with the East (another questionable cultural construct). The premodern East was nostalgically painted as a pristine and "authentic" past that was, in his view, coherent and congenial, almost idyllic.

In Al-e Ahmad's conspiratorial worldview, aside from the sacred history of Islam and the Shi'i clerical establishment, few historical forces and actors remained unscathed. Culprits included movements of dissent from the Isma'ilis of Alamut to the Sufis, the Noqtavis, new schools of thought including Safavid philosophers of the seventeenth century, and religious minorities including the Jews and the Baha'is. Political powers from the Abbasid caliphate to Turkish dynasties of the Islamic Middle Ages, the Mamluks of Egypt, the Ottomans, the Safavids and Qajars, and even the nomads of the Iranian interior were seen as creatures or collaborators or as unintended victims of sinister Christian powers that, ever since the inception of Islam, had been hatching plots against Muslims and especially against the people and culture of Iran. Their ranks included the Byzantines, the Crusaders, the Vatican, the Venetians and the Genoans, European trading companies, Christian missionaries, European travelers, and the more predictable nemeses, such as colonial empires of the nineteenth century, oil companies, US spy agencies, and the economic and cultural long arms of Yankee imperialism.

In this cosmic onslaught of evil against the good, even the Mongols of the Gobi Desert and the Uighurs of Eastern Turkistan were not spared. European Christians not only had provoked the Crusades and the Mongol and Timurid invasions but also somehow instigated the Sunni-Shi'i conflict between the Ottomans and Safavids. Later in the twentieth century the failure of pan-Islamism was considered the outcome of European plots. These were conspiracies to destroy the solidarity of the Muslims, taint their "pure" culture, and lay hands on their material resources. In Al-e Ahmad's customary self-righteous tone and abbreviated style, this litany of assertions was appealing to his young and historically uninformed readership and soothing to their injured sentiments. His rendering of the Islamic past triggered a sense of victimization inherent in the Shi'i narrative and conveniently placed the fault of Muslim "decline" squarely on the shoulders of hostile others.

Al-e Ahmad's paranoid history aside, in many respects his *Gharbzadehgi*, though rushed and polemical, anticipated not only critiques of Orientalism in the 1970s but also the world-system and dependency theories of the 1980s. Here, emphasis on the wholesale import of the West's material culture and ideas, adopting the so-called *montage* mentality, and relying on a rentier oil economy, was novel. It contested the Pahlavi modernism project and posed a counterargument to the modernization theory in its heyday, when "underdeveloped" countries were demanded by the likes of the World Bank to resort to heavy industry, a planned economy, and wholesale overhaul of their agrarian economies. By contrast, Al-e Ahmad questioned the kind of rushed "progress" that summed up the shah's White Revolution that emerged shorty after and the mentality of the technocrats who presided over it. Before his eyes, Al-e Ahmad could see the dismantling of the village economies and village communities, growth of overpopulated and badly organized cities, and a way of life and an identity about to be wiped out. Yet despite the advocacy of cultural authentic-ity, Al-e Ahmad also believed that "inventing the machine" would remedy the maladies of the developing societies. Though informed by the then fashionable discourse of *machinisme,* it is curious that he also subscribed to the modern-ization theory as a means of liberation from Western economic and cultural hegemony.

Deeper still in Al-e Ahmad's *Gharbzadehgi* was a fear of an alien intrusion revoking a Shi'i-Iranian dichotomy of the "chaste" body versus the alien "pol-luting" agents. It was as if the satanic forces had invaded the "pure" core of believers. That is what brought Al-e Ahmad, and a generation of like-minded intellectuals, to the bosom of an idealized Islamic alternative. A popular slogan of revolutionary days: "Neither Western nor Eastern [but] the Islamic Repub-lic" (*na sharghi, na gharbi, jomhuri-ye Islami*) aptly resonated, Al-e Ahmad's lasting mark on shaping the Islamic Revolution. It is highly doubtful, however, that Al-e Ahmad himself would have survived that revolution even in its initial stages.

SHARI'ATI'S REVOLUTIONARY ISLAM

Of comparable standing to Al-e Ahmad in the shaping of a nativist Islamic dis-course was 'Ali Shari'ati (1933–1977), another generational icon with an eclec-tic worldview. In the late 1960s his fiery sermons, numerous popular books, pamphlets, and cassette recordings made him a new prophet of revolutionary Shi'ism. Like Al-e Ahmad, who had an early influence on him, Shari'ati too was born to a religious family from a village around Sabzevār, an old stronghold of Shi'ism, to Mashhad, where his father, a lay preacher of some fame, ran a religious center with a revivalist agenda. As with Al-e Ahmad, the National Movement of the early 1950s and the dissident political culture that followed it into the 1960s also shaped Shari'ati. He, too, was a high school teacher and supporter of the National Front. His path diverted, however, once he moved to France on a government fellowship, where he earned a *doctora de l'université* from the Sorbonne in sociology of religion. The not-so-rigorous degree, then acquirable with a modicum of academic effort, was good enough to land him on the faculty of Mashhad University. His dissertation, a run-of-the-mill textual analysis of a Persian mystical text, was of no scholarly value.

While in France, Shari'ati became interested in politics of the left, and especially in the Algerian Revolution, then in the late 1950s in full swing. He supported the Islamic wing of the movement and sympathized with its anticolonial objectives, searching all the while for new readings of Islam through the prism of sociology of religion, then an academic novelty. George Gurvitch (1894–1965), the Russian-born French sociologist and a strong advocate of Algerian independence, impressed Shari'ati and helped him contextualize Islam not merely as a system of beliefs and rituals but as a socioreligious movement. He may have also been inspired by Louis Massignon's 1922 *La passion d'al Hallaj*, a seminal study of the life and time of the early Shi'i Sufi martyr. The young Shari'ati could not have missed Massignon's personal history (1883–1962) and his inspirational neo-Catholicism, with its ecumenical tilt toward Islam and with a growing fascination with the Shi'i myth of martyrdom.

The greatest influence on Shari'ati, however, came from the Caribbean-born Frantz Fanon (1925–1961) and his revolutionary anticolonial thesis then in vogue among intellectuals of the left. Fanon, a Francophone intellectual, became almost a role model for Shari'ati, who translated into Persian his *The Wretched of the Earth* (*Les damnés de la Terre*) soon after it was published in 1961. Through Fanon, Shari'ati came to view the struggle against colonialism, then epitomized by the Algerian Revolution, as an existential struggle for human liberation in which suffering and sacrifice of the oppressed were to restore not only political freedom but also human dignity and moral responsibility. Fanon had become the voice of passionate intellectuals and activists of the so-called third world, a term widely employed to define a geography of deprivation and dependency on the West. Still socialist in its core, Fanon's anticolonialism went beyond Marxian class struggle to emphasize national, cultural, ethnic, and religious ties. These he held as crucial tools for struggle, even armed struggle, to cast off alien ideologies on both sides of the global divide. Shari'ati absorbed that message but refashioned it to fit his own mytho-historical reading of Shi'ism.

Returning to Iran in 1964, he was inevitably harassed by Savak and detained for his dissident activities abroad, but soon, possibly after giving assurances, he was allowed to hold his university position teaching sociology of religion and history in Mashhad University. He made a name for himself as a motivated teacher with radical views about Islamic history and setting it in a novel context for his growing audiences. His intellectual brinkmanship made him tolerable to the regime so long as he observed his rhetorical limits. Moving to Tehran a couple of years later, he soon became the most prominent public voice in Hosainiyeh-e Ershad, where he came to be known as an inspirational speaker who understood the younger generations of alienated Iranians.

Hosainiyeh-e Ershad was a modern religious institution in northern Tehran established in 1964 to promote a fresh Islamic perspective palatable to mostly university students and educated professionals. Reminiscent of Catholic establishments in France or Evangelical halls in the United States, or closer to home to Tehran's former Baha'i center, it was entirely different from the familiar environment of mosques and traditional takkiyehs where Muharram mourning ceremonies were held. It was a domed structure with Persian tile work that covered a spacious hall equipped with auditorium seats, air-conditioning, an audio system, a library, and exhibition space. Qur'anic verses in colorful tilework decorated the hall's center stage. For Shari'ati this offered the right ambiance to preach, for nearly a decade, his massage of Islamic rediscovery and Shi'i activism in a language of restrained metaphors. For audiences who came in droves to listen to him, Ershad's surroundings presented something modern, bright, and dignified, an ideal setting for a charming lecturer, handsome, well dressed in suit and tie, shaved, smiling, and speaking with a trace of a delightful Khorasani accent. He was a novelty even secularized middle-class Iranians could not ignore.

Shari'ati's style was sentimental, even melodramatic, and intense. He loved preaching, understood his audiences, and knew which sympathetic chords to strike. Though long winded to the point of being loquacious, repetitive, and declamatory, he was not boring, at least not to his young and dedicated followers who regularly attended his lectures, listened to his cassette tapes, and studiously devoured his growing oeuvre in print. His writing style was equally rambling, emotional, and intense, fitting the quasi-mystical and entirely ahistorical message that he was preaching. Sensational mytho-history was at the core of his popularity.

Considering himself a theistic existentialist, Shari'ati sought a massage of liberation in the Qur'anic narrative and in the Shi'i past. He was not interested in the empirical, factual history of Islam, which he dismissed as irrelevant and misleading, produced by oppressive powers and Westerners. Rather, he sought in the early Shi'i sacred past archetypes for his vision of revolt against political and religious oppressions. In his message there existed a potent amalgam of Fanon, Sartre, and Massignon, alongside Marx, Mosaddeq, Algeria's National Liberation Front, and Al-e Ahmad, not to mention Shari'ati's own father and his advocacy of "true" Islam. Such characters were synthesized and amalgamated in Shari'ati's mind to make his early Islamic heroes speak his revolutionary message. They ranged from 'Ali, Hosain, and Fatima to such early companions of the Prophet as the emaciated Abyssinian slave Bilal and the pro-'Alid figures Abu-Dharr al-Ghifari and 'Ammar ibn Yasir. In the vocal and written universe of

'Ali Shari'ati they turned into champions of social justice, self-sacrifice (*ithar*), and revolt against the oppressors. The early deniers of the Prophet among the Quraysh and their Umayyad descendants, Mu'awiya and his son Yazid, were predictable villains. They were timely signifiers who pointed to the Pahlavi regime.

In this sacred past, the age of the early believers, Shari'ati imagined a dynamic course when the pure, egalitarian, and self-sacrificing Imams and their companions actively resisted their corrupt oppressors. This he called the age of 'Alid Red Shi'ism. Here in the House of the Prophet, the so-called Five of the Mantle (of the Prophet), more popularly known as the Five Bodies (*panj tan*) — namely Mohammad, 'Ali, Fatima, Hasan, and Hosain, and their loyal supporters — he sought a "religion of protest." In this narrative of revolutionary Shi'ism, Shari'ati was a modern "promoter" (*maddah*) and a contemporizing "reciter of the sufferings" who assigned to his "wronged" heroes the urgent task of revolutionary rebellion against their oppressive villains. By contrast, his "Safavid Black Shi'ism" stood for clerical conservatism, which he characterized as compromising, pedantic, and rapacious. The dichotomy of the two forms of 'Alid and Safavid Shi'ism was devoid of plausible historical reference. Furthermore, he believed that the rise of Safavid Shi'ism against the Sunni Ottomans was the outcome of a conspiracy to divide Islamic unity, a conspiratorial perspective he shared with Al-e Ahmad. Yet his mytho-history was electrifying to his audiences, who could contrast Shari'ati and his seemingly valiant and dynamic Islam to the stagnant world of turbaned Shi'ism.

Shari'ati's criticism of the Pahlavi regime was understandably implicit, though not entirely veiled. Nor were his allusions beyond the grasp of the Savak agents who routinely monitored his activities and occasionally harassed him. Despite much disruption by Savak, and a break with Mortaza Motahhari (1919–1979), a representative of the less rigid clerical wing of Qom who also was active in Ershad. Shari'ati went on lecturing and publishing until the closure of Ershad in 1972. His publications, widely available to people from all walks of life, was a source of anxiety to the regime. Yet the fact that he was not completely silenced, one may surmise, was because the regime valued him as an effective counterweight to a fast-radicalizing clerical opposition in Qom. Only in 1972, at the height of urban guerrilla clashes, Shari'ati was seen as a serious threat. He was accused of collaboration with the People's Mojahedin and subsequently spent eighteen months in solitary confinement, before being released with the shah's consent when international publicity for his release were loud enough to make the shah realize the disadvantage of keeping a popular figure like Shari'ati in detention. For two yeas after his release he lived under virtual house arrest with his health in serious decline. In early 1977 he was allowed to leave the country after Savak forced him to publish, or forged on his behalf, a statement in praise of the White Revolution. When he arrived in England in March, he was suffering from depression and other ailments. Soon after he died of a massive heart attack in a hospital in Southampton. Oddly enough, the circumstances surrounding his death did not alarm the British authorities enough to hold an inquest. Regardless, Shari'ati was to be remembered by the Iranian opposition as another victim of the Savak, even though his premature death, like that of Al-e Ahmad, was due to health reasons, most likely heavy smoking.

DISARRAY IN A CULTURAL SPACE

Nearly two decades of state patronage had opened a wider and more exciting cultural space in Iran. Media, especially television, artistic venues, the press and book publication, and growing viewership and readership offered intellectuals and artists a broader market and greater recognition. These happened despite the shrinking political horizons and the state's obsessive efforts to silence all forms of dissent or coopt willing partners. Voices of dissent survived, however veiled, in the state's broadcasting network, in cinema, and in various cultural and public institutions. Insofar as giving Iranians a more articulate sense of themselves, the state was able to reap the fruits of a half century of Pahlavi nationalist policies. But as it remained closely identified with a vision of positivist progress and Westernizing modernity, it also set in motion a quest for "authenticity" and cultural sovereignty. Palpable in many quarters, among writers, poets and filmmakers, the return to the authentic self had an irresistible lure. Popular music, even artists whose prosperity was indebted to middle-class stability under the Pahlavi rule, could occasionally sing ballads of heroic fall, alienation, and martyrdom.

Intellectuals and activists who remained outside the state's reach had their own possibilities. Such figures as Al-e Ahmad, Shamlu, and later Shari'ati were able to frequent their own circles and speak, write, translate, and publish so long as they avoided taboos. Overt criticism was out of the question, but political symbolism of all sorts and allusions to political repression and social ills were not entirely silenced despite censorship and intimidation (fig. 12.12). Metaphors, hints, and literary brinkmanship had long been familiar in the Persian milieu, and unsurprisingly they became second nature to the post-1953 generation. Under censorship, strategies of dissent thrived, ensuring greater originality and innovation. The audiences, too, shared in the codified language of dissent and took pleasure in unraveling literary cryptograms and political clues. A

Figure 12.12. A thinly veiled critical view of the shah and Pahlavi statesmen
by the gifted satirist Ardeshir Mohassess. In this 1977 portrayal of a public
audience, Mohammad 'Ali Shah Qajar, with his Kayanid crown, substitutes
for Mohammad Reza Shah Pahlavi during the last years of his rule.
"The existence of a suspicious cabinet minster was reported to the king," *Life in Iran*,
collection of drawings, Library of Congress, CD 1—Mohassess, no. 34.

prevailing culture of resentment that was mastered by intellectuals and artists
was well suited to a language of allusions and symbols and to the recycling of
old paradigms of Shi'i Islam in a new activist guise.

High but sanitized culture came to serve a purpose: releasing excessive social
pressures created by a booming economy and autocratic rule. While the secularized middle classes could, and partially did, become absorbed into the cultural milieu, the lower middle classes, the urban migrants, and the traditional
sectors of Iranian society by and large remained outside the state's reach. The
state's cultural policies were largely geared to absorb the intellectual left rather
than the forces of religious dissent. The former could relay cryptic message
of dissent, as much as possible, and hope for better days. The latter enjoyed
fewer forums and had to rely mostly on its own traditional venues. The closure of Hosainiyeh-e Ershad ironically diverted more energies and attention to
mosques, Qur'an study classes, and inspirational preaching presided over by
activist clergy who were not patronized by the state.

Part Four

A CONTESTED REVOLUTION AND THE RISE OF THE ISLAMIC REPUBLIC

The tumultuous events that led to the revolution of 1979 and the establishment of the Islamic Republic of Iran were a classic example of modern popular revolution. A momentary confluence of forces of discontent, which mostly relied on mobilizing urban lower middle classes and the grassroots bazaar, succeeded in bringing down the Pahlavi regime and dismantling its power structure. Out of a broad alliance of Islamic tendencies there emerged a militant clerical leadership, led by Ayatollah Khomeini. Over the course of the following decade, Khomeini played a decisive part in defining the Islamic Republic, as well as its ideology and institutions. Even though the revolution had its roots in Iran's experience of the past seven decades, the rise and the consolidation of the new regime caused huge contentions and conflicts.

Prevailing over its opponents at home largely by coercion and violence, and despite setbacks in the prolonged war against its Iraqi neighbor, by 1989, when Ayatollah Khomeini died, the Islamic regime had been able, it was evident, to put down roots. Yet the years that followed revealed ideological chasms and political tensions within the Islamic Republic that echoed the demands of younger generations of Iranians for social freedoms, democracy, and an end to international isolation. Independent of the Islamic regime's nepotism, ideological blind spots, and socioeconomic quagmires, Iranian society did fundamentally evolve. It created its own space and its own culture and artistic imagination. Two decades after the Islamic Revolution prevailed, the 2009 Green Movement revealed profound discontent and disillusionment within Iranian society.

13

THE MAKING OF THE ISLAMIC
REVOLUTION (1977–1979)

Between August 1978 and February 1979, a period of less than seven months, Iran witnessed a revolution that brought down the Pahlavi regime and abolished the institution of monarchy, wiped out the privileges of the Pahlavi elite, and significantly weakened its secularized middle classes. In its stead Ayatollah Khomeini and his associates created the Islamic Republic, which aimed to establish the "Guardianship of the Jurist" (*welayat-e faqih*) as the only legitimate model of governance. The Islamic Revolution, as it soon came to be known inside Iran and out, was backed by Islamic activists, many of them radicals, the urban poor, merchants of the bazaar, and, for a while at least, by the youth, the university students, lower-ranking government employees, and men and women of modest urban backgrounds. It was financed, at least at the outset, by sympathizers in the bazaar community and by other religiously inclined people in Tehran and other major cities and through dues paid to local mojtaheds or representatives of Khomeini.

Ideologically, it was a strange mix of return to pristine Islam, the shari'a-laden worldview of Khomeini and his cohorts in Qom, notions of Islamic modernity (as understood by tie-wearing Islamists such as Mahdi Bazargan), dormant Shi'i messianic aspirations, rampant anti-Westernism, and anti-Pahlavi sentiment. It demonstrated in its earlier stages genuine aspirations for democracy, freedom of speech, and human rights but also exhibited shades of leftist ideas as seen through the prism of the secular and the Islamic guerrilla organizations and their sympathizers and soon the sympathizers of the revived Tudeh Party. Coming in the wake of major twentieth-century revolutions in Russia and China, the Islamic Revolution was informed as much by third-world postcolonial discourse as by the radicalizing experience of the Cuban Revolution, the Vietnam

War and the unfolding tragedy of the Palestinian liberation movement. It soon evolved into a textbook revolution with momentous domestic and international repercussions.

In its historical context, the Islamic Revolution proved far more encompassing, though much less "innocent," than the Constitutional Revolution seven decades earlier. And, as it turned out, it was far less loyal to its own democratic and liberalizing promises than the Constitutional Revolution. By some stretch of historical rationale it was also a rebellious child of the National Movement of the Mosaddeq era. It inherited from that era not only street politics, on a much larger scale, but also a sense of defiance vis-à-vis the great powers. In its social exposure it was more widespread than both the Constitutional Revolution and the National Movement, and in certain ways it tried to complement the unfulfilled aspirations of both those events. Without falling victim to historical teleology, one can draw a line—a zigzagging and broken but nevertheless traceable one—from the *mashru'eh* demand of the constitutional period to the extremism of the Fada'iyan-e Islam of the postwar era and the ideology of the Islamic Revolution.

Across the wider span of the Iranian past, the Islamic Revolution may be compared in its intensity with the rise of the Safavid state and the establishment of Shi'ism as the official creed. More immediately, it was perhaps less decisive for Iran than the rise of Pahlavi state had been half a century earlier. Yet it was far more instrumental in its long-term social and demographic impact. The Islamic ideology and its beneficiaries aside, the revolution also released an unprecedented reservoir of creative energies at what may be called the social peripheries of the Iranian society. Insofar as its regional and global impact, the Islamic Revolution is the first, and so far the only, popular movement in the Muslim World that has sustained and successfully driven forward its ideological agenda. The establishment of the Islamic Republic, it can be argued, reinvigorated Islamist activism throughout the Muslim world and propelled it beyond the postcolonial nationalist and socialist aspirations or Salafi obscurantism of earlier decades. It is the potency of this brand of politicized Islam, and its Shi'i underpinnings, that transformed Iran's manifold strands of opposition into a monolithic revolution. It affected, moreover, the Islamically inspired movements of the early 1980s in neighboring Iraq and, to a lesser extent, Afghanistan, Pakistan, Lebanon, and Syria.

Like any major revolution, the true beginnings of the Islamic Revolution were debated as much as its outcomes. With the benefit of hindsight we can identify a number of systemic problems in the late Pahlavi era, especially from the mid-1970s on, which were at the root of the early protests and revolutionary impulses. The socioeconomic, demographic, and cultural changes of the late Pahlavi era sharpened social divisions and contributed to public discontent. By 1976, the fall in Iran's oil revenue and subsequent budgetary shortfall had slowed down the shah's overambitious development projects. Perennial repression, at the same time, eroded support among the middle classes and even alienated the elite.

These were ingredients capable of igniting some form of social protest, but are perhaps not enough to explain the potency of the forthcoming revolution and its swift success. In the mid-1970s, and as late as 1977, only the most radical trends on the Iranian left, such as the Fada'iyan-e Khalq and Mojahedin-e Khalq guerilla organizations, yearned for a revolution on the Marxist model, a prospect unforeseen at the time even by the most astute observers. The near vanquishing of urban guerrilla organizations by the mid-1970s relegated that project to the distant future, though no doubt sharpened public resentment among a younger generation of Iranians. The road to revolution was to be paved, however, not by guerrilla warfare but by mass support for a prophetic figure, the likes of whom Iran had rarely seen in its recent past. Ayatollah Khomeini and his cohorts, who reaped the fruits of many decades of fury, benefited from a unique opportunity to build their own monopoly on power.

FIRST SPARKS

Signs of political protest came rather unexpectedly with a change in the international climate. During the US presidential campaign in the fall of 1976, Jimmy Carter, the Democratic candidate, made human rights and free speech the major concern of his foreign policy. The worldwide echo quickly reached Iran and raised new hopes. Though primarily aimed at the Soviet Union and the Eastern Bloc, Carter's advocacy, even before assuming office in January 1977, sent a positive signal to Iranian liberal opposition, including veterans of the former National Front, lawyers, intellectuals, journalists, and dormant revolutionaries from the olden days. Encouraged by Carter's initiative, a reversal of Nixon's support for pro-US dictators worldwide, in early 1977 individuals and small groups began writing open letters addressed to Premier Hovayda and to the shah, criticizing human rights violations and demanding greater accountability. They also raised concerns about the state's flawed economic policies, wasteful and mismanaged development projects, nepotism and corruption in high office, dysfunctional bureaucracy, culture of subservience and sycophancy, alienating social policies, and ill effects of the shah's autocratic style. These voices, audible after years of silence, were a refreshing breeze in a climate of royal adulation and chronic subservience. Hovayda's premiership, after thirteen dreary years of holding office, seemed vulnerable. In his familiar fashion, the shah, who was the root cause of many of the state's failed polices, began to point the finger of blame at his subordinates. And Hovayda was the first to go.

Open letters, having been widely circulated in intellectual and clerical circles by means of photocopies and word of mouth, however, held responsible not only Hovayda but implicitly the shah. These were the first critical statements not retaliated by the Savak, at least not immediately. The mellow response was bound to be interpreted by the still amorphous opposition as a sign of the shah's readjustment to the new US administration. On June 12, 1977, when an open letter addressed to the shah by Karim Sanjabi, Dariush Foruhar, and Shapur Bakhtiar was first circulated, neither the authors nor the recipient or readers could have perceived the enormity of the upheavals that eighteen months later would bring the Pahlavi regime to its knees. The authors warned the shah:

> At this juncture when we submit this letter, the country is at the brink of an abyss, all efforts have reached a dead-end, public necessities—and particularly the price of foodstuffs and housing—have swollen tremendously and caused shortages; agriculture and livestock have reached near extinction; budding national industries and human resources are in crisis and on shaky grounds, and the trade imbalance reflecting an import-export discrepancy is startling. The oil [revenue], this God-given blessing, has been seriously mismanaged and programs that were presented under the rubric of reform and the [White] revolution, have remained unfulfilled. Worst of all, the disregard for human rights and personal and social liberties, a breach of the very foundation of the constitution, together with signs of extreme terror, growing corruption, decadence, and sycophancy, have brought national morale to its lowest ebb.

The unusually blunt tone, reflecting the angry mood of the time, was complemented by a plea that the shah take a conciliatory course before it became too late:

> The only road to salvation and relief from the current difficulties and pitfalls that threaten the future of Iran is to abandon autocratic rule, fully comply with the values of the constitutional regime [*mashrutiyat*], restore the rights of the people, truly respect the Constitution and the Universal Declaration of Human Rights, set aside the one-party system, allow freedom of the press and freedom of association, free political prisoners and political exiles, and establish a regime based on elected representatives of the people, who according to the Constitution are accountable for the conduct of the government.[1]

It is wrong to believe that President Carter's advocacy of human rights was solely responsible for raising such voices or for the shah's greater latitude. By 1977 the effects of mismanagement, corruption in state projects, and unpopular price stabilization measures were palpable enough to prompt protest. The global recession and the ensuing revenue shortfall caused by the glut in the oil market further slowed government projects. The perennial criticism from international human rights organizations, Amnesty International in particular, over military tribunals, mock trials, and treatment of political prisoners darkened the regime's image. President Carter's human rights policy thus was more of a stimulant than a prime cause, a conduit through which the subterranean reservoir of social discontent found its way to the surface and soon erupted in a revolutionary movement.

The shah's health also had some bearing on the rapidly shifting climate. In the early 1970s he had been diagnosed with a mild case of lymphoma, a condition that for years was guarded with the utmost secrecy. For the first few years, evidently in a state of denial, he conceived of no realistic plans for the transfer of power. He did appoint Queen Farah as viceroy to the minor crown prince Reza, but this was for the most part a formality. In a male-dominated Pahlavi court where all matters great and small hinged on royal approval—even minute details of military and civilian affairs—the shah could not afford to be seen as a cancer patient or a dying man. The entire system relied on the royal persona exuding an image of resolve and confidence.

Yet that was exactly what seemed to have been missing. By 1977 when his cancer was no longer in remission, it seemingly impaired the shah's ability to make crucial decisions. His appetite for European prostitutes remained intact, as his court minister and confidant Asadollah Alam noted in his secret diaries. Though the shah still promised his people an impending arrival at the "gates of the great civilization," though in a tone more subdued than before, there was a noticeable anxiety in his conduct. He forecast "dark days" ahead if people were to be lured by what he labeled "the coalition of the red and black reactionaries," a not-so-subtle code for the radical left and clerical dissenters.

Soon after, officials held responsible for the mismanagement of the state projects were dismissed. The appointment of Jamshid Amuzegar (1923–2016) on August 7, 1977, as the new prime minister was seen as the regime's clear response to the restive popular mood. In retrospect, it was also the shah's first in a series of grave, possibly irrevocable, errors of judgment. Amuzegar was an American-educated economist with a doctorate from Cornell University. He was untainted by rampant venalities and dutiful in his professional conduct. For a long time he had served as the finance minister and as Iran's chief negotiator at OPEC. The skeptical general public nevertheless could not see him as any-thing but the shah's loyal servant and facilitator, an image reaffirmed by the fact that he was the leader of the Rastakhiz Party's so-called progressive wing. His choices of cabinet ministers, with a few exceptions, were also mere window-dressing. They were predictable faces that had caressed the royal ego and fol-lowed his wishes uncritically, even slavishly. Amuzegar's public statements only imbued a massage of conformity. At a time when criticism of the regime was on the rise, he was content to highlight "cumbersome bureaucracy" and "lack of coordination" as primarily responsible for public frustration. The contrived image of a "progressive" wing of the Rastakhiz Party proved even more of a li-ability as Amuzegar, concurrent with his premiership, was appointed to the post of secretary-general of that crumbling party.

On balance, Amuzegar's yearlong government that was meant to be a calm-ing breeze only fueled the revolutionary fires. He managed to secure a limited degree of nominal freedom for the press and political activities. He even man-aged to restrict some of Savak's most egregious practices of illegal arrests and torture. Yet the release of political prisoners, which began in his time, an end to the secret military tribunals that had sent so many dissidents to prison, and lowering of the deafening tone of state propaganda all relayed to the animated general public a message of the state's weakness, and even desperation. Concil-iatory gestures triggered further protests in the universities and soon thereafter in venues dominated by radical activists. By September 1978 the public shift from acts of protest to a revolutionary mode was palpable. If there had indeed been a flicker of hope for the Amuzegar government to rescue the troubled regime from the verge of a revolutionary inferno, this was dashed by frequent mass demonstrations, acts of sabotage by the Islamic extremists, and crippling strikes by workers in the public sector and the oil industry.

In June 19, 1977, the death of 'Ali Shari'ati was believed by many among his supporters to be because of foul play. Three months later news of the death of Mostafa Khomeini (1930–1977), the ayatollah's older son, was also received by the public, similar to Shari'ati's death, almost as a martyrdom. Though he had died of illness, somehow his death was seen as instigated by the sinister regime. In a closed society where the leader of the country, most members of its political elite, and some leading intellectuals were openly subscribing to con-spiratorial theories, it was quite plausible that many nonelite would entertain similar ideas. Demonstrations in Tehran University among the growing ranks of Shari'ati's followers, which coincided with a deluge of condolences from all quarters forwarded to Khomeini, shared a common sentiment of holding the regime responsible for the death of both figures.

After fourteen years of exile in Najaf, Khomeini once more was about to reemerge as the most relentless critic of the Pahlavi state. He enjoyed support not only from among his clerical and lay followers but also within the general public, who hailed him as a champion of resistance. Yet by no means was he yet viewed as the sole leader of the protest movement, or even as the man at its forefront. Exiled but not forgotten, he patiently had waited out years in the social wilderness, perhaps with little hope of ever going back to Iran, let alone leading a revolution. For younger generations of Iranians Ayatollah Khomeini was a figure of the opposition from the past who had returned to the political stage. An opportune moment seemed to have miraculously propelled him to the forefront of a powerful movement and despite his best of expectations, his image would soon be surrounded by an aura of sanctity.

On September 14, 1977, the congregational prayer for the feast of Fitr, at the end of the fasting month of Ramadan, was attended by tens of thousands of worshippers in the neighborhood of Qaytariyeh, at an open space in the north of the capital that was chosen by Khomeini's supporters for the occasion. An orderly congregation for the first time exhibited the new organizing capabilities of the Islamic activists. Shortly thereafter, a largely obscure group of activists known as Iran's Militant Clerics (Ruhaniun-e Mobarez-e Iran), all former students of Khomeini, went on to announce that the Iranian "Muslim nation" would not cease its struggle until the crumbling foundations of the current regime were supplanted by an Islamic "unitarian society." This was an unveiled challenge to the shah and his government, displaying clear solidarity with the exiled ayatollah.

The ten evenings of poetry reading by well-known Iranian literary figures, mostly dissident intellectuals and some Tudeh sympathizers, held in October 1977 in Tehran's Goethe Institute was a match to the show of Islamic sentiments. Among them were the poets Mahdi Akhavan-Sales and Hushang Ebtehaj, the novelist Simin Daneshvar, and the playwright Gholam-Hosain Sa'edi. The experience of listening to the icons of modern Persian poetry and prose reciting poems and passages brimming with symbolic references to repression, resistance, and rebellion was highly inspiring to the animated audience which were estimated to be a few thousand on the opening night. The subtext of the event, and the thrilling mood among the packed crowds that attended the Nights of Poetry, was predictably anti-Pahlavi but hardly pro-Islamic. The sheer excitement of uttering long-withheld feelings of discontent, mostly through the powerful medium of poetry, was empowering, especially in an atmosphere of fear of the regime's retaliation. Though apprehensive of the radical clergy and their growing ambition, the intellectuals and their audiences showed their implicit solidarity with other voices of opposition, which included the supporters of Ayatollah Khomeini.

SHEDDING TEARS FOR THE ISLAND OF STABILITY

By the fall of 1977 the protest movement had moved beyond Iranian cities to become more tangible to the world beyond. Rallies held by dissident Iranian students during the shah's visit to the United States exposed the depth of anti-Pahlavi sentiments. Since the early 1960s thousands of Iranian students abroad—then one of the largest contingents of foreign students in Europe and the United States—had posed vocal opposition to the shah and protested his autocratic rule, mostly under the umbrella of the Confederation of Iranian Students. An influential contingent within this confederation consisted of sympathizers of the Tudeh Party. Maoists and independent Marxists were also active. Others were affiliated with the National Front or had no political affiliation. A much smaller contingent consisted of Islamic student associations. Idealistic and ideologically divided, except in their opposition to the shah, the Confederation gained greater visibility in the early 1970s. Through pamphlets, public campaigns on university campuses, demonstrations, sit-ins, shows of solidarity with other student organizations, and the occasional takeover of Iranian consulates in Europe, the confederation had become a force to be reckoned with. A source for embracing the Iranian regime and a thorn in the side of the Pahlavi narrative of serenity and splendor, the confederation remained vocal despite a few defections to the regime's side.

A test of the shah's unpopularity with the opposition abroad became more visible in a violent demonstration in front of the US White House in November 1977 when the Iranian monarch was on a state visit. Divided up into numerous splinter groups, the confederation nevertheless managed to marshal about one thousand members and affiliates for a rally. In turn, the Iranian embassy in Washington, under ambassador Ardeshir Zahedi, arranged for nearly five thousand pro-regime students from all over North America. They were to be reimbursed for their travel expenses and with pocket money thrown in. The showdown between the two sides could not have come at a less opportune moment for President Carter and his royal guest. The anti-shah demonstrators, in sympathy with the striking students in the Iranian universities, clashed with the police as they crossed the police lines and attacked their opponents near the White House.

A few hundred yards away, on the south lawn, the shah and President Carter, accompanied by Queen Farah and Rosalind Carter, were standing on a raised platform erected for the occasion (fig. 13.1). They were putting on public view a solid alliance between the two countries. Yet their speeches through the public address system were barely audible against the loud anti-Pahlavi slogans in the background. The demonstrators called the shah a "murderous dictator," a "US puppet," and a "corrupt squanderer of the nation's wealth." Still worse, the ceremony had to be cut short when smoke from the teargas canisters deployed by Washington police to disperse the crowd inadvertently reached the royal guests and their hosts. Tears were running down their cheeks in front of television cameras as the indignant shah reached into his pocket and brought out his handkerchief. The accidental tears were not merely shed in a moment of disgrace; they were an ominous preview of what was to come in the months ahead.

The shah's customary pilgrimage to Washington upon the arrival of any new administration—Carter's being the seventh since 1949—was intended to receive US blessings as a "vital strategic ally," even though misgivings about his domestic policies remained at an all-time high. Misgivings aside, in the eyes of the Carter administration, the shah was too important an ally to be quickly abandoned, or chastised, merely on his human rights records and his repression at home, even if disturbing reports of unrest in Iran and the student rally in Washington bluntly showcased his unpopularity. After initially giving him the cold shoulder, the administration began to somewhat warm up to the shah and tried to gratify his insatiable appetite for military hardware. To repair the shah's bruised image as a US-backed potentate, his friends and supporters in Washington had already launched a rehabilitation campaign. Former vice president

Figure 13.1. President Carter and the shah with Queen Farah and Rosalind Carter on the South Lawn of the White House, November 1977.
Courtesy of Jimmy Carter Presidential Library.

Nelson Rockefeller, and soon after Henry Kissinger, both longtime advocates of the Pahlavi crown, visited Tehran to assuage the royal mind and assuring the shah of solid support among the Republican ranks.

As a gesture of goodwill toward Iran, after months of resistance, on the eve of the 1977 royal visit, the US Congress ratified the sale of $1.2 billion in airborne early warning and control system (AWACS) aircraft, then the cutting-edge of reconnaissance technology. The sale was meant to equip Iran—and in effect to enable the US government that received security intelligence through Iran—with a powerful tool along its common borders with the Soviet Union. Mending fences with the shah also was desirable at that time, on the eve of the peace negotiations between Egypt and Israel, a process in which the shah had acted as an important early mediator between the prime minister of Israel, Golda Meir, and the Egyptian president. Three days after the shah's Washington visit, President Anwar al-Sadat of Egypt arrived in Jerusalem for the first round of face-to-face talks with Israeli leaders.

On the other side of the troubled region, the fall of the Pakistani president Zulfikar Ali Bhutto in July 1977 after a military coup that brought to power General Muhammad Zia-ul-Haq alarmed both Washington and Tehran. For years the shah had backed Bhutto with military and financial support in the hopes that he could stay in power and remain a friendly secular ally and neighbor. General Zia, on the other hand, reacted tamely to US interests but appeased the Pakistani Islamist parties. His takeover was the first symptom of a worrying shift toward Islamism that soon was to become a hallmark of Pakistani politics and inevitably the shah had to act as a US surrogate in stabilizing Pakistan. Finally, declining oil demand in the world markets was a serious concern for both sides. The shah advocated greater price stabilization so as to secure funds for his ambitious military and civilian projects and to bring vitality to Iran's stagnant economy.

Soon after his return to Iran the shah, having been reassured of US moral and material support, staged a show of power. Even though Savak's wings were somewhat clipped by the Amuzegar government, and eventually in June 1978 a new chief was appointed in place of General Nasiri to reform the organization, it was still unrestrained enough to retaliate against sporadic trouble spots throughout the country. Savak agents carried out an attack on a meeting called by the newly revived National Front in a private garden near Karaj, in the vicinity of Tehran, and hundreds were indiscriminately beaten up and arrested. They were mostly secular intellectuals and university students. A follow-up crackdown on university students aimed to quash months of protests and clashes with the police. The clampdown proved an obvious misjudgment—the first in a series of tactical errors by the security forces—for it only solidified the forces of opposition.

Yet during his short stay in Tehran on New Year's Eve of 1978, President Carter, at a banquet given in his honor, toasted the shah and declared Iran "an island of stability" in the troubled Middle East. A misstatement that was destined to gain some notoriety, it appeared in the official reports along with pictures of President Carter holding a glass of champagne and flanked by Princess Ashraf, who at the time was perhaps the most unpopular member of the Pahlavi family. Only two days prior to President Carter's arrival (accompanied on the trip by Secretary of State Cyrus Vance and National Security Adviser Zbigniew Brzezinski) the American-Iranian Cultural Center building in Tehran, a hub of American-inspired cultural activities and language learning, was bombed by the Fada'iyan-e Khalq guerrillas.

The opposition condemned the miscalculated American gesture as an affront to the Iranian people. But the US apparent insensitivity was only topped eight months later by a visit by the premier of the People's Republic of China. Hua Guofeng's state visit to Iran in September 1978 came at time when the revolutionary firestorm, in which Iranian Maoists were an integral part, were about to consume the very survival of the Pahlavi regime. It was as if neither the US nor the Chinese could yet grasp the force of the revolution in offing.

TOWARD A REVOLUTIONARY COURSE

By late 1977 the regime's response to street protests was to use the liberalized press to its own advantage. Already in August an article attacking Mosaddeq appeared on the anniversary of the 1953 coup, presumably to counterbalance the rising pro–National Front sentiments. A week after Carter's departure, and buoyed by the presumed US blessing of the shah, the Rastakhiz Party held a convention in Tehran that hosted ten thousand strong from all over the country. In its resolution, the convention declared all-embracing combat against "colonialism," euphemism in the Pahlavi parlance for the politicized Shi'i clergy and their alleged ties to the British in colonial times. A predictable and baseless ploy, it was rooted in the British authorities' distribution of the proceeds of the Awadh Endowment (*pul-e Hend*) and similar Indian endowments among the Shi'i mojtaheds in Ottoman Iraq and later during the British Mandate.

The next propaganda volley that followed proved an utter disaster. On January 8, 1978, an article appeared in the daily *Ettela'at*, often the mouthpiece of Pahlavi establishment, attacking Ayatollah Khomeini in spiteful terms. Apparently planted by the Ministry of the Court against the wishes of the paper's editor and using a pseudonym, the article condemned the "alliance of the red and the black reactionaries" and denounced Khomeini, and the Shi'i clerical leadership, as turbaned servants of colonialism who had clung to a reactionary worldview and a corrupt culture. Khomeini was accused of being an opium addict who was assigned by his masters to incite sedition and derail Iran's march to progress and prominence. "He was an adventurer, a faithless and ambitious man associated with and subservient to colonial powers," stated the invective article. "A man with a mysterious past who was attached to the most reactionary colonial elements. Since he failed to acquire a status among the country's most senior clergy—despite all the suspicious support that he had received—he sought for an opportunity to make a name for himself by mean of inciting a political adventure."[2] Outraged by the *Ettela'at* article, a day later, on January 9, 1978, supporters of Khomeini, mostly seminarians, rallied in the city of Qom and clashed with security forces. As many as six of the protesters were killed and more were injured. The Qom riot in retrospect triggered a turning point in the calendar of the Islamic Revolution, for it launched a whole year of rallies, strikes, and violence, resulting in a steady waning of state's power in all major cities. By January 1978 the revolutionary course, with its thrill and terror, had hit full stride, with the militant clergy about to appear at the helm.

The revolutionary course, moreover, compelled more senior clerical figures almost grudgingly to declare their support for Ayatollah Khomeini. One after another, the Qom *marja's* were obligated to issue statements giving their mandate and condemning the crackdown by the security forces. Up until then most *marja's* had viewed Khomeini as a troublemaker and feared his threat to their authority. Even moderate ayatollahs, such as Mohammad-Kazem Shari'atmadari (1905–1986), could no longer remain equivocal. Senior students of Khomeini, among them Hosain 'Ali Montazeri (1922–2009), were instrumental in elevating Khomeini to a status above others and above the *marja'iyat* status. Though not yet fully spelled out, the notion of *welayat-e faqih* was beginning to place Khomeini far above his cohorts not merely as a jurist but also as a savior of the nation.

By January 18, Tabriz, then the second-largest Iranian city, was the scene of a violent two-day uprising with many casualties. The angry crowd burned down banks, government buildings, provincial headquarters of the Rastakhiz Party, cinemas, and a Pepsi-Cola bottling facility. Once the unrest continued into the second day, the government declared martial law in Tabriz and brought troops into the streets. This was the first time since the uprising of June 1963 that martial law had been declared, hence adding to the public anxiety and fear that worse things were to come. Further unrest in Ahwaz, Mashhad, Yazd, and Isfahan turned the crisis national and gave it the appearance of ominous regularity.

Throughout 1978 demonstrations recurred on the fortieth mourning commemoration (*arba'in*) of the "martyrs" who had fallen in the earlier round of clashes. This began with a remembrance for Qom and Tabriz victims and soon gained a fixed rhythm, with unmistakable hinting at the Shi'i tragedies of Karbala. The numbers of victims almost invariably were exaggerated in the same way that government's punitive actions were overstated. Rallies throughout the country, leading to fresh clashes with the police, and soon with the armed forces, coincided with debilitating strikes in the public sector, among teachers, students and university professors, government employees, factory workers, public utility workers, and even the civilian cadres of the armed forces. Sit-ins at universities and government offices and collective hunger strikes, called political fasting, were the order of the day.

The demands listed by demonstrators ranged from tangible grievances and realistic objectives such as salary raises, job benefits, and the meeting of housing needs to political demands rooted in decades of discontent. These ranged from the unconditional release of all political prisoners, an end to press censorship, and prosecution of corrupt officials to the more idealistic calls inspired by left: an end to plundering Iran's natural resources, liberating the Iranian currency from the financial hegemony of the US dollar, and ending all the so-called *montage* industries. The latter was a reference to assembly plants manufacturing mostly Western consumer goods under license, enterprises dismissed by armchair revolutionaries who probably had read too much Al-e Ahmad as somehow inauthentic and useless. In the mosques the radicalized clergy preached from the pulpits, and in the hastily set-up "Islamic associations" in factories, government offices, universities, schools, and private firms, overnight activists demanded the swift exercise of "Islamic justice" and the removal from power of agents of the "idol" (*taghut*), a Qur'anic term euphemized to stand for the shah and the Pahlavi elite.

In university rallies, where the left held the upper hand, cries of victory to peoples (*khalq-ha*) of Iran and an end to the "exploitation of the masses" were audible. Still more widespread, the supporters of the People's Mojahedin, the fastest-growing political movement among youth, called for victory of the "disinherited of the earth" (*mostaza'fin-e arz*) and the establishment of a "classless" Islamic society. A language of political Islam inherited from likes of 'Ali Shari'ati quickly shaped the revolutionary discourse. With great speed the lists of demands, and the radical slogans that went with them, traveled from one protest camp to another, adding to the excitement of the multitudes whose forbidden sentiments were finally spilling out after years of silence.

During the month of Ramadan, the protest movement gained new momentum. On August 11, 1978, following clashes with police in Isfahan, the angry crowd set fire to cinemas, liquor stores, banks, government buildings, and Rastakhiz headquarters. Even trees along sidewalks of the historic Chahar Bagh were uprooted to block the advancing security force. In response, the Amuzegar government declared martial law in the city. As if that was not enough, nine days later, on August 19, coinciding with the anniversary of the 1953 coup, a horrendous tragedy in Abadan reversed the course of the protests in favor of the Islamic militants. An act of arson in the Rex Cinema resulted in the death of 377 men, women, and children. They were burned to death or died of asphyxiation behind the locked doors of the movie hall. Ironically, the movie on the screen, *Gavazn-ha* (The Deer, 1976), by the Iranian director Mas'ud Kimiya'i, almost anticipated the coming of a revolution. It was about solidarity of the underclasses—portrayed in a thief and a drug addict—whose desperate rebellion against social injustices brought them to a violent showdown with security forces. The movie received a screening permit from Savak with great difficulty and only after substantial reediting.

From what is known, the Rex Cinema's exit doors were intentionally locked. Widespread rumors at the time held Savak and the pro-government agents provocateurs responsible. Yet the arson was consistent with a pattern of Islamic activists' setting ablaze cinemas and other venues of supposed Western decadence for more than a decade. As was witnessed in many instances of arson that destroyed cinemas, first in Qom and later in other cities, the Rex Cinema incident displayed the perpetrators' utter lack of moral scruples, as became evident in the course of their trial a few months later. The Islamic opposition, however, stood to reap major propaganda advantages from the tragedy in the prevailing environment of suspicion and anger.

The Amuzegar government faced intense criticism for mishandling both the Isfahan riots and the Rex Cinema incident. Criticism came not only from the general public but also from the Majles as well, whose deputies, having serious credibility issues, tried hard to behave as the people's genuine representatives. Amuzegar's resignation on August 27 was a serious blow to the regime's hope for stabilizing the restive climate. His resignation proved that a smooth reform movement by a chosen member of the Pahlavi technocracy could not remedy many years of absolutist rule. It was too little and too late. Plunged into a deeper crisis of confidence, the shah appointed as new prime minister Ja'far Sharif-Emami, who twice had served in the same office in the late 1950s. This proved another misstep, one even graver than Amuzegar's appointment a year earlier.

Sharif-Emami, the president of the Senate (and concurrently head of the Pahlavi Foundation and a member of the board of various private enterprises) was a quintessential insider. He was too closely associated with the shah and the upper echelons of the Pahlavi elite to have any chance of withstanding the revolutionary storm that was sweeping the country. A wheeler and dealer and a facilitator of high-stakes foreign and domestic deals, his public image left much to be desired. His only perceived credentials in the eyes of the shah and his advisers were that he was from a well-known clerical family and a devout Muslim who held ties in clerical circles. His "national reconciliation" government, as he liked to call it, comprised predictable Pahlavi officials who aimed to mend fences with the moderate clergy through persuasion and appeasement. By doing so he hoped to isolate Khomeini and his supporters and open up, at least partially, the political space.

That the shah at the time did not opt for a more credible figure from among veteran statesmen suggested that even by August 1978 he had difficulty grasping the depth of the revolutionary realities. He still entertained conspiratorial fantasies about Khomeini and the clerical radicals around him, whom he continued to label as "black reactionaries," as if they were somehow creatures of a British plot or even the American CIA. Opting for a moderate figure from among the liberal opposition may have been the only hope to realistically preserve the constitutional monarchy, if not the shah himself on the throne. That option, of course, required a near-complete delegation of authority by the shah to a reasonably credible government, holding of a free and fair election, and even the shah's peaceful abdication in favor of his son and successor. At the time these were concessions the shah had great difficulty granting. Nor were they palatable to the senior generals of his army or the security apparatus that he had fostered for long. His record of thirty-seven years on the throne showed little evidence that he would ever be willing to make such concessions.

Stressing his independence and calling for an end to royal meddling in the affairs of the government, Sharif-Emami nevertheless embarked on a series of remedies and a morality campaign to assuage public opinion. He abolished the imperial calendar (Shahanshahi) initiated by the shah two years earlier and reverted back to the customary Iranian solar calendar that started with the Hijra. He closed down nightclubs and casinos and introduced anticorruption and austerity measures. He raised the salaries of the discontented government employees, released a number of activist clerics from prison and returned others from internal exile, and forced into retirement a handful of senior army officers with reputations for fraud. He relaxed censorship of the press and the media, accepted the existence of multiple political parties, and, by doing so, put an effective end to the Rastakhiz Party. Even the Tudeh Party reemerged after a quarter of a century of surviving in exile.

In response Ayatollah Shari'atmadari cautiously welcomed the measures introduced by Sarif-Emami's government and offered a three-month window to implement other public demands. The newly revived National Front issued a twelve-point declaration calling for restoration of the Constitution, free press and free elections, and dissolution of the Savak. Yet the appeasement policy generated the reverse effect. It emboldened the opposition and under popular pressure compelled the *marja's* of Qom to further support Khomeini and his increasingly militant statements from Najaf and soon after from Paris. Khomeini labeled the government measures as nothing short of "hypocrisy." A massive rally of hundreds of thousands across the length of the capital from north to south was followed by a congregational prayer held in the middle of a public square. It displayed, with an impressive show of discipline, public solidarity with Khomeini and his cohort.

The organizing capabilities of the Islamic opposition were on display only three days later, on September 4, 1978, when more than two hundred thousand marchers in Tehran carried thousands of placards with Khomeini's portrait and banners openly hostile to the regime. They rallied to Shahyad Square, soon to be renamed Freedom Square, crying out "death to the shah" and calling for "sovereignty, freedom, and Islamic government." Fraternizing with the troops who were brought to the streets in anticipation of violent clashes, protesters placed roses and carnations in the rifle barrels of the troops—apparently inspired by the 1974 Carnation Revolution in Portugal. The gesture soon became commonplace. Rhymed slogans filled the air: "My brother in uniform; why fratricide?" (*Baradar-e arteshi! Chera baradarkoshi?*). Made up mostly of conscripts carrying out their military service, many of the troops were sympathetic to the protestors' emotional pleas.

BLACK FRIDAY AND ITS AFTERMATH

Deeply troubled by widespread protests and paralyzing strikes, and fearing worse, the Sharif-Emami government extended martial law to Tehran and eleven other major cities in the country. Backed by elements within the army, and no doubt with the shah's blessing—and the knowledge of the American and British envoys who regularly were consulted by the shah—General Gholam 'Ali Ovaysi (1918–1984), the commander in chief of the army and a staunch

Pahlavi loyalist, was appointed military commander of the capital. These draconian measures were meant to nip the revolutionary movement in the bud. As it turned out, the last-ditch effort instead sealed the fate of the shah and the Pahlavi rule.

On September 8, a day after the declaration of martial law, a large crowd gathered in Jaleh Square, the core of a religious middle-class neighborhood in east-central Tehran that had been the scene of repeated demonstrations since the beginning of the unrest. Defiant, and possibly unaware that martial law had just been declared, demonstrators ignored repeated warnings to disperse. Sniper shots from the leftist elements in the crowd, who evidently were members of former guerrilla organizations, further unnerved the troops. In a tense moment the troops opened fire on the panicked crowd. The two-hour street battle that followed left behind as many as ninety-five dead and many wounded, including women and children. Other clashes around the capital resulted in even more casualties.

The emotional impact of these events, which soon was marked on the calendar of the Islamic Revolution as Black Friday, was greater even than the loss of human lives. It further alienated the regime and set the revolution almost on a course of no return. If there had been a hope among members of the secular opposition to end the shah's autocratic rule but preserve the constitutional monarchy, that was diminished. The clerical activists, backed by the Qom *marja's*, capitalized on the Jaleh Square massacre to paint the regime as brutal and illegitimate. Aided by a rumor-mongering machine that became fully operational in the absence of reliable media and news reporting, the number of casualties, the "martyrs" on the path of Islam, was inflated to thousands, and the troops who opened fire on them were labeled as Israeli mercenaries who were brought in to crush the revolution. There was a decided loss of confidence among the military personnel, both officers and troops. They were reluctantly dragged into the midst of a revolutionary struggle and asked to defend an unpopular regime and shoot at ordinary Iranians like themselves. Events of the next seven months clearly illustrated the security forces' moral conundrum and their diminishing appetite to save the Pahlavi regime, especially in the absence of a resolute royal master.

Facing violent defiance in the streets and the army's failure to effectively enforce martial law, the Sharif-Emami government looked elsewhere for help. Reacting to a flurry of smuggled cassette tapes with fiery messages from Khomeini calling on the Iranian people to rise up and oust the shah, the Iranian government could only plead with Saddam Hussein to remove Khomeini from Najaf. Once he was banished from his base, it was naively hoped, the troublesome cleric would lose contact with his constituency in Iran and eventually wither into oblivion. For Saddam Hussein, too, who by 1978 as vice president had solidified his control over the Baʻath Party of Iraq, Khomeini appeared more of a liability inside Iraq than an asset against Iran. Even considering the grudge Saddam nursed against the shah and the Iranians, this was a request that he could not have easily turned down given the Baʻathist antagonism toward the restive Iraqi Shiʻis. Khomeini, Saddam feared, was a dangerous role model for the Iraqi clerical activists, such as Mohammad Baqer Sadr (1935–1980), with whom Khomeini maintained close ties.

On Saddam's orders, Khomeini was forced out of Najaf and unceremoniously dumped at the Kuwaiti border. Once refused entry into Kuwait, he considered Lebanon, Libya and Algeria but decided against them out of fear of civil war in the former and manipulation by dictators in the latter. He then was persuaded by some of his aides to go to France. The role of Sadeq Qotbzadeh (1936–1982), a longtime activist and avid supporter of Khomeini, was instrumental in the choice of the land of Farangis. France was a safe haven even for a steadfast Shiʻi jurist, not only because the shariʻa allowed for taking refuge at perilous times in the land of unbelievers but also because it allowed him to resume his struggle free of harassment. On October 6, 1978, he flew to Paris and shortly afterward took up residence in a small villa in Neauphle-le-Château, a middle-class suburb of Paris. Sufficiently austere and frugal, the rented red bungalow was close enough to the French capital to allow for accessibility to a string of visitors who soon crowded the modest resident. He found himself surrounded by a host of aides and supporters, mostly laymen, as well as members of the Iranian opposition, his former students, and enthusiastic scholars and intellectuals who came to pay homage. Television personalities, press correspondents, and freelance writers from all over Europe and the United States also began to arrive.

To the delight of the ayatollah and his aides, and to the disgust of the Iranian authorities, his stay in Paris offered Khomeini an unprecedented three months of free exposure to world media and sympathetic visitors, who almost invariably treated him with awed deference. Sitting cross-legged and leaning against an apple tree in the small courtyard of his residence, which became an open-door public space for his frequent audiences and daily prayers, clad in traditional Shiʻi clerical attire—a black turban and a black robe over a long white shirt—the white bearded but robust ayatollah appeared to most of his Iranian visitors to be a fatherly figure and a national savior (pl. 13.1). To most Westerners he appeared a curious, if not exotic, dissident from another time and place.

His austere demeanor, and his piercing gaze, confirmed an uncompromising message of solidarity and defiance. Facing the media, Khomeini skillfully handled the press by answering prepared questions cautiously and concisely. Television interviewers, correspondents from the *New York Times*, *Le Monde*, and *The Guardian*, as well as freelancers, were often bewildered as they tried to read into Khomeini's ascetic facade and deceptively brief answers. They often went away with implicit praise for a man who had resolutely defied the shah's autocratic rule.

To the anxious members of the Iranian secular opposition as well as Western journalists, he portrayed the revolt against the Pahlavi regime as an all-embracing liberation movement under the banner of Islam while remaining deliberately equivocal on his perceived Islamic utopia. While painting a rosy picture of justice and equity under the "Islamic republic," he at the same time stressed that the mandate of the people of Iran would determine the shape of the future order. He further stressed that the envisioned Islamic republic would treat all its citizens as equals, including Jews, Christians (*Nasranian*, or "the Nazarenes") and other "lawful" minorities. The clergy, who had the loftier task of offering moral guidance to the nation, would refrain from political ambitions and monopolizing power. The future for Islamic Iran would include the coexistence of all groups and tendencies while preserving Islam at the core of its sovereignty and religious identity. Whether these were sincere pronouncements, wishfully embellished by his advisers, or deceptive tactics to lessen anxieties in Iran and internationally at the prospect of an Islamic theocratic state, was a matter left to individuals' judgments. What was clear, however, was that contrary to the Iranian government's hopes, Khomeini's defiant tone and message of rebellion found a far greater audience in Iran and recognition abroad.

The remaining months of Sharif-Emami's government were riddled with more violent clashes and angry demonstrations. Debilitating strikes spread through the public sector from the oil fields and refineries to banks and radio and television broadcasting and to the gas and electric supplies. Pressure on state coffers became more tangible once the government raised salaries and pensions in the vain hope of placating the voice of the opposition. It also tried, but with little success, to appease the more conservative *marja's* in Qom and Najaf as a counter to Khomeini. Under pressure, the government also sacked a number of senior government employees with shady reputations, detained former ministers and high officials, and brought corruption charges against them. It blacklisted yet others and banned their travel abroad, and it imposed stringent regulations, though difficult to enforce, on the flight of capital abroad. Electricity and fuel shortages, a predictable outcome of the strike in the energy sector, only added to popular discontent.

The anticorruption measures and the government's tone of appeasement only emboldened the opposition, which was succeeding in mobilizing new followers through the mosques and Muharram associations. Elements from among the Fada'iyan-e Khalq and Mojahedin-e Khalq also were lending their support to what they perceived to be an impending armed struggle. Paying lip service to Khomeini, the left was hard at work recruiting, especially among high school and university students. Many from Tudeh backgrounds and other leftist tendencies aligned themselves with their families' past affiliations. They viewed the rise to prominence of Khomeini and the Islamist fervor as a transient phase that would pave the way for the rule of the masses. Others in the liberal nationalist camp perceived some form of future power sharing with the Islamists, hoping that Khomeini's leadership would champion a free and fair constitutional regime—admittedly with a thin Islamic veneer. As it turned out, both the left and the liberals grossly underestimated Khomeini's shrewd maneuvering and the extent of popular support he had mustered.

On November 5, 1978, widespread riots in the streets of the capital brought the crisis to the boiling point. Rioters set fire to at least four hundred bank branches around town and destroyed numerous government buildings, movie theaters, liquor stores, restaurants, businesses, and other real or imagined symbols of Pahlavi affluence. The security forces ostensibly were absent from the streets, thus allowing the protesters to inflict maximum damage. Whether this was a preconceived Savak operation, as was alleged then, or the work of Islamic radicals with a record of incendiary sabotage remained a matter of speculation. What was clear was that the riots succeeded in bringing the shaky government of Sharif-Emami to its knees.

The next day, on November 6, 1978 accepting the premier's resignation, the shah in desperation appointed a military government headed by the chairman of the Joint Chiefs of Staff, Gholam-Reza Azhari (1912–2001), a mild-mannered general and a devout practicing Muslim with little political or strategic acumen. It was as if the shah decided on Azhari in a delusional haze atypical of his controlling habits. The military government was appointed with the naive hope of peacefully ending the strikes and bringing the economy back to normal. Azhari took office, understandably, with a degree of reservation as how to govern an almost ungovernable nation. The proactive wing of the Carter administration headed by Brzezinski, backed Ardeshir Zahedi, a close confidant of the shah and Iran's ambassador to the United States, were convinced that only a firm military stance could end the revolution and rescue the regime. What ominously seemed a reenactment of the 1953 coup, however, proved to be, citing Marx's famous saying, a "second-time farce." Facing millions in the streets, Azhari was not in the mood to stand for such a spectacle.

Sensing the gravity of the situation, and under enormous psychological pressure, even the shah didn't have faith in the success of a military government. His ambivalence doubtlessly trickled down through the upper echelons of the military command. Troubled by the rapid course of events, the murky prospects of his dynasty, and the conflicting messages from Washington, the shah was unwilling to allow a draconian measure that might result in another bloodbath like Jaleh Square. To his credit, bewildered and demoralized though he was, he recognized that by sheer force he no longer could quell a popular revolt led by a determined and charismatic leader and backed by millions in the streets.

Prior to Azhari's appointment, the shah had offered the premiership to 'Ali Amini, who, emerging from the political wilderness after nearly two decades, wisely turned it down primarily because of the shah's refusal to relinquish control of the military. This was one prerogative that he had jealously guarded all of his career and was not willing, even at the perilous moment of a revolution in making, to relinquish to someone he could barely trust. He also declined Amini's other condition that he leave the country with the prospect of abdicating in favor of his son. Such parallels with Mosaddeq's demands in 1953 were too obvious for the shah to comply with. He evidently still contemplated some future means of restoring his power.

The army, it soon became apparent, lacked experience in civil affairs as much as it lacked the resolve to face a restive public. For all the years since 1953 the shah, and before him his father, assiduously had kept the army officers firmly under their thumbs. Both father and son demanded from all military personnel, and senior officers in particular, nothing short of blind obedience to the person of the monarch in exchange for material privileges and their generous purchases of military hardware. He had engendered in their ranks a sense of order and discipline and a pride in the uniform. Even hard-line generals like Ovaysi, who from the beginning of the unrest had called for a systematic crackdown, were quickly forced to retire without much remonstrance from them or their cohorts in uniform. In addition to a culture of blind dependency, the shah had used as his effective weapon petty rivalries among senior officers and held them at the mercy of his whims and wishes. In doing so he had deprived the army of a spirit of institutional self-reliance and independent identity.

One other systemic factor barring the officers from acting like a military junta was a justifiable fear of disloyalty from within their own lower ranks. When it came to enforcing law and order in the streets, the top-heavy officer corps relied essentially on unskilled conscripts in their two-year military service. The soldiers were often villagers and urban immigrants who, though sufficiently indoctrinated in the barracks, were unprepared to face an angry crowd. Even less so were they willing to shoot at men and women essentially like themselves who were protesting under the banner of Islam and the country.

Already by October 1978 warning signs of troop absenteeism and defection were rife. By the end of the year these were aggravated further into disobedience. On December 14, 1978, in the Lavizan barracks north of Tehran, where the regiments of the Imperial Guard were stationed, a serious case of mutiny unfolded whereby soldiers shot and killed some twelve of their commanding officers, presumably in retaliation for their antirevolutionary sentiments. The air force cadets known as Homafars, the ground support for the Iranian air force, were among the first to break ranks and openly support the revolution. They initially were vocal in demanding higher wages and better terms of employment, but soon, in February 8, 1979, they spearheaded mass defection within the air force personnel. On the eve of the revolution's success, the Homafars took to the streets of the capital and fought on the side of the revolutionaries, not entirely unlike the Kronstadt sailors during the 1917 Bolshevik Revolution.

The Azhari government's lukewarm start continued to be crippled by self-doubt, and it ended with remorse. To start with, on the same day General Azhari was appointed, the shah himself undermined his mandate by appearing on television declaring that "the revolution of the Iranian people cannot fail to have my support as the monarch of Iran" and that he had "heard the message of the revolution" from his people. As the "guardian of the constitutional monarchy"—a divine "gift entrusted to the shah by people"—he pledged "not to allow the past mistakes to occur or unlawful conduct, oppression and corruption to recur." He further reassured the utterly incredulous public that the military government was a mere caretaker and that he was compelled to appoint it in light of his unsuccessful efforts to form any coalition government representing the nation's will.[3]

For a public accustomed to decades of royal pomposity descending upon it from the "Sunlight of the Aryans" this was an astonishing admission bordering on cynicism. It was a deathbed confession at best and at worst a pitiable scheme to cling to power under the guise of a constitution for which the shah had shown little respect in the past. The emphasis on the transitory role of the military government severely weakened the chances of its survival. The new government, at first manned entirely by the generals, shortly afterward appointed the predictable faces of former civilians. For a few weeks it managed to return to the streets a semblance of normalcy, ending the most acute strikes and even attempting to place some restrictions on the flurry of Khomeini's fiery cassette-tape pronouncements. Treading down the path of appeasement, it was obliged also to detain, with the shah's blessing, on November 9 sixty officials and officers, including the former prime minister Hovayda, former head of the Savak General Nasiri, and a number of ministers of Hovayda's government. They were detained under the general rubric of corruption, misappropriation of public funds, and even implicit charges of treason. The arrests had the immediate impact of eroding the confidence of the Pahlavi elite who until then had rested their hopes on the person of the shah and the support of the army. If the shah no longer was able to protect his own loyal prime minister and chief security officer, and willing to sacrifice them for the sake of his own survival, it was thought, other members of the elite may well be the next victims to be sent down to the revolutionary den. Bonds of loyalty that had long held together the Pahlavi regime were about to be quickly unraveled.

SEARCHING FOR A VIABLE PREMIER

By December 1978 Azhari's government, military in name only, had become a subject of public ridicule on account of its inability to restore order. In a report to the Iranian Senate Azhari famously claimed that the repeated cries of "*Allah'u akbar*" (God is great) that were audible in the dead of night from city rooftops were mere cassette recordings. Soon tens of thousands of marchers in the streets of Tehran shouting "*Allah'u akbar*" supplemented their cries with a slogan: "O miserable Azhari! Dare say it again! Is this a [cassette] tape? Tape doesn't have hands; tape doesn't have legs." The proof provided by the marchers was thousands of revolutionary graffiti slogans, including abuses of the shah, Azhari and his government, sprayed all around the massive base of the Shayhad monument and continuing way up the tower.

Bloody clashes between demonstrators and security forces made the former more resolute and the latter weary and weak. All over the country, even in smaller towns, the growing number of dead and injured on both sides brought about an alarming state of siege and inevitable international concern for the plight of the Iranian people. The four centers of the revolution—the bazaar, the mosque and the Moharram committees, the university campuses, and the oil industry—were by now unanimous in denouncing the Pahlavi rule. Notably, they were, among other things, still divided over the degree of their compliance with Khomeini's leadership. Beyond unanimity in rejecting the status quo, ominous ideological chasms divided the opposition.

The Moharram of year 1399 of the Islamic calendar, falling in December 1978, was bound to carry an even greater emotional weight than the usual commemoration of the Karbala martyrs. The forthcoming turn of the fifteenth Islamic century, and its messianic undertone for the advent of a "renovator

[*mojadded*] at the turn of the century," a dormant trait in the history of messianic Islam, had found an apt candidate in the person of Ayatollah Khomeini.
The release from prison of Ayatollah Mahmud Taleqani (1911–1979), a longtime political activist and a relatively independent-minded cleric close to the
religiously inclined Freedom Movement, added further weight to the clerical
leadership. His call for another rally on the day of 'Ashura (December 11, 1978)
to commemorate martyrs of the revolution—its numbers reaching perhaps no
more than a few hundred—brought to Shahyad (Azadi) Square a crowd that
was reported to be a million strong. The seventeen demands set forth by demonstrators included an end of the Pahlavi regime and the formation of an Islamic order under Ayatollah Khomeini. They also called for political freedom
and civil rights, social justice, and the end of imperialist hegemony, presumably
that of the United States. Here the dichotomy in denouncing the shah as traitor
and welcoming Khomeini as savior pointed to a sad irony in a political culture
that could only demand the removal of one autocrat by welcoming another,
even though the latter was still in making.

Internationally, support for the regime was dwindling fast. Veteran US Republicans were unwavering in their support for the shah, as evidenced by
statements issued by Henry Kissinger and former presidents Gerald Ford and
Richard Nixon. Whether out of expediency or moral conviction, however, the
Carter administration gradually moved away, at least on the surface, from unconditional backing of the shah. When on December 7 President Carter was
asked about the chances of the shah's survival, he said: "I don't know. I hope
so. This is something that is in the hands of the people of Iran." Ambivalence
and confusion persisted. The State Department, under Cyrus Vance, was cautiously inching toward accepting the revolution as an unpleasant but unavoidable reality. As prescribed by William Sullivan (1922–2013), the US ambassador
in Tehran, establishing contact with the revolution's clerical and lay leadership
was inevitable. Sullivan identified Mahdi Bazargan, the head of the Freedom
Movement, and Mohammad Beheshti (1928–1981), an influential member of
the organization of the Militant Clerics, as the most plausible candidates. Hard-
liners in the US National Security Council, headed by Brzezinski, however,
hadn't entirely given up on the Iranian military even though they now viewed
the shah as a redundancy. They were even contemplating a military takeover
independent of the shah to contain the revolutionary course, preserve a semblance of Pahlavi rule, and support an eventual return to normalcy. With the
threat of Soviet intervention in the picture, Iran loomed too crucial on the US
strategic horizon to be abandoned to a revolutionary crowd led by a militant
mullah. Sullivan seemed more confirmed in his opinion when he encountered

General Azhari in late December 1978 coming down the steps of the Niavaran Palace after an audience with the shah. He detected in him a depressed and exhausted man hardly capable of rendering the task Brzezinski and others in Washington expected of him. He had just submitted his resignation to the shah and agreed to be a caretaker until a new premier is appointed.

By mid-December the shah had come to the realization that his only viable option was to call on a handful of veteran nationalists of earlier decades to form a government. After decades of dismissing them as nonentities and leaving them on the political sidelines, his appeal seemed ironic, if not outright absurd. Karim Sanjabi, a statesman of the Mosaddeq era and a leader of the revived National Front who has been released from Savak's temporary detention a week earlier, turned down the shah's offer with little hesitation. His condition, reflecting the overwhelming urgency that the revolution had brought upon even its moderate players, was that the shah leave the country for an indefinite period and delegate all affairs of the state to a privy council to be convened from among credible personalities. In the volatile climate Sanjabi's hope was to utilize the limited resources at his disposal to secure a constitutional middle ground between waning Pahlavi rule and the sweeping storm of the Islamic Revolution. As in his earlier negotiation with 'Ali Amini, again the shah was unwilling to entertain such an option. He most probably feared, even at this late stage, not only the end of his own rule but also the end of the Pahlavi monarchy.

Already on November 3, more than a month before his meeting with the shah, Sanjabi had flown to Paris to meet with Khomeini and try to arrive at an understanding over the future course of the revolution. Despite a courteous exchange, Khomeini clearly was not in the mood to accommodate a secular nationalist. He warned that he would denounce and "expel from the revolutionary movement" anyone who negotiated with the shah. The three-clause declaration authored by Sanjabi at the conclusion of the meeting mirrored the shifting balance of power in favor of the ayatollah and his Islamic agenda. It condemned the shah's dictatorial rule as unconstitutional and against individual freedoms, and hence devoid of legal and Islamic legitimacy. It further denounced any collaboration with the regime so long as it continued to act undemocratically. Finally, it called for Iran's future political order to be determined by a popular referendum.

Given the circumstances, Sanjabi's Paris visit and the widely publicized three-point declaration was seen as a success and hailed as such, for it gave the impression of solidarity between liberal nationalists and the Islamists without making too many concessions to the latter. Despite much disingenuous publicity by the royalists in later years denouncing the declaration as a sellout to Khomeini, short of an innocuous reference to Islam, the declaration simply reiterated the National Front's positions long publicized in statements and speeches by Sanjabi and by others. It also expressed the aspiration of all those who had long been critical of the shah's dictatorial conduct, desiring a return to constitutional order. Yet there was an ominous ring to the very act of seeking an open alliance with Khomeini, for it showed the secular opposition's loss of momentum, a bitter reality that became even more evident when the ayatollah insidiously received the signed declaration from Sanjabi and pushed it under the blanket he was sitting on without ever putting his own signature on it.

In the following days after the unsuccessful meeting with Sanjabi the shah was compelled to realize that his days on the throne were numbered. In search of a solution, and no longer sure of the United States' support for his rule, he approached Gholam-Hosain Sadiqi, another veteran of the Mosaddeq era who was no longer associated with the new National Front. Sadiqi, too, promptly turned down the shah's offer but for a different reason. He was forewarned by the opposition figures that under the circumstances accepting the premiership would be a serious breach of the revolutionary solidarity. The shah also refused Sadiqi's condition that he remain in the country, rather than going abroad, and relinquish all power, including control of the armed forces. Sadiqi's demand was presumably grounded in his justified fear that once the shah left the country, the army would cave under the weight of the revolution. He proved correct. In his bewildered state of mind the shah, however, had declined both the offer to leave and the offer to stay, an indecision that implied to both veterans of the Mosaddeq era, Sanjabi and Sadiqi, a hidden agenda, perhaps to buy time and stage a military coup.

In late December 1978, having received two negative responses, the shah began to negotiate in secret with Shapur Bakhtiar, another National Front member and leader of the newly revived Iran Party. Unbeknownst to his longtime colleagues, and contrary to Sanjabi's pledge not to spoil the opposition's barely sustained unanimity, on December 29, 1978, Bakhtiar accepted the premiership. He did so at a time when it was obvious that political odds were dead set against any secularist who did not at least have Khomeini's implicit consent. By moving away from his comrades, and in effect working against them, Bakhtiar willingly trapped himself in an impossible political corner. He also eroded the meager chances that a united secular front might have had to revive constitutional monarchy while withstanding Khomeini and his radical following. Desperate though it seemed to others, to Bakhtiar his acceptance of the premiership appeared a heroic act of patriotism against the threat of Islamic fanatics and the dark future they promised to bring to the country.

To his critics Bakhtiar's move was motivated by quixotic ambition for high office. He was duly expelled from the National Front and from his own Iran Party, an action that barely concerned him at the time but that later he claimed to be a contributing factor to his downfall. Thereafter, most nationalists could see no recourse but to comply with the revolution's Islamic course, while others like Sadiqi preferred to stay completely out of the game. Bakhtiar, and handful of the halfhearted ministers in his cabinet, clung to the implausible chance that through an alliance with the army they would prevail. He had asked and received assurance from the shah that he would temporarily leave Iran, that Savak would be disbanded, and that Bakhtiar would be in charge of both the military and foreign affairs.

Unfortunate for Bakhtiar, the tone of the protest movement had taken a decidedly more radical and a more Islamic turn. Calls for the downfall of the Pahlavi "dictatorship" were no longer followed by demands to restore the 1906 constitution, but to end the "despotic" institution of monarchy and return to the "Islamic justice," and soon after to establish an "Islamic government" (*hokumat-e eslami*) and eventually an Islamic Republic (*jomhuri-ye eslami*). The shift from political reforms to an Islamic order meant an adamant rejection of a liberal democratic alternative. In many slogans and on thousands of placards carried in rallies, the tone of the revolution had turned in favor of Khomeini and his evolving ambitions to create a new Islamic order.

The general enthusiasm for this Islamic alternative was as spontaneous as it was contagious. Half a century of Pahlavi rule and its state-initiated monotony had heightened the yearning for an alternative face and an alternative message. To many Iranians this idealized, politicized, and radicalized Islam—a construct that had gestated for many decades—became more appealing, especially in its revolutionary garb. Not only the bazaar merchants and poorer urban and urbanizing Iranians but also people of secular or semisecular upbringing, especially among youth, were thrilled by Khomeini and his promises. Often alien to the clergy's earlier image as reactionaries opposed to secular values, the Iranian youth were ready to accept the "Imam" of the revolution in place of Pahlavi shah and its excesses.

BAKHTIAR'S IMPLAUSIBLE QUEST

The timing of Bakhtiar's premiership proved particularly unfortunate for those who were still hoping to maintain a middle ground between Khomeini and the Pahlavi regime. By January 1, 1979, while the United States was declaring its support for the Bakhtiar government, the new premier was denounced by Khomeini and his own appointed revolutionary provisional government as illegal and was subsequently boycotted. In the course of the first few crucial days, as the shah's uncertainties became more manifest, Bakhtiar's government appeared to be far less viable. The Carter administration's poor handling of Iran's affairs further reduced the frail chance of stopping Khomeini's ascendancy. The Bakhtiar interlude, like Kerensky's interim government in 1917 Russia, seemed the catalyst for the regime's ultimate downfall.

Two days after Bakhtiar took office with the mandate to contain (or accommodate) the army, General Oveysi resigned as chief of the army and head of the Tehran military command, leaving the country in haste. He had waited in vain for the US blessing, which eventually went to Bakhtiar; but even with US backing, it was highly unlikely that Ovaysi would have succeeded. The chairman of the Joint Chiefs of Staff, General 'Abbas Qarabaghi (1918–2000), a French-educated career officer and a devout Muslim, on the other hand, was a noninterventionist. He was persuaded by the Americans to work with Bakhtiar's "virtual" government to steer an impossible course that would return the country to normalcy after the shah's departure. By the same token, the National Front and its affiliated secular allies were also deprived of their valued weapon to halt Khomeini's meteoric rise. By giving advance notice to Khomeini of the possibility of a military coup—had Oveysi remained in office—the leaders of the National Front were hoping to persuade the turbaned revolutionaries to abide by their mediatory role in resolving Iran's crisis. Bakhtiar's move clearly robbed the National Front of that chance.

Bakhtiar was a cultured Francophile and a political maverick from a tribal aristocracy that had been defanged by the Pahlavis decades earlier. He had fought against Franco in the Spanish Civil War, later volunteered for the French army during World War II, and had served in the French Resistance. By keeping the shah away, Bakhtiar hoped that he could deploy the army to harness the revolution and restore Iran's constitutional regime. By implementing drastic reforms and carrying out an anticorruption campaign, he hoped to disarm Khomeini and force him to negotiate. Yet in the coming weeks, despite fulfilling some of his promises, such as lifting all restrictions on the press, Bakhtiar's government proved utterly incapable of restoring the status quo. Popular outbursts of protest and paralyzing strikes swept away the last vestiges of the premier's authority, along with his miniscule power base. In his speech to the Majles—at a time when that institution itself was fast losing its relevance—after announcing his fourteen-point program, Bakhtiar poetically concluded that he was a thunderbird (*morgh-e tufan*) ready to face the storm of the revolution. As if he saw a huge gamble ahead, in which all of his political credibility and even his life were at stake, he recited a verse from the poet Nima:

I am a thunderbird, I am not afraid of the storm,
I am a wave, but not that rolls back to the sea.

On the morning of January 16, 1979, the shah finally left the country for Egypt for an extended "vacation." Accompanied by Queen Farah and a small entourage, he left behind nearly all of his possessions and, for the Iranians, mixed memories. Walking across the tarmac to his private aircraft, he was captured in a memorable photograph. Tears running down his cheeks, the shah was bending forward to prevent a uniformed officer of the Eternal Guard from bowing down to kiss his feet—a last show of loyalty at a time when the entire nation seemed to have rejected their king. The headlines in the extras that day, printed in huge typeface, simply read: "Shah left" (*shah raft*). The two words expressed the feelings of exuberance and triumph of hundreds of thousands Iranians who rushed into the streets, joyfully, dancing and honking car horns. Boxes of candies were placed in front of stores, flowers were offered to passersby, and people greeted one another. It was as if the gates of a utopian epoch had finally opened widely.

More than a quarter of a century after his surreptitious departure for Rome in August 1953, the shah's departure this time around promised a different end, a sorrowful journey all the way to the grave. It seemed as if his end were a replication of Jamshid's legend in the *Shahnameh* and his loss of royal glory to pride and vanity. It is sobering to note that the shah's exile was the fourth in a row for Iranian rulers in the twentieth century, coming in the wake of two revolutions in 1909 and 1979 and two coups, one in 1921 and one in 1953. Over a broader historical span, since the turn of the eighteenth century, that is, when Shah Solayman of the Safavid dynasty died in 1694, for more than 275 years of Iran's political history, thirteen major rulers came to power. Of those only four died a natural death while still on the throne. Of the remaining nine, one was executed, four assassinated, and four exiled. Mohammad Reza Shah's exile, seventy years after the forced abdication and exile of Mohammad 'Ali Shah Qajar, also promised a blossoming era of freedom and democracy. In an ironic turn of fortune, the shah's departure brought to a virtual end the institution of the Persian kingship only seven years after the shah had celebrated 2,500 years of Iranian monarchy. The public sentiment in that short time had almost entirely turned against him (pl. 13.2 and pl. 13.3).

Coinciding with the shah's departure, the rapid unraveling of the entire Pahlavi order seemed inevitable. To appease the public, Bakhtiar soon presided over dismantling the Savak at a time when its officers and agents were on the defensive, incapable of withstanding revolutionary pressure. The Privy Council had barely convened before its chairman, who was hoping to negotiate with Khomeini, flew to Paris and, having been denied even a meeting with him, ignominiously handed in his resignation. Adding to his desperation, some ministers of Bakhtiar's government resigned even before taking office. Those who did venture to serve were refused entry by the staff of their assigned ministries.

Despite setbacks, Bakhtiar continued as if his passion for the office did not allow him to see the bleak prospects ahead. He declared the end of censorship, as well as freedom of the press and political parties, and he released the remaining political prisoners. Yet his shaky base never solidified. Even a rally of tens of thousands of supporters of the constitution in the Baharestan Square on January 25, 1979, mostly members of the secular middle classes terrified of the prospects of a theocracy under Khomeini, could not tilt the balance in his favor. Despite all his efforts, the focus of public attention was the much-anticipated arrival of Ayatollah Khomeini. Bakhtiar's waning fortune and the army's uncertain prospects boosted the chances of Khomeini's return, which was set for January 26.

Figure 13.2. Frequent rallies, like this one in January 1979, contested Bakhtiar's shaky government. Placards represented diverse ideologies and political demands.
Maryam Zandi, *Enqlab-e 57* (Tehran: Nazar Publishers, 1393/2014), 83.

Figure 13.3. The reopening of Tehran University in January 1979, after
months of closure, further boosted public morale. The growing number
of participants in the demonstrations reflected the accelerating pace of
revolution, and the absence of placards implied fleeting unity.
Maryam Zandi, *Enqlab-e 57* (Tehran: Nazar Publishers, 1393/2014), 34.

This was exhilarating to the multitudes who regularly took part in rallies in his
support (fig. 13.2 and fig. 13.3).

Adding to the complexity was the Carter administration's difficult adjustment
to Iran's fast-changing reality. Already on January 8, while the shah was still
in Iran, General Robert Huyser (1924–1997), the deputy commander in chief
of the US European Command, was assigned by the White House (despite
the angry objections of his superior, General Alexander Haig) to visit Iran and
facilitate, presumably in the absence of the shah, a collaboration between the
ranking military and Bakhtiar's government. In reality his task, if there was an
unambiguous one, was to prepare the army, in the likely event of Bakhtiar's fall,
to stage a takeover, a quasi-military coup.

Huyser faced a demoralized officer corps with fast-vanishing loyalty among its lower ranks and senior officers unwilling to confront revolutionary crowds. He was sensible enough to recognize that 1953-type adventurism was no longer in the cards. No matter how desperately Carter's security adviser and his ally Ardeshir Zahedi, by then ousted as Iranian ambassador to Washington, would have wished, the chance of coming up with another General Zahedi was slim. The idea was too far-fetched and at any rate too late. As Huyser put it, the mission "started with desperation and disunity and ended in disaster." Bakhtiar's virtual government was no less doomed. The only outcome was that the army chiefs were convinced to stay out of the revolutionary trouble, start negotiating with Mahdi Bazargan, the prime minister of the provisional government, and with Khomeini's clerical representatives, and eventually return to the barracks.

DOWNFALL OF PAHLAVI RULE

Another huge rally on January 26, 1979, in Tehran and other cities showed the futility of a military option. Though Khomeini and his coterie in Paris, wary of a military coup, were debating the auspicious moment for his return, it was clear that in essence nothing could upset his chances, not even Bakhtiar's temporary closure of Tehran's Mehrabad Airport. The closure of the airport came after Khomeini soundly rejected Bakhtiar's offer to resign within four months, during which he would conduct a referendum to determine people's choice between a monarchy and a republic. At the age of seventy-nine, after fourteen years in exile, Khomeini's reappearance as the triumphant champion of the revolution was certain—something that a few months earlier he himself probably could not have imagined.

On February 1, 1979, when he walked up the staircase of an Air France charter flight that brought him to Tehran with his aides and a host of journalists, he was still mindful of a murky course ahead. Upon arrival in Tehran and all along the twenty-mile route to section 17 of the Behesht Zahra public cemetery south of Tehran, where he headed to pay his homage to the martyrs of the revolution, millions of well-wishers stood for hours to get a glance of his motorcade, some touching the bumpers of the SUV in which he sat as it slowly made its way through the crowd. Listless and stone faced, he gazed at the welcoming crowds, awkwardly waving his hand from the front passenger seat. Aboard the aircraft that brought him home, he had already replied to a Western journalist who asked about his momentary "feelings." He had none, he said. A predictable response, one might assume, from a man untouched by bourgeois sensibilities.

In his fiery sermon at the cemetery, the first in a repertoire that lasted a decade, he called the Bakhtiar government, the Majles, and the Senate illegitimate; he called Reza Shah a usurper who illegally came to power and Mohammad Reza Shah a puppet of foreign powers. He accused the Pahlavi regime of corruption and nurturing prostitution, appealed to people's power and pledged on the blood of the martyrs to appoint a legitimate Islamic government to eradicate the seeds of oppression. Appealing to the army generals, he said:

> We call on those who have not yet joined [the revolution] to follow the rest [of the army personnel]. For you Islam is better that disbelief; nation is better than the aliens. . . . Abandon him [the shah] and don't think that if you abandoned him, we will execute you. These are things [i.e., rumors] made up by you or by others. . . . We want the country to be strong. We want the country to have a powerful army. We don't intend to disturb the army. We want the army to survive but an army rooted in the nation and in service of the nation. . . . I will appoint the government! I will spurn this government [i.e., Bakhtiar's]! With the support of you people, I will appoint a [new] government![4]

As it became abundantly clear some two weeks later, the soft gesture toward the army chiefs and senior officers was nothing but a cynical ploy to break up what little was left of the corps' solidarity and loyalty to the shah.

During the following ten days, from February 1–11, 1979, revolution struck its final blows upon the dying Pahlavi regime and heralded the birth of a new one. "Ten days that shook the world," to borrow from John Reed's famous narrative of the Bolshevik Revolution. Mindful of a military coup, less than three weeks before his arrival, on January 12, Khomeini had appointed a semiclandestine Islamic Revolutionary Council (*shura'-ye enqelab*) with an undisclosed membership. It was established primarily to counter both the shaky Privy Council appointed by the shah and the Iranian legislature. The Revolutionary Council was the first of the institutions to be born of the yet amorphous revolution. The shifting membership, as it later came to be known, consisted of an odd bunch of militant clergy and Khomeini loyalists, some old-timers and some overnight converts with blueprints for instant Islamification.

On February 5, five days after his arrival—and while the Bakhtiar government was still in office—Khomeini appointed Mahdi Bazargan as the head of the provisional government. The former member of the National Front of the Mosaddeq era and a longtime leader of the Freedom Movement, which he cofounded in 1961, Bazargan was imprisoned for five years in the early 1960s for opposition to the shah and support for Khomeini. As the informal spokesman for the Revolutionary Council, Bazargan's mandate, as Khomeini's "decree" asserted, not only was to form a government and supervise the affairs of the state but also to conduct a referendum determining the nature of the new regime, a formality as it turned out, to publically sanctify the birth of an Islamic republic. The provisional government was also mandated to supervise the election of a constituent assembly and frame a new constitution. Finally, it was to supervise the election of the first Majles under the new regime (fig. 13.4 and fig. 13.5).

Below the solemn surface of what appeared an orderly transition, there were complex and tumultuous undercurrents. Driven by sheer revolutionary spirit, multitudes of marchers in the street seemed unwilling to go home and settle for a mere transition in the civilian government. With the departure of the shah and the termination of the old regime, the scramble for power had only started. At the top, senior officers of the headless armed forces were becoming quickly frustrated with Bakhtiar's toothless promises. The chances for a military takeover, too, were rapidly fading. Most commanding officers viewed a violent encounter with the revolutionary crowds as nothing short of suicide. Instead they hoped to come to terms with Khomeini's provisional government, so long as the armed forces would remain untouched. Bazargan and the Revolutionary Council, even Khomeini himself, shared such a prospect. By the first week of February, judging by statements issued from both sides, the army chief of com-

Figure 13.4. Tehran public seeking Khomeini's blessing,
February 3, 1979, at 'Alavi School.
Maryam Zandi, *Enqlab-e 57* (Tehran: Nazar Publishers, 1393/2014), 126.

Figure 13.5. Flanked by his aides Sadeq Qotbzadeh (*right*)
and Ibrahim Yazdi (*left*), Khomeini attended his first press conference in
Tehran on February 3, 1979, at 'Alavi School.
Maryam Zandi, *Enqlab-e 57* (Tehran: Nazar Publishers, 1393/2014), 122.

mand and Khomeini's provisional government, the parties were on the verge of
a compromise for a bloodless transition.

The departure of the US special emissary, General Huyser, on February 6, after a month of fruitless negotiation with his Iranian counterparts to preserve the
military, was a step in that direction. It concurred with the appointment of Bazargan's government. Washington's indecision, and the push and pull between
hawks and doves in the Carter administration, finally seems to have weighed
not only on the side of abandoning the shah but also on the unfeasibility of a
military initiative. Washington, along with most of its European allies, seemed
to have come to terms with the rude reality of a popular revolution. A summit
of Western leaders—United States, Britain, France, and West Germany—in
the Caribbean island of Guadeloupe a month earlier, having faced wild vicis-
situdes in global oil supplies and the consequent likelihood of rising prices,
stressed the need to maintain diplomatic and economic ties with the future
Iranian regime. As he flew out of his capital into an uncertain future, the shah
had quickly turned into a crownless ghost of his imperial past. He would have
been overshadowed by the turbulence of a revolution in the making had it not
been for the fact that his ghost was needed to vilify real and imagined enemies
of the revolution.

Despite a gloomy forecast by the British foreign secretary David Owen and
other sporadic voices warning of darker days ahead, the Western world became
increasingly resigned to Iran's unstoppable course. Taken by surprise, the Soviet

authorities also viewed with reservation the shaping on their southern border of an Islamic revolution led by a radical ayatollah. Following the incident in which the revolutionary crowd set fire to the chancery of the British embassy in Tehran, the British government opted for a noncommittal posture, a low profile that would soon change into de facto acceptance of the new regime. The Israelis sent off their own undercover emissary to persuade Bakhtiar to persevere, but to no avail. No longer in denial, Bakhtiar made secret contacts with his old friend Bazargan in the hope of arriving at an acceptable exit strategy. In public, however, even as late as February 10, Bakhtiar insisted that neither Bazargan's call for his resignation nor the near takeover of police and the army barracks by revolutionaries would have any effect on him.

Yet despite hopes for a peaceful transition, on February 9 the restive air force cadets, the Homafars, shifted complete loyalty to Khomeini and the revolution. Their mutiny disturbed the fragile accord between Bazargan's provincial government and the army's joint chief of staff. The next day, when a battalion of Imperial Guards was sent off to quell the mutineers at Farahabad air force base on the eastern outskirts of the capital, the army command's intention, at least among the more level-headed generals, was to preserve the integrity of the armed forces rather than crush Khomeini loyalists. The ever-present protesters in the street saw the army's ambivalence as a heinous overture to a military coup.

Almost spontaneously the crowd barged on the barracks, attacking and occupying the police stations and soon confronting auxiliary troops that were dispatched to the aid of the Imperial Guard. Spearheading clashes with the security forces, the Marxist Fada'iyan-e Khalq and their Islamic counterpart, Mojahedin-e Khalq, saw a golden chance to fulfill their long-awaited dream of dismantling the Pahlavi power. More than any other party, they were instrumental in the final collapse of the armed forces. This was an ominous overture to the left's initiatives glorifying violence and enticing Khomeini supporters to go to extremes.

Just after the first street clashes, a chain reaction was set in motion that had unanticipated consequences. In a desperate move, on February 10 the Tehran military command, alarmed by chaos and dissension within its ranks, issued a communiqué extending curfew hours throughout most of the day and into the night. The angry crowd viewed the move as the start of a military coup. Almost instantaneously, on February 10 Khomeini issued a strongly worded statement urging the public to "pour into the streets" in defiance of martial law. The bold tone of the statement, perhaps one of the most decisive in Khomeini's career, swayed the crowd toward a bolder move, even though it had stopped short of a general plea for occupying police and military installations.

On February 11, the security forces faced greater resistance in the streets, makeshift barricades, and attacks on police stations. In response, the military Supreme Council, consisting of all commanding officers and chiefs of the three forces, swiftly issued another communiqué declaring the army's neutrality in the ongoing crisis. It further declared that the army was on the side of the people and the revolution, and, most crucially for the outcome of the revolution, it called on all military units to withdraw from the streets and return to the barracks. The military command was under the wrong impression that troop withdrawal would facilitate an easy transition from the hapless Bakhtiar government to the provisional government of Mahdi Bazargan.

The conciliatory gesture, however, proved detrimental to the very survival of the most powerful and most symbolic institution of Pahlavi rule. Almost immediately after the withdrawal, the ecstatic crowd of demonstrators stormed the seemingly impenetrable army barracks throughout the capital. The crowd looted not only caches of light weapons but also tanks, armored vehicles, and heavy machine guns (fig. 13.6 and fig. 13.7). At an amazingly fast pace the imperial army turned into a submissive shadow of itself and never recovered from that shock. To their utter bewilderment, droves of generals were arrested while

Figure 13.6. Revolutionary youth with ransacked rifles
guarding the streets of Tehran, February 12, 1979.
Maryam Zandi, *Enqlab-e 57* (Tehran: Nazar Publishers, 1393/2014), 163.

Figure 13.7. Triumphant revolutionaries climbed an army tank
in Saltanatabad military barracks, February 17, 1979.
Maryam Zandi, *Enqlab-e 57* (Tehran: Nazar Publishers, 1393/2014), 161.

still in their offices. Other were caught in civilian clothes and while on the run. On the same day Bakhtiar resigned from his post and went into hiding. Reportedly with the help of Mahdi Bazargan, he escaped the country and surfaced in Paris some months later. Bazargan's provisional government, a mix of Khomeini sympathizers, National Front leaders, and independent opposition figures with some Islamic affinity officially took over. Yet almost immediately it became apparent that an orderly transfer of power belonged more to the realm of ideals than realities.

Remarkably, the "victory" of the revolution on February 11, 1979 (22 Bahman 1357 of the solar Iranian calendar), came not with a smooth transfer of power, as intended by the provisional government, but with riotous clamor and popular insurgency. That was a surprise even to Khomeini and his devotees, if not to the remnants of guerrilla organizations and their sympathizers. That Khomeini successfully navigated the tumultuous course, rather than lagging behind the left and the angry masses who took over the barracks and overpowered the police, was early evidence of his political sorcery. Here, and repeatedly in the coming months and years, he opted for the most radical of the choices before him and rapidly appropriated it as one of his own. Keeping up with the momentum, often at the expense of the moderate wing of the revolution, kept him in favor not only with his rapidly radicalized clerical base but also with the underprivileged multitudes who yearned for leadership.

WAS THE REVOLUTION AVOIDABLE?

For the secular middle classes, at home or in exile, who saw themselves as victims of the Islamic Revolution, for the disillusioned revolutionaries soon to be cast aside, and for many observers wishful for a better turn of events, one question persisted: Was the revolution, or rather the Islamic Revolution and the way it prevailed, avoidable? The short answer to this seemingly ahistorical question is a cautious no. It can be argued that in August 1978 the appointment of the Sharif-Emami government removed the last chance for adopting an evolutionary rather than a revolutionary course. Without dabbling too much in such a virtual course, it could be argued that an evolutionary process probably was untenable at the time not so much because of the potency of the opposition or the shah's aversion for the democratic process but because of long-term dynamics already in place.

A quarter of a century of autocratic rule since 1953 had effectively demolished the political infrastructure on which a democratic regime and a sound civil society could be built. Even as late as 1975 if—instead of creating the bogus Rastakhiz Party the Pahlavi regime had allowed some measure of liberalization and had permitted moderate but genuine political parties to emerge—there still would have been a chance. Instead of deafening propaganda campaigns glorifying the Sunlight of the Aryans, if the shah had permitted some measure of free speech and free press, an evolutionary process still would have been plausible. If Savak had not engendered an atmosphere of fear and intimidation, of arrest and torture, of military courts, of repeatedly crushing student protests and completely suppressing any independent voice, there could have been a different political outcome.

Instead, the shah's regime inadvertently paved the way for a popular revolution as the only alternative to his autocratic conduct, especially during the 1970s. In the absence of genuine political institutions and the growth of a middle class devoid of political agency, the rise of a populist demi-prophet like Khomeini is understandable. He was a mirror image of the shah in his undemocratic outlook, though distinct from the Pahlavi ruler in every other respect. The regime over the years had recklessly facilitated the growth of leftist extremism and clerical loyalties by virtually eliminating all moderate alternatives. But the radical left was the victim not only of the Pahlavi regime but also of its own naïveté, ideological alienation, and cult of martyrdom. It had little popular support. The Qom clerical movement, in contrast, proved resilient, shrewd, and capable of building grassroots support.

Over a longer historical span, the march toward a revolutionary upheaval arguably was set as early as 1953, when the last chance for a democratic process was lost, or was taken away, depending on how we would look at it. One might even trace the origins of the revolutionary quest further back, to the aftermath of the Constitutional Revolution and the rise of the Pahlavi modernity, when maturation of the nascent political process effectively came to a standstill. Yet seminal to the causes of the 1979 revolution, even more than 1921 or 1953, were the developments of the 1960s, when the land reform freed generations of land-bound villagers from rural Iran and brought them into the cities. These new-comers fueled a popular revolution that came to fruition in large part because of their sheer multitude.

That the 1979 revolution was destined to acquire an "Islamic" face is another debatable issue. *Islamic*, as it became blatantly clear, meant not merely respect for Islamic moral values in a secular constitutional framework. Nor did it mean merely honoring a national icon in the person of Ayatollah Khomeini. As the revolution unfolded and turned into an Islamic Republic, it became pain-fully clear that *Islamic* meant something more: a radical state with theocratic underpinnings, or more accurately, a hierocracy headed by an authoritarian guardian jurist and buttressed by an oligarchy with militant clergy at its core. Utilizing modern means of ascendency and control, the republic's clerical elite and subservient lay cohort quickly deployed weapons of intimidation and vio-lence. They added to this concoction a generous dose of anti-Westernism and Islamist idealism, the former largely a legacy of people like Al-e Ahmad and the latter, that of Islamists like Shari'ati.

Beyond these considerations, one can identify structural underpinnings that for centuries helped shape Shi'i Iran. That the Pahlavi secular project even-tually gave way to a religiously defined revolution cannot be viewed in isola-tion from a century-long rift between the state and the Shi'i establishment. Nor can one ignore the widening gap dividing the Iranian secular from the religious worldview, a gap that the state-sponsored modernity could not suc-cessfully bridge. Moreover, the revolution can be fully understood only if we take into account dormant messianic traits in Iranian Shi'ism, which periodi-cally revolted against the state and religious establishment. The 1979 revolution demonstrated a remarkable affinity with these features while operating almost entirely on a different trajectory, as became more apparent in the decade after the revolution.

14

THE GUARDIAN JURIST AND
HIS ADVOCATES

That Ayatollah Khomeini and his cohorts put their mark on the Islamic
Revolution was more than an accident of history. At least since 1961, and with
a greater resolve since 1970, clerical Shi'ism explored ideological Islam and
contemplated juridical authority as an alternative to secular power. Although
political activism was well-trodden territory, contemplating a conscious, if not
consistent, political theory was new to the clerical experience. Shi'i jurists by
and large remained loyal to the idea of political nonintervention.

The shift in political climate required a new approach and new rhetoric.
To secure the loyalties of their followers and to remain relevant to a changing society, the clergy could no longer cling to merely promoting devotional
acts and intricate details of jurisprudence. Mobilizing urban multitudes, even
the bazaar constituency, called for a proactive role. Competitions from lay Islamists, such as Shari'ati, and from Mojahedin Khalq added to the urgency, not
to mention competition from the secular left. Even in Qom, to preserve loyalties of the clerical core, the leadership could no longer remain indifferent to the
outside world, especially to anticolonial struggles and postcolonial discourse in
the greater Islamic world. Isolation in the clerical teaching circles, the *howzeh*,
no longer paid off, and Khomeini and his students and supporters began to fill
the gap as a voice of radical dissent against the Pahlavi state.

GUARDIAN OF THE ISLAMIC NATION

Already in 1969 in Najaf, Khomeini had delivered a series of lectures on the
subject of the governance of the jurist, a pivotal notion that came to define the
ideology of the revolution. *Welayat* (or, in Arabic, *wilaya*) is a broad and complex

term with multiple legal, mystical, and historical nuances. As a legal principle in Shiʻi jurisprudence, it entrusted the jurist (s. *fqih*; pl. *foqaha*) with a set of legal supervisory duties to serve as a guardian, a custodian, a legatee, or a public advocate. In its broadest sense these duties are roughly equivalent of those of an attorney general or a public advocate in a modern legal system, though largely devoid of the latter's centralized and hierarchical structure. These duties included custodianship of minors, orphans, the mentally incapacitated, and such who were deemed incapable of looking after their own affairs and lacked other guardians. The jurist also acted as the trustee of charitable endowments that lacked a named trustee and undertook fair allocation of unclaimed inheritance. By any standard, the question of *wilayat* was viewed as a dry academic debate in the books of jurisprudence. It had preserved its arcane character since the tenth century with little change.

A few jurists in the Safavid period entertained, in theory, that guardianship of the jurist could mean something beyond such fiduciary duties. More specifically, they saw a public duty for the jurist on behalf of the community and in its dealings with the state. The mainstream Shiʻi jurists, however, made only passing references, if any at all, to the public aspect of *welayat* and never established a framework for it. Nor did it serve, it is important to note, as legal ground for any form of political action or a springboard for the clergy's opposition to the state in the Qajar or Pahlavi eras. Contrary to what has often been claimed, the most widely quoted source on the subject of guardianship, Mulla Ahmad Naraqi (1772–1829), an Usuli jurist of early nineteenth-century Kashan, never explicitly claimed *welayat* as ground for jurists' political authority. On the contrary, he was known for his firm support for the Qajar state and his advocacy of the separation of clerical from temporal duties. Likewise, Sayyed Mohammad Baqer Shafti, another powerful contemporary of Naraqi, clearly observed such a division.

Khomeini's novel reading of the notion of guardianship of the jurist as the only legitimate alternative to "unjust" temporal rule was at odds with the traditional Shiʻi aversion toward political power, avoiding government offices, and, for the most part, engaging in state affairs (except the mostly hereditary post of serving as leaders of Friday congregational prayers in major cities). Shiʻi law generally held the position that in the absence of the Imam of the Age, any form of government, presumably even a government led by the jurists, is fundamentally "unjust" and therefore theoretically illegitimate. Only the savior Mahdi—in Twelver Shiʻism, the Twelfth Imam who is considered to be in occultation—upon his return to the material world at the outset of a process that leads to the End of the Time will, with divine blessing, restore justice and equity to earth and establish the utopian society (or dystopian, if we consider its apocalyptic finale) that was lost with the death of the Prophet of Islam. While the Twelfth Imam is absent (i.e., in occultation), any form of temporal power, including kingship, is essentially unsanctified and hence "tyrannical."

Aside from historical circumstances that led to such a drastic, almost anarchistic, position, in practice the Shi'i jurists were generally accommodating toward temporal rulers, even if the sultans and the shahs were not particularly known for their religiosity or fair treatment of their subjects. They had established a kind of *modus vivendi* loyal to the old Persian sisterhood pact of kingship and "good religion" that had survived for more than a millennium in the Persianate world. In the case of the Safavid shahs, whose private lives were scandalously negligent of shari'a obligations, this ancient alliance was as applicable as in the case of the seemingly God-fearing Qajar rulers. Rulers, even unjust rulers, were to be abided, even though they were not legally legitimate, so long as they confessed to be Muslims. The idea of resisting "oppressive" rulers was a mere philosophical ideal foreign to the mostly sheepish jurists taking refuge in the madrasa.

Even the rulers' essential duties of defending the realm of Islam against foreign intrusion, maintaining security and order in the community, and enforcing the laws of the shari'a were treated with great latitude. Shi'i jurists were content with virtually any form of temporal power so long as it remained mindful of their jealously guarded clerical privileges and their shari'a legal domain. They were generally complimentary, if not always laudatory, toward the Safavid and the Qajar shahs, for these rulers honored a division between the authority to rule (*wilayat-e hokm*), which was the domain of the rulers, and the authority to judge (*wilayat-e qada*), which was that of the jurists. Even if in practice the latter authority was curtailed by the state, in and of itself it hardly ever established the grounds for disqualifying temporal power. The doctrine of confessional disguise (*taqiyya*) in Shi'ism always allowed jurists, under the pretext of self-preservation, to conveniently dodge the state's harshest treatments. Even in the Pahlavi era, when clerical power and privileges were curtailed or assumed by the state, the clerical establishment before Khomeini, despite its deep resentments, did not contemplate an Islamic alternative, let alone the political guardianship of the jurist.

The strongest precedent for conceptualizing clerical authority, perhaps, was the notion of the *mashru'eh* (i.e., a system of government compliant with principles of the shari'a), advanced by Shaykh Fazlollah Nuri and his supporters during the Constitutional Revolution. Nuri, who eventually abandoned the *mashru'eh* and turned into a staunch royalist supportive of Mohammad 'Ali

Shah's anticonstitutional regime, demanded, at most, compliance with the shari'a in framing the constitution and insisted on a supervisory role for the mojtaheds in the Majles. His end at the gallows silenced his supporters, although his ambitions for restoring some measure of clerical agency were never discarded. Khomeini's guardianship of the jurist can be viewed as an indirect descendant of Nuri's *mashru'eh*.

By contrast, Mohammad Hosain Na'ini, a contemporary of Nuri, offered a new reading of the shari'a whereby, in the absence of the Imam of the Age, popular representation and a democratic constitutional regime (*mashruteh*) could be considered the legitimate, and expedient, form of government. He was backed for a while by a minority of mojtaheds in Najaf and Iran. Yet in the aftermath of the Constitutional Revolution, senior jurists, even Na'ini himself, frustrated with the outcome of the revolution, rejected democratic representation, and the *mashruteh* as a whole, essentially because it proved unmindful of their corporate authority. Once the ramifications of a constitutional order in any form became more apparent, the clerical desire to create even a shari'a-based alternative, namely the *mashru'eh*, subsided. What remained was passive but nontheoretical resistance to the Pahlavi state by some activist jurists.

Khomeini's "governance of the jurist" (a more apt translation for *welayat-e faqih*, in the political context) thus was a drastic departure from the Shi'i jurists' political quietism. He argued that contrary to the conventional view held by conservative and pro-regime jurists, in the absence of the Imam of the Age it is the inalienable duty of the jurists to try to erect a relatively just Islamic government. As jurists, he stressed, they possessed "accredited guardianship" (*welayat-e e'tebari*), parallel to that of the Prophet and the Shi'i Imams, to discharge public duties necessary to defend the bastion of Islam against foreign intruders. This was a controversial view, for it substituted, in effect, the divine mandate with human agency. He insisted that "belief in the necessity of establishing the [Islamic] government and creating its executive and administrative components, are parts of the *welayat* and struggle toward establishing it also requires belief in the *welayat*":

> Remember you are obligated to establish the Islamic government. Have self confidence and know that you will be able to do it. The colonizers laid the ground for three or four hundred years; they started from zero until they arrived here. We too will start from zero. Do not be intimidated by the uproar of a few western-stricken (*gharbzadeh*) individuals and servial lackeys of colonialism. . . . If you don't interfere with the colonizers' schemes and [instead] consider Islam only the [devotional] acts that you [i.e., the traditional jurists]

always discuss and never go beyond them, they too don't ever bother you. You perform as much prayer as you like [but] they want your oil; what do they care about your prayers? They want your mines; they want our country to be the market for their products. It is by this rationale that their [subservient] client states prevent us from becoming industrialized; they build instead assembly factories and dependent industries. They don't wish to see us as human beings, since they are afraid of humans.

As if referring to his own defiance against the conservative clergy and the shah's government, Khomeini's tone turns sharper. "They would say this clergyman [*akhund*] is political. So was the Prophet [of Islam]. Such fabrications comes from political agents of colonialism in order to drive you out of politics and prevent you from engaging in social issues and prevent you from struggling against traitorous governments and [their] anti-nationalist and anti-Islamic designs so as to allow them to do whatever they wish and whatever damned thing they want [to achieve] and no one can stop them."[1]

In Khomeini's view the Western colonial powers (which in his eye were not different from his contemporary Western superpowers) entertained conspiratorial designs to subjugate all Muslims in cultural, economic, and political spheres. In due course, he believed, they intended to destroy the very essence (*bayzeh*, or "seed") of Islam. Since the holders of temporal power, he asserted, were facilitators of such hegemonic designs, they were no longer capable of discharging their traditional duty to defend the Muslim community. They were, he asserted, guilty of collaborating with the infidels in plundering the realms of Islam, and Iran in particular, of its riches, violating Islam's chastity and honors (*navamis*), and displaying servitude toward Western masters. They had encouraged immorality, irreligion, and corruption on earth and had weakened the foundations of the clerical establishment, the last bastion of true Islamic values.

Khomeini's provocative tone appeared in his *Hokumat-e Islami* (Islamic Government), laced with a conspiratorial worldview and curious antimodern anxieties. The work stood at the center of his radical theocracy. Originally a series of Persian lectures on the subject of guardianship in Shi'ism given at the behest of his clerical and lay loyalists in Najaf, it was published as a booklet first in Beirut in 1970 and clandestinely distributed in Iraq and Iran. His views were primarily indicative of a grudging rage that had accumulated toward Reza Shah and his successor, a rage that later burst into the open in the isolation of exile in Najaf (fig. 14.1). In his *Hokumat-e Islami*, a manifesto of the sort, he painted a bleak picture of Pahlavi Iran while displaying a sense of victimization and a disdain toward dissipation of clerical solidarity. He relied heavily on the Qur'anic

Figure 14.1. Khomeini in Najaf, c. 1976.
Contemporary photograph, Jamaran.ir. http://www.jamaran.ir/
PhotoNews-gid_72547–id_80875.aspx.

verses, the prophetic *hadith*, citations from the Shi'i Imams, and the works of medieval Shi'i scholars—mostly out of context—to underscore the duty of the jurists to defend the community against alien intrusions. Jurists, he claimed unabashedly, are the most virtuous, and hence the most eligible, to uphold justice and communities' moral standards. Legally the most qualified leaders of the community, he prescribed, the jurists must aspire toward the creation of an Islamic government.

Responding no doubt to his clerical critics, Khomeini elaborated on the necessity of *welayat* of the jurist to establish the Islamic government. "To further clarify I ask this question":

From the time of the minor occultation [of the Shi'i Twelfth Imam; i.e., 784] more than one thousand and few hundred years have passed and it may not be expedient for him [the Mahdi] to return for another hundred thousand years. In such a long period of time are the teachings of Islam supposed to remain ignored and unenforced? And do people allowed to do whatever they wish? Is there going to be a state of chaos? . . . Such beliefs are worse than confessing to the annulment of Islam. [But] no one can say that it is unnecessary to defend the frontiers of the Islamic homeland and its territorial integrity or not collect the taxes, the poll tax [*jiziya*, from the "nonbelievers"], the land tax, the one-fifth tax [*khoms*] and religious alms or [say] that Islamic punitive laws and obligations and laws of retribution [*qesas*] should be abandoned.

> Anyone who asserts that establishing the Islamic government is not necessary, [if effect] rejects the need to enforce the Islamic law and denies the universality and eternity of the blessed Islamic teachings.[2]

In Khomeini's view the secular rulers are unlikely candidates to enforce Islamic law because:

> If the ruler is not knowledgeable about [Islamic] legal affairs, he is not fit to rule for if he would just follow ([*taqlid*] a jurists), his authority will be wrecked. And if he doesn't follow [a jurist], he cannot enforce the Islamic law. It is an obvious fact [therefore] that "the jurists are rulers over the sultans" [*al-fuqaha hukkam ala al-salatin*]. If the sultans are obedient to Islam, they must abide by the jurists and ask them about laws and injunctions in order to enforce them. In that case the jurists are the true ruler and therefore authority to rule [*hakemiyat*] must officially rest with them and not with those who because of their ignorance of the [Islamic] law must abide by the ruling of the jurists.[3]

In a worldview such as this there were many enemies with evil designs lurking in every corner. These enemies were not only the corrupt rulers—a reference to the Pahlavi regime in everything but name—but also their presumed masters: the United States and Britain being the most obvious, but also Jews, Christian missionaries, the Freemasons, and the Baha'i. His condemnation of the Jews, a term he conflated indiscriminately with Zionists, for contemplating world hegemony echoed anti-Semitic literature such as the turn-of-the-century Russian *Protocol of the Elders of Zion*. Traditional tirades were not rare either: "May God curse them" is how Khomeini addressed the Jews. The establishment of the state of Israel, of course, loomed large as a prelude to this colonial master plan for Jewish hegemony. Coming in the wake of the 1967 Arab-Israeli War, Khomeini's allegation of Jewish hegemony implied a broader concern. Since in his view the entire Muslim world was in danger, the bar dividing Shi'i and Sunni was to be lowered, if not fully crossed.

In the opening page of *Hokumat-e Islami* Khomeini states: "Islamic movement from the outset encountered the Jews and they were the first to spread anti-Islamic propaganda and hatch intellectual conspiracies. And as you can see these continued to the present. Then it came the turn of those who in some way more sinister than the Jews. From three hundred year ago or earlier they in the guise of colonizers penetrated into the Islamic countries and to achieve their colonial objectives, they found it necessary to prepare the grounds for destruction of Islam. . . . They realized that what stands against their vested interests and their political domination is Islam, its teachings and people's faith in Islam. So through different means they propagated and conspired against Islam."[4]

The *Hokumat-e Islami* saw the United States in particular as the archenemy, though not yet as the "Great Satan." In this designation one could sense not only shades of third-worldist ideology, and the unavoidable bitter aftertaste of 1953 and 1963 events, but also the United States' unconditional support for Israel and Israel's oppressive treatment of Palestinians in the Occupied Territories. Wider coverage of the Palestinians' plight in the Arabic press and the aftershocks of the 1967 disaster no doubt also caught his attention while in Najaf. His disillusionment at the time with the rhetoric of the leadership in the Arab world, above all Nasser's brand of Arab nationalism, along with increased anti-Westernism among Iranian intellectuals of the left and their greater awareness of political Islam all served as a backdrop to Khomeini's evolving political outlook and his doctrine of an Islamic government. Likewise, the increased presence of the United States in Iran throughout the 1960s, a major target of his criticism, also played a role in his ideological formation.

In assigning to the United States the primary blame for the sad state of affairs in the Muslim world and elsewhere, *Hokumat-e Islami* was a blueprint for what was to come less than a decade later during the Islamic Revolution. Here the "guardian jurist" was portrayed as the supreme head of the clerical pyramid, which is collectively empowered to conduct the affairs of the Islamic state. Quite tellingly, the text refrained from any reference to the *marja'-e taqlid* (the supreme exemplar) and other customary clerical titles, as if bypassing the Shi'i informal hierarchy by envisioning an inherently all-encompassing office superior to the negotiated authority of the *marja's*. Moreover, much of what later gained currency in the revolution was presaged in Khomeini's manifesto, as were key concepts and institutions of the future Islamic Republic. From the recruitment (*basij*) of an Islamic army (*sepah-e Islam*) to characterization of the shah and the ruling elite as idol worshippers (*taghuti*) and to those condemned in the revolutionary courts as corruptors of the earth (*mufsid fi'l-ard*), all were anticipated in the text.

In many respects Khomeini's outlook in the *Hokumat-e Islami*, his frequent calls for the return to an "authentic Islam," reveal a subtle affinity with the Sunni Salafi views widespread for at least two centuries before his time. Despite sharp attacks in his earlier writings on the Wahhabi teachings and those who echoed these teachings in a Shi'i guise—such as Shari'at Sangelaji, Khomeini essentially approved of a trait of activist Islam that intended to replicate an early Islamic community albeit a Shi'i one. In this he was conceptually ahistorical and politically radical. This activist Islam imagined a theocratic state on the model of 'Ali's caliphate, but one that would be presided over by the jurists. It is likely that he was familiar not only with lives and works of such figures as his countryman Jamal al-Din Asadabadi (better known as Afghani) but also with the influential Syrian writer and theologian Rashid Rida (1865–1935) and the Egyptian founder of the Muslim Brothers, Hasan al-Banna (1906–1949). The radical theoretician of the Muslim Brothers, Sayyid Qutb, and Abul 'Ala Mawdudi (1903–1979), the Pakistani Islamist and founder of Jamaat-e Islami, both could have influenced Khomeini in his formative years and helped him articulate his own model of an Islamic revolution and an Islamic government.

The idea of creating an Islamic government, or even the denial of the temporal state, it is important to note, came late in Khomeini's career. Up to the 1970s he still was abiding by the Shi'i principle that in the absence of the Imam of the Age, the community could refrain from allowing oppressive rulers or at the most could advise and admonish. In the early 1960s Khomeini was still doing just that when he rebuked Mohammad Reza Shah for not listening to the clergy, the *ruhaniyun* (the spiritual authorities, as they came to be known in the Pahlavi era), and accused him of collaborating with Western enemies of Islam. Hosain-'Ali Montazeri, an early student close to Khomeini recalls that once, presumably in the early 1960s, he and Moretza Motahhari, another early student of Khomeini, debated the question of leadership of the community in the absence of the Imam of the Age: "We finally came to the conclusion that in the age of occultation the leadership of the community will be rested on the choice of the people but according to the principles and values defined by Islam. And this is not contrary to the Shi'ism." When they raised the issue with Khomeini and emphasized that in their view the "elected Imam should be an all-embracing qualified mojtahed," he begged to differ. "In Shi'ism the Imam must be infallible and designated [by another Imam]. At the time of occultation it is people's fault that Imam is in in occultation. . . . It is because we don't deserve him that the Imam is in occultation and it is on us to prepare the ground for the Imam of the Age to come." When they pointed out that as such occultation is the age of chaos, Khomeini replied: "This is people's own fault. God has provided us with the [divine] favor but we should make ourselves worthy of the Imam to return." At that time, Montazeri recalls, Khomeini "did not make any reference to guardianship of the jurist."[5]

The emerging idea of the Islamic government, which he embraced from 1970 on, in part was to satisfy the radical trends in his own camp. He also was frustrated with how "dear Islam," a catchphrase of his, was being pummeled under the feet of heedless Pahlavi secularism. Invariably, Khomeini also shared with many Islamist thinkers a sense of decline in the community, moral decrepitude, intrusion of alien powers, and an urgency to reconstruct an Islamic state. Like his cohorts elsewhere in the Islamic world, Khomeini also rejected temporal powers as weak and immoral, incapable of defending Islam against domestic corruption and foreign encroachments, and like them, he also prescribed a radical break from the secular state and the Western model of political change. Commonality with Sunni Islamist trends, however, did not devalue Khomeini's scheme or diminish the place of the Shi'i victimization narrative of Islamic past, of the caliphate of 'Ali, the first Imam, and the revolt of Hosain ibn 'Ali the Third Imam. He, moreover, deeply adhered to a Shi'i juristic tradition as it developed over the course of a millennium. Yet these ideals meant to him something diametrically opposed to the conservative Shi'i jurists of Qom, let alone the Pahlavi secular values against which he had revolted. The dawn of the revolution reassured Khomeini of his political convictions and for the first time gave him a realistic hope of implementing some of the views he articulated in the Hokumat-e Islami. That throughout the years of his exile he had remained in contact with his senior students and lay supporters and preserved a network of patronage and exchange of ideas made him all the more reassured.

THE MAKING OF REVOLUTIONARY MULLAHS

A number of Khomeini's former students were indeed crucial in organizing support and articulating his message throughout the 1970s. Among them Mortaza Motahhari, a teacher of Islamic philosophy and a prolific religious writer, was the most rigorous. For years he had advanced a revamped version of Shi'i theology, as understood by the Qom madrasas, with a pedestrian modernist veneer. Like Shari'ati, though somewhat less of a populist, he strived to "enlighten" the youth from the tribune of Hosainiyeh Ershad by highlighting Islam's "true" humanitarian vales and its solution for the problems of modern times. Staying away from Khomeini's doctrine of the guardianship of the jurist, at least on the surface, Motahhari was in favor of peacefully incorporating Islamic values into the Iranian cultural landscape rather than conspiring for the downfall of Pahlavi regime and its replacement with an Islamic alternative. His subtext of Islamist dissent was partially tolerated by the Pahlavi regime because he maintained sufficient rapport with the Islamically inclined cultural figures of the late Pahlavi era.

Yet by 1977, Motahhari, typical of Khomeini's students in the middle ranks of the Qom hierarchy, was carried away by revolutionary momentum and tilted more forcefully toward the radical Islamic alternative. The author of a vast number of semischolarly works in theology, ethics, and other Islamic topics, often in the form of lecture series and proceedings from his study groups, they represented a rationalized approach to Islam that was attractive to a religiously inclined younger audience. Offering a more palatable Islam in modern guise, he borrowed concepts and terminology from Western philosophy and social sciences and engaged secular modernists, a bridge between Qom madrasa culture and lay Islamist such as Shari'ati and Mahdi Bazargan.

Motahhari was not the only one to undergo a metamorphosis toward radical Islam. More typical among Khomeini's students was Mohammad Beheshti (1929–1981), arguably the chief strategist of the clerical wing of the revolution. He, too, had exposure to the world outside Qom's conservative enclosure and acquired a somewhat modernist outlook. In the early 1960s he had spent five years in Germany as the clerical resident in the Islamic Center in Hamburg, a Shi'i institution. Like Motahhari, he held a PhD from the School of Religious Sciences of Tehran University, but more than his colleague he was inclined toward political activism. On and off he was detained by the Savak, often more as a precaution than punishment. He was in contact with Khomeini during his exile and more regularly after the start of the unrest in 1977. Likewise, Mohammad Mofatteh (1928–1979), another product of the Qom seminary with a doctorate in philosophy from Tehran University came to the forefront of pro-Khomeini activists in the late 1970s. Preaching an antiregime message in a Tehran mosque, Mofatteh was sent to internal exile in 1978 but was freed soon enough to play his part in the early stages of the protests along with his two better-known cohorts.

The three stood at the forefront of the Islamic protest movement in 1977 while most other pro-Khomeini clergy were either in detention or in exile. Educated and relatively nuanced they projected an alluring image of political Islam: cordial, inclusive, and in essence Iranian nationalist. By implication they also projected an amiable image of Khomeini as a spiritual guide who was reluctant, even unwilling, to hold the reins of political power and was tolerant of most, if not all, political outlooks. Tellingly, all three were early victims of the postrevolutionary scramble, having been assassinated during the first twenty-five months after the victory of the revolution. Had they survived, it may be argued, the revolutionary course could have taken a different trajectory, even though such a prospect was fairly dim given Khomeini's towering presence and his resolute, almost innate, appetite for making a tilt toward greater militancy. Beheshti's own conduct during the two years after the revolution was far from moderate and, as has often been noted, rather devious.

Beyond this, a larger number of clerical and lay supporters made up of Khomeini's former students and loyalists spread the message of revolution. They were mostly from Khomeini's days in Qom, and less so in Najaf. They also included those who aligned themselves rather opportunistically with his brand of Islam. Most prominent were the anti-Pahlavi activists who had been harassed by the Savak for their fiery sermons. Yet there were others who all the way up to the dawn of the revolution were political quietists and coexisted with the regime. Even the militant clergy who were sent into internal exile or imprisoned seldom were treated by the shah's regime as harshly as the Marxist guerrillas or other lay critics of the Pahlavi regime.

The shield of clerical immunity inherent to Iranian Shi'i society protected them even at the height of Pahlavi power. Many during internal exile sustained their social status in the community and even thrived once the Savak's restrictions were relaxed. Inadvertently, it was as if banishment to remote towns and cities of Iran was a blessing in disguise, for it allowed them access audiences who had otherwise remained untouched by the message of religious dissent. Case in point were the future president of the Islamic Republic, Akbar Hashemi Rafsanjani (1934–2017); the chief judge of the Islamic Revolutionary Courts, Sadegh Khalkhali (1926–2003); and the future leader (*rahbar*) of the Islamic Republic, Sayyed 'Ali Khamenei. They were younger than their aforementioned cohorts and more extreme in their ideologically orientation.

The turbaned advocates of Khomeini were mostly from rural or low-income urban backgrounds. They often had a combined, and at times simultaneous, secular public education and madrasa training. Those of the older generation more likely had only received a madrasa education, but they were not entirely devoid of secular Pahlavi education. Nor were they sanguine toward the use of modern means for radical ends. The most senior among them, including Borujerdi, recalled the troubled postwar years and had witnessed, on the sidelines, the early 1950s struggle under Mosaddeq. As a wary observer of the National Movement Khomeini, and many like him in the *howzeh*, were supporters of Kashani and backed his break with Mosaddeq. Only a handful of the clergy, among them Sayyed Reza Mowsavi Zanjani (1902–1983) and the young Mahmud Taleqani, remained loyal to Mosaddeq's camp and later cofounded with Mahdi Bazargan the Freedom Movement. Yet even they were not fully adherent to liberal nationalism of the National Movement.

Only gradually and from the early 1960s the activists among the clergy subscribed to the anti-imperialist message of the Mosaddeq era and came to see themselves as victims of the Pahlavi regime. Only a few were deprived of their social network and material benefits that the majority of the clergy came to enjoy in the years of economic growth under the shah. Their dual education prepared them for an activist life beyond the madrasa and made them better informed on domestic and international affairs, ideologies of the left, and anticolonial popular struggles abroad, ranging from Nasser and Egypt during the Suez Crisis to the Algerian Revolution, the Vietcong, and the most lasting, the Palestinian struggle (fig. 14.2).

These events helped shape their anti-Western convictions. Nasser, in particular, was favored for his open attack on the shah and his anti-Western posture, despite the Egyptian president's autocratic rule and enmity toward the Muslim Brothers. Likewise, the Vietnam War was crucial in sharpening the clergy's anti-American sentiments. Mostly through Iranian and Arabic presses but also through the radical literature of the Arab world, especially publications of the Muslim Brothers, as well as Persian broadcasts of Radio Moscow and clandestine publications of the Marxist and Islamic guerrilla organizations, they acquired a more sophisticated and radical perspective of global affairs. Even Colonel Qaddafi of Libya in his earlier years was revered as an anticolonial champion. His support for radical Islamic movements, including the Mojahedin-e Khalq, as well as some radical seminarians in Qom, sidelined his eccentricities, his

Figure 14.2. Yasser Arafat (*center front*), chairman of the Palestinian Liberation Organization, was the first foreign visitor to revolutionary Iran in February 1979. He was received warmly by Khomeini and his clerical supports, including (*front row from right*) Mohammad Beheshti, Akbar Hashemi Rafsanjani, Hosain-Montazeri, and Abol-qasem Lahuti.
© A. Abbas/Magnum Photos. Arafat in Tehran, 1979 (PAR232690).

unconventional interpretation of Islam in his Green Book, and his ruthless suppression of critics at home.

Not only in outlook but also in style, Khomeini's students represented a new hybrid. In contrast to the often coarse and ungrammatical Persian of most mullahs of the older generation—often heavily Arabicized, culturally alienated, and of arrogant demeanor—the new generation of clergy, thanks to the Persian they learned in the state schools of the Pahlavi era, could communicate to their audiences with grater proficiency. Their fiery sermons and politicized theology, orally and in writing, were more palatable and easier to grasp by the younger audiences in mosques and rallies. They handled themselves with greater ease and confidence as advocates of a proactive Islam and eventually as leaders of a revolutionary movement. Encounters with lay Islamists such as Shari'ati and taking part in debates in Hosainiyeh Ershad and other forums deepened their grasp of the public mode and honed their rhetorical style. Their hybrid training and their humble social background gave the new mullahs an edge over their ideological contenders on the left and the mostly affluent liberal veterans of earlier years. Far more effective than children of the middle and lower-middle classes who were captivated by the lure of the guerrilla movements, the younger clergy were able to share on the pulpit of mosques their veiled narrative of deprivation, criticism of the Pahlavi state and call for social justice.

During the 1960s mosque congregations steadily grew in size as urban populations grew. Along with the prosperity that came with the oil price hikes, the senior clergy also acquired greater economic benefits and expanded their networks through the collection of alms and other religious dues. New mosques were built, or enlarged and improved, in poorer neighborhoods. By broadening their social network of schools with Islamically inclined curricula and staff, they also added to their followers. And this was at the time when the Savak was busy harassing intellectuals and university students. The more senior among the clergy in provincial centers often curried favor with their politically active devotees while maintaining an uneasy coexistence with the government and its agencies. Though a majority was discontented with the regime, only a small number of clergy were vociferous and hence sustained the brunt of the pressure from the security forces.

One such example, Hosein-'Ali Montazeri, senior among Khomeini's former students, was from a small and religiously conservative town of Najafabad nineteen miles west of Isfahan. He was born to a peasant family, had studied mostly jurisprudence and usul al-fiqh in Isfahan, and later in Qom under Borujerdi, and later in his career he gravitated toward Khomeini. Like many of his cohort, he was the product of the Hawzeh-ye 'Elmiyeh Qom, a conglomerate of seven teaching circles established in 1922 under 'Abd al-Karim Ha'eri, Khomeini's teacher and patron. Fayziyeh, a madrasa from the early Safavid period, thrived in the postwar era under Borujerdi and became a core to the Shi'i studies only second to Najaf (pl. 14.1). The Qom *howzeh* was a new notion in Shi'i Iran, aiming to bring some centrality and academic discipline to the otherwise dispersed Shi'i madrasas and teaching curricula. In essence, it resembled the original notion of the university, consisting of mostly independent colleges (and itself probably influenced by the early Islamic teaching institutions such as the Isma'ili al-Azhar in tenth-century Fatimid Egypt and the Sunni-Ash'ari Nizamiya network created by Nezam al-Molk in the eleventh-century Saljuq domains). Yet in practice, Qom *howzeh* under Ha'eri and Borujerdi only partially succeeded in homogenizing clerical education in Qom and other cities.

Montazeri's activist career began in earnest in the 1950s with anti-Baha'i campaigns in his hometown Najafabad. At Borujerdi's behest he repeatedly called on Najafabad believers to impose sanctions on the Baha'i "heretics" and demanded concerted anti-Baha'i action in Isfahan and other places. Like many mullahs of that era anti-Baha'i campaign was the point of departure for Montazeri's activism and a communal and doctrinal challenge to his clerical core. Like many Qom students, too, Montazeri's initial training was largely focused on the intricacies of the Islamic law. Under Khomeini's influence, perhaps, he later developed an interest in a "reformed" theology that relied more on Islamic philosophy, which largely aimed to buttress the otherwise paralyzed Shi'i scholasticism of the era. In the early 1940s Montazeri attended in Qom Khomeini's teaching circle:

> For us his class had a great appeal. . . . Of course in his teaching of ethics there was much about mysticism. He discussed some of the litanies of Khwajeh 'Abdollah Ansari [the eleventh century Sufi of Heart]. His articulation was fascinating. He elaborated on themes of repentance, supplication and the Day of Return is such manner that many would weep. For us his lessons were very attractive and very constructive. My acquaintance with him started there. He also taught philosophy but I was not attending that class. . . . He was not then teaching jurisprudence and *Usul (al-Fiqh)*. His ethics class was for the public; a group of well-known bazaaris regularly attended and so did many of the preachers of Qom.[6]

In later years anti-Pahlavi activism rather than ethics or close examination of the Shi'i *fiqh* became Montazeri's preoccupation. What made sense to him, and to many of his cohort, was to render a political reading of Islam rather than reexamine the tenets of the Islamic law, and its inadequacies in the face of modern challenges, something that normally should have fallen within a jurist's area of expertise. For politically engaged students, his criticizing the shah and the Pahlavi regime, its excesses, and its alleged anti-Islamic stance were far more appealing than the dispassionate study of the modern applicability of Islamic law. As a critic of the Pahlavi regime and supporter of Khomeini, Montazeri was repeatedly arrested, sent to internal exile, and imprisoned. Between 1966 and 1975 he was exiled to five different parts of Iran: Masjed Soleiman in Khuzestan, Najafabad in Isfahan, Tabas in the central Iranian desert, Khalkhal at the western edge of Gilan province, and Saqqez in the Iranian Kurdistan. He was at last released from a four-year term in the months leading to the revolution.

Nearly all of Montazeri's works before 1979 were on arcane treatment of such aspects of Shi'i jurisprudence as religious alms, religious taxes, religious punishments and unlawful gains. He uncritically complied lectures of his teachers Ayatollah Borujerdi and Ayatollah Khomeini on roots of jurisprudence (*usul al-fiqh*) as well as on the Friday prayers and on travelers' devotional obligations. He also published an anti-Baha'i polemic indicative of his strong anti-Baha'i sentiments. None of these works, published or unpublished, dwelled in the realm of politics. Before the revolution his political activism was more on the pulpit than in writing. It was only in the years leading to the Islamic Revolution that he and like-minded jurists of his generation fully engaged in the discourse of political Islam. His lectures on legal foundations of the doctrine of the guardianship of the jurist, which was rendered in Arabic and later translated into Persian, was one of several works articulated immediately after the revolution with clear political connotations. His extensive commentary on *Nahj al-Balagha*, a series of lectures on the sermons attributed to 'Ali, the First Imam, was another. They indicated a shift from earlier studies of jurisprudence and his preoccupation with ritualistic aspects of Shi'i Islam.

As one of the framers of the 1979 constitution and as the designated successor to "Imam Khomeini," Montazeri played an important part in the early consolidation of the Islamic Republic (fig. 14.3). Only isolation in the years following his fall out with Khomeini in 1988-1989 and the experience of harassment by hard-liners brought Montazeri to a more tolerant legal and moral perspective atypical of Qom's clerical activists of his time.

Of the same generation as Montazeri, and equally instrumental in the early consolidation of the Islamic regime, was Mahmud Taleqani. He was a cleric of radical convictions but with a wider horizon than his cohorts. His atypical interest in writing a Qur'anic commentary with a politico-moral message was reminiscent of Sayyid Qutb. Born to a family of village mullahs in the Tale-

Figure 14.3. Hosain-'Ali Montazeri as leader of Friday prayer, Tehran University,
c. 1980. The poster calls on university students, as the arm of the great
Islamic power, to liberate the deprived people of the world. A rifle with
bayonet represents the military authority of the Islamic state.
Made by Jihad-e Sazandegi (The crusade for construction), c. 1981. Middle Eastern
Posters. Collection, Box 4, Poster no. 25, Special Collections Research Center,
University of Chicago Library.

qan region in northwestern Iran, Taleqani, too, was a product of Fayziyeh. A
onetime supporter of the Fada'iyan-e Islam, in 1953 he harbored their leader,
Navvab Safavi, and later in 1965 helped fund the assassination of the premier
Hasan-'Ali Mansur. As a vocal member of Mahdi Bazargan's Freedom Movement, he was detained, convicted by a military court, and spent long years in
jail. More as a collaborator than a follower of Khomeini, he was sympathetic
to the Mojahedin-e Khalq, with whom he spent time in prison. His relatively
independent stance in the postrevolutionary days briefly made him a champion
of the moderate Islamists and a fatherly figure for the Mojahedin-e Khalq.

Taleqani's study of the concept of property in Islam displayed his faint socialist sympathies, an aspect that set him apart from mainstream Qom authorities.
After the victory of the revolution, his pluralist approach and greater tolerance
for other readings of Islam and secular ideologies were increasingly at odds with
Khomeini's exclusivist brand. His death from a heart attack in September 1979,
in the heat of the postrevolutionary struggle, was the first of several losses that

deprived the Islamic Republic of its relatively moderate and broader-minded leaders. If he had survived, he could have potentially served as a counterweight to Khomeini's radicalizing agenda, even though in his first public face-off with the leader of the revolution, when he criticized the arrest of some sympathizers of the Mojahedin-e Khalq, he quickly yielded to Khomeini's reverse decision.

Of the second tier of students loyal to Khomeini were Akbar Hashemi Rafsanjani and Sayyed 'Ali Khamenei. Their numbers exceeded no more perhaps than a half dozen, but they constituted a core for wider support within and beyond the clerical establishment. Rafsanjani, who was born to a family of landowning pistachio growers in Bahreman, a small village forty-five miles north of Rafsanjan in Kerman province, had never traveled beyond the vicinity of his village until he was fourteen years old, when in the fall of 1948 he first traveled to Qom to receive clerical training. "Listening to radio was not conventional. . . . Before leaving my village, I had never seen a receiver," recalled Rafsanjani. "This was my first trip outside my village. Before then I only once had travelled about one *farsakh* [four miles] outside. From the village to the main road we ride on a donkey. There were no cars in our village. . . . I guess we waited [in another village close to the main road] for three days for a truck to appear. . . . We sat atop the cargo."[7]

In Qom, young Rafsanjani gravitated toward antiregime dissent and became one of the founders of the journal *Maktab-e Tashayyu'* (the school of Shi'ism), one of the two major journals in Qom that since 1959 debated modern themes from an Islamic perspective with the hope of engaging a wider religiously inclined readership outside Qom. In contrast to the better-known *Maktab-e Islam*, which since 1958 had appeared as the organ of the Qom *howzeh* and enjoyed the patronage of Borujerdi and later Ayatollah Shari'atmadari, the *Maktab-e Tashayyu'*'s approach was proactive and mildly critical of the regime. When Rafsanjani and his colleagues appealed to Khomeini for his patronage, he declined, no doubt to the great disappointment of the contributors, many of them later among supporters of Khomeini and active in the revolution. Decades later, Rafsanjani went to a great length to justify Khomeini's inaction:

> All in all, we had a well-rounded impression of the Imam [Khomeini]. We could not spot any weakness or fault in him. Even if there were some issues, which were contrary to our expectation, such as his reclusive predisposition, reluctance to appear on the stage and take a stance in such political currents as the oil [nationalization] movement and [support for] Fada'iyan-e Islam, later it became clear that he was right. If he acted in accordance with our wishes, perhaps it would have left some ill impression on others. Besides, at

the time of Ayatollah Borujerdi, honoring his wishes was a necessity; without his consent no movement in Qom would have fully succeeded.[8]

Like Montazeri, here Rafsanjani's portrayal of Khomeini is reverential and yet indicative of his reluctance to politically engage. Further, in their accounts both authors attribute Khomeini's quietism to attacks that he was sustaining at the time from the ultraconservative quarters in Qom who objected his interest in philosophy and mysticism, and especially in the great thirteenth-century Andalusian mystic Muhi al-Din Ibn al-'Arabi. Only in the years following the death of Borujerdi and with the completion of moderate *marja's* in Qom and Najaf did Khomeini begin to draw the support of such radicalized clergy as Montazeri, Rafsanjani, Motahhari, and Beheshti and emerge as the only outspoken Qom critic of the Pahlavi state.

In contrast to the small-town and village backgrounds of Montazeri and Rafsanjani, another student of Khomeini, Sayyed 'Ali Khamenei, was born in 1939 in the city of Mashhad to a middle-ranking clerical family. He received most of his clerical education there before going to Najaf for a brief period and then in 1958 to Qom, where he studied under Borujerdi and Khomeini. He returned to Mashhad some years later and taught there for some time. In the aftermath of the 1963 uprising, Khamenei's activism let to his brief detention in 1966 in Birjand, in central Khorasan, and later in Tehran. Not known for his scholarship, Khamenei came to be known for his translations from Arabic into Persian. Among them were a number of works by Sayyid Qutb, whose impression of Khamenei's worldview cannot be denied. He had a side interest in Persian poetry as well not only Mohammad Iqbal's Persian poems but also works of some of the new-wave Iranian poets. Only in the months leading to the Islamic Revolution, however, did Khamenei gain some visibility in Khomeini's inner circle as a skilled orator capable of articulating his mentor's message.

These students in one way or another shared the marginality of the madrasa environment. Donning clerical garb, a stigma of a sort in the age of Pahlavi secularism, set them apart from the majority. Experiences of interrogations, exile, and detention, though seldom severe for clerics, also gave them a sense of solidarity with one another. These experiences allowed them to forge ties with other political tendencies in prison and in exile and helped sharpen their rhetorical skills in encounters with the Mojahedin, Marxists, and other shades of political dissent while absorbing many of the themes and arguments proposed by other forces of opposition and making them their own.

Khomeini's revolutionary bandwagon in the days leading to 1979 also had a network of middle and upper clerical ranks. Even during his Najaf exile

Khomeini had preserved an impressive array of agents in Iranian towns and cities, another testimony to Savak's misplaced focus on the left rather than the radical clerical circles. These agents collected alms and religious dues on Khomeini's behalf and soon became conduits for spreading his words orally and in print and on cassette tapes. They often were at the forefront of the protest rallies and responsible for recruiting lay followers to the revolutionary cause. A growing number of these clerical activists served as the backbone of the revolutionary institutions that would soon take root in the Islamic Republic.

BAZAAR FOLLOWERS OF THE IMAM

Beyond his clerical following, Khomeini relied primarily on the bazaar for moral and financial support and for manning his revolutionary ranks. In the urban economy in the 1960s and 1970s much of the large-scale business and international trade gradually moved out of the bazaar and into the streets. The new middle classes who generally ran big businesses generally had little or no traditional ties to the bazaar. Deprived of much of its economic muscle, the bazaar's mostly small merchants and wholesalers all over the country survived, and even occasionally thrived. The bazaar also preserved some of its traditional functions. The export of Persian carpets, textiles, and commodities, as well as wholesale trade and retail sales of domestic and imported consumer goods, small-scale workshops, and a host of intermediaries and dealers in promissory notes still served a sector of the middle class and poorer urban populations. The *bazaaris* who ran large wholesale and petty businesses in the bazaar's stores and caravansaries within a sprawling cloister of roofed space or its virtual extensions in adjacent low-income neighborhoods had preserved professional loyalties. They also held ties with the clerical establishment and contributed, at times generously, to their coffers. They made up the mosque congregations, funded the Muharram mourning associations, and their rank and file packed Muharram and Ramadan events.

The neighborhood associations, in and out of the bazaar, often named "association of mourners of Hosain" or after other Shiʻi saintly patrons or after "His Majesty the Imam of the Age" represented indigenous civic organizations. Financed and often supervised by neighborhood elders, they organized the Muharram procession (*dasteh*) and were responsible for the upkeep of the takki-yehs and mosques. They allowed men, and especially youth, to uphold a group identity and were fertile ground for Islamist activism. The novelty of the revolution, and the thrill of massive marches, distribution of clandestine tracts, and street clashes with the police and the troops excited the youth, especially when invoking paradigms of sacrifice and martyrdom rooted in Iran's Shiʻi culture.

Disgruntled with years of Pahlavi disdain toward the bazaar, many petty merchants and retailers alike sought in the revolution a message of deliverance and social mobility. To those who were brought up in the closely knit and religiously conscious environment of the bazaar, or in poorer neighborhoods associated with the bazaar, the Pahlavi economy had offered relative prosperity but did not engender political loyalty to the regime in power. Ties to the mosques and to the mullahs in charge of the mosques were made through the payment of religious dues and new recruits to clerical ranks from the children of the bazaar's petty merchants. The memory of the bazaar as a political powerhouse challenging the state was still alive, even though the bazaar's ability to effectively shut down the cities' economies was far smaller than before.

The Coalition of Mourning Associations (Hay'atha-ye Mow'talefeh), crucial in mobilizing mass support, was first formed in the early 1960s in the Tehran bazaar and adjacent neighborhoods, and later in religious centers such as Qom, Kashan, Isfahan, and Yazd. Some of the members had been active since the 1940s as supporters of Ayatollah Abol-Qasem Kashani and affiliates of Fada'iyan-e Islam, and later in the 1960s acted as the mobilizing arm of Khomeini's protest movement. In 1960 they backed Khomeini's leadership and encouraged him to produce a "treatise" (*resaleh*) on intricate details of jurisprudence, a prerequisite for *marjaʻiyat* leadership. As much as they were eager to turn a mystical philosopher like Khomeini into a mainstream faqih, the leaders of the coalition were keen to sharpen his political rhetoric as well. Leaders of the coalition, among the small merchants in the Tehran bazaar, such as Habibollah ʻAskarawladi (1932–2013) and Mahdi ʻEraqi (1930–1979), had close ties with the Fada'iyan-e Islam and were convicted and incarcerated for taking part in the 1965 assassination of Hasan-ʻAli Mansur. In the 1963 uprising, as in 1979, they helped organize rallies; they produced placards, posters, and tracts; and they disseminated Khomeini's cassette messages. During Khomeini's exile ʻAskarawladi also served as Khomeini's agent, collecting religious dues from his followers. The bazaar survival as a cloister of religio-political loyalties buttressed the morale of Khomeini and his lieutenants and topped up their coffers throughout the revolt.

THE UNDOING OF MODERATE ISLAMISTS

Khomeini's message was alluring to an assortment of lay Islamists who served him in the early days of the revolution but were mostly disillusioned shortly

afterward. They felt they had been used by Khomeini and abused by his clerical clique. To Khomeini and his turbaned cohorts, these tie-wearing advocates
of the revolution were ultimately outsiders and therefore more readily dispos-
able, even though they had paved the way for him, idealized him as a national
liberator, and worked hard to make him acceptable to the middle classes as the
"spiritual father" of the revolution.

Mahdi Bazargan, the prime minister of the provisional government appointed by Khomeini in February 1979, and his colleagues in the Freedom
Movement, were prime examples of this brand of Islamic modernism embellished with rationalized religiosity and a positivist outlook. The Freedom Movement was a league independent of Khomeini's cohorts that had loomed on
the horizon for some time. Bazargan, a longtime advocate of a new reading of
Islam and a supporter of constitutional democracy with an Islamic coloring,
was born in 1908 in Tehran to a bazaar merchant family with firm religious ties.
He was among the first group of Iranian students who in 1927 under Reza Shah
received a scholarship to pursue his higher education in France. He completed
his studies in thermodynamics in Paris in 1934 before joining the School of
Engineering of the newly established Tehran University. Despite his impressive
academic and administrative record, Bazargan was first detained for his close
collaboration with Mosaddeq after the 1953 coup, and again in the aftermath of
the 1963 uprising when he sustained five years imprisonment and internal exile
together with other members of the Freedom Movement. Besides the Freedom
Movement he was also pivotal in founding the Islamic Association (*anjoman-e
Islami*) at Tehran University as well as several Islamic associations for teachers,
engineers, and physicians.

Bazargan's "scientific" reading of Islamic doctrines and practices may well
be attributed to his exposure to the revival of neo-Catholicism in France in the
interwar period. What may appear to a secular mind as an outlandish take on
Islamic faith were to Bazargan, and his school of thought, "scientific" evidence
of Islam's veracity, its endurance, and its applicability to the needs of modern
societies. His articulation of the existence of God based on the laws of quantum
physics and his advocacy of the aerobic benefits of setting the daily prayers five
times were just two examples. As early as 1936 he published the earliest version
of his *Namaz* (Prayer), on scientific functions of daily prayer in Islam that went
through numerous editions. Rationalizations such as these went a long way
toward assuring like-minded people of the infallibility of Islam as a comprehensive system of beliefs and practice. A prolific writer, beyond publications in his
own field, Bazargan published more than 230 books and pamphlets of varying
size and quality on diverse religious, social, and political topics from an Islamic

perspective, including *Religion in Europe* in 1942, *Conversion Ratio between Materialism and Spirituality* in 1943, *Islam and Pragmatism* in 1949, *Love and Worship or Human Thermodynamics* in 1953, a guide to the study of the Qur'an between 1959 and 1964 in six volumes, and *Boundaries between Religion and Politics* in 1962.

A veteran of the National Movement of the Mosaddeq era, Bazargan capitalized on his past association and his record of resistance and arrest under the shah to make the image of a firebrand Khomeini more agreeable to ambivalent middle classes. Yet Bazargan and his colleagues were the first to go. Though respectful of Khomeini, Bazargan was a critic of the postrevolutionary excesses. Not surprisingly, his tumultuous relations with Khomeini and his cohorts led to his resignation eight months after assuming office.

Bazargan's colleague Ibrahim Yazdi (b. 1931), a member of the Freedom Movement and another early aide to Khomeini, was instrumental in promoting his cause first within the university Islamic associations in the United States. In Paris he served as a prominent though informal spokesman for Khomeini (especially in dealings with the English-speaking media). He became minister of foreign affairs in April 1980, after Karim Sanjabi resigned his post in protest, but he was forced to resign his post seven months later at the outset of the hostage crisis, along with the rest of the Bazargan cabinet. He was sidelined in the turbulent years that followed to the point of becoming an outcast and was labeled along with Bazargan as a "compromising liberal" (*liberal-e sazeshkar*).

Abol-Hasan Banisadr (b. 1933), the first president of the Islamic Republic who earlier had hosted Khomeini in Paris and served as his French-speaking facilitator, fared even less favorably. Coming from an old clerical family in Hamadan, he had earned a law degree from Tehran University and was active in the second National Front. His Islamic orientation soon turned him into an advocate of Khomeini during and after 1963. His advocacy of a unitarian (*tawhidi*) economy and society was a syncretic notion rooted in the socialist reading of Islamic doctrines then in vogue among the Islamic left. With Khomeini's implicit blessing, in February 1980 he was elected as first president of the Islamic Republic, only to be ousted in disgrace sixteen months later and driven out of the country into exile in France.

Sadeq Qotbzadeh (1936–1982), an activist in the early days of the Confederation of Iranian Students (and reportedly at one time a student in the Georgetown School of Foreign Service), had an idealized view of political Islam that was dismissive of the conservative clergy. As a longtime advocate of Khomeini, and his fashionable facade for the Western media, he gained prominence after the revolution as the head of the NRTI broadcasting services and later as minister of foreign affairs; but he, too, soon witnessed his downfall. He was sent to the gallows in September 1982 on charges of conspiracy to stage a coup.

These and a host of other lay supporters of Khomeini mostly had tinkered with their own version of Islamic discourse in the semisecular milieu of exile in Europe and the United States. Despite serious differences among themselves, these advocates of revolution shared varying degrees of aversion toward the *akhund* element, as the clergy somewhat pejoratively were known. They also were critical of the clergy's populism, rather unflatteringly in popular parlance called *akhund-bazi.* Secular Iranians viewed these lay advocates of the Islamic cause as a cunning bunch who had found their place in the sun, a place that, though unstable, was the only chance to save the revolution from the mullahs. But no love was lost between them and the clerical camp, which was anxious to see their rapid downfall. The mullahs viewed the Islamic modernists as a convenient ladder for ascending to power, or as opportunists who rode to office at the back of the revolution.

At stake was not merely a struggle for popular support but warring ideological worldviews in which the radical clerics and their allies, now to be defined as Khomeinists by their critics, held the upper hand. Contrary to the mullahs, the Islamic opposition of Bazargan's brand believed in evolutionary, step-by-step change. They barely upheld their inner cohesion either, which in turn made them susceptible to Khomeini's whims and wishes and dependent on his diminishing favor. They were crucial, no doubt, in the transition period and deemed indispensable in the early days of the Islamic Republic. They mellowed Khomeini's image, ran the provisional government, and gave the inexperienced clergy and their allies time to whet their political appetite and learn about the machinery of the state. Their sad fate clearly showed how expendable they were to Khomeini. They were outsiders no matter how regularly they said their prayers in public or how studiously they demonstrated Islamic loyalty to the Imam of the revolution.

The downfall of the "compromising liberals" came about in part also because of a host of other lay Islamists loyal to Khomeini camp. Serving as technocrats and advisers to the clergy, the latter group filled the place of the lay moderates. Mohammad Ali Raja'i (1933–1981), a high school teacher and Islamic activist, was typical of the Khomeinists at odds with the revolution's moderate wing, and was rapidly propelled to power as second president of the Islamic Republic. Mir Hosein Musavi (Moussavi; b. 1942), who had studied interior design at the Tehran School of Design and pursued that subject further in England, became a long-serving prime minister in the early 1980s during the difficult years of the Iran-Iraq War. Mostafa Chamran (1932–1981), a former member of

Bazargan's Freedom Movement and a Berkeley-educated electrical engineer who, for some years in the 1960s, had worked in various US research institutes, was another example.

Driven by the success of the Cuban Revolution and the revolutionary spirit of the period, in the early 1960s Chamran moved to Cuba and later to Nasser's Egypt to be trained in guerrilla warfare. In 1971, at the outset of Lebanon's civil war, he moved to Beirut. By then he had become a de facto leader of an Islamic "international brigade" that helped organize dissidents in Syria and Palestine, mostly under Nasser's auspices. In Lebanon he collaborated with the Iranian-born cleric Musa Sadr, the charismatic leader of the Shi'is of Lebanon, and was instrumental in the founding of the Shi'i Amal movement (whose radical wing later evolved into Hezbollah of Lebanon). Upon his return to Iran at the outset of the revolution, Chamran was appointed an early leader of the Revolutionary Guards and the Islamic Republic's first minister of defense. In 1981, in the early stages of the Iraq-Iran War, when he was leading Revolutionary Guards in the battlefield, he died from shrapnel wounds. As a martyr of the "Holy Defense" against the Iraqi aggressor, Chamran occupies an iconic place in the narrative of the Islamic Revolution. As a loyal soldier of the revolution appearing in military fatigues, his image in gigantic murals in Iranian cities is often interspersed with those of clerical martyrs of the revolution, presumably to highlight clergy-lay symbiosis.

What differentiated Chamran and other lay activists from Bazargan and Banisadr were not only their willingness to comply with the emerging hierocracy under Khomeini and go along with its radical course but also a generation gap. Whereas Bazargan and his cohorts were shaped by the National Movement of the 1940s and 1950s, the younger activists mostly remembered and idealized the revolt of the 1960s led by Khomeini and were motivated by the 1960s guerilla warfare and radical trends in the Arab world.

AN IMAM FOR THE DISINHERITED

Beyond the circle of aides and cohorts with similar worldviews, Khomeini's appeal extended to the urban lower middle classes and the poor neighborhoods in big cities as well as in smaller towns. The "disinherited" (*mostaz'afin*) of the land, at least a good portion of them, began to view him as a liberator who would improve their lot in a fast-changing society. It was these multitudes and their strength in numbers that kept him in power despite all odds.

Originally a Qur'anic concept (e.g., 28:5–6), "disinherited of the earth" became a current in Khomeini's speeches and among the advocates of the Islamic Revolution. They consciously used it to supplant the favored catchphrase of the left: the "deprived masses." The term has gone through a metamorphosis since it was first used by 'Ali Shari'ati to reconceptualize Frantz Fanon's "wretched of the earth," a notion he may well have taken from the first line of "The Internationale": "Stand up, damned of the Earth!" In the early 1970s the term quickly was sponged into the lexicon of Ayatollah Khomeini, where it found currency for years to come. The merger of the Qur'an and socialism via Fanon, Shari'ati, and Khomeini became a signifier of class to be applied to the urban poor living in the slums of southern Tehran and on the fringes of Iran's rapidly growing provincial centers. It was meant to define those who were down and out among the rural immigrants and dismayed by the affluent lifestyle of the elite: the unskilled construction laborers, factory workers and small workshop apprentices, the lowly of the bazaar, menial wage earners, and the growing body of unemployed youth. The downtrodden aside, the term also included the somewhat better-off but still discontent sectors of the lower middle classes: shopkeepers, public school teachers, technicians, and low-paid government employees.

The men and women who were motivated through mosques and mourning associations were led to believe that Islam, and especially Shi'i Islam, packaged as an ideological miracle pill for all of Iran's ills, was not primarily a set of monotheistic beliefs, devotional acts, and moral principles, nor even loyalty to the House of the Prophet and belief in the coming of the Mahdi, but instead a religion of protest and political action against oppression and exploitation, monarchical power, and its global allies. It was among these awakened multitudes that Khomeini shrewdly managed to harness energies for his revolutionary cause. He repeatedly paid homage to what he called "our valiant Islamic nation" and invariably acted on a presumed mandate on behalf of the disinherited to further the "true" (rastin) objectives of his "dear Islam."

Inimical to the "disinherited of the earth" in Khomeinists' emerging revolutionary universe and the manic rhetoric that erupted with the revolution stood the "arrogant" (mostakbarin)—the other end of the binary derived from another Qur'anic reference to the "unheeded" people of privilege who succumb to idolatrous tyrants (2:87). The taghut of the Qur'an (4:51) were idol worshippers who rebelled against God and by implication denoted all transgressors unafraid of God's ultimate vengeance. In the language of revolutionary Iran, taghuti thus became a code word for the Pahlavi regime and its associated elites. They were enemies of true Islam who were about to be purged in the punitive inferno of the revolution so as to pave the way for restoring just rule and returning to the disinherited of the earth what justly belonged to them. Not only did the revolution unseat the taghut and its domestic cliques at home; it also promised to deter the forces of "global arrogance" (estekbar-e jahani), a code for global hegemony.

A range of newly coined expressions brought to the surface the perception of a battle of good versus evil, a faint reflection, perhaps, of the old dichotomy inherent to Iranian culture. By underscoring this dichotomy, Khomeini and his supporters consciously aimed to dismantle the Marxist-inspired vocabulary of dissent, which the left perceived as an inevitable outcome of the revolution. In contrast to the left's vision of a class struggle, Khomeinists advocated a moral struggle along the path of God, a struggle that shaped history of humanity, a sacred movement driven by faith and by "commitment" (*ta'ahhod*).

The "hope of the disinherited" of course was "Imam Khomeini," as he quickly came to be known weeks after his advent in Paris. His hybrid of Shi'i jurisprudence, precepts of Greco-Islamic philosophy, mystical outlook with a neo-Platonic flavor, and radical political viewpoint influenced by ideologies of the left and fused into an Islamic agenda, were combined to bring out in him an enduring leadership. A shrewd, almost cunning man, he enjoyed an extraordinary gift for identifying and taking advantage of opportunities. Assertive and intimidating, he was a quick study, adjusting to new realities, negotiating when the situation called for it, and persuading others by means of coercion, intrigue, and charm. Seemingly distant but seductive, in his advanced age he was resolute, confident, and mostly uncompromising. Discreet, emotionally detached, and ruthless when need be, he mesmerized his audiences and won them over with seeming effortlessness.

Added to these complexities were his stern appearance in clerical garb and his imposing comportment. Wearing a black turban and a white beard, in his late seventies he was unapologetically distinct from conventional images of twentieth-century revolutionary leaders ranging from Lenin, Trotsky and Stalin to Mao, Castro, and Che Guevara. To most Iranian people, who for decades had not seen a turbaned man in a position of power, Khomeini appeared unique. Often unsmiling, his piercing eyes underneath frowning eyebrows, his monotonous but solemn voice—which betrayed a central Persian countryside accent with an Arabicized mullah intonation—spawned an image of an ascetic from bygone times. To many of his countrymen, such unconventionality was awe inspiring, even terrifying, and yet appealing. His austerity, fearless and fierce, stood in stark contrast to the formalistic militarism of the Pahlavi era and especially to the shah's royal opulence. In his plain cloak, he appeared deceivingly authentic in contrast to the shah's dazzling appearance in military uniform, rich with fringes and accoutrements.

The ayatollah's coterie was smart enough to capitalize on this image, and Khomeini cleverly allowed them to do so. No one seemed to have been able to resist the rising star of the new political prophet—not the self-deceiving liberal nationalists, the rationalizing intellectuals, the radicalized left and guerillas with Kalashnikovs, the intimidated pro-Pahlavi middle class, the shah's army and Savak, or even the Islamically correct Freedom Movement. Listening to the mood in the Iranian streets and cleverly negotiating the unique window of opportunity opened before him, Khomeini stressed national unity and Islamic solidarity against the "corrupt and repressive" Pahlavi idol and the "idol-worshiping" institution of kingship itself.

References to an alternative political order, an Islamic republic, soon made their entry into his many statements and public addresses. In a matter of months, in mid-1978 explicit demands for an Islamic republic became an integral part of the street slogans and revolutionary rallies: "Sovereignty, Freedom, the Islamic Republic" (*esteqlal, azadi, jomhuri-e eslami*). As if a utopia were being ushered in before their eager eyes, the marching crowds echoed the rhymed slogans that called on the Imam, the "savior," to lift tyranny and lead them to a promised land. The Shi'i messianic motifs behind Khomeini's image as "imam of the community" (*imam-e ommat*) were unmistakable—motifs that inspired millions to call on him to save the country and the world.

Sovereignty, on the other hand, harkening back to memories of the postwar National Movement for control of Iran's oil resources, found in the revolutionary imagination a new lease on life a quarter of a century later. Revolutionaries began to see the United States rather than Britain as the prime culprit responsible for Iran's economic dependency and presumed subservience. The concept of freedom (*azadi*), too, gained prominence among its proponents who were mindful of half a century of Pahlavi autocracy. They demanded an open political space and aspired to a just and tolerant society. Khomeini and his cohorts were riding on the back of these ideals, all the while pushing the project of the Islamic Republic and thrusting it forth into the still-amorphous revolutionary sphere. The nature of the Islamic government was ambiguous, at least to the majority who called for it, and perhaps even to its chief advocates.

How spontaneous Khomeini's Islamic message was remains a matter of debate. There is little doubt that his idea of a revolution with Islam as its defining principle substantially changed along the way from Najaf to Paris to Tehran. Even more than other classic revolutions, the dynamics of the popular movement in Iran had not been set at the outset by any one individual or ideological trend. It was more the outcome of a turbulent push and pull. To a great extent, Khomeini's talent for adjusting to different situations, incorporating multiple concepts, adopting various strategies, and utilizing various political tools allowed him to glean current ideas and vocabularies from diverse quarters—the radical left, dissident intellectuals, Islamic radicals, the media, and even army jargon—so as to tinker his own ideology.

It is possible to speculate, on the basis of Khomeini's statements and conduct, that in early 1977 he had hoped for the political space to open up and Iran's constitutional order to be redeemed. At the time, he probably was satisfied with Qom's greater say in the affairs of the country and greater respect for conservative Islamic values. Encouraged by the rapid course of events, he later that year may have started envisioning the departure of the shah and investiture of an emasculated constitutional monarch, though he hardly could have hoped for or predicted the collapse of the Pahlavi order.

By the beginning of 1978, however, he began to contemplate a greater role for himself as the prime mover behind a revolution mandated by the Iranian people and governed by Islamic principles. By then the senior clergy, too, almost unanimously had joined the revolutionary fold and were willy-nilly rallying behind him. Earlier on, Khomeini preferred to speak of a movement (*nahzat*) rather than a revolution (*enqelab*), the latter being a modern notion still alien to his conservative tastes. He had his moments of hesitation, no doubt, but was adamant about his immediate objectives. "He must go" (*bayad beravad*) was his call for the shah to abdicate, which he relentlessly demanded despite the many cautionary messages from his own advisers. To this end he called for solidarity (*vahdat*) among all popular forces. "All together" (*hamah ba-ham*) became his catchphrase calling for a united front that ranged from the liberal nationalists to Islamic reformists, diverse clerical tendencies, disgruntled intelligentsia, secular or Islamist intellectuals, the Mojahedin-e Khalq, and even various shades of Marxist. To such a diverse assortment, he was careful to convey a tantalizingly simple message of unity that ordinary people could easily grasp. After years of silence, the thrill of enormous multitudes, hundreds of thousands, if not millions, crying out, "Neither Eastern nor Western [but] the Islamic Republic!" (*na sharqi, na gharbi, Jomhuri-e Islami*), was intoxicating even if the true ramifications of an Islamic republic were not yet understood even by Khomeini's close allies.

That Khomeini became the Imam of the Islamic Revolution and its "guardian" (*wali*) was particularly remarkable, given the connotations of both terms in the Shi'i messianic context. In the long history of Shi'ism, no other mojtahed or any other mainstream figure had ever assumed the title of *imam* or was referred to as such by his following. Imam in Twelver Shi'ism was exclusively reserved for the Twelve Imams, whom the Shi'is considered loci of divine inspiration and true successors to the Prophet of Islam. In effect, Khomeini no longer was a mere jurist or a *marja'*; he appropriated qualities of a "deputy" of the Shi'i Mahdi. He theoretically was assumed to be a "deputy of the Imam" (*na'eb-e Imam*), yet he was routinely addressed as *imam* in everyday parlance, and that was what mattered in a revolutionary environment. Even claim to individual deputyship on behalf of the Imam of the Age (as opposed to the collective authority of the mojtaheds) was pure novelty. No established authority since the ninth century had ever claimed to be the deputy of the Imam. Even 'Abd al-'Ali Karaki's claims in the sixteenth century were coached in a cautious legal language that limited the implication of jurists' deputyship. Ironically, any such claims by messianic prophets stood to be denounced by the mojtaheds and gravely punished as in the case of nineteenth-century Sayyed 'Ali Mohammad the Bab.

Likewise, the term *wali* and *welayat* with historical reference to 'Ali ibn Abi-Talib, the Fourth Caliph and the First Shi'i Imam, connoted a politico-moral authority for the guardian jurist and a true vicarage of that community. The mystical undertone associated with the idea of *welayat* in Sufism, particularly Shi'i Sufism, injected an element of the sacred to the otherwise worldly office. In effect, it may be argued, the revolution finally brought the messianic process within Shi'ism to a head. The Mahdi paradigm was employed not by a charismatic prince-warrior like Islam'il I, the founder of the Safavid Shi'i state. Nor did an antinomian Noqtavi Qalandar claim it or Sayyed 'Ali Mohammad Shirazi, the Bab. Rather, here a representative of the jurist orthodox establishment, a mojtahed and a *marja'*, crossed the long-protected boundaries of normative and messianic Shi'ism to appropriate the mantel of the prophet and become the savior of an Islamic revolution.

15

CONSOLIDATION OF THE
ISLAMIC REPUBLIC (1979–1984)

In less than a year after victory of the revolution in February 1979, the new regime managed to consolidate its base, build new institutions, and eliminate its contenders for power. It conducted a referendum on the change of regime to an Islamic republic, ratified a new constitution, elected a parliament, elected a president to office, and established revolutionary courts, the Revolutionary Guards Corps, the Guardian Council, and the Assembly of Experts. All the while the newly established republic was engaged in major domestic and international crises that threatened its very existence. In the eighteen months between February 1979 and September 1980, it faced serious challenges from the left, significantly from the Mojahedin-e Khalq and the Fada'iyan-e Khalq; a brief but bloody confrontation with the autonomy-seeking movements in Kurdistan, Khuzestan, and the Turkmen region of the northeast; a powerful face-off with the rival Muslim People's Republican Party; a major international row with the United States over a hostage crisis that lasted for nearly fifteen months; a military coup in the making; several assassination attempts against revolutionary leaders by the shadowy Marxist-Islamic Forqan group; and finally the Iraqi invasion of Iran, which led to a protracted and ruinous war that lasted eight years.

Moreover, internal divisions between moderate and radical wings of the revolution led to resignations, clashes, arrests, and defections. A little over seven months after the founding of the Islamic Republic, Khomeini dismissed Mahdi Bazargan, the prime minister of the provisional government who had facilitated the birth of the new regime. Less than two years later, hard-line supporters of Khomeini not only forced out the relatively moderate first president of the Republic, Abol-Hasan Banisadr, and his allies but also wiped out nearly all the forces of the left. The republic, moreover, banned or marginalized all moderate clerical and secular voices and purged, jailed, or executed real or imagined supporters of the old regime. It forced hundreds of thousands of members of the middle classes into self-imposed exile. Conducting a "cultural revolution" of its own, the regime purged thousands from universities and research institutes and tried to redefine education and cultural discourse on its own terms. By all accounts, this was an impressive performance, irrespective of how oppressive and violent it turned out to be.

What was behind the Islamic Republic's apparent success, and more specifically, how was it that the influence of Khomeini and his cohorts did not wither? Contrary to the wishful predictions of the Pahlavi sympathizers, the intellectuals on the left and other early optimists, Khomeini and his associates managed to frame a new order, put it in place, and sustain it against all odds. It was quite possible, given Iran's earlier experiences in the twentieth century that the popular mandate supporting Khomeini could have evaporated once it reached a peak. The revolution's Islamic fervor also could have subsided. Once the regressive features of the Islamic revolution were fully exhibited, they were prone to criticism, and even ridicule, at least by conventional standards. Charismatic leadership, too, often seen as Khomeini's innate asset, could have dissipated or been diluted, despite propaganda that trumpeted the "demi-prophetic" (*payambar-guneh*) qualities of the "Imam" as guardian of the Islamic nation. Yet popular support remained strong, and his personal appeal did not degenerate. The powerful Shi'i paradigm of sacred leadership no doubt was at work. Yet contrary to its basic premises, Khomeini was neither martyred nor persecuted. On the contrary, his proved a story of unparalleled success. Perhaps no other prophetic figure in the course of Iran's religious history, not even Isma'il I, the founder of the Safavid dynasty, was as triumphant.

A convincing explanation for this success is perhaps to be found in the very dynamic of the revolution and the way powerful energies erupted to resolve enormous contentions in favor of Khomeini and his republic. The hostage crisis gave the new regime a much-needed propaganda tool to claim triumph over a superpower now labeled as the source of "universal arrogance" and the "Great Satan." The Iraqi invasion, in contrast, rallied the Iranian public behind the regime and enabled it to wage a patriotic war, at least in the early stages. The Islamic Republic also thrived all along by confronting its domestic contenders, especially when it produced martyrs from its "committed" (*mote'ahhed*) ranks. The assassinations of prominent figures such as Motahhari and Beheshti offered the regime a chance to appear victimized while giving it license to act more vehemently.

CRUSHING THE PAHLAVI IDOLS

The first to face the thrust of the revolutionary violence were "collaborators" of the Pahlavi regime. These "idol worshippers" (*taghuti*), a substantial number of former ministers, senior army officers, deputies of the Majles, senators, associates of the Pahlavi court, and senior government officials, as well as prominent businessmen, industrialists, and professionals suspected of having ties with the former regime, were rounded up and brought before the Islamic revolutionary courts. Though there are no reliable figures, by 1983, four years into the revolution, there were upward of sixty thousand prisoners in the capital alone.

In the chaos of the postrevolutionary days, any affluent, secular member of society was a potential suspect. The distance between suspicion and accusation was short, and not much farther from arrest and imprisonment—the latter often for a long duration without trial. A thick "Islamic" beard or even a week of stubble could help for a while to cover past "un-Islamic" lifestyles, especially if worn along with a threadbare buttoned-up white shirt over tattered pants, unkempt appearance, and plastic slippers. For women such an overnight metamorphosis was not optional but mandatory and with dire consequences. Soon cries in the streets of "either cover or suffer" (*ya rusari ya tusari*) forced women to adopt "Islamic attire," a large scarf knotted under the chin over a shapeless, ankle-length overcoat in "modest" dark colors (which came to be known as Islamic overalls, or *manteau*). Those who resisted were harassed, arrested, and lashed (fig. 15.1).

Soon revolutionary committees (*komitehs*) and revolutionary courts, and their members, intruded deep into many private lives and laid their hands on many houses and properties, personal belongings—even women's lingerie—family heirlooms, book collections, and family photo albums. Everything was up for grabs, and everything was evidence of betrayal if one happened to be on the wrong side of the revolutionary divide. The *komitehs* that soon popped up in every neighborhood, in government departments, airports, factories, and business offices carried the self-assumed task of "defending" the revolution. In reality, these were sorting houses for a crude revolutionary justice and even cruder redistribution of wealth. Vigilantes from all walks of life who joined revolutionary *komitehs* were hardly answerable to anyone but the local mullah, who served as honorary head, or an overnight convert to the revolution with shady credentials.

Some *komiteh* members, including young seminarians and adventurous youth, were sincere in their sense of duty toward the revolution and content with the thrill of holding Kalashnikovs and wearing trench coats. Revolution

Figure 15.1. Women protesting the imposition of
the hijab at Tehran University, March 1979.
Maryam Zandi, *Enqlab-e 57* (Tehran: Nazar Publishers, 1393/2014), 206.

empowered them and made them tolerably reckless. There were also thugs and racketeers who saw an opportunity to control the *komitehs*; relics of the *lutis* of the older days, perhaps, but certainly minus their chivalry. They soon began to act as police and security forces, and in the absence of both they controlled neighborhoods in the name of revolutionary justice. Confiscating and coercing, arresting and beating on behalf of the "disinherited," was not an uncommon occurrence.

From the perspective of the victims, those who were harassed and detained, and whose belongings were confiscated, *komitehs* were synonymous with terror and intimidation. Rumors were rife of *komiteh* chiefs taking kickbacks, small and large, in exchange for currying favors. Punishments were a stark reality, including lashes, severe beatings, and extortion, inflicted often for such unproven charges as failure to put on proper hijab, drinking or smelling of alcohol, and appearing to be affluent or therefore "antirevolutionary." The behavior of the *komitehs*, of course, was not unknown to the revolutionary leadership, though they quickly realized their inability to fully check their unruly conduct; nor was it to the advantage of the evolving leadership of the revolution, especially the clergy, to do so. In the volatile environment of the time, any attempt to curb the activities of the *komitehs*, even serious criticism of their conduct, ran the risk of jeopardizing the revolutionary credentials of the leadership. These spontaneous grassroots cells facilitated clerical ascendency and served as a voluntary arm of the revolutionary courts. Some mullahs were behind *komitehs'* egregious conduct, and others partook in their spoils. The *komitehs* soon provided fertile ground for a more organized force in service to the revolution, and to the displeasure of moderates, Khomeini did not hesitate to endorse them.

The launching of the Revolutionary Guards Corps (Sepah-e Pasdaran-e Enqelab-e Islami) in May 1979 was a shrewd move to tap into the energies of the youth sparked by the revolution and especially into the still-decentralized *komitehs*. The Revolutionary Corps was organized not only to purge membership of the *komitehs* of the undesirable elements of the lefts but also, more important, to act as a counterweight to the regular Iranian armed forces, or what was left of them. The Khomeinists in power, being distrustful of the army and fearing a coup of some sort, needed a loyal force to counter not only the perceived threat of the royalists but also an assortment of the armed militias controlled by or loyal to the left.

The new Revolutionary Guards Corps was crudely organized and inexperienced. Yet by late 1981, it had proved its worth when it managed to quash the Mojahedin opposition in the earliest street clashes in the capital. By 1983, hundreds of young Mojahedin, male and female, were killed and thousands more were arrested, tortured, and executed in the prisons of the Islamic Republic. The symbiosis of the mullahs and Revolutionary Guards also worked well in the course of the war with Iraq, whereby the latter served as a parallel force to the regular army, however unprofessionally. In return, a vast treasure trove of "nationalized" industries and confiscated land and properties of the Pahlavi state and its elite soon came under the control of the Revolutionary Guards. The conglomerates of agricultural estates and other economic resources kept them content and in comportment with the wishes of the ruling mullahs. Even after the war, the Guards served as the single most effective guarantor of the regime's survival.

Parallel with the Revolutionary Guards and complementary to their mission of combatting so-called antirevolutionary forces, the Islamic revolutionary courts (*dadgahha-ye enqelab-e Islami*) were established immediately after the victory of February 1979. They were presided over by clerical judges appointed in most cases by Khomeini and functioned under the close supervision of his clerical allies. With singular ferocity the revolutionary courts exercised their version of the Islamic justice. "God's vengeance," by which they often legitimized their verdicts, was clear and simple, irrespective of the complexity of the cases before them or a complete lack of viable evidence. Independent of Bazargan's provisional government, the mission of the revolutionary courts was to eliminate the "enemy," imprison, confiscate, intimidate, and quash the "antirevolution," which meant any voice or force deemed to be against the regime's hegemony.

In nearly all cases, the judges were acting also as prosecutors. There were no juries or defense lawyers, due process was almost nonexistent, procedures were chaotic, and summary verdicts were often final and irreversible, at least in the earlier years. Charges were vague and unsubstantiated, and at times mere accusations brought forward by a dubious "revolutionary" party and members of the "disinherited" class. The unwritten code of conduct behind erratic judgments, if there was one, consisted of the judges' own interpretations of arcane and uncodified Shi'i penal injunctions. The carefully crafted civil and penal codes of the Pahlavi era were categorically thrown out, to be replaced by "pristine justice," presumably, from the time of 'Ali's caliphate. Yet if compassion—what traditionally is associated with 'Ali's image as a just ruler—was missing in the courtrooms, there was plenty of folly and vengefulness to turn judges into the most callous face of the Islamic Republic. If other acts of lawlessness and violence could be attributed to the chaotic climate of the postrevolutionary era, the verdicts of the revolutionary courts became the most deliberate means of legitimizing violence and sustaining the regime's coercive conduct.

The victims of the courts were as diverse as the judges were monolithic. The first to be brought before a makeshift tribunal were a group of senior officers of the armed forces. They and a host of other victims during the first few weeks were executed by firing squad on the roof of the building adjacent to the 'Alavi school, where Khomeini had first made his residence and headquarters. In the early hours of the morning when he was setting his dawn prayers, he must have heard the shots from the nearby building. Later in the day when he was waving listlessly from a small window to thousands of visitors who came to pay their homage to him, the corpses were taken down and sent off to the city morgue to be photographed and publicized in national dailies. Almost simultaneously, during February 1979, some three hundred generals, the entire senior officer corps of the Iranian armed forces above the rank of lieutenant general, were forced to retire by Khomeini's order. Many later found themselves in the Islamic Republic's jails. By early 1980, some 7,500 military personnel had been purged, and by the beginning of the war with Iraq that figure reportedly had exceeded 12,000.

It took a little while before reality dawned on the thousands who in the following months and years hoped for justice, if not mercy, from the revolutionary courts. One example was the summary trial of Amir 'Abbas Hovayda, the shah's premier for thirteen years. He had been detained during the Azhari government and reportedly refused to escape his detention in the chaotic hours following the fall of Pahlavi rule. He seemed to have had misplaced faith in revolutionary justice when in April 1979 he appeared before the revolutionary tribunal. It was presided over by Sadeq Khalkhali (1926–2003), the notorious judge and head of the revolutionary courts (dubbed by the Western press as the "Hanging Judge"). Hovayda even prepared a reasonably detailed defense against an array of charges that included treason, corruption, mismanagement, and repression. He declared innocence, arguing that he was merely a diligent statesman, not responsible for the repressive conduct of the shah's security police. His defense did not even receive a summary response from the judges. After several days of hearings, unusual for Khalkhali's courts, the court delivered a verdict of execution but out of public sight. Reportedly, though, even before reaching the firing squad, a firebrand cleric, Hadi Ghaffari (b. 1950), known for his volatile rhetoric as much as for his love of the machine gun, approached Hovayda from behind and shot him twice in the head with his revolver.

Hovayda's life indeed had come to an ironic end. A literary dilettante, once a member of Sadeq Hedayat's circle of friends, his long journey from Beirut's *lycée français* and Parisian intellectual circles in the 1940s and 1950s to the inner circles of Pahlavi politics in the 1960s and 1970s could not have ended more tellingly than in Sadeq Khalkhali's court. A quintessential militant mullah, Khalkhali came from the opposite end of the Iranian social spectrum. He was a former student and devotee of Khomeini of humble village origin and a typical product of Qom's radicalized climate (fig. 15.2). Unlike Hovayda, he

Figure 15.2. Sadeq Khalkhali in his office in the Islamic Revolutionary Courts. Sadeq Khalkhali, *Khaterat*, 2nd ed. (Tehran: Sayeh Publishers, 1379/1990), 528.

dabbled not in André Gide and André Malraux but in dry texts of jurisprudence and Arabic grammar. His political credentials included an affiliation with the Fada'iyan-e Islam and some years of internal exile by Savak. His vengeful verdicts in the early years of the revolution gave him a reputation as a psychopath with a clownish demeanor and a devilish sneer. Personality aside, he symbolized the revolution's rapid tilt toward systemic violence.

Khalkhali's victims ranged far and wide, from former Pahlavi officers and officials, whom he invariably stamped as "corrupters of the earth," to all shades of the left, as well as secular nationalists, ethnic nationalists, the Baha'is, and other nonpolitical victims who fell pray to revolutionary courts. In the first twenty-two months of the revolution, he sent before firing squads hundreds of autonomy-seeking Kurdish and Turkmen activists, all condemned with the one-size-fits-all charge of "corrupting the earth and combatting God," a charge of Qur'anic origin. When the wife of one of the victims of his summary executions in Kurdistan complained to Khalkhali that her husband was utterly innocent, he cynical responded: "If he was guilty he would go to hell; if innocent, he would end up in heaven." The victim was one in a group of eight executed before the general hospital on August 28, 1979 (fig. 15.3).

Figure 15.3. Kurdish dissidents before the Islamic Republic's firing squad after a thirty-minute trial, Paveh, Iranian Kurdistan, August 28, 1979.
© Jahangir Razmi/Magnum Photos, 1979 (NYC67478) (RAJ1979006W00001/01).
First published in *Ettela'at*, Tehran, August 29, 1979.

Khalkhali's domain soon extended beyond "political" prisoners to include alleged or real drug dealers, female and male prostitutes, and homosexuals and other moral "deviants" whom he duly dispatched to the firing squad or to the gallows, whichever was more terrifying to the Iranian public, who followed with horror the latest of his exploits. It is difficult to believe, as he repeatedly stated in later years in his memoirs, that Khalkhali's verdicts against the enemies of the revolution, including executions of ranking officers and Hovayda, were carried out without the full approval of Ayatollah Khomeini.

Khalkhali was no less active in the realm of cultural hatemongering. In his vast catalog of corrupters of the earth, he reserved a place for rulers of Iran's pre-Islamic past. He wrote an essay condemning Cyrus the Great, the founder of the Achaemenid Empire of the fifth century BCE, accusing him not only of being a despot and liar but also of being a sexual pervert. In the early days of the revolution, Khalkhali intended to bulldoze Persepolis and other ancient Iranian monuments of the pre-Islamic era. His campaign was stopped, miraculously, because of local resistance. Reportedly, even Ferdowsi's tomb made it onto Khalkhali's demolition wish list. Yet he managed only to muster enough mob support, and backing from Khomeini, to destroy the mausoleum of Reza Shah, the archnemesis of Khalkhali's teacher and patron. Completed in 1950 near the shrine of Shah 'Abd al-'Azim south of Tehran, the massive structure designed in the modern style was a fine example of Iran's contemporary architecture. It invoked a message of secular grandiosity, holding at its core Reza Shah's embalmed remains encased in a glass casket. With great difficulty the edifice was razed to the ground, thanks to dynamite and the immense horsepower of bulldozers. Khalkhali's intent was to build in its stead public lavatories, but the location was eventually devoted to an Islamic seminary, part of the shrine complex.

FRAMING THE ISLAMIC CONSTITUTION

By the summer of 1979, through months of chaos and conflict, four interrelated themes began to emerge that helped shape revolutionary Iran. First and foremost was the rise of the pro-Khomeini clergy and their lay supporters to the top of the revolutionary pyramid, sanctified by a deeply Islamicized constitution. The Khomeinist bloc was built on a cult of personality, held at its core an old sense of Qom solidarity, backed by the newly established Revolutionary Guards and was in alliance with other pro-Khomeini forces in the bazaar and elsewhere. It shared an acute sense of survival at any cost. Second, a decisive turn toward greater militancy, encouraged as much by the Islamic regime as by the radical left, drove moderates out of the political process, eventually dismantled the bourgeoning press and closed down most political parties. Third, an outburst of anti-Western sentiments that culminated in a hostage crisis and vilification of the United States as the Great Satan created a much-needed hostile Other in Iran's revolutionary rhetoric and in its dealings with the outside world. Finally, the creation of an ever-growing state economy through expropriation and nationalization increased the power of the revolutionary re-gime beyond proportion.

The forging of the Islamic constitution (*qanun-e asasi*) helped bolster the regime's institutional tenacity and move toward greater monopoly of power, even though at the outset such intentions were not fully evident. In the early months of the republic, Khomeini, mindful of earlier promises, was content with a draft of the constitution prepared by Bazargan's aides. He reportedly only altered two points: he barred women from judgeships and from the presidency. The rest, mostly a revision of the 1906–1907 constitution, with changes inspired in part by the French presidential model, did not attract much of his scrutiny at the outset. There was a large-enough dose of homage to Islam as its guiding principle to make the essentially secular document palatable.

Two influential advisers to the Imam preferred a plebiscite for acquiring a popular mandate. Banisadr, an advocate of his own brand of egalitarian Is-lamism, and Mohammad Beheshti, the brains behind the clerical bloc, were momentary allies. The idea of a referendum, however, met resistance from the Bazargan government and its allies who, honoring their earlier promises, insisted on convening a constituent assembly. The radical left, too, with their predictable blind spot for moderation, deemed the draft document a product of the liberal bourgeoisie and therefore inherently "unprogressive." Demanding an elected constituent assembly, they entertained the naive hope that through a popular vote they would control the assembly and refashion the draft constitu-tion to their own liking, which they equated to the "will of the masses."

An Islamic constitution was a relatively recent concept, especially in the Shi'i political context. Advocates of the *mashru'eh* at the time of the Constitutional Revolution, for instance, viewed shari'a as an all-encompassing corpus unfet-tered by human legislation. In the 1950s and 1960s the idea of an Islamic con-stitution raised some clerical interest, often tracing the origins for it in such documents as the Prophet's "Constitution of the Medina" and 'Ali's letter of instructions to Malik al-Ashtar al-Nakha'i, his appointed governor of Egypt in 657 CE. At no time, however, in the history of Shi'ism did followers (*moqa-lleds*) perceive the idea of electing mojtahids to any collective body. Nor did Khomeini's own writings anticipate the forging of an Islamic constitution or constituent assembly.

Despite initial uncertainties, the Assembly of Experts (Majles Khebrehgan) was nevertheless elected in August 11, 1979, to draft a new constitution. Despite Bazargan government's promise of a free and fair election, during the contested election, a number of candidates from among the left and the liberals were virtually barred from campaigning, and some twenty parties and groups boycotted the election altogether. Out of the total of seventy-three seats, sixty were captured by Khomeinists, of whom eighteen were ayatollahs and twenty of the lower clerical ranks (fig. 15.4). Earlier, the first draft of the constitution had acknowledged Khomeini as the leader of the revolution but did not mention the guardianship of the jurist as an office, let alone elevate the clerical establishment to a theocratic elite. The ultimate authority rested with a popularly elected president whose executive function was delegated to a prime minister. Yet the deliberation of the Assembly of Experts, dominated by candidates of the newly founded Islamic Republican Party, took a very different approach by producing a document much more authoritarian in substance than the first draft, Islamicized in language, and patriarchal in orientation. It recognized the supreme authority of the guardian jurist and in effect ratified the primacy of the clergy above all others (fig. 15.5).

At the core of the new draft, ratified in November and overwhelmingly approved in a plebiscite on the December 3, 1979, was the supreme authority of the guardian jurist, an office above the president and above the Islamic Consultative Assembly. Though he was to be designated by the clergy-dominated

Figure 15.4. A cartoon in the pro-Tudeh satirical journal *Ahangar* lampoons the election of the Council of Experts. Banisadr, along with Qotbzadeh and Yazdi, is at the front of the club-wielding thugs, labeling the left as "antirevolutionary" and "hypocritical." Bazargan wistfully observes, and the clergy are entirely absent.
Year 1, no. 15, 9 Mordad 1358/August 1, 1979. Courtesy of Siavush Ranjbar-Daemi.

Figure 15.5. The future president Abol-Hasan Banisadr (*left*) with Mahmud Taleqani on the floor of the former Iranian Senate, where the Assembly of Experts held its sessions in the summer of 1979. The two moderates reluctantly abided by the constitutional article that recognized the supreme authority of the guardian jurist. Pars News Agency, Tehran, Iran (now dissolved). https://commons.wikimedia.org/wiki/File:Banisadr_and_Taleghani.jpg.

Assembly of Experts, he was not accountable to any other elected body—a free agent with almost a divine mandate. Article 5 asserted that in the absence of the Hidden Imam, "in the Islamic Republic the guardianship of the cause [of God] [*welayat-e amr*; i.e., the authority to rule] and leadership of the community are assumed by a jurist who is just, virtuous, conscious of the [needs of the] time, valiant, capable and astute."[1] Article 57 initially granted the guardian jurist the authority to "supervise" the three branches of government while leaving "coordination" among the three branches to the president of the republic. Such a blurred division of labor, echoed in other articles of the constitution, resembled inconsistencies about the prerogatives of the monarch in the 1906 constitution. The constitutional revision of 1989, upon Khomeini's death, conveniently resolved that problem by granting the guardian jurist "absolute guardianship (*welayat-e motlaqeh*) over coordination of three powers and resolving their differences.

Article 110 also included among the guardian jurist's responsibilities the appointment of the Guardian Council (*shura-ye negahban*), responsible for overseeing Majles legislation and compliance with Islamic shari'a, and the head of the judiciary. As commander in chief of the armed forces, the guardian jurist also would appoint the chiefs of the three forces, the police, and the Revolutionary Guards. He was further granted authority to declare war and peace, to endorse the elected president of the republic, and—if need be—to dismiss him at his own behest. As if this were not sufficient for defining a highly authoritarian office, when article 110 was amended in 1989, it further granted the guardian jurist power to define and supervise all general policies of the Islamic Republic of Iran (as well as appointing the head of the national government-controlled broadcasting service).

The preamble to the constitution left no doubt about its theocratic grounding: all institutions of the state, the whole "community" of Iran, was to be ideologically Islamic (*maktabi*). Here, the term *Iranian community* (*ommat-e Iran*), with obvious Islamic universalistic overtones had replaced the familiar and explicit *Iranian nation* (*mellat-e Iran*). With the "Imam" at the center, the new constitution asserted, the "militant clergy" led an Islamic movement that first ignited in June 1963 against an "American conspiracy" called the "White Revolution." The Islamic Revolution, it went on to claim, left behind sixty thousand martyrs and at least one hundred thousand injured and invalid. (These, of course, were hugely exaggerated figures.) The objective of such a sacrifice, the preamble declared, was to establish a "united universal community" of the "disinherited," who by reembracing Islam would vanquish the "arrogant" hegemonic global forces. In a "movement toward Allah" they would create an "exemplary society" that would give substance to doctrinal principles of revolutionary Islam and support for Islamic movements worldwide. In this society only those who are morally merited would conduct public affairs under the severe and sustained supervision of the guardian jurist and the "just jurists" who are guarantors against deviation from Islamic duties.

In this highly authoritarian and indoctrinated constitutional framework, the economy is not an objective but a tool: an "Islamic economy" that seeks equal opportunities for work and for distribution of benefits. Women who were exploited by the corrupt consumer culture of the Pahlavi regime, the document declared, would be restored to their virtuous standing so they could perform their sacred "motherly duty." Only in such an order would humanity's "sublime virtue" manifest itself. Bureaucratic obstacles would be cast aside, the committed armed forces and the Revolutionary Guards would discharge their ideological mission of jihad in the path of God, the judiciary would preempt any ideological deviation, and the mass media, under the continuous watch of faithful officials, would advocate a thriving Islamic culture free from "un-Islamic" blemishes.

Despite the full theocratic grounding of the constitution, affirmed by the clerically dominated Assembly of Experts, ample contradictions pervaded the text. Article 4, for instance, grudgingly fulfilled the long-desired Islamic supervision over all legislations of the Islamic Majles: "All civilian, financial, economic, administrative, cultural, military, political and other laws and regulations must be based on Islamic principles. . . . Determining this issue (i.e., compatibility with Islamic principles) is upon the jurists of the Guardian Council." It was bestowed with the authority to veto any legislation it deemed un-Islamic and contrary to the shari'a. This meant that an uncodified corpus of Shi'i opinions, prone to wild interpretation by the council, was to serve as the standard for endorsing or rejecting any piece of legislation. Other articles further buttressed the monopolizing power of the guardian jurist and the Guardian Council.

Article 6 of the constitution recognized the Islamic Consultative Assembly, a replacement for the National Consultative Assembly (Majles) of the past, as a popularly elected body whose deputies were to be representatives of the people and its laws the manifestation of the will of the nation and the source of all laws of the land. Articles 3 and 9 allowed for "political liberties within the law," "equality before the law," and inalienable "legitimate freedoms." Under no circumstances could these be suspended or removed. In reality, however, such lofty statements seemed utterly hollow, given the Islamic Majles's incapacity to pass legislation contrary to the wishes of the guardian jurist and the Guardian Council.

A contrast between theocratic and democratic features of the constitution was undeniable, and perhaps irreconcilable. The evident supremacy of clerical authority over the legislature and over personal and political liberties were too manifest to be missed by the framers of the constitution. More likely, it reflected the revolution's inner tension between the long-denied democratic aspirations of the Iranian people and the theocratic authoritarianism of a new elite. The legalist culture grounded in the concept of *ejtehad*, or making legal opinions by means of deduction from principles of the Islamic law, made it quite permissible for the politicized Qom-trained ideologues to view their own understanding of the constitution as superior to that of the general public.

Superiority of Shi'i Islam was visible in other areas of the constitution as well. Article 12, for instance, not unlike the 1906 constitution, declared Shi'ism as being "eternally" the official creed of the country, thus recognizing its supremacy over other religious beliefs: "Iran's official creed is Islam of the Twelver Ja'fari [Shi'i] school and this article is eternally unalterable." While the same article recognizing Sunni schools of Islamic law, article 13 recognized only three religious minorities as "official": Zoroastrianism, Judaism, and Christianity, excluding most significantly and predictably the Baha'i faith. Iran's largest non-Muslim community was destined to remain "heretical" and a "despicable sect" (*ferqah-ye zallah*) and would face dire consequences. Conveniently, the

Islamist-dominated legislators accepted the old regime's discriminatory laws. The "reformed elections law" of 1911, for instance, similarly recognized the three official religions at the expense of the others.

Article 14 made it a duty to display "noble conduct," equanimity and justice toward all non-Muslims, and respect for "human rights" (*hoquq-e ensani*). Likewise, pledges for equal rights of all ethnicities, equal protection before the law, and protection of life and property of all citizens against illegal intrusions of all sorts (articles 19, 20 and 22) proved sheer rhetoric when thousands were illegally arrested and imprisoned on flimsy charges and their properties confiscated by order of the revolutionary courts. The ethnic Kurd, Turkmen, and Arab minorities were harassed, and many were persecuted and fell victim to the regime's denial of their demands.

Rights of women, which received some attention throughout the text, revealed familiar features of male superiority, as evident particularly among the clergy. The preamble to the constitution, which devoted a section to women, promised that "because in the idle-worshiping regime women sustained greater oppression, reclaiming their rights deserves a priority." It is in the framework of the family, it further specifies, "that women will no longer be objects or tools disseminating consumerism and exploitation." By "rediscovering their critical and precious duty of motherhood, women will be forebears in the active field of life [giving] so as to produce together with their male fellow warriors ideologically committed [*maktabi*] humans." Discharging this duty "in Islamic perspective enjoys highest value and blessing." The trendy revolutionary language aside, the clerical framers of the constitution here defined women's "function" essentially the same as in traditional Shi'i jurisprudence where women primarily recognized as reproductive unites. Article 21 furthermore obliged the state to prepare suitable grounds for realizing all aspects of women's rights "according to Islamic guidelines." Among these rights, "qualified" women were granted custodianship of their children only when no other "legal guardian" could be appointed, so as to avoid women's mental agony. In reality, this invariably meant giving priority to the divorced husband or male relatives of the deceased husband.

Numerous articles (23, 24, 26, and 27) of the constitution also meant to safeguard civil and political liberties and freedom of expression, even though, in one way or another, all of them were burdened by compliance with "Islamic values" (article 26). Soon even compliance with Islamic values did not guarantee immunity from the state's long and repressive arm. Character assassination of political figures, routine intimidation, unqualified intolerance of any criticism of militant mullahs and their violent means, attacks by club-wielding

"Hezbollah" mobs on political rallies and political party headquarters, and forced closure of nearly all organized political and civil activities further undermined the lofty civil liberties provisioned in the constitution. Likewise, there were provisions prohibiting torture (article 38) and demanding humane treatment of all detainees and prisoners (article 39). Yet in practice, from the outset these provisions were routinely breached in the sprawling prisons and secret detention facilities of the Islamic Republic. Real and mock executions, all manner of torture and rape of prisoners, prolonged detention without credible charges, psychological and ideological pressures for political prisoners to "confess" and "repent," televised show trials, and public confessions of the repentants—all made a mockery of the constitution. These violations were often made with full knowledge of the "experts," who had pontificated on such articles in the Islamic constitution.

Of some consequent gravity for Iran's future were articles concerning the perceived Islamic economic model for the Islamic Republic. Most palpable was an unresolved tension between a centralized and bureaucratized state-dominated economy with quasi-socialist characteristics, on the one hand, and a free market economy supposedly adherent to principals of Islamic law, on the other. Also palpable were the influence of the left and its demands, even if its candidates were largely barred from the Constituent Assembly. Eastern European and Chinese models of centralized economies seemed to have influenced the framers of the Islamic constitution. Article 43 prohibited any form of economic "monopoly"; in clear contrast, article 44 called for state ownership of all heavy and "mother" industries, foreign trade, mining, banking, insurance, energy, dams, irrigation, mass media, communication, airlines, shipping, and railroads. Vast and unchecked monopolies were granted to the state at a time when, in the late 1970s, state-controlled economies had already proved elsewhere, even in the communist bloc, to be inefficient and outdated. Beyond state monopolies, "cooperatives" were to control the remaining parts of the public sector, a provision largely abandoned at the outset of the republic. The private sector, the third and most inferior in the constitution's economic scheme, was to engage in farming, animal husbandry, small industries, trade, and services. To add to the state's vast economic control, the constitution also allowed for "expropriation" (*mosadereh*) of all properties of the "usurpers," such as usurers, corrupt contractors, and uncultivated and unclaimed land. In reality, as in most totalitarian regimes, the state's vast constitutional power meant appropriation of any property that it wished to possess, including industries, businesses, and residential properties.

On the whole, the constitution of the Islamic Republic proved ideologically too burdened, conceptually too inconsistent, and practically too nonfunctional to guide, oversee, and regulate the emerging institutions of the state. It was still-born, it can be argued, offered by the "experts" to the high altar of the guardian jurist. As article 56 asserted, with a puzzling rationale, since God has "absolute authority" over the universe and over the humanity, therefore humanity in effect has sovereignty over its own social destiny. This inalienable right was to be implemented only through "absolute guardianship" (*welayat-e motlaqeh*) of the divine cause by the Imam of the community (article 57). The tortured language of this article demonstrated the framers' semantic juggling to confine human rights by the shackles of autocratic theology. Remarkably, the revised article 57 (in 1989) clarified any such ambiguity by granting the guardian jurist "absolute guardianship" over all affairs of the state and, by implication, any other article of the constitution.

It was a sad irony that less than a year after the collapse of the Pahlavi regime, dubbed in revolutionary lingo as "idol-worshipping tyranny," Iranians were to be subjected to a theocracy with far broader constitutional powers compared to what assigned to the monarch in the old constitution even after the 1948 amendment. Now in power, the clergy replicated an autocratic model that they long had opposed, at least rhetorically. As much as they employed means of modernity, first to shape and then to convey their revolutionary message, they also utilized the constitution and other democratic trappings to give the illusion of an Islamic utopia, as if it were impossible to cast off a political culture that had long honored authority by means of control and coercion. A leap from the shah's "Great Civilization" to the Islamic Republic could be achieved only through an even stronger state, now adorned with a new veneer of sanctity.

THE UNRAVELING OF THE ECONOMY

Debate about the constitution carried on amid domestic turmoil, with crucial international repercussions. Under pressure the Bazargan government under-took a grave initiative with lasting, and largely disastrous, effects on the weaken-ing Iranian economy. Responding to the radical mood of the time, persistent demands of the radical left, and backed by a constitution that essentially called for a state-run economy, in July 1979, on the spur of the moment, the provi-sional government "nationalized" (or more appropriately, confiscated) fifty-one of Iran's largest private industries, businesses, and agricultural conglomerates. All banks and insurance companies were also declared nationalized. More an act of desperation than conviction, Bazargan's government inherited these businesses almost by default. Owners of major industries either had left the country or were languishing in prisons or simply had disowned the entities for fear of confrontation with workers or arrest by the revolutionary committees. Strikes and labor unrest, intimidation and threats to management, shortages of raw materials and of spare parts and electricity, and a breakdown of the production network put many industries in a state of hibernation, if not closing them down entirely. Maladies of the earlier years—the price stabilization campaign, the oil glut, and overreliance on foreign technologies and skills—further aggravated the postrevolutionary crisis.

Workers' demands for better wages, benefits, and work conditions added to the mix. The absence of genuine labor unions and professional organizations had quickly turned the shop floor and office space into recruitment grounds for the Fada'iyan, the Mojahedin, the reinvigorated Tudeh Party and Islamic associations. Claims of "collective" management councils (*shura'i*) and communal ownership, inspired by the Bolshevik model, were rife and alluring. The councils empowered the workers, technicians, and low-ranking management of larger factories, especially the labor-intensive textile mills, and medium-sized workshops, offering them an agency they never had under the previous regime. Yet the dream of collective management proved fleeting, not least because the revolutionary regime did not remain favorably disposed toward such potentially dangerous experiments. The regime soon moved in, bolstering the competing Islamic associations and appointing so-called Islamically committed managers. Though often inexperienced and inept, these managers had the backing of the Mostaz'afan Foundation and similar revolutionary institutions.

Founded by Khomeini's decree in March 1979, the Mostaz'afan Foundation grew into a giant enterprise in charge of hundreds of public and private properties, ranging from the assets of the defunct Pahlavi Foundation, the Pahlavi family and the state-owned industries to privately owned manufacturing and industrial entities, businesses, agricultural conglomerates, transportation, insurance and communication firms, houses, plots of privately owned land, banks and financial institutions, bank accounts, bonds and stocks, and any other asset, small or large, summarily confiscated by the revolutionary courts or appropriated by the revolutionary committees. Overnight, the foundation turned into Iran's second-largest economic entity (after the Iranian National Oil Company) and soon after became one of the largest enterprises in the Middle East. By 1989 it "supervised" at least 1,024 entities with an estimated value of $20 billion. The companies under its control included some 140 factories, 470 agricultural businesses and farms, 100 construction firms, 64 mines, and 250 commercial companies. Although its proceeds were earmarked for the support of the "disinherited," in reality it provided vital sustenance for the new regime and its associates, and especially the Revolutionary Guards.

Entrusted with this instantaneous megawealth, and obviously caving under its weight, the foundation came to be known for its wasteful and inept management and for its nepotism. In the years immediately after the revolution, many of the manufacturing industries and large agricultural concerns under its tutelage fell into decay or were entirely ruined. Poor management, low morale, and low efficiency turned numerous factories into industrial wastelands, with cannibalized machinery, dilapidated buildings, derelict infrastructure, a discontented workforce, and cynical management. Industries in the vicinity of the sprawling cities, in particular, soon fell victim to land speculation and makeshift housing projects that aimed to accommodate the extraordinary population growth but also to line pockets of the new regime's cronies. The emerging elite were in the main children and relatives of the ayatollahs, relatives of ministers and ranking officials, affiliated *bazaari* activists, soon the Iran-Iraq War veterans, and men with a convincing-enough Islamic lineage.

The massive shift of the private wealth of the Pahlavi era to state ownership or to semipublic entities, and to individuals with ties to the regime, was barely admissible by even a radical interpretation of the provisions of Islamic law or the constitution of the Islamic Republic. The revolutionary courts that were supposed to uphold the spirit and the letter of the Islamic law in their judgments barely bothered to substantiate their rulings with textual evidence of Shi'i jurisprudence. Such a task would have been particularly arduous, if not impossible, given the sanctity of ownership in Islamic law. Centuries of Shi'i jurisprudence, and scrutiny over the details of property laws, were astonishingly overlooked—violated—by revolutionary judges. Revolutionary fervor and ideological turpitude quickly overcame any concern for restraint (*ehtiyat*), a principle often emphasized in Islamic law, especially with reference to people's lives and properties.

Amassing new wealth, though nominally earmarked as charity for the benefit of the underprivileged and the poor, had the noticeable effect of making the clergy financially autonomous from their traditional sources of income. In doing so, it helped loosen old ties with the bazaar, its major source of economic support, or income from the charitable endowments. As the bazaar continued to lose ground to the street and become marginalized, more so in the decades to come, its economy transformed. It primarily housed a network of wholesalers and small-scale retailers. The Islamic state, however, moved to the economic center stage, not only intervening in the national economy but also shaping it even more drastically than its Pahlavi predecessor had. The bazaar's grass roots continued, at least for a decade or two, to produce dependable manpower for the Islamic Republic's sprawling bureaucracy, but as a vibrant economic space, it no longer carried any significant weight with the country's new masters.

The public sector controlled not only all the infrastructure and service industries, including energy, water, communication, and transportation, but also, in the fashion of socialist centralized economies, it owned and operated a wide range of industries, from steel and petrochemicals to food, distribution networks, and retail. Predictably, the Islamic state in return promised a range of services and welfare schemes to its underprivileged citizens, at times completely devoid of planning or mindful of long-term repercussions. A case in point was the promise of free amenities, including electricity, water, and gas, to all citizens of Iran—a wishful commitment first promised by the Imam in the early days of the revolution, but one that soon had to be withdrawn when the cost and potential for such a generous offer became apparent. Subsidies for petrol and basic food items, however, continued for decades, placing a huge burden on state expenditures and causing serious setbacks in the performance of a national economy addicted to subsidies.

More detrimental to a manageable pattern of urban growth were the Islamic Republic's promises to provide free housing for the poor, a remedy to the sprawling shantytowns that had grown around the capital and major provincial centers in the 1970s. Presided over in the early days of the revolution by two fiery mullahs, two self-styled housing organizations laid their hands on a vast number of privately owned houses, apartments, and plots of land in large cities. The seizure had no legal grounds, having occurred even before any ruling by the revolutionary courts. They invited the disinherited to apply for ownership and subsequently settled hundreds of thousands into confiscated properties. The prospect of free housing proved an incentive for the poor and lower middle classes to migrate to larger cities. Far more than could have been realistically accommodated, there were so many applicants that the free housing scheme turned into a fiasco. Even the Revolutionary Guards were wary of how to maintain order and security. Multitudes of unlucky applicants had to settle for less in the poor neighborhoods that quickly swelled in the capital and provincial centers. In a short span, overenrolled schools, pressure on utilities, congested traffic, and air pollution became a fact of postrevolutionary urban life. Unregulated building permits granted to speculating building contractors aggravated the sprawl.

Dismantling the Pahlavi business and industrialist class and the associated secular and semisecular middle classes, however, did not instantly result in a new class of the same size and financial acumen. For years to come the state remained the powerful economic player, to the detriment of private sector, which continued to haphazardly operate within an inefficient economy. Even more than in the Pahlavi era, the new business sector was subject to the whims and wishes of the state and its fickle economic behavior, which often revolved around cronyism, connection, or extortion.

Beyond holding to the amenities and vital services, the new regime gradually adopted a haphazard privatization practice, whereby it parceled out some of its profitable assets to people with connections in very favorable terms as a reward for their loyalty; individuals and families the regime considered as its own, the insiders (*khodi*). The most obvious candidates were ayatollahs' offspring and their cronies. The closer to the center of power, the better their chances were for building new business empires, ranging from manufactured goods, textiles, and food industries to banking, shipping, heavy industry, auto manufacturing, and import-export. Also favored as insiders were former members of the Revolutionary Guards, veterans of the Iraq-Iran War with notable loyalty to the regime, and families of the war martyrs who became clients of the powerful ayatollahs. The shady fashion in which wealth and property transferred from government hands to private hands, at times in several stages, was the state's easy solution to cover up its managerial ineptitude in handling the enormous wealth it had confiscated from the Pahlavi elite. Redistributing resources, especially after 1989, was an informal means of rewarding loyalty rather than concerns for managerial skills and economic expediency.

BANISADR'S CRUCIBLE

By early 1980, despite the regime's consolidation, economic turmoil and revolutionary disarray had not subsided. The hostage crisis of November 1979, whereby sixty-six diplomats and staff of the American embassy in Tehran were held captive by revolutionary students for nearly fifteen months (they were later released in two stages), was the final straw for the provisional government. Its resignation on November 3, 1979, was a turning point. It illustrated the failure of the liberal Islamist narrative, a legacy of the National Movement of the earlier decades, in harnessing the revolution's contentious forces. Within the volatile environment of the time, these forces were to soon erupt, leading to clashes within the regime and outside it. The election of Abol-Hasan Banisadr in January 25, 1980, as the first president of the Islamic Republic appeared to be a step toward stability. The immediate power struggle that came in its wake, however, proved otherwise. Six months later in September 1980 a fierce Iraqi invasion across the southwestern and western borders shattered Iran's defenses and took the nascent Islamic Republic completely by surprise. The combination of the hostage crisis, the ongoing power struggle in the regime, and the Iraqi invasion posed a severe ordeal to an infant regime already suffering from international isolation. In retrospect, these crises helped further solidify the hard-liners' hold over the revolution and its emerging organs of coercion and control.

With a mandate of eleven million votes, more than 75 percent of the voting public, and Khomeini's blessings, who then was recovering in hospital from a mild heart attack, Banisadr's presidency seemed to be trouble-free. Yet from the outset he faced systematic, albeit covert, opposition from a wide spectrum of radical Khomeinists, clerical and lay, centered primarily in the newly established Islamic Republican Party. Founded by Beheshti and Rafsanjani, among others, the party's objective was to consolidate the Islamic Republic's grass roots. It enjoyed Khomeini's blessing, too. Yet contrary to the monolithic model of the communist bloc, the creation of a regime-sponsored Islamic Republican Party was bound to clash with a president who was neither endorsed nor tolerated by the hard-line bloc. The clash between the two interpretations of the revolution soon rose to the surface, despite Khomeini's early efforts to reconcile the opposing parties. In effect, it showed that the hard-liners, and especially the clerical bloc within the Islamic Republican Party, had enough clout to undermine a popularly elected president and even go against the wishes of the leader of the revolution.

Though Banisadr was a longtime supporter of Khomeini, in his own right he was an advocate of a peculiarly utopian outlook that fell between Islamic activism and liberal nationalism with a socialist coloring. Born to a clerical family, he witnessed in his youth the turbulent years of the National Movement and was inspired by Mosaddeq's struggle. Later, as a university student in the early 1960s, he was active in the second National Front, and during the June 1963 uprising he was arrested and briefly imprisoned. Later in voluntary exile in Paris, he joined the Confederation of Iranian Students and became a vocal critic of the shah's regime. Taking some courses in economics at the Sorbonne toward a doctorate degree, which he never completed, his time was spent mostly in the isolation of his apartment articulating what he defined as "unitarian" economics (*eqtesad-e tawhidi*). An Islamic take on socialist economic theories popular in the 1960s, his pièce de résistance was to reject profit making as prime motive for human economic activities.

When he returned to Tehran in February 1979 alongside Khomeini, the radical Khomeinist clique viewed him from the outset as a power-hungry outsider and treated him with suspicion. Khomeini viewed him with a kinder eye. An alternative to Bazargan's now-defunct step-by-step approach to accomplish the revolution's objectives, Banisadr promised a revolutionary makeover with a democratic face but also ample Islamic veneer. As a civilian capable of articulating a vision, he seemed to Khomeini to be a viable choice having still been concerned with the future of the revolution and fearing public resistance to clerical monopoly (pl. 15.1).

In his frequent public talks, press conferences, and interviews, Banisadr came across as sincere and forbearing, yet loquacious and self-congratulatory. A political loner, his odd mélange of Islamic ideology, the by-product of years of self-absorption, advocated an Islamic society in which "committed" citizens strive for the sake of God, rather than for their own personal gain, to improve the lot of others. Economy, he believed, was a path to salvation and service to God and that modern socioeconomic quandaries worldwide were to be resolved only through Islamic devotion to others and self-sacrifice. Ambiguous and self-assured, he came across as obsessed with categorization, often excessive, and with ready-made solutions to everything large and small, from unemployment to military strategy and from Western ideologies to history of Islam. He contested the unrestrained ambitions of his clerical opponents and at times even was reluctant to shower unqualified adulation on the guardian jurist. Readily engaging his opponents on the left in television debates and in his newspaper's columns, he was more of an intellectual with an Islamic bent than a Qom-oriented insider with a network of devout supporters.

Once Banisadr failed to take advantage of the momentum of the first month or two of his presidency, when he still had a chance to turn the popular tide against the stifling political space, he became a target of many justified and unjustified attacks. Soon he appeared more like the leader of a rowdy and dissatisfied opposition party than the president of the republic. With so many urgent issues to tackle, his chances for success appeared slim. Unrest in Kurdistan and Azarbaijan—turning almost into a civil war—provocations of the left on shop floors, in universities and in government offices, revolutionary courts averse to any government control, and the demands of a revolutionary-ridden economy required acumen and resolve. Lacking coherent organization and grassroots support, he could only rely, beyond Khomeini's quivering support, on long-winded public speeches and a small but devoted staff of aides and advisers, unmatched in number to the multitudes of his enemies.

The election of the first Islamic Consultative Assembly in March 15, 1980—with the majority of deputies unfavorable toward the president—deepened the rift between Banisadr and the hard-liners. Of the total of 243 deputies who were confirmed (out of the total of 270), 115 were independents, 85 belonged to

Khomeinists' grand coalition, 33 were from a coalition of Banisadr supporters, and 20 belonged to the Freedom Movement coalition. Secular parties were intentionally sidelined. Only 3 percent belonged to the National Front and 4 percent to the Tudeh Party. Supporters of the Mojahedin-e Khalq were entirely excluded. Following the highly contested election, a commission was set up by the Revolutionary Council to address a wave of protest by political parties and candidates who alleged widespread fraud. The commission examined 40 out of 173 cases and annulled the election results in 24 of them. Yet fearing loss of control, the clerics of the Revolutionary Council sought and received Khomeini's help. He decreed that the election complaints should be the affair of the Majles itself, "of which the majority of elected members so far are, God be praised, Islamic and committed." The commission was thus overruled, the protests were ignored, and the complaints were shelved.

Shortly afterward in a meeting with the newly elected deputies, Khomeini tried to mend fences between the majority hard-liners from the Islamic Republican Party and minority supporters of Banisadr. "If we want victory for our country and for Islam," he cautioned, "we should stop bickering. We should all have one voice. Guidance is one thing and backstabbing is another. . . . If the president undermines the Majles, he would collapse before the Majles does. If some in the Majles weaken the president, and those who are in the executive (branch), they too will be weakened. And today this is not expedient. . . . Today this is a major crime." Turning the sharp edge of his criticism toward the "nationalists," by whom he meant the members of the National Front, he continued: "From these nationalists [melliyun] we haven't seen anything except sabotage. Not a single one of them I have seen to be correct and Islamic."[2] This was an ominous response to the protests lodged by the National Front, whose handful of deputies was disqualified by the Majles hard-liners. It was also a warning to Banisadr to distance himself from the National Front, whose future seemed increasingly gloomy, and to return to the Khomeinists' fold.

The bone of contention, soon after the Majles was in session, was in the appointment of a prime minister, who, according to the constitution, was to be nominated by the president and ratified by the Majles. In the months that followed, the tug-of-war between the two sides revealed an ideological chasm that degenerated into a full-blown constitutional crisis. Khomeini astutely allowed the contest to come to its own end. A case in point was ambiguity in the constitution concerning the authority of the president versus the prime minister, and the level of the Majles's supervision. The function of the prime minister, the chief executive officer of the government, and the degree of his autonomy in appointing ministers were interpreted by the Islamic Republican Party's deputies in the Majles as something independent of the president. The latter was treated almost like a ceremonial head of the state. Banisadr contested this, arguing that not only the choice of the premier and his ministers but also the broad contours of the government's policies were to be set, or as a last resort approved, by the president. Below the constitutional quarrel, deeper threads of ideological division were palpable.

After months of wrangling, in August 1980 Banisadr yielded. With visible reluctance and after rejecting less desirable candidates for the post, he condoned the choice of Mohammad 'Ali Raja'i, a hard-line activist and earlier minister of education under Bazargan. He held the right credentials for the rapidly polarizing politics of the time: a fully "committed" Khomeinist, his upbringing and class status contrasted Banisadr's. Born in Qazvin, he began his career as a schoolteacher of humble background who had suffered Savak's imprisonment and torture. His father, a modest haberdasher in the bazaar, was among the founders of the Society of Expectants for the Advent of the Mahdi, devoted to combatting communists and Baha'is. The young Mohammad 'Ali himself recited Shi'i mourning eulogies (*nawheh*) in the Moharram processions. Immigrating to the capital in late 1940s, where he eked out a menial livelihood as a store apprentice in the bazaar, for a while as a peddler of cheap utensils in poor neighborhoods, he later became civilian personnel in the Iranian air force. During the heyday of religious activism in the early 1950s, he was recruited by an Islamic association, drawn into the sermons of Mahmud Taleqani and Mahdi Bazargan, and soon after affiliated with Fada'iyan-e Islam. After 1953, while serving as a schoolteacher in one of Tehran's a poor neighborhood, he continued as an Islamic activist, engaging Baha'is in religious debates. Soon he became an advocate of Khomeini, which landed him in prison for a few years.

Raja'i had a blunt and furious style and a supply of anti-Western rhetoric distinct from the refined but dreary tone of his embattled superior. Though the intrigue and squabbling ebbed momentarily with the breakout of war with Iraq, by no means did it end the regime's inner quarrels. It was clear that the relatively restrained brand of Islamism of Banisadr, and other modernist blends and flavors in his camp, were bound to face stiff resistance from the better-organized clerical quarters. Frustration with the opposition in Tehran and the looming prospects of war with Iraq, meanwhile, drew Banisadr's attention and his energies away from the capital and to the front. Frequently traveling to Khuzestan and other war-torn provinces, he tried to put a brave face on his crumbling presidency. He was steadily marginalized in Tehran and failed to make any decisive inroads at the war's front. Setback on the front and Banisadr's favored defensive strategy, especially in the Battle of Susangerd in January 1981, further gave an opportunity to his clerical opponents to tarnish his reputation. They made Khomeini clearly furious and distrustful of the president's capabilities. Banisadr's criticism of the excesses of the revolutionary courts and his calls for a peaceful end to the hostage crisis did not improve his standing with the Imam and his hard-line followers. Seeking a counterweight to the Islamic Revolutionary Party, Banisadr gradually tilted toward the Mojahedin camp, then still a force to be reckoned with, and embraced their anticlerical stand, a move that proved fatal to his presidency and his political career.

Banisadr's speech at a rally at Tehran University on March 5, 1981, the anniversary of Mosaddeq's death, more clearly revealed the irreconcilable rift with the Khomeinist camp. An army of club-wielding (*chomaqdar*) saboteurs who came to disrupt the rally clashed with oppositional forces, including Mojahedin-e Khalq and the National Front, who as a last resort had gathered around Banisadr. During a lengthy speech that was repeatedly interrupted by pro- and anti-Banisadr slogans, he paid homage to Mosaddeq's Islamic principles and touched on the government's inefficiency, heroic resistance in the war with Iraq, and the absence of judicial security, by which he meant the willful conduct of the revolutionary courts and the hostage takers. He then went on to say:

> The job of the president is to disclose the truth and raise people's awareness and strive to maintain the sense of unity in the country. . . . We must investigate and get to the bottom of everything in order to return security to our country. If your president who comes to deliver a speech [here] is to encounter armed men with club and firearms, that is not a republic that can survive. . . . If they exchange their clubs with thinking with their brains, then the social atmosphere will heal and purify. By God's grace and your selfless support we shall overcome perils and be triumphant.[3]

Banisadr's aspirations proved misplaced. The rally, and the clashes between supporters and opponents of Banisadr received a wide negative coverage in the hard-line press and in pro-Khomeini circles that no longer had any reservation to openly attack the president. The retaliatory course that followed eventually brought about Banisadr's downfall. Within weeks it became apparent that he lacked the popular backing strong enough to withstand the barrage of attacks in the press, in the broadcasting services and in mass rallies accusing him of being "compromising liberal," a collaborator with the domestic and foreign enemies of the revolution and for mismanagement of the war with Iraq. His relatively tolerant and inclusive interpretation of the new Islamic order seems to have been no longer palatable to the radicalized supporters of the Imam, or indeed to the Imam himself.

PURGING THE ISLAMIC OPPOSITION

In June 1981, when the war with Iraq was at a critical stage, the Iranian forces were demoralized, and popular enthusiasm for the regime was dwindling, the Majles moved to impeach Banisadr on charges of incompetence, ill intentions, and defiance toward the guardian jurist, all charges carrying a subtext of treason. In an orchestrated move Khomeini duly dismissed his first president only fifteen months after blessing his election to the office. Shortly before his dismissal, Banisadr had already been removed by Khomeini's order from the post of commander in chief of the armed forces, a position the Imam had bestowed on him at the beginning of the war. Weeks earlier, the Khomeinist press and media sharpened their attacks on the president and his supporters, accusing him of compromise and deviating from the revolutionary path.

But more was in the offing. Fearing the perils ahead, Banisadr had already gone into hiding in Tehran in the house of Mas'ud Rajavi (1948–2016?), a leader of the Mojahedin-e Khalq. A change in climate in favor of the Khomeinists was clearly palpable. The radicals had gathered enough acumen in a short span of time not to leave the job of governing to the outsiders, nor were they willing to tolerate "compromising liberals" lecturing on the splendors of democracy or the "deviating" People's Mojahedin selling their "classless society." Soon after Banisadr's downfall, a new presidential election brought Raja'i to office with a margin that claimed to be even larger than Banisadr's. Khomeini, too, astutely recognized that hard-liner loyalty was far more vital to him than sustaining a doomed presidency.

Forty-three days after his disappearance, in a dramatic escape Banisadr resurfaced in Paris, along with Mas'ud Rajavi, who had survived the anti-Mojahedin purges. They flew in disguise aboard an air force 707 flown by a colonel who formerly served as the shah's personal pilot. Banisadr's disguise cost him his famous mustaches, though in Paris he soon returned to his former self, minus, of course, the cachet as the Islamic Republic's first president. His reliance on the Mojahedin, though largely tactical, came at an expense not only to him but also to the Mojahedins' rank and file. The collapse of Banisadr triggered a "reign of terror" that soon engulfed all nonaffiliated revolutionary and nonrevolutionary political organizations that the Islamic regime viewed as real or imagined competition.

Besides the Mojahedin, who were the crackdown's main target and most numerous victims, the purge extended to the Marxist Fada'iyan and the Maoist Paykar. Even moderates such as the National Front and Freedom Movement were not spared. By February 1983, four years into the Islamic Republic, the raging flames even caught up with the Tudeh Party, which despite its consistent pandering at Khomeini's gate and praising the "progressive" virtues of the Islamic Revolution, was soon subject to arrest and eventual elimination. The ten-month-long coup de grace of 1981–1982 can thus justifiably be seen as the third stage of the revolution. While February 1979 brought down the Pahlavi ancien régime and the hostage crisis wiped out the "step-by-step" Bazargan model, the fall of Banisadr and the purging of the opposition—coinciding with mass mobilization for the war with Iraq—brought the greatest concentration of power into the hands of the hard-liner Khomeinists.

At the core of the anti-Banisadr camp was Mohammad Beheshti, chief of the judiciary and the most influential leader of the Islamic Republican Party. Behind him was Rafsanjani, then the speaker of the Majles and an up-and-coming enabler of clerical supremacy. Others outside the party, such as Khalkhali, the head of the revolutionary courts, were no less hostile, and Khomeini himself required little persuasion. Banisadr's tacit pact with the Mojahedin-e Khalq was sufficiently vilifying. From the early days of the Islamic Republic, Khomeini and his disciples had looked upon the Mojahedin with a mix of suspicion, fear, and resentment. Mojahedin's flirting in the early months of the revolution with "Father Taleqani," as they referred to their presumed patron, did not help remedy doctrinal differences with the Khomeinists or conceal mutual enmities between them. The Mojahedin's widespread recruitment of young men and women, mostly high school and university students, their well-organized and disciplined cadres, and their program of ideological indoctrination turned them into a formidable force ahead of all other brands of opposition.

Mojahedin's amalgam of idealized but selective Islamic teachings, romantic readings of early Shi'i history drenched in martyr worship, via 'Ali Shari'ati, and a watered-down Marxist-Leninist theory of class struggle with a veneer of a socialist political economy was appealing. Despite being cultish and hierarchical, to the point of a resembling a fascist party, the Mojahedins' appeal to young women and men lay in their seemingly liberating message, which contrasted starkly with the male-dominated, paternalistic Islam of the Khomeinists. In reality, the Mojahedin had become an Islamicized answer to the demands of a younger generation for agency. Breaking gender barriers and allowing a greater mix of the sexes under an Islamic canopy and a collectivized morality code was the key. While it required headscarves for women and button-down shirts for men, it allowed for a brotherly-sisterly interaction and instilled a strong spirit of sacrifice, armed struggle, and hero worship. It provided a ready-made package of doctrinaire answers to complex questions posed by the revolution.

Even before Banisadr's flight, the pro-regime militias—soon to be labeled "Hezbollahis" (from the Qur'anic *hizb-Allah*, or "party of God") armed with sticks and clubs interrupted opposition rallies, especially of the Mojahedin. In a matter of weeks such clashes turned into bloody street battles between the Revolutionary Guards and the armed cadres of the Mojahedin, resulting in hundreds dead and thousands, perhaps as many as five thousand, arrested. The Mojahedin supporters were mostly from urban lower-middle classes with religious backgrounds. Fired with revolutionary zeal and too anxious to resort to armed struggle, they carried the legacy of the older generation of the Mojahedin leadership. In Pahlavi prisons they honed their "dialectical" rationale that made them adamant, as they frequently claimed, that they are the only "alternative" to the reactionary Khomeinists. Under Rajavi and his cohort, Musa Khiabani (1943–1982), the People's Mojahedin grew to be a formidable paramilitary force with a wide network, safe houses, a cache of weapons looted from the army barracks in February 1979, and a steadfast cadre of young men and women with some experience in urban warfare. Resorting to an armed insurgency thus seemed to them inevitable when they effectively were pushed out of the political process along with all other forces of opposition—a deadly miscalculation for which they paid dearly.

In clashes that lasted through early 1982, small Mojahedin cells operating in the capital and provincial cities lost most of their recruits in street battles. Frequently, clashes occurred when a Mojahedin safe house was identified, leaving them no choice but to defend themselves. The alternative was torture and often death in detention. Daring and brave, they nevertheless were outgunned and outmaneuvered by the Revolutionary Guards. In a déjà vu reminiscent of the Pahlavi era, the Mojahedin proved utterly wrong in assuming that the bold act of resistance would miraculously prompt a public uprising against the regime.

Armed clashes came with a barrage of anti-Mojahedin propaganda from the Islamic Republic. Their label as "eclectics" (*elteqati*) in the early days of the revolution, for their Islamo-Marxist doctrine, soon was degraded to "hypocrites" (*monafeqin*), a Qur'anic reference denoting those who accepted Islam outwardly but inwardly retained their pagan beliefs. When confrontations turned to armed clashes, the Mojahedin were declared outright infidels (*kafer*), which allowed the Islamic regime to deal with them on the harshest of terms. Hundreds of Mojahedin, along with Fada'iyan and Paykar, and their sympathizers, were summarily tried and sent before firing squads or hanged inside the Evin prison and other detention centers.

Those who were spared did not find life in prison any easier. Under the gaze of a notorious revolutionary judge, Mohammad Mohammadi Gilani (1928–2014), and chief prosecutor and prison warden, Asadollah Lajevardi (1935–1998), known as the "Butcher of Evin," the inmates, men and women, were systematically tortured and humiliated, placed in long-term solitary confinement, and forced to confess their "mistakes" in front of television cameras. Women were forced to seek penance by sitting on their knees for hours on end in pigeonhole partitions and in total silence. Everyone had to repent and be subjected to "reeducation," or face more torture or possible execution. "Recanting" their earlier political affiliations under pressure, whether Mojahedin, Fada'iyan, or others on the left, they were labeled as *tawabin* (repentants), a term historically denoting those who after the Battle of Karbala in 680 renounced their allegiance to the House of Umayyads. Not unlike the style of the Khmer Rouge, the inmates at Evin "university" were subject to a program of Islamic "rehabilitation," which in reality amounted to full indoctrination, open displays of loyalty to the Imam and the Islamic regime, and complete collaboration by disclosing the identities of their comrades and locations of safe houses. Even then some remained suspect, were accused of insincerity, and in due course, were retried and executed.

Outmaneuvering Khalkhali, the revolutionary judge Gilani gained notoriety not only for his cold-blooded verdicts that sent hundreds, if not thousands to the gallows, but for his television program in which he articulated intricate points of Shi'i jurisprudence often with sexual undertones pertaining to temporary marriage, incest, and sodomy. His dispassionate legalistic tone, seeming at times even leisurely, stood in surreal contrast to his death verdicts, which by 1988 had acquired the definition of mass murder. His aloof clinical approach in blending ruthlessness on the judicial bench with an almost comical television performance spoke volumes of a humanistic disconnect that was the prevailing character of Qom legalism. In September 1981 in an interview with the daily *Kayhan*, he declared: "Those who are arrested during street armed clashes can be lined up against the wall and shot on the spot. The wounded can also be finished off on the spot. From a religious point of view, there is no need to bring such people to court, because they have waged war on God."[4] By October he felt the need to further clarify his legal reasoning when in an interview with the daily *Ettela'at* he pointed out, "According to Islam, even if they [i.e., Mojahedin] die under torture, no one is held accountable. This is the precise decree of the Imam."[5] Two of Mohammadi Gilani's sons, who earlier had joined the People's Mojahedin, were among the victims of the regime. Escaping the country, close to the Turkish border they were caught by the Revolutionary Guards. Anticipating the outcome of their arrest, they committed suicide with cyanide capsules. Their father confirmed that if they were brought before his court, they would have received death sentence.

Others among the Khomeinists did not display as much zeal as Gilani, though they were not far behind in their line of reasoning. Serving as shari'a judges, prosecutors, prison wardens, and—among the higher ranks—as head of the judiciary, ministers of information and justice, leaders of Friday prayers appointed by Khomeini, and his representatives in the Revolutionary Guards, armed forces, and other sensitive organs of the government, they abided by the same guidelines. Thousands were purged, imprisoned, and executed once any affiliation with the mostly imagined forces of opposition was detected. Many sympathizers of the left were arrested on such minor charges as befriending an activist, possessing a revolutionary tract, or attending informal gatherings suspected of leftist tendencies. By mid-1982, the tail end of the Mojahedin insurgency, the regime's draconian measures had successfully created an environment of terror detrimental to any show of sympathy toward any popular cause, let alone those initiated by the left.

The Mojahedin and their associates did not remain entirely passive to the regime's design to destroy them. On June 28, 1981, a week after Banisadr's downfall and the start of serious street clashes, a massive explosion in the headquarters of the Islamic Republican Party killed more than seventy, including the secretary-general of the party, Mohammad Beheshti. The loss of government ministers, officials, and party activists inflicted the gravest blow to the regime's leadership since the start of the revolution. The seventh of the month of Tir 1360 thus became a new red dot on the martyrdom calendar. In particular the loss of Beheshti, eulogized as the "tulip of the paradise" (*laleh-ye behesht*), deprived the clerical hierarchy of one of its most astute operators. Despite his pivotal role in establishing the Islamic Republican Party and the ousting of Banisadr, Beheshti was distinct from a host of Khomeinists in appreciating the complexity of the political process.

More than two months later, in the last days of August 1981, another massive bomb went off in the office of the president, killing Mohammad 'Ali Raja'i, two weeks after he had been elected president. He was killed along with his newly appointed prime minister Mohammad Javad Bahonar (1933–1981), a founding member of the Islamic Republican Party and the first cleric to hold an important ministerial post. The two bombings, coming at short intervals, were shocking displays of the regime's faulty security and infiltration by foes. A series of assassinations and attempted assassinations against pro-regime elements aggravated fears. Among them, Sayyid 'Ali Khamenei, future president and Supreme Leader, was the target of a bomb blast in June 1981 while preaching in a Tehran mosque. The bombings, carried out presumably by Mojahedin agents, had an enormous adverse effect on the political climate, for they tilted public sympathies toward the Khomeinists. It also alerted the regime to the lethal threat to its very survival. In return, it unleashed the harshest clampdown so far on the opposition.

CRUSHING THE SECULAR DISSENT

Crushing the Mojahedin served as a pretext to eradicate all other forms of dissent. Earlier on, after months of insinuations, in a fiery speech in June 1981, Khomeini had denounced the National Front leadership as "apostates," primarily for calling a rally to protest the passage by the Majles of the law of Islamic retribution (*qesas*). The law, that replaced the penal code of the Pahlavi era, inculcated such ancient punishments as stoning married woman for extramarital affairs, cutting off limbs for theft and other serious offences, and determining life or death of murderers and other culprits by the mere consent of relatives of the victim, whom the new law defined as "custodians of the [victim's] blood" (*awliya-e damm*). On a broader scheme, the National Front was being punished for holding Khomeini accountable for the climate of intimidation and terror. By the summer of 1982, most leaders of the National Front either had fled the country into permanent exile or had ended up in the prisons of the Islamic Republic. Not entirely devoid of potential middle-class support, the National Front nevertheless found itself in no position to withstand Khomeini's rage or the terror of the club-wielding Hezbollah and their paymaster in the Islamic Republican Party. The Freedom Movement had been saved only barely by renouncing its old comrades in the National Front.

This was a humiliating fate for a movement that had stood for national sovereignty and political freedom for three decades. Khomeini and his turbaned clique never really trusted or cared for the tie-wearing, liberal nationalists. Nor did Khomeini ever acknowledge Mosaddeq as a national leader or subscribe to his path. It was largely the misplaced hopes of the liberal nationalists in the early days of the revolution that made them believe Khomeini was their partner in democracy, an error they quickly began to regret. As Karim Sanjabi, the leader of the National Front, once said: "Now it is the mullahs' sleepers who replaced military boots." Fearing for his life, in July 1981 Sanjabi went into hiding before leaving for Paris and soon after retiring in the United States.

Likewise, the National Democratic Front, a competing political coalition loyal to Mosaddeq's memory, was labeled heretical. Established in March 1979 by intellectuals and activists unexcited by the National Front's old-style liberalism, they advocated a secular socialist outlook. After the daily *Ayandegan*, affiliated with the Democratic Front, was closed in August 8, 1979, most leaders were harassed and driven into exile. In Paris, the Democratic Front's leadership collaborated with the Mojahedin and other oppositional elements associated with Banisadr to create the National Council of Resistance. For a short while the council was a promising voice of opposition abroad, though in practice it proved a liability for secular intellectuals unaccustomed to the Mojahedin's authoritarian outlook and paramilitary conduct. Once the latter's collaboration with the Iraqi Ba'athist regime became too embarrassing for any self-respecting Iranian nationalist, the council virtually dissolved.

The last of the political parties to go was the Tudeh Party. Despite the devious pretentions of its leadership, insisting that they were loyal to the people's revolution, declaring that socialist principles are in harmony with revolutionary Islam, and saluting Khomeini as an anti-imperialist champion, they scarcely overcame Khomeini's innate mistrust of the left. Nor did it remain immune to the regime's wrath, despite careful treading down a tactical path or collaborating with the regime on issues of intelligence and security. From the early days of the revolution the Tudeh recruited from among the old comrades but also the ideologically inclined younger generations. It also embraced a merger with the so-called Majority (*aksariyat*) faction of the Fada'iyan-e Khalq. Not the least remorseful of its past history, the Tudeh leadership steadfastly followed a pro-Soviet party line. Entertaining high hopes for their future, it infiltrated the middle ranks of the regime's nascent security and intelligence apparatus, evidently counting on long-term gains once the "inept mullahs" handed them the reins of power in desperation.

Major figures such as Ehsan Tabari (1917–1989), a respected theoretician of the party and a historian of some weight; Nur al-Din Kianuri (1915–1999), the party's general secretary, notorious for his checkered record before 1953; and Maryam Firuz (1913–2008), the most prominent woman among the Tudeh ranks, were survivors of the party's cadre who escaped to Soviet Union and Eastern Europe in the late 1940s and early 1950s. They returned to Iran after decades of exile, bringing experience and discipline but also a doctrinaire brand of Marxism that tried hard to comply with the rhetoric of the radical clergy and their spirit of militancy. Like many on the left, including liberal intellectuals, the Tudeh naively assumed that the days of the mullahs were numbered. Like many "progressives," the Tudeh, too, relished the "historical necessity" of revolutionary action against the "degenerate" Pahlavi monarchy, and often sneered at such "bourgeois" values as human and civil rights (unless they were in their favor). If not in words at least in deeds, nearly all means were legitimate if they were serving their end and fulfilling their lofty dream of the masses' one day casting off the threadbare cloak of religious "superstitions."

The Tudeh woke up to a nightmare, however, when the Islamic regime began a massive crackdown that lasted until 1984. Despite the Tudeh's unreserved support for the Islamic Revolution in its publications and rallies, the regime's deep suspicion of the party and its activities never truly abated. Revelations of the KGB spymaster Vladimir Kuzichkin, a onetime Soviet station chief in Tehran who defected to Britain in 1982, confirmed these fears. In his interviews with CIA officers, Kuzichkin not only revealed the identities of almost the entire Tudeh leadership but also their infiltrators and the party's close ties to the KGB. In early 1983 the CIA secretly shared these details with the Iranian intelligence, an early gift from the agency's chief, William Casey, in the hopes that by courting Iran, the United States would be able to check presumed Soviet influence. This was at a time when the Reagan administration was about to adopt a policy of counterbalancing its massive assistance to Iraq in its war with Iran. Offering incidental intelligence to Iran and consignments of weaponry constituted a series of covert measures that eventually culminated in 1985 in the Iran-Contra Affair.

Widespread arrests of Tudeh members by the hundreds in Tehran and the provinces were followed by their torture, long prison sentences, and executions. Soon after, in 1985, a series of "panel interviews," a euphemism for forced televised confessions, brought Tudeh Party leaders before the cameras, where they expressed remorse for a life of communist deceit and subservience to foreign powers. They praised the Imam for his true revolutionary qualities and bowed down in servility to Islam and the revolution as the true path to salvation. Intimidation, torture, and Soviet-inspired interrogation techniques cast long and ominous shadows over these interviews.

Also notable were the aftershocks of a crumbling ideological worldview. Thereafter came the "memoirs" and more "interviews" by well-known Tudeh leaders, including Tabari and Kianuri, in which the aged leaders, then in their seventies, again praised Khomeini and confessed to a life of political errors. The authenticity of these publications was deeply suspect, no doubt choreographed under duress and threat of further torture. Some of the heinous interrogators were themselves former Tudeh members and sympathizers. Now in the service of the regime's Ministry of Information, a reincarnation of Savak, they were responsible for the post-torture interrogation, when victims were "broken" and ready to say or write whatever pleased their captors. Of all the reversals that the Iranian people witnessed following the revolution, the confessions of the Tudeh leadership probably were the most sobering.

Coinciding with massive crackdowns on Banisadr and Mojahedin, in April 1982 the security forces arrested Sadeq Qotbzadeh, once a senior member of Khomeini's camp and at one time his minister of foreign affairs. He was detained, brought to trial, and forced to make a television confession. Like Banisadr, he was instrumental to Khomeini's rise to prominence and, like him, was to become another devoured offspring of the revolution. He was accused of plotting a coup to assassinate Ayatollah Khomeini and topple his clerical regime. After an unusually long trial of twenty-six days, and after securing Khomeini's consent, in September 15, 1982, a military revolutionary tribunal convicted him of the highest treason and sent him to the gallows.

Qotbzadeh reportedly "confessed" to a plot that implicated culprits inside and outside Iran, ranging from the CIA and the Bakhtiar opposition in Paris to royalists in exile, the Socialist International, military officers, and clerical and lay figures associated with Ayatollah Shari'atmadari and the Muslim People's Republican Party. If the KGB officer Kuzichkin is to be believed, Qotbzadeh's removal was in part aided by the KGB, who presumably loathed him for his anti-Soviet and anti-Tudeh sentiments. According to this version, KGB agents planted in Qotbzadeh's house a forged secret message from the CIA that implicated him in a largely spurious antiregime plot. Whatever the reality, Qotbzadeh was a victim of his refusal to be resigned to his political fate. A maverick with a trait of eccentricity, like many revolutionaries of his persuasion, he was rudely awakened to the fact that he had been overrun by a circle of clerical insiders who were cohesive, single-minded, and ruthless. In February 1979, as the head of Iran's broadcasting services, when he expressed disgust with clerical reactionary measures, using the popular pejorative expression *akhund-bazi* (i.e., mullah's conduct), he probably never imagined the grim implications of the expression.

The Muslim People's Republican Party, a once-powerful rival to the ruling Islamic Republican Party, was another victim. Its moderate program of reform with elements of socialist economics appealed to the middle classes wary of the speedy rise of the Khomeinists. Backed by Ayatollah Mohammad-Kazem Shari'atmadari, a moderate *marja'* from Iranian Azarbaijan, and one time the most respected authority in Qom, the party hoped to create a wider constituency despite open hostility of the hard-liners. When large rallies organized in Tabriz and other cities of Azarbaijan sufficiently worried the regime, a club-wielding mob readily assigned to sabotage rallies and trigger violence. In the meantime the leadership was called a stooge of the Americans and the party was duly crushed to oblivion.

Soon after Qotbzadeh's execution, and in the context of the alleged plot, Khomeini ordered Shari'atmadari to be "defrocked" (*khal'-e lebas*) and kept under house arrest for the rest of his life. A highly unusual measure, even for Khomeini, to mistreat a fellow ayatollah, particularly a man who once in 1962 mediated on his behalf with the shah and probably saved Khomeini from death, it reflected the gravity of the situation in which the regime found itself. The Center for Islamic Publication and Teaching, one of the oldest in Qom created under Shari'atmadari's watch, was closed down, along with its journal *Maktab-e Islam*, long a voice of Islamic nonrevolutionary persuasion. Members of Shari'atmadari's family were arrested and tortured. Accused of collaboration with plotters, the aging Shari'atmadari, then a dignified figure of seventy-seven, was beaten and manhandled by the minister of information and chief henchman of the Islamic Republic, Mohammad Rayshahri (b. 1946). To complete his public humiliation, he, too, was brought before television cameras to read a statement apologizing for his misdeeds (fig. 15.6).

The "defrocking" of a recognized *marja'*, clearly an invented reprimand inspired by the Vatican, was an unprecedented intrusion into the recognized safe space of a high-ranking mojtahed. It was meant to exhibit Khomeini's hierarchical superiority over other *marja's*, especially if they didn't bow publically to his status as Imam and the guardian jurist. This was the first time in the history of clerical Shi'ism that an institutional hierarchy was set with punitive repercussions for violating it. Other *marja's* dully followed the lead. Save for Ayatollah Hosain-'Ali Montazeri, a chief lieutenant and designated successor

Figure 15.6. Khomeini and Shari'atmadari meet in Qom in 1979.
Relations quickly turned sour as the two *marja's* took distinct paths.
Imam Khomeini. http://www.imam-khomeini.ir/fa/c201_30173. Public domain.

to Khomeini (who in 1989 was to face a fate comparable to Shari'atmadari), few audible objections came from Qom or other major Shi'i centers.

Another casualty of the purge, though less severe, was the Hojjatiyeh Society (also known as *anjoman-e zedd-e Baha'iyat*, or the Anti-Baha'i Society) founded in 1953 in the aftermath of the coup. Shaykh Mahmud Halabi (1900–1998), a madrasa cohort of Khomeini who established the society and became its leader, viewed anti-Baha'i activities—including harassment of individual members of that faith and disrupting their gatherings—as a duty of committed Muslims in anticipation of the coming of the Hidden Imam or the Proof (*Hojjat*; hence *Hojjatiyeh*, meaning "party of the Proof of God, i.e., the Mahdi"). The society's latent messianism was a response to the Baha'is' post-Islamic belief. On the eve of the revolution and continuing through the postrevolutionary days, the Hojjatiyeh had emerged as a cohesive nonclerical network advocating a messianic interpretation of the Islamic Revolution as a preparatory stage for the Advent of the Imam of the Age. "Until Mahdi's revolution," declared a favorite slogan of the Hojjatiyeh, "the movement continues," implying that the Islamic Revolution was a prelude to the Advent of the Imam of the Age. In response, those supportive of Imam Khomeini cried out, "Khomeini! Khomeini! You are a manifestation of the Imam [of the Age]," a clear emphasis on the authority of the guardian jurist as "deputy" of the Hidden Imam. For a while Hojjatiyeh was tolerated by its opponent, but eventually in a 1983 speech, Khomeini banned the society's activities, fearing its rising influence among the new elite. A vast number of the "committed" in the Islamic Republic's cadre were former Hojjatiyeh and silently remained, even after Khomeini's ban, loyal to its memory and its objectives.

AN ISLAMIC CULTURAL REVOLUTION

Removing the remnants of the Pahlavi past and, more urgently, obliterating the regime's ideological nemesis on the left and even within the Islamic fold called not only for a takeover of political power but also for closure of newspapers and publications run by the secular opposition. Independent newspapers such as the left-leaning *Ayandegan*, which had mustered an impressive following and rendered higher standards of reporting and editorship, were the first to go. The closure of *Ayandegan*, which had been in print since 1967 and had covered the prerevolutionary and revolutionary course of events from the vintage point of the intellectuals of the left, was an ominous reminder to a generation of activists of the liberal left who embraced the revolution as a paragon of an open society and freedom of press. The confiscation of the paper's offices by the order of the attorney general of the Islamic Republic, and after the passage of a highly restrictive press law in August 1979, made it clear that the Islamic authorities had no stamina for even tamed criticism of the regime's excesses.

Ayandegan was the first among other newspapers and journals that either brought into silence in the following months and years or completely taken over by supporters of Khomeini. If the stringent monitoring of the Ministry of Islamic Guidance was not sufficient to intimidate journalist and force them to silence, the Hezbollah vigilantes and the *komitehs'* "shock troops" were. The two major national dailies were simply taken over at the outset of the revolution and nationalized. After a thorough purge of the staff, control of these papers was entrusted to Khomeini's aides or to the most egregious hard-liners. The official organ of the Islamic Republican Party and other well-funded government journals and newspapers also had their share in the Islamification of the press. By 1983, the forced closure of almost all independent newspapers and journals left a faint shadow of the burgeoning press, which had exceeded one hundred periodicals in 1980 (fig. 15.7).

Along with the press, educational and cultural institutions were obvious targets of a regime with a pronounced cultural agenda. Purging all "uncom-

Figure 15.7. Ambivalence about the chances for the growth of a free press in the shadow of machine guns is evident in this enigmatic poster produced in October 1979. Designed by Kurosh Shishehgran. *Honar-e Enqlab, 57 Poster az Enqelab-e 57*, ed. Rasul Ja'farian (Tehran: Kitabkhaneh, Muzeh va Markaz-e Asnad-e Majles-i Shura-ye Islami, 1390/2011), 24.

mitted" faculty, staff, and students from institutes of higher education and Is-
lamization of education at all levels soon became a major preoccupation of the
Islamic Republic. At the core of what came to be known as the Cultural Revolution (Enqelab-e Farhangi) stood a deep resentment of the secular educational
system that had emerged since the turn of the twentieth century. Such a vindictive attitude may be attributed to the past belittling, even denial, of the brand
of knowledge often viewed by the Pahlavi rule as arcane and backward—in
contradistinction to what was revered in the Shiʻi teaching circles of Qom and
Najaf. Though in most respects the radical clergy camp and their lay associates
viewed modern technical, scientific, and medical education as realities congruent with Islamic teaching, they felt that traditional brands of Islamic knowledge,
especially jurisprudence, were unjustly ignored and even ridiculed.

More so, especially since the 1960s they felt that the university environment
was tainted with moral laxity and Western depravity, including various flavors
of Marxist ideology, and that the Pahlavi cultural elite for long nursed a deep
grudge against anything associated with traditional Shiʻi education. This is
what the Islamic authorities and its civil agents aimed to transform. The discourse of "Westoxication" (*gharbzadehgi*), a legacy of Al-e Ahmad, also had its
place. And so did Shariʻati's idealized radical Islamism. Both contributed to an
air of moral indignation adopted by Ayatollah Khomeini and his commissars
of the Cultural Revolution who frequently characterized universities as dens
of disbelief where students are conditioned to disdain Islam and its teachings.
Class disparity also played a part. Purging the venerable faculty with obvious
grudge, often by revolutionary agents of lower social standing, symbolized a
victory over the old educational elite. The extent of the purge, and its centrality to the regime's ethos, is also evident in what can be described only as the
conquest of Tehran University. As in other universities and institutes of higher
education, Tehran University in the early days of the revolution had turned
into a bastion of the Fadaʼiyan and Mojahedin organization and recruitments,
another motive for the "forces of the Hezbollah" to take over campuses all over
the country and purge undesired elements from among students and faculty
(fig. 15.8 and fig. 15.9).

Immediately after the victory of the revolution, every week thousands of supporters of the regime occupied the Tehran University's soccer field at the center of the campus to set Friday congregational prayers. The symbolic gesture,
complete with the leader of the prayer delivering hellfire sermons (*khotbeh*)
with a G3 rifle in hand, denouncing domestic and foreign enemies of Islam,
was meant to underscore the regime's Islamic sovereignty in a venerable center
of educational modernity. As if a ritual, the audience responded with salutes

Figure 15.8. Ferdowsi's statue in front of the School of Letters, Tehran
University, March 1979. Posters, graffiti, and notices, including a portrait
of Arani, were predominantly by the Fada'iyan and the Mojahedin.
Maryam Zandi, *Enqlab-e 57* (Tehran: Nazar Publishers, 1393/2014), 103.

to the Prophet and his progeny followed by "death to America," "death to idol
worshippers," "death to hypocrites"—and death to other flavors of the week.

That Friday prayer was to be held on the campus of an institution that for
nearly half a century had been a vital source for training Iran's professional
elite and a center of political dissent exhibited a meaningful mix of intents.
It displayed the desire of the Qom *howzeh* to "Islamicize," as Khomeini often stressed, the heathen world of the university. "Crossbreeding the university
with the *howzeh*" became a priority of the regime. The Friday congregation
was also meant to overpower with sheer numbers (and loudspeakers) all other
voices, especially the left, which since the victory of the revolution had taken
shelter inside university campuses. That Friday prayers continued to be held at
Tehran University for more than three decades despite the availability of larger
sites speaks of the Islamic Republic's existential anxiety. To withdraw from the
campus of Tehran University in effect signaled a retreat from the revolution's
Islamicizing crusade, a concession the regime was, and still is, unwilling to
grant at any cost.

Other symbolic gestures, benign as they may have appeared at the outset,
followed. Iran's Cultural Revolution initiated by Khomeini's decree in June

Figure 15.9. On the eve of the revolution, curbside booksellers offered
an assortment of long-censored books, pamphlets, and snapshots that had
surfaced around Tehran University. Among the favorites were leftist literature,
including Stalinist and Maoist tracts, and works by Shari'ati and Al-e Ahmad.
Maryam Zandi, *Enqlab-e 57* (Tehran: Nazar Publishers, 1393/2014), 90.

1980 was the start of a widespread purge (*paksazi*; literally, "purification") of
suspect elements at all levels, from elementary schools to universities. Probably inspired by the Chinese Cultural Revolution — a torrent of intimidation,
terror, massacre, and destruction of mostly academics and intellectuals that
consumed Mao Zedong's China between 1966 and 1976 — the Iranian version
was far tamer, less bloody, and largely concerned with control of educational
levers at all levels. It was nevertheless deeply damaging to the fabric of Iranian
education, professional fields, technological skills, and most of all, branches
of the humanities. The Supreme Council of the Cultural Revolution, consisting of Khomeini's appointees from among hard-liners, took its cues from the
guardian jurist's directives and furious public speeches. He repeatedly urged
the council to rid the universities of all un-Islamic elements and at all costs. By
mid-1981, in actions parallel to ousting Banisadr and crushing Mojahedin, mobs
in Tehran and other provinces randomly attacked university campuses, beating
up and injuring students, driving out the left from their offices and paramilitary
bases, and in turn occupying campuses. To complete their task, on June 4, 1980,
the council ordered the closure of the universities nationwide. They remained

closed for the following three years to give ample time to systematically cull undesirable elements. A few days later Ayatollah Khomeini's directive confirmed the closing of the universities:

> The need for Cultural Revolution, which is an Islamic issue and demand of the Muslim nation, has been recognized for sometimes. . . . The Muslim nation is worried that God forbid the opportunity is missed and no positive action has yet been taken and the culture remains the same as the time of the corrupt regime when the uncultured officials put these important centers under the disposal of colonialists. Continuation of this disaster, which unfortunately is the objective of groups guided by foreign interests will strike a heavy blow on the Islamic Revolution and the Islamic Republic and any indifference towards this vital issue would be an act of great treason to Islam and the Islamic country.[6]

Under the rubric of reevaluation, thousands were expelled or subjected to Islamic ideological tests or sent off to revolutionary courts. The adverse effects of depriving universities of some of their most skilled and qualified faculty, who were labeled "antirevolutionary," "idol worshippers," and "decadent," soon became apparent at all levels. Intimidated and weary of the ponderous Islamicizing measures, thousands resigned and left Iran or went into businesses or private practice. Professors of humanities and social sciences, in particular, were targets of academic cleansing, having been accused of facilitating a Western "cultural onslaught" (*tahajom-e farhangi*) or entertaining an "un-Islamic" lifestyle. Also subject to great scrutiny were faculty with left-leaning affinities, records of currying favor with the old regime, or Baha'is identified as members of the "devious sect."

Classrooms and curricula also bore the burnt of the Cultural Revolution. Classes were segregated by gender and, though still under the same roof, were under the watchful eyes of zealous "security" (*herasat*) agents. Instructors who survived the purges had to meander through ideological minefields when teaching such areas as evolutionary theory, sociology of religion, civil law, and various fields of humanities. History, both modern and premodern, was embattled by an indoctrinated reading of the past. Being "Islamically correct" soon became the order of the day. After the universities reopened in the fall of 1984, "committed" students, many from among the war veterans or favored insiders, were admitted mostly on the basis of their zeal and connections rather than their scholarly merits. They weren't shy about challenging their professors, and if necessary, they harassed them in and out of the classroom or reported them to universities' Islamic associations. A spirit of fear and suspicion quickly set in, diminishing any drive for independent inquiry and academic objectivity. Even the exact sciences were to comply with Islamic "ideological" values.

The students' fervor, however, subsided with time and gave way in many instances to cynicism or sheer utilitarian motives. Acquiring a degree to excel in the regime's technocracy or improve one's chances for immigration prevailed. The regime's grip over the educational system, and especially over higher education, steadily grew and became further institutionalized over the coming decades. "Committed" cadres trained under the new system gradually replaced the older generation of instructors and university professors, though even then the spirit of dissent and skepticism did not entirely evaporate. The maturing of a new generation of academics had its surprises. While seemingly subordinate to the ideological dictates of the regime, many were critical of the narrow-minded superficiality imposed on higher education and at times courageous enough to question the mainstream.

Even more drastic was the Islamification of the curricula, the other urgent task of the Cultural Revolution. A fair amount of mandatory "Islamic" education was injected into the system at all levels, including devotional acts, rudimentary Shi'i jurisprudence, and theology. A systematic effort was also made to substantially revise and rewrite textbooks in the humanities, most notably history, philosophy, and literature. Relying heavily on the Shi'i narrative, new textbooks presented the Islamic Revolution embedded within a salvation narrative—a liberating struggle, as it were, that restored two and a half millennia of Iranian history gone awry. It aimed to supplant the Pahlavi nationalistic histories of the latter half of the twentieth century with an Islamicized version of its own, displaying familiar symptoms: ideologically driven, naive, self-righteous, always pitting good versus evil, and xenophobic.

With the emphasis on Islamic history, the Pahlavi promotion of the ancient Iranian past of the Achaemenid and Sassanian periods did not receive the same preferential treatment. With a twist, perhaps borrowed from the Soviet-inspired Tudeh literature, the power and glory of those eras was attributed to the toiling masses who built empires under the yoke of oppressive King of Kings. The real glories were reserved for the Islamic era, particularly for early Shi'i history. A facile hagiography of the Shi'i Imams, mostly based on popular legends filtered through Qom clerical channels, offered a sanctimonious narrative in which persecution and suffering was blended with a largely imagined political activism. This was a picture as unfitting to the Shi'i Imams' mostly docile lives as it was disingenuously ideological. The updated language and vocabulary injected into the otherwise arcane narratives, as in the Shi'i books of mourning (*mas'eb va marasi*), appeared surreal, if not absurd.

The greatest distortions were rendered in the story of modern Iran as a prelude to the Islamic Revolution. Loyal to the narrative of moral decadence, the history textbooks of the Islamic Republic portrayed Qajar rulers as ignorant, oppressive and hedonistic, and responsible for Iran's territorial losses to the rapacious European powers. Devoid of any political agency, with few exceptions Qajar statesmen were depicted as puppets stranded between British and Russian insatiable greed. Predictably, the loss of the precious Caucasian provinces as well as Herat and Marv were bemoaned in a tone that betrayed a veiled expansionist complex. Lamenting the fate of the Constitutional Revolution, the new Islamic narrative accused secular constitutionalists of selling out virtuous Islamic ideals to alien liberal ideologies. It portrayed statesmen of the period as deviant Westernizers. By contrast, Shaykh Fazlollah Nuri was celebrated as the true champion of the Constitutional Revolution, a victim of his Islamic convictions, and a forerunner of an Islamic movement that eventually came to fruition under Ayatollah Khomeini. The only other hero of early Qajar era was Mirza Taqi Khan Amir Kabir. He received an equally idealized treatment, one that was inherited from nationalistic narrative in earlier decades. He was portrayed as an unblemished anti-imperialist champion whose murder at the hands of heinous Qajars robbed Iran of its only chance for reform and progress.

The greatest villain of the Islamic Republic's grand narrative, however, was Reza Shah, or Reza Khan, as he was contemptuously referred to in the language of the Islamic Revolution. Portrayed as the puppet of British mischief, the much-favored conspiratorial theory of his rise to power painted him—and of course, Pahlavi reforms—with a vindictive brush. It was as if the entire era had been nothing but a grand betrayal of the spirit of true Islam and the Shi'i clergy, a modernistic aberration with no positive value to Iranian state and society. Predictably, such a narrative found in Hasan Modarres, by then elevated to ayatollah status, not a political maneuverer but an innocent martyr of Pahlavi's anti-Islamic tyranny. He was another precursor to the Islamic Revolution. The Reza Shah era, the prevailing narrative of the Ministry of Education of the Islamic Republic assured students, had no benefit; rather, it had caused Iran's educated middle classes to deviate from the path of Islam. Ironically, the authors of these textbooks and a whole host of the radical Khomeinists were the ungrateful by-products of this same middle class.

By the same token, Mohammad Reza Shah's era received an utterly Manichaean treatment, contrasting the forces of Islamic good under the auspices of Ayatollah Khomeini against the evils of a "treasonous" Mohammad Reza Shah and the greed, oppression, and subservience he brought to the country. Not surprisingly, Mohammad Mosaddeq (often referred to by his Qajar title,

Mosaddeq al-Saltaneh, to stress his aristocratic lineage) emerged in this narrative not as champion of the oil nationalization movement but as its accidental leader. And like liberal constitutionalists before him, he, too, was doomed to fail once he parted ways from the true Islamic leader of his time, Ayatollah Kashani, another turbaned precursor in the sacred genealogy of the Islamic Revolution. A succession of encounters between clerical activism and secular modernity, always corrupt and deviant, offered a modern version of a Shi'i passion play (*ta'ziyeh*) with a providential touch, one that was destined to bring Ayatollah Khomeini to the stage as the ultimate savior of centuries of clerical service and sacrifice.

TOWARD COMPLETE SUPREMACY

By late 1983 the regime had succeeded in silencing virtually all voices of political opposition that had helped bring it to power only four years earlier. All autonomy-seeking ethnic voices in the country including Kurdish, Azari, Turkmen, and Sunni Arab natives of Khuzestan, were efficiently extinguished. The magnitude of the crackdown becomes even more striking when we take into account Iran's successes during 1982 and 1983 in repelling Iraqi offensives. Compared to the experiences of earlier revolutionary regimes in Europe and elsewhere, the Islamic Republic's success was impressive. Four years into the 1789 French Revolution, and two years before the Reign of Terror, the revolutionary process in France was largely unsolidified and the fate of the revolutionary regime undetermined. By 1921 the Russian Revolution still had a long way to go, having been fighting a widespread civil war that cast doubt on the Bolsheviks' very survival. Even the Chinese Revolution of 1949, with popular support for Mao Zedong, was not fully capable of eliminating its Nationalist nemesis.

The key to this remarkable sustenance may be attributed to the crucial presence of Khomeini as a revolutionary prophet. He brought to bear, above all, a high degree of group cohesion—to borrow Ibn Khaldun's famous '*asabiyya* theory of the rise and fall of empires—among his clerical and lay followers with resolve and unmerciful acumen. When necessary, he forfeited even his closest aides or highest-ranking clerical rivals. The clerical network over which he presided had little doubt as to who was an insider and who was not, and in a short time, the eventful course of the revolution made this differentiation even sharper. Saving the "self" and purging the "other" quickly became a matter of survival. While the "old regime" was almost completely wiped out, the participants in the revolution were swiftly sifted through for their doctrinal (*maktabi*) loyalty.

Group cohesion was complemented by organization and leadership of a strong state. Though revolutionary institutions were chaotic and clerical leadership decentralized, and even flawed, there was enough organization and financial resources, thanks to income from soaring oil prices in the early 1980s, to allow the new regime to consolidate. By trial and error Ayatollah Khomeini and the Khomeinist elite learned the art of survival and its accompanying need for coercion and terror. Their "Qomified" style of politics quickly taught them the intricacies of mass politics, honed their talents for intimidation and control, enriched their radical rhetoric and propaganda skills, indulged their fascination for new technologies—much of which had originated in the land of the Great Satan—enhanced their skills in the face of international isolation, and above all convinced them that it was their moment to transform society to their image and ethos.

This was a Qom-based style of rule because it was grounded in centuries of madrasa solidarity and decades of isolation from sources of political power, a world steeped in inner rivalries and factionalism but also unified against the common enemy of Pahlavi secularity. Qom was as much a physical space as it was a mental state, a complex and multifaceted labyrinth with its own moral economy based on the madrasas' frugal life and the clergy's connection with the larger community of believers through mosques, shrines, sermons, and the Moharram mourning ritual. This was the culture now projected onto the larger political stage.

In resilience or shrewdness this clerical community had no rivals, not even the Mojahedin who nurtured unquestioned organizational loyalties and doctrinal certitude. The latter's leadership, and the leadership of the Fada'iyan, were as ideologically naive and politically imprudent as the Tudeh was subservient to its Marxist-Leninist idols. Veteran liberal nationalists, either of the Islamist or the secular type, still dwelled in paradigms of the Mosaddeq era. They were barely equipped, nor could ever have been, to truly fathom Khomeini and the new brand of radicalized clergy around him. Their uneasy partnership, based on an assumption on their part that divisions of labor were to be observed between the clerical and political wings of the new revolutionary order, proved utterly outdated. Beyond the initial task of facilitating their rise to power, the mullahs had little use for the mild-mannered, democratically inclined men of the past generation. When these veterans chose not to accommodate the hierocracy in power, it was too late.

Solidarity and manipulation aside, the new regime benefited tremendously from public support and patriotic sympathies generated by the war against Iraq. The Khomeinists were not shy in acknowledging that the hostage crisis and war with Iraq were indeed blessings for their survival, once Iranians with diverse sympathies chose in the course of the war to put the defense of their country ahead of their preference for the emerging political order. Popular sentiments were still too raw, and resentment for the previous regime too intense, to allow for dispassionate political discretion. In particular, most Iranians saw Khomeini as the only legitimate leader who could steer their country through the treacherous waters to victory over a menacing Iraqi invader and its real or imagined Western backers.

16

FACING THE FOE: THE HOSTAGE CRISIS, THE IRAQ-IRAN WAR, AND THE AFTERMATH (1979–1989)

All the while that the Council of Experts deliberated over the articles of the Islamic constitution and the supreme authority of the guardian jurist, a crisis of great magnitude was in progress, one that shook Iran's relations with the outside world and initiated an adversarial encounter with the United States that shaped their relationship for decades to come. The hostage crisis of November 1979 started an international tremor that for the following fourteen months would enrage the United States, preoccupy world media, appall public opinion worldwide, and irreparably damage the image of the Islamic Republic. A devastating conflict with the Ba'athist regime in neighboring Iraq compounded Iran's external troubles. While the first event offered the Islamic regime a chance to symbolically engage a superpower, the prolonged war with Iraq proved a calamity that adversely affected lives of Iranians and Iraqis alike. As in most revolutions, domestic turmoil found an adversarial projection beyond its borders, even though neither of the two events, the hostage crisis or the Iraqi invasion, was entirely unavoidable.

Yet both events boosted Khomeini's uncompromising stance and helped consolidate his Islamic order at the expense of his contenders. What he proudly labeled the "second revolution" was an attempt to eradicate not only the remnants of what his camp labeled as "royalist sedition" but also the "compromising liberals." Khomeinists exploited the hostage crisis, and the assumed threat of "world-devouring" America (*emrika-ye jahan-khawar*), to steal the show from the left, the first to "expose" (*efshagari*) the great powers' "sinister imperialist plots." The war, in contrast, helped silence any contestation of clerical supremacy by labeling it "traitorous." The experience of defending the "Islamic homeland," moreover, gave new legitimacy to the regime, which basked in its patriotic glow, and helped raise a generation of veterans tied to the Islamic Republic through sacrifice and blood.

EXORCISING THE GREAT SATAN

On November 4, 1979, a group of young hard-liners who called themselves Students Following the Line of the Imam (Daneshjuyan-e Payro-e Khatt-e Imam) in a dramatic move took over the compound of the American Embassy in Tehran. They seized sixty-six US diplomats and staff and held them hostage, presumably demanding the shah's repatriation by the United States to stand trial in a revolutionary court. A week earlier, in late October 1979, the shah, by then a ghost of his past, had arrived in New York to receive urgent treatment for his cancer. Having approached his influential friends for an entry visa to the United States, among them Henry Kissinger and Nelson Rockefeller, his arrival in New York aroused further suspicions in the conspiracy-infested climate of the revolution in Iran. The bitter memories of the US intervention in the coup of August 1953 fueled a sense of déjà vu that was highly opportune for whoever wished to exploit it.

The 444-day hostage crisis proved as beneficial to Khomeini's camp as it was damaging to Iran's international standing. Immediately after the seizure, a few of the US embassy staff were paraded before cameras, an audacious gesture to gain publicity that was amply covered by world media. Images of blindfold and terrified Americans (some of them taken from behind their consulate desks where they had been issuing visas to terrified Iranians seeking residence in the United States) soon turned into iconic markers of American humiliation in the hands of vengeful fanatics.

Furthering the demand for the shah's return, the Students of the Imam Line, as they came to be known, alleged that the embassy of the world-devouring superpower was a "spy den" (*laneh-ye jasusi*) conspiring against the revolution, aiding "idol worshippers," and somehow aiming to stage a coup and restore the shah to power. In Iran's revolutionary atmosphere "exposing" such mischiefs, no doubt, could arouse huge popular sentiment. If further conspiratorial pretexts were needed, they were readily offered by meetings between members of the provisional government and the American diplomats and statesmen. Already, occasional meetings between Bazargan and William Sullivan (1922–2013), the American ambassador in Tehran, were portrayed in the leftist and Islamic hard-line presses as compromising and suspicious. A meeting between Ibrahim Yazdi and the US secretary of the state at the time, Cyrus Vance (1917–2002), during the UN General Assembly in New York, aggravated the charges of conspiracy.

A meeting between Bazargan and Zbigniew Brzezinski, the US national security adviser, during the anniversary celebration of Algerian independence in late October 1979 added fuel to the paranoiac climate. Though all negotiations revolved around mutual concerns and the need to revamp US-Iran relations in the aftermath of the revolution, and even sought remedies for excesses of the Pahlavi era, this apparently was not enough to vindicate Bazargan in the eye of his radical critics. Soon these contacts became a major part of the "exposés" by the hostage takers to discredit the provisional government.

The intention to take over the embassy was a familiar part of the radical left's agenda, rehearsed earlier and unsuccessfully staged. No less than three times before the takeover by the Students of the Imam Line, the US embassy had been attacked by leftist militias—first on Christmas 1978 and again on February 13, 1979, two days after the victory of the revolution. The second assault by the People's Fada'iyan was deflected with the cooperation of Ibrahim Yazdi and the provisional government. Later, a self-styled revolutionary *komiteh* was stationed in the embassy and headed by a thug-turned-revolutionary—who evidently was on the embassy's payroll. A further attempt by the Mojahedin paramilitary took place weeks before November 1979. All attempts evidently were meant to be symbolic and gain publicity for the perpetrators, but thanks to the radical left, lessons in hostage taking were quickly learned by the Islamic understudies.

The terminology of the hostage crisis, too, part of the widespread neology of the early revolutionary days, was a joint product of the left and the Khomeinists. The "line" (*khatt*) indicative of an ideological line evidently came from the Marxist milieu and was quickly spread in the linguistically contagious environment of the time eager to differentiate one "position" from another. "Clarify your position!" was a common cautionary message at a time when minute ideological variances separated the Marxist from the Marxist Islamic and both of them from the radical Islamist line. Occupying the US embassy was a bold move by the Students of the Imam Line to outmaneuver competing trends on the fast-changing revolutionary stage. That they were of the "Imam's line" implied a certain personal loyalty to the leader of the revolution, though, as it turned out, not entirely to the clerical or lay Khomeinist factions around the Imam. Acting as a free agent, the students were a handful of young and idealistic men and women of mostly middle or lower middle classes motivated by the anti-imperialist discourse and in solidarity with world liberation movements (fig. 16.1). Such sentiments were rampant in the Islamic associations in universities, often in competition with the leftist publicity. The sense of urgency attached to the seizure of the embassy was meant to be dramatic, even theatrical.

Expressions of moral indignation throughout the crisis were a powerful propaganda weapon in the hands of the Students of the Imam Line forcing all other

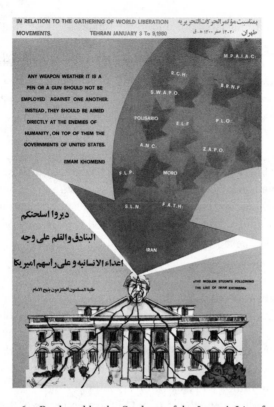

Figure 16.1. Produced by the Students of the Imam's Line for the
World Liberation Movements conference in Tehran in January 1980,
the poster in English and Arabic shows Iran spearheading the struggle
against the United States. Its citation by Khomeini was the inspiration
for nasty anti-American propaganda during the hostage crisis.
Middle Eastern Posters. Collection, Box 2, Poster no. 49, Special Collections Research Center,
University of Chicago Library.

revolutionaries to jump on the bandwagon. The seizure turned into a crisis of
unprecedented scale. To the surprise of many, Bazargan included, Khomeini
unabashedly backed the takeover of the embassy not only as a valiant move
by the committed Islamic youth but also a preemptive measure to "expose"
the American "satanic" plots in the hand of "spies" masked as diplomats. Still
residing in Qom, Khomeini on the surface was reluctant to intervene in the
affairs of the provisional government, while he actually routinely and overtly
undermined it, often with undisguised relish. He gave inflammatory interviews
to international media calling on Islamic militants worldwide to rise up against
world-devouring superpowers, he appointed radical clergy critical of Bazargan

to executive and judiciary posts and to the offices of Imam Jom'eh (leader of Friday prayers) in every city, and extolled rabble-rousers and their maverick behavior. If he needed any pretext to rule by decree, the constitution was about to award it to him. Soon his escalating militancy became all the more apparent to all who hoped for a quick end to the hostage crisis and revolutionary chaos. As Bazargan had once noted, the Imam himself proved the most potent source of confusion. He resembled Iran to "a city of hundred mayors" and his own government a "knife without a handle."

The first victim of the hostage crisis, predictably, was the provisional government. It resigned on November 5, a day after the seizure, and Khomeini eventually accepted the resignation a few days later. By late October, though, it had been largely paralyzed and ready to quit. It faced harassment not only from the unruly *komitehs* backed by Khomeinists and the revolutionary courts but also from the free-agent Revolutionary Council, with its semiclandestine and revolving membership. The council was set up by Khomeini almost as a parallel authority to the provisional government, as if from the start he intended to pull off all the authority from under the government and put all the blame for chaos and contention on its shoulder. Bazargan was attacked both by Marxists and the Islamic left, who accused him of sheltering "dependent" (*vabasteh*) capitalists and actively collaborating with the United States and its agents. Bazargan's "step-by-step" transition had clearly run aground.

After veraciously digging the remnant of the documents in the embassy, the "revelations" (*efsha-gari*) made of the Students of the Imam Line revealed few earth-shaking spy stories. Though they landed 'Abbas Amir Entezam (b. 1933), the spokesman of the then-defunct provisional government, in prison on charges of collaborating with the US embassy, there was little substance to the charges of American meddling in Iran's internal affairs. What seemed to be routine intelligence gathering by embassy staff, handicapped by lack of credible sources, appeared to the embassy invaders as undeniable evidence of the superpower's design to destroy the Islamic Revolution. With unparalleled obsession, the students pored over thousands of embassy files in search of agents and spies, plots for assassination and overthrow, and enemies within. They even pasted together, unbelievably though it may sound, thousands of classified documents that were hurriedly shredded by the American staff minutes before the embassy's complete takeover. The Herculean act of document recovery, however, did not reveal much of a conspiracy.

What eventually did emerge out of this frantic exercise in exposing "malicious imperialist intrigues" were many published volumes of *Asnad-e Laneh-ye Jasusi* (Documents from the Den of Spies), demonstrating years of close US monitoring of Iran's domestic affairs and regional developments. What every in-telligence unit of any embassy in any country around the world would routinely perform appeared to the wide-eyed Students of the Imam's Line as undeniable proof of US espionage. The documents revealed a high level of attention to detail but also a bureaucratic sense of benign negligence toward the bigger picture and the underlying revolutionary pressures that were building up under the glittery surface of Pahlavi regime.

As far as the postrevolutionary period was concerned, beyond the nitty-gritty who's who and the means of establishing contacts with new authorities, the US diplomacy and intelligence gathering appeared to be less concerned with the makeup of the revolutionary regime and activist Islam. Rather, the US embassy was engaged with repercussions of the new regime domestically and for the region: the potential Soviet benefits from the fall of the shah, security of the Per-sian Gulf, and consequences of the reactivation of the Tudeh Party and various other brands of Marxism in Iran. Khomeini was seen more as a rabble-rouser than a potent nemesis, and Bazargan as a potential fellow traveler on the road to diplomatic normalization. There was little admission of past mistakes, and even less about ways to offset the loss of a valuable ally such as the shah. The Islamic Revolution was seen as a regional headache, yet to be figured out and dealt with.

For the students and the captivated Iranian public, the hostage episode first appeared as a triumph, a preemptive move to avert another 1953 coup, so it seemed, thanks to revolutionary alertness of the young and unblemished stu-dents. But from the start the crisis decidedly tilted the political discourse toward greater militancy as the students successfully adopted the rhetoric and tech-niques of the left. Not only they were empowered by the fall of the provisional government, they persuaded Khomeini and his allies to place higher ideologi-cal bets. The slogan "Neither East nor West but the Islamic Republic" had to be amended with a more potent "anti-imperialist" label. Now the frequently uttered slogan in the rallies, "Death to America" (*marg bar Amrika*), a relic of the Tudeh slogans of the 1950s, was matched by Khomeini's fiery denunciation of America as the "Great Satan" (*shaytan-e bozorg*)

Almost becoming a voodoo-like invocation, the satanic attribute, first uttered in November 1979 by Khomeini in a routine diatribe against the United States, may have been rooted more in Cold War propaganda than in an Islamic no-tion of Satan. To be sure, the Qur'an does have its Great Satan leading an army of smaller demons. Yet Satan was barely ever perceived beyond the context of worldly temptations and an agency for personal damnation. He is a fallen angel capable of mischief and deceit but devoid of dark destructive powers. Applying this to the United States as a demonic superpower, with an almost apocalyptic connotation, seems to have been inspired by more mundane sources. In the new Islamic garb, demonizing America went beyond the Cold War invective. It came to predicate an ultimate act of "othering," as if in cosmic combat the Islamic Revolution was leading the forces of good against the evil armies of hegemony and decadence. That such a dichotomy appeared in a land that once nurtured the Zoroastrian belief in eternal war between good and evil is striking.

In a more historical Iranian experience, however, one can only draw a parallel with Safavid Shi'ism. The cursing of the Caliphs and other desecrations of Sunni symbols were rooted in the vulnerability of the new Shi'i state versus the military might of the Ottoman Empire in the sixteenth and seventeenth centuries. Anti-Sunni propaganda not only reflected anxiety about Ottoman hegemony but also generated legitimacy for the new Safavid state. It consolidated its social base and allowed it to eliminate its real and potential rivals. "Curse and rebuke" (*sabb va la'n*) of the first three Righteous Caliphs, scandalizing 'Aisha, the wife of the Prophet and leader of anti-'Ali revolt during the first civil war, even the ritualistic burning of the effigy of the second caliph 'Umar (*'Omar-koshan*), cursing of the first Umayyad caliph Mu'awiya, his son Yazid and some of the celebrated figures of early Islamic history, and steady harassment of the Sunni and crypto-Sunni population of Iran helped consolidate the Safavid base, especially among the restive Qezilbash. For centuries to come, the Shi'i propaganda generated a powerful counternarrative to Sunni history, with a lasting impact on Iran's identity.

With some historical latitude, it may be argued that the modern Students of the Imam Line in their praise of the Imam were not unlike the Qezilbash of the Safavid era. Nor was the cursing of the American demon entirely unlike the damning of the Ottoman Sunnis. And Khomeini was as much a prophet for the Islamic Revolution as Isma'il was for the Safavid revolution. Such a parallel, ahistorical as it may seem, is sociologically constructive. To define its identity in moments of crisis, Shi'ism has relied on an element of social cohesion, charismatic leadership, a persecution narrative, and an external Other, real or imagined. Here in the Islamic revolution, the alien Other reappeared as a demonized United States so as to allow for the political legitimacy of the Shi'i clerical body and secure its ascendency. Students of the Line of the Imam hence facilitated a leap to a new era of international animosity, severing the Islamic Republic from the Pahlavi past.

To this end there was no dearth of enthusiasm. In front of the embassy, along Roosevelt Avenue (renamed Mofatteh), there was a spirit of fanfare: thousands gathered everyday to take part in anti-American and anti-Israeli rallies or to witness the spectacle. "Committed" graffiti artists were hard at work depicting on the outer walls of the embassy ad hoc scenes of American crimes and graphic expressions of revolutionary victory. Sayings of the beloved Imam were painted in huge size, including *Emrika hich ghalati nemitavanad bekonad* (roughly, "America can't do a damn thing"), an assurance from Khomeini that despite much talk in the media, the United States was in no position to take any military action against Iran. There were vendors selling their goods: grilled corncobs, fresh walnuts, and oven-roasted beets, all delicacies of the poor now brought to the affluent neighborhood in north Tehran. In the aftermath of the Camp David accords and the subsequent Egypt-Israeli peace treaty signed in March 1979, young peddlers in front of the US embassy were selling crude string puppets of the "three corruptors: Carter, Sadat, and Begin." The Tudeh Party, too, had to make its presence felt. Every morning a large bouquet of flowers was delivered to the front gate of the embassy as a token of Tudeh appreciation of the heroism of the students.

The street culture of the hostage crisis also brought street booksellers to the thoroughfare in front of the US embassy (renamed "Den of Spies") offering "blank cover" clandestine translations of Russian Marxist-Leninist pamphlets along with popular writings on Islamic ideology; works of Al-e Ahmad, Shari'ati, and Taleqani; hasty translations of popular histories about US crimes in Vietnam, international Zionism, and crimes of Israel against Palestinians; pamphlets published by Fada'iyan and Mojahedin; and portraits of Mosaddeq, Mirza Khuchak Khan, and martyrs of the Islamic Revolution. The small collection of books and posters was an iconic representation of a revolutionary culture in the making, with its diverse origins and curious readership in search of a political identity.

As if he were a clairvoyant, Khomeini's assurance about the US inability to do any harm proved true on April 24, 1980, when Operation Eagle Claw undertaken by the US Army Delta Force in collaboration with other units of the US armed forces attempted to rescue the hostages. The operation was a total failure. In a highly elaborate, multistage military plan, US troops first were to land on a deserted airstrip in the middle of the central Iranian desert, then fly some four hundred miles north with helicopters to a secure base near the capital, then storm the embassy compound, and after releasing hostages, drive them over to an airstrip near the capital and fly them back to safety abroad.

The operation, however, was aborted halfway through because of logistical problems and while troops were still landing in the inhospitable Lut desert south of the oasis town of Tabas. In a frantic move to return to their base, three

US helicopters crashed with a huge C-130 military transport aircraft, resulting in the death of eight servicemen. The failure was caused by no less a biblical calamity (more accurately, a Qur'anic one) than a momentary sandstorm. This was a huge discredit to President Carter and the Carter administration even though in retrospect it displayed his sound judgment to abort the operation. The perception of divine intervention projected a sense of invincibility onto Khomeini's image and vastly boosted his revolutionary resolve. Soon after, when Khalkhali rushed to the scene of the crash, where charred bodies of the victims were still exposed, his jubilant sneer against the backdrop of the empty desert appeared grossly surreal. In front of Iranian TV cameras he irreverently kicked their remains with his shoes as if he were raking through the ruins of a forlorn empire. To many Iranian revolutionaries the debacle was a living testimony that the United States indeed could not "do a damn thing."

BA'ATHIST MENACE REVISITED

The Iraqi invasion of Iran in September 1980 was a rude awakening for the Islamic Republic and an unexpected retreat from the empty rhetoric of the hostage taking and the pretensions of "bringing the United States to its knees." Reminiscent of earlier episodes from Iran's long history, here, too, turmoil at the center encouraged intrusion into the vulnerable periphery. At the end of the Safavid era, when Iran's western frontiers were overrun by Ottoman armies and those in the north by Russian troops, or in the postconstitutional era when turmoil in Tehran invited occupations from all directions, were two distinct reminders of past vulnerabilities going back to the Roman-Parthian and Byzantine-Sasanian times. The Iraqi regime's aggression, however, added an ideological facet to the ancient border tension along the Zagros range.

For Saddam Hussein and his Ba'athist cohorts there was an added ideological facet. Arab nationalism, in its Ba'athist permutation east of Damascus, suffered from a sense of insecurity toward Iran that was fueled as much by Iraq's own religious and ethnic complexities as by Saddam's skewed, and barely concealed, ambitions to become champion of the Arab cause. The postcolonial complex of Ba'athist nationalism was bound to invent its own demons nearby. Saddam's Tikrit clique, in particular, was brimming with racial and cultural hatred for "Persians" ('Ajam). They were viewed as historical enemies of the "Arabs," who, despite defeat and humiliation in the early days of the Islamic era, according to the Ba'athist narrative, persisted over the centuries and encroached on Iraq's Arab supremacy. The time had come to put the enemy in its place, not through a war of propaganda but through the barrel of a gun. Invoking the early history of Islamic conquests (*al-Futuh*) and Arab armies routing Sassanian defenses in successive battles, Saddam hoped for a quick victory. Ominously, he named the Iraqi offensive Qadisiya after the decisive battle in 636 fought on the west bank of Euphrates. In that battle, the Iranian loss opened Mesopotamia to armies of Islam and soon after brought the loss of Ctesiphon, the capital of the Sasanian Empire (north of today's Baghdad), and the beginning of its rapid downfall.

Iran's historical claims over the Shi'i holy sites and the Shi'i community of Iraq added to the Ba'athist resentment. Capture of Baghdad in 1508 and in 1638 under the Safavids, Nader Shah's occupation of the shrine cities of Iraq in 1743, and Karim Khan's occupation of Basra in 1775, though distant memories, had not entirely lapsed from the modern Iraqi narrative. Fierce Wahhabi anti-Shi'i campaigns in southern Iraq and the sack of Karbala in 1802, on the other hand, incensed Iranians. The aborted campaign in 1821 by the Qajar prince-governor of western Iran, Mohammad 'Ali Mirza Dowlatshah, in part was motivated by concern for protection of the Shi'i community. Even though the conclusion of the 1823 and 1847 Perso-Ottoman border treaties stabilized the frontiers and diminished both the Ottoman and the Iranian territorial ambitions, Qajar moral authority over Shi'i Iraq endured throughout the nineteenth century.

The unfavorable treatment of the Shi'i community, once the Mamluk dynasty of Iraq was supplanted in 1831 by Ottoman direct rule, rekindled Iranian resentment. Yet Naser al-Din Shah's 1871 visit and his cordial reception by the Ottomans was but one example of how the Iranian state tried to reassert its authority albeit symbolically. Predominance of the ulama and of the seminarians of the Iranian origin in the teaching circles of Najaf and Karbala has in effect made these centers inseparable part of Iran's religious fabric. A steady stream of Iranian pilgrims to southern Iraq and a large community of Iranian permanent residents in the shrine cities bonded the two countries even after the formation of modern Iraq. That by the 1960s and 1970s tens of thousands of Shi'is with dual Iranian-Iraqi identities were residing in the pilgrimage cities of southern Iraq further injured Ba'athist sensibilities.

The ethnically diverse population of Iraq that had been glued together under the British mandate now had to be tied up by a police state wallowing in its oil wealth. Saddam saw revolution-stricken Iran both as a threat and an opportunity. Iraq's 1975 territorial compromise with the shah over demarcation of the Shatt al-Arab waterway (or what Iranians knew as Arvand Rud) had wounded his ego and whetted his expansionist appetite. In July 1980, a week after the shah's death in a Cairo hospital, Saddam appeared on Baghdad television denouncing the earlier settlement with Iran and shredding the Algiers Declaration. Shatt al-Arab, he claimed, was in Iraqi territory in its entirety. Sole access to the

two-hundred-mile waterway not only offered Iraq strategically secure access to
the Persian Gulf but also exacted a major blow on Iran's commercial shipping
and access to the Persian Gulf along its southeastern province of Khuzestan.

Saddam also entertained other ambitions. With purges of Iranian armed
forces after the revolution, and the ensuing chaos in Iranian defense, he saw a
golden opportunity to "annex" Iran's oil-rich Khuzestan province, or what the
Iraqi regime called Arabistan, to the "Arab motherland"—a Ba'athist dream of
an Anschluss. With about 40 percent of the Khuzestan population then con-
versing in an Arabic dialect or of some Arab descent, Saddam believed he had a
popular base inside Iran. Although a leftist-inspired and Iraqi-sponsored secessionist movement known as Jibhat al-Tahrir (liberation front) flickered briefly
in the early months of the revolution, there was virtually no support inside
Khuzestan for Saddam or Ba'athism, even among Sunnis of the province.

Only weeks after the victory of the revolution, the ethnic Arab activists in
Khorramshahr led by pro-Ba'athist Jibha al-Tahrir and its left-leaning associates
put out a list of three demands. They called for cultural autonomy and adoption
of Arabic as the official language of the Khuzestan province, use of Iran's oil
revenue as a first priority, and an exclusive Arabic-speaking cohort to govern the
province. Months of negotiations with representatives of the provisional government and with Khomeini and his aids reached a deadlock and eventually led to
an armed confrontation in Khorramshahr on May 29, 1979. The commander
of the Iranian Navy, Admiral Ahmad Madani (1928–2006), a popular National
Front figure, led the government forces that crushed the secessionist rebellion.
There were at least fifty-five dead and many injured. The Khorramshahr incident, the first of several ethnic rebellions in other provinces, demonstrated the
Islamic Republic's commitment to a strong and centralized state, a policy that
in Baghdad's view reaffirmed Iranian hegemony of the Pahlavi era.

Beside Khorramshahr incident, Saddam's fear of a Shi'i revolution in Iran
had deeper roots. Although in early 1979 he had congratulated Khomeini for
the revolution's success and even invited Bazargan to Baghdad, his shift to a
hostile posture came after Khomeini and his hard-line supporters called for
the "export" of the Islamic Revolution to neighboring Iraq. The Islamic Da'wa
Party, a cleric-dominated Shi'i revolutionary organization active since the 1960s,
emerged as an eager partner. The Da'wa Party was responsible for a Shi'i uprising in Najaf in 1977 that had been brutally put down by the Ba'athist regime. In
the absence of secular parties, Da'wa epitomized Shi'i grievances and years of
repression, torture, and killing.

The Iranian revolutionary message was carried not merely over the airwaves
and through clerical channels, but also by provocative acts that made Saddam

even more concerned with a recurring Shi'i rebellion in the south at a time when prospects of a second Kurdish revolt in the north were not far off. Following two assassination attempts against senior Ba'athist figures, by April 1980 Saddam was anxious enough to go as far as detaining and then executing Muhammad Baqir al-Sadr (1935–1980), the most visible leader of the Da'wa, on charges of support for the Islamic Revolution and attempts to replicate it in Iraq. His sister Amina bint Huda al-Sadr (1937–1980) was tortured and killed before his eyes. Muhammad Baqir al-Sadr, a respected theologian and author of a trilogy expounding on political, economic, and philosophical dimensions of his perceived Islamic order, had already spent time in Saddam's jail on charges of sedition.

These executions, followed by more arrests and executions, were warning signals to Khomeini and his Iraqi sympathizers. His years of exile in Najaf made Khomeini a familiar face among the Shi'i clerical leadership of Iraq, who viewed him with a mix of awe and fear. Baghdad's extreme measures had the reverse effect, for it heightened anti-Ba'athist sentiments in revolutionary Iran and further blackened Saddam's image as a brutal tyrant. As it turned out, the Shi'is of Iraq were not entirely sold on Khomeini's revolution. Despite sympathy for the Islamic Revolution, droves of them recruited into the Iraqi army fought against Iran and died for their country. Yet hatred for Saddam and the Ba'athist regime persisted. It was too deep to be diminished even by the horrifying experience of an eight-year war with Iran. Shi'is continued to be discriminated against, intimidated, and kept out of the ruling circles in Iraq. These were conditions that swayed the Iraqi Shi'is toward clerical leadership and its Islamic political alternative.

Saddam's blend of anxiety and expansionism was further fed by Iranian opposition figures in exile, an all-too-familiar phenomenon in history of revolutions. With the demise of the shah, senior Pahlavi army officers in exile, such as General Gholam-'Ali Oveysi, viewed Saddam as a potential ally. They were apparently in cahoots with Shapur Bakhtiar, then in exile in Paris, who unmindful of Ba'athist ambitions, viewed Saddam as a valuable counterbalance to the harm brought by Khomeini. The hostage crisis, the fall of Bazargan's provisional government, and the shah's demise consolidated the Islamic Republic's stance. Even in the early months of the war, there were nebulous hopes among opponents of the Islamic regime that the Iraqi invasion would weaken Khomeini and open a road to Pahlavi restoration. Four months into war with Iraq, and as late as January 1981, the hostage crisis was still in progress, adding uncertainty to the future of the Iranian revolution. These were incentives to engage in a conflict, hoping that Iran's anti-American belligerence and the general anti-Iranian climate in the West would work in their favor.

A SACRED DEFENSE

Despite many months of hostile exchanges over the airwaves and at border posts, the full-scale Iraqi invasion came as a surprise. On September 22, 1980, Iraqi air strikes targeted Iranian air force bases deep inside the country (map 16.1). Concurrently, the Iraqi infantry and amphibious forces crossed the Shatt al-Arab, and breaking through the southwestern and western borders, they infiltrated deep inside Iran's strategic positions. With unconcealed desire, the invading army aimed to occupy the oil-rich province of Khuzestan. Pushing back feeble Iranian defenses all along the western borders, and as far north as Kermanshahan province, the Iraqis' rapid gains within the first few weeks of the conflict were significant. Claiming the entire Shatt al-Arab waterway, the Iraqi siege of Khorramshahr, Iran's most important commercial port in the Persian Gulf, and near destruction of the nearby city of Abadan, Iran's most important oil refinery, were severe blows to Iran's defense, economy, and morale. Iraq's control of the Zagros heights along the Luristan and Kurdistan frontiers, moreover, meant the loss of a crucial natural strategic advantage that had protected Iran through the ages.

Yet Iraqi gains proved transient. When the first shock of the invasion had passed, Iranian resistance and its reconstituted defenses, despite the huge odds, were effective enough to withhold Iraqi advances. In a matter of weeks, the Iranian armed forces—or what was left of them—along with the Revolutionary Guards, disorganized and inexperienced but steadfast, and soon after with the help of the Basij volunteer militia, managed to bring the Iraqi advances to a near halt. In less than a year Saddam's army was in retreat. A foreign intrusion in the midst of the revolution brought most Iranians behind the Islamic regime, and soon the war became a unifying cause despite its many domestic divisions. As it turned out, the "sacred defense" (*defa'-e moqaddas*), as it soon was labeled, became a blessing to a regime then in the throes of a deadly domestic struggle versus the People's Mojahedin and other opposition forces. Incredible feats of sacrifice by hundreds of thousands of young Iranians fighting and dying at the front electrified Iranian society. Despite Iran's many instances of civil war and wars of succession and despite two rounds of occupation by European powers, this was the first time since the Russo-Persian wars of the early nineteenth century that Iranians had experienced a full-scale invasion. Remarkably, with the exception of the People's Mojahedin, whom Saddam harbored in 1986, throughout the course of the conflict there was no known case of collaboration with the enemy or defection to the Iraqi side. Even the few senior officers of the shah's army who have set their hope in Saddam's victory quickly gave up.

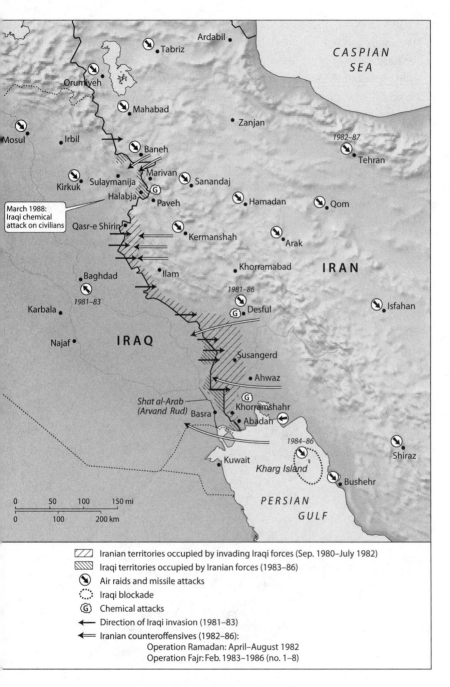

Map 16.1. Iraq-Iran War, 1980–1988

Legend:

- Iranian territories occupied by invading Iraqi forces (Sep. 1980–July 1982)
- Iraqi territories occupied by Iranian forces (1983–86)
- Air raids and missile attacks
- Iraqi blockade
- Chemical attacks
- Direction of Iraqi invasion (1981–83)
- Iranian counteroffensives (1982–86):
  Operation Ramadan: April–August 1982
  Operation Fajr: Feb. 1983–1986 (no. 1–8)

Map labels:

CASPIAN SEA

Ardabil
Tabriz
Orumiyeh
Mahabad
Zanjan
Mosul
Irbil
Baneh
1982–87
Tehran
Marivan
Kirkuk
Sulaymanija
Sanandaj
Halabja
Paveh
Hamadan
Qom
March 1988: Iraqi chemical attack on civilians
Qasr-e Shirin
Kermanshah
Arak
IRAN
Baghdad
Ilam
Khorramabad
1981–83
1981–86
Desful
Isfahan
Karbala
Najaf
IRAQ
Susangerd
Ahwaz
Shat al-Arab (Arvand Rud)
Basra
Khorramshahr
Abadan
1984–86
Kuwait
Kharg Island
Shiraz
Bushehr
PERSIAN GULF

0   50   100   150 mi
0   100   200 km

By late November 1980 Iran had amassed some two hundred thousand regular troops and one hundred thousand Revolutionary Guards and volunteers on its southwestern front. Iranian special forces, moreover, with naval and air support, attacked the Iraqi oil export terminals on the southern tip of the Faw peninsula. The Iraqi defensive posture changed the course of the war and forced the invading army to dig in along its advanced lines. Thus began trench warfare that lasted for nearly eight years, at huge human cost to both sides. Iranian counteroffensives in January 1981 in the Battle of Susangerd, forty miles northwest of Khuzestan's provincial capital, Ahwaz, was the first of many that came in its pace (see map 16.1). Banisadr, who at the time also served as commander-in-chief of the Iranian armed forces, oversaw an operation that proved ineffective and caused massive casualties. Dejected and tired of animosities in Tehran, he spent the greater part of his time behind the front lines, preoccupied with the course of the war, hence lost more ground to his many nemesis in the capital (fig. 16.2). He was perhaps unfairly blamed for the failure of the first Iranian counteroffensive. The operation was marred by rivalries between the regular armed forces and the Revolutionary Guards and by the aftereffects of heightening political quarrels in Tehran. Both the command and the rank and file had to adjust to new realities: revolutionary turmoil, multiple sources of power within the regime, and the dictates of a total war.

Figure 16.2. Banisadr visiting the front (Susanged?), c. January 1981.
Kaveh Golestan and Alfred Yaghoubzadeh, *Jang: Do Gozaresh az Jang-e Iran-Iraq*, 1359 (Tehran, 1360/1981), 50 (photographed by Alfred Yaghoubzadeh).

After the ousting of Banisadr in June 1981 and the takeover by the Supreme Defense Council, appointed by Khomeini and headed jointly by two of his senior clerical aides, Akbar Hashemi Rafsanjani and 'Ali Khamenei, there was a semblance of greater coordination. The Revolutionary Guards called in September 1980 to fight alongside the embattled Iranian armed forces learned to be more practical in driving the enemy back. Though untried and hardly battle-worthy, the challenge of the war built up the spirit of the Guards, solidified their ranks, and raised their prestige, sometimes unfairly at the expense of the regular forces. The propaganda machine of the Islamic Republic invariably gave preference in its coverage to the Guards and credited them with major gains. Soon emerging as a powerful arm of the Islamic state, the Revolutionary Guard Corps relied on its militia spirit and organizational spontaneity, extensive indoctrination, and generous state funding to compensate for the lack of experience and training of its new recruits. In Khuzestan, together with the Basij paramilitary force, the Guards staunchly resisted Iraqi offensives, and in joint operations with the regular army managed to push the Iraqis behind the border. On the southwestern front, and especially in the Battle of Khorramshahr in the fall of 1980, the Guards fought valiantly, sustaining massive losses.

By September 1981, the Iranians forced the Iraqis to lift the siege of Abadan, and by December, the Iranian regular army units had pushed back the Iraqi army along the western and northwestern fronts. Fighting pitched battles, by May 1982 Iranian Guards and Basij volunteer units finally recaptured the ruined port of Khorramshahr at huge human cost (see map 16.1). The Battle of Khorramshahr—dubbed "Khunin-shahr" (city of blood), claimed thousands of young Iranian lives. It was a drama of blood and martyrdom that boosted Iranian morale rather than having huge strategic value. The Iraqi retreat behind Khuzestan's borders, and from most other sectors of occupied Iranian territory, was an undeniable victory for Iran. This was despite Iranian military and economic disadvantages, and despite regional and international isolation, a turning point after nearly two years of carnage and destruction. Having recovered its losses, Iran stood at a clear advantage to end the war in its own terms. Yet the war continued for reasons beyond defense of the "Islamic motherland," as Iran labeled it in the Iranian media.

CULTURE OF THE WAR

Stories of bravery and resistance by regular army recruits, purged officers returning to service—some directly from the jails of the Islamic Republic—the

Revolutionary Guards, and Basij volunteers moved millions of their compatriots. The "human waves"—or "cannon fodder" as cynics called it—mostly consisted of young volunteers spearheading counterattacks, or, more accurately, sent off on suicidal missions by Revolutionary Guard commanders and low-ranking clergy who served as the "ideological-devotional" commissars behind the lines (fig. 16.3 and fig. 16.4). With astounding audacity some of the volunteers crossed Iraqi lines and with grenades in hand went under Iraqi tanks. The Islamic regime saw such sacrifice as the edifying fruit of the revolution. War unified the society against a foreign intruder, giving it unprecedented resilience. The siege of Khorramshahr in September and October 1980 was particularly galvanizing. Although Iranian resistance failed and the ruined city fell into Iraqi hands, acts of endurance boosted Iranian morale and heralded eventual victory over the Iraqis.

Young volunteers were mostly a by-product of Iran's demographic revolution that had started in the early 1970s. These were teenagers who at times, despite their parents' wishes, escaped home, buying one-way tickets to the front on the

Figure 16.3 and Figure 16.4. Luring children to the front was one objective
of the state-sponsored cult of martyrdom. The extra push up the hill (*left*) is
symbolic. The message on the wall (*right*) has Khomeini saying, "Our leader is
a twelve-year-old who throws himself under the tank with a grenade in hand."
(*Left*) Kaveh Golestan and Alfred Yaghoubzadeh, *Jang: Do Gozaresh az Jang-e Iran-Iraq*, 1359
(Tehran, 1360/1981) (photographed by Kaveh Golestan). (*Right*) Middle Eastern Posters. Collection,
Box 4, Poster no. 208, Special Collections Research Center, University of Chicago Library.

intercity bus services. Others took their school textbooks with them to the front to study in their spare time. Still others, with the blessing of their family, left for the front as if going on an outdoor excursion, taking with them rugs, bedding, and samovars. Once there, a few received sufficient military equipment or protective clothing. Often they had very little or no training. After each operation, thousands of corpses lay rotting on the parched plains of Khuzestan, amid dust, mud, and heat, some run over by tanks or smashed to pieces by shrapnel.

Those bodies that could be identified and sent back to their families occupied rows of humble graves in overflowing local cemeteries. Every town and village soon had its own martyrs' section (or "flower garden of martyrs," as they were named) with tombstones adorned with framed youthful portraits and heartbreaking epithets. These were recruits of what Khomeini called the Army of the Twenty Million. Tehran's Behesht-e Zahra cemetery, where the largest number of war victims was laid to rest, displayed the state's appropriation of the cult of martyrdom. Red-colored water falling through spouts into large decorative pools, a reminder of the blood of the martyrs, welcomed visitors. These were Iran's sites of memory. On religious holidays the martyrs' section, with its ever-expanding rows of fresh graves, awaited the relatives who came to listen to prayers for the dead and sermons in praise of martyrdom.

Beyond television and radio coverage and military communiqués, frequent encounters with popular symbols of sacrifice reinforced shared sentiments. Hundreds of bridal canopies, known as *hejleh*, were set up wherever a young unmarried war victim lived, often in low-income neighborhoods. A glittering structure of mirrors, lamps, feathers and flowers, often plastic, and parchment with Qur'anic verses and Shi'i martyrdom poetry, these canopies were meant to celebrate the figurative wedding of a fallen warrior, a moving reference to Shi'i lore visualizing the unconsumed wedding of Qasim, the young son of Hasan ibn 'Ali, the Second Imam, who fell in the Battle of Karbala in 680. A whole mournful funerary cult enveloped war martyrdom reflected in posters, films, and propaganda literature (pl. 16.1).

The outpouring of emotions was further aggravated as the war raged bloodier and casualties became more numerous. Visual representations of the war emphasized the recurrence of the suffering of early Shi'i history. Huge makeshift murals in the streets, in public places, and in barracks behind the front lines depicted scenes of Karbala with injured bodies of Hosain ibn 'Ali, his companions, and his loyal double-winged horse Dhul-Janah. Painted in dramatic settings and bright colors, they evoked a cross between popular narrative paintings (carried by dervish storytellers) and the publicity murals made for low-priced movies of the prerevolutionary cinema. Yet in other murals, subtle emphasis was placed on blending the paradigmatic tragedies of the Shi'i past with sacrifices of the present, and at times with a messianic undertones.

A sentimental visual language and iconography was visible in the blooming red tulips and roses that signified the blood of the fallen heroes in the garden of martyrs, a familiar theme in Shi'i mourning imagery. A blazing horizon was reminiscent of the Karbala-like struggle and sacrifices on the model of Hosain, and the green color in warriors' headbands and on their flags hinted at their acquired sacredness. Captions were further reminders of the sacred narrative. One mural showed in the foreground a fallen Hosain ibn 'Ali and his fatally injured horse at the close of the Battle of Karbala on the day of 'Ashura, the most sacred date in the Shi'i calendar. The background showed a modern battlefield as if a scene of the war with Iraq. The caption in Arabic complimented the moving iconography: "All lands are Karbala, all days are 'Ashura" (pl. 16.2).

Another mural, to be repeated on the streets of the capital, showed a luminous holy figure with covered face—presumably Hosain ibn 'Ali—holding to his bosom a young fallen hero in military uniform, a Revolutionary Guard or Basij, no doubt. It was as if the "King of the Martyrs" were offering his blessing to his contemporary emulators, a message underscored by the caption "Martyrdom is an honor inherited from the House of the Prophethood and Guardianship [nubowwat va wilayat] by their followers." Playing on the theme of welayat and its contemporary heir, numerous other murals embedded Khomeini's portrait and cited his sayings in support of the "sacred defense" (pl. 16.3).

Beyond murals, war propaganda elevated martyrdom to a new eschatological plane. To further dramatize the messianic connotation of the "battle of good versus evil," reportedly the warriors in the wake of major counteroffensives were allowed to see on the horizon an apparition of the Mahdi, the Imam of the Age, clad in white and on the back of a white horse. Even if this was a mere wartime myth, its wide reportage by word of mouth implied an implicit desire to elevate the war to a messianic cause, which soon became characteristic of the second stage of the conflict.

A common venue for such sentiments was in martyrs' last testaments (vasiyat-namehs), which appeared in newspapers and propaganda publications of the Islamic Republic. Almost a genre of folk literature, they followed a set pattern, with predictable catchwords, a melodramatic style, and pedestrian syntax. Over the years the frequent publication of these testaments made their content more predictable as if they were produced as a routine obligation. Although they were to be read by members of the author's family, especially mothers and fathers, they frequently addressed the general public, referring to them as Islamic brothers and sisters. That these last testaments were to appear in newspapers or be collected and preserved by authorities added incentive to their production. Mostly written by the Basij recruits in their late teens and early twenties, they imbued innocence but also fascination with the battlefield.

Often written before the volunteers left for the front or while at the front, the authors testified, as was customary, to their belief in God, the Prophet of Islam, and the Qur'an, but they also expressed glowing commitment to the revolution and to the "sacred defense." Almost invariably they saluted Khomeini in exaggerated terms, calling him a prophetlike Imam, light of God and his spirit—the latter a wordplay on Khomeini's first name, Ruhollah. References to his radiant face, his steely willpower, and his mesmerizing words were not uncommon. Invariably, they affirmed faith in Hosain, the Third Imam, as lord of the martyrs. The cult of Hosain was omnipresent. Some authors expressed their gratitude to God, or to Khomeini, for granting them the chance to sacrifice themselves for the cause of Islam while others revered Hosain and the heroic story of Karbala as their inspiration. Preoccupation with blood, sacrifice, and martyrdom was often couched in a crypto-mystical language rife with such catchphrases as wishing to "ascend to the heavens" and "see the divine countenance." The authors begged forgiveness from their parents for often undefined, perhaps uncommitted, sins and thanked them for their selfless labor. They were proud to denounce any material attachment. Absolute obedience to the Imam and to the exalted goals of the revolution was frequent advice offered to fellow warriors and the public. Doing good and trying to be honest and kind were among other counsel. To women, often addressed as "Islamic sisters," the key advice was to live chaste lives and observe the hijab. Saluting the fallen soldiers in the "war of the good against the evil" was also a common assertion, perhaps camouflaging anxieties for the unknown challenges ahead.

THROUGH KARBALA TO QUDS

June 1982 marked the end of the first phase of the war in Iran's favor. Despite political and strategic advantages, however, Iran adamantly refused the offer of a cease-fire set forth by a number of mediators who had Saddam Hussein's blessing. After tens of thousands of lives were lost and many more injured, and at the cost of billions of dollars in material and military losses, the tyrant of the Euphrates had apparently come to his senses. He realized that annexation of Khuzestan, let alone the collapse of the Islamic Republic, was an awful and costly nightmare. The Imam of Jamaran, as Khomeini was labeled by his opponents, turned down the peace offer. From Jamaran (a hamlet on the slopes of the central Alborz in the affluent Shemiran suburb north of the capital), where

Khomeini took residence after his return from Qom to Tehran, he continued exhorting his revolutionary fighters to vanquish the intruding enemy and his satanic backers. He also called on the "slum dwellers" (*kukh-neshinan*) to take their revolutionary reprisal from the "mansion dwellers" (*kakh-neshinan*). The two calls to vanquish the enemy and to take reprisal were intertwined.

Rejecting the cease-fire, Iran's new offensive posture set in motion the second phase of the war. The momentum, driven by general euphoria after pushing back the Iraqis, served as a vehicle for Khomeini to project his revolutionary vision beyond his own country. Operation Ramadan, in July 1982, when tens of thousands of poorly trained and poorly equipped volunteers were sent off to face Iraqi armored units, was an intensification of the "human waves." The casualties were staggering. By February 1983 some two hundred thousand "last reserve" Revolutionary Guards and the Basij descended on Iraqi defenses along a twenty-five-mile stretch on the shore of the Tigris River near 'Amara, thirty-five miles into Iraqi territory. In just one day at least six thousand were killed, though little territory was solidly gained.

By the end of 1983 an estimated 120,000 Iranians and 60,000 Iraqis had been killed in battle, stunning losses for both countries. This was also reflective of the Iranian resolve to push ahead at almost any cost. Iraq's huge advantages included billions of dollars of financial support from conservative Arab states wary of the threat of the Islamic Revolution. Saudi Arabia contributed as much as US$30 billion to Saddam's war chest, while Kuwait and the United Arab Emirates contributed in excess of $8 billion each. The Iraqi army, moreover, received massive military hardware from the United States, France, Britain, and West Germany. The Ba'athist regime enjoyed the general blessing of countries of the Western bloc throughout the war and in contrast to a spirit of belligerence aimed at Iran. A surfeit of financial and military and moral support nevertheless kept the Iraqi positions only barely defensible. By early 1984 Iran had managed to gain the upper hand not merely by fielding greater numbers of troops or superior strategy but also by high morale and sheer sacrifice. Deceived by its momentary successes, however, soon the Iranian leadership, and above all Khomeini, had to face the harsh reality as the Iraqis' revived spirit of resistance countered Iran's repeated offensives inside Iraq. Military and civilian casualties, too, were quickly rising.

As Iran shifted from defense to the offensive, the war had turned bloodier and the carnage heavier. Early in 1984, for the first time Iraqis began deploying chemical weapons against Iranian troops and later against Kurdish Iraqi civilians in the north. The use of mustard gas and nerve gas were flagrant violations of the 1925 Geneva Protocol that prohibited the deployment of chemical and biological weapons. Yet the countries of the Western world did not condemn

Saddam's criminal act outright. In a ludicrous charade, the US administration and its European allies instead pointed their finger of blame toward Iran, if not as a chief culprit, at least as a co-offender of the chemical ban. Both the Reagan administration and Margaret Thatcher's Conservative government surreptitiously facilitated, directly or through a third party, the sale to Iraq of material for production of chemical weapons, including a factory for manufacturing chlorine, the chief ingredient in the production of chemical weapons. Thousands of Iranian soldiers died a painful death or were permanently injured after exposure to poisonous fumes. Though chemical weapons had limited logistical use, their effect on Iranian morale was lasting and helped slowing down troop maneuvers. Gruesome scenes of victims of gas attacks with advanced skin burns, fatal respiratory problems, or total or partial blindness were eerily reminiscent of World War I chemical warfare. Use of deadly gases, however, did not substantially change the Iranians' resolve to abandon its offensive.

Disregard for the use of chemical weapons was an example of the sustained Western bias in favor of Iraq, especially after 1984, and indifference to the fact that Saddam was the aggressor who started the war. As Iranian attacks intensified inside Iraq, so grew Western support for Saddam as a tactical ally against Iran's export of its Islamic revolution. That was despite the Iraqi regime's dark record of human rights abuses, expansionist drive, and near-psychopathic behavior of the men at the top. The warming up in relations with Iraq came at the time when the Ba'athist regime's genocidal campaigns in the operation code name al-Anfal (literally, "spoils" of the war, and more broadly "total decimation of the enemy") had begun. In a prolonged operation that lasted five years, the Iraqi forces demolished thousands of Iraqi villages near the Iranian border and other targeted areas and forcefully removed its Kurdish and Turkmen inhabitants. They resettled Kurdish cities and villages with Arabic-speaking populations and engaged in repeated mass killing of mostly innocent Kurdish villagers. Between 1984 and 1989, al-Anfal cost at least one hundred thousand Iraqi Kurdish and Turkmen lives and the destruction of about four thousand villages, together with their associated institutions, schools, and public amenities. Reminiscent of the Armenian genocide during World War I, though not on the same massive scale, or of Stalin's mass movement of the Chechen and other ethnic populations in the Caucasus to Central Asia and Siberia, at the time, al-Anfal received little attention in the Western media, even in human rights circles.

In March 1988 the Iraqi regime broadened its use of chemical weapons against its own civilian population. The town of Halabja in Iraqi Kurdistan near the Iranian border was the chief target. Using nerve gas as a punitive measure for Kurds' alleged collaboration with the enemy, it resulted in at least four thousand deaths and eight thousand serious injuries of men, women, and children (see map 16.1). Despite all the evidence pointing to the Iraqi crime, the Western media and the US administration raised doubts about the true identity of the perpetrator of that tragedy. Iran's disclaimer throughout the war—that it did not deploy chemical weapons—was treated with deep skepticism, while the menacing silence from Iraq was hardly ever taken as an admission of guilt.

A series of eight offensives throughout 1984 and early 1985 known as wa'l Fajr (meaning "dawn") brought an estimated two hundred thousand Iranian troops, Revolutionary Guards, and volunteers to within a short distance of the Basra-Baghdad road and a covetous distance from the Shi'i holy cities of southern Iraq. In one of the largest operations of the entire war, in early March 1984 a clash of the two armies reportedly left behind twenty-five thousand casualties, with no tangible advantage for the Iranians. They managed to capture parts of the oil fields of the Majnoon Islands, in the marshes of southern Iraq near the head of the Persian Gulf, but Iraqi air and ground defenses retaliated causing heavy Iranian losses (see map 16.1). In another offensive at least five Iranian brigades with a total of fifteen thousand men reportedly perished in the operation. With little advance on either side, both parties were forced to return to their trenches. The war of attrition that continued for another four years brought both armies to a gloomy stalemate: futile operations followed by seemingly unending carnage. Iraq's renewed efforts to negotiate a cease-fire for the second time failed, and in April 1984, Khomeini rejected outright a face-to-face meeting with Saddam.

Even if up to the end of 1984 the Iranian war effort appeared justified on the grounds of defending the homeland and punishing the aggressor, from that point on there was no acceptable rationale for it. The war efforts were primarily motivated by Khomeini's wish to uproot the Ba'athist regime altogether. The hard-liners in his circle fully abided by that objective, at least until 1987, as if they, too, were expecting a miracle that would bring down Saddam, similar to that which earlier had toppled the Pahlavi ruler. By late 1984 there was virtually no viable ground for Iran to prolong the war—strategically, politically, or morally—except Khomeini's call to "liberate" the heartland of Shi'ism from the yoke of the "godless" Ba'athists. His messianic vision perhaps called for advancing to the lands beyond in the hopes of liberating the Quds, as the Holy Land is known to Muslims, from Zionist occupation. Though never part of the official Iranian war objectives or war propaganda, the longing for such a move was in the air. Numerous war murals, posters, and signposts along the front read "Through Karbala to Quds."

The Iranian refusal to negotiate came despite a casual offer of Saddam's Arab backers—Kuwait, Saudi Arabia, and the United Arab Emirates—to pay Iran a hefty war indemnity, which in effect was an admission of Iraqi guilt. Even though the offer was never solid enough, the climate was decidedly in Iran's favor to press for monetary reparations and boundary amendments. Yet from Khomeini's perspective, and that of his advisers, so much was invested in the war that it was formidable, if not impossible, for Iran to accept even a favorable cease-fire. The blood of martyrs, lofty Islamic ideals, and material destruction of a large portion of the southwest were but one concern. Anti-Saddam propaganda—he was the "Minor Satan" in the service of the Great Satan—was another.

In Khomeini's eyes, the odds were greatly in favor of his revolutionary crusade, and the prospect of victory for his "dear Islam" was high. To him, annihilation of the Iraqi regime, despite numerous setbacks, was an unavoidable task to be fulfilled, even at the cost of tens of thousands of casualties and further material losses. In his narrative, the unfolding destiny of the Islamic Revolution had anticipated such a miracle. The whole process over the previous five years from his hermetic seclusion in Najaf to the suburbs of Paris, his triumphant return to Iran, the collapse of the mighty Pahlavi regime and the shah's pitiful demise in exile, the apparent despair of the Great Satan throughout the hostage crisis, the crushing of his numerous opponents at home, and successful deflecting of Iraqi aggression—all were chapters of a sacred drama. The end game, therefore, could not have been an inconclusive peace with the enemy; rather, it was the capture of the holy Shiʻi sites of Karbala, Kufa, and Najaf, where the mytho-historical narrative of Shiʻism was first conceived. With the Iranian forces in early 1984 within tantalizing distance of these cities, what was the worth of human lives in order to vanquish a satanic enemy, even if superpowers stood behind it?

Even as late as March 19, 1987, more then six years into the war, when Iranian forces launched operation waʼl-Fajr 10, with no decisive results, Khomeini, in his message to the commander of the Revolutionary Guards, still called for further sacrifice. "With the blessing of God almighty and support of his great messenger" he saluted his "resilient and sacrificing nation and the valiant warriors of Islam for their great and thunderous victory":

> For sure this divine gift . . . is the fulfillment of the [Qurʼanic verse] "support God and God supports you and solidifies your pace." This is the outcome of the unique resistance of this great nation against [Saddam's] cowardly onslaughts and his bombing of the [Iranian] cities. The news of the epic victories of the Islamic warriors not only cheered the hearts of our people, but those of all disinherited and deprived. It also grieved Saddam . . . and his protectors and masters, especially America and Israel.

Saluting the people of the liberated Iraqi cities, no doubt a reference to Halabja, Khomeini urged them to see "how insanely Saddam targeted you and

your cities with chemical and cluster bombs and witness how the world devouring [powers] in their poisonous propaganda ignored our great victories and
overlooked the crimes of Saddam's armies." He then urged the "gallant youth of
the proud Islamic land of Iran to rush to the fronts" and "suffocate the defeated
and desperate" forces of Saddam.[1]

THE UNITED STATES AND THE FORTUNES OF WAR

Despite Khomeini's lofty wishes, the fate of the war shifted once more in favor
of Iraq. In the third and final stage of the war, between 1985 and 1988, Saddam
began for the first time since 1982 a new offensive in which he was not alone.
He continued to receive generous funding from the oil-rich countries of the
Persian Gulf as well as Western powers and the Soviet bloc. The Soviet Union,
Iraq's chief supplier in the past, initially observed an arms embargo, perhaps in
the hope of encouraging Iran's neutrality, if not cooperation, in its increasingly
troubled occupation of Afghanistan and with an eye toward Tudeh support for
the Iranian regime. From 1986, however, the Soviets were back in business supplying their old Iraqi ally. The Iraqi forces, regrouped and refurbished, began
firing their Soviet-made Scud missiles with horrifying frequency at Iranian cities, and Iranians retaliated in kind, with the North Korean version of Scuds,
though theirs were far fewer in numbers. It was a bitter irony that both sides
were using Soviet and American weaponry against each other with no ideological tag attached to the hardware and no scruples on the side of the suppliers.

In what came to be known as the "War of the Cities," thousands were killed
on both sides, and tens of thousands turned into internally displaced refugees
(see map 16.1). With Mirage fighter-bombers purchased from France, Iraqis
could reach targets deep inside Iran, and American-made combat helicopters
offered them visual advantage on the battlefield. In an increasingly vicious war,
both sides had little compunction about harming civilians. In the course of the
war, the Iraqis fired more than three hundred Scud and other missiles on urban
targets in Iran, and Iranians retaliated with more than seventy. The exchange
of missiles had limited military significance, but its psychological impact on
the general public was substantial. For the first time since the early days of the
war, ordinary people felt that the war was no longer an affair fought off in the
distance but a tangible reality.

Iranians began frantically searching for arms to purchase, not only on the
treacherous black market at outrageous prices but also through state suppliers
ranging from China, North Korea, and Libya (which sold them Scud missiles
purchased from the Soviet Union) to backdoor deals with the United States

and its allies, including Israel, for spare parts and antitank weapons. Though much smaller in scale and effectiveness, the Israeli and American weapon consignments that came through Israel, with the approval of the Reagan administration, or directly through CIA channels, as it turned out, had a scandalous fallout. Israel's motive was simple. It viewed Saddam's victory a cause for Arab solidarity and with Saddam at the helm. Given that the Palestinian leadership under Yasser Arafat had shifted sides, from praise for Khomeini in the early days of the revolution to praise for Saddam during the later stages of the war, such a security concern hit closer to home. It is hard, moreover, not to detect in Israel's move a desire to see both sides—Iraq and Iran—militarily exhausted and bankrupt.

The US record of support for Saddam's war efforts, however, was far more problematic. It was probably among the most appalling in the history of American aid to villainous dictators. While the hostage crisis was still going on, the Carter administration hinted at thawing diplomatic relations with Iraq, a reversal of a policy that for years had treated the Ba'athists as pariahs. At the outset this seemed a plausible course to counterbalance Iranian success while returning Iran's anti-Americanism in kind. Yet US support for Ba'athists did not stop at the level of diplomacy. Though the Reagan administration had declared neutrality in the Iraq-Iran War, soon it relapsed into a proactive course, especially after 1984, when the US government began to view Iran's advances detrimental to American interests in the region. US assistance to Iraq ranged from the direct and indirect sale of weapons and export of raw materials for manufacturing chemical and biological weapons to extensive sharing of military intelligence, CIA and Pentagon operational support on the battlefield, training of Iraqi military personnel, and vast sums of credit for Iraqi purchases of weapons, agricultural needs, and other necessities, as well as tacit or explicit backing for Iraq in the United Nations and other international forums.

Fearing the collapse of the Iraqi regime, late in 1983 and again in March 1984, two delegations headed by then US special envoy to the Middle East, Donald Rumsfeld, visited Baghdad to normalize relations and offer help in Iraq's war efforts. The warming of relations began just at the time when Iraq was extensively using mustard gas and nerve gas against Iranian troops. Iraq's "struggle for survival," as Washington expressed it, soon gave rise to officers from the US Defense Intelligence Agency making available to the Iraqis satellite and airborne early warning and control (AWACS) intelligence on Iran's troop movements as well as helping directly with military operations. The US personnel in effect helped plan and execute the war on a daily basis and advised Iraqi air attacks and shelling Iranian targets. Assistance from the United States proved essential in destroying much of the Iranian military, which had been built so painstakingly by the shah with US hardware and technical support. Anxiety over the potential fall of the Iraqi regime went so far as to persuade the United States to bring Iraqi personnel to Fort Bragg in North Carolina, where, among taking other courses, they were trained in insurgency tactics in the event of an Iranian victory.

Most controversial was the US role in facilitating Iraq's chemical and biological weapon programs. It has been reported that at least seventy shipments of US raw materials for manufacture of chemical and biological weapons were sent to Iraq between 1984 and 1987. This was in addition to the sale of the same materials from German and British private and government sources. It is difficult to determine how much the US matériel went toward the actual manufacture of Iraqi chemical weapons, but there is little doubt that the United States deemed it unavoidable that the banned weapons be used against Iranian troops. In March 1984 the US delegation to the United Nations even went so far as to collude with Iraq in defeating an Iranian resolution in the Security Council that condemned Iraq's use of chemical weapons on the battlefield. Later, in the wake of the Halabja mass killing in 1988, the Reagan administration woefully pointed the finger of suspicion at Iran, presumably knowing full well the extent of Saddam's al-Anfal operation and his vengeance toward the Kurdish population.

Later in the course of the conflict, the United States also played a pivotal role in the so-called Tanker War of 1984–1988, aimed to escort Kuwaiti (and later Saudi and Iraqi) vessels under the US flag to protect them against Iranian amphibian attacks in the Persian Gulf. The internationally accepted pretext of keeping the shipping lanes open, and hence the supply of oil through the Strait of Hormuz uninterrupted, had the intended effect of providing Iraq and its regional allies with a revenue stream from the sale of their oil for the duration of the conflict while the revived Iraqi air force, with the aid of the Americans and their allies, repeatedly pummeled Iranian oil export terminals on Kharg Island. Even US outrage over the Iraqi bombing of the USS *Stark* in May 17, 1987, which resulted in the loss of thirty-seven American sailors, was contained once Iraq lodged a formal apology admitting its error.

By April 1988 US support for Saddam had effectively changed the fortune of the war in favor of Iraq and brought it closer to an end. Had it not been for the United States and its European allies, it may be argued, the war probably would have ended in 1984 or 1985 with a serious weakening, or possibly collapse, of the Ba'athist regime. The United States' national interests to some degree may have vindicated a balancing in the critical struggle between an expansionist and a revolutionary regime with an avowed anti-American ideological bent. Yet by no stretch of realpolitik can one vindicate the US condoning of Iraq's use of chemical weapons or coordinating of a counteroffensive by a belligerent maverick whose hands were red with the blood of his own people.

Realistic casualty figures for the eight-year war period are difficult to come by. By early 1988 the estimated war casualties had reached at least 300,000 dead on the Iranian side and 250,000 on the Iraqi side. Hundreds of thousands more were injured and disabled in what came to be probably the longest war of the twentieth century and one of the most ferocious. Exhausted, demoralized, and internationally isolated, Iran slowly came to realize that it no longer could sustain high casualties and the huge economic costs of the war without the risk of renewed internal dissent. Iraqi missile attacks on Iranian cities added to the public distress, especially when combined with the loss of oil revenue, growing numbers of internal refugees, and troop exhaustion. Equally grave was the possibility of a serious confrontation with the United States in the Persian Gulf once the Tanker War had escalated by early 1988. If not Khomeini himself, some of his advisers in charge of the war, most significantly Rafsanjani, came to realize the long-term dangers of engaging a superpower.

The downing of an Iran Air passenger Airbus on July 3, 1988, by the USS *Vincennes*, a guided missile cruiser, resulting in the loss of 290 civilian lives, was an ominous sign. The incident presumably was caused by the US cruiser mistaking the passenger airliner as an approaching Iranian fighter jet, a questionable judgment, perhaps, given Iran's poor air force capabilities at the time and the USS *Vincennes*'s advanced radar and intelligence equipment. The incident, Iran's first and only direct military engagement with the United States, reflected the growing tension that had built up between the two countries ever since the hostage crisis. The United States barely expressed regret for the incident, blaming it on the roguery of the Iran Air pilot. Eight years later, when the United States agreed to pay only minimal reparations to the victims' relatives, this was interpreted as a further mark of the United States trying to humiliate Iran.

On July 20, 1988, shortly after the downing of its aircraft, Iran finally accepted the UN Security Council Resolution 598, initially adopted in July 20, 1987, calling for an end to hostilities between Iraq and Iran and the withdrawal of all forces to "internationally recognized boundaries without delay." Although the resolution requested the UN secretary-general to explore "the question of entrusting an impartial body with inquiring into responsibilities for the conflict," and although it deplored in strongest terms "heavy loss of human life and material destruction," it did not call for any form of war reparation or condemnation of the belligerent party. It went only as far as expressing conviction that "a comprehensive, just, honorable and durable settlement should be achieved between Iran and Iraq." One of the decisions attached to the text of the resolution also expressed deep dismay based on the "unanimous conclusion of the specialists that there has been repeated use of chemical weapons against Iranian forces by Iraqi forces," and that "civilians in Iran also have been injured by chemical weapons, and that Iraqi military personnel have sustained injuries from chemical warfare agents."[2]

By August 20, 1988, although both countries observed a cease-fire on all fronts, Iraq refused to evacuate from the frontier territories it had captured in the last years of the war. That was in clear breach of the resolution's call upon both parties to "withdraw all forces to the internationally recognized boundaries without delay." Other articles of the resolution such as a call on both sides for the release of all prisoners of war, and the demand that the UN secretary-general facilitate a lasting settlement between the countries, remained unaddressed. As it turned out, the Iraqi regime did not abide by any of the additional terms of the resolution. By 1988 Iran's international isolation, its loss of any strategic advantage over Iraq in the battlefield, and its inaptitude to effectively argue its case, compelled it to accept the cease-fire from a position of weakness and without any explicit UN recognition of Iraq's belligerence.

In a rare admission of remorse, Khomeini declared that he had succumbed to the cease-fire as if drinking a "chalice of poison" (*jam-e zahr*), a tantalizing reference perhaps to Socrates's death when condemned by the Athenian court. Coming from a man who was once a teacher of philosophy in Qom with a passion for Greek philosophers, the phrase contained oblique nuances. Accepting the cease-fire was an admission of humiliating defeat while defying, as did the Greek philosopher, the morality of "might makes right." The sum total of eight years of suffering and carnage for Iran was not only the loss of territory to Iraq along its western border but also, more important, succumbing to a cease-fire with an Iraqi tyrant who won the war with the military backing of a superpower. His decision, Khomeini stressed, was in consultation with his trusted advisers, and that he took into account the best interest of the country and the revolution. "By God," he went on to say:

> If it was not because of concerns for all of our credibility, honor and expediency for the cause of Islam and the Muslims, I would have never condoned to this act since death and martyrdom is sweeter to me. But what alternative do we have but to abide by the divine will? No doubt our heroic and valiant nation has and will abide by it. . . . In future some individuals may intentionally or unintentionally raise doubt as to the fruit of all the blood and sacrifice. They obviously are unaware of the invisible worlds [of the hereafter] and of

the philosophy of martyrdom. . . . Beyond doubt the blood of the martyrs is insurance for revolution and Islam. . . . Blessed you the nation! Blessed you women and men! Blessed you the martyrs and the captives, those who are lost in action, and families of the glorious martyrs! And woe on me for being still alive drinking the poisonous callous of this resolution. I feel humbled before all the sacrifice and glory of this great nation.[3]

Yet no amount of verbiage, sophistry, and emotional manipulation could conceal the magnitude of the disaster for which the guardian jurist of the Islamic Republic was largely responsible.

Over a longer historical span, the Iran-Iraq War can be seen as a clash of two ideologies, both manifestations of an evolving modern Middle East. Saddam's Ba'athism had all the symptoms of an extreme state-based pan-Arabism rooted in the post–World War I territorial settlements, unfulfilled national aspirations, volatility within the Iraqi polity, tensions with the Shi'i and the Kurdish communities of Iraq, and conflict with the neighboring Iran. The Islamic Revolution, by contrast, was based on a revolutionary ideology, a later phase of a new Islam that rejected, at least on the surface, the secular model of nationalism that for more than a century had transformed the region. On the Iranian side, these revolutionary sentiments were deeply ingrained with patriotic feelings, reaffirming a national identity within its historical boundaries. Once these sentiments acquired an invasive posture, however, outside traditional Iranian borders, beyond Zagros and into the Mesopotamian lowlands, they proved ineffective, despite the shared Shi'i religious heritage of the two countries. As in the past such ambitions under the Islamic Republic did not, and perhaps could not, bear any fruit.

Ethnic loyalties and collective memories played their parts in the Iraq-Iran conflict, but what really fueled the war and enabled both sides to fight long and hard was the availability of economic resources generated in the main by oil revenues, despite the damages to both countries' oil installations. Both regimes were able to quell the opposition and tighten their monopoly of power. In effect, the world's energy needs, and the ensuing strategic concerns of Western powers, facilitated intervention in the conflict, albeit covertly. Interventions in the conflict secured, first and foremost, the flow of oil through the Persian Gulf, but also aimed to maintain the upper hand in the region against a potential Soviet threat, especially after the Soviet occupation of Afghanistan. Yet the war did not settle the main territorial issue that contributed to the prolonged conflict. Sovereignty over Shatt al-Arab remained unresolved at least officially. The humiliating end to the war, moreover, did not bring down the

Iranian regime or even sap the revolutionary zeal of its leadership. In part, this can be explained by an effective purge of Iran's political dissent throughout the war and after. Though never reaching the scale and ferocity of the police state in Saddam's Iraq, silencing domestic opposition in Iran under the pretext of security and war priorities secured the regime enough synergy to last even after the demeaning final settlement. War, in effect, vastly helped the Islamic Republic consolidate its military, propaganda and policing apparatuses, close constitutional loopholes, and increase ideological and economic control over society. In this respect, although the war was a net defeat with huge casualties, material ruination, and temporary territorial loss, it was a "blessing" in disguise, as was repeatedly acknowledged by the regime's clerical leadership. Irrespective of what the regime claimed as its popular mandate, the experience of the war and memories of sacrifice, life in the trenches, bombing of the cities, rationing, and economic hardship were all ingredients for a trial by fire that contributed to shaping postrevolutionary Iran.

On the Iraqi side the Ba'athist euphoria ended soon in a new disaster. As it turned out, soon after Saddam's armies paraded under the Qadisiya victory arch, built in a gruesome design using helmets of perished Iranian troops as decoration, and shortly after he was hailed by the press in the Arab world as a hero, his expansionist ambitions brought about another adventure. Iraq's invasion of Kuwait in August 1990, on another territorial pretext, may in part be attributed to the six years of US fraternization with Saddam and accommodation of his ambitions. Even a few weeks before Saddam's onslaught against Kuwait—his financial backer during the war with Iran—he still received indecisive messages from the US State Department, which may well have persuaded him to imagine that this time his adventure would be trouble-free.

AVENGING DEFEAT AT HOME

The eighty-six-year-old Imam of the Revolution's admitting of even a relative defeat did not come without terrible retaliation against his domestic opponents, real or potential. Unforeseen developments during the last days of the war deepened the regime's fears of renewed discontent, public unrest, and armed rebellion. The humiliating end to the war added an almost psychopathic urgency for another round of purges. A sequence of events taking place in less than a year between the cease-fire in July 1988 and Khomeini's death in June 1989 offers a clue to his motivation, if not a rationale. The systematic execution in secret of at least 4,500 political prisoners through the latter part of 1988 was one manifestation of the regime's insecurity and its unexhausted reservoirs of violence.

Four days after Iran accepted the cease-fire, on July 26, 1988, an estimated force of seven thousand Mojahedin Khalq equipped with heavy weaponry by the Iraqis and based inside Iraq made a surprise attack fifty miles into the western Iranian province of Kermanshahan. Backed by Iraqi air and logistical support, the Mojahedin operation, named Forugh-e Javidan (Eternal glory), was meant to liberate Iran from its clerical regime. After a crushing setback in 1982 and a respite in France, the Mojahedin leadership and their loyal comrades-in-arms took refuge in Saddam's Iraq and settled in a military base they called Camp Ashraf 67 miles north of Baghdad and 110 miles west of the Iranian frontier. By doing so, the desperate Mojahedin turned into Saddam's pawn, a fifth column of sorts that justified collaboration through a culture of indoctrination and iron-fisted conformity. Hoping to gain further advantage from the Iranian regime while it was down, Saddam let the Mojahedin launch their attack on Iranian soil just after the cease-fire came into effect.

The Mojahedin operation, however, proved neither eternal nor glorious. It went terribly wrong. Under international pressure, Saddam was soon obligated to withdraw air cover, exposing the Mojahedin to Iranian fighter jets and soon to the Revolutionary Guards' airborne units landing behind their lines. Cut off from their base and with limited firepower, the inexperienced Mojahedin force was completely routed four days after their initial assault. At least two thousand Mojahedin were killed in action, and reportedly more than four hundred Iranian troops and Guards perished. To the limited extent that the Mojahedin advanced inside Iran, the civilian population did not receive them as liberators. Nor would they have been accorded a warm reception given the extensive damage they had inflicted on Shahabad Gharb (now Islamabad Gharb), the only town they occupied on the Iranian western border. The remnants of the Mojahedin and those who managed to flee back to the Iraqi camp suffered the defeat with pitiful complacency.

Irrespective of their defeat, the thrust of the regime's anti-Mojahedin grudge had already resurfaced in mass executions inside the Islamic Republic's prisons. On July 19, 1988, on the eve of the cease-fire, and four days before the start of the Mojahedin's operation, Khomeini issued a fatwa-like executive order declaring members of the People's Mojahedin already in prisons of the Islamic Republic to be "active combatants (against Islam; i.e., *mohareb*) and [thus] condemnable to death." He justified this extraordinary ruling on the grounds that the "hypocrites" were not believers in Islam, had committed apostasy (*ertedad*), had actively engaged in a "classic war" along Iranian frontiers, had collaborated with the Ba'athist regime and spied for them against "our Islamic nation," and were in contact with the "universal arrogance" (*estekbar-e jahani*), a reference to the United States and its allies. Despite the shari'a-sounding rationale, Khomeini's instructions were aimed not at the combatants in the battlefields but at the thousands of political prisoners he stigmatized in his executive order as those "insisting on their hypocrisy." The Qur'anic reference to hypocrites (*monafeqin*) was a convenient shortcut to a vengeful mass killing.[4]

Khomeini's ruling, which must have been in the making for a while, was only reaffirmed by the Mojahedins' action and gave the Khomeinist hard-liners an ideal excuse to empty the prisons of thousands of victims. Immediately, a three-men clerical tribunal appointed by Khomeini and aided by some of his most trusted henchmen meticulously went through the roster of Evin and other prisons and detention centers in Tehran and the provinces, selecting and segregating thousands of "suspects," both men and women. They were individually brought before a tribunal to answer a set of questions, and though this action appeared to be consistent with the Islamic law of apostasy, it was in fact a sinister ploy to remove almost any chance of acquittal for the victims.

Many of the suspects, teenagers or in their early twenties, had been arrested years earlier and had already been tried and given prison sentences. They were originally accused of such crimes as being members of the Mojahedin and Fada'iyan, distributing their tracts, attending demonstrations, "sympathizing" with the left, and other charges entirely inconsistent with the charge of apostasy, or actively warring against Islam or collaboration with enemy. Even some of the most ardent "repentants" (*tawwabin*) who were "reeducated" in prison and actively practicing Islamic rituals under the watchful eyes of the prisons' "ideological-religious commissars" or inmates who had completed their terms or were near completion, were not spared.

Unaware of why they were brought before the tribunal or unaware of the charges, the defendants had to confirm or deny belief in Islam; whether they were practicing Muslims; if they were prepared to reveal the identity of other "hypocrites," sympathizers, and false repentants; if they were willing to go before television cameras to repent; and if they were prepared to fight on the front and pass over minefields. After the first or the second question, usually, the tribunal passed its judgment. Victims were then asked to write their last will and immediately were sent off in groups of six to the gallows. In compliance with Islamic law, in most cases the victims were hanged so that they would suffer a slow death, rather than going before a firing squad.

Most victims were the Mojahedin and their sympathizers, followed by the Fada'iyan, the Tudeh, Paykar, and other leftist parties. Female members of the Mojahedin and other parties were forced to repent, severely beaten, received a lashing, and were kept in solitary confinement. A few were executed or died under torture. In the nearly six months between July and December 1988, executions went on around the clock and almost in total secrecy. The regime's denial of any executions was only occasionally countered by the pleas of anxious but terrified families, who were banned even from gathering before the prison gates. Bodies of the victims were not returned to their relatives, contrary to usual practice in the Islamic Republic of returning slaughtered bodies in exchange for the price of bullets. Those executed in the Evin prison were dumped in secrecy in mass graves in an undisclosed location in the vicinity of the capital. The location of the graves, which the regime dubbed "Kofrabad" (abode of infidelity) and "La'nat-abad" (abode of damnation), were revealed to the families only a year later. They were permitted to visit the ramshackle site only if they observed a total ban on memorial gatherings of any sort. In the cemetery in southwestern Tehran, later known as Khavaran, the mass graves of the 1988 victims were shared with graves of the Baha'is, the other "infidels" of the Islamic Republic. Even as late as 2009 the regime's anxieties were not entirely abated; Khavaran was bulldozed so as to remove even the makeshift marks made by the families of the dead. These were Iran's other sites of memory, unmarked and unattended.

The executions elicited virtually no criticism within the regime's inner circles except for one important exception, Ayatollah Hosain-'Ali Montazeri. And he paid dearly for raising his voice. The majority of high-ranking mullahs and their associates who were aware of the mass killings, or came to know of them in the following months, were either in favor of this atrocity or did not dare to raise an objection. The rotating membership of the "Death Committee," as the three-man tribunal came to be known, included some of the most notorious revolutionary judges and perpetrators of political crimes in the Islamic Republic. Their verdicts, grounded in a meticulous reading of Khomeini's directive, revealed a culture of brutality at odds with the idealized image of Khomeini as the kindhearted father of the revolution. Like the massacre of the Banu-Qurayza in seventh-century Medina, which Khomeini was fond of recalling as a model for dealing with charges of treason, the judges saw no grounds for mercy or fairness.

BAHA'IS AS THE OTHER

Aside from political opponents, the Islamic Republic, and more specifically its anti-Baha'i activists, continued to harass and persecute Baha'is. In the months following the victory of the revolution, other non-Muslim communities — Jews, Armenians, and Zoroastrians, as well as Sunni Muslims, Sufis, the

Ahl-e Haqq, and Shaykhis—did not remain untouched by the new regime's rigorous segregationist policies. Non-Muslims were banned from government employment, their community school curricula were Islamicized, community activities controlled, and for a while Jews were banned from traveling abroad. The thrust of this systematic persecution, however, was directed against the "devious sect" (*ferqeh-e zalleh*), a familiar euphemistic label for the Baha'is.

The renewed persecution was a culmination of anti-Baha'i sentiments common to Iranian society since the very inception of the new faith in the mid-nineteenth century. In the first decade of the Islamic Republic, more than two hundred Baha'i women and men were executed, not only elected members of Baha'i national and local administrative bodies but ordinary Baha'is in towns and villages around the country. They were executed merely for being Baha'i. Others were abducted and killed in secret. 'Ali-Morad Davudi (1922–1979), a professor of philosophy at Tehran University and a Cartesian of some repute, was abducted and killed in November 1979 after he penned a succinct response to anti-Baha'i smears. Manuchehr Hakim (1910–1981), a professor of medicine at Tehran University and a pioneer of free medical clinics, was attacked and slaughtered in his office. Among those executed between February 1980 and June 1981 either by order of the revolutionary courts or without any court proceedings were Zhinus Mahmudi (1925–1981), dean of Iran's School of Meteorology; her husband, Hushang Mahmudi, a well-known TV personality of children's programs; and a number of lawyers, physicians, career engineers and contractors, army officers, as well as homemakers.

Among numerous executions ordered by the revolutionary courts was the case of the Baha'i women of Shiraz. In June 1983 ten Baha'i woman in that city, mostly in their twenties, were arrested on the charge of teaching principles of their faith to Baha'i children in Friday classes held in houses of the Baha'is. They were summarily tried, and despite excessive pressure, they refused to repent their faith. They were condemned of being "agents of the Zionists entity" and executed. Before execution some were reportedly raped in prison on the grounds that the Shi'i shari'a requires, as the revolutionary judge interpreted it, that virgins be "deflowered" before execution so as to prevent their salvation in the hereafter. The head of the Shiraz revolutionary court, a certain Hujjat al-Islam Qaza'i, later implied in a newspaper interview that he condemned to death twenty-two Baha'i women and men because they remained steadfast in their faith. He threatened that all deviant Baha'is must repent if they wish to avoid Muslim's "religious obligation" to destroy all infidels.

Altogether in the first decade of the Islamic Republic upward of two hundred Baha'is were executed and thousands more in urban and rural communities throughout Iran were imprisoned and tortured. Tens of thousands were harassed, looted, purged from government posts, barred from universities, had their livelihoods confiscated by the revolutionary courts, were forced to repent their faith under duress, lost their retirement pensions, or were forced out of their towns and villages. As the largest non-Muslim community in Iran, Baha'is had a remarkable nationwide geographical and class distribution that included villagers (some established at the inception of the Babi movement in remote regions), residents of small towns and working classes in large cities, teachers, bureaucrats, small business owners, as well as professionals and members of the affluent middle classes.

The Islamic Revolution had been a major blow to the community as a whole. While many, including most affluent Baha'is, soon emigrated to Europe and North America, others, mostly lower-income Baha'is, stayed behind only to face increasing restrictions and humiliation. Vile anti-Baha'i campaigns in the press and media, lies and fabrications in history textbooks, and economic loss and general social demotion were accompanied by losses of educational opportunities for the younger generations. The unaccredited Baha'i Institute of Higher Education in Tehran, a semiclandestine institution but effective in countering the official ban on higher education for Baha'is, faced repeated onslaughts by security forces. Bans on Baha'i administration, public gatherings, and publications, as well as the destruction of Baha'i cemeteries all over Iran and the confiscation, desecration, and demolition of sacred and historic Baha'i sites, among them, the best-preserved examples of Qajar domestic architecture, all became everyday facts of life. These actions represented a program of intolerance and intimidation aimed at suffocating to extinction a community considered by the Islamic Republic heretical and treasonous. Despite all pressures, few among the Iranian Baha'is denied their religious identity.

Baha'is did not present a political threat to the Islamic Republic. Yet they were increasingly perceived as a potent internal enemy, especially when other political contenders had been effectively quashed. Accusations against them followed a historical pattern. Whereas in earlier times the charges were mostly of heresy and apostasy, by the mid-twentieth century the accusations had become exceedingly political and conspiratorial. In earlier times the old charge of sexual revelry, especially clandestine sexual transgressions (*abaha*), was leveled against them. This was a smear as old as the history of persecuted Jewish, Christian, and Manichaean minorities in ancient times. Even early Islamic societies accused nonconformists of forbidden sexual transgressions. Popularized relics of such smears found a new lease on life in the fertile imagination of the anti-Baha'i polemicists. Yet even the charge of immorality gradually faded, giving way to charges of disloyalty, spying, and treason.

Political allegations were the by-product of a climate of paranoid fears and conspiracy theories, an obsession with the hidden hand of European colonialism. In this representation, Baha'is were viewed as puppets of a sinister Western power whose identity kept evolving with time. One prevalent narrative originating in the 1930s was presented in the form of a fraudulent "memoir" of a Russian diplomat, Prince Dolgrouki, a composite figure of a sort, attributing the "creation" of the Baha'i "pseudoreligion" to Russian imperial ambitions in the nineteenth century. Later, however, the same narrative was amended by a new epilogue in which the Russian imperialists, once they no longer had a use for the Baha'is, generously handed over control of them to British colonialists. Given the potency of British "hidden hands" in the Iranian popular imagination, such a charge carried grave consequences throughout the 1950s and 1960s. Yet the evolutionary mutation in the life of this deception did not end with the British. In the 1960s Baha'is were further accused of being not merely "British lackeys" but simultaneously agents in the service of US imperialism and the CIA, and soon after, coinciding with the Islamic Revolution and the rise of anti-Zionist sentiments, as agents and spies of world Zionism.

The latter allegation brought many Baha'is, men and women, before the revolutionary courts even in remote towns and villages of Iran and led to numerous executions and long-term imprisonment during the first decade of the revolution and later. That the Baha'i world center and Baha'i sacred sites were located in Haifa and 'Akka, in today's Israel, itself the outcome of a long-term banishment of Baha'ullah (founder of the Baha'i faith) to Ottoman Palestine seven decades before the creation of the state of Israel, was more than sufficient proof in the eyes of its accusers of Baha'i complicity in a British-American-Zionist collusion. Somehow they were all instruments of the sinister "colonialists" and agents of a global ploy hatched by "universal arrogance" to destroy the Islamic Republic and Islam as a whole.

If further proof was needed, the accusers could always resort to the record of the Baha'i leader, Mirza 'Abbas Nuri, better known as 'Abdul-Baha, who in 1921 accepted British knighthood presumably for his peaceful efforts toward the success of Allied operation in Palestine following the collapse of the Young Turks regime and the end to their atrocities in Syria and Palestine. In the eyes of the Islamic Republic, this was tantamount to Baha'i subservience to British imperialism and later to the "Zionist entity," as Israel was referred to in the Islamic Republic.

The Baha'i experience in the Pahlavi era exposed the community's own shortcomings to communicate more effectively with Iranian society at large. Throughout the postconstitutional period and into the early Pahlavi era, a sector of the urban Baha'is excelled in socioeconomic terms in part because of decreased harassment and discriminations. They also advanced because they were welcomed into a benign partnership in the early Pahlavi project of modernity and were part of its flourishing middle classes. Yet with time, the Baha'is gradually lost much of their appeal as harbingers of religious modernity. Relative prosperity brought social isolation from society at large. Success, empowered by education and capital, widened the gulf between Baha'is and traditional Muslim sectors and sharpened differences with Islamic opponents. Both the clergy and anti-Baha'i activists, such as the Hojjatiyeh Society, bemoaned the Baha'is' acquired freedoms to preach their message, limited though they were. In effect, their enemies viewed Baha'is as a new challenge to Islamic superiority. The Hojjatiyeh Society, perhaps the largest Islamic organization before the revolution, was almost solely devoted to anti-Baha'i activities.

Yet heated engagements with Islamic clergy and lay activists over arcane points of theology and acrobatics of messianic prophecies not surprisingly made the Baha'i message stagnant and their approach outmoded and intellectually timid. Because the Baha'is maintained a doctrine of political noninterference, a relic of the nineteenth century, they were unfairly suspected as complaisant, even collaborating with the Pahlavi regime. By the mid-1970s, like any other isolated minority under a repressive regime, the Baha'is were accused of monopolizing "key positions" in the Pahlavi regime. The premier Amir 'Abbas Hovayda, in particular, was rumored to be a Baha'i only because at some stage in the distant past his father, an Iranian diplomat, was a member of the Baha'i community, though he later withdrew from it altogether. Baha'is were accused of pulling the strings, running the Savak and torturing its victims, monopolizing wealth and privilege through their intimate connections with sources of power, and liaising in dirty deals with the British intelligence services, the CIA, and the Israelis. Venomous rumors such as these thrived in the late Pahlavi era while Baha'is carefully tried to stay away from the raging flames of the revolutionary movement. Under the Islamic Republic these rumors were quickly upgraded to unquestionable facts and turned into evidence for charges of treason and conspiracy.

Deeper than doctrinal differences or conspiratorial obsessions, however, antagonism toward the Baha'i was representative of a shared heritage not only among Islamists but also among many intellectuals on the left, academics, and the public at large. The search for an enemy within, on whose shoulder could be placed all the faults of the past and fears for the future, was an exercise in self-indulgence familiar to cultures of victimization. The Baha'is were cohesive and resilient but increasingly introverted. Standing their ground and refusing to doctrinally assimilate made them a target of suspicion and animosity. If the revolutionary regime in its quixotic battle could no longer defeat the Great Satan, it could harass a vulnerable enemy within.

DEAL WITH THE GREAT SATAN

Revelations in November 1986 concerning an Iranian arms deal with the United States, using Israel as an intermediary, triggered a full-scale political scandal between August 1985 and March 1987 in Washington, known as the Iran-Contra Affair, with serious repercussions for the Reagan administration. The course of events that shaped the affair exhibited how the United States, despite a history of rancorous relations with Iran, was prepared to engage Iran by supplying it with arms and spare parts, albeit for its own covert operation. Even more troubling was the fact that despite the Islamic Republic's public denouncement of Israel, it had no compunction in using Israel as intermediary in the arms deal, all the while persecuting Baha'is in towns and villages of Iran on charges of espionage for the Great Satan and the Zionist entity.

In the years leading to Iran-Contra, Iran was enlisted by the United States among the "rogue" states sponsoring terrorism and subject to an arms embargo and other sanctions. The secret arms deal thus promised to provide Iran with much-needed material in the war with the minor Satan, as Saddam ranked in the demonology of the Islamic Republic. Whatever the Reagan administration's justifications for the arms deal with Iran, including raising funds needed for a covert operation against Nicaragua, facilitating the release of American hostages who were in the custody of the Hezbollah of Lebanon, and a good-will gesture with the remote hope of rekindling relations with revolutionary Iran, the initiative eventually backfired. It blew up into a major embarrassment on several counts and received enormous publicity worldwide. In addition to breaching the arms sanctions against Iran, the White House security adviser stood accused of breaking a congressional ban on assistance to Contra forces fighting the Nicaraguan revolutionary regime.

The Iranian side of the deal was arranged by a shady Iranian arms dealer Manuchehr Ghorbanifar (b. 1945), once a Savak agent and partner in an Israeli-Iranian shipping company. He claimed to have contacts with influential "moderates" in the Iranian regime. On the American side was maverick staff member of the National Security Council, Lieutenant Colonel Oliver North (b. 1946). The prospect of reopening relations with Iran was intriguing to the American administration. Not only the national security adviser Robert McFarlane (b. 1943) but also the CIA chief William Casey, as well as other senior White House officials and President Reagan himself, were optimistic enough to approve the sale of more than 2,500 American-made TOW antitank missiles to Iran over two years. The Israelis delivered early consignments of missiles and spare parts after they scratched off the tracing numbers and Hebrew letters presumably saving the Iranian regime from the embarrassment of sending Israeli equipment to their warriors in the "battlefields of the good versus the evil," as war with Iraq was labeled in the Iranian revolutionary propaganda. From the outset, Iranians had no illusions as to where the weapons had originated and at what overblown price. Later consignments were directly shipped from the United States.

Encouraged by the release of some hostages in Lebanon through Iranian mediation, the Reagan administration was thrilled enough to dispatch to Iran in May 1986 a mission headed by McFarlane and including North, a host of other American officials, and Amiram Nir (1950–1988), the chief Israeli agent in charge of the deal. They were aboard an Israeli aircraft that also carried a planeload of missiles and military spare parts for delivery to Iran. Upon arrival in Tehran, the uninvited mission soon realized they were unwelcome. Even a copy of the Bible signed by the US president as a goodwill gesture and a cake brought over in the shape of a key did not open any friendly doors. The mission returned to the United States hastily and in disgrace.

What was remarkable about the whole affair was the degree of naïveté displayed by the White House in assessing the complexity of the Iranian situation and its predicament. It was even more curious that Americans assumed that Iranians would not see through so obvious a ploy as luring Iran to normalization when at the very same time the US administration, as part of its two-track policy, was offering military assistance and reconnaissance to Saddam's Iraq. Under such circumstances, it was quite possible that Iranians, even the "moderates" imagined by the arms-selling intermediary, were not prepared to risk years of investing in the "Great Satan" rhetoric, a cornerstone of Islamic Republic's international posture, for the sake of an arms deal with a superpower clearly opposed to their ideological standing. They were willing to purchase arms from the United States and Israel so long that things stay at that level.

What was also remarkable was how shrewdly the leadership of the Islamic Republic managed to wave the scandalous aftereffects of Iran-Contra. The fact that Iran struck a secret deal with the Great Satan, and even with the "Zionist entity," was no small matter at a time when echoes of "Death to America" and "Death of Israel" were audible in every Friday prayer throughout Iran. Such temerity was typical of the regime's political culture. Any regime, it may be argued, in the throes of a deadly war would strike a deal with a power capable of delivering the necessary hardware. Yet purchasing arms from the United States and Israel to fight a Muslim neighbor could be swallowed by the Iranian public only with a great deal of ideological grease, as when only a few years earlier, in 1982, the Israeli invasion of Lebanon claimed eighty thousand Shi'i Lebanese and Palestinians victims.

Concerned with the damage that exposure of the arms deal can cause, in September 1987 the Iranian security forces arrested Mehdi Hashemi (1946–1987), a close aide to Montazeri and in control of a militia loyal to him, on the charge of treason. A seminarian of militant convictions and a lifetime client of Montazeri, Hashemi in 1977 was tried in a Pahlavi court and sentenced to life imprisonment on the charge of assassinating a prominent ayatollah in Isfahan. Hashemi was the ringleader of a terrorist group known as the Hadafis (those who believed in Shi'ism's political objective), which was inspired by the publication of a controversial book, *Shahid-e Javid* (The eternal martyr). It argued that Hosain, the Third Shi'i Imam, sacrificed himself for a proactive political cause rather than sheer moral endeavor.

After the victory of the revolution and release from prison, Hashemi gravitated toward the idea of exporting the revolution and especially to Shi'i communities abroad, which in turn drew him into the factional politics of the then evolving Lebanese Hezbollah. Opposed to the secret arms deal with the United States in exchange for the release of American hostages in Lebanon, Hashemi disclosed the secret deal to the Lebanese weekly *al-Shira'*. Outraged by the imminent disclosure, in October 1986 the Iranian security forces arrested Hashemi and forty of his associates shortly before the publication of the damaging revelations in *al-Shira'* on November 3, 1986. After lengthy detention, torture, and a forced television interview, in which he "confessed" to his crime of collaborating with the Great Satan, Hashemi was eventually put on trial in the clergy's special court. He was executed in November 1987. Silencing Hashemi, and in turn Montazeri, only partially diverted the bewildered Iranian public. Other pretexts were needed to distract attention to another direction.

It was not mere coincidence, therefore, that at the tail end of the Iran-Contra Affair and shortly after Hashemi's execution, Khomeini should engage in a seemingly unnecessary crisis. What came to be known as the Rushdie affair inflicted further damage to Iran's already-battered image abroad, yet it handsomely paid off, saving Khomeini's image at home as an uncompromising Islamic crusader. On February 14, 1989, he issued a famous fatwa accusing Salman Rushdie, the British writer of Muslim Indian descent and author of *The Satanic Verses*, of blasphemy. The fatwa called on "all valiant Muslims" to kill the author and all the editors and publishers who were aware of the novel's content, wherever they found them and without delay, "so that no one will dare insult the sacred beliefs of Muslims henceforth. And whoever is killed in this cause will be a martyr."[5]

The fatwa, while elevating postwar turmoil inside Iran to a new height, also triggered a wave of condemnation in the West toward Khomeini and his Islamic regime. From the perspective of Khomeini and his officials and aides, who in the days following the issuance of the fatwa announced a $6 million award for Rushdie's assassination, the fatwa was an affordable tool of brandishing the regime's comparative brand in a fast-growing international market of Islamic militancy even if the cost would be a break in diplomatic relations with Britain, where Rushdie was residing.

Less than four months before Khomeini's death from terminal cancer, which had already been diagnosed at the time, one might attribute his stirring up the Rushdie controversy primarily to leave behind a legacy of unbending militancy. The grievous end to the war and the unraveling of his vision to export the revolution may well have given him the impression that condemning Rushdie would ensure his legacy. Placing himself in a primary role in the anti-Rushdie protest movement that stretched from Britain to Pakistan and beyond guaranteed that. As he saw it, in the scheme of things, the issuance of a death fatwa was a religious duty, especially when coming from the guardian jurist of the Islamic Republic. Jumping on the bandwagon of anti-Rushdie mania, no doubt, also secured the intended publicity at home as well. A hefty award brazenly placed on Rushdie's head gave the affair an extra flavor of bounty-hunting justice.

Whatever the offensive content of the novel *The Satanic Verses*, the fatwa constituted serious harassment of a gifted writer with great cultural sensibilities. It also undermined provisions in Islamic law regarding cases of blasphemy and the evidentiary and procedural grounds for issuing a legal opinion. For one thing, it can be argued that a work of fiction with a phantasmagoric style and with such ambiguous characters as the story's Mahound can hardly be accepted as evidence for blasphemy. According to such a yardstick, many Sufi aphorisms and some in the corpus of Persian and Arabic poetry would be heretical. It is also debatable whether the penal provisions of Islamic law are binding by anyone beyond the jurisdiction of Dar al-Islam, if for no other reason than that the accused must first be brought before a shari'a court presided over by one or more jurists who are qualified to study the text in question, or rely on unbiased and trusted experts. By calling on the "brave Muslims of the world" it was as if Khomeini instantaneously expanded the "abode of Islam" globally, a trend that was soon to be emulated by Muslim militants everywhere. Yet there is near consensus that no opinion can be issued by an Islamic court before the accused is cross-examined in person, admitting or denying a charge of blasphemy brought against him or her. The text by itself, according to most jurists, does not carry sufficient weight for the issuance of a fatwa of blasphemy, let alone a death sentence, the execution of which at any rate cannot be delegated to an anonymous individual. That the author apologized, or "repented," did not alter Khomeini's or his clerical followers' opinions even though an overwhelming majority of Muslim jurists admit that repentance for first-time offenders is adequate grounds for recalling a death sentence, even in grave blasphemy cases.

Khomeini's fatwa thus appeared to be serving other purposes than a mere discharge of juristic obligation, given the glaring legal breaches that must have been known to him and his cohorts. That the intense publicity in the Iranian media portrayed publication of *Satanic Verses* as a Western conspiracy against Islam, moreover, pointed to a skillful masking of the realties of the postwar era. The gloomy realities included the return home of hundreds of thousands of disillusioned and disabled war veterans, rows of graves in overcrowded "martyr cemeteries," tens of thousands of detainees kept in ghastly Iraqi prisoner-of-war camps, and difficulties in fulfilling promises made to families of martyrs. The anti-Rushdie crusade also served to soften contention within the leadership at a critical juncture when Khomeini's death loomed large. The designation of the next guardian jurist appeared to be in trouble.

DISMISSAL OF THE DESIGNATED HEIR

The state-sponsored public clamor demanding Rushdie's assassination was loud enough to swamp Montazeri's call for moderation. In an atmosphere of adulation for the great leader and an imagined Western conspiracy to blemish and ridicule Islam, Montazeri dared to say that the people of the world thought of Iran as just in the business of killing people. No other ranking clergy raised any concern, at least in public, over the validity of Khomeini's fatwa, let alone concern with free speech or Iran's image abroad. As in the case of the 1988 executions, here too, bowing blindly before the guardian jurist had become a norm in the Islamic Republic with no parallel in the Shi'i past—and for good reason, as Montazeri's fate soon demonstrated.

As designated heir (*janeshin*) to the Imam, and probably the most prominent jurist in Khomeini's inner circle and an early advocate of *welayat-e faqih*, Montazeri has kept a healthy distance from the internal quarrels and controversial decisions. Earlier he had criticized the way the hard-liners shunned Bazargan and his colleagues as "compromising liberals," and in 1981 he even attempted, unsuccessfully, to broker peace with the Mojahedin. In his typical plain language, he occasionally mentioned the regime's harsh treatment of his opponents, touching at times innocuously on Khomeini's positions. In turn, he was gradually cut off from the decision-making circle around the Imam of the revolution. Equally worrisome was the regime's fear of a domestic source of dissent similar to the leftist militias and close to the Mojahedin's anticlerical positions, especially if it had the blessing of an important clerical authority such as Montazeri. His implicit rebuke of how revolutionary ideals were being compromised with the growth of financial corruption in high circles and widespread political repression added to the rift.

Already distraught by Hashemi's execution, by mid-1988 Montazeri was voicing his abhorrence at the reports of mass executions of political prisoners. In a number of cautionary notes addressed to Khomeini, he considered such killings neither consistent with the shariʻa nor justified by human rights standards. He openly reiterated his earlier demands to reassess failures of the revolution and open up the political space, demands that stood little chance of seeing Khomeini's compliance. This was the first, and the only, public confirmation of the mass killings coming from a senior figure. Coinciding with the anti-Rushdie campaign came the revelation of Montazeri's note to Khomeini dating August 1, 1988, cautioning against prison executions on Islamic and human rights grounds. "About your honor's recent order pertaining to the execution of the hypocrites [i.e., the Mojahedin] who are already in prisons," wrote Montazeri,

> The execution of those who were detained after the recent incident [i.e., Mojahedin's offensive in western Iran in July 1988], nation and the society will accept it and apparently it will not have a negative repercussion. But executing those who were already in prisons [beforehand], first of all will be interpreted under the present circumstances as an act of vengeance and reprisal. . . . What have we gained so far from killings and violence except increasing adverse publicity against ourselves while adding to the appeal of the hypocrites and antirevolutionaries? It is now the time to act for a while with compassion and benevolence.[6]

By early 1989 Montazeri had gone so far as to implicitly criticize Khomeini in public for denying people their rights and disregarding the revolution's true values. He called on the "leader" to allow for a political and ideological reassessment. By the standards of the Islamic Republic, this was an unprecedented reproach of Khomeini and his radical allies. Montazeri's revelation and criticisms of the guardian jurist predictably further enraged Khomeini and vexed his associates, among them Sayyid ʻAli Khamenei, president of the Islamic Republic since 1981 and soon to be Supreme Leader of the Republic. An enforcer of Khomeini's whims and wishes, and the chief implementer of Khomeini's war strategy, he appeared to have been instrumental in staging the last scene of the anti-Montazeri coup de grace.

The Council of Experts, entirely peopled by ranking mullahs loyal to Khomeini, had already begun revisiting the qualifications for the guardian jurist in the Islamic Republic's constitution while contemplating the choice of the next leader. By March 1989, when Khomeini openly disowned Montazeri, his once-close comrade, it was more for public consumption than to alert the Council of Experts of Montazeri's undesirability. In March 28, 1989, two days after a taunting speech by Khomeini, Montazeri quietly resigned. He also accepted with dignity the restrictions placed on him by the regime for the following two decades of his life. Residing in his house in Qom, he continued teaching a small circle of students and gave occasional interviews before his statements subjected him to house arrest and a complete ban on interviews. Not long afterward, he was erased (not unlike in the Soviet Union of the Stalin era) entirely from public view and the official revolutionary narrative.

During Mohammad Khatami's presidency (1997–2005), his house arrest was partially relaxed, though he remained an outsider deprived of public speeches, travel, and publication of any political statement. Contesting the restrictions despite his ailments, he expressed views and issued opinions antithetical to some repressive polices of the regime and reflective of his moderating outlook. His re-issuance of a fatwa in May 2008 in response to renewed persecutions of Baha'is of Iran reflected Montazeri's courageous stance. The members of the "Baha'i sect," he stressed, "don't have a divine scripture" and are not "considered a religious minority, but since they are citizens of this country, they have indigenous rights [*haqq-e ab va gel*] and are entitled to rights of citizenship. Moreover, they should benefit from Islamic compassion as emphasized in the Qur'an and by guardians of [our] faith."[7] His death in December 19, 2009, stirred much public sympathy in Tehran, Qom, Isfahan, and elsewhere. Coming in the aftermath of the June 2009 Green Movement, the regime imposed a near-total ban on any commemorative gathering.

Montazeri's fall was the last of the purges of Khomeini's era and emblematic of the Islamic Republic's relentless quest for regimented uniformity. That the clerical establishment, with few exceptions, rallied behind Khomeini on this issue, was not merely due to a climate of coercion and a demand for total loyalty. The ruling clergy was also responsible for trading its customary judicial and academic autonomy in exchange for new privileges under the republic's hierarchy. They took advantage of the opportunity to monopolize political power and solidify privileges at the price of depreciating *ejtehad* as a tool of judicial independence. Slavish subservience to *welayat-e faqih* superseded even the authority of *marja'iyat*.

END OF AN ERA

On June 3, 1989, Ayatollah Khomeini died of terminal cancer at the age of eighty-seven. His funeral brought hundreds of thousands of mourners into the streets of the capital along the road to his burial place fifteen miles south of Tehran on the road to Qom. A memorable event in the calendar of the Islamic Revolution, crowds of mourners were comparable in size only to Khomeini's reception upon arrival from exile a decade earlier. The two events in effect marked the beginning and the end of the first phase of the Islamic Revolution during which Khomeini's leadership was central and enduring.

The mourners, spontaneous in their emotions and visibly overcome with grief, brought the funeral to a standstill, broke through the procession, and struggled to reach the casket and touch Khomeini's shroud. The pandemonium that followed long delayed the interment. The outpouring of emotions carried an underlying message. It was as if the public were not only mourning the loss of the Imam but also burying with Khomeini's remains the revolutionary passions that had motivated a generation, brought people into the streets, and forever transformed Iranian society. It was a subtle message from an exhausted public to leave behind protest rallies and sacrifice in the battlefield and move ahead toward greater normalcy.

Even Khomeini's mausoleum, hastily designed and hurriedly built, seemed to carry a message of finality. The gilded dome, minarets, the inner structure (*zarih*), and the niche (*mehrab*) clearly called for a return to the sacred Shi'i past. At the terminus of a Tehran underground line, the "Imam's Mausoleum" seemed to emphasize, symbolically, an end point along the revolution's mental itinerary. The building in effect beatifies Khomeini in a space meant to be superior to the nearby Shah 'Abd al-'Azim shrine and on par with such sites as the shrines of Qom and even Mashhad. It also was a symbolic reference, albeit in reverse, to the demolished Reza Shah mausoleum that had once been located not far away.

The inscription above an entrance to the interior of the mausoleum carries a short passage from Khomeini's "political-divine testament." It assures visitors: "By God's grace, it is with a serene soul, a confident heart, an elated spirit and a hopeful conscience that I now bid farewell to my sisters and brothers and travel to my eternal resting place."[8] It is quite remarkable that being for a decade at the helm of a ferocious course of events that claimed hundreds of thousands of lives in the battlefields, in prisons, and on the streets, the guardian jurist of the revolution could still entertain such cheerful aspirations.

With the benefit of hindsight, it is possible to say that by 1989 the charismatic phase of the revolution had decidedly come to an end. During the decade under Khomeini, the revolution effectively dismantled not only the Pahlavi political and technocratic elites but also a large sector of the Pahlavi middle classes. During the same period, the new regime effectively suppressed competing sources of dissent, from the radical left to liberals and clerical moderates, and regional and ethnic resistance. Despite serious setbacks, it also managed to deter a formidable aggressor in neighboring Iraq while taking on a superpower, the United States, in an egregious, though largely symbolic, contest. Through the hostage crisis and war with Iraq, and a host of other challenges, the Islamic Republic under Khomeini solidified its base and created political and security institutions to preserve its economic and financial monopolies.

Like a host of twentieth-century revolutionary leaders, from Lenin and Mao to Ho Chi Minh, and possibly even Gandhi, Khomeini was crucial in the shaping of a mass revolution. His prophetic acumen, however, neither entirely replicated the revolutionary and messianic examples of the past nor was a mere by-product of modern ideologies and their postcolonial reverberations. He relied instead on a normative Islam and the clerical establishment that represented it. Ruthless and resolute, he successfully transformed the shari'a-based clerical establishment into a powerful tool to mobilize the less-privileged sectors of society without ever fully breaking from traditional Islamic values or offering a coherent program of socioeconomic and cultural change. His fascination with an idealized and largely ahistorical "true Islam," though not entirely devoid of elements of modernity, remained by and large regressive in its outlook and conduct.

Khomeini's most tangible and enduring contribution, however, was his success in putting into practice the long-speculated-on idea of political Islam. The Islamic republic that he helped found was the first to emerge out of an ideological revolution, something that perhaps could emerge only in Shi'i Iran. Yet as a militant and a revolutionary promoting the paradigm of an Islamic state, Khomeini's influence has been well evident throughout the Muslim world since the 1980s. In that regard at least, in modern times no other Muslim thinker, activist, or revolutionary can match his record. Irrespective of their brand of Islamic activism, it can be argued that none of the modern Muslim thinkers and revolutionaries, from Mohammad ibn 'Abd al-Wahhab in the eighteenth century to Jamal al-Din Asadabadi and Mohammad 'Abdu in the nineteenth century to Rashid Rida, Hasan al-Banna, Sayyid Qutb, and Abul-'Ala Mawdudi in the twentieth century, are comparable to Khomeini insofar as their regional or global impact.

At least three characteristics qualify the Islamic Revolution as a major revolutionary movement in modern times. First, it was based on mass mobilization and large-scale popular participation. It was unprecedented not only in Middle East history but also in the sheer number of participants—perhaps one of the largest in modern history. The revolutionary movement was comprehensive and decisive in ousting the old political order and dismantling its associated political and economic elites. Second, in a remarkably short time, the Islamic Revolution managed to establish a new political order, nurture a new sociopolitical elite, and institutionalize its hierocracy despite serious domestic and external challenges. The incipient Islamic Republic violently surpassed all other real or potential contenders. In this respect it demonstrated a consistent drive toward greater monopoly of power. This was in common with most totalitarian regimes intolerant of dissent even within their own ranks. War in particular greatly contributed to the Islamic Republic's grassroots support as much as to its ability to crush its opposition. Third, the Islamic Revolution offered a cultural program that included a curious mix of hard-line conservatism, anti-imperialist rhetoric, selective modernity, and conscious antisecularism. In practice, it showed no hesitation in employing modern means of repression, control, and propaganda. Nor did it show hesitation to adopt modern programs of economic development and social welfare, so long they could be safely Islamicized. In this respect, too, despite many signs of anachronism, the Islamic Republic put into practice a program of social engineering with enduring results.

17

SOCIETY AND CULTURE UNDER THE ISLAMIC REPUBLIC

The revolution that brought to power a new regime and a new polity also left its profound imprint on Iran's society, economy, and culture. By the end of the first decade of the revolution, the privileged upper and middle classes of the Pahlavi era had been forced out of the political process and gradually replaced in the economic sector as well. Hundreds of thousands of people were purged from the workforce or retired early or lost access to sources of power and capital. Even those who remained relatively untouched by the first wave of the revolution had to refashion their economic resources and lifestyle and try, often unsuccessfully, to renegotiate with the regime control over their wealth and businesses. They were admittedly a thin layer in Iranian society of the 1970s and 1980s but vital because of their predominance in the educational, economic, and technocratic structures of the Pahlavi era. Hundreds of thousands immigrated to North America, Western Europe, and Australia to start new lives.

In place of the old elite, the new regime relied primarily on "traditional" middle and lower-middle classes loyal to the revolution. They were mostly from families of religious orientation (*mazhabi*) with clerical or bazaar backgrounds, especially small retailers, and first- and second-generation rural migrants in Tehran and the provincial centers. Gradually, more were recruited or rose in the ranks from smaller towns and villages or from urban working classes or low-income government families. They were educated in state schools, including a large number of the middle-aged clergy (who had modern schooling before entering the madrasa or concurrent with their *howzeh* education). Some members of the older middle classes survived as government employees and carried on with their official duties but never at the helm. There was also a smaller group of "born-again" Islamists, who remained in government service, though were never fully trusted by the regime or given sensitive posts, at least not public ones. The extensive purges and the climate of terror throughout the 1980s put many member of the middle classes out of government employment and drove them to the private sector.

The new state elite in the main belonged to a network that Khomeini and his associates had managed to foster in the 1960s and 1970s while he was in exile. Crucial to their rise was the agility of the new social classes that propelled them forward, their rapid learning curve, and their sense of group solidarity, soon rewarded with high offices and in due course economic privileges. At the pinnacle of the new hierarchy were the Khomeinist clergy and the laymen close to them. Though a relatively tiny and often quarrelling group, they were conscious of their power and determined to preserve it. They held high offices such as speaker of the Majles, head of the judiciary, head of the security, judges in the revolutionary courts, Imam Jum'as of the major provincial centers, clerical members of the Guardian Council, representatives of Khomeini in the military and security forces, in economic and educational institutions and various lucrative subsidiaries of the state-run foundations. The lower ranks of the hierarchical structure, manned by a mix of trusted laymen and clergy, held technocratic and bureaucratic posts, including oversight of second-tier ministries, banks and financial institutions, and provincial governorships, and army officers and Revolutionary Guard chiefs heading the armed forces. The deputies of the Islamic Majles constituted a category of their own. Some deputies had formerly served in government, in the Revolutionary Guard Corps, and in government-owned concerns. Others were Islamic activists from lower-income neighborhoods in larger cities or from small towns who had climbed up the political ladder because of their credentials as war veterans or as clients of an influential Khomeinist in their constituency.

A privileged group in the new elite, though often behind-the-curtain, included the children and close relatives of the ayatollahs, who, as ultimate "insiders," stood to reap vast political and economic benefits. Referred to, somewhat sarcastically, as *aqazadehs* (offspring of [clerical] masters), these were characteristically laymen with modicum of education who came to overseeing the "house" (*bayt*; i.e., the bureau) of their fathers or fathers-in-law; a role equivalent, perhaps, to a chief of staff. Management, predictably, involved a wide and often lucrative range of activities from facilitating deals, lobbying, and influence peddling to investment and financial management of religious texts, endowments, and acquired wealth and properties (more likely confiscated); activities that their direct supervision were incongruent with an ayatollah's public image as man of God detached from worldly affairs. The monopoly of important offices by some clergy, as if they had lifetime appointments, further empowered *aqazadehs* as the aging ayatollahs heavily relied on their advice and influence. Competing with the *aqazadeh* elite for privilege and power were the newcomers who earned their insider status through revolutionary credentials. Mostly from urban working classes and rural origins, they were veterans of the Iraq-Iran War who often served as commanders of Revolutionary Guard and *basij* units, or revolutionaries in the formative years of the revolution who proved their radical merits and their loyalty to the regime. It was this class of war veterans, former revolutionaries, and family of the martyrs that provided a human reservoir for the Islamic Republic's expanding bureaucracy and, to lesser extent, to replenish its leadership ranks. To be a successful candidate, one had to, above all, display Islamic "commitment" (*ta'ahud*): zealous loyalty to the leadership and its political objectives. Only a smaller percentage from this group felt obliged to acquire a level of "expertise" (*takhassos*), as the postrevolutionary jargon had it, through some form of university education. From the late 1980s, the Islamic Republic established quotas for the higher education of the war veterans, which in practice allowed them, and relatives of the martyrs, to enter universities with academic aptitude significantly less than accepted standards. Even postrevolutionary Iranian society remained deferential toward university titles, which in turn heightened the urge for doctoral and engineering degrees, at times irrespective of any rigorous training.

Yet despite the regime's success in building a new elite with an exclusionary mind-set, it was not as successful in creating a totalitarian state on the classical model. In part, one may attribute this to the inherent complexity of the new elite, particularly the political maneuverability of the clergy, their shifting bonds, and their skills in rhetorical juxtaposition, all of which they honed in the madrasas of Qom, with its complex pedagogic practices and clerical politics. They projected this "Qomified" political culture into the higher echelons of the state machinery and with predictable outcomes—a sustained internal rivalry, even chaos, within the inner circles and between offices over tutelage, while also professing loyalty to the guardian jurists and the core ideologies of the regime. The dangerous challenges to the very survival of the Islamic Republic during the formative years of the revolution no doubt helped solidify bonds of loyalty and means of defiance. The inner complexity of the regime, and its drive toward hegemony, required more time beyond Khomeini's era. Decades after his demise the regime witnessed tension, primarily within its own ranks, between the hard-liners, steadfast in their support for the Supreme Leader, 'Ali Khamenei, and the "reformists," hopeful to introduce a more inclusive outlook.

The composition of the new elite and its hierarchy clearly demonstrated the Islamic Republic's reluctance to broaden the political spectrum through free and popular representation and by means of uncontrolled democratic institutions. Contrary to the promises of the revolution, political leadership by most standards remained oligarchic; a relatively coherent structure that vetted admission to the system by such institutional means as the Guardian Council (shura-ye negahban). Even though ideological and factional tensions within the ruling elite at times have brought about surprising results, by and large the insider versus outsider divide has remained intact. Compared to the Pahlavi era, it can be argued, the polity of the Islamic Republic is more exclusive and more doctrinaire, even though it is closer to its grass roots and at times even more outspoken.

A DEMOGRAPHIC REVOLUTION

Beyond the emerging political order, but not unrelated to it, the first decade after the revolution witnessed demographic explosion with lasting consequences. As the latest stage in Iran's rapid population growth that began in the 1960s, and as part of a pattern throughout the Middle East in the late twentieth century, the country's total population between 1976 and 1986 grew from 33.7 million to 49.4 million, an annual increase of 9.3 percent, the largest in recent Iranian history. At the turn of the twentieth century, Iran's estimated population was 8 million, and by 1956 it had reached 18.9 million. Remarkably, by the beginning of the twenty-first century it exceeded 68 million, a more than eleven-fold increase throughout the twentieth century. In 2010 the birthrate officially stood at 1.8 percent, far below the 1980s rate of 4.2 percent.

Between 1975 and 1985 Iranians younger than twenty years of age constituted more than 50 percent of the total population, one of the youngest in the region, a pattern that continued for another decade before dropping to below 35 percent by the beginning of the twenty-first century. Equally noteworthy, in 1966, at the height of the White Revolution and the land reform, 37 percent of the population was urban, a major increase from the mid-1950s, when less than 25 percent of the population was urban. By 1976, just before the start of the Islamic Revolution, the urban population rose to 46 percent, a decade later had reached 54 percent, and it has continued to increase ever since. By 2012, of a total population of 78 million, 71 percent were urban, of which 30 percent lived in five major cities (18 percent in greater Tehran and another 12 percent in four major provincial centers). Urbanization inevitably increased literacy rates while pushing down birthrates. In 1976 only 44 percent of the population older than six years of age was literate; by 1986 the literacy rate had reached 54 percent, and by 2015 as many as 97 percent of young adults were literate. This is far higher than the 65 percent for the remaining Middle East.

Population growth and urbanization were vital forces in the shaping of the Islamic Revolution and how it evolved in its first decade of consolidation. The multitudes that rallied against the shah and later for the Islamic Republic (as well as the rank and file of the radical left who opposed the Islamic regime) were mostly younger than twenty-five years of age. Most of the army conscripts, the Revolutionary Guards, and the Basij volunteers who fought during the Iraq-Iran War, too, were predominantly from the same under-twenty-five age group. At the outset of the revolution, the youthful age of the population proved an indispensible boon because of their agility, ideological commitment, and demands for greater political agency and equity in distribution of wealth and privileges. Ideals such as these were barely fulfilled for the Iranian population at large, but they benefited a small sector that remained adamantly loyal to the regime's leadership.

On a broader scope, it is important to note that at no time in Iran's past half millennium had there been more favorable demographics for a revolutionary change: a reservoir of a vigorous urban population ready to rise for a cause. Neither in sixteenth-century Tabriz of Isma'il's era, nor in Tehran and Tabriz of the Constitutional era or in Tehran and other provincial centers during the National Movement of the early 1950s did such a demographic concentration with a thirst for political participation exist. Throughout the 1970s and 1980s a vast number of immigrants who came from the countryside and smaller cities to Tehran and to provincial centers brought with them a culture of multiple births and life in large, often extended, families. These factors may explain the rapid growth of the cities in the 1970s and beyond. It took a generation, at least, for this new urbanized population to adopt the nuclear family model, with fewer children, mostly reliant on the income of one parent and somewhat independent of the multigenerational families of their grandparents. Still, from a long-term point of view, it is remarkable how swiftly the emerging middle classes under the Islamic Republic cast off the traditional familial patterns in favor of new values and a new lifestyle, but with their own demands and dynamics.

The Islamic regime relied heavily on the youthful generations and their aspirations to succeed, yet it also denied them their political agency in no small measure. It failed to meet their yearning for a pluralistic, and socially tolerant, society. Islamification, as an ideologically driven course, endorsed and implemented by the revolutionary elite—with a diametrically different lifestyle and life experience—held a distinct perspective and had a different set of priorities. To the extent the new regime attempted to address leisure and social freedoms, as well as gender equality, religious toleration, and other nonpolitical needs of Iran's new society—education, health, employment, and housing—its long-term record was at best mixed and more often abysmal.

AFTER KHOMEINI'S DEMISE

At the outset, the Islamic Republic's development plan proved a relative success, despite international isolation and a repressive civic record. During the presidency of Akbar Hashemi Rafsanjani (1989–1997) the state engaged in an impressive set of infrastructural, urban, educational, and industrial projects. In the postwar period, known as the Construction Era (*dowran-e sazandegi*), Iran witnessed the building of large-scale road and communication networks, new airports, dams, irrigation, power plants and energy-harnessing projects, heavy and light industry, automobile manufacturing, and food and chemicals production. These enterprises were largely owned and operated by the state, in an increasingly public-sector economy, though less ambitious projects were undertaken in the private sector. Some were incomplete projects from the previous regime and others were on the model, and used the blueprint, of Pahlavi development plans. Yet others were precipitous, and impulsive, initiatives. The country's overall workforce grew rapidly, especially in the industrial, semi-industrial, and service sectors.

In June 1979 creation of the Jihad-e Sazandegi (or the Construction Crusade), a revolutionary organization that intended to utilize engineering and technological expertise among the university faculty and students, engaged in an ambitious number of developmental and public construction projects in remote, often impoverished, towns and villages of Iran. The Crusade, somewhat inspired by the White Revolution of the Pahlavi era but with a thin luster of idealism perhaps borrowed from Maoist ideology, engaged in a heroic campaign that was barely backed with thorough planning and use of resources. Yet it soon found itself during the Iraq-Iran War on the war front answering the urgent military engineering needs. The prolonged experience of the war gradually changed the mission and the structure of the Crusade and in due course allowed it in the postwar era to be incorporated into the state bureaucracy—a clear example of transient top-down revolutionary development model captivated with the vision of modernization. As it turned out, the Construction Crusade, by building roads and enhancing communications, virtually paved the way for the faster movement of population from countryside to cities.

Increasingly, urban development, new housing projects, and better urban amenities made Iranian cities oases of greater prosperity, absorbing people with higher education who were unwilling and unable to work in smaller and less developed towns. Agricultural output grew in the mid-1990s, bringing Iran to the verge of self-sufficiency in wheat and other major cereals and fulfilling, briefly, one of the revolution's promises. Food production methods improved, and agriculture became almost fully mechanized, hence driving the larger surplus village population to cities.

The state's near monopoly on resources, and revenues from oil and natural gas in particular, combined with its centralized economy, heavily bureaucratized government structure, and poor policy making, were all reminiscent of planned economies of the 1950s and 1960s. The Islamic Republic in effect augmented manifold the malaise of the Pahlavi state and its economy. Despite industrialization, the Iranian economy became even more dependent on oil income, which further increased the concentration of capital and decision making in the hands of the state and its agencies. With the increase in oil prices in international markets from 1980s on, an unprecedented treasure trove of unearned income poured into state coffers. Public projects funded by state capital became channels of favoritism, corruption, and amassing wealth that trickled down a chain of nepotism and network connections. This was true under Rafsanjani's presidency, which brought massive financial benefits to a network of his relatives, allies, and cronies.

The election of Mohammad Khatami (b. 1943) to the presidency in June 1997 and his promises of civil society, rule of law, tolerance, and sociocultural openness was in effect a response to the wishes of younger Iranians who were disillusioned with the rhetoric and realities of the Islamic leadership. His victory was a huge upset to the regime's insider candidate, who had been anointed by the Supreme Leader, 'Ali Khamenei. Many who campaigned for Khatami—and came to be identified as Dovvom-e Khordadi (in reference to the election day, June 23, 1997, which corresponds in the Iranian solar calendar to the second of Khordad 1376)—typically were sobered revolutionaries. They were bruised by the excesses of the regime and discontent with the plutocracy associated with the Rafsanjani clique.

Enjoying the momentum, these "religious reformers," as they generally defined themselves, were revisionists who believed that the Islamic Republic could be a more tolerant and pluralistic space answerable to law, social freedoms, and sounder governance. A surprise by-product of the revolution, they were symptoms of a crisis within the revolutionary ranks. Often from religious backgrounds and themselves active in the revolution, they developed new interests and engaged in intellectual and cultural trends beyond the barren ideological confines. In Khatami they searched for a bridge connecting the ideals of the Islamic Revolution, as they experienced it, and the realities of a more pluralistic modernity. Khatami's intellectual makeup and amicable personality were a far cry from the frowning tedium of the clerical oligarchy. In domestic affairs he seemed to be breaking new ground, moving away from the menacing vagaries of earlier years. In foreign policy, too, he inclined toward an end to isolation and antagonism. His program of reform, though vague and indecisive, was enough to momentarily mobilize vast support for him. It was a breath of fresh air, especially during the first year or so of his first term when the conservatives were in temporary retreat and Khatami was more attuned to the hopes of his constituency. In 1997 in an election that brought 80 percent of the eligible voters to the voting stations, Khatami was elected to office with 70 percent of the votes. His impressive performance, even in conservative constituencies such as the city of Qom, ushered a new political era.

For a moment it seemed as if the days of the hard-liners were numbered. Khatami's success soon gave expression to a range of intellectual and cultural activities. Liberal dailies with a critical perspective appeared on the newsstands, books whose publications were long delayed or banned saw the light of the day, new films portraying social ills and implicitly critical of the revolution were produced and some screened, and the overall political climate improved noticeably. Yet Khatami's victory proved a mirage. Alarmed by the contagious spirit of openness, the hard-liners, turbaned and unturbaned, rallied behind the Supreme Leader and archconservatives such as Ayatollah Mohammad-Taqi Mesbah-Yazdi (b. 1935). Soon winds of reaction were blowing full force. In a systematic move to restrain the restive public and quell its democratic demands, the Majles, under the control of the hard-liners, impeached Khatami's minister of the interior, 'Abdollah Nuri (b. 1950) and soon thereafter indicted him on charges of anti-Islamic offenses, sentencing him to five years in jail. Perhaps the most outspoken insider of the Islamic Republic, and earlier a close aide to Khomeini, Nuri, himself a cleric, had turned critical of clerical excesses, defended Montazeri, and criticized the suffocating lack of individual and political freedoms, as well as the seemingly unlimited authority of the guardian jurist. He even questioned Islam's undisputed validity as the sole source of political order.

By the end of his second term in 2005, Khatami was largely isolated, his program of reforms was blocked, and his close aides and supporters had been checked. Although the eight years of his presidency were a respite of sorts from the social pressures imposed on Iranian society, he was constantly under attack from his opponents. Despite Khatami's political integrity and intellectual sophistication, the end result of his presidency can be defined only as a setback of his initial objectives—a déjà vu, perhaps, of Banisadr's presidency sixteen years earlier. This may be attributed to Khatami's tactical hesitancy or lack of political acumen, which from the outset kept him from leveraging his huge popular mandate to check his hard-liner opponents. Obstacles on his way to implement the rule of law (*qanun-mandi*), his favorite catchphrase, and "institutionalize" respect for human and civil rights, however, can be attributed to the inherent superior powers of his opponents. While Khatami enjoyed a popular mandate, his was a soft power, and his presidency flaccid and amorphous. His conservative opponents, however, controlled most institutional levers except the presidency. Not only was Khamenei willing and able to exert his constitutional prerogative as Supreme Leader to cut the president to size or bypass him altogether; the Majles, and even more so the Guardian Council, and the judiciary remained in conservative hands. The leadership of the Revolutionary Guards, the media, the police, and the armed forces, and much of the clerical establishment, including leaders of Friday prayers, were also firmly in the conservative camp.

For most Iranians, and the middle classes in particular, the failure of the Khatami experiment, insofar as it could be assessed, was a major setback but not a crushing end. Modern Iranian history is littered with political upsets that led to long episodes of political silence. This time around under Khatami, the experiment proved to have far less finality than, for instance, the closure of the Majles in 1911, the coup of 1953, or the fall of the provisional government in 1979. Nevertheless, the election of Mahmud Ahmadinejad (b. 1956) to the presidency in August 2005, which aimed to reverse the liberalizing trends of the Khatami era, was deeply felt by the reformist milieu. It was a triumph for the new wave of hard-liners, whether through the ballot box or by marshaling their popular supporters or by way of intimidation and fraud. It was an outright reversal of the civil and political process under Khatami and his conciliatory course in foreign policy. In terms of personality, too, Ahmadinejad and his cohorts stood in sharp contrast to Khatami and his allies.

At least at the outset Ahmadinejad carried populist appeal, especially among the less privileged classes who were disappointed with the economic performance of the Khatami era. This is well evident in Ahmadinejad's everyman demeanor, his frugal attire, sharp tongue, deceptive promises, maverick maneuvers, and reckless boasting on sensitive issues of foreign policy. Reclaiming the radical spirit of the revolution's early days, he hoped to shift Iran's political discourse toward radical lines and, in effect, return Iran to its great revolutionary days. His messianic yearning for the imminent advent of the Imam of the

Age pointed at a demagogic mind-set. Coupled with a fiery rhetoric, his desire for a secure power base among lower-class youth paid off at least for a while.

Complementing his messianic aspirations were the wasteful, incompetent, and corrupt hordes who formed his administration. Under the guise of upholding "Islamic revolutionary justice," Ahmadinejad and his cohorts squandered tens of billions of dollars of oil revenue, perhaps the largest amount ever in modern Iranian history, only to bring the economy to the brink of insolvency. With the full blessing of the "beloved Supreme Leader," Ahmadinejad's government made millions of Iranians more dependent on menial state-distributed cash handouts, known as *yaraneh*. Hooked to a miserable culture of dependency, even some sectors of the middle classes began to taste an unprecedented level of poverty and deprivation.

Along the same path, he reinstituted the largely inactive Basij militia as a paramilitary force. The indoctrinated youth, enthralled by weapons and a common hatred of domestic and foreign enemies, posed a new menace. Nearly three decades after the Islamic Revolution, the appeal of Islamic activism had not entirely ceased. At least until the 2009 presidential election, when obvious vote rigging reinstated Ahmadinejad to office, the Basij option continued to appeal to youth if not out of sheer conviction, at least for access to economic privilege. Numerically and doctrinally, though, the Basij had lost steam. Ahmadinejad's antics and the ineptness of his government became apparent even to regime insiders.

Yet Khamenei's support for Ahmadinejad, at least until 2010, when serious rift began to occur between them, may be viewed as a continuum of Ayatollah Khomeini's strategy to opt for the most radical. By adopting a similar course since 1989, the Supreme Leader has exerted detrimental influence over the overall orientation of the Islamic Republic. This he did in the face of the Iranian public, who on more than one occasion rejected his advocacy for radicalism and isolation. And despite setbacks, such as after the first presidential election of Mohammad Khatami in June 1997, or during the Green Movement in June 2009, he doggedly fought to reassert his authority even by means of coercion and intrigue.

In pursuit of his hard-line course, Khamenei had to secure the loyalty of the Revolutionary Guard Corps, the state-controlled media, the Guardian Council and the clerical establishment, and an assortment of hard-liners in the Islamic parliament. Through patronage and moral support he was able to acquire, at least temporarily, the allegiance of the madrasas in Qom and elsewhere, the Islamic propaganda organizations that mushroomed around the county, and editors of the hard-line press. They were the recipients of his institutional and personal blessing and financial largesse, in return for their advancement of his ideological line and political agenda. He has also acted as a shield, covering up enormous financial misappropriations and mismanagement of those close to his inner circle. The nouveau-riche plutocracy that emerged on Iran's economic horizon, especially during the presidency of Ahmadinejad, continues to operate under his wing. Many cronies of the "leader's house," as his core headquarters is known, were among the beneficiaries of the financial boom that came with high oil prices and international sanctions.

The steady growth of the Revolutionary Guard Corps in areas of defense, security, and economic activities exemplifies Khamenei's purposeful patronage. In 1989, in the postwar construction era, a new economic arm of the Revolutionary Guard, known as Qarargah-e Sazandegi-e Khatam al-Anbiya (the Khatam al-Anbiya construction military base), gradually took over the most lucrative state development projects. In the following decades Qarargah, an expanding economic conglomerate with numerous subsidiaries, acquired a near monopoly over major engineering, energy transmission, oil and gas, hydrological, and telecommunications projects. Being an integral part of the Revolutionary Guards' command structure and operating on a military model, the Qarargah may be compared to similar military-economic conglomerates elsewhere in Egypt, Thailand, and Myanmar. In the Islamic Republic the reciprocal arrangement between the clerical wing of the leadership, headed by the Supreme Leader, and the Revolutionary Guards, as the military guarantor of the regime, cannot be missed. In exchange for noninterference in the political sphere, the Revolutionary Guard is granted extensive economic monopolies to assure its institutional wellbeing and welfare of its personnel.

The excesses and adventurism of Ahmadinejad era were serious enough to bring even Khamenei to his senses. His implicit consent with the Guardian Council to hold a relatively fair presidential election in 2013 that brought Hasan Rouhani (b. 1948), a middle-of-the-road insider, to power was one manifestation of Khamenei's a conciliatory course, one motivated by expediency rather than radical ideology. Two years later his "heroic flexibility," as he justified his consent for concluding a nuclear deal with the Five plus One (the permanent members of the Security Council plus the European Union) is another example. For Khamenei, condoning the terms of the agreement, signed on July 14, 2015, to dismantle Iran's nuclear program, known as the Joint Comprehensive Plan of Action (JCPOA; the Persian acronym is *barjam*), signaled a shift in direction, one that can be compared to Khomeini's drinking from a "poisoned chalice." The agreement imposed on Iran a highly restrictive and intrusive regime of inspections and verifications, one that Iran has never before experienced in the course of its long and eventful modern history. For a regime that for more than three decades made the cause of "combatting the intrusions of the universal arrogance" its existential crusade, accepting the terms of JCPOA was a particularly humiliating experience. Yet contrary to Khomeini, who at least accepted the humiliating terms of the 1988 cease-fire, Khamenei did not feel even obligated to acknowledge a complete reversal of the nuclear policy.

Yet to its credit, the Islamic Republic for nearly four decades since its inception, and despite all its domestic and international challenges, was able to provide Iran with security at its borders and a remarkable degree of internal stability. This at the time when the whole region stretching from Pakistan and Afghanistan to Iraq, Syria and Palestine experienced domestic conflict, civil war, military invasions by superpowers, and prolonged and oppressive occupation. Despite all the hostile rhetoric that accused Iran of being the "threat to the security of the region" and "greatest sponsor of terrorism," it is important to note that four decades after President Carter declared Iran an "island of stability in one of the more troubled areas of the world," his words still bear some validity. Such stability, however, came at the price of domestic repression, social chasms, and boiling discontent that periodically has erupted and is likely to erupt again. But as the celebrated Iranian thinker Mohammad Ghazzali (1058–1111) put it nine centuries ago, "a hundred years of oppression is better than a day of chaos."

A SOCIETY IN TRANSITION

With better roads and communications and with changes in the pattern of agriculture invariably came changes in the relationship between city and countryside. Village life began to transform—with even greater rapidity than before the revolution. The extensive network of villages, hamlets, and oases across the plains, deserts, mountain slopes, river valleys, forests, and costal regions of Iran diminished in both number and population. They were all part of a precious habitat that had survived several millennia of earthquakes, drought, military campaigns, and maltreatment by the state and absentee landlords. Yet they were vulnerable to the potent nemesis of modernization, first in the Pahlavi era and then under the Islamic Republic. With the slow demise of Iran's basic rural social fabric, the idyllic village setting, with its distinctive architecture, also began to vanish gradually, giving way to mundane Western-inspired buildings with somewhat better construction and sanitation but often devoid of ecological or climatic rationales. Also vanishing were the *qanats*, the irrigation ponds, and the walled gardens indigenous to the Iranian landscape, the beasts of burden and cattle, species of plants and shrubs, even flocks of sheep and goats. Even more rapidly forgotten were village crafts and skills, regional dialects, folktales, ceremonies and rituals, and the diversity of clothing worn by people from different regions. With maddening speed Iran forged its path to uniformity, a path paved with fervor, damaging on its way much of the country's natural resources, wildlife and diverse habitats, and idyllic beauty. This ironically happened under the watch of a revolutionary regime that had called for "authenticity" and the preservation of Iran's unspoiled Islamic heritage.

At the edge of Iranian deserts, as remote villages were depopulated and their cultivation declined, soil erosion brought greater desertification. With the loss of their ancient function, many oases disappeared. They paid the price for the demise of the caravan trade and the end to the subsistence village economy, a process that had started decades earlier. Changes in old irrigation techniques, too, accelerated the villages' demise. Most notably, new deep-well pumping, which came to be extensively used in mechanized agriculture in the central Iranian plains, increased agricultural output but at a high cost. Not only did deep wells dangerously lower the water tables in subterranean aquifers; they also hastened a water shortage into a national crisis. Villages and their agricultural hinterlands that were in the vicinity of the growing cities, in particular, were eaten up piecemeal by land speculators and developers. They became victims of shoddy housing projects, treeless and birdless, which provided housing for the urban migrants from towns and villages near and far.

With few exceptions major Iranian cities, even more than in the Pahlavi era, began to suffer from a process of modernization gone awry. They grew haphazardly, short on amenities, vulnerable to earthquakes and other natural and manmade disasters, and some suffered from extreme levels of air pollution. Ineffective environmental control, substantial loss of green spaces in and around cities, and above all an unbridled cult of the car contributed to the degradation of urban life. Cars and small trucks, in particular, intruded into all public spaces and most private spaces at the expense of individuals and their privacy, devouring even pedestrian pavements, the front yards of houses, most green dividers in streets and boulevards, and any pathway possible or potentially possible. For many, vehicles were not merely means of transportation but tools of empowerment when their individual liberties have been curbed or taken away altogether.

A pattern of social ills, rampant from the early 1990s, complemented the failure of the state's social policies. Widespread drug addiction, prostitution networks, abused and abandoned children, teenagers escaping home, battered women and murdered spouses—all weakened society's moral fabric. These were compounded by huge discrepancies in wealth, high unemployment, and health and environmental problems. The new generations of urban Iranians under the Islamic Republic, frustrated by a regime that deprived them of political and social liberties and tired of the Islamic Republic's outmoded radicalism and incessant, almost maniacal, propaganda, adopted a double life of outward compliance and inward illicit leisure.

Drug addiction, in particular, became more widespread among the urban middle classes. While smoking opium was a declining recreational habit during the Pahlavi era, it gained a new lease of life under the Islamic Republic. More worrying, heroin addiction became dangerously rampant among youth. A ban on the cultivation of opium and the anti-addiction campaigns of the 1950s, one of the success stories of the Pahlavi era, had helped control opium addiction and drug abuse. With the rise of the Islamic Republic, however, it was as though the social stigma had been lifted and all moral barriers had crumbled. Even though the government of the Islamic Republic continued to enforce the ban on drugs and built up a substantial force to fight drug trafficking on its southeastern borders with Afghanistan and Pakistan, opium and purified heroin continued to be smuggled across the Baluchistan border in large quantities, despite the Revolutionary Guards' routine clashes with armed drug traffickers.

By the 1990s heroin, as a cheap and accessible drug, was available not only on the street but also in high schools and universities. Young victims from both sexes and every social class multiplied in large numbers, turning addiction into a major cause for the growth of underaged prostitution, both male and female, juvenile delinquency, and petty and organized crime. Addiction in Iran had deep historical roots, though perhaps not any more prevalent than in other societies exposed to rapid urban change. Yet addiction was emblematic of the failure of the revolutionary regime to fulfill its declared mission to eradicate "moral turpitude" through Islamic chastity and changes in the decadent lifestyles of the Pahlavi era.

The lure of illicit drugs was—and still is—that it allows for a temporary escape from the grim realities of life in postrevolutionary Iran. It was perhaps the most extreme manifestation of a subculture, confined and clandestine, that began to flourish in the 1980s among disillusioned and often cynical youth of the middle and lower-middle classes. Engrossed in Western-inspired fads, especially in larger cities and among the more affluent, it expressed itself in clothing and hairstyles, excessive partying, curious lingos, and a new middle-class cult of "child ingratiation" fostered by guilt-ridden parents anxious to make up for the state-imposed social and moral restrictions. The postrevolutionary youth of the 1990s and beyond even coined a term for this identity: the "burnt generation" (*nasl-e sukhteh*) summed up their unfulfilled aspirations and lost opportunities, audible in Iran's underground music and the lyrics of Iranian rappers.

An even more pronounced feature of the silent rejection of the Islamic Republic's dystopia was a contagious urge among many, and especially among the educated classes, to leave Iran and settle elsewhere. A sense of entrapment in their own country, coupled with an unrealistic, almost philistine, perception of the world beyond, was responsible for the departure from Iran of hundreds of thousands to uncertain futures. Iranian émigrés in increasing numbers were to be found wandering in low-income neighborhoods in Istanbul and Izmir awaiting entry visas to the United States and European countries, or in the shopping malls in Dubai and other UAE countries, in Greek port cities near the harbor preparing for crossing to other European destinations, in detention centers as far east as in Malaysia, Indonesia, Australia, and New Guinea, and as undocumented émigrés everywhere and many in detention centers and refugee camps. At no time in Iran's recent history has there been such a desperate movement of the population. The closest, the immigrant workers to Baku oil fields in the early decades of the twentieth century or to Kuwait in the 1960s, were temporary guest workers in much smaller numbers and invariably limited to unskilled workers from the Iranian countryside.

The Islamic Republic remained altogether indifferent to this massive brain drain. Propelled by the growth in the numbers of university graduates and professional classes who were unable to find gainful employment at home or unwilling to bow to unwelcome social pressures, the by-products of Iran's demographic revolution were to the regime more of a potential liability than a precious workforce necessary to build Iran's future. It was as if the boundary lines between the self and the other in the Islamic Republic were drawn in such a fashion as to protect an elite minority, loyal to the regime but inferior in education and skills, at the expense of repelling a far larger segment of the population who was educated and skilled but ideologically uncommitted to the emerging Islamic order. "Commitment [*ta'ahhod*] over expertise [*takhassos*]" was a favorite slogan that cost the Iranian economy dearly.

POLICING GENDER ROLES

A major thrust of the Islamic Republic's social and moral mission was to police gender roles. Despite paying lip service to women's elevated status in the constitution and widespread rhetoric about "restoring women's sublime motherly status," the Islamic Republic essentially viewed women with a patriarchal eye and treated them accordingly, or at least tried to. The male-favoring standards of the enforced shari'a, as interpreted by the regime and its jurists, consciously resisted gender equality. Uninformed and unaffected by the discourse of feminism, these standards came to determine not only women's physical appearance but also their social and familial roles, legal status, and civil rights. The ultimate marker for the new Islamic gender, predictably, was the mandatory use of the hijab and the regime's obsessive enforcement of chastity standards.

Threatened with the pain of humiliating arrests, detention, lashing, and monetary penalties, women, the younger generations in particular, were forced to abide by the redefined standards of Islamic modesty. Wearing the hijab, as murals and banners cautioned the public in the streets, stores, and restaurants, was "a religious duty upon which was erected the foundation of the Islamic Revolution." Under the rubric of "restoring women's dignity" and "rescuing them from the superficiality of Pahlavi pseudomodernity," a set of frequently repeated clichés in the regime's antimodernity rants aimed at associating secularized women with stereotypes of immodest attire, garish makeup and sexual laxity. In this fixated outlook, sexuality became the cornerstone of any male-female relationship. Any retreat of the headscarf showing a dash of women's hair, any shrinking in the length of the "Islamic" overalls (*rupush*), a touch of bright color, any showing of the natural female contour, the use of cosmetics—even nail polish—all were seen as potent mediums for arousing uncontrollable male sexuality. Hence they were subject to strict policing.

All through the first two decades of the Republic, the morality police, the dreaded "Patrol of God's Vengeance" (Gasht-e Sar-Allah), terrorized women in the capital and larger cities. They detailed a litany of moral transgressions that included the length of fingernails, the height of heels, and shades of hair highlighting. The never-ending chastity-enforcement campaigns not only revealed a fetishistic obsession with the female body but also an element of class warfare, for they set up poorer people with religious proclivities to inspect and correct the "vices" of a secularized middle class. A sense of empowerment was well evident in the conduct of the chastity police when encountering their terrified detainees. Nonconformity with the Islamic Republic's morality code, nonetheless, persisted among many women and men. Undeterred by prospects of humiliation and punishment, they hailed passive resistance as an article of faith against absurd practices of the Islamic regime.

Obsession with the human body, especially the female body, had a deep history in the Shi'i jurisprudence, for it served as the regulatory principle for enforcing hijab, gender segregation, and other controlling practices in the Islamic Republic and in its courts, schools, offices, and prisons. Shi'i jurisprudence viewed the vagina (*rahem*) as primal unit for kinship and family loyalties and legal rights, and henceforth demanded from the male members of the family and clan that they safeguard it. The ayatollahs' detailed descriptions in their books of "explication of problems" (*tawdih al-masa'il*), a dissertation-like requirement for acquiring *marja'iyat* in the twentieth century, in part spelled out intricate rules conducive to such a defense. For the general public these were the most accessible juristic production coming out of madrasas of Qom and Najaf. Aimed to regulate the lives of the "followers," they were unapologetic representations of male superiority formed in a male-only public environment. Among other means, these books of explication offered meticulous instructions about female reproductive organs, virginity, menstrual cycles, rules of sexual intercourse, manners of male penetration, ejaculation, and the handling of bodily fluids. They were also concerned with dress code and head covering for men and women, rules of intimacy, lawful interaction with the opposite sex, gender boundaries, segregation rules, and methods of sheltering women in residential confinement and outside. In all, the "explication" genre revealed deep anxieties about the human body and the dangers of allowing it to become undisciplined. The moral code it advanced was the guiding principle behind the Gasht-e Sar-Allah and similar shari'a-inspired moral policing.

Beyond enforcing a shari'a-prescribed bodily code, the essentially misogynistic clerical culture of Qom embarked on a systematic rewriting of women's civil and legal rights in the Islamic Republic. It reversed much of the achievements of the late Pahlavi era. Marriage and family laws were drastically rewritten along old patriarchal lines. Uninhibited polygamy was reintroduced, the age of marriage for females was lowered according to the dictates of the shari'a, under most circumstances divorce was redefined as the sole prerogative of the husband, and children's custodianship was primarily granted to the husband and paternal relatives. Compliance (*tamkin*) with the husband's sexual desires and abiding by his patriarchal superiority, rules that were endorsed by legislation and backed by the shari'a, turned women, at least on the surface, into objects of control and instruments of pleasure.

Restrictions on the social life of women and men, severe though they were, soon were to be balanced by deeper currents in Iranian society and outbursts of generational energies. Most remarkable, perhaps, was the growth and greater democratization of higher education, an unexpected outcome, as far as the Islamic Republic was concerned, of the demographic shifts of the 1970s and 1980s. Building new universities, institutes of higher education, and medical and vocational schools were among the Islamic Republic's priorities. Higher education, far more accessible than the Pahlavi era to both men and women, created a new college-educated generation, which, though energetic and ambitious, could not be absorbed promptly into the workforce. Despite restrictions on choice of professional field, women excelled in higher education because, by contrast to men, who were expected to entered the job market and support their family, women were able to continue their education, at times despite pressures to marry at an early age. The rapid growth of the universities, whether public, semiprivate, or private, increased the available opportunities. The Azad University system, a private institution with the state's informal backing, championed the new trend. Branching out in large cities and small towns throughout the country, its often small campuses had low budgets and were ill equipped, but they enabled, for a fee, hundreds of thousands of students to receive higher education who otherwise would have had little chance of entering more established universities. With flexible curricula and makeshift staffing, these private universities brought unprecedented geographical and, in effect, social mobility.

Young women and men enrolled in universities far away, moved out of their homes and hometowns, and learned to live independently along with cohorts from other towns and provinces. The separation from family and late absorption into the workforce facilitated a break from what had become provincial cocoons and, for women in particular, an escape from patriarchal bonds. The widening of intellectual horizons created new lifestyles and new expectations for careers and marriage. In larger cities, while the marriage age gradually rose as birthrates declined, the new middle classes felt even more starkly the absence of employment and career opportunities. By 1986 only about 6 percent of women were employed outside the home, and women's literacy rate stood at 65 percent, a discrepancy more pronounced in the mid-1990s, when the percentage of women in Iranian universities surpassed 50 percent of the total student body (and afterward steadily grew). More visible and more confident, younger women of postrevolutionary generations constituted a voiceless but palpable source of social discontent, at odds with the male-dominated elite of the Islamic Republic and their desire to keep women on the margins of, if not entirely outside, the public space. In some respects the societal dynamics of the postrevolutionary era gave younger women far greater agency than today's clerical elite ever anticipated.

VOICES AND VISIONS OF DISSENT

A stable but repressive order did not remain free of voices of dissent. As a space of resistance, one can detect in the emerging culture of the postrevolutionary times a degree of continuity with the 1960s and 1970s. Despite the state's stark intrusions through censorship, restrictions and manipulation—innocuously called Islamic guidance—culture and art remained bastions of Iranian individuality.

Music, cinema, visual arts, poetry, and fiction not only survived waves of Islamification but almost miraculously thrived. They managed to bypass, often in a
language of symbolism, the die-hard obscurantism and ideological hurdles of the
state's cultural bureaucracy and mirror, with subtlety, the untold sentiments of
their eager audiences. The palpable vitality of this eventful era complemented
the reformist aspirations that brought Khatami to powers but with deeper roots.

In the early days of the revolution, when high hopes for a new liberating
space were not yet entirely lost, a large sector of younger Iranians, and some
veterans of earlier political struggles, could rejoice in a momentary "dawn" of
freedom. In October 1979 the Persian lyricist Hushang Ebtehaj (b. 1928), with
the sobriquet "Sayeh" (shadow), composed a poignant *ghazal* entitled *Sepideh*
(the dawn) to be recited in the joyous *mahur* mode by the master of Persian classical music Mohammad Reza Shajarian (b. 1940). Performed in a public concert attended by thousands, and soon distributed nationwide on cassette tapes,
the lyrics and music captured the mood of the time. Just as he was achieving
new heights in his amazingly long singing career, Shajarian, along with some
of the best instrumentalists of the time, led by the composer and *tar* virtuoso
Mohammad Reza Lotfi (1947–2014), conveyed Ebtehaj's nostalgic message to
a new generation (pl. 17.1). Underscoring continuity with the past, the poet
stressed that the success of the revolution was indebted to the long and painful
struggle of past generations:

> Time has drawn your name in the new lot of Fortune,
> Be Joyful! The world is now turning in your favor.
> Oh, in this air how breaths are so full of fire, and yet joy!
> For this is the fragrant incense of our hearts that fills your nostrils.
> Remember the furnace of our burning breasts!
> Where in the fire of our hearts your raw clay was baked.
> The glow of one diamond from the treasure box of our hearts,
> Is now the morning light dawning upon your rooftops.
> It was through the mirror-like virtue of those who rise at dawn,
> That the sun's radiant visage was cast upon your night sky.
> Time is now handing you the reins of Fortune,
> For you are reined by the hands of wisdom.
> The Bird of Fortune that was fleeing the earth,
> Has landed and is pecking seeds in the safety of your net.
> Saddle the horse of Fortune under your questing loins,
> For you've tamed the heavens as you did the beast of the earth.
> Revel now in freedom's pleasure palace with *Sayeh*'s lyrics,
> So that your cups may brim with the wine of joy![1]

To the bitter disappointment of the poet's audiences, for most Iranians there was little "wine of joy," nor was there a "pleasure palace" of freedom, and certainly not any flight of the "Bird of Fortune." The "mirror-like virtue of those who rise at dawn," presumably a veiled reference to Khomeini and the religious message of the revolution, proved wishful thinking. Yet there were plenty of "burning breasts" within which to bake the "raw clay" of new generations of Iranians.

Modern Persian poetry, of which Ebtehaj offered some of the best in the neoclassical genre, however, was passed over as the predominant medium of artistic expression. Along with it was eclipsed a messianic yearning for a redemptive revolution. Modern poetry since Nima's time, despite masterful refinement, seems to have reached its limits even if great poets of the 1960s generation such as Forugh, Akhavan-Sales, Shamlu, Sepehri, and Mohammad-Reza Shafi'i Kadkani (b. 1939) making great poetry. A long poem by Akhavan-Sales in the classic genre of *qasideh*, with the opening line "Of the absurdity of the world if anything I love. You, my old homeland, you I love!," marked a new height in the neoclassical style. Composed in the postrevolutionary years, it illustrated the intricacies of Akhavan's style, his masterful yet accessible language, and the richness of his nostalgia for his country's past and for its fast-changing culture and natural environment, a poetic maturity that went beyond chauvinism and ideology. Whether modern or classic, however, it seemed as if a millennium-old tradition of Persian poetry were about to give way to a new medium of images. A verbal revolution of sorts had gradually dried up poetic creativity, even though appreciation of select modernist and classics such as Ferdowsi and Hafez remained strong.

Instead the growing fascination with cinematic imagery in the postrevolutionary era reflected a new artistic dynamism. Although Iran had a film industry since the 1930s, the new shift to cinematic language reflected a desire to move beyond words, whether poetry or prose. Fascination with cinema also reflected an earlier appeal of foreign films, ranging from Italian neorealism to highbrow cinemas of India and Japan and to Hollywood extravaganzas. Enthusiastic filmmakers and movie buffs, despite the severe ban on "corrupting" foreign films, turned to cinema as an effective means of cultural interconnectedness. The wider availability of videocassettes starting in the mid-1980s and a robust underground distribution network made this possible. The focus of Iranian art-house filmmakers, however, was somewhat different from contemporary currents outside Iran. A new sense of cultural confidence among younger filmmakers allowed for an endogenous cinematic language to grow. Iranian independent filmmakers exerted torturous effort to cope with the mandatory Islamic code for the performing arts and to pass the absurd censorship so as to get across their poignant message of social criticism or philosophical musings.

With a refreshing honesty that characterized much of Iranian cinema's "new wave," the filmmakers' cameras subtly but unapologetically examined taboos that had barely been touched on in Iranian films or any other media. Issues such as the plight of women in a patriarchal society, children's deprivation, violence and socioethnic biases, drug addiction, prostitution, and the underworld, as well as class divides and poverty, the dreariness of everyday life, double standards and muddled ethics, shades of religiosity, intellectual despair and the search for alternatives, and even clerical hypocrisy became powerful counterweights to the regime's deceptive portrayal of the pious life in the paradise of the Islamic Republic.

By far neorealism ruled supreme among Iranian filmmakers of the 1980s and 1990s, even though they were mostly obliged to work within the genre of children's films to secure funding and pass the censors. The film department of the Organization for the Intellectual Development of Children and Young Adults, one of the more successful institutions established in 1965 with the patronage of Queen Farah, had a lasting impact on filmmakers of the next generation. *Bashu* (1986, released in 1989) by the gifted playwright and filmmaker Bahram Bayzai (b. 1938) and produced by the Children and Young Adults Organizations, was one of the first in the postrevolutionary era to address the delicate issue of ethnic diversity and national integrity while the Iraq-Iran War was raging.

The main character, Bashu, "a little stranger" as the subtitle informs us, is a dark-skinned teenage Arab-Iranian refugee from the war-torn Persian Gulf provinces who, having lost his family in Iraqi raids, in distress climbs in the back of a passing truck that brings him the next day to a serene but alien village in the Caspian province of Gilan. Given shelter by a woman villager, Na'i, who takes pity on him, they bond in near silence, despite their own doubts and each other's suspicions. Bashu does not understand the Gilaki dialect of northern Iran, nor does Na'i comprehend the Arabic dialect of the south. The drama reaches a climax when Na'i's husband returns. He is a disabled war veteran (who apparently by dictate of the censor was portrayed as returning from a failed job search in the city), a male symbol who is absent throughout the story but appears at the end as a nuisance, resisting the true mother-child bond that has developed against all odds between one from the north and one from the south.

The thinly veiled patriotic message of the movie is devoid of any Islamic component and free of Tehran-centric sentiments, even though Persian is the only means of communication. The unifying message of the film: Iranians moving beyond ethnicity, language, and race (and presumably religion, if Bashu is to be considered a Sunni) may well be interpreted as Bayzai's foresight about Iran's emerging society, when the demographic melting pot of the postwar era dissolves regional barriers and removes hollowed and soulless, yet terrifying, symbols of authority. In the last scene, Bashu, along with other village boys, runs across the rice fields assailing a black scarecrow, which symbolizes throughout the film the intimidating male power of the state.

'Abbas Kiarostami (1940–2016), another filmmaker of the 1970s who started with children's films, left his lasting mark on postrevolutionary cinema but also became a major cultural figure of the period. His poetic-philosophical approach to cinema, both in subject and in technique, offered an inward view. His existential soul-searching with a touch of humor, palpable even in his treatment of social themes, was followed by other filmmakers inspired by his enigmatic message. Creating a pictorial rendering of Persian mystical poetry, he portrayed with a stoic eye the rhythm of the ordinary lives of the people of towns and villages, which are fast disappearing. Theirs, he reminds his viewers, has a subtle existential endurance that is missing in the anguished lives of the sophisticated middle classes and agonized intellectuals.

Even in *Close-Up* (1990), where he makes a powerful statement about the younger generation's fascination with cinema, we can detect threads of innocence gone astray. The leading character in the film, Hosain Sabzian, an impostor who plays himself in this reconstruction of a true story, is on trial for pretending to be the well-known film director of the time, Mohsen Makhmalbaf (b. 1957). An affable man of humble background, Sabzian has gone so far as to convince members of an affluent but naive middle class family, also playing themselves, to finance his next imaginary film project. He has also motivated the family's young son, who is dreaming about becoming a filmmaker. In dissecting the narrative, Kiarostami carries viewers with him to share an insight into Sabzian's mind. The impostor did not wish to be wealthy or powerful or even famous. Rather, he aspired to a cultural sophistication that would allow him to convey his vision through films much as his hero did. Sabzian's quest was symbolic of a generation enamored of cinema because it is an escape from the harsh, almost surreal, realities of postrevolutionary times.

In *The Circle* (2000) by Ja'far Panahi (b. 1960), the inescapabilty of the vicious cycle of everyday life becomes ever more apparent, especially for its younger victims of the society's harsh and unfair realities. It juxtaposes the lives of six young women in Tehran of the 1990s and their struggles in the face of misogynistic mores, family tyranny and, above all, the long arm of the state. The film's female characters represent a cross-section of crushed lives as these fellow travelers endure deprivation across a sea of fear and denial. This is an acciden-

tal sisterhood whose members understand one another's unwanted and undeserved fates. What is remarkable is that they are not devoid of human agency
and are not merely passive recipients of what society or authorities impose on
them. Yet by escaping their homes in search of freer lives, they encounter severe
desperation that drives them to prostitution, unavoidable abortion, abandonment of their children, and jail (repeatedly). Such is the outcome, as *The Circle*
powerfully underscores, of three decades of morality police and the project of
Islamification.

Equally poignantly, women directors dealt with the plight of women with
a naked realism and palpable rage. *Two Women* (1999) by Tahmineh Milani
(b. 1960), one of several movies she produced with feminist themes, narrates
the lives of two young women over a period of fourteen years at the outset of
the Revolution. Out of economic desperation and under family pressure, the
talented but unprivileged character quits school during the Cultural Revolution and under pressure enters into a marriage that exposes her to her husband's
tyranny and abuse. The Islamic legal code is squarely in the husband's favor,
leading to a tragic ending for which Milani condemns male-dominated society
and its failings. Yet similar to the characters of *The Cycle*, the women resist becoming objectified and passive—an aspiration rather than reality, perhaps, but
emblematic nevertheless of the changing female awareness at all levels.

In *Under the Skin of the City* (2000) Rakhshan Bani Etemad (b. 1954), another talented woman director with an impressive cinematic record, portrays
the sufferings of a humble textile worker, who besides the absence of an oppressive husband is subject to destructive forces beyond her control. Here, an
unhappy daughter with an abusive husband, a dissident son on the run, another
son who desires to leave Iran at any cost—even at the cost of ransoming the
family house to loan sharks and later, in desperation, smuggling heroin—brings
the mother to utter despair. Such a profusion of social troubles may seem rather
forced if we overlook the urgency by which Bani Etemad brings her symbolic
message home.

As much as the new wave of Iranian cinema reflected social ills and personal
anguish, it also pointed at an emerging Iranian identity decidedly separate from
the ideals of the state. The popular appeal of most of these movies beyond highbrow viewers and international festivals, where they received many awards and
accolades, points to the public's desire to see their reality unmasked and their
agonies surface even if the censorship does not permit its full exposure. Such a
collective wish elevated the role of cinema in Iran beyond entertainment and
leisure into a powerful instrument of dissent, unmatched in its scope and impact by literary or other modes of cultural expression. The potency of this mes-

sage of dissent played a major part in elevating Iranian cinema—as early as the 1960s but more poignantly since the Islamic Revolution—to internationally acknowledged standards. Asghar Farhadi's *A Separation* (2011) clearly relayed such a message to audiences at home and abroad.

A Separation is about the painful divorce of a young middle-class Tehran couple, Nader and Simin, whose daughter is involuntarily caught in their wrangling over custody. Simin wishes to leave Iran and settle abroad, whereas Nader does not wish to sever ties, emotional and familial, to his country. The couple's motive for separation, to which Farhadi (b. 1971) clearly alludes, is more societal than personal; it is as if they have been left no choice but to part ways. To take care of his elderly father who suffers from dementia, Nader hires a caretaker. As much as the father's situation is a very real human one, he is also a metaphor for the burden of a rapidly vanishing past. The caretaker is a working-class woman with an outlook shaped by the traditional Shi'i code of conduct, one that is blessed by the Islamic Republic. The complex plot revolves around the suspicion of theft, for which the caretaker is subjected to an act of alleged violence by Nader. The ambiguity surrounding the event involves the caretaker's husband, an unemployed worker with nervous demeanor who takes upon himself the mission of protecting his wife and preserving his honor. The story masterfully portrays generational, class, cultural, and gender tensions in today's Iran while also depicting the multiplicity of reality and ambiguities surrounding human relationships. One of the most important features of the film is its ability to humanize the Iranian society's dilemmas and tensions. The film's enthusiastic reception worldwide (which included being awarded the Golden Bear at the Berlin International Film Festival, a Golden Globe Award, and Academy Award for Best Foreign Language Film in 2011) denoted its universal appeal, for it was able to present the Iranian couple not in an exceptional Iranian light but as a microcosm of a global phenomenon.

As much as cinema appealed to younger Iranians, classical Persian music and its remarkable revival in the postrevolutionary era projected the other side of the quest for cultural autonomy. Reclaiming the Persian musical tradition in the face of the Islamic state's initial rejection was not only an act of defiance but also a window onto a fascinating world where the confluence of music and poetry brought back to the present centuries of collective memory. Persian lyrical poetry combined with songs of the constitutional and early Pahlavi eras and examples of Kurdish, Luri, and other pastoral melodies, served as a cultural ground for this recovered cultural past.

A number of musicians and composers with roots in the prerevolutionary era contributed to the flourishing musical scene. Great virtuosi of the Pahlavi era aside, among the younger artists, Hossein Alizadeh (b. 1951) followed a well-trodden path in Iran's musical modernity by employing Persian melodies to compose brilliant ensemble music and film music. His work proved on par with the best of contemporary classical music worldwide. His 1983 *Naynava*, a concerto for the Persian *nay* (reed pipe) and string orchestra consisting of five interconnected pieces based on melodies (*gushehs*) in the *Nava* mode combined Persian and Western string instruments to deliver a melodically absorbing and technically intricate composition. Reminiscent of the famous opening passage of Rumi's *Masnavi*, it is a melodic conversation between the string orchestra, representing the vibrating human vocal chords, and the sound of the *nay*, representing the inspired melody that, according to the Sufi thought, is divinely embedded in the human chest. The riveting finale, "Raqs o Sama'" (Dance and music) is inspired by the ecstatic dance and music of Sufi gatherings.

A prolific artist, Alizadeh also composed the 1989 *Torkaman*, a set of instrumental pieces for the Persian *setar*. In the fourteen improvised pieces that constitute *Torkaman*, Alizadeh employed the Persian *radif* system to capture melodies, sounds, and sceneries of Iran's northeastern frontier of Torkaman Sahra. With a rare technical ability, he explores *setar*'s possibilities of producing a range of musical impressions, from galloping horses in the steppe to the wailing of Turkmen mourners. Alizadeh is versatile in utilizing folk melodies and local musical instruments from all over Iran, features that made his music daring and innovative. As in Bayzai's *Bashu* or Kiarostami's trilogy on Iranian village life, and Akhavan-Sales's *qasideh* eulogizing Iran, many of Alizadeh's compositions are tributes to Iran's vanishing ethnic and regional diversity, a subconscious effort, perhaps, to withstand forces of cultural homogeneity.

Mohammad Reza Lotfi and Parviz Meshkatian (1955–2009) also utilized rural and nomadic tunes to capture the revolutionary spirit of their time and compose some of the most memorable songs of the era. The tangible absence of female performers and vocalists, however, because of the Islamic Republic's ban on women performing in public, exposed a major lacuna. Yet the ban did not deter women from excelling in Persian music in private. Vocalist Parisa was among the best of her generation in mastering classical *radif* and offering new renderings of the old Qajar songs. Some of her early concerts in the Shiraz Arts Festival adhered to the *radif* performance as pioneered a half a century earlier by Qamar al-Moluk Vaziri, who was among the first women to record Persian classical music in the 1920s and 1930s.

Perhaps the most distinguished figure of Persian musical revival since the 1970s, however, is Mohammad Reza Shajarian, a master vocalist of remarkable quality and range. His popularity over the years has given him an iconic position, free of state patronage and immune to its infringement. Born in 1931 in Mashhad to a religious family—his father was a teacher and professional reciter (*qari*) of the Qur'an—he grew up to be not only a marvelous reciter of the Qur'an, and for a while an elementary school teacher in villages of northern Khorasan, but also a serious student of Persian *radif*. Initially a self-taught vocalist, he listened to radio broadcasts and musical records made by former masters before receiving any systematic training. Overcoming the traditional stigma of becoming professional singer, he performed first in Radio Mashhad and from 1966 on Radio Iran's celebrated *Golha* program, where he had his first national exposure. His career spanning more than forty years made him an undisputed master of Persian music and a symbol of artistic integrity. Having been able to perform in the prerevolutionary era, during the revolution, and later under an Islamic regime that frowned upon, if not outright banned, the production and performance of music outside its official domain. He gleaned from most of the masters of his time a vast repertoire of melodies and singing techniques, intricate details of *tasnifs*, diverse folk music of Iran (especially Khorasan), and music of the Shi'i mourning rituals.

With a fine taste for selecting Persian poetry for his concerts and albums, Shajarian has conveyed with subtlety his messages in carefully composed performances. Refusing to perform on the Islamic Republic's radio and television networks in protest to their miscasting of his music, in a 1982 concert he recited a well-known *ghazal* of Hafez. This concert, released on a 1986 album, was titled "Bidad" (Injustice), a play on a *gusheh* in the Homayun mode. Hafez's *ghazal*, wistfully reminiscing an idyllic past, well fit the mood of Shajarian's audiences discouraged by the strange turn of revolution's fortune:

Friendship I see naught, what befallen to friends?
When affection came to pass? What happened to lovers? . . .
No jewel unearthed from the mine of camaraderie for years,
What happened to the heat of the sun, the might of the wind and the rain?
Ours was the land of companions [*shahr-e yaran*] and the soil of sun priests
     [*mehr-banan*],
When did camaraderie [*mehrbani*] end? Where are the princes of the realm
     [*shahryaran*]?
Hundreds of thousands of flowers bloomed and not a single bird sang,
What happened to the nightingales, where are the songsters? . . .
Silent O Hafez! No one knows mysteries of the providence,
From whom do you ask what befell at the turns of the Time?[2]

References to camaraderie lost, to his barren land that once belonged to sun priests—an allusion to the ancient Zoroastrians in Fars province, to perished princes of the realm (another allusion to a princely patron of the poet), to silent nightingales (probably the poet-singer himself), and finally to mysterious turns of fortune deeply resonated with audiences, who may have identified with Hafez's allusions to "injustices" of their own time and misfortunes of the revolutionary course.

In his 1999 Ahang-e Vafa (Song of faithfulness) Shajarian included an old song with lyrics by Bahar, the poet of the Constitutional Revolution and composed by the celebrated Gholam-Hosain Darvish (1872–1926), possibly in 1915, when most of Iran had come under Russian and British occupation. The message resonated with Shajarian's audiences eight decades later:

> It is all gloom and doom,
> Will a dawn to our night ever bloom?
> Our homeland has no other cure,
> But to wait and endure.
> Poor Bahar stop moaning,
> For there is no use in sobbing and sighing.

Shajarian had to add a note to the album's leaflet, presumably at the request of the Ministry of Islamic Guidance, stressing that the song "was composed at the end of the Qajar era and reflects conditions of that time." He also dropped the final line in Bahar's lyric:

> From both directions they smack on her head [i.e., Iran],
> She who doesn't have a double-edged blade.[3]

A GREEN SEDITION

In June 2009 the Green Movement (jonbesh-e sabz) brought to the surface among the urban middle classes these undercurrents of discontent with the Islamic Republic and its devious ways. Triggered by the presidential election campaigns of two opposition candidates, Mir Hosein Musavi (b. 1942) and Mahdi Karrubi (b. 1937), who were running against the incumbent President Ahmadinejad, the Green Movement brought millions to the streets of the capital and provincial centers. They were the largest demonstrations that Iran has seen since the early days of the revolution three decades earlier. Both challenging candidates were among the regime's insiders—Musavi being the former prime minister between 1981 and 1989, and Karrubi a ranking cleric who served a number of times as speaker of the Majles—they were hailed by the public and welcomed as realistic alternatives to Ahmadinejad's presidency. What motivated the campaign rallies to transform into a mass protest movement, more than the relative credibility of the opposition candidates, was Ahmadinejad's disastrous presidency, Khamenei's flawed judgment, and the Islamic Republic's fearful elite.

The vote rigging in favor of Ahmadinejad that reinstated him in office were followed in succeeding days by the Supreme Leader's endorsement of the rigged election. His approval, coming after an equally flawed inquiry by the Guardian Council, confirmed the regime's audacity to enforce a lie. The subsequent clampdown on the rallies, mass arrests of protesters, barbaric torture in detention centers, and secret murders of detainees further displayed a willingness to use whatever means were at the regime's disposal to crush any voice of opposition. The mass trials in front of television cameras, when large numbers of "leaders of sedition" (*saran-e fetneh*) were tried and given heavy sentences, were reminiscent of the Soviet-style trials of the Stalin era. The Green Movement, named after the green color adopted by the protesters, above all demonstrated popular demand for liberalization, democracy, and accountability. It revealed to the Islamic regime, to the international community, and to the hundreds of thousands who gathered in Maydan Azadi in Tehran, in Maydan Naqsh-e Jahan in Isfahan, and elsewhere in Iran the existence of popular dissent among the predominantly young middle classes (pl. 17.2). After thirty years of the regime's Islamification, failed economic policies, international isolation, and ethnic, religious, and cultural repression, people had not sunk into submission. Although the Green Movement was crushed, the hope for change is unabated: there is hope for a more open and more tolerant state that allows for its citizens to flourish, to emerge from deacades of isolation, and for the revolution to bear unspoiled fruits.

Soon after the authorities labeled the Green Movement as a *fetneh* (Arabic *fitna*, meaning "sedition") so as to discredit it in the eye of the public as an act of rebellion against the just cause of the Islamic government. Yet seemingly unbeknownst to the regime, the concept of *fetneh* in Islamic history, and even with the greater resonance in Iran's historical experience, carried an intricate subtext. As much as in the hand of the authorities *fetneh* could be used to denounce and to stamp out the dissent, *fetneh* also conveys a sense of rebellion against the unjust rule, a notion perhaps closest to the modern concept of a popular revolution. Even in Shi'i apocalyptic prophecies the advent of the

Mahdi, the Lord of the Time, is preceded by a *fetneh*—one that eventually topples the dark age of the antichrist, known as the Dajjal, and paves the way for the establishment of the Mahdi's "just and equitable order." It was as if three decades of resting in power had made the authorities in the Islamic Republic forget not only the fact that the 1979 revolution was a *fetneh* but also the very Shi'i prophecies that they had studied, or ought to have studied, in the madrasas of Qom.

EPILOGUE

The Islamic Revolution of 1979 and its aftermath not only brought down the Pahlavi regime and dismantled its elite; it also allowed, for the first time in Iran's long history, the Shiʻi clerical establishment to assume political power. The magnitude of this paradigmatic shift, and the way a conservative Shiʻi establishment transformed into a radical force of dissent, becomes all the more striking when we set the Islamic Revolution in the broader political and cultural contexts of the past five centuries.

The unraveling of the ancient pact between religion and state, the pillars of an ancient social order with a conservative worldview, did not occur in a vacuum. As discussed in Part III, it was the outcome of a project of the state's secular modernity that since the early decades of the twentieth century had shaped Pahlavi Iran; the trajectory, which gave the state far greater economic and political autonomy in implementing a top-down program of secularizing and centralizing reforms, gradually alienated the bazaar and the clergy, which in turn eroded Iran's delicate sociocultural balance. In the middle decades of the century the quest for economic sovereignty and the National Movement under Mosaddeq did not succeed in dislodging Pahlavi because of foreign intervention, but more so because state-religion ties endured. The Shiʻi clerical establishment in effect was the beneficiary of the Pahlavi restoration; it consolidated without giving full allegiance to the state.

To understand how a program of state modernization in the Pahlavi era could be carried through independently of the religious establishment but also independently of a grassroots democratic process, we must look back at the circumstances in the nineteenth century, as discussed in Part II, whereby a number of factors, including the meager economic resources at the government's disposal,

897

made even selective reforms a formidable task. Long-standing geopolitical pressures from neighboring empires, suppression of indigenous ideas of reform and renewal (as in the Babi movement), and the aborted state-sponsored reform under Amir Kabir—all hindered Iran's process of modernity. The experience of the Constitutional Revolution clearly demonstrated domestic and foreign obstacles to forging a constitutional regime. While the indigenous dissidents among the preachers and their bazaar support successfully challenged both the Qajar state and the authority of the conservative clergy, they succumbed to the interests of the landed nobility, to imperial vested interests, and eventually to the contingencies of security and territorial integrity that brought Reza Khan and his military cohort to power.

Despite demographic and economic deficiencies, ineffective institutional reforms, and resistance to European intrusions, the geopolitical equilibrium that prevailed in the Qajar period allowed Iran to survive the direct onslaughts of its neighbors. This was not merely because of European imperial deigns to preserve Iran as a buffer state, but more so because of renewed societal bonds and revival of a political culture that relied on the Persian model of kingship and appealed to the imperial memory of the Safavid past. The Safavid and the post-Safavid experiences, as discussed in Part I, made Shi'ism a defining character of the state and a source of social cohesion and national identity. Resistance against hostile pressures on its frontiers and the forging of new commercial and diplomatic connections with the outside world helped tie the Safavid Empire to the Iranian plateau and set it apart from its Sunni nemesis to the west and east. To incorporate numerous regional entities into the Guarded Domains of Iran, the Safavid project of empire building also required a confederacy of the Qezilbash tribes, a political construct that in long run generated new tensions between the political center and its periphery. After the collapse of the Safavid Empire, at least two attempts to restore the Safavid order were inconclusive, largely because the Afshars and to some extent the Zands aimed to substitute the Shi'i solidarity and renewal of the state-religion bonds with other sources of loyalty.

Beyond this sketch, looking for patterns over the course of half a millennium between the rise of the Safavid dynasty and the shaping of the Islamic Republic is a formidable task, and possibly a hazardous one. Long-term historical trends, the *longue durée*, are subject to many exceptions in time and space. Yet they help place the seemingly fragmented course of events into a relatively coherent landscape. Iran has preserved its territorial integrity since the sixteenth century despite domestic ups and downs and losses along its periphery; its political sovereignty endured, as well, against many odds. Military threats from mighty neighboring empires and nomadic and seminomadic incursions along its frontiers were not rare. The Guarded Domains of Iran, as it was traditionally known, survived in part because of a degree of decentralization along its provincial, ethnic, communal, and linguistic divides.

The Iranian state and social order were fragile, and the forces in the periphery frequently resisted domination by the state. Yet they contributed to a relatively cohesive cultural and religious core. In the Persian political culture, maintaining the balance between "the inland and the border" (Persian: *bum va bar*; and its synonym *marz va bum*: "the frontier and the inland") was key to the security and prosperity of the Guarded Domains. The delicate balance between the sedentary center and the mobile periphery depended on "justice" (Persian *dad*; Arabic *'adl*), an ancient principle of government and one of the five fundamental beliefs in Shi'ism. The "injustice" (*bidad*), as the *Shahnameh* frequently reminds its readers, destroys both the center and the frontier. Modern nationalism reinforced centralization and fostered greater social cohesion. The relative absence of ethnic hostilities since the early decades of the twentieth century, in contrast to civil wars and sessions elsewhere in the postcolonial era, contributed to Iran's greater homogeneity. Using a tangible, though imperfect, analogy, Iran stood like an old mansion in the midst of a redeveloped neighborhood in which the plots have been awkwardly divided and the neighbors were, and still are, uncomfortable in their dwellings.

The state continued to seek legitimacy by relying on memories of an imperial past and through claims to be the defender of the land of Islam and the Shi'i creed. It endured by maintaining an elaborate court, demonstrating the royal might, exemplary punishments, displays of generosity, and patronage of the religious establishment, as well as arts and poetry. A class of landed nobility who held ministerial posts in the divan, and, to a lesser extent, those who enjoyed semiautonomous tribal power, also sustained the state. Defeat in war and loss of territory in the early nineteenth century, however, diminished the Qajar state's prestige and tarnished its image. Through consent and occasional coercion the state had to negotiate with urban notables, the ulama, the landed class, and the tribal khans, to preserve a precarious equilibrium. The most persistent obstacle, however, was lack of a rational division of labor between the court (*dargah*) and the divan. The interplay between the court and the bureaucratic elite was never fully regulated, despite repeated attempts to reform the system. Ministers never managed to secure their place at a safe distance from the rulers and often suffered from the insecurity of their high office. It was to remedy this dysfunctional relation between court and bureaucracy that the discourse of reform was first introduced. Plans to restructure the state, a preoccupation of a Westernizing minority within the Qajar elite, were never detached from a sense of decline that prevailed in the late nineteenth century, particularly as a material gap in comparison with Europe became more apparent and the weakening of the domestic economy more tangible.

The urban elites, including members of the divan, and the tribal khans controlled most of Iran's agrarian economy, which remained the most important source of wealth and state revenue before the twentieth century. The land tenure system was a major tool of state patronage, but in the late nineteenth and early twentieth centuries, private land ownership by the members of the divan, affluent merchants, and even wealthy ulama was not uncommon. Throughout the period, but more visibly since the seventeenth century, Iran's subsistence agrarian economy was complemented by the introduction of cash crops, which changed the patterns of Iran's foreign trade. Silk, cotton, and—later in the Qajar period—opium and tobacco, were exports that injected revenue into the Iranian economy and paid for the increasing volume of imports from neighboring lands and overseas.

Despite Iran being at a migratory, commercial, and cultural crossroads in Eurasia, changes in the Central Asian caravan routes, the rise of the Uzbek Empire and other nomadic barriers, and the opening of new maritime routes to China brought Iran's ancient trade with East Asia to a virtual standstill. Iran's access to the Mediterranean and the Black Sea, too, was restrained, though never fully abandoned, after the rise of the Ottoman Empire and later because of the Shi'i-Sunni conflict. The decline of the Mediterranean route and the Central Asian route in turn contributed in the eighteenth century to Iran's economic isolation and had a direct effect on the diminished wealth and the prosperity of its cities. In the nineteenth century the Persian Gulf, and the Caspian and Black Sea routes nevertheless revitalized foreign trade and brought greater prosperity to long-distance merchants and their associates. From late antiquity Iran has always been an active partner in the Indian Ocean trade, but from the seventeenth century onward through the southern maritime route, it gained access to European and East Asian markets and exported a variety of commodities, including silk, opium, tobacco, and carpets, and eventually oil in the twentieth century . Yet for reasons of geography—the difficult terrain, which made access to the interior cumbersome—the Persian Gulf and Caspian ports seldom sustained a powerful mercantile presence like that of Aleppo, Alexandria, Istanbul, or Mumbai. Iranians never became a serious seafaring nation in modern times partly because of a lack of forests in the south to supply timber for shipbuilding. As a land-bound power, Iran had no navy to speak of and nurtured no maritime commercial or colonial ambitions.

Iran, moreover, did not seriously industrialize before the middle of the twentieth century. Like other non-Western countries, Iran was further incorporated into the world market in the latter part of the nineteenth century. It supplied the European industrial powerhouses with cash crops while increasingly becoming a market for Western manufactured goods. Iran's international trade in the nineteenth century mostly benefited the mercantile classes at the expense of local manufacturers. The most important of the export items, petroleum, however, was developed in the twentieth century by the British almost as if it were a colonial plantation commodity, with no direct Iranian input except unskilled labor. The urbanized mercantile classes by and large remained commodity traders rather than industrial manufacturers, but the Iranian bazaar remained a powerful site of their political protest.

The Safavid Empire and its successors also relied on their subjects' loyalty through a state-enforced creed. By the middle of the eighteenth century, if not earlier, Iran had become not only a Shi'i state but also a Shi'i society. Nader Shah's failure to revert back to the Sunni fold (or even position Shi'ism as an accepted creed within the Sunni realm) proved the depth of Iran's Shi'i conviction. As much as the majority of Iranians became more loyal to their faith, even as early as the middle of the sixteenth century, their Sunni neighbors were adamant to keep them as their heretical "other." More than any other unifying force, what held together the sinews of Iranian ruling classes—the kingship, the nobility, the divan, the religious establishment, the large landowners, the urban notables, and even the tribal khans—proved to be the Shi'i religion. Shi'ism also served as the most important ingredient bonding the majority population in the cities and the countryside to the state and its ruling elites. The Safavids and the Qajars, and to a lesser extent the dynasties in between, posed as "defenders of the faith."

In reality, this meant that the state had to accommodate a clerical class, which by the nineteenth century came to acquire a semiautonomous status. The sisterhood of the religious establishment and the temporal state (*din va dowlat*), which was at the heart of Persian political culture at least since the Sasanian era, only renewed in the Safavid era, and then again in the Qajar period. Up to the middle of the twentieth century, the clergy remained in partnership, at least implicitly, with the dynastic state and the nobility. They coexisted, despite inherent tensions. Shi'ism as a national creed came to reinforce communal identity while avoiding active political involvement. Judicial authority did not rest solely with either the clerical establishment or the state. The blurred boundaries between the shari'a and customary laws were never straightened out before the implementation of modern legal codes during the Constitutional Revolution and later under early Pahlavi rule.

The dual existence of the Mahdi in Shi'i beliefs and in Shi'i concept of authority, that he was presumed to be alive and yet hidden, proved a major obstacle to temporal legitimacy. The existence of the Mahdi not only potentially challenged the validity of the temporal state, and any theoretical possibility of a just and equitable rule, but also gave the clerical establishment a collective authority on behalf of the Imam of the Age. Before the latter half of the twentieth century, Shi'ism never articulated a workable theory of government that reconciled temporal power with the utopian kingdom of the Mahdi. It never explicitly denied the validity of the institution of kingship either. The ulama always remained indebted to the state for support and patronage. Instead, they invariably labeled anticlerical and messianic movement as heretical, and helped to silence them, although they could not stamp them out altogether or stop prophetic expressions that were inspired, directly or indirectly, by the messianic legacy inherent to the Iranian environment. The dynamics of priests versus prophets, to borrow a Weberian concept, proved one of the most enduring. The clerical authorities were never able to fully eradicate prophetic, speculative, philosophical, and mystical trends, either. Nor were they in full control of folk Shi'ism or popular beliefs, also inherent to the Iranian environment and often the breeding ground for messianic aspirations. Despite a sustained air of intolerance, an uneasy equilibrium allowed for both formal and informal religions to coexist and even thrive.

Movements of protest thus remained an integral part of the religious landscape and increasingly came to represent in the nineteenth and twentieth centuries socioeconomic discontent. Starting with the Safavi order itself in the fifteenth century and followed by the Noqtavi, Sufi Ne'matollahi, the Shaykhi doctrine and later the Babi movement, the Mahdi cult in Shi'ism contested clerical authority and its overly legalistic reading of religion. The antinomian ideas ingrained in all these movements sought an apocalyptic end to the shari'a, implicitly and at times explicitly. The dual existence of the Imam of the Age and the possibility of his advent, posed a unique tension within Shi'ism that went beyond mere theology. Despite a powerful appeal to the disenchanted, to the ordinary folks, and to communities on the religious fringe, messianic trends seldom withstood the onslaught of the state-ulama symbiosis. Though they had survived in the Iranian world for centuries, they could convert only within clandestine networks. At the turn of the twentieth century, the Constitutional Revolution, a form of secularized messianism, was an exception. And that succeeded only to a limited extent.

Despite the state-clergy symbiosis that ensured some stability in the Qajar era, the structural handicaps of the Iranian political system paved the way for new outside challenges. Virtually throughout the period under consideration, Iranian borders, and at times the state's very existence, were threatened by geopolitical threats and foreign invasions. The dual Ottoman and the Uzbek threats up to the middle of the eighteenth century forced Iran into a two-front defense strategy. Any imperial expansion beyond Iran proper, such as Nader Shah's expedition to Iraq and Hindustan, therefore proved ephemeral and unsustainable. From the early nineteenth century the competing strategies of the two European empires, Russia and Britain, introduced a north-south polarity into the region within which Iran stood as a "buffer."

The two European powers interfered with Iran's domestic affairs and compromised its sovereignty. Yet their strategies did not result in the Iranian state's total loss of political agency. It can be argued that Iran took advantage of its buffer status to stabilize and recover from devastation caused by political strife in the eighteenth century. Even though it lost territory and prestige, in the long run Iran managed to gain strategically by acquiring a recognized status in the European imperial vista as a sovereign state. Iranians learned to confirm their survival not by means of confronting mighty armies in the battlefield but by negotiation, backdoor deals, and even playing the European powers against one another. Despite lack of clear foreign policy and a paucity of administrative and economic resources before the Pahlavi era, Iran did not entirely succumb even to Europe's informal colonialism. The so-called Persian Question in late-nineteenth-century diplomacy can be read as a prelude to Iran's fragmentation, as the 1907 agreement between Russia and Britain confirmed. Yet it could also be seen as the success of Iran's foreign policy in keeping the two powers at bay.

During the Constitutional Revolution both the Western-inspired reform and the indigenous messianic trends converged into a relatively coherent discourse giving voice to an emerging urban intelligentsia and their demands to end arbitrary rule, open the political space, and create modern legislative and judicial institutions. The Constitutional Revolution should be seen as a moment in Iran's modern history when Western-inspired institutions of democracy, division of powers, popular representation, and individual freedoms were adopted into the Iranian environment and fused with aspirations for justice and renewal. Constitutionalism, moreover, was perceived as the key to material progress, secularism, centralization, and state-implemented reforms. The Constitutional Revolution weakened the Qajars' arbitrary rule but ironically opened the way for the landowning nobility and their vested interests to gain more power without making the new democratic institutions any more effective. They in turn witnessed in the person of Reza Shah and his cohorts the making of a strong state, one of the chief objectives of the Constitutional Revolution. In the aftermath of the Constitutional Revolution and at the end of the World War I, a large sector of the Iranian middle class and its intelligentsia by and large acquiesced to autocratic Pahlavi modernism as the only viable option for restoring Iran's threatened sovereignty and implementing long-awaited reforms.

The rise of the Pahlavi state in the 1920s changed the patterns that had been set at least since the rise of the Safavids. State centralization reduced tribes' political and military power, marginalized the clerical establishment and eventually dismantled the landowning class's hold over Iran's agrarian regime. With the aid of a nontribal army, the Pahlavi state forever emasculated the nomadic periphery and in effect removed tribes as the most powerful player in the political life of the Iranian plateau. Forced sedentarization and, more important, the growth of urbanization transformed a highly mobile nomadic population. This was in consequential contrast to the survival of tribes and tribal networks in neighboring Afghanistan, Pakistan, Iraq, Saudi Arabia, and parts of Central Asia. A socioethnically amalgamated Iran at least since the 1960s, by coercive or by peaceful means, never again would experience a tribal resurgence.

The double-edged sword of state modernization transformed the economy and infrastructure, built a new middle class, and reasserted Iran's sovereignty. These were the nonpolitical objectives of the Constitutional Revolution. But it also built an oppressive autocracy that, backed by an effective army and police, was able to dismantle the political achievements of the Constitutional era. Sustaining such a regime was greatly facilitated by Iran's oil revenue, a small portion of the Anglo-Persian Oil Company's total income, but enough to make the Pahlavi project a success. The Pahlavi ideology also facilitated, through the discovery of a new source of legitimacy by greater reliance on Iran's ancient past. Though Iran's national awareness and its sense of mytho-historical continuity had never faded, the new nationalist narrative of the Pahlavi era was keen to contrast the glories of distant past with the perceived decadence of the Qajar era. These notions of glory and decadence laid the foundation for a national memory that has lasted up to the present. Reza Shah's resolute personality also contributed to transforming Iran beyond anything it has experienced at least since the rise of the Qajars.

The material success of Pahlavi modernity demonstrated the importance of oil revenue as a transformative commodity. But unlike coal in nineteenth-century European industrialization, oil revenue proved a blessing toward the creation of a stronger state with an extracting economy rather than a resource for growth of the national bourgeoisie. Since 1953, oil revenue, irrespective of

Iran's share of the proceeds and its legitimate claims for control of its natural resources, further strengthened the state at the expense of its citizens' political and civil rights. Undermining old political checks and balances, the monopoly of the oil income, which had sharply increased over decades, gave the Iranian state a unique opportunity to implement top-down modernization projects. It also provided the state with more tools of repression and control. The Islamic Republic only reaffirmed that pattern of political coercion that had been set during the Pahlavi rule.

Growth of the population, urbanization, secular education, modern communication, and to some degree industrialization crated new sociopolitical dynamics. In the aftermath of World War II, demands for economic sovereignty and nationalization of the oil industry echoed the discourse of decline and renewal, but also the political demands of the Constitutional era. The downfall of Mosaddeq in 1953, a critical moment in Iran's collective memory, denoted not only a showdown with Western geopolitical and economic interests but also an old struggle between ministers and rulers. The defeat of the nationalization movement, at least in the way it was perceived by its chief actors, further traumatized the Iranian collective memory, for it denoted to the Iranian intelligentsia the ominous collusion of foreign and domestic forces working to quash Iran's legitimate demands. That it happened in the context of the Cold War and with the United States as the chief sponsor of the Pahlavi regime disillusioned a whole generation of intellectuals and sympathizers of the left. Control of natural resources continued to erode the state's accountability, reduce its compliance with people's political demands, and create in effect a rentier state with its own privileged class.

The Islamic Revolution, in a way, was the final stage in a process that started in the Constitutional Revolution, continued in the postwar era with the National Movement, and later was redefined in the land reforms of the 1960s. The ideological element aside, the Islamic Revolution completed the dismantling of the old landed elites. More important, it diminished in size and influence a secularized middle class that was the backbone of the Pahlavi project of modernity. Yet the emerging middle classes under the Islamic Republic continued to follow the path of their predecessors. Even the inner clique of the Islamic regime, despite its ideological posturing and conspiratorial worldview, by and large has complied with the dictates of global markets and global communications. Despite an early claim of Islamic compassion, the revolution promptly employed all modern means of coercion and control even more intrusively.

With the Islamic Revolution another long-term historical process came to a head. Whereas the clerical establishment under the Safavids and their

successors was nurtured by the state and patronized by it, in the postconstitutional era and under Pahlavi rule, it lost much of its institutional privileges
and social prestige. Intellectually outcast and socially isolated, by the 1960s a
new generation of clerics, mostly from humble backgrounds, began to attract
a wider popular constituency mostly by advocating a politicized interpretation
of Islam. Aided by a radical ideology, it first opposed the Pahlavi state and later
transformed into a revolutionary force. Ayatollah Khomeini and his militant
clique borrowed elements of their ideology and rhetoric from the radical left as
much as they did from Islamic populists and repenting intellectuals of the left
and combined it with politicized readings of the Shi'i narrative. Yet the potency
of Khomeini's message, and key to his success, was his ability to appropriate the
messianic spirit inherent to the Shi'i heterodox milieu and exploit its martyrdom paradigm in his own favor.

Yet despite the Islamic Revolution's fervor and ideological mission, it did not
essentially transform the state's interaction with society at large. The Islamic Republic shared too many authoritarian traits with its predecessor, in theory and
practice, to be able to dislodge the state's institutional hegemony. But almost
in all respects it superseded its predecessor. It upheld the monopoly on power,
repression of essential liberties, propaganda and indoctrination, nepotism and
corruption, and control of the economy and natural resources in manners almost unprecedented in Iran's past. It also displayed conspiratorial traits to justify
its militancy and monopoly of power. The conspiratorial approach to politics
and history allowed for an easy escape from the painful realities and from having to assume responsibility for failures. Far more agency was given to the evil
other, the *aniran* of the Iranian mythology, than to the immaculate self. Self
could be celebrated only as victim and martyr. Repeated conspiracies from 1911
to 1953 and military occupations in the course of two world wars no doubt offered (and still offer) ample fodder for such a confined and fearful outlook.

Postrevolutionary Iranian society nevertheless appears to have a different perspective from that of the state. There is a vibrant and eager younger generation
better informed about the world outside and by and large immune to the state's
militant ideological hegemony. The state's systematic efforts to reconstruct Iran
in its own Islamic image have had mixed results. Despite a consistent effort, and
billions invested and wasted, the Iranian society has not turned, conceptually
speaking, into a greater Qom. Nor are the prospects for such a metamorphosis is very bright. Representations of an Islamic identity are amply displayed
and Islamification policies resolutely enforced in schools, workplaces, and the
public space. Yet under the surface, a tenacious quest for alternative identity

motivates a vast sector of Iranians, especially urban youth. Disillusioned with the revolution's unfulfilled promises and frustrated with the harsh realities of everyday life, most Iranians are in search of an alternative. However nebulous, the postideological ideals that younger Iranians are looking for seem to be culturally more sophisticated, and more pluralist, as became amply evident during the 2009 Green Movement.

The emerging generations, who are products of Iran's demographic revolution, are better nurtured, better educated, and often less romantically nationalist. They are by and large cynical about the regime's xenophobic outlook and its isolationist policies. The age of Westoxification and imagining a strict bipolarity between the East and the West seems to be over. The mystique of another revolution that could bring about an ideological utopia is also safely dispelled. Yet the women and men whose future now hangs in the balance are often disillusioned by the prospect of ever freeing themselves from the shackles placed on them by an indoctrinating regime. Whether they succumb to the mold stamped on their society or succeed in redefining Iran in their own image as an open and pluralistic society remains to be seen.

What is undeniable is that for five centuries Iran produced paintings, music, and architecture, fine craftsmanship, sustainable, horticulture, irrigation, and habitats, as well as poetry and philosophy, history and narratives, and—more recently—theater and cinema, to reflect on, or perhaps to escape from, the cruelty, intolerance, and fetters of conformity. Though in the past the best of these creative expressions were patronized by the state, they were shaped by motifs and memories of a complex cultural legacy, whether legendary, lyrical, or religious. The sense of nationhood that consciously emerged in the twentieth century and enforced by the state, Pahlavi or Islamic Republic, aimed to make the ethnic, linguistic, religious, and regional diversity of the past conform to a generic nation of compliance and docility. Yet the collective memory that was passed along through generations persisted and helped define and redefine a national identity defiant of repressive authorities. Expressions of political discontent, utopian ideals, and heretical visions often were couched in the language of metaphor that withstood censorship and pressure. Quests for alternative values, for cultural authenticity, and for moral change were seldom fulfilled, at least not in ways that their initiators intended or idealized them. However, grieving the loss of golden opportunities, disillusionment and anguish over what went wrong, resenting the abuses of power and mourning for lost chances have always been the stuff of Iranian intellectual and artistic creativity. These were voices that endured despite suffering and material defeat and empowered the

Iranian peoples. When Forugh Farrokhzad wrote, "It is only the sound that endures" (*tanha sedast keh mimand*), she probably was pointing to this long and complex culture, perhaps the sum total of the best Iran ever offered. In this respect she was echoing Hafez's memorable verse nearly six centuries earlier:

Anything sweeter than the sound of love I haven't heard.
Memorable echoes remain under this revolving dome.

Under Iran's revolving dome sounds of memories are still echoing.

NOTES

1. SHI'ISM AND THE SAFAVID REVOLUTION (1501–1588)

1. Hasan Rumlu, *Ahsan al-Tawarikh*, ed. C. N. Seddon (Baroda, India: Oriental Institute, 1931), 1:60–61 (in Persian).
2. V. Minorsky, "The Poetry of Shah Isma'il I," *Bulletin of the School of the Oriental and African Studies* 10, no. 4 (1942): 1031a and English translation at 1042–43 (with my modifications).
3. Tahmasp's *farman* (firman) is cited in Mirza 'Abdollah Afandi Isfahani, *Riyad al-'ulama wa hayaz al-fudala*, 5 vols. (Qom, AH 1401/1980 CE), 3:455–60. "AH," for *Anno Hegirae*, refers to the year in the Islamic lunar calendar.
4. Rumlu, *Ahsan al-Tawarikh*, 353.
5. Iskandar-beg Munshi Turkaman, *'Alamara-ye 'Abbasi*, ed. I. Afshar, 2 vols. (Tehran and Isfahan: Amir Kabir and Ketabforushi-ye Ta'id, 1335/1956), 1:228 (I have simplified and summarized the passage).

2. THE AGE OF 'ABBAS I AND THE SHAPING OF THE SAFAVID EMPIRE (1588–1666)

1. Pietro Della Valle, *Viaggi di Pietro Della Valle il pellegrino, descritti da lui medesimo in lettere familiari all'erudito suo amico Mario Schipano, divisi in tre parti cioè: La Turchia, la Persia e l'India* (Torino, 1843), letter 4, vol. 1; translated into Persian by M. Behforuzi, 2 vols. (Tehran, 1380/1991), vol. 1, 651–52, 667–68.

3. THE DEMISE OF THE SAFAVID ORDER AND THE UNHAPPY INTERREGNUMS (1666–1797)

1. Mohammad Hashem Asaf, Rostam al-Hokama, *Rostam al-Tawarikh*, ed. Mohammad Moshiri, 2nd ed. (Tehran: Taban, 1352/1973), 307–17, 342.

2. Shaykh Mohammad 'Ali Hazin, *Tarikh va Safarnameh*, ed. 'Ali Davani (Tehran: Markaz-e Asnad, 1375/1996), 240–41.
3. Shaykh Mohammad 'Ali Hazin, *Divan*, ed. Z. Sahebkar (Tehran: Nashr-e Sayeh, 1374/1995), 724.
4. 'Abbas Eqbal, ed., *Ruznameh-e Mirza Mohammad Kalantar-e Fars* (Tehran: Yadegar, 1325/1946), 89–90.

4. THE MAKING OF THE QAJAR ERA (1797–1852)

1. J. Malcolm, *Sketches of Persia*, 2nd ed. (London: John Murray, 1845), 222–23.
2. J. C. Hurewitz, *The Middle East and North Africa in the World Politics*, 2 vols., 2nd ed. (New Haven, CT: Yale University Press, 1975), 1:200.
3. A. Amanat, ed., *Cities and Trade: Consul Abbott on the Economy and Society of Iran, 1847–1866* (London: Ithaca Press, 1984), xv–xvi; see also C. Issawi, ed., *The Economic History of Iran, 1800–1914* (Chicago: University of Chicago Press, 1971), 259.
4. Amanat, *Cities and Trade*, xv.

5. NASER AL-DIN SHAH AND MAINTAINING A FRAGILE BALANCE (1848–1896)

1. Statistics are based on data collected by Justin Sheil and published as "Additional Notes" to Lady Mary Sheil, *Glimpses of Life and Manners in Persia* (London, 1856), 380–402.
2. Mirza Malkom Khan, "Resaleh-ye Ghaybiyeh," *Rasalehha-ye Mirza Malkom Khan Nazem al-Dowleh*, ed. Hojjatollah Asil (Tehran: Nashr-e Nay, 1381/2002), 27; also cited in translation in A. Amanat, *Pivot of the Universe: Nasir al-Din Shah Qajar and the Iranian Monarchy, 1931–1896* (Berkeley: University of California Press, 1997), 360.
3. Nasir al-Din Shah Qajar, *The Diary of H.M The Shah of Persia during His Tour through Europe in A.D. 1873*, trans. J. W. Redhouse (London: John Murray, 1874), 199–200.
4. Iraj Afshar, ed., *Ruznameh-e Khaterat-e E'temad al-Saltaneh* (Tehran: Amir Kabir, 1345/1966), 141.

6. THE CONSTITUTIONAL REVOLUTION

1. Edward Granville Browne, *The Persian Revolution of 1905–1909* (Cambridge: Cambridge University Press, 1910), 354.
2. Ibid., 373.
3. William Morgan Shuster, *The Strangling of Persia* (New York: Century Co., 1912), xiv.
4. *Divan-e Mirza Abolqasem 'Aref Qazvini*, ed. Sayf Azad (Berlin: Sharqi, 1924), supplement (songs), 20–21. For an earlier English translation, see Edward Granville Browne, *The Press and Poetry of Modern Persia* (Cambridge: Cambridge University Press, 1914), 250–52.
5. Shuster, *Strangling of Persia*. 204.

6. Ibid., 204.
7. Mohammad Taqi Bahar Malek al-Sho'ara, *Divan-e Ash'ar*, ed. M. Bahar, 5th ed. (Tehran: Entesharat Tus, 1368/1984) 1:261–62.
8. 'Aref Qazvini, *Divan*, 14–25.
9. Ibid., 176–77.
10. Browne, *Press and Poetry*, 195–96.
11. Edward Granville Browne, A *Literary History of Persia* (Cambridge: Cambridge University Press, 1959) 4:472–74.

7. THE GREAT WAR AND THE RISE OF REZA KHAN (1914–1925)

1. 'A. Mostawfi, *Sharh-e Zendegani-ye Man ya Tarikh-e Ejtema'i va Edari-ye Dowreh-ye Qajariyeh*, 3 vols., 2nd ed. (Tehran: Zavvar, 1343/1964), 3:215, published in English as A. Mustawfi, *The Administrative and Social History of the Qajar Period*, trans. N. Mostofi-Glenn, 3 vols. (Costa Mesa, CA, 1977).
2. "Agreement: Great Britain and Persia, 9 August 1919," in Hurewitz, *The Middle East*, 2:182–83.
3. Ibid., 2:240–45.
4. *Divan-e 'Eshqi va Sharh-e Hal-e Sha'er*, ed. 'A. Salimi (Tehran: Shafaq, 1308/1929), 197–98.
5. Mostawfi, *Sharh-e Zendegani-ye Man*, 3:601.
6. Bahar, *Divan-e Ash'ar*, 1:356–58.

8. REZA SHAH AND THE PAHLAVI ORDER (1925–1941)

1. *Kolliyat-e Divan-e Iraj Mirza* (Tehran: Mozaffari, n.d.), 166–67.

9. CHAOTIC DEMOCRACY, OIL NATIONALIZATION, AND DENIED HOPES (1941–1953)

1. Manucher Farmanfarmaian, *Blood and Oil: Inside the Shah's Iran* (New York: Random House, 1997), 184–85.
2. Mostafa Fateh, *Pajah Sal Naft-e Iran* (Tehran: Chehr, 1335/1956), 525.
3. W. O. Douglas, *The Douglas Letters: Selections from the Private Papers of Justice William O. Douglas*, ed. M. Urofsky (Bethesda: Adler and Adler, 1987), 282.

10. THE WHITE REVOLUTION AND ITS OPPONENTS (1953–1963)

1. "Letter From President Kennedy to the Shah of Iran," August 1, 1962, in *Foreign Relations of the United States, 1961–1963*, vol. 18, *Near East, 1962–1963* (Washington, DC: Government Printing Office, 1995–1996), 11.
2. "Special National Intelligence Estimate," September 7, 1962, in *Foreign Relations of the United States, 1961–1963*, vol. 18, *Near East, 1962–1963* (Washington, DC: Government Printing Office, 1995–1996), 35.

3. "Payam beh Mellat-e Iran," Ordibehesht 2, 1323/April 22, 1944, in Ruhollah Khomeini, *Sahifeh-e Imam: Majmu'eh-e Asar-e Imam Khomeini,* 5th ed. (Tehran: Moasseseh-e Tanzim va Nashr-e Asar-e Imam Khomeini, 1389/2010), 1:21–23.
4. Qom, Farvardin 26, 1343/April 16, 1964, in Khomeini, *Sahifeh-e Imam,* 1:415–23.
5. Qom, Aban 4, 1343/November 26, 1964, in Khomeini, *Sahifeh-e Imam,* 1:415–23.
6. Syrus Tahbaz, ed., *Majmu'eh-e Asar-e Nima Yushij: Daftar-e Avval, She'r* (Tehran: Nasher, 1364/1985), 555.
7. Mahdi Akhavan-Sales (M. Omid), *Akir-e Shahnameh: Majmu'eh-e She'r* (Tehran: Zaman, 1338/1959), 19–25. Composed in April 1956.
8. Ibid., 79–86. Composed in October 1957.
9. Forugh Farrokhzad, *'Esyan* (Tehran, 1336/1957), 8–28.
10. Forugh Farrokhzad, *Tavallodi Digar* (Tehran: Morvarid, 1342/1963), 148–57.
11. Forugh Farrokhzad, *Iman Biavarim be Aghaz-e Fasl-e Sard* (Tehran: Morvarid, 1352/1973), 30–35.
12. Ahmad Shamlu, *Ayda, Derakht, Khanjar va Khatereh,* 2nd ed. (Tehran: Morvarid, 1344/1965), 125–37. Composed in February 1965.

11. DEVELOPMENT, DISARRAY, AND DISCONTENT (1963–1977)

1. *Telegram from the Department of State to the Embassy in Iran,* US National Archives, RG 59, Central Foreign Policy Files, P850017-2033.
2. Memorandum from Vernon Walters, acting director of Central Intelligence to Henry Kissinger, the president's assistant for national security affairs, October 7, 1974. Library of Congress, Manuscript Division, Kissinger Papers, Box CL-152, Iran, Chronological File, 6 October–30 December 1974, Secret. The CIA agent is not identified.

12. CULTURES OF AUTHORITY AND CULTURES OF DISSENT

1. Monday 27 Bahman 1349/February 15, 1971, *Yaddashtha-ye 'Alam,* ed. 'Ali-Naqi 'Alikhani (Bethesda, MD: Iranbooks, 1993), 2:168.
2. *Hajm-e Sabz* (Tehran: Rowzan, 1346/1967), 20–23.
3. *Gharbzadehgi* (Tehran, 1341/1962), 16.

13. THE MAKING OF THE ISLAMIC REVOLUTION (1977–1979)

1. Cited in Karim Sanjabi, *Omidha va Naomidiha* (Hopes and despairs) (London: Nashre Ketab, 1368/1989), 441–42.
2. *Ettela'at,* no. 15506, 17 Day 1356.
3. 14 Aban 1357/November 6, 1978, cited at http://jamejamonline.ir/ayam/1709458624 889167071.
4. Speech in Behesht-e Zahra, February 1, 1979, available at http://imam-khomeini.com/web1/persian/showitem.aspx?cid=957&pid=1042.

14. THE GUARDIAN JURIST AND HIS ADVOCATES

1. Ruhollah Khomeini, *Welayat-e Faqih: Hokumat-e Islami* (Tehran: Amir Kabir, 1357/1978), 23–25.
2. Ibid., 30–31.
3. Ibid., 60.
4. Ibid., 6–7.
5. *Khaterat-e Ayatollah Montazeri* (Essen, Germany: Entesharat-e Enqlab-e Islami, 2001), 86.
6. Ibid., 30.
7. Akbar Hashemi Rafsanjani, *Dowran-e Mobarezeh* ed. Mohsen Hashemi (Tehran: Daftar-e Nashr-e Ma'aref-e Enqlab, 1376/1997), 1:62–64.
8. Ibid., 105.

15. CONSOLIDATION OF THE ISLAMIC REPUBLIC (1979–1984)

1. "Qanun-e Asasi-ye Jomhuri-e Islami-e Iran," Markaz-e Pazhuheshha-ye Majles-e Shura-ye Islami, http://rc.majlis.ir/fa/content/iran constitution. All future references are to this source.
2. Ruhollah Khomeini, "Speech to the Deputies on the Occasion of the First Session of the Islamic Consultative Assembly," Jamaran, 3 Khordad 1359/May 25, 1980, *Sahifeh-e Imam*, 12:347.
3. *Enqlab-e Islami*, 14 Esfand 1359/March 5, 1981.
4. *Kayhan*, 29 Shahrivar 1360/September 20, 1981, p. 4.
5. *Ettela'at*, 10 Mehr 1360/October 3, 1981, p. 2.
6. Ruhollah Khomeini, "Decree Establishing the Executive Committee of the Cultural Revolution," Jamaran, 23 Khordad 1359/June 12, 1980, *Sahifeh-e Imam*, 12:431.

16. FACING THE FOE

1. Letter to Mohsen Reza'i, Jamaran, Ruhollah Khomeini, *Sahifeh-e Imam*, 20:501–2.
2. "Security Council Resolution 598: Iraq-Islamic Republic of Iran," July 20, 1987 cited in United Nations Peace Agreements Database, at peacemaker.un.org/iraqiran-resolution598.
3. "Message to the Nation on the Occasion of the Anniversary of the Bloody Massacre of Mecca," 29 Tir 1367/July 20, 1988, Jamaran, Khomeini, *Sahifeh-e Imam*, vol. 21 (in http://www.jamaran.ir).
4. Hosain-'Ali Montazeri, *Khaterat*, p. 302, suppl. 152 (and facs. no. 152-1).
5. Jamaran, 25 Bahman 1367/February 14, 1988, Khomeini, *Sahifeh-e Imam*, 21:263.
6. Montazeri, *Khaterat*, 303–4.
7. Fereydun Vahman, *Yeksad va shast sal mobarezeh ba diyanat-e Baha'i* (Darmstadt, Germany: Asr-e Jadid, 2009), 657.
8. Ruhollah Khomeini, "Vasiyat-nameh-e siyasi-elahi," Jamaran, 19 Azar 1366/December 11, 1987, *Sahifeh-e Imam*, 21:391–451 (499).

17. SOCIETY AND CULTURE UNDER
THE ISLAMIC REPUBLIC

1. Hushang Ebtehaj (H. A. Sayeh), *Siah Mashq* (Tehran: Nashr-e Karnameh, 1378/1999), 11–12. The title of the *ghazal* in this collection is "Beh nam-e shoma" (In your name). The musical album *Sepideh* (Tehran: Ava-ye Shayda, n.d.) is a recording of the original concert in Iran National University (renamed Shahid Beheshti University) in December 1979.

2. Hafez, *Divan*, ed. Parviz Natel Khanlari, 3rd ed. (Tehran: Khwarazmi, 1362/1983), 1:344–45, no. 164. On the album *Bidad* by 'Aref and Shayda Ensembles (Tehran: Del Avaz, 1364/1985), Shajarian is accompanied by Lotfi and Meshkatian, among others.

3. Bahar, *Divan*, 2:1322. On the album *Ahang-e Vafa* (Tehran: Del Avaz, 1999), Mohammad Reza Shajarian and Homayun Shajarian are accompanied by the Ava Ensemble.

FURTHER READINGS

Studies cited here cover Western languages and predominantly are in English. Scholarship in Persian is outside the scope of this survey. Works aimed at specialists are generally excluded, but some important primary sources in translation are included. Introductory literature on Iran is too extensive and easily accessible to require inclusion here. Many entries in *Encyclopedia Iranica* (hereafter *EIr*) on history and culture of the period— including personalities, events, places, and themes—provide an excellent assessment of the available scholarship.

1. SHI'ISM AND THE SAFAVID REVOLUTION (1501–1588)

Safavid Iran has received a fair amount of modern scholarly attention since the 1930s. *The Cambridge History of Iran: Timurid and Safavid Periods*, vol. 6, ed. P. Jackson and L. Lockhart (Cambridge: Cambridge University Press, 1986), is an extensive survey of the Safavid period. Among many important contributions to that volume, see H. R. Roemer, "Safavid Period," which provides the dynastic history. R. Savory, *Iran under the Safavids* (Cambridge: Cambridge University Press, 1980), is a general history with chapters on economic, social, and intellectual aspects and relations with Europe. The rise of the Safavid state has been the subject of several studies, though most of the scholarship has emphasized the religious dimension. M. Hodgson, *The Gunpowder Empires and Modern Times*, volume 3 of *The Venture of Islam* (Chicago: University of Chicago Press, 1977), especially the prologue and chapter 1; and S. Dale, *The Muslim Empires of the Ottomans, Safavids, and Mughals* (Cambridge: Cambridge University Press, 2010), provide a broader context. S. A. Arjomand, *The Shadow of God and the Hidden Imam: Religion, Political Order, and Societal Change in Shi'ite Iran from the Beginning to 1890* (Chicago: University of Chicago Press, 1984), is an insightful work of historical sociology utilizing a range of primary sources. A. Newman, *Safavid Iran: Rebirth of a Persian Empire* (London: I. B. Tauris, 2006), explores the foundations of the Safavid socioreligious order and the causes of its eventual downfall. See also five collections of essays on aspects of Safavid politics, society, culture, and foreign relations: J. Calmard, ed., *Études Safavides* (Paris: Institut Français de Recherche en Iran, 1993); C. Melville, ed., *Safavid Persia: The History and Politics of an Islamic Society* (London: I. B. Tauris, 1996); M. Mazzaoui, ed., *Safavid Iran and Her*

Neighbors (Salt Lake City: University of Utah Press, 2003); A. Newman, ed., *Society and Culture in the Early Modern Middle East: Studies on Iran in the Safavid Period* (Leiden: Brill, 2003); and C. P. Mitchell, ed., *New Perspectives on Safavid Iran: Empire and Society* (New York: Routledge, 2011). For the prelude leading to the rise of the Safavids, see Walter Hinz, *Irans Aufstieg zum Nationalstaat im Fünfzehnten Jahrhundert* (Berlin: Walter de Gruyter, 1936); and J. Woods, *The Aqquyunlu: Clan, Confederation, Empire* (Minneapolis: Bibliotheca Islamica, 1976; new ed., Salt Lake City: University of Utah Press, 1999). They examine the century between the decline of the Ilkhanids and the rise of the Ottomans. D. Morgan, *Medieval Persia, 1040–1797*, 2nd ed. (New York: Routledge, 2016), places the Safavids in a broader historical perspective.

On early Safavid messianic Shi'ism, see Mazzaoui, *The Origins of the Ṣafawids: Shi'ism, Sufism, and the Gulat* (Wiesbaden: F. Steiner, 1972); and J. Aubin, "L'avènement des Safavides reconsidéré (Études Safavides 3), *Moyen Orient et Océan Indien* 5 (1988): 1–130. K. Babayan, *Mystics, Monarchs and Messiahs: Cultural Landscape of Early Modern Iran* (Cambridge, MA: Harvard University Center for Middle Eastern Studies, 2003), explores the cultural and intellectual milieu of the early Safavid era. See also S. Bashir, "Shah Isma'il and the Qizilbash: Cannibalism in the Religious History of Early Safavid Iran," *History of Religions* 45 (2006): 234–56; J. Cole, "Millenarianism in Modern Iran History," in *Imagining the End, Visions of Apocalypse from the Ancient Middle East to Modern America* (London: I. B. Tauris, 2002), 282–311. For a biography of Shah Isma'il, we still rely on G. Sarwar, *History of Shah Isma'il Safawi* (Aligarh, 1939). C. Mitchell, *The Practice of Politics in Safavid Iran: Power, Religion and Rhetoric* (London: Tauris Academic Studies, 2009), explores state-sponsored rhetoric from the time of Isma'il to the reign of 'Abbas I. Two studies, one by J. J. Reid, *Tribalism and Society in Islamic Iran, 1500–1629* (Malibu, CA: Undena Publications, 1983), and another by M. Haneda, *Le châh et les Qizilbāš: Le système militaire safavide* (Berlin: Schwarz, 1987), examine the Qezilbash *oymaq* system and the structure of the early Safavid armies.

The administrative history of the Safavid period is examined in two articles by R. Savory: "The Principal Offices of the Ṣafawid State during the Reign of Isma'il I (907–30/1501–24)," *Bulletin of the School of Oriental and African Studies* 23, no. 1 (1960): 91–105, and "The Principal Offices of the Ṣafawid State during the Reign of Ṭahmāsp I (930–84/1524–76)," *Bulletin of the School of Oriental and African Studies* 24, no. 1 (1961): 65–85, as well as in his "The Safavid Administrative System" in *Cambridge History of Iran*, vol. 6. W. Floor, in *Safavid Government Institutions* (Costa Mesa, CA: Mazda Publishers, 2001), and in his "The Ṣadr or Head of the Safavid Religious Administration, Judiciary and Endowments and Other Members of the Religious Institution," *Zeitschrift Der Deutschen Morgenländischen Gesellschaft* 150 (2000): 461–500, further explores the subject. Three manuals of the late Safavid administration are available in English translation: *Tadhkirat al-Mulūk, a Manual of Ṣafavid Administration (circa 1137/1725)*, Persian text and translation with extensive notes by V. Minorsky, Gibb Memorial Series (London: Luzac, 1943); Mirza Rafi'a, *The Dastur al-Moluk: A Safavid State Manual*, trans. and ed. W. Floor and M. H. Faghfoory (Costa Mesa, CA: Mazda Publishers, 2006); and Mirza Naqi Nasiri, *Titles & Emoluments in Safavid Iran: A Third Manual of Safavid Administration*, trans. W. Floor (Washington, DC: Mage Publishers, 2008).

The diplomatic history of the period is discussed in an early work by K. Bayani, *Les relations de l'Iran avec l'Europe occidentale à l'époque Safavide* (Paris: Les Presses Modernes, 1937); and L. Lockhart's chapter in the *Cambridge History of Iran*, vol. 6. W. Floor and E. Herzig, eds., *Iran and the World in the Safavid Age* (London and New York: I. B. Tauris,

2012), presents recent scholarship on Safavid foreign relations and the challenges of geographical and religious isolation. A. Allouche, *The Origins and Development of the Ottoman-Safavid Conflict (906–962/1500–1555)*, (Berlin: K. Schwarz Verlag, 1983), and P. Brummett, *Ottoman Seapower and Levantine Diplomacy in the Age of Discovery* (Albany: State University of New York Press, 1994), are two studies on less explored Safavid-Ottoman relations.

2. THE AGE OF 'ABBAS I AND THE SHAPING OF THE SAFAVID EMPIRE (1588–1666)

The reign of 'Abbas I witnessed the production of numerous chronicles and court histories of a greater variety than earlier Safavid rulers, most of which remain available only in Persian. Two notable exceptions are Iskandar Beg Munshi, *The History of Shah 'Abbas the Great*, trans. and abridged by R. Savory, 2 vols. (Boulder, CO: Westview Press, 1978); and Fazli Beg Khuzani Isfahani, *A Chronicle of the Reign of Shah 'Abbas*, ed. C. Melville and K. Ghereglou (Cambridge: Gibb Memorial Trust, 2015). See also S. Quinn and C. Melville "Safavid Historiography," *History of Persian Historiography*, ed. C. Melville, vol. 10 of *A History of Persian Literature*, ed. E. Yarshater (London: I. B. Tauris, 2011); and S. Quinn, *Historical Writing during the Reign of Shah 'Abbas: Ideology, Imitation, and Legitimacy in Safavid Chronicles* (Salt Lake City: University of Utah Press, 2000). For an introduction to the artistic efflorescence during the reign of 'Abbas I and his successors, see B. Gray, "The Arts in the Safavid Period," and R. Hillenbrand, "Safavid Architecture," in the *Cambridge History of Iran*, vol. 6. More recently, S. Canby, ed., *Shah 'Abbas and the Treasures of Imperial Iran* (London: British Museum, 2009), provides an overview. K. Rizvi's *The Safavid Dynastic Shrine: Architecture, Religion and Power in Early Modern Iran* (London: I. B. Tauris, 2011), uses the architecture of the Shaykh Safi al-Din shrine in Ardabil to explore the political authority and religious piety of early Safavid rulers. Two studies by D. Roxburgh—*Prefacing the Image: The Writing of Art History in Sixteenth-century Iran* (Leiden: Brill, 2001), and *The Persian Album, 1400–1600: From Dispersal to Collection* (New Haven: Yale University Press, 2005)—explore the collection and recording of material culture. For Isfahan under 'Abbas I, see S. Babaie, *Isfahan and Its Palaces: Statecraft, Shi'ism and the Architecture of Conviviality in Early Modern Iran* (Edinburgh: Edinburgh University Press, 2008); S. P. Blake, *Half the World: The Social Architecture of Safavid Isfahan, 1590–1722* (Costa Mesa, CA: Mazda Publishers, 1999); and his "Shah 'Abbas and the Transfer of the Safavid Capital from Qazvin to Isfahan," in A. Newman, ed., *Society and Culture in the Early Modern Middle East: Studies on Iran in the Safavid Period* (Leiden: Brill, 2003). For textile arts, see C. Bier, *Woven from the Soul, Spun from the Heart: Textile Arts of Safavid and Qajar Iran (16th–19th Centuries)*, (Washington, DC: Textile Museum, 1987). On the development of Nast'aliq calligraphy, see S. Blair, *Islamic Calligraphy* (Edinburgh: Edinburgh University Press, 2008). Two studies by M. Shreve Simpson—*Sultan Ibrahim Mirza's Haft Awrang: A Princely Manuscript from Sixteenth-Century Iran* (New Haven: Yale University Press, 1997) and *Princeton's Great Persian Book of Kings: The Peck Shahnama* (Princeton, NJ: Princeton University Art Museum, 2015)—draw attention to Safavid patronage and the art of bookmaking.

There are several significant studies on the history of trade and economics—and by extension diplomacy—during the reigns of 'Abbas I and his successors. For an overview, see R. Ferrier, "Trade from the Mid-14th Century to the End of the Safavid Period," in *Cambridge History of Iran*, vol. 6. R. Matthee, *The Politics of Trade in Safavid Iran: Silk for Silver, 1600–1730* (Cambridge: Cambridge University Press, 1999), is an excellent study of the political economy of the Safavid period with special reference to Safavid silk production and European trading companies. It relies on extensive archival sources. Two studies, by I. B. McCabe, *The Shah's Silk for Europe's Silver: The Eurasian Trade of the Julfa Armenians in Safavid Iran and India, 1530–1750* (Atlanta: Scholars Press, 1999), and S. Aslanian, *From the Indian Ocean to the Mediterranean: The Global Trade Networks of Armenian Merchants from New Julfa* (Berkeley: University of California Press, 2011), using rare primary sources to examine the vast network of the Armenian merchants of Isfahan. An in-depth study of the social history, leisure, consumption, and commodities of the Safavid era, relying on Persian and European sources, is R. Matthee, *The Pursuit of Pleasure: Drugs and Stimulants in Iranian History, 1500–1900* (Princeton, NJ: Princeton University Press, 2005). M. Keyvani, *Artisans and Guild Life in the Later Safavid Period* (Berlin: Klaus Schwarz Verlag, 1982), is a pioneering study with valuable appendices. Two studies—W. Floor, *A Fiscal History of Iran in the Safavid and Qajar Periods, 1500–1925* (New York: Bibliotheca Persica Press, 1998), and more recently, R. Matthee, W. Floor, and P. Clawson, *The Monetary History of Iran, From the Safavids to the Qajars* (London: I. B. Tauris, 2013)—review the monetary system of the Safavid era, with special attention to the drainage of precious metals.

L. Lockhart, "European Contacts with Persia, 1350–1736," in the *Cambridge History of Iran*, vol. 6, provides an overview of this topic. The accounts of numerous European travelers to Safavid Iran, including the Sherley brothers, Pietro della Valle, Don Garcia de Silva y Figueroa, John Chardin, Jean Thevenot, Jean-Baptiste Tavernier, Raphael du Mans, Adam Olearius, Engelbert Kaempfer, Pedros Bedik, and Cornelis de Bruyn, illuminate various aspects of society, culture, and politics. W. Floor and M. H. Faghfoory used Dutch archival sources in *The First Dutch-Persian Commercial Conflict: The Attack on Qeshm Island, 1645* (Costa Mesa, CA: Mazda Publishers, 2004). A rare account of a Safavid mission to the court of Siam appears in *The Ship of Sulaiman*, trans. John O'Kane (New York: Columbia University Press, 1972). The portion of Evilya Çelebi's famous travelogue related to Safavid Iran has been published as *Travels in Iran and the Caucasus in 1647 and 1654*, trans. and annotated by W. Floor (Washington, DC: Mage Publishers, 2010).

The intellectual trends of the Safavid period have received a fair amount of attention. H. Corbin, *En Islam iranien: Aspects spirituels et philosphiques*, vol. 4, *L'École d'Ispahan* and *Le Douzième Imâm* (Paris: Gallimard, 1972), and his "Confessions extatiques de Mir Damad: Maître de théologie à Ispahan," in *Mélanges Louis Massignon*, ed. H. Massé (Damascus: Institut Français de Damas, 1956), are among pioneering studies. A. Newman, *Safavid Thinkers: The Intellectual Creators of Iran's Renaissance in the Early Modern Period* (London: I. B. Tauris, 2012), offers an overview of jurists, theologians and philosophers, and historians of the period. See also S. H. Nasr, "The School of Iṣpahān," in *A History of Muslim Philosophy*, ed. M. M. Sharif (Wiesbaden: Harrassowitz, 1966), 1:904–32. For studies on Mulla Sadra, see F. Rahman, *The Philosophy of Mullā Ṣadrā* (Albany: State University of New York Press, 1975); and S. Rizvi, *Mullā Ṣadrā Shīrāzī: His Life and Works and the Sources for Safavid Philosophy* (Oxford: Oxford University Press, 2007). For a translation of Mulla Sadra's well-known work, see *The Wisdom of the Throne: An Introduction to the Philosophy of Mulla Sadra*, trans. J. W. Morris (Princeton, NJ: Princeton University Press, 1981). Two other translations of Mulla Sadra's works are *Divine Manifestations Concerning the Secrets of the Perfecting Sciences*, transl. F. Asadi Amjad and M. Dasht Bozorgi (London: ICAS Press, 2010) and *Metaphysical Penetrations*, transl. S. H. Nasr (Provo, UT: Brigham Young University Islamic Translation Series, 2014). The *Anthologie des phi-*

losophes iraniens depuis le XVIIᵉ siècle jusqu'à nos jours, ed. H. Corbin and J. Ashtiyani, 4 vols. (Tehran, 1971–1979), offers specimens of the philosophical writings of the period. See also H. Corbin, *Spiritual Body and Celestial Earth: From Mazdian Iran to Shi'ite Iran*, trans. N. Pearson (Princeton, NJ: Princeton University Press, 1977), chaps. 5–8. R. Pourjavady, *Philosophy in Early Safavid Iran: Najm al-Dīn Maḥmūd al-Nayrīzī and His Writings*, is a case study of a lesser-known philosopher. H. J. J. Winter, "Persian Science in Safavid Times," in *Cambridge History of Iran*, vol. 6, provides a general survey.

On religious trends, see R. Abisaab, *Converting Persia: Religion and Power in the Safavid Empire* (London: I. B. Tauris, 2004), which examines the emergence of Twelver Shi'ism, and the Arab-Persian clerical establishment and its relations with the Safavid state and society. Three widely read Persian works in Shi'i theology and ethics by Muhammad Baqir Majlisi (Mohammad Baqer Majlesi), are available in English translation: *Haqul Yaqeen (Haqq al-Yaqin): A Compendium of Twelver Shia Religious Beliefs*, trans. S. A. H. Rizvi (Mumbai: Jafari Propagation Center, 2013); *Hayat al-Qulub: Stories of the Prophets, Characteristics and Circumstances of the Prophets and Their Successors*, trans. S. A. H. Rizvi (Qom: Ansariyan Publications, 2007); and *Ain-al Hayat ('Ayn al-Hayat): The Essence of Life*, trans. S. T. Bilgrami (Qom: Ansariyan Publications, 2014). See also D. J. Stewart, *Islamic Legal Orthodoxy: Twelver Shiite Responses to the Sunni Legal System* (Salt Lake City: University of Utah Press, 1998); and A. Amanat, "Meadow of the Martyrs: Kashifi's Persianization of the Shi'i Martyrdom Narrative in Late Timurid Herat," in *Apocalyptic Islam and Iranian Shi'ism* (London: I. B. Tauris, 2009), 91–110.

For an overview of Safavid literature, see Z. Safa, "Persian Literature in the Safavid Period," in the *Cambridge History of Iran*, vol. 6; and E. Yarshater, "Safavid Literature: Progress or Decline," *Iranian Studies* 7, nos. 1–2 (1974): 217–70. For poetic trends, see E. Yarshater, "Persian Poetry in the Timurid and Safavid Periods," *Cambridge History of Iran*, vol. 6; P. Losensky, *Welcoming Fighānī: Imitation and Poetic Individuality in the Safavid-Mughal Ghazal* (Costa Mesa, CA: Mazda Publishers, 1998); and Losensky, "'The Equal of Heaven's Vault': The Design, Ceremony, and Poetry of the Ḥasanābād Bridge," in *Writers and Rulers: Perspectives from Abbasid to Safavid Times*, ed. B. Gruendler and L. Marlow (Wiesbaden: Ludwig Reichert Verlag, 2004). On Judeo-Persian literature of the period, see V. B. Moreen, *In Queen Esther's Garden: An Anthology of Judeo-Persian Literature* (New Haven: Yale University Press, 2000).

3. THE DEMISE OF THE SAFAVID ORDER AND THE UNHAPPY INTERREGNUMS (1666–1797)

The eighteenth century is among the least studied in early modern Iranian history and the secondary literature on the period is thin. The seminal study of the collapse of the Safavid Empire is L. Lockhart, *The Fall of the Safavi Dynasty and the Afghan Occupation of Persia* (Cambridge: Cambridge University Press, 1958). M. Dickson's long review, "The Fall of the Safavi Dynasty," *Journal of the American Oriental Society* 82, no. 4 (December 1962): 503–17, provides a critique and serves as a helpful companion to Lockhart's book. R. Matthee, *Persia in Crisis: Safavid Decline and the Fall of Isfahan* (London: I. B. Tauris, 2012), reassesses the demise of the Safavid Empire by putting greater emphasis on the syphoning of precious metals and the monetary crisis, military disloyalties, and administrative corruption rather than moral decay. J. Foran, "The Long Fall of the Safavid Dynasty: Moving beyond the Standard Views," *International Journal of Middle East*

Studies 24, no. 2 (May 1992): 281–304, also explores economic factors contributing to the Safavid downfall. For a comparative perspective, see R. D'Souza, "Crisis before the Fall: Some Speculations on the Decline of the Ottomans, Safavids and Mughals," *Social Scientist* 30, nos. 9–10 (September–October 2002): 3–30, which offers a nuanced critique of C. A. Bayly's interpretation of the decline of the three empires in his *Imperial Meridian: The British Empire and the World 1780–1830* (London: Routledge, 1989).

Studies on the Afghan interlude are few, primarily because of the lack of sources. There are, however, a few accounts written by people who lived through the period. Judas Thaddaeus Krusinski was a Jesuit employed in the service of the Catholic bishop in Isfahan, lived in Iran for twenty years, and witnessed the Afghan invasion. His *An Historical Account of the Revolutions in Persia in the Years 1722, 1723, 1724, and 1725* (London: J. Roberts, 1727), provides an European's perspective on the years immediately following the collapse of Safavid rule. Similarly, *A Chronicle of the Carmelites in Persia and the Papal Mission of the XVIIth and XVIIIth Centuries*, 2 vols. (London: Eyre & Spottiswoode, 1939; reprint: London: I. B. Tauris, 2012), is a valuable source. Mohammad Hazin's memoirs were translated and published by F. C. Belfour, *The Life of Sheikh Mohammed Ali Hazin* (London: J. Murray, 1830). For the post-Safavid claimants to the throne, see J. Perry, "The Last Safavids, 1722–1773," *Iran: Journal of the British Institute of Iranian Studies* 9 (1971): 59–69; and G. Rota, "The Man Who Would Not Be King: Abu'l-Fath Sultan Muhammad Mirza Safavi in India," *Iranian Studies* 32, no 4 (1999): 513–35.

There are contemporary Armenian and European accounts of the rise and rule of Nader Shah. Three Armenian accounts are available in English translation: Abraham of Crete, *The Chronicle of Abraham of Crete*, trans. and annotated by G. A. Bournoutian (Costa Mesa, CA: Mazda Publishers, 1999); Arak'el of Tabriz, *Book of History*, trans. and with an introduction by G. A. Bournoutian (Costa Mesa, CA: Mazda Publishers, 2010); and Abraham of Erevan, *History of the Wars: 1721–1736*, trans. and annotated by G. A. Bournoutian (Costa Mesa, CA: Mazda Publishers, 1999). J. Fraser, *The History of Nadir Shah Formerly Called Thamas Kuli Khan, the Present Emperor of Persia* (London: A. Millar, 1742), was published while Nader was in power. William Jones translated Mirza Mohammad Mahdi Astarabadi, *Tārīkh-i Jahān-Gushā-yi Nādirī* to French as *Histoire de Nader Chah* (London, 1770). This was in turn translated into English a few years later as *The History of the Life of Nader Shah* (London: J. Richardson, 1773). Also useful is J. Hanway, *An Historical Account of the British Trade over the Caspian Sea . . . to Which Are Added, the Revolutions of Persia during the Present Century, with the Particular History of the Great Usurper, Nadir Kouli*, 4 vols. (London, 1753). L. Lockhart's two studies on Nader Shah are important for their time: *The Navy of Nadir Shah* (London: Iran Society, 1936); and *Nadir Shah: A Critical Study Based Mainly upon Contemporary Sources* (London: Luzac, 1938). W. Floor collected Dutch East India Company reports on Nader Shah in *The Rise and Fall of Nader Shah: Dutch East India Company Reports, 1730–1747* (Washington, DC: Mage Publishers, 2009). E. Tucker, *Nadir Shah's Quest for Legitimacy in Post-Safavid Iran* (Gainesville: University Press of Florida, 2006), and M. Axworthy, *Sword of Persia: Nader Shah, from Tribal Warrior to Conquering Tyrant* (London: I. B. Tauris, 2006), explore new dimensions of Nader's life and era.

The most comprehensive study of Karim Khan Zand and his era remains J. Perry, *Karīm Khān Zand: A History of Iran, 1747–1779* (Chicago: University of Chicago Press, 1979), which covers his campaigns and state-building efforts. Perry also wrote the essay on the Zand period in *Cambridge History of Iran*, vol. 7, *From Nadir Shah to the Islamic Republic* (Cambridge: Cambridge University Press, 1991). T. M. Ricks, *Notables, Merchants,*

and Shaykhs of Southern Iran and Its Ports: Politics and Trade of the Persian Gulf Region,
AD 1729–1789 (Piscataway, NJ: Gorgias Press, 2012), is another valuable study of the socioeconomic history of the period with special reference to the Persian Gulf. For two German
monographs on the Zand period, see M. Roschanzamir, *Die Zand-Dynastie* (Hamburg:
H. Lüdke, 1970), and P. Rajabi, *Iran unter Karim Han (1752–1779)*, (Göttingen, 1970).

T. Naff and R. Owen, eds., *Studies in Eighteenth Century Islamic History* (Carbon-
dale: Southern Illinois University Press, 1977), includes two pertinent contributions, one
by A. K. S. Lambton, "The Tribal Resurgence and the Decline of the Bureaucracy in
Eighteenth-Century Persia," and another by H. Algar, "Shi'ism in Iran in the Eighteenth
Century." For a history of the Usuli-Akhbari conflict that places the religious leaders within
their social and economic context, and provides an alternative to Algar's above chapter,
see J. Cole, "Shi'i Clerics in Iraq and Iran, 1722–1780: The Akhbari-Usuli Conflict Reconsidered," *Iranian Studies* 18, no. 1 (Winter 1985): 3–34. For revival of the Sufi orders in the
Qajar era, see L. Lewisohn, "An Introduction to the History of Modern Persian Sufism,
Part I: The Ni'matullāhī Order: Persecution, Revival and Schism," *Bulletin of the School
of Oriental and African Studies* 61, no. 3 (1998): 437–64.

4. THE MAKING OF THE QAJAR ERA (1797–1852)

Modern studies on Qajar Iran appeared as early as 1890s but greater attention to this period
began in earnest in the 1960s. There are several collections of articles and essays that serve
as general studies and introductions to the Qajar period. The chapters related to the Qajar
period in *Cambridge History of Iran*, vol. 7, ed. P. Avery, G. Hambly, and C. Melville
(Cambridge: Cambridge University Press, 1991), survey aspects of the history of the period.
A. K. S. Lambton, *Qajar Persia: Eleven Studies* (London: I. B. Tauris, 1987), brings together her valuable articles on the Qajar era in one volume. Lambton's pioneering *Landlords and Peasants in Persia: A Study of Land Tenure and Land Revenue Administration*
(London: Oxford University Press, 1953) devotes several chapters to the Safavid and Qajar
periods. *Qajar Iran: Political, Social, and Cultural Change, 1800–1925*, ed. C. Bosworth
and C. Hillenbrand (Edinburgh: Edinburgh University Press, 1983), comprises twenty-
one articles on the political, cultural, and social history of period. *Religion and Society
in Qajar Iran*, ed. R. Gleave (London: Routledge, 2005), addresses the question of the
relationship between religion and society. Two other collections of articles also provide
useful introductions to the Qajar period: *Society and Culture in Qajar Iran: Studies in
Honor of Hafez Farmayan*, ed. E. L. Daniel (Costa Mesa, CA: Mazda Publishers, 2002),
and *War and Peace in Qajar Persia: Implications Past and Present*, ed. R. Farmanfarmaian
(London: Routledge, 2008).

The early history of the Qajar period, including the rise of the dynasty and the con-
solidation of power, remains less studied. G. Hambly's essays in the *Cambridge History of
Iran*, vol. 7 ("Āghā Muhammad Khān and the Establishment of the Qājār Dynasty" and
"Iran during the Reigns of Fath 'Alī Shāh and Muhammad Shāh"), are the best introduc-
tions. See also *EIr:* "Fath-'Ali Shah" (A. Amanat). L. Diba's article "Introducing Fath 'Ali
Shah: Production and Dispersal of the *Shahanshahnama* Manuscripts," in *Shahnama
Studies*, ed. C. Melville (Cambridge: Centre of Middle Eastern and Islamic Studies, Uni-
versity of Cambridge, 2006), 1:239–58, demonstrates how Fath 'Ali Shah styled himself
as a king along a traditional Persian model. A. Amanat, "The Kayanid Crown and Qajar
Reclaiming of Royal Authority," *Iranian Studies* 34, nos. 1–4 (2001): 17–30, explores Qajar

legitimacy strategies through the lens of art history and material culture. A. Ashraf, "The Politics of Gift Exchange in Early Qajar Iran, 1785–1834," *Comparative Studies in Society and History* 58, no. 2 (April 2016), 550–76, underscores the significance of gift giving in early Qajar political culture. Ahmad Mirza 'Azod al-Dowleh's important *Tarikh-e 'Azodi* is translated as *Life at the Court of the Early Qajar Shahs*, trans. and ed. M. M. Eskandari-Qajar (Washington, DC: Mage Publishers, 2014). Two Qajar chronicles are available in translation: H. J. Brydges, *The Dynasty of the Kajars* (London: J. Bohn, 1833), and *History of Persia under Qajar Rule*, trans. H. Busse (New York: Columbia University Press, 1972). R. G. Watson, *A History of Persia* (London: Smith, Elder and Co., 1866), is partially based on Persian contemporary chronicles.

Several studies have explored the role of Iran in the entangled politics of European powers. J. B. Kelly, *Britain and the Persian Gulf, 1795–1880* (Oxford: Clarendon Press, 1968); E. Ingram, *Britain's Persian Connection 1798–1828: Prelude to the Great Game in Asia* (Oxford: Clarendon Press, 1992); M. Yapp, *Control of the Persian Mission, 1822–36* (Birmingham, UK: University of Birmingham, 1960); and Yapp, *Strategies of British India: Britain, Iran, and Afghanistan, 1798–1850* (Oxford: Clarendon Press, 1980)—all study British political, economic, and diplomatic interests in Iran and Persian Gulf. M. Afchar, *La politiques européenne en Perse* (Berlin: Librairie Orientale Iranschahr, 1921), is still a useful source for the diplomacy of the nineteenth century. F. Adamiyat, *Bahrein Islands: A Legal and Diplomatic Study of the British-Iranian Controversy* (New York: F. A. Praeger, 1955), addresses similar questions but with greater use of Persian-language sources. I. Amini, *Napoleon and Persia: Franco-Persian Relations under the First Empire* (Richmond, UK: Curzon, 1999), is a pioneering study of the subject.

The best known among the numerous European travelogues from the first decades of the nineteenth century are those by Edward Scott Waring, Pierre-Amédée Jaubert, Harford Jones Bridges, John Malcolm, James Morier, William Ouseley, Robert Ker Porter, James Baillie Fraser, Henry C. Rawlinson, Gaspard Drouville, Adrien Dupré, and Alfred Gardane. Translations of early Qajar travels abroad include Abol-Hassan Shirazi (Ilchi), *A Persian at the Court of King George, 1809–10: The Journal of Mirza Abul Hassan Khan*, ed. and trans. M. Morris Cloake (London: David and Charles, 1989); and Najaf Kuli Mirza, *Journal of Residence in England and of a Journey from and to Syria of . . . Reeza Koolee Meerza, Njaf Koolee Meerza, and Taymour Meerza of Persia*, trans. A. Y. Khayyat (London: W. Tyler, 1939). For a study of British diplomats, travelers, missionaries, and officers, see D. Wright, *The English amongst the Persians during the Qajar Period, 1787–1921* (London: Heinemann, 1977), and his study of Persian visitors to Britain, *The Persians amongst the English* (London: I. B. Tauris, 1985). His collected essays appear as *Britain and Iran, 1790–1980* (London: Iran Society, 2003). N. Green, *The Love of Strangers: What Six Muslim Students Learned in Jane Austen's London* (Princeton, NJ: Princeton University Press, 2015), offers an imaginative portrayal of Iranian students of the early Qajar era in 1815 England. H. McKenzie Johnston, *Ottoman and Persian Odysseys* (London: British Academic Press, 1998) is a biography of James Morier and provides some details on the production of *Hajji Baba of Ispahan*.

M. Atkin, *Russia and Iran, 1780–1828* (Minneapolis: University of Minnesota Press, 1980) studies Russo-Persian relations and the origins of the conflict in the late eighteenth and early nineteenth centuries. Essays in the *Cambridge History of Iran*, vol. 7, by F. Kazemzadeh, "Iranian Relations with Russia and the Soviet Union, to 1921," and S. Shaw, "Iranian Relations with the Ottoman Empire in the Eighteenth and Nineteenth Centuries," offer general introductions. Other studies include P. W. Avery,

"An Enquiry into the Outbreak of the Second Russo-Persian War, 1826–28," ed. C. E. Bosworth, in *Iran and Islam* (Edinburgh: Edinburgh University Press, 1971), 17–46; F. Mostashari, *On the Religious Frontiers: Tsarist Russia and Islam in the Caucasus* (London: I. B. Tauris, 2006); and L. Kelly, *Diplomacy and Murder in Tehran: Alexander Girboyedov and Imperial Russia's Mission to the Shah of Persia* (London: I. B. Tauris, 2002). See also M. L. Entner, *Russo-Persian Commercial Relations, 1828–1914* (Gainsville: University Press of Florida, 1965); G. A. Bournoutian, *The Khanate of Erevan Under Qajar Rule, 1795–1828* (Costa Mesa, CA: Mazda Publishers, 1992); and Bournoutian, *From Tabriz to St. Petersburg: Iran's Mission of Apology to Russia in 1829* (Costa Mesa, CA: Mazda Publishers, 2014). Bournoutian has also published several collection of documents and translations of local histories, including Jamal Javanshir Qarabaghi, *Tarikh-e Qarabagh*, trans. and annotated by G.A. Bournoutian (Costa Mesa, CA: Mazda Publishers, 1994); *Russia and the Armenians of Transcaucasia, 1797–1889* (Costa Mesa, CA: Mazda Publishers, 1998); and *The 1823 Russian Survey of the Karabagh Province: A Primary Source on the Demography and Economy of Karabagh in the Early 19th Century* (Costa Mesa, CA: Mazda Publishers, 2011). A. Amanat, "'Russian Intrusion into the Guarded Domain': Reflections of a Qajar Statesman on European Expansion," *Journal of the American Society of Oriental Studies* 113, no. 1 (1993): 35–56, explores responses among the Qajar elite to Russian expansion.

The history of the Qajar clerical establishment is the focus of H. Algar, *Religion and State in Iran, 1785–1906: The Role of the Ulama in the Qajar Period* (Berkeley: University of California Press, 1969). J. Cole, "Shi'i Clerics in Iraq and Iran, 1722–1780: The Akhbari-Usuli Conflict Reconsidered," *Iranian Studies* 18, no. 1 (1985): 3–34, provides an alternative socioreligious perspective. Essays in *Authority and Political Culture in Shi'ism*, ed. S. A. Arjomand (Albany: State University of New York Press, 1988), also examine the institutionalization of Shi'ism from the sixteenth to nineteenth centuries and provide useful documents and primary sources. The volume includes A. Amanat, "In Between the Madrasa and the Marketplace: The Designation of Clerical Leadership in Modern Shi'ism." S. A. Arjomand, *The Shadow of God and the Hidden Imam*, also provides a sociological reading of the Qajar hierocracy. J. Cole, *Roots of North Indian Shi'ism in Iran and Iraq: Religion and State in Awadh, 1722–1859* (Berkeley: University of California Press, 1988), offers a comparative perspective on the development of Shi'ism in the early nineteenth century. M. Litvak, *Shi'i Scholars of Nineteenth Century Iraq: The 'Ulama of Najaf and Karbala'* (Cambridge: Cambridge University Press, 1998) is a study of patronage and scholarship and the ulama network in Iran and India. M. Tavakoli-Targhi, *Refashioning Iran: Orientalism, Occidentalism, and Historiography* (New York: Palgrave, 2001), employs eighteenth- and nineteenth-century Indo-Persian texts to demonstrate how vernacular forms of Indo-Iranian modernity evolved in the eighteenth and nineteenth centuries.

The development of messianic Shi'ism and its encounter with the Qajar clerical establishment, with special reference to the Babi movement, is studied in A. Amanat, *Resurrection and Renewal: The Making of the Babi Movement in Iran, 1844–1850* (Ithaca: Cornell University Press, 1989). D. MacEoin, *The Messiah of Shiraz: Studies in Early and Middle Babism* (Leiden: Brill, 2009), also traces the evolution of Shaykhism into the Babi movement and its development after 1850. For a collection of Western accounts of the Babi and Baha'i religions, see M. Momen, *The Babi and Baha'i Religions, 1844–1944: Some Contemporary Western Accounts* (Oxford: George Ronald, 1981). See also his "The Social Basis of the Babi Upheavals in Iran (1848–53): A Preliminary Analysis," *International Journal of Middle East Studies* 15, no. 2 (May 1983): 157–83. A number of translations and edited volumes by E. G. Browne on the history of the Babis and Baha'is include *A Travellers Narrative Written to Illustrate the Episode of the Bab*, 2 vols. (Cambridge: Cambridge University Press, 1891); *The Tarikh-i-Jadid or New History of Mirza 'Ali Muhammad the Bab* (Cambridge: Cambridge University Press, 1893); and *Materials for the Study of the Babi Religion* (Cambridge: Cambridge University Press, 1918). His *A Year amongst the Persians* (London: A. and C. Blake, 1893), provides a unique window onto the heterodox milieu of the time. See also H. M. Balyuzi, *Edward Granville Browne and the Baha'i Faith* (London: George Ronald, 1970). T. Lawson, *Gnostic Apocalypse and Islam: Qur'an, Exegesis, Messianism, and the Literary Origins of the Babi Religion* (London: Routledge, 2012) is the only detailed study of Babi hermeneutics.

5. NASER AL-DIN SHAH AND MAINTAINING A FRAGILE BALANCE (1848–1896)

The second half of the nineteenth century has received greater scholarly attention. A. Amanat, *Pivot of the Universe: Nasir al-Din Shah Qajar and the Iranian Monarch, 1831–1896* (Berkeley: University of California Press, 1997), serves as a biography and a critical analysis of the institution of monarchy in Iran. M. Ekhtiar, *Modern Science and Education in Qajar Iran: the Dar al-Funun* (London: RoutledgeCurzon, 2003); J. Lorentz, "Iran's Great Reformer of the Nineteenth Century: An Analysis of Amir Kabir's Reforms," *Iranian Studies* 4, nos. 2–3 (Spring 1971): 85–103, and A. Amanat, "The Downfall of Mirza Taqi Khan Amir Kabir and the Problem of Ministerial Authority in Qajar Iran," *International Journal of Middle East Studies* 23 (1991): 577–99, are among the few available studies on Amir Kabir era in Western languages. Two studies on government administration and reform in the Naseri period — S. Bakhash, *Iran: Monarchy, Bureaucracy, and Reform Under the Qajars: 1858–1896* (London: Ithaca Press, 1978); and A. R. Sheikholeslami, *The Structure of Central Authority in Qajar Iran, 1871–1896* (Atlanta: Scholars Press, 1997) — rely on an array of Persian and European primary and archival sources. G. Nashat, *The Origins of Modern Reform in Iran, 1870–80* (Urbana: University of Illinois Press, 1982), is the only book-length publication on the age of Moshir al-Dowleh.

C. Issawi, *The Economic History of Iran, 1800–1914* (Chicago: University of Chicago Press, 1971), provides an overview of major trends in Iran's economy and trade through a collection of mostly English-language primary sources. An earlier article by Issawi, "The Tabriz-Trabzon Trade, 1830–1900: Rise and Decline of a Route," *International Journal of Middle East Studies* 1, no. 1 (1970): 18–27, examines an important overland trade route. A. Amanat, *Cities and Trade: Consul Abbott on the Economy and Society of Iran, 1847–1866* (London: Ithaca Press, 1983), contains three substantial reports with details of urban and rural population, trade and guilds, and local crafts and industries. S. Mahdavi, *For God, Mammon, and Country: A Nineteenth-Century Persian Merchant, Haj Muhammad Hassan Amin Al-Zarb (1834–1898)*, (Boulder, CO: Westview Press, 1999), is a study of one of the nineteenth century's prominent merchants. W. Floor, *Agriculture in Qajar Iran* (Washington, DC: Mage Publishers, 2003); *Guilds, Merchants, and Ulama in Nineteenth-Century Iran* (Washington, DC: Mage Publishers, 2009); and "Tea Consumption and Imports in Qajar Iran," *Studia Iranica* 33 (2004): 47–111, provide useful leads on sources and potential avenues for future research. His *A Fiscal History of Iran in the Safavid and Qajar Periods, 1500–1925* (New York: Bibliotheca Persia Press, 1998), is a survey of four hundred years of Iran's economy. A three-part study by M. Nouraei and V. Martin, "The Role of the

'Karguzar' in the Foreign Relations of State and Society of Iran from the Mid-Nineteenth Century to 1921," *Journal of the Royal Asiatic Society* 15, no. 3 (2005): 261–77; 16, no. 1 (2006): 29–41; and 16, no. 2 (2006): 151–63, examines the evolution of this important office. On banking in Qajar Iran, see G. Jones, *Banking and Empire in Iran: The History of the British Bank of the Middle East*, vol. 1 (Cambridge: Cambridge University Press, 1986). On British economic interests in Iran and in the Persian Gulf, including the Karun navigation concession, see S. Shahnavaz, *Britain and South-West Persian 1880–1914: A Study of Imperialism and Economic Dependence* (London and New York: Routledge, 2014). See also A. Amanat, *EIr*: "British Influence in Persia: Qajar Period."

Ulrich Marzolph, in his *Narrative Illustrations in Persian Lithographic Books* (Leiden and Boston: Brill, 2001), and in his numerous other publications, examines the lithographic literature and print culture of Qajar Iran. P. Avery, "Printing, the Press and Literature in Modern Iran," in *Cambridge History of Iran* (Cambridge: Cambridge University Press, 1991), 7:815–69, offers an overview. *At the Gate of Modernism: Qajar Iran in the Nineteenth Century*, ed. E. M. Jeremiás (Piliscsaba, Hungary: Avicenna Institute of Middle Eastern Studies, 2012), is a collection of essays on modernity and encounters with Europe. A seminal study on medicine in Qajar Iran is J. E. Polak, *Persien: Das Land und seine Bewohner* (Leipzig: Brockhaus, 1865). For a study of the author and his work, see A. Gäuchter, *Briefe aus Persien: Jacob E. Polaks Medizinische Berichte* (Vienna: New Academic Press, 2013). F. Speziale, *Hospitals in Iran and India, 1500–1950s* (Leiden: Brill, 2012), is a novel study of coexistence of traditional medicine and modern hospitals.

M. Volodarsky, "Persia's Foreign Policy between the Two Herat Crises, 1831–56," *Middle Eastern Studies* 21, no. 2 (1985): 111–51, is among the few studies using Russian archives on the Herat crisis. Other studies include H. W. C. Davis, *The Great Game in Asia (1800–1844)*, (London: Oxford University Press, 1927); P. M. Sykes, *A History of Afghanistan*, 2 vols. (London: Macmillan & Co., 1940); and P. Hopkirk, *The Great Game: The Struggle for Empire in Central Asia* (New York: Kodansha International, 1992), which discuss the Herat crisis in the context of broader geopolitics and the emergence of the so-called Persian Question. G. Curzon's highly informative *Persia and the Persian Question*, 2 vols. (London: Longmans, Green & Co., 1892) is a clear demonstration of British imperial anxieties over Iran. Studies on Russo-Persian and Anglo-Persian diplomatic rivalry in the latter half of the nineteenth century include F. Kazemzadeh's seminal *Russia and Britain in Persia, 1864–1914: A Study in Imperialism* (New Haven: Yale University Press, 1968), as well as R. L. Greaves, *Persia and the Defense of India 1884–1892* (London: Athlone Press, 1959); more recently L. Stebbins, *British Imperialism in Qajar Iran: Consuls, Agents and Influence in the Middle East* (London: I. B. Tauris, 2017). Most of the scholarship on German and Austrian relations with Iran during the nineteenth century is in German, with the notable exception of B. G. Martin, *German-Persian Diplomatic Relations 1873–1912* (London: Mouton and Co., S-Gravenhage, 1959). A. Yeselson, *United States-Persian Diplomatic Relations, 1883–1921* (New Brunswick, NJ: Rutgers University Press, 1956), is a pioneering study about the topic in the English language. Perso-Ottoman frontiers in the Qajar period are studied in S. Ateş, *Ottoman-Iranian Borderlands: Making a Boundary, 1843–1914* (Cambridge: Cambridge University Press, 2015).

Studies of new political, religious, and social trends during the Naseri period include N. R. Keddie, *Sayyid Jamāl ad-Dīn "al-Afghānī": A Political Biography* (Berkeley: University of California Press, 1972); M. Bayat's pioneering *Mysticism and Dissent: Socioreligious Thought in Qajar Iran* (Syracuse: Syracuse University Press, 1982); J. Cole, *Modernity and the Millennium: The Genesis of the Baha'i Faith in the Nineteenth-Century Middle*

East (New York: Columbia University Press, 1998); and H. Algar's highly partisan *Mirza Malkum Khan: A Study in the History of Iranian Modernism* (Berkeley: University of California Press, 1973). On the Jewish community in Iran and its relations with religious authorities, see D. Tsadik, *Between Foreigners and Shi'is: Nineteenth-Century Iran and Its Jewish Minority* (Stanford, CA: Stanford University Press, 2007).

M. Momen, *The Baha'i Communities of Iran, 1851–1921*, vol. 1: *The Northern Iran* (Oxford, UK: George Ronald, 2015), studies social history of transformation of the Babi communities into the Baha'i faith. Y. Ioannesyan, *The Development of the Babi/Baha'i Communities: Exploring Baron Rosen's Archives* (Abingdon, UK: Routledge, 2013), provides new Russian archival material on the Baha'is in the late nineteenth century. A. Amanat and F. Vahman, *Az Tehran ta 'Akka: Babiyan va Baha'iyan dar Asnad-e Dowran-e Qajar* (Copenhagen: Ashkaar Publishers, 2016), is a documentary history of the Babis and Baha'is in mid-nineteenth-century Ottoman exile and in Iran. A. D. Becker, *Revival and Awakening: American Evangelical Missionaries in Iran and Origins of the Assyrian Nationalism* (Chicago: University of Chicago Press, 2015) is an excellent study of the role of the missionaries in development of ethnic nationalism.

Studies on the social history of the period include five book-length studies of cities. H. Walcher, *In the Shadow of the King: Zill al-Sultan and Isfahan under the Qajars* (London: I. B. Tauris, 2008), studies the politics of notables, minorities, missionaries, and European representatives during the long tenure of Zell al-Soltan. C. Werner, *An Iranian Town in Transition: A Social and Economic History of the Elites of Tabriz, 1747–1848* (Wiesbaden: Harrassowitz, 2000), covers the first half of the century using *waqf* documents. J. Clark, *Provincial Concerns: A Political History of the Iranian Province of Azerbaijan, 1848–1906* (Costa Mesa, CA: Mazda Publishers, 2006); C. Adle and B. Hourcade, *Téhéran: Capitale bicentenaire* (Paris: Institute Français de Recherche en Iran, 1992), partially examines history of the Iranian capital in the Qajar period. J. M. Gustafson, *Kirman and the Qajar Empire: Local Dimensions of Modernity in Iran, 1794–1914* (New York: Routledge, 2015), mostly examines urban notables of Kerman. See also C. E. Davies, "Qajar Rule in Fars Prior to 1849," *Iran* 25 (1987), 125–53. On tribes and forces of modernity in the Qajar era, see A. Khazeni, *Tribes and Empires on the Margins of Nineteenth-Century Iran* (Seattle: University of Washington Press, 2010); and G. R. Garthwaite, *Khans and Shahs: A History of the Bakhtiyari Tribe in Iran*, 2nd ed. (London: I. B. Tauris, 2010).

N. R. Keddie, *Religion and Rebellion in Iran: The Tobacco Protest of 1891–1892* (London: Cass, 1966), provides a pioneering study of the tobacco protest using a variety of sources, including the British National Archives. J. de Groot, *Religion, Culture and Politics in Iran: From the Qajars to Khomeini* (London: I. B. Tauris, 2007), offers a perceptive study of culture and religion in the Qajar and Pahlavi periods, with an emphasis on Iran's tradition of social protest. More recently, R. Kazemi, "The Tobacco Protest in Nineteenth-Century Iran: The View from a Provincial Town," *Journal of Persianate Studies* 7, no. 2 (2014): 251–95, has contributed to our knowledge of how the protest unfolded in Shiraz. J. D. Gurney and M. Sifatgul, *Qum dar Qaḥṭī-i Buzurg-i 1288 Qamarī* (Qom: Kitabkhanah-i Buzurg-i Hazrat Ayatullah al-'Uzma Mar'ashi Najafi, 2008), brings to light an extraordinary first-person account of the Great Famine in Qom and its effects.

On the history of women and gender, A. Najmabadi, *Women with Mustaches and Men without Beards: Gender and Sexual Anxieties of Iranian Modernity* (Berkeley: University of California Press, 2005), explores how Western notions of modernity spurred changes in Iranian gender and sexual norms. W. Floor, *A Social History of Sexual Relations in Iran* (Washington, DC: Mage, 2008), devotes sections to the Qajar period. *The Education of Women and the Vices of Men: Two Qajar Tracts*, trans. and with an introduction by H. Javadi and W. Floor (Syracuse, NY: Syracuse University Press, 2010), presents a fascinating debate on the sexes in the late Qajar era. M. M. Ringer, *Education, Religion and the Discourse of Cultural Reform in Qajar Iran* (Costa Mesa, CA: Mazda Publishers, 2001), surveys military educational reforms, missionary schools, and modern curricula through the nineteenth and early twentieth centuries. V. Martin, *The Qajar Pact: Bargaining, Protest and the State in Nineteenth-Century Persia* (London: I. B. Tauris, 2005), sheds light on the nonelite, including women and slaves. On slavery in Iran and the Persian Gulf, see also B. A. Mirzai, *A History of Slavery and Emancipation in Iran, 1800–1929* (Austin: University of Texas Press, 2017); J. Zdanowski, *Slavery and Manumission: British Policy in the Red Sea and the Persian Gulf in the First Half of the 20th Century* (Reading, UK: Ithaca Press, 2012); and A. Amanat and A. Khazeni, "The Steppe Roads of Central Asia and the Captivity Narrative of Mirza Mahmud Taqi Ashtiyani," in *Writing Travel in Central Asian History*, ed. N. Green (Bloomington and Indianapolis: Indiana University Press, 2014), 113–34.

Studies on travel literature include N. Sohrabi, *Taken for Wonder: Nineteenth-Century Travel Accounts from Iran to Europe* (Oxford: Oxford University Press, 2012) and *A Shi'ite Pilgrimage to Mecca (1885–1886): The Safarnameh of Mirza Mohammad Hosayn Farahani*, ed. and trans., and with annotations by, H. F. Farmayan and E. L. Daniel (Austin: University of Texas Press, 1990). Two travel diaries of Naser al-Din Shah are available in translation: *The Diary of H.M. The Shah of Persia: During His Tour through Europe in A.D. 1873*, trans. J. Redhouse (London: J. Murray, 1874; reprint, Costa Mesa, CA: Mazda Publishers, 1995); and *A Diary Kept by His Majesty, the Shah of Persia during His Journey to Europe in 1878*, trans. J. W. A. H. Schilndler and Baron L. de Norman (London: Richard Bentley and Son, 1879). Zayn al-'Abdedin Maragheh'i's fictional travelogue is translated as *Travel Diary of Ebrahim Beg*, trans. J. D. Clark (Costa Mesa, CA: Mazda Publishers, 2006).

Art and architecture of the Qajar period as of late received the deserved attention. See B. W. Robinson's pioneering "Persian Painting under the Zand and Qajar Dynasties," in *Cambridge History of Iran* (Cambridge: Cambridge University Press, 1991), 7:870–89; L. Diba and M. Ekhtiar, eds., *Royal Qajar Paintings: The Qajar Epoch, 1785–1925* (London: I. B. Tauris, 1999), a collection of essays accompanying the catalog of an exhibition at Brooklyn Museum; A. Amanat, "Court Patronage and Public Space: Abu'l-Hasan Sani' al-Mulk and the Art of Persianizing the Other in Qajar Iran," *Court Cultures in the Muslim World, Seven to Nineteenth Centuries*, ed. A. Fuess and J. Hartung (London: Routledge Taylor and Francis, 2011), 408–44; and M. Ritter, *Moscheen und Madrasabauten in Iran, 1785–1848* (Leiden: Brill, 2006). On early photography in Qajar Iran, see P. Khosronejad, *Untold Stories: The Socio-Cultural Life of Images in Qajar Era Iran* (Berlin: LIT Verlag, 2015); A. Behdad, *Camera Orientalis: Reflections on Photography of the Middle East* (Chicago: University of Chicago Press, 2016); and S. G. Scheiwiller, *Liminalities of Gender and Sexuality in Nineteenth-Century Iranian Photography: Desirous Bodies* (New York: Routledge, 2017).

6. THE CONSTITUTIONAL REVOLUTION

There is a large body of literature on the Constitutional Revolution in European languages. E. G. Browne, *The Persian Revolution of 1905–1909* (London, 1910), is the earliest account in English conveying the voices of the Iranian revolutionaries. See the new edition with an introduction by A. Amanat (Washington, DC: Mage Publishers, 1995). A. Kasravi, *History of the Iranian Constitutional Revolution*, trans. E. Siegel (Costa Mesa, CA: Mazda Publishers, 2006), is the only Persian general account of the revolution available in English translation. The multiauthored entry "Constitutional Revolution" in *Encyclopedia Iranica* (by A. Amanat, V. Martin, S.A. Arjomand, M. Ettehadiyeh-Nezam-Mafi, S. Sirjani and S. Soroudi) offers a succinct survey of the intellectual trends, events, a summary of the Constitution of 1906–1907 and other aspects. Modern book-length studies of the revolution include V. Martin, *Islam and Modernism: The Iranian Revolution of 1906* (London: I. B. Tauris, 1989), which highlights the role of the 'ulama; M. Bayat, *Iran's First Revolution: Shi'ism and the Constitutional Revolution of 1905–1909* (New York: Oxford University Press, 1991), which stresses the place of freethinkers and nonconformists; and J. Afary, *The Iranian Constitutional Revolution, 1906–1911: Grassroots Democracy, Social Democracy, and the Origins of Feminism* (New York: Columbia University Press, 1996), which offers a class analysis and focuses on the role of women and the underprivileged. A collection of essays—*Iran's Constitutional Revolution: Popular Politics, Cultural Transformations and Transnational Connections*, ed. H. Chehabi and V. Martin (London: I. B. Tauris, 2010), and N. Sohrabi, *Revolution and Constitutionalism in the Ottoman Empire and Iran, 1902–1910* (Cambridge: Cambridge University Press, 2011)—provide a comparative perspective. See also N. R. Keddie, "Iranian Revolutions in Comparative Perspective," *American Historical Review* 88 (1983): 579–98; and *Iran's Constitutional Revolution of 1906 and Narratives of the Enlightenment*, ed. A. Ansari (London: Gingko Library, 2017).

On women in the constitutional era, A. Najmabadi, *The Story of the Daughters of Quchan: Gender and National Memory in Iranian History* (Syracuse, NY: Syracuse University Press, 1998), portrays the plight of captives abducted and the resonance of this over time. A. Amanat, "Memory and Amnesia in the Historiography of the Constitutional Revolution," in *Iran in the 20th Century: Historiography and Political Culture*, ed. T. Atabaki (London: I. B. Tauris, 2009), highlights the Babi background of popular leaders of the revolution. R. M. Afshari, "The Historians of the Constitutional Movement and the Making of the Iranian Populist Tradition," *International Journal of Middle East Studies* 25, no. 3 (1993): 477–94, also touches on the same issues. H. Berberian, *Armenians and the Iranian Constitutional Revolution of 1905–1911: "The Love for Freedom Has No Fatherland"* (Boulder, CO: Westview Press, 2001), discusses Armenian politicization and participation in the Constitutional Revolution. On Jewish conversions and fluid identities, especially in the late Qajar era and the early Pahlavi period, see M. Amanat, *Jewish Identities in Iran: Resistance and Conversion to Islam and the Baha'i Faith* (London: I. B. Tauris, 2011). D. Tsadik, "The Legal Status of Religious Minorities: Imāmī Shī'ī Law and Iran's Constitutional Revolution," *Islamic Law and Society* 10, no. 3 (Leiden: Brill, 2003): 376–408, examines the legal ambivalence toward Iranian religious minorities in the constitutional period. On Jewish communities in modern Iran, see H. M. Sarshar, *Esther's Children* (Philadelphia: Jewish Publication Society, 2002). On Baha'i education and communities in the constitutional era, see S. Shahvar, *The Forgotten Schools: The Baha'is and Modern Education in Iran, 1899–1934* (London: I. B. Tauris, 2009), and Shahvar's collection of letters and reports of Russian officials, *The Baha'is of Iran, Transcaspia and Caucasus*, 2 vols. (London: I. B. Tauris, 2011–2012).

For the clerical attitude toward the Constitutional Revolution, in addition to the aforementioned, see "Two Clerical Tracts on Constitutionalism," trans. H. Dabashi, in S. A. Arjomand, ed., *Authority and Political Culture in Shi'ism*, which provides an overview of Shaykh Fazlollah Nuri's anticonstitutional position. C. Kurzman, ed., *Modernist Islam, 1840–1940: A Sourcebook* (Oxford: Oxford University Press, 2002), includes Mohammad Hosain Na'ini's theory of Islamic governance, translated and edited by M. Sadri. M. M. Farzaneh, *The Iranian Constitutional Revolution and the Clerical Leadership of Khurasani* (Syracuse, NY: Syracuse University Press, 2015), is a study of the renowned Najaf-based *marja's* and their support for the Iranian constitutionalists. See also A. Fathi, "Ahmad Kasravi and Seyyed Jamal Waez on Constitutionalism in Iran," *Middle Eastern Studies* 29 (1993): 702–13.

W. M. Shuster's *The Strangling of Persia: A Record of European Diplomacy and Oriental Intrigue* (London: T. F. Unwin, 1912), reveals how British and Russian interests in Iran crushed the fledgling constitutional democracy there. See also R. A. McDaniel, *The Shuster Mission and the Persian Constitutional Revolution* (Minneapolis: Bibliotheca Islamica, 1974). For an extensive study on British interests and opposition to the imperial intervention in Iran, see M. Bonakdarian, *Britain and the Iranian Constitutional Revolution of 1906–191: Foreign Policy, Imperialism, and Dissent* (Syracuse, NY: Syracuse University Press and Iran Heritage Foundation, 2006). A. Destrée, *Les fonctionnaires belges au service de la Perse* (Leiden: Brill Publishers, 1976), also examines the constitutional period. D. Fraser, *Persia and Turkey in Revolt* (London: W. Blackwood and Sons, 1910), is a hostile treatment of the Iranian Constitutional Revolution by a conservative correspondent of the *Times* of London. H Javadi, ed., *Letters from Tabriz: The Russian Suppression of the Iranian Constitutional Movement*, translated from the Persian by E. G. Browne (Washington, DC: Mage Publishers, 2008), should be considered a supplement to Browne's *The Persian Revolution*.

E. G. Browne, *The Press and Poetry of Modern Persia* (Cambridge: Cambridge University Press, 1914), is a pioneering study based on Persian sources of the role of the press in the period. See also S. Balaghi, "Print Culture in Late Qajar Iran: The Cartoons of *Kashkūl*," *Iranian Studies* 34 (2001): 165–81. E. G. Browne, *A Literary History of Persia*, vol. 4 (Cambridge: University Press, 1928), and B. Alavi, *Geschichte und Entwicklung der modernen persischen Literatur* (Berlin: Akademie-Verlag, 1964), survey the literature of the Constitutional period. See also H. Kamshad, *Modern Persian Prose Literature* (Cambridge: Cambridge University Press, 1966); S. Soroudi, "Poet and Revolution: The Impact of the Iranian Constitutional Revolution on the Literary and Social Outlook of the Poet," *Iranian Studies* 12, nos. 1–2 (1979): 3–41 and also 12, nos. 3–4 (1979): 239–73; A. Bausani, "Europe and Iran in Contemporary Persian Literature," *East and West* 11 (1960): 3–14; and F. Machalski, *La littérature de l'Iran contemporain*, vol. 1, *La poésie persane de l'époque de "réveil des iraniens" jusqu'au coup d'état de Reḍā Ḫān, environ 1880–1921* (Warsaw: Narodowy im. Ossolińskich, 1965).

7. THE GREAT WAR AND THE RISE OF REZA KHAN (1914–1925)

The literature on the impact of World War I on Iran has received a fair amount of attention. O. Bast's *La Perse et la Grande Guerre* (Tehran: Institut Français de Recherche en Iran, 2002), is a valuable study of the war and diplomacy of the period. T. Atabaki, ed., *Iran and the First World War: Battleground of the Great Powers* (London: I. B. Tauris, 2006), includes a number of important essays on the secret activities of Ottomans in Iran during the war, the Kurdish tribes along the Iran-Ottoman border, and the establishment of the

Communist Party in Iran. There are three studies on Anglo-Iranian relations during World War I and the postwar era: N. S. Fatemi, *Diplomatic History of Persia, 1917–1923: Anglo-Russian Power Politics in Iran* (New York: Russell F. Moore, 1952); W. J. Olson, *Anglo-Iranian Relations during World War I* (London: F. Cass, 1984); and H. Sabahi, *British Policy in Persia, 1918–1925* (London: Frank Cass, 1990). For Sykes and the South Persian Rifles, see A. Wynn, *Persia in the Great Game: Sir Percy Sykes, Explorer, Consul, Soldier, Spy* (London: John Murray, 2003). See also P. Sykes, "Persia and the Great War," *Journal of the Royal Central Asian Society* 9, no. 4 (1922): 175–87; Sykes, "South Persia and the Great War," *Geographical Journal* 58, no. 2 (1921): 101–16; and Sykes, "The British Flag on the Caspian: A Side-Show of the Great War," *Foreign Affairs* 2, no. 2 (1923): 282–94. F. Safiri's doctoral dissertation, "The South Persian Rifles" (University of Edinburgh, 1976), is the only scholarly study in English on the subject (available only in Persian translation). See also C. J. Edmonds, *East and West of Zagros; Travel, War, and Politics in Iraq and Persia*, ed. Yann Richard (Leiden: Brill, 2010).

For a survey of the beginning of the oil exploration, see R. W. Ferrier, *The History of the British Petroleum Company: The Developing Years, 1901–1932*, vol. 1 (Cambridge: Cambridge University Press, 1982); H. Nabavi, "D'Arcy's Oil Concession of 1901: Oil Independence, Foreign Influence and Characters Involved," *Journal of South Asian and Middle Eastern Studies* 33, no. 2 (2010): 18–33; and chapters in Khazeni, *Tribes and Empires*. For the Anglo-Persian Agreement of 1919, see H. Katouzian, "The Campaign against the Anglo-Iranian Agreement of 1919," *British Journal of Middle Eastern Studies* 25, no. 1 (May 1998): 5–46; and W. J. Olson, "The Genesis of the Anglo-Persian Agreement of 1919," in *Towards a Modern Iran: Studies in Thought, Politics, and Society*, ed. E. Kedourie and S.G. Haim (London: Frank Cass & Co., 1980): 184–216. On the Khayabani revolt, see H. Katouzian, "The Revolt of Shaykh Muḥammad Khiyābānī," *Iran* 37 (1999): 155–72.

On German-Iranian relations, see O. Bast, *Les Allemands en Perse pendant la première guerre mondiale d'après les sources diplomatiques françaises* (Paris: Peeters, 1997), using German and French diplomatic sources. See also U. Gehrke, *Persien in der deutschen Orient-Politik während des Ersten Weltkrieges*, 2 vols. (Stuttgart: W. Kohlhammer, 1960), and his "Germany and Persia up to 1919," in *Germany and the Middle East, 1835–1939*, ed. Jehuda Lothar Wallach (Tel Aviv: Tel Aviv University, 1975). See also the entry by O. Bast in *EIr*: "Germany, i. German-Persian Relations" and the bibliography. C. Sykes's *Wassmuss, the German Lawrence* (New York: Longmans, Green, 1926), is a popular biography of this intriguing figure. On the influence of Bolshevism and European revolutionary ideologies on Iranian politics, see related essays in S. Cronin, ed., *Iranian-Russian Encounters: Empires and Revolutions since 1800* (New York: Rutledge, 2013). C. Chaquèri's *The Soviet Socialist Republic of Iran, 1920–1921: Birth of the Trauma* (Pittsburgh: University of Pittsburgh Press, 1995), is the only book-length study in English of the Jangal movement and its relations with the Bolsheviks. See also P. Dailami, "The Bolshevik Revolution and the Genesis of Communism in Iran, 1917–1920," *Central Asian Survey* 11, no. 3 (1992): 51–82; Dailami, "The Bolsheviks and the Jangali Revolutionary Movement, 1915–1920," *Cahiers du Monde Russe et Soviétique* 31, no. 1 (1990): 43–60; J. Afary, "The Contentious Historiography of the Gilan Republic in Iran: A Critical Exploration," *Iranian Studies* 28 (1995): 3–24; and A. Arkun, "Armenians and the Jangalis," *Iranian Studies* 30 (1997): 25–52. Utilizing mostly Russian sources, F. Kazemzadeh, *The Struggle for Transcaucasia, 1917–1921* (New York: Philosophical Library, 1951), examines the impact of the Russian Revolution on the political realities in the Caucasus. Ottoman-Iranian relations during World War I remain largely underexplored. See J. P. Luft, "The Iranian Nationalists in

Istanbul during World War I," in C. Hillenbrand, ed., *Studies in Honour of Clifford Ed-mund Bosworth* (Leiden: Brill, 2000).

On the rise of Reza Shah, see C. Ghani, *Iran and the Rise of Reza Shah: From Qajar Collapse to Pahlavi Rule* (London: I. B. Tauris, 1998); S. Cronin, *The Army and the Creation of the Pahlavi State in Iran, 1910–1926* (London: I. B. Tauris, 1997); and M. P. Zirinsky, "Imperial Power and Dictatorship: Britain and the Rise of Reza Shah, 1921–1926," *International Journal of Middle East Studies* 24 (November 1992): 639–63. Largely relying on British sources, they offer complementary insights into the rise of the Pahlavi order.

8. REZA SHAH AND THE PAHLAVI ORDER (1925–1941)

For an overview and introduction to the Pahlavi period, see essays in *Cambridge History of Iran*, vol. 7 (Cambridge, Cambridge University Press: 1991), especially chapter 6, "The Pahlavi Autocracy: Riza Shah, 1921–1941," by G. Hambly. See also D. Wilber, *Riza Shah Pahlavi: The Resurrection and Reconstruction of Iran 1878–1944* (Hicksville, NY: Exposition Press, 1975). Two edited volumes—T. Atabaki and E. Zürcher eds., *Men of Order: Authoritarian Modernization under Atatürk and Reza Shah* (London: I. B. Tauris, 2004), and S. Cronin, *The Making of Modern Iran State and Society under Riza Shah, 1921–1941* (London: Routledge Curzon, 2003), explore political, social, and cultural aspects of Reza Shah's rule. A. Banani, *The Modernization of Iran, 1921–1941* (Stanford, CA: Stanford University Press, 1961), represents an early interpretation of modernization as the triumph of secular nationalism. S. Cronin has also written two other valuable studies on the Reza Shah period: *Tribal Politics in Iran: Rural Conflict and the New State, 1921–1941* (London: Routledge, 2007), and *Soldiers, Shahs and Subalterns in Iran: Opposition, Protest and Revolt, 1921–1941* (New York: Palgrave Macmillan, 2010). Part 2 of Lambton, *Landlords and Peasants*, is devoted to the study of agrarian relations in the early Pahlavi era. On the most influential statesman of the period, see M. Rezun, "Reza Shah's Court Minister: Teymourtash," *International Journal of Middle East Studies* 12 (1980): 119–37.

The rise of nationalist ideology during the Reza Shah period has received ample scholarly attention. R. W. Cottam, *Nationalism in Iran* (Pittsburgh: University of Pittsburgh Press, 1964), examines the impact of nationalism on Iranian political culture. More recently, F. Kashani-Sabet, *Frontier Fictions: Shaping the Iranian Nation, 1804–1946* (Princeton, NJ: Princeton University Press, 1999), draws attention to the significance of land and boundaries. F. Vejdani, *Making History in Iran: Education, Nationalism, and Print Culture* (Stanford: Stanford University Press, 2014), examines historical writing, textbooks, and educational curricula and their significance in the shaping of national identity. Vejdani's "Appropriating the Masses: Folklore Studies, Ethnography, and Interwar Iranian Nationalism," *International Journal of Middle East Studies* 44, no. 3 (2012): 507–26, explores the preoccupation with popular culture. A. Marashi, *Nationalizing Iran: Culture, Power, and the State, 1870–1940* (Seattle: University of Washington Press, 2008), examines the role of print capitalism, state monuments, and Iran's cultural heritage in the shaping of Iranian nationalism. His "Imagining Hafez: Rabindranath Tagore in Iran, 1932," *Journal of Persianate Studies* 3, no. 1 (2010): 46–77, draws on the Indo-Iranian connection. For a survey of nationalist trends during the 1920s, see also H. Katouzian, "Nationalist Trends in Iran, 1921–1926," *International Journal of Middle East Studies* 10, no. 4 (November 1979): 533–51. A. Ansari's excellent study, *The Politics of Nationalism in Modern Iran* (New York: Cambridge University Press, 2012), locates Reza Shah in the context of the "enlightenment nationalists" of the Constitutional Revolution. A. Marashi and K. Aghaie, eds., *Rethinking Iranian Nationalism and Modernity* (Austin: University of Texas Press, 2014), includes a number of essays addressing the contingent nature of nationalism.

On the discourse of national identity, see also A. Ashraf, "The Crisis of National and Ethnic Identities in Contemporary Iran," *Iranian Studies* 26 (1993): 159–64, and A. Amanat, "Iranian Identity Boundaries: A Historical Overview," in *Iran Facing Others*, ed. A. Amanat and F. Vejdani (New York: Palgrave Macmillan, 2012), 1–39. M. Vaziri's controversial argument in *Iran as Imagined Nation: The Construction of National Identity* (New York: Paragon House, 1993), underscores the European conception of Iran. For the significance of archeology in the emergence of nationalist discourse, see K. Abdi's "Nationalism, Politics, and the Development of Archaeology in Iran," *American Journal of Archaeology* 105 (2001): 51–76, and *Ernst Herzfeld and the Development of Near Eastern Studies, 1900–1950*, eds. Ann Gunter and S. Hauser (Leiden: Brill, 2004).

For early Pahlavi social, economic and cultural developments, see, for instance, P. Clawson, "Knitting Iran Together: The Land Transport Revolution, 1920–1941," *Iranian Studies* 26 (1993): 235–50; M. Koyagi, "The Vernacular Journey: Railway Travelers in Early Pahlavi Iran, 1925–1950," *International Journal of Middle East Studies* 47, no. 4 (November 2015): 745–63; and E. Ehlers and W. Floor, "Urban Change in Iran, 1920–1941," *Iranian Studies* 26, nos. 3–4 (1993): 251–75. H. Chehabi's extensive studies on dress code and culinary practices of the period include "Staging the Emperor's New Clothes," *Iranian Studies* 26, nos. 3–4 (Summer–Fall 1993): 209–33; "The Westernization of Iranian Culinary Culture," *Iranian Studies* 36, no. 1 (March 2003): 43–61; and "Dress Codes for Men in Turkey and Iran," in *Men of Order*, ed. T. Atabaki and E. Zürcher (London: I. B. Tauris, 2004), 209–37. For the Pahlavi state and the clerical establishment up to the end of World War II, see Y. Richard, "Shari'at Sangalaji: A Reformist Theologian of the Riza Shah Period," in *Authority and Political Culture in Shi'ism*, ed. S. A. Arjomand (Albany: State University of New York Press, 1988), 159–77; and M. H. Faghfoory, "The Ulama-State Relations in Iran: 1921–1941," *International Journal of Middle East Studies* 19, no. 4 (1987): 413–32.

J. Perry, "Language Reform in Turkey and Iran," *International Journal of Middle East Studies* 17, no. 3 (1985): 295–311; and R. Matthee, "Transforming Dangerous Nomads into Useful Artisans, Technicians, Agriculturists: Education in the Reza Shah Period," *Iranian Studies* 26, nos. 3–4 (1993): 313–36, offer glimpses of educational policies. S. Cronin's 2003 *The Making of Modern Iran* also includes essays by H. Chehabi, J. Rostam-Kolayi, and S. Mahdavi on the banning of the veil, family law, and the expansion of women's rights, respectively. The same volume also includes valuable essays on tribes and Reza Shah's tribal policy by K. Bayat, R. Tapper, and Cronin herself. See also J. Rostam-Kolayi, "Origins of Iran's Modern Girls' Schools: From Private/National to Public/State," *Journal of Middle East Women's Studies* 4, no. 3 (2008): 58–88. B. Devos and C. Werner, *Culture and Cultural Politics under Reza Shah: The Pahlavi State, New Bourgeoisie and the Creation of a Modern Society in Iran* (London: Routledge, 2014), explores the role of nonstate actors in the creation of the Pahlavi state. C. Schayegh, *Who Is Knowledgeable, Is Strong: Science, Class, and the Formation of Modern Iranian Society, 1900–1950* (Berkeley: University of California Press, 2009), calls attention to the intersection of science, medicine, and the emergence of a middle class in the Pahlavi period. H. Enayat, *Law, State, and Society in Modern Iran: Constitutionalism, Autocracy, and Legal Reform, 1906–1941* (New York: Palgrave McMillan, 2013), is a pioneering study of legal reforms and modern codifications from the constitutional era to the end of Pahlavi period.

9. CHAOTIC DEMOCRACY, OIL NATIONALIZATION, AND DENIED HOPES (1941–1953)

There is a lacuna in the social, economic, and political historiography of Iran during World War II. The causes and circumstances of the Allied invasion is studied in R. A. Stewart, *Sunrise at Abadan: The British and Soviet Invasion of Iran, 1941* (New York: Praeger, 1988); C. Skrine, *World War in Iran* (London: Constable & Co., 1962); and F. Eshraghi, "The Immediate Aftermath of Anglo-Soviet Occupation of Iran in August 1941," *Middle Eastern Studies* 20, no. 3 (July 1984): 324–51. Aspects of the politics of the period are covered in E. Abrahamian, "Factionalism in Iran: Political Groups in the 14th Parliament (1944–46)," *Middle Eastern Studies* 14, no. 1 (January 1978): 22–55; L. P. Elwell-Sutton, "Political Parties in Iran, 1941–1948," *Middle East Journal* 3, no. 1 (January 1949): 45–62; and Elwell-Sutton, "The Iranian Press, 1941–1947," *Iran* 6 (1968): 65–104. C. M. Amin "Selling and Saving 'Mother Iran': Gender and the Iranian Press in the 1940s," *International Journal of Middle East Studies* 33, no. 3 (August 2001): 335–61, looks at political cartoons during the Allied occupation of Iran.

For an overview of the Iranian left during the 1940s and early 1950s, see E. Abrahamian's seminal study *Iran between Two Revolutions* (Princeton, NJ: Princeton University Press, 1982); S. Zabih, *The Communist Movement in Iran* (Berkeley: University of California Press, 1966). See also Abrahamian, "The Strengths and Weaknesses of the Labour Movement in Iran 1941–53," in *Modern Iran: The Dialectics of Continuity and Change*, ed. N. R. Keddie and M. Bonine (Albany: State University of New York Press, 1981), 181–202; M. Behrooz, "Tudeh Factionalism and the 1953 Coup in Iran," *International Journal of Middle East Studies* 33, no. 3 (2001): 363–82; and C. Chaqueri, "Did the Soviets Play a Role in the Founding of the Tudeh Party in Iran?," *Cahiers Monde Russe* 40, no. 3 (July–September 1999): 497–528. Cronin's edited volume, *Reformers and Revolutionaries in Modern Iran: New Perspectives on the Iranian Left* (New York: Routledge Curzon, 2004), also deals with the historical transformation of the left.

The Azarbaijan crisis has been the subject of three studies: T. Atabaki, *Azerbaijan: Ethnicity and the Struggle for Power in Iran*, rev. ed. (London: I. B. Tauris, 2000); Jamil Hasanli, *At the Dawn of the Cold War: The Soviet-American Crisis over Iranian Azerbaijan, 1941–1946* (Lanham, MD: Rowman and Littlefield, 2006); and L. L. Estrange Fawcett, *Iran and the Cold War: The Azerbaijan Crisis of 1946* (Cambridge: Cambridge University Press, 2009). On Kurdish autonomy and Mahabad Republic, see W. Eagleton, *The Kurdish Republic of 1946* (London: Oxford University Press, 1963); and F. Koohi-Kamali, *The Political Development of the Kurds in Iran* (New York: Palgrave MacMillan, 2003).

For the emergence of an independent left, see, for instance, H. Katouzian, "Khalil Maleki: The Odd Intellectual Out," in N. Nabavi, ed., *Intellectual Trends in Twentieth-Century Iran* (Gainesville: University Press of Florida, 2003), 24–52. A decidedly Marxist interpretation of the history of the left appears in B. Jazani, *Capitalism and Revolution in Iran* (London: Zed Books, 1980). Trade unions and labor movement in this period are studied in H. Lodjevardi, *Labor Unions and Autocracy in Iran* (Syracuse, NY: Syracuse University Press, 1985); and R. C. Elling, "On Lines and Fences: Labour, Community and Violence in an Oil City," in *Urban Violence in the Middle East: Changing Cityscapes in the Transition from Empire to Nation-State*, ed. U. Freitag, N. Fuccaro, N. Gherawi, and C. Nafi (Oxford: Berghahn Books, 2015), explores the oil city of Abadan during and after World War II.

The premiership of Mohammad Mossadeq, the oil nationalization movement, and the 1953 coup have been the subject of considerable historical scholarship. For Mosaddeq's memoirs, see *Musaddiq's Memoirs*, ed. and trans. S. H. Amin and H. Katouzian (London: Jebheh National Movement of Iran, 1988). For his biography, see H. Katouzian, *Musaddiq and the Struggle for Power in Iran* (London: I. B. Tauris, 1990), and F. Diba, *Mohammad Mossadegh: A political biography* (London: Routledge Kegan & Paul, 1986). F. Azimi, *Iran: The Crisis of Democracy* (New York: St. Martin's Press, 1989), offers the most scholarly political history of the period based on extensive archival sources. Other studies include S. Siavoshi, *Liberal Nationalism in Iran: The Failure of a Movement* (Boulder, CO: Westview, 1988), and two collection of essays: J. A. Bill, and W. R. Louis, eds., *Musaddiq, Iranian Nationalism, and Oil* (Austin: University of Texas Press, 1988); and M. Gasiorowski and M. Byrne, eds., *Mohammad Mosaddeq and the 1953 Coup in Iran* (Syracuse, NY: Syracuse University Press, 2004). The overthrow of Mosaddeq is also the subject of M. Gasiorowski, "The 1953 Coup d'État in Iran," *International Journal of Middle East Studies* 19, no. 3 (1987): 261–86; and E. Abrahamian, *The Coup: 1953, the CIA, and the Roots of Modern U.S.-Iranian Relations* (New York: New Press, 2013). See also Y. Richard, "Ayatollah Kashani: Precursor of the Islamic Republic," in *Religion and Politics in Iran: Shi'ism from Quietism to Revolution*, ed. N. R. Keddie (New Haven: Yale University Press, 1983); and M. Yazdi, "Patterns of Clerical Behaviors in Postwar Iran, 1941–1953" *Middle Eastern Studies* 26, no. 3 (1990): 281–307.

S. Kinzer, *All the Shah's Men: An American Coup and the Roots of Middle East Terror* (Hoboken, NJ: John Wiley & Sons, 2003); and K. Roosevelt, *Countercoup: The Struggle for Control of Iran* (New York: McGraw-Hill, 1979), provide popular yet valuable accounts. For the relationship between the United States and Iran in the years preceding the coup, see M. H. Lytle, *The Origins of the Iranian-American Alliance, 1941–1953* (New York: Holmes & Meier, 1987). On the oil dispute, see M. A. Heiss, *Empire and Nationhood: The United States, Great Britain, and Iranian Oil, 1950–1954* (New York: Columbia University Press, 1997); M. Elm, *Oil, Power, and Principle: Iran's Oil Nationalization and Its Aftermath* (Syracuse, NY: Syracuse University Press, 1992); L. P. Elwell-Sutton, *Persian Oil: A Study in Power Politics* (London: Lawrence and Wishart, 1955); R. W. Ferrier and J. H. Bamberg, *The History of the British Petroleum Company*, vol. 2: *The Anglo-Iranian Years, 1928–1954* (Cambridge: Cambridge University Press, 2000) and vol. 3: *British Petroleum and Global Oil, 1950–1975* (Cambridge: Cambridge University Press, 2000); M. Farmanfarmaian, *Blood and Oil: Inside the Shah's Iran* (New York: Random House, 1997); and relevant chapters in D. Yergin, *The Prize: The Epic Quest for Oil, Money and Power* (New York: Free Press, 1991). On the American development projects in Iran, see W. E. Warne, *Mission for Peace: Point Four in Iran* (Indianapolis: Bobbs-Merrill Co., 1956).

10. THE WHITE REVOLUTION AND ITS OPPONENTS (1953–1963)

The political trends of the 1950s and early 1960s are discussed in L. Binder, *Iran: Political Development in a Changing Society* (Berkeley: University of California Press, 1964). M. Gasiorowski, *U.S. Foreign Policy and the Shah: Building a Client State in Iran* (Ithaca, NY: Cornell University Press, 1991), also covers this period, though the thrust of his book is later decades. Two studies — M. Zonis, *The Political Elite of Iran* (Princeton, NJ: Princeton University Press, 1971), and J. A. Bill, *The Politics of Iran: Groups, Classes, and Moderniza-*

tion (Columbus, OH: Charles Merril, 1972)—offer some insight into the Iranian political and intellectual elites.

S. Akhavi, *Religion and Politics in Contemporary Iran: Clergy State Relations in the Pahlavi Period* (Albany: State University of New York Press, 1980), provides an overview of the 1960s and the 1970s. M. J. Fischer, *Iran from Religious Dispute to Revolution* (Madison: University of Wisconsin Press, 1980) is particularly insightful for the author's fieldwork in Qom. See also J. Foran, ed., *A Century of Revolution: Social Movements in Iran* (Minneapolis: University of Minnesota Press, 1994), and especially the essay by M. Parsa, "Mosque of Last Resort: State Reform and Social Conflict in the Early 1960s," 135–59. For the anti-Baha'i campaigns of the mid-twentieth century, see M. Tavakoli-Targhi, "Anti-Baha'ism and Islamism in Iran"; H. Chehabi, "The Anatomy of Prejudice: Reflections on Secular Anti-Baha'ism in Iran"; and A. Amanat, "The Historical Roots of the Persecution of Babis and Baha'is in Iran," all in *The Baha'is of Iran: Socio-Historical Studies*, ed. S. Fazel and D. Brookshaw (New York: Routledge, 2008). See also F. Vahman, *160 Years of Persecution: An Overview of the Persecution of the Baha'is of Iran* (Spanga, Sweden: Baran, 2010).

Land reform has been the subject of a number of monographs. A. K. S. Lambton, *The Persian Land Reform, 1962–1966* (Oxford: Clarendon Press, 1969), is an early example. Other studies include H. Katouzian, "Land Reform in Iran: A Case Study in the Political Economy of Social Engineering," *Journal of Peasant Studies* 1, no. 2 (1974): 220–39; E. J. Hooglund, *Land and Revolution in Iran, 1960–1980* (Austin: University of Texas Press, 1982); A. Najmabadi, *Land Reform and Social Change in Iran* (Salt Lake City: University of Utah Press, 1987); and I. Ajami, *Agrarian Reform and Institutional Innovation in the Development of Agriculture in Iran* (Madison: University of Wisconsin Press, 1977). For a more general assessment of economic development in Iran during the twentieth century, see J. Bharier, *Economic Development in Iran, 1900–1970* (London: Oxford University Press, 1971). K. S. McLachlan, *The Neglected Garden: The Politics of Ecology and Agriculture in Iran* (London: I. B. Tauris, 1988), is an important study of the changing agriculture in Pahlavi era and the resulting environment constraints.

For literary and artistic trends in the Pahlavi era, see M. Ghanoonparvar, *In a Persian Mirror: Images of the West and Westerners in Iranian Fiction* (Austin: University of Texas Press, 1993); K. Talatoff, *The Politics of Writing in Iran: A History of Modern Persian Literature* (Syracuse, NY: Syracuse University Press, 2000); I. Parsinejad, *A History of Literary Criticism in Iran* (Bethesda, MD: Ibex Publishers, 2003); A. Karimi-Hakkak, *Recasting Persian Poetry: Scenarios of Poetic Modernity in Iran* (Salt Lake City: University of Utah, 1995); and A. Karimi-Hakkak and K. Talatoff, eds., *Essays on Nima Yushij: Animating Modernism in Persian Poetry* (Leiden: Brill, 2004). For studies of Sadeq Hedayat, see H. Katouzian, *Sadeq Hedayat, the Life and Legend of an Iranian Writer* (New York: I. B. Tauris, 2000), and the edited volume *Sadeq Hedayat: His Work and His Wondrous World*, ed. H. Katouzain (New York: Routledge, 2008). M. Beard's *Hedayat's Blind Owl as a Western Novel* (Princeton, NJ: Princeton University Press, 1990), locates Hedayat's work in a broader Western context. For studies of Forugh Farrokhzad, see M. C. Hillmann, *A Lonely Women: Forugh Farrokhzad and Her Poetry* (Washington, DC: Mage Publishers, 1987); M. C. Hillmann, ed., *Forugh Farrakhzad: A Quarter Century Later* (Austin: University of Texas Press, 1998), and D. P. Brookshaw and N. Rahimieh, eds., *Forugh Farrokhzad, Poet of Modern Iran: Iconic Woman and Feminine Pioneer of New Persian Poetry* (London: I. B. Tauris, 2010), contribute to our understanding of Forugh in contemporary Persian poetry.

For two valuable anthologies of modern Persian prose and poetry see H. Moayyad, *Stories from Iran: A Chicago Anthology, 1921–1991* (Washington, DC: Mage Publishers, 1992) and N. Mozaffari (and A. Karimi Hakkak), eds., *Strange Times, My Dear: The Pen Anthology of Contemporary Iranian Literature* (New York: Arcade, 2005). For a translation of some of Ahmad Kasravi's work, see M. R. Ghanoonparvar, trans., *On Islam and Shi'ism* (Costa Mesa, CA: Mazda Press, 1990).

11. DEVELOPMENT, DISARRAY, AND DISCONTENT (1963–1977)

Mohammad Reza Shah Pahlavi's biography has received ample attention in M. Zonis, *Majestic Failure: The Fall of the Shah* (Chicago: Chicago University Press, 1991); G. R. Afkhami, *The Life and Times of the Shah* (Berkeley: University of California Press, 2009); and A. Milani, *The Shah* (New York: Palgrave Macmillan, 2011). Mohammad Reza Shah Pahlavi, *Mission for My Country* (New York: McGraw-Hill, 1961), sketches his public persona. The shah's *Answer to History* (New York: Stein & Day, 1980), completed shortly before his death, is a vindication of his career and indictment of his real and imagined nemesis. An abridged edition of the secret diaries of his influential prime minister, and later the court minister, A. Alam, *The Shah and I: the Confidential Diaries of Iran's Royal Court, 1969–1977*, ed. and trans., and with an introduction by, A. Alikhani (London: I. B. Tauris, 1991), opens a window onto the shah's private life, worldview, and inner politics of the Pahlavi court. A. Saikal, *The Rise and Fall of the Shah* (Princeton, NJ: Princeton University Press, 1980), gives an account of the shah's policies and reliance on the United States. A. Milani, *The Persian Sphinx: Amir Abbas Hoveyda and the Riddle of the Iranian Revolution: A Biography* (Washington, DC: Mage Publishers, 2004), is a nuanced biography of the longest-serving premier of the Pahlavi period. Ashraf Pahlavi's *Faces in a Mirror: Memoirs from Exile* (New York: Prentice Hall Trade, 1980), offers the story of the shah's influential twin sister. W. Shawcross, *The Shah's Last Ride: A Cautionary Tale* (London: Chatto & Windus, 1988), is a popular account of the shah's last days in exile.

For state and society in the late 1960s and 1970s, see, for instance, H. Katouzian, *The Political Economy of Modern Iran: Despotism and Pseudo-Modernism, 1926–1979* (New York: New York University Press, 1981); R. Ramazani, *Iran's Foreign Policy, 1941–1973: A Study of Foreign Policy in Modernizing Nations* (Charlottesville: University Press of Virginia, 1975); and D. Menashri, *Education and the Making of Modern Iran* (Ithaca, NY: Cornell University Press, 1992). See also M. P. Mini, "A Single Party State in Iran, 1975–1978: The Rastakhiz Party," *Middle East Studies* 38, no. 1 (2002): 131–68.

For the prerevolutionary trends of the 1960s and 1970s, see E. Abrahamian, *The Iranian Mojahedin* (New Haven: Yale University Press, 1989); and Abrahamian, "The Guerrilla Movement in Iran, 1963–77," in *Iran: A Revolution in Turmoil*, ed. H. Afshar (Albany: State University of New York Press, 1985), 149–74; A. Matin-Asgari, *Iranian Student Opposition to the Shah* (Costa Mesa, CA: Mazda, 2001); and H. Algar, "The Oppositional Role of the Ulama in Twentieth-Century Iran," in *Scholars, Saints, and Sufis: Muslim Religious Institutions in the Middle East Since 1500*, ed. N. R. Keddie (Berkeley: University of California Press, 1972). For 'Ali Shariati, see A. Rahnama, *An Islamic Utopian: A Political Biography of Ali Shariati* (London: I. B. Tauris, 2000); M. Bayat-Philip, "Shi'ism in Contemporary Iranian Politics: The Case of Ali Shari'ati," in *Towards a Modern Iran: Studies in Thought, Politics, and Society*, ed. S. Haim and E. Kedouri (London: Frank Cass, 1980), 155–68.

12. CULTURES OF AUTHORITY AND CULTURES OF DISSENT

The cultural patronage of the Pahlavi state in the 1960s and 1970s, specifically the use of music, architecture, visual arts, and media, is studied in T. Grigor, *Building Iran: Modernism, Architecture, and National Heritage under the Pahlavi Monarchs* (New York: Prestel, 2009). H. Chehabi, "Sport and Politics in Iran: The Legend of Gholamreza Takhti," *International Journal of the History of Sport* 12, no. 3 (1995): 48–60, and his "Annotated Bibliography of Sports and Games in the Iranian World," *Iranian Studies* 35, no. 4 (2002): 403–19, provide useful resources. Farah Pahlavi's memoirs, *An Enduring Love: My Life with the Shah* (New York: Miramax, 2004), are devoted in part to her patronage of cultural projects during the Pahlavi era. See also R. Gluck, "The Shiraz Arts Festival: Western Avant-Garde Arts in 1970s Iran," *Leonardo* 40, no. 1 (2007): 20–28. For Persian music, see Jean During, *The Art of Persian Music* (Washington, DC: Mage, 1991); C. Nelly and D. Safvate, *Iran: Les traditions musicales* (Paris: Buchet-Chastel, 1966); and E. Zonis, "Contemporary Art Music in Persia," *Musical Quarterly* 51 (1965): 636–48. On traditional Persian theatrical arts and ta'ziyeh, see Peter Chelkowski, *Ta'ziyeh: Ritual and Drama in Iran* (New York: New York University Press, 1979); and W. Floor, *The History of Theater in Iran* (Washington, DC: Mage Publishers, 2005). On painting and sculpture, see H. Keshmirshekan, "Neo-Traditionalism and Modern Iranian Painting: The *Saqqa-khaneh* Scool in the 1960s," *Iranian Studies* 38 (2005): 607–30.

Studies by M. Boroujerdi, *Iranian Intellectuals and the West: The Tormented Triumph of Nativism* (Syracuse, NY: Syracuse University Press, 1996); A. Gheissari, *Iranian Intellectuals in the Twentieth Century* (Austin: University of Texas Press, 1998); and A. Mirsepassi, *Intellectual Discourse and the Politics of Modernization: Negotiating Modernity in Iran* (Cambridge: Cambridge University Press, 2000), focus on modern and contemporary intellectual and literary trends. N. Nabavi, ed., *Intellectual Trends in Twentieth-Century Iran* (Gainesville: University Press of Florida, 2003), also deals with intellectuals of the period. Jalal Al-e Ahmad's influential work "Westoxification" has been translated into English, see *Gharbzadegi*, ed. J. Green and A. Alizadeh (Lexington, KY: Mazda, 1982), and *Occidentosis: A Plague from the West*, R. Campbell (Berkeley, CA: Mizan, 1984). See also M.C. Hillmann, ed., *Iranian Society: An Anthology of Writings by Jalal Al-e Ahmad* (Lexington, KY: Mazda, 1982).

Iranian cinema has garnered much scholarly attention. A comprehensive study is H. Naficy, *A Social History of Iranian Cinema*, 4 vols. (Durham: Duke University Press, 2011–2012). See also H. Dabashi, *Close Up: Iranian Cinema, Past Present and Future* (London: Verso, 2001); H. R. Sadr, *Iranian Cinema: A Political History* (New York: I. B. Tauris, 2006); S. Mirbakhtyar, *Iranian Cinema and the Islamic Revolution* (Jefferson, NC: McFarland Publishers, 2006); N. Mottahedeh, *Displaced Allegories: Post-revolutionary Iranian Cinema* (Durham, NC: Duke University Press, 2008); R. Tapper, *The New Iranian Cinema: Politics, Representation and Identity* (London: I. B. Tauris, 2002); Saeed Zeydabadi-Nejad, *Politics of Iranian Cinema: Film and Society in the Islamic Republic* (London and New York: Routledge, 2010); M. M. J. Fischer, *Mute Dreams, Blind Owls, and Dispersed Knowledges: Persian Poesis in the Transnational Circuitry* (Durham, NC: Duke University Press, 2004); G. Rekabtalaei, "Cinematic Revolution: Cosmopolitan Alter-cinema of Pre-revolutionary Iran," *Iranian Studies* 48, no. 4 (2015): 567–89; and A. Sreberny and A. Mohammad, *Small Media, Big Revolution: Communication, Culture, and the Iranian Revolution* (Minneapolis: University of Minnesota Press, 1994), and P. Decherney and B. Atwood, *Iranian Cinema in a Global Context: Policy, Politics, and Form* (New York: Routledge, 2014) examine Iranian cinema from global and interdisciplinary perspectives.

13. THE MAKING OF THE ISLAMIC REVOLUTION (1977–1979)

There is a large and diverse body of studies on the Iranian revolution. S. Bakhash, *The Reign of the Ayatollahs: Iran and the Islamic Revolution* (New York: Basic Books, 1984), is a pioneering narrative of the early stages of the revolution. R. P. Mottahedeh, *The Mantle of the Prophet: Religion and Politics in Iran* (New York: Simon & Schuster, 1985), masterfully places the story of a semifictional madrasa student within many episodes of the intellectual, cultural, and social history of premodern and modern Iran. Other studies include S. A. Arjomand, *The Turban for the Crown: The Islamic Revolution in Iran* (New York: Oxford University Press, 1988) and N. R. Keddie, *Modern Iran: Roots and Results of Revolution* (New Haven: Yale University Press, 2006). F. Azimi, *The Quest for Democracy in Iran: A Century of Struggle Against Authoritarian Rule* (Cambridge: Harvard University Press, 2008) is an insightful treatment of Iran's sociopolitical history at a critical juncture. Three accessible narratives are by R. Kapuściński, *Shah of Shahs* (New York: Random House, 1982); Michael Axworthy, *Revolutionary Iran: A History of the Islamic Republic* (New York: Oxford University Press, 2013); and J. Buchan, *Days of God: the Revolution in Iran and Its Consequences* (London: John Murray, 2013). Among the works highlighting specific aspects of prerevolutionary or revolutionary processes are H. Chehabi's insightful *Iranian Politics and Religious Modernism: The Liberation Movement of Iran under the Shah and Khomeini* (Ithaca, NY: Cornell University Press, 1990), and S. Akhavi, *Religion and Politics in Contemporary Iran: Clergy-State Relations in the Pahlavi Period* (Albany: State University of New York Press, 1980). See also H. Algar, *The Roots of the Islamic Revolution* (London: Open Press, 1983); H. Dabashi, *Theology of Discontent: The Ideological Foundations of the Islamic Revolution in Iran* (New York: New York University Press, 1993); V. Martin, *Creating an Islamic State: Khomeini and the Making of a New Iran* (London: I. B. Tauris, 2000); and A. Amanat, *Apocalyptic Islam and Iranian Shi'ism* (London: I. B. Tauris, 2005). H. Enayat, *Modern Islamic Political Thought* (Austin: University of Texas Press, 1982), provides a concise introduction to Islamic political trends across a broad Muslim geographic setting.

The socioeconomic dimensions of the revolution are discussed in F. Kazemi, *Poverty and Revolution in Iran: The Migrant Poor, Urban Marginality, and Politics* (New York: New York University Press, 1980); C. Kurzman, *The Unthinkable Revolution in Iran* (Cambridge, MA: Harvard University Press, 2004); M. Parsa, *Social Origins of the Iranian Revolution* (New Brunswick, NJ: Rutgers University Press, 1989); M. Moaddel, *Class, Politics, and Ideology in the Iranian Revolution* (New York: Columbia University Press, 1992); M. M. Milani, *The Making of Iran's Islamic Revolution: From Monarchy to Islamic Republic* (Boulder, CO: Westview Press, 1988); S. Zubaida, "Classes as Political Actors in the Iranian Revolution," in *Islam, the People, and the State: Political Ideas and Movements in the Middle East* (London: I. B. Tauris, 2009); and A. Ashraf, "From the White Revolution to the Islamic Revolution," in *Iran after the Revolution: Crisis of an Islamic State*, ed. S. Rahnema and S. Behdad (London: I. B. Tauris, 1995), 21–44. See also N. Mazaheri, "State Repression in the Iranian Bazaar, 1975–1977: The Anti-Profiteering Campaign and an Impending Revolution," *Iranian Studies* 39, no. 3 (2006): 401–14.

The active role played by women in the revolutionary movement is the subject of H. Moghissi, *Populism and Feminism in Iran: Women's Struggle in a Male-Defined Revolutionary Movement* (New York: St. Martin's Press, 1996), and G. Nashat, ed., *Women and Revolution in Iran* (Boulder, CO: Westview Press, 1983). Two works by P. Paidar—*Women and the Political Process in Twentieth-Century Iran* (New York, Cambridge University

Press, 1995) and *Gender of Democracy: the Encounter between Feminism and Reformism in Contemporary Iran* (Geneva: UN Research Institute for Social Development, 2001)—examine Iranian women and gender in a broader perspective.

M. Behrooz, *Rebels with a Cause: The Failure of the Left in Iran* (London: I. B. Tauris, 1999), and S. Zabih, *The Left in Contemporary Iran: Ideology, Organization, and the Soviet Connection* (London: Croom Helm, 1986), address the dismantling of the left after the revolution. J. Afary and K. Anderson, *Foucault and the Iranian Revolution: Gender and the Seductions of Islamism* (Chicago: University of Chicago Press, 2005), focuses on the French philosopher's encounter with the Islamic Revolution in Iran.

14. THE GUARDIAN JURIST AND HIS ADVOCATES

Some of Ayatollah Khomeini's works have been translated into English: *Islamic Government*, trans. Joint Publications Research Service of the US Government (New York: Manor Books, 1979); *Islam and Revolution: Writings and Declarations of Imam Khomeini*, transl. H. Algar (Berkeley: Mizan Press, 1981); and *A Clarification of Questions: an Unabridged Translation of Resaleh Towzih al-Masael*, trans. J. Borujerdi with a foreword by M. M. J. Fischer and M. Abedi (Boulder, CO: Westview, 1984). B. Moin, *Khomeini: Life of The Ayatollah* (London: I. B. Tauris, 1991), provides an accessible account. A. Sachedina, *The Just Ruler in Shi'ite Islam: The Comprehensive Authority of the Jurist in Imamite Jurisprudence* (Oxford: Oxford University Press, 1988), is an attempt to evaluate Khomeini's theory of governance. For a critical revision, see H. Modarressi, "The Just Ruler of the Guardian Jurist: An Attempt to Link Two Different Shi'ite Concepts," *Journal of American Oriental Society* 111, no. 3 (1991): 549–62. See also H. Enayat, "Iran: Khumayni's Concept of the Guardianship of the Jurist," in *Islam in the Political Process*, ed. J. Piscatori (New York: Cambridge University Press, 1983); and A. Amanat, "From Ijtihad to Wilayat-i Faqih: The Evolution of Shiite Legal Authority to Political Power," in *Apocalyptic Islam and Iranian Shi'ism* (London: I. B. Tauris, 2009). *Lessons in Islamic Jurisprudence: Muhammad Baqir as-Sadr*, trans. with an Introduction by R. P. Mottahedeh (Oxford: One World, 2003) provides a valuable translation and commentary on the work of a major Shi'i scholar of the twentieth century. Essays by S. Akhavi, "Shi'ite Theories of Social Contract," and S. A. Arjomand, "Shari'a and Constitution in Iran: A Historical Perspective," in *Shari'a: Islamic Law in the Contemporary Context*, ed. A. Amanat and F. Griffel (Stanford: Stanford University Press, 2007), offer new insights. S. Akhavi, "Contending Discourses in Shi'ite Law on the Doctrine of Wilayat al-Faqih," *Iranian Studies* 29, nos. 3–4 (Summer–Fall 1996): 229–68; and K. Amirpur, "A Doctrine in the Making? Velayat-e Faqih in Post-Revolutionary Iran," in *Speaking for Islam: Religious Authorities in Muslim Societies* (Leiden: Brill, 2006), also survey the evolving nature of the Guardianship of the Jurist in its political context.

For Hosain-'Ali Montazeri, see Sussan Siavoshi, *Montazeri: The Life and Thought of Iran's Revolutionary Ayatollah* (New York: Cambridge University Press, 2017); R. Hajatpour, "Reflections and Legal Analysis of the Relationship between 'Religious Government and Human Rights' from the Perspective of Grand Ayatollah Muntaziri," *Die Welt Islams* 51 (2011): 382–408; S. Akhavi, "The Thought and Role of Ayatollah Hossein'ali Montazeri in the Politics of Post-1979 Iran," *Iranian Studies* 41, no. 5 (2008): 645–66; and G. Abdo, "Rethinking the Islamic Republic: A 'Conversation' with Ayatollah Hossein 'Ali Montazeri," *Middle East Journal* 55, no. 1 (2001): 9–24. For a selection in

English of Mahmud Taleqani's work, see "The Characteristics of Islamic Economics," in *Islam in Transition: Muslim Perspectives*, ed. J. Donohue and J. Esposito (New York: Oxford University Press, 1982).

15. CONSOLIDATION OF THE ISLAMIC REPUBLIC (1979–1984)

Few historians have yet explored the early years of the Islamic Republic. E. Abrahamian, *Khomeinism: Essays on the Islamic Republic* (London: I. B. Tauris, 1993), contains glimpses of political and ideological trends in postrevolutionary Iran, including "The Paranoiac Style of the Iranian Politics." Other works, including R. Ramazani, *Revolutionary Iran: Challenge and Response in the Middle East* (Baltimore, MD: Johns Hopkins University Press, 1986); Ramazani, *Iran's Revolution: The Search for Consensus* (Bloomington: Indiana University Press, 1990); S. Hunter, *Iran after Khomeini* (New York: Praeger, 1992); N. R. Keddie and E. J. Hooglund, eds., *The Iranian Revolution and the Islamic Republic* (Syracuse, NY: Syracuse University Press, 1986), explore the consolidation of political power in the Islamic Republic.

The framing of the constitution of the Islamic Republic, and constitutional politics, have been the subject of A. Schirazi, *The Constitution of Iran: Politics and the State in the Islamic Republic* (London: I. B. Tauris, 1998). Extensive works by S. A. Arjomand on the subject include "Shi'ite Jurisprudence and Constitution Making in the Islamic Republic of Iran," in *Fundamentalisms and the State: Remaking Polities, Economies and Militancy*, ed. M. E. Marty and R. S. Appleby (Chicago: University of Chicago Press, 1993); "Authority in Shi'ism and Constitutional Developments in the Islamic Republic of Iran," in *The Twelver Shia in Modern Times: Religious Culture & Political History*, ed. W. Ende and R. Brunner (Leiden: Brill, 2000). For a comparative perspective, see also S. A. Arjomand and N. Brown, eds., *The Rule of Law, Islam, and Constitutional Politics in Egypt and Iran* (Albany: SUNY Press, 2013); and S. Zubaida, "The Politics of Sharia in Iran" in *Law and Power in the Islamic World* (London: I. B. Tauris, 2003).

Elite factionalism in the postrevolutionary period has also received some scholarly attention in B. Bakhtiari, *Parliamentary Politics in Revolutionary Iran: The Institutionalization of Factional Politics* (Gainesville: University Press of Florida, 1996); M. Moslem, *Factional Politics in Post Khomeini Iran* (Syracuse, NY: Syracuse University Press, 2002); D. Menashri, *Post Revolutionary Politics in Iran: Religion, Society, and Power* (New York: Routledge, 2001); and S. Akhavi, "Elite Factionalism in the Islamic Republic of Iran," *Middle East Journal* 41, no. 2 (1987): 181–201.

J. A. Bill, *The Eagle and the Lion: The Tragedy of American-Iranian Relations* (New Haven: Yale University Press, 1988), extensively covers American-Iranian relations from the 1940s through the Iran-Contra Affair with greater emphasis on the last years of the shah and the rise of the Islamic Republic. P. Chelkowski and H. Dabashi, *Staging a Revolution: The Art of Persuasion in the Islamic Republic of Iran* (New York: New York University Press, 1999), highlight the role played by graphic arts in the creation of the Islamic Republic. M. Kazemzadeh, *Islamic Fundamentalism, Feminism, and Gender Inequality in Iran under Khomeini* (Lanham, MD: University Press of America, 2002), assesses the impact of Khomeini's gender policies.

16. FACING THE FOE

Among studies of the Iraq-Iran War are S. Chubin and C. Tripp, *Iran and Iraq at War* (Boulder, CO: Westview Press, 1991), which provides a thorough political history and the leadership on both sides of the conflict. R. Varzi, *Warring Souls: Youth, Media, and Martyrdom in Post-Revolution Iran* (Durham, NC: Duke University Press, 2006), is an anthropological study of the effects of the war, specifically its visual and cultural memory. Other works include F. Rajaee, *The Iran-Iraq War: The Politics of Aggression* (Gainesville: University Press of Florida, 1993); and L. G. Potter and G. Sick, *Iran, Iraq and the Legacies of War* (New York: Palgrave, 2004). The latter volume includes an essay by S. Bakhash: "The Troubled Relationship: Iran and Iraq, 1930–1980." For an exploration of Arab-Persian relations and notions of identity, see H. Chehabi, "Iran and Iraq: Intersocietal Linkages and Secular Nationalisms," in A. Amanat and F. Vejdani's *Iran Facing Others: Identity Boundaries in a Historical Perspective* (New York: Palgrave, 2012). On the culture of the Iraq-Iran War, see P. Khosronejad, ed., *Unburied Memories: The Politics of Bodies of Sacred Defense Martyrs in Iran* (New York: Routledge, 2013); and D. R. Khoury, *Iraq in Wartime: Soldiering, Martyrdom, and Remembrance* (New York: Cambridge University Press, 2013).

The vast body of literature on the hostage crisis includes accounts of a former hostage, C. Scott, *Pieces of the Game: The Human Drama of Americans Held Hostage in Iran* (Atlanta: Peachtree Publishers, 1984), and the American charge d'affaires in Tehran, B. Laingen, *Yellow Ribbon: The Secret Journal of Bruce Laingen* (New York: Brassey's, 1992). G. Sick, *All Fall Down: America's Tragic Encounter with Iran* (New York: Random House, 1985); D. P. Houghton, *U.S. Foreign Policy and the Iran Hostage Crisis* (Cambridge: Cambridge University Press, 2001); and K. Pollack, *The Persian Puzzle: The Conflict between Iran and America* (New York: Random House, 2004), provide readable accounts of the crisis and the many dilemmas faced by the Carter administration. W. O. Beeman, *The Great Satan versus the Mad Mullahs: How the United States and Iran Demonize Each Other* (Chicago: University of Chicago Press, 2005), examines how Iran and the United States perceived and represented each other.

A vast literature also exists on Iran's human rights record. E. Abrahamian, *Tortured Confessions: Prisons and Public Recantation in Modern Iran* (Berkeley: University of California, 1999), and R. Afshari, *Human Rights in Iran: The Abuse of Cultural Relativism* (Philadelphia: University of Pennsylvania Press, 2011), examine various dimensions and highlight the mass executions of 1988. D. Rejali, *Torture and Modernity: Self, Society, and the State in Modern Iran* (Boulder, CO: Westview Press, 1994), places the Iranian case in the broader context of states' disciplinary mechanisms. W. Buchta, *Who Rules Iran: The Structure of Power in the Islamic Republic* (Washington, DC: Washington Institute for Near East Policy, 2000); and "Taking Stock of a Quarter Century of the Islamic Republic of Iran," *Islamic Legal Studies Program Harvard Law School Occasional Publication* 5 (2005), emphasize political oppression in the context of the organization of the Islamic state. The aforementioned edited volume, *The Bahai's of Iran: Socio-Historical Studies*, includes two relevant essays by E. Sanasarian, "The Comparative Dimension of the Baha'i Case and Prospects for Change in the Future," and by R. Afshari, "The Discourse and Practice of Human Rights Violations of Iranian Baha'is in the Islamic Republic of Iran." See also M. Amanat, "Set in Stone: Homeless Corpses and Desecrated Graves in Modern Iran," *International Journal of Middle East Studies* 44 (2012): 257–83. E. Sanasarian,

Religious Minorities in Iran (Cambridge: Cambridge University Press, 2006), is a thorough treatment of state-minority relations focusing on the decade after 1979. Since its foundation in 2004, the Iran Human Rights Documentation Center has produced extensive and well-documented reports (available online), on a wide range of human rights violations in Iran against ethnic and religious minorities, political and nonpolitical prisoners, political dissidents, journalists, human rights activists, women's rights groups, gays, lesbians, and transgendered men and women, as well as widespread torture, forced confessions, show trials, political assassinations abroad, press and Internet censorship, and the Islamic Republic's intelligence apparatus.

17. SOCIETY AND CULTURE UNDER THE ISLAMIC REPUBLIC

Since the onset of the Islamic Revolution, there has been a proliferation of studies concerning life in postrevolutionary Iran. For a general overview of the political, social, and economic landscape in contemporary Iran, see E. J. Hooglund, ed., *Twenty Years of Islamic Revolution: Political and Social Transition in Iran since 1979* (Syracuse, NY: Syracuse University Press, 2002); S. Rahnema and S. Behdad, *Iran after the Revolution: Crisis of an Islamic State* (London: I. B. Tauris, 1995); and S. A. Arjomand, *After Khomeini: Iran Under His Successors* (Oxford: Oxford University Press, 2009). C. Rundle, *Reflections on the Iranian Revolution and Iranian-British Relations* (Durham, UK: University of Durham Centre for Middle Eastern and Islamic Studies, 2002), focuses on postrevolutionary Iran. A. Shakoori, *The State and Rural Development in Post-Revolutionary Iran* (New York: Palgrave, 2001), examines development policies under the Islamic Republic. A. Keshavarzian, *Bazaar and State in Iran: The Politics of the Tehran Marketplace* (Cambridge: Cambridge University Press, 2007), is an important study of the bazaar network and shifting political loyalties under the Islamic Republic. F. Nomani and S. Behdad, *Class and Labor in Iran: Did the Revolution Matter?* (Syracuse, NY: Syracuse University Press, 2006), explores the reconfiguration of Iran's working class. A. Bayat, *Street Politics: Poor People's Movements in Iran* (New York: Columbia University Press, 1997), is a pioneering study detailing grassroots political movements in Iran from the mid- to late twentieth century, with a chapter on the squatter riots of the early 1990s.

There are also numerous scholarly works concerning the intellectual life in the postrevolutionary era, most of which highlight the question of what it means to be "modern" under the Islamic regime. See, for example, F. Jahanbakhsh, *Islam, Democracy and Religious Modernism in Iran, 1953–2000: From Bazargan to Soroush* (Leiden: Brill, 2001); F. Vahdat, *God and Juggernaut: Iran's Intellectual Encounter with Modernity* (Syracuse, NY: Syracuse University Press, 2002), which looks at the question of subjectivity and ideology from the perspective of sociological philosophy; and F. Adelkhah, *Being Modern in Iran* (New York: Columbia University Press, 2004). *Civil Society and Democracy in Iran*, ed. R. Jahanbegloo (Lanham: Lexington Books, 2012) includes a number of insightful essays. For a critical assessment of the debate of modernity versus tradition, see also S. A. Arjomand, "The Reform Movement and the Debate on Modernity and Tradition in Contemporary Iran," *International Journal of Middle East Studies* 34 (2002): 719–31. The complex relationship between Islam and democracy is studied in A. Gheissari and V. Nasr, *Democracy in Iran: History and the Quest for Liberty* (New York: Oxford University Press, 2006); A. Bayat, *Making Islam Democratic* (Stanford: Stanford University Press, 2007);

Z. Mir-Hosseini and R. Tapper, *Islam and Democracy in Iran* (London: I. B. Tauris, 2004); and A. Mirsepassi, *Political Islam, Iran, and the Enlightenmen: Philosophies of Hope and Despair* (New York: Cambridge University Press, 2010), and *Democracy in Modern Iran: Islam, Culture, and Political Change* (New York: New York University Press, 2011). A. Amanat, "The Study of History in Post-revolutionary Iran: Nostalgia, Illusion, or Historical Awareness?," *Iranian Studies* 22, no. 4 (1989): 3–18, explores major historiographical issues in the postrevolutionary era and their earlier origins. A. Mirsepassi, *Transnationalism in Iranian Political Thought: The Life and Times of Ahmad Fardid* (New York: Cambridge University Press, 2017), is a study of a controversial student of philosophy and his influence in postrevolutionary Iran.

The role of women in the postrevolutionary era, as well as the broader issues of gender and sexuality, have received ample scholarly attention. P. Paidar, *Women and the Political Process in Twentieth-Century Iran* (Cambridge: Cambridge University Press, 1995), and J. Afary, *Sexual Politics in Modern Iran* (Cambridge: Cambridge University Press, 2009), provide *longue durée* perspectives on women's participation in politics and sexual politics in Iran. P. Mahdavi, *Passionate Uprisings: Iran's Sexual Revolution* (Stanford: Stanford University Press, 2008), examines changing sexual mores. Other notable examples are N. Naghibi, *Rethinking Global Sisterhood: Western Feminism and Iran* (Minneapolis: University of Minnesota Press, 2007); Z. Mir-Hosseini, *Islam and Gender: The Religious Debate in Contemporary Iran* (Princeton, NJ: Princeton University Press, 1999); M. Moallem, *Between Warrior Brother and Veiled Sister: Islamic Fundamentalism and the Politics of Patriarchy in Iran* (Berkeley: University of California Press, 2005); and R. Bahramitash and H. Salehi Esfahani, *Veiled Employment: Islamism and the Political Economy of Women's Employment in Iran* (Syracuse, NY: Syracuse University Press, 2011). A. Najmabadi, *Professing Selves: Transsexuality and Same-Sex Desire in Contemporary Iran* (Durham, NC: Duke University Press, 2014), explores spaces of transsexuality in contemporary Iran.

Persian music and arts in postrevolutionary Iran has been the subject of a few studies. Most recently N. Siamdoust, *Soundtrack of the Revolution: The Politics of Music in Iran* (Stanford: Stanford University Press, 2017) covers culture and the politics of music in contemporary Iran. *Music and Society in Iran* is a valuable selection of essays and a bibliography published as a special issue of *Iranian Studies* 38 (2005): 367–512. See also A. Movahed, "Religious Supremacy, Anti-Imperialist Nationhood and Persian Musicology after 1979 Revolution," *Asian Music* 35 (2003): 85–113; and two studies by R. Simms and A. Koushkani: *Mohammad Reza Shajarian's Avaz in Iran and Beyond* (Lanham, MD: Lexington Books, 2012), and *The Art of Avaz and Mohammad Reza Shajarian: Foundation and Contexts* (Lanham, MD: Lexington Books, 2012). On modern sculpture, see L. Fischman and S. Balaghi, *Parviz Tanavoli* (Wellesley, MA: Davis Museum, 2015). On graphic arts, see P. Tanavoli, *An Introduction to the History of Graphic Design in Iran* (Tehran: Nazar, 2015). On painting, see H. Keshmirshekan's "Discourse of Postrevolutionary Iranian Art: Neotraditionalism during the 1990s," *Muqarnas* 23 (2006): 131–57, and "Contemporary Iranian Art: The Emergence of New Artistic Discourses," *Iranian Studies* 40 (2007): 335–66.

The wave of Iranian émigrés who left after the revolution produced a corpus of memoirs and personal accounts. See, for example, A. Nafisi, *Reading Lolita in Tehran: A Memoir in Books* (New York: Random House, 2003); R. Hakakian, *Journey from the Land of No: A Girlhood Caught in Revolutionary Iran* (New York: Crown Publishers, 2004); and F. Keshavarz, *Jasmine and Stars: Reading More Than Lolita in Tehran* (Chapel Hill: University of North Carolina Press, 2007). H. Dabashi, *Iran: A People Interrupted* (New York:

New Press, 2007), combines a personal story with the broader political, intellectual, and social history of Iran. A fair number of accounts written by women journalists include two accounts based on firsthand observations by E. Sciolino, *Persian Mirrors: The Elusive Face of Iran* (New York: Free Press, 2000), and R. Wright, *The Last Great Revolution* (New York: Random House, 2001). A. Moaveni's insightful *Lipstick Jihad: A Memoir of Growing Up Iranian in America and American in Iran* (New York: Public Affairs, 2005) and M. Satrapi, *Persepolis 2: The Story of a Return* (New York, Pantheon Books, 2004), offer personal narratives of postrevolutionary Iran.

Following the 2009 presidential elections and the ensuing Green Movement, those who were released from detention in the Islamic Republic wrote about their experiences. See, for example, R. Saberi, *Between Two Worlds: My Life and Captivity in Iran* (New York: Harper, 2010), and M. Bahari and A. Molloy, *Then They Came for Me: A Family's Story of Love, Captivity, and Survival* (New York: Random House, 2010). For critical, scholarly assessments of the Green Movement, see K. Harris, "The Brokered Exuberance of the Middle Class: An Ethnographic Analysis of Iran's 2009 Green Movement," *Mobilization: An International Journal* 17, no. 66 (2012): 435–55; and C. Kurzman, "The Arab Spring: Ideals of the Iranian Green Movement, Methods of the Iranian Revolution," *International Journal of Middle East Studies* 44, no. 1 (2012): 162–65. Accessible accounts of the events leading up to the Green Movement is presented in S. Peterson, *Let the Swords Encircle Me: Iran, a Journey Behind the Headlines* (New York: Simon and Schuster, 2010).

Social, economic, and environmental issues in postrevolutionary era have been the subject of a few studies. J. Amuzegar, *The Islamic Republic of Iran: Reflections on an Emerging Economy* (New York: Routledge, 2014), complements his earlier study *The Dynamics of the Iranian Revolution: The Pahlavis' Triumph and Tragedy* (Albany: State University of New York, 1991). S. Maloney, *Iran's Political Economy since the Revolution* (New York: Cambridge University Press, 2015), examines the adverse impact of revolution, ideology, and war on the Iranian economy and society. D. Brumberg and F. Farhi, eds., *Power and Change in Iran: Politics of Contention and Conciliation* (Bloomington: Indiana University Press, 2016), and P. Alizadeh and H. Hakimian, eds., *Iran and the Global Economy: Petro Populism, Islam and Economic Sanctions* (New York: Routledge, 2014), are both valuable collections of essays that examine, among other topics, public policy, education, rule of law, institutional changes, and impact of the sanctions. R. Wright, ed., *The Iran Primer: Power, Politics and U.S. Policy* (Washington, DC: United States Institute of Peace Press, 2010), is a useful collection of essays by a longtime observer that survey Iran's domestic politics, military, opposition, economy, and regional tensions. A. Amanat and M. Tahbaz, eds., "Environment in Iran," in *Iranian Studies* 49 (2016): 925–1099, provide an overview of Iran's water crisis, air pollution, forestry and wildlife conservation, and aspects of environmental history and culture.

INDEX

Page numbers in *italics* indicate figures.

oil concession, 521, 531–32; and assassination attempt on shah, pl. 9.3, 523; government crackdown on, 523; Razmara and, 524–26; anti-US demonstrations by, 533, 546; opposing Mosaddeq, 534–35 (535); and clashes with Sumka, 535; Third Force splinter group, 535–36; protesting Mosaddeq's ouster, 540, 552, 553, 560; CIA and, 548, 552–53; supporting a republic, 552; arrests after 1953 coup, 557–58; Reza Shah's purge, 565, 566; and US embassy takeover, 827; under Islamic Republic, 781, 783, 790; purge of, 800, 805–7

Turkey, Republic of: abolition of caliphate, 433; declaration of, 415, 430–31. *See also* Ottoman Empire

Turkmens, 137, 260, 817; Aqa Mohammad Khan/Shah and, 162, 166–67, 169, 217; culture and traditions, 42–43; Fada'iyan-e Khalq and, 659; Hosain-Qoli Khan Qajar and, 161; Islamic Republic suppression of, 780; Isma'il and, 33, 60–61; Khalkhali and, 780; Kurdish border protection against, 14–15; Mohammad 'Ali Shah and, 369; Mohammad Khan Salar and, 251; Nader-Qoli and, 142–43, 146, 150, 157; Qajars and, 217–18, 264; Qezilbash confederacy and, 78; Saddam's chemical warfare against, 840–42; as Safavid slaves, 74; Salim's massacre of, 55; Shah-Qoli Baba messianic movement, 52; territory of, 15. *See also* Ahl-e Haqq; Nader Shah Afshar; Qezilbash confederacy

Twelfth Imam. *See* Mahdi

Twelver Shi'ism, 46; beliefs of, 34; and End of Time, 744–45; Isma'il I's promotion of, 46, 49, 60, 75; Khomeini and, 744–45, 771; Moharram rituals, 63, 291, 483, 492, 592, 595, 725, 797, 818; as official religion of Iran, 340, 786; and Qezilbash headgear, 43; Safavid jurists and, 113, 147; and Sunni identity, 75;

under Tahmasp, 63; *taqlid* (practice of emulation), 64; ulama as trustees of, 63. *See also* Shi'ism

Two Women (Milani), 890

Under the Skin of the City (Bani Etemad), 890

United Nations Security Council, 517, 533–34, 847

United States, 645–49, 749–50, 770; early mention of in foreign news, 253; Truman administration, 544–48, 557; alliance (1950s and 1960s), 563–66, 573–75, 582–84, 599, 621, 628–30, 633; recommending Shuster, 367–68; alliance (1970s), 562, 627, 640; Kennedy administration, 474, 476, 576–77, 584–85, 668; Johnson administration, 599–600; Nixon administration, 565–66; Ford administration, 632; Carter administration, 646, 705, 707, 710–13 (711), 726, 729–30, 737, 820, 824–28, 845, 879; objections to Anglo-Persian Agreement, 406; Point Four Program, 646–47; Reagan administration, 806, 840–41, 844–47, 858–60; and Imbrie Affair, 437–38; military aid to Iran, 522

urban planning/public spaces, 15–19 (18); Pahlavi demolition and reconstruction, 456–60 (459); of Fath 'Ali Shah, 184–87 (185, 186), 219–20, 294; Isfahan, 83–91 (83, 90), 115–16; under Islamic Republic, 879–81; Naqsh-e Jahan Square, pl. 2.1; of Naser al-Din Shah, 289–95 (290–91); New Julfa, 95 (96); pavilion at Paris Exposition, 282 (282); public square (*maydan*), 17, 18; Tehran, 200, 255, 256, 458–60 (459), 666–67 (667), pls. 5.4, 8.1, 17.2; walled gardens, 23, 24; Zand Shiraz, 154–57 (155), 219–20 (220); effects of motor vehicles on, 456. *See also* architecture; land reform (*eslahat-e arzi*)

USS *Vincennes* downing of airliner, 847